THE
AMERICAN
PROMISE

A HISTORY OF THE UNITED STATES

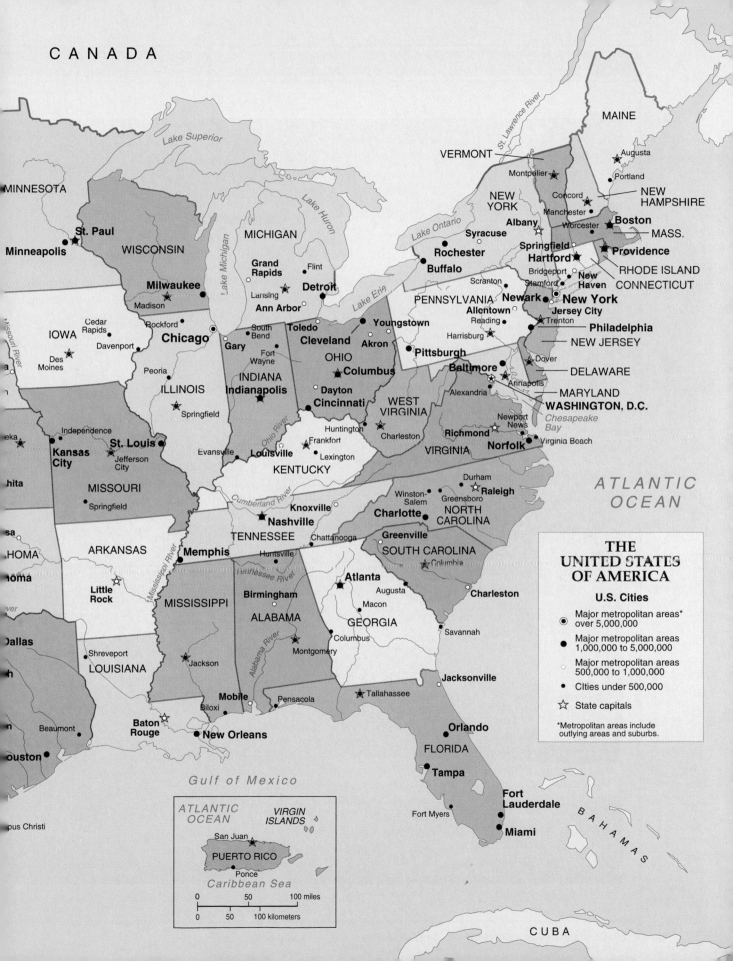

SALEM COMMON ON TRAINING DAY *by George Ropes, 1808. Peabody Essex Museum.*

THE AMERICAN PROMISE

A HISTORY OF THE UNITED STATES

Volume I: To 1877

JAMES L. ROARK
Emory University

MICHAEL P. JOHNSON
Johns Hopkins University

PATRICIA CLINE COHEN
University of California at Santa Barbara

SARAH STAGE
Arizona State University, West

ALAN LAWSON
Boston College

SUSAN M. HARTMANN
The Ohio State University

BEDFORD BOOKS ⚞ Boston

For Bedford Books

President and Publisher: Charles H. Christensen
General Manager and Associate Publisher: Joan E. Feinberg
History Editor: Katherine E. Kurzman
Project Manager: Tina Samaha
Developmental Editors: Louise D. Townsend and Barbara Muller
Editorial Assistant: Thomas Pierce
Managing Editor: Elizabeth M. Schaaf
Production Assistants: Ellen C. Thibault and Deborah A. Baker
Copyeditor: Barbara G. Flanagan
Proofreaders: Mary Lou Wilshaw and Lisa Wehrle
Text Design: Wanda Kossak
Photo Researcher: Pembroke Herbert/Sandi Rygiel, Picture Research Consultants & Archives, Inc.
Cartography: Mapping Specialists Limited
Page Layout: DeNee Reiton Skipper
Indexer: Steve Csipke
Cover Design: Wanda Kossak
Cover Art: Collection of the Philadelphia Contributionship for the Insurance of Houses from Loss by Fire (The Contributionship), Philadelphia, Pa./Photo by Steven Goldblatt.
Composition: York Graphics Services, Inc.
Printing and Binding: R. R. Donnelley & Sons

Library of Congress Catalog Card Number: 97–72376

2 1 0 9 8
f e d c b

For information, write: Bedford Books, 75 Arlington Street, Boston, MA 02116 (617–426–7440)

ISBN: 0-312-09525-2 (hardcover)
ISBN: 0-312-11196-7 (paperback Vol. 1)
ISBN: 0-312-11197-5 (paperback Vol. 2)

Cover art: Painted ceremonial hat, about 1850, of the Mount Airy, Pennsylvania, Fire Company. The hat, worn in dress parades, shows Liberty wearing the Stars and Stripes, holding a shield and the Liberty Cap and pole. The date on the back of the hat, 1804, refers to the founding of the company.

BRIEF CONTENTS

CONTENTS

CHAPTER 6

The British Empire and the Colonial Crisis, 1754–1775   197

CHAPTER 7

The War for America, 1775–1783   239

CHAPTER 14

The House Divided, 1846–1861

519

CHAPTER 15

The Crucible of War, 1861–1865

561

SPECIAL FEATURES

A NOTE FROM THE PUBLISHER
PRESENTING *THE AMERICAN PROMISE*

YOU ARE HOLDING IN YOUR HANDS an innovative new text for the American history survey course. Carefully developed with the needs of students foremost in mind, *The American Promise* deftly wraps the inherently interesting but loose strands of social history around the more formal structure of political history. It is born of two convictions: (1) faced with an overwhelming amount of information, students need help determining what's important and (2) students won't get anything out of a textbook unless it's interesting and enjoyable. The design and art program represents an attempt to rethink the "look" of a textbook, fashioning every element from running-heads to captions to serve a pedagogical function or to further the narrative.

The next few pages offer an overview of the book and introduce its student-focused features. We urge you to take a few minutes to see how we've tried to improve on what has come before us. When you're finished, we hope you'll agree with us that *The American Promise* does more for students than any other survey of American history.

EASY-TO-FOLLOW CHAPTER STRUCTURE

The authors have sought to avoid an encyclopedic approach to American history in favor of building understanding through extensive examination of only the most important events and developments. The architecture of individual chapters is carefully designed to present information in a logical and ordered fashion that emphasizes major themes in history while incorporating individual accounts to maintain students' interest. Common to each chapter is a set of features—vignette, call-outs, conclusion, chronology, and bibliography—that provide useful guides to the narrative.

Opening vignettes

Every chapter begins with an engaging anecdote that eases readers into its major themes while immersing them in a specific historical moment.

(The complete example is found on page 605.)

(The complete example is found on page 605.)

RECONSTRUCTION,
1863-1877

16

Whem the war was over, swarms of northern journalists and government officials rushed to the South to see what four years of fighting had accomplished. Ugly stories of stiff-necked defiance toward Yankees and brutal violence toward ex-slaves had drifted northward. Andrew Johnson, Abraham Lincoln's successor in the White House, asked General Carl Schurz to undertake a special fact-finding tour to assess conditions in the ex-Confederate states. Schurz, a leading antislavery lecturer and Union general, arrived in Charleston, South Carolina, the "Queen City of the South," in July 1865.

Charleston greeted the visitor with an empty harbor, rotting wharves, and gutted buildings. The city looked, Schurz observed, as if it had been struck with "the sudden and irresistible force of a thunderbolt." Cattle grazed in its weed-filled streets. Schurz met former cotton kings and rice barons who could not afford to buy breakfast. Ex-slaves, now Union soldiers, patrolled the city's streets. Schools overflowed with African American children whom it was formerly considered a crime to educate. The Citadel, the state's military school, where once "the chivalric youth of South Carolina was educated for the task of perpetuating slavery by force of arms," now ho___d the Fifty-fourth ___assachusetts Colored Re___ment.

Two-tiered running heads

Double bars at the top of every page let students know where they are in the book, and where they are in the chronology of American history.

Call-outs

While northern resolve to defend black freedom withered, southern commitment to white supremacy intensified.

Throughout each chapter, occasional brief passages have been pulled from the main text to highlight important points, focus readers' attention, and convey the liveliness of the narrative.

Conclusions

Each chapter ends with a brief conclusion that summarizes the narrative's main points, analyzes their significance, and discusses their consequences.

(The complete example is found on page 639.)

Conclusion: "A Revolution but Half-Accomplished"

In 1865, when General Carl Schurz visited the South at President Andrew Johnson's behest, he discovered "a revolution but half-accomplished." Defeat had not prepared the South for an easy transition from slavery to free labor, from white racial despotism to equal justice, and from white political monopoly to biracial democracy. The old elite wanted to get "things back as near to slavery as possible," while ex-slaves and whites who had lacked power in the slave regime were eager to exploit the revolutionary implications of defeat and emancipation.

Chronologies

A chronology at the close of each chapter provides a handy review of the most important dates and events.

(For the complete chronology, see pages 640–641.)

CHRONOLOGY

1863	**December.** Lincoln issues Proclamation of Amnesty and Reconstruction.
1864	**July.** Congress offers more stringent plan for reconstruction, Wade-Davis bill.
1865	**January.** General William T. Sherman sets aside land in South Carolina for black settlement.
	March 4. Lincoln sworn in for second term as president of United States.
	March. Congress establishes Freed-

April 14. Lin
15, is succeed
Andrew John
Fall. Souther
criminatory b
December. T
ment abolishi
of U.S. Const
1866 **April.** Congre
Amendment
blacks Ameri

Bibliographies

Each chapter includes an up-to-date list of recommended works of scholarship. These bibliographies begin with general references for the period with the remainder of the titles organized under subheadings that closely correspond to the chapter's major sections.

(For the complete bibliography, turn to page 641.)

BIBLIOGRAPHY

GENERAL WORKS

W. E. B. Du Bois, *Black Reconstruction in America* (1935).

Eric Foner, *Reconstruction: America's Unfinished Revolution, 1863–1877* (1988).

John Hope Franklin, *Reconstruction after the Civil War* (1961).

James M. McPherson, *Ordeal by Fire: The Civil War and Reconstruction* (1982).

Rembert W. Patrick, *The Reconstruction of the Nation* (1967).

J. G. Randall and David Donald, *The Civil War and Reconstruction* (1967).

WARTIME RECONSTR

Richard H. Abbott, *Th*
lican Party and the S

Herman Belz, *Emancip*
Constitutionalism in t

Ira Berlin et al., eds.,
Emancipation, 1861–

Louis S. Gerteis, *From*
icy toward Southern b

Peyton McCrary, *Abra*
Louisiana Experiment

STRIKING VISUAL FEATURES

Beautifully designed and illustrated, *The American Promise* is replete with visual elements that expand upon—rather than merely decorate—the narrative. Every image has been chosen for its ability to enhance an understanding of the past.

Comprehensive illustration program with extensive captions

Hundreds of fresh images (many of them published in a survey text for the first time) dramatize and extend the story in the text. Unusually full captions—many of which include quotations, questions, or comparisons with other images—draw readers into active engagement with this visual material.

(This illustration is found on page 87.)

Chapter-opening artifacts

To emphasize the importance of material culture in studying the past, each chapter opens with a full-page reproduction of a contemporary cultural artifact, such as clothing, books, musical instruments, or political emblems. Informative captions provide background information and invite readers to consider the artifact's historical implications.

(This chapter-opening artifact is found on page 238.)

TOBACCO ADVERTISEMENT
This ad for "Kositzky's Best Virginia" tobacco illustrates a colonial planter and tobacco merchant examining the quality of a sample of leaves from an open cask waiting to be shipped to London, while an onlooker samples the leaves more thoroughly, by smoking. To smooth the transaction an Afri

PAINTED DRUM
Drums were essential military equipment in eighteenth-century wars. Small to carry but loud in use, they provided a percussive beat that penetrated the din of the battlefield to signal troop advances, retreats, or other field movements. Drummers often stood right behind soldiers in firing formation, regulating the timing of each volley of shots. The eagle painted on this Revolutionary-era drum from Fort Ticonderoga in New York holds a banner inscribed "Sons of Liberty," a name adopted in 1765 to distinguish protesters of British policies toward the colonies.
Fort Ticonderoga Museum.

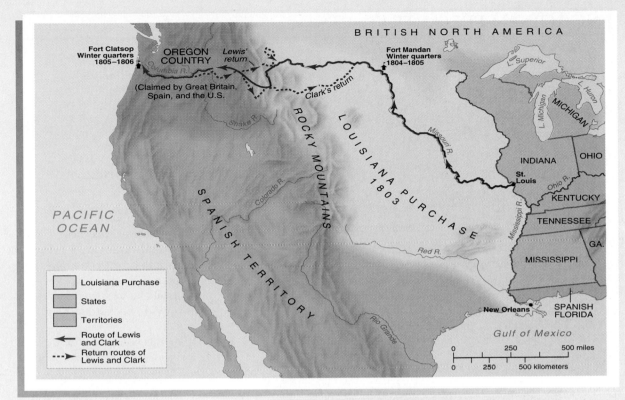

Lewis and Clark and the Louisiana Purchase

Extensive map and graphics program

The American Promise includes numerous four-color maps that provide a visual representation of historical data. Attractively designed tables, charts, and graphs throughout the book reinforce and expand on information in the text. An accompanying workbook — available free of charge with copies of the text — provides additional opportunities to expand on themes relating to the historical significance of geography using maps from the textbook.

(This map is found on page 354. Turn to page 567 for this graph.)

Resources of the Union and the Confederacy

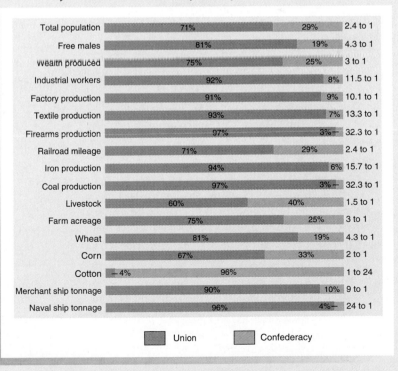

	Union	Confederacy	
Total population	71%	29%	2.4 to 1
Free males	81%	19%	4.3 to 1
Wealth produced	75%	25%	3 to 1
Industrial workers	92%	8%	11.5 to 1
Factory production	91%	9%	10.1 to 1
Textile production	93%	7%	13.3 to 1
Firearms production	97%	3%	32.3 to 1
Railroad mileage	71%	29%	2.4 to 1
Iron production	94%	6%	15.7 to 1
Coal production	97%	3%	32.3 to 1
Livestock	60%	40%	1.5 to 1
Farm acreage	75%	25%	3 to 1
Wheat	81%	19%	4.3 to 1
Corn	67%	33%	2 to 1
Cotton	4%	96%	1 to 24
Merchant ship tonnage	90%	10%	9 to 1
Naval ship tonnage	96%	4%	24 to 1

ENGAGING SPECIAL FEATURES

The narrative in *The American Promise* is augmented with three kinds of special features to highlight the kinds of evidence and issues that fascinate even the casual reader. Providing students a moment to pause in the great sweep of coverage, these documents and mini-essays allow a focus that is not possible within the main narrative.

TEXTS IN HISTORICAL CONTEXT

The Panic of 1837

The panic of 1837 brought fright and hysteria to city after city. Crowds of hundreds thronged the banks during the spring to get their money out. Business came to a standstill and many merchants appeared to be ruined overnight. Whig leaders were certain that the crisis could be traced to President Jackson's antibank and hard money policies, but others blamed it on what they saw as an immoral frenzy of greed and speculation that had gripped the nation for the preceding few years.

Harriet Martineau traveled throughout the United States and described booming land sales in the infant city of Chicago in 1836.

DOCUMENT 1. An English Visitor Describes the "Mania" for Speculation

I never saw a busier place than Chicago was at the time of our arrival. The streets were crowded with land speculators, hurrying from one sale to another. A negro, dressed up in scarlet, bearing a scarlet flag, and riding a white horse with housings of scarlet, announced the times of sale. At every street-corner where he stopped, the crowd flocked round him; and it seemed as if some prevalent mania infected the whole people. The rage for speculation might fairly be so regarded. As the gentlemen of our party walked the streets, store-keepers hailed them from

some reas[...]
of the lots[...]
risks from[...]
from othe[...]
profits, ur[...]
within so[...]
would ser[...]
of purchas[...]
on the ba[...]
was sellin[...]
improved[...]
Mohawk,[...]
is already[...]
amount of[...]
be the suf[...]
no one v[...]
unfortuna[...]
delusion,[...]
spirited, [...]
simple se[...]
knaves.

*Philip [...]
taste of [...]
failed in N[...]
term.*

Saturday,[...]
son's adn[...]

Texts in Historical Context

A variety of primary documents —letters, diaries, speeches, memoirs and testimony—bring students into direct contact with the human impact of major historical events and issues. Headnotes provide background and context.

(For this complete Texts in Historical Context, turn to pages 420–421.)

Historical Question

These interpretive essays address specific historical questions likely to be of intrinsic interest to students. Among the topics discussed are: How Could a Vice President Get Away With Murder?, and Why Did the Allies Refuse to Bomb the Death Camps? Historical Questions single out issues of ongoing interest, providing answers in greater detail than possible in the narrative.

(For this complete Historical Question, turn to pages 594–595.)

HISTORICAL QUESTION

Why Did So Many Soldiers Die?

FROM 1861 TO 1865, Americans killed Americans on a scale that had never before been seen. Not until the First World War, a half century later, would the world match (and surpass) the killing fields at Shiloh, Antietam, and Gettysburg. Why were the totals so appallingly large? Why did 260,000 rebel soldiers and 373,000 Union soldiers die in the Civil War?

The balance between the ability to kill and the ability to save lives had tipped disastrously toward death. The sheer size of the armies — some battles involved more than 200,000 soldiers — ensured that battlefields would turn red with blood. Moreover, armies fought with antiquated strategy. In the

casualty l
Confedera
with skirr
had no ar
the battle
liver ther
ment, w
Union ho
something
beds." It
compel re
that the S
and South
corps, bu
and nurse

Soldi
portation
As one U
tle than t
the lines.
vanced to
in the da

Technology in America

Recognizing that the impact of technologies is of particular interest and relevance today, these brief (150–300 words) illustrated essays examine the ramifications —positive and negative—of specific technological changes.

(For this complete Technology in America, turn to page 186.)

TECHNOLOGY IN AMERICA
The Printing Press

In the eighteenth century, colonial printers began to publish newspapers. Since the 1630s, printers had used presses much like the one shown here to churn out

in 1704 with the appearance of the *Bos*
usually printed on both sides of a sing
smaller than conventional typing pape
News-Letter contained reprints of articl
peared in English newspapers along w
of local news such as deaths, fires, stor
rivals. For years, the audience for such
mained small; the editor complained i
could not sell three hundred copies of
Nonetheless, a competing newspaper,
Gazette, began publication in that year.
by James Franklin on his press, showr
had brought from England. Both the *C*
News-Letter submitted their copy to the
official approval before the newspaper
Frustrated by this official scrutiny, Fra
new paper, the *New England Courant*, v
thumb its nose at officialdom, both go
religious. The *Courant* pledged "to ent
with the most comical and diverting l
mane Life" and to "expose the Vice ar
sons of all Ranks and Degrees." Frank
broadcast to the reading public dissen
that previously one had to hear (or ov
vate conversations. When the old tech
ing was used in fresh ways to publish
all kinds of information and ideas beg
more readily beyond official channels
public opinion. Eighteenth-century ne
bined old printing technology with th

INNOVATIVE APPENDICES

A three-part appendix serves as a convenient repository of important documents, historical data, and research resources. As with every other part of *The American Promise*, we have endeavored to enhance the usefulness of this critical material in new ways.

Documents

In addition to the complete texts of the Declaration of Independence and the Constitution, this section features unique annotations that provide appropriate background to the twenty-seven constitutional amendments—plus six that didn't make it into the final document.

(The annotated amendments are on pages A-10–A-23.)

Amendment IV

The right of the people to be secure in their persons, houses, papers, and effects, against unreasonable searches and seizures, shall not be violated, and no warrants shall issue but upon probable cause, supported by oath or affirmation, and particularly describing the place to be searched, and the persons or things to be seized.

◆ ◆ ◆

In the years before the Revolution, the houses, barns, stores, and warehouses of American colonists were ransacked by British authorities under "writs of assistance" or general warrants. The British, thus empowered, searched for seditious material or smuggled goods that could then be used as evidence against colonists who were charged with a crime only after the items were found.

Facts and Figures

This uniquely abundant collection of political, economic, and demographic information supplements the statistical data in the text on everything from population to education. It also includes summaries of twenty-four significant Supreme Court cases.

(For Facts and Figures, see pages A-24–A-26.)

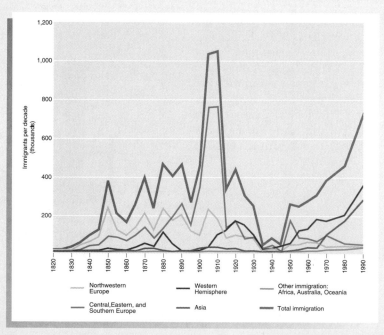

Research Resources in U.S. History

Located on pages A-67–A-69, this annotated list of reference materials and Internet offerings provides a handy starting point for research papers, with extensive suggestions for locating many kinds of primary and secondary sources.

American Memory: Historical Collection from the National Digital Library Program. <http://rs6.loc.gov/amhome.html> An Internet site that features digitized primary source materials from the Library of Congress, among them African American pamphlets, civil war photographs, documents from the Continental Congress and the Constitutional Convention of 1774–1790, materials on woman suffrage, and oral histories.

Directory of Scholarly and Professional Electronic Conferences. <http://n2h2.com/KOVAKS/>. A good place to find out what electronic conversations are going on in a scholarly discipline. Includes a good search facility and instructions on how to connect to e-mail discussion lists, newsgroups, and interactive chat sites with academic content. Once identified, these conferences are good places to raise questions, find out what controversies are currently

User-friendly Index

Knowing that students use indexes primarily as study aids, the index in *The American Promise* is designed to make people, events, topics, and concepts as easy to locate as possible. Page numbers for a topic's main coverage are indicated in boldface; entries for significant people and events include dates; listings of important images, maps, and graphics are provided; and cross-references highlight related subjects.

NOTE TO INSTRUCTORS

The American Promise is accompanied by an unusually full complement of ancillaries. Available for student purchase are a documents reader, a study guide, and titles from the Bedford Series in History and Culture. For teachers, we offer an instructor's manual, a testbank, a guide for teaching assistants, and a large transparency set that includes images not found in the text and a guide with teaching suggestions. Also available to be packaged free with the textbook is a two-volume map workbook with exercises based on maps drawn from every chapter in the text. For complete descriptions of each of these ancillaries, please refer to the Preface for Instructors.

PREFACE FOR INSTRUCTORS

We set out to write *The American Promise* because, as longtime teachers of the survey course, we felt that other texts simply didn't reflect what works in our classrooms. Most survey texts emphasize either a social or a political approach to history; by focusing on one, they inevitably slight the other. In our classrooms, students need *both* the structure a political narrative provides and the insights gained from examining social and cultural experiences. In our view, the story of politics is an account not merely of parties and presidents but also of the public arena in which issues of power, interest, culture, ideology, and identity are contested. In our effort to write a comprehensive account of American history, we have focused on the public arena—as the place where politics comes together with social and cultural events—to show how Americans lived within their political culture and confronted the major issues of their times.

We have worked to keep our writing clear, direct, and interesting, never losing sight of our obligation to engage our readers and offer them guidance. Because students in the introductory course often complain that they have difficulty figuring out what they need to know and why they need to know it, we deliberately avoided unnecessary detail so that we could offer more fully developed discussions of the major political, social, cultural, and economic changes that students should understand and remember when they've completed the course.

In our view, history is the story of human agency. To show students that history was made by *people*, we have included the voices of contemporaries who confronted the issues and events of their day. Every chapter includes numerous quotations from the famous and forgotten, taken from their journals, speeches, and letters. Vignettes open every chapter, spotlighting individuals like Benjamin Franklin, Frederick Douglass, and Jane Addams who worked for change in their day and whose efforts still affect our lives. More than a dozen document features demonstrate the impact of major historical events on individuals.

The American Promise also aims to demonstrate that history is both a body of knowledge and an ongoing process of investigation. Too many beginning students believe that historians simply gather facts and string them together into a chronological narrative: that what historians write, students must memorize. To show that the story of history is a reflection of questions historians consciously pose of the past, recurring interpretive essays illustrate how contemporary curiosity shapes historical inquiry and introduce students to a more textured understanding of the discipline.

Features

The narrative in *The American Promise* is buttressed by a number of features that address the concerns most frequently voiced by teachers: that students often find history boring and difficult. Every feature has been conceived and developed with one of these two elemental problems in mind.

We have tried to make American history as accessible as possible for students. In addition to stressing the most important historical developments, each chapter is clearly structured to reinforce the essential people, events, and themes of the period. Innovative **call-outs**—attention-grabbing passages pulled from the main narrative and set in larger type—help students focus. At the close of each chapter, **conclusions** summarize the main themes and events and provide a bridge to upcoming material, **chronologies** provide a handy review of significant events and dates, and extensive **bibliographies** provide an up-to-date listing of recommended works of scholarship for additional reading and research.

Because students learn more when they're interested in the subject matter, we've made a special effort to incorporate features that bring American history to life. **Chapter-opening vignettes** invite students into the narrative with a compelling account of a person or event that embodies some of the chapter's main themes. **Historical Questions** pose and investigate specific questions of continuing interest to demonstrate to students the depth and variety of possible answers. **Texts in Historical Context** reprint primary documents that illustrate the social impact of major events and issues, and **Technology in America** highlights the ramifications that new inventions and processes—most of which we now take for granted—had when they were introduced.

Finally, we are especially proud of our art program. The publisher has provided **an impressive collection of illustrations**—many of them never published before in a survey text—that supplement the narrative, drawing students in and encouraging them to engage the visual material. Rather than leave students to make what they can from these illustrations, we offer a lot of guidance. **Comprehensive captions** unpack the layers of meaning in the pictures, supplement the information in the chapter, raise questions that challenge students to use their historical imaginations, and help students view the images analytically.

Our title, *The American Promise*, reflects our conviction that American history is an unfinished story. From the beginning, Americans have differed profoundly over the meaning of the nation's promise. Yet few doubted that unusual opportunities beckoned in America. In many ways, these potential opportunities intensified conflict over the direction of change, as Americans sought to realize a measure of the promise they sensed around them. For millions, the nation held out the promise of a better life, unfettered worship, representative government, democratic politics, and other freedoms seldom found elsewhere on the globe. But none of these promises came with guarantees. And promises fulfilled for some meant promises denied to others. As we see it, much of American history is a continuing struggle over the definition and realization of the nation's promise. Abraham Lincoln, in the midst of what he termed the "fiery trial" of the Civil War, pronounced the nation "the last best hope of Earth." That hope, kept alive by countless sacrifices, has been marred by compromises, disappointments, and denials, but it lives still. Ideally, *The American Promise* will help students become aware of the legacy of hope bequeathed to them by previous generations of Americans stretching back nearly four centuries, a legacy that is theirs to preserve and to build upon.

Supplements

A comprehensive collection of supplements, every one of them created specifically to accompany *The American Promise*, provides an integrated support system for classroom success. All of the expected elements are included, but in every case we have tried to raise the bar a notch higher, adding new features to help instructors teach and students learn American history. We've also provided some new items: a guide for teaching assistants, an unusually full set of transparencies accompanied by teaching suggestions, and a map workbook that provides in-depth exercises on maps in the text.

For Students

Reading the American Past: Selected Historical Documents. This affordable two-volume collection of primary sources—selected and edited by Michael P. Johnson (Johns Hopkins University) specifically to accompany *The American Promise*—permits students to go beyond the textbook narrative and puzzle out the meanings of historical documents. Paralleling the organization of the text, each chapter includes substantial passages from several documents—including presidential speeches, court records, estate inventories, private diaries, personal letters, and oral histories. Each document is introduced by a brief headnote and followed by questions that help students understand both what the document says and what its historical significance is.

Making the Most of THE AMERICAN PROMISE: A Study Guide. This essential supplement for students, prepared by John Moretta and David Wilcox (both of Houston Community College), provides practice opportunities to reinforce the main themes and ideas from the text's narrative. For each chapter in *The American Promise*, a corresponding chapter in the study guide includes learning objectives, a brief summary, a timeline with questions on important dates, a glossary of terms, map exercises with location and analysis questions, multiple-choice questions, and essay questions. An answer key allows students to test themselves.

Mapping THE AMERICAN PROMISE: Historical Geography Workbook. Prepared by Mark Newman (University of Illinois, Chicago), this stand-alone supplement provides additional exercises using maps drawn from *The American Promise*. Because a knowledge of geography is crucial to understanding the way our country has grown over five hundred years, we make this supplement available to students free with the purchase of the text. Each exercise asks students to label landmarks on the American continent and then analyze the significance of geography in the unfolding of historical events.

Working to suggest the implications of geography for history, these exercises also reinforce basic place names in a way that helps students remember them and understand why they should.

The Bedford Series in History and Culture. Any of the volumes from this highly acclaimed series of brief, inexpensive, document-based supplements can be packaged with *The American Promise* at a reduced price. More than forty titles include *The Sovereignty and Goodness of God, The Interesting Narrative of the Life of Olaudah Equiano, The Autobiography of Benjamin Franklin, Narrative of the Life of Frederick Douglass, The Souls of Black Folk, Plunkitt of Tammany Hall,* and many more.

For Instructors

Teaching THE AMERICAN PROMISE: A Hands-On Guide for Instructors. Written by Michael Gagnon (Emory University) and Sarah E. Gardner (Mercer University), this practical two-volume guide provides myriad suggestions and resources for teaching *The American Promise.* Each of its thirty-two chapters includes an outline (in the form of questions) of the text's narrative, three lecture strategies, multiple-choice questions, a list of video and film resources, and suggestions for incorporating sources from *READING THE AMERICAN PAST* or from the Bedford Series in History and Culture. A particularly useful new feature for first-time teachers anticipates some of the most common misconceptions undergraduates have about each chapter's topics.

Testbank to Accompany THE AMERICAN PROMISE. Written by two longtime teachers of the American history survey, John Moretta and David Wilcox (both of Houston Community College), this set provides 70–80 multiple-choice, true/false, short-answer, identification, and essay questions for each of the thirty-two chapters in *The American Promise.* The testbank is available either on disk (Macintosh and Windows), with a function that allows users to customize the exams, or in booklet form.

Discussing THE AMERICAN PROMISE: A Survival Guide for First-Time Teaching Assistants. Tied directly to *The American Promise,* this unique resource provides a wealth of practical suggestions to help first-time teaching assistants develop their skills and succeed in the classroom. Written by experienced TA adviser Michael A. Bellesiles (Emory University), this brief supplement offers concrete advice on teaching from *The American Promise,* working with professors, dealing with difficult students, running discussion sections, designing assignments, grading tests and papers, relating research to classroom experience, overcoming common problems, and more.

Transparencies to Accompany THE AMERICAN PROMISE (with Teaching Suggestions). More than 150 images are available as full-color acetates to adopters of *The American Promise.* For each chapter a set of five transparencies has been assembled to highlight the chapter-opening artifacts, important maps and graphs, and striking illustrations. We have also selected additional illustrations that are not included in the text. To assist teachers in presenting these images, a guide provides background and elaborates on teaching possibilities.

Acknowledgments

We owe a great debt to the community of scholars who took time away from their own teaching and research to help us complete *The American Promise*. Many people have read chapters and offered valuable criticism; others have listened patiently and provided important advice. The authors would like to express their gratitude to:

Katherine G. Aiken, University of Idaho
Todd Beekley
Kathleen Christine Berkeley, University of North Carolina—Wilmington
John C. Burnham, The Ohio State University
Vernon Burton, University of Illinois, Urbana
Victoria Byerly
Victor Chen
Peter Coclanis, University of North Carolina at Chapel Hill
Joseph Cugini
Leonard Dinnerstein, University of Arizona, Tucson
Laura F. Edwards, University of South Florida
Joseph J. Ellis, Mount Holyoke College
Lancelot Farrar
Elizabeth Feder, Rhodes College
Dan Feller, University of New Mexico
Alan Gallay, Western Washington University
Mark Gelfand, Boston College
William Graebner, State University of New York, Buffalo at Fredonia
Michael D. Green, University of Kentucky
Jack Greene, Johns Hopkins University
Thomas Hartshorne, Cleveland State University
Ronald Howard, Mississippi College
George Juergens, Indiana University
Wilma King, Michigan State University
Barbara Loomis, San Francisco State University
George McJimsey, Iowa State University
Melinda McMahon, University of California, Santa Barbara
John Moon, Fitchburg State University
Roger L. Nichols, University of Arizona, Tucson
Donald K. Pickens, University of North Texas
John O. Pohlman
Theda Perdue, University of Kentucky
David Rankin, University of California, Irvine
Herbert Rissler, Indiana State University
Dave Roediger, University of Minnesota
Carole Srole, California State University, Los Angeles
Thomas Terrill, University of South Carolina
Daniel H. Usner, Jr., Cornell University

A project as large and as complex as this requires the talents of many individuals. The authors would like to thank Pembroke Herbert and Sandi Rygiel of Picture Research Consultants, Inc., whose research and imagination are responsible for the fine illustrations. Thanks are also due to Barbara Muller, whose accomplished editing and sage advice improved volume 1 in countless ways, and to Lynne Weiss for her extensive work on the appendix materials. Michael Gagnon of Emory University and Sarah Gardner of Mercer University drew deeply on their own experience to write the Instructor's Manual, and Michael Bellesiles of Emory University turned his talents to the TA guide. John Moretta and David Wilcox of Houston Community College combined their skills to produce the study guide and testbank. Mark Newman of the University of Illinois at Chicago developed the very useful map workbook. Thanks also to Gerry McCauley, who represents us as literary agent.

Finally, we would like to thank the many people at Bedford Books who have been crucial to this project. We are grateful to Katherine Kurzman and to Ellen Kuhl for their tireless efforts marketing the book, and to Charisse Kiino, who worked on the ancillary program. No one has carried more of the burden than our editor, Louise Townsend. Her skill, composure, and endurance brought the project from an incomplete draft to a finished work. With great skill and professionalism, Tina Samaha, our project manager, pulled all the pieces together. She kept her head when the rest of us were in danger of losing ours. Managing Editor Elizabeth Schaaf oversaw production of the book, while Ellen Thibault, Deborah Baker, and Thomas Pierce helped out on myriad editorial tasks. Copyeditor Barbara Flanagan's sharp eye improved our best efforts and made the entire book better. Charles Christensen, publisher, and Joan Feinberg, general manager, have taken a personal interest in this project from the first and have guided it through every stage of development.

THE
AMERICAN
PROMISE

A HISTORY OF THE UNITED STATES

SALADO RITUAL FIGURES

About 1350 — more than a century before Columbus arrived in the New World — these figures were carefully wrapped in the reed mat (shown in the back, on the right) and stored in a cave in a mountainous region of New Mexico by people of the Salado culture, descendants of the Mimbres, who had flourished three centuries earlier. Presumably used for sacred rituals, the effigies suggest the place of humans in the cosmos, where snakes inhabit the subterranean world, mountain lions roam the earth, and birds soar across the sky. The haunting human figures display the high artistry of ancient Americans. Adorned with vivid pigments, cotton string, bright feathers, and stones, the effigies hint at the objects the Salado and other ancient Americans used and valued in their daily lives.

The Art Institute of Chicago.

ANCIENT AMERICA
Before 1492

1

GEORGE MCJUNKIN WAS AN AFRICAN AMERICAN COWBOY who worked on a ranch near Folsom, New Mexico. Born a slave in Texas in 1851, McJunkin grew up around cowboys. The name and identity of his mother are unknown, although she must have been a slave. His father was a free black man who worked as a blacksmith; his white customers called him Shoeboy because he shoed their horses, but his real name is unknown. The younger McJunkin learned to ride wild horses as a boy and soon after he obtained his freedom in 1865 at the end of the Civil War, he worked at ranches in Colorado and New Mexico. In 1891, he became manager of the Crowfoot Ranch outside Folsom.

In August 1908, a violent storm ripped through Folsom and the surrounding countryside, causing a devastating flood. After the flood subsided, McJunkin rode out to mend fences and to look for cattle that had been killed or injured. As he rode along he noticed that the floodwaters had gouged a dry gulch named Wild Horse Arroyo eight or nine feet deeper than he had ever seen it. As he glanced around for signs of missing cattle, he noticed a deposit of stark white bones in the bank of the arroyo, about ten feet below the surface. Curious, he dismounted and chipped away at the deposit with heavy wire cutters. He continued to scrape until he had exposed an entire fossilized bone. McJunkin had seen the parched skeletons of many range cattle and buffalo in his day, but this bone fossil was far larger than those. He strapped the fossil to his saddle and took it back to his room at the ranch.

Over the next few years, McJunkin kept an eye on what he called the "Bone Pit" in Wild Horse Arroyo. He showed the huge bone he had excavated to his cowboy friends, but they had little interest in strange fossils. In 1912, McJunkin met Carl Schwachheim, a white blacksmith in Raton, New Mexico, who shared his curiosity about fossils. McJunkin told Schwachheim about the Bone Pit, but since Schwachheim had little free time and neither a horse nor a car, he could not get out to the Crowfoot Ranch to take a look for himself. When McJunkin died in 1922, Schwachheim had not yet seen the Bone Pit. A few months after McJunkin's death, Schwachheim organized an expedition to the Bone Pit. With some friends, one of whom had a car, Schwachheim went out to Wild Horse Arroyo, dug out enough bones to fill a gunnysack, and brought them back to Raton, where he and his friends examined them and argued about them. But they could not identify the animals the bones had come from.

Four years later, Schwachheim had a job delivering some cattle to the stockyards in Denver, and he carried along some of the old bones. He took them to the Denver Museum of Natural History and showed them to J. D. Figgins, a paleontologist who was an expert on fossils of ancient animals. Figgins immediately recognized the significance of the bones and a few months later began an excavation of the Folsom Bone Pit. He then hired Schwachheim to do much of the digging. In

GEORGE MCJUNKIN
This photo of McJunkin was taken a few years after he discovered the Folsom site, but about fifteen years before the significance of his discovery was understood by anyone. He appears here on horseback in his work clothes, as he probably was when he made the discovery. The fossilized bones he discovered belonged to an extinct bison species that was much larger than modern bison; the horns of the ancient animal often spanned six feet, wide enough for McJunkin's horse to have stood sideways, as it appears in the photo, between the tips of the horns.
Eastern New Mexico University, Blackwater Draw Site, Portales, New Mexico 88130.

the course of the excavation, Figgins and his associates revolutionized knowledge about the first Americans.

When Figgins began his dig at the Folsom site, archaeologists (individuals who study the artifacts of prehistoric peoples) believed that Native Americans had arrived relatively recently in the Western Hemisphere, probably no more than three or four thousand years earlier when, the experts assumed, they had crossed the icy waters of the Bering Strait from what is now Russia in small boats. Although plenty of evidence of ancient American civilizations existed in the enormous burial mounds east of the Mississippi and in the pueblos of the Southwest, few Americans saw a connection between these structures and those of contemporary Native Americans. Instead, scholars attributed the ancient ruins to people who had mysteriously vanished long before the appearance of contemporary Indians. Despite the abundant physical evidence of ancient human habitation, a general consensus existed that Indians were recent arrivals in the New World. This conventional wisdom had to be tossed on the aca-

demic trash heap once the Folsom discoveries came to light.

At Folsom, Figgins found the bones of twenty-three giant bison, a species known to have been extinct for at least 10,000 years. McJunkin had been right that these were no ordinary, modern-day buffalo bones. Far more startling were nineteen flint projectile points (Folsom points, they have since been called) associated with the bones, proof that human beings had been alive at the same time as the giant bison. Skeptics claimed that earth slides, water, or some other natural process might have accidentally pushed the man-made flint points into the vicinity of the fossils. But even skeptics were convinced by the discovery of one flint point firmly stuck between two rib bones of a giant bison, just where a Stone Age hunter had plunged it more than 10,000 years earlier. No longer could anyone doubt that human beings had inhabited the New World for at least ten millennia.

Through their curiosity and perseverance, George McJunkin, Carl Schwachheim, and J. D. Figgins rediscovered the first Americans more than four hundred years after Columbus had arrived and thousands of years after the continent was first inhabited by humans. The Folsom discovery sparked other major finds of ancient artifacts, pushing back the date of arrival of the first Americans. The artifacts make clear that 95 percent of human history in America occurred before the arrival of Columbus. Since the 1930s, scholars have tried to piece together this history, making connections between the hunters who killed giant bison with flint points, their descendants who built southwestern pueblos and eastern burial mounds, and *their* descendants among the Native Americans who live throughout the Western Hemisphere today.

Unlike Columbus and the European settlers who followed him after 1492, the first Americans did not leave written accounts of their discovery and settlement of the Western Hemisphere. Their encounters with the New World occurred long before recorded history. No documents preserve their languages or their names. No letters or poems describe their thoughts or emotions. But millions of artifacts survive that document their creativity and artistry. Clever and resourceful archaeologists have tried to reconstruct as much of the history of ancient Americans as can be gleaned from the artifacts. Instead of reading words in documents written by persons in the past—as historians normally do—archaeologists try to decipher the meaning of the ruins, garbage dumps, mummified skeletons, baskets, pots, stone blades, charred bones, and other remains left by prehistoric peoples. The story they have assembled is, of course, incomplete. Mysteries abound. Most artifacts that scholars would like to study rotted away millennia ago. Even the artifacts that have survived the millennia can be interpreted in different ways. Consequently, much of what is known about ancient America remains controversial. Nonetheless, scholars have learned enough about ancient Americans to bring into focus who they were, where they came from, and some of the most important features of their history in the thousands of years that stretched between their arrival in the New World and that moment in 1492 when Columbus stepped ashore on a small island in the Caribbean.

FOLSOM POINT AT WILD HORSE ARROYO
In 1927, paleontologist J.D. Figgins found this spear point (subsequently named a Folsom point) at the site discovered by George McJunkin. Embedded between the fossilized ribs of a bison that had been extinct for ten thousand years, this point proved that ancient Americans had inhabited the hemisphere at least that long. The importance of this find led one paleontologist to hold up several Folsom points and proclaim, "In my hand I hold the answer to the antiquity of man in America." Although he exaggerated (since Folsom was only part of the answer), the Folsom discovery stimulated archaeologists to rethink the history of ancient Americans and to uncover fresh evidence of their many cultures.

The First Americans

Human beings existed elsewhere in the world long before they reached the Western Hemisphere. The first human beings *(Homo erectus)* evolved in Africa about 1.5 million years ago. Modern humans *(Homo sapiens)* appeared later still, within the last 350,000 years. Archaeologists have found fossil remains of these ancient humans in Africa, Europe, and Asia, but not in America. For hundreds of thousands of years after human beings inhabited the rest of the

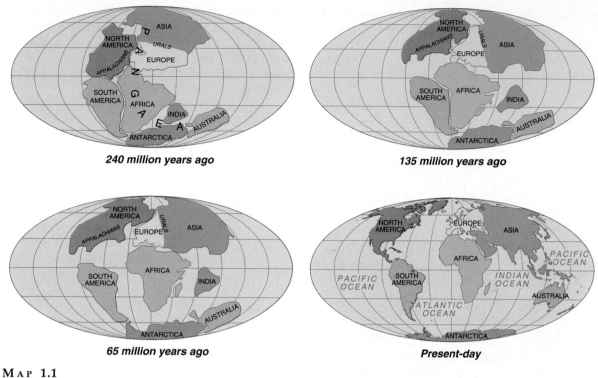

240 million years ago

135 million years ago

65 million years ago

Present-day

MAP 1.1
Continental Drift
Massive geological forces separated North and South America from other continents eons before human beings evolved in Africa in the last 1.5 million years. This continental drift explains why human life developed elsewhere on the planet for hundreds of thousands of years before the first person entered the Western Hemisphere during the last fifteen thousand years.

earth, the New World remained untouched by humankind.

The basic reason for the absence of human life from the Western Hemisphere for such a long time is that millions of years before human beings came into existence the American landmass became detached from Africa, Europe, and Asia. About 240 million years ago, North and South America were attached to Europe, Asia, and Africa in a gigantic continent scientists now call Pangaea. Slowly over the next 150 million years, powerful forces deep within the earth pushed the continents apart to approximately their present positions. This process of continental drift encircled the land of the Western Hemisphere with large oceans and isolated it from the other continents. Over 100 million years after continental drift had disrupted Pangaea, human beings evolved in Africa and eventually migrated throughout Europe and Asia. For almost 95 percent of the time *Homo sapiens* have existed on the face of the globe, no one set foot in America.

Asian Origins

Two major developments made it possible for human beings to migrate to the Western Hemisphere. The first development was humans' successful adaptation to the frigid environment near the Arctic Circle. The second was a change in the earth's climate that reconnected the land of the New World to that of the Old World.

By about 25,000 years ago, humans had learned to use bone needles to sew animal skins into warm clothing similar to that still worn by Eskimos. These snug garments permitted humans to become permanent residents of extremely cold regions like northeastern Siberia. Today the Bering Strait, a body of water about sixty miles wide, separates easternmost Siberia from westernmost Alaska. In the dead of winter the strait freezes, and a person can sometimes make the hazardous journey across the ice. Conditions now, however, are much different than they were when humans first came to America.

We live in a relatively warm period of the earth's climatic history. The last great cold spell—which scientists call the Wisconsin glaciation—endured from about 80,000 years ago to about 10,000 years ago. The colder temperatures during this era meant that snow piled up in glaciers that did not melt and release water back into the sea; the glaciers grew and the sea level dropped as much as 350 feet below its current level. When that happened, the seafloor that is now submerged 120 feet below the surface of the Bering Strait became dry land. It formed what is often called a "land bridge" between Asian Siberia and American Alaska. The word *bridge,* however, is misleading. The exposed land was not a narrow passageway. Instead, it was more like a small continent about a thousand miles wide, roughly the distance from New Orleans to Minneapolis. Scientists refer to it as Beringia.

There is abundant evidence that the first Americans were nomadic hunters whose primary source of food was the meat of large mammals that grazed on the tundra in the interior of Beringia. Their Asian origins seem beyond dispute.

Periodically, Beringia sank beneath the waves when the globe experienced a warm snap for a few thousand years and the glaciers began to melt. But for most of the Wisconsin glacial period, Beringia stood above sea level. Because it received little snow, it had few glaciers. Grasses and small shrubs covered much of the land and supported herds of mammoth, bison, and horses. Smaller animals like seals, birds, and fish could also be found.

Siberian hunters presumably roamed into Beringia for thousands of years in search of game animals, especially mammoths. Some may have hopscotched along the southern coast of Beringia in small boats, establishing settlements and living off fish, waterfowl, and sea mammals until they reached the shores of Alaska, Canada, and the Pacific Northwest. No conclusive evidence has been found of such a seaborne migration of the first Americans. If it occurred, the traces of it have been submerged since the end of the Wisconsin period about 10,000 years ago when glaciers melted and Beringia once again disappeared beneath the sea, where it has remained ever since.

There is abundant evidence, however, that the first Americans were nomadic hunters whose primary source of food was the meat of large mammals that grazed on the tundra in the interior of Beringia. Archaeologists speculate that hunters trekked around Beringia in small bands of perhaps twenty-five people. How many such bands arrived in the New World before water once again covered Beringia will never be known. It may have been as few as one or two or three. When they arrived in the Western Hemisphere is hotly debated by ex-

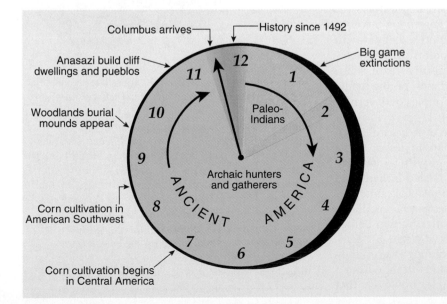

FIGURE 1.1
Human Habitation of the Western Hemisphere
This clock face illustrates the long history of ancient Americans. If the total period of human life in the New World is converted from millenia to a twelve-hour clock, then all history since Columbus occupies only the last half-hour. Ancient American history makes up the first eleven and a half hours.

perts. It is safe to say that the first migrants arrived sometime after 15,000 years ago. Several tantalizing discoveries hint at earlier dates, but professional archaeologists strongly disagree about how to interpret these finds. None disagree that by 12,000 years ago—and possibly earlier—after human life had existed for hundreds of thousands of years, human beings had finally come to America.

The precise identity of these people can never be known. Archaeologists refer to them and their descendants for the next few millennia as Paleo-Indians. Their Asian origins seem beyond dispute. Siberians hunted large mammals such as mammoths, and Beringia provided a mammoth-hunting ground that reached all the way to the Western Hemisphere, a wide avenue that existed for no other humans at the time. Furthermore, Native Americans today still share certain obvious physical characteristics of Asians, including straight black hair, light brown skin, relatively sparse facial and body hair, and incisor teeth that often have shovel-shaped indentations on their inner surface. Detailed analyses of Native American languages and of certain blood proteins provide additional compelling evidence of Asian origins.

Paleo-Indian Mammoth Hunters

When the first humans arrived in Alaska, massive glaciers covered most of Canada. A narrow corridor not entirely obstructed by ice ran along the eastern side of the Canadian Rockies, and most archaeologists believe that Paleo-Indians filtered through it fairly quickly in pursuit of mammoths. At the southern edge of the massive glaciers, Paleo-Indians entered a hunters' paradise. The enormous territory of North, Central, and South America teemed with wildlife that had never before confronted wily two-legged predators armed with deadly, razor-sharp spears. Presumably, the abundance of big game made hunting relatively easy. Ample food permitted the Paleo-Indian population to grow in numbers, perhaps more rapidly than ever before. Good hunting also allowed Paleo-Indians to diffuse to the outermost limits of the hemisphere with remarkable speed. Within a thousand years, Paleo-Indians had reached the southern tip of South America and virtually everywhere else in the Western Hemisphere.

It may seem unlikely that after human beings had failed to migrate to the New World for hundreds of thousands of years, once they arrived they rushed from coast to coast, top to bottom, within a thousand years. Experts estimate, however, that

even if only one band of twenty-five people crossed Beringia to the Western Hemisphere, their descendants could have numbered about a million within 350 years—an assumption that an abundance of food makes feasible. Since the actual population of Paleo-Indians in the entire hemisphere probably never exceeded one million, a thousand years was plenty of time for descendants of the original migrants to be born in sufficient numbers. Likewise, the descendants did not have to sprint to spread throughout the hemisphere in a millennium; instead, they needed to migrate fewer than twenty miles a year, a speed consistent with the assumption that they moved to maintain contact with animals who had seldom or never seen a hunter.

Paleo-Indians used a distinctively shaped spearhead known as a Clovis point, named for the place in New Mexico where it was first excavated. The discovery of Clovis points throughout North

CLOVIS POINTS
These Clovis points were found in a fossilized mammoth carcass discovered at Naco, Arizona. The large number of points hints that the mammoth may have escaped from its hunters, who then failed to recover their points when the animal died. Although the points are different sizes, note the similarity in shape and workmanship, the telltale characteristics of Clovis points. Contrast these points with the smaller, more finely worked Folsom point (page 5). The size of the Clovis points also suggests the danger Paleo-Indian hunters encountered when they attacked a mammoth, using weapons tipped with these small flakes of stone against an animal almost as big as a modern African elephant.
Arizona State Museum/University of Arizona.

and Central America in sites dated between 11,500 and 11,000 years ago (9500–9000 B.C.) is powerful evidence that these nomadic hunters shared a common ancestry and way of life. Clovis hunters probably staked out a watering hole, watched for an opportunity to isolate a mammoth from a herd, and then attacked it by repeatedly stabbing their spears into the animal. The hunters probably also used a spear-thrower, called an atlatl, to hurl their spears with greater force and over a longer distance. A Clovis point probably was fastened to a tip (called a foreshaft) that detached from the spear shaft inside the animal, so that the hunter could withdraw the spear shaft and reload it with another pointed foreshaft to defend against the wounded animal and inflict another wound. Typically, an excavation of a Clovis mammoth kill uncovers one or two points, suggesting that the hunters worked in small groups of two or three. One mammoth carcass discovered in Arizona, however, has eight Clovis points, suggesting a larger hunting group and—evidently—a very tough mammoth.

The Paleo-Indians who used Clovis points to kill big animals probably also hunted smaller animals, but the artifacts that have survived the millennia indicate that they specialized in big mammals. One mammoth kill, for example, supplied meat for weeks or, if dried, for months. In addition, the hide could be used for clothing and shelter. Bones and tusks could be used to erect a framework for small, hide-covered dwellings, fashioned into a variety of useful tools, or even burned for fuel. Fatty deposits and internal organs that were not eaten could become fuel for cooking or for lamps.

About 11,000 years ago (9000 B.C.) Paleo-Indians confronted a major crisis. The big-game animals they hunted for food became extinct. Throughout the hemisphere, mammoths and other large mammals disappeared, along with certain species that preyed on them, such as saber-toothed tigers. Scientists are not completely certain why the extinction occurred, although the changing environment probably was the trigger. About this time the earth began to warm, the Wisconsin glacial period came to an end, glaciers melted, and sea levels rose. Large mammals became extinct presumably because they had difficulty adapting to the warmer climate. Many archaeologists also believe that Paleo-Indian hunters contributed to the New World extinctions by killing animals more rapidly than they could reproduce.

Paleo-Indians adapted to the extinctions by making at least two important changes in their way of life. First, throughout the hemisphere hunters focused their attention on smaller animals that did not become extinct. Second, Paleo-Indians also devoted more energy to foraging, that is, to collecting wild plant foods such as roots, seeds, nuts, berries, and fruits. When Paleo-Indians made these changes, the apparent uniformity of the mammoth-oriented Clovis culture* was replaced by great cultural diversity. Clovis points disappear from the archaeological record about the time of the extinctions. When hunters had to survive by gathering plant foods and by killing many small animals instead of a few big ones, they adapted to the natural environments throughout the hemisphere. The immense variety of natural settings—from icy tundra to steamy jungles—meant that remarkably diverse cultures came into existence. Compelling evidence of these adaptations to local environments is that after about 11,000 years ago, archaeological artifacts display great variety rather than Clovis-like uniformity.

About 11,000 years ago (9000 B.C.) Paleo-Indians confronted a major crisis. The big-game animals they hunted for food became extinct.

Post-Clovis adaptations to local environments were the origins of the astounding variety of Native American cultures that existed when Columbus arrived in 1492. By then, adaptations that had occurred for more than ten millennia caused tribes to differ from each other in languages, customs, religions, and ways of life. In 1492, more than three hundred major tribes and hundreds of lesser groups inhabited North America alone; hundreds more lived in Central and South America. Tribes spoke different languages, practiced different religions, lived in different dwellings, followed different subsistence strategies, and observed different rules of

---

*The word *culture* is used here as an all-encompassing term that connotes what is commonly called "way of life." It refers not only to how a group of people supplied themselves with food and shelter but also to their family relationships, social groupings, religious ideas, and every other feature of their way of life. In most cases—as for the Clovis people—more is known about food or shelter than about other features of prehistoric cultures because of the artifacts that have survived. Ancient Americans' ideas, assumptions, hopes, dreams, and fantasies were undoubtedly important, but we know little or nothing about them.

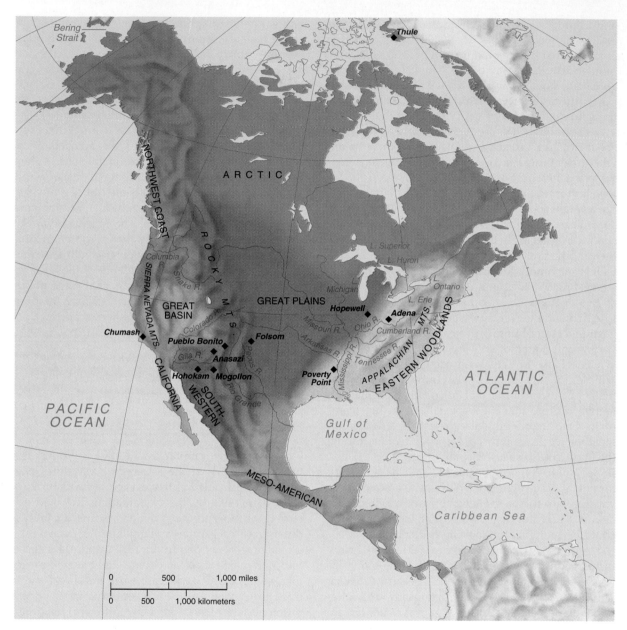

MAP 1.2
Native North American Cultures
Environmental conditions defined the boundaries of the broad zones of cultural similarity among
ancient North Americans. Using the map, try to specify the crucial environmental features that
set the boundaries of each cultural region. The topography indicated on Map 1.3,
"Native North Americans about 1500," may be helpful.

kinship and inheritance. During the long millennia that stretched between the end of the Wisconsin glacial period and the arrival of Columbus, hundreds of other ancient American cultures disappeared or transformed themselves as their members constantly adapted to changing environmental conditions.

A full account of those changes and the cultural diversity they created is beyond the scope of this introductory textbook of United States history. But we cannot ignore the most important changes and adaptations made by ancient Americans in the centuries between 9000 B.C. (that is, 11,000 years ago) and A.D. 1492. Any such survey necessarily oversimplifies the amazing variety of human experience in ancient America. The absence of written records makes it impossible to identify the individuals or groups responsible for the changes that occurred and makes oversimplification of complex changes unavoidable. Nonetheless, the remarkable human creativity demonstrated by the variety and longevity of ancient American cultures makes it far preferable to oversimplify their history than to overlook it.

Archaic Hunters and Gatherers

Archaeologists use the term *Archaic* to describe the many different hunting and gathering cultures that descended from Paleo-Indians. *Archaic* is a somewhat confusing term because it is used to describe both this great variety of cultures as well as the long period of time when those cultures dominated the history of ancient America, roughly from 8000 B.C. to somewhere between 2000 and 1000 B.C. Neither the cultural nor the chronological boundaries of the Archaic are sharply defined. Great Plains bison hunters, for example, did some foraging, but unlike most other Archaic peoples, they depended primarily on big-game hunting. Bison hunters and other Archaic cultures, especially those west of the Rocky Mountains, continued to thrive long after 1000 B.C. and even long after A.D. 1492. The term *Archaic* is nonetheless useful. It describes the important era in the history of ancient America that followed the Paleo-Indian mammoth hunters and preceded the development of agriculture. It also denotes a hunter-

gatherer way of life that persisted throughout most of North America during these millennia and well into the era of European settlement.

The term Archaic *describes the important era in the history of ancient America that followed the Paleo-Indian mammoth hunters and preceded the development of agriculture.*

Like their Paleo-Indian ancestors, Archaic Indians hunted with spears; but they also took smaller game with traps, nets, and hooks. Unlike Paleo-Indians, most Archaic peoples used a variety of stone tools to prepare food from wild plants; a characteristic Archaic artifact is a grinding stone used to pulverize seeds of wild plants into edible form. Most Archaic Indians migrated from place to place. The availability of plants to harvest appears to have played a larger part in their movements than access to animals to hunt. Migrating with the seasons, they usually did not establish permanent villages, although they often returned to the same river valley or fertile meadow from year to year to take advantage of abundant food resources. In certain regions where resources were especially rich—such as California and the Pacific Northwest—permanent settlements developed. Some Archaic cultures also built large mounds of earth and performed elaborate burial rituals. Many Archaic groups became highly proficient basket makers, but few made pottery. Above all, Archaic folk did not depend on agriculture for food. Instead of growing food crops, they gathered wild plants and hunted wild animals. These general traits of Archaic peoples appeared in various distinctive ways in the major environmental regions of North America.

Great Plains Bison Hunters

Big-game hunting did not end with the extinction of mammoths. Instead, Paleo-Indian hunters began to concentrate on bison. Huge herds of bison survived the post-glaciation extinctions. They grazed the grassy, arid plains that stretched for hundreds of miles east of the Rocky Mountains. For almost a thousand years after 9000 B.C., Paleo-Indians hunted bison with Folsom points (named for the site of the discoveries made by George McJunkin).

BISON KILL SITE

About eighty-five hundred years ago at this kill site near Kit Carson, Colorado, hunters stampeded a bison herd into an arroyo. By carefully studying the jumbled animal bones, archaeologists have been able to reconstruct numerous details about the hunt. Many of the carcasses lay where the animals fell, facing south, suggesting that the wind blew from the south on the day of the hunt, as the hunters stayed downwind and maneuvered the herd toward the arroyo. Cooperation among the hunters was necessary for the stampede and for the subsequent heavy labor of butchering. In all, the hunters butchered about three-fourths of these bison, feasting on bison tongues as they worked. From this hunt they obtained many valuable hides and enough meat to sustain more than one hundred people for at least a month.

Joe Ben Wheat photo, University of Colorado Museum.

Like their predecessors, Folsom hunters were nomads who moved constantly to maintain contact with their prey. Often two or three hunters from a band of several families would single out a few bison from a herd and creep up close enough to spear them. Always the hunters were on foot. The ancient horses that had once existed in the New World were extinct; from 9000 B.C. to after A.D. 1500, bison hunters walked to work. They developed techniques of trapping that made it easier to kill groups of bison. At the original Folsom site, careful study of the bones McJunkin found suggests that early one winter hunters drove bison into the arroyo and speared twenty-three of them. Most likely such kills involved cooperation by hunters from several bands. At many other sites, hunters stampeded large numbers of bison over a cliff, killing some and injuring others, which could then be readily dispatched by waiting hunters. At the well-named Head-Smashed-In site in Alberta, Canada, hunters carefully piled up stone markers to maneuver a bison herd slowly along the five-mile path toward the deadly jump-off point. Deep deposits of bison bones at the base of the Head-Smashed-In cliff demonstrate that hunters returned to the site repeatedly for more than 7,000 years.

Each band of hunters most likely included at least one shaman, who could enter a trance and communicate with the supernatural spirit world. Shamans used their powers to treat the sick, predict events, and aid hunters by appeasing or enticing animal spirits. At one kill site in Colorado, an archaeologist discovered an antler flute and other artifacts near the location of a posthole that may have held a perch for a shaman whose supernatural powers attracted bison to the kill. This interpretation is plausible because 10,000 years later Europeans observed Plains Indian shamans perched on poles and playing flutes to whistle bison toward their deaths.

Bows and arrows reached the Great Plains by A.D. 550 and largely replaced spears, which had been the hunters' weapon for more than 10,000 years. Bows permitted hunters to strike an animal from farther away, and arrows made it easy to shoot repeatedly. Also, arrow points could be crafted from stone that was more readily available than the stones required to make the larger, stronger spear points. These new weapons did not much alter the age-old techniques of bison hunting that had been developing since the Folsom era. The bison-hunting tradition continued on the Great Plains until long after the arrival of Columbus. The bison hunters were perhaps the clearest example of the continuity between the Paleo-Indians who first inhabited the continent and the numerous Native American peoples in A.D. 1492.

Great Basin Cultures

Archaic peoples in the Great Basin between the Rocky Mountains on the east and the Sierra Nevada on the west inhabited a region of great environmental diversity. During wet periods, large marshes and lakes formed in low-lying areas and many Great Basin Indians lived along the shores. Other cultures survived in the foothills of mountains, a zone between the arid, blistering heat on the desert floor and the cold, rocky, treeless mountain heights. These broadly defined zones of habitation changed constantly depending largely on the amount of rainfall. Archaic cultures in the Great Basin had to adapt to the diverse and changeable environment and be prepared for rapid and unpredictable fluctuations in the availability of food.

Much of the information about Great Basin cultures has come from cave sites, particularly in Utah, that have remained extremely dry for thousands of years. The dry conditions preserved numerous fragile artifacts that rotted away in the wetter climates prevailing elsewhere in North America. In addition,

GREAT BASIN DUCK DECOYS
These decoys were crafted about two to three thousand years ago by observant ancient Americans who resided in the Great Basin. Discovered in a cave in the arid environment of west-central Nevada, the decoys show that the ancient Great Basin environment was sometimes marshy. The decoys, skillfully constructed of shoreline plants, were presumably used to attract waterfowl toward hunters hiding among reeds in what amounted to an ancient duck blind.
Courtesy of the National Museum of the American Indian, Smithsonian Institution.

the arid climate of the caves preserved thousands of human coprolites (the dried remains of human feces), from which archaeologists can reconstruct with great accuracy what Great Basin Indians ate.

Despite the variety and occasional abundance of animals, plants were the most important source of food for Great Basin Archaic cultures.

Hunters took deer, antelope, and sometimes bison, as well as smaller game like rabbits, rodents, and snakes. Some cultures used brush fires to drive animals toward a net or into a dead end where they were easily captured. They set traps and snares made from twisted plant fibers for unwary game. At sites near water, Great Basin peoples hunted waterfowl with well-crafted decoys made of reeds. When unsuspecting ducks approached a group of decoys, lurking hunters grabbed their feet underwater or tossed a net over them before they could fly away. These people also ate fish of every available size and type, taking them with bone hooks as well as with nets.

Despite the variety and occasional abundance of animals, plants were the most important source of food for Great Basin Archaic cultures. Unlike animal food, plant food could be collected in large quantities in years of abundance and then stored in baskets for long periods to protect against shortages caused by the fickle rainfall. Baskets for food gathering and storage appear in Great Basin sites well before 7000 B.C. Piñon nuts became a dietary staple for many Great Basin peoples. Great Basin sites typically include grinding stones used to pulverize wild seeds into a coarse flour. By diversifying their food sources and migrating to favorable locations, Great Basin peoples adapted to environmental challenges and maintained their basic hunter-gatherer way of life until long after A.D. 1492.

Pacific Coast Cultures

The distinctive Archaic cultures along the Pacific coast—from southern California to the Pacific Northwest—adapted to an enormously rich marine environment. The abundance of fish, shellfish, and marine mammals such as seals, sea lions, sea otters, and whales supported comparatively large and long-lived settlements.

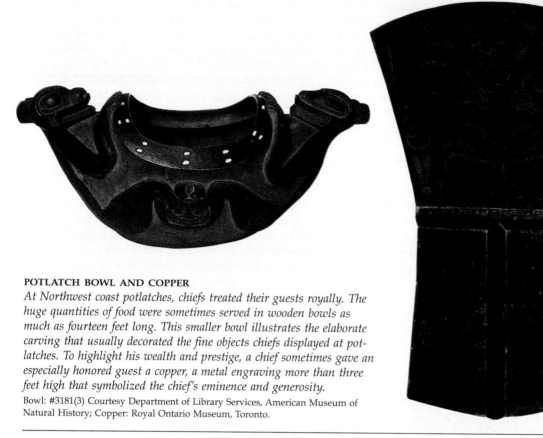

POTLATCH BOWL AND COPPER
At Northwest coast potlatches, chiefs treated their guests royally. The huge quantities of food were sometimes served in wooden bowls as much as fourteen feet long. This smaller bowl illustrates the elaborate carving that usually decorated the fine objects chiefs displayed at potlatches. To highlight his wealth and prestige, a chief sometimes gave an especially honored guest a copper, a metal engraving more than three feet high that symbolized the chief's eminence and generosity.
Bowl: #3181(3) Courtesy Department of Library Services, American Museum of Natural History; Copper: Royal Ontario Museum, Toronto.

The richness of the California environment made the region the most densely settled in all of ancient North America. The climate permitted agriculture, but the natural environment offered such ample food that California groups remained hunters and gatherers for hundreds of years after A.D. 1492. Although anchored to the Pacific Ocean, California cultures also exploited the diverse inland environments, from the foothills of the mountains to the marshes of the great central valley, from dry canyons in the south to damp forests in the north. The diversity of California's environment encouraged corresponding diversity among the native peoples. By A.D. 1492 the complex mosaic of settlements in California included about five hundred separate tribes speaking some ninety languages, each with many local dialects. No other region of comparable size in North America exhibited such cultural variety.

Near Santa Barbara about 3000 B.C. emerged the origins of what became the Chumash culture, which lasted long after A.D. 1492. Chumash peoples hunted land animals like deer and bears, but they also preyed on sea mammals like seals, usually clubbing them while they were asleep on the shore. Chumash groups built large canoes from wooden planks and used them to fish in coastal waters and to travel along the coast and to offshore islands. They also collected plant foods, especially acorns. Over the millennia, the bounty of food evidently supported a growing population. After about 1000 B.C. the Chumash and other California cultures devoted increasing attention to gathering acorns, probably in response to the growing population and the greater need for food. Stone mortars and pestles used to grind acorns into meal have been found at sites throughout California. Since acorn meal contains toxins, Archaic Californians leached the meal with water and then boiled it to make it safe to eat. Chumash and other California cultures stored and processed acorns in finely crafted baskets rather than in pottery.

The plentiful food resources permitted Chumash peoples to establish relatively permanent villages. At the time of European contact, some villages contained a thousand people living in large dome-shaped dwellings constructed of wooden poles covered by reeds. Typically a large central village headed by a chief was surrounded by several smaller villages subordinate to the chief. After about 2000 B.C. the Chumash developed an elaborate currency system, using beads made from shells as a form of money and a status marker. Conflict frequently broke out among Chumash villages, and skeletons from prehistoric burials document a notable proportion of violent deaths. Archaeologists believe that such conflicts arose in part from efforts by Chumash villages to restrict access to their valuable acorn-gathering territory. Although few other California cultures achieved the population density and cultural complexity of the Chumash, all shared the hunter-gatherer way of life and reliance on acorns as a major source of food.

The richness of the California environment made the region the most densely settled in all of ancient North America.

Another rich natural environment lay along the Pacific Northwest coast from the California border north to Alaska. The abundance of fish and marine life permitted the ancient Americans who lived in that region to devote substantial time and energy to activities other than hunting and gathering. Especially after about 3500 B.C. they concentrated on catching large quantities of salmon, halibut, and other fish, which they dried to last throughout the year. With time free from the demands of food gathering, Northwest peoples developed sophisticated woodworking skills. They fashioned huge canoes, some big enough to hold fifty people, which they used to fish and to hunt sea mammals using artfully crafted bone harpoons. They also employed the canoes to conduct warfare against neighboring tribes. Much of the conflict among Archaic northwesterners seems to have arisen from attempts to defend good fishing sites from incursions by outsiders.

Like the Chumash, the Northwest peoples built more or less permanent villages. They constructed large, multifamily houses from cedar planks. Beginning around A.D. 500 they often adorned their houses with totems, elaborately carved images of animals, supernatural beings, or their own ancestors (it is quite possible that similar carvings were made much earlier but have simply disintegrated in the damp climate). These carvings, some of which Europeans later called "totem poles," honored the lineage of the family clan in a dwelling and displayed the clan's wealth and status. Northwest peoples enjoyed displaying their wealth; but they also liked to give it away. These cultures instituted the potlatch, a ceremony that featured a feast after which the host gave the guests as many fine things as possible. Potlatches served to redistribute wealth from the richest families to those less well off. They also reinforced the hierarchy that ascribed to certain clans the status of nobles and consigned others to lesser, common ranks. Maintaining such social distinctions was probably a principal function of the many artistic carvings that have survived to the present.

Arctic Cultures

In the Arctic environment of most of Alaska and northern Canada, the harsh, bitterly cold climate prohibited gathering plants for almost the entire year. Therefore, from Paleo-Indian times to long after A.D. 1492, Arctic peoples subsisted by hunting. They preyed on caribou that grazed on the short grasses of the Arctic tundra, and they also hunted seals, walruses, whales, and other sea mammals. Arctic hunters concentrated on these animals rather than on fish because fish contained too little of the fat that was necessary in human diets to maintain health in the polar climate. By adapting to the forbidding environment, Archaic cultures in the Arctic differed substantially from those elsewhere in North America.

Descendants of Paleo-Indians probably inhabited Alaska until around 4000 B.C. Sometime before about 2000 B.C. a new group appears to have migrated into Alaska, probably from Siberia. Although the archaeological evidence is sketchy and can be interpreted in conflicting ways, these new migrants were probably the ancestors of the Inuit (or Eskimos), whose culture came to dominate the entire Arctic. Within two or three hundred years, these newcomers had migrated east all the way to the Atlantic coast, hunting as they went. They built winter houses from blocks of hard-packed snow and obtained heat and light by burning seal fat in stone lamps. They also were the earliest ancient Americans to use bows and arrows, which are found in

Archaic Arctic sites dating to roughly 1500 B.C. Apparently they brought bows and arrows with them from Siberia; those weapons did not appear in other North American cultures until about A.D. 500, evidently the result of slow diffusion southward.

About A.D. 1000, Thule people began to spread east from Alaska to the Atlantic coast. They developed especially effective weapons for hunting sea mammals like seals, walruses, and whales far from shore: bone and ivory harpoons combined with skillfully made kayaks constructed of animal hides. Thule folk also developed dogsleds for long-distance travel across snow and ice. These Thule innovations established the basic technology used by their Inuit descendants. Thule people were probably the first ancient Americans to encounter Europeans. At a Thule site on Ellesmere Island in far northeastern Canada, archaeologists have excavated chain mail and other iron objects that demonstrate contact with Vikings who settled Greenland a few years before A.D. 1000.

Eastern Woodlands Cultures

East of the Mississippi River, the climate supported a forest environment dominated in most regions by oak and hickory trees. With the warming trend that followed the Paleo-Indian period, the deciduous forest slowly crept northward, encroaching upon the pine forests that had previously covered the northernmost regions and eventually replacing them. This Eastern Woodlands environment had numerous local variants. Among the most important were in the major river valleys, especially the Mississippi, Ohio, Tennessee, and Cumberland; the Great Lakes region; and along the Atlantic coast. Archaic peoples in these and other locales developed distinctive artifacts that demonstrated the great variety of their adaptations to the Woodlands environment. Underlying that variety, however, were certain basic similarities among all Woodlands cultures.

Deer were the most important prey of nearly all Woodlands hunters. At one Archaic dwelling site in Tennessee dating from 5000 to 3500 B.C., deer accounted for 90 percent of the excavated bones. Woodlands hunters also took bears, turkeys, opossums, raccoons, and smaller animals using spears and spear-throwers like their Archaic counterparts in other regions. If they lived near rivers, lakes, or the sea, they usually fished with bone hooks, nets, or traps and gathered shellfish. But everywhere the deer that thrived in the Woodlands remained the hunters' primary target. In addition to food, deer supplied hides and bones that were crafted into many useful items such as clothing, weapons, needles, and other tools.

Like Archaic peoples elsewhere, Woodlands Indians gathered edible plants, seeds, and especially nuts. Hickory nuts were the most commonly gathered plant food, but pecans, walnuts, acorns, and hazelnuts were also collected. Stones for grinding nuts appear in Woodlands sites as early as 7500 B.C. and they remained a basic food processing tool until long after A.D. 1492.

Woodlands groups migrated with the seasons to favorable gathering and hunting locations. After about 4000 B.C. the Woodlands climate stabilized and, it appears, some Woodlands peoples established more or less permanent settlements in locations that offered a wide variety of plant and animal resources. These Woodlands settlements were usually near a river or lake and typically included from 25 up to about 150 people. Around 5500 B.C. Woodlands folk at a site in southern Illinois built rectangular houses roughly twenty-five feet by fifteen feet. They placed large wooden poles in the ground around the perimeter of each house and filled in the space between the poles with sticks and mud. These houses were the earliest to be constructed in all of North America, experts believe. Woodlands folk used similar building techniques for millennia afterward.

The existence of semipermanent settlements has permitted archaeologists to locate numerous Archaic burial sites that provide fascinating insights into the character of Woodlands cultures. At one burial site in Tennessee, half the women had died before the age of thirty, many of them evidently succumbing to the high risks of childbirth. In contrast, almost a fifth of the men lived to the ripe old age of sixty. At the Indian Knoll site in western Kentucky, which dates to about 2500 to 2000 B.C., archaeologists found 1,100 burials that allowed them to calculate the life expectancy at birth for these Woodlands people to be slightly over eighteen years. Some graves contained shell and copper goods that demonstrate the existence of long-distance trade, although just how the trade worked remains unknown. Some burials contain evidence of violent death; one skeleton, for example, has a spear point embedded in the rib cage. Archaeologists speculate that Woodlands groups sometimes fought over access to desirable hunting and gathering grounds.

TECHNOLOGY IN AMERICA
Weaver's Workbasket

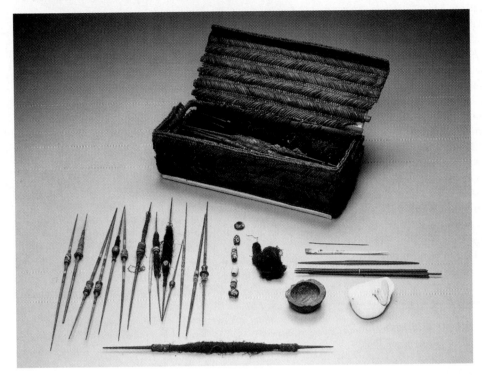

This workbasket of a master weaver illustrates the technology of ancient American textile production. Found in a woman's grave in the Andes dating from five hundred years before the arrival of Columbus, the workbasket contains the simple tools that, when combined with the experience, skill, ingenuity, and creativity of the weaver, were used to create intricate weavings like that on page 28 of this chapter. The basket contains tools for every stage in the process of textile production. The weaver took fiber from cotton plants or animal wool (such as llama or alpaca) and spun it into thread. For colored threads, the weaver dyed the fibers before spinning, using different vegetable and mineral concoctions. The pointed sticks wrapped with thread (left center) are spindles on which the weaver spun. She used the small ceramic cup to hold one end of the spindle while she twisted the fiber through her fingers to create strong, thin thread. She used the two pieces of chalk (to the right of the ceramic cup) to make a powder that lubricated her fingers, allowing the thread to pass smoothly onto the spindle. Skeins of finished thread removed from their spindles are just to the left of the ceramic cup. This small workbasket contained more than 150 spindles for the many varieties of thread a master weaver made and used. The beadlike objects at the center are whorls the weaver placed on spindles to anchor the thread and for decoration; the designs on the whorls probably had religious meaning. On the right, above the chalk and ceramic cup are bobbins used to pass the thread through the weaving, a bone pick with fine teeth to press down on the closely woven threads and tighten the weave, and a long spine needle with a tiny hole, used for sewing and for embroidery. Mastery of this technology presumably took years of training and experience. Most likely, a master weaver passed on her skill and knowledge to her daughters or other kinswomen.

Gift of Charles H. White. Courtesy, Museum of Fine Arts, Boston.

Some experts also believe that burials were a way to stake a claim to specific territory by making it literally the land of one's ancestors.

Around 2000 B.C. two major changes occurred among Woodlands cultures. First, some groups began to cultivate plants for food. Gourds and pumpkins that originated in Mexico were grown in parts of Missouri and Kentucky before 2000 B.C. After the introduction of these Mexican crops, Woodlands peoples began to cultivate local species such as sunflowers and other seed-bearing plants. It is likely that Woodlands folk also grew tobacco, an import from South America, since stone pipes for smoking appeared by 1500 B.C. and became common by 500 B.C. Corn, the most important plant food in Mexico, did not begin to be cultivated by Woodlands groups until about 300 B.C. and did not become a significant food crop until more than a thousand years later. Cultivated crops added to the quantity, variety, and predictability of Woodlands food sources, but they did not fundamentally alter the hunter-gatherer way of life.

Around 2000 B.C. two major changes occurred among Woodlands cultures. First, some groups began to cultivate plants for food. Second, Woodlands peoples incorporated pottery in their basic hunter-gatherer cultures.

ANCIENT CORN POPPER
Long before movies and microwave ovens, ancient Americans munched popcorn. This corn popper comes from the Mochica culture, which thrived on the northern coast of Peru for about six hundred years after the birth of Christ. The Mochica presumably nestled the popper on a bed of coals with the opening facing up, placed corn inside, and covered the opening with a lid (not shown) while the kernels popped. The Mochica and other ancient Americans did not pop most of the corn they grew. Instead, they ground it into cornmeal, which they incorporated in a wide variety of dishes, probably including ancient counterparts of modern tortillas.
The Field Museum #A112961c, Chicago. Photographer: Diane Alexander White.

The second major change after about 2000 B.C. was the introduction of pottery. Techniques for making ceramic pots probably also originated in Mexico and may have been brought north along with Mexican seeds. Pots were used for food storage and preparation. Woodlands peoples incorporated pottery, as they did agriculture, into their basic hunter-gatherer cultures, which persisted in most areas to A.D. 1492 and beyond.

Perhaps the most spectacular Archaic Woodlands site was Poverty Point near the Mississippi River in northeastern Louisiana. The Poverty Point culture existed from about 1700 B.C. to 700 B.C. It appears to have emerged from peoples indigenous to North America rather than being a cultural outpost of Central American peoples. Poverty Point folk constructed an enormous earthworks consisting of six concentric half-circles more than a half-mile in diameter; each ring was built of dirt piled nine feet high and twenty-five feet wide. The purpose of this huge earthworks is unknown. It may have been used for astronomical observations since it seems to be aligned to view the spring and fall equinoxes. The labor and organization required to build such massive earthworks suggest that important ceremonies were conducted at the site. The complex may also have served as a meeting place for traders who exchanged items that were common in one place but exotic in others. At least a thousand people and perhaps several times that many lived in dwellings near the earthworks. Nearly one hundred smaller villages clustered here and there in the surrounding countryside. The marked differences between the large central site and the smaller surrounding settlements seem to indicate a recognition of social hierarchy. Details about this and many other features of Poverty Point culture remain unknown.

Southwestern Cultures

In southwestern America—roughly including Arizona, New Mexico, and southern portions of Utah and Colorado—Archaic peoples developed distinctive cultures characterized by agriculture and eventually by multiunit dwellings called pueblos. The southwestern environment is generally arid; rainfall varies greatly from season to season and year to year. Water is more plentiful along the major rivers of the region, particularly the Colorado, Rio Grande, Pecos, and Gila. Like Archaic peoples elsewhere in North America, southwestern groups developed a wide variety of cultures adapted to local environmental circumstances. All southwestern cultures, however, confronted the challenge of a dry climate and unpredictable fluctuations in rainfall that made the supply of wild-plant food very unreliable for subsistence. These ancient Americans probably adopted agriculture in response to this basic environmental condition of the Southwest.

Corn, supplemented by squash and beans, became the staff of life of ancient southwesterners.

Until about 3000 B.C. the population of the Southwest appears to have been extremely sparse. Geographically the region lies between the Great Basin and northern Mexico, and some features of cultures from both regions exist in such artifacts as spear points and seed-grinding stones that date to the two millennia after 3000 B.C. Sometime within a few centuries of 1500 B.C. southwestern peoples began to cultivate their signature food crop, corn (as it is called in North America; elsewhere it is called maize). The date of the introduction of corn cultivation and the motivations for it are subjects of intense debate among archaeologists. The debate is important for many reasons, among them that by A.D. 1492 corn had become the basic cultivated food crop for Native American peoples throughout North America (and it remains one of the most productive food crops in the world today). It appears safe to say, however, that Southwestern peoples began to cultivate corn in a conscious attempt to provide themselves with a more predictable source of food in a highly unpredictable environment.

Corn was one of the most important developments in the history of world agriculture. Before 5000 B.C. somewhere in Central or South America, people began to cultivate seeds of the wild grass teosinte, the ancient ancestor of modern corn. Within a few centuries, selective cultivation of the bigger and more productive seeds led to progressively bigger ears of corn and progressively larger numbers of kernels harvested per kernel planted, although these prehistoric corn ears were much smaller than modern corn. Central and South American peoples grew corn for millennia before the crop made its way to southwestern America. Since ancient corn possessed enormous genetic diversity, southwestern cultures were able to select seeds and thereby develop corn varieties that would tolerate the arid, relatively short growing season of the Southwest, despite the plant's origins in wetter and warmer climates farther south.

By about 1000 B.C. southwestern folk also grew squash, and by 500 B.C. beans appeared in their gardens. Like corn, both squash and beans had traveled north from Mexico. Corn, supplemented by squash and beans, became the staff of life of ancient southwesterners. The demands of corn cultivation encouraged southwestern hunter-gatherers to restrict their migratory habits and to settle near ground that would support the growth of the crop. A vital consideration was access to water. Southwestern Indians became experts at conserving water from streams, springs, and rainfall and at distributing available water through irrigation. The adoption of agriculture and of more or less permanent settlements did not occur overnight. The process waxed and waned over the centuries depending on the availability of alternative food sources, among other considerations. The long-term trend, however, clearly pointed toward sedentary villages that depended on growing corn.

Between about A.D. 200 and 900, small settlements appeared throughout southern New Mexico marking the emergence of the Mogollon culture. Typically a Mogollon settlement included between three and fifteen pit houses made by digging out a rounded pit about fifteen feet in diameter and a foot or two deep and then erecting poles to support a roof of branches or dirt. These small clusters of pit houses probably housed members of a family. Mogollon people began to make pottery about A.D. 200, and they also engaged in trade since seashells, turquoise, and other luxuries from far away appear

MIMBRES BOWLS

Mimbres people left a vivid record of their culture on bowls like these, which were found in their graves. They punched a hole in the bottom of a decorated bowl and then placed the inverted bowl over the face of the corpse. The hole was obviously quite important in the burial ritual, but exactly what it meant is unknown. The decoration may have depicted a characteristic of the dead person. The bowls shown here, made between A.D. 1000 and 1150, illustrate the differing activities of Mimbres men and women. It is likely that Mimbres women made and decorated the bowls.

Al Ligrani Photograph, Museum of Western Colorado; Transfer, Department of Anthropology, University of Minnesota.

in these sites. Larger villages usually had one or two pit houses that were bigger than conventional dwellings and may have been used for trade or ceremonial purposes. These larger pit houses may have been the predecessors of the circular kivas, the partially underground ceremonial rooms that became a characteristic of nearly all southwestern settlements. About A.D. 1000, Mogollon culture began to decline, for reasons that remain obscure. Among their descendants were the Mimbres people in southwestern New Mexico, who produced spectacular pottery with characteristic designs that often portrayed human and animal forms. By about A.D. 1150, the Mimbres culture also disappeared.

About A.D. 500, people who appear to have emigrated from Mexico established the distinctive Hohokam culture in southern Arizona. Hohokam peoples made extensive use of irrigation to plant and harvest twice a year. The comparatively high crop yields made possible by irrigation allowed the Hohokam population to grow and seek out more land to irrigate and settle. They also built pit houses, although theirs were more rectangular than those in Mogollon villages. Hohokam culture continued to be strongly influenced by Mexican cultures. The people built sizable platform mounds and ball courts characteristic of cultures to the south. The Hohokam culture declined about A.D. 1400, for unknown reasons.

North of the Hohokam and Mogollon cultures, in a region that encompassed southern Utah and Colorado and northern Arizona and New Mexico, the Anasazi culture developed during the first century A.D. The early Anasazi built pit houses and used irrigation much like their neighbors to the south. However, since many Anasazi settlements were on mesas high above riverbeds, the people built reservoirs to capture rainwater and melted snow and then channeled the runoff to fields on the mesa and to terraces on the steep mesa walls. Beginning around A.D. 1000, for reasons that remain unclear, the Anasazi began to move their dwellings off the mesa tops. They built large, multistory cliff dwellings whose spectacular ruins can still be seen at Mesa Verde, Colorado, and Canyon de Chelly, Arizona. Other Anasazi communities, like the one whose impressive ruins can be visited at Chaco Canyon, New Mexico, erected huge, stone-walled pueblos with enough rooms to house the entire population of the settlement. Pueblo Bonito at Chaco Canyon, for example, contained more than eight hundred rooms. Anasazi pueblos and cliff dwellings typically contained one or more kivas used for secret ceremonies, restricted to men, that sought to communicate with the supernatural world.

Pueblo Bonito stood at the center of a dozen large pueblos in or near Chaco Canyon that developed between A.D. 900 and 1150. Scattered over some 25,000 square miles were scores of smaller pueblos that were linked to Chaco Canyon and to the central site of Pueblo Bonito by an amazing system of roads. Some roads were nearly thirty feet wide and extended straight from Chaco Canyon for sixty-five miles, sometimes including stairs and footholds carved in rock cliffs that threatened to interrupt a straight-line passage. Remnants of the roads are still visible today. The immense labor required to construct these roads suggests their importance, although the reason for their size remains mysterious since the Anasazi traveled exclusively on foot. The inhabitants of Chaco Canyon engaged in an extensive trade network involving turquoise, pottery, seashells, baskets, ritual items of many sorts, and even macaws—tropical birds valued for their brightly colored feathers. Around A.D. 1130, drought began to plague the region; it lasted for half a century, triggering the disappearance of the Chaco culture.

By A.D. 1200 the large Anasazi pueblos had been abandoned, for reasons that are not entirely clear. The prolonged drought may have intensified conflict among pueblos and rendered ineffective the agricultural methods that had been developed in earlier centuries. Some Anasazi migrated toward regions with more reliable rainfall and settled in Hopi, Zuñi, and Acoma pueblos that their descendants in Arizona and New Mexico have occupied ever since.

Burial Mounds and Chiefdoms

Beginning around 500 B.C., Archaic Woodlands cultures throughout the vast drainage of the Mississippi River began to build burial mounds that indicate new forms of social and political organization. The size of the mounds, the labor and organization required to erect them, and the differences in the artifacts buried with certain individuals suggest the existence of a social and political hierarchy that archaeologists term a chiefdom. Typically a chief was a man who inherited his status and who was believed to have some supernatural authority. The burial mounds suggest that a chief could command the labor and respect of many people who were not members of his immediate family.

The size of the burial mounds, the labor and organization required to erect them, and the differences in the artifacts buried with certain individuals suggest the existence of a social and political hierarchy that archaeologists term a chiefdom.

Adena and Hopewell Cultures

Between about 500 B.C. and 100 B.C., hundreds of burial mounds were built within a 150-mile radius of Chillicothe, Ohio, by the Adena peoples. The Adena were Woodlands hunter-gatherers who supplemented wild resources by cultivating some tobacco and perhaps a few local plants, but they did not grow corn. They lived in small settlements and migrated to obtain food, as did previous Woodlands cultures. But from time to time, presumably when an important person died, small groups coalesced into large gatherings that performed burial ceremonies involving the construction of mounds. Often they also built circular mounds surrounding or near the burial mound. These "sacred circles" may have been ritualistic gathering places for the deceased's clan or kin.

Normally, Adena people constructed a burial house, where the dead may have been kept until decay exposed the skeleton, permitting the bones to be coated with red pigment. The burial house was usually burned down before the body or skeleton

MOUND EXCAVATION

During the nineteenth century, long before archaeologists developed scientific methods of excavation, curious Americans dug into ancient mounds. Dr. Munro Dickeson (holding a notebook at the bottom center of the painting) excavated hundreds of mounds and gave lectures about his discoveries to audiences throughout the Midwest. Dickeson used this painting of a mound he excavated in Louisiana during the 1840s as a backdrop for his lectures. Part of a canvas almost 350 feet long, the painting illustrates the way mounds were constructed with alternating strata of burials and dirt. Can you detect in the painting hints of the burial rituals enacted at this site? Note that African Americans — presumably slaves — did the physical labor of this excavation.
The Saint Louis Art Museum. Purchase: Eliza McMillan Fund.

was covered with a mound of earth. Sometimes two or three individuals—presumably of high status—were placed in log tombs before the mound was built. With the bodies, the Adena people usually deposited a wide variety of grave goods—spear points and stone pipes as well as decorative and ritualistic items such as thin sheets of mica (a glasslike mineral) crafted into naturalistic shapes, copper ornaments like bracelets and pendants, or headdresses made from the skulls of deer. Men, evidently of high status, sometimes were buried with a skull, perhaps of an enemy or an ancestor; the surface of some such skulls is polished, suggesting that it was an important object that was handled frequently for a long time before burial. Grave goods were not restricted to the burials of important men. In fact, children's graves often included grave goods. Once the body and grave goods were in place, dirt was piled into a mound one basketful at a time. Sometimes mounds were constructed all at once, but often they were built up over many years after many burials.

About 100 B.C., Adena culture evolved into the more elaborate Hopewell culture, which lasted until about A.D. 400. It too was centered in Ohio but it extended throughout the Ohio and Mississippi valleys. Hopewell people built larger mounds and filled them with more magnificent grave goods than had their Adena predecessors. A typical Hopewell mound was 100 feet in diameter and 30 feet high. Some mounds had geometrical designs; others were shaped like animals. The immense Serpent Mound, a likeness of a snake over 1,200 feet long, can still be visited in Ohio. Like Adena people, however, Hopewell folk remained hunter-gatherers who lived in small villages and did not grow corn. Burial rituals appear to have brought many people together to honor an important personage. Some Hopewell sites contain mounds that resemble the Adena sacred circles.

Burial was probably reserved for the most important members of Hopewell groups. Most people were cremated. Careful analysis of skeletons in one Hopewell mound suggests that the more important graves contained men who were hunters; they tended to have arthritis of the elbow associated with stress to the elbow joint from using spear-throwers. Men in lesser graves showed evidence of arthritis of the wrist, perhaps associated with handwork. The men with arthritic elbows were also taller than those with arthritic wrists, suggesting that high status may have been related to stature.

Grave goods at Hopewell sites were often lavish. In one burial a young man and woman lay side by side, each wearing many items of copper jewelry, necklaces of grizzly bear teeth, and artificial copper noses; the woman was surrounded with thousands of buttons and pearl beads. Large deposits of mica, obsidian, and other valuable resources were buried with certain men; perhaps they were artisans who worked with such materials. Certainly Hopewell sites testify to the high quality of their crafts. They included objects similar to those at Adena sites, but finer, more decorative, more exquisite.

Hopewell grave goods also demonstrate the existence of a wide-ranging trade network. Sites in Ohio contain obsidian from the Yellowstone Park region of Wyoming; other stones originating in Missouri, Illinois, North Dakota, and Canada; shells and alligator teeth from the Florida and Gulf coasts; mica and minerals from North Carolina; and copper from near Lake Superior. Likewise, artifacts evidently exported from Hopewell centers appear at faraway sites in the Southeast, Northeast, and Midwest. Hopewell burial practices also spread through much of the trading area. It may be that the chiefs buried in Hopewell mounds played an important role in the vast interregional trade. Some archaeologists believe that chiefs may have used their access to trade to elevate their own status.

After about A.D. 400, Hopewell culture declined, for reasons that are obscure. Some archaeologists believe that the adoption of the bow and arrow and of increasing reliance on agriculture may have made small settlements more self-sufficient and weakened their dependence on central chiefs.

HOPEWELL EFFIGY PIPE

Hopewell burial mounds often contain effigy pipes in the shape of animals. This coyote pipe was carved from pipestone between about 200 B.C. and A.D. 100. To smoke the pipe, a Hopewell person would tamp tobacco into a bowl hollowed from the back of the coyote (not visible in the photo) and then light the pipe, perhaps with a flaming splinter. Facing the effigy, the smoker would inhale through the hole at the right end of the curved platform, under the coyote's nose. The coyote was probably more than simply an attractive decoration for a pipe, but what it signified remains unknown.

Photograph © 1996 The Detroit Institute of Arts, Dirk Bakker Collection of Ohio Historical Society, Columbus.

Mississippian Culture

About A.D. 800, another mound-building culture flourished. The Mississippian culture emerged in the floodplains of the major Southeastern river systems and lasted until about A.D. 1500. Mississippian peoples practiced agriculture, growing corn, squash, and beans. They also continued to hunt, fish, and gather wild plants. Major Mississippian sites include not only burial mounds but huge mounds with platforms on top for ceremonies and for the residences of great chiefs. The largest Mississippian site was Cahokia, Illinois, just across the Mississippi River from St. Louis, Missouri. Other important Mississippian centers were at Moundville, Alabama; Etowah, Georgia; and Spiro, Oklahoma.

At Cahokia, more than one hundred mounds of different sizes and shapes were grouped around large open plazas. Monk's Mound, the largest, covered sixteen acres at its base and was one hundred feet tall. Spreading far beyond the mounds and plazas were dwellings that at one time covered five square miles and may have housed as many as thirty thousand inhabitants, easily qualifying Cahokia as the largest settlement in North America and comparable to major centers of the era in Central America. At Cahokia and other Mississippian sites, people evidently worshiped a sun god; perhaps the mounds were a way to elevate elites nearer to the sun.

One Cahokia burial mound suggests the authority associated with a great chief. One man—presumably the chief—was buried on a platform composed of twenty thousand shell beads. Buried near him, evidently at the same time, were the dismembered bodies of several people, perhaps enemies or slaves; three men and three women of high status, perhaps relatives of the chief, accompanied by eight hundred arrowheads, numerous sheets of mica and copper, and fifteen polished stone disks used in a spear-throwing game; four men, perhaps servants or guards, whose heads and hands had been cut off; and fifty young women between the ages of eighteen and twenty-three who had evidently been strangled. Such a mass sacrifice suggests the power a Cahokian chief wielded and the obedience he commanded. However, details about how Mississippian chiefs exercised their powers remain mysterious. The sacrifices associated with the burials suggest that ordinary Mississippians may have had reason to fear their chiefs.

Cahokia and other Mississippian sites had dwindled by 1500. On the eve of European contact, most of the descendants of Mississippian cultures lived in small dispersed villages supported by agriculture, hunting, and gathering.

By 1500, all these Archaic cultures were either extinct or in decline, for reasons that are not well known. However, their monuments, dwellings, and artifacts survived, as did various remnants of their cultural practices. On the eve of European conquest, North American tribes had incorporated and adapted many of the cultural achievements of their ancestors. The rigors of the natural environment required that they continue to make cultural adaptations.

MEXICAN CEREMONIAL SKULL
This human skull, decorated by Mexican artisans with a mosaic of turquoise, jet, and shell, represented Tezcatlipoca, the supreme Mexican deity who governed human fate. Every eighteen months, a handsome young man was selected for the great honor of impersonating Tezcatlipoca for the next eighteen months. Montezuma gave the impersonator riches and privileges of all sorts, including allowing him to rule Tenochtitlán for the last five days of his life. On the last day, the impersonator climbed the steps of a temple where priests cut out his heart and decapitated him. This skull from the Tezcatlipoca ceremony presumably belonged to one of the impersonators. The skull is said to have been a gift from Montezuma to Cortés.
British Museum.

Native Americans in 1492

In the vast Eastern Woodlands region, tribes clustered into three major groups. Algonquian tribes inhabited the Atlantic seaboard from Virginia through Maine and the Great Lakes region and much of the upper Midwest. The relatively mild climate along the Atlantic permitted the coastal Algonquians to grow corn and other crops as well as to hunt and fish. Around the Great Lakes and in northern New England, however, cool summers and severe winters made agriculture impractical. Instead, the Abenaki, Penobscot, Chippewa, and other tribes hunted and fished, using canoes both for transportation and for gathering wild rice.

Inland from the Algonquians were the territories of the Iroquoian tribes, centered in Pennsylvania and upstate New York. The Iroquoian peoples also inhabited the hilly upland regions of the Carolinas and Georgia. Several features distinguished Iroquoian tribes from their neighbors. First, their success in cultivating corn and other crops allowed them to build permanent settlements, usually consisting of several bark-covered longhouses up to one hundred feet long and housing five to ten families. Second, Iroquoian societies were thoroughly matriarchal. Property of all sorts, including land, children, and inheritance, belonged to women. Women headed family clans and even selected the chiefs (normally men) who governed tribes. Third, for purposes of war and diplomacy, the Seneca, Onondaga, Mohawk, Oneida, and Cayuga tribes formed the League of Five Nations, an Iroquoian confederation that remained powerful well into the eighteenth century.

Muskogean peoples were spread throughout the Southeast, south of the Ohio River and east of the Mississippi. Including Creek, Choctaw, Chickasaw, and Natchez tribes, the Muskogean Indians inhabited a bountiful natural environment that provided abundant food both from agriculture and from hunting and gathering. Remnants of the Mississippian culture existed in the religious rites common among the Muskogean. They all practiced a form of sun worship, and the Natchez even built temple mounds modeled after those of their Mississippian ancestors.

West of the Mississippi River, Great Plains Indians straddled the boundary between the Eastern Woodlands and the western tribes. Plains Indians lived in much of the enormous region drained by the Missouri River. Many of the tribes had migrated to the Plains within the century or two before 1500, forced out of the Eastern Woodlands by Iroquoian and Algonquian tribes. They were in the process of increasing their reliance on buffalo, although some tribes—especially the Mandan and Pawnee—were successful farmers, growing both corn and sunflowers as major food crops. The Teton Sioux, Blackfeet, Comanche, Cheyenne, and Crow on the northern Plains and the Apache and other nomadic tribes on the southern plains depended on buffalo. They migrated with the huge herds that grazed the rich prairies. Lacking horses before the arrival of the Spaniards, these Indians hunted on foot with the techniques in use since human beings first came to America.

By the time Columbus arrived, the comparatively small Indian settlements in North America supported a population estimated to be about 4.5 million, slightly less than the population of the British Isles at the time and roughly half that of Spain and Portugal combined.

In the Southwest, descendants of the Anasazi, Hohokam, and Mogollon cultures lived in settled agricultural communities, many of them pueblos. However, a large number of warlike Athapascan tribes had invaded the area within the two hundred years before 1500. The Athapascans—principally Apache and Navajo—were hunters and gatherers who preyed on the sedentary pueblo Indians. They did not engage in agriculture themselves. Instead they specialized in the skills and traditions of warfare that made their raids successful and permitted them to enjoy the fruits of agriculture without the work of farming.

Tribes in the Great Basin region, such as the Comanche and Shoshone, continued to follow the subsistence practices of earlier Great Basin cultures. Likewise, Pacific coast cultures continued their distinctive hunter-gatherer ways of life.

By the time Columbus arrived, the comparatively small Indian settlements in North America supported a population estimated to be about 4.5 million, slightly less than the population of the

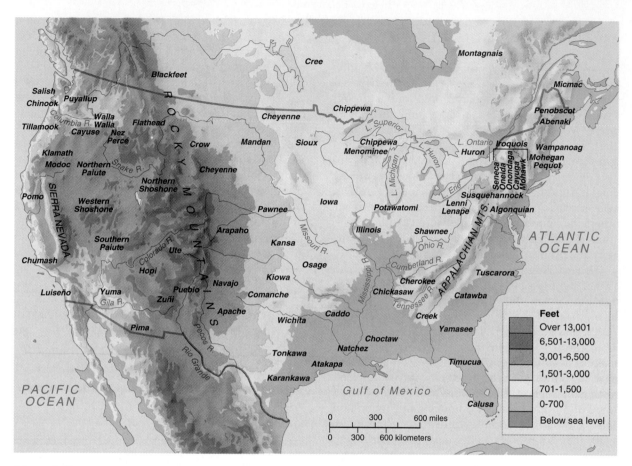

MAP 1.3

Native North Americans about 1500

Distinctive Native American peoples resided throughout the area that, centuries later, would be-
come the United States. This map indicates the approximate location of some of the larger tribes
about 1500. In the interest of legibility, many other peoples who inhabited North America at the
time are omitted from the map.

British Isles at the time and roughly half that of Spain and Portugal combined. All of the Indian peoples depended on hunting wild game and gathering wild seeds, nuts, and plants for a major portion of their food. Most of them also practiced agriculture, some far more than others. All of them used bows and arrows, as well as other weapons, for hunting and warfare. None of them employed writing, but they expressed themselves in many other ways. They made drawings on stones, wood, and animal skins; wove patterns in baskets and textiles; painted designs on pottery; and crafted beadwork,

pipes, and other decorative items. They danced, sang, and played music. They performed elaborate burial ceremonies and other religious rites.

Although they had rich and varied cultural resources, they lacked certain common conveniences found in late-fifteenth-century Europe: They did not use wheels; sailing ships were unknown; they had no large domesticated animals like horses, cows, or oxen; their use of metals was restricted to copper; and metallurgy did not exist in North America. However, the absence of these European conveniences was profoundly irrelevant to ancient North

Americans. Their tribal cultures, in all their varieties and similarities, had developed as adaptations to the natural environment local to each tribe. That was the great similarity that underlay all the cultural diversity among native North Americans.

The Mexica: A Meso-American Culture

The ancient peoples of Central and South America were far more numerous than their North American cousins. They too lived in a natural environment of tremendous diversity. They too built impressive civilizations and great monuments. They too developed hundreds of tribal cultures, far too numerous to catalog here. But among all the Central and South American cultures the Mexica (often called Aztecs, a name they did not use) stood out. They were the most powerful Indians in the entire New World at the moment of European contact. Their empire stretched from coast to coast across central Mexico, encompassing as many as 25 million people. We know more about the fifteenth-cen-

tury Mexica than about any other Native American society of the same time. Their significance in the history of the New World after 1492, especially in the Spanish empire that shaped the expectations of other Old World colonizers, dictates a brief consideration of their culture and society.

The Mexica began their rise to prominence about A.D. 1325 when small bands settled on an unpromising marshy island in Lake Texcoco, the site of the future city of Tenochtitlán. Resourceful, courageous, cold-blooded warriors, the Mexica were often hired as mercenaries by richer, more settled tribes. The Mexica survived and prospered by making alliances with far more powerful neighboring tribes who were eager to have the fierce Mexican warriors on their side. By 1430, the Mexica succeeded in asserting their dominance over their former allies and leading their own military campaigns in an ever-widening arc of empire building. Certain tribes battled the Mexica to a standoff and managed to preserve their independence. The Tlaxcalans, the most notable of these holdouts, eventually became allies of the European conquerors. Despite these pockets of resistance, by 1500 the Mexica ruled an empire that covered more land than Spain

MEXICAN CALENDAR
The Mexican system of writing used glyphs, pictorial representations of gods, objects, and ideas. Some of the writing from before the arrival of Europeans has survived in the form of books, called codices. (Soon after the conquest, Spaniards burned all the codices they could find.) This preconquest codex is a calendar of the 260-day religious year. The central figure on each page is Tlaloc, the rain god. The glyphs along the bottom of each page represent specific days; the symbols along the top indicate the sky and rain. Tlaloc priests used the calendar for many purposes, including setting the dates of major religious rituals.
Lee Boltin.

PERUVIAN WEAVING
Ancient American women wove a dazzling variety of textiles, including this spectacular cloth made by a weaver of the Paracas people, who inhabited the southern coast of Peru from about 700 B.C. to A.D. 200. This weaving wrapped a Paracas mummy, presumably a person of high status. The jewellike quality of the cloth suggests the artistry of the weavers and the Paracas's appreciation of design, color, and exquisite workmanship in their everyday lives.
Denman Waldo Ross Collection. Courtesy, Museum of Fine Arts, Boston.

and Portugal combined and contained almost three times as many people.

The empire exemplified the central values of Mexican society. The Mexica worshiped the war god

> *Despite pockets of resistance, by 1500 the Mexica ruled an empire that covered more land than Spain and Portugal combined and contained almost three times as many people.*

Huitzilopochtli, who they believed repaid their reverence with victories. Warriors held the most exalted positions in the Mexican social hierarchy, even above the priests who performed the sacred ceremonies that won Huitzilopochtli's favor. In the almost constant battles necessary to defend and ex-

tend the empire, young Mexican men could exhibit the courage and daring that would allow them to rise in the carefully graduated ranks of warriors. The Mexica considered capturing prisoners the ultimate act of bravery. The captives were usually turned over to the priests, who sacrificed them to Huitzilopochtli by cutting out their hearts.

The empire contributed far more to Mexican society than victims for sacrifice. At the most basic level, the empire was a military and political system for collecting tribute from subject peoples. The Mexica forced conquered tribes to pay tribute in goods, not money. Tribute included everything from candidates for human sacrifice to basic food products like corn and beans as well as exotic luxury items like gold or turquoise jewelry and rare bird feathers. The total annual tribute collected by the Mexica was enormous. One scholar has estimated that it included more than 200,000 cloaks, about 650 elaborate warriors' costumes, 16,000 bales of cotton, about 5,000 large pieces of lumber (wood was scarce on the Mexica's heavily populated islands), almost 30,000 bowls made of gourds or wood, some 240 large gold disks, as well as huge quantities of corn, beans, cacao beans, chiles, tomatoes, and tropical fruits and millions of brightly colored feathers, thousands of animal skins, and other special items like wild ocelots, jaguars, snakes, and caged birds.

Tribute redistributed to the Mexica a major fraction of the goods produced by conquered tribes. Farmers and artisans in subjugated territories were required to pay in tribute as much as a third (and sometimes more) of what they produced. The Mexica employed a sizable army of tribute collectors who made certain that each conquered settlement was paid in full. On the whole, the Mexica did not

INCA MUMMY

Many ancient American peoples practiced human sacrifice as a sacred rite of communion with the gods. In the Inca ritual of capac hucha, each village sent one or two especially beautiful children between the ages of six and ten to the capital, where they were honored in religious ceremonies and then taken back to their homes in a procession of priests and villagers. After joyous festivities, the children chosen for sacrifice were given an intoxicating drink and then buried in a prepared tomb, where they died. This mummy was probably a child sacrificed in the capac hucha ritual sometime around A.D. 1500. Discovered in Chile at an altitude of about 20,000 feet, where the dry, intense cold preserved the body, the mummy was accompanied by a female votive figure wrapped in finely woven cloth and capped with a bright feather headdress, a llama figurine, a bag of coca leaves, and other objects.
Loren McIntyre.

GOLD SHAMAN FIGURE

Gold signified sacred and secular power in many Central and South American societies. The only gold artifacts to survive the plunder of the Spanish conquest — like this shaman figure — were those that had been hidden away, usually buried, often with a powerful chief. (Spaniards typically melted down any gold objects they found.) This shaman was crafted by a goldsmith of the Diquís people, who resided in Costa Rica and Colombia in the centuries just before the arrival of Europeans. The shaman's supernatural powers are suggested by the aura of crocodile heads that surround him (facing up on his shoulders and arms and down on his thighs) and by his indifference to the dangers of holding the tail of a poisonous snake in his mouth while beating a drum. Ritualistic ingestion of hallucinogens often heightened the perception that a shaman could merge human and animal forms and access the realms of cosmic mystery.

No. BCCR-963 Central Bank Museums, Costa Rica.

much interfere with the internal government of conquered regions. Instead, they usually permitted the traditional ruling elite to stay in power—so long as their tribute was paid on time. For their efforts, the conquered provinces received very little from the Mexica, except immunity from punitive raids by the dreaded Mexican warriors.

Tribute reflected the fundamental relations of power and wealth that pervaded the Mexican empire. The relatively small nobility of Mexican warriors, supported by a still smaller priesthood, possessed the military and religious power to command the obedience of thousands of nonnoble Mexica and of millions of other non-Mexica in subjugated provinces. The Mexican elite exercised their power to obtain tribute and thereby to redistribute wealth from the conquered to the conquerors, from the commoners to the nobility, from the poor to the rich. This redistribution of wealth made possible the achievements of Mexican society that eventually amazed Europeans: the temples, markets, bridges, waterworks, gardens, and zoos, not to mention the storehouses stuffed with gold and other treasures.

The empire did not permit conquered peoples to participate as full-fledged citizens of Mexican society. Instead, the empire treated the inhabitants of conquered territories as subjects. Subjugated communities felt exploited by the constant payment of tribute to the Mexica. Rather than identifying with the magnificent achievements of the empire, subject peoples felt oppressed. By depending on military conquest and constant collection of tribute, the Mexica failed to create among their subjects a belief that Mexican domination was, at some level, legitimate and equitable. The high level of discontent among subject peoples comprised the soft, vulnerable underbelly of the Mexican empire. Instead of making friends for the Mexica, the empire created many bitter and resentful opponents, a fact Spanish conquerors eventually discovered.

Conclusion: The Legacy of Ancient America

In 1492, the total indigenous population of the New World was roughly 80 to 100 million, about the same as the population of Europe. Until then, ancient Native Americans shaped the history of human beings in the New World. Much of their history remains irretrievably lost. But much can be pieced together from the artifacts they left behind over the millennia. They succeeded in establishing continuity of human habitation in the hemisphere from the time the first big-game hunters crossed Beringia until 1492 and beyond. They achieved their success through resourceful adaptation to the hemisphere's many, ever-changing natural environments. They also adapted to social and cultural changes caused by human beings—such as marriages, deaths, political struggles, and warfare—but the sparse evidence that has survived renders those adaptations almost entirely unknowable. Their creativity and artistry are unmistakably documented in the artifacts they left behind at kill sites, camps, and burial mounds. Those artifacts limn the only likenesses of ancient Americans we will ever have—blurred, shadowy images that are indisputably human but forever silent.

In the five hundred years after 1492—barely 4 percent of the time human beings have inhabited the Western Hemisphere—Europeans and their descendants began to shape and eventually to dominate American history. Native American peoples continued to influence major developments of American history from 1492 to the present. But the new wave of immigrants that at first trickled and then flooded into the New World from Europe and from Africa forever transformed the peoples and places of ancient America.

CHRONOLOGY

c. 80,000–10,000 B.C.	Wisconsin glaciation exposes Beringia, "land bridge" between Siberia and Alaska.
c. 13,000–10,000 B.C.	First humans arrive in North America.
c. 9500–9000 B.C.	Paleo-Indians in North and Central America use Clovis points to hunt big game.
c. 9000 B.C.	Mammoths and many other big-game prey of Paleo-Indians become extinct.
c. 8000–1000 B.C.	Archaic hunter-gatherer cultures dominate ancient America.
c. 7500 B.C.	Grinding stones for food processing appear in Eastern Woodlands.
c. 5000 B.C.	Corn cultivation begins in Central or South America.
c. 2000 B.C.	Some Eastern Woodlands people grow gourds and pumpkins and begin making pottery.
	Chumash in southern California develop currency based on shell beads.
c. 1700–700 B.C.	Poverty Point culture flourishes in Louisiana.
c. 1500 B.C.	Southwestern cultures begin corn cultivation.
	Bows and arrows appear among Arctic peoples.
	Stone pipes for tobacco smoking appear in Eastern Woodlands.
c. 500 B.C.	Eastern Woodlands cultures start to build burial mounds.
c. 500–100 B.C.	Adena culture develops in Ohio.
c. 300 B.C.	Some Eastern Woodlands peoples begin to cultivate corn.
c. 100 B.C.–A.D. 400	Hopewell culture emerges in Ohio and Mississippi valleys.
c. A.D. 200–900	Mogollon culture emerges in New Mexico.
c. A.D. 500	Bows and arrows appear in North America south of the Arctic.
	Pacific Northwest cultures denote wealth and status with elaborate wood carvings.
c. A.D. 500–1400	Hohokam culture develops in Arizona.
c. A.D. 800–1500	Mississippian culture flourishes in Southeast.
c. A.D. 1000	Thule people contact Vikings in northeastern Canada.
c. A.D. 1000–1150	Anasazi peoples build cliff dwellings at Mesa Verde, Colorado, and pueblos at Chaco Canyon, New Mexico.
	Mimbres culture thrives in New Mexico.
c. A.D. 1325–1500	Mexica conquer neighboring peoples and establish Mexican empire.
A.D. 1492	Columbus arrives, beginning European conquest of New World.

BIBLIOGRAPHY

GENERAL WORKS

Karen Olsen Bruhns, *Ancient South America* (1994).

Michael D. Coe, *Mexico: From the Olmecs to the Aztecs* (4th ed., 1994).

Michael Coe, Dean Snow, and Elizabeth Benson, *Atlas of Ancient America* (1986).

E. James Dixon, *Quest for the Origins of the First Americans* (1993).

Brian M. Fagan, *The Journey from Eden: The Peopling of Our World* (1990).

Brian M. Fagan, *Ancient North America: The Archaeology of a Continent* (1991).

Brian M. Fagan, *Kingdoms of Gold, Kingdoms of Jade: The Americas before Columbus* (1991).

Stuart J. Fiedel, *Prehistory of the Americas* (2nd ed., 1992).

Franklin Folsom and Mary Elting Folsom, *America's Ancient Treasures: A Guide to Archeological Sites and Museums in the United States and Canada* (4th ed., 1993).

Donald K. Grayson, *The Establishment of Human Antiquity* (1983).

Francis Jennings, *The Founders of America: How Indians Discovered the Land, Pioneered in It, and Created Great Classical Civilizations; How They Were Plunged into a Dark Age by Invasion and Conquest; and How They Are Now Reviving* (1993).

Jesse D. Jennings, *Prehistory of North America* (1974).

Jesse D. Jennings, ed., *Ancient North America* (1983).

Alvin M. Josephy Jr., *America in 1492: The World of the Indian Peoples before the Arrival of Columbus* (1992).

Richard J. Shutler Jr., ed., *Early Man in the New World* (1983).

Richard Townsend, ed., *The Ancient Americas: Art from Sacred Landscapes* (1992).

Gordon R. Willey and Jeremy A. Sabloff, *A History of American Archaeology* (2nd ed., 1980).

NORTH AMERICAN CULTURES

Mary J. Adair, *Prehistoric Agriculture in the Central Plains* (1988).

David G. Anderson, *The Savannah River Chiefdoms: Political Change in the Late Prehistoric Southeast* (1994).

Alex W. Barker and Timothy R. Pauketat, eds., *Lords of the Southwest: Social Inequality and the Native Elites of Southeastern North America* (1992).

Timothy G. Baugh and Jonathan E. Ericson, eds., *Prehistoric Exchange Systems in North America* (1994).

John Howard Blitz, *Ancient Chiefdoms of the Tombigbee* (1993).

Roy Carlson, ed., *Indian Art Traditions of the Northwest Coast* (1983).

Jefferson Chapman, *Tellico Archaeology* (1985).

Linda S. Cordell, *Prehistory of the Southwest* (1984).

Linda S. Cordell and George R. Gumerman, eds., *Dynamics of Southwest Prehistory* (1989).

David Damas, ed., *Handbook of North American Indians,* vol. 5, *Arctic* (1984).

Warren L. D'Azevedo, ed., *Handbook of North American Indians,* vol. 11, *Great Basin* (1986).

Don Dumond, *Eskimos and Aleuts* (2nd ed., 1987).

Thomas E. Emerson and R. Barry Lewis, eds., *Cahokia and the Hinterlands: Middle Mississippian Cultures of the Midwest* (1991).

Brian M. Fagan, *The Great Journey: The Peopling of Ancient America* (1987).

J. D. Figgins, "The Antiquity of Man in America," *Natural History* 27 (1927):229–39.

William Fitzhugh, ed., *Crossroads of Continents: Cultures of Siberia and Alaska* (1988).

William W. Fitzhugh and Valerie Chaussonnet, eds., *Anthropology of the North Pacific Rim* (1994).

Franklin Folsom, *Black Cowboy: The Life and Legend of George McJunkin* (1992).

Nelson Foster and Linda S. Cordell, eds., *Chilies to Chocolate: Food the Americas Gave to the World* (1992).

Kendrick Frazier, *People of Chaco: A Canyon and Its Cultures* (1986).

George C. Frison, *Prehistoric Hunters of the High Plains* (2nd ed., 1991).

George Gumerman, *A View from Black Mesa* (1984).

George Gumerman, ed., *Themes in Southwest Prehistory* (1994).

Robert F. Heizer, ed., *Handbook of North American Indians,* vol. 8, *California* (1978).

June Helm, ed., *Handbook of North American Indians,* vol. 6, *Subarctic* (1981).

R. Douglas Hurt, *Indian Agriculture in America: Prehistory to the Present* (1987).

Barry L. Isaac, ed., *Prehistoric Economies of the Pacific Northwest Coast* (1988).

Sissel Johannessen and Christine A. Hastorf, eds., *Corn and Culture in the Prehistoric New World* (1994).

Roger G. Kennedy, *Hidden Cities: The Discovery and Loss of Ancient North American Civilization* (1994).

Ruth Kirk, *Hunters of the Whale* (1975).

Theodora Kroeber, *Ishi in Two Worlds* (1965).

Steven A. LeBlanc, *The Mimbres People: Ancient Pueblo Potters of the American Southwest* (1983).

Ronald J. Mason, *Great Lakes Archaeology* (1981).

R. G. Matson, *The Origins of Southwestern Agriculture* (1991).

William E. McGoun, *Prehistoric Peoples of South Florida* (1993).

Jerald T. Milanich, *Archaeology of Precolumbian Florida* (1994).

Michael J. Moratto, *California Archaeology* (1984).

Jon Muller, *Archaeology of the Lower Ohio Valley* (1986).

Alfonso Ortiz, ed., *Handbook of North American Indians*, vol. 9, *Southwest* (1979).

Alfonso Ortiz, ed., *Handbook of North American Indians*, vol. 10, *Southwest* (1983).

Timothy R. Pauketat, *The Ascent of Chiefs: Cahokia and Mississippian Politics in Native North America* (1994).

Karl H. Schlesier, *Plains Indians*, A.D. *500–1500: The Archaeological Past of Historic Groups* (1994).

Lynne Sebastian, *The Chaco Anasazi: Sociopolitical Evolution in the Prehistoric Southwest* (1992).

Lynda Shaffer, *Native Americans before 1492: The Moundbuilding Centers of the Eastern Woodlands* (1992).

Bruce D. Smith, ed., *The Mississippian Emergence* (1990).

Dean Snow, *The Archaeology of New England* (1980).

Katherine A. Spielmann, *Interdependence in the Prehistoric Southwest: An Ecological Analysis of Plains-Pueblo Interaction* (1991).

Stuart Struever and Felicia Holton, *Koster: Americans in Search of Their Prehistoric Past* (1979).

Kenneth B. Tankersley and Barry L. Isaan, eds., *Early Paleoindian Economies of Eastern North America* (1990).

Bruce G. Trigger, *The Children of Aataentsic: A History of the Huron People to 1660* (1972).

Bruce G. Trigger, *Natives and Newcomers* (1985).

Bruce G. Trigger, ed., *Handbook of North American Indians*, vol. 15, *Northeast* (1978).

J. A. Tuck, *Onondaga Iroquois Prehistory* (1971).

William Snyder Webb, *The Adena People* (1974).

Randolph J. Widmer, *The Evolution of the Calusa: A Nonagricultural Chiefdom on the Southwest Florida Coast* (1988).

THE MEXICA

Frances Berdan, *The Aztecs of Central Mexico: An Imperial Society* (1982).

David Carrasco, *Quetzalcoatl and the Irony of Empire: Myths and Prophecies in the Aztec Tradition* (1992).

Inga Clendinnen, *Aztecs: An Interpretation* (1991).

Brian M. Fagan, *The Aztecs* (1984).

Ross Hassig, *War and Society in Ancient MesoAmerica* (1992).

Richard F. Townsend, *The Aztecs* (1992).

Muriel Porter Weaver, *The Aztecs, Maya, and Their Predecessors: Archaeology of Mesoamerica* (1981).

Eric Wolf, *Sons of the Shaking Earth* (1959).

TAINO ZEMI BASKET
This basket is an example of the effigies Tainos made to represent zemis, their deities. The effigy illustrates not only the artistry of the basket maker — probably a Taino woman — but also the basket maker's incorporation of European mirrors into a sacred object. Crafted sometime between 1492 and about 1520, the effigy suggests that Tainos readily adopted goods obtained in contacts with Europeans without altering their own traditional beliefs.
Archivio Fotografico del Museo Preistorico Etnografico L. Pigorini, Roma.

EUROPEANS AND THE NEW WORLD

1492–1600

2

A HALF HOUR BEFORE SUNRISE ON AUGUST 3, 1492, Christopher Columbus commanded three ships to catch the tide out of a harbor in southern Spain and sail west. Barely two months later, in the predawn moonlight of October 12, 1492, Columbus glimpsed an island on the western horizon. At last, he believed, he had found what he had been looking for, a western route across the Atlantic Ocean to Japan, China, and India. For almost three hours—probably the longest three hours in Columbus's life—the little fleet lay offshore, awaiting daylight. To negotiate with the Muslim traders he soon expected to encounter, Columbus had brought along a translator who spoke Arabic, among other languages. At daybreak, Columbus could see people gathered on the shore of the island; they had spotted his ships. Columbus and several of his crew rowed ashore. As the curious islanders crowded around to watch, Columbus claimed possession of the land for Ferdinand and Isabella, king and queen of Spain, who had sponsored his voyage. He named the island San Salvador, in honor of the Savior, Jesus Christ.

A day or two afterward, Columbus described that first encounter with the inhabitants of San Salvador in an extensive diary he kept during his voyage. He called these people Indians (*yndios* in the original Spanish), assuming that their island, which they called Guanahani, lay somewhere in the East Indies near Japan or China. They did not seem to possess the riches Columbus expected to find in the East. "It seemed to me that they were a people very poor in everything," he wrote. He and his men gave them red caps, glass beads, small bells, and other trinkets, "in which they took so much pleasure and became so much our friends that it was a marvel," he noted. As a sign of friendship, the Indians "brought us parrots and cotton thread in balls and javelins and many other things."

The Indians were not dressed in the finery Columbus expected to see adorning people in the East. "All of them go around as naked as their mothers bore them; and the women also," he observed. Their skin color was "neither black nor white." They adorned themselves with black, white, or red pigment. He judged these people "very well formed, with handsome bodies and good faces." Their hair was "coarse—almost like the tail of a horse—and short." They were not familiar with the Spaniards' weapons. "I showed them swords," Columbus wrote, "and they took them by the edge and through ignorance cut themselves." He explained that "they have no iron. Their javelins are shafts without iron." He noted that some of the Indians had scars from wounds and he "made signs to them asking what [the scars] were; and they showed me how people from other islands nearby came there and tried to [kidnap] them." This first encounter led Columbus to conclude, "They should be good and intelligent servants, for I see that they say very quickly every-

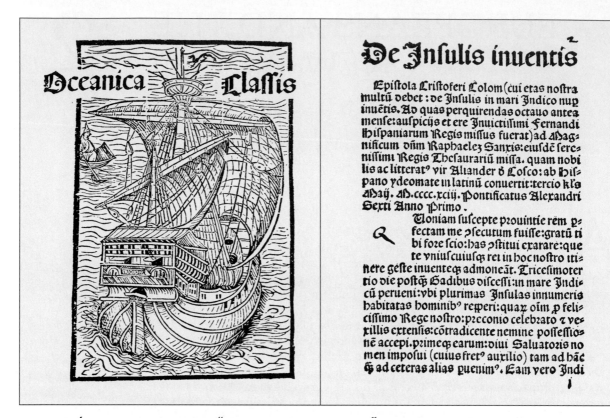

COLUMBUS'S LETTER ANNOUNCING "THE DISCOVERED ISLANDS"
*Shortly after Columbus arrived back in Lisbon in 1493, he rushed a letter — written in Latin —
to Ferdinand and Isabella with the good news of his discoveries across the Atlantic. His news
spread quickly. In less than three months, by the time Columbus had traveled to Barcelona and
reported personally to the Spanish monarchs, his letter had already been published in Spain and
was soon reprinted in other countries. In the edition shown here, published in Switzerland in
1493, the ship under the Latin heading "Ocean Fleet" is the* Santa María, *which had in fact run
aground in the Caribbean on Christmas Eve 1492. Columbus had dismantled it and used its timbers to build a fort for the sailors he did not have room to take back to Spain on his remaining
two ships.*
Special Collections, New York Public Library.

thing that is said to them; and I believe that they
would become Christians very easily, for it seemed
to me that they had no religion."

The people Columbus called Indians called
themselves Tainos. To them, *Taino* meant "good" or
"noble," and it distinguished them from the hostile
Caribs who were responsible for the scars Columbus noticed. Tainos inhabited most of the islands
Columbus visited on his first voyage, as had their
ancestors for more than two centuries. Other ancient
peoples had lived on the islands since 5000 B.C.
Tainos were an agricultural people. Their principal

food was cassava, a nutritious root that women
grated and ground into flour. They also grew sweet
potatoes, corn, cotton, tobacco, and other crops. To
fish and to travel from island to island, the Tainos
built canoes by hollowing out logs, some big
enough to hold fifty people.

Taino villages usually contained one or two
thousand people who lived in round wooden
houses with thatched roofs. Each village was ruled
by a chief who owed allegiance to a higher chief
who governed several villages. A chief could be either a woman or a man. Tainos traced their lineage

through their mothers rather than their fathers. This matrilineal system determined how property, social status, and the position of chief were inherited. Tainos worshiped gods they called zemis. Zemis included the spirits of ancestors and of natural objects like trees or stones. Tainos made effigies that represented their zemis and performed rituals to honor them. Of utmost interest to Columbus, Tainos mined gold in small quantities.

What the Tainos thought about Columbus and his men we can only surmise from what Columbus wrote. At first, Columbus believed that the Tainos thought the Spaniards came from heaven. Two days after the initial encounter, he noted that several Tainos swam out to the Spaniards' ships and called out to others on the shore, "Come see the men who came from the heavens." What these Tainos really said cannot be known. After six weeks of additional experience with Tainos, Columbus was no longer confident that he understood them. Late in November 1492, he wrote that "the people of these lands do not understand me nor do I, nor anyone else that I have with me, them. And many times I understand one thing said by these Indians . . . for another, its contrary." Clearly, the translator's knowledge of Arabic did not help communicate with these "Indians."

The confused communication between Europeans and Tainos suggests how different, how strange, each group seemed to the other. For example, Columbus's observation that the Tainos had "no religion" meant no religion that he recognized. We can only imagine what the Tainos thought about the Europeans' religion; presumably they saw it as different from their worship of zemis. Columbus's perceptions of Tainos were shaped by European ideas, attitudes, and expectations, just as Tainos' perceptions of Europeans were colored by their own culture and heritage. Yet the word that Columbus coined for the Tainos—"Indians," a word that originated in a colossal misunderstanding—hinted at the direction of the future. To Europeans, "Indians" came to mean all native inhabitants of the New World. After 1492, the perceptions and cultures of Europeans began to exert a transforming influence on the New World and its peoples.

Long before 1492, certain Europeans restlessly expanded the limits of the world known to them. Their efforts made possible Columbus's encounter with the Tainos. In turn, Columbus's landfall in the Caribbean not only changed the history of the Tainos; it also changed the history of Europe and the rest of the world. After 1492, Europeans slowly began to grasp that Columbus had located what they called a New World, a Western Hemisphere containing enormous lands separated by vast oceans from the Old World of Europe, Asia, and Africa. After 1492, neither the New World nor the Old would ever be the same.

Europe in the Age of Exploration

Europeans first encountered the New World about five hundred years before Columbus arrived on San Salvador. Around the year 1000, Norse who had ventured across the North Atlantic to Iceland and Greenland founded a small fishing settlement in North America at L'Anse aux Meadows on the tip of Newfoundland. Excavations by modern archaeologists have disclosed that the Norse occupied the fifteen or so dwellings at the site intermittently for about ten years. After 1000, the Viking expansionism that had driven the Norse to the shores of Newfoundland began to decline as the world's climate cooled, choking the North Atlantic with ice and making it impassable. Viking sagas memorialized the Norse "discovery," but it had virtually no other impact in the New World or in Europe.

Historically, the East—not the West—attracted Europeans. In 1096, Christian Crusaders set out for the Middle East to "liberate" the Holy Lands from their Muslim rulers. The Crusaders returned to the Middle East twice during the next century, but they never accomplished their religious and political goal of establishing a permanent Christian stronghold in the heart of Islamic territory. They did, however, stimulate trade in eastern goods.

Wealthy Europeans developed a taste for luxury goods from Asia and Africa, and merchants competed to satisfy that taste. The profits to be made lured ambitious Europeans to find new ways to expand trade of all kinds. As Europeans traded with the East and with one another, they developed new information about the world they inhabited. One of the things some learned was that the known world was not all there was to know. A few people —sailors, merchants, aristocrats—took the risks of venturing beyond the limits of what was known. Those risks were genuine and could be deadly. But sometimes they paid off in new information, new opportunities, and eventually in the discovery of a New World entirely unknown to Europeans.

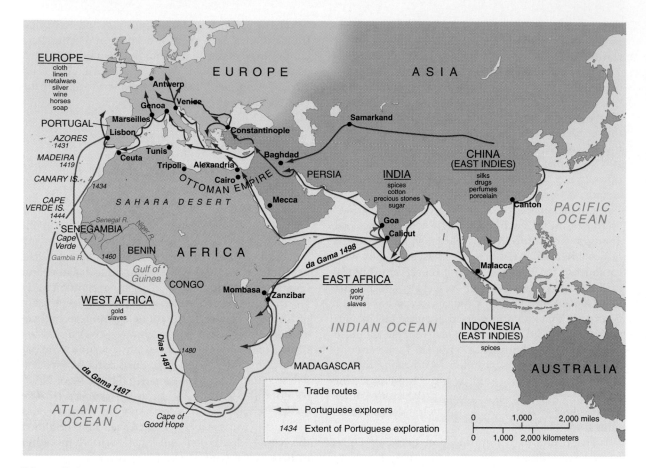

MAP 2.1

European Trade Routes and Portuguese Exploration in the Fifteenth Century

The strategic geographical position of Italian cities as a conduit for overland trade from Asia was slowly undermined during the fifteenth century by Portuguese explorers who hopscotched along the coast of Africa and eventually found a sea route that opened the rich trade of the East to Portuguese merchants.

Mediterranean Trade and European Expansion

From the twelfth century through the fifteenth century, spices, silk, carpets, ivory, gold, and other exotic goods traveled overland from Persia, Asia Minor, India, and Africa and then funneled into continental Europe through Mediterranean trade routes. Dominated primarily by the Italian cities of Venice, Genoa, and Pisa, this lucrative trade enriched Italian merchants and bankers who had been doing business with the East since the Crusades. Rival merchants and financiers in other European cities coveted a share of the Mediterranean trade.

But the Italians battled fiercely to protect their near-monopoly of access to eastern goods. Instead of trying to displace the Italians, merchants in other European countries chose the far safer alternative of trading with them.

Late in the thirteenth century a fleet of Genoese ships opened a new phase of the Mediterranean trade by venturing through the Strait of Gibraltar into the stormy waters of the North Atlantic, bringing goods from southern Europe to markets in northern Europe. Ocean-borne access to North Atlantic ports allowed Mediterranean traders to carry much larger quantities much less expensively than in the old overland trade. The vitality of the

Mediterranean trade in the fourteenth and fifteenth centuries gave merchants and governments who participated in the trade few reasons to look for fresh alternatives. New routes to the East and the discovery of new lands entirely unknown to Europeans were the stuff of fantasy.

The preconditions for turning fantasy into reality existed in fifteenth-century Europe. In the mid-fourteenth century, Europeans suffered a catastrophic epidemic of bubonic plague. The Black Death, as it was called, killed about a third of the European population, a greater disaster than anything in Europe before or since. This devastating pestilence had repercussions that lasted for more than a century. The drastic depopulation, along with other developments, disrupted the old institutions of medieval Europe. So many people died that the pressure of population on Europe's food resources was significantly eased. Survivors, many of whom had inherited property from those who died, had greater opportunities for advancement. Many peasants moved from village to village and even to cities. The experience of disruptive change undermined the traditional belief that one's place in the world was fixed and unchangeable.

Most Europeans, however, did not view these changes in positive terms. Instead, they perceived the world as a place of alarming risks where the delicate balance of health, harvests, and peace that sustained life could quickly be tipped toward disaster by epidemics, famine, and violence. A history of the world written in the late fifteenth century reflected this widespread sense of uncertainty and insecurity by referring to "the calamity of our time." Most Europeans resolved to protect themselves from what they perceived as the constant threat of calamity by worshiping the supernatural, by living amid kinfolk and friends, and by maintaining good relations with those who were richer and more powerful. Curiously, the insecurity and uncertainty of fifteenth-century life encouraged a few to take greater risks. A sailor's willingness to embark on a dangerous sea voyage through uncharted waters to points unknown was one of many European responses to the risks and opportunities of fifteenth-century life.

Some aristocrats, members of the most powerful class in European society, had reasons to hazard the risks involved in exploration. Voyages of exploration provided a convenient outlet for the military energies of lesser members of the nobility and those who aspired to noble rank. Many explorers were young sons of aristocratic families who had fallen on hard times. Others, like Columbus, were not of noble birth but hoped to gain entrance to the aristocracy as a reward for their daring achievements. By taking the risks of exploration outside Europe, explorers sought to win recognition and rewards within European society.

The insecurity and uncertainty of fifteenth-century life encouraged a few Europeans to take great risks, such as embarking on a dangerous sea voyage through uncharted waters to points unknown.

Scientific and technological advances also helped set the stage for exploration. The invention of movable type stimulated the diffusion of information among literate Europeans. In the last half of the fifteenth century, printing presses churned out thousands of books a year, accelerating the spread of fresh ideas. Columbus, like many other Europeans, bought books, read them, and grappled with them, making detailed notes in the margins of pages. Improvements in navigation made it possible for Columbus and other mariners to better determine their ship's direction, speed, and location, even when out of sight of land. By the end of the fourteenth century, the crucial navigational aids employed by explorers were already available. Compasses were in widespread use. Hourglasses allowed fairly precise determination of elapsed time, useful in estimating speed. The astrolabe and the quadrant, devices for determining latitude, were beginning to be adopted by sailors. However, the difficulty of standing on the pitching deck of a ship at sea and sighting the star Polaris while simultaneously measuring the angle it formed with the horizon often made the readings worthless. Even experienced sailors sometimes became hopelessly lost. Charts called portulanos helped them find their way if they were within sight of land. Portulanos included detailed drawings of the shoreline and compass settings for sailing from one point to another. Fifteenth-century merchant ships designed for the Mediterranean trade to the North Atlantic were built to carry heavy cargoes long distances in stormy seas—qualities as useful for exploration as for trade.

These and other technological advances were known to many people throughout fifteenth-century Europe. The Portuguese intentionally seized them to blaze a trail beyond the limits of the known world.

A Century of Portuguese Exploration

In many ways, Portugal was an unlikely candidate to take the lead in exploration. A small country, Portugal was populated by poor peasants governed by a tiny minority of noble families. Europe's richest courts and most brilliant thinkers were elsewhere, especially in Italy. Yet Portugal, with less than 2 percent of the population of Christian Europe, devoted far more energy and wealth to the geographical exploration of the world between 1415 and 1460 than all the other countries of Europe combined.

Facing the Atlantic on the Iberian peninsula, the Portuguese lived on the fringes of the thriving Mediterranean trade. During the fourteenth century, merchants and sailors in Lisbon gained valuable experience in the extensive North Atlantic trade that Italians still controlled at its eastern source. As a Christian kingdom, Portugal cooperated with Spanish monarchs in the Reconquest, the centuries-long drive to expel Muslims from their residence on the Iberian peninsula. The religious zeal that propelled the Reconquest also justified continued expansion into what the Portuguese considered heathen lands. The key victory came in 1415 when Portuguese forces conquered Ceuta, a Muslim bastion at the mouth of the Strait of Gibraltar. After 1415, Muslim enemies no longer blocked Portugal's access to the Atlantic coast of Africa.

The Portuguese government actively encouraged exploration. The most influential advocate was Prince Henry the Navigator. The third son of the Portuguese king, Henry channeled his energy and ambition into sponsoring voyages of exploration and conquest. From 1415 until his death in 1460, he stood at the forefront of Portuguese expansion, collecting the latest information about sailing techniques and geography, advocating new crusades against the Muslims, encouraging fresh sources of trade to fatten Portuguese pocketbooks, and pushing explorers to go farther and farther still.

Henry had the backing of the king and the pope to extend the Reconquest down the African coast. Missionaries were essential passengers aboard the explorers' ships. However, economic motives fueled Portuguese exploration. Conquests along the African coast promised to wrest wheat fields from their Moroccan owners and secure Portugal's food supply. Africa also supplied most of Europe's gold. Produced in mines along the headwaters of the Niger, Senegal, and Gambia Rivers, African gold passed through the hands of Mali traders, who took it by caravan across the Sahara Desert to the east-

BENIN BRONZE
This bronze was crafted in the sixteenth century by a highly skilled artist of the Benin people of western Africa. The bronze shows a Benin chief flanked by two of his warriors (lower left and right) and a Portuguese man (upper right). The Portuguese figure holds a gold spiral in his hand, presumably obtained in trade with Africans. In turn, the chief wears coral beads obtained in trade with the Portuguese on the African coast. The heavily armed chief and warriors suggest one reason why the Portuguese confined their activities to the coast. Note that the Portuguese figure does not have a weapon, clearly indicating the artist's sense of who had the upper hand.
British Museum.

ern Mediterranean. Rumors of the wealth of Mali raced through Europe after a Mali ruler made a pilgrimage to Mecca in 1324 and distributed lavish gifts transported by more than eighty camels, each of them carrying three hundred pounds of gold. Gold was the basis of currency in European trade and it was scarce in the fifteenth century. The accelerating pace of commerce increased the need for currency in Europe, while purchases in the East drained gold away from European markets.

At first, the possibility of opening a sea route to the rich trade of the East was unimaginable. It played no part in Portuguese calculations until the 1440s, about thirty years after their African explorations had begun. When the word *discovery* first entered the Portuguese language, it meant pushing back the boundaries of the Mediterranean world and penetrating the mists that had caused sailors to name the ocean off the south coast of Morocco the Sea of Darkness. Portuguese sailors slowly learned how to sail through those mists and take advantage of the winds and currents of the mid-Atlantic, laying the foundation of expertise and confidence that ultimately permitted Columbus to dream of going west.

Neither the Portuguese nor anybody else in Europe knew how big Africa was. At first, Portuguese mariners cautiously edged into the Sea of Darkness along the African coast, seldom venturing beyond sight of land. By 1434, they had reached the northern edge of the Sahara Desert, where strong westerly currents swept them far out to sea. Within the next few years they learned how to ride the powerful westerly currents far away from the coast before sailing back toward land, a technique that allowed them to reach Cape Verde by 1444.

To stow the supplies necessary for long periods at sea and to withstand the battering of ocean waves, the Portuguese developed the caravel, a sturdy ship that became the workhorse of exploration. The caravel enabled Portuguese sailors to round Cape Verde by first sailing hundreds of miles west into the Atlantic before catching favorable trade winds and currents that swung them back along the African coast. Navigating these huge westward loops into the Atlantic, Portuguese caravels sailed into and around the Gulf of Guinea and as far south as the Congo by 1480.

Portuguese explorations paid off handsomely in trade with Africans. Although fierce African resistance confined the Portuguese to coastal trading posts, Portuguese traders bartered successfully for gold, slaves, and ivory. African rulers controlled the African interior and, to a large degree, the terms of trade on the coast. The Portuguese tried to stay on good terms with the leaders of such powerful societies as the Wolof of Senegambia and the Obas of Benin. Portuguese merchants learned that relatively peaceful trading posts were far more profitable than violent conquests and attempts at colonization. In the 1460s, the Portuguese employed African slaves to develop sugar plantations on the Cape Verde Islands, inaugurating an association between African slaves and plantation labor that would flourish in the New World in the centuries to come.

About 1480, the Portuguese began a conscious search for a sea route to Asia. Sailors now had to navigate enormous westward loops, this time into the South Atlantic, to avoid the strong northerly currents streaming around the Cape of Good Hope at the southern tip of Africa. In 1488, Bartolomeu Dias sailed around the Cape far enough to discover that the African coast finally turned north. He hurried back to Lisbon with the exciting news that it appeared to be possible to sail on to India and China. In 1498, after ten years of careful preparation, Vasco da Gama commanded the first Portuguese fleet that sailed to India. Da Gama learned about the potential profits of seaborne trade with the East. Pepper, for example, could be purchased in Calicut for 96 percent less than in Venice. Portugal quickly capitalized on the obvious commercial potential of da Gama's new sea route.

Within a few years, the Portuguese established and defended trading posts in India and pushed on to Indonesia and China (collectively referred to as the East Indies). By the early sixteenth century, the Portuguese commanded a far-flung empire in the East Indies. Portuguese officials administered local governments, and Catholic missionaries baptized thousands of Asian Christians. But the lifeblood of the empire was commerce. The new sea route to the East eliminated overland travel and the numerous intermediate merchants and their markups, integral parts of the old Mediterranean trade routes. As a result, Portuguese merchants could set a much lower price on eastern goods. Lower prices allowed Europeans to purchase more eastern goods than ever before, to the great profit of Portuguese traders.

By a century of African explorations, Portugal broke the monopoly of the old Mediterranean trade with the East, dramatically expanded the known world, established a network of missions and trading posts in Africa and Asia, and developed methods of sailing the high seas that Columbus employed on his revolutionary voyage west.

A Surprising New World in the Western Atlantic

In many ways, the Portuguese were the logical candidates to discover America. They had pioneered the frontiers of seafaring, exploration, and geography for almost a century. However, the knowledge and experience that led them around the Cape of Good Hope discouraged them from trying to sail across the Atlantic. They knew better than to undertake such a risky venture. The discovery of America required someone bold enough to believe that the experts were wrong, that despite the best available scientific knowledge, it was possible to reach the East Indies by sailing west. That person was Christopher Columbus.

Born in 1451 into the family of an obscure master weaver in Genoa, Italy, Columbus received a practical education at his father's woolen looms, in the streets, and along the wharves of the city. The allure of ships from remote Mediterranean ports proved irresistible to Columbus. Like thousands of other Genoese boys, he went to sea when he was about fourteen. Crisscrossing the Mediterranean as a sailor, he learned the arts of navigation, although he continued to work as a weaver. About 1476, Columbus moved to Lisbon and two or three years later married Felipa Moniz. Felipa gave Columbus valuable connections to Portugal's royal court. Her father, Bartolomeu, had been raised in the household of Prince Henry the Navigator and had retained close ties to the prince. Bartolomeu helped conquer the Madeira Islands, where he became a prominent merchant deeply involved in the Portuguese voyages to the African coast. Although Bartolomeu died long before Felipa's marriage, Columbus inherited his maps and papers crammed with information about the currents and winds of the Atlantic gathered from innumerable Portuguese sailors. Columbus himself sailed frequently to the Madeira Islands and at least twice all the way to the coast of central Africa. He learned firsthand about the westward loops into the Atlantic that took advantage of prevailing winds and currents. By the mid-1480s, he had become obsessed with the idea of reaching Asia by continuing to sail west instead of turning back toward the African coast.

The Explorations of Columbus

Like other Europeans, Columbus believed that the earth was a sphere. Theoretically, they felt, it was possible to reach the East Indies by sailing west. Ancient scientists whose writings were revered by contemporary Renaissance scholars disagreed about the practicality of the idea. Both the philosopher Aristotle and the geographer Strabo suggested it could be done. Ptolemy, an ancient geographer whose writings were considered the final authority by most fifteenth-century Europeans, concluded that the earth was simply too big to make it feasible to sail west from Europe to Asia. Sailors would die of thirst and starvation before they reached the East Indies.

Columbus rejected this conventional Ptolemaic wisdom. He preferred the estimate of the earth's size worked out by a medieval Muslim geographer. With a series of flawed calculations converting Arabic miles to nautical equivalents, Columbus estimated the circumference of the earth at a little over 16,000 nautical miles, a good 25 percent smaller than it really is. Columbus reasoned that Asia lay about 2,500 miles from the westernmost boundary of the known world, a shorter distance than Portuguese ships routinely sailed between Lisbon and the African Congo. In fact, the shortest distance to Japan from Europe's jumping off point in the Canary Islands was almost 11,000 miles. Convinced that his misguided calculations were correct, Columbus became obsessed with a scheme to prove he was right.

Columbus tried to convince the Portuguese king to sponsor an expedition west. But his peculiar notions about geography did not divert the Portuguese monarchy from its lucrative African explorations. Disappointed by the Portuguese, Columbus moved to Spain in 1485 and sought backing from King Ferdinand and Queen Isabella. Experts on geography and navigation advised the monarchs that Columbus's plan violated the basic precepts of contemporary knowledge and had little to recommend it. He continued to lobby for his plan in Spain and even tried to interest the royal courts of England and France. He obtained only polite skepticism and a few modest but encouraging grants—until 1492, when Ferdinand and Isabella finally agreed to finance most of the journey. The monarchs saw Columbus's venture as an inexpensive gamble: If it failed, not much was lost; if it succeeded, a great deal might be gained. In addition to money and their royal blessing, the monarchs gave Columbus a letter of introduction to the Grand Khan of the Mongols, whom Columbus expected to meet soon after he arrived in China.

After barely three months of hurried preparation, Columbus and his small fleet—the *Niña* and *Pinta,* both caravels, and the *Santa María,* a larger merchant vessel—embarked for the Canary Islands along the westerly route into the Atlantic that Portuguese sailors had pioneered seventy-five years earlier. When he cast off from the Canaries, he did not head for the coast of Africa; instead he kept sailing west. Six weeks later, he landed on a tiny Caribbean island (probably Watling Island), which he named San Salvador.

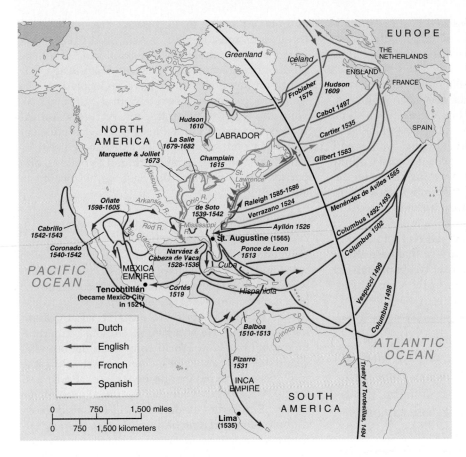

MAP 2.2
European Explorations in Sixteenth-Century America
This map illustrates the approximate routes of early European explorations of the New World. Note that — with the exception of the voyage of John Cabot — English, French, and Dutch explorers were late-comers. What accounts for their tardiness?

Columbus and his men understood that they had made a momentous discovery. Yet they found it frustrating. Although the Tainos proved friendly and accommodating, they possessed little gold and none of the riches Columbus expected to find in the East. For three months Columbus cruised from island to island, looking for the king of Japan and reconnoitering these strange new lands.

In mid-January 1493, he started back, taking seven Tainos with him. Blown off course by storms, he landed first in Portugal, where he was obliged to report his exciting news to the king. The Portuguese found nothing astounding about Columbus's discovery. They believed he had simply found some new islands far out in the Atlantic. When Columbus finally managed to reach Isabella and Ferdinand in mid-March, they were overjoyed by his news. With a voyage that had lasted barely eight months, Columbus appeared to have catapulted Spain from a secondary position in the race for a sea route to Asia into that of a serious challenger to Portugal, whose explorers had not yet sailed to India or China. Columbus and his Taino companions became the toast of the royal court. Columbus was appointed Admiral of the Ocean Sea, viceroy and governor of the islands he had discovered, and a member of the hereditary nobility, and he was permitted to use the royal insignia on his coat of arms. All seven Tainos were baptized as Christians, Ferdinand and his son serving as their godfathers.

The Spanish monarchs, following Portuguese precedent, rushed to the pope to obtain confirmation of their claim to Columbus's discoveries. Pope Alexander VI, a Spaniard, complied. In May 1493, he issued the decree *Inter caetera* granting to Spain all land discovered west of an imaginary line lying 300 miles west of the Azores. The decree alarmed the Portuguese, who believed that it violated their rights under previous papal grants. To protect their African claims, the Portuguese negotiated with Spain the Treaty of Tordesillas in 1494. The treaty shifted the imaginary line to 1,100 miles west of the Canary Islands. Land discovered west of the line belonged to Spain, while Portugal claimed land to the east. In effect, the treaty reassured Portugal and allowed Spain to follow up Columbus's discovery without being threatened by the menacing Portuguese navy.

In the fall of 1493, Isabella and Ferdinand sent Columbus back west to locate the Asian mainland. This time he commanded a fleet of seventeen ships and more than one thousand men, who planned to settle, explore, find gold, and get rich. Near the end of his first voyage, a shipwreck had forced Columbus to leave behind thirty-nine of his sailors on the island of Hispaniola. When Columbus returned in 1493, he learned that his men had terrorized the Tainos, kidnapped local women, and held them in harems; in retaliation, Taino chiefs had killed all of the Spaniards. The brief history of that first group of Spaniards to reside in the New World prefigured much of what was to happen in the years ahead.

With a voyage that had lasted barely eight months, Columbus appeared to have catapulted Spain from a secondary position in the race for a sea route to Asia into that of a serious challenger to Portugal, whose explorers had not yet sailed to India or China.

Columbus and other Spaniards sailed from island to island. Some gold turned up, but just enough to keep the Spaniards looking for more. The settlers quarreled among themselves and brutalized the Indians. Before long, prospects of beating the Portuguese to Asia began to dim along with the hope of finding vast hoards of gold. Before Columbus died in 1506, he had returned to the New World two more times (1498–1500 and 1502–1504) without relinquishing his belief that the East Indies were there, someplace. Explorers continued to search for a passage to the East or some other source of profit. But for a generation after 1492, the meager results disappointed the Spanish crown.

Nonetheless, Columbus's discoveries forced sixteenth-century Europeans to think about the world in new terms. Columbus proved that it was possible to sail from Europe to the western rim of the Atlantic in six or seven weeks and to get back to Europe. His superior navigational skills set the standard route and time of passage that prevailed for two centuries. Columbus also made clear that beyond the western shores of the Atlantic lay lands entirely unknown to Europeans. The belief that those lands must be part of Asia fired Columbus's imagination. Without this geographical fantasy he would never have undertaken his first voyage; certainly no monarch would have sponsored it. The Asian trade dangled like a tempting carrot just beyond the reach of fifteenth-century rulers and explorers. For many years after 1492, it was not clear whether Columbus had in fact discovered the Atlantic coast of Asia, as he continued to believe, or a barrier to the riches of the East, as he refused to admit.

The Geographic Revolution

Peter Martyr, a priest and humanist scholar who was Queen Isabella's chaplain, was present in 1493 when Columbus first described his discovery to the queen. Soon afterward, Peter Martyr began to use the phrase "New World" to describe what Columbus had found. He accepted Columbus's interpretation that this New World comprised the outlying islands of the East Indies. The truth slowly came into focus as explorers probed to the north and south. Within thirty years of Columbus's initial discovery, Europeans' understanding of world geography underwent a revolution. Of course most Europeans, isolated in rural villages, remained ignorant of the revolution. An elite of perhaps twenty thousand people surrounding the royal courts and trading centers of western Europe had access to information about the new geography of the world. Before 1492, they could not imagine the existence of a New World. It took a generation of additional exploration before they could comprehend the general contours of what Columbus had found.

In 1497, King Henry VII of England, who had spurned Columbus's request for sponsorship a decade earlier, sent another Genoese sailor, John Cabot, to look for a passage to the Indies across the North Atlantic. Cabot managed to reach the tip of Newfoundland, which he too believed was part of Asia. Cabot hurried back to England, assembled a small fleet to follow up his discovery, and returned in 1498. But he was never heard from again. Three thousand miles to the south, in 1498 Columbus touched the mainland of Venezuela, near the mouth of the Orinoco River. A year later, another Spanish expedition landed about six hundred miles farther south, accompanied by Amerigo Vespucci, an Italian businessman whose avocation was geography. In 1500, Pedro Álvars Cabral commanded a Por-

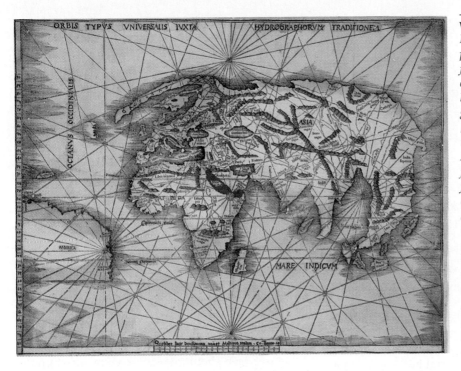

WALDSEEMÜLLER MAP

In 1507, Martin Waldseemüller prepared this map, carefully conforming to the accepted wisdom of the ancient geographer Ptolemy except, he wrote "as regards the new lands." "Hitherto [the world] has been divided into three parts, Europe, Africa, and Asia," Waldseemüller explained, following Ptolemy. "Now, a fourth part has been discovered. . . . The first three parts are continents, while the fourth is an island. . . ." The map showed that the "new lands" were not connected to Asia, but it left vague the western shores of the "island" he named America.

Courtesy of the John Carter Brown Library at Brown University.

tuguese fleet bound for the Indian Ocean; as it looped westward into the Atlantic, it made a landfall on the coast of Brazil. The next year the Portuguese sent Vespucci west to determine whether Cabral's discovery lay on their side of the Tordesillas line, as in fact it did.

By the beginning of the sixteenth century, it was clear that several large chunks of land cluttered the western Atlantic. A few cartographers speculated that these chunks were connected to one another in a continent that was not Asia. In 1507, Martin Waldseemüller, a German cartographer, published the first map that showed the New World as a continent separate from Asia; he named the continent America, in honor of Vespucci. Waldseemüller's geography did not convince everybody. Other contemporary maps continued to show a water route to Asia across the Western Hemisphere. In 1516, even Waldseemüller retreated and published a revised map that portrayed America jammed against Asia.

Two additional discoveries confirmed Waldseemüller's initial speculation. In 1513, Vasco Núñez de Balboa crossed the isthmus of Panama and reached the Pacific Ocean. Clearly, more water lay between the New World and Asia. How much water Ferdinand Magellan discovered when he set out to circumnavigate the globe in 1519. Sponsored by King Charles I of Spain, Magellan sailed first to the New World. He rounded Cape Horn at the southern tip of South America through what became known as the Straits of Magellan and entered the Pacific late in November 1520. Crossing the Pacific took almost four months. When he reached the Philippines, his crew had been decimated by extreme hunger and thirst. Magellan himself was killed by Philippine tribesmen. A remnant of his expedition continued into the Indian Ocean and managed to transport a cargo of spices back to Spain in 1522.

Magellan's voyage left no doubt that America was a continent separated from Asia by the enormous Pacific Ocean. The voyage made clear that Columbus was dead wrong about the identity of what he had discovered.

In most ways Magellan's voyage was a disaster. One ship and 18 men managed to return from an expedition that had begun with five ships and more than 250 men. But the geographic information it provided left no doubt that America was a conti-

Justifying Conquest

A few individual Spaniards raised their voices against the brutal treatment of Indians in Spanish colonial America. In 1511, a Dominican friar named Antón Montesino delivered a blistering sermon that astonished the Spaniards gathered in the church in Santo Domingo, headquarters of the Spanish Caribbean.

DOCUMENT 1. Excerpt from Montesino's 1511 Sermon

Your greed for gold is blind. Your pride, your lust, your anger, your envy, your sloth, all blind. . . . You are in mortal sin. And you are heading for damnation. . . . For you are destroying an innocent people. For they are God's people, these innocents, whom you destroyed. By what right do you make them die? Mining gold for you in your mines or working for you in your fields, by what right do you unleash enslaving wars upon them? They have lived in peace in this land before you came, in peace in their own homes. They did nothing to harm you to cause you to slaughter them wholesale. . . . Are you not under God's command to love them as you love yourselves? Are you out of your souls, out of your minds? Yes. And that will bring you to damnation.

Montesino returned to Spain to bring the Indians' plight to the king's attention. In 1512 and 1513, King Ferdinand met with philosophers, theologians, and other advisers and concluded that the only justification for conquest was to spread the Christian faith. To but-tress this claim, the king had his advisers prepare the Requerimiento. Conquistadors were commanded to read the Requerimiento to Indians before any act of conquest. Beginning in 1514, they routinely did so, reading aloud in Spanish while other Spaniards brandishing unsheathed swords stood nearby.

DOCUMENT 2: Excerpt from the *Requerimiento*

On the part of the king . . . [and] queen of [Spain], subduers of the barbarous nations, we their servants notify and make known to you, as best we can, that the Lord our God, living and eternal, created the heaven and the earth, and one man and one woman, of whom you and we, and all the men of the world, were and are descendants. . . .

God our lord gave charge to one man called St. Peter, that he should be lord and superior to all the men in the world, that all should obey him, and that he should be the head of the whole human race, wherever men should live . . . and he gave him the world for his kingdom and jurisdiction.

And he commanded him to place his seat in Rome, as the spot most fitting to rule the world from. . . . This man was called Pope, as if to say, Admirable Great Father and Governor of men. The men who lived in that time obeyed that St. Peter and took him for lord, king, and superior of the universe. So also they have regarded the others who after him have been elected to the pontificate, and so has it been continued even till now, and will continue till the end of the world.

One of these pontiffs, who succeeded that St. Peter as lord of the world . . . made donation of these islands and mainland to the aforesaid king and queen [of Spain] and to their successors. . . .

---

nent separated from Asia by the enormous Pacific Ocean. The voyage made clear that Columbus was dead wrong about the identity of what he had discovered. Furthermore, while the voyage proved it was possible to sail west to reach the East Indies, it also demonstrated that that was a terrible way to go. Some sixteenth-century explorers continued to hope that a water passage across the American landmass might still be located. But most Europeans who sailed west after Magellan had their sights set on the New World, not on Asia.

Columbus's arrival in the Caribbean anchored the western end of what might be imagined as a sea bridge that spanned the Atlantic, connecting the New World to Europe. That sea bridge ended the separation of the hemispheres and opened a pathway for exploration, conquest, settlement, and commerce that has never since been disrupted. The Europeans who first ventured across that bridge carried with them the legacy of centuries of European expansion, trade, and intellectual awakening. The Native Americans they confronted on the west-

So their highnesses are kings and lords of these islands and mainland by virtue of this donation; and . . . almost all those to whom this has been notified, have received and served their highnesses, as lords and kings, in the way that subjects ought to do, with good will, without any resistance, immediately, without delay, when they were informed of the aforesaid facts. And also they received and obeyed the priests whom their highnesses sent to preach to them and to teach them our holy faith; and all these, of their own free will, without any reward or condition have become Christians, and are so, and the highnesses have joyfully and graciously received them, and they have also commanded them to be treated as their subjects and vassals; and you too are held and obliged to do the same. Wherefore, as best we can, we ask and require that you consider what we have said to you, and that you take the time that shall be necessary to understand and deliberate upon it, and that you acknowledge the Church as the ruler and superior of the whole world, and the high priest called Pope, and in his name the king and queen [of Spain] our lords, in his place, as superiors and lords and kings of these islands and this mainland by virtue of the said donation, and that you consent and permit that these religious fathers declare and preach to you. . . .

If you do so . . . we . . . shall receive you in all love and charity, and shall leave you your wives and your children and your lands free without servitude, that you may do with them and with yourselves freely what you like and think best, and they shall not compel you to turn to Christians unless you yourselves, when informed of the truth, should wish to be converted to our holy Catholic faith. . . . And besides this, their highnesses award you many privileges and exemptions and will grant you many benefits.

But if you do not do this or if you maliciously delay in doing it, I certify to you that with the help of God we shall forcefully enter into your country and shall make war against you in all ways and manners that we can, and shall subject you to the yoke and obedience of the Church and of their highnesses; we shall take you and your wives and your children and shall make slaves of them, and as such shall sell and dispose of them as their highnesses may command; and we shall take away your goods and shall do to you all the harm and damage that we can, as to vassals who do not obey and refuse to receive their lord and resist and contradict him; and we protest that the deaths and losses which shall accrue from this are your fault, and not that of their highnesses, or ours, or of these soldiers who come with us.

Indians who heard the Requerimiento *could not understand Spanish, of course. No native documents survive to record the Indians' thoughts upon hearing the Spaniards' official justification for conquest, even when it was translated into a language they understood. But one conquistador reported that when the* Requerimiento *was translated for two chiefs in Colombia, they responded that if the pope gave the king so much territory that belonged to other people, "the pope must have been drunk."*

Document 1. Zvi Dor-Ner, *Columbus and the Age of Discovery* (New York: William Morrow, 1991), 220–21. Copyright 1991 by William Morrow. Reprinted with permission.

Document 2. Adapted from A. Helps and M. Oppenheim, eds., *The Spanish Conquest in America and Its Relation to the History of Slavery and to the Government of Colonies,* 4 vols., (London and New York, 1900–1904), I, 264–67.

ern shores were biological cousins but cultural strangers. For almost a generation after 1492, Europeans straggled across the sea bridge, not quite sure what to make of these alien peoples and their world. That question was settled forever in the years just after 1519, as Spaniards pushed into the interior of Mexico. What they found there established a two-way traffic across the sea bridge that helped make Spain the most powerful country in both Europe and the New World over the course of the sixteenth century.

Spanish Exploration and Conquest

During the sixteenth century, Spain established its supremacy over the indigenous peoples of Central and South America. In the initial Caribbean phase of conquest (1492–1519), Spanish expeditions reconnoitered the islands, scouted stretches of the mainland coast, and placed settlements on the large islands of Hispaniola, Puerto Rico, Jamaica, and

Cuba. Spanish settlers subjugated island tribes, enslaved their people, and put them to work growing crops and mining gold. But the profits from these early ventures barely covered the costs required to maintain the settlers. After almost thirty years of exploration, the promise of Columbus's discovery seemed illusory.

Soon after 1519, however, that promise was fulfilled, spectacularly. The mainland phase of exploration began in 1519 with Hernán Cortés's march into Mexico and lasted until about 1545, when Spanish conquests extended from northern Mexico to southern Chile, and New World riches filled Spanish treasure chests. Cortés's expedition served as the model for all the rest.

The Conquest of Mexico

Hernán Cortés, who would become the richest and most famous conquistador (conqueror) of all, arrived in the New World in 1504, an obscure nineteen-year-old Spaniard seeking adventure and the opportunity to make a name for himself. He fought in numerous campaigns against the Caribbean Indians and participated in the conquest of Cuba. In 1519, the governor of Cuba authorized Cortés to organize an expedition to investigate rumors of a fabulously wealthy kingdom somewhere in the interior of the mainland. A charming, charismatic leader, Cortés quickly assembled a force of about six hundred men, including soldiers and assorted friars, artisans, and hangers-on. The governor of Cuba soon had second thoughts about entrusting the expedition to a magnetic and unpredictable man like Cortés, and he withdrew permission for the campaign. Characteristically, Cortés ignored the governor, loaded his ragtag army aboard eleven ships, and set out on his freelance crusade, confident that the legal niceties could be sorted out later.

Cortés's confidence that he could talk his way out of most situations and fight his way out of the rest fortified the small band of Spaniards. Landing first on the Yucatán peninsula, Cortés had the good fortune to be given a gift by a Mayan chief: a young woman named Malinali who spoke both Mayan and Nahuatl, the language of most people in Mexico and Central America. Malinali, whom the Spaniards called Marina, soon learned Spanish and became Cortés's interpreter. (She also became one of Cortés's mistresses and bore him a son.) Marina served as the essential conduit of communication between the Spaniards and the Indians. With her help, Cortés talked and fought with Indians along the Gulf coast of Mexico, trying to discover the location of the fabled kingdom.

In Tenochtitlán, the capital of the Mexican empire, the emperor Montezuma heard about some strange creatures along the coast. (Montezuma and his people are often called Aztecs, but they never used that term; they called themselves Mexica.) He feared that the strangers were led by the god Quetzalcoatl, who was returning to Tenochtitlán as predicted by the Mexican religion. Montezuma sent emissaries, carrying gifts appropriate for a god, to meet with the intruders.

When the emissaries arrived, Cortés and his men showed little interest in the dazzling featherwork and other paraphernalia suitable for Quetzalcoatl and other Mexican deities. Cortés inquired about the great emperor who had sent the emissaries, where he lived, and whether he had gold. Cortés obliged the visitors and donned the regalia they had brought, almost certain proof to the Mexica that he was indeed Quetzalcoatl. For their part, the Spaniards astounded the emissaries by blasting their cannon, showing off their iron swords and armor, and exhibiting their horses, which the Mexica had never seen and which they considered a species of supernatural deer.

The emissaries hurried back to Montezuma with their amazing news. Montezuma decided he must welcome Quetzalcoatl with food and hospitality, which he also hoped would postpone (and perhaps prevent) the god's arrival in Tenochtitlán. Montezuma arranged for large quantities of food to be brought to the coast for Cortés and his army. In addition, since Quetzalcoatl presumably hungered for blood, Montezuma sent numerous hostages for sacrifice. Before the food was served to the Spaniards, the Mexica sacrificed the hostages and soaked the food in their blood. This fare sickened the Spaniards and, alone, might have been enough to turn them back to Cuba. However, along with these divine victuals, the Mexica also brought a gift, a "disk in the shape of the sun, as big as a cartwheel and made of very fine gold," as one Mexican recalled. Here was conclusive evidence that the rumors heard by Cortés and his army had some basis in fact.

In August 1519, Cortés embarked on a march to find Montezuma. Leading about 350 men armed with swords, lances, and muskets and supported by ten cannon, four smaller guns, and sixteen horses, Cortés had to live off the land, making friends with the indigenous tribes when he could and killing them when he had to, and often when he did not

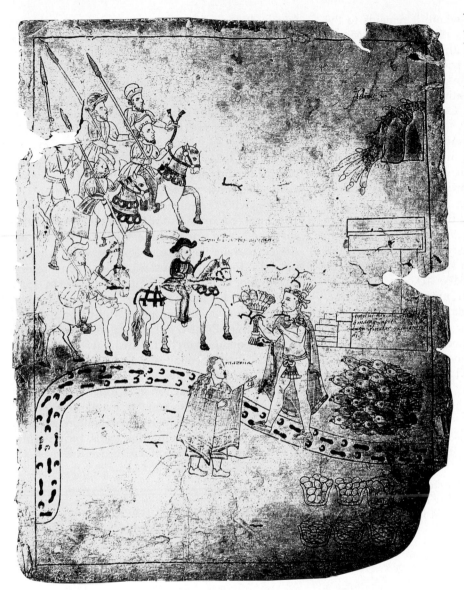

have to. In the grueling and bloody expedition, Cortés's soldiers usually slept in their armor, their swords at their sides. Cortés never wavered in his determination to find Montezuma, and his diplomacy and leadership in battle inspired his men to continue, even though they did not know where they were going or how to get there.

On November 8, 1519, Montezuma came out to meet Cortés on a causeway leading into Tenochtitlán. After presenting Cortés with bouquets of flowers, golden necklaces, and other gifts, Montezuma welcomed Cortés and his army to the royal palace and showered them with the lavish hospitality the Mexican tribute system put at his disposal. Quickly, Cortés took Montezuma hostage and held him under house arrest, hoping thereby to make him a puppet through which the Spaniards could rule the Mexican empire. This uneasy peace existed for several months until, after a brutal massacre of many Mexican nobles by one of Cortés's subordinates, the population of Tenochtitlán revolted, murdered Montezuma, and mounted a ferocious assault on the Spaniards. On June 30, 1520, Cortés and about a hundred other Spaniards fought their way out of Tenochtitlán; the gold they had confiscated weighed them down so much they had to drop most of it in the lake and abandon it (where it remains to this day, buried somewhere in the middle of Mexico City) in order to escape with their lives. Cortés retreated to Tlaxcala, where friendly Indians allowed him to regroup, obtain reinforcements, and plan a strategy to conquer Tenochtitlán.

In the spring of 1521, Cortés mounted a complex campaign against the Mexican capital. The Spaniards and tens of thousands of Indian allies laid siege to the city. They advanced slowly along the causeways leading into the city, systematically reducing to rubble every structure in their path in order to deny the Mexica any cover when they counterattacked and forced the Spaniards to retreat, as they often did. This relentless, scorched-earth strategy, a blockade of the city's food and water supplies, and protection from sailboats the Spaniards built and launched on Lake Texcoco to defend against Mexican attacks from canoes finally succeeded in defeating the last Mexican defenders on August 13, 1521. The great capital of the Mexican empire "looked as if it had been ploughed up," one of Cortés's soldiers remembered. A few years later, one of the Mexica described the utter despair of the defeated:

Broken spears lie in the roads;
we have torn our hair in grief.
The houses are roofless now, and their walls
are red with blood.

Worms are swarming in the streets and plazas,
and the walls are splattered with gore.
The water has turned red, as if it were dyed,
and when we drink it,
it has the taste of brine.

We have pounded our hands in despair
against the adobe walls,
for our inheritance, our city, is lost and dead.
The shields of our warriors were its defense,
but they could not save it.

We have chewed dry twigs and salt grasses;
we have filled our mouths with dust and bits of
    adobe;
we have eaten lizards, rats, and worms . . .
everything that once was precious was now
    considered worthless.

The Search for Other Mexicos

When Cortés conquered Tenochtitlán, he and his men hoped to find more gold. Cortés was quoted as telling the Mexica, "I and my companions suffer from a disease of the heart which can only be cured with gold." One of the Mexica who watched the Spaniards loot and pillage commented later that they "lusted for gold. Their bodies swelled with greed . . . they hungered like pigs for that gold."

Lured by their insatiable appetite for gold, conquistadors quickly fanned out from Tenochtitlán in search of other Mexicos. To the south, Guatemala, El Salvador, and Nicaragua came under Spanish control by 1524. The Mayan tribes of the Yucatán peninsula did not succumb for another twenty years. The most spectacular prize fell to Francisco Pizarro, who conquered the Inca empire in Peru. The Incas controlled a vast, complex region that contained more than nine million people and stretched along the western coast of South America for more than two thousand miles, from present-day Quito, Ecuador, to Santiago, Chile. In 1532, Pizarro and his army of fewer than two hundred men captured the Inca emperor Atahualpa and held him hostage. Pizarro demanded ransom, and the Incas responded with by far the largest treasure yet produced by the conquests: gold and silver worth 1.5 million pesos, equivalent to half a century of precious-metal production in Europe. With the ransom safely in their hands, the Spaniards executed Atahualpa. Although periodic rebellion plagued Spanish rulers in Peru until the 1570s, Inca treasure proved that at least one other Mexico did exist.

Lured by their insatiable appetite for gold, conquistadors quickly fanned out from Tenochtitlán in search of other Mexicos.

In the north, Juan Ponce de León, who had coasted around the Florida peninsula in 1513, was encouraged by Cortés's success to return to Florida in 1521, where he was killed in a battle with Calusa Indians. In 1525, Lucas Vázquez de Ayllón led an expedition that explored the Atlantic coast north of Florida to South Carolina. A year later, Ayllón established a small settlement on the Georgia coast that he named San Miguel de Gualdape, the first Spanish attempt to create a town in what is now the United States. Within a few months most of the settlers, including Ayllón, became sick and died, and the few survivors beat a retreat back to the Caribbean. In 1528, Pánfilo de Narváez surveyed the Gulf coast, moving west from Florida to Texas.

The Narváez expedition floundered badly and came to a disastrous end on the Texas coast, near Galveston, where the few survivors were enslaved by coastal Indians. After several years of enslavement, four Spaniards managed to escape and began to try to find their way back to Mexico. Led by Cabeza de Vaca, the Spaniards convinced local tribes that they were holy men who possessed the power to cure the sick. In 1536, Cabeza de Vaca and his companions, accompanied by about six hundred Indians who worshiped them, stumbled upon a group of Spanish slave hunters in northern Mexico and were finally rescued. Cabeza de Vaca's account of his amazing experiences, eventually published in Spain in 1542, stimulated additional interest in exploring the lands north of Mexico.

In 1539, Hernando de Soto, a seasoned conquistador who had taken part in the conquest of Peru, set out with nine ships and more than six hundred companions to find another Peru in North America. Landing in Florida, de Soto literally slashed his way through much of the southeastern United States for three years, employing the conquistadors' methods of brutality to find the rich, majestic civilizations he knew had to be there. After many battles and much hardship, de Soto became sick and died in 1542, and his men buried him in the Mississippi River before turning back to Mexico, disappointed.

Tales of the fabulous wealth of the mythical Seven Cities of Cíbola also lured Francisco Vásquez de Coronado to search the Southwest and Great Plains of North America. In 1540, Coronado left northern Mexico with more than three hundred Spaniards, a thousand Indians, fifteen hundred horses, and a guide named Marcos de Niza, a priest who claimed to know the way to what he called "the greatest and best of the discoveries." Cíbola turned out to be a small Zuñi pueblo of about a hundred families. When the Zuñi shot arrows at the Spaniards, Coronado attacked the pueblo and routed the defenders after a hard battle. Convinced that the rich cities must lie somewhere over the horizon, Coronado sent out scouting parties. One traveled to the edge of the Grand Canyon in northern Arizona. Coronado went east to pueblos near Albuquerque, where the residents soon rebelled against the Spaniards, who had confiscated their food, clothing, and women. Again Coronado conquered the pueblos and again he kept moving all the way to central Kansas before deciding in 1542 that the rumors he had pursued were just that, nothing more.

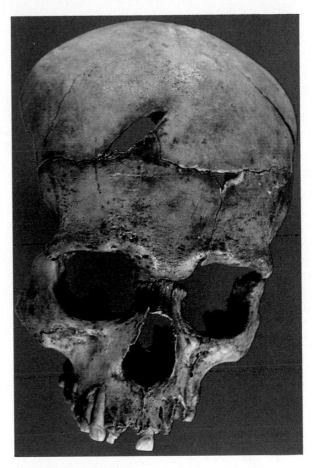

A SIGN OF CONQUEST
This skull was recently excavated by archaeologists from the site of a native American village in northwest Georgia visited by de Soto's expedition in 1540. The skull is that of an Indian man in his fifties who suffered a fatal sword wound above his right eye. Combined with slashed and severed arm and leg bones from the same site, the skull offers compelling proof of the brutality de Soto employed against indigenous peoples on his expedition through the Southeast. No native weapons were capable of inflicting the wounds indelibly marked on this skull and other bones.
Dr. Robert L. Blakely.

Farther west, Juan Rodríguez Cabrillo, an experienced conquistador like Hernando de Soto, led an expedition in 1542 that sailed along the coast of California. Cabrillo died on Santa Catalina Island, offshore from present-day Los Angeles, but his men sailed on to the border of Oregon, where a ferocious storm forced them to turn back toward Mexico.

Why Did Cortés Win?

By CONQUERING MEXICO, Hernán Cortés demonstrated that Columbus had in fact discovered a New World of enormous value to the Old. But why did a few hundred Spaniards so far away from home defeat millions of Indians fighting on their home turf?

First, several military factors favored the Spaniards. They possessed superior military technology. They fought with weapons of iron and steel against the Mexica's stone, wood, and copper; they charged on horseback against Mexican warriors on foot; they ignited gunpowder to fire cannon and muskets toward the attacking Mexicas, whose only source of power was human muscle. However, the Mexica's immense numerical superiority partially offset the Spaniards' weaponry.

The Spaniards also enjoyed superior military organization, although it was hardly a spit-and-polish hierarchy. Cortés's army was composed of soldiers of fortune, young men who hoped to fight for God and the king and to get rich. Far from a highly disciplined, professional fighting force, they were governed by the force of Cortés's personality, by their own desire for glory and riches, and by fear of the consequences of not following orders. The unsteady discipline among the Spaniards is suggested by Cortés's decision to beach and dismantle the ships that had brought his small army to the Mexican mainland—after that, the only way for his men to go was forward.

The Spaniards were a well-oiled military machine compared with the Mexica. The Mexica tended to attack from ambush or in waves of frontal assaults, with great courage but little organization or discipline. They seldom sustained attacks, even when they had the Spaniards on the run. In the siege of Tenochtitlán, for example, the Mexica often paused to sacrifice any Spanish soldiers they had captured, taking time to skin "their faces," one Spaniard recalled, "which they afterward prepared like leather gloves, with their beards on." Spanish tactics, in contrast, emphasized concentrating their soldiers to magnify the effect of their firepower and to maintain communication in the thick of battle.

But perhaps the Spaniards' most fundamental military advantage was their concept of war. The Mexican concept of war was shaped by the nature of their empire. They fought to impose their tribute system on others and to take captives for sacrifices. From their viewpoint, war made their adversaries realize the high cost of continuing to fight and gave them a big incentive to surrender and pay tribute. For the Spaniards, war meant destroying the enemy's ability to fight. In short, the Spaniards sought total victory; the Mexica sought surrender. All these military factors weakened the Mexica's resistance to the Spaniards, but they were insufficient to explain Cortés's victory.

Disease played a major part in the Mexica's defeat. When the Mexica confronted Cortés, they were not at full strength. An epidemic of smallpox and measles had struck the Caribbean in 1519, arrived in Mexico with Cortés and his men, and lasted through 1522. Thousands of Indians died, and many others became too sick to fight or help resist the invaders. When the Spaniards were regrouping in Tlaxcala, after their disastrous evacuation of Tenochtitlán, a great plague broke out in the Mexican capital. As one Mexica explained to a Spaniard shortly after the conquest, the plague lasted for seventy days, "striking everywhere in the city and killing a vast number of our people. Sores erupted on our faces, our breasts, our bellies; we were covered with agonizing sores from head to foot. The illness was so dreadful that no one could walk or move. The sick were so utterly helpless that they could only lie on their beds like corpses, unable to move their limbs or even their heads. A great many died from this plague, and many others died of hunger. They could not get up to search for food, and everybody else was too sick to care for them, so they starved to death in their beds."

The sickness was not confined to Tenochtitlán. It also killed and weakened people in the areas surrounding the city, spreading back along the network of trade and tribute that fed the city, reducing its food supply, and further weakening the survivors. While the Mexica were decimated by their first exposure to smallpox and measles, the Spaniards were for all practical purposes immune, having previously been exposed to the diseases. European viruses probably played at least as large a role in the conquest as weapons and military tactics.

Religion also contributed to the Mexica's defeat. Mexica religious doctrine led Montezuma to be hesitant and uncertain in confronting the Spaniards during the months when they were most vulnerable. While Cortés marched toward Tenochtitlán, it was not at all clear to the Indians that the Spaniards and their horses were mortals. Cortés worked hard

CONQUEST WARFARE

This postconquest painting by a sixteenth-century Mexican artist is one of a series illustrating crucial battles in the ultimate defeat of the Mexica. Here Mexican warriors are attacking the conquistadors shortly before the Spaniards retreated from Tenochtitlán and regrouped for the final siege. The distinctive shields and costumes of the Mexica signify their military status, which was based on their battlefield prowess. The Spaniards, in contrast, wear gray metal armor, their crossbows and guns pitted against the Mexica's spears. The Mexica won this particular battle, a point the artist suggests by making the Mexican warriors appear bigger while the massed conquistadors lean slightly backward.
Oronoz.

to maintain the illusion, hiding Spaniards who died. But by the time Cortés retreated from Tenochtitlán, the Mexica knew that the Spaniards could be killed, and their resistance stiffened accordingly.

While the Mexica's religion reduced their initial resistance to the conquistadors, Christianity strengthened the Spaniards. The Spaniards' Christianity was a confident, militant, and ruthless faith that commanded its followers to destroy idolatry, root out heresy, slay infidels, and subjugate nonbelievers. Their religious certainty had been honed for centuries in the battles of the Reconquest that recaptured the Iberian peninsula from the Muslims. Christianity was as much a part of the conquistadors' armory as chain mail and gunpowder.

Mexican military commanders often turned to their priests for military guidance. Although the Spaniards routinely celebrated mass and prayed before battles, their military and diplomatic decisions were not made by friars, but by Cortés and his subordinates, tough, practical, wily men. When the Spaniards lost battles, they did not worry that God had abandoned them. However, when the Mexica lost battles advised by their priests, they confronted the distressing question of the power of their gods. Their gods no longer seemed to listen to them. The

deadly sickness sweeping through the countryside also seemed to show that their gods had abandoned them. "Cut us loose," one Mexican pleaded, "because the gods have died."

Finally, political factors proved decisive in the Mexica's defeat. Cortés shrewdly exploited the tensions between the Mexica and their subjects. With skillful negotiation and diplomacy, Cortés obtained the cooperation of thousands of Indian soldiers, porters, and food suppliers. These Indian allies were the crucial ingredient in the Spaniards' success. Besides actually fighting alongside Cortés, the Spaniards' Indian allies provided the invaders with a fairly secure base from which to maneuver against the Mexica's stronghold. Cortés's small army fought alongside thousands of Indians who were eager to seek revenge against the Mexica. Hundreds of thousands of other Indians helped the Spaniards by not contributing to the Mexica's defense. These passive allies of the Spaniards sat on their hands, preventing the Mexica from fully capitalizing on their overwhelming numerical superiority. In the end, although many factors contributed to the conquest, Cortés won because the Mexican empire—the source of the Mexica's impressive wealth and power—was their Achilles heel.

These probes into North America by de Soto, Coronado, and Cabrillo persuaded Spaniards that, while enormous territories stretched northward, their inhabitants had little to loot or exploit. After a generation of vigorous exploration, Spaniards concluded that there was only one Mexico and one Peru.

New Spain in the Sixteenth Century

For all practical purposes, Spain dominated the New World in the sixteenth century. Portugal claimed the giant territory of Brazil under the Tordesillas treaty, but during most of the sixteenth century the Portuguese were far more concerned with exploiting their hard-won trade with the East Indies than in colonizing the New World. England and France envied the Spanish discoveries in the Western Hemisphere, especially after 1519, but they were absorbed in the affairs of Europe and largely lost interest in America until late in the century. In the decades after 1519, Spaniards created the distinctive colonial society of New Spain that gave other Europeans a striking illustration of how the New World could be made to serve the purposes of the Old.

Spaniards' economic, religious, and political dominance relegated Indians to an inferior status in New Spain, inaugurating a racial hierarchy of white supremacy that—in one way or another—was replicated endlessly in subsequent New World colonies. Spaniards forced Indians to work for them in the fields and mines that enormously enriched colonists and the Spanish monarchy. Spanish missionaries worked zealously to convert Indians to Christianity. Spanish colonial policies and European diseases had catastrophic consequences for Indians, who lost control of their world after 1492. Only on the fringes of New Spain—including the area of the present-day United States—did Native American societies elude the control of Spanish colonists. Spain established scattered outposts of settlement in North America to buttress its territorial claims, but the heartland of New Spain remained in Central and South America.

From Conquistadors to Colonists

The conquest of Mexico and the rest of New Spain had been organized and paid for by individual investors, men who hoped to find riches that would repay their investment manyfold. The soldiers who fought with Cortés, for example, purchased their own weapons, armor, and supplies. They were entrepreneurs of conquest, anticipating a high return from their high-risk venture. The Spanish monarchy, which claimed ownership of most of the land in the Western Hemisphere, gave the conquistadors permission to undertake their speculative forays. In return, the crown received the "royal fifth," that is, one-fifth of any loot confiscated by the conquerors. Virtually every expedition of conquest included a representative of the crown with the responsibility to make certain that the royal fifth was skimmed off the top of any plunder. When the conquering Spaniards captured golden artifacts made by indigenous people, they usually melted them, in part to allow the royal fifth to be assessed immediately.

> In the decades after 1519, Spaniards created the distinctive colonial society of New Spain that gave other Europeans a striking illustration of how the New World could be made to serve the purposes of the Old.

Although the crown got paid first and in full, when the remaining treasure was finally divided up, the conquistadors themselves received very little, in most cases far less than they invested. For example, a horseman who accompanied Cortés and earned a share of the booty of Tenochtitlán received one hundred gold pesos, which was only about one-fifth of the man's investment in his own horse. The share of a foot soldier was even less. After almost three years of bloody, hand-to-hand combat, such token payments did not make Cortés's soldiers happy.

Luckily for Cortés and the Spanish crown, the conquistadors found something far more valuable than gold as they pillaged Tenochtitlán, room by room. The Spaniards seized the Mexica's tribute rolls, documents that pictured exactly what each town in the Mexica empire paid in tribute. They showed that 370 towns paid one-third or more of their total production in tribute to the Mexica. This knowledge, along with their lust for gold, spurred Cortés's men to split up into smaller groups and extend the conquest throughout the reaches of the Mexican empire. They found some gold, but not nearly enough to satisfy them. Cortés, aware of the

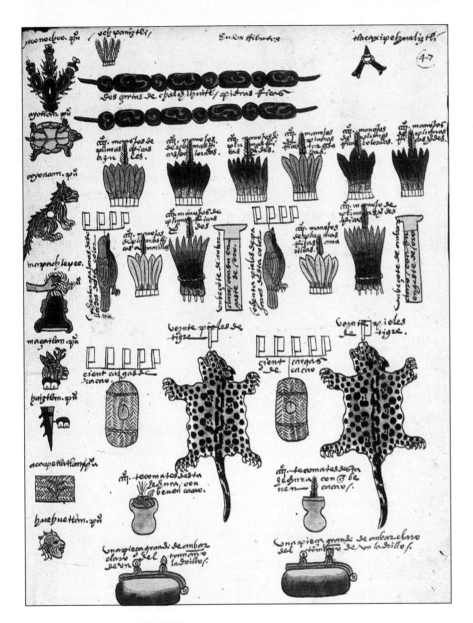

MEXICAN TRIBUTE ACCOUNT

This page from the Codex Mendoza *records the tribute paid to the Mexican capital by the Xoconochco province, a tropical region along the Pacific coast near the Guatemalan border (present-day Chiapas). Prepared by a Mexican artist around 1540 for the viceroy of New Spain, the* Codex Mendoza *provides an inventory of the tribute exacted by the Mexican empire. Most Mexican provinces paid tribute in food or textiles, but Xoconochco contributed, as this account specifies, "first, two large strings of green stones, rich stones; also one thousand four hundred bundles of rich feathers of blue, red, green, turquoise-blue, . . . which are drawn in six bundles; also eighty complete bird skins, of*

rich turquoise-blue feathers and purple breasts, of the colors drawn; also another eighty complete skins of said birds; also eight hundred bundles of rich feathers; also eight hundred bundles of rich long green feathers . . . ; also two lip plugs of clear amber decorated with gold; also two hundred loads of cacao; also forty jaguar skins . . . ; also eight hundred rich bowls for drinking cacao; also two large pieces of clear amber of the size of a brick — all of which they gave in tribute every six months." In the Mexican capital, artists crafted the exotic feathers and skins into elaborate cloaks and the stones and amber into fashionable jewelry. The cacao was brewed into a mildly intoxicating beverage.*

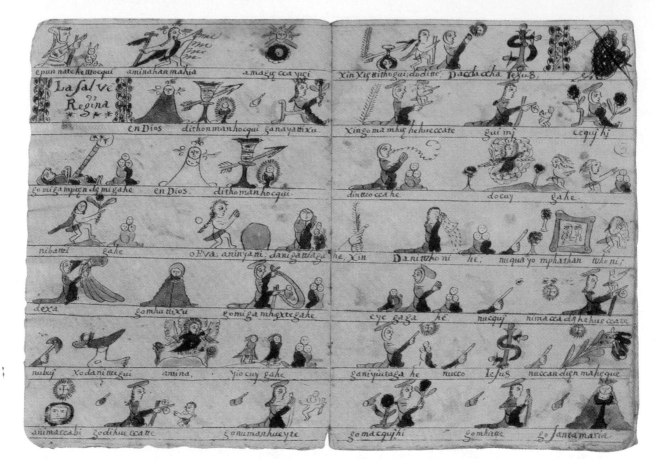

MISSIONARY CATECHISM

In the 1540s, Franciscan missionaries tried to teach basic Christian rituals by using pictures that somewhat resembled the glyphs in pre-Columbian codices (see page 27), hoping to appeal to the Mexica's respect for the power of ancient texts. Known as Testerian manuscripts, these catechisms were read from left to right across two facing pages and then back from right to left on the next line, and so on. This catechism illustrates the prayer "Salve Regina"; the words below the pictures are in the Otomi language. Can you puzzle out some of the symbols that were intended to communicate the words of the prayer? Begin with the title, "La Salve Regina," at the far left of the second line: "Hail to the Queen who reigns above / Mother of clemency and love! / Hail, thou our hope, life, sweetness! We / Eve's banished children cry to thee. / We, from this wretched vale of tears, / Send sighs and groans unto thy ears; / Oh then, sweet advocate, bestow / A pitying look on us below! / After this exile let us see / Our blessed Jesus, born of thee. / O merciful, O pious Maid / O gracious Mary, lend thy aid."
Bibliothèque Nationale, Paris/Arch. Photeb.

risks to him and the monarchy posed by poor, disgruntled, battle-hardened conquistadors, decided to compensate his men by giving them the towns the Spaniards had subdued.

The distribution of conquered towns institutionalized the system of *encomienda,* which empowered conquistadors to rule the Indians and the lands in and around one or more towns. The concept of encomienda was familiar to the Spaniards since they had employed it to govern regions recaptured from the Muslims during the Reconquest of the Iberian peninsula, and they had adopted it when they colonized the Caribbean. In New Spain, encomienda transferred to the Spanish *encomendero* (the man who "owned" the town) the tribute that the town had previously paid to the Mexica. In theory, encomienda involved a reciprocal relationship between the encomendero and "his" Indians. In return for the tribute and labor of the Indians, the encomendero was supposed to encourage the Indians to convert to Christianity, to be responsible for their material well-being, and to guarantee order and justice in the town. The theory of encomienda was an idealized version of the relationship between lord and peasant in medieval Europe. It illustrates how institutions, relationships, and ideas that were decaying in Europe were revitalized in the New World and imposed on subject peoples.

Catholic missionaries labored earnestly to convert the Indians to Christianity. Franciscan friars arrived in Mexico in 1524, and they were followed in a few years by Dominicans and Augustinians. At first, the missionaries enjoyed great success. The Indians welcomed these men who, in contrast to the despotic conquistadors, were relatively humble and kind. The friars baptized tens of thousands of Indians. "We are much busied with great and constant labor to convert the infidel," the newly appointed bishop of Mexico, Juan de Zumárraga, reported in 1531. He boasted of "five hundred [Indian] temples razed to the ground, and twenty thousand idols of the devils worshiped [by the Indians] smashed and burned." However, the missionaries soon discovered that the Indians had merely added the Christian God to their own deities, whom they continued to worship, even with human sacrifice. Some friars began to realize that authentic conversions could take place only if the Spaniards first learned exactly what the Indians did believe. A few missionaries studied Indian languages and culture; Fray Bernardino de Sahagún conducted extensive interviews with the Mexica and, over forty years, compiled a systematic firsthand account of Mexican society, *General History of the Things of New Spain.* Most friars, however, focused their efforts on instructing Indian children in the religious and other ways of the Spaniards. They did not hesitate to resort to whippings, imprisonment, and even executions to emphasize their message. They enlisted the labor of Indian converts to build numerous schools, convents, and churches. By midcentury, nearly twelve hundred missionaries toiled in Mexico and Peru. By then, most of them had come to believe that the Indians were lesser beings inherently incapable of fully understanding the mysteries of Christian faith.

The behavior of the encomenderos also departed from the assumptions of reciprocity between Indians and Spaniards. In practice, encomienda placated the conquistadors. By the 1550s, some 130 encomenderos in Mexico controlled more than 180,000 Indians. However, the encomenderos were far more interested in what the Indians could do for them than in what they could or should do for the Indians. Encomenderos subjected Indians to chronic overwork, mistreatment, and abuse. They forced them to do labor of every sort without recompense. As one Spaniard remarked, "Everything [the Indians] do is slowly done and by compulsion. They are malicious, lying, thievish. . . . They are very ungrateful. . . . They are capital enemies of the Spaniards." Encomenderos collected tribute from the Indians, then forced them to buy it back at wildly inflated prices. They confiscated Indian possessions, ravaged the women, beat them, imprisoned them, and turned dogs loose to tear at them. The encomenderos were responsible for the brutal deaths of thousands of Indians.

Economically, however, encomienda recognized a fundamental reality of New Spain. The most important treasure the Spaniards could plunder from the New World was not gold, but Indian labor. The central economic question for the rulers of New Spain was how to exploit Indian labor, the hemisphere's richest natural resource. Encomienda answered that question by giving encomenderos the right to force Indians to work when, where, and how the Spaniards pleased.

Encomienda recognized a fundamental reality of New Spain. The most important treasure the Spaniards could plunder from the New World was not gold, but Indian labor.

Encomienda engendered two groups of influential critics. A few of the missionaries were horrified at the brutal mistreatment of the Indians. The cruelty of the encomenderos made it difficult for the priests to persuade Indians of the tender mercies of the Spaniards' God. Fray Bartolomé de Las Casas pointedly criticized the treatment of the Indians. "What will [the Indians] think about the God of the Christians," he asked, when they see their friends "with their heads split, their hands amputated, their intestines torn open? . . . Would they want to come to Christ's sheepfold after their homes had been destroyed, their children imprisoned, their wives raped, their cities devastated, their maidens deflowered, and their provinces laid waste?" Las

quintlatique.

Casas vigorously defended the humanity of the Indians, arguing that they were just as much children
of God as their Spanish overlords.

Las Casas and other outspoken priests softened
few hearts among the encomenderos, but they did
win some sympathy for the Indians from the Spanish monarchy and royal bureaucracy. Brutality toward the Indians seemed excessive and somewhat
embarrassing to the government in Spain. Royal officials, however, interpreted the encomenderos'
treatment of the Indians as part of a larger general
problem: the autonomy of the encomenderos. The
Spanish monarchy sought to abolish the encomienda in an effort to undermine the authority of
the encomenderos, to take the government of New
Spain away from swashbuckling old conquistadors,
and to put it in the hands of report-writing bureaucrats who answered to the crown.

The transition from encomienda to a crown-
controlled bureaucracy was a long, slow process because of the local power of the encomenderos, the

difficulty of efficiently projecting royal authority
across the Atlantic, and the unwillingness of the
monarchy to allow reforms to interrupt the very tangible rewards that flowed from New Spain. One of
the most important blows against the encomienda
was the imposition in 1549 of a reform called the
repartimiento. The repartimiento limited the labor an
encomendero could command from his Indians to
forty-five days per year from each adult male. While
the repartimiento stripped the encomenderos of
their right to force Indians to work all the time, it
did not challenge the principle of forced labor nor
did it prevent encomenderos from continuing to
cheat, mistreat, and overwork their Indians. Enforcement was haphazard. As the old encomenderos
died, however, the crown refused to allow their
children to inherit the privileges of encomienda,
and repartimiento slowly replaced encomienda as
the basic system of exploiting Indian labor.

The central fact of the labor system of New
Spain during the sixteenth century under both en-

comienda and repartimiento was that Spaniards forced Indians to work for them. Indians did not work for wages set by a competitive labor market. They worked because their Spanish rulers forced them to, punished them if they hesitated, enslaved them if they resisted, and killed them if they proved too much of a problem. The system of coerced labor in New Spain grew directly out of the Spaniards' assumption that they were superior to the Indians. As one missionary put it, the Indians "are incapable of learning. . . . The older they get, the worse they behave. . . . The Indians are more stupid than asses and refuse to improve in anything." Therefore, most Spaniards assumed, the Indians' labor should be organized by and for their conquerors.

The Economy and Society of New Spain

In New Spain the bulk of agricultural production was consumed by the local population. Unlike the colonies that developed elsewhere in the New World in the next century, agriculture in New Spain was not devoted to production of an export crop for sale on the world market. Instead, the major crops grown throughout New Spain were the same ones grown for centuries before the Spanish arrived: corn, beans, and squash.

The Spaniards introduced a number of European crops, but only one—sugar—became an important export in the sixteenth century. The Spaniards grew sugar, mostly on islands in the Caribbean. By the end of the sixteenth century, sugar was the fourth leading export from New Spain, but it represented only the start of the sugar boom that would take place in the next century.

The Spaniards also introduced livestock to New Spain. Before the conquest, dogs and turkeys were the most important animals domesticated by the Indians. The Spaniards brought not only horses, so important in battles of conquest; but, of greater significance for the economy of New Spain, they also brought cattle. By the middle of the sixteenth century, an extensive ranching and herding economy had developed in northern Mexico. Meat from the animals was used for domestic consumption, and hides were exported to tanneries and leather shops in Spain. Hides were the second most important export from New Spain in the sixteenth century, worth twice as much as sugar. While agriculture occupied the overwhelming majority of the population of New Spain and provided a few valuable exports to Spain, crops were not what made the riches of New Spain legendary in Europe.

From the viewpoint of Spain, the single most important economic activity in New Spain was silver mining. Gold exports from the New World were

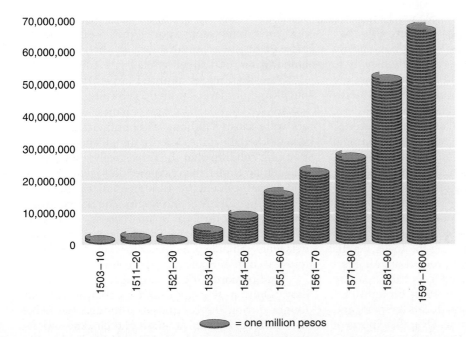

FIGURE 2.1
New World Gold and Silver Imported into Spain during the Sixteenth Century, in Pesos
Spain imported more gold than silver during the first three decades of the sixteenth century, but the total value of this treasure was quickly eclipsed during the 1530s and 1540s when rich silver mines were developed. Silver accounted for most of the enormous growth in Spain's precious metal imports from the New World.

AFRICAN SLAVES MINING GOLD
This sixteenth-century illustration provides a simplified view of African slaves mining gold in New Spain. Spaniards imported African slaves in substantial numbers after the native American population had been decimated by conquest and disease. The two slaves on the right dig ore, from which the gold is separated by the slave in the center and then washed in hot water over the fire, before the clean nuggets are given to the Spaniard, who carefully weighs them and sets them aside. How did the artist emphasize the differences between the Spaniard and the slaves? Is it possible to detect the artist's point of view about who was more "civilized"?

The Pierpont Morgan Library. MA 3900, f.100.

substantial early in the sixteenth century, as the conquistadors filled treasure chests with any gold they could find. During the 1520s, as the loot, mostly gold, from the conquest of Mexico made its way to Spain, the value of New World treasure amounted to about 1.4 million ducats (a unit of Spanish currency). During the 1530s, with the conquest of Peru, the treasure imported to Spain swelled to about 6.7 million ducats. Nonetheless, before 1533, the annual value of gold exports from New Spain did not exceed what the Portuguese brought to Europe from the west coast of Africa. The bonanza for the Spanish came from silver mines. With the discovery of the major silver deposits at Potosí, Bolivia, in 1545 and Zacatecas, Mexico, in 1546, imported bullion rose to 12.5 million ducats during the 1540s. As the mines swung into large-scale production, an ever-growing stream of silver flowed from New Spain to Old. During the 1590s, treasure fleets brought precious metals worth 83.5 million ducats to Spain, and the riches promised to continue. Overall, exports of precious metals during the sixteenth century were

worth about twenty-five times more than hides, the next most important export. From the perspective of Spain, its colony on the western shores of the Atlantic was a solid-silver asset.

The silver mines required large capital investments and numerous miners. Typically, a mine was supervised by a handful of Spaniards, and the miners were mostly Indians, although African slaves also worked the mines later in the sixteenth century. Working conditions in the mines were abominable, worse than under the encomienda system. But the mines exemplified the fundamental relationships between the colonists and Spain. The native Indian miners worked for local Spanish bosses to produce silver for export to Spain. The mines and their products were valuable principally for their contribution to the wealth of Spain, not the colony.

For Spaniards, life in New Spain was relatively easy. Only a few thousand Spaniards actually fought during the conquests. Although the riches the survivors won fell far short of their expectations, the benefits of encomienda provided a comfortable,

MIXED RACES

Residents of New Spain maintained a lively interest in each person's racial lineage. These eighteenth-century paintings illustrate three forms of racial mixture common in the sixteenth-century. In the first painting, a Spanish man and an Indian woman have a mestizo son; in the fourth, a Spanish man and a woman of African descent have a mulatto son; in the fifth, a Spanish woman and a mulatto man have a morisco daughter. The many racial permutations of parents caused residents of New Spain to develop an elaborate vocabulary of ancestry. The child of a morisco and a Spaniard was a chino; the child of a chino and an Indian was a salta abas; the child of a salta abas and a mulatto was a lobo; and so on. Can you detect hints of some of the meanings of racial categories in the clothing depicted in these paintings?
Bob Schalkwijk/INAH.

Español con India, Mestizo.

Mestizo con Española, Castizo.

Castizo con Española, Español.

Español con Mora, Mulato.

Mulato con Española, Morisco.

Morisco con Española, Chino.

Chino con India, Salta atras.

Salta atras con Mulata, Lobo.

leisurely existence that was the envy of many poorer noblemen in Spain. The success of the conquest and the opportunity to spend less time in a workshop or behind a plow and more time in a hammock or on a shaded patio attracted many Spaniards to the New World. As one colonist wrote his brother back in Spain, "Don't hesitate [to come]. . . . This land [of New Spain] is as good as ours [in Spain], for God has given us more here than there, and we shall be better off."

During the century after 1492, about 225,000 Spaniards came to settle in the colonies. Virtually all of them were poor young men of common (nonnoble) lineage who came directly from Spain. Laborers and artisans made up the largest proportion, but soldiers and sailors were also numerous. Throughout the sixteenth century, men vastly outnumbered women among the Spanish immigrants, although the proportion of women grew from about one in twenty before 1519 to nearly one in three by the 1580s.

The gender and number of Spanish settlers shaped two fundamental features of the society of New Spain. First, despite the thousands of immigrants, Europeans never made up more than 1 or 2 percent of the total population of New Spain. Although Spaniards ruled New Spain, the population was almost wholly Indian. Second, the shortage of Spanish women meant that a great deal of concubinage and intermarriage took place between Spanish men and Indian women.

The highest social status in New Spain was reserved for natives of Spain, *peninsulares* (people

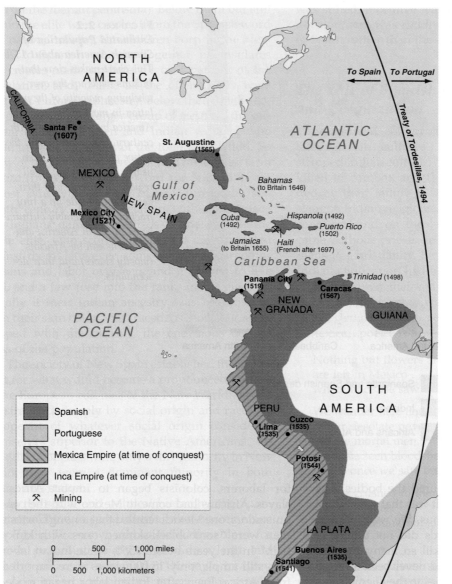

MAP 2.3
New Spain in the Sixteenth Century
Spanish control spread throughout Central and South America during the sixteenth century, with the important exception of Portuguese Brazil. North America, although claimed by Spain under the Treaty of Tordesillas, remained peripheral to Spain's New World empire.

made by the pope in 1493. By the mid-sixteenth century, however, France openly challenged Spain's claim and the papacy began to backpedal, pointing out that Spain did not have exclusive rights to North America since it had not yet been discovered in 1493. The Spanish monarchy insisted that a few settlements be established in North America to give some tangible reality to its legalistic claims. Settlements in Florida would have the additional benefit of protecting Spanish ships from pirates and privateers who lurked along the South Atlantic coast. Winds and currents in the Caribbean made the route of the Spanish treasure fleet quite predictable; the

ships rode the Gulf Stream along the east coast of Florida until they could catch favorable winds, usually off South Carolina, that propelled them toward Spain. Foreign raiders watched, waited, and attacked with great success, a practice that alarmed the monarchy.

In 1565, the Spanish king sent Pedro Menéndez de Avilés to create settlements along the Atlantic coast. In early September, Menéndez founded St. Augustine and within a few weeks mounted a deadly attack that eliminated a nearby French settlement. Menéndez established a series of small outposts along the Florida coast. In 1567 he founded the town of St. Elena, on what is now Parris Island, South Carolina.

In 1570, Menéndez sent an expedition to settle on the Chesapeake Bay, but within a few months the settlers were killed by local Indians. The Spaniards' translator, a young Algonquian whom they had captured on an earlier scouting party in the region, led the Indian attack. The young man had been sent to Mexico, where he had learned Spanish and had been given the name Luis de Velasco by his patron, the viceroy of Mexico. Among his fellow Algonquians, Luis de Velasco became known as Opechancanough, or "He Whose Soul Is White." In years to come, Opechancanough would surprise English settlers of the region, much as he did the Spaniards.

Antagonisms between Spaniards and native peoples plagued the Florida outposts. In 1576, an Indian attack forced evacuation of St. Elena. Eleven years later, the Spaniards concluded that St. Elena could not be defended from hostile Indians and marauders like the English privateer Francis Drake, who had sacked and burned St. Augustine in 1586. Spanish officials destroyed St. Elena themselves in 1587 and fell back to St. Augustine, where they dug in. St. Augustine was the first permanent European settlement within what became the United States. By 1600, the garrison town had a population of about five hundred, mostly men (although women and children lived there too), mostly soldiers, and mostly there because military orders kept them from leaving. The small town was a token Spanish presence on the vast Atlantic shoreline of North America.

More than 1,600 miles west of St. Augustine, another Spanish outpost was founded in 1598. During the 1580s, the Mexican mining frontier extended far into northern Mexico, and rumors of fabulous riches to be found just over the northern horizon still circulated, as they had in Coronado's time forty years earlier. In 1598, Juan de Oñate led an expedition of about five hundred people to settle New Mexico and develop the booty that supposedly awaited. Oñate had impeccable credentials for both conquest and mining. He came from a wealthy mining family; his father had helped discover the bonanza silver mines of Zacatecas. His wife was Isabel Tolosa Cortés Montezuma, the granddaughter of Cortés—the conqueror of Mexico—and the great-granddaughter of the Mexican emperor Montezuma. Despite the previous forays of Coronado, Oñate and other officials in New Spain had only a hazy understanding of the geography of the American Southwest. Oñate, for example, planned to supply New Mexico by sea; he requested and received permission to bring two ships a year to the new settlement.

In the spring of 1598, Oñate and his companions set out from Mexico across the Rio Grande and after two months reached a pueblo near present-day Albuquerque, where Oñate solemnly convened the pueblo's leaders in a kiva and, to his satisfaction, received their oath of loyalty to the Spanish king and the Christian God. Oñate repeated these ceremonies at additional pueblos as he made his way to a pueblo that he named San Gabriel, north of present-day Santa Fe. He soon sent out scouting parties to find the legendary treasures of the region and to locate the ocean, which he reasoned had to be nearby. Meanwhile, a large contingent of his soldiers planned to mutiny, and relations with the pueblo Indians deteriorated. When the Acoma pueblo revolted, Oñate ruthlessly suppressed the uprising, killing some eight hundred men, women, and children. Although Oñate reconfirmed the Spaniards' military superiority, he did not bring peace or stability to San Gabriel. Another pueblo revolted in 1599, and many of Oñate's settlers returned to Mexico, disillusioned. A few held on, deserting San Gabriel early in the seventeenth century for the greater security of Santa Fe. New Mexico was so marginal to New Spain that officials talked repeatedly of abandoning it, but they did not. Instead New Mexico lingered as a small, dusty token of Spanish claims to the North American Southwest.

The New World and Europe

The riches of New Spain helped make the sixteenth century Spain's Golden Age. After the death of Queen Isabella (in 1504) and King Ferdinand (in 1516), their sixteen-year-old grandson became King Charles I of Spain. Charles used the wealth of the Indies to pursue his vast ambitions in the fierce dynastic and religious battles of sixteenth-century Europe. Through the power of Spain, the New World had a major impact on Europeans.

In 1519, while Cortés made his way into Mexico, Charles I used judicious bribes to secure his selection as Holy Roman Emperor. At the age of nineteen the new Holy Roman Emperor now became Charles V (Charlemagne, who founded the Holy Roman Empire seven hundred years earlier, had prior claim to the title Charles I). His empire encompassed more than that of any other European monarch. With ambitions that matched his sprawling empire, Charles V planned to expand his empire in western Europe and defend its eastern boundary from the advances of the Ottoman Turks. Unexpectedly, Martin Luther, an obscure Catholic priest in central Germany inaugurated a new challenge that commanded the attention of the young emperor.

The Protestant Reformation and the European Order

In 1517, Martin Luther initiated the Protestant Reformation when he nailed his famous ninety-five theses on the door of the Castle Church in Wittenberg, Germany, publicizing some of his criticisms of the Catholic church. Luther's ideas, although shared by many other Catholics, were considered extremely dangerous by church officials and by many monarchs like Charles V who believed firmly that, just as the church spoke for God, they ruled for God. Although a full account of Luther's doctrines and their contribution to the complex history of the Reformation is beyond the scope of this book, it is easy to understand why the church and monarchs were alarmed.

Luther preached a doctrine known as justification by faith: Individual Christians could obtain salvation and life everlasting only by faith that God would save them; giving offerings to the church, following the orders of the priest, or participating in many church rituals did not get believers one step closer to heaven. The only true source of information about God's will, Luther argued, was not the church, but the Bible. By reading the Bible, any Christian could learn as much about God's commandments as any priest. Indeed, Luther called for a priesthood of all believers.

Martin Luther hoped his ideas would reform the Catholic church, but instead they ruptured forever the unity of Christianity in western Europe.

Nearly five centuries later, it may be difficult to appreciate the subversive implications of these ideas. In effect, Luther charged that the Catholic church, which had been the only Christian church in Europe for centuries, was in many respects fraud-

ulent: Contrary to the church's claims, priests were unnecessary for salvation and actually hindered salvation by engaging in religious practices not specifically commanded by the Bible; the church should focus not on playing a major role in the worldly realm of kings and wars and politics—as it had done for centuries—but on aiding individual Christians to understand the spiritual realm, the realm of faith revealed to them in the Bible. Although Luther hoped his ideas would reform the Catholic church, instead they ruptured forever the unity of Christianity in western Europe.

Official recognition of the rupture came in 1521 when Charles V presided over an official interrogation of Luther (who already had been excommunicated by the pope) and commanded him to recant his views. Luther refused and was banned from the empire. Witnessing Luther's intransigence, Charles V pledged to devote all his efforts to exterminate the Protestant heresies.

The wealth pouring into Spain from the New World fueled the determination of Charles V to defend against the Protestant challenge to the Catholic faith, against Muslim enemies in eastern Europe, and against any nation bold or foolhardy enough to contest Spain's supremacy. As the wealthiest and most powerful monarch in Europe, Charles V (who ruled until 1556) and his son and successor Philip II (who ruled until 1598) assumed responsibility for upholding the existing order of sixteenth-century Europe.

New World Treasure and Spanish Ambitions

During the sixteenth century, Spain received gold and silver from New Spain worth well over 1.5 trillion dollars (in 1990 terms). The value of this trade was so great that it paid for all Spanish exports to New Spain and all the costs of colonial administration in the New World and still left staggering sums for the Spanish monarchy to spend.

Both Charles V and Philip II fought wars throughout the world during the sixteenth century. The royal bureaucracy collected revenues from the New World and spent them to pay for military expeditions to defend Catholicism and Spain's empire. Mexican silver funneled through the royal treasury into the hands of military suppliers, soldiers, and sailors wherever in the world Spain's forces happened to be fighting at the time. New World treasure was dissipated in military adventures that served the goals of the monarchy but did little to benefit most Spaniards.

COLUMBIAN EXCHANGE

The arrival of Columbus in the New World initiated the transatlantic exchange of goods, people, and ideas that has continued ever since. Spaniards brought domesticated animals common in the Old World, including horses, cattle, goats, chickens, cats, and sheep. The novelty of such animals is demonstrated by the Nahua words the Mexican people initially used to refer to these strange new beasts: for horses, they used the Nahua word for deer; a cow was "one with horns"; a goat was "a bearded one with horns"; a chicken was a "Spanish turkey hen"; a cat was a "little cougar"; a sheep was referred to with the word for cotton, linking the animal with its fibrous woolen coat, which was somewhat akin to native cotton. Spaniards brought many other alien items such as cannon, which the Nahua at first termed "fat fire trumpets," and guitars, which the Nahua called "rope drums." Smuggled along unknowingly were also unseen animals, Old World microorganisms that caused devastating epidemics of smallpox, measles, and other diseases. Ancient American goods, people, and ideas made the return trip across the Atlantic. Columbus's sailors became infected with syphilis in sexual encounters with New World women and then unwittingly carried the deadly parasite from the Caribbean back to Portugal and Spain. New World tobacco, like that in the cigar smoked by the ancient Mayan lord crowned with a deer headdress, created a European rage for smoking that has yet to abate. Europeans were also introduced to such vital New World crops as corn and potatoes as well as exotic items like the pineapple, a fruit the Europeans named for its resemblance to the pinecone.

The Bancroft Library; Arxiv Mas; Francis Robicey.

In a sense, American wealth made the Spanish monarchy too rich and too powerful among the states of Europe. The ambitions of Charles V and Philip II were so great that the expenses of constant warfare far outstripped the revenues arriving from New Spain. To help maintain military expenditures, both kings continually raised taxes in Spain. Between 1527 and 1598, taxes levied on Spaniards increased more than fivefold. In accordance with the principle of privilege, the nobility—by far the wealthiest class in Spain—was completely exempt from direct taxation, so the increasing tax burden was collected mostly from the peasantry. Thus, escalating taxation, required to pursue the ambitions of the monarchy, further impoverished the vast majority of Spain's population. To the extent that New

World treasure contributed to the kings' ambitions, it indirectly resulted in making most Spaniards poorer.

New World treasure stimulated the ambition of the Spanish monarchy to exercise its great-power status on a scale that brought Spain to the brink of economic bankruptcy. Even though tax rates in Spain were ten times greater than in England, the Spanish crown did not have enough funds to fight its wars. The only alternative was to borrow, principally from Italian, German, and Flemish bankers. The drain of constant military expenditures drew the monarchy deeper and deeper into debt. By the end of the century, paying interest on debts swallowed two-thirds of the crown's annual revenues. For Spain, the riches from New Spain proved a short-term blessing but a long-term curse.

> *New World treasure stimulated the ambition of the Spanish monarchy to exercise its great-power status on a scale that brought Spain to the brink of economic bankruptcy.*

But sixteenth-century Spaniards did not see it that way. At the beginning of the sixteenth century, Spaniards and other Europeans looked at the New World through the eyes of people who venerated the ancient authorities of classical Greece and Rome. They had trouble believing that a New World really existed, in considerable measure because ancient traditions made no mention of such a thing. By the end of the sixteenth century, Spaniards had added enormously to their knowledge. They had discovered staggering riches and built mines, cities, churches, and even universities on the other side of the Atlantic. As they looked at their accomplishments in the New World, they saw what appeared to them unmistakable signs of progress. Their own efforts were responsible for these achievements. Experience had proved a far better guide to success and progress than ancient tradition. Their military, religious, and economic achievements gave them great pride and confidence in themselves and their abilities.

Europe and the Spanish Example

The lessons of sixteenth-century Spain were not lost on Spain's European rivals. Spain proudly displayed the fruits of its New World conquests. In 1520, for instance, Charles V exhibited some of the gifts Montezuma had presented to Cortés. After seeing the objects, the German artist Albrecht Dürer wrote in his diary of his amazement at "the things which were brought to the King from the New Golden Land: a sun entirely of gold, a whole fathom [six feet] broad; likewise a moon, entirely of silver, just as big; likewise sundry curiosities from their weapons, armour, and missiles; very odd clothing, bedding and all sorts of strange articles for human use. . . . I have never seen in all my days what so rejoiced my heart, as these things. For I saw among them amazing objects, and I marvelled over the subtle ingenuity of the men in these distant lands."

Dürer's reaction illustrates the excitement the New World generated among some Europeans. But the most exciting thing about "the men in these distant lands" was that they could serve the interests of Europeans, as Spain had shown. With a few notable exceptions, Europeans saw the New World as a place for the expansion of European influence, a place where—as one Spaniard wrote—Europeans could "give to those strange lands the form of our own." Spain's success in doing just that in New Spain held irresistible allure for its European competitors.

Spain's example proved that an empire in the New World could make a major contribution to a nation's power and prestige in Europe. It also illustrated the profits that could be made in a new arena for commerce across the Atlantic. The thousands of Spaniards who emigrated to the New World found opportunities for work and comfort that far surpassed what Europe offered them, and they encouraged their friends and relatives to follow. Spain benefited, some Europeans observed, by sending to New Spain those Spaniards who would make trouble at home. But the most important lesson Europeans learned from Spain's example was that the New World was a source of fabulous riches.

France and England tried to follow Spain's example. Both nations warred with Spain in Europe, preyed on Spanish treasure fleets, and ventured to the New World, where they too hoped to find an undiscovered passageway to the East Indies or another Mexico or Peru.

In 1524, France sent Giovanni da Verrazano to scout the Atlantic coast of North America from North Carolina to Canada, looking for a northern route to the East Indies, referred to as a Northwest Passage. Eleven years later, they probed farther north with Jacques Cartier's voyage that ventured

CAROLINA ALGONQUIAN MOTHER AND DAUGHTER

When the English artist John White visited the coast of present-day North Carolina in 1585 as part of Raleigh's Roanoke expedition, he painted this watercolor portrait of the wife and daughter of a local Algonquian chief. This and White's other portraits are the only surviving likenesses of sixteenth-century North American Indians that were drawn from direct observation in the New World. The young girl holds a doll and copies her mother by suspending her right wrist from her necklace. The mother's clothing and body paint or tattoos may signify her status as a mature woman and a chief's wife.
British Museum.

up the St. Lawrence River. Encouraged, Cartier returned to the region with a group of settlers in 1541, but the colony they established—like the search for a Northwest Passage—came to nothing. In 1564, a group of French Huguenots (Protestants fleeing from persecution in Catholic France) established a settlement near present-day Jacksonville, Florida, that was soon eliminated by Spaniards led by Pedro Menéndez de Avilés. French interest in North America did not revive until the seventeenth century.

English attempts to mimic Spain were slower but equally ill-fated. Not until 1576, almost eighty years after John Cabot's voyages, did the English try again to find a westward route to the East Indies. This time Martin Frobisher sailed into the frigid waters of northern Canada; his sponsor was the Cathay Company, which hoped to open trade with China. Like many other explorers who preceded and followed him, Frobisher was mesmerized by the Spanish example and was sure he had found gold. The tons of "ore" he hauled back to England proved worthless, the Cathay Company collapsed, and English interests shifted southward.

English attempts to establish North American settlements were no more fruitful than their search for a northern route to China. Sir Humphrey Gilbert, a soldier-adventurer who had won his reputation in Ireland, led an expedition in 1578 and another in 1583 that made feeble efforts to found colonies in Newfoundland, until Gilbert himself vanished at sea. In 1585, Sir Walter Raleigh organized an expedition to settle Roanoke Island off the coast of present-day North Carolina. The explorers collected valuable information about the region and its native inhabitants. The artist John White, for example, made virtually the only eyewitness drawings that exist of sixteenth-century North American Indians. Although the first group of explorers left no colonists on the island, two years later Raleigh sent a contingent of more than a hundred settlers to Roanoke under John White's leadership. White left the settlers and returned to England for supplies to keep the colony provisioned. White and the supply fleet did not return to Roanoke until 1590. By then, the Roanoke colonists had disappeared, leaving only the word "Croatoan" (whose meaning is unknown) carved on a tree. Although the fate of the Roanoke colonists remains a mystery, they most likely died from a combination of natural causes and unfriendly Indians. In any case, by the end of the sixteenth century England had failed to secure a New World beachhead.

Conclusion: The Legacy of the Sixteenth Century

The sixteenth century in the New World belonged to the Spanish, who had employed Columbus, and the Indians, who had greeted him as he stepped ashore. Spanish explorers, conquistadors, and colonists forced the Indians to serve the interests of Spanish settlers and the Spanish monarchy. Spaniards brought with them things that were novelties in the New World but were commonplace in sixteenth-century Europe, including Christianity, iron technology, sailing ships, firearms, wheeled vehicles, horses, and deadly diseases. They took back to Spain cargoes of New World silver, gold, and hides as well as crops like corn, potatoes, and tobacco that had been grown for millennia in the New World but were novelties in Europe. Historians have termed this transfer of goods, ideas, foods, and diseases the "Columbian exchange." The exchange illustrated one of the most important legacies of the sixteenth century: After millions of years, the Atlantic no longer was an impermeable barrier separating the Eastern and Western Hemispheres. After the voyages of Columbus, European sailing ships regularly bridged the Atlantic and transferred an unending stream of people, products, and ideas from one shore to the other. No European monarch could forget the seductive lesson about this transfer taught by Spain's example: The New World could vastly enrich the Old. Spain remained a New World power for almost four centuries, and its language, culture, and institutions left a permanent imprint. By the end of the sixteenth century, however, other European monarchies began to contest Spain's dominion in Europe and to make forays into the northern fringes of Spain's New World preserve. They sought to reap some of the benefits the Spaniards enjoyed from their New World domain. But to do so they had to learn a difficult lesson: how to deviate from Spain's example. That discovery lay ahead.

CHRONOLOGY

1415	Portugal conquers Ceuta at Strait of Gibraltar, gaining access to western coast of Africa.
1444	Portuguese explorers reach Cape Verde.
1451	Columbus born in Genoa, Italy.
1480	Portuguese ships reach Congo.
1488	Bartolomeu Dias rounds Cape of Good Hope.
1492	Columbus lands on Caribbean island that he names San Salvador.
1493	Columbus makes second voyage to the New World.
1494	Portugal and Spain negotiate Treaty of Tordesillas to divide New World between them.
1497	John Cabot searches for Northwest Passage.
1498	Columbus makes third voyage to New World and lands in Venezuela.
	Vasco da Gama sails to India.
1500	Pedro Álvars Cabral makes landfall in Brazil.
1507	German mapmaker Waldseemüller names New World America.
1513	Vasco Nuñez de Balboa crosses isthmus of Panama.
1517	Protestant Reformation begins in Europe.
1519	Hernán Cortés leads expedition to find and conquer Mexico.
	Ferdinand Magellan sets out to sail around world.
	Charles I of Spain becomes Holy Roman Emperor Charles V.

1521	Cortés conquers Mexica at Tenochtitlán.
	Juan Ponce de León lands in Florida.
1524	Guatemala, El Salvador, and Nicaragua come under Spanish control.
	Franciscan missionaries arrive in Mexico.
1526	Lucas Vázquez de Ayllón establishes San Miguel de Gualdape on Georgia coast.
1528	Pánfilo de Narváez leads expedition to survey Gulf coast from Florida to Texas.
1532	Francisco Pizarro begins conquest of Peru.
1539	Hernando de Soto launches exploration of Southeast.
1540	Francisco Vásquez de Coronado starts to explore Southwest and Great Plains.
1542	Juan Rodríguez Cabrillo explores California coast.
1549	Repartimiento reforms begin to replace encomienda.
1565	Pedro Menéndez de Avilés establishes St. Augustine, Florida.
1587	English colonists settle Roanoke Island.
1598	Juan de Oñate leads expedition into New Mexico.

BIBLIOGRAPHY

GENERAL WORKS

Alfred W. Crosby Jr., *The Columbian Exchange: Biological and Cultural Consequences of 1492* (1972).

Zvi Dor-Ner, *Columbus and the Age of Discovery* (1991).

J. H. Elliott, *The Old World and the New, 1462–1650* (1970).

Felipe Fernández-Armesto, *Before Columbus: Exploration and Colonization from the Mediterranean to the Atlantic, 1229–1492* (1987).

J. A. Levenson, *Circa 1492: Art in the Age of Exploration* (1991).

D. W. Meinig, *The Shaping of America* (1986).

Samuel E. Morison, *The European Discovery of America: The Northern Voyages, A.D. 500–1600* (1971).

Samuel E. Morison, *The European Discovery of America: The Southern Voyages, A.D. 1492–1616* (1974).

John H. Parry and Robert G. Keith, eds., *New Iberian World: A Documentary History of the Discovery and Settlement of Latin America to the Early Seventeenth Century,* 5 vols. (1984).

William D. Phillips and Carla Rahn Phillips, *The Worlds of Christopher Columbus* (1992).

David B. Quinn, *North America from Earliest Discovery to First Settlements* (1977).

David B. Quinn, ed., *New American World: A Documentary History of North America to 1612,* 5 vols. (1970).

A. J. R. Russell-Wood, *A World on the Move: The Portuguese in Africa, Asia, and America, 1415–1808* (1992).

Hugh Thomas, *Conquest: Montezuma, Cortés, and the Fall of Old Mexico* (1993).

John Thornton, *Africa and Africans in the Making of the Atlantic World, 1400–1680* (1992).

David J. Weber, *The Spanish Frontier in North America* (1992).

EXPLORERS AND EMPIRES

Charles Boxer, *The Portuguese Seaborne Empire, 1415–1825* (1969).

Lorenzo Camusso, *Travel Guide to Europe, 1492: Ten Itineraries in the Old World* (1990).

Nicholas P. Canny, *The Elizabethan Conquest of Ireland* (1976).

Philip Curtin et al., *African History* (2nd ed., 1995).

Jan De Vries, *The Economy of Europe in an Age of Crisis, 1600–1750* (1976).

William Eccles, *Canadian Frontier, 1534–1760* (1969).

Paul Hulton, *America, 1585: The Complete Drawings of John White* (1984).

Karen Ordahl Kupperman, *Roanoke: The Abandoned Colony* (1984).

Peggy K. Liss, *Isabel the Queen: Life and Times* (1992).

John Lynch, *Spain, 1516–1598: From Nation State to World Empire* (1992).

Harry A. Miskimin, *The Economy of Later Renaissance Europe, 1460–1600* (1977).

John H. Parry, *The Spanish Seaborne Empire* (1966).

David B. Quinn, *England and the Discovery of America, 1481–1620* (1974).

David B. Quinn, *Set Fair for Roanoke* (1985).

David B. Quinn, ed., *North American Discovery, 1000–1612* (1971).

Carl O. Sauer, *The Early Spanish Main* (1966).

Carl O. Sauer, *Sixteenth-Century North America: The Land and the People as Seen by the Europeans* (1971).

A. C. de C. M. Saunders, *A Social History of Black Slaves and Freedmen in Portugal, 1441–1555* (1982).

Roger C. Smith, *Vanguard of Empire: Ships of Exploration in the Age of Columbus* (1993).

Robert S. Weddle, *The Gulf of Mexico in North American Discovery, 1500–1685* (1985).

EUROPEANS ENCOUNTER THE NEW WORLD

James Axtell, *Beyond 1492: Encounters in Colonial North America* (1992).

Robert F. Berkhofer Jr., *The White Man's Indian: Images of the American Indian from Columbus to the Present* (1978).

Philip P. Boucher, *Cannibal Encounters: Europeans and Island Caribs, 1492–1763* (1992).

Nicholas Canny and Anthony Pagden, *Colonial Identity in the Atlantic World, 1500–1800* (1987).

Rebecca Catz, *Christopher Columbus and the Portuguese, 1476–1498* (1993).

Fredi Chiappelli et al., *First Images of America: The Impact of the New World on the Old*, 2 vols. (1976).

Alfred W. Crosby, *Ecological Imperialism: The Biological Expansion of Europe, 900–1900* (1986).

Alfred W. Crosby, *Germs, Seeds, and Animals: Studies in Ecological History* (1994).

Oliver Dunn and James E. Kelley Jr., trans., *The Diario of Christopher Columbus's First Voyage to America, 1492–1493* (1988).

William W. Fitzhugh, ed., *Cultures in Contact: The Impact of European Contacts on Native American Cultural Institutions, 1000–1800* (1985).

Valerie J. Flint, *The Imaginative Landscape of Christopher Columbus* (1992).

Antonello Gerbi, *Nature in the New World: From Christopher Columbus to Gonzalo Fernández de Oviedo*, trans. Jeremy Moyle (1986).

Anthony Grafton, *New Worlds, Ancient Texts: The Power of Tradition and the Shock of Discovery* (1992).

Stephen Greenblatt, *Marvelous Possessions: The Wonder of the New World* (1991).

Stephen Greenblatt, ed., *New World Encounters* (1993).

David Henige, *In Search of Columbus: The Sources for the First Voyage* (1991).

Hugh Honour, *The New Golden Land: European Images of America from the Discoveries to the Present Time* (1975).

Peter Hulme, *Colonial Encounters: Europe and the Native Caribbean, 1492–1797* (1986).

Peter Hulme and Neil L. Whitehead, eds., *Wild Majesty: Encounters with Caribs from Columbus to the Present Day* (1992).

William F. Keegan, *The People Who Discovered Columbus: An Introduction to the Prehistory of the Bahamas* (1992).

Kenneth Nebenzahl, *Atlas of Columbus and the Great Discoveries* (1990).

Anthony Pagden, *The Fall of Natural Man: The American Indian and the Origins of Comparative Ethnology* (1981).

Anthony Pagden, *European Encounters with the New World: From Renaissance to Romanticism* (1993).

Anthony Pagden, *Lords of All the World: Ideologies of Empire in Spain, Britain, and France, 1500–1800* (1995).

Irving Rouse, *The Tainos: Rise and Decline of the People Who Greeted Columbus* (1992).

David Hurst Thomas, ed., *Columbian Consequences*, 3 vols. (1991).

Samuel M. Wilson, *Hispaniola: Caribbean Chiefdoms in the Age of Columbus* (1990).

CONQUEST AND NEW SPAIN

Ida Altman, *Emigrants and Society: Extremadura and Spanish America in the Sixteenth Century* (1989).

Kenneth J. Andrien and Rolena Adorno, eds., *Transatlantic Encounters: Europeans and Andeans in the Sixteenth Century* (1991).

Frances Berdan, *The Aztecs of Central Mexico: An Imperial Society* (1982).

Frances F. Berdan and Patricia Rieff Anawalt, eds., *The Codex Mendoza*, 4 vols. (1992).

Peter J. Blackwell, *Silver Mining and Society in Colonial Mexico: Zacatecas, 1546–1700* (1971).

Peter J. Blackwell, *Miners of the Red Mountain: Indian Labor in Potosí, 1545–1650* (1984).

Frederick P. Bowser, *The African Slave in Colonial Peru, 1524–1650* (1974).

Gordon Brotherston, *Image of the New World: The American Continent Portrayed in Native Texts* (1979).

Louise M. Burkhart, *The Slippery Earth: Nahua-Christian Moral Dialogue in Sixteenth-Century Mexico* (1989).

Lawrence A. Clayton, Vernon James Knight Jr., and Edward C. Moore, eds., *The de Soto Chronicles: The Expedition of Hernando de Soto to North America in 1539–1543,* 2 vols. (1993).

Inga Clendinnen, *Aztecs: An Interpretation* (1991).

David Noel Cook, *Demographic Collapse: Indian Peru, 1520–1620* (1981).

David Noel Cook and W. George Lovell, eds., *"Secret Judgments of God": Old World Disease in Colonial Spanish America* (1991).

Cyclone Covey, trans., *Cabeza de Vaca's Adventures in the Unknown Interior of America* (1961).

Kathleen A. Deegan, ed., *America's Ancient City: Spanish St. Augustine, 1565–1763* (1991).

Bernal Díaz, *The Conquest of New Spain,* trans. J. M. Cohen (1963).

Charles Gibson, *The Aztecs under Spanish Rule* (1964).

Charles Gibson, *Spain in America* (1966).

Serge Gruzinski, *Painting the Conquest: The Mexican Indians and the European Renaissance* (1992).

Serge Gruzinski, *The Conquest of Mexico: The Incorporation of Indian Societies into the Western World, Sixteenth–Eighteenth Centuries* (1993).

Ramon A. Gutiérrez, *When Jesus Came, the Corn Mothers Went Away: Marriage, Sexuality, and Power in New Mexico, 1500–1846* (1991).

Lewis Hanke, *All Mankind Is One: A Study of the Disputation between Bartolomé de Las Casas and Juan Ginés de Sepúlveda in 1550 on the Intellectual and Religious Capacity of the American Indians* (1974).

Robert T. Himmerich, *The Encomenderos of New Spain, 1521–1555* (1991).

Paul E. Hoffman, *A New Andalucía and a Way to the Orient: The American Southeast during the Sixteenth Century* (1990).

Robert H. Jackson, ed., *Indians, Franciscans, and Spanish Colonization: The Impact of the Mission System on California Indians* (1995).

Andrew L. Knaut, *The Pueblo Revolt of 1680: Conquest and Resistance in Seventeenth-Century New Mexico* (1995).

James Lang, *Conquest and Commerce: Spain and England in the Americas* (1975).

Clark Spencer Larsen and George R. Milner, eds., *In the Wake of Contact: Biological Responses to Conquest* (1994).

Bartolomé de Las Casas, *In Defense of the Indians,* trans. Stafford Poole (1974).

Miguel Leon-Portilla, *Aztec Thought and Culture: A Study of the Ancient Nahuatl Mind* (1963).

Miguel Leon-Portilla, ed., *The Broken Spears: The Aztec Account of the Conquest of Mexico* (1962).

James Lockhart, *The Nahuas after Conquest: A Social and Cultural History of the Indians of Central Mexico, Sixteenth through Eighteenth Centuries* (1992).

James Lockhart, ed., *We People Here: Nahuatl Accounts of the Conquest of Mexico* (1993).

James Lockhart and Enrique Otte, eds., *Letters and People of the Spanish Indies: Sixteenth Century* (1976).

James Lockhart and Stuart B. Schwartz, *Early Latin America: A History of Colonial Spanish America and Brazil* (1983).

Lyle N. McAlister, *Spain and Portugal in the New World, 1492–1700* (1984).

Sabine McCormack, *Religion in the Andes: Vision and Imagination in Early Colonial Peru* (1991).

Bonnie G. McEwan, *The Spanish Missions of la Florida* (1993).

Jerald T. Milanich, *Florida Indians and the Invasion from Europe* (1995).

Jerald T. Milanich, ed., *Earliest Hispanic/Native American Interactions in the American Southeast* (1991).

Jerald T. Milanich and Charles Hudson, *Hernando de Soto and the Indians of Florida* (1993).

Jerald T. Milanich and Susan Milrath, eds., *First Encounters: Spanish Explorations in the Caribbean and the United States* (1989).

Colin A. Palmer, *Slaves of the White God: Blacks in Mexico, 1570–1650* (1976).

Carroll L. Riley, *Rio del Norte: People of the Upper Rio Grande from Earliest Times to the Pueblo Revolt* (1995).

Fray Bernardino de Sahagún, *General History of the Things of New Spain,* ed. Arthur J. O. Anderson and Charles E. Dibble, 13 vols. (1982).

Robert Silverberg, *The Pueblo Revolt* (1994).

Steve J. Stern, *Peru's Indian Peoples and the Challenge of Spanish Conquest: Huamanga to 1640* (1982).

David Hurst Thomas, *St. Catherines: An Island in Time* (1988).

David Hurst Thomas, ed., *Ethnology of the Indians of Spanish Florida* (1991).

David Hurst Thomas, ed., *The Missions of Spanish Florida* (1991).

Tzvetan Todorov, *The Conquest of America: The Question of the Other* (1984).

John W. Verano and Douglas H. Ubelaker, eds., *Disease and Demography in the Americas* (1992).

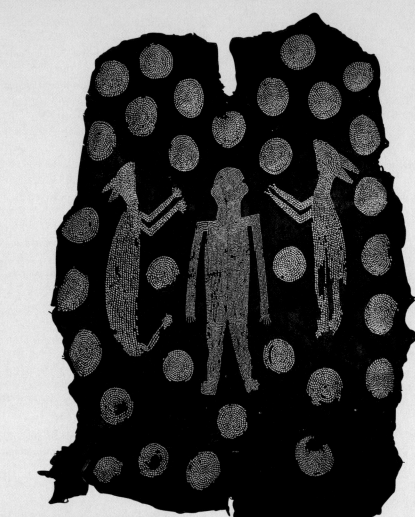

VIRGINIA ALGONQUIAN TOTEM

*This object was made by one of Powhatan's peo-
ple, probably a woman skilled in sewing small shell beads
into intricate patterns. Soon after it appeared in England about 1630, it was called
"Powhatan's mantle," a name still used for it. It is large, more than six feet long and four feet
wide, constructed of four deer hides sewn together. The hides and the decorative shells used
conclusively establish its Virginia Algonquian origins, although there is no firm evidence that
it actually belonged to Powhatan or that it was used as a mantle or cloak. What looks like a
neck opening is simply an unfinished seam between two deerskins. Furthermore, there is no
record of a Virginia Algonquian wearing a cloak suspended from the neck. Cloaks worn by
Powhatan, described by Captain John Smith and other settlers, evidently had fringe or animal
tails dangling from them, unlike this object. A modern expert has concluded that this object
was probably an image kept in a treasure house where chiefs stored their valuables. The large
human figure, the deer on the right, the mountain lion on the left, and the thirty-four concentric circles probably served as totems, what Smith called "sentinels," linking the chief, the
valuable objects in the treasure house, and the spirits that animated the world.*

Ashmolean Museum, Oxford.

THE SOUTHERN COLONIES IN THE SEVENTEENTH CENTURY

3

1601–1700

EARLY IN 1607, POWHATAN RULED an Algonquian chiefdom on the brink of a strange new world, a world in which white people from England would become a permanent and growing presence in North America. In Central and South America, other chiefdoms had entered this new world a century earlier when newcomers from Spain had arrived, plundering, praying, and staying. The conquistadors de Soto and Coronado made forays into North America in the 1540s. Decades later, the colonizers Menéndez and Oñate established small, struggling outposts of New Spain in Florida and New Mexico. Elsewhere in North America, no Europeans established a permanent settlement. Explorers, missionaries, fishermen, pirates, and others cruised along the Atlantic coast from time to time before 1607 and made an occasional landing. But they did not stay or, if they tried to stay —as at Roanoke—they did not survive. In 1607, all that was about to change. The Powhatan chiefdom was the first Native American group in North America to encounter the new English world that would eventually engulf them all.

Powhatan was the supreme chief—in his language, the *mamanatowick*—of about 14,000 Algonquian people who inhabited the coastal plain of present-day Virginia, near the Chesapeake Bay. Powhatan's people belonged to more than thirty subordinate chiefdoms, each headed by its own chief, called a *werowance*. Powhatan, who was probably born in the 1540s, inherited leadership of six of these subordinate chiefdoms. The others he systematically added to his chiefdom by conquest or threat. By 1607, the werowances beholden to Powhatan governed about 140 settlements scattered along the banks of the four major rivers that drained into Chesapeake Bay. Most werowances inherited their positions from female ancestors. Women sometimes served as werowances; the woman Opussunoquonuske was werowance of a town of the Appamatucks.

Hostile tribes surrounded Powhatan's chiefdom, and intertribal warfare occurred constantly. Men aspired to be courageous warriors who excelled at killing their enemies. One of Powhatan's duties as mamanatowick was to travel from village to village and listen to men boast of their heroic feats in battle. His visits energized the warrior ethic and strengthened his chiefdom. The emphasis on warfare arose partly from increased competition for access to prime deer-hunting lands caused by a growing Native American population. Another purpose of warfare was to capture women and children who could be then incorporated into Powhatan's chiefdom. Captured male children would grow into valuable warriors, and their

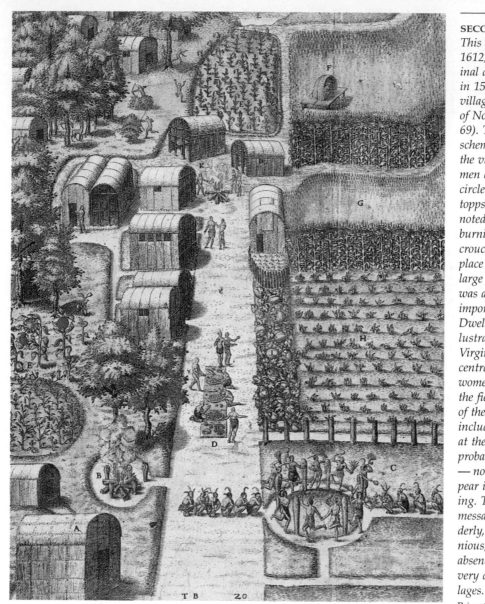

SECOTAN VILLAGE
This engraving, published in 1612, was copied from an original drawing John White made in 1585 when he visited the village of Secotan on the coast of North Carolina (see page 69). The drawing provides a schematic view of daily life in the village. In the lower right, men dance and sing around a circle of "posts carved on the topps lyke mens faces," White noted on the original. The fire burning behind the line of crouching men he labeled "the place of solemne prayer." The large building in the lower left was a tomb where the bodies of important leaders were kept. Dwellings similar to those illustrated on Smith's map of Virginia (see page 78) lined a central space, where men and women ate. Corn is growing in the fields along the right side of the village. The engraver has included hunters shooting deer at the upper left; hunting was probably never so convenient — no such hunters or deer appear in White's original drawing. This portrait conveys the message that Secotan was orderly, settled, religious, harmonious, and peaceful (note the absence of fortifications), and very different from English villages.
Princeton University Libraries.

mothers and sisters would give birth to still more warriors while performing valuable labor.

The arts of war were similar in many ways to the skills of hunting, the basic subsistence activity of Powhatan's men. Hunters took small game of all sorts. They hooked, netted, and trapped fish in the region's many streams and rivers. Deer were their most important prey, supplying not only meat but also hides, bones, and antlers that were crafted into clothing, tools, weapons, and decorative objects. Successful hunters who kept their families well supplied with meat were accorded high status. A young hunter who wished to marry a young woman offered gifts of meat to her as proof of his hunting skills.

Men hunted not only for food but also because Powhatan required each of his werowances to pay him an annual tribute in the form of deer hides. Powhatan collected many other forms of tribute, including turkeys, fish, shellfish, beads, copper, and especially corn. Corn was such a vital crop that Powhatan's people divided their year into five seasons: fall, winter, spring, summer, and the season when ears appeared on the corn.

Powhatan stored the hides and other goods in huge storehouses and used them to reward favorites and to provide gifts to the parents of the young women he took as wives. On his journeys from village to village, he surveyed the young virgins and selected the most desirable to be his wives. He had well over fifty wives in all; at any one time, a dozen or more lived with him. Typically, after a wife bore him a child he sent her back to her home village and kept the child to be raised in his settlement. This practice interlaced the dispersed villages in Powhatan's chiefdom with ties of kinship and loyalty to the mamanatowick. Werowances also often had more than one wife, but usually not many more since they lacked the wealth Powhatan obtained from tribute.

Women's responsibility for the essential food that came from foraging and agriculture underscored their importance and status in Powhatan's communities. Women in the chiefdom planted crops using sticks or deer bones to dig holes for seeds. They harvested, processed, stored, and cooked the produce. Cultivated crops supplied about a quarter of their families' diet. Women obtained other plant food by foraging. They also wove baskets and mats, fashioned various bone utensils, and kept the home fires burning. When an important man visited a settlement, the werowance usually assigned a woman to sleep with the visitor. If her husband consented, as many men did, a married woman could have sexual relations with other men. A man who was caught having unauthorized sex with another man's wife was killed.

By 1607, Powhatan had heard about white men who appeared from time to time. His brother Opechancanough had told him about the Spaniards' plans for a Chesapeake settlement thirty years earlier. Powhatan's warriors probably helped kill the last survivors of England's abortive Roanoke settlement. Powhatan posted scouts along the Atlantic coast to watch for white people and their "floating islands," a term one Indian coined for ships. Confident of his formidable power, Powhatan was not afraid of these white intruders. In fact, they might make useful allies against enemy tribes.

In the century after 1607, Powhatan's people were decimated by English settlers and the diseases they inadvertently brought with them. The English newcomers had different ideas about how to organize their communities, what crops to plant, what rulers to obey, what labor to perform, and why. During the seventeenth century, English notions about these matters came to dominate the coastal plain bordering the Chesapeake that had been Powhatan's chiefdom for decades before 1607. In the decades after 1607, English immigrants built a new world of permanent colonies in North America, initiating the sporadic, long-term decline of Powhatan's chiefdom and others like it. A world of Stone Age hunters and gatherers began to be replaced by a New World of farmers with tools, weapons, and ideas unknown to Powhatan.

An English Colony on the Chesapeake

By 1600, King James I of England eyed North America as a possible location for English colonies. He understood that North American colonies could extend English power across the Atlantic and might become the foundation of an English empire in the New World. Although Spain claimed all of North America under the 1494 Treaty of Tordesillas with Portugal, Spain's claim meant little if it could not be defended. In 1588, when King Philip II of Spain had sent a large fleet, the Armada, to invade England and attempt to place him on the English throne, English forces soundly defeated the Armada, demonstrating that England was capable of checking Spanish ambitions. It seemed likely that England could also prevail against Spain in North America, a distant hinterland of Spain's stoutly defended colonial heartland in Mexico and South America. Maybe England could encroach on the outskirts of Spain's New World empire, start colonies, and defend them. Maybe England could prevail against Spain's claims to North America by seizing the opportunity for colonization and daring Spain to intervene.

Colonization was an expensive undertaking. It required raising funds to purchase supplies, obtain ships and crews, and keep colonies provisioned until they became self-sufficient. Colonization was also risky. If a colony collapsed, the investments would be lost. But as the Spaniards had shown during the sixteenth century, expensive and risky as colonization was, it could also be enormously profitable. English merchants had used joint stock companies for many years to pool capital and share risks in trading voyages to Europe, Africa, and Asia. The tantalizing Spanish example lured certain Englishmen, with King James's blessing, into creating a joint stock company for the purposes of colonizing North America.

JOHN SMITH'S MAP OF VIRGINIA
In 1612, John Smith published a detailed map of early Virginia that showed not only geographical features but also the limits of exploration (indicated by small crosses), the locations of the houses of the Indian "kings" (indicated by dwellings that look like quonset huts), and "ordinary houses" of indigenous people (indicated by dots). The map shows the early settlers' intense interest in knowing where the Indians were — and were not. Note the location of Jamestown (upriver from Point Comfort) and of Powhatan's residence at the falls (just to the right of the large P outside the hut portrayed in the upper left corner). The drawing of Powhatan surrounded by some of his many wives (upper left corner) was almost certainly made by an English artist who had never been to Virginia or seen Powhatan but who tried to imagine the scene as described by John Smith. Princeton University Libraries.

In 1606, a number of "knightes, gentlemen, merchauntes, and other adventurers of our cittie of London" organized the Virginia Company of London and petitioned King James to grant them permission to establish a colony in North America. The king gave the company a charter authorizing the group to settle a colony on the coast of Virginia and to possess "all the landes, woods, soile, groundes, havens, ports, rivers, mines, mineralls, marshes, waters, fishinges, commodities and hereditamentes [anything inheritable] whatsoever" that lay within fifty miles north and south of the coastal settlement and one hundred miles inland (later extended to the Pacific). James boldly granted the Virginia Company over six million acres and everything they might contain, in large measure because they were not his to grant. In effect, the charter was a royal license to poach on Spanish claims and on Powhatan's chiefdom.

> *English merchants had used joint stock companies for many years to pool capital and share risks in trading voyages to Europe, Africa, and Asia. The tantalizing Spanish example lured certain Englishmen into creating a joint stock company for the purposes of colonizing North America.*

The adventurers in the Virginia Company hoped to found an empire that would strengthen England not only overseas but also at home. Richard Hakluyt, a strong proponent of colonization, argued that a colony would provide a convenient outlet for the swarms of poor "valiant youthes rusting and hurtfull by lacke of employement" in England. As colonial settlers, these jobless Englishmen would be put to work, producing goods that England currently had to import from other nations. They would also provide a ready market in the colony for English woolens. But the main reason the Virginia Company adventurers were willing to risk (or "adventure") their capital in Virginia was not to reduce unemployment in England or provide overseas markets for English textiles. Instead, they fervently hoped for quick profits.

Virginia Company investors did not know exactly how they could make money in the colony. Enthusiastic reports from the Roanoke voyages twenty years earlier claimed that in Virginia "the earth bringeth foorth all things in aboundance, as in the first creation, without toile or labour." Perhaps some valuable exotic crop could be grown in this Eden. Maybe the virtually limitless timber could be exploited to produce pitch and tar, those essentials for watertight ships. Or perhaps deposits of gold, silver, or other precious minerals awaited discovery. Another, more certain source of riches lay in Spanish treasure ships as they cruised up the North American coast to catch the trade winds that sped them home. Perhaps, the adventurers reasoned, an occasional raid on the Spanish fleet would yield quick and relatively easy returns. One way or another, Virginia promised to reward the adventurers. Or so they thought.

The Fragile Jamestown Settlement

In December 1606, the *Susan Constant, Discovery,* and *Godspeed* carried 144 Englishmen toward Virginia. Delayed by storms and a stopover in the West Indies, where they picked up plants that might prove hardy in Virginia, they arrived at the mouth of the Chesapeake Bay on April 26, 1607. That night while the colonists rested onshore, one of them later recalled that a band of Indians "creeping upon all foure, from the Hills like Beares, with their Bowes in their mouthes," attacked and dangerously wounded two men. The attack gave the colonists an early warning that the North American wilderness was not quite the paradise described by the Virginia Company's publications in England. For the next three weeks, the 105 colonists (39 had died at sea) explored the bay for a suitable place to settle. On May 14, they put ashore on a small peninsula in the James River, about sixty miles from the coast, in the midst of Powhatan's chiefdom. With the memory of their first night in America fresh in their minds, they quickly built a fort, the first building in the settlement they named Jamestown.

The fort accurately conveyed the colonists' belief that they needed to protect themselves from Indians and Spaniards. They worried that Spain might try to eliminate their fledgling colony before it got established. Spaniards did employ spies who kept them well informed about events in Virginia, and they even planned an expedition to wipe out Jamestown. But, like many other Spanish plans in the seventeenth century, this one never got beyond the planning stage. Powhatan's people, however, could not afford to be lackadaisical about defending their homeland. The Jamestown fort showed that, despite Spanish claims, English ambitions, and

the king's charter, the colonists knew that native peoples were prepared to defend Virginia as their own.

During May and June 1607, the settlers and Powhatan's warriors skirmished repeatedly. English muskets and cannon repelled Indian attacks on Jamestown, but the Indians' superior numbers and knowledge of the Virginia wilderness made it risky for the settlers to venture far beyond the Jamestown peninsula. Late in June, Powhatan sensed a stalemate and made peace overtures.

The settlers soon discovered that they confronted a far more dangerous, invisible threat: disease. For six weeks during the summer, many of the Englishmen lay "night and day groaning in every corner of the Fort most pittiful to heare," wrote George Percy, one of the settlers. By September, fifty of the colonists had died. "Our men were destroyed with [such] cruell diseases as Swellings, Fluxes, Burning Fevers, and by [Indian] warres, and some departed suddenly, but for the most part they died of meere famine," Percy recalled. "There were never Englishmen left in a forreigne Countrey in such miserie as wee were in this new discovered Virginia."

The colonists also made themselves miserable by constant bickering and plotting. While real and imaginary conspiracies occupied the attention of Jamestown's leaders, crops went unplanted and food supplies dwindled.

Powhatan's people came to the rescue of the weakened and distracted colonists. Early in September 1607, they began to bring corn to the colony for barter. When that was insufficient to keep the colonists fed, the settlers sent Captain John Smith to trade for corn with tribes upriver from Jamestown. More soldier than merchant, Smith did not hesitate to take hostages and shoot to kill when Indians were reluctant to trade away their corn. His efforts managed to keep 38 of the original settlers alive until a fresh supply of food and 120 more colonists arrived from England in January 1608.

Smith himself barely managed to survive that first year. Late in December, when he was on one of his trading forays, Powhatan's warriors captured him and brought him before the powerful chief. Smith wrote that Powhatan "feasted him after their best barbarous manner." Then, after the chief had consulted with his men, "two great stones were brought before Powhatan: then as many [Indians] as could layd hands on [Smith], dragged him to [the stones], and thereon laid his head, and being ready with their clubs, to beate out his braines." At that moment, Pocahontas, Powhatan's young daughter, rushed forward and "got [Smith's] head in her armes, and laid her owne upon his to save him from death." Powhatan spared Smith and, with a promise of friendship, released him to return to Jamestown.

Smith's famous Pocahontas story is almost too good to be true. Although Smith himself is the source of the story, it probably happened about as he claimed. Certainly he was captured and released by Powhatan; and certainly Pocahontas was friendly with the colonists—she eventually married the

SATIRICAL PLAYING CARD
Horrifying tales that filtered back to England contradicted the claims of promoters that settlers would find an idyllic land of milk and honey in Virginia. This English playing card makes fun of rich investors who "fool away A Sporting Sum in North America," getting shares of stock that will be honored only by "Asses Ears." The card hints that investing in overseas colonies made less sense than gambling — which was presumably how this card was used. What does the drawing suggest about those who became settlers rather than simply shareholders in a joint stock company?
Bodleian Library, Oxford.

Englishman John Rolfe and moved to England, where she died in 1617. Making allowances for Smith's flair for self-dramatization, the Pocahontas story emphasizes two central themes of Jamestown's first year: the colonists' dependence on the Indians and Powhatan's reluctance to drive away the struggling English settlers while he had the chance. Those themes remained central to Virginia's history for almost twenty years.

It is difficult to exaggerate the precarious state of the early Jamestown settlement. Although the Virginia Company sent hundreds of new settlers to Jamestown each year, few survived. During the "starving time" winter of 1609–10, food was so short that one or two famished settlers resorted to eating their recently deceased neighbors. When Sir Thomas Gates, the first governor of Jamestown, arrived in 1610, he found only about 60 of the 500 settlers alive. The survivors were "full of misery and misgovernment," wrote William Strachey, who accompanied Gates. They were so demoralized that, rather than "step into the Woods a stone's cast off . . . to fetch other firewood," they ripped apart the dead settlers' empty houses. When Gates announced that he would take the survivors back to England if he could not feed them from the supplies in his ship, they responded with "a general acclamation, and shoute of joy." No cheers were recorded when a shipload of fresh supplies arrived from England just in time for the survivors to prolong their flirtation with death. Although the company continued to pour new settlers into Virginia, most of them went to an early grave. In the three years from 1619 through 1621, for example, the company sent 3,570 people to Virginia to supplement the 700 settlers already there. By 1622, however, only 1,240 of the 4,270 were still alive.

Encounters between Natives and Newcomers

In retrospect, the weakened condition of the settlers raises the question of why Powhatan did not strike to eliminate them. Of course, we cannot be certain about Powhatan's motives. Since Indians relied on spoken rather than written language, they left no documents that record their ideas. All our information about them comes filtered through the distorting lenses of English eyes. However, we can be certain about what the Indians did. They vacillated. They maintained contact with the English settlers, most of the time peaceful contact. But they also kept their distance.

Becaufe many doe defire to know the manner
of their Language, I haue inferted thefe few words.

KA katorawincs yowo. What call you this.
Nemarough, a man.
Crenepo, a woman.
Marowancheffo, a boy.
Yehawkans, Houfes.
Matchcores, Skins, or garments.
Mockafins, Shooes.
Tuffan, Beds. *Pokatawer,* Fire.
Attawp, A bow. *Attonce,* Arrowes.
Monacookes, Swords.
Aumouhhowgh, A Target.
Pawcuffacks, Gunnes.
Tomahacks, Axes.
Tockahacks, Pickaxes.
Pamefacks, Kniues.
Accowprets, Sheares.
Pawpecones, Pipes. *Mattaßin,* Copper
Vffawaffin, Iron, Braffe, Silver, or any white mettall. *Muffes,* Woods.
Attaffkuff, Leaues, weeds, or graffe.
Chepfin, Land. *Shacquohocan.* A ftone.
Wepenter, A cookold.
Suckahanna, Water. *Noughmaff,* Fifh.
Copotone, Sturgeon.
Weghfhaughes, Flefh.
Sawwehone, Bloud.
Netoppew, Friends.
Marrapough, Enemies.
Maskapow, the worft of the enemies.
Mawchick chammay, The beft of friends
Cafacunnakack, peya quagh acquintan vitafantafough, In how many daies will there come hither any more Englifh Ships.
Their Numbers.
Necut, 1. *Ningh,* 2. *Nuff,* 3. *Yowgh,* 4.
Paranske, 5. *Comotinch,* 6. *Toppawoff,* 7
Nuffwafh, 8. *Kekatawgh,* 9. *Kaskeke* 10
They count no more but by tennes as followeth.
Cafe, how many.
Ninghfapooeksku, 20.
Nuffapooeksku, 30.

Yowghapooeksku, 40.
Parankeftaffapoockfku, 50.
Comatincktaffapooekfku, 60.
Nuffswafhtaffapooekfku, 70.
Kekataughtaffapooekfku, 90.
Necuttoughtyfinough, 100.
Necuttwevnquaough, 1000.
Rawcofowghs, Dayes.
Kefkowghes, Sunnes:
Toppquough. Nights.
Nepawwefhowghs, Moones.
Pawpaxfoughes, Yeares.
Pummahumps, Starres.
Ofies, Heavens.
Okees, Gods.
Quiyoughcofoughs, Pettie **Gods, and** their affinities.
Righcomoughes, Dcaths.
Kekughes, Liues.
Mowchick woyawgh tawgh noeragh kaqueremecher, I am very hungry? what fhall I eate?
Tawnor nehiegh Powhatan, Where dwels Powhatan.
Mache, nehiegh yourowgh, Orapaks. Now he dwels a great way hence at Orapaks.
Vittapitchewayne anpechitchs nehawper Werowacomoco, You lie, he ftaid ever at Werowacomoco.
Kator nehiegh mattagh neer vttapitchewayne, Truely he is there I doe not lie.
Spaughtynere keragh werowance mawmarinough kekatë wawgh peyaquaugh. Run you then to the King Mawmarynough and bid him come hither.
Vtteke, e peya weyack wighwhip, Get you gone, & come againe quickly.
Kekaten Pokahontas patiaquagh niugh tanks manotyens neer mowchick rawrenock audowgh, Bid Pokahontas bring hither two little Baskets, and I will giue her white Beads to make her a Chaine. *FINIS.*

JOHN SMITH'S DICTIONARY OF POWHATAN'S LANGUAGE
In 1612, John Smith published this list of the English equivalents of words used by Powhatan's people, almost the only record of the coastal Algonquian language that exists. Smith probably compiled this list by pointing and listening carefully. Can you find any of Powhatan's words that made their way into common English usage? What do the words in the list suggest about Smith's encounters with Powhatan's people? What interested Smith? What compelled the interest of his informants?
Princeton University Libraries.

The Virginia Company boasted that the settlers bought from the Indians "the pearles of earth [corn] and sell to them the pearles of heaven [Christianity]." In fact, few Indians converted to Christianity, and the English devoted scant effort to encouraging them. Intermarriage between Indian women and English men was also rare, despite the acute shortage of English women in Virginia in the early years. One of the few settlers who troubled to learn the Indians' language was Captain John Smith. From Smith's notes on Indian vocabulary, we know that the settlers quickly adopted the Virginia Algonquian

Why Did English Colonists Consider Themselves Superior to Indians and Africans?

A YOUNG VIRGINIAN
In 1645, the Dutch artist Wenceslaus Hollar drew this portrait of a twenty-three-year-old Indian from Virginia. The young man had evidently been brought to London, where he posed for this likeness. Hollar portrayed his exotic adornment — the animal claw headband, shell earrings, and necklace, facial markings, Mohawk haircut, and bare-chested torso. Yet these distinctly non-European features did not cause Hollar to compromise his humane, dignified depiction of this man whose gaze seems to be fixed steadily and shamelessly upon the observer. If this young Virginian had been back in the Chesapeake rather than in London, he probably would have been engaged in the deadly warfare triggered by Opechancanough's 1644 uprising. One might imagine how this portrait would be different if it were drawn by a Virginia colonist in 1645. British Museum.

Were seeds of the racial prejudice that has been such a powerful force in American history planted in the seventeenth-century Chesapeake? To answer that question, historians have paid close attention to the words the colonists used to describe Indians, Africans, and themselves.

In the mid-1500s, the English adopted the words *Indian* and *Negro* from Spanish, where they had come to mean, respectively, an aboriginal inhabitant of the New World and a black person of African ancestry. Both terms were generic, homogenizing an enormous diversity of tribal affiliations, languages, and cultures. Neither term originated with the people to whom it referred. The New England clergyman Roger Williams, who published a book on Indian languages in 1643, reported, "They have often asked mee, why we call them *Indians*," a poignant question that reveals the European origins of the term.

After *Indians,* the word the settlers used most frequently to describe Native Americans was *savages.* The Indians were savages, in the colonists' eyes, because they lacked the traits of English civilization. As one Englishman put it in 1625, the natives of Virginia were "so bad a people, having little of humanitie but shape, ignorant of Civilitie, of Arts, of Religion; more brutish than the beasts they hunt, more wild and unmanly than that unmanned wild countrey, which they range rather than inhabite; captivated also to Satans tyranny in foolish pieties, mad impieties, wicked idlenesse, busie and bloudy wickednesse." Some English colonists counterbalanced this harsh indictment with admiration for certain features of Indian behavior. They praised Indians' calm dignity and poise, their tender love and care for family members, and their simple, independent way of life in apparent harmony with nature.

Color was not a feature of the Indians' savagery. During the seventeenth century colonists never referred to Indians as "red." Instead, they saw Indians' skin color as tawny or tanned, the "Sun's livery," as one settler wrote. Many settlers held the view that Indians were innately white like the English but in every other way woefully un-English.

In effect, the English colonists defined the Indians as "them," not "us." "Us" and "them" did not

AFRICAN MAN AND WOMAN

Albrecht Dürer, the foremost German artist of the Renaissance, drew these portraits early in the sixteenth century. They are among the first portraits of Africans to be made in Europe. Dürer drew Katarina, who was the servant of a Portuguese merchant Dürer visited in the Netherlands, in the spring of 1521. The portrait of the unidentified man was done several years earlier, but exactly when is unknown; the date 1508 was added after the portrait was completed. In any case, both portraits were completed before the Atlantic slave trade had begun to boom but well after Portuguese merchants had brought thousands of African slaves to Europe. Dürer's meticulously observed portraits betray no trace of racial prejudice. Both Katarina and the man appear to wear European clothing and to be depicted with the same respect and dignity Dürer accorded his European subjects. One might imagine how these portraits would be different if they had been executed by an artist in the southern colonies of North America in the late seventeenth century.

Foto Marburg/Art Resource, NY.

merely connote the differences between colonists and Native Americans. The colonists assumed that those differences expressed a hierarchy of power and status: "We" are superior and should be dominant; "they" are inferior and should be subordinate. The English enforced that distinction ferociously. In the early years of settlement, the colonists allowed a few young men to live for a while in Indian villages to learn native languages and then serve as interpreters. However, settlers who deserted English settlements in preference for Indian ways were punished with a vengeance. (*Continued*)

The colonists identified Africans quite differently. Only a few Africans lived in the Chesapeake early in the seventeenth century. The first recorded arrival of Africans occurred in 1619, when a Dutch man-of-war brought to Virginia "20. and odd Negroes," as John Rolfe wrote. Rolfe's usage illustrates the colonists' most common term for Africans: *Negroes*. But the other word the colonists frequently used to refer to Africans was not *savage* or *heathen*, but *black*. What struck English colonists most forcefully about Africans was not their un-English ways but their un-English skin color.

Black was not a neutral color to the colonists. According to the *Oxford English Dictionary* (which catalogs the changing meaning of words), *black* meant to the English people who settled the Chesapeake "deeply stained with dirt; soiled, dirty, foul . . . having dark or deadly purposes, malignant; pertaining to or involving death, deadly; baneful, disastrous, sinister . . . foul, iniquitous, atrocious, horrible, wicked." Black was the opposite of white, which connoted purity, beauty, and goodness—attributes the colonists identified with themselves. In fact, by the middle of the seventeenth century, the colonists referred to themselves not only as English but also as free, implying that people who were not English were not free. After about 1680, the colonists stated that implication in racial terms by referring to themselves as white. By the end of the seventeenth century, blacks were "them"—un-English, unwhite, and unfree.

A few of the English dissented from such views. Thomas Phillips, a slave ship captain, declared in 1694 that he could not "imagine why they [blacks] should be despis'd for their colour, being what they cannot help, and the effect of the climate it has pleas'd God to appoint them. I can't think there is any intrinsick value in one colour more than another, nor that white is better than black, only we think it so because we are so, and are prone to judge favourably in our own case, as well as the blacks, who in odium of the colour, say, the devil is white, and so paint him."

Virginians did not legally define slavery until 1660, but the sparse surviving evidence demonstrates that they practiced slavery long before that. Although there is no way to be certain, it is likely that the "20. and odd Negroes" who arrived in 1619 were slaves. And the punishments handed out to blacks who broke the law usually took for granted that their servitude could not be extended by several years, as was the case with white servants.

The debased status of slavery strengthened the colonists' prejudice toward blacks, just as racial prejudice buttressed slavery. A Virginia law of 1662, for instance, provided that "if any christian shall committ Fornication with a negro man or woman, hee or shee soe offending" had to pay a double fine. The law also demonstrates that, despite racial prejudice, sexual relations between white and black settlers were prevalent enough to attract the attention of the legislature.

For most of the seventeenth century, possession of a black skin did not automatically and necessarily condemn one to the status of slave in the eyes of whites. Some Africans in the Chesapeake served for limited periods of time like white servants, became free like white servants, and even acquired land, reared families, and participated in local affairs like former white servants. In fact, white colonists' prejudice against blacks represented an extreme form of wealthy colonists' attitudes toward servants and other poor white people. White servants, like blacks, were often considered "the vile and brutish part of mankind" by their masters.

The colonists hardened and exaggerated English attitudes about social hierarchy, about "us" and "them." Part of the reason is that, when colonists left England, they worried that they were separating themselves from "us"—the English—and risking becoming "them"—those uncivilized people found in the colonial wilds. To temper those fears and reduce those risks, colonists defined "us" and "them" in terms that emphasized their own Englishness in both color and civilization, providing a fertile seedbed for the growth of racial prejudice.

words *tomahawk* and *moccasin*. But since Smith's writings contain almost all we know about Virginia Algonquian (the language is now extinct), we remain ignorant of English words that may have entered the Indians' vocabulary. It is safe to speculate that such words were few, given the cultural distance the Indians maintained.

Powhatan's people regarded the English with suspicion, and for good reason. While the settlers often exhibited friendship toward the Indians, they did not hesitate to use their superior weapons— muskets, swords, and cannon—to enforce English notions of proper Indian behavior. More than once the Indians refused to trade corn to the settlers, evidently hoping to starve them out. But each time, the English broke the boycott by pillaging uncooperative villages and confiscating their corn.

The Indians retaliated against English violence, but for fifteen years they did not organize an all-out assault on the European intruders. Several considerations probably caused their hesitation. Although the Indians felt no attraction to Christianity, they were impressed by the power of the settlers' God. One chief put it succinctly when he told John Smith that "he did believe that our God as much exceeded theirs as our guns did their bows and arrows." The settlers not only had guns. They had sailing ships that mysteriously arose from the eastern horizon on a regular basis. They had abundant supplies of glass beads that appeared to be crystals of divine origin. These powerful strangers would make better allies than enemies, Powhatan and his werowances probably concluded. Powhatan dealt with the settlers much as he might have done with an alien tribe, one that he could ally with and use to his own advantage, with proper diplomacy.

As allies, the English not only strengthened Powhatan's dominance over the tribes in the region. They also supplied his people with European goods, usually in exchange for corn. Although the native Virginians possessed copper before the English arrived, they immediately recognized the superiority of the settlers' iron and steel weapons and tools, and they could not get enough of them. An important reason Powhatan's people did not launch a full-scale attack against the settlers for fifteen years after 1607 was that the English possessed axes, swords, pots, and other goods that the Indians wanted.

The trade that supplied Indians with European conveniences provided the English settlers with a prime necessity: food. But why did the settlers prove unable to feed themselves for more than a decade?

First, as the staggering death rate suggests, many settlers were too sick to be productive members of the colony. They evidently succumbed to New World pathogens. Their weakened condition after their long, hazardous sea voyage increased their susceptibility to disease. Although news of the deadly conditions in Virginia filtered back to England, the Virginia Company published pamphlets that denied the worst reports, offered incentives to prospective colonists, and promoted continued settlement. A 1609 tract promised that "the general sort that shall goe to bee planters [settlers], bee they never so poore, so they be honest, and painefull [diligent], the place will make them rich." However, during the first ten years, most settlers died and the company failed to make any profit, despite huge investments. The economic failure increased the company's desire to realize some gain from the enterprise. Neither the company nor most of the settlers fully grasped that Jamestown's first priority had to be survival, not profit.

The trade that supplied Indians with European conveniences provided the English settlers with a prime necessity: food.

A second reason the colonists failed to grow sufficient food had to do with their social origins in England. Very few farmers came to Virginia in the early years. Instead, the largest group of newcomers was gentlemen and their servants, men who— in John Smith's words—"never did know what a day's work was." Except for a small number of carpenters and blacksmiths, Smith wrote, "all the rest were poor gentlemen, tradesmen, and serving men, libertines, and such like, ten times more fit to spoil a commonwealth than . . . begin one or . . . help to maintain one." In fact, the proportion of gentlemen in Virginia in the early years was six times greater than in England, a reflection of the Virginia Company's urgent need for both investors and settlers. Instead of seeing gentlemen as a liability to the colony, the company tried to attract them. In a 1610 pamphlet, the company declared that nobody should believe that Virginia "excludeth Gentlemen, whose breeding never knew what a daies labour meant; for though they cannot digge, use the square, nor practise the axe and chizell, yet [they know] . . . how to employ the force of knowledge, the exercise of counsell, the operation and power of their best breeding and qualities."

In Virginia, however, breeding and quality were worthless for growing corn, catching fish, or even hunting deer. Nevertheless, the colonists clung to English notions of hierarchy and gentle breeding. Consider the procession to Jamestown's church in 1610: Each Sunday, William Strachey observed, the governor marched from his house to church accompanied by all the captains and officers and all the gentlemen, followed by an honor guard of fifty soldiers wearing "his Lordship's Livery, faire red cloakes." The governor sat in the choir of the church, surrounded by the captains and officers, and knelt for prayer on a special velvet cushion resting on a table. After church, the worthies reassembled in the order in which they had come and marched back to the governor's home.

These weekly rituals reassured English gentlemen that they were upholding proper standards of social hierarchy in the wilderness. By those same standards, gentlemen were not supposed to work with their hands and tradesmen were not supposed to work at trades for which they had not been trained. Adherence to these English attitudes about the proper subdivision of leisure and work prevented the settlers from squarely confronting the absolute requirement for the colony's survival: labor. John Smith repeatedly pointed out that in Virginia "there is no country to pillage . . . all you [can] expect from thence must be by labor." For more than a decade, however, most of the settlers who survived clung to ideas about labor that made more sense in labor-rich England than in labor-poor Virginia. In the meantime, they depended on the Indians' corn for food.

The persistence of the Virginia colony, precarious as it was, created difficulties for Powhatan's chiefdom. As the population of the colony slowly grew, some settlers moved to farms a few miles away from Jamestown, encroaching on Indian lands. The steady contact between natives and newcomers spread European viruses among the Indians, who suffered deadly epidemics in 1608 and between 1617 and 1619. While epidemics devastated the Indian population, trade with the settlers distorted Indian culture. Virginia Indians readily incorporated English trade goods into their traditional ways, but the constant English demand for corn required Indians to produce a large surplus. If the Indians produced only enough corn for self-

sufficiency, as they had for centuries, they risked famine when the English commandeered it to feed the settlers. The need to produce a sizable corn surplus for their own survival, as well as for trade, probably introduced tensions within Powhatan's villages, increasing the significance of agriculture and women's work. But from the Indians' viewpoint, the most important fact about the Virginia colony was that it was surviving. Instead of a temporary outpost, it was proving to be a permanent settlement.

Powhatan died in 1618, and his brother Opechancanough replaced him as mamanatowick. In 1622, Opechancanough organized an all-out assault on the English settlers. Striking on March 22, the Indians killed 347 settlers, nearly a third of the English population. But the attack failed to dislodge the Virginia colonists. In the aftermath, the settlers unleashed a murderous campaign of Indian extermination that in a few years pushed Indians beyond the small circumference of white settlement. Before 1622, the settlers knew that the Indians, though dangerous, were necessary to keep the colony alive; after 1622, the settlers concluded that the life of the colony required the death of the Indians, at least in the vicinity of white settlement. After 1622, most colonists considered Indians their perpetual enemies.

From Private Company to Royal Government

The 1622 uprising came close to achieving Opechancanough's goal of pushing the colonists back into the Atlantic—so close that it prompted a royal investigation of affairs in Virginia. The investigators discovered that the appalling mortality among the colonists was caused by disease and mismanagement more than by Indian raids. In 1624, King James revoked the charter of the Virginia Company and made Virginia a royal colony, subject to the direction of the royal government rather than to the company's private investors, an arrangement that lasted until 1776.

The king now appointed the governor of Virginia, but most features of local government established under the Virginia Company remained intact. In 1619, for example, the company had inaugurated the House of Burgesses, an assembly of representatives (called burgesses) elected by the colony's inhabitants. (Historians do not know which settlers were considered inhabitants and were thus qualified to vote for burgesses.) The company authorized the burgesses to propose laws that, when approved by company officials in London, would become enforceable. Under the new royal government, proposed laws had to be approved by the king's bureaucrats in England rather than by the company. Otherwise, however, the House of Burgesses continued as before, acquiring distinction as the oldest representative legislative assembly in the British colonies. In addition, under the royal government in Virginia, all free adult men could vote for burgesses, giving the House of Burgesses a far broader and more representative constituency than the English House of Commons.

In 1624, King James revoked the charter of the Virginia Company and made Virginia a royal colony, subject to the direction of the royal government rather than to the company's private investors, an arrangement that lasted until 1776.

The demise of the Virginia Company marked the end of the first phase of colonization of the Chesapeake. From the 105 adventurers who had landed in 1607 and the hundreds more who followed, the population had grown to about 1,200 by 1624. The Indians who had first been a necessary source of support were now considered deadly enemies. Despite its promises, the Virginia Company never paid a dividend to its investors and delivered most settlers to their graves. But by 1624 it was clear that the English were in Virginia to stay. Mortality rates among newcomers continued at levels higher than those in the worst epidemics in London, but new settlers still arrived. Their arrival and King James's willingness to take over the struggling colony signaled a fundamental change under way in Virginia. After years of fruitless experimentation, it was becoming clear that English settlers could make a fortune in Virginia by growing tobacco.

TOBACCO ADVERTISEMENT
This ad for "Kositzky's Best Virginia" tobacco illustrates a colonial planter and tobacco merchant examining the quality of a sample of leaves from an open cask waiting to be shipped to London, while an onlooker samples the leaves more thoroughly, by smoking. To smooth the transaction, an African — presumably a slave — offers a glass of wine. One way the English artist emphasized the differences between the African and the other men was giving the African a skirt of leaves; it is doubtful that any slaves in the Chesapeake wore such a skirt. How else did the artist highlight differences? Kositzky must have traded in other goods; the insignia at the top features scythes used for cutting grain but useless in harvesting tobacco, perhaps a hint of ignorance common in London about how tobacco was produced in the Chesapeake.
Arents Collection, New York Public Library.

A Tobacco Society

Tobacco grew wild in the New World, and Native Americans used it for thousands of years before Europeans arrived. *Tobacco*, in fact, was a Caribbean Indian word that referred not to what we know as the tobacco plant, but to a leaf of the plant rolled into a cigarlike shape. Indians inserted the lit cigar into a nostril and inhaled, a practice Columbus observed in Cuba on his first journey of discovery. Many sixteenth-century European explorers commented on the Indians' odd habit of "drinking smoke."

By the late sixteenth century, smoking was popular enough among Europeans that the word *tobacco* first entered the English language (via Spanish) and pipes began to be commonplace in England. Before the seventeenth century, however, tobacco imported from the Spanish colonies remained an expensive luxury in the Old World.

Tobacco did not figure in the plans of the Virginia Company. In 1609, a company pamphlet listed more than twenty crops that might profitably be cultivated in Virginia, but tobacco was not among them. "As for tobacco," John Smith wrote later, "we never then dreamt of it." John Rolfe, Pocahontas's husband-to-be, began to plant West Indian tobacco seeds in 1612. His experiments demonstrated that the plant could be grown successfully in Virginia. The first commercial shipment of tobacco to England left the colony in 1617. When it sold for a handsome price, the same Virginia colonists who had difficulty growing enough corn to feed themselves quickly tried to learn how to grow as much tobacco as possible. In a sense, that first commercial cargo was a pivot on which Virginia turned from a colony of rather aimless adventurers into a society of dedicated tobacco planters.

> *The first commercial shipment of tobacco to England in 1617 was a pivot on which Virginia turned from a colony of rather aimless adventurers into a society of dedicated tobacco planters.*

Dedicated they were. In 1620, with fewer than a thousand colonists, Virginia shipped 60,000 pounds of tobacco to England. By 1630, the population had grown to 2,500 while tobacco exports mushroomed to 350,000 pounds. More than a million pounds entered English markets in 1640, and even that was only the beginning. By 1700, tobacco exports from the Chesapeake region (encompassing Virginia and Maryland) topped 35 million pounds. By then, over 98,000 colonists lived in the region, and they had learned a thing or two about growing tobacco. Per capita tobacco exports were about 70 pounds in 1620; by 1700, they exceeded 350 pounds. This fivefold growth in productivity demonstrates that Chesapeake colonists mastered the demands of growing tobacco. To a large degree, the "Stincking Weede" (a seventeenth-century Marylander's term for tobacco) also mastered the Chesapeake colonists. The routines of tobacco agriculture structured daily life on Chesapeake farms. Tobacco planters' endless need for labor attracted droves of indentured servants from England to work in tobacco fields and settle the Chesapeake.

LEARNING TO INHALE
It took a while for Europeans to master the many refinements of smoking. This Dutch ceramic tile made early in the seventeenth century shows a smoker accomplishing the remarkable feat (at that time) of blowing smoke through his nose. Europeans rhapsodized about the many virtues of smoking. A seventeenth-century Dutch print of two men relaxing with their pipes was captioned "Vita est Fumus" — Life is Smoke.
Niemeyer Tabaksmuseum.

Tobacco Agriculture

Tobacco was a demanding crop. It required close attention and a great deal of hand labor year-round. Early each spring, colonists sowed the tiny seeds in specially prepared beds for sprouting. In June, when a good rain moistened the fields, workers hurried to transplant the sprouts to mounds of earth spaced about three feet apart. Then they had to hoe the fields to eliminate weeds and to protect the roots of the plants, a routine that continued throughout the summer. As the plants grew, they had to be tended carefully to produce marketable leaves. When the leaves began to yellow in the early fall, the stalks were cut and the plants left in the fields to wither.

Colonists then gathered the plants and strung them up in sheltered areas to dry and cure, usually for the winter. During moist weather the following spring, when the dried leaves became pliable, the workers stripped the leaves from the stalks and tightly packed them into a hogshead (a large barrel) for shipment to market. By the time one year's crop was being packed, the next year's crop was already in the ground.

Primitive tools and methods made this intensive cycle of labor even more taxing. Like the Indians, the colonists "cleared" fields not by chopping down trees but by stripping a ring of bark from each tree (known as girdling), thereby killing it. Dead trees and stumps usually studded a cleared field, making the use of plows and draft animals impractical. Instead, colonists tilled the ground with heavy hoes. To plant, a visitor noted, they "just make holes [with a stick] into which they drop the seeds," much as the Indians did. In addition to planting tobacco, the colonists grew corn and other food crops—after all, tobacco is miserable food. Work on food crops had to be done in the midst of the tobacco crop cycle, leaving little time for idleness. But in spare moments colonists enjoyed the fruits of their labor. As a traveler observed, "Everyone smokes while working or idling . . . men, women, girls, and boys from the age of seven years."

English settlers were willing to work hard because they could expect to do much better in the Chesapeake than in England. One colonist declared that "the dirt of this Province affords as great a profit to the general Inhabitant, as the Gold of Peru doth to . . . the Spaniard." Although that observation was exaggerated, it was true that a hired man would have to work two or three years in England to earn as much as he could in Chesapeake tobacco fields in just one year. Better still, in Virginia even common laborers could hope to obtain land. Land was so abundant that, by English standards, it was extremely cheap. In the mid-seventeenth century Chesapeake, a colonist could buy one hundred acres of land for less than a laborer's annual wages—an utter impossibility in England. New settlers who paid their own transportation to the Chesapeake received free land. Each such settler received a grant of fifty acres of free land (a headright), a policy begun by the Virginia Company and continued by the royal government to encourage settlement.

A Servant Labor System

Headrights, cheap land, and high wages gave poor English folk powerful incentives to immigrate to the New World. Despite the incentives, many potential immigrants could not scrape together the fare to sail across the Atlantic. Their poverty and the colonists' crying need for labor formed the basic context for the creation of a servant labor system.

Today, people tend to think of the colonial South as a slave society. The seventeenth-century Chesapeake, however, was fundamentally a servant society. Twenty Africans arrived in Virginia in 1619 and more came in subsequent years. But until the last quarter of the seventeenth century, only a small number of slaves labored in Chesapeake tobacco fields. (Large numbers of slaves came later, as chapter 5 explains.) About 80 percent of the immigrants to the Chesapeake during the seventeenth century were indentured servants. In large measure, colonists in the Chesapeake were servants, former servants, and descendants of servants. Along with tobacco, the servant labor system profoundly influenced nearly every feature of Chesapeake society.

The seventeenth-century Chesapeake was fundamentally a servant society, not a slave society. In large measure, colonists in the Chesapeake were servants, former servants, and descendants of servants.

To buy passage aboard a ship bound for the Chesapeake, an English immigrant had to come up with about £5, roughly a year's wages for an English servant or laborer. Saving a year's wages then was no easier than it is now. Many laborers, servants, and artisans did not even have steady work throughout the year. Opportunities for work were shrinking in seventeenth-century England. Many country gentlemen fenced fields they had formerly planted with crops and began to pasture sheep in the enclosures. Keeping sheep required only a few of the laborers who had previously been hired to cultivate crops; the other farmhands had to find work elsewhere, if they could. Even if they found other jobs, the purchasing power of their wages slowly deteriorated as England's population grew faster than its food supply, causing prices to rise.

A SERVANT'S INDENTURE
This document indentured the servant Richard Lowther to a Virginia master in 1627. As a written contract, an indenture specified the agreement between servant and master and could be used in court to help settle disputes. No such contract detailed the relationship between master and slaves.
Virginia Historical Society.

Unemployed servants, laborers, and tradesmen wandered from village to village looking for work. Many of them drifted to seaports like Bristol, Liverpool, and especially London. As they searched for jobs in the cities, they heard of the opportunities in the colonies, where jobs were abundant and workers were scarce.

Lacking the money to get across the Atlantic, poor immigrants entered an agreement with a local shopkeeper, mariner, or merchant. The terms of the agreement were spelled out in a contract called an indenture. The indenture specified that the local merchant would pay for the immigrant's transportation to the Chesapeake. In return, the immigrant agreed to work for a period—usually four to seven years—without pay. During this period of indentured servitude, the immigrant received food and shelter from the employer in the colonies. When the indenture expired, the employer was required to give the former

servant "freedom dues," usually three barrels of corn and a suit of clothes.

In effect, indentures allowed poor immigrants to trade their most valuable asset—their ability to work—for a trip to the New World. The English shopkeepers and merchants who signed them to indentures and paid their fare to the colonies owned the rights to their labor. When the indentured immigrants arrived in the Chesapeake, ship captains arranged to sell those rights to tobacco planters who needed some hands in the fields or rough carpenters to bang together a shed. Most planters were willing to pay about twice the cost of transportation for the right to four to seven years of an immigrant's labor. Normally, a planter literally paid with tobacco, the legal tender of the Chesapeake region. Most of the planter's payment was returned as a handsome profit to the English merchant who had indentured the immigrant and paid his or her fare.

Planters were eager to purchase as many indentured servants as they could afford. As one Virginia planter noted, "our principall wealth . . . consisteth in servants." More servants meant more hands to grow more tobacco. More servants also meant more land. For every servant purchased, a planter received from the colonial government a headright of another fifty acres of land. Even without the land, a servant was a good investment for a planter. A new servant cost about one thousand pounds of tobacco. The first year the servant worked for a planter, he or she could be expected to grow between one and two thousand pounds of tobacco plus enough corn to feed himself or herself. The servant's labor for the subsequent years of the indenture gave the planter a substantial return on his investment.

At least it did if all went well. Bad weather, crop disease, or insect pests could ruin a harvest. But the biggest risk to both the planter and the servant was that the servant would get sick and die before serving out the term of the indenture. Mortality remained at very high levels in the Chesapeake through the middle decades of the seventeenth century. About half of all children born in the Chesapeake died before they reached adulthood. A person who survived to age twenty could expect to live only twenty-five more years. Life expectancy had improved so little by 1687 that a thirty-six-year-old planter remarked, "Now I look upon myself to be in my declining age."

As immigrants to the Chesapeake, servants had a slimmer chance of surviving—the prerequisite for them to receive a payoff from their servitude. Among one group of 275 servant men who arrived in Maryland before midcentury, 40 percent died before their servitude ended. Of the survivors, another 40 percent died or moved away within ten years of obtaining their freedom. Less than a third of the original group remained in the colony for ten years after their indentures expired. Eight out of ten of these men managed to acquire small farms, and a few possessed servants of their own. For this minority, the bargain struck by signing an indenture proved hard, but real. For the vast majority of servants, the bargain was just hard.

The mayor of Bristol, England, observed that of the servants leaving for the colonies, "some are husbands that have forsaken their wives, others wives who have abandoned their husbands; some are children and apprentices run away from their parents and masters; oftentimes unwary and credulous persons have been tempted on board [ships] by men-stealers, and many [servants] . . . have been pursued by hue-and-cry for robberies, burglaries, or breaking prison." The mayor was correct that some servants came from each of these groups. For the most part, however, servants were simply poor young English men seeking work.

More than two-thirds of the servants were between the ages of fifteen and twenty-five when they came to the Chesapeake. Many of them were orphans. Typical in his desperate situation was sixteen-year-old Francis Haires, who indentured himself for seven years because "his father and mother and All friends [are] dead and he [is] a miserable wandering boy." Like Francis, most indentured servants had no special training or skills, although the majority had some experience with agricultural work. "Hunger and fear of prisons bring to us," a Virginia planter complained in 1662, "onely such servants as have been brought up to no Art or Trade." Planters were eager for skilled carpenters, blacksmiths, and coopers (barrel makers). However, only about one indentured servant in five had some training at a skilled trade, and many had apprenticed in trades with little usefulness in the Chesapeake, like button mold making or hemp dressing. With a valued skill, a servant could obtain a shorter indenture; had Francis been an experienced carpenter, he might well have served four instead of seven years. Nonetheless, few skilled craftsmen risked coming to the colonies unless they were down on their luck and, like Francis, had few prospects at home.

Women were almost as rare as skilled craftsmen in the Chesapeake and more ardently desired. In the early days of the tobacco boom, the Virginia Company tried to reduce the scarcity of women by shipping unattached young women to the colony as prospective wives for male settlers willing to pay "120 weight [pounds] of the best leaf tobacco for each of them." The company reasoned that, as one official wrote in 1622, "the plantation can never flourish till families be planted, and the respect of wives and children fix the people on the soil." The company's efforts as a marriage broker proved no more successful than its other ventures. Men continued to outnumber women by a wide margin until late in the seventeenth century.

The servant labor system perpetuated the gender imbalance. Although female servants cost about the same as males and generally served for the same length of time, only about one indentured servant in four was a woman. Planters preferred male servants for field work, although many women also hoed tobacco fields. Most women servants, however, did household chores such as cooking, washing, cleaning, gardening, and milking.

Servant life was harsh by the standards of seventeenth-century England and even by the rougher, frontier standards of the Chesapeake. In England, laborers sold their services to their masters at annual hiring fairs; in the Chesapeake, servants were bought and sold more or less like livestock. Unlike their English counterparts, Chesapeake servants had virtually no control over who purchased their labor—and thus them—for the period of the indenture. A servant might be bought and sold several times before the indenture expired. One servant wrote from Virginia in 1623 that his master "hath sold me for £150 sterling like a damnd slave." The colonial practice of treating servants as property alarmed some Englishmen. In 1625, a ship captain refused to transport servants to Virginia because "servants were sold heere upp and downe like horses, and therefore he held it not lawfull to carie any." The colonists' need for labor and the profits to be made in supplying it quickly muffled such qualms. But in England rumors persisted that, as one contemporary wrote, Chesapeake masters "abuse their servantes there with intollerable oppression and hard usage."

Some former servants argued against the scuttlebutt that indentured servitude bordered on slavery. George Alsop, who served as an indentured servant in Maryland, wrote that "the four years I served there were not to me so slavish, as a two years Servitude of a Handicraft Apprenticeship was here in London." According to Alsop, servants in the colonies had "the least cause to complain, either for strictness of Servitude, want of Provisions, or need of Apparel." Women servants, he said, "are no sooner on shoar, but they are courted into a Copulative Matrimony." Overall, Alsop argued, Chesapeake servants "live well in the time of their Service, and by their restrainment in that time, they are made capable of living much better when they come to be free."

Most servants who came to the Chesapeake probably hoped their experience would match Alsop's claims. If so, most learned otherwise. James Revel, an eighteen-year-old thief who was punished by being transported to Virginia, where he was indentured to a tobacco planter, described experiences common to most servants. In verse, Revel chronicled what happened when he arrived at his new master's plantation:

My Europian clothes were took from me,
Which never after I again could see.
    A canvas shirt and trowsers then they gave,
With a hop-sack frock in which I was to slave:
No shoes nor stockings had I for to wear,
Nor hat, nor cap, both head and feet were bare.
    Thus dress'd into the Field I next must go,
Amongst tobacco plants all day to hoe,
At day break in the morn our work began,
And so held to the setting of the Sun.
        My fellow slaves were just five Transports
            more,
With eighteen Negroes, which is twenty four:
Besides four transport women in the house,
To wait upon his daughter and his Spouse,
    We and the Negroes both alike did fare,
Of work and food we had an equal share. . . .
Six days we slave for our master's good,
The seventh day is to produce our food.
        Sometimes when that a hard days work
            we've done,
Away unto the mill we must be gone;
Til twelve or one o'clock a grinding corn,
And must be up by daylight in the morn. . . .
    And if we offer for to run away,
For every hour [away] we must serve a day;
For every day a Week, They're so severe,
For every week a month, for every month a year.
But if they murder, rob, or steal when there,
Then straightway hang'd, the Laws are so severe;
For by the Rigour of that very law
They're much kept under and to stand in awe.

Severe laws were designed to keep servants in their place in more ways than one. Punishments for petty crimes like running away or stealing a pig stretched servitude far beyond the terms of indenture. Servant Christopher Adams, for example, had to serve three extra years for running away for six months; Richard Higby received six extra years of servitude for killing three hogs. Just after midcentury, the Virginia legislature added at least three years to the servitude of most servants by requiring them to serve until they were twenty-four years old.

Women servants were subject to special restrictions and risks. They were prohibited from marrying until their servitude had expired. A servant woman, the law assumed, could not serve two masters at the same time: one who owned her indentured labor and another who was her husband.

TOBACCO PLANTATION

This print illustrates the tobacco harvest on a seventeenth-century plantation. Workers cut the mature plants and put the leaves in piles to wilt (left foreground and center background). After the leaves had dried somewhat, they were suspended from poles in a drying barn (right foreground), where they were seasoned before being packed in casks for shipping (see page 87). Sometimes they were also dried in the fields (center background). The print suggests the labor demands of tobacco by showing twenty-two individuals, all but two of them actively at work with tobacco. The one woman depicted (hand in hand with a man in the left foreground) may be on her way to work in the harvest, but it appears more likely that she and the man are overseeing the labor of their servants or employees.

From "About Tobacco" Lehman Brothers.

However, the overwhelming predominance of men in the Chesapeake population inevitably pressured women to engage in sexual relations. The pressure was strong enough that about a third of immigrant women were pregnant when they got married. Pregnancy and childbirth sapped a woman's strength, and a new child diverted her attention, reducing her usefulness to her master. Thus for a servant woman, pregnancy meant punishment: As a rule, if a woman servant gave birth to a child, she had to serve two extra years and pay a fine. When servant Ann Parke had a baby, a local court simply doubled her remaining period of servitude.

Such punishments reflected four fundamental realities of the servant labor system. First, masters'

hunger for labor led them to demand as much work from their servants as possible, and they did not hesitate to devise legal ways to extend the period of servitude. Second, servants did not share masters' interest in maximum labor. Instead, servants hoped to survive their period of servitude and then use their freedom to start a family and obtain land. This conflict of interest made servants somewhat reluctant, grudging laborers. They worked as hard as they had to rather than—as their masters wanted—as hard as they could. Third, servants did not always comply meekly with their masters' demands for obedience. They saw themselves as free people in a temporary status of servitude, and they frequently resisted their masters' orders. Fourth, both servants and masters put up with this contentious arrangement because the alternatives were less desirable. Masters could not hire free men and women because few were willing to work for wages. Land was so readily available that those who were free preferred to work on their own land, for themselves. Furthermore, most masters could not depend on much labor from family members, especially sons. The skewed sex ratio among servants and in the general population meant that families were few, were started late, and thus had few children. And, until the 1680s and 1690s, slaves were expensive and hard to come by. Before then, masters who wanted to expand their labor force and grow more tobacco had few alternatives to buying indentured servants.

The Evolution of Chesapeake Society

The colonists' incessant desire to grow more tobacco propelled the evolution of Chesapeake society. The requirements of tobacco agriculture shaped patterns of settlement, making the landscape of the English colonies in the Chesapeake quite different from that of rural England. English colonists professed the Protestant and Catholic faiths, but they governed their daily lives less by the dictates of religious doctrine than by the demands of tobacco cultivation.

English colonists professed the Protestant and Catholic faiths, but they governed their daily lives less by the dictates of religious doctrine than by the demands of tobacco cultivation.

Success in the tobacco economy—whether through hard work, shrewd judgments, political favoritism, or sheer good luck—elevated some colonists far above others in wealth and status and in the capacity to grow still more tobacco. The success of some colonists was built on the indentured servitude of others, sharpening inequality in Chesapeake society by the mid-seventeenth century. Social and political polarization culminated in 1676 when Bacon's Rebellion convulsed the Chesapeake. The rebellion ultimately prompted reforms that stabilized relations between elite planters and their lesser neighbors and paved the way for a social hi-

erarchy based less overtly on land and wealth than on race. Amidst this social and political evolution, one thing did not change: the dedication of Chesapeake colonists to growing tobacco.

Life, Faith, and Labor

Villages and small towns dotted the rural landscape of seventeenth-century England, but colonists did not reproduce that English pattern in the Chesapeake. Colonial leaders tried to promote the development of towns, but they failed, with the exception of the town surrounding the capital at Jamestown. The Chesapeake landscape was not made up of cultivated fields punctuated here and there by small villages. Instead, acres of wilderness were interrupted here and there by tobacco farms. This landscape of widely scattered farms arose from the settlers' determination to profit from tobacco, even at the expense of patterns of community life they had been accustomed to in England.

Tobacco was such a labor-intensive crop that one field worker could tend only about two acres of the plants in a year (an acre is slightly smaller than a football field). A family farmer needed to devote a few more acres to food crops, but a total of five or ten acres under cultivation sufficed to make a working tobacco farm. However, a successful farmer needed a great deal more land because tobacco quickly exhausted the fertility of the soil. Freshly cleared land produced good tobacco harvests for only three or four years. To maintain yields, farmers let depleted fields lie fallow (unplanted) and cleared new land. Although this practice appeared wasteful from the perspective of land-scarce English agriculture, land was so abundant in the Chesapeake that farmers found it easier to plant new fields than to fertilize old ones. Thus, a farmer who ran a small, family operation needed 150 to 200 acres of land. A planter who employed eight or ten indentured servants required 1,000 acres or more. Since each farmer would cultivate only 5 or 10 percent of his land at any one time, a "settled" area comprised pockets of cultivated land surrounded by virgin forest.

Arrangements for marketing tobacco also contributed to the dispersion of settlements. Ideally, tobacco planters sought land that fronted a navigable river. Oceangoing ships could then dock at the planter's doorstep, minimizing the work of transporting and loading the heavy hogsheads of tobacco leaves. To obtain these prized riverfront locations, new settlers pushed inland along watercourses, venturing as far as they dared into Indian territory. As the population grew, these riverside settlements reached the limits of navigable water. A settled region resembled a lacework of farms stitched around waterways.

On individual farmsteads, farmers built their houses from beams and planks hewn from felled timber. Although serviceable, the houses were by no means grand, imposing, or even particularly sturdy. A typical seventeenth-century tobacco farmer lived with his family and servants (if he had them) in a one- or two-room box of about four hundred square feet. A wattle and daub chimney stood at one end of the house. A few windows—without glass—let in light and air when the shutters that normally covered them were thrown open. Dried mud chinked the gaps between wall planks. Bare earth served as the floor. Of the thousands of such structures built in the seventeenth-century Chesapeake, none has survived. Such houses accurately reflected the colonists' desire for plain shelter while they tried to make a living growing tobacco.

Most Chesapeake colonists were nominally Protestants. For most of the seventeenth century, attendance at Sunday services and conformity to the doctrines of the Church of England were required of all English men and women. As much as possible, Chesapeake settlers adhered to these practices in the American wilderness. They built churches, required weekly attendance, and, when they could find a minister, heard sermons. However, clergymen were difficult to attract to the Chesapeake. Many of those who came were no more pious, righteous, or godly than their parishioners. Certainly some colonists took their religion seriously. Church courts punished fornicators, censured blasphemers, and served notice on those who spent Sundays "goeing a fishing." But on the whole, religion did not awaken the zeal of Chesapeake settlers, certainly not as it did their counterparts who settled New England in these same years (see chapter 4). Virginians went to church and enjoyed the socializing before and afterward. But what quickened the pulse of most Chesapeake folk was a close-run horse race, a bloody cock fight, a high-stakes dice game, or—most of all—an exceptionally fine tobacco crop. The religion of the Chesapeake colonists was Anglican, but their faith lay in the turbulent, grasping, competitive, high-stakes gamble of survival as tobacco planters.

The history of the Catholic colony of Maryland provides a good illustration of that faith. In 1632, King Charles I (who had succeeded James I in 1625)

INSIDE A POOR PLANTER'S HOUSE
The houses of seventeenth-century Chesapeake settlers were typically "earth-fast" — that is, the structural timbers that framed the house were simply placed in holes in the ground and the floor was packed dirt. No seventeeth-century house was substantial enough to survive today. This photo shows a carefully documented historical reconstruction of the interior of a poor planter's house at St. Mary's City, Maryland. The wall of this one-room dwelling with a loft features a window with a shutter, but no glass; when the shutter was closed, the only source of light would be a candle or a fire. Note the rustic, unfinished bench, table, and walls. These meager furnishings were usually accompanied by a storage chest and some bedding, but not a bed. If and when the planters became more prosperous, they often made a bed their first acquisition, suggesting that the lack of a good night's sleep was one of their major discomforts.
Paul Leibe, Historic St. Mary's City.

granted his Catholic friend Lord Baltimore about six and a half million acres in the Chesapeake. In return, the king specified that Lord Baltimore pay him a rent of "two Indian arrowheads" each year during Easter week. Lord Baltimore intended to use his American domain to create a refuge for Catholics,

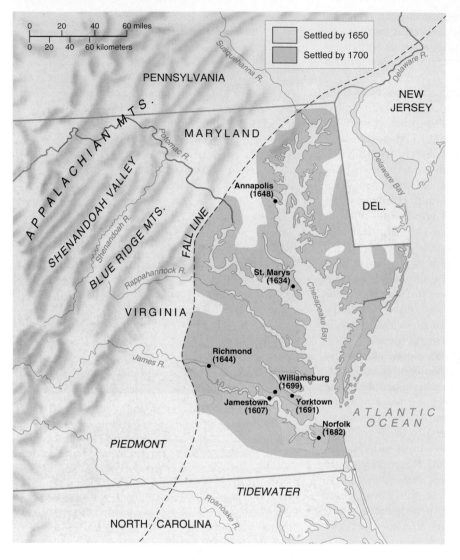

MAP 3.1

The Chesapeake Colonies in the Seventeenth Century

The intimate association of land and water in the settlement of the Chesapeake in the seventeenth century is illustrated by this map. Why was access to navigable water so important?

who suffered severe discrimination in England. He fitted out two ships, the *Ark* and the *Dove,* gathered about 150 settlers, and sent them to the new colony, where they arrived on March 25, 1634. However, the population of Maryland grew very slowly for the next twenty years, and most settlers were Protestants rather than Catholics. While England seethed with the religious turmoil of the Puritan Revolution (discussed in chapter 4), religious tension spilled across the Atlantic, creating conflict between Maryland's few Catholics—most of them wealthy and prominent—and the Protestant majority, few of whom were either wealthy or prominent. During the 1660s, however, Maryland at last began to attract settlers as readily as Virginia, most of them

Protestants. Like the Virginians, they came to grow tobacco. Although Catholics and the Catholic faith continued to exert influence in Maryland, the colony's society, economy, politics, and culture were virtually indistinguishable from Virginia's. Both colonies shared a common devotion to tobacco, the true faith of the Chesapeake.

Tobacco was a good poor man's crop. With land, know-how, and the labor of their own hands, colonists could produce a salable commodity. Special tools or expensive equipment were unnecessary. In the early years of the tobacco boom, when the weed commanded high prices in English markets, colonists hoped to get rich. Most tobacco plantations, however, were small operations run by one planter and two or three servants. A few elite planters had larger estates and commanded ten or more servants. But mortality in the Chesapeake was so high for the first thirty or forty years that few men lived long enough to accumulate a fortune sufficient to set them much apart from their neighbors. One historian has aptly termed this the era of the yeoman planter (that is, a farmer who owned a small plot of land sufficient to support a family and tilled largely by family members and perhaps a few servants).

Until midcentury, the principal division in Chesapeake society was less between rich and poor planters than between free farmers and unfree servants.

Until midcentury, the principal division in Chesapeake society was less between rich and poor planters than between free farmers and unfree servants. While these two groups contrasted sharply in their legal and economic status, their daily lives had many similarities: Most of them worked at the same tasks in the same fields, ate the same food, often at the same table, and slept in the same house. Although servants were required to be subordinate, they nonetheless looked forward to the time when their indentures would expire and they would cross the threshold of freedom. Once free, they usually had to work several more years as hired hands or tenant farmers to earn enough to buy land. Nonetheless, they readily assimilated into free society. For example, among 155 freed servants in Charles County, Maryland, in the first half of the seventeenth century, two-thirds became landowners, a third obtained servants, and almost all married, had families, and participated in the affairs of local government. On the whole, a rough, frontier equality characterized free families in the Chesapeake until about 1650.

Three major developments splintered that equality during the third quarter of the seventeenth century. First, as tobacco production increased, prices declined. In the Old World, lower prices meant that more people could afford to smoke Chesapeake tobacco. In the colonies, cheap tobacco reduced planters' profits. It became more difficult —though still not impossible—for freed servants to save enough to become landowners. While the door

to freedom remained open for servants, landownership became more difficult to attain. Second, because the mortality rate dropped, more and more servants survived their indentures and joined the swelling ranks of freemen seeking land. However, the lower prices of tobacco limited their chances of realizing their ambitions of landownership. In Northampton County, Virginia, for instance, only about a quarter of the freemen who paid taxes between 1664 and 1677 ever obtained land there. Landless freemen became more numerous and more discontent. Third, declining mortality also encouraged the formation of a planter elite. By living longer, the most successful planters compounded their success. They not only earned more from their larger tobacco crops; they also acquired more land and more servants. The wealthiest planters also began to serve as merchants, marketing crops for their less successful neighbors, importing English

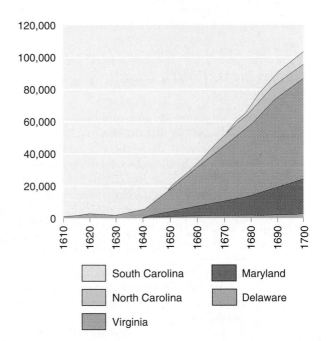

F I G U R E 3.1

Population of the Southern Colonies in the Seventeenth Century

About 1630, more than twenty years after the founding of Jamestown, the population of the southern colonies began to grow rapidly and steadily. The Chesapeake accounted for all but a tiny fraction of the population of the seventeenth-century southern colonies; for the most part, the inhabited regions of both North Carolina and Delaware were outgrowths of the Chesapeake's tobacco economy.

goods for sale, and above all giving credit to hard-pressed customers. In planter-merchant ledgers, the profits of trade added to the proceeds from tobacco.

By the 1670s, the social structure of the Chesapeake became polarized. Landowners—the planter elite and the more numerous yeoman planters—clustered around one pole. Landless colonists, mainly freed servants, gathered at the other extreme. Each group eyed the other with suspicion and mistrust. Looking down, planters saw a dangerous rabble. Looking up, landless freemen saw greedy exploiters. When a Dutch invasion threatened Virginia in 1673, the social tensions within the colony made Governor William Berkeley apprehensive about arming troops for defense. Of the men he could muster, Berkeley wrote, "at least one third are Single freemen (whose Labor will hardly maintaine them) or men much in debt, both [of] which wee may reasonably expect upon any Small advantage the Enemy may gaine upon us, wold revolt to them in hopes of bettering their Condicion by Shareing the Plunder of the Country with them."

Government, Politics, and Polarization

In general, government and politics amplified rather than reduced the distinctions in Chesapeake society. The most vital distinction separated servants and masters, and the colonial government enforced it with an iron fist. In 1624, when Richard Barnes made "base and detracting" remarks about the governor of Virginia, the governor's council ordered that Barnes "be disarmed, and have his armes broken and his tongue bored through with a awl [and] . . . pass through a guard of 40 men and . . . be butted by every one of them" in addition to being banished and prohibited from ever enjoying "the priviledge of freedome of the countrey." Quick to prosecute critics, the council hesitated to censure masters who brutalized their servants. When servants Elizabeth Abbott and Elias Hinton died after beatings inflicted by their masters John and Alice Proctor, the council did not punish the Proctors, despite the testimony of witnesses that Hinton had been beaten with a rake and that Abbott had received five hundred lashes that left "her body full of sores and holes very dangerously raunckled and putrified both above her waist and upon her hips and thighes." Members of the council believed that the government should make sure that servants obeyed their masters, no matter what. No wonder

poor men like William Tyler complained that "nether the Governor nor Counsell could or would doe any poore men right, but that they would shew favor to great men and wronge the poore."

The poor had plenty of ammunition for such views. Men from the planter elite monopolized the seats in both the governor's council and the House of Burgesses. After 1640, no former servant ever served in either body. Former servants participated in county government as jurors and in other minor offices. Members of the governor's council, however, were typically the wealthiest and most prominent planters. They were appointed by the king, usually on the recommendation of the governor, to advise the governor about colonial policies. Burgesses were chosen by popular election. Until 1670, all freemen could vote, and they routinely elected prosperous planters to the legislature. Most Chesapeake colonists, like most Europeans, assumed that the responsibilities of government were best borne by men of wealth and status.

In the 1660s and 1670s, colonial officials began to lose confidence that that assumption provided sufficient security from the growing discontent of the poor. Beginning in 1661, for example, Governor Berkeley did not call an election for the House of Burgesses for fifteen years. In 1670, the House of Burgesses limited voting rights to landowners and householders. Poor men with neither land nor homes were prohibited from voting since, the burgesses explained, "haveing little interest in the country [they] doe oftener make tumults at the election to the disturbance of his majesties peace, then by their discretions in their votes provide for the conservasion thereof."

The governor and other colonial officials did not simply administer government; they exploited their offices to make a profit. Tax agents, for example, received a slice of the revenues they collected. The secretary of the colony received fees for each document filed in official records: A land patent brought him eighty pounds of tobacco; a marriage license, forty pounds. Few governors were as brazen in their take-the-money-and-run attitude as Lord Thomas Culpepper. During his seven years as governor of Virginia, he lived in England for all but nine months, pocketed the governor's £2,000 annual salary, and hired a substitute to do the dirty work of governing the colony. Other governors spent more time in the colony, but, like Culpepper, they expected to make their office pay.

In 1660, the king himself began to collect substantial revenue from the Chesapeake. The Navigation Act passed that year required all tobacco and other colonial products (referred to in the act as "enumerated articles") to be sent only to English ports. The act supplemented laws of 1650 and 1651 that specified that colonial goods had to be transported in English ships with predominantly English crews. These regulations were designed to funnel the colonial import trade exclusively into the hands of English merchants, shippers, and seamen. A 1663 law extended that design to exports by stipulating that all goods sent to the colonies must pass through English ports and be carried in English ships by English sailors. Together, these regulations reflected the English government's assumptions about the colonies, assumptions subsequently termed "mercantilist": namely, that the colonies should benefit the mother country. What was good for England as a nation and for English people as individuals should determine policies toward the colonies.

These mercantilist assumptions underlay the import duty on tobacco inaugurated by the 1660 Navigation Act. The law assessed a duty of two pence on every pound of colonial tobacco imported into England. Two pence per pound was about the price a Chesapeake tobacco farmer received at the time; later, the price dropped lower (although of course the duty raised the price of the weed for consumers in England and on the continent). Regardless of the price planters received, the king collected his two-pence duty on imports. In fact, after 1660 a tobacco planter in Virginia earned at least as much for the king every year as he did for himself. The duty gave the king a major financial interest in the size of the tobacco crop. In the 1660s, tobacco revenues amounted to about one-quarter of all English customs duties and 5 percent of total government income, and they continued to grow.

Hierarchy permeated all levels of government and politics, from the relation between king and colonies to that between master and servant. Inequality was the organizing principle of these relationships. At every level, rulers expected to rule and to be obeyed; subjects expected to be ruled and to be punished for disobeying. To our ears, these expectations sound like a recipe for tyranny. In the seventeenth century, however, they were counterbalanced by other expectations that moderated the severity of hierarchical rule. Both rulers and subjects expected government to be administered for the good of the society as a whole. Rulers were supposed to keep in mind what was best for their subjects, and vice versa. Opinions differed—among rulers, between rulers and subjects, and among sub-

jects—about what actually was the best policy. A wise ruler steered a course that took account of conflicting opinions and that minimized the use of raw military force to crush dissenters. However, if rulers violated these precepts, the widely shared assumption that government should work for the benefit of all also provided the justification for subjects to rebel. In general, rebellions did not contest the principles of inequality and hierarchy. Instead, rebels lashed out against what they considered their rulers' failure to govern for the general good. In a sense, rebellions were directed against too much of what even the rebels conceded was a good thing: too much inequality; too much hierarchy.

In the Chesapeake after midcentury, government and politics contributed to the polarization of society and made the region ripe for rebellion. Small-scale servant rebellions broke out sporadically in the 1660s and 1670s. Sometimes the rebellious servants demanded better treatment; other times they organized plots to seize their freedom by running away. Vigilant masters, with the cooperation of the government, stifled the rebellions and conspiracies. When six servants who tried to run away from their master's plantation were captured, the court deciding on their punishment worried about "a dangerous precedent for the future time if [the servants were] left unpunished." Accordingly, the court sentenced Christopher Miller, the ringleader of the group, to "whipping . . . [with] thirty stripes and so [to] be burnt in the cheek with the letter R and to work with a shackle on his legg for one whole year and longer if said master shall see cause, and after his full time of service is Expired with his said master, to serve the colony for seven whole years." Miller's comrades received similar, though lesser, punishments. While the servant labor system continued to produce millions of pounds of tobacco that enriched the king, English traders, and colonial masters, it also produced the political crisis of the seventeenth-century Chesapeake.

Bacon's Rebellion

In 1676, Bacon's Rebellion erupted in the Chesapeake. A political upheaval that verged on civil war, the rebellion began as a dispute over Indian policy. Before it was over, however, the rebellion convulsed Chesapeake politics and society, leaving in its wake death, destruction, and a legacy of hostility between the great planters and their lesser neighbors.

Opechancanough, the old chief who had led the Indian uprising of 1622, tried again in 1644. In a surprise attack, Opechancanough's warriors killed about five hundred colonists in two days. During the next two years of bitter fighting, the colonists eventually gained the upper hand. They captured Opechancanough, jailed him, and murdered him in his cell. The peace treaty that concluded the war established policies toward the Indians that the government tried to maintain for the next thirty years. The Indians relinquished all claims to land already settled by the English. Wilderness land beyond the fringe of English settlement was supposed to be reserved exclusively for Indian use. The government's objective was to minimize contact between settlers and Indians and thereby maintain the peace.

Had the Chesapeake population remained constant, the policy might have worked. But the number of land-hungry colonists, especially poor, recently freed servants, continued to multiply. In their quest for land, they pushed beyond the treaty limits of English settlement and encroached steadily on Indian land. During the 1660s and 1670s, violence between colonists and Indians repeatedly flared along the advancing frontier. The government, headquartered in the tidewater region near the coast, far from the danger of Indian raids, took steps to calm the disputes and reestablish the peace. Frontier settlers condemned such niceties. They thirsted for revenge against what their leader, Nathaniel Bacon, termed "the protected and Darling Indians." Bacon minced no words about his intention: "Our Design [is] not only to ruine and extirpate all Indians in Generall but all Manner of Trade and Commerce with them." In 1676, Bacon and his followers demanded government support for their deadly plan.

Indians were not the only enemies Bacon and his men singled out. Bacon appealed to all colonists to consider the "nature of their Oppressions" and to investigate "by what Caball and mistery the designes of many of those whom wee call great men have been transacted and caryed on." Bacon urged the colonists to "see what spounges have suckt up the Publique Treasure and wither it hath not bin privately contrived away by unworthy Favourites and juggling Parasites whose tottering Fortunes have bin repaired and supported at the Publique chardg." In sum, Bacon charged that "Grandees," or elite planters, operated the government for their private gain, a charge that made sense to many colonists.

By most measures, Bacon himself was one of the grandees. The son of an English country gen-

tleman, Bacon came to Virginia in 1674 at the age of twenty-seven to make his fortune. A cousin of Governor Berkeley and a relative of other colonial officials, Bacon was quickly appointed to the governor's council. However, like other newcomers and most freemen, he remained outside the inner circle of established planters who ran things in Jamestown and in local government. He claimed land on the frontier near the fall line, the place where falls and rapids made Chesapeake rivers unnavigable. Within two years, he had crystallized the grievances of the lesser planters and poor farmers against both the Indians and the colonial rulers in Jamestown.

At first, Bacon simply insisted that Governor Berkeley commission him to lead a campaign against the Indians. Berkeley refused, hoping to maintain the fragile peace on the frontier. The governor expelled Bacon from the council, denounced him as a rebel, and threatened to punish him for treason. The council charged that Bacon and his supporters were a "Rabble Crue" that included "only the Rascallity and meanest of the people . . . there being hardly two amongst them that we have heard of who have Estates or are persons of Reputation and indeed very few who can either read or write." To isolate Bacon and his followers, Berkeley also called for elections for burgesses, hoping to divert the colonists' grievances into channels that he controlled.

The tactic worked better than Berkeley expected. Only five of the forty burgesses who had held office for the previous fifteen years were returned to their seats. All the other new burgesses were men who were prominent at the local level, most of them as justices of the peace. And, to Berkeley's surprise, Bacon was among the newly elected burgesses. The legislature was now in the hands of minor grandees who, like Bacon, chafed at the rule of "these men in Authority and Favour to whose hands the dispensation of the Countries wealth has been commited."

In June 1676, the new legislature passed a series of reform measures known as Bacon's Laws. Among other changes, the laws gave local settlers a voice in setting tax levies, forbade colonial officials from demanding bribes or other extra fees for carrying out their duties, placed limits on holding multiple official positions, required officials to be native-born or resident for at least three years, and restored the vote to all freemen. In late June 1676, when Bacon marched into Jamestown at the head of five hundred armed men demanding a commission to fight the Indians, Berkeley sensed that it was time to compromise. He pardoned Bacon, returned him to the council, and commissioned him to recruit additional troops for his campaign against frontier Indians.

Bacon called for and received the support of local militia units and then trekked off to the frontier in search of Indians. While he was away, several of the elite planters convinced Berkeley that it was extremely dangerous to have hundreds of armed men marauding through the countryside. What if they should decide to plunder the estates of the grandees? What if they should call for servants—who made up about half the population—to join them? They were desperate men, the secretary of the colony pointed out, "a Rabble of the basest sort of People," nearly all of them men who "were Idle and will not worke, or such whose Debaucherie or Ill Husbandry has brought [them] in Debt beyond hopes or thought of payment." Berkeley agreed. He nullified Bacon's commission and proclaimed him a rebel once again.

In late July 1676, when Bacon learned that his status as traitor had been renewed, he declared war against Berkeley and his supporters among the grandees. For three months, contingents of Bacon's forces combined fighting Indians with sacking and looting the plantations of Berkeley's men, and Berkeley's loyalists plundered the homes of Bacon's supporters in retaliation. To obtain fresh recruits, both Bacon and Berkeley promised freedom to servants and slaves who would aid their cause. In mid-September, Bacon marched on Jamestown, routed Berkeley's forces, and burned the town. The plunder continued until late in October, when Bacon unexpectedly died of a "Lousey Disease" known as "Bloody Flux," most likely dysentery. The arrival of several armed ships from England also bolstered Berkeley's forces, and Bacon's supporters dissipated. Back in power, Berkeley sent several of Bacon's allies to the gallows and revived the plunder of their plantations.

In the end, Bacon's Rebellion was not a revolt of the have-nots against the haves. Bacon's supporters included planters and small farmers as well as landless freemen. On the whole, they probably were less wealthy than Berkeley's allies. However, the crucial distinction between Bacon's rebels and Berkeley's loyalists was less between poor and rich than between outsiders and insiders. Bacon and other leading outsiders redirected the social and economic grievances of poor men toward a challenge to the rule of insider grandees. Bacon did not intend to overturn the hierarchy of Chesapeake politics and society. Instead, he challenged the ruthless and callous exploitation of the many outsiders by the few insiders.

Bacon's Rebellion did not dislodge the grandees from their seats of power. If anything, it strengthened their position. When the king learned of the turmoil in the Chesapeake and its devastating effect on tobacco exports, he ordered an investigation. The royal officials replaced Berkeley with a governor more attentive to the king's interest in increasing tobacco exports, nullified Bacon's Laws, and instituted an export tax on every hogshead of tobacco as a way of paying the expenses of government without having to obtain the consent of the tightfisted House of Burgesses. In a sense, the grandees of the Chesapeake were put in their place by still grander royal officials.

Bacon did not intend to overturn the hierarchy of Chesapeake politics and society. Instead, he challenged the ruthless and callous exploitation of the many outsiders by the few insiders.

The suppression of Bacon's Rebellion did not end turmoil in the Chesapeake. In 1682, for example, depressed tobacco prices led numerous farmers to try to reduce production by destroying the plants thriving in their neighbors' fields. Although these tobacco riots had little impact on production and petered out when prices improved, they expressed the colonists' dependence on the world market for tobacco. When prices were good, the Chesapeake prospered; when prices fell, it suffered. The tobacco riots illustrate that Chesapeake colonists in the late seventeenth century came to realize that they were not only wedded to tobacco but were shackled to it by the world market and the growing assertion of royal authority over both political and commercial affairs.

In the aftermath of Bacon's Rebellion, political stability slowly returned to the Chesapeake. Tensions between great planters and small farmers gradually lessened. By 1700, the new export duty on tobacco allowed the government to cut other taxes to just one-fourth what they had been in 1660, a move welcomed by all freemen. In the long run, however, the most important contribution to political stability was the declining importance of the servant labor system. During the 1680s and 1690s, fewer servants arrived in the Chesapeake, partly because of improving economic conditions in England. Accordingly, the number of poor, newly freed servants also declined, reducing the size of the lowest stratum of free society. In 1700, as many as one-third of the free colonists still worked as tenants on land owned by others, but the social and political distance between them and the great planters—enormous as it was—did not seem as profound as it had been in 1660. The main reason was that by 1700 the Chesapeake was in the midst of transition to a slave labor system that minimized the differences between poor farmers and rich planters and magnified the differences between whites and blacks.

Toward a Slave Labor System

The Spaniards and Portuguese engaged in an extensive African slave trade in the sixteenth century, and they established slavery as an important form of coerced labor in the New World. In the seventeenth century, British colonies in the West Indies followed the Spanish and Portuguese examples and developed sugar plantations with slave labor. In the British North American colonies, however, a slave labor system did not develop until the last quarter of the seventeenth century. During the 1670s, settlers from Barbados brought slavery to the new English mainland colony of Carolina, where the imprint of the West Indies remained strong for decades. In Chesapeake tobacco fields at about the same time, slave labor began to replace servant labor, marking the transition toward a society of freedom for whites and slavery for Africans.

The West Indies: Sugar and Slavery

The most profitable part of the British New World empire in the seventeenth century lay in the Caribbean. The tiny island of Barbados, colonized in the 1630s, was the jewel of the British West Indies. The island's economy appeared at first to be moving along the path blazed by English settlers in the Chesapeake: The early Barbadian colonists grew tobacco and cotton on small farms worked by family members and indentured servants. During the

1640s, however, the island's economy swerved away from the Chesapeake pattern and became the prototype of West Indian colonies. Barbadian planters began to grow sugarcane, with such success that a colonial official proclaimed Barbados "the most flourishing Island in all those American parts, and I verily beleive in all the world for the production of sugar." Sugar commanded high prices in England, and planters rushed to grow and sell as much as they could. By midcentury, annual sugar exports from the British Caribbean totaled about 150,000 pounds; by 1700, exports nearly reached 50 million pounds.

Sugar transformed Barbados and other West Indian islands. Starting a sugar plantation required substantial capital. Poor farmers could not afford the expensive machinery that extracted and refined the sugarcane juice; as sugar production boomed, their prospects plummeted. So many farmers left Barbados in quest of better opportunities that the white population in 1700 was only half what it had been in 1650. Planters who remained and had the necessary capital to grow sugar got rich. By 1680, a group of 175 planters owned over half the total wealth of Barbados. On the average, each of them was worth four times more than the richest tobacco grandees in the Chesapeake. The sugar grandees differed from their Chesapeake counterparts in another crucial way: The average sugar baron in Barbados in 1680 owned 115 slaves.

During the 1670s, settlers from Barbados brought slavery to the new English mainland colony of Carolina. In Chesapeake tobacco fields at about the same time, slave labor began to replace servant labor, marking the transition toward a society of freedom for whites and slavery for Africans.

African slaves planted, cultivated, and harvested the sugarcane that made planters wealthy. For planters, slaves were a good buy. A planter could recover the cost of buying an African with the sugarcane the slave could be expected to grow in one year. Beginning in the 1640s, Barbadian planters purchased thousands of slaves to work their plantations, and the African population on the island mushroomed. During the 1650s, when blacks made

SUGAR MILL
*This seventeenth-century drawing of a Brazilian sugar mill highlights the heavy equipment
needed to extract the juice from sugarcane. A vertical waterwheel turns a large horizontal gear
that exerts force on the jaws of a press, which squeezes the cane. Workers constantly remove
crushed cane from the press and replenish it with freshly harvested cane as it is unloaded from an
oxcart. Note that except for the overseer (just to the right of the waterwheel), all of the workers
are black, presumably slaves from Africa, as suggested by their clothing. All of the mill workers
appear to be men, a hint of the predominance of men among newly imported African slaves.*
Musées Royaux des Beaux-Arts de Belgique.

up only 3 percent of the Chesapeake population, they had already become the majority on Barbados. By 1700, blacks, nearly all of them slaves, constituted more than three-fourths of the island's population. The island was literally a slave society that belonged to white men.

For slaves, work on a sugar plantation was a life sentence to brutal, unremitting labor. The sentence did not last long for many slaves. Planters were so eager for maximum production that they drove cane field slaves to the limits of endurance and beyond. Although precise data are lacking, it is clear that slaves' life expectancy was short and their death rate high. Furthermore, since slave men outnumbered slave women two to one, the vast majority of slaves could not form a family and have children. The unbalanced sex ratio and the high mortality rate meant that in Barbados and else-

where in the West Indies, the slave population did not grow by natural reproduction. Instead, planters had to continue to purchase slaves from Africa in order to maintain their slave force. For the most part, then, slaves on sugar plantations were African-born men and women who remembered when they had been free at home on the other side of the Atlantic. They tended to be bitter, unruly, and hostile, making sugar planters all the more ruthless in enforcing obedience.

As the sugar boom moved from island to island in the Caribbean, this distinctively West Indian colonial society was reproduced repeatedly. Although sugar plantations did not gain a foothold in North America in the seventeenth century, the West Indies nonetheless exerted a powerful influence on the development of slavery in the mainland colonies to the north.

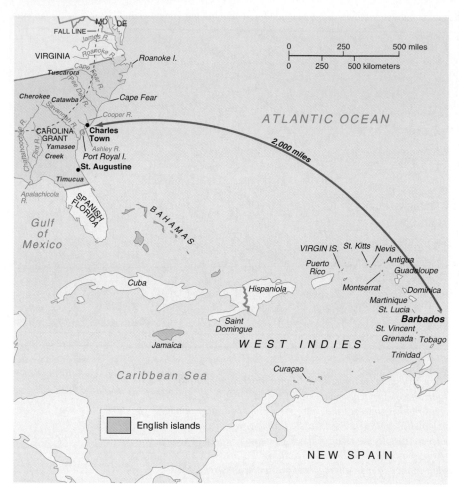

MAP 3.2
*Carolina and the West
Indies in the Seventeenth
Century*
*Although Carolina was geo-
graphically closer to the
Chesapeake colonies, it was
culturally closer to the West
Indies in the seventeenth century since its early settlers —
both blacks and whites —
came from Barbados. South
Carolina retained close ties to
the West Indies for more than
a century, long after many of
its subsequent settlers came
from England, Ireland, France,
and elsewhere.*

Carolina: A West Indian Frontier

The early settlers of what became South Carolina
were emigrants from Barbados. By 1680, the island
was the most densely settled British colony in the
New World. More colonists inhabited the island's
160 square miles than the hundreds of thousands of
square miles in the Chesapeake. The governor of
Barbados explained to his superiors in London that
the shortage of land meant that "people no longer
come to Barbados, many having departed to Carolina, Jamaica, and the Leeward Islands in hope of
settling the land which they cannot obtain here."

In 1663, a Barbadian planter named John Colleton and a group of seven other men obtained a
charter from King Charles II to establish a colony
south of the Chesapeake. Settlers from Virginia had
already begun to migrate south searching for good
tobacco land around the Albemarle Sound, in what
would become (in 1712) the colony of North Car-

olina. Colleton and his colleagues, known as the
"proprietors," had their sights set farther south, in
the vast region north of the Spanish territories in
Florida. The proprietors' motives were commercial.
They hoped to siphon settlers from Barbados and
other colonies and encourage them to develop a
profitable export crop comparable to West Indian
sugar and Chesapeake tobacco.

Following the Chesapeake example, the proprietors offered headrights of up to 150 acres of land
for each settler. During the 1660s, they sponsored
several settlements in Carolina, but none survived.
In 1670, they established the first permanent English beachhead in the colony, at a site on the west
bank of the Ashley River, just across from the peninsula where the king's namesake city, Charles Towne
(later spelled Charleston), was founded.

As the proprietors had planned, most of the settlers were from Barbados. In fact, Carolina was the
only seventeenth-century English colony to be set-

tled principally by colonists from other colonies rather than from England. The Barbadian immigrants brought their slaves with them. More than a fourth of the early settlers were black, and, as the colony continued to attract settlers from Barbados, the black population multiplied. By 1700, blacks made up about half of the population of Carolina.

Both economically and socially, seventeenth-century Carolina was a frontier outpost of the West Indian sugar economy.

Although few plantations existed in Carolina before 1700, the racial composition of the colony began to resemble Barbados more closely than it resembled Virginia or Maryland. English officials associated the colony so closely with Barbados that as late as 1700 they referred to "Carolina in ye West Indies."

The Carolinians experimented with tobacco, cotton, indigo, olives, and rice as potentially prof-

itable export crops. But until the end of the seventeenth century, the experiments proved disappointing. Finally, in the mid-1690s, colonists identified a hardy strain of rice and worked out successful methods of cultivation that inaugurated a flourishing rice industry in the years to come. During the first generation of settlement in the seventeenth century, however, Carolina remained an economic colony of Barbados. The king himself pointed out that "Barbados and ye rest of ye Caribee Islands . . . have not food to fill their bellies." Carolinians sniffed a market for their livestock—cattle and swine that roamed and grazed freely in Carolina's woodlands. Settlers looked after the animals and then sold them to hungry Barbadians. Since the trees on Barbados had been cut to make room for sugar plantations, Carolinians took advantage of their dense forests and exported wood, especially staves for making the barrels used to ship sugar products. Carolina settlers also exploited another "natural resource": They captured and enslaved several thousand local Indians and sold them to

LONDON COFFEEHOUSE
By the mid-seventeenth century, English merchants began to meet in coffeehouses like this one to swap gossip about colonial commerce and to make deals. Sipping coffee, puffing pipes, and comparing notes, these bewigged gentlemen may also have indulged in the amorous attention of prostitutes, as suggested by the portrait over the mantel. The female proprietor of this coffeehouse may have purveyed nothing more than coffee, tobacco, and good cheer, but her reputation may still have been sullied by the common presumption that a woman who worked in this type of male enclave must be up to no good.
E.T. Archive.

Caribbean planters. Both economically and socially, seventeenth-century Carolina was a frontier outpost of the West Indian sugar economy.

The Chesapeake: Tobacco and Slaves

By 1700, more than eight out of ten people in the southern colonies of British North America lived in the Chesapeake. Until the 1670s, almost all Chesapeake colonists were white people from England. In 1700, however, one out of eight people in the region was a black person from Africa. Although a few blacks had lived in the Chesapeake since the 1620s, the black population increased fivefold between 1670 and 1700 as tobacco planters made the transition from servant to slave labor.

At bottom, the shift to slave labor occurred simply because hundreds of individual Chesapeake planters began to purchase slaves rather than servants to work in their tobacco fields. For planters, slaves had several obvious advantages over servants. Although slaves cost three to five times more than servants, slaves did not become free after several years of servitude. They were slaves for life. By the 1680s, the mortality rate among immigrants to the Chesapeake had declined significantly, and planters could reasonably expect slaves to live far longer than a servant's period of indenture. Better yet from the planters' point of view, slaves promised to be a perpetual labor force. Children of slave mothers inherited the status of slavery. When William Fitzhugh, a wealthy Chesapeake planter, placed his order for slaves with a slave ship captain in 1682, he revealed the logic common to many other planters. Fitzhugh told the slave trader that he would "give 3000 lb. Tobo. [tobacco] for every Negro boy or girl, that shall be between the age of seven & eleven years old, . . . 4000 lb. Tobo. for every youth or girle that shall be between the age of 11 & 15 & . . . 5000 lb. Tobo. for every young man or woman that shall be above 15 years of age, & not exceed 24." Like other planters, Fitzhugh valued young slaves not simply because they would probably live and work longer than either servants or older slaves. He pointed out to a friend that his "Negroes increase being all young, & a considerable parcel of breeders, will keep that Stock [of slaves] good for ever."

For planters like Fitzhugh, slaves had another important advantage over servants: They could be controlled politically. Servants came to the Chesa-

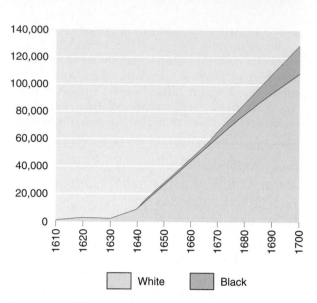

FIGURE 3.2
White and Black Populations in the Southern Colonies in the Seventeenth Century
Although the first Africans arrived in the southern colonies in 1619, Africans and their descendants remained a small fraction of the population throughout the seventeenth century. What features of this chart reflect the servant labor system, the transition to slave labor, and the settlement of Carolina?

peake expecting to become free, obtain land, and participate in colonial society. Bacon's Rebellion had demonstrated how disruptive former servants could be when their expectations were not met. Planters in the Chesapeake, like those in Barbados and Carolina, had no intention of permitting African slaves the luxuries of freedom and assimilation into free society. They determined that slaves would be a permanent laboring class excluded from the privileges of freedom expected and demanded by seventeenth-century English men and women. A slave labor system promised to avoid the political problems caused by the servant labor system. Slavery kept discontented laborers in permanent servitude, and their color was a badge of their bondage. All whites, not just the planters who owned slaves, were officially given the duty to keep blacks in their place. Slaves were even prohibited from defending themselves. A 1680 Virginia law provided that "any negroe or other slave [who] shall presume to lift up his hand in opposition against any christian" would be punished with "thirty lashes on his bare back well laid on."

The slave labor system polarized Chesapeake society along lines of race and status: All slaves were black and nearly all blacks were slaves; almost all free people were white and all whites were free or only temporarily bound in indentured servitude. Unlike Barbados, however, the Chesapeake retained a vast white majority. Among whites, huge differences of wealth and status still existed. In fact, the emerging slave labor system sharpened the economic differences among whites since only prosperous planters could afford to buy slaves. By 1700, more than three-quarters of white families had neither servants nor slaves. They grew tobacco with family labor. Nonetheless, unlike the swelling slave population, poorer white farmers enjoyed the privileges of free status. They could own property of all sorts; they could marry, have families, and bequeath their property and free status to their descendants; they could move when and where they wanted; they could associate freely with other people; they could serve on juries, vote, and even hold political office; they could work, loaf, or sleep as they chose. All these privileges and more were prohibited to slaves. These very real distinctions between slaves and free people made lesser white folk feel they had a genuine stake in the existence of slavery, even if they did not own a single slave. By emphasizing the privileges of freedom shared by all white people, the slave labor system reduced the tensions between poor folk and grandees that had plagued the Chesapeake in the 1670s.

The slaves purchased by Chesapeake planters in the seventeenth century came mostly from the West Indies. As the acting governor of Virginia wrote in 1708, "What negroes were brought to Virginia were imported generally from Barbados for it was very rare to have a Negro ship come to this Country directly from Africa." In the applications for headrights filed by masters who imported slaves, names like "Barbados Mary" appear repeatedly, an index of the link between the island and the mainland. While the demand for slaves was growing in the Chesapeake late in the seventeenth century, the market among tobacco planters was still small compared with that in the West Indies or Brazil, where African slave ships preferred to sell their human cargo. While Barbados annually imported an average of more than 1,300 slaves directly from Africa, the Chesapeake imported only about 250 to 300 slaves a year during the peak years of the 1690s. Chesapeake planters made the transition to slave labor with native-born Africans who had already been "seasoned," that is, acclimated to the natural environment of the New World and the repressive confines of slavery. Many of the slaves probably had already learned some English. The Chesapeake eased into the slave labor system at a relatively leisurely pace. The transition was still under way in 1700, but by then, although servants continued to arrive in the Chesapeake area, the majority of laborers found in Chesapeake tobacco fields were slaves.

The slave labor system polarized Chesapeake society along lines of race and status: All slaves were black and nearly all blacks were slaves; almost all free people were white and all whites were free or only temporarily bound in indentured servitude.

Slaves performed the same tasks on tobacco plantations that servants had done previously. Unlike sugar plantations, Chesapeake tobacco plantations were small operations. Often, as James Revel described in his verse (see page 92), slaves and servants worked side by side in the fields. Slave owners made up only a minority of tobacco planters, and most of them owned just a few slaves. On their farms, the white owner and his family members usually worked shoulder to shoulder with their slaves. A few wealthy planters owned twenty, thirty, or more slaves, permitting greater specialization of labor and more pronounced social distance between blacks and whites on the plantation, but nothing akin to the situation on sugar plantations, with more than a hundred slaves. In contrast to Barbados, most slaves in the seventeenth-century Chesapeake colonies had frequent and close contact with white people.

For slaves, work on a tobacco plantation was less onerous than on a sugar plantation. But the small size of tobacco farms and slaves' constant exposure to white surveillance made Chesapeake slavery especially confining. Slaves took advantage of every opportunity to slip away from white supervision and seek out the company of other slaves. Since, for the most part, few slaves lived on any one plantation, slaves who sought the companionship of the opposite sex had to "go abroad," that is, visit slaves on neighboring plantations. Planters did not like such visiting, since it loosened their control over their slaves. Nonetheless, they occasionally and grudgingly permitted slaves to spend a few hours with friends on other farms. More than once, slaves turned such seemingly innocent social pleasures to political ends, either to run away or to conspire to strike against their masters. In 1680, for example, Virginia planters uncovered a "Negro Plott, formed . . . for the Distroying and killing his Majesties Subjects . . . with a designe of Carrying it through the whole Collony of Virginia." The committee that investigated the conspiracy concluded that "the great freedome and Liberty that has beene by many Masters given to their Negro Slaves for Walking on broad on Saterdays and Sundays and permitting them to meete in great Numbers in makeing and holding of Funerals for Dead Negroes gives them the Opportunityes under pretention of such publique meetings to Consult and advise for the carrying on of their Evill and Wicked purposes and Contrivances." It became clear that slaves were no more content with their servitude than servants had been.

While slavery resolved the political unrest caused by the servant labor system, it also created new political problems. By the end of the seventeenth century, the bedrock political issue in the Chesapeake was keeping slaves in their place, at the business end of a hoe in a tobacco field. By 1700, the Chesapeake was well on its way to developing a slave labor system that stood midway —both geographically and socially—between the sugar plantations and black majority of Barbados to the south and the small farms and homogeneous villages that developed in seventeenth-century New England to the north.

Conclusion: Staple Crops, Coerced Labor, and Racial Hierarchy in the Southern Colonies

By 1700, the colonies of Virginia, Maryland, and Carolina were firmly established. The staple crops they grew for export provided a livelihood for many, a fortune for a few, and valuable revenues for shippers, merchants, and the English monarchy. Their societies differed markedly from England in most respects, yet the colonists considered themselves English people who happened to live in North America. They claimed the rights and privileges of English men and women while they denied those rights and privileges to Native Americans and African slaves. The English colonies also differed from the sixteenth-century example of New Spain. Large quantities of gold and silver never materialized in the Chesapeake. The system of encomienda was never adopted because Indians were too few and too hostile and their communities too small and decentralized, compared with those of the Mexica. Yet forms of coerced labor and racial distinction that developed in New Spain had North American counterparts, as English colonists employed servants and slaves and defined themselves as superior to Indians and Africans. By 1700, only the remnants of Powhatan's people survived. As English settlement pushed out north, west, and south of the Chesapeake, the various Indian tribes were faced with the New World that Powhatan encountered in 1607. By 1700, few doubted that the new English world in North America was there to stay.

CHRONOLOGY

1588 England defeats Spanish Armada.

1606 Virginia Company of London receives royal charter to establish colony in North America.

1607 English colonists found Jamestown settlement.

1609 Starvation plagues Jamestown.

1612 John Rolfe begins to plant tobacco in Virginia.

1617 First commercial tobacco shipment leaves Virginia for England.
Pocahontas dies in England.

1618 Powhatan dies and is replaced by Opechancanough.

1619 First Africans arrive in Virginia.
House of Burgesses begins to meet in Virginia.

1622 Opechancanough leads Indian uprising against Virginia colonists.

1624 Virginia becomes royal colony.

1632 King Charles I grants Lord Baltimore land for colony of Maryland.

1634 Colonists begin to arrive in Maryland.

1644 Opechancanough leads Indian uprising against Virginia colonists.

1660 Navigation Act requires colonial tobacco to be shipped to English ports and to be assessed customs tax.

1663 Carolina proprietors receive charter from King Charles II for Carolina colony.

1670 Charles Towne, South Carolina, is founded.
Slave labor system emerges first in Carolina and more gradually in Chesapeake colonies.

1676 Bacon's Rebellion convulses Virginia.

BIBLIOGRAPHY

GENERAL WORK

Kenneth R. Andrews, *Trade, Plunder, and Settlement: Maritime Enterprise and the Genesis of the British Empire* (1984).

Bernard Bailyn and Philip D. Morgan, eds., *Strangers within the Realm: Cultural Margins of the First British Empire* (1991).

Robert M. Bliss, *Revolution and Empire: English Politics and the American Colonies in the Seventeenth Century* (1990).

Wesley Frank Craven, *The Southern Colonies in the Seventeenth Century, 1607–1689* (1949).

K. G. Davies, *The North Atlantic World in the Seventeenth Century* (1974).

Richard Beale Davis, *Intellectual Life in the Colonial South, 1585–1763*, 3 vols. (1978).

Lewis Cecil Gray, *History of Agriculture in the Southern United States to 1860*, 2 vols. (1933).

Jack P. Greene and J. R. Pole, eds., *Colonial British America: Essays in the New History of the Early Modern Era*, (1984).

Winthrop D. Jordan, *White over Black: American Attitudes towards the Negro, 1550–1812* (1968).

John J. McCusker and Russell R. Menard, *The Economy of British America, 1607–1789* (1985).

Edmund S. Morgan, *American Slavery, American Freedom: The Ordeal of Colonial Virginia* (1975).

Gary B. Nash, *Red, White, and Black: The Peoples of Early America* (1982).

James F. Shepherd and Gary M. Walton, *The Economic Rise of Early America* (1979).

John R. Stilgoe, *Common Landscape of America, 1580–1845* (1982).

INDIANS

James Axtell, *The European and the Indian: Essays in the Ethnohistory of Colonial North America* (1981).

James Axtell, *The Invasion Within: The Contest of Cultures in Colonial North America* (1985).

Philip L. Barbour, *Pocahontas and Her World* (1970).

Kathryn E. Holland Braund, *Deerskins and Duffels: The Creek Indian Trade with Anglo-America, 1685–1815* (1993).

Wesley Frank Craven, *White, Red, and Black: The Seventeenth-Century Virginian* (1971).

Charles Hudson and Carmen Chaves Tesser, eds., *The Forgotten Centuries: Indians and Europeans in the American South, 1521–1704* (1994).

Karen Ordahl Kupperman, *Settling with the Indians: The Meeting of English and Indian Cultures in America, 1580–1640* (1981).

J. A. Leo Lemay, *Did Pocahontas Save Captain John Smith?* (1992).

James H. Merrell, *The Indians' New World: Catawbas and Their Neighbors from European Contact through the Era of Removal* (1989).

Helen C. Rountree, *The Powhatan Indians of Virginia: Their Traditional Culture* (1989).

Helen C. Rountree, *Pocahontas's People: The Powhatan Indians of Virginia through Four Centuries* (1990).

Helen C. Rountree, ed., *Powhatan Foreign Relations, 1500–1722* (1993).

Bernard W. Sheehan, *Savagism and Civility: Indians and Englishmen in Colonial Virginia* (1980).

Timothy Silver, *A New Face on the Countryside: Indians, Colonists, and Slaves in South Atlantic Forests, 1500–1800* (1990).

Peter H. Wood, Gregory A. Waselkov, and M. Thomas Hatley, eds., *Powhatan's Mantle: Indians in the Colonial Southeast* (1989).

CHESAPEAKE SOCIETY

Charles M. Andrews, ed., *Narratives of the Insurrections, 1675–1690* (1915).

Philip L. Barbour, ed., *The Complete Works of Captain John Smith,* 3 vols. (1986).

Warren M. Billings, *The Old Dominion in the Seventeenth Century: A Documentary History of Virginia, 1606–1689* (1975).

Warren M. Billings, John E. Selby, and Thad W. Tate, *Colonial Virginia: A History* (1986).

Carl Bridenbaugh, *Jamestown, 1544–1699* (1980).

Philip Alexander Bruce, *Economic History of Virginia in the Seventeenth Century,* 2 vols. (1896).

Lois Green Carr, Russell R. Menard, and Lorena S. Walsh, *Robert Cole's World: Agriculture and Society in Early Maryland* (1991).

Lois Green Carr, Philip D. Morgan, and Jean B. Russo, eds., *Colonial Chesapeake Society* (1988).

Richard Beale Davis, ed., *William Fitzhugh and His Chesapeake World, 1676–1701* (1963).

James Deetz, *Flowerdew Hundred: The Archaeology of a Virginia Plantation, 1619–1864* (1993).

Carville Earle, *The Evolution of a Tidewater Settlement System: All Hallow's Parish, Maryland, 1650–1783* (1975).

Clayton Colman Hall, ed., *Narratives of Early Maryland, 1633–1684* (1910).

James Horn, *Adapting to a New World: English Society in the Seventeenth-Century Chesapeake* (1994).

David William Jordan, *Maryland's Revolution of Government, 1689–1692* (1974).

David W. Jordan, *Foundations of Representative Government in Maryland, 1632–1715* (1987).

Aubrey C. Land, *Colonial Maryland: A History* (1981).

Aubrey C. Land, Lois Green Carr, and Edward C. Papenfuse, eds., *Law, Society, and Politics in Early Maryland* (1977).

Kenneth A. Lockridge, *The Diary, and Life, of William Byrd II of Virginia, 1674–1744* (1987).

Gloria Lund Main, *Tobacco Colony: Life in Early Maryland, 1650–1720* (1982).

Edwin J. Perkins, *The Economy of Colonial Ameria* (1980).

James Perry, *The Formation of a Society on Virginia's Eastern Shore, 1615–1655* (1990).

Jacob M. Price, *Perry of London: A Family and a Firm on the Seaborne Frontier, 1615–1753* (1992).

Darrett B. Rutman and Anita H. Rutman, *A Place in Time: Middlesex County, Virginia, 1650–1750,* 2 vols. (1984).

James F. Shepherd and Gary M. Walton, *Shipping, Maritime Trade, and the Economic Development of Colonial North America* (1972).

Thad W. Tate and David L. Ammerman, eds., *The Chesapeake in the Seventeenth Century: Essays on Anglo-American Society* (1979).

SERVANTS AND SLAVES

Philip D. Curtin, *The Atlantic Slave Trade: A Census* (1969).

David W. Galenson, *White Servitude in Colonial America: An Economic Analysis* (1981).

David W. Galenson, *Traders, Planters, and Slaves: Market Behavior in Early English America* (1986).

Henry A. Gemery and Jan S. Hogendorn, eds., *The Uncommon Market: Essays in the Economic History of the Atlantic Slave Trade* (1979).

Marcus W. Jernegan, *Laboring and Dependent Classes in Colonial America, 1607–1783* (1931).

Herbert S. Klein, *The Middle Passage: Comparative Studies of the Atlantic Slave Trade* (1978).

Paul E. Lovejoy, ed., *Africans in Bondage: Studies in Slavery and the Slave Trade* (1986).

Richard B. Morris, *Government and Labor in Early America* (1946).

James A. Rawley, *The Transatlantic Slave Trade: A History* (1981).

Abbot Emerson Smith, *Colonists in Bondage: White Servitude and Convict Labor in America, 1607–1776* (1947).

CAROLINA SOCIETY

Alan Vance Briceland, *Westward from Virginia: The Exploration of the Virginia-Carolina Frontier, 1650–1710* (1987).

Converse D. Clowse, *Economic Beginnings in Colonial South Carolina, 1670–1730* (1971).

Leland G. Ferguson, *Uncommon Ground: Archaeology and Early African America, 1650–1800* (1992).

Thomas M. Hatley, *The Dividing Paths: Cherokees and South Carolinians through the Era of the American Revolution* (1993).

Daniel C. Littlefield, *Rice and Slaves: Ethnicity and the Slave Trade in Colonial South Carolina* (1981).

Alexander S. Salley Jr., ed., *Narratives of Early Carolina, 1650–1708* (1911).

Aaron M. Shatzmann, *Servants into Planters: The Origin of an American Image: Land Acquisition and Status Mobility in Seventeenth-Century South Carolina* (1989).

Richard Waterhouse, *A New World Gentry: The Making of a Merchant and Planter Class in South Carolina, 1670–1770* (1989).

Robert M. Weir, *Colonial South Carolina: A History* (1983).

Peter H. Wood, *Black Majority: Negroes in Colonial South Carolina from 1670 through the Stono Rebellion* (1974).

THE WEST INDIES

Carl Bridenbaugh and Roberta Bridenbaugh, *No Peace beyond the Line: The English in the Caribbean, 1624–1690* (1972).

Michael Craton, *Sinews of Empire: A Short History of British Slavery* (1974).

Richard S. Dunn, *Sugar and Slaves: The Rise of the Planter Class in the English West Indies, 1624–1713* (1972).

Jerome S. Handler and Frederick W. Lange, *Plantation Slavery in Barbados* (1978).

Kenneth F. Kiple, *The Caribbean Slave: A Biological History* (1984).

Herbert S. Klein, *African Slavery in Latin America and the Caribbean* (1986).

Sidney W. Mintz, *Sweetness and Power: The Place of Sugar in Modern History* (1985).

Richard B. Sheridan, *Sugar and Slavery: An Economic History of the British West Indies, 1623–1775* (1974).

Eric Williams, *From Columbus to Castro: The History of the Caribbean, 1492–1969* (1970).

GREAT CHAIR

This thronelike chair belonged to Michael Metcalf, a teacher in seventeenth-century Dedham, Massachusetts. The oldest known piece of New England furniture inscribed with a date, 1652, the chair was made in Dedham specifically for Metcalf (note the initials flanking the date), who turned sixty-six in that year. Metcalf stored books, presumably including a well-thumbed Bible, in the enclosed compartment under the seat. No overstuffed recliner, the chair is suited less for a relaxing snooze than for alert concentration. The panels under the arms served to block chilly drafts. Otherwise, the chair shows few concessions to comfort or ease. The carved back—rigidly upright—displays motifs often found on Puritan tombstones. The grand austerity of the chair hints at the importance of serious Bible study and unflinching introspection in Puritan New England.

Dedham Historical Society/photo by Forrest Frazier.

THE NORTHERN COLONIES IN THE SEVENTEENTH CENTURY

4

1601-1700

I N 1630, AN OFFICIAL OF THE CHURCH OF ENGLAND FILED CHARGES against Reverend Charles Chauncy, a minister in the small village of Ware, a few miles north of London. Chauncy had sworn obedience to the doctrines of the Church of England, but church officials found him alarmingly disobedient.

The list of Chauncy's transgressions was long and detailed. During worship services, he refused to read aloud certain required passages from the Book of Common Prayer. He announced that "people have been deluded" by the Book of Common Prayer and the Church of England. Such speeches brought "the Book of Common Prayer and the Liturgy of the Church into contempt amongst the people," the church officials declared. But that was only the beginning of Chauncy's deviations from prescribed practices. He refused to make the sign of the cross in baptisms and marriage ceremonies. He refused to give the required lessons in church doctrine before launching into his sermon. He refused to hold worship services on the special holy days appointed by the Church of England. He preached, for example, "that there be many thousand souls damned in hell for their gaming and reveling in twelve days at Christmas time, and that the damned in hell do curse the birth of our Savior Christ and the Church for instituting the celebration thereof." Chauncy believed that the celebration of Christmas was sinful because it was not mentioned in the Bible.

That was only one of what the Church of England considered his "uncouth and strange opinion[s]." He also caused "much strife, heartburning, and dissension . . . amongst the inhabitants in Ware" by preaching constantly that "the Sabbath doth begin every Saturday at sunset." If Chauncy was correct, then innocent Saturday night pleasures were sins. Anybody in Ware who spent a few hours singing, dancing, drinking, or even working on Saturday night was violating the Sabbath—the Sabbath was for worship, not work or fun.

Chauncy "terrified the people," the Church of England asserted, by preaching that "idolatry was admitted into the Church." From the pulpit Chauncy declared "that there never [was] so much atheism, popery . . . and heresy in our Church as at this time." He said that the Church of England lacked "men of spirit and courage" who would point out the church's errors and evils. Instead, he said with "great scorn and contempt," the Church of England had too many "rotten divines and . . . pot [contemptible] ministers." Chauncy claimed that if worshipers followed the dictates of the Church of England, they sinned and would be punished in eternity.

Not surprisingly, the Church of England took the opposite view. "You have most grossly and contemptuously neglected your duty, both to God and the Church wherein you live," church officials charged Chauncy. Furthermore, they declared that "under a false pretence of zeal and purity in religion," Chauncy "would seem to be more precise than other men, and in very truth you do affect the name of Puritan."

Chauncy was indeed a Puritan, and proud of it. He warned his parishioners that "the preaching of the Gospel would be suppressed, and that some families are preparing to go for New England." Chauncy's warnings, the Church of England asserted, "caused a great distraction and fear amongst the people, . . . making them believe that there would forthwith ensue some alteration of religion."

Chauncy was correct that Puritanism was being suppressed, as the church's charges against him demonstrated. The Church of England was correct that Chauncy refused to perform his duty as defined by the church because he was a Puritan. As he saw it, his duty was defined by the Bible, the Word of God. The confusion and worry among Chauncy's parishioners are also understandable: Did they sin if they followed Chauncy or if they conformed to the Church of England? The "alteration of religion" they feared—and much more—was in fact on the historical horizon. Within a few years, Chauncy spent several months in prison in England before leaving to preach in New England.

The charges against Chauncy illustrate the religious, social, and political turmoil that pervaded England in the first decades of the seventeenth century. Puritans like Chauncy both responded to that turmoil and helped create it. Most Puritans and their followers stayed in England where, in the 1640s, they fought the battles of the Puritan Revolution. In the years before the revolution, however, thousands of other Puritans like Chauncy immigrated to New England. In the wilderness on the western shores of the Atlantic, they aspired to build a new, godly society purged of the idolatry, heresy, and corruption of England. They intended to remake England, not by revolution at home but by reconstruction abroad. The architect of their new England, they believed, was neither the king of England nor the archbishop of Canterbury, but God himself. Their blueprints for a society of saints guided their efforts to establish a new England in North America. The New England colonies reflected the rigor and discipline of their Puritan founders and the tensions within their faith.

During the seventeenth century, however, colonial experiences tempered Puritan zeal, and the goal of founding a holy new England faded. Late in the century, new colonies were founded in the mid-Atlantic region of North America. These middle colonies—New York, Pennsylvania, and New Jersey—differed sharply from the ideals and realities of New England. Despite these differences, by the end of the seventeenth century, all the North American colonies—New England as well as the middle and southern colonies—were tied more firmly to the English empire.

Puritan Origins: The English Reformation

The origins of Puritanism trace back to the English Reformation in the sixteenth century. In 1500, the church in England, like the church in other European countries, owed allegiance to the pope in Rome. The Roman church was a catholic, or universal, church. It had a monopoly on religious life in western Europe. It was also a unified church. But when the Protestant Reformation arose in Germany in 1517 and spread to other countries soon afterward, that unity shattered forever.

During the early years of the Reformation, the English church remained within the Catholic fold. King Henry VIII, who reigned from 1509 to 1547, was such a loyal Catholic that the pope bestowed on him the honorific title Defender of the Faith. Henry's faith, like that of other European monarchs, was strongly influenced by political considerations. He witnessed the bitter religious disputes and rampant popular unrest the Reformation brought to the European continent, and he hoped to prevent both from spreading to England. He also understood that in the right hands—his own—the Reformation offered a golden political opportunity. A break with the church in Rome would allow him to take control of the church in England. Taxes that English Christians paid to the pope would be redirected to Henry's treasury; the enormous landholdings of the church in England would belong to him; the power to appoint priests, bishops, and archbishops in England would be his; and the prestige and majesty of the church would be identified with the English monarchy. In short, Henry VIII realized that a rupture with the Catholic Church could make the church in England serve his purposes.

PERSECUTION OF ENGLISH PROTESTANTS
This sixteenth-century drawing shows the persecution of Protestants in England during the reign of Queen Mary, a staunch Catholic. Here Protestant prisoners are being marched to London to be tried for heresy. This pro-Protestant drawing emphasizes the severity of royal tyranny by depicting four well-armed guards, two of them mounted, escorting some fifteen prisoners, including at least five women, who are roped together, although they do not appear to be menacing or likely to run away. The guards seem to be necessary less to maintain order among the prisoners than to prevent sympathetic citizens from rushing toward the marchers and freeing them. The drawing assumes that most citizens opposed the queen's persecution of Protestants. The Bible verse from the book of Matthew underscores Protestants' fealty to Christ rather than mere "Princes and Rulers" like Queen Mary.
Folger Shakespeare Library.

The pretext for the breach with Rome was Henry's desire for a divorce from his wife, Catherine of Aragon, the daughter of Ferdinand and Isabella of Spain. Their marriage had cemented a close relationship between the kings of England and Spain, but by the mid-1520s Henry was becoming alarmed at the increasing power of the Spanish monarchy, fueled in part by New World treasure. Henry was also disappointed that Catherine had failed to give birth to a male heir; of their six children, only their daughter, Mary, survived infancy. Furthermore, Henry had become enamored of a young woman named Anne Boleyn and in 1527 he asked the pope to annul his marriage to Catherine so that he could marry Anne. The pope, who happened to be Catherine's relative, showed little inclination to grant Henry's request.

When Henry assembled Parliament in 1532, the members presented him with a long list of grievances against the Catholic Church. The grievances directly challenged the pope's supremacy by stipulating that the king must approve any religious legislation promulgated by the pope or the church hierarchy. This threat did not budge the pope from his refusal to annul Henry's marriage. In 1533, with Parliament's blessing, Henry had his marriage to Catherine annulled by his own nominee for archbishop of Canterbury, the top official in the English church, and secretly married Anne Boleyn—who was already pregnant with their daughter, Elizabeth. He was quickly excommunicated by the pope.

In 1534, Henry completed the break with Rome and formally initiated the English Reformation. At his insistence, Parliament passed the Act of Supremacy, which outlawed the Catholic Church and proclaimed the king "the only supreme head on earth of the Church of England." The vast properties of the Catholic Church in England were now the king's, as was the privilege of appointing bishops and other members of the governing hierarchy of the church. But Henry had no desire to restructure or reform the church. He wanted to control the church, not change it. Protestant doctrines advocated by Martin Luther and his followers held no attraction for him. In almost all matters of theology and religious practice, Henry remained an orthodox Catholic.

In the short run, the English Reformation allowed Henry VIII to achieve his political goal of bringing the church under the dominion of the monarchy. In the long run, however, the English Reformation brought to England the political and religious turmoil that Henry had hoped to avoid. For more than a century after 1534, English politics revolved around the question of the extent and character of the English Reformation. Henry himself sought no more than a halfway Reformation. Many English Catholics wanted no Reformation at all; they hoped to return the Church of England to the pope and to maintain Catholic doctrines and ceremonies. But many other English people insisted on a genuine, thoroughgoing Reformation; these people came to be called Puritans.

During the sixteenth century, Puritanism was less an organized movement than a set of ideas and religious principles that appealed strongly to many dissenting members of the Church of England. Puritans adhered to the doctrines of Protestantism developed by Luther and others on the European continent. They sought to purify the Church of England by eliminating what they considered the offensive features of Catholicism. For example, they demanded that the church hierarchy be abolished and that ordinary Christians be given greater control over religious life. They called for a reformed clergy composed of educated and moral men dedicated to the spiritual life of their parishioners. Many Puritans also believed that ministers should be appointed by their congregations. Puritans wanted to eliminate the ceremonies and displays of Catholic worship. They emphasized an individual's personal relationship with God developed through Bible study, prayer, and introspection. They also believed that the sermons of well-trained ministers could help them understand the Bible. They insisted that religious faith should have a powerful influence on the daily lives of individual Christians, disciplining them to think and act according to God's biblical commandments. Although there were many varieties and degrees of Puritanism, all Puritans shared a desire to carry the Reformation to its logical Protestant conclusion.

In the short run, the English Reformation allowed Henry VIII to achieve his political goal of bringing the church under the dominion of the monarchy. In the long run, however, the English Reformation brought to England the political and religious turmoil that Henry had hoped to avoid.

When Henry VIII died in 1547, the advisers of the new king, Edward VI—Henry's nine-year-old son by his third wife, Jane Seymour—initiated religious reforms that moved in a Protestant direction. The tide of reform reversed in 1553 when Edward died and was succeeded by Mary I, the daughter of Henry and Catherine of Aragon. Mary had remained a steadfast Catholic, and shortly after she became queen, she married Europe's most powerful guardian of orthodoxy, Philip II of Spain. Mary attempted to turn back the clock of the English Reformation to a pre-Reformation Catholic Church. She outlawed Protestantism and persecuted those who refused to conform, sentencing almost three hundred to burn at the stake.

The tide turned again in 1558 when Mary died and was succeeded by Elizabeth I, the daughter of Henry and Anne Boleyn. Elizabeth tried to consolidate the English Reformation midway between the extremes of Catholicism and Puritanism. She legalized Protestantism, reaffirmed the breach with Rome, and asserted her control over the Church of England. Like her father, she was less concerned with theology than with politics. Above all, she desired a church that would strengthen the monarchy and the nation. Late in the sixteenth century, the threat from Catholic Spain made Protestantism patriotic in England. By the time Elizabeth died in 1603, many people in England looked on Protestantism as a defining feature of national identity.

Shortly after Elizabeth's successor, James I, came to the throne, English Puritans petitioned for further reform of the Church of England, or Anglican-

Church. The king authorized a new translation of the Bible, known ever since as the King James version. However, neither James I nor his son Charles I, who became king in 1625, were receptive to the ideas of Puritan reformers. Increasingly hostile to both Puritans and Parliament, James and Charles moved the Church of England away from Puritanism rather than toward it. They enforced conformity to the Church of England and punished dissenters, both ordinary Christians and ministers like Charles Chauncy. The monarchy's anti-Puritan policies made many English Puritans despair that they would be permitted to live and worship in peace. A few Puritans decided to remove themselves from the political and religious repressions they suffered in England. They sought a refuge where they could build a society in harmony with their beliefs.

Puritans and the Settlement of New England

The Puritan emigration to New England resulted from the religious and political turbulence created by the Reformation during the sixteenth century. Puritans who emigrated to Plymouth colony or the much larger Massachusetts Bay settlement aspired to escape the turmoil of England and to build a new, orderly society that conformed to God's plan for humankind. Their faith shaped the colonies they established in New England in virtually every way. Some New Englanders never were Puritans, and their numbers increased during the seventeenth century. Nonetheless, Puritanism remained the paramount influence in New England not only in religion but also in politics and community life.

The Pilgrims and Plymouth Colony

One of the earliest groups to emigrate, known subsequently as Pilgrims, left their homes in Scrooby, a village in northern England, and moved to Holland in 1608. They enjoyed the Dutch republic's toleration of Protestant dissenters, but by 1620 life in exile threatened to undermine the small Pilgrim community. William Bradford, a leading member of the group, recalled that "of all the sorrows most heavy to be borne, was that many of their children, by . . . the great licentiousness of youth in that country, and the manifold temptations of the place, were

drawn away by evil examples into extravagant and dangerous courses, getting the reins off their necks and departing from their parents." The Pilgrim elders looked for a way to protect their children's piety and to preserve their community. "The place they had thoughts on," Bradford wrote, "was some of those vast and unpeopled countries of America, which are fruitful and fit for habitation, being devoid of all civil inhabitants, where there are only savage and brutish men which range up and down, little otherwise than the wild beasts." The Pilgrims had confidence that if they were the only "civil inhabitants" of someplace in America, they could preserve their vision of an uncorrupted, godly society, a society that looked like a Puritan version of England, a new England.

The Pilgrims obtained permission to settle in the extensive lands granted to the Virginia Company. To finance their journey, they formed a joint stock company with London investors. The investors provided the capital; the Pilgrims, their labor and lives. The Pilgrims agreed to share all profits with the investors for seven years. Following months of delay in Holland and England, 102 prospective settlers finally boarded the *Mayflower* in August 1620. After eleven weeks at sea, all but one of them arrived at the outermost tip of Cape Cod, in present-day Massachusetts.

The Pilgrims realized immediately that they had landed far north of the Virginia grant and had no legal authority from the king to settle in the area. However, the long, stormy voyage and the wet, bitterly cold November weather gave the Pilgrims no choice. They had to find a place to stay in what Bradford called the "hideous and desolate wilderness." To help protect themselves from the wilderness they could see and the desolation they could imagine, the Pilgrims drew up the Mayflower Compact on the day they arrived. They agreed to "covenant and combine ourselves together into a civil Body Politick, for our better Ordering and Preservation." The signers (all men) agreed to enact and obey necessary and just laws. With this pact, the Pilgrims hoped to provide order and security as well as a claim to legitimacy until the king granted them legal rights.

Early in December, the Pilgrims chose to settle at Plymouth, a site recommended by a small bay and by abandoned fields that had been cleared by Patuxet Indians, who had been decimated by an epidemic in 1617. The Pilgrims exercised their self-proclaimed political authority by electing William

PLYMOUTH FORT AND MEETINGHOUSE

This building is a careful historical reconstruction of a fort built by the Plymouth settlers in 1622, shortly after hearing of Powhatan's uprising against English colonists in Virginia (discussed in chapter 3). It is adapted from the traditional design of a seventeenth-century granary, but the ports lining the second story are not for stacking sheaves of grain but for firing on attacking Indians or on hostile Spaniards or Frenchmen. In fact, no attack ever came. The Pilgrims nonetheless made good use of the fort as a meetinghouse. Sermons, prayers, and worldly testimony—not cannon—echoed through the fort. Colonists gathered on the first floor for church services and court sessions. The building evokes the Plymouth colonists' military vulnerability and religious security.

Courtesy of Plimoth Plantation, Inc., Plymouth, MA USA/Ted Curtin.

Bradford as their governor, a position he held almost continuously until his death in 1657. That first winter "was most sad and lamentable," Bradford wrote later. "In two or three months' time half of [our] company [including Bradford's wife] died . . . being the depth of winter, and wanting houses and other comforts [and] being infected with scurvy and other diseases."

Having succeeded in founding a small Puritan haven from the religious corruptions of England and the secular temptations of Holland, the Pilgrims saw their colony as an example to the world.

In the spring, Indians rescued the floundering Plymouth settlement. First Samoset, then Squanto —both of whom had learned English from fishermen and sailors who had visited the region— befriended the settlers. Samoset arranged for the Pilgrims to meet and establish good relations with Massasoit, the chief of the Wampanoags, whose territory included Plymouth. Squanto, Bradford recalled, "was their interpreter and was a special instrument sent of God for their good beyond their expectation. He directed them how to set their corn, where to take fish, and to procure other commodities, and was also their pilot to bring them to unknown places." With Squanto's help and their own hard labor, the Pilgrims managed to store enough food to guarantee their survival through the coming winter, an occasion they celebrated in the fall of 1621 with a thanksgiving feast attended by Massasoit and many of his warriors. Despite the celebration, the colony's status remained precarious. Only seven dwellings had been erected that first year, half the original colonists were dead, and a new group of thirty-six threadbare, sickly settlers arrived in November 1621, requiring the colony to adopt stringent food rationing.

The Plymouth colony struggled to survive. The colonists quarreled with their London investors, who became frustrated and abusive when the colony failed to produce the expected profits. Additional settlers arrived periodically and the colony's population slowly grew to about four hundred. By 1630, Plymouth had become a permanent settlement, and the Pilgrims lived quietly and simply. They coexisted in relative peace with the Indians by using diplomacy and cash payments to Massasoit when settlers gradually encroached on Wampanoag territory.

Having succeeded in founding a small Puritan haven from the religious corruptions of England and the secular temptations of Holland, the Pilgrims saw their colony as an example to the world. "As one small candle may light a thousand," Bradford wrote, "so the light here kindled hath shone unto many, yea in some sort to our whole nation." But Plymouth's beacon of light did not attract many other English Puritans. The Pilgrims' desire to separate themselves from the Church of England—a heresy known as separatism and punished severely in England—destined Plymouth to become a backwater in seventeenth-century New England. That did not alarm the Pilgrims. They had given up on reforming the English church and wanted simply to live their lives as they saw fit.

The Founding of Massachusetts Bay Colony

During the 1620s, most English Puritans considered the American wilderness more ominous than the mounting religious and political unrest in England. But in 1629, King Charles I dissolved Parliament—where Puritans were well represented—and appointed the aggressive anti-Puritan William Laud as bishop of London (and later archbishop of Canterbury). Many Puritans despaired about continuing to defend their faith in England and began to make plans to emigrate. Some left for Europe, others for the West Indies. The largest number set out for New England.

In 1629, shortly before the dissolution of Parliament, a group of Puritan merchants and country gentlemen obtained a royal charter for the Massachusetts Bay Company. The charter provided the usual privileges granted to joint stock companies. It granted land for colonization from sea to sea, including the present-day states of Massachusetts, New Hampshire, Vermont, and Maine and upstate New York. The charter also bestowed the right to trade in such native commodities as furs, fish, and timber. In addition, the charter contained a unique provision that allowed the government of the company to be located in the colony rather than in England. Exactly how the Massachusetts Bay Company slipped this innovation past the king's advisers remains unknown. But the Puritans understood its significance. With royal permission to transfer the company's government to the colony, the Puritans had a golden opportunity to put the Atlantic between themselves and the hostile rule of King Charles and Bishop Laud. They could exchange their position as a harassed minority in England for self-government in Massachusetts—which, in practice, meant Puritan government.

To lead the emigrants, the stockholders of the Massachusetts Bay Company elected John Winthrop to serve as governor. Like many other English Puritans, Winthrop came from the rural gentry. He owned Groton Manor, a handsome estate composed primarily of land that Henry VIII had confiscated from a Catholic monastery and sold for a bargain price to Winthrop's grandfather. A prosperous and respected lawyer, Winthrop had much to lose. He thought long and hard before deciding to leave the comforts of his estate and risk the perils of founding a settlement in the New World. A deliberate man, he carefully listed the reasons that persuaded him, and presumably his fellow Puritans, to take the risk.

In England, things were not as they should be. "This land grows weary of her inhabitants," Winthrop wrote, "so as man who is the most precious of all creatures is here more vile and base than the earth we tread upon, and of less price among us than a horse or a sheep." Children, servants, and neighbors, "if things were right," should "be the chiefest earthly blessing"; instead, "it is come to pass that . . . especially if they be poor, [they] are counted the greatest burden." Wealthy men, Winthrop observed, indulge in the "height of intemperance" until "no man's estate almost will suffice to keep sail with his equals, and he who fails . . . must live in scorn and contempt." Men who succeed carry on their business in a "deceitful and unrighteous" manner, while "it is almost impossible for a good and upright man to maintain his charge and live comfortably." With these examples constantly before them, "most children (even the best wits and fairest hopes) are perverted, corrupted and utterly overthrown." The wickedness of English society invited God's wrath, especially since most churches did little to set things right and much to make things worse. "Who knows," Winthrop asked, "but that God hath provided . . . [New England] to be a refuge for many whom he means to save out of the general calamity?"

Hundreds of Puritans concluded that, indeed, there was no better work than building churches in the wilderness, where, according to Winthrop, the Lord "will provide a shelter and hiding place for us and ours." They settled their affairs at home and collected the supplies necessary for starting a new life in America. Winthrop assembled the largest fleet ever to embark for an English colony. In March 1630, eleven ships crammed with seven hundred (mostly Puritan) passengers and assorted livestock, tools, and food sailed for Massachusetts; six more ships and another five hundred emigrants followed a few months later.

Winthrop's flagship, the *Arbella*, and three others arrived in Massachusetts Bay in early June, and the other ships straggled in soon afterward. A precursor of the Massachusetts Bay Company had established a small fishing and trading settlement at Salem in 1628, but the new arrivals looked elsewhere for a suitable settlement site. They did not want to be associated with the struggling separatist colony of Pilgrims at Plymouth. Instead, Winthrop and a small group moved to the peninsula that became Boston, while other settlers clustered at promising locations nearby.

In a sermon to his companions aboard the *Arbella* while they were still at sea—probably the most famous sermon in American history—Winthrop explained the cosmic significance of their journey. The Puritans had "entered into a covenant" with God to "work out our salvation under the power and purity of his holy ordinances," Winthrop proclaimed. This sanctified agreement with God meant that "the Lord will [not] bear with such failings at our hands as he doth from those among whom we have lived" in England. Having entered a covenant with the Puritans, God "looks to have it observed in every article," Winthrop warned. The Puritans had to make "extraordinary" efforts to "bring into familiar and constant practice" religious principles that most people in England merely preached. To do so, the Puritans had to subordinate their individual interests to the common good. "We must be knit together in this work as one man," Winthrop declared. "We must delight in each other, make others' conditions our own, rejoice together, mourn together, labor and suffer together, always having before our eyes . . . our community as members of the same body." To do otherwise discredited God in the eyes of humankind, jeopardized his plan for the world,

ENGLISH GENTLEMAN
This portrait of an English gentleman, painted a few years before the Puritan migration to New England, reveals the appearance considered the height of fashion among wealthy English men and women but condemned by Puritans as a vain, sinful focus on outward appearance. From head to toe, this clothing displayed intricate workmanship and artfully composed embellishment, all designed—Puritans declared—to win approving glances from other humans rather than from the Almighty.
By Courtesy of National Portrait Gallery, London.

and would surely cause him to "break out in wrath against us." The stakes could not be higher, Winthrop told the emigrants surrounding him on the deck of the *Arbella* somewhere in the North Atlantic. "We must consider that we shall be as a city upon a hill. The eyes of all people are upon us."

The whole world was not watching the settlement at Massachusetts Bay, of course. Nonetheless, that belief shaped seventeenth-century New England as profoundly as tobacco shaped the Chesapeake. The vision of a city on a hill announced the Puritans' fierce determination to keep their covenant and live according to God's laws, unlike the backsliders, trimmers, and compromisers who accommodated to the Church of England. The Puritans believed that God had one perfect plan, and they resolved to do their best to discover it through prayer, Bible study, and church attendance. Because they knew that their understanding of God's plan was imperfect, they constantly looked for evidence of God's judgment of their behavior. Surely, the Puritans reasoned, if they built a new society according to God's plan, he would be pleased and would favor them with peace, plenty, and good fortune. If, instead, the colonists experienced strife, shortage, or disaster, that might mean that God was punishing them for departing from his plan and warning them to make the necessary corrections. Or it could mean that Satan was alarmed that God's plan was being so closely followed and that he was fighting back by subjecting the Puritans to an extra dose of evil. The Puritans' determination to adhere strictly to God's plan charged nearly every feature of life in seventeenth-century New England with a distinctive, high-voltage piety.

The new colonists, as Winthrop's son John wrote later, had "all things to do, as in the beginning of the world." At first, the Puritans' high aspirations confronted the rigors of survival in the Massachusetts environment. Unlike the early Chesapeake settlers, the first Massachusetts Bay colonists encountered few Indians because the local population had been almost exterminated by an epidemic more than a decade earlier. Still, the colonists had more than enough to do building shelters, planting crops, and trying to harvest them before the bitter New England winter set in. As in the Chesapeake, the colonists fell victim to deadly ailments. More than two hundred settlers died during the first year, including one of Winthrop's sons and eleven of his servants. About the same number decided by the spring of 1631 that they had had enough and returned to England aboard the first outbound ship. But Winthrop remained confident. "I like so well to be heer," he wrote his wife, "as I doe not repent my comminge. . . . I would not have altered my course, though I had forseene all these Afflictions."

Winthrop's confidence proved more infectious than the discouraging news the returning colonists took back to England. Each year from 1630 to 1640, ship after ship followed in the wake of Winthrop's fleet. In all, more than twenty thousand new settlers came, their eyes fixed on the Puritans' city on a hill. These people differed from the thousands of other English settlers during the same years whose gaze was drawn instead to the high-risk lottery of the Chesapeake tobacco economy.

SEAL OF MASSACHUSETTS BAY COLONY
In 1629, the Massachusetts Bay Company designed this seal depicting an Indian man inviting English settlers to "Come Over and Help Us." Of course, such an invitation was never issued. Instead, the seal attempted to lend an aura of altruism to the Massachusetts Bay Company's colonization efforts. In English eyes, the Indian man obviously needed help. The only signs that he was more civilized than the pine trees flanking him were his girdle of leaves, his bow and arrow, and his miraculous use of English. In reality, colonists in Massachusetts and elsewhere were far less interested in helping Indians than in helping themselves. For the most part, that suited Indians just fine, since they did not want the colonists' "help."
Courtesy of Massachusetts Archives.

English Puritans continued to come to New England for the same reasons that had attracted Winthrop. The exact number of Puritans among the settlers cannot be determined, but there is no doubt that ships bound for Massachusetts were as full of Puritans as vessels headed toward Virginia were of indentured servants. Often, when the Anglican Church cracked down on a Puritan minister in England, he and all those in his flock who could take the risk uprooted and moved together to New England. Fragments of Puritan congregations, even of villages, moved from one side of the Atlantic to the other. By 1640, New England had one of the highest ratios of preachers to population in all of Christendom: 129 preachers had settled in New England, among them such eminences of Puritanism as John Cotton, Richard Mather, Thomas Shepard, and Thomas Hooker. But the ratio was still not high enough to provide a trained minister for every band of settlers, causing a colonist to complain that ordinary "fellowes which keepe hogges all weeke preach on the Saboth." That preachers with such unpromising credentials drew an audience indicated the colonists' hunger for religious instruction.

The vision of a city on a hill announced the Puritans' fierce determination to keep their covenant and live according to God's laws, unlike the backsliders, trimmers, and compromisers who accommodated to the Church of England.

The occupations of the New England immigrants reflected the social origins of English Puritans. On the whole, the immigrants came from the middle ranks of English society. Few representatives of the nobility or the gentry came to Massachusetts; Winthrop was an exception. Likewise, few common laborers arrived in New England. Instead, the vast majority of immigrants were either farmers or tradesmen, including carpenters, tailors, textile workers, and many others. Servants, whose numbers dominated the Chesapeake settlers, accounted for only about a fifth of those headed for New England. Most of the New England immigrants had paid their way to Massachusetts, even though the journey often took their life savings. To such people, reports like the one Winthrop sent his son must have been encouraging: "Here is as good land as I have seen there [in England], but none so bad as there. Here is sweet air, fair rivers, and plenty of springs, and the water better than in England. Here can be no want of anything to those who bring means to raise out of the earth and sea."

Family ties stitched one immigrant to another. In contrast to the Chesapeake—where immigrant women and children were nearly as rare as atheists in Boston—immigrants to New England usually arrived as part of a family. In fact, more Puritans came with family members than did any other group of immigrants in all of American history. The ship that left Weymouth, England, in 1635 carrying 106 passengers included the minister Joseph Hull and his fellow Puritans and neighbors, 98 of whom belonged to one of the 14 families aboard, typically a husband, wife, and children, sometimes accompanied by a servant or two. In Hull's group, one out of five passengers was an adult woman; two out of five were youngsters; together, women and children made up a solid majority.

These families were not democracies, of course. Fathers and husbands who headed the immigrant families expected to rule them. As Winthrop reminded the first settlers in his *Arbella* sermon, God "hath so disposed of the condition of mankind, as in all times some must be rich, some poor, some high and eminent in power and dignity, others mean and in subjection." All the immigrants understood that each father and husband—regardless of his wealth or status—expected to be considered "high and eminent" by his wife and children. Each family was a "little commonwealth" that mirrored the hierarchy among all God's creatures, Puritans believed. Just as humankind was subordinate to God, so young people were to be subordinate to their elders, children to their parents, and wives to their husbands. The immigrants' family ties reinforced their religious beliefs with an effective and universally understood form of government. While immigrants to the Chesapeake were disciplined mostly by the coercions of servitude and the caprices of the tobacco market, immigrants to New England entered a social order defined by the interlocking institutions of family, church, and community.

The Evolution of New England Society

The New England colonists did not scatter isolated farmsteads across the land like their counterparts in the Chesapeake. Instead, they settled in small towns

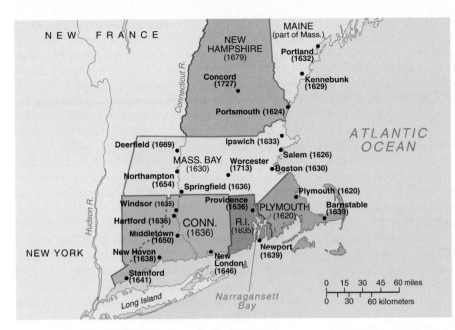

MAP 4.1
New England Colonies in the Seventeenth Century
New Englanders spread across the landscape town by town during the seventeenth century. (For the sake of legibility, only a few of the more important towns are shown on the map.) Why were towns so much more important in seventeenth-century New England than in the Chesapeake?

located either on the coast or on a river, ensuring good access to water. Massachusetts Bay colonists founded six towns in 1630 and nearly two dozen within the first decade, including several quite remote from Boston in present-day New Hampshire, Connecticut, and Rhode Island. During the entire seventeenth century, they established 133 towns. Each town had one or more churches organized by Puritan believers who had entered a covenant with God and with each other to follow God's orders. Church members' fervent piety, buttressed by the institutions of local government, enforced remarkable religious and social conformity in the small New England settlements. But the tensions within the Puritan faith and changes in New England communities during the seventeenth century splintered Puritan orthodoxy and weakened Puritan zeal. Nonetheless, by the end of the seventeenth century, Puritanism maintained a distinctive and unmistakable influence in New England.

Church, Covenant, and Conformity

At the center of each Puritan community stood the church. Often the building occupied literally the geographic center of the town; if it was not at the center, it was within walking distance of the town's residents. These buildings did not look like churches in seventeenth-century England or like the churches in New England towns today. Typically, they were unadorned wooden structures housing a simple

meeting room with wooden benches for fifty or one hundred or more. The buildings were also used for many other gatherings, such as courts and town meetings. They had no stained glass, no organs, not even any heat. At the front stood a table and a lectern or an elevated pulpit. To our eyes, the building would appear to be a plain lecture hall.

That was precisely what the Puritans intended. God's word—not music or art—was the focus of their religious services. Nothing about the meeting room should interfere with the congregation's concentration on the sermon. And it took concentration. Each Sunday, ministers preached for five or six hours, interrupted by a noontime break. A minister's prayer alone often lasted an hour. The elders (respected leaders of the congregation) sat with their backs to the preacher while they monitored the congregation's reception of his sermon. During the frigid New England winter, the people's fingers, toes, and cheeks grew numb while the communion bread and baptismal water froze solid. Whatever the weather, each town required every inhabitant to attend sermons on Sundays and usually on Thursdays too. They came, and they listened. On cold days, they could almost see God's word as the preacher's breath turned white in the icy air.

To the Puritans, however, the church was not the building where the services were held. Instead, the church was composed of men and women who had entered a solemn covenant with each other and with God. Winthrop and three other men had signed the original covenant of the first Boston church, agreeing to "Promisse, and bind our selves, to walke in all our wayes according to the Rule of the Gospell, and in all sincere Conformity to His holy Ordinaunces, and in mutuall love, and respect to each other, so neere as God shall give us grace." Church membership was restricted to men and women who entered such a covenant. A new member not only had to agree to the terms of the covenant but also had to persuade existing members that she or he had fully experienced conversion. The fervent Puritans among the early colonists, whose faith had been tempered by persecution in England and by the journey to Massachusetts, had little difficulty meeting the test of covenant membership. By 1633, the Boston church had added 132 names to the four original subscribers to the covenant; by 1635, that covenant had more than 250 members.

Church members' fervent piety, buttressed by the institutions of local government, enforced remarkable religious and social conformity in the small New England settlements.

Puritan views on church membership derived from John Calvin, the Protestant theologian of sixteenth-century Geneva, Switzerland, who insisted that Christians discipline their worldly behavior to conform strictly to their religious ideas. Calvin stressed the doctrine of predestination, which held that before the creation of the world, God chose a few human beings to receive salvation. These fortunate individuals—the "elect" or "invisible saints" —were predestined for eternal life. But only God knew who they were. Each person had no way to know for certain whether she or he was bound for heaven with the few or for Hades with the many. Nothing a person did could change God's inscrutable choice.

Puritans believed that if one were among the elect, one would surely act like it. To a certain extent, one's sainthood would become visible in one's behavior, especially if one were privileged to know God's Word as revealed in the Bible. Humans' inherent and overpowering tendency to sin made saintly behavior extremely difficult to maintain. Therefore, Puritans believed, one's ability to live a rigorously and consistently godly life—and overcome the constant temptations to sin—was proba-

bly a sign, a hint, that one might be among the elect. However, the connection between sainthood and saintly behavior was far from firm. Some members of the elect, for example, had never heard God's Word and did not know how to manifest their sainthood in their behavior. One reason the Puritans required all town residents to attend church services was to enlighten invisible saints who remained ignorant of God's Truth. Other people might act as if they were saints, yet in fact not be one of the chosen few. God gave no guarantee that pious behavior was a sign of salvation; the identity of the invisible saints remained forever unknowable. But the Puritans thought that passing the demanding test of membership in one of their churches was a promising clue that one was in fact among God's elect. Puritan church members considered it quite possible that they were visible saints, that is, members of God's invisible elect who could be identified by their highly visible godly behavior.

Members of Puritan churches ardently hoped that they were visible saints and tried to act that way. Their covenant bound them to help each other attain this lofty goal. Their covenant also required them to discipline the entire community by saintly standards. Church members kept an eye on the behavior of everybody in town. Infractions of morality, order, or propriety were reported to the elders, who summoned the wayward to a church inquiry. The Dorchester church, for example, examined Robert Spur for his offense of "giving entertainment in his house [to] loose and vain persons," Mrs. Clark for "her reproachful and slanderous tongue," and Samuel Blake for "his sin of fornication before marriage." Failure to attend sermons, drunkenness, oath swearing, disobedience to superiors, covetousness—all these and more could cause a person to be called before the elders and, if found guilty, punished. Hardly anything escaped the gaze of righteous scrutiny. When a church member chided William Hibben for "calling one of my Brethren 'sir' instead of 'brother,'" Hibben asked the Boston church to forgive him for using "an expression unsuitable for the covenant I am in." The watchfulness that set the tone of life in Puritan communities is suggested by a minister's note that "the church was satisfied with Mrs. Carlton as to the weight of her butter." By saintly surveillance of everything, including Mrs. Carlton's butter, church members enforced a remarkable degree of righteous conformity in Puritan communities.

Like churches, towns chose their residents with care and refused to accept individuals who dissented from Puritan orthodoxy. The founders of Dedham, for example, covenanted that "we shall by all means labor to keep off from us all such as are contrary minded, and receive only such unto us as may be probably of one heart with us." People who refused to conform were advised to leave town; if they did not take the advice, they were forced to leave.

THE
World turn'd upside down:
OR,
A briefe defcription of the ridiculous Fafhions of thefe diftracted Times.

By T.J. a well-willer to King, Parliament and Kingdom.

London : Printed for *John Smith*. 1647.

THE PURITAN CHALLENGE TO THE STATUS QUO
This title page of The World Turn'd Upside Down *satirizes the Puritan notion that the contemporary world was deeply flawed. Printed in London in 1647, the pamphlet refers to the "distracted Times" of the Puritan Revolution in England. The drawing ridicules criticisms of English society that were also common among New England Puritans. The drawing shows at least a dozen examples of the conventional world of seventeenth-century England turned upside down. Can you identify them? Puritans, of course, would claim that the drawing had it wrong, that instead the conventional world turned God's order upside down. How might the drawing have been different if a devout Puritan had drawn it?*
British Library.

Despite their centrality, churches had no direct role in the civil government of New England communities. The Puritans did not want to emulate the Church of England, which they considered a puppet of the king rather than an independent church that served the Lord. They were determined to insulate New England churches from the contaminating influence of the civil state and its merely human laws. Although ministers were the most highly respected figures in New England towns, they were prohibited from holding government office. The ban guaranteed that Puritan ministers, unlike Bishop Laud, answered only to the laws of God.

Although they deplored the influence of the English government on the Anglican Church, the Puritans had no qualms whatsoever about their own churches influencing New England governments. Following Calvin, they expected the civil government to be subordinate to the church. As John Cotton said, "it is better that the commonwealth be fashioned to the setting forth of God's house, which is His church, than to accommodate the church in the civil state." Like Calvin, the Puritans believed that the government should support and reinforce God's laws.

In England, the Anglican Church had censured Charles Chauncy for his "strange opinion" that the Sabbath began at sunset on Saturday evening. In New England, Chauncy's strange opinion was the rule, except for those who believed that the Sabbath began even earlier. Winthrop, for example, presumed that the Sabbath started about three o'clock Saturday afternoon. The question was no mere theoretical concern. After the Sabbath began, townsfolk could not work, play, or travel. Fines for Sabbath breaking were issued for such transgressions as playing a flute, smoking a pipe, and visiting neighbors. When two young boys fell through the ice of a Cambridge pond and drowned, Cotton Mather, the Puritan minister, concluded that they had become victims of God's punishment for ice skating on the Sabbath.

Besides strict observance of the Sabbath, the Puritans mandated other purifications of what they considered corrupt English practices. They refused to celebrate either Christmas or Easter. They changed the names of the months from such pagan names as January and February to simple numerals. They outlawed religious wedding ceremonies; couples were married by a magistrate in a civil ceremony—the first Massachusetts wedding to be performed by a minister did not occur until 1686. They prohibited elaborate, colorful clothing, censuring such fineries as lace trim, short sleeves ("whereby the nakedness of the arm may be discovered"), and long hair. Wearing a wig was forbidden since, as one minister explained, "for a man to be discontented with his own hair which God made for him and gave to him, and to covet another's hair which God made for another and gave to another . . . is a sin of the same kind with coveting our neighbor's house or his wife." Cards, dice, shuffleboard, and other games of chance were banned, as were music and dancing. The distinguished minister Increase Mather explained that "Dancing, or Musick, or Singing are [not] in themselves sinful," but he insisted that "Mixt or Promiscuous Dancing . . . of Men and Women" could not be tolerated since "the unchaste Touches and Gesticulations used by Dancers have a palpable tendency to that which is evil." On special occasions, Puritans proclaimed days of fasting and humiliation, which, as one preacher boasted, amounted to "so many Sabbaths more." As much as possible, the Puritans brought public life into conformity with their view of God's law.

Government by Puritans for Puritanism

It is only a slight exaggeration to say that seventeenth-century New England was governed by Puritans for Puritanism. The charter of the Massachusetts Bay Company empowered the company's stockholders (known as freemen) to meet and make the laws to govern the company's affairs. The colonists transformed this arrangement for running a joint stock company into a structure for governing the colony. In 1631, the General Court expanded the small number of original stockholders by admitting almost 120 settlers to the status of freemen. At the same time, the court ruled that freemen must be male church members. Only freemen had the right to vote for governor, deputy governor, and other colonial officials. In addition, all the freemen met together as the General Court to enact laws for the colony. In the first decades of settlement, about half of the adult men in each town became freemen. When new settlers continued to be admitted as freemen, the number became too large to meet conveniently. In 1634, the freemen in each town agreed to send two deputies to the General Court to act as the colony's legislative assembly.

By restricting freemanship to male church members, the General Court hoped to assure that godly men would decide government policies. Even when church membership was not required, as in

Connecticut—which restricted freemanship to those who owned property worth £30 sterling—almost all freemen were church members anyway. Men had to apply to the General Court to gain the rights of freemen, and the court carefully weighed each man's qualifications. The court described one successful applicant for freemanship as a "settled inhabitant . . . orthodox in religion [and] of pious and laudable conversation."

New England town meetings routinely practiced a level of popular participation in political life that was unprecedented elsewhere during the seventeenth century.

Some male church members never applied for freemanship, evidently to avoid such troublesome duties as attending meetings, serving on juries, and mustering with the militia. As the decades passed, fewer men became church members and the growing population of New England made the duties of freemen more time-consuming, causing the number of freemen to shrink to roughly one in three adult men by the end of the seventeenth century.

All other men were classified as "inhabitants," and they had the right to vote, hold office, and participate fully in town government. A "town meeting," composed of all the town's inhabitants and freemen, chose the selectmen and other officials who administered local affairs. New England town meetings routinely practiced a level of popular participation in political life that was unprecedented elsewhere during the seventeenth century. Almost every adult man could speak out in town meetings and fortify his voice with a vote. However, town meetings were far from democratic. All women—even church members—were prohibited from voting, and towns did not permit "contrary-minded" men to become or remain inhabitants. New England towns were composed of people who agreed on a broad range of fundamentals, Puritan doctrine above all else. Of course, town meetings wrangled from time to time; Dorchester, for example, took steps to prevent "the disorderly jarring of our meetings, and the intemperate clashings, and hasty, undigested, and rash votes" that had "been grievous and justly offensive unto many." Despite such disagreements, widespread political participation in town meetings reinforced conformity to Puritan ideals.

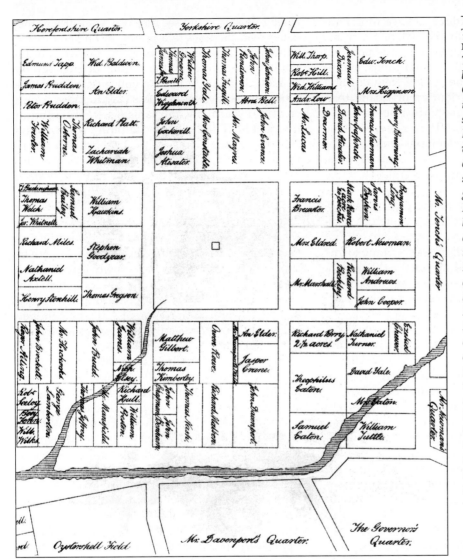

The following text appears within the map image:

Herefordshire Quarter.   Yorkshire Quarter.

Edmund Tapp.   Wid. Baldwin.
James Prudden.   An Elder.
Peter Prudden.
William Fowler.   Thomas Osborne.   Richard Platt.   Zachariah Whitman.

Thomas Fugill.   Thomas Yale.   Thomas Welch.   John Brockett.
John Budd.   Abra. Bell.
John Cockerill.   Mr. Mansel.
Joshua Atwater.   Mr. Gibbard.   John Evance.

Will. Thorp.   Jeremiah Dixon.   Edw. Tench.
Rob. Hill.
Wid. Williams.   Mrs. Higginson.
Andr. Low.
Mr. Lucas.   Demor.   Francis Newman.   John Caffinch.   David Atwater.   Henry Browning.

T. Buckingham   Samuel Bayley.   William Hawkins.
Thomas Welch.
Jer. Whitnell.
Richard Miles.   Stephen Goodyear.
Nathaniel Axtell.
Henry Stonhill.   Thomas Gregson.

Francis Brewster.   Mark Pierce   George King.   John Punderson.   Benjamin Ling.
Mrs. Eldred.   Robert Newman.
Mr. Marshall.   Richard Beckley.   William Andrews.
John Cooper.

Roger Alling.   John Brockett.   Mr. Nicholas.   John Budd.   William Ives.   Nich. Elsey.   Richard Hull.   George Lamberton.   Thomas Jeffry.   William Preston.   Thomas Fugill.
Rob. Seeley.
Benj. Fenn.
Will. Wilkes.

Matthew Gilbert.   Owen Rowe.   An Elder.   Jasper Crane.
Thomas Kimberley.   Mr. Newman.   John Davenport.   Thomas Nash.

Richard Perry 2½ acres.   Nathaniel Turner.   Ezekiel Cheever.
David Yale.
Theophilus Eaton.   Mr. Eaton.
Samuel Eaton.   William Tuttle.

Mr. Jenck's Quarter.

Mr. Newman Quarter.

Oystershell Field.   Mr. Davenport's Quarter.   The Governor's Quarter.

TOWN PLAN OF NEW HAVEN

This drawing shows the distribution of land in New Haven, Connecticut, in 1641. Although the church was the spiritual center of each New England town, New Haven was unusual in having the church (indicated by the small square) located literally at the geographical center. New Haven was founded in 1638 by the wealthy Puritan merchant Theophilus Eaton and the Puritan minister John Davenport. The town plan contains clear evidence of their leadership. Can you locate it? In New Haven as in other New England towns, land was distributed according to status and need. The town plan therefore provides a revealing map of New Haven's social structure. Try to identify the lots of the leading families and of the lesser folk. What does the town plan suggest about the character of New Haven society?

New York Public Library.

One of the most important functions of town government was distributing land among the inhabitants. Under the charter of the Massachusetts Bay Company, the General Court controlled unsettled land. Settlers who desired to establish a new town entered a covenant and petitioned the General Court for a grant of land. The court granted to suitably pious petitioners town sites that ranged from 40 up to 250 square miles. The court did not allow settlement until the Indians who inhabited a grant agreed to relinquish their claim to the land, usually in exchange for various manufactured goods, especially iron tools and utensils. In a typical transaction, William Pynchon purchased the site of Springfield, Massachusetts, from the Agawam Indians for "eighteen fathams [arm's lengths] of

Wampam, eighteen coates, 18 hatchets, 18 hoes, [and] 18 knives."

Having established their claim, the town founders would apportion the granted land among themselves and any newcomers they permitted to join them. Normally, each family received a house lot large enough for an adjacent garden as well as one or more strips of agricultural land on the perimeter of the town. Most of the house lots in a town were about the same size, between 1 and 5 acres. Agricultural land, however, was distributed according to the wealth and status of the inhabitants. Ministers and men who had contributed disproportionately to the purchase of the land from the Indians received the largest allocations, sometimes as much as 1,000 acres but usually much less. Common laborers received as little as 10 acres. Most families received more, typically 50, 100, or 150 acres. Although there was a considerable difference between the largest and smallest grants, most allocations clustered in the middle, giving New England a more homogeneous distribution of wealth than the Chesapeake. Towns usually distributed only a fraction of their total grant. They reserved some common land, which all inhabitants could use for grazing livestock and cutting wood, and saved the rest for new settlers and the descendants of the founders.

The details of land tenure and cultivation varied widely from town to town. As much as local conditions permitted, settlers adapted agricultural techniques they had used in England. Some towns enclosed fields; others used an open field system, which entailed greater cooperation in planting, cultivating, and harvesting the crops of wheat, oats, and barley.

Physically, towns were as different as the local terrain, sometimes meandering along a stream, other times rimming a bay or crisscrossing a meadow or rich valley. House lots were typically clustered in an inner core, surrounded by agricultural strips. Colonists walked from their houses to their fields and back again, with one or two trips a week to the meeting house for sermons and lectures and daily visits to neighbors. The physical layout of the towns encouraged settlers to look inward toward their neighbors, multiplying the opportunities for godly vigilance. Although the forest lay within a few hundred yards of every settler's house, most people considered it an alien environment dotted here and there with those oases of civilization, towns. The footpaths connecting one town with another were so rudimentary that even John Winthrop once got lost within a half mile of his house and spent a sleepless night in the forest, circling the light of his small campfire and singing psalms.

The Splintering of Puritanism

One voice singing psalms in the wilderness is a good metaphor for what the Puritans believed they should do in New England. And in large measure, they did it, especially for the first thirty or forty years. But almost from the beginning, Winthrop and other leaders discovered that Puritans sang with more than one voice. Puritans insisted that the Bible spelled out God's Way for humankind and that individual believers, with the guidance of an edu-

cated minister, could see that Way as clearly as they could read the lines of a psalm. In England, persecution as a dissenting minority unified Puritan voices in opposition to the Church of England. But in New England, different interpretations of the Bible, different views of God's Way, found voice and created disharmony. Puritanism's emphasis on individual Bible study led the faithful to discover not God's Way but God's Ways. Yet each Puritan remained convinced that God had only one Way. Puritan leaders interpreted dissent as an error caused either by a misguided believer or by the malevolent power of Satan. Whatever the cause, errors could not be tolerated. As one Puritan minister proclaimed, "God doth no where in his word tolerate Christian States, to give Tolerations to . . . adversaries of his Truth, if they have power in their hands to suppress them. The Scripture saith . . . there is no Truth but one." In New England, Puritan leaders had the power to suppress adversaries of their view of the Truth, even when the adversaries were themselves Puritans.

Among the immigrants who arrived in Massachusetts in 1630 was Roger Williams, a lively young minister who had trained at Cambridge University and who counted Winthrop and other Puritan elders among his friends. From the start, Williams needled the colony's leadership with his outspoken views that their church was fatally impure. He refused to accept the invitation to preach in Boston, since people who were not full church members were required to attend sermons. Such a policy "stinks in God's nostrils," Williams said. The only way to preserve the purity of the church was to exclude everyone but church members from sermons. Williams believed that the act of worship should be kept so utterly pure that even family prayers were sinful, unless all family members were visible saints (as they rarely were). Worse from the viewpoint of Winthrop and other Puritan leaders, Williams declared that the government of Massachusetts contaminated the purity of the church. He demanded that the state be kept completely separate from the church. For the church to rely in any way on the state to uphold religion—as it did, of course, in Massachusetts—defiled the church with the squalor of worldly affairs, Williams asserted. For these opinions and others, Massachusetts banished Williams in 1635. He moved to Narragansett Bay, where he established the town of Providence and helped found the colony of Rhode Island as a refuge for dissenters from Puritan orthodoxies. Williams's heresy carried one strain of Puritanism to a logical conclusion that challenged the legitimacy of the emerging Puritan order.

Another early immigrant pushed Puritan doctrines in a different direction. In 1634, Anne Hutchinson arrived in Massachusetts with her husband and their family. A brilliant woman, Hutchinson had received an excellent education from her father. The mother of fourteen children, she also served her neighbors as a skilled midwife. Most of all, she was an ardent Puritan, steeped in Scripture and absorbed by sermons, especially those of John Cotton. On board the ship to Massachusetts, Hutchinson often met with other immigrants to discuss the sermons of the minister who accompanied the group, whom Hutchinson considered second-rate. The meetings continued after the Hutchinsons settled into their home in Boston. At first, mostly women gathered at Hutchinson's home to hear her Thursday lectures on Cotton's most recent sermons. As the months passed, the meetings increased to twice a week and the crowds grew to sixty or eighty, including many of Boston's most prominent citizens, female and male.

The sermons of Hutchinson's favorite minister, John Cotton, emphasized that individuals could be saved only by God's grace in choosing them to be predestined members of the elect, a doctrine Cotton termed the "covenant of grace." Cotton contrasted this familiar Puritan tenet with the "covenant of works," the erroneous belief that one's behavior— one's works—could win God's favor and, ultimately, salvation. Belief in the covenant of works was a heresy known as Arminianism. One of the worst insults that could be leveled at a Puritan was to call her or him an Arminian; it accused the person of believing that the behavior of human beings could influence God's will. Cotton's sermons strongly hinted that many Puritans, even ministers, leaned toward Arminianism, and Anne Hutchinson agreed. It must have been easy to get that impression in the pious atmosphere of Massachusetts Bay. Hutchinson's lectures stressed that many of the leaders of the colony, under the delusion of a covenant of works, believed that their godly behavior moved them closer to heaven. Hutchinson, like Cotton, avowed that only God's gift of grace could do that. In effect, Hutchinson amplified Cotton's somewhat muted message that the leaders of the colony were repudiating the marrow of Puritan faith, and she did so without the protection of Cotton's status as a minister and a man.

The meetings at Hutchinson's alarmed her nearest neighbor, John Winthrop. He believed that Hutchinson was subverting the good order of the colony. Winthrop held conventional notions about the inferiority and necessary subordination of women: Women should stay in their place and listen to their husbands, not give lectures that both men and women find compelling. In 1637, Winthrop arranged to have formal charges brought against Hutchinson, and he confronted her in court as her chief accuser. Winthrop denounced Hutchinson's lectures as "not tolerable nor comely in the sight of God nor fitting for your sex." As the two squared off in court—Bible to Bible—he was no match for Hutchinson's learning, wit, and insight. Hutchinson gave far better than she got. She pointed to passages in the Bible that instructed women to meet and teach one another. When Winthrop claimed those Scriptures did not apply to her, she asked him, "Must I shew my name written therein?" Besides, she replied, if it is "not lawful for me to teach women . . . why do you call me to teach the court?" Outsmarted and off-balance, Winthrop pressed forward with the investigation, fishing for some heresy that he could pin on Hutchinson.

Winthrop and other elders referred to Hutchinson and her followers as "Antinomians," that is, people who opposed the law. Hutchinson's opponents charged that she believed that Christians could be saved by faith alone, that they did not need to act according to God's law in the Bible as interpreted by the colony's leaders. In her scriptural duel with Winthrop in court, Hutchinson nimbly defended herself against this accusation. Yes, she believed that men and women were saved by faith alone; but no, she did not deny the need to obey God's law. "The Lord hath let me see which was the clear ministry and which the wrong," she said. Finally, her interrogators cornered her. How could she tell which was which? "By an immediate revelation," she replied, "by the voice of [God's] own spirit to my soul." Here was the crime Winthrop had been searching for, the heresy of prophecy, the erroneous claim that God revealed his will directly to a believer instead of, as every good Puritan knew, exclusively through the Bible.

In 1638, the Boston church formally excommunicated Hutchinson. The minister decreed, "I doe cast you out and . . . deliver you up to Satan that you may learne no more to blaspheme to seduce and to lye. . . . I command you . . . as a Leper to withdraw your selfe out of the Congregation." Banished, Hutchinson and her family moved first to Rhode Island and then to Long Island, where she and her family, except for her ten-year-old daughter, were killed by Indians.

Hutchinson's admission of divine revelation was a departure from standard Puritan belief. Yet by directing believers to search for evidence of God's grace, Puritanism encouraged the faithful to listen for a whisper from God that they were among the elect. Puritanism was a volatile combination of rigid insistence on conformity to God's law and aching uncertainty about how to identify and act upon it. Despite the best efforts of Winthrop and other leaders to render God's instructions in no uncertain terms, Puritanism inspired believers to draw their own conclusions and stick to them. In this sense, Anne Hutchinson was more a product of Puritanism than a dissenter from it.

Such strains within Puritanism caused it to splinter repeatedly during the seventeenth century. The prominent minister Thomas Hooker, for example, clashed with Winthrop and Cotton over the composition of the church. Hooker argued that men and women who lived godly lives should be admitted to church membership, even if they had not experienced conversion. This question, like most others in New England, had both religious and political dimensions, since only church members could vote in Massachusetts. In 1636, Hooker led an exodus of more than eight hundred colonists from Massachusetts to the Connecticut River valley, where they founded Hartford and neighboring towns. In 1639, the towns adopted the Fundamental Orders of Connecticut, a quasi-constitution that could be altered by vote of the freemen, who did not have to be church members, although nearly all of them were.

Puritan churches divided and subdivided throughout the seventeenth century as acrimony developed over doctrine and church government. After Charles Chauncy came to New England, the colonists learned that he firmly believed that infants should be baptized by immersion rather than by mere sprinkling, a practice that—needless to say—alarmed parents; it did, however, ultimately earn him a safe appointment as president of Harvard College, which was founded in 1636. Other divisions occurred over questions of church government. Most churches followed the congregational practice, whereby individual congregations selected and dismissed ministers on their own. Some leaned toward a presbyterian structure, by which ministerial associations (or synods) set ecclesiastical policy

and influenced the selection of ministers by individual churches. Sometimes churches split over the appointment of a controversial minister. Sometimes families who had a long walk to the meeting house simply decided to form their own church nearer their houses. The schism of Puritan churches arose from the ambiguities and tensions within Puritan belief. As the colonies matured, other tensions developed as well.

Growth, Change, and Controversy

In England, Puritans led a parliamentary challenge to royal authority. King Charles I dissolved Parliament in 1629, vowing to rule without parliamentary advice. He succeeded until 1640 when, desperately in need of money to repel an invasion from Scotland, he reconvened Parliament. Members of Parliament immediately attacked the king's absolutist policies. In 1642, the political conflict escalated to civil war, known as the Puritan Revolution. The Cavaliers (the name given the king and his supporters) were defeated both politically and militarily by the parliamentary forces (known as Roundheads because of their short hair), led by the staunch Puritan Oliver Cromwell. In 1649, Cromwell's forces crowned their victories by executing Charles I and proclaiming a Puritan Republic. From 1649 to 1660, England's rulers were not monarchs who tried to suppress Puritanism but believers who tried to champion it. In a half century, English Puritans rose from a harassed group of religious dissenters to a dominant power in English government.

Such a revolutionary transformation in the fortunes of English Puritans had profound consequences in New England. In 1640, when the Puritan Revolution began, the stream of immigrants to New England dwindled to a trickle. The end of immigration brought hard times to the colonists. They could no longer consider themselves a city on a hill setting a godly example for humankind. English society was being reformed by Puritans in England, not New England. Furthermore, during the 1630s the steady current of immigrants had stimulated the New England economy. A vigorous trade developed between the latest arrivals and those who had preceded them. Newcomers brought money and English goods to exchange for the food, supplies, and services they needed to put down roots in New England. When that immigrant trade came to a halt in 1640, the colonists faced sky-high prices for scarce English goods and few customers for their plentiful colonial products. As they searched for a re-

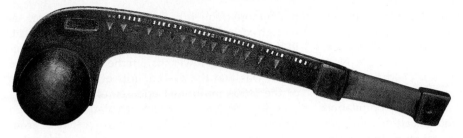

WAMPANOAG WAR CLUB
*This Wampanoag war club vividly illustrates the potency of a traditional weapon made of wood.
A swing of the club generated tremendous force because of the heavy wooden ball at the end. The
club could easily smash bones; even a glancing blow could knock a victim senseless. The weapon
was most effective, however, only at very close range—essentially hand-to-hand combat. While
these weapons were still used during King Philip's War, the Wampanoags and other native
peoples inflicted far more damage with European firearms obtained in colonial trade.*
Courtesy of the Fruitlands Museum, Harvard, Massachusetts.

placement for the immigrant trade, they marked out the basic patterns of the New England economy.

New England's rocky soil and short growing season ruled out cultivating the common colonial crops of tobacco, sugar, and rice that found a ready market in Atlantic ports. Instead of commercial crops for export, New England farmers planted food crops for home consumption. Towns usually granted each family enough land to grow sufficient grain, vegetables, and fruit to keep food on the table. With the labor of family members and perhaps a servant or hired hand, farmers often had a modest surplus of one thing or another—apples or eggs, milk or butter—and they eagerly sought to sell it to or barter it with their neighbors. This brisk local market linked neighbor to neighbor in a dense network of exchange, but it seldom extended much beyond town boundaries.

Exports that New Englanders could not get from the soil they took instead from the forest and the sea. During the first decade of settlement, colonists traded with Indians for animal pelts much in demand in Europe as fashionable apparel. By the 1640s, so many fur-bearing animals had been trapped that pelts became scarce unless traders ventured far beyond the frontiers of English settlement. Trees from the seemingly limitless forests of New England proved a longer-lasting resource. Masts for ships and staves for barrels of Spanish wine and West Indian sugar were crafted from New England timber. But the most important New England export was fish. During the religious and political turmoil of the 1640s, English ships withdrew from the rich North Atlantic fishing grounds and New Eng-

land fishermen quickly took their place. Dried, salted codfish found markets in southern Europe and, increasingly, in the West Indies. The fish trade also stimulated colonial shipbuilding and trained generations of fishermen, sailors, and merchants. By 1660, New England fishermen dominated the North Atlantic fishing grounds and New England merchants sailed from port to port throughout the colonies trading fish for Virginia tobacco, Carolina rice, and West Indian sugar. The commercial network they built endured for more than a century.

Under the pressures of steady population growth and integration into the Atlantic economy, New England society maintained the outward features that had been established by Winthrop's generation. But the white-hot piety of the founders cooled during the last half of the seventeenth century.

Merchants prospered in the export trade, and coastal towns catered to sailors and fishermen. But the export economy remained peripheral to most New England colonists. Their lives revolved around their farms, their churches, and their families.

Families were the source of one of the most important long-term changes in seventeenth-century New England. Although immigration came to a standstill in 1640, the population continued to boom, doubling every twenty years. In contemporary England, more than a quarter of the population never married. But in New England, nearly everybody married, men at about twenty-six, women at about twenty-three. Typically, a New England woman had eight or nine children, spaced about two years apart. Universal marriage and frequent births created an ever-growing population because New England enjoyed a healthful environment. Long, cold winters eliminated the warm-weather ailments that plagued the Chesapeake and the Carolinas. Low population density and the relative isolation of towns minimized the spread of diseases. Puritan habits of order, tidiness, and watchfulness probably helped. Men and women lived longer in New England; grandparents became relatively common in families by midcentury, though they remained rare elsewhere. Even more important to population growth, New England children survived the hazards of infancy and childhood

much more frequently than children elsewhere. Although early death remained an ever-present threat, in the seventeenth century death rates in New England were much lower than in the Chesapeake. The result was that the descendants of the immigrants of the 1630s multiplied and remultiplied, quickly boosting the New England population to a rough equality with that of the southern colonies. From 1640 almost to 1700, New Englanders constituted about forty-five out of every hundred British colonists in North America, southern colonists contributed another forty-five, and the remainder inhabited the middle colonies.

Under the pressures of steady population growth and integration into the Atlantic economy, New England society maintained the outward features that had been established by Winthrop's generation. But the white-hot piety of the founders cooled during the last half of the seventeenth century. New England churches and towns continued their strict observance of God's laws, but ministers accused their congregations of a decline from the passionate faith of the founders. "The truth is," Roger Williams declared, "the great Gods of this world are God-belly, God-peace, God-wealth, God-honour, God-pleasure . . . [and] God Land."

After the 1630s, the population grew faster than church membership. All residents attended sermons on pain of fines and punishment, but many could not find seating room in the meeting houses. Boston's two churches in 1650 could house only about a third of the population. An increasing fraction of the population, men especially, practiced what one historian has called "horse-shed Christianity." They attended sermons but loitered outside (near the horse shed) as long as possible, gossiping about the weather, their corn crop, a big fish, or the scandalous behavior of Goodman Such-and-Such and Goodwife So-and-So. Their bodies came to church but their minds lingered on the profane gods described by Roger Williams. By the 1680s, women were the majority among full church members throughout New England. In some towns, only 15 percent of the adult men were church members. Puritan minister Michael Wigglesworth asked

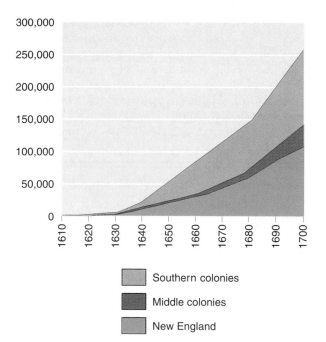

FIGURE **4.1**
Population of British North American Colonies in the Seventeenth Century
The colonial population grew at a steadily accelerating rate during the seventeenth century. On the whole, New England and the southern colonies each comprised about half the total colonial population until after 1680, when the growth in Pennsylvania and New York contributed to the surge in the population of the middle colonies.

How is it that I find
    In stead of holiness Carnality,
In stead of heavenly frames an Earthly mind,
    For burning zeal luke-warm Indifferency,
For flaming love, key-cold Dead-heartedness,
    For temperance (in meat, and drink, and
        cloaths) excess?

Whence cometh it, that Pride, and Luxurie
    Debate, Deceit, Contention, and Strife,
False-dealing, Covetousness, Hypocrisie
    (With such Crimes) amongst them are so rife,
That one of them doth over-reach another?
    And that an honest man can hardly trust his
        Brother?

How is it, that Security, and Sloth,
    Amongst the best are Common to be found?
That grosser sins, instead of Graces growth,
    Amongst the many more and more abound?

Most alarming to Puritan leaders, the children of visible saints often failed to experience conversion and attain full church membership. Puritans tended to assume that sainthood was inherited—that the children of the elect were probably also among the elect. Acting on this premise, churches permitted saints to baptize their babies, symbolically cleansing the infants of their contamination with original sin. Yet during the 1640s and 1650s, children of the visible saints outwardly conformed to God's laws but seldom experienced the inward transformation that signaled conversion and qualification for church membership. The problem became urgent during the 1650s when the children of saints—people who had grown to adulthood in New England—began to have children themselves. These babies, the grandchildren of visible saints, could not receive baptism and the protection it afforded against the terrors of an early death.

Puritan churches debated what to do. To allow anyone—even the child of a saint—to become a church member without conversion was an unthinkable retreat from the most fundamental Puritan doctrine. To allow the children of the unregenerate to be baptized flung open the door of church membership to any and all—another unthinkable affront to Puritan faith. In 1662, a synod of Massachusetts ministers reached a compromise known as the Halfway Covenant. The unconverted children of saints were permitted to become halfway church members. They could baptize their infants, but they could not participate in communion or have the voting privileges of church membership. The Halfway Covenant generated a controversy that sputtered through Puritan churches for the remainder of the century. Opponents protested the "many chaffy hypocrites" the compromise brought into the covenant, if only halfway. Defenders argued that "the Lord hath not set up Churches onely that a few old Christians may keep one another warm while they live, and then carry away the Church into the

A NEW ENGLAND CHILD
Young Alice Mason, who appears to be five or six years old in this 1668 painting, shows little of the lightheartedness or endearing vulnerability we might expect in a child today. Instead, she fixes the viewer with a confident, steady gaze that suggests that she had few doubts about what she should do and that, in fact, she did it. The painting illustrates the drift away from the intense piety and plain dress of New England's founding generation. The elaborately decorated dress, especially the slashed sleeves, reflects the prosperity that some New Englanders had achieved by the 1660s, prosperity they displayed in their clothing and homes in ways the founders would have deemed profane. Alice stands on a floorcloth painted to resemble tile, suggesting that her family could afford to cover drab wooden floors with canvas but not with genuine tile or fine carpets that adorned the homes of a wealthy few. Adams National Historic Site.

cold grave with them when they dye." Instead, the Halfway Covenant permitted the church to "*nurse up* still successively *another Generation* of Subjects to Christ . . . so he might have a People and Kingdome successively continued to him from one Generation to another." With the Halfway Covenant, Puritan churches came to terms with the replacement of

Why Were Some New Englanders Accused of Being Witches?

Almost everybody in seventeenth-century North America—whether Native American, slave, or colonist—believed that supernatural spirits could cause harm and misfortune. Outside New England, however, few colonists were legally accused of being witches, persons who had become possessed by evil spirits. More than 95 percent of all legal accusations of witchcraft in the North American colonies occurred in New England. In 1691 and 1692, an epidemic of witchcraft accusations broke out in Salem, Massachusetts, and more than one hundred individuals were accused. Many other New Englanders may have been called witches privately, but historians do not know about them because legal charges were never filed. After all, to charge a person with witchcraft was a serious matter. As a 1641 Massachusetts law stated, "If any man or woman be a witch . . . they shall be put to death." The other New England colonies had identical laws. During the seventeenth century, courts carried out the letter of the law: Thirty-four accused witches were executed, nineteen of them during the Salem outbreak.

To understand the peculiar New England preoccupation with witchcraft, historians have gathered a great deal of information about accused witches and the dark deeds their accusers attributed to them. Almost anyone could be accused of being a witch, but 80 percent of the accusations were leveled against women. About two-thirds of the accused women were over forty years old, past the age of childbearing. About half the men who were accused as witches were relatives of accused women. Normally one family member did not accuse another. Nor did accusers single out a stranger as a witch. Instead, accusers pointed to a neighbor they knew well, typically a woman.

Almost always the accused witch denied the charge. Occasionally, the accused confessed. A confession could sometimes win sympathy and a reduced punishment from officials. During the Salem witch-hunt, those who confessed usually saved their own skins by naming other people as witches. The testimony of the confessed witch was then used to accuse others. At Salem, authorities sought to obtain a confession from accused witch Giles Corey by piling stones on his chest until he was crushed to death.

Accusers of all descriptions stepped forward to testify against alleged witches. Witchcraft investigations often stretched over weeks, months, or even years as courts accumulated evidence against (and sometimes in favor of) the accused. About 90 percent of accusers were adults, about six out of ten of them men. Young women between the ages of sixteen and twenty-five made up almost all of the remaining 10 percent of accusers; they claimed to be tortured by the accused witches.

At Salem, for example, afflicted young girls shrieked in pain, their limbs twisted into strange, involuntary contortions. The young women pointed out the witches who tortured them. At the trial of accused witch Bridget Bishop in Salem, the court record noted that if Bishop "but cast her eyes on them [the afflicted], they were presently struck down. . . . But upon the touch of her hand upon them, when they lay in their swoons, they would immediately revive." The bewitched girls testified that "the shape of the prisoner did oftentimes very grievously pinch them, choke them, bite them, and afflict them; urging them to write their names in a book," the devil's book.

Such sensational evidence of torture by a witch was relatively rare in witch-hunts and trials. Usually, accusers attributed some inexplicable misfortune they had suffered to the evil influence of an accused witch. In Bridget Bishop's trial, for instance, one man testified that when he bought a pig from Bishop's husband, Bishop became angry because she "was hindered from fingering the money," and soon afterward the pig—obviously bewitched— "was taken with strange fits; jumping, leaping, and knocking [its] head against the fence." Another woman accused a witch whom she feared would "smite my chickens," and "quickly after [the suspected witch went away] one chicken died." One woman testified against a witch who had bewitched her cow, causing it to give discolored milk. A man was accused as a witch because his "spirit bewitched the pudding," which was inexplicably "cut lengthwise . . . as smooth as any knife could cut it." Mary Parsons testified that she suspected her hus-

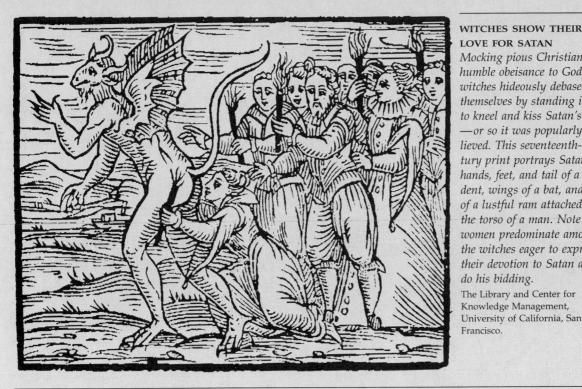

WITCHES SHOW THEIR LOVE FOR SATAN
Mocking pious Christians' humble obeisance to God, witches hideously debased themselves by standing in line to kneel and kiss Satan's butt —or so it was popularly believed. This seventeenth-century print portrays Satan with hands, feet, and tail of a rodent, wings of a bat, and head of a lustful ram attached to the torso of a man. Note that women predominate among the witches eager to express their devotion to Satan and to do his bidding.
The Library and Center for Knowledge Management, University of California, San Francisco.

band, Hugh, of being a witch "because almost all that he sells to anybody does not prosper."

The list of misfortunes that accusers attributed to witches went on and on. From our perspective in the late twentieth century, the accusers seem to have been victims not of witches but of simple accidents, of overheated imaginations, or—in the case of the possessed young women—of emotional distress. But why did seventeenth-century New Englanders find the testimony of accusers persuasive?

Seventeenth-century New Englanders believed that almost nothing happened by chance. Supernatural power—whether God's or Satan's—suffused the world and influenced the smallest event, even the death of a chicken. When something bad happened, an unhappy God may have caused it to show his displeasure with the victim, who had perhaps sinned in some way. But maybe the victim was not responsible for the misfortune; maybe Satan, acting through a witch, had caused it. If misfortunes could be pinned on a witch, the accuser was absolved from responsibility; the accuser became a

helpless victim rather than a guilty party. Witches were an explanation for the disorder that continually crept into New England communities, an explanation that attributed the disorder not to chance or to the faults of the community but to the witches' evil purposes.

Accusers usually targeted a vulnerable neighbor, such as an older woman. Historians have noted that accusers often complained that accused witches were quarrelsome, grumbled about being mistreated, muttered vague threats about getting even, and seemed to be dissatisfied with their lives. Researchers have pointed out that many New Englanders had such feelings after about 1650, but most people did not express them openly or, if they did, felt guilty about doing so. Accused witches often expressed and acted on feelings that other people shared but considered inappropriate, shameful, or sinful in their zeal to lead the saintly lives prescribed by their Puritan religion. Witches made it somewhat easier for New Englanders to consider themselves saints rather than sinners.

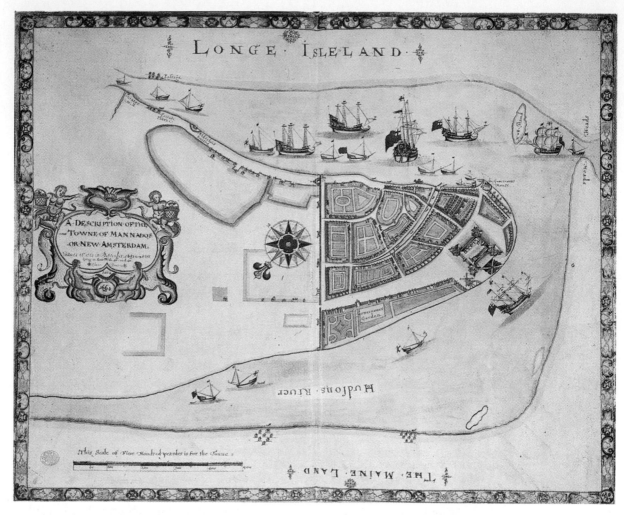

NEW AMSTERDAM, NEW YORK
This map was made for the Duke of York, whose small fleet seized New Amsterdam in 1664. The map reflects the early transition from Dutch to English rule. Although the map still uses the Dutch name New Amsterdam, the fort at the tip of Manhattan ("the Towne of Mannados") flies an English flag, as do at least six ships in the harbor, making clear that the colony is New York in all but name. Already Manhattanites were seeking refuge in the suburbs, indicated here as the enclosures along the top of the peninsula, to the left of the city wall (the vertical line dividing city streets from the wilds of upper Manhattan).
British Library.

Although few in number, the New Netherlanders were remarkably diverse, especially compared with the homogeneous English settlers to the north and south. Religious dissenters trickled in from other North American colonies. Immigrants from Holland, Sweden, France, Germany, and elsewhere made their way to the colony. Merchants and sailors in the West Indies trade stopped over in New Amsterdam and ended up staying. In 1646, the gover-

nor of New Netherland told a visitor that the colonists spoke eighteen different languages. A few years later, a minister of the Dutch Reformed Church complained to his superiors in Holland that several groups of Jews had recently arrived, adding to the religious mixture of "Papists, Mennonites and Lutherans among the Dutch . . . [and] many Puritans . . . and many other atheists and various other servants of Baal . . . who conceal themselves under the name of Christians." Spiritually, the polyglot society of New Netherland could qualify as a New England Puritan's nightmare. One minister reported that in several New Netherland villages there were as many religious opinions as residents, while the preacher in another settlement was reported to be a "man of impious and scandalous habits, a wild, drunken, unmannerly clown, more inclined to look into the wine can than into the Bible."

The West India Company struggled to govern the motley colonists for its own purposes. Under the stern leadership of Peter Stuyvesant, who served as governor from 1647 to 1664, the population slowly grew, but it remained intractable. Stuyvesant pointed out to company officials in Holland that "the *English* and *French* colonies are continued and populated by their own nation and countrymen and consequently [are] bound together more firmly and united, while your Honors' colonies in New-Netherland are only gradually and slowly peopled by the scrapings of all sorts of nationalities (few excepted), who consequently have the least interest in the welfare and maintenance of the commonwealth." Stuyvesant tried to enforce conformity to the Dutch Reformed Church, but the company—eager for more immigrants—ordered him to "shut your eyes" to the many dissenting faiths. The company added that "the consciences of men should be free and unshackled," making a virtue of New Netherland necessity. The company never permitted the "scrapings" who settled in the colony to form a representative government. Instead, the company appointed government officials who set policies, including taxes, which many colonists deeply resented.

Spiritually, the polyglot society of New Netherland could qualify as a New England Puritan's nightmare.

In 1664, New Netherland became New York. Charles II, who became king of England after the monarchy was restored in 1660, gave his brother James, the Duke of York, an enormous grant of land that included New Netherland. Of course, the Dutch colony did not belong to the king of England and was not his to give away. But that legal technicality did not impede the king or his brother. The duke quickly organized a small fleet of warships, which soon appeared off Manhattan Island in late summer 1664, and demanded that Stuyvesant surrender. With little choice, he did.

As the new proprietor of the colony, the Duke of York exercised almost the same unlimited authority over the colony as had the West India Company. He could appoint government officers, make laws, regulate trade, and adjudicate all matters without the bother (to him) of representative assemblies. The duke himself never set foot in New York, but his governors struggled to impose order on the unruly colonists. Like the Dutch, the duke permitted "all persons of what Religion soever, quietly to inhabit . . . provided they give no disturbance to the publique peace, nor doe molest or disquiet others in the free exercise of their religion." This policy of religious toleration was more a sober recognition of reality than a farsighted affirmation of liberty of conscience. It arose from the government's grudging accommodation to the difficulties of bringing order to the most heterogeneous colony in seventeenth-century North America.

New Jersey and Pennsylvania

The creation of New York led indirectly to the founding of two other middle colonies, New Jersey and Pennsylvania. In 1664, the Duke of York subdivided his grant and gave the portion between the Hudson and Delaware Rivers to two of his friends at court. The proprietors of this new colony, New Jersey, soon discovered that Puritan and Dutch settlers already in the region stubbornly resisted paying taxes and declaring their loyalty to the new government. The continuing strife in New Jersey discouraged immigration and persuaded one of the proprietors to sell his share to two Quakers. When the two Quaker proprietors began to quarrel, they called in a prominent English Quaker, William Penn, to arbitrate their dispute. Penn eventually worked out a settlement that continued New Jersey's proprietary government but did little to end the conflict with the settlers. In the process, Penn became intensely interested in what he termed a "holy experiment" of establishing a genuinely Quaker colony in America.

Unlike most other Quakers, William Penn came from an eminent family. His father served as an admiral under both Cromwell and Charles II and had been knighted. The younger Penn trained for a military career, but the ideas of dissenters from the reestablished Anglican Church appealed to him. His father attempted to cool Penn's religious enthusiasm by sending him to Oxford University and on a tour of the continent, but by 1667—when he was twenty-three years old—Penn had become a devout Quaker.

In England, the Quakers' inner light appeared most brightly to men and women of humble origins. Tradesmen, farmers, and laborers were drawn to the Quaker teaching that God loved them and revealed his grace directly to them through the inner light. The Quakers' concept of an open, generous God who made his love equally available to all people manifested itself in unusually egalitarian religious services and social behavior that continually brought Quakers into conflict with the government.

Quaker meetings consisted of quiet meditation interrupted by spontaneous testimony from any member of the meeting who felt moved to expound on religious or moral issues. Quaker leaders were ordinary lay men and women, not specially trained preachers. More than any other seventeenth-century sect, Quakers allowed women to assume positions of religious leadership. "In souls there is no sex," they said. Since all people were equal in the spiritual realm, Quakers considered the conventional social hierarchy of their day false and evil. Like the Puritans, they condemned the ornate costumes and elegant flattery fashionable in late seventeenth-century England. Instead, they dressed in plain, somber clothing and spoke in plain, honest language. They refused to observe the prevailing etiquette that required men to remove their hats and women to curtsy when in the presence of someone of higher rank and to address their superiors in terms of respect such as "lord" or "lady," "sir" or "madam." They insisted on calling everyone "friend" and on shaking hands instead of curtsying or removing their hat—even when meeting the king. These customs enraged many non-Quakers and provoked innumerable beatings and worse. Thousands of Quakers were imprisoned and hundreds were killed during the 1660s and 1670s in England (as they were, on a smaller scale, in New England). Penn himself was jailed four times, once for nine months.

Penn was one of the most outspoken and prominent Quakers in England. By 1680, he had published fifty books and pamphlets and spoken at countless public meetings, but he appeared no closer to realizing his goal of toleration for Quakers. A Quaker colony in America held out the promise not just of toleration but of a society constructed on Quaker principles, a possibility Penn found irresistible. Despite his many run-ins with the government, Penn remained on good terms with

WILLIAM PENN
This portrait of William Penn was drawn about a decade after the founding of Pennsylvania. At a time when extravagant clothing and fancy wigs proclaimed that their wearer was an important person, Penn was portrayed informally, lacking even a coat, his natural hair neat but undressed—all a reflection of his Quaker faith. Penn's full face and double chin show that his faith did not make him a stranger to the pleasures of the table. No hollow-cheeked ascetic or wild-eyed enthusiast, Penn appears sober and observant, as if sizing up the viewer and reserving judgment. The portrait captures the calm determination, anchored in his faith, that inspired Penn's hopes for his new colony.
Historical Society of Pennsylvania.

Charles II, and he asked the king for a grant of land to found his colony. The king had begun a policy of tightening royal control of the English colonies in America, but he greeted Penn's request as an opportunity to rid England of the troublesome Quakers. In 1681, he made Penn the proprietor of 45,000 square miles for his new colony of Pennsylvania.

"The service of God first, the honor and advantage of the king, with our own profit, shall I hope be the result of all our endeavors," Penn wrote soon afterward. Penn planned to profit by selling some of his vast dominion. Although he eventually sold over 700,000 acres, profits eluded him and he remained perpetually in debt. He was far more successful in serving God by building his colony on a Quaker foundation.

Toleration and Diversity in Pennsylvania

When Penn announced the creation of his new colony, Quakers flocked to English ports in numbers exceeded only by the great Puritan migration to New England fifty years earlier. Between 1682 and 1685, nearly eight thousand immigrants came to Pennsylvania, most of them Quakers from England, Ireland, and Wales. They represented a cross section of the artisans, farmers, and laborers who predominated among English Quakers. But they also included poor men and women whose way to Pennsylvania was paid by their Quaker meetings in England. In addition, Quaker missionaries encouraged immigrants from Europe, and many came, giving Pennsylvania greater ethnic diversity than any English colony other than New York. In 1685, Penn wrote that the settlers were "a collection of Divers Nations in Europe: as, French, Dutch, Germans, Swedes, Danes, Finns, Scotch, French and English, and of the last equal to all the rest."

Despite its toleration and diversity, Pennsylvania was as much a Quaker colony as New England was a stronghold of Puritanism.

Penn was determined to live in peace with the Indians who inhabited the region he had been granted. Penn's Indian policy expressed his Quaker ideals and contrasted sharply with the hostile policies of the other English colonies. On the eve of colonization, he explained to the chief of the Lenni Lenape (or Delaware) Indians that "God has written his law in our hearts, by which we are taught and commanded to love and help and do good to one another, and not to do harm and mischief one unto another . . . [and] this great God has been pleased to make me concerned in your parts of the world, and the king of the country where I live has given unto me a great province therein, but I desire to enjoy it with your love and consent." Penn instructed his agents to obtain the Indians' consent by purchasing their land, respecting their claims, and dealing with them fairly. The Delawares readily cooperated with Penn, partly because they welcomed English allies against their own traditional enemies, the much stronger Iroquois confederation.

Penn declared that the "First Fundamental of the government of my country" was that every settler would "enjoy the free possession of his or her

faith and exercise of worship towards God." Accordingly, Pennsylvania tolerated Protestant sects of all kinds as well as Roman Catholics. Likewise, the government did not compel settlers to attend religious services or to pay taxes to maintain a state-supported church. Religious liberty was not absolute, however. It extended only to Christians "who confess and acknowledge the one almighty and eternal God to be the creator, upholder, and ruler of the world." All voters and officeholders had to be Christians.

Come all ye Saints that would for little Buy ,
Great Tracts of Land, and care not where they lye ,
Deal with your Quaking Friends, they're Men of Light,
The Spirit hates Deceit and Scorns to Bite .

MAKING FUN OF LAND SPECULATORS
This playing card satirizes greedy "Saints" in England who "for little" money buy "Great Tracts of Land" from the Pennsylvania Company without knowing or caring "where they lye." Don't worry, the card gibes at the gullible men lining up to purchase land from the representatives of the Pennsylvania Company, you can trust "your Quaking Friends, they're Men of Light."—The card illustrates the skepticism common in England about colonial promoters' tantalizing schemes of quick and easy wealth. Bodleian Library, Oxford.

Despite its toleration and diversity, Pennsylvania was as much a Quaker colony as New England was a stronghold of Puritanism. "Government seems to me a part of religion itself," Penn wrote, "for there is no power but of God. The powers that be, are ordained of God: whosoever therefore resists the power [of government], resists the ordinance of God." Penn believed that government had two basic purposes: "to terrify evildoers . . . [and] to cherish those that do well." He had no hesitation about using civil government to enforce religious morality. One of the colony's first laws provided that "all such offenses against God, as swearing, cursing, lying, profane talking, drunkenness, drinking of healths, obscene words, incest, sodomy, rapes, whoredom, fornication, and other uncleanness . . . all prizes, stage plays, cards, dice, May games, gamesters, masques, revels, bull-baitings, cockfightings, bear-baitings, and the like, which excite the people to rudeness, cruelty, looseness, and irreligion, shall be . . . discouraged and severely punished." The ethnic and religious diversity of Pennsylvania prevented the strict enforcement of these prohibitions. But these Quaker expectations of godly order and sobriety nonetheless set the tone of Pennsylvania society.

Penn's Quaker principles shaped not only the colony's government and society but also its capital city, Philadelphia. Penn carefully planned the orderly grid of streets on the peninsula at the confluence of the Schuylkill and Delaware Rivers. Philadelphia soon rivaled New York—though not yet Boston—as a center of commerce. By the end of the seventeenth century, the city's five thousand inhabitants participated in a thriving trade exporting food products, especially flour, to the West Indies and importing textiles and manufactured goods. Quaker habits of industry and sobriety contributed to the prosperity of numerous merchants and tradesmen. In less than two decades, Philadelphia had become one of the most important cities in British North America.

Penn thought a great deal about how to structure the colony's government. As proprietor he had extensive power, subject only to review by the king. But he did not want a proprietary government in which "the will of one man may . . . hinder the good of an whole country." Penn proposed instead to appoint a governor who would maintain the proprietor's power to veto any laws passed by the colonial council. The members of the council were elected by property owners who possessed at least one hundred acres of land or who paid taxes. (In other colonies, the council was appointed by the governor.) The council had the power to originate laws and administer all the affairs of government. An elected assembly served as a check on the council; its members had the authority to reject or approve laws framed by the council, but otherwise it had little influence.

Penn stressed that the exact form of government mattered less than the men who served in it. "Governments, like clocks, go from the motion men give them; . . . governments rather depend upon men than men upon governments. Let men be good, and the government can't be bad. . . . But if men be bad, let the government be never so good; they will endeavor to warp and spoil it to their turn." Penn himself stayed in Pennsylvania only from 1682 to 1684 before he returned to England to defend Quakers from persecution and to lobby on behalf of his colony. But in Penn's eyes, "good men" staffed Pennsylvania's government. Despite the colony's diversity, Quakers dominated elective and appointive offices. Quakers, of course, differed among themselves. Members of the assembly struggled to win the right to debate and amend laws, especially tax laws. They finally won the battle in 1701 when a new Charter of Privileges gave the proprietor the power to appoint the council and in turn stripped the council of all its former powers and gave them to the assembly, which became the only unicameral legislature in all the British colonies.

The Colonies and the British Empire

The creation of proprietary colonies permitted the king to reward his friends with faraway lands to which he had tenuous claims and over which he exercised almost no real control. From the king's point of view, the proprietary grants were, in a sense, cheap gifts. As the colonies grew, however, the gifts became more valuable. During the last third of the seventeenth century, the crown moved, at first slowly, to exert its own proprietorship over all the English colonies. After the restoration of the monarchy in 1660, the king took initiatives to channel colonial trade through English hands and to consolidate royal authority over colonial governments. These initiatives defined the basic relationship between the colonies and England that endured until the American Revolution.

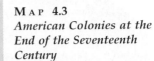

MAP 4.3
American Colonies at the End of the Seventeenth Century
By the end of the seventeenth century, settlers inhabited a narrow band of land that stretched more or less continuously from Boston to Norfolk, with pockets of settlement farther south. The colonies' claims to enormous tracts of land to the west were contested by Native Americans as well as the ambitions of France and Spain.

Royal Regulation of Colonial Trade

English economic policies toward the colonies were designed to yield customs revenues for the monarchy and profitable business for English merchants and shippers. In addition, the policies were intended to divert the colonies' trade from England's enemies, the Dutch and the French.

The Navigation Acts of 1650, 1651, and 1660 set forth two fundamental regulations governing colonial trade. First, all colonial goods imported into England had to be transported in English ships; the same held true for ships involved in the coastal trade from one colonial port to another. The law defined an English ship as one in which the captain and three-fourths of the crew were English. Since the Navigation Acts defined colonists as English, ships owned by colonial merchants and crewed by

colonial sailors could continue to carry colonial products to England. No longer, however, could colonists legally ship their goods to England aboard Dutch, French, or Spanish ships.

Second, the Navigation Acts "enumerated" (listed) specific colonial products that could be shipped only to England or to other English colonies. Initially, tobacco was the only export of the British North American colonies among the enumerated products; most, like sugar, were exports of the West Indies. While enumeration prevented Chesapeake planters from shipping their tobacco directly to the European continent, it did not interfere with the commerce of New England and the middle colonies. Their principal exports—fish, lumber, and flour—were not enumerated and could still be shipped to their most important market in the West Indies.

PINE TREE SHILLING

Currency was in short supply in the colonies. Since England prohibited the export of its coins, the precious currency circulating in the North American colonies tended to be Spanish, Dutch, French, or Portuguese. In violation of English rules that forbade colonies from issuing their own currency, John Hull, a wealthy Boston merchant and shipowner, began to mint coins in 1652. Shown here is one of his pine tree shillings, boldly announcing its Massachusetts origins. A shilling was worth twelve pennies; twenty shillings equaled a pound sterling. Despite Hull's attempt to ease the currency shortage, the legal tender most colonists used consisted of such commonly available items as bushels of corn or wheat, skins of beaver or deer, or—following the Native American practice—wampum.

Courtesy of the Museum of the American Numismatic Association.

The Staple Act of 1663 imposed a third regulation on colonial trade. It required all goods imported into the colonies to pass through England. Goods manufactured in France or Italy, for example, had to be shipped first to England, unloaded and taxed, and then reloaded in English ships before they could be sent to the colonies. The Staple Act gave English merchants a monopoly on exports to the colonies and, by raising the prices of non-English goods, gave English manufacturers a competitive edge in colonial markets.

After the restoration of the monarchy in 1660, the king took initiatives to channel colonial trade through English hands and to consolidate royal authority over colonial governments. These initiatives defined the basic relationship between the colonies and England that endured until the American Revolution.

Colonial merchants found ways to evade these regulations. The Plantations Duty Act of 1673 attempted to reduce the evasions by requiring customs duties to be paid when goods left the colonies and by providing for customs agents to collect the duties and enforce the trade laws. Colonial merchants still managed to smuggle in non-English goods and to trade with other nations. Colonial juries routinely winked at the merchants' infractions. The Navigation Act of 1696 responded to such "Frauds and . . . Abuses" by creating seven vice-admiralty courts staffed by royal appointees to try violators of the trade laws. The crown also expanded the customs service, gave agents greater power to search ships and warehouses for illegal goods, and set up the Board of Trade to rigorously supervise and administer colonial commerce.

By the end of the seventeenth century, colonial commerce flowed in channels defined by the regulations of the British Empire. The regulations raised the price colonists paid for imports and subjected merchants and shippers to royal supervision. They also benefited colonists engaged in commerce by giving them access to markets throughout the British Empire on the same terms as residents of England. In addition, colonial commerce came under the protective umbrella of the British navy, the world's strongest. Commercial regulations also poured cash into the British treasury and into the pockets of British merchants. By 1700, colonial goods (including those from the West Indies) accounted for one-fifth of all British imports and for two-thirds of all goods reexported from England to the continent. In turn, the colonies absorbed more than one-tenth of British exports. The commercial regulations gave economic meaning to England's proprietorship of American colonies.

Consolidation of Royal Authority

The monarchy also took steps to exercise greater control over colonial governments. Virginia had been a royal colony since 1624; Maryland, South Carolina, and the middle colonies were proprietary colonies with close ties to the crown. The New England colonies possessed royal charters, but they had developed their own distinctively Puritan governments. Charles II, whose father, Charles I, had been executed by Puritans in England, took a particular interest in harnessing the New England colonies more firmly to the British Empire. The occasion was a royal investigation following a series of battles between colonists and Indians known as King Philip's War.

> By the end of the seventeenth century, colonial commerce flowed in channels defined by the regulations of the British Empire.

In 1675, warfare between Indians and colonists erupted in the Chesapeake and in New England. Almost a half-century earlier, in 1637, Massachusetts settlers had massacred hundreds of Pequot Indians, nearly exterminating the tribe and establishing more or less peaceful relations with the more potent Wampanoags. During the subsequent decades, New Englanders encroached steadily on Indian lands and, in 1675, the Wampanoags struck back with attacks on settlements in western Massachusetts. Metacomet—whom the colonists called King Philip—was the chief of the Wampanoags and the son of Massasoit, who had befriended William Bradford and his original band of Pilgrims. Metacomet probably neither planned the attacks nor masterminded a conspiracy with the Nipmucks and the Narragansetts, as the colonists feared. But when militias from Massachusetts and other New England colonies counterattacked all three tribes, a deadly sequence of battles killed over a thousand colonists and thousands more Indians. The Indians

utterly destroyed thirteen English settlements and partially burned another half-dozen. By the spring of 1676, Indian warriors ranged freely within seventeen miles of Boston. The colonists finally forced the Indians to stop fighting, principally with a scorched-earth policy of burning their food supplies. The war left the New England colonists with an enduring hatred of Indians, a large war debt, and a devastated frontier. And in 1676, Edward Randolph, an agent of the king, arrived to investigate whether New England abided by English laws.

Not surprisingly, Randolph found all sorts of deviations from English rules, which he duly reported to the king along with the suggestion that troops be used "to reduce Massachusetts to obedience." The English government decided instead to govern New England more directly. Randolph went back to New England as a customs agent, where he met only slightly less hostility than a Narragansett

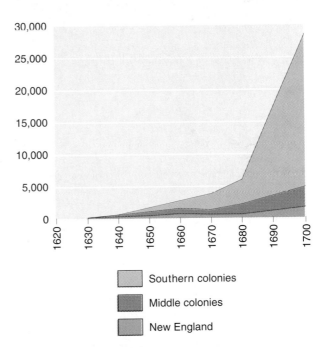

F I G U R E 4.2
African American Population in the Seventeenth Century
The African American population in the colonies grew dramatically after about 1680, especially in the southern colonies where the overwhelming majority of blacks resided after about 1660. Since slavery was legal throughout the colonies, why did the black population grow more slowly in New England and the middle colonies than it did in the South?

INDIANS VISIT JESUIT MISSION
While English colonies developed along the Atlantic coast, French explorers and missionaries established outposts on the St. Lawrence River and at strategic locations near the Great Lakes. This seventeenth-century drawing by a Jesuit priest shows three Indians trekking across the snow toward the mission at Sault St. Louis, not far from Montreal. Try to identify features of both Native American and European cultures displayed in the drawing.

Archives Departmentales de la Gironde, France.

Indian. In 1684, an English court revoked the Massachusetts charter, the foundation of the distinctive government built by the Puritan founders. Two years later, royal officials incorporated Massachusetts and the other colonies north of Maryland into the Dominion of New England.

To govern the dominion, the English sent Sir Edmund Andros to Boston. Some New England merchants cooperated with Andros, but most colonists were offended by his flagrant disregard of such Puritan traditions as keeping the Sabbath—one Sunday he held a fireworks show in honor of the king. Worst of all, the Dominion of New England invalidated all land titles held under the old

Massachusetts charter. Every landowner in New England faced the horrifying prospect of losing his or her land.

Events in England, however, permitted Massachusetts colonists to overthrow Andros and retain title to their property. When Charles II died in 1685, he was succeeded by his brother James II, a zealous Catholic. James's aggressive campaign to appoint Catholics to government posts engendered such unrest that in 1688 a group of Protestant noblemen invited the Dutch ruler William of Orange—who was married to James's daughter Mary, a Protestant—to claim the English throne. When William landed in England at the head of a large army, James fled to France and William became King William III in the bloodless Glorious Revolution. Rumors of the revolution raced across the Atlantic and emboldened colonial uprisings in Massachusetts, New York, and Maryland.

In Boston, the colonists seized Andros, Randolph, and other English officials and tossed them in jail. The rebels reestablished the government that had existed under the old Massachusetts charter, destroying the Dominion of New England. New Yorkers followed the Massachusetts example. Under the leadership of Jacob Leisler, rebels seized the royal governor and ruled the colony for more than a year. When King William's new governor arrived in 1691, Leisler relinquished control of the government without violence, but the governor executed him and one of his subordinates for treason. In Maryland, the Protestant Association, led by John Coode, overthrew the colony's pro-Catholic government in 1689, fearing it would not recognize the new Protestant king. Coode's men ruled until the new royal governor arrived in 1692 and ended both Coode's rebellion and Lord Baltimore's proprietary government.

The events that followed the Glorious Revolution proved that the colonists were capable of taking power into their own hands and that they were incapable of holding it. The trend toward consolidation of royal authority over the colonies continued during the 1690s, but the colonial governors accommodated somewhat more to the needs and sensitivities of local colonial elites. The colonists, in turn, adjusted to royal control, especially since royal protection came with it.

During the 1690s, the northern colonists valued English protection against threats from the French. Since the 1660s, French explorers and Jesuit priests had established outposts along the Great Lakes and explored the vast watershed of the Mississippi River. The French succeeded in establishing a lucrative and far-flung fur trade, draining pelts away from the mighty Iroquois, the most powerful Indians in eastern North America. In 1689, Andros encouraged the Iroquois to mount an offensive against French settlements along the Canadian border. While the colonies were distracted by the Glorious Revolution, French forces counterattacked against villages in New England and New York. Known as King William's War, the conflict with the French was a colonial outgrowth of William's war against France in Europe. The war dragged on until 1697 and ended inconclusively in both Europe and the colonies. But it made clear to many colonists that along with English royal government came a welcome measure of military security.

In Massachusetts, John Winthrop's city on a hill became another royal colony in 1691, when a new charter was issued. Under the charter, the governor was appointed by the king rather than elected by the colonists' representatives. The governor appointed judges and militia officers, but not members of the council or General Court, as in other royal colonies. Instead, colonists were permitted to elect their own representatives to the General Court, which advised the governor and served as an upper house of the legislature. But perhaps the most unsettling change was the new qualification for voting. Possession of property worth £40 sterling replaced church membership as a prerequisite for voting in colony-wide elections. Wealth replaced God's grace as the defining characteristic of Massachusetts citizenship.

Conclusion: The Seventeenth-Century Legacy of English North America

By the end of the seventeenth century, the diverse English colonies in North America had developed along lines quite different from the example New Spain had set in 1600. In the North American colonies, English immigrants and their descendants predominated, but many other settlers came from Europe, and a growing number of Africans arrived in bondage. Economically, the English colonies thrived on agriculture and trade, exporting crops of the soil and sea rather than silver and gold. Protestantism prevailed in the English colonies, relaxed in some colonies and militant in others, but religious diversity and religious indifference were growing and, in some colonies, tolerated. Politics and government differed from colony to colony, but everywhere local settlers—at least those who were free, white, adult men—had an extraordinary degree of political influence. The new world that Columbus could not imagine, that Powhatan only glimpsed, had been firmly established by 1700. During the next half-century in North America, that world would undergo surprising new developments that built upon the indelible legacies of the seventeenth-century colonies.

CHRONOLOGY

1534	Henry VIII breaks with Roman Catholic Church and initiates English Reformation.
1609	Henry Hudson searches for Northwest Passage for Dutch East India Company.
1620	English Puritans found Plymouth colony.
1626	Peter Minuit purchases Manhattan Island for Dutch West India Company and founds New Amsterdam.
1629	Massachusetts Bay Company receives royal charter for colony.
1630	John Winthrop leads Puritan settlers to Massachusetts Bay.
1635	Roger Williams, banished from Massachusetts, establishes Rhode Island colony.
1636	Thomas Hooker leaves Massachusetts and helps found Connecticut colony. Harvard College founded.
1637	Anne Hutchinson accused of Antinomianism, excommunicated from Boston church.
1642	Civil war inflames England, pitting Puritans against royalists.
1649	English Puritans win civil war and execute King Charles I.
1656	Quakers arrive in Massachusetts, are persecuted.
1660	Monarchy restored in England; Charles II becomes king. Navigation Act requires colonial goods to be shipped in English vessels through English ports.
1662	Many Puritan congregations adopt Halfway Covenant.
1663	Staple Act requires all colonial imports to come from England.
1664	English seize New Netherland colony from Dutch, rename it New York. Duke of York subdivides his colony, creating new colony of New Jersey.
1673	Plantations Duty Act attempts to reduce smuggling and evasion of Navigation Acts.
1675	Indians and colonists clash in King Philip's War.
1681	King Charles II grants William Penn charter for colony of Pennsylvania.
1686	Royal officials create Dominion of New England.
1688	James II overthrown by Glorious Revolution; William III becomes king.
1691	Massachusetts becomes royal colony.
1692	Witch trials flourish at Salem.
1696	Navigation Act creates vice-admiralty courts and Board of Trade to oversee colonial commerce.

BIBLIOGRAPHY

This bibliography excludes pertinent sources listed in chapters 2 and 3. Please consult the bibliographies of those chapters for additional suggested readings.

GENERAL WORKS

Patricia U. Bonomi, *Under the Cope of Heaven: Religion, Society, and Politics in Colonial America* (1986).

Jon Butler, *Awash in a Sea of Faith: Christianizing the American People* (1990).

Lawrence A. Cremin, *American Education: The Colonial Experience, 1607–1783* (1970).

David Hackett Fischer, *Albion's Seed: Four British Folkways in America* (1989).

Stephen Foster, *The Long Argument: English Puritanism and the Shaping of New England Culture, 1570–1700* (1991).

Jack P. Greene, *Pursuits of Happiness: The Social Development of Early Modern British Colonies and the Formation of American Culture* (1988).

David D. Hall, *Worlds of Wonder, Days of Judgment: Popular Religious Belief in Early New England* (1989).

Alan Heimert and Andrew Delbanco, eds., *The Puritans in America: A Narrative Anthology* (1985).

Peter Charles Hoffer, *Law and People in Colonial America* (1992).

Stephen Innes, *Creating the Commonwealth: The Economic Culture of Puritan New England* (1995).

David S. Lovejoy, *Religious Enthusiasm in the New World: Heresy to Revolution* (1985).

Perry Miller, *The New England Mind: The Seventeenth Century* (1939).

Perry Miller, *The New England Mind: From Colony to Province* (1953).

Helena Wall, *Fierce Communalism: Family and Community in the American Colonies in the Seventeenth Century* (1990).

ENGLISH BACKGROUND

Kenneth R. Andrews, Nicholas P. Canny, and Paul E. H. Hair, eds., *The Westward Enterprise: English Activities in Ireland, the Atlantic, and America, 1480–1650* (1979).

Joyce Appleby, *Economic Thought and Ideology in Seventeenth-Century England* (1978).

Patrick Collinson, *The Religion of Protestants: The Church in English Society, 1559–1625* (1982).

Patrick Collinson, *The Birthpangs of Protestant England: Religious and Cultural Change in the Sixteenth and Seventeenth Centuries* (1988).

Jan de Vries, *The Economy of Europe in an Age of Crisis, 1600–1750* (1978).

Dewey D. Wallace Jr., *Puritans and Predistination: Grace in English Protestant Theology, 1525–1695* (1982).

Michael Walzer, *The Revolution of the Saints: A Study in the Origins of Radical Politics* (1965).

Peter O. G. White, *Predestination, Policy, and Polemic: Conflict and Consensus in the English Church from the Reformation to the Civil War* (1992).

Keith Wrightson, *English Society, 1580–1680* (1982).

INDIANS

James Axtell, *The Indian Peoples of Eastern America: A Documentary History of the Sexes* (1980).

Colin G. Calloway, *The Western Abenaki of Vermont, 1600–1800: War, Migration, and the Survival of an Indian People* (1990).

William Cronon, *Changes in the Land: Indians, Colonists, and the Ecology of New England* (1983).

Matthew Dennis, *Cultivating a Landscape of Peace: Iroquois-European Encounters in Seventeenth-Century America* (1993).

Carol Devens, *Countering Colonization: Native American Women and Great Lakes Missions, 1630–1900* (1992).

Francis Jennings, *The Ambiguous Iroquois Empire: The Covenant Chain Confederation of Indian Tribes with English Colonies from Its Beginnings to the Lancaster Treaty of 1744* (1983).

Yasughide Kawashima, *Puritan Justice and the Indian: White Man's Law in Massachusetts, 1630–1763* (1986).

James W. Mavor, *Manitou: The Sacred Landscape of New England's Native Civilization* (1989).

H. C. Porter, *The Inconstant Savage: England and the North American Indian, 1500–1660* (1979).

Daniel K. Richter, *The Ordeal of the Longhouse: The Peoples of the Iroquois League in the Era of European Colonization* (1992).

Daniel K. Richter and James H. Merrell, *Beyond the Covenant Chain: The Iroquois and Their Neighbors in Indian North America, 1600–1800* (1987).

Neal Salisbury, *Manitou and Providence: Indians, Europeans, and the Making of New England, 1500–1643* (1982).

Alden T. Vaughan, *New England Frontier: Puritans and Indians, 1620–1675* (3rd ed., 1995).

Richard White, *The Middle Ground: Indians, Empires, and Republics in the Great Lakes Region, 1650–1815* (1991).

NEW ENGLAND

David Grayson Allen, *In English Ways: The Movement of Societies and the Transferal of English Local Law and Custom to Massachusetts Bay in the Seventeenth Century* (1981).

Virginia Dejohn Anderson, *New England's Generation: The Great Migration and the Formation of Society and Culture in the Seventeenth Century* (1991).

Bernard Bailyn, *The New England Merchants in the Seventeenth Century* (1955).

Paul Boyer and Stephen Nissenbaum, *Salem Possessed: The Social Origins of Witchcraft* (1974).

Paul Boyer and Stephen Nissenbaum, eds., *Salem Village Witchcraft: A Documentary Record of Local Conflict in Colonial New England* (1972).

Theodore Dwight Bozeman, *To Live Ancient Lives: The Primitivist Dimension in Puritanism* (1988).

T. H. Breen, *Puritans and Adventurers: Change and Persistence in Early America* (1980).

Francis J. Bremer, *Shaping New Englands: Puritan Clergymen in Seventeenth-Century England and New England* (1994).

Richard Bushman, *From Puritan to Yankee: Character and the Social Order in Connecticut, 1690–1765* (1967).

Jonathan M. Chu, *Neighbors, Friends, or Madmen: The Puritan Adjustment to Quakerism in Seventeenth-Century Massachusetts Bay* (1985).

Charles Lloyd Cohen, *God's Caress: The Psychology of Puritan Religious Experience* (1986).

David Cressy, *Coming Over: Migration and Communication between England and New England in the Seventeenth Century* (1987).

Bruce C. Daniels, *The Connecticut Town: Growth and Development, 1635–1790* (1979).

Bruce Colin Daniels, *Puritans at Play: Leisure and Recreation in Colonial New England* (1995).

Andrew Delbanco, *The Puritan Ordeal* (1989).

John Demos, *A Little Commonwealth: Family Life in Plymouth Colony* (1970).

John Putnam Demos, *Entertaining Satan: Witchcraft and the Culture of Early New England* (1982).

Stephen Foster, *Their Solitary Way: The Puritan Social Ethic in the First Century of Settlement in New England* (1971).

Gordon E. Geddes, *Welcome Joy: Death in Puritan New England* (1981).

Richard P. Gildrie, *The Profane, the Civil, and the Godly: The Reformation of Manners in Orthodox New England, 1679–1749* (1994).

Richard Godbeer, *The Devil's Dominion: Magic and Religion in Early New England* (1992).

Charles S. Grant, *Democracy in the Connecticut Frontier Town of Kent* (1961).

Philip J. Greven Jr., *Four Generations: Population, Land, and Family in Colonial Andover, Massachusetts* (1970).

Philip Gura, *A Glimpse of Sion's Glory: Puritan Radicalism in Seventeenth-Century New England, 1620–1660* (1984).

David D. Hall, ed., *The Antinomian Controversy, 1636–1638* (1968).

David D. Hall, ed., *Witch-Hunting in Seventeenth-Century New England: A Documentary History, 1638–1692* (1991).

David D. Hall and David Grayson Allen, eds., *Seventeenth-Century New England* (1984).

Michael G. Hall, *The Last American Puritan: The Life of Increase Mather, 1639–1723* (1988).

Stephen Innes, *Labor in a New Land: Economy and Society in Seventeenth-Century Springfield* (1983).

Sydney V. James, *Colonial Rhode Island: A History* (1975).

Carol F. Karlsen, *The Devil in the Shape of a Woman: Witchcraft in Colonial New England* (1987).

Karen Ordahl Kupperman, *Providence Island, 1630–1641: The Other Puritan Colony* (1993).

Benjamin Labaree, *Colonial Massachusetts* (1979).

George D. Langdon, *Pilgrim Colony: A History of New Plymouth, 1620–1691* (1966).

Kenneth A. Lockridge, *A New England Town: The First Hundred Years, Dedham, Massachusetts, 1636–1736* (1970).

Kenneth A. Lockridge, *Literacy in Colonial New England: An Enquiry into the Social Context of Literacy in the Early Modern West* (1974).

Jackson Turner Main, *Society and Economy in Colonial Connecticut* (1985).

Bruce H. Mann, *Neighbors and Strangers: Law and Community in Early Connecticut* (1987).

Carolyn Merchant, *Ecological Revolutions: Nature, Gender, and Science in New England* (1989).

Perry Miller, *Errand into the Wilderness* (1956).

Perry Miller and Thomas H. Johnson, eds., *The Puritans*, 2 vols. (1963).

Edmund S. Morgan, *The Puritan Dilemma: The Story of John Winthrop* (1958).

Edmund S. Morgan, *Visible Saints: The History of a Puritan Idea* (1963).

Edmund S. Morgan, *Roger Williams: The Church and the State* (1967).

Edmund S. Morgan, ed., *The Diary of Michael Wigglesworth, 1653–1657: The Conscience of a Puritan* (1946).

James G. Mosely, *John Winthrop's World: History as a Story, the Story as History* (1992).

Carla Gardina Pestana, *Quakers and Baptists in Colonial Massachusetts* (1991).

Amanda Porterfield, *Female Piety in Puritan New England: The Emergence of Religious Humanism* (1992).

Sumner C. Powell, *Puritan Village: The Formation of a New England Town* (1963).

Michael J. Puglisi, *Puritans Besieged: The Legacies of King Philip's War in the Massachusetts Bay Colony* (1991).

Howard S. Russell, *A Long, Deep Furrow: Three Centuries of Farming in New England* (1976).

Darrett B. Rutman, *Winthrop's Boston: Portrait of a Puritan Town, 1630–1649* (1965).

Darrett B. Rutman, *The Husbandmen of Plymouth: Farms and Villages in the Old Colony, 1620–1692* (1967).

Timothy J. Sehr, *Colony and Commonwealth: Massachusetts Bay, 1649–1660* (1989).

Kenneth Silverman, *The Life and Times of Cotton Mather* (1984).

Richard C. Simmons, *Studies in the Massachusetts Franchise, 1631–1691* (1989).

David E. Stannard, *The Puritan Way of Death: A Study in Religion, Culture, and Social Change* (1977).

William K. B. Stoever, *"A Faire and Easie Way to Heaven": Covenant Theology and Antinomianism in Early Massachusetts* (1978).

Harry S. Stout, *The New England Soul: Preaching and Religious Culture in Colonial New England* (1986).

Robert J. Taylor, *Colonial Connecticut: A History* (1979).

Laurel Thatcher Ulrich, *Good Wives: Image and Reality in the Lives of Women in Northern New England, 1650–1750* (1982).

Robert E. Wall Jr., *Massachusetts Bay: The Crucial Decade, 1640–1650* (1972).

Avihu Zakai, *Exile and Kingdom: History and Apocalypse in the Puritan Migration to America* (1992).

MIDDLE COLONIES

Thomas J. Archdeacon, *New York City, 1664–1710: Conquest and Change* (1976).

Patricia U. Bonomi, *A Factious People: Politics and Society in Colonial New York* (1971).

Thomas J. Condon, *New York Beginnings: The Commercial Origins of New Netherland* (1968).

Richard S. Dunn and Mary Maples Dunn, eds., *The World of William Penn* (1986).

Joseph E. Illick, *Colonial Pennsylvania: A History* (1976).

Michael G. Kammen, *Colonial New York: A History* (1975).

Sung Bok Kim, *Landlord and Tenant in Colonial New York: Manorial Society, 1664–1775* (1978).

Donna Merwick, *Possessing Albany, 1630–1710: The Dutch and English Experiences* (1990).

David E. Narrett, *Inheritance and Family Life in Colonial New York City* (1992).

Gary B. Nash, *Quakers and Politics: Pennsylvania, 1681–1726* (1968).

Thomas Eliot Norton, *The Fur Trade in Colonial New York, 1686–1776* (1974).

John E. Pomfret, *Colonial New Jersey: A History* (1973).

Oliver A. Rink, *Holland on the Hudson: An Economic and Social History of Dutch New York* (1986).

Robert C. Ritchie, *The Duke's Province: A Study of New York Politics and Society, 1664–1691* (1977).

Jean R. Soderlund, ed., *William Penn and the Founding of Pennsylvania, 1680–1684: A Documentary History* (1983).

Allen Tully, *Forming American Politics: Ideals, Interests, and Institutions in Colonial New York and Pennsylvania* (1994).

Stephanie Grauman Wolf, *Urban Village: Population, Community, and Family Structure in Germantown, Pennsylvania, 1683–1800* (1976).

"DUMMY BOARD" OF PHYLLIS, A NEW ENGLAND SLAVE

This life-size portrait of a slave woman named Phyllis, a mulatto who worked as a domestic servant for her owner, Elizabeth Hunt Wendell, was painted sometime before 1753. Known as a "dummy board," the painted wood was evidently propped against a wall or placed in a doorway. Its function is not known. Perhaps Wendell displayed the dummy board to show visitors that she possessed a servant woman. Maybe Phyllis herself moved the board from place to place in Wendell's house to indicate where she was working at the time. Or possibly the portrait was painted in recognition of some unknown special relationship between Phyllis and Wendell. Phyllis is shown as a demure, well-groomed woman whose dress and demeanor suggest that she was capable, orderly, and efficient. Although tens of thousands of slaves were brought to the British North American colonies during the eighteenth century, it does not appear that Phyllis was one of them. Instead, she was probably born in the colonies of mixed white and black parentage. Like thousands of other slave women who labored in the homes of prosperous white families, Phyllis illustrates the integration of the mundane tasks of housekeeping with the shifting currents of transatlantic commerce.

Courtesy of the Society for the Preservation of New England Antiquities/photo by David Bohl.

COLONIAL AMERICA IN THE EIGHTEENTH CENTURY

5

1701–1760

ARLY ON A SUNDAY MORNING IN OCTOBER 1723, young Benjamin Franklin stepped from a wharf along the Delaware River onto the streets of Philadelphia. As he wrote later in his autobiography, "I was dirty from my Journey; my Pockets were stuff'd out with Shirts and Stockings; I knew no Soul, nor where to look for Lodging. I was fatigu'd with Travelling, Rowing and Want of Rest. I was very hungry."

Born in 1706, Benjamin Franklin grew up in Boston, where his father, Josiah—a Puritan—had emigrated from England in 1683. Josiah Franklin worked as a tallow chandler in Boston, making soap and candles for the city's families. The father of seventeen children, he provided a modest but stable living for his large family. He made certain each of his sons served an apprenticeship to learn a trade.

When Benjamin was ten years old, Josiah put him to work in his own shop, where, Benjamin recalled, "I was employed in cutting Wick for Candles, filling the Dipping Mold, and the Molds for cast Candles, attending the Shop, going of Errands, &c." Benjamin was bored stiff. He stole time to indulge his passion for reading, even on Sunday. He admitted "evading as much as I could the common Attendance on publick Worship," for which his father scolded him. His "Bookish Inclination . . . determin'd my Father to make me a Printer." After some hesitation, the twelve-year-old Benjamin signed an indenture to serve until he was twenty-one as an apprentice to his brother James.

James Franklin, nine years older than Benjamin, had recently returned to Boston from England, where he had learned the printer's trade. He opened a shop in the city, where his young apprentice learned how to set type, compose a page, and operate the press. Benjamin also had access to the latest books and pamphlets, and he read everything he could get his hands on.

In 1721, James inaugurated the *New England Courant,* only the fourth newspaper to be published in the colonies. The articles in the *Courant,* as one of Franklin's friends said, were written "in a very easy and familiar manner, so that the meanest ploughman, the very meanest of God's people may understand them." Before long, the sixteen-year-old printer's apprentice secretly wrote fourteen essays under the pseudonym of a New England widow, Silence Dogood—a sly reference to Puritan minister Cotton Mather's work *Essays to Do Good*—and slipped them under the door of the print shop during the night.

Benjamin's responsibilities grew quickly after James aroused the ire of the government with an article that denounced men who "*dissemble* and *lie, snuffle* and

PHILADELPHIA WHARF

This early-nineteenth-century drawing of the Arch Street wharf in Philadelphia approximates the world Benjamin Franklin entered when he stepped ashore in 1723. The wharf was a center of purposeful movement, of industrious activity; almost everyone depicted appears to be working or making profitable use of their leisure (by fishing, for example). The pulse of Atlantic commerce propels casks of products from the deck of the small local sailboat (right) toward the hold of large oceangoing ships (center) bound for England and Europe. The small rowboat carrying four people (just to the right of the large ships) is probably similar to the boat Franklin rowed to the city. Coordinating the complicated comings and goings of people and goods that moved through the wharf rewarded individuals who combined intelligence, energy, and discipline with efficiency, reliability, and trustworthiness—traits Franklin and other eighteenth-century colonists sought to cultivate.

Rare Book Department, The Free Library of Philadelphia.

whiffle . . . [and who] will overreach and defraud all who deal with them," proclaiming that of all such knaves, "the *religious knave* is the worst." The Massachusetts government found public ridicule of religion intolerable and ordered James to submit all future issues of the *Courant* for censorship. Rather than comply, James evaded the order by making his seventeen-year-old brother the new publisher of the *Courant,* but requiring him to continue to serve out his apprenticeship.

Benjamin published the paper for several months, but he chafed under his brother's supervision. "Tho' a Brother, he [James] considered himself as my Master, and me as his Apprentice," Benjamin remembered; "and [he] accordingly expected the same Services from me as he would from another; while I thought he demean'd me too much. . . . My Brother was passionate and had often beaten me, which I took extreamly amiss." Benjamin resolved "to assert my Freedom." The young printer-author-publisher "inclin'd to leave Boston" and bought passage aboard a ship to New York, unbeknown to his brother or his father.

After three days at sea, he arrived in New York, nearly three hundred miles from anyone he knew. When he could not find work, he sailed to the New

Jersey shore and then walked fifty miles west to a town on the Delaware River upstream from Philadelphia. While strolling along the riverbank in the evening, he talked his way aboard a small boat heading down the river toward Philadelphia. After rowing half the night, Franklin and the other exhausted travelers floated up to a wharf about eight o'clock the next morning.

Franklin went straight to a bakery, ordered three cents worth of bread, and was surprised to be given "three great Puffy Rolls." He began to eat one and, "having no Room in my Pockets," which were stuffed with shirts and socks, he "walk'd off, with a Roll under each Arm." He went back to the wharf to wash down the bread with "a Draught of the River Water. . . . Thus refresh'd I walk'd again up the Street, which by this time had many clean dress'd People in it who were all walking the same Way; I join'd them, and thereby was led to the great Meeting House of the Quakers. . . . I sat down among them, and . . . I fell fast asleep, and continu'd so till the Meeting broke up."

Franklin's account of his early life in Boston and his arrival in Philadelphia is probably the most well known portrait of life in eighteenth-century colonial America. It illustrates the everyday experiences that an obscure but extraordinary printer's apprentice shared with many others in the colonies: a large family; short schooling; long hours of labor as a subordinate to the authority of a superior, whether a parent, relative, or employer; and a restless quest for something better, for escape from the ties that bound, for freedom. Franklin's account hints at other, less tangible trends: an ambition to make something of oneself in this world rather than worry too much about the hereafter; an eagerness to subvert the domination of ministers and government officials by publishing dissenting opinions expressed in simple, clear language understandable by "the meanest ploughman"; a confidence that, with a valued skill and a few coins, a young man could make his way in the world, a confidence few young women could dare assert; and a slackening of religious fervor displayed in open dissent and in Franklin's snooze during the Quaker meeting.

The simple story of Franklin's first day in Philadelphia introduces some of the major changes under way in eighteenth-century America. Those changes affected all the colonies in British North America, but they did not erase the fundamental differences among New England, the middle colonies, and the southern colonies. Instead of becoming more alike, the three regions became more

sharply differentiated. While social and economic changes tended to underscore the diversity among the colonies, important cultural and political developments tugged in the opposite direction, creating common experiences, aspirations, and identities. In 1776, when *E Pluribus Unum* (Latin meaning "From Many, One") was adopted as the motto for the Great Seal of the United States, the *Pluribus* referred to the dominant legacy from the eighteenth-century colonies. But changes in eighteenth-century America that strengthened *Pluribus* also planted the seeds of *Unum.*

A Growing Population and Expanding Economy

The most important fact about eighteenth-century colonial America was its phenomenal population growth. In 1700, colonists numbered barely more than 250,000; by 1770, they tallied well over 2 million. The eightfold growth of the population of the British North American colonies between 1700 and 1770 was unequaled in the eighteenth century. In England, by comparison, the population grew only about 40 percent in the same period, from 5 million to over 7 million. An index of the emerging significance of colonial America is that in 1700 there were 19 people in England for every American colonist, whereas by 1770 there were only 3.

The dramatic growth of the colonial population signaled the maturation of a distinctive colonial society. That society was by no means uniform or homogeneous. It encompassed the regional diversity of climate and natural environment that extended inland along the Atlantic coast from Maine to Georgia. Colonists of different ethnic groups, races, and religions lived under thirteen different colonial governments, all of them under the umbrella of the British Empire, which encouraged immigration to the colonies.

In general, the growth and diversity of the eighteenth-century colonial population derived from two sources: immigration and natural increase (that is, growth through reproduction). Natural increase contributed about three-fourths of the population growth, immigration about one-fourth. Immigration did more than boost the colonial population. New settlers from the Old World poured into the colonies in such unprecedented numbers that they changed the face of the population. They shifted the ethnic and racial balance among the colonists, making them by 1770 less English and less white than ever before. During the entire seventeenth century, about 200,000 people arrived in the mainland British colonies; 80 percent of them came from England and another 5 percent from Africa, nearly all of the latter slaves. In contrast, from 1700 to the eve of the American Revolution in 1776, almost 800,000 newcomers streamed into the colonies. Fewer than 10 percent came from England; about 36 percent were Scots-Irish, mostly from northern Ireland; 33 percent came from Africa, again almost all of them slaves; nearly 15 percent came from the many German principalities (the nation of Germany did not exist until 1871); and almost 10 percent came from Scotland. This massive influx of new colonists profoundly altered the composition of the colonial population in the century between 1670 and 1770. In 1670, more than 9 out of 10 colonists were of English ancestry, and only 1 out of 25 was of African ancestry. By 1770, only about half the colonists were of English descent, while more than 20 percent descended from Africans. By 1770, the people of the colonies had a distinctive *colonial*—rather than English—profile.

The booming population of the colonies hints at a second major feature of eighteenth-century colonial society: an expanding economy. Today, societies with rapidly growing populations often suffer from poverty and overpopulation. They have more people than they can adequately feed; or, put another way, they have a high ratio of people to land. In the eighteenth-century colonies, very different conditions prevailed.

In 1700, after almost a century of settlement, nearly all the colonists lived within 50 miles of the Atlantic coast, on the edge of a vast wilderness peopled by native Indians and a few trappers and traders. The population was overwhelmingly rural. Only about 1 colonist in 20 lived in a town of 2,500 or more, a fraction that hardly changed during the eighteenth century. The wilderness so dominated the colonies that even in the 1750s sailors approaching the American mainland could begin to smell pine trees when they were 180 miles from shore. The almost limitless wilderness gave the colonies an extremely low ratio of people to land, which had far-reaching economic consequences.

For one thing, it meant that land was cheap. Of course, it was never so cheap that every colonist owned some. But it was cheap enough that every colonist who wanted to own land had a much better chance of doing so than in eighteenth-century

MAP 5.1
Europeans and Africans in the Eighteenth Century
This map illustrates regions where Africans and certain immigrant groups clustered. It is important to avoid misreading this map. Predominantly European regions, for example, also contained colonists from other places. Likewise, regions where African slaves resided in large numbers also included many whites, their masters among them. The map suggests the polyglot diversity of eighteenth-century colonial society.

England or continental Europe. Land in the colonies commonly sold for a fraction of its price in the Old World, often for only a shilling an acre, at a time when a carpenter could earn three shillings a day. Along the frontiers of settlement, newcomers who lacked the money to buy land often lived as squatters on unoccupied land, hoping it might somehow eventually become theirs. Legally or otherwise, land was so readily available that colonial governors had difficulty recruiting soldiers during the 1740s and 1750s, since the hungry, landless men from whom armies were recruited in Europe were hard to find in large numbers in the colonies.

Without labor, land was almost worthless for agriculture. The abundance of land in the colonies made labor precious, and the colonists always needed more. The colonists' insatiable labor demand was the fundamental economic environment that sustained the mushrooming population.

The unusually low ratio of people to land in the colonies—with all that meant about access to land and demand for labor—made it possible for the colonial population to grow rapidly without producing widespread poverty. Starvation in the eighteenth-century colonies was confined to isolated catastrophes, and famine was unknown. For most colonists, food was simple but ample enough to go around. Indeed, travelers marveled that settler families often invited strangers to share the families' food and seldom asked for payment, a good sign that settlers hungered for news and companionship more than they worried about another mouth to feed.

The dramatic growth of the colonial population signaled the maturation of a distinctive colonial society. That society was by no means uniform or homogeneous.

Economic historians estimate that the standard of living of free colonists (that is, those who were not indentured servants or slaves) actually improved during the eighteenth century: The colonial economy grew fast enough not just to keep up with an eightfold increase in population, but to surpass it. By 1770, most free colonists had a higher standard of living than the majority of people elsewhere in the Atlantic world. That did not mean that most colonists were rich; far from it. Economic expansion engendered glaring inequities. Instead, it meant that the colonies' abundance of land, demand for labor, and supply of food created a rare social and economic environment that, in general, permitted free colonists to live well. Many colonists did get rich during the eighteenth century. But the unique achievement of the eighteenth-century colonial economy was less the wealth of the most success-ful colonists (plenty of Europeans were much, much richer) than the modest economic welfare of the vast bulk of the free population. In Europe, pinnacles of wealth stood on foundations of poverty; in the eighteenth-century colonies, the pyramid of wealth was impressive not for its height but for its broad, solid base in the free population.

These general, large-scale trends in the eighteenth-century colonies evolved in distinctive patterns in New England, the middle colonies, and the southern colonies.

New England: From Puritans to Yankee Traders

The New England population grew sixfold during the eighteenth century, but it lagged behind the growth in the other colonies. The main reason New England failed to keep pace was that most immigrants steered clear of Massachusetts and Connecticut. They chose other destinations partly because Puritan orthodoxy—atrophied though it was by the eighteenth century—made these colonies comparatively inhospitable for both religious dissenters and those indifferent to theology. In 1734, for example, residents of Worcester, Massachusetts, literally demolished a new Presbyterian church built by a group of recent Scots-Irish immigrants. Rhode Island's tolerance encouraged religious heterodoxy, but its tiny land area discouraged immigrants. However, the most important reason immigrants avoided New England was that the growth of population there gave it a higher and less desirable ratio of people to land than the other colonies. As the population grew, many settlers dispersed from towns to individual farms, and Puritan communities lost much of their cohesion. Nonetheless, networks of economic exchange laced rural settlers to their neighbors, local market towns, Boston merchants, and the broad currents of Atlantic commerce. In many ways, trade became a faith that competed strongly with the traditions of Puritanism.

Natural Increase and Land Distribution

The New England population grew mostly by natural increase, much as it had during the seventeenth century. Nearly every adult woman married. The widespread expectation that women would and should marry caused unmarried adult women to be considered a little peculiar. Predictably, married women had children, and, thanks to the relatively low New England mortality rate, often many children. The perils of childbirth gave wives a shorter life expectancy than husbands, but wives often lived to have six, seven, or eight babies. When a wife died, her husband usually remarried quickly. A wife's labor and companionship were too vital for a farm family to do without. Often, a widowed husband had still more children with a second or third wife. Benjamin Franklin's father had seven children with his first wife and ten (including Benjamin) with his second. Such large families rapidly multiplied the New England population, especially since—unlike in England—most children survived to adulthood when, as husbands and wives, they made their own hearty contributions to the population.

In many ways, trade became a faith that competed strongly with the traditions of Puritanism.

The burgeoning New England population pressed against a limited amount of land. The interior of New England, bounded by the Hudson River on the west and the St. Lawrence River to the north, was smaller than that of colonies farther south. Furthermore, as the northernmost group of colonies, New England had a contested northern and western frontier. Powerful Indian tribes—especially the Iroquois and Mahicans—jealously guarded their territories. When provoked by colonial or European disputes, the French (and Catholic) colony of Quebec also menaced the English (and Protestant) colonists of New England. But the main reason New Englanders were pinched for land during the eighteenth century was what they chose to do with the land they had available.

During the seventeenth century, New England towns parceled out land to individual families. In most cases, the land allotments proved large enough to permit the original settlers to practice partible inheritance (that is, to subdivide the land more or less equally among sons). By the eighteenth century, the original land allotments had to be further subdivided to accommodate grandsons and great-grandsons, and many plots of land became too small for a family to make a living. Sons who could not hope to inherit a livable farm (like Ben-

jamin Franklin) had several options. They could find a trade or a profession in one of the scores of villages that dotted the New England countryside. Or they could try their luck in Boston, the region's one metropolis, which housed about 16,000 souls by midcentury. But if they wanted to farm, as 8 out of 10 New Englanders did, they had to move away from the town where they were born.

During the eighteenth century, colonial governments in New England abandoned the seventeenth-century policy of granting land to towns. Needing revenue, the governments of both Connecticut and Massachusetts sold land directly to individuals, including speculators. This new land policy undermined the powerful influence churches and towns had exerted over New Englanders during the seventeenth century. Now, money rather than membership in a community knit together in a church covenant determined whether a person could obtain land.

The new land policy also caused the disintegration of the seventeenth-century pattern of settlement. As New Englanders moved into western Massachusetts and Connecticut and north into New Hampshire and Maine, they tended to settle on individual farms rather than in the towns and villages that characterized the seventeenth century. New Englanders still depended on their relatives and neighbors for help in clearing land, raising a house, worshiping God, and having a good time. But far more than in the seventeenth century, they regulated their behavior in newly settled areas by their own individual dictates. A telling measure of the decline in Puritan watchfulness that accompanied the settlement on individual farms was the rising rate of premarital pregnancy. Historians have discovered that in the seventeenth century, fewer than one New England bride in ten was pregnant when she married; by the mid-eighteenth century, one-third of New England brides were pregnant, and in some communities nearly half were.

Farms, Fish, and Trade

The relative scarcity of land in New England (compared with the middle colonies and the southern colonies) encouraged agricultural diversification. New England farmers grew food for their families, but their fields did not produce a huge marketable surplus. In fact, New England farms could not grow enough wheat to feed the population, partly because of the diminished fertility of the soil and partly because a plant disease withered the wheat.

New England had to import wheat from Pennsylvania, New York, Maryland, and Virginia. Without one big crop, farmers grew many small ones and, if they had extra, sold to or traded with neighbors. Interwoven networks of local exchange reached only a few miles from each farm. Poor roads made travel difficult, time-consuming, and expensive, especially with bulky and heavy agricultural goods. The one major agricultural product the New England colonies exported—livestock—walked to market on its own four legs. A New England farm was a place to get by, not to get rich. By 1770, New Englanders had less wealth per capita than residents of the middle colonies and only one-fourth as much as free colonists in the southern colonies.

As consumers, New England farmers made up the foundation of a diversified commercial economy that linked remote farms to markets throughout the world. Although farmers had little to sell on world markets, the cash they earned in local markets they took to stores in nearby villages and towns where they could buy Chinese tea, English textiles, ceramics, tobacco, and metal goods, or possibly a newspaper, a collection of sermons, or a handy almanac. Merchants large and small stocked mostly imported goods. But farmers' needs for sturdy shoes, a warm coat, a sound cart, a tight barrel, or a solid building supported local shoemakers, tailors, wheelwrights, blacksmiths, carpenters, masons, and coopers. In the larger towns and especially in Boston, such specialized artisans as cabinetmakers and silversmiths could be found, along with tallow chandlers and printers, like Benjamin Franklin's father and brother. Skilled tradesmen made up about a third of Boston's adult men, and most of them managed to make a decent living. Shipbuilders tended to do better than other artisans because they served the most dynamic sector of the New England economy.

As consumers, New England farmers made up the foundation of a diversified commercial economy that linked remote farms to markets throughout the world.

As they had since the seventeenth century, New Englanders made their fortunes at sea. Fishermen salted and sold some of their catch to their fellow colonists, but most was exported to markets in southern Europe or, principally, the West Indies,

NATHANIEL HURD, A BOSTON ARTISAN
Like Benjamin Franklin, Nathaniel Hurd was born into an artisan family in Boston. With a tailor great-grandfather, a joiner grandfather, and an accomplished silversmith father, Hurd apprenticed with his father and became an expert engraver, designing bookplates as well as various commercial and social notices, such as loan certificates and wedding invitations. This portrait was painted in 1765 by John Singleton Copley, the most accomplished American artist of the time. Hurd's fine clothing illustrates the prosperity a highly skilled artisan in a good trade could achieve. His open collar and plain cuffs show that he was no idle gentleman; the prominence of his hands suggests their centrality in his life and work. Although Hurd's trade made him dependent on the orders of his customers, he does not appear to be obsequious; instead, he seems to be secure, even independent, though not haughty or overbearing.
© The Cleveland Museum of Art, Gift of the John Huntington Art and Polytechnic Trust, 1915.534

---

where sugar plantation slaves ate cheap New England cod. Fish accounted for more than a third of New England's exports, with livestock and timber making up another third. The West Indies absorbed two-thirds of all New England's exports, while almost all the rest went to England and continental Europe. This Atlantic commerce benefited the entire New England economy, providing jobs for la-

BOSTON COMMON IN NEEDLEWORK

This exquisite needlework was embroidered by Hannah Otis in 1750 when she was eighteen years old. Her picture illustrates the semirural character of one of the largest colonial cities. She showed the Boston Common as if the city's bustling streets and wharves were behind the viewer. Her cityscape is populated by more animals than people and covered by plants rather than paving stones. From the perspective of the late twentieth century, the scene gives few hints of a city. Try to adopt the perspective of the mid-eighteenth century and imagine how the picture might be different if it showed rural Massachusetts. Or, conversely, what features would suggest a city to an eighteenth-century viewer? The large house (center right) belonged to the Hancock family; John Hancock, who later signed the Declaration of Independence, is shown on horseback in the foreground. Does it appear that the Hancocks farmed their land? Note that Otis did not fail to show that wealthy Bostonians were familiar with slavery.

Courtesy, Museum of Fine Arts, Boston.

borers and tradesmen such as sailors, stevedores, and rope makers as well as for ship captains, clerks, and merchants of all kinds.

Merchants dominated the commercial economy of New England. Whether in inland communities like Springfield, Massachusetts, or Hartford, Connecticut, or seaports like Marblehead, Massachusetts, New London, Connecticut, or Providence, Rhode Island, merchants stood at the hub of trade between local folk and the international market. The largest and most successful merchants lived in Boston, where they not only bought and sold imported goods but also owned and insured the ships that carried the merchandise. On the whole, the New England merchants and shippers did not take part in the lucrative tobacco, sugar, and rice trade from the plantation colonies, which tended to be re-

served for British merchants. As British colonists, they benefited from the protection of the Royal Navy, but they seldom hesitated to evade imperial trade regulations when a good profit could be made. For example, although the colonists were prohibited from purchasing tea in Amsterdam—where it was much cheaper than in London, because the Dutch did not tax it as heavily as the English did—New England merchants often bought tea illegally in the Dutch West Indies and sold it back home at a lower price than English tea but with a higher margin of profit for themselves. Merchants also profited from privateering—preying on French and Spanish ships during the intermittent warfare between those nations and England during the eighteenth century.

By the 1760s, the richest Boston merchants built elegant mansions, imported ornate carriages, and had servants (often slaves) dressed in livery. When John Adams—a New England lawyer who became a leader during the American Revolution and ultimately president of the United States—was invited to a wealthy Boston merchant's home, he was stunned by its magnificence. It was a house "for a noble Man, a Prince," he wrote; "the Turkey Carpets, the painted Hangings, the Marble Tables, the rich Beds with crimson Damask Curtains and Counterpins, the beautiful Chimney Clock, the Spacious Garden, are the most magnificent of any Thing I have ever seen." The contrast Adams noted between the luxurious home of this merchant prince and the lives of other New Englanders indicates the polarization of wealth that occurred in Boston and other seaports during the eighteenth century. The thriving commercial activity concentrated wealth in the hands of the most successful merchants. In the late seventeenth century, the richest 5 percent of Bostonians owned about a third of the city's wealth; by 1770, they owned about half. At the other end of the spectrum, the share of the city's wealth possessed by the poorest two-thirds of the population declined from about one-sixth to less than one-tenth.

The rich got richer, and everybody else had a smaller share of the total wealth, but the incidence of genuine poverty did not change much. Roughly 5 or 6 percent of the New England population qualified for poor relief throughout the eighteenth century. Nonetheless, the colony's growing population increased the sheer numbers of unemployed or sick men, widows, orphans, and elderly or disabled people. Boston and other New England towns struggled to provide relief for them in families or in almshouses. To minimize the taxes required to support these relief efforts, Boston and other towns built workhouses during the eighteenth century, hoping to force able-bodied poor folk to earn something for their keep. But compared with the poverty in England, the colonists were better off. As a Connecticut traveler wrote from England in 1764, "We in New England know nothing of poverty and want, we have no idea of the thing, how much better do our poor people live than 7/8 of the people on this much famed island."

The contrast with English poverty had meaning since the overwhelming majority of New Englanders traced their ancestry to England, making the region more English and more homogeneous than any other. The population of African ancestry in the region remained small. Several merchants specialized in the African slave trade and often brought a few slaves back from their voyages to the West Indies or the southern colonies and readily sold them in New England. New Englanders had no hesitation about acquiring slaves, and many Puritan ministers, including Cotton Mather, owned one or two. But except for the Narragansett region of Rhode Island, where numerous slaves worked raising livestock, New England's family farms were unsuited for slave labor. Instead, New England's slaves concentrated in towns, especially Boston, where most of them worked as domestic servants and laborers. Although the black population of New England grew from less than 2,000 in 1700 to over 15,000 by 1770, it barely diluted the region's 97 percent white, mostly English, majority.

By 1770, the population, wealth, and commercial activity of New England differed from what they had been in 1700. Ministers still enjoyed high status in New England, but the Yankee trader had replaced the Puritan divine as the symbolic New Englander.

The Middle Colonies: Immigrants, Wheat, and Work

During the eighteenth century, the population of the middle colonies (Pennsylvania, New York, New Jersey, and Delaware) grew faster than that of New England. At the beginning of the century, almost twice as many people lived in New England as in the middle colonies. But by 1770, the population of the middle colonies had multiplied tenfold—mainly from an influx of German, Irish, Scotch, and other immigrants—and nearly equaled the population of New England. Pennsylvania received more immigrants than any other middle colony; its population grew thirteenfold between 1700 and 1770. In 1700, Pennsylvania was the sixth largest colony in British North America; by 1770, Pennsylvania's population surpassed that of every colony but Virginia.

Immigrants made the middle colonies a uniquely diverse society. The population was less English than either New England or the South. By the end of the eighteenth century, barely one-third of Pennsylvanians and less than half the total population of the middle colonies traced their ancestry to England.

NEW YORK STREET SCENE
This painting depicts John Street, a residential neighborhood of New York, in 1768, as recalled by artist Joseph B. Smith early in the nineteenth century. The painting highlights the urbane pleasures of casual encounters and friendly conversations on the street. Unlike urban streets today, noise on John Street was limited to human voices, a few yipping dogs, and the clip-clop of horses' hooves. The street appears safe and secure; the people show no sign of caution about theft or assault, nor do they appear to be in a hurry to seek refuge indoors. What do the various clusters of people suggest about patterns of sociability on John Street in the eighteenth century? Standing at the door of Wesley Chapel (the first Methodist church building in America) is Peter Williams, an African American who served as sexton of the church. Williams later earned enough money buying and selling tobacco to help build New York's first African American Methodist church. Old John Street United Methodist Church.

German and Scots-Irish Immigrants

Germans made up the largest contingent of migrants from the European continent to the middle colonies. In 1683, a small group of Quaker and Mennonite families from Germany founded Germantown, Pennsylvania. (Like Quakers, Mennonites were sober pacifists, persecuted for their strict piety.) Not until the first decade of the eighteenth century, however, did ships crowded with German settlers begin to dock at Philadelphia wharves. By 1770, more than 100,000 had arrived in the colonies. Their fellow colonists often referred to them as "Pennsylvania Dutch," an English corruption of the German word the immigrants used to describe themselves and their native language, *Deutsch.*

Most German immigrants came from a region along the Rhine River in southwestern Germany called the Palatinate, although some hailed from German-speaking parts of Switzerland, Austria, and the Netherlands. Families, neighbors, and sometimes whole villages uprooted to escape harsh conditions that had become intolerable. Throughout Europe, peasants suffered from exploitation by landowners and governments, and they had few opportunities to improve their lives. Palatine peasants in particular, one observer noted, were "not as well off as cattle elsewhere." Devastating French invasions of the Palatinate during Queen Anne's War (1702–1713) made ordinarily bad conditions even worse and triggered the first large-scale migration. German immigrants to the middle colonies included numerous artisans and a few merchants, but the great majority were farmers and laborers. Economically, they represented "middling" folk, neither the poorest (who could not afford the trip) nor the better off (who did not want to leave).

By the 1720s, Germans who had established themselves in the colonies wrote back to their friends and relatives, as one reported, "of the civil and religious liberties [and] privileges, and of all the goodness I have heard and seen." Such reports prompted still more Germans to pull up stakes and embark for America. Dutch shipping firms employed agents, known as "Newlanders," to amplify these messages and advertise the virtues of the colonies as they traveled the Rhine valley. Newlanders earned a small fee for every passenger they persuaded to depart for America. One disillusioned immigrant referred to Newlanders as "thieves of human beings . . . trafficking in human flesh." Others probably discounted the glowing reports from Newlanders and even the more temperate letters from those already settled in the colonies. But they left anyway, because—as several travelers told one of their stay-behind compatriots—they "preferred being slaves in America to being free townsmen" in Germany. That statement expressed the immigrants' overpowering desire to exchange the miserable certainties of their lives in Germany for the uncertain attractions of life in the colonies.

Similar motives propelled the Scots-Irish, who outnumbered German immigrants by more than two to one. The term *Scots-Irish,* like *Pennsylvania Dutch,* was a misleading label coined in the colonies. Immigrants labeled Scots-Irish actually hailed from the north of Ireland (Ulster Scots), Scotland, and northern England. Some of the Scots-Irish were Irish natives who had no personal or ancestral connection whatever with Scotland. This somewhat confusing mixture of peoples shared traits that made them recognizable to other colonists and gave rise to the umbrella term *Scots-Irish.*

Unlike the Germans, the Scots-Irish spoke English, but with a distinctive accent that set them apart. Like the Germans, the Scots-Irish were Protestants, but with a difference. Most German immigrants worshiped in Lutheran or German Reformed churches; many others belonged to dissenting sects like the Mennonites, Moravians, Dunkers, Schwenkfelders, and Amish, whose adherents sought relief in the colonies from persecution they had suffered in Europe for their refusal to bear arms and to swear oaths, beliefs they shared with Quakers. In contrast, the Scots-Irish tended to be militant Presbyterians who seldom hesitated to swear oaths or bear arms, often in that order. Also, like German settlers, Scots-Irish immigrants were clannish, residing when they could among relatives or neighbors from the old country.

Immigrants made the middle colonies a uniquely diverse society. By the end of the eighteenth century, barely one-third of Pennsylvanians and less than half the total population of the middle colonies traced their ancestry to England.

Scots-Irish immigrants trickled into the colonies during the seventeenth century. In the eighteenth century, wave after wave of Scots-Irish immigrants arrived, beginning in 1717, cresting every twelve or fifteen years thereafter, and culminating in a flood of immigration in the years just before the American Revolution. The timing of the waves was determined by deteriorating economic conditions in northern Ireland, Scotland, and England. Most of the immigrants were farm laborers or tenant farmers squeezed by landlords who sought profits by raising rents and thereby reducing tenants' income

and standard of living. Handloom weavers fled the collapsing linen industry in northern Ireland, especially after 1770. Droughts, crop failures, high food prices, and genuine famine pushed many others to depart for the colonies. An Ulster Scot remarked that "oppression has brought us" to the "deplorable state . . . [that] the very marrow is screwed out of our bones." By 1773, British officials became so concerned about the drain of people to the colonies that they began to quiz prospective settlers about why they were leaving. The answers the Scots-Irish gave echoed the motives of their predecessors in previous decades: "out of work"; "poverty"; "could not earn bread sufficient to support family"; "tyranny of landlords"; "high rents and oppression"; and to "do better in America."

Both Scots-Irish and Germans probably heard the common saying that "Pennsylvania is heaven for farmers [and] paradise for artisans," but they almost certainly did not fully understand the risks and rigors of their decision to leave their native lands. Gottfried Mittelberger, a musician who traveled from Germany to Philadelphia in 1750, described the grueling passage to America commonly experienced by eighteenth-century emigrants. Mittelberger's trip down the Rhine River from his home village to the port of Rotterdam took seven weeks because the boat had to stop at thirty-six customs houses of German principalities along the river, each of which took its time to inspect papers and baggage and to collect a fee. Mittelberger reckoned that the trip to Rotterdam cost four times more than the trip from Rotterdam to Philadelphia. Many German emigrants who set out with what they believed to be plenty of money arrived in Rotterdam with empty pockets. They still needed to maintain themselves for five or six weeks in Holland until the ship was fully loaded and ready to depart. Scots-Irish emigrants usually avoided expensive delays before sailing simply because they lived nearer the coast.

Nearly two-thirds of all German emigrants arrived at their port of departure with no money to stock up on extra provisions for the trip or even to buy a ticket. Likewise, they could not afford to go back home. Ship captains, aware of the hunger for labor in the colonies, eagerly signed up the penniless emigrants as "redemptioners," a variant of the more common arrangement for indentured servants. A captain would agreed to provide transportation to Philadelphia, where redemptioners would obtain the money to pay for their passage from a friend or relative who was already in the colonies or, as most did, by selling themselves as servants. Impoverished Scots-Irish emigrants, especially the majority who traveled alone rather than with families, typically paid for their passage by contracting to become indentured servants before they sailed from the British Isles, as English emigrants had been doing since the seventeenth century.

Mittelberger enjoyed the amenities of food and cabin service reserved for passengers who paid their way to Pennsylvania, but he witnessed the distress among the four hundred other Germans aboard his ship, most of them redemptioners. They were packed, he wrote, "as closely as herring," in bunks two feet by six feet. Seasickness compounded by exhaustion, poverty, poor food, bad water, inadequate sanitation, and tight quarters encouraged the spread of disease. Dozens died; on Mittelberger's ship, thirty-two children were buried at sea. "Groaning, crying, and lamentation go on aboard day and night," Mittelberger reported; "many people . . . become homesick at the thought that many hundreds of people must necessarily perish, die, and be thrown into the ocean in such misery. And this in turn makes their families, or those who were responsible for their undertaking the journey, oftentimes fall almost into despair—so that it soon becomes practically impossible to rouse them from their depression." The emigrants' misery continued for the seven or eight weeks usually required to sail to the colonies. Scattered evidence suggests that the dismal conditions on Mittelberger's ship were not unusual. One historian has noted that on the sixteen emigrant ships arriving in Philadelphia in 1738, over half of all passengers died en route.

When his ship finally approached land, Mittelberger explained, "everyone crawls from below to the deck . . . and people cry for joy, pray, and sing praises and thanks to God." Unfortunately, their troubles were far from over. Once the ship docked, passengers who had paid their fare could go ashore, as could redemptioners who could provide the captain some collateral while they tried to raise the funds for their passage. All the other redemptioners and indentured servants—the majority of passengers—had to stay on board until someone came to purchase them (or, more precisely, to purchase their labor). Captains advertised the sale of redemptioners and servants, and the prospects of cheap labor attracted buyers. Unlike indentured servants, redemptioners negotiated independently with their purchasers about their period of servitude. Typically, a healthy adult redemptioner agreed to four years of servitude. If a family member had died at sea, the surviving members of the family still had to pay the deceased's fare by agreeing to longer periods of servitude. Indentured servants commonly served five, six, or seven years, as did weaker, sicker, younger, and less skilled redemptioners. Children ten years old or younger usually had to become servants until they were twenty-one.

Pennsylvania: "The Best Poor [White] Man's Country"

New settlers, whether free or in servitude, poured into the middle colonies because they perceived unparalleled opportunities. Hired workers could get wages three or four times higher than in England. Pennsylvania deserved its reputation as "the best poor Man's Country in the World," indentured servant William Moraley wrote in 1743. Although Moraley reported that "the Condition of bought Servants is very hard" and masters often failed to live up to their promise to provide decent food and clothing, opportunity abounded because there was more work to be done than workers to do it.

Most servants toiled in Philadelphia, New York City, or one of the smaller towns or villages. Only a minority—roughly one-third—labored on farms. Artisans, small manufacturers, and shopkeepers prized the labor of male servants. Female servants made valuable additions to households, where nearly all of them worked cleaning, washing, cooking, and minding children. From the masters' viewpoint, servants were a bargain. A master could purchase five or six years of a servant's labor for approximately the wages a common laborer would earn in four months. Wage workers could walk away from their jobs when they pleased, and they did so often enough to be troublesome to employers. Servants, however, were legally bound to work for their masters until their terms expired. The restrictions and confinements of bondage were genuine, and they were vigorously enforced. But for servants, bondage was temporary. Much like Benjamin Franklin's service as an apprentice, it carried no lasting stigma.

A few black slaves worked in shops and homes in Philadelphia and New York City. For example, after Benjamin Franklin became prosperous, he purchased slaves named Peter, Jemima, King, Othello, and George. Since a slave cost at least three times as much as a servant, only affluent colonists could afford the long-term investment in slave labor. While the population of African ancestry (almost all

BENJAMIN FRANKLIN
This is the earliest known portrait of Benjamin Franklin. Painted by Robert Feke in about 1748 when Franklin was in his early forties, the portrait illustrates Franklin's status as an aspiring printer, merchant, and citizen of Philadelphia. To the late-twentieth-century eye, Franklin appears prim, foppish, and mannered, with an elaborately curled wig framing a composed, satisfied face. However, compare Franklin's demeanor and dress with that of Nathaniel Hurd (page 159) and of Mrs. Barnard Elliott (page 180). Franklin appears more pretentious than Hurd and less elegant than Elliott, a rough index of his in-progress social mobility from a hardworking printer to a prominent and wealthy thinker and statesman.
Courtesy of the Harvard University Portrait Collection, Bequest, Dr. John C. Warren, 1856.

seventeenth century when New York was a Dutch colony. The Dutch, unlike the Quakers in seventeenth-century Pennsylvania, encouraged the importation of slaves because New Amsterdam had difficulty attracting white settlers and because the slave trade profited the Dutch West India Company.

During the eighteenth century, most slaves came to the middle colonies as they did to New England, in ships returning from the West Indies. Enough arrived to prompt colonial assemblies to pass slave codes that punished slaves much more severely than servants for the same transgressions. "For the least trespass," servant Moraley reported, slaves "undergo the severest Punishment." As Moraley noted, the law permitted runaway slaves to be "unmercifully whipped." In practice, both servants and slaves were governed more by their masters than by the laws. But in cases of abuse, servants had legal protections that slaves did not. Servants could and did charge masters with violating the terms of their indenture contracts. The terms of a slave's bondage were set forth in a master's commands, not in a written contract.

Small numbers of slaves managed to obtain their freedom, especially in New York City. But free African Americans did not escape whites' firm convictions about black inferiority and white supremacy. Those convictions lay at the foundation of the slave codes. Blacks worked alongside white servants and tradesmen, nursed white babies, cooked meals for white families, drank toasts with whites in taverns, and gambled with whites at horse races and fist fights. But few whites doubted that people of African ancestry should be where they were, at the bottom of the social pyramid. Whites' racism and blacks' lowly social status made African Americans scapegoats for European Americans' suspicions and anxieties. In 1741, when arson and several unexplained thefts plagued New York City, officials suspected a murderous slave conspiracy. On the basis of little more than evidence of slaves' "insolence" (that is, refusal to conform fully to whites' expectations of servile behavior), city authorities had thirteen slaves burned at the stake and eighteen others hanged. Although slaves were certifiably poor (they usually had no property whatever), they were not included among the poor for whom the middle colonies were reputed to be the best country in the world.

The reason more slaves were not brought to the middle colonies was that farmers, the vast majority of the population, had little use for them. Most farms operated with family labor. Wheat, the most

slaves) in the middle colonies grew from about 3,000 in 1700 to over 30,000 in 1770, it represented only about 7 percent of the total population, and in most of the region much less. People of African ancestry made up less than 3 percent of the population of Pennsylvania for most of the eighteenth century. In New York, blacks were much more common, accounting for nearly 15 percent of the population, more than in any other colony north of the Chesapeake. This pattern had been established during the

BETHLEHEM, PENNSYLVANIA

*This view of the small community of Bethlehem, Pennsylvania, in 1757 dramatizes the profound
transformation of the natural landscape in the eighteenth century by highly motivated human
labor. Founded by Moravian immigrants in 1740, Bethlehem must have appeared at first like the
dense woods on the upper left horizon. In fewer than twenty years, precisely laid-out orchards
and fields had replaced forests and glades. Carefully penned livestock (lower center right) and
fenced fields (lower left) kept the handiwork of farmers separate from the risks and disorders of
untamed nature. Not only individual farmsteads (lower center), but impressive multistory brick
town buildings (upper center) combined the bounty of the land with the delights of community
life. Few eighteenth-century communities were as orderly as Bethlehem, but many effected a comparable transformation of the environment.*

Miriam and Ira D. Walsh Division of Art, Prints, and Photographs, New York Public Library. Astor, Lenox, and
Tilden Foundations.

widely grown crop, did not require more labor than
farmers could typically muster from relatives,
neighbors, and a hired hand or two.

Immigrants swarmed to the middle colonies because of the availability of land to farm. The Penn
family encouraged immigration to bring in potential buyers for their enormous tracts of land in Pennsylvania. Owners of the huge estates in New York's
Hudson valley preferred to rent rather than sell
their land, making it more difficult for them to at-

tract immigrants. During the seventeenth century,
Pennsylvania had promoted immigration by offering a headright of fifty acres of land to servants who
completed their terms. In the eighteenth century,
servants' freedom dues were limited to two suits of
clothing, one new and one old, and some farm tools,
perhaps a hoe and a shovel, but no land. Nonetheless, the desire for farmland still tugged immigrants
to Philadelphia and other seaports and then scattered them to the ever-expanding periphery of set-

tlement, invigorating the demand for still more immigrants.

The price of farmland varied depending on soil quality, access to water, distance from a market town, and the extent of improvements. One hundred acres of improved land that had been cleared, plowed, fenced, ditched, and perhaps had a house and barn built on it might cost three or four times more than the same acreage of uncleared, unimproved land. Since the cheapest unimproved land always lay at the margin of settlement, would-be farmers tended to migrate to promising areas just beyond already improved farms. From Philadelphia, settlers moved north along the Delaware River and west along the Schuylkill and Susquehanna Rivers. By midcentury, settlement had reached the eastern slopes of the Appalachian Mountains, and newcomers spilled down the fertile valley of the Shenandoah River into western Virginia and the Carolinas. Thousands of settlers migrated from the middle colonies through this back door to the South. In 1765, for example, a young Scots-Irishman named Andrew Jackson and his wife, Elizabeth, migrated with their two young sons from northern Ireland to Pennsylvania and then trekked down the Shenandoah valley to South Carolina, where their third son, Andrew—the future president of the United States—was born in 1767.

From the beginning, Pennsylvania followed a policy of negotiating with Indian tribes to purchase additional land. This policy greatly reduced the violent clashes that flared along the frontier of settlement elsewhere in the colonies. The relative weakness of local tribes made negotiations easier for Pennsylvanians. The Susquehannocks in western Pennsylvania, for example, had been drubbed repeatedly by their powerful Iroquois enemies to the north, so it was attractive to them to sell off rights to land they could not defend very well in any case. Yet the Penn family did not shrink from pushing its agreements with Indian tribes to the limit and beyond. In a dispute with tribes on the northern Delaware in 1737, the Penn family pulled out a 1686 deed that showed that local tribes had then granted the Penns land that stretched as far as a man could walk in a day and a half. Under the terms of this infamous "Walking Purchase," the Penns sent out three runners, two of whom collapsed before the thirty-six hours expired. The third runner managed to cover sixty miles of wilderness, approximately doubling the size of the Penns' claim.

Few colonists drifted beyond the northern boundaries of Pennsylvania. The Iroquois dominated the lucrative fur trade of the St. Lawrence valley and eastern Great Lakes, and they had the political and military strength to defend their territory from colonial encroachment. They enforced their dominance through alliances with less mighty tribes and by clever diplomatic maneuvers that played the French colonists in Montreal, Canada, against the British colonists in Albany, New York, both of whom were eager to trade for Iroquois furs. Few settlers wanted to risk having their scalps lifted by Iroquois warriors in northern New York when they could choose to settle instead in the comparatively safe environs of Pennsylvania.

Farmers made the middle colonies the breadbasket of North America. They planted a wide variety of crops to feed their families, but they grew wheat in abundance. Flour milling was the number one industry and flour the number one export of the middle colonies. Wheat—whether as grain or flour—comprised nearly three-fourths of all exports from the middle colonies and connected Pennsylvania farmers to economic developments in the nations that rimmed the Atlantic. Pennsylvania flour fed residents in other colonies, in southern Europe, and—above all—in the West Indies. For farmers, the world grain market proved risky but profitable. Grain prices rose steadily after 1720; by 1770, a bushel of wheat was worth twice (in real terms, that is, adjusted for inflation) what it had been fifty years earlier. The ready market for surplus wheat allowed farmers to pay off debts; buy land, livestock, farm tools, and imports such as textiles, metalware, ceramics, tea, coffee, and sugar; and even to squirrel away a few shillings for a rainy day.

Prosperity and Poor Richard

The standard of living in rural Pennsylvania was probably higher than in any other agricultural region of the eighteenth-century world. Compared with their counterparts in cities, the rural South, or Europe, the wealthiest Pennsylvanians had a smaller share of the colony's total wealth. In midcentury Chester County, Pennsylvania, for example, the top 10 percent of taxpayers owned about a quarter of all wealth, the middle 40 percent possessed about half the wealth, and the bottom 50 percent had the remaining quarter. While wealth distribution in Chester County and elsewhere in the rural middle colonies was far from equitable, it contrasted sharply with such cities as Philadelphia, where the top 10 percent of the population in 1767 owned two-thirds of the wealth while the poorest half of the population had only 5 percent. The comparatively widespread prosperity of the middle colonies permitted residents to indulge in a half-century shopping spree for English imports. The middle colonies' per capita consumption of imported goods from England more than doubled between 1720 and 1770, far outstripping the per-capita consumption of English goods in New England and the southern colonies.

At the crossroads of trade in wheat exports and English imports stood Philadelphia. In the four decades after 1730, fifty-two new towns sprang up in Pennsylvania, and almost all channeled their trade through Philadelphia. The city's population grew steadily during the eighteenth century, eclipsing New York City by 1740 and Boston by 1750 to reach a population of about 40,000 by 1770. By 1776, Philadelphia had a larger population than any other city in the entire British Empire except London, which dwarfed all other cities with its 750,000 inhabitants.

Merchants occupied the top stratum of Philadelphia society. They made fortunes in trade, ship-

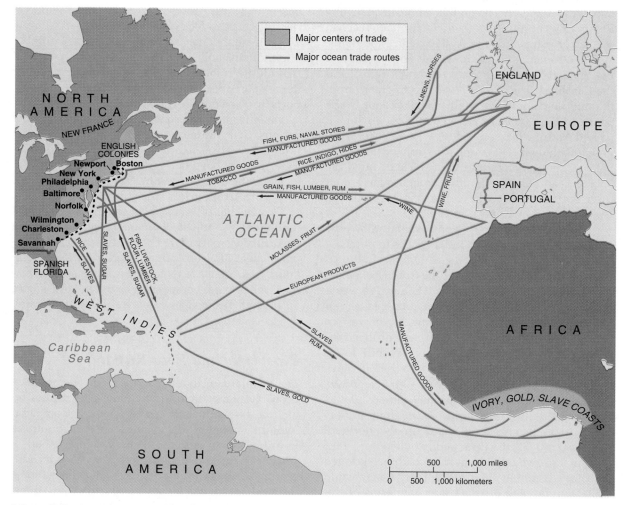

MAP 5.2
Atlantic Trade in the Eighteenth Century
This map illustrates the economic outlook of the colonies in the eighteenth century: that is, east toward the Atlantic world rather than west toward the interior of North America. The long distances involved in the Atlantic trade and the uncertainties of seaborne travel suggest the difficulties Britain experienced governing the colonies and regulating colonial commerce.

POOR RICHARD'S ALMANACK

This illustration from Poor Richard's Almanack *celebrates the virtues of work and the vices of sloth. Unlike the industrious farmers, lazy sluggards put off until tomorrow what they might do today. They will be forced to buy corn rather than growing enough to eat and to sell. However pleasant it might seem in the short run to sleep late and dillydally, in the long run lazy folk will be miserable, Poor Richard counseled. In fact, they will be like the sheep being sheared at the right: Their loss will be the gain of hard workers. One of Poor Richard's central messages was the likelihood of long-term gain in repayment for the certainty of the short-term pain of labor. Poor Richard's maxim assumed that, on the whole, workers received the fruits of their labor, an assumption that made more sense for landowning farmers or artisans like Franklin than for wage laborers, women workers, or slaves.*

Courtesy, American Antiquarian Society.

ping, insurance, land, and law. They dominated the wealthy oligarchy that governed the city. Only 2 percent of the city's residents owned enough property (£50) to qualify to vote. They built grand homes with elaborate formal gardens on the outskirts of Philadelphia. They sent their sons to England and the continent for education and refinement; their daughters learned enough at home, they believed. They tried their best to follow European fashions, succumbing, one observer noted, to "the evil Itch of overvaluing Foreign parts."

The ranks of merchants reached downward to aspiring tradesmen like Benjamin Franklin. After he started to print the *Pennsylvania Gazette* in 1728, Franklin opened a shop to sell stationery. Run mostly by his wife, Deborah, the shop soon branched out to sell a little bit of everything: cheese, codfish, goose feathers, sealing wax, coffee, chocolate, soap, and now and then a slave. In 1733, Franklin began to publish *Poor Richard's Almanack*, a calendar of weather predictions, astrological alignments, and pithy epigrams. The *Almanack* sold thousands of copies, quickly becoming Franklin's most profitable product. As Franklin's prosperity grew, he devoted his energies to civic improvement projects, organizing fire companies, police squads, and a subscription library. He continued to identify himself as a "leather apron man" (a tradesman), but by 1740 the ambitious, upwardly mobile printer could not resist concocting a Franklin coat of arms

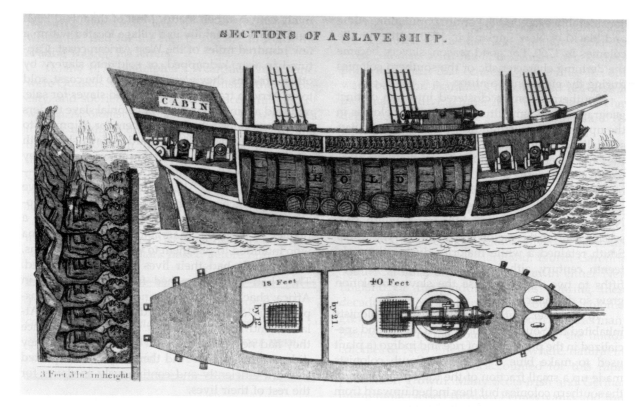

SLAVE SHIP

Newly enslaved Africans made the Middle Passage crammed belowdecks on a slave ship like this one, sitting upright in a space just over three feet high. Other ships installed an intermediate shelf, forcing slaves into a reclining position with barely enough vertical space to turn from side to side. Profit calculations dictated carrying as many slaves as possible to offset the fixed costs of the ship, insurance, supplies, and crew. But security precautions were the prime consideration in confining slaves to unhealthy, tight quarters belowdecks. Slaves vastly outnumbered the crew aboard the ship, and crew members justifiably feared a slave uprising. Note that the cannon on deck (pointing at one of the hatches over the slave quarters) swiveled to permit shooting at mutinous slaves as well as unfriendly ships.

British Library.

continually, and for several days did not eat anything but what they forced into my mouth."

During the next six or seven months, Equiano was sold to several different African masters, each of whom moved him closer to the coast. One evening Equiano's sister was brought to the house where he was being kept. That night, Equiano remembered, "the man to whom I supposed we belonged lay with us, he in the middle while she and I held one another by the hands across his breast all night; and thus for a while we forgot our misfortunes in the joy of being together." The next morning his sister was taken away, and he never again saw her, his parents, or any of his villagers.

When Equiano arrived at the coast, a slave ship waited offshore. The ship and its sailors terrified Equiano. He feared that he had "gotten into a world of bad spirits," that he was going to be killed and "eaten by those white men with horrible looks, red faces, and loose hair." He fainted when he was first brought on board the slave ship. Once he revived, the crew confined him belowdecks where "with the loathsomeness of the stench and crying together, I became so sick and low that I was not able to eat . . . [and] now wished for the last friend, death, to relieve me." When he refused the food the slavers offered him, they "flogged me severely. I had never experienced anything of this kind before." The beatings continued for Equiano and others who did not eat. When Equiano located other slaves aboard the ship who spoke Ibo, as he did, and heard from them that they were being taken to the whites' country, where they would be made to work, he felt somewhat relieved. But he still feared that he would be killed, since "the white people looked and acted . . . in so savage a manner" toward the slaves and each other.

Once the ship set sail, the slaves were confined to the hold, which "became absolutely pestilential." Many slaves died from sickness that swept below the deck where they were chained, crowded together in suffocating heat fouled by filth of all descriptions. "The shrieks of the women and the groans of the dying rendered the whole a scene of horror almost inconceivable," Equiano recalled. He "was soon reduced so low" that the sailors brought him on deck in hopes of keeping him alive. Others were "almost daily brought upon deck at the point of death" and died. Equiano "envied them the freedom they enjoyed, and as often wished I could change my condition for theirs."

The ship finally arrived in Barbados, and merchants and planters came on board to examine the slaves. "We thought . . . we should be eaten by these ugly men," Equiano wrote. That evening, when the slaves were confined again belowdecks, "there was much dread and trembling among us, and nothing but bitter cries to be heard all the night from these apprehensions." To calm the newly arrived slaves, "some old slaves from the land" were brought on board. They told Equiano and his shipmates that they would not be eaten but would instead work alongside "many of our country people . . . [which] eased us much." In a few days, white masters in Barbados had purchased most of Equiano's shipmates, but he and a few others "were not saleable." These leftovers "were shipped off in a sloop for North America."

The sloop sailed to Virginia and up a river some distance from the sea. There Equiano "saw few or none of our native Africans and not one soul who could talk to me." Soon, all the other slaves had been sold "and only myself was left. I was now exceedingly miserable and thought myself worse off than any of the rest of my companions, for they could talk to each other, but I had no person to speak to that I could understand. In this state I was constantly grieving and pining and wishing for death." After "some time in this miserable, forlorn, and much dejected state," Equiano was sold to a white man, the captain of a tobacco ship bound for England.

Some of the slaves brought into the southern colonies came as Equiano did, aboard ships from the West Indies. Merchants in the North American colonies often specialized in this trade; Equiano himself was owned for several years by a Quaker merchant from Philadelphia who traded exten-

OLAUDAH EQUIANO

This portrait of Olaudah Equiano was painted by an unknown English artist about 1780, when Equiano was in his mid-thirties, more than a decade after he had bought his freedom. The portrait evokes Equiano's successful acculturation to the customs of eighteenth-century England. His clothing and hairstyle reflect the fashions of respectable young Englishmen. In his Interesting Narrative, *published in 1789, Equiano explained that as a slave he had learned to speak and understand English. "I now not only felt myself quite easy with these new countrymen but relished their society and manners," he wrote. "I . . . looked upon them . . . as men superior to us [Africans], and therefore I had the stronger desire to resemble them, to imbibe their spirit and imitate their manners; I therefore embraced every occasion of improvement, and every new thing that I observed I treasured up in my memory." Equiano's embrace of English culture did not cause him to forsake his African roots. In fact, he honored his dual identity by campaigning against slavery. His* Narrative *was one of the most important and powerful antislavery documents of the time.*
Royal Albert Memorial Museum, Exeter, England.

sively with the West Indies. But slaves arriving from the West Indies accounted for only about 15 percent of all the Africans brought into the southern colonies during the eighteenth century. All the rest came directly from Africa on ships that specialized in the slave trade and carried an average of two hundred slaves each. Almost all these ships (roughly 90 percent) belonged to British merchants.

Equiano accurately described the horrendous conditions aboard these ships. The slaves were wedged into only half as much space as white convicts or soldiers were assigned in eighteenth-century ships. Children under the age of fourteen, like Equiano, were relatively rare, typically no more than 10 or 15 percent of a cargo. Most slaves on board were young adults, men usually outnumbering women two to one.

Mortality during the Middle Passage varied considerably from ship to ship. On average, about 15 percent of the slaves died, but sometimes half or more perished. The average mortality among the white crew of slave ships was often nearly as bad. In general, the longer the voyage, the larger the number of deaths. Recent studies suggest that many slaves succumbed not only to virulent epidemic diseases such as smallpox and dysentery but also to acute dehydration caused by fluid loss from heavy perspiration, vomiting, and diarrhea combined with a severe shortage of drinking water to replace the lost fluids.

Although slave ship captains did not understand the dangers of dehydration, they knew about the risks of epidemics, filth, and polluted water, and they certainly wanted to keep slaves alive—a dead slave, after all, took money from their pockets. But captains tolerated the deplorable conditions aboard their ships because they feared rebellion if slaves were not kept chained belowdecks. Slave ship crews never forgot that slaves had little to lose. At bottom, the brutalities of the Middle Passage arose from the violent imperatives of slavery.

Normally an individual planter purchased at any one time a relatively small number of newly arrived Africans, or "new Negroes," as they were called. The number of slaves a planter bought reflected in part the comparatively high price of slaves. In the Chesapeake in 1735, for example, a healthy adult slave cost about the same as nineteen head of cattle. Slave prices escalated with surging demand for their labor; by 1770, a comparable slave cost as much as thirty head of cattle. Only relatively prosperous planters could afford the investment in slaves. Poor families struggling to make ends meet

TABLE 5.1	
SLAVE IMPORTS, 1451-1870	
Estimated Slave Imports to the *Western Hemisphere*	
1451-1600	275,000
1601-1700	1,341,000
1701-1810	6,100,000
1811-1870	1,900,000

thought twice before buying a slave. In 1735, they could buy one hundred acres of decent land for the price of one good slave. Well-off planters often bought slaves on credit, hoping to pay off their debt with the boost in production they anticipated from their new laborers.

Another reason planters preferred to purchase small groups of newly arrived Africans was to permit the newcomers to be trained by the planters' other slaves. Like Equiano, newly arrived Africans were often profoundly depressed, demoralized, and disoriented. They did not understand English. They could not know where they were or what their future held. Planters counted on their other slaves—either those who had been born into slavery in the colonies (often called "country-born" or "creole" slaves) or Africans who had arrived earlier—to help new Negroes become accustomed to their strange new surroundings on a tobacco farm in Virginia or a rice plantation in South Carolina.

Planters' preferences for slaves from specific regions of Africa aided the process of acculturation (or "seasoning," as it was called) to the routines of slave life in the southern colonies. The slaves on any given slave ship usually came from several African societies and spoke a number of different languages, partly because of the vagaries of the enslavement process in the interior of Africa and partly because slave ship captains feared the heightened prospect of slave rebellion if most of the captives aboard a vessel spoke the same language. A slave purchased by a master in the southern colonies might speak any one of the several hundred Mande, Gur, Kwa, Adamawa, Bantu, or other languages. Nonetheless, Chesapeake planters preferred slaves from Senegambia, the Gold Coast, or—like Equiano—the Bight of Biafra, the origin of 40 percent of all Africans imported to the Chesapeake. South Carolina planters favored slaves from the central African Congo and Angola regions, the origin of about 40 percent of the African slaves they im-

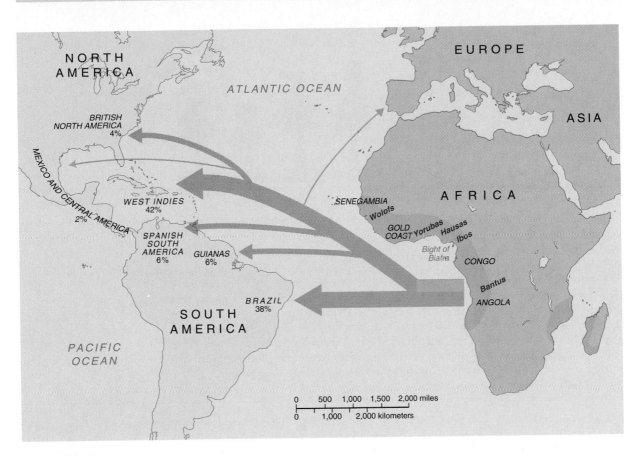

M A P 5.3
The Atlantic Slave Trade
Although the Atlantic slave trade endured for more than four centuries, the heyday of the trade occurred during the eighteenth century, when the vast majority of African slaves were imported to the New World. Only a small fraction of the African slaves imported to the Western Hemisphere were taken to British North America; most went to sugar plantations in Brazil and the Caribbean (see Table 5.1). Why were so many more African slaves sent to the West Indies and Brazil than to British North America?

ported. Although slaves within each of these regions spoke many different languages, enough linguistic and cultural similarities existed that they could communicate with other Africans from the same region. The high concentration of Africans in the slave-dense low country of South Carolina permitted the development of a distinctive pidgin language, Gullah, an amalgam of English, Hausa, Ibo, Yoruba, and other West African tongues that can still be heard among some longtime residents of the sea islands along the coast of South Carolina and Georgia. The linguistic and cultural overlap among African societies from the same region permitted slaves already in the southern colonies to ease some-

what the dehumanizing process of seasoning confronted by new arrivals.

Seasoning acclimated new Africans to the physical as well as the cultural environment of the southern colonies. Slaves who had just endured the Middle Passage were often poorly nourished, weak, and sick. In this vulnerable state of health they encountered the alien diseases of North America without having developed a biological arsenal of acquired immunities. As many as 10 or 15 percent of newly arrived Africans died during their first year in the southern colonies, and sometimes more. One Virginia planter bought thirty-two Africans in an eight-year period, and eight of them died within a year

THOMAS JEFFERSON'S CHESS SET

These pieces from Thomas Jefferson's chess set illustrate the unmistakable African presence in the eighteenth-century South, as tens of thousands of newly imported slaves flooded into the region. The origin of these chess pieces is unknown; they may have been crafted by ivory carvers in Africa and brought to Virginia with a shipment of slaves. Note that the white king has African features, unlike the other white pieces. All the dark pieces appear African, although the dark queen wears a European dress (the white queen has been lost). Imagine Jefferson and his slave-owning friends maneuvering these tiny statues of Europeans and Africans, seeking to achieve victory and avoid defeat. In many ways, the chessboard was a genteel reflection of the harsh, utterly unequal real-world contests between white masters and their black slaves.
Monticello/Thomas Jefferson Memorial Foundation.

of their purchase. Respiratory diseases proved especially deadly. New arrivals who survived for a year or two were considered seasoned. In practice, that meant they were still alive and had learned to do the work their masters commanded.

While newly enslaved Africans poured into the southern colonies, slave women made an even greater contribution to the growth of the black population. Both country-born women and seasoned Africans gave birth to slave babies, who caused the slave population to mushroom. Country-born slave women tended to have more children than seasoned Africans principally because they did not undergo the physical and emotional stresses of enslavement described by Equiano. They became mothers for the first time at a younger age and therefore had a longer period of childbearing and more children. Slaveowners profited from these births, of course. Thomas Jefferson explained, "I consider the labor of a breeding [slave] woman as no object, that a [slave] child raised every 2 years is of more profit than the crop of the best laboring [slave] man." The birth and survival of a growing number of slave babies set the southern colonies apart from other New World slave societies, which experienced natural *decrease*; that is, slave deaths exceeded births. The high

rate of natural increase in the southern colonies meant that by the 1740s the majority of southern slaves were country-born. But the large numbers of newly enslaved Africans who continued to arrive made the influence of African culture in the eighteenth-century South stronger than ever before—or since.

Slave Labor and African American Culture

Planters purchased slaves to employ them in the tobacco fields of the Chesapeake and the rice fields of South Carolina. Planters expected slaves, both men and women, to work from sunup to sundown and beyond. George Washington wrote that his slaves should "be at their work as soon as it is light, work til it is dark, and be diligent while they are at it." Masters had difficulty imposing these expectations on their slaves. The conflict between the masters' desire for maximum labor and the slaves' reluctance to do more than necessary made the threat of physical punishment a constant for eighteenth-century slaves. Eighteenth-century masters preferred black slaves over white indentured servants not just because slaves served for life rather than for a limited term and because their servitude was inherited rather than contractual, but also because colonial laws did not limit the force masters could use against slaves, as it did against servants.

Newly enslaved Africans often prompted masters on eighteenth-century plantations to reach for their whips, or worse. As a traveler observed in 1740, "A new negro . . . will require more discipline than a young spaniel . . . let a hundred men show him how to hoe, or drive a wheelbarrow; he'll still take the one by the bottom and the other by the wheel and . . . often die before [he] . . . can be conquered." Slaves, the traveler noted, were not stupid or simply obstinate; despite the inevitable punishment, they resisted their masters' demands because of their "greatness of soul," their stubborn unwillingness to conform to their masters' definition of them as merely slaves.

Some slaves escalated their acts of resistance to direct physical confrontation with the master, mistress, or an overseer. A hoe raised in anger, a punch in the face, or a desperate swipe with a knife led to swift and predictable retaliation by whites. Throughout the eighteenth-century southern colonies, the balance of physical power rested securely in the hands of whites. The likelihood of brutal retaliation made most slaves cautious about venting their hostility toward whites.

Rebellion occurred, however, at Stono, South Carolina, in 1739. Before dawn on a September Sunday, a group of about twenty slaves, mostly Angolans, attacked a country store, killed the two storekeepers, confiscated the store's guns, ammunition, and powder, and set out along the road south toward Spanish Florida after pausing to set the severed heads of the storekeepers on the store's front steps. Enticing other rebel slaves to join the march south, the group plundered and burned more than a half-dozen plantations and killed more than twenty white men, women, and children. As their numbers grew, the rebels stopped in a field to rest, to beat drums to signal still more slaves to join them, and to dance and sing in celebration. A mounted force of whites, gathered by an alarm raised by a government official who had encountered the rebels and managed to escape, attacked the exultant slaves and killed many of them. They placed rebels' heads atop mileposts along the road, grim reminders of the consequences of rebellion. At least thirty rebels fled the attack, to be hunted down by the end of the week; a few rebels remained at large for months. The Stono rebellion illustrated that eighteenth-century slaves, no matter how determined, had no

chance of overturning slavery, and very little chance of defending themselves in any bold strike for freedom. After the Stono rebellion, South Carolina legislators enacted repressive laws designed to guarantee that whites would always have the upper hand (see Texts in Historical Context, page 178). For slaves, open rebellion was a more or less rapid form of suicide. No other similar uprising occurred in South Carolina or elsewhere during the colonial period.

Day-to-day experience convinced most slaves that survival lay within the boundaries of slavery. But slaves did not readily accept their masters' definition of those boundaries. They maneuvered constantly to shift the boundaries in their favor, to protect themselves, and to gain a measure of autonomy. In the Chesapeake, close white supervision gave most slaves little autonomy at work. Most masters owned ten or fewer slaves and often worked in the tobacco fields alongside them. On larger tobacco plantations, slaves often toiled in work gangs, but almost always under the watchful eye of a white overseer. In the lower South, rice and indigo plantations were worked by groups of fifty or more slaves. Many rice planters assigned each adult slave a task, typically defined as a certain area of ground to be planted, cultivated, and harvested or a specific job to be completed. The task system reduced the need for close white supervision; planters often assigned supervisory responsibilities to slaves known as "drivers." The task system gave lower South slaves some control over the pace of their work for their master and some discretion in the use of the rest of their time. If a slave could complete the task before the end of the day, he or she could use the remainder of the day to work in a garden plot, fish, hunt, spin, weave, sew, or cook. When a master sought to increase productivity by changing the plantation's definition of tasks, slaves did their best to defend customary practices.

Eighteenth-century slaves planted the roots of African American lineages that branch out to the present.

Eighteenth-century slaves planted the roots of African American lineages that branch out to the present. Historians are only beginning to explore the kin networks eighteenth-century slaves built within the confines of bondage; much remains unknown. But it is clear that slaves valued family ties

Tobacco, Rice, and Prosperity

Slaves' labor bestowed prosperity on their masters, British merchants, and the monarchy. Rice exports from the lower South exploded from less than half a million pounds in 1700 to eighty million pounds in 1770, virtually all of it grown by slaves. Exports of indigo—another product of low country slaves—also boomed. Together, rice and indigo made up three-fourths of lower South exports, nearly two-thirds of them going to England and most of the rest to the West Indies, where sugar-growing slaves ate slave-grown rice. Tobacco exports from the Chesapeake did not accelerate as rapidly as rice exports, but they still leaped from about thirty million pounds in 1700 to a hundred million pounds in 1770. Many slaveless small farmers in the Chesapeake grew a little tobacco, but slaves produced the bulk of tobacco exported. Tobacco was by far the most important export from British North America; by 1770, it represented almost a third of *all* colonial exports and three-fourths of all Chesapeake exports. And under the provisions of the Navigation Acts (see chapter 4), nearly all of it went to England, where the monarchy collected a lucrative tax on each pound. British merchants then reexported over 80 percent of the tobacco to the European continent, pocketing a nice markup for their troubles. From the British viewpoint, the southern colonies were the export capital of North America: they supplied 90 percent of all North American exports to England; only about 10 percent of North American exports to England came from New England and the middle colonies combined.

These products of slave labor made the southern colonies by far the richest in North America. The per capita wealth of free whites in the South was four times greater than that in New England and three times that in the middle colonies. In the Chesapeake, about six out of ten white families owned slaves by 1770 and, of course, they reaped more profit than families without slaves. In one tobacco county, for example, white families with land and slaves had four times more wealth than families with land but no slaves and forty-five times more wealth than tenant families who owned neither land nor slaves.

At the top of the wealth pyramid stood the rice grandees of the lower South and the tobacco gentry of the Chesapeake. These elite families commonly resided on estates of a thousand or more acres adorned by handsome brick mansions and luxurious gardens, maintained and supported by

PLANTATION MISTRESS
The wife of a wealthy South Carolina rice planter, Mrs. Barnard Elliott displays the opulence made possible by the soil of plantations and the toil of untold slaves. Mrs. Elliott appears to be a discriminating consumer. Although she probably made most of her purchases in the best Charleston shops, her custom-made fashions would not have been out of place in the drawing rooms of the English gentry. Sensuous textiles, billowing lace-encrusted sleeves, a daring neckline, and dazzling jewels demonstrate Mrs. Elliott's cosmopolitan tastes despite her colonial residence. Her formal, almost regal pose evokes the enormous distance between the luxurious refinements of elite planters and the workaday plantation realities that gilded their world. Contrast the appearance of Mrs. Elliott with that of her approximate contemporary, the New England household slave Phyllis (page 152).
The Gibbes Museum of Art, Carolina Art Association.

several hundred slaves. The extravagant lifestyle of one gentry family astonished a young tutor from New Jersey who noted with amazement that during the winter months the family kept twenty-eight large fires roaring, requiring six oxen to haul in a heavy cartload of slave-cut wood four times a day. (Yeoman families—those that supported themselves on a small plot of land with no slaves—normally warmed themselves around one fire.) Slave-grown tobacco and rice were not the only sources of gentry wealth. The gentry speculated in western lands, acquiring title to huge tracts in the southern backcountry and selling off parcels as land-hungry settlers moved south from Pennsylvania or west from the coastal regions. Many wealthy planters kept stores on their plantations stocked with textiles, pots and pans, rum, and other delicacies, which they sold to their neighbors or, more often, traded for tobacco. Affluent planters also made loans to their lesser neighbors, collecting both interest payments and deference from their debtors. Land sales, store trade, and loans combined with such favors as help with marketing tobacco, sending medicine to a sick child, or sharing a toddy during a neighborly conversation laced the southern gentry to white yeomen and tenants.

The products of slave labor made the southern colonies by far the richest in North America. The per capita wealth of free whites in the South was four times greater than that in New England and three times that in the middle colonies.

The vast differences in wealth among white southerners engendered envy and occasional tension between rich and poor, but remarkably little open hostility. The gentry looked down upon the "meaner sort" and spoke of them disparagingly in private. In public, the planter elite acknowledged humble whites as their equals, at least in belonging to the superior—in their minds—white race. Looking upward, white yeomen and tenants sensed the gentry's condescension and veiled contempt. But they also appreciated the gentry for granting favors, upholding white supremacy, and keeping slaves in their place. Curiously, while racial slavery made a few whites much richer than most others, it also gave those who did not get rich a powerful reason to feel similar (in race) to those who were so different (in wealth).

The slaveholding gentry dominated politics as well as the economy of the southern colonies. In Virginia, only adult white men who owned at least one hundred acres of unimproved land or twenty-five acres of land with a house could vote. This property-holding requirement prevented about 40 percent of white men in Virginia from voting for representatives to the House of Burgesses. In South Carolina, only fifty acres of land were required to vote, and most adult white men qualified. But in both colonies, voters elected members of the gentry to serve in the colonial legislature. And they elected them again and again and again. The gentry passed political offices from generation to generation, almost as if they were hereditary. Between 1725 and 1773, for example, nearly half of the men elected from southern Maryland to serve in the colonial legislature followed in the footsteps of their fathers, who had served in the same offices; almost as many of these men had grandfathers who had preceded them in office. Politically, the gentry built a self-perpetuating oligarchy—rule by the elite few—with the votes of their many humble neighbors.

The gentry also set the cultural standard in the southern colonies. They bought wines from France, fashions and books from London. They entertained lavishly, dancing minuets and jigs while their tables groaned under the best game and produce their slaves could prepare. They attended the Anglican Church for the twenty-minute sermon and the subsequent two hours of conversation with neighbors about crops, horses, politics, and scandals. They gambled on races, cards, cockfights, and other blood sports. Above all they cultivated a life of leisurely pursuit of happiness. They did not condone idleness; far from it. Their pleasures and their responsibilities kept them busy. Thomas Jefferson, an obsessively busy and phenomenally productive member of the gentry, recalled that his earliest childhood memory was of being carried on a pillow by a family slave—a powerful image of the slave hands beneath the gentry's leisure and achievement.

Unifying Experiences

While the societies of New England, the middle colonies, and the southern colonies became more sharply differentiated during the eighteenth century, colonists throughout British North America shared certain unifying experiences. The first was economic: The economies of all three regions had their roots in agriculture. The seasonal rhythms of plant life marked time for nearly everyone. But the tempo of commerce quickened during the eighteenth century. Colonists sold their distinctive products in markets that, in turn, offered to consumers throughout the colonies a more or less uniform array of goods. A second unifying experience was a decline in the importance of religion. Religious diversity increased dramatically during the eighteenth century, propelled by immigrants faithful to one or another of the many varieties of Protestantism. Throughout the colonies, some settlers drifted away from piety while others called for a revival of religious intensity. Yet religion mattered less, the affairs of the world more, than they did in the seventeenth century. Third, white inhabitants throughout North America in the eighteenth century became aware that they shared a distinctive identity as British colonists. Thirteen different governments presided over the North American colonies, but all of them answered to the British monarchy. Enemies the colonists perceived around them—French to the north and west, Spaniards to the south, and Indians almost everywhere—strengthened the colonists' allegiance to England. While royal officials expected loyalty from the colonists, they often had difficulty obtaining obedience to dictates from England. The North American colonists stood under the umbrella of the British Empire and asserted their prerogatives as British subjects to defend their special colonial interests.

Commerce and Consumption

Eighteenth-century commerce whetted the appetite to consume. Colonial products spurred the development of mass markets throughout the Atlantic world. A preacher in New England, a printer in Pennsylvania, a planter in South Carolina, or a merchant in London could munch a cracker made with flour from the middle colonies, sip tea from colonies in the East Indies sweetened by sugar from colonies in the West Indies, and smoke a pipe of tobacco from the Chesapeake. Massive increases in the supply of colonial products brought the price of these small luxuries within reach of nearly everyone, at least from time to time. Colonial goods brought into focus an important lesson of eighteenth-century commerce. Ordinary people, not just the wealthy elite, would buy things they desired, not only what they absolutely needed. The realm of desire, unlike the arena of need, had almost no limits. In England, for example, the per capita consumption of tea rose fifteenfold during the eighteenth century. With the appropriate stimulus to desire, markets seemed unlimited.

Eighteenth-century merchants and manufacturers catered to their customers' desires. In advertisements in the newspapers that became common-

place in the eighteenth century, in handbills distributed on street corners and posters plastered on walls, and in attractive shop window displays, merchants strove to make consumers feel that they needed what they desired, namely the items merchants had for sale. Manufacturers specialized in producing mundane goods people used daily—pots and pans, dishes, textiles, pins and needles—and in making them durable, attractive, and desirable.

Colonial goods brought into focus an important lesson of eighteenth-century commerce. Ordinary people, not just the wealthy elite, would buy things they desired, not only what they absolutely needed.

The Atlantic commerce that took colonial goods to markets in England brought these objects of consumer desire back to the colonies. English merchants and manufacturers recognized that colonists made excellent customers, and the Navigation Acts gave English exporters privileged access to the colonial market. English manufacturers boosted their output to keep up with colonial demand as the colonial market grew more rapidly than the English domestic market. By midcentury, export-oriented industries in England were growing ten times faster than firms attuned to the home market. Of course, most English exports went to the vast European market, where potential customers outnumbered those in the colonies by more than one hundred to one. But as European competition stiffened, colonial markets became even more important to English exporters. British colonies consumed about one-fifth of all English exports by 1750; twenty years later, they absorbed more than two-fifths.

North American colonists bought their share and more. British exports to North America multiplied eightfold between 1700 and 1773. For the first half of the century, exports to North America grew apace with the colonial population. After midcentury, colonists upped their purchases of English exports, and by 1760 the colonists' per capita consumption of exports had leaped 75 percent above the level of 1740. After 1750, the colonists' eagerness to consume exceeded their ability to pay, and English exporters willingly extended credit. As colonists put more of their purchases on the tab, their debts to English exporters soared.

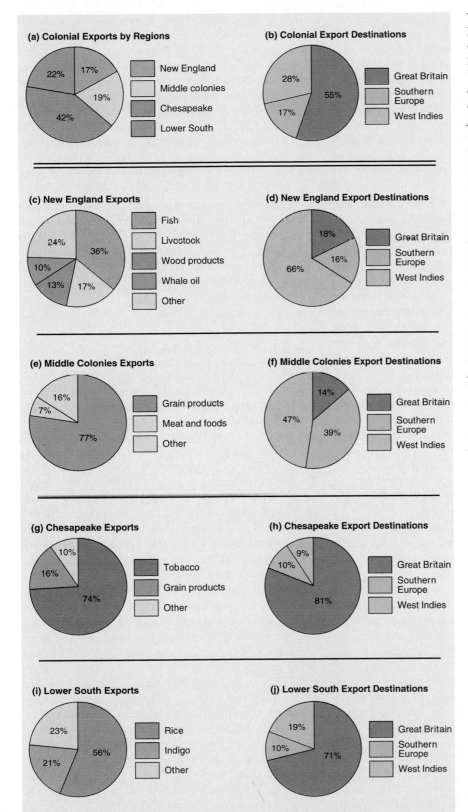

(a) Colonial Exports by Regions

17%
19%
42%
22%

- New England
- Middle colonies
- Chesapeake
- Lower South

(b) Colonial Export Destinations

55%
28%
17%

- Great Britain
- Southern Europe
- West Indies

(c) New England Exports

36%
24%
10%
13%
17%

- Fish
- Livestock
- Wood products
- Whale oil
- Other

(d) New England Export Destinations

18%
16%
66%

- Great Britain
- Southern Europe
- West Indies

(e) Middle Colonies Exports

16%
7%
77%

- Grain products
- Meat and foods
- Other

(f) Middle Colonies Export Destinations

14%
47%
39%

- Great Britain
- Southern Europe
- West Indies

(g) Chesapeake Exports

10%
16%
74%

- Tobacco
- Grain products
- Other

(h) Chesapeake Export Destinations

9%
10%
81%

- Great Britain
- Southern Europe
- West Indies

(i) Lower South Exports

23%
21%
56%

- Rice
- Indigo
- Other

(j) Lower South Export Destinations

19%
10%
71%

- Great Britain
- Southern Europe
- West Indies

FIGURE 5.1
*Colonial Exports,
1768–1772*
These pie charts provide an overview of the colonial export economy in the 1760s. The first two show that almost two-thirds of colonial exports came from the South and that the majority of the colonies' exports went to Great Britain. The remaining charts illustrate the distinctive patterns of exports in each colonial region. Fish, livestock, and wood products were New England's most important exports; they were sent primarily to the West Indies, only a small fraction going to Great Britain. From the colonial breadbasket in the middle colonies, grain products made up three-fourths of all exports, most of which went to the West Indies or to southern Europe. The Chesapeake also exported some grain, but tobacco accounted for three-fourths of the region's export trade, nearly all of it bound for Great Britain as mandated by the Navigation Acts. Rice and indigo comprised three-fourths of the exports from the Lower South, the bulk of which was sent to Great Britain. Taken together, these charts reveal Britain's economic interest in the exports of the North American colonies.

The flood of exports spread throughout the colonies, from Maine to Georgia, from gentry mansions to humble farmsteads. For years after he was married, Benjamin Franklin ate his breakfast of bread and milk (he considered tea too expensive) with a pewter spoon from a cheap earthenware bowl. The "first Appearance of Plate and China in our House," he recalled later, occurred one morning in the 1730s when his wife surprised him with breakfast served "in a China Bowl with a Spoon of Silver," the first of numerous purchases. Only the affluent could afford fine silver tableware, but cheaper imports were within reach of many. The German musician and traveler Gottfried Mittelberger reported from the middle colonies in the 1750s that "it is really possible to obtain all the things one can get in Europe in Pennsylvania, since so many merchant ships arrive there every year." The currents of consumption swept into the homes of backcountry farmers. In rural Massachusetts in the mid-seventeenth century, for example, knives and forks could hardly be found; most tables were set with thick wooden spoons. By the mid-eighteenth century, about one-third of New England farmers ate with knives and forks, most of them stamped out in an English factory. Farmers, like other colonists, succumbed to the seductions of desire. In the mid-seventeenth century, mirrors hardly existed in poor households; farmers and their families glimpsed their reflections in the placid surface of water in a bowl or bucket. By the mid-eighteenth century, nearly half of poor New England farmsteads possessed a mirror.

Imported mirrors, silver plate, spices, bed and table linens, clocks, tea services, wigs, books, and more infiltrated parlors, kitchens, and bedrooms throughout the colonies. Despite the many differences among the colonists, the consumption of English exports built a certain material uniformity across region, religion, class, and status. Some mirrors were small and plain, others large and ornately decorated; but all mirrors permitted colonists to scrutinize their appearance, to see themselves as others saw them. Consumption of English exports did not simply tie the colonists to the British economy. It also made the colonists look and feel more British, even though they lived at the edge of a wilderness an ocean away from England.

The rising tide of colonial consumption had other less visible but no less important consequences. Because consumption so often arose from desire rather than necessity, it presented colonists —both women and men—with a novel array of choices. In many respects the choices were small, seemingly trivial: whether to buy knives and forks, teacups, or a clock. But such small choices confronted eighteenth-century consumers with a big question: "What do you want?" That question did not simply ask about desires; it also identified who defined those desires: each person. As colonial consumers defined and expressed their desires with greater frequency during the eighteenth century, they became accustomed to thinking of themselves as individuals who had the power to make decisions that influenced the quality of their lives. Merchants worked constantly to ensure that those decisions led to still more consumption. The merchants' efforts emphasized that ordinary men and women exercised power and made important decisions—messages of considerable significance in the hierarchical world of eighteenth-century British North America.

Religion, Enlightenment, and Revival

Eighteenth-century colonists could choose from almost as many religions as consumer goods. Virtually all of the bewildering variety of religious sects represented some form of Christianity, almost all of them Protestant. Roman Catholics concentrated in Maryland as they had since the seventeenth century, but even there they were outnumbered by Protestants, whose suspicions about a conspiracy by the Roman Catholic Church kept Catholics on the defensive. Slaves made up the largest group of non-Christians. A few slaves converted to Christianity in Africa or after they arrived in North America, but for the most part, slaves did not flock to Christ's sheepfold. The haunting silence of the historical record limits our knowledge of most slaves' religious beliefs. Some professed Islam. Most, it seems clear, continued to embrace elements of indigenous African religions rather than the Christian faith of their masters.

The varieties of Protestant faith and practice ranged across an extremely broad spectrum. In such isolated communities as Ephrata, Pennsylvania, adherents of Baptist and Quaker sects tried to live a holy life untainted by profane corruptions. Throughout the plantation South and in urban centers like Charleston, New York, and Philadelphia, prominent colonists attended the Anglican Church, conforming to the rituals and relaxed worldliness of the king's faith. In New England, old-style Puritanism splintered into strands of Congregationalism that differed over fine points of theological doctrine. The thousands of immigrants in the middle colonies and the southern backcountry included militant Baptists and Presbyterians. Huguenots who had fled persecution in Catholic France peopled congregations in several cities. Some colonists ignored doctrinal distinctions and frequented several churches: If one church was good, why weren't two or more that much better?

In New England, the Congregational Church was the official established church and all residents paid taxes for its support. In the South, Anglicans enjoyed a similar status as the established state church. But in both regions, dissenting faiths grew, much as they did in colonies without a state-supported religious establishment. In New England and the South, Baptists, Quakers, Presbyterians, and others eventually won the right to worship publicly, although the established churches retained official sanction.

Rivalry and competition for converts often developed among churches. When the Anglican missionary Charles Woodmason ventured into the South Carolina backcountry in the 1760s he received a less than hearty welcome. The colonists there "wanted no D——d Black Gown Sons of Bitches [Anglican ministers] among them," he was told. Woodmason accused Presbyterians and Baptists of resorting to dirty tricks to foil his efforts: They distributed two barrels of whiskey before one service, urging the drunks to begin "firing [guns], hooping and hallowing like Indians" while Woodmason tried to administer communion; another group brought to church "57 Dogs (for I counted them) which in Time of Service they set fighting"; after communion one Sunday, some men "got into the Church and left their Excrements on the Communion Table"; others stole Woodmason's clerical robe one night and draped it over a man who slipped into the bed of a sleeping woman, "making her give out next day, that the Parson came to Bed to her."

The bickering and dissension that often tore at eighteenth-century churches grew out of the fundamental convictions of Protestantism. A faith that affirmed the priesthood of all believers (in Martin Luther's famous phrase) empowered Christians to look into their Bibles and their hearts to find God's Way. Not surprisingly, faithful and well-meaning Protestants identified different Ways, each of which had its defenders who claimed it as the one true Way while denouncing the others as misguided heresies. The strife engendered by the core of Protestant belief led many colonists to favor toleration of religious differences and peaceful coexistence among disputing churches.

Many educated colonists became deists, looking for God's plan in nature more than in the Bible. They believed in God, but they avoided becoming mired in hair-splitting arguments about whether it was the Presbyterians' God, the Anglicans' God, the Congregationalists' God, or the Quakers' God. They commonly expressed doubts about such important Christian doctrines as original sin or Christ's divinity. But they usually had no difficulty supporting the general moral precepts of more orthodox Christians. When deist Benjamin Franklin drew up his plan "for arriving at moral Perfection" a few years after he arrived in Philadelphia, it featured a list of thirteen virtues quite compatible with Protestant morality. But a devout Protestant probably would have reordered Franklin's list. Franklin's thirteenth virtue—after temperance, silence, order, resolution, frugality, industry, sincerity, justice, moderation, cleanliness, tranquillity, and chastity— was humility, which meant to Franklin "Imitate Jesus and Socrates." Pairing Jesus with a pagan philosopher and honoring both for their meekness rather than for their message aptly illustrated deists' point of view.

Deists shared the ideas of eighteenth-century European Enlightenment thinkers, who believed that science and reason could disclose God's laws in the natural order. During the seventeenth century, Isaac Newton, the brilliant English scientist, demonstrated that all physical objects obeyed precise mathematical laws, such as the law of gravity. Newton's ideas suggested a new vision of the universe and the place of human beings in it, a vision Enlightenment thinkers found compelling. In the Newtonian universe, order was maintained not by the constant intervention of God but by basic mathematical laws. God had presumably created those laws and set the universe in motion, but then he had stepped back to observe his handiwork. God, many eighteenth-century thinkers believed, was like a watchmaker who assembled a watch from sprockets, gears, and springs and then let it run. The concept of a watchmaker God made God seem more distant from the world, less interested in the minutiae of each person's vices and virtues. In addition, a watchmaker God was not arbitrary, capricious, or vengeful, plaguing the world with floods, famine, or fires to express his displeasure. Instead, God was orderly and predictable, although still mysterious

TECHNOLOGY IN AMERICA
The Printing Press

In the eighteenth century, colonial printers began to publish newspapers. Since the 1630s, printers had used presses much like the one shown here to churn out books, pamphlets, broadsides, government announcements, legal forms, invitations, and even promissory notes. The innovation of compiling newsworthy information and publishing it on a regular schedule began in 1704 with the appearance of the *Boston News-Letter*, usually printed on both sides of a single sheet of paper smaller than conventional typing paper. Each week the *News-Letter* contained reprints of articles that had appeared in English newspapers along with a few tidbits of local news such as deaths, fires, storms, and ship arrivals. For years, the audience for such information remained small; the editor complained in 1719 that he could not sell three hundred copies of each issue. Nonetheless, a competing newspaper, the *Boston Gazette*, began publication in that year. It was printed by James Franklin on his press, shown here, which he had brought from England. Both the *Gazette* and the *News-Letter* submitted their copy to the governor for official approval before the newspapers were printed. Frustrated by this official scrutiny, Franklin started a new paper, the *New England Courant*, which set out to thumb its nose at officialdom, both governmental and religious. The *Courant* pledged "to entertain the Town with the most comical and diverting Incidents of Humane Life" and to "expose the Vice and Follies of Persons of all Ranks and Degrees." Franklin's press broadcast to the reading public dissenting opinions that previously one had to hear (or overhear) in private conversations. When the old technology of printing was used in fresh ways to publish unofficial news, all kinds of information and ideas began to diffuse more readily beyond official channels and to help form public opinion. Eighteenth-century newspapers combined old printing technology with the new currents of commerce, dissent, and enlightenment, creating a novel awareness of the problems and possibilities of public life.

Newport Historical Society.

---

because the deepest underlying principles of his order remained unknown.

Although human beings seemed to matter less to the Newtonian God, they had an important role to play. First, they needed to study nature to discover the basic principles of God's order. Second, they must clear away any obstacles that impeded the smooth functioning of the natural order. Some obstacles were false ideas, such as that the Bible or the church was the final authority on God's truth. Other obstacles were social or political institutions that violated natural laws. For example, in Newton's universe the same physical laws applied to all matter. The underlying concept of equality in the Newtonian universe suggested that human beings should try to eliminate social distinctions that violated the principles of the divine order.

The ideas associated with a Newtonian universe percolated through the Atlantic world during the eighteenth century, influencing devout Christians as well as skeptical deists. In the colonies as well as in Europe, Enlightenment ideas encouraged people to study the world around them, to think for themselves, and to ask whether the disorderly appearance of things masked the principles of a deeper, more profound order. Throughout the colonies, curious individuals collected specimens of odd plants and animals; experimented with seeds, grafts, and potions; and kept detailed notes on astronomy, weather patterns, topography, vegetation, and much more. From New England towns to southern drawing rooms, individuals met to discuss such matters. Philadelphia was the center of these scientific conversations, especially after the formation of the American Philosophical Society in 1769, an outgrowth of an earlier discussion group organized by Benjamin Franklin. The American Philosophical Society fostered communication among leading colonial thinkers; Benjamin Franklin was its first president, Thomas Jefferson its third. Among the purposes of these scientific discussions was to find ways to improve society. Franklin declared that the Philosophical Society would be a forum for "all philosophical experiments that let light into the nature of things, tend to increase the power of man over matter, and multiply the conveniences or pleasures of life." Franklin's interest in electricity, stoves, and eyeglasses exemplified the quest for useful knowledge. His focus on the conveniences and pleasures of life indicates the way Enlightenment ideas shifted the gaze of many eighteenth-century colonists from heaven to the here and now.

Most eighteenth-century colonists went to church seldom or not at all, although they probably vaguely considered themselves Christians. A minister in Charleston observed that on the Sabbath "the Taverns have more Visitants than the Churches." In the leading colonial cities, church members were a small minority of eligible adults, no more than 10 or 15 percent. Anglican parishes in the South rarely claimed more than one-fifth of eligible adults as members. In some regions of rural New England and the middle colonies, church membership embraced two-thirds of eligible adults, while in other areas only one-quarter of the residents belonged to a church. Women were the majority of New England church members; they tended to join in their early twenties, about the time they got married. Few unmarried New England men joined churches, and married men usually delayed joining until they were in their thirties or forties. Considering the colonies as a whole, the dominant faith was religious indifference. As a late-eighteenth-century traveler observed, "Religious indifference is imperceptibly disseminated from one end of the continent to the other." The competing varieties of Protestant faith did not persuade most colonists to lift their eyes from their worldly preoccupations.

The spread of religious indifference among most colonists, of deism among many educated leaders, of denominational rivalry, and of comfortable backsliding among the faithful profoundly concerned many ministers. A few despaired that, as one wrote, "religion . . . lay a-dying and ready to expire its last breath of life." To combat what one preacher called the "dead formality" of church services, some ministers set out to convert the unchurched and to revive the piety of the faithful with a new style of preaching that appealed more to the heart than the head. Historians have termed this wave of revivals the "Great Awakening." In Massachusetts during the mid-1730s, the fiery Puritan minister Jonathan Edwards reaped a harvest of souls by reemphasizing traditional Puritan doctrines of humanity's utter depravity and God's vengeful omnipotence. The title of Edwards's most famous sermon, "Sinners in the Hands of an Angry God," conveys the flavor of his message. Edwards's sermons, a member of his congregation noted, caused "great moaning and crying through the whole house [church]—What shall I do to be saved—oh I am going to Hell . . . the shrieks and cries were piercing and amazing." In Pennsylvania and New Jersey, Presbyterian William Tennent and his four minister sons led revivals dramatizing conventional appeals for spiritual rebirth with accounts of God's miraculous powers—such as his raising William Tennent Jr. from the dead. Strangers flocked to the Tennents' revivals to hear about such supernatural visitations and came away, Gilbert Tennent wrote, "much affected . . . the Tears trickling down their Cheeks like Hail."

Most eighteenth-century colonists went to church seldom or not at all, although they probably vaguely considered themselves Christians.

The most famous revivalist in the eighteenth-century Atlantic world was George Whitefield. An Anglican, Whitefield preached well-worn messages of sin and salvation to large audiences in England using his spellbinding, unforgettable voice that bespoke sincerity, urgency, and utter conviction. Newspapers in England and the colonies printed reports of Whitefield's revivals, building anticipation and curiosity about him and his oratory. Whitefield visited the North American colonies seven times, staying for more than three years during the mid-1740s and attracting tens of thousands in his travels. His sermons transported many in his audience to emotion-choked states of religious ecstasy. At one revival, he wrote, "the bitter cries and groans were enough to pierce the hardest heart. Some of the people were as pale as death; others were wringing their hands; others lying on the ground; others sinking into the arms of their friends; and most lifting

GEORGE WHITEFIELD
This portrait of George White-field preaching emphasizes the power of his sermons to trans-port his audience to a revived awareness of divine spiritual-ity. Light from above gleams off Whitefield's forehead. His crossed eyes and faraway gaze suggest that he spoke in a semihypnotic trance. Note the absence of a Bible at the pul-pit. Rather than elaborating on God's word as revealed in Scripture, Whitefield speaks from his own inner awareness. The young woman bathed in light below his hands appears transfixed, her focus not on Whitefield but on some inner realm illuminated by his words. Her eyes and White-field's do not meet, yet the author's use of light suggests that she and Whitefield see the same core of holy Truth. The other people in Whitefield's audience appear not to have achieved this state. They re-main intent on Whitefield's words, failing so far to be ig-nited by the divine spark.
National Portrait Gallery, London.

their eyes to heaven, and crying to God for mercy. They seemed like persons . . . coming out of their graves to judgment." Whitefield impressed even those he did not convert. The slave Olaudah Equiano attended one of Whitefield's sermons and was "much struck and impressed" by "this pious man exhorting the people with the greatest fervour and earnestness, and sweating as much as I ever did while in slavery." Equiano disclosed the source of Whitefield's magnetic appeal with his observation that "I thought it strange I had never seen divines exert themselves in this manner before, and was no longer at a loss to account for the thin congregations they preached to."

Whitefield's successful revivals spawned many lesser imitators. Itinerant preachers, many of them poorly educated, toured the colonial backcountry after midcentury, mimicking Whitefield's medium and message as best they could. Educated and established ministers often regarded them with distaste and even disgust. Charles Woodmason considered "most of those Preaching fellows . . . most notorious Thieves, Jockeys, Gamblers." Re-vival meetings appeared to Woodmason "a Gang of frantic Lunatics."

In fact, the revivals that Woodmason deplored attracted many to Christianity. Revivals awakened and refreshed the spiritual energies of thousands of colonists struggling with the uncertainties and anxieties of eighteenth-century America. The conversions at revivals did not substantially boost the total number of church members, however. After the revivalists moved on, the routines and pressures of everyday existence reasserted their primacy in the lives of many converts. But whether revivals were held in a well-appointed church building in New York City or a wilderness clearing in the Virginia backcountry, they imparted an important message to colonists, both converted and unconverted. The revivals communicated that every soul mattered, that men and women could choose to be saved, that individuals had the power to make a decision for everlasting life or death. Colonial revivals expressed in religious terms many of the same democratic and egalitarian values expressed in economic terms by colonists' patterns of consumption. One colonist noted the analogy by referring to itinerant revivalists as "Pedlars in divinity." Like consumption, revivals contributed to a set of common experiences that bridged colonial divides of faith, region, class, and status.

Bonds of Empire

The plurality of peoples, faiths, and communities that characterized the North American colonies arose from the somewhat haphazard policies of the eighteenth-century British Empire. Since the Puritan Revolution of the mid-seventeenth century, British monarchs had valued the colonies' contributions to trade. The propensity of colonists to enrich the mother country by exchanging colonial products for English consumer goods led royal officials to encourage the growth and development of the colonies. Unlike the French—whose policy of excluding Protestants and foreigners kept the population of its territory tiny—the British kept the door to their colonies open to anyone. The open door boosted the population of the British Empire as tens of thousands of non-British immigrants crossed the threshold of the North American colonies, settled, and raised families. The open door did not extend to trade, however, as the seventeenth-century Navigation Acts restricted colonial trade to British ships and traders. These policies did not spring from wise foresight and shrewd planning by British policymakers. Instead, British policies toward the colonies evolved during the eighteenth century because they served the interests of the monarchy and of influential groups in England and the colonies and be-

cause no group of powerful, determined opponents emerged. The policies of empire also provided the colonists a common framework of political expectations and experiences.

At a minimum, British power defended the colonists from foreign enemies. Each colony organized a militia, and privateers sailed from every port to prey on foreign ships. But the British navy and army bore responsibility for colonial defense. Royal officials warily eyed the settlements of New France and New Spain for signs of threats to British colonies, but Spanish outposts at St. Augustine and elsewhere in Florida did not significantly menace the British North American colonies. Standing on the northeastern frontier of New Spain, the Florida settlements served principally to protect Spanish treasure fleets from the depredations of other European powers, especially the British. Planters in South Carolina feared that runaway slaves would find a haven among Spanish colonists, but only a few did. Likewise, the far-flung settlements of New France scattered across the vast drainages of the St. Lawrence and Mississippi Rivers posed no imminent threat to British North America. French trappers and traders lived in Indian villages, learned native languages, and often married Indian women. In large measure, the acculturation of French settlers to Indian ways arose from the social and military weakness of New France, which was designed not to build a colonial society in the New World but principally to block British advances to the north and to divert North American furs to Paris markets. Alone, neither New France nor Spanish Florida jeopardized British North America, but with Indian allies they became a potent force that kept colonists on their guard.

The policies of the British Empire provided the colonists a common framework of political expectations and experiences.

All along the ragged edge of settlement, colonists encountered Indians. Population growth and land hunger propelled the colonists toward the Indians. Indians' impulse to defend their territory from colonial incursions warred with their desire for knives, axes, fishhooks, traps, pots, blankets, rum, guns, powder, and bullets, which tugged them toward the settlers. The fur trade was the principal medium of exchange between the two groups. To trade for goods manufactured largely by the British, Indians trapped animals throughout the interior of the continent, from north of the Great Lakes to the Gulf of Mexico, from the Appalachian slopes to the edge of the Great Plains. Colonial traders competed for Indian furs. British officials monitored the trade to prevent French, Spanish, and Dutch competitors from deflecting the flow of hides toward their own markets. Indians took advantage of this competition to improve their own prospects, playing one trader off against another. And Indian tribes and confederacies competed against each other for favored trading rights with traders from one colony or another, a competition colonists encouraged.

The shifting alliances and complex dynamics of the fur trade struck a fragile balance along the frontier of colonial settlement. The threat of violence from all sides was ever present, and the threat became reality often enough for all parties to be vigilant and prepared for the worst. Did a shot mean that a raiding party—colonial or Indian—was on its way? Was a skirmish merely the first wave of a concerted attack by British, French, or Spanish troops and their Indian allies? In the Yamasee War of 1715, for example, Yamasee and Creek Indians—with French encouragement—mounted a coordinated attack against colonial settlements in South Carolina and inflicted heavy casualties. The Cherokees, traditional enemies of the Creeks, refused to join the attack. Instead, they protected their access to British trade goods by allying with the embattled colonists and turning the tide of battle, thus triggering a murderous rampage of revenge by the colonists against the Creeks and Yamasees.

The details of relations between Indians and the colonists differed from colony to colony and from year to year. But the colonists' nagging perception of menace on the frontier kept them continually hoping for help from the British in keeping the Indians at bay and in maintaining the essential flow of trade goods. In 1754, the colonists' endemic competition with the French flared into the French and Indian War, which would inflame the frontier for years. Before the 1760s, neither the colonists nor the British developed a coherent policy toward Indians. But both colonists and British shared the view that Indians made profitable trading partners, powerful allies, and deadly enemies.

British attempts to exercise their political power in colonial governments confronted obstacles almost as implacable as those preventing peace on the frontier. British efforts to govern the colonists' trade

HURON BONNET
This dazzling bonnet illustrates the trade between Native Americans and colonists. Beads of Venetian glass were one of the many items colonists imported from Europe specifically to exchange for animal skins offered by Indian hunters and trappers. Native American women in turn incorporated these European beads into designs they had previously wrought with porcupine quills, shells, bones, and other natural objects. European needle and thread were also used to craft this bonnet. Native American artistry transformed these simple trade goods into a beautiful bonnet useful and valuable in Huron society.
Musée de l'Homme.

met with success so long as British officials were on or very near the sea. Colonists acknowledged—although they did not always readily comply with—British authority to collect customs duties, inspect cargoes, and oversee the enforcement of trade regulations. But when royal officials tried to wield their authority on land, in the internal affairs of colonies, they invariably encountered obstreperous colonial resistance. A governor appointed by the king in each of the nine royal colonies (the two royal chartered colonies of Rhode Island and Connecticut selected their own governors) or by the proprietors in each of the two proprietary colonies (Maryland and Pennsylvania) headed the government of each colony. The British tended to envision colonial governors as mini-monarchs able to exert influence in the colonies much as the king did in eighteenth-century England. But colonial governors were not kings and the colonies were not England.

Most colonial governors were appointed to their posts because of their influence with the

BEAVER HAT
European colonists, like Native Americans, adapted items obtained in trade to their own purposes. The beaver hat shown here is a careful reproduction of a seventeenth-century design. Although a colonial hatmaker pressed and molded beaver skin in the process of manufacture, the animal origins of the hat were still evident in the finished product. A good beaver hat like this one was sturdy, water-repellent, and warm. But compared to the Huron bonnet opposite, it was drab and utilitarian. Women colonists sewed garments of all kinds, but they did not create intricate designs of beadwork on hats or other items.
Pilgrim Society.

British monarchy rather than with the colonists. Eight out of ten colonial governors had been born in England, not in the colonies. They lacked the knowledge about people and issues more common among native-born colonists, although American birth did not guarantee success as a colonial governor. Some governors—like the two men who served as governor of Virginia for the first half of the eighteenth century—stayed in England, close to the source of royal patronage, and delegated the grubby details of colonial affairs to subordinates. Even the best-intentioned colonial governors had difficulty developing relations of trust and respect with influential colonists because their terms of office averaged just five years and could be terminated upon the arrival of the latest instructions from London. In England, politicians cemented political alliances with the careful distribution of patronage, a clerkship here, a treasury post there. But colonial governors did not have access to many patronage positions to secure political friendships. The officials

who administered the colonial customs service, for example, received their positions through patronage networks that centered in England rather than in the hands of the colonial governors. But from the standpoint of patronage, colonial governors were more like puppets than puppeteers, a situation that severely limited their ability to govern. Hamstrung by their meager resources for political persuasion, the governors received instructions from the colonial office in England detailing what must be done, now.

In obedience to their instructions, colonial governors fought incessantly with the colonists' representatives in the colonial assemblies. They battled repeatedly over the governors' veto of colonial legislation, removal of colonial judges, creation of new courts, dismissal of the representative assemblies themselves, and other local issues. Some governors developed a working relationship with the assemblies. But by the eighteenth century, the assemblies had developed the upper hand.

British policies did not clearly define the powers and responsibilities of colonial assemblies. In effect, the assemblies made many of their own rules and, by successfully defending them, established a strong tradition of representative government analogous—in their eyes—to the English Parliament. Voters often returned representatives to the assemblies year after year, building continuity in power and leadership that far exceeded that of the governor. Early in the eighteenth century, colonial assemblies won the power to initiate legislation, including tax laws and authorizations to spend public funds. Although all laws passed by the assemblies (except in Maryland, Rhode Island, and Connecticut) had to be approved by the governor and then by the Board of Trade in England, the difficulties of maintaining communication about complex subjects over long distances effectively ratified the assemblies' decisions. Years often passed before a law was repealed, and in the meantime the assemblies' law prevailed.

The heated political struggles between royal governors and colonial assemblies that occurred throughout the eighteenth century taught colonists a common set of political lessons. Colonists learned to employ traditionally British ideas of representative government to defend their own interests. They learned to resist the definition of colonial interests issued by colonial governors and other royal officials. They learned that power in the British colonies rarely belonged to the British government.

Conclusion: The Dual Identity of British North American Colonists

During the eighteenth century, a distinctive society emerged in British North America, a society that was both distinctively colonial and distinctively British. Tens of thousands of immigrants and slaves gave the colonies an unmistakably colonial complexion. People of different ethnicities and faiths sought their fortunes in the colonies, where land was cheap and labor was dear. Indentured servants and redemptioners risked a temporary period of bondage for the potential reward of better opportunities than on the Atlantic's eastern shore. Slaves endured lifetime servitude that they neither chose nor desired, and their masters benefited. Identifiably colonial products from New England, the middle colonies, and the southern colonies flowed across the Atlantic. Back came unquestionably British consumer goods along with fashions in ideas, faith, and politics. The bonds of the British Empire required colonists to think of themselves as British subjects and, at the same time, encouraged them to consider their status as colonists. By the 1750s, colonists could not imagine that their distinctively dual identity—as British and as colonists—would soon become a source of intense conflict. But by 1776, colonists in British North America had to choose whether they were British or American.

CHRONOLOGY

1702	Queen Anne's War triggers large German immigration to American colonies.
1717	Scots-Irish immigration to American colonies begins to increase.
1733	Benjamin Franklin begins to publish *Poor Richard's Almanack.*
1739	Slave insurrection occurs at Stono, South Carolina.
1740s	George Whitefield preaches revival of religion throughout colonies.
1754	French and Indian War begins.
1769	American Philosophical Society founded in Philadelphia.

BIBLIOGRAPHY

This bibliography excludes pertinent sources listed in chapters 2, 3, and 4. Please consult the bibliographies of those chapters for additional suggested readings.

GENERAL WORKS

Bernard Bailyn, *The Peopling of British North America* (1986).

Bernard Bailyn, *Voyagers to the West: A Passage in the Peopling of America on the Eve of the Revolution* (1986).

Carl Bridenbaugh, *Cities in the Wilderness: The First Century of Urban Life in America, 1625–1742* (1938).

Richard D. Brown, *Knowledge Is Power: The Diffusion of Information in Early America, 1700–1865* (1989).

R. J. Dickson, *Ulster Immigration to Colonial America, 1718–1775* (1966).

A. Roger Ekirch, *Bound for America: The Transportation of British Convicts to the Colonies, 1718–1775* (1987).

Jack P. Greene, *The Intellectual Construction of America: Exceptionalism and Identity from 1492–1800* (1993).

Richard Hofstadter, *America at 1750: A Social Portrait* (1971).

Alice Hanson Jones, *Wealth of a Nation to Be: The American Colonies on the Eve of the Revolution* (1980).

Nancy F. Koehn, *The Power of Commerce: Economy and Governance in the First British Empire* (1994).

Douglas Edward Leach, *Arms for Empire: A Military History of the British Colonies in North America, 1607–1763* (1973).

Robert D. Mitchell, *Appalachian Frontiers: Settlement, Society, and Development in the Preindustrial Era* (1991).

Gary B. Nash, *The Urban Crucible: Social Change, Political Consciousness, and the Origins of the American Revolution* (1979).

A. G. Roeber, *Palatines, Liberty, and Property: German Lutherans in Colonial British America* (1993).

Carole Shammas, *The Pre-Industrial Consumer in England and America* (1990).

NEW ENGLAND

John L. Brooke, *The Heart of the Commonwealth: Society and Political Culture in Worcester County, Massachusetts, 1713–1861* (1989).

Richard Bushman, *From Puritan to Yankee: Character and the Social Order in Connecticut, 1690–1765* (1967).

Charles E. Clark, *The Eastern Frontier: The Settlement of Northern New England, 1610–1763* (1970).

David W. Conroy, *In Public Houses: Drink and the Revolution of Authority in Colonial Massachusetts* (1995).

Edward M. Cook Jr., *Fathers of the Towns: Leadership and Community Structure in Eighteenth-Century New England* (1976).

Jay Coughtry, *The Notorious Triangle: Rhode Island and the African Slave Trade, 1700–1807* (1981).

Bruce C. Daniel, *Dissent and Conformity on Narragansett Bay: The Colonial Rhode Island Town, 1635–1790* (1979).

David E. Van Deventer, *The Emergence of Provincial New Hampshire, 1623–1741* (1976).

Toby L. Ditz, *Property and Kinship: Inheritance in Early Connecticut, 1750–1820* (1986).

Christine Leigh Heyrman, *Commerce and Culture: The Maritime Communities of Colonial Massachusetts, 1690–1750* (1984).

Christopher Jedrey, *The World of John Cleaveland: Family and Community in Eighteenth-Century New England* (1979).

Douglas Lamar Jones, *Village and Seaport: Migration and Society in Eighteenth-Century Massachusetts* (1981).

James W. Jones, *The Shattered Synthesis: New England Puritanism before the Great Awakening* (1973).

Paul R. Lucas, *Valley of Discord: Church and Society along the Connecticut River, 1636–1725* (1976).

Jackson Turner Main, *Society and Economy in Colonial Connecticut* (1985).

William E. Nelson, *Dispute and Conflict Resolution in Plymouth County, Massachusetts, 1725–1825* (1981).

Gregory H. Nobles, *Divisions throughout the Whole: Politics and Society in Hampshire County, Massachusetts, 1740–1775* (1983).

William D. Piersen, *Black Yankees: The Development of an Afro-American Subculture in Eighteenth-Century New England* (1988).

Patricia J. Tracy, *Jonathan Edwards, Pastor: Religion and Society in Eighteenth-Century Northampton* (1979).

Lynne Withey, *Urban Growth in Colonial Rhode Island: Newport and Providence in the Eighteenth Century* (1984).

Robert M. Zemsky, *Merchants, Farmers, and River Gods* (1971).

MIDDLE COLONIES

Ronald W. Clark, *Benjamin Franklin* (1983).

Thomas J. Davis, *A Rumor of Revolt: The "Great Negro Plot" in Colonial New York* (1985).

Thomas M. Doerflinger, *A Vigorous Spirit of Enterprise: Merchants and Economic Development in Revolutionary Philadelphia* (1986).

Benjamin Franklin, *The Autobiography of Benjamin Franklin*, ed. Leonard W. Labaree et al. (1964).

Douglas Greenberg, *Crime and Law Enforcement in the Colony of New York, 1691–1776* (1976).

David Freeman Hawke, *Franklin* (1976).

Arthur L. Jensen, *The Maritime Community of Colonial Philadelphia* (1963).

Sung Bok Kim, *Landlord and Tenant in Colonial New York: Manorial Society, 1664–1775* (1978).

Susan E. Klepp and Billy G. Smith, eds., *The Infortunate: The Voyage and Adventures of William Moraley, an Indentured Servant* (1992).

Jessica Kross, *The Evolution of an American Town: Newtown, New York, 1642–1775* (1983).

Ned C. Landsman, *Scotland and Its First American Colony, 1683–1765* (1985).

James T. Lemon, *The Best Poor Man's Country: A Geographical Study of Early Southeastern Pennsylvania* (1972).

James H. Levitt, *For Want of Trade: Shipping and the New Jersey Ports, 1680–1783* (1981).

Stephen L. Longenecker, *Piety and Tolerance: Pennsylvania German Religion, 1700–1850* (1994).

Edward J. McManus, *A History of Negro Slavery in New York* (1970).

Peter C. Mancall, *Valley of Opportunity: Economic Culture along the Upper Susquehanna, 1700–1800* (1991).

Gary B. Nash, *Quakers and Politics: Pennsylvania, 1681–1726* (1968).

Gary B. Nash and Jean R. Soderlund, *Freedom by Degrees: Emancipation in Pennsylvania and Its Aftermath* (1991).

Thomas Eliot Norton, *The Fur Trade in Colonial New York, 1686–1776* (1974).

Paul F. Paskoff, *Industrial Evolution: Organization, Structure, and Growth of the Pennsylvania Iron Industry, 1750–1860* (1983).

Sharon V. Salinger, *"To Serve Well and Faithfully": Labor and Indentured Servitude in Pennsylvania, 1682–1800* (1987).

Sally Schwartz, *"A Mixed Multitude": The Struggle for Toleration in Colonial Pennsylvania* (1987).

Mary M. Schweitzer, *Custom and Contract: Household, Government, and the Economy in Colonial Pennsylvania* (1987).

Beverly Prior Smaby, *The Transformation of Moravian Bethlehem: From Communal Mission to Family Economy* (1988).

Billy G. Smith, *The "Lower Sort": Philadelphia's Laboring People, 1750–1800* (1990).

Merrill D. Smith, *Breaking the Bonds: Marital Discord in Pennsylvania, 1730–1830* (1991).

Jean R. Soderlund, *Quakers and Slavery: A Divided Spirit* (1985).

Frederick B. Tolles, *Meeting House and Counting House: The Quaker Merchants of Colonial Philadelphia* (1948).

Alan Tully, *William Penn's Legacy: Politics and Social Structure in Provincial Pennsylvania, 1726–1755* (1977).

Peter O. Wacker, *Land and People: A Cultural Geography of Preindustrial New Jersey* (1975).

SOUTHERN COLONIES

Richard R. Beeman, *The Evolution of the Southern Backcountry: A Case Study of Lunenburg County, Virginia, 1746–1832* (1984).

T. H. Breen, *Tobacco Culture: The Mentality of the Great Tidewater Planters on the Eve of the Revolution* (1985).

Carl Bridenbaugh, *Myths and Realities: Societies of the Colonial South* (1952).

Edward J. Cashin, *Lachlan McGillivray, Indian Trader: The Shaping of the Southern Colonial Frontier* (1992).

Edward J. Cashin, *Governor Henry Ellis and the Transformation of British North America* (1994).

David R. Chesnutt, *South Carolina's Expansion into Colonial Georgia, 1720–1765* (1989).

Paul G. E. Clemons, *The Atlantic Economy and Colonial Maryland's Eastern Shore: From Tobacco to Grain* (1980).

Kenneth Coleman, *Colonial Georgia* (1976).

Philip D. Curtin, *The Rise and Fall of the Plantation Complex: Essays in Atlantic History* (1990).

Harold E. Davis, *The Fledgling Province: Social and Cultural Life in Colonial Georgia, 1733–1776* (1976).

A. Roger Ekirch, *Poor Carolina: Politics and Society in Colonial North Carolina, 1729–1776* (1981).

Allan Gallay, *The Formation of a Planter Elite: Jonathan Bryan and the Southern Colonial Frontier* (1989).

Jack P. Greene, *Landon Carter: An Inquiry into the Personal Values and Social Imperatives of the Eighteenth-Century Virginia Gentry* (1967).

Gwendolyn Midlo Hall, *Africans in Colonial Louisiana: The Development of Afro-Creole Culture in the Eighteenth Century* (1992).

Joseph E. Inkiori and Stanley L. Engerman, eds., *The Atlantic Slave Trade: Effects on Economies, Societies, and Peoples in Africa, the Americas, and Europe* (1992).

Rhys Isaac, *The Transformation of Virginia, 1740–1790* (1982).

Alan L. Karras, *Sojourners in the Sun: Scottish Migrants in Jamaica and the Chesapeake, 1740–1800* (1992).

Marvin L. Michael Kay, *Slavery in North Carolina, 1748–1775* (1995).

Allan Kulikoff, *Tobacco and Slaves: The Development of Southern Cultures in the Chesapeake, 1680–1800* (1986).

Robin Law, *The Slave Coast of West Africa, 1550–1750: The Impact of the Atlantic Slave Trade on an African Society* (1991).

Hugo Prosper Leaming, *Hidden Americans: Maroons of Virginia and the Carolinas* (1995).

Jan Lewis, *The Pursuit of Happiness: Family and Values in Jeffersonian Virginia* (1983).

Ronald L. Lewis, *Coal, Iron, and Slaves: Industrial Slavery in Maryland and Virginia, 1715–1865* (1979).

Paul E. Lovejoy, *Transformations in Slavery: A History of Slavery in Africa* (1983).

Gloria L. Main, *Tobacco Colony: Life in Early Maryland, 1650–1720* (1982).

Patrick Manning, *Slavery and African Life: Occidental, Oriental, and African Slave Trades* (1990).

Harry Roy Merrens, *Colonial North Carolina in the Eighteenth Century* (1964).

Joseph C. Miller, *Way of Death: Merchant Capitalism and the Angolan Slave Trade, 1730–1830* (1988).

Robert L. Mitchell, *Commercialism and Frontier: Perspectives in the Early Shenandoah Valley* (1977).

Gerald W. Mullin, *Flight and Rebellion: Slave Resistance in Eighteenth-Century Virginia* (1972).

Michael Mullin, *Africa in America: Slave Acculturation and Resistance in the American South and the British Caribbean, 1736–1831* (1992).

Paul David Nelson, *William Tryon and the Course of Empire: A Life in British Imperial Service* (1990).

Jacob M. Price, *France and the Chesapeake: A History of the French Tobacco Monopoly, 1674–1791, and of Its Relationship to the British and American Tobacco Trades* (1973).

Jacob M. Price, *Capital and Credit in the British Overseas Trade: The View from the Chesapeake, 1700–1776* (1980).

John C. Rainbolt, *From Prescription to Persuasion: Manipulation of Eighteenth-Century Virginia Economy* (1974).

Robert W. Ramsey, *Carolina Cradle: Settlement of the North Carolina Frontier, 1747–1762* (1964).

Edward Miles Riley, ed., *The Journal of John Harrower: An Indentured Servant in the Colony of Virginia, 1773–1776* (1963).

A. G. Roeber, *Faithful Magistrates and Republican Lawyers: Creators of Virginia Legal Culture, 1680–1810* (1981).

Daniel Blake Smith, *Inside the Great House: Planter Family Life in Eighteenth-Century Chesapeake Society* (1980).

Mechal Sobel, *The World They Made Together: Black and White Values in Eighteenth-Century Virginia* (1987).

Barbara L. Solow, ed., *Slavery and the Rise of the Atlantic System* (1991).

Donna Spindel, *Crime and Society in North Carolina, 1663–1776* (1989).

Gregory A. Stiverson, *Poverty in a Land of Plenty: Tenancy in Eighteenth-Century Maryland* (1977).

Charles S. Sydnor, *Gentleman Freeholders: Political Practices in Washington's Virginia* (1952).

Daniel B. Thorp, *The Moravian Community in Colonial North Carolina: Pluralism on the Southern Frontier* (1989).

Dell Upton, *Holy Things and Profane: Anglican Parish Churches in Colonial Virginia* (1986).

Betty Wood, *Slavery in Colonial Georgia, 1730–1775* (1984).

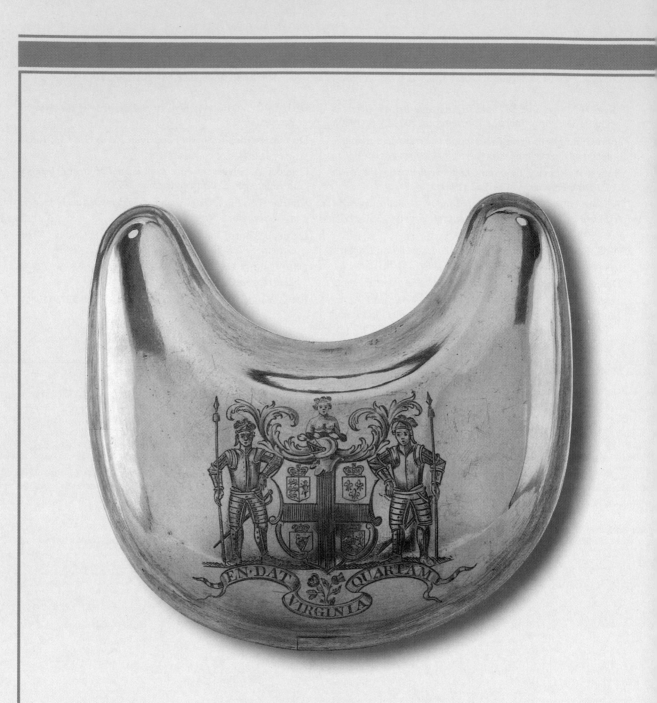

GILDED BRASS GORGET

George Washington wore this small brass gorget during the French and Indian War. It symbolized, in miniature, the throat piece of a medieval suit of armor. Eighteenth-century gorgets probably did not stop many Indian arrows, but they reminded officers of their noble loyalty to their monarch. The inscribed Latin motto, En Dat Virginia Quartam, boasts that Virginia is fourth in importance in the British Empire, after England, Scotland, and Ireland—and therefore first among the many American colonies.

Courtesy of the Massachusetts Historical Society ©.

THE BRITISH EMPIRE AND THE COLONIAL CRISIS

6

1754–1775

THOMAS HUTCHINSON WAS A FIFTH-GENERATION DIRECT DESCENDANT of Anne Hutchinson, the woman of conscience who so rattled the Puritan town of Boston in the 1630s. Thomas Hutchinson likewise was a man of conscience, but there the resemblance to his famous ancestor ended. He was a Harvard-educated member of the Massachusetts elite, from a family of successful merchants. He shared the family propensity for rigorous bookkeeping, tracking every penny and shilling in daily account books. Hutchinson was a measured and cautious man. "My temper does not incline to enthusiasm," he once wrote, in a shrewd self-assessment.

Hutchinson entered politics at a young age and in 1758 was appointed lieutenant governor after two decades of faithful service to the crown in the Massachusetts general assembly. In 1771, with Boston politics a powderkeg, he agreed to become the royal governor, knowing full well the risks. Hutchinson was one of the rare native-born royal governors, with deep roots in his home community; most of the other colonies were ruled by men British born and bred. But those deep roots did not ensure that Hutchinson would side with Americans when they began opposing British policies in the 1760s and 1770s.

Hutchinson had the misfortune to preside over the most tumultuous years in Massachusetts history. His love of order and tradition inclined him to unconditional support of the British Empire and away from the contagious enthusiasms of rebellion. Remaining loyal to England was no easy thing to do in Boston after 1765; to defend the existing order took courage and exposed Hutchinson to dangerous situations. He personally faced agitated and threatening crowds during demonstrations over the Stamp Act, the Townshend duties, the Boston Massacre, and the Boston Tea Party, all landmark events on the road to the American Revolution. Privately he lamented the stupidity of the British acts that provoked trouble, but the poker-faced, humorless administrator in him kept him from any public deviation from loyalty to the crown.

As early as anyone, Thomas Hutchinson reflected on the difficulties of maintaining full rights and privileges for Americans so far from their supreme government, the king and Parliament in England. In 1769, soon after British troops had come to occupy and pacify Boston, he wrote to a friend in England, "There must be an abridgment of what are called English liberties. . . . I doubt whether it is possible to project a system of government in which a colony three thousand miles distant from the parent state shall enjoy all the liberty of the parent state." What he could not imagine was the possibility of giving up the parent state altogether.

Others in America would draw the opposite conclusion by 1775: If the distance of governance precludes full participation in liberties, then perhaps it is time to change the government and bring it closer to home.

A sympathetic view of Hutchinson sees him as a tragic figure, a competent colonial administrator just trying to do his job, which was to defend royal policies that he knew were misguided. A less principled man would have taken the first opportunity to resign; an English-born governor would have longed to go home, to England. But Boston was Hutchinson's home, and he dug in. The more he dug in, the more his opposition flourished. Boston deserved its reputation as the leading edge of the colonial rebellion. Hutchinson gave Bostonians an immediate target, a man to vilify for defending British policies. The man not inclined to enthusiasm unleashed popular enthusiasm all around him. He never appreciated that irony.

Thomas Hutchinson was a loyalist; in the 1750s, probably most English-speaking inhabitants of the colonies would have considered themselves affectionately loyal to England. But the French and Indian War, which England and its colonies fought together as allies, shook that affection, and imperial policies in the decade following the war (1763–1773) shattered it completely. Over the course of that decade serious questions about American liberties and rights were raised insistently and repeatedly. Despite sharing a common language, the British and the colonists only slowly discovered that they sometimes meant fundamentally different things when they used words like *liberty* and *representation*. Each side in the imperial conflict was certain it was right, and that certainty limited the chances for compromise and peaceful solutions.

Many on the American side came to believe what Thomas Hutchinson could never credit, that a tyrannical Britain had embarked on a course to enslave the colonists by depriving them of their traditional English liberties. A liberty was a right, a freedom to act with independence and without coercion, and the liberty of taxation was the primary right Americans wanted to control. The opposite of liberty was slavery, a condition of unfreedom and of coercion. Political rhetoric about liberty, tyranny, and slavery heated up emotions during the many crises of the 1760s and 1770s. It was very effective as a call to arms, as a way of persuading others that very basic and significant issues were involved in the struggle with England. But this rhetoric turned out to be a two-edged sword. The call for an end to

THOMAS HUTCHINSON
The only formal portrait of Thomas Hutchinson still in existence shows an assured young man in ruffles and hair ribbons. Decades of turmoil in Boston failed to puncture his self-confidence. Doubtless he sat for other portraits, as did all the Boston leaders in the 1760s to 1780s, but no other likeness has survived. Hutchinson was hated; any portrait that fell into his enemies' hands would probably have been mutilated.
Courtesy of the Massachusetts Historical Society ©.

tyrannical slavery meant one thing when sounded by Boston merchants whose commercial shipping rights had been revoked; the same call meant something quite different when sounded by black Americans in 1775, locked in the bondage of perpetual slavery.

The French and Indian War

Whenever England was at war with France or Spain, the colonists in America also got drawn in. For twenty-two of the first fifty years of the eighteenth century, England was at war, mostly with France, and the colonists who felt it most acutely and continuously were the ones in frontier New

England, sharing an uncertain and dangerous border with the French in Quebec and Montreal and their Indian allies. A significant and costly victory in 1745—the capture by Massachusetts soldiers of the French fortress Louisbourg in Nova Scotia—held promise of cutting off all the French inland settlements to access to the Atlantic Ocean. But the Treaty of Aix-la-Chapelle in 1748 inexplicably returned the fortress to the French, a major blunder in New Englanders' eyes.

From 1754 to 1763, British and American soldiers shared the hardships of battle and the glory of victory over the French and their Indian allies.

In the 1750s, tensions returned to full force, as the French boldly extended their empire south from Canada into lands that some British colonists now eyed with desire, anticipating westward expansion. The result was the French and Indian War. From 1754 to 1763, British and American soldiers shared the hardships of battle and the glory of victory over the French and their Indian allies. But the expense of the war abruptly plunged the British and the colonists into their most serious disagreement yet.

French-English Rivalry in the Ohio Valley

The French used the period of peace after 1748 to advance south into Indian territory in the western regions of present-day New York and Pennsylvania. They also moved north and east from forts along the Mississippi River. Through strategic trade connections with Indian tribes, they planned to secure a western barrier to British-American expansion. Their goal was a solid French presence connecting New Orleans with its Canadian outposts.

But the French had competition. A well-organized group of Virginians had designs on what was called the Ohio valley. Virginia had long had an exaggerated idea of its territory, claiming its original charter included all lands west to the Mississippi River and far north to Lake Superior. In 1747 some wealthy Virginians, including the brothers Lawrence and Augustine Washington, formed the Ohio Company and obtained a grant from the king to some 200,000 acres of forests in the region of the Monongahela, Allegheny, and Ohio Rivers. The Vir-

ginians were interested in profits from the eventual resale of the land; the British government was more interested in blocking the advances of the French. The crown promised even more free acreage if the Ohio Company could launch a settlement of one hundred families and a fort. By 1753, the enterprising Virginians had blazed an eighty-mile road into their land grant and set up a trading post near present-day Pittsburgh. The French, meanwhile, were moving troops south from Lake Erie, strewing their path with iron tablets that announced French ownership of the land. The Virginia governor, Robert Dinwiddie, himself a major shareholder in the Ohio Company, sent a messenger to warn the French that they were trespassing on Virginia land.

The man who volunteered to be the messenger on this dangerous mission was George Washington, younger half-brother of the Ohio Company leaders.

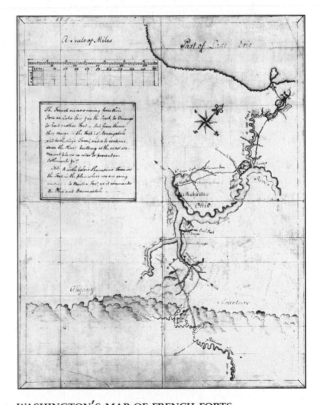

WASHINGTON'S MAP OF FRENCH FORTS
Washington's surveying skill was essential to his 1753–1754 journey to the French forts. His map combines an artistic perspective of the Allegheny Mountains as seen from the Virginia tidewater with a roughly accurate aerial map showing French troop encampments in western Pennsylvania.
British Library.

TABLE 6.1
EUROPEAN WARS OF EMPIRE

European Name	American Name	Years	Summary
War of the League of Augsburg	King William's War	1689–1697	Treaty of Ryswick signed. France and England surrender all American territory gained during war. Colonial possessions remain almost unchanged.
War of Spanish Succession	Queen Anne's War	1702–1713	Treaty of Utrecht signed. France surrenders to England the Hudson Bay region, Newfoundland, and Nova Scotia region of Acadia. France returns two major colonies of New France; Canada and Louisiana.
War of Austrian Succession	King George's War	1744–1748	Treaty of Aix-la-Chapelle signed. England and France give back territory won in the war, including return of fortress of Louisbourg to French.
Seven Years' War	French and Indian War	1754–1763	Treaty of Paris signed. England gains Canada, Spanish Florida, and most French possessions east of Mississippi River. Spain receives all French territory west of the Mississippi and New Orleans. France's empire in North America reduced to West Indian islands of Martinique, Guadeloupe, St. Domingue, and tiny islands of St. Pierre and Miquelon off Newfoundland.

Although he was only twenty-one, Washington was an ambitious youth whose imposing height (six foot three) and air of silent competence convinced the governor he could do the job. And Washington was eager to volunteer. As the middle child in a family of eight, he could not count on inheriting wealth. When George was eleven, his father had died, and his landholdings had been fragmented among his sons. George's mother could not afford to send him to England for classical schooling, as his half-brothers had enjoyed. Instead George learned geometry and trigonometry and with this relatively uncommon skill had found steady employment as a surveyor. But his path upward, he knew, required that he cultivate the Virginia elite. Leading a mission to the French would give him the kind of visibility he craved.

Washington took Governor Dinwiddie's letter to the French commander's headquarters near Lake Erie. While he waited for the official response, he counted the French soldiers, made sketches of their forts, and picked up boasts from French soldiers of their goal to capture all the land west of the Appalachians and drive out the few English traders and settlers already there. This information led the Virginia governor to appoint Washington to raise troops against the French. In the spring of 1754, a small military force numbering less than a hundred men moved west searching for nine hundred French troops said to be encamped along the Ohio River. Washington recruited Indian support as well, and a small group of Mingos, fewer than two dozen, joined him. But after an initial skirmish with about forty French soldiers—in the opening battle of what came to be called the French and Indian War—in May 1754, the Indians dropped out, realizing the Virginians would be greatly outnumbered. The Virginians built a flimsy fortification, called Fort Necessity, and in early July the nine hundred French troops stormed and took it. Washington was captured and then sent back to his governor carrying a new message: The French had no intention of departing from the disputed territory.

Thus began the French and Indian War, just six years after the end of the last war. Unlike earlier French-British conflicts, this one started in America, and its battles would be centered there. By 1756, the war had escalated to include a half dozen European countries, and battles had occurred in the Caribbean and in Europe. To the Europeans, the war was known as the Seven Years' War, once it concluded in 1763. But for Americans, with their two-year head start, it actually lasted nine years.

The Albany Congress and Intercolonial Defense

To succeed in even a limited war, the British needed coordinated support from the American colonists as well as some way to woo Indians at least into neutrality. Requisitioning soldiers and supplies from each individual colonial government was time-consuming and also difficult, since not every colony cared about French movements into the Ohio valley. So London officials instructed the colonies from Virginia north to send delegates to a meeting in Albany, New York. One goal of the Albany Congress was to construct an intercolonial agency to provide for the mutual defense of the colonies. A second and perhaps more crucial goal was to attempt to persuade some of the key Indian tribes of the powerful Iroquois Nation of western New York to support the English, or at least to promise neutrality in the war with the French.

PORTRAIT OF GEORGE WASHINGTON, BY CHARLES WILLSON PEALE

In 1772, George Washington posed for the artist Charles Willson Peale in his splendid uniform from the French and Indian War. Note the ornamental gorget (see page 196), the graceful sash, and the brass vest buttons that still meet buttonholes over the Virginian's forty-year-old girth. Washington's pocket contains an "Order of March," implying that military duty still lies ahead. Peale captured Washington's grandeur in his clothes but not his face, which appears plain and simple. Washington wrote a friend that he was "in so grave—so sullen a mood" and often so sleepy "that I fancy the skill of this gentleman's pencil will be hard put to it, in describing to the world what manner of man I am."
Washington and Lee University

In June 1754, twenty-four delegates from seven colonies met in Albany, among them Benjamin Franklin of Pennsylvania and Thomas Hutchinson of Massachusetts, two men in their mid-forties who were rising political stars in their home colonies. For several years Franklin had urged closer connections among the colonies because he feared the military alliance of the French and Native American peoples in the west. Hutchinson was more generally in favor of restructuring and streamlining imperial authority. At Albany, the two men drew up the Albany

Plan of Union. No radical desire for increased colonial power motivated them; the Plan of Union humbly reaffirmed Parliament's authority over the colonies. The plan proposed a new top layer of colonial government consisting of a president general, appointed by the crown, and a grand council, with members selected by the colonial assemblies. The president and the council would have powers only in the areas of defense and Indian affairs.

Despite Franklin's best efforts to publicize the Albany Plan, not a single colony ever approved it. The Massachusetts assembly feared it was nothing but "a Design of gaining power over the Colonies," especially the power of taxation. Others suspected that the colonies could never agree on policies toward hundreds of quite different Indian tribes. Oddly enough, the British government never backed the Albany Plan either, which perplexed both Franklin and Hutchinson, who were earnestly trying to solidify British authority. England in 1754 was not yet ready to press for more control. Some forty years later, long after the Revolution, Franklin almost wistfully reflected that if the Albany Plan "had been adopted and carried into Execution, the subsequent Separation of the Colonies from the Mother Country might not so soon have happened." The irony was, said Franklin, that "the Crown disapprov'd it, as having plac'd too much Weight in the democratic Part; and every Assembly as having allow'd too much to Prerogative," that is, to the king's rights.

Representatives of the Iroquois League, embracing the Seneca, Mohawk, Onondaga, Cayuga, Oneida, and Tuscarora tribes, also attended the Albany Congress. They collected thirty wagon loads of gifts and made ambiguous promises to the colonists but then left without actually pledging to fight the French. The Iroquois preferred to stall and play off the English against the French, for their best interests were served by being on the winning side, which in 1754 looked as if it might well be the French. Not until 1759, when the tide turned in the war, would the Iroquois deliver on their vague promise of support for the British colonies.

The War Heats Up

By 1755, Washington's frontier skirmish had turned into a major mobilization of British and American troops against the French. At first the British government hoped for quick victory by throwing armies at the French in three strategic places. General Edward Braddock from England was sent to at-

tack the French at Fort Duquesne at the confluence of the Ohio, Allegheny, and Monongahela Rivers. In Massachusetts, Governor William Shirley raised a force of colonial militiamen to take Fort Niagara, critically located at the narrow land neck between Lakes Erie and Ontario. And finally, William Johnson of New York, a wealthy and influential Indian trader, was charged with leading troops to unseat the French at Lake Champlain and push them back to Canada.

Unfortunately for the British, a French spy in England learned details of the plans, so the French were ready. In July 1755, General Braddock set out from Virginia with more than two thousand regular army troops to clear the French out of Fort Duquesne. Washington and several hundred Virginia militiamen accompanied him. But a day short of their objective, they were ambushed by a combined French and Indian force, and 976 British were killed or wounded. The British redcoats, said Washington, "broke and ran as sheep pursued by dogs." Washington was unhurt, though two horses in succession were shot from under him; Braddock was killed. For the second time in the young man's short military career, Washington returned to Virginia to report defeat. But this time, the news of his valor on the field of battle caused the governor to promote him to commander of the Virginia army. At age twenty-two, Washington was beginning to realize his ambitions.

News of Braddock's defeat alarmed the other two armies, then hacking their way through dense New York forests. Shirley's forces simply turned back and did not try to capture Niagara. William Johnson's troops were attacked and put on the run by the French before they ever got to Lake Champlain. For the next two years, the British stumbled badly on the American front of a war that was quickly expanding to sites in Europe and the Caribbean. British political leaders were initially unwilling to commit large reserves of troops to the

MAP 6.1
European Areas of Influence and the French and Indian War, 1754–1763
In the mid-eighteenth century, France, England, and Spain claimed vast areas of North America, many of them already inhabited by various Indian peoples. The early flash points of the French and Indian War occurred in regions of disputed claims where the French had allied with powerful native groups—the Iroquois and the Algonquin —to put pressure on the westward-moving English.

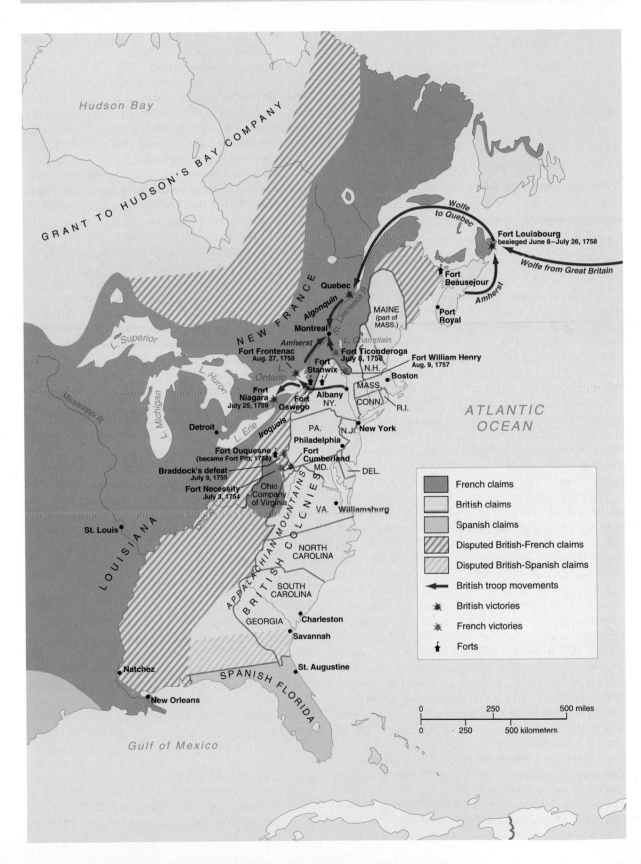

Hudson Bay

GRANT TO HUDSON'S BAY COMPANY

NEW FRANCE

L. Superior

L. Huron

L. Michigan

Mississippi R.

L. Erie

Detroit

Iroquois

Algonquin

Quebec

St. Lawrence R.

Montreal

Amherst

Fort Frontenac
Aug. 27, 1758

L.
Ontario

Fort
Stanwix

Fort Ticonderoga
July 8, 1758

L. Champlain

MAINE
(part of
MASS.)

Wolfe
to Quebec

Fort Louisbourg
besieged June 8–July 26, 1758

Fort
Beausejour

Amherst

Port
Royal

Wolfe from Great Britain

Fort William Henry
Aug. 9, 1757

N.H.

Boston

MASS.

Fort
Niagara
July 25, 1759

Fort
Oswego

Albany
N.Y.

CONN.

R.I.

ATLANTIC
OCEAN

PA.

Philadelphia

Fort
Cumberland

N.J.

New York

Fort Duquesne
(became Fort Pitt, 1758)

MD.

DEL.

Braddock's defeat
July 9, 1755

Fort Necessity
July 3, 1754

Ohio
Company
of Virginia

Ohio R.

VA.

Williamsburg

St. Louis

LOUISIANA

APPALACHIAN MOUNTAINS

BRITISH COLONIES

NORTH
CAROLINA

SOUTH
CAROLINA

GEORGIA

Charleston

Savannah

Natchez

SPANISH FLORIDA

St. Augustine

New Orleans

Gulf of Mexico

French claims

British claims

Spanish claims

Disputed British-French claims

Disputed British-Spanish claims

British troop movements

British victories

French victories

Forts

0   250   500 miles

0   250   500 kilometers

struggle, while the various colonies perversely refused to coordinate their military strategies. The French sat tight in their western forts, and all the major Indian tribes in the frontier rushed to ally themselves with what they anticipated would be the winning side.

William Pitt, the king's leading minister, recklessly declared, "I know that I can save this country and that no one else can," and then committed a massive infusion of troops and money to an all-out war effort.

What finally turned the war around was the rise to power in 1757 of William Pitt, the king's leading minister. Pitt operated beyond the bounds of reasonable confidence; he recklessly declared, "I know that I can save this country and that no one else can," and then committed a massive infusion of troops and money to an all-out war effort. He sent the best generals with large, well-equipped armies to America in 1757. In 1758, he sent a large naval fleet up the St. Lawrence River to threaten French cities. Pitt also pried American troops out of the colonial assemblies with promises to reimburse the colonies later.

Within two years, Pitt's strategy resulted in a string of resounding successes. In 1758, Louisbourg was recaptured by English and Massachusetts soldiers led by Sir Jeffrey Amherst. The British advanced on Fort Duquesne again, and again George Washington traveled with them, in a reprise of the Braddock campaign. But this time the French abandoned the fort without a fight, and the victorious British renamed it Fort Pitt, in honor of the unstinting minister. In 1759, Fort Niagara was taken by William Johnson, with the help of a thousand Iroquois, who by now recognized the shifting balance of power and were ready to throw their weight to the English. Next the fort at Ticonderoga on Lake Champlain was taken by Amherst's forces without a shot fired; the French were scrambling north to defend Montreal. With Niagara and Ticonderoga gone, and the British navy advancing up the St. Lawrence River, the French cities of Montreal and Quebec were isolated from help.

The decisive victory in the war was the capture of Quebec in September 1759. Led by the young General James Wolfe, British ships had, since midsummer, threatened the fortress city, located on a seemingly invincible rocky cliff. The opposing French general, the marquis de Montcalm, defended it with his outnumbered army. Wolfe bombarded the city with cannon fire and devastated large areas of the surrounding countryside, burning fourteen hundred farmhouses and all the crops in a campaign of sustained terror.

But by fall, Wolfe had still not budged Montcalm from the city, so he resorted to an unlikely direct attack. In the dead of night he led a small initial force of men up a very steep hill along the St. Lawrence River. At dawn, Montcalm learned of the British troops amassing on the open space at the top of the bluff, called the Plains of Abraham. Unaccountably, Montcalm delayed his response until more British troops ascended the cliff and positioned themselves advantageously. He then attacked, but in less than thirty minutes his outnumbered troops were a mangled mess, and he—and Wolfe as well—lay dying on the field of battle. Montcalm signed a full surrender of the city and died several minutes later.

The backbone of the French in North America was broken by the fall of Quebec. The victory was completed by the surrender of the French at Montreal to Amherst in late 1760. American colonists rejoiced, but the French and Indian War was not officially over yet. Battles continued in the Caribbean, where the French sugar islands Martinique and Guadeloupe fell to the English in 1762, and in Europe and India. France finally capitulated, and the Treaty of Paris was signed in 1763.

Consequences of the War

The triumph of victory was sweet but unfortunately short-lived. Much of what England should have won in this expensive and spectacular war was given away at the peace negotiations, because of the inexperience of the minister who replaced William Pitt. The map of North America was redrawn, but Americans were surprised at the outcome. France relinquished its Canadian territory and its claim to forts from Montreal to the Ohio valley, so at least the French threat from the north and west was gone. But all French territory west of the Mississippi River, including New Orleans, was now transferred to Spain, as compensation for its assistance to France during the war. Stranger still, Martinique and Guadeloupe, the Caribbean islands captured

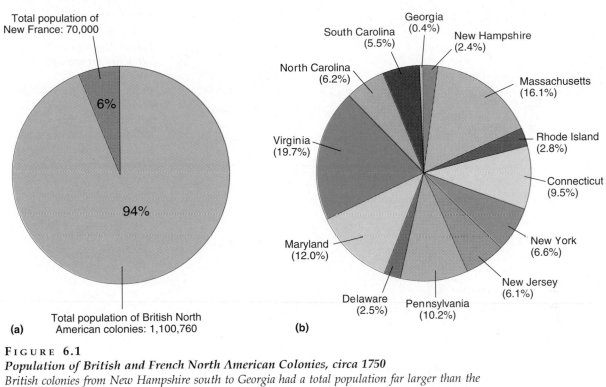

FIGURE 6.1

Population of British and French North American Colonies, circa 1750

British colonies from New Hampshire south to Georgia had a total population far larger than the number of French settlers in New France (Quebec and Montreal). In fact, more than half of the colonies each had a larger population than New France. However, the French army in the French and Indian War had unnumbered Indian allies to draw upon for aid: war with England was therefore not a foolish enterprise for them.

late in the war, were returned to France. Older Americans who remembered the Aix-la-Chapelle treaty of 1748, which ended the last war, bitterly wondered whether Louisbourg and perhaps all of Canada might be returned again to the enemy. Some shrewd colonists deduced an indirect advantage to England in allowing France to keep its sugar islands: A French presence might worry Americans and keep them dependent on England for protection.

In truth, the French islands in the Caribbean were hardly a threat to Americans, for they provided a brisk and profitable trade in smuggled molasses. The main threat to the safety of colonists came instead from Indians disheartened by England's victory. The Treaty of Paris dictated terms for the European powers but completely ignored the Indians. Indian lands were "won" and assigned to English rule on the map, but of course there was no way to compel the native inhabitants to vacate. With the French gone, the Indians had lost the advantage

of having two opponents to play off against each other, and they now had to cope with the westward-moving Americans. Indian policy would soon become a serious bone of contention between the British government and the colonists.

England's version of the victory of 1763 awarded all credit to the redcoats of the British army. In this version, ungrateful colonists had dragged their feet in providing troops for a war fought to save them from the French. More worrisome still, reliable reports reached England about business-as-usual smuggling. An illegal trade in beaver pelts, conducted by Albany merchants with French fur traders, was not dented in the least by the war, and neither was the illegal molasses trade in the Caribbean. An informant counted more than a hundred American ships anchored at one of the French islands, no doubt picking up cargoes of cheap molasses. American traders, grumbled the British leaders, were really traitors. William Pitt was convinced that the illegal trade "principally, if not

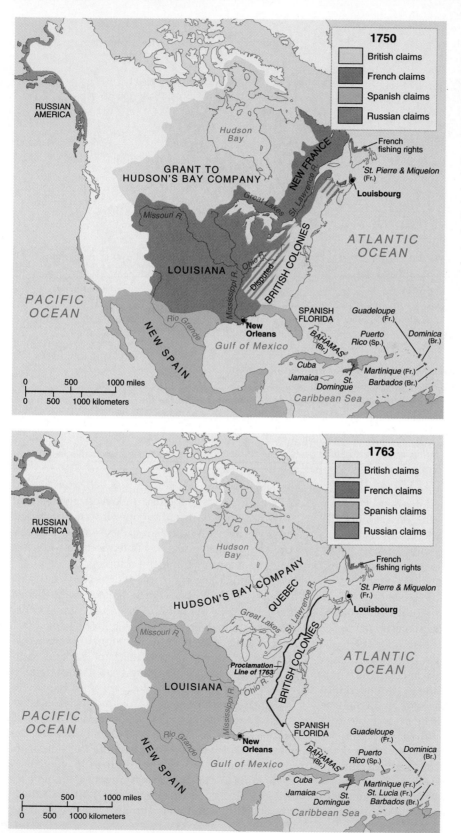

MAP 6.2
North America before and after the French and Indian War, 1750–1763.
In the peace treaty of 1763, France ceded its interior lands but retained fishing rights and tiny islands in the far north, and, more important, several sugar islands in the Caribbean. A large part of France's claim —to land called Louisiana west of the Mississippi River —went not to England but to Spain.

alone, enabled France to sustain and protract this long and expensive war."

Colonists, of course, read the lessons of the war differently. What they remembered were the British redcoats under Braddock, a professional army incompetent to fight Indians. American militia units turned out in force, but the troops had been relegated to second-rate status by arrogant British military leaders, who assigned them arduous trench-digging duties and made them haul the cannons. General Braddock had confidently predicted to Benjamin Franklin that "these savages may, indeed, be a formidable enemy to your raw American militia, but upon the king's regular and disciplined troops, sir, it is impossible they should make any impression." Braddock's defeat "gave us Americans," Franklin wrote, "the first suspicion that our exalted ideas of the prowess of British regulars had not been well founded." Yet four years later in the war, the British still had not altered their negative impressions. The impetuous General Wolfe had been heard to remark that the Americans were nothing but "contemptible dogs," and Americans believed that his prejudice was widely shared yet completely undeserved.

The human costs of the war were also etched sharply in the minds of New England colonists, who had contributed most of the colonial troops. About one-third of all Massachusetts men between age fifteen and thirty had seen service. Many families had suffered death and disease, the ultimate sacrifices of war, and this cost would not soon be forgotten.

The enormous expense of the war cast another huge shadow over the victory. Pitt's no-holds-barred military strategy was effective but costly. By 1763, England's national debt, double what it had been when Pitt took office, posed a formidable challenge to the next decade of leadership in England. At the heart of the matter was disagreement about the relative responsibility the colonists should bear in helping to pay off that debt.

From 1754 to 1763, power alignments had sharply shifted in America. The French-Indian alliance had posed a serious threat to a rapidly expanding British-American population, but with defeat came the virtual disappearance of the French. For the winners, mutual misgivings and suspicions immediately marred the satisfactions of the victory and set England and its colonies on a collision course. The Indians would soon find they had new allies, the British, to help them dam the flow of westward-moving settlers.

Tightening the Bonds of Empire

Throughout the 1760s, inconsistent leadership in England pursued a hodgepodge of policies toward the colonies. A new and inexperienced king had gained the throne in 1760, and he spent the next ten years searching for a prime minister he could trust. Nearly half a dozen ministers in succession took their turns formulating policies designed to address one basic, underlying British reality: A huge war debt needed to be serviced, and the colonists, as British subjects, should expect to have to pay. From the American side, however, these policies deeply violated what colonists perceived to be their rights and liberties as British subjects.

British Leadership and the Indian Question

In 1760, in the middle of the French and Indian War, George III, age twenty-two, came to the British throne, quite underprepared for his monarchical duties. The grandson of the previous king, George II, he had not been trained for leadership because it was assumed that his father would inherit the crown first. But the father unexpectedly died when George was thirteen, and the new heir-apparent emerged quickly from an unhappy childhood to undergo a crash course in kingship. When he assumed power nine years later, he was timid and insecure; he trusted only his tutor, John Stuart, earl of Bute, a Scotsman who was an outsider to power circles in London. George III therefore installed Bute in his cabinet of ministers.

Bute opposed Pitt's strategy on the war in America as "too bloody and expensive." He next squandered England's war victory by negotiating the unfavorable Treaty of Paris. Within two years the best talents in the cabinet had resigned, leaving Bute isolated. In his short remaining time in office, Bute made one other significant decision—to keep a standing army in the colonies. In terms of money and political tension, this was a costly move.

The ostensible reason for keeping ten thousand British troops in America was to maintain the peace between the colonists and the Indians. This was not a misplaced concern. Three months after the Treaty of Paris was signed, Pontiac, chief of the Ottawa tribe in the northern Ohio region, seized the moment to attack the westernmost settlers. A British trader in the region called Pontiac "a shrewd, sen-

sible Indian of few words, who commands more respect amongst these nations than any Indian I ever
saw could do amongst his own tribes." From spring
until fall 1763, Pontiac's uprising visited destruction
on isolated settlements in far western Pennsylvania,
the Ohio country, and north into the Great Lakes region. Pontiac mobilized the Chippewa, Huron,
Delaware, and Seneca tribes and captured all but
three British forts in the region. More than two thousand colonists were killed or taken captive. Scots-
Irish men in the town of Paxton, in western Lancaster County, decided that the Pennsylvania
assembly was shirking its responsibility to defend
against Pontiac's warriors, and they descended on
two nearby Indian settlements—inhabited by
friendly Conestoga Indians, as it happened—and .
murdered twenty of them. Several hundred men
from Paxton then marched on Philadelphia to demand better protection and a larger voice in the
state assembly; they were never punished for their
murderous vigilante injustice to the Conestoga.
Pontiac's uprising was quelled in December 1763
by the combined efforts of British and colonial soldiers, plus the news that French aid to the Indians
would not materialize. Pontiac later wrote to the
British, "All my young men have buried their
hatchets."

The potential for continued and costly wars
with the Indians, so well illustrated by Pontiac's uprising, caused the British government to issue an
order, called the Proclamation of 1763, which forbade colonists to settle west of a line drawn from
Canada to Georgia along the crest of the Appalachian Mountains. The ten thousand British troops
were to police this line. Meant as a temporary expedient rather than a permanent boundary, the line
promised to provide a reserve to protect in the short
run not only the Indians but also the lucrative fur
trade, now in British rather than French hands. But
the pressure of frontier population meant that the
proclamation line would be very difficult to enforce.
Settlers had already moved into the western regions
of Pennsylvania and Virginia, and they were now
instructed to return east of the mountains. During
Pontiac's uprising, many of these settlers had fled
east, but they had no intention of permanently
abandoning their farmlands and were swiftly moving back in 1764. The proclamation line had also
been breached by land speculators, such as those of
Virginia's Ohio Company. For them, a restriction on
westward movement would severely limit their opportunities for profitable resale of their claims.

MOHAWK WARRIOR
*This rear view of a Mohawk warrior highlights clothes
and body decoration: arm and ankle bracelets, earrings, a
hair ornament, and body paint. An important element of
frontal display is included by the English watercolor
artist — the warrior's tomahawk.*
Ville de la Rochelle.

Bute's decision to leave a standing army in the
colonies was thus cause for concern for western settlers and speculators alike.

Growing Resentment of British Authority

The mission of George Grenville, the king's next
chief minister, was to tackle the problem of the war
debt, which in 1763 amounted to £123 million, a
shockingly high figure that grew larger every day
because of the continued expenses of maintaining

the standing army. The annual interest alone on the debt was nearly £5 million, owed to edgy London bankers.

Grenville's attention first alighted on the customs service, a division of the government that stationed customs officers in British and American ports. Their job was to monitor the flow of ships and goods and to collect the customs duties on specified items. But the customs service was in a sorry state. Grenville found that the total sum paid as salary to the officers was four times larger than the total revenue collected in duties. One reason for this imbalance was that some customs officers in effect sold their jobs: An officer would stay in England and hire someone at a lesser salary to work in his place in the distant colonies. The replacement person on the smaller stipend was thus a susceptible target for bribes to augment his income, and some shippers found it more convenient to pay the officer directly in bribe money than to pay duties. Grenville ordered absentee customs officers to stop this practice, and he demanded rigorous attention to paperwork and a strict accounting of collected duties.

For the most part, American shippers did abide by the various navigation acts and customs duties regulating trade. But one trade law in particular, the Molasses Act of 1733, presented a hardship for Americans in the Caribbean trade, so through long tradition they simply ignored it and smuggled molasses into the country. The Molasses Act imposed a stiff duty on any molasses purchased from non-British sources. The idea was to encourage trade with the British islands by making French molasses more expensive. Without the tax, French molasses was cheap. A by-product of sugar production, molasses was a key ingredient in making rum, a drink the French scorned. So French planters on Martinique and Guadeloupe were willing to sell it to the rum-loving Americans on extremely favorable terms.

American shippers had long flouted the Molasses Act, even during the French and Indian War. Grenville's goal was to capture the revenue lost to smuggling, and his ingenious solution was to lower the duty on French molasses, to make it more attractive to obey the law, at the same time raising penalties for smuggling. Whereas the Molasses Act required a duty of six pence per gallon on non-British molasses, the new Revenue Act of 1764 (popularly dubbed the Sugar Act) lowered the tax to three pence. It passed Parliament with no opposi-tion, for it seemed to be a clear example of navigation legislation designed to regulate trade. But Grenville had added a new twist: His actual intent was to raise a revenue, not redirect trade. He was using an established form of law for new ends, and he was doing it by the novel means of lowering a duty.

The Sugar Act set out tougher enforcement policies. From now on, Grenville announced, British naval crews could act as impromptu customs officers, boarding ships suspected of smuggling and seizing cargoes found to be in violation. (The enthusiasm of the captains and crews of the naval ships was secured by a provision that they all earned a share of the profits in seized cargoes.) American smugglers caught without proper paperwork would be prosecuted for their offense, not in a friendly civil court with a local jury, but in a vice-admiralty court located in Halifax, Nova Scotia, where a single judge presided without a jury. The implication was that justice would be more sure and severe.

Grenville hoped that his tightening of the customs service and the lowered duties of the Sugar Act would reform American smugglers into law-abiding shippers and in turn generate income for the empire. Unfortunately, the decrease in duty was not sufficient to offset the attractions of smuggling, and the new vigilance in enforcing the act annoyed American shippers and created ill feeling. The presence of new personnel in the customs service made it harder for shippers to rely on the old smooth-working system of bribery, and several ugly confrontations occurred in key port cities such as Newport, Rhode Island, and New York City. But in general, larger political questions about the power of taxation lay hidden in the Sugar Act, and they stayed hidden. Americans who objected to the law came from the seacoast cities, and their objections were based on the financial damage the act caused them personally. Mainly, they tried to evade the law by carrying forged papers or by unloading cargoes at night in small harbors.

One other new act engineered by Grenville added to the growing resentment of British authority. The Currency Act of 1764 flatly prohibited the colonies from issuing any more paper money. Paper money had been issued frequently in the colonies during the emergency of the French and Indian War. Assemblies used it to finance war-related expenses, allowing it to circulate briefly as a medium of exchange and then be retired as payment for taxes. In

PAPER CURRENCY OF THE 1750S TO 1770S
Colonial paper currencies contained text that stipulated the legality and value of the money, accompanied by elaborate designs that discouraged counterfeiting. Handwritten numbers and signatures authenticated each paper. Parliament's Currency Act of 1764 prohibited paper money, but some colonies continued to print it, and it returned with force in 1775 when the Continental Congress began printing dollars (lower left).
Courtesy of the Decorative & Industrial Arts Collection of the Chicago Historical Society.

the short run, paper money in modest issues lubricated the economy by increasing the volume of money in a society that was always short of adequate silver and gold coins. But London merchants squawked about not getting full value for their goods, and Grenville persuaded Parliament to ban new paper money, a dire solution indeed because it left the colonial governments with no short-term financing flexibility and a reduced flow of money.

From the British point of view, the 1763 Proclamation Act, the Sugar Act, and the Currency Act all seemed to be reasonable efforts to administer the colonies. British leaders were looking for ways to consolidate their empire and bring the colonies under closer economic supervision. From the American point of view, however, the British supervision appeared to be a disturbing intrusion into colonial practices.

The Stamp Act Crisis

By his second year in office, Grenville had made almost no dent in the national debt. Continued evasion prevented the Sugar Act from becoming the moneymaker he had hoped it would be. So in February 1765, he significantly escalated his revenue program by securing passage of the Stamp Act in Parliament. He thus precipitated the first major, open conflict between England and the colonies over Parliament's right to tax. The crisis generated a second and much more surprising result: It politicized many colonists who had not before participated in politics in the eighteenth century.

Taxation and Consent

The Stamp Act imposed a tax on various colonial documents—newspapers, pamphlets, contracts, court documents, licenses, deeds, wills, ships' bills of lading—and required that a special stamp be embossed on the documents proving that the tax had been paid. Unlike the Sugar Act, which was part of a trade regulation system, the Stamp Act broke new ground. It instituted a tax whose purpose was plainly and simply to raise money. Grenville was not trying to encourage or discourage the use of paper. He was out to raise cash, and, what is more, the tax had to be paid in sterling silver, a condition that made the Stamp Act even more unpopular, because hard money was in short supply.

Grenville was no fool, and he anticipated that some Americans might be leery of the stamp tax. He therefore decided that the administration of the act should be delegated to Americans themselves, to avoid the problem of hostility to British enforcers, an unfortunate feature of the Sugar Act. He let it be known that in each colony, native stamp distributors would be hired at a handsome salary of 8 percent of the revenue collected.

The passage of the Stamp Act in 1765 precipitated the first major, open conflict between England and the colonies over Parliament's right to tax.

Benjamin Franklin was working in London that winter as the official agent (or lobbyist) of the Pennsylvania government. Franklin was not enthusiastic about the Stamp Act, and he and three other colonial agents met with Grenville personally to warn him that Americans favored taxing themselves. But Franklin nonetheless nominated a friend of his to be the Philadelphia stamp distributor, and the Connecticut agent who accompanied Franklin put forth his own name. Obviously they underestimated just how unpopular the Stamp Act would prove to be.

Grenville had other warnings that this tax might be extremely unpopular. Thomas Hutchinson, lieutenant governor of Massachusetts, wrote to his colony's London agent to urge him to lobby against the tax. Hutchinson immediately appreciated the key legal issue at stake. Aside from the navigation acts, which were intended to regulate trade and not make money, Parliament had levied no taxes on the colonists before this. Hutchinson warned that the colonies could reasonably conclude that Parliament had conceded to them the right to tax themselves, after all these years of no taxation by Parliament. On practical grounds, Hutchinson also urged the British officials to consider potential disruptions to trade if the colonists tried to evade the use of stamped customs documents. The disruptions might well cost more than the revenue the act generated, Hutchinson noted. But Hutchinson's warnings went unheeded.

The colonists, of course, paid taxes to support their local governments, but the taxing bodies were always the colonial assemblies, composed of elected representatives. A long English tradition held that taxation was a gift of the people to the king offered by the people's representatives. This view of taxes, as a freely given gift, preserved an essential concept of English political theory, the idea that citizens have the liberty to enjoy and use their property without fear of confiscation. The king could not simply demand money; only the House of Commons could grant it. Grenville himself completely agreed

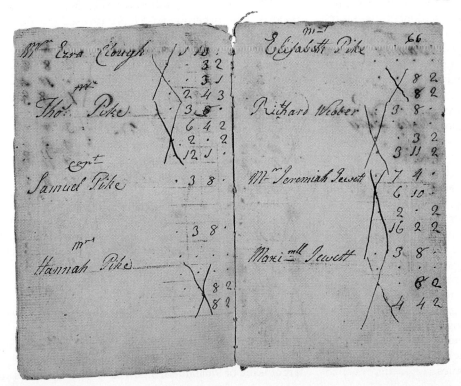

TAX ASSESSMENT BOOK
American colonists routinely paid property taxes to local authorities. This 1772 tax book from Rowley, Massachusetts, records amounts due in pounds, shillings, and pence. The several entries for each name indicate assessments on real estate, personal property, and a poll (per head) tax. Notice that two women owe taxes. Since married women by law owned no property, we can conclude that these were widows. Several numbers are frequently repeated; what might that suggest? Chicago Historical Society.

with this concept. He openly supported the colonists' privilege "of being taxed only with their own Consent." But, he argued, they were already "virtually" represented in Parliament, just as citizens in the new factory towns of Birmingham and Leeds in England were virtually represented, electing no member to Parliament on their own. All members of the House of Commons represented all British subjects, wherever they were. This British view of representation was emphatically rejected by colonial leaders. A Maryland lawyer named Daniel Dulany wrote a best-selling pamphlet explaining that virtual representation, while it might perhaps work within England, could not withstand the stretch across the Atlantic to the colonial dependencies. The flaw consisted in the fact that Parliament might well levy special taxes on the colonies —like, for example, the Stamp Act—whereas taxes within England were likely to be more uniform. Voters in Anne Arundel County, Maryland, denounced Grenville's reasoning as illusory: "The MINISTER'S *virtual Representation* in Support of the TAX on us is fantastical and frivolous."

Resistance Strategies

The Stamp Act passed Parliament with a November 1, 1765, start-up date. News of the act first reached the colonies in April 1765, so the colonists had a space of seven months to contemplate a response. Colonial governors might have argued for repeal, but since most of them owed their office to the king, they were unwilling to challenge the law. The colonial assemblies were another potential source of leadership on the issue, and eight of them did discuss objections to the Stamp Act. The assembly in Massachusetts met to denounce it, but Lieutenant Governor Hutchinson persuaded the legislators to moderate their outrage and humbly petition Parliament to indulge them in the privilege —not the right—of taxing themselves. Hutchinson privately thought the Stamp Act was bad policy— "happy would it have been for us if it had not passed"—but he was simply by nature incapable of publicly defying a British law. (Hutchinson also knew that his brother-in-law Andrew Oliver had been appointed stamp distributor for Massachusetts.) As in Massachusetts, all of the other colonial assemblies had a hard time grappling with the logical consequences of objecting the Stamp Act, for any consideration of Parliament's right to tax Americans soon led to the question of Parliament's general authority over the colonies.

Virginia's assembly, the House of Burgesses, waded into the implications of objecting to the Stamp Act and learned where that road led. The burgesses were at first not willing to object very loudly, but at the very end of their May 1765 sitting, when two-thirds of the members had already left town to go home, a twenty-nine-year-old lawyer named Patrick Henry, a newly elected member, presented a series of resolutions on the Stamp Act that were debated and passed, one by one. They came to be called the Virginia Resolves.

The drift of Henry's successive resolutions inched the assembly toward radical opposition to the Stamp Act. The first two resolutions merely affirmed that Virginians were British citizens with all the same rights and privileges they would have in England. The third resolution identified self-taxation as one of those rights, and the fourth stated the simple fact that Virginians had always taxed themselves, via their representatives in the House of Burgesses. The fifth resolution took the radical leap, by pushing the other four unexceptional statements to one logical conclusion—that the Virginia assembly alone had the sole right to tax Virginians. Henry persuaded the small group of burgesses present to endorse this declaration, but the ebbing numbers of positive votes indicated shrinking support for the implications of these resolutions.

Two more fiery resolutions were debated, but majority support eroded as Henry pressed the logic of his case to the extreme. The sixth resolution denied any legitimacy to a tax law originating outside Virginia, and a seventh boldly called anyone who disagreed with these propositions an enemy of Virginia. Such rhetoric was inflammatory, but Henry's logic, through the sixth resolution, was controlled and persuasive. However, it was too much for the burgesses. They backed away from resolutions six and seven and the following day, after Henry had left, retreated on number five as well, voting to rescind it.

Their caution hardly mattered, however, because newspapers in other colonies printed the whole set of seven Virginia Resolves, yielding the impression that a daring first challenge to the Stamp Act had taken place in Virginia. This made it easier for other assemblies to adopt more radical positions.

By fall 1765, the colonial assemblies were sufficiently emboldened to take a step together. In October, nine assemblies sent delegates to a meeting in New York City called the Stamp Act Congress. The delegates were extremely cautious about the larger issue of Parliament's power over the colonies and instead focused narrowly on the Stamp Act. The outcome of the congress was a polite petition sent to Grenville that affirmed the colonies' subordination to Parliament and asked for repeal of the Stamp Act.

Individual colonial assemblies beyond Virginia and Massachusetts debated the Stamp Act, and several finally confronted the larger question at stake: By what authority could Parliament legislate for the colonies without taxing them? No one disagreed, in 1765, that Parliament was the supreme body ruling the colonists, who were, after all, British subjects. But several assemblies developed the argument that there was a distinction between *external* taxes, those imposed on foreign trade to regulate it, and *internal* taxes, such as a stamp tax or a property tax, that in the long English tradition could only be self-imposed. So long as Americans were not represented in Parliament, internal taxes had to be managed by the colonial assemblies, they argued.

Crowd Politics

Besides the governors and the assemblies, there was a third arena for response to the Stamp Act: the local community. Every person whose livelihood required the use of official paper had to decide whether to comply with the act. Noncompliance could come in three forms. First, each individual could avoid using any stamped paper. But the cost of avoidance might be prohibitively large; if enough people ceased using stamped paper, the information network of newspapers, the legal system, and the world of trade might grind to a halt. A second option was to continue business as usual and ignore the required stamp. The risk here was that such an action was plainly illegal, and violators, if few in number, might be identified and fined or jailed. A third option thus seemed all the more attractive: to destroy the stamped paper or prevent its distribution at the source, before the law took effect; this tactic would ensure universal noncompliance.

The capital of Massachusetts was Boston, a port city of about seventeen thousand people packed into a square-mile peninsula jutting into a large bay. Virtually all of Boston's major occupational groups —lawyers and politicians, merchants and shipowners, tradesmen and artisans, dockworkers and sailors—depended on official papers to conduct business. In June 1765, the *Boston Gazette* denounced the response of the Massachusetts assembly to the Stamp Act as "tame" and "insipid." In contrast, it offered its readers the Virginia Resolves, all seven

SAMUEL ADAMS
Samuel Adams consented to pose for Boston artist John Singleton Copley in 1770. The portrait highlights Adams's face, which projects a dramatic intensity and dominates the bulky body, subdued by dark clothes. Adams stares thoughtfully and silently at the viewer and points to important legal documents before him, including the Massachusetts charter of 1689. Wealthy merchant John Hancock commissioned the portrait, which hung in his house. Copley painted scores of Boston's leaders in the 1760s, both loyalists and patriots. He maintained neutrality until 1773, when his father-in-law became an official East India tea distributor. Copley's home was threatened by a crowd, and he left for England in 1774.
Deposited by the City of Boston, Museum of Fine Arts, Boston.

of them, as an example of a "spirited" response. The *Gazette* did not shy away from appropriating the language of the seventh resolution and calling anyone who agreed that Parliament could tax Massachusetts "AN ENEMY TO THIS HIS MAJESTY'S COLONY." Left unreported in the *Gazette* was the news of the Virginia burgesses' own timidity in rejecting the sixth and seventh resolutions and rescinding their approval of the fifth. The royal governor of Massachusetts, Francis Bernard, feared that the Virginia Resolves were "an Alarm bell to the disaffected."

Over the summer a plan took shape to head off the Boston stamp distribution at its source. The leadership behind the plan came from a small group of shopkeepers, master craftsmen, distillers, and the printer of the *Boston Gazette*, Benjamin Edes, working closely with Samuel Adams, a forty-three-year-old town politician. Together they formed the core of the Boston Sons of Liberty. Adams, the son of a prosperous brewer, attended Harvard College in his youth and from an early age showed an interest in politics. His graduating thesis at Harvard was an essay on the question "Whether it be lawful to resist the Supreme Magistrate if the Commonwealth cannot otherwise be preserved?" Adams's carefully reasoned reply was yes. In the 1760s, Adams had settled into an unrewarding occupation, that of town tax collector. In distinct contrast to Thomas Hutchinson, Adams cared nothing for status, exalted office, or fine material goods. He was oblivious to his daily clothing, a matter that occasionally distressed his friends. Adams devoted himself not to appearances but to politics in the town meeting, Boston's arena of local government, and in the Massachusetts assembly. He had shrewd political instincts and a gift for organizing.

Both his contemporaries and later historians have portrayed Adams in a multitude of ways. Critics (like Hutchinson) viewed him as a troublemaker, the devil incarnate, or a puppeteer who craftily manipulated ordinary men into doing his bidding. Others have seen him as a man of the people or a man of vision who was among the first to favor independence from England. A distant and much younger cousin, John Adams, later wrote that Samuel Adams's character "will never be accurately known to posterity, as it was never sufficiently known to its own age." The consummate politician ensured that he would be a mystery man by burning or shredding much of his correspondence over his long lifetime. "None of my friends shall ever suffer by my negligence," he wrote.

The plan hatched by Samuel Adams and others in August 1765 called for a street demonstration to convince Andrew Oliver, the stamp distributor, that his personal safety would best be served by resigning. With no stamp distributor, there could be no stamps sold. Adams enlisted as demonstrators men from craft and artisan groups, as well as a shoemaker named Ebenezer MacIntosh, the leader of a South End gang of laborers, apprentices, and sailors, who forged their identity in opposition to the rival North End gang. The two groups staged ritual mock battles every year on Guy Fawkes Day,

a century-old British anti-Catholic celebration falling in early November. They were already experienced in the ways of symbolic action and costumed street theater, just the sort of behaviors that might throw a scare into Andrew Oliver.

On the morning of August 14, an effigy (stuffed dummy) of Oliver was found hanging from a tree. Governor Bernard met with Hutchinson and the governor's council and decided to take no action, in an effort to keep tensions under control. In the evening, a large crowd of two to three thousand people paraded the effigy around town, using it as a prop in short plays demonstrating the dangers of selling the stamps. The crowd then pulled down a small building on Oliver's dock, reported to be the future stamp office. Next, at Oliver's house, they beheaded and burned the effigy and broke some windows. The flesh-and-blood Oliver was in hiding; the next day he resigned his office in a well-publicized announcement.

There were lessons from the August 14 demonstration for everyone. Oliver learned that stamp distributors would be very unpopular people. Bernard and Hutchinson learned the limitations of their own powers to govern, with no police to call on. Hutchinson had attempted to confront the crowd at Oliver's house at eleven at night and learned that his personal authority meant nothing. The demonstration's leaders learned that street action was very effective. And hundreds of laborers, sailors, and apprentices learned what the Stamp Act was all about and, what is more, learned that some of their customary behaviors could have political significance.

Twelve days later a second crowd action, more properly termed a riot, showed just how well some of these lessons had been learned. On August 26, a crowd assembled and visited the houses of four detested officials. One was a customs officer, and two others were officers of the admiralty courts, where smugglers were tried; windows were broken and wine cellars raided. The fourth house was the finest dwelling in Massachusetts, owned by the stiff-necked Thomas Hutchinson. Rumors abounded that Hutchinson had urged Grenville to adopt the Stamp Act. In fact, he had done the opposite, but he refused to set the record straight, saying curtly, "I am not obliged to give an answer to all the questions that may be put me by every lawless person." His family fled the house, but Hutchinson stood his ground until his daughter returned and begged him to leave. Shortly after, the crowd attacked and worked all night to destroy his house, leaving only the exterior walls standing.

The destruction of Hutchinson's house brought a halt to crowd activities in Boston for a while. The Boston town meeting issued a statement of sympathy; but a reward of £300 for the arrest and conviction of riot organizers failed to produce a single lead. The emerging Sons of Liberty denied planning the event.

Essentially, the opponents of the Stamp Act in Boston had won the day; no one volunteered to replace Oliver as distributor. When November 1 arrived, the day the Stamp Act took effect, the customs officers in Boston allowed ships to pass through the harbor without properly stamped clearance papers. They had little choice; they simply did not have the staff to force the ships to halt. Hutchinson in his role as chief justice of the Massachusetts court could not tolerate this defiance of the law, nor could he bring the lawbreakers to justice in his court. So he did the only thing he could do as a principled man: He resigned his judgeship. Hutchinson was far from out of hot water, however. He was still the lieutenant governor, and within five years he would agree to become the royal governor.

Liberty and Property

Boston's crowd actions of August sparked similar eruptions by groups calling themselves the Sons of Liberty in virtually every colony. In New York City, the stamp distributor quit on August 22, as soon as he heard the details of Oliver's humiliation. In September, October, and into November, stamp distributors in nearly every colony hastened to resign. By the end of the year, fifty towns had witnessed demonstrations. The New Hampshire distributor resigned three times in public places, to make sure that the word got out. The Connecticut colonial agent in England who had snapped up a distributor's office even as he told Grenville how unwise the tax was, returned to his colony from England to face an angry crowd for whom simple resignation was not enough. The people were not satisfied until he also threw his hat and powdered wig in the air and shouted a cheer of "Liberty and property!" But this man fared much better than another Connecticut stamp agent, who was nailed in a coffin and lowered in the ground by the Sons of Liberty. Only when the thuds of dirt sounded on the box did he have a sudden change of heart and shout out his resignation to the crowd above. Luckily he was heard. In the South too, Sons of Liberty emerged. In Charleston, South Carolina, the stamp distributor resigned in late October after crowds burned effi-

SEAL OF ANDREW OLIVER
This amethyst seal suggests that important business was a routine event for its owner, Bostonian Andrew Oliver. Long before he became the unfortunate stamp distributor in 1765, Oliver held a succession of offices—overseer of the poor, collector of taxes, member of the provincial council, and secretary of Massachusetts. He thus had many occasions to press the unique seal into melted wax to authenticate documents. The stone bears the tough-minded motto Pax Quaeritur Bello *(Peace Is Obtained by War), an appropriate maxim for the man willing to become the royal lieutenant governor of Massachusetts in 1770.*
Collection of the Oliver Family, photo by Clive Russ.

gies and chanted "Liberty! Liberty!" But when a crowd of Charleston blacks paraded with similar shouts of "Liberty!" a few months later, the town militia turned out in a hurry to break up the demonstration.

The rallying cry of "Liberty and property" made perfect sense to many white Americans of all social ranks who feared that their traditional rights as English subjects were threatened by the Stamp Act. Englishmen claimed liberty as a birthright, meaning that they had a right to be free from interference by other people. The opposite of liberty was slavery, the condition of being under the total control of someone else. Civil society required some interference to perfect freedom in the form of laws, but Englishmen preserved liberty by making sure that only representative governments passed the laws. Up to 1765, Americans consented to accept Parliament as a body that in some way represented them, at least for purposes of legislation. But the right to own property was a special kind of liberty, requiring even stricter safeguards, given the likelihood that powerful rulers might become greedy and try to deprive citizens of their property. It was for this reason that the tradition arose that only a directly representative body could tax British subjects, so that taxation could be said to be truly self-imposed.

One Pennsylvania pamphlet writer asserted that the Stamp Act threatened to plunge the colonies into "a state of slavery." A Maryland writer warned that if the colonies lost "the right of exemption from all taxes without their consent," that loss would "deprive them of every privilege distinguishing freemen from slaves."

To Americans, the Stamp Act violated this principle of liberty and property, and some Americans began to speak and write about a plot by British leaders to enslave them. One Pennsylvania pamphlet writer asserted that the Stamp Act threatened to plunge the colonies into "a state of slavery." A Maryland writer warned that if the colonies lost "the right of exemption from all taxes without their consent," that loss would "deprive them of every privilege distinguishing freemen from slaves." The oppositional meanings of *liberty* and *slavery* were utterly clear to white Americans' minds; but they stopped short of applying similar logic to the one million black Americans they held in bondage.

The Declaratory Act

It was not colonial demonstrations and noncompliance alone that undermined the Stamp Act; the merry-go-round of British ministers contributed as well. In the summer of 1765, Grenville fell out of favor with George III and was dismissed. The new prime minister, Charles Watson-Wentworth, the marquess of Rockingham, was much less determined to force the Stamp Act on Americans. London merchants had besieged the government for repeal of the measure, in fear of disastrous disruptions in trade. Rockingham's dilemma was to find a way

out of the Stamp Act, without conceding the Americans' claim that Parliament could not tax them.

Rockingham's strategy was to secure the repeal of the Stamp Act by emphasizing the economic hardships suffered by British merchants. Unluckily for Rockingham, both William Pitt and George Grenville sat in Parliament, and neither one could let go of the larger principle. Pitt electrified—and confused—the other members by essentially agreeing with the American view of taxation. "It is my opinion that this kingdom has no right to lay a tax upon the colonies," he said. "At the same time, I assert the authority of this kingdom over the colonies, to be sovereign and supreme, in every circumstance of government and legislation whatsoever." In other words, Parliament ruled the colonies, but it could not tax them. Pitt clung to the ancient presumption that the gift of taxation could be granted only by a people's representatives, and Americans had no such representatives in Parliament. One member who was very impressed with Pitt's argument struggled to reconstruct it for a friend and gave up: "If you understand the difference between representative and legislative capacity it is more than I do, but I assure you it was very fine when I heard it."

Grenville was angered by Pitt's speech and responded with a stirring condemnation of American ingratitude. Grenville offered his listeners the example of the familiar arrangements of patriarchal power to help them understand the colonial relationship: "Protection and obedience are reciprocal. Great Britain protects America; America is bound to yield obedience." Grenville then challenged the defiance of the colonies: "When they want the protection of this kingdom, they are always ready to ask for it. . . . The nation has run itself into an immense debt to give them their protection; and now [when] they are called upon to contribute a small share towards the public expence, an expence arising from themselves, they renounce your authority, insult your officers, and break out, I might almost say, into open rebellion."

Ultimately Rockingham succeeded in sidestepping these two elder statesmen. In March 1766, the Stamp Act was repealed, but Parliament at the same time passed the Declaratory Act, which asserted the principle that Parliament had the right to legislate for the colonies "in all cases whatsoever." Perhaps the stamp tax had been inexpedient, but the power to tax—one prime case of a legislative power—was stoutly upheld.

Over the year-long period of the Stamp Act crisis, Americans had confronted a fundamentally new assertion of British control, the power to tax. They had challenged that control, through statements of defiance from the Virginia House of Burgesses followed by milder requests from an unprecedented body, a colony-wide Stamp Act Congress. As the crisis deepened, many thousands of ordinary Americans, unused to any regular political role, demonstrated a newfound competence to ponder questions of political authority and to protest grievances. News of the repeal of the Stamp Act set off celebrations in America, some restrained and others more carnival-like, with firecrackers and public drinking. But the general sense of celebration could not erase the growing uneasiness that the Declaratory Act marked the beginning, not the end, of trouble.

The Townshend Acts and Economic Retaliation

Rockingham did not last long as prime minister. By the summer of 1766, George III had persuaded William Pitt to return to office. Pitt appointed other new ministers, among them Charles Townshend, who served as chancellor of the exchequer, the chief financial minister in the government. Townshend assumed the upper hand in formulating colonial policy when Pitt became ill and incapacitated in the spring of 1767. As the chief financial minister, Townshend was still struggling to solve the old war debt problem. The continuing costs of the British army in America suggested again the idea of deriving revenue in some way from the colonies. Townshend's knowledge of the developing political climate in the colonies was unfortunately limited; his simple idea to raise revenue turned quickly into a major blunder.

The Townshend Duties

Townshend proposed new taxes in the old form of a navigation act. Officially called the Revenue Act of 1767, it established new duties on tea, glass, lead, paper, and painters' colors imported into the colonies, to be paid by the importer but surely passed on to consumers in the retail price. A year before, the duty on French molasses had been re-duced from three pence down to one pence per gallon, and finally the Sugar Act was pulling in a tidy revenue of about £45,000 annually, so it was not unreasonable to suppose that new duties might also improve the cash flow. Townshend and others in the ministry were proceeding on the assumption that external taxes—that is, duties levied on the transatlantic trade—would be more acceptable to Americans than internal taxes, such as the stamp tax. During the turmoil of 1765, several American essayists and politicians had drawn this distinction, and in a calculating fashion Townshend was seizing on it to smooth the path for his new tax scheme. At the same time, he also beefed up the customs service to improve the collection of the duties. Townshend established a five-man American Board of Customs Commissioners whose members would now reside in the colonies, the better to oversee the customs service. Townshend picked Boston for the board's home base, a decision that yet again showed he was not very shrewd about colonial protest politics.

"We are taxed without our consent . . . We are therefore—SLAVES," wrote Philadelphia lawyer John Dickinson, calling for "a total denial of the power of Parliament to lay upon these colonies any 'tax' whatever."

The Townshend duties by themselves were not especially burdensome, but the principle they embodied—taxation extracted through trade duties—looked different to the colonists now, when seen against the backdrop of the Stamp Act crisis. If there had ever been a clear distinction between external taxes and internal taxes, that distinction was wiped out by the realization that the Townshend duties were flatly intended to raise money. John Dickinson, a Philadelphia lawyer, articulated this view in a series of articles titled *Letters from a Farmer in Pennsylvania*, widely reprinted in colonial newspapers and pamphlets in the winter of 1767–68. To pretend that the new taxes were merely a form of trade regulation, he wrote, would permit "a new servitude" to be slipped upon unwary Americans. "We are taxed without our consent. . . . We are therefore—SLAVES." Dickinson called for "a total denial of the power of Parliament to lay upon these colonies any 'tax' whatever."

Unlike the Stamp Act, the Townshend duties directly affected few people. Sleepy country villages woke up for the Stamp Act, but they were lulled back to local affairs in the wake of the Stamp Act's repeal and were unlikely to recognize a tax on painters' colors and lead as a momentous outrage. What made the duties a red flag for the colonies was a second key provision, which directed that some of the income generated would be used to pay the salaries of the royal governors and judges. The prevailing practice had been for each local assembly to set and pay the salaries of its own officials, which in effect gave the assemblies a measure of influence over crown-appointed officeholders. But the assemblies seemed to Townshend to be getting out of hand, and he wanted to strengthen the independence of the governors.

In New York, for example, the assembly had refused to enforce a rule of 1765 called the Quartering Act, which directed the colonies to provide shelter and firewood, drink, salt, and candles for the British army, and the royal governor seemed unable to make them comply. Part of the army had been stationed in the west near the Proclamation Line since 1763, but in 1766 units were being moved to New York City in the wake of the crowd actions protesting the Stamp Act. The New York assembly, deeply unhappy about the arrival of the troops, argued that the Quartering Act was really a tax measure since it required New Yorkers to pay money by order of Parliament. Townshend came down hard on the New York assembly: He orchestrated a parliamentary order, the New York Suspending Act, which declared all of the assembly's acts null and void until it met its obligations to the army.

Both these measures—the new way to pay royal officials' salaries and the suspension of the governance functions of the New York assembly—struck a chill throughout the colonies. Many Americans wondered if their legislative government was at all secure.

The Massachusetts assembly quickly took the lead in protesting the Townshend duties by issuing a circular letter (so called because it was widely circulated) to all the other assemblies in early 1768. Samuel Adams, a member from Boston, drafted the letter, which argued that any form of parliamentary taxation was unjust because Americans were not represented in Parliament and that the new way to pay the royal officials' salaries subverted the proper relationship between the people and the rulers. Adams urged the other assemblies to officially endorse the circular letter. Not since the Stamp Act Congress of 1765 had there been any similar attempt to coordinate the response of the colonies to British measures.

When the circular letter reached the British ministry, there was yet again a new man in charge of colonial affairs, Wills Hill, Lord Hillsborough, appointed to a newly created post, secretary of colonial affairs. Hillsborough fired back his own circular letter to the assemblies, telling them to treat the Massachusetts document, which he termed seditious, "with the contempt it deserves." He instructed the Massachusetts governor, Francis Bernard, to dissolve the assembly if it refused to rescind its statement. The assembly refused to rescind, by a vote of 92 to 17, and Governor Bernard carried out his instruction. In the summer of 1768, Boston was in an uproar.

Nonconsumption and the Daughters of Liberty

The Boston town meeting had already passed resolutions, termed "nonconsumption agreements," calling for the boycott of British-made goods. Nearly three dozen other New England towns passed similar resolutions in 1767, and by 1768 nonconsumption as a tactic against the Townshend duties was widespread. The town of New Haven, Connecticut, for example, listed prohibited purchases, which included carriages, house furniture, hats, clothing, shoes, gold, silver, lace, iron plate, clocks, jewelry, textiles, furs, toys, velvets, linseed oil, malt liquors, and cheese. The idea was to encourage home manufacture of such items and to hurt trade with Britain, causing London merchants to pressure Parliament for repeal of the duties.

The trouble with nonconsumption agreements as a strategy was that they were very hard to enforce. With the Stamp Act, there was one hated item, a stamp, and a limited number of official distributors. Choking off the supply of stamps was a straightforward strategy. But an agreement to boycott British goods was extremely diffuse, and it also required serious personal sacrifice. Many merchants were wary of nonconsumption because it hurt their pocketbooks. Many continued to import British goods, to be ready for the day nonconsumption ended, or indeed to sell to people choosing to ignore nonconsumption. In Boston, such merchants found themselves blacklisted in newspapers and broadsides.

A more direct blow to trade came from nonimportation agreements, but it proved even more dif-

EDENTON TEA LADIES

American women in many communities renounced British apparel and tea during the early 1770s. Women in Edenton, North Carolina, publicized their pledge and drew hostile fire in the form of a British cartoon. The cartoon's message is that brazen women who meddle in politics will undermine their femininity. Neglected babies, urinating dogs, wanton sexuality, and mean-looking women are some of the dire consequences, according to the artist. The cartoon works as humor for the British because of the gender inversions it predicts and because of the insult it poses to American men.

Library of Congress.

ficult to get merchants to agree to these. There was always the risk that merchants in other colonies might continue to trade and thus receive handsome profits if neighboring colonies prohibited trade. Not until late 1768 could Boston merchants agree to suspend trade through nonimportation agreements. Sixty men signed the agreement, to be in effect exactly one year—from January 1, 1769, to January 1, 1770. New York merchants soon followed suit, as did Philadelphia and Charleston merchants in 1769.

Planters in Virginia were more eager than merchants to join the boycott. George Washington and George Mason spearheaded the formation of the As-

sociation for Non-Importation in 1769. When the royal governor dissolved the Virginia House of Burgesses because it issued a strong condemnation of the Townshend duties, eighty-nine burgesses walked down the street from the capitol to the Raleigh Tavern in Williamsburg and drew up the nonimportation agreement. Washington hoped for a second major benefit from nonimportation, beyond the pressure on British merchants. Extravagant living had brought some Virginia planters to the brink of ruin because they owed large debts to British merchants for luxury purchases. Nonimportation would provide "a pretext to live within bounds," Washington felt.

Doing without British products, whether they were luxury goods or basics such as tea or textiles, no doubt was a hardship for the American population. But it also presented an opportunity, for many of the British goods specified in nonconsumption agreements were household items and goods traditionally under the control of women. By 1769, male leaders in the patriot cause clearly understood that women's cooperation in nonconsumption and home manufacture was essential. The Townshend duties thus provided an unparalleled opportunity for developing and showcasing female patriotism. During the Stamp Act crisis, Sons of Liberty took to the streets in protest. During the difficulties of 1768–1769, the phrase "Daughters of Liberty" emerged and gave shape to a new idea—that women could play a role in public affairs.

Any individual woman could express affiliation with the colonial protest by complying with the nonconsumption agreements and by taking up home manufacture of items previously imported from England. One young Philadelphia woman inscribed some "patriotic poesy" in her commonplace book in 1768, the gist of which was that women can take up the patriotic cause even if men falter and stumble: "If the Sons (so degenerate) the Blessing despise, / Let the Daughters of Liberty nobly arise, / And tho' we've no Voice, but a negative here, / The use of the Taxables, let us forbear, / (Then Merchants import till yr. Stores are all full / May the Buyers be few and yr. Traffick be dull.) / Stand firmly resolved and bid Grenville to see / That rather than Freedom, we'll part with our Tea." On a more organized level, women in some towns met to sign nonconsumption agreements. Three hundred women in Boston drew up a petition agreeing to abstain from tea, "sickness excepted," to protest the duty on tea. A similar group in Edenton, North Carolina, agreed to forgo tea and found themselves

THE BLOODY MASSACRE PERPETRATED IN KING STREET, BOSTON, ON MARCH 5, 1770
This mass-produced engraving by Paul Revere sold for six pence per copy. In this patriot version, the soldiers fire on an unarmed crowd under orders of their captain. The tranquil dog is an artistic device to signal the crowd's peaceful intent; not even a deaf dog could actually hold that pose during the melee. Among the five killed was Crispus Attucks, a black dock worker, but Revere shows only whites among the casualties.
Anne S. K. Brown Military Collection, Providence, R.I.

ridiculed in an English political cartoon that depicted bad women—sexually loose, neglectful of children—signing a boycott petition.

Homespun cloth became a prominent badge of patriotism. In the latter half of 1769, dozens of towns organized public spinning "frolicks" or bees—women dusted off their spinning wheels and looms (dusty with disuse over the previous two decades of textile importation) and gathered for daylong competitions in spinning and weaving. Local newspapers publicized the "frolicks" and reported on the yards of cloth produced, thus further encouraging participation in the boycotts. Cloth making was no longer simply a chore of family service, but a task invested with political content. A Connecticut girl who spun ten knots of wool in one day proclaimed in her diary that her work made her feel "Nationly." Said the editor of the Boston *Evening Post,* "The industry and frugality of American ladies must exalt their character in the Eyes of the World and serve to show how greatly they are contributing to bring about the political salvation of a whole Continent."

On the whole, the year of boycotts was a success. British imports fell by more than 40 percent, and British merchants felt the pinch.

Military Occupation and "Massacre" in Boston

By the summer of 1768, the turmoil in Boston thoroughly alarmed Governor Bernard. Townshend's new customs commissioners had been forced to flee to an island in Boston harbor for safety. After Bernard dissolved the assembly, men from ninety-six Massachusetts towns staged a convention (a gathering closely resembling the dissolved assembly) to appeal—unsuccessfully—for reinstatement. On August 15, a rollicking anniversary celebration of the Stamp Act demonstration of 1765 put crowds in the street and apprehension in the hearts of Governor Bernard and Lieutenant Governor Hutchinson. With no police force and no reasonable hope of controlling the town militia, Bernard concluded that he needed British soldiers to help keep the peace.

Four regiments of troops from a garrison at Halifax, Nova Scotia, arrived in the fall of 1768, packing a total of three thousand uniformed soldiers into Boston. They camped out on the Boston Common and in rented warehouses, turning Boston into an occupied city. The soldiers conspicuously drilled on the Common, played loud band music on the Sabbath, set up a sentry point at the narrow Boston neck (the only entry to the city by land), and in general grated on the nerves of Bostonians. To occupy their spare time, some soldiers took casual day-labor work, putting themselves in direct competition with the laboring men of the town for low-wage jobs.

Although the situation was frequently tense, there were no major troubles during that winter and into the spring of 1769. In May, two of the four regiments departed, and in July Governor Bernard himself left for England, having been recalled by the king. Wild celebrations in Boston marked his departure, including massive bonfires and ceremonial bell ringing, no compliment to his years of rule. Thomas Hutchinson, the lieutenant governor, assumed the acting governorship.

At the very end of 1769, Boston's year-long nonimportation agreement drew to a close. The ban on British goods had been enforced by public pressure, but as January 1 approached, it was clear that some merchants could no longer be kept in line. Hutchinson's two sons, for example, were both importers hostile to the boycott, and they had already ordered new goods from England, anticipating a return to business as usual. The early months of 1770 were thus bound to be an eventful and conflict-ridden period in Boston.

Serious troubles began in January. The Hutchinson sons prepared to sell imported tea, and their shop was visited by a crowd that smeared "Hillsborough paint," a potent mixture of human excrement and urine, on the door. In mid-February another shopowner, who had complained that the nonimportation movement was akin to coercive lawmaking without his consent, found tar and feathers slapped on his storefront. The next day, a crowd surrounded the house of Ebenezer Richardson, a cranky, low-level customs official. Richardson panicked and pulled out his musket to defend his house and family. But when he fired it, the shot struck an eleven-year-old boy on the fringes of the crowd; he died within hours. The Sons of Liberty orchestrated an impressive funeral procession, with two lines of five hundred schoolboys accompanying the coffin and two thousand men and women trailing through Boston streets. This was the first instance of violent death in the struggle with England.

For the next week the mood was especially tense in Boston. Soldiers and young laborers engaged in brawls, typically over the odd-job employment sought by moonlighting soldiers. The climax came on Monday evening, March 5, 1770. Townsmen roved the streets, taunting soldiers on guard duty. One sentry guarding the entrance to the customs house on King Street was subject to verbal abuse from a growing crowd. Among other things, he was called a "damned rascally Scoundrel Lobster Son of a Bitch." (The red uniforms of the British were often likened to lobsters.) The sentry threatened to respond with force, but being vastly outnumbered, he hesitated to act. About 8:30 P.M., the town bells mysteriously began to ring, drawing more citizens into the streets. British Captain Thomas Preston decided to send a seven-man guard to join the lone sentry. The soldiers fended off the hostile crowd with loaded and raised muskets. Onlookers threw snowballs and chunks of ice, daring the soldiers to fire. Preston restrained his men, but finally one of the soldiers, hit by a piece of ice, slipped to the ground and rose up with a blast from his gun. After a second's pause, the other soldiers fired as well. Eleven men in the crowd were hit, five of them fatally. The victims had funerals befitting martyrs, with elaborate orations by leaders of the Sons of Liberty about the threat to all Americans posed by the British army.

The Boston Massacre, as it quickly became called, was over in minutes, but its repercussions were serious and long-lasting. In the immediate aftermath, Acting Governor Hutchinson showed courage in confronting the crowd personally, from the balcony of the customs house. By daybreak of March 6, he accepted the necessity of removing the full two regiments to an island in the harbor to prevent further bloodshed. Hutchinson also jailed Preston and the eight soldiers, as much for their own protection as to appease the townspeople, and promised they would be held accountable for their actions. But he also postponed their trial for nearly eight months, in the hope that angry tempers would subside.

Preston and the soldiers came to trial in the fall of 1770, defended by two young attorneys, John Adams and Josiah Quincy. Because Adams and Quincy had direct ties to the leadership of the Boston Sons of Liberty, their decision to defend the British soldiers at first seems odd. The thirty-five-year-old John Adams had recently become a member of the Massachusetts assembly, in an election engineered by his distant cousin and ally Samuel Adams. John Adams had a thriving legal practice in Boston, and, in his view, Preston sought out his services because he was simply the best lawyer in town. Adams was deeply committed to the idea that even unpopular defendants deserve a fair trial. Throughout his long public life, he was never shy

Who Got Tarred and Feathered, and Why?

TARRING AND FEATHERING as a form of vigilante brutality has long been associated with the American Revolution. British political cartoons gave wide currency to images of befeathered victims in humiliating postures. Boston loyalist Peter Oliver (brother-in-law of Thomas Hutchinson) claimed that tarring and feathering was an American invention and supplied shocked British friends with the "recipe," as he termed it:

> First, strip a Person naked, then heat the Tar untill it is thin, & pour it upon the naked Flesh, or rub it over with a Tar Brush, *quantum sufficit*. After which, sprinkle decently upon the Tar, whilst it is yet warm, as many Feathers as will stick to it. Then hold a lighted Candle to the Feathers, & try to set it all on Fire; if it will burn so much the better.

Both the cartoon depictions and Oliver's recipe for this messy ritual must be taken cautiously, however, for they were promulgated by pro-British men who had a stake in portraying Americans as barbarians. How often did tarring and feathering really occur? Who were the victims? Was actual harm done? Answers to such questions allow historians to evaluate the role of violence and terrorism as tactics of revolutionary struggle.

Recorded incidents of tarring and feathering do not support Oliver's assertion that the practice was frequent. Probably fewer than a dozen instances occurred between 1765 and the outbreak of war in April 1775. The practice peaked in popularity in the turbulent year 1775, making a total of perhaps two to three dozen cases in all the colonies.

Tarred and feathered victims were *not* British officials. For a person openly identified with British authority, the ritual of choice was hanging or burning an effigy of their body or conducting a mock funeral. Such dramatic representations of crowd dis-

pleasure made a chilling point without doing any physical harm. Ceremonies with effigies released anger, tempered by a measure of restraint.

Tarring and feathering pushed the boundaries of restraint, for the act involved considerable bodily discomfort. Victims of the sticky, feathery assault were usually community members suspected of being informers, violators of agreements to spurn British goods, or men conspicuous for their animosity toward the revolutionary point of view. They were men *of* the community who had to be rit-

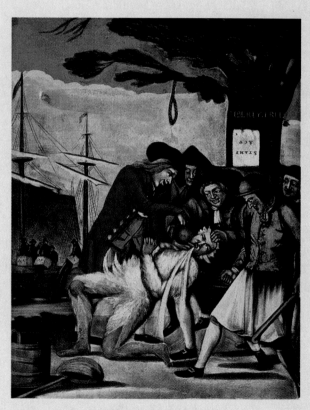

TAR AND FEATHERING CARTOON
John Malcolm, a customs official in Boston, becomes a feathery chicken forced to drink tea. A tar bucket and brush are in the left foreground; the Boston Tea Party— in reality ten months before the cartoon was published— proceeds in the rear. The Liberty Tree has become a gallows; posted to it is the Stamp Act, upside down.
Courtesy of John Carter Brown at Brown University.

ually distanced from the community for breaking a moral code, not a law. The standard treatment for lawbreakers was a flogging, fine, or jail, imposed by a judge. Moral code transgressors, in contrast, got symbolic punishments from their neighbors on the local committee of public safety, without benefit of legal procedures.

Tarring and feathering was a severe variant in a long tradition of ritual humiliations for transgressive people. Typical humiliations imposed on fornicators, adulterers, or other deceivers included dressing victims in clothes of the opposite sex, riding them around town backward on an ass, or making them stand in public wrapped in white sheets. The object was to shame them into apologizing for their bad behavior as a condition of acceptance back into the community. Tarring and feathering introduced a new variation on the theme: A person was rendered into an animal—a fowl or chicken—and paraded around in a state of near nakedness, the better to garner public shame.

For example, in 1771 a Providence, Rhode Island, man suspected of informing on smugglers was stripped, tied up, painted with warm tar, and feathered, after which dirt was thrown in his face. A man in Charleston, South Carolina, snarled, "Damnation to the Committee and their proceedings" and was soon tarred and feathered for his outburst. A New Jersey artisan who reviled the Continental Congress in late 1775 was set upon by townsmen, stripped, tarred and feathered, and paraded in a wagon for a half hour until he begged pardon. Probably the most famous case occurred in 1774, involving the Bostonian John Malcolm, a dishonest customs collector who extorted extra money from shippers. Malcolm's horrid fate was immortalized in a London cartoon showing five cruelly gleeful Americans forcing tea into his mouth, yanking his hair, and terrorizing him with a noose about his neck.

Peter Oliver's assertion that feathers were set on fire was a serious exaggeration. Hot tar of course hurt, and the eventual removal of the suit of feathers posed the risk of additional pain. It mattered what feathers were used. Soft goose down was an expensive household item in the eighteenth century; few revolutionary women would relinquish treasured quilts and pillows easily. A more prevalent source of feathers, scratchy ones at that, was the chicken coop. Powerful humiliation, not serious injury, was the goal. In one of the few known instances of a female-inspired sticky assault, girls at a quilting frolic in a small Hudson River village in fall 1775 reportedly stripped to the waist a young man of loyalist sympathies and adorned him with molasses and weeds.

In one unusual case, British soldiers in Boston in March 1775 turned the tables and attacked a rural man who had tried to buy a gun from a soldier. The man was stripped, tarred, feathered, and hauled around on a cart, with a sign affixed to his back proclaiming "American Liberty, or a Specimen of Democracy"—meaning, a sorry specimen. A fife and drum accompanied him, playing "Yankee Doodle" to irritate the Bostonian onlookers, and twenty bayonet-bearing British soldiers surrounded him, to prevent a rescue attempt. The soldiers' inversion fundamentally changed the ritual: No longer community-confirming, the event became in their hands a mockery of the civilian population.

Tarring and feathering was not practiced often. Other tactics involving less personal violence were more frequently used: publishing offenders' names in the newspaper, boycotting businesses, intimidating their families, and breaking windows. Sometimes just the threat of a tar and feather treatment was sufficient, as when a Pennsylvania loyalist had his nose pushed up to a barrel of tar or when a warning directed at an individual mysteriously appeared in a newspaper, signed by a fictional "Committee for Tarring and Feathering."

Peter Oliver did not think so, but historians generally agree that the years of revolutionary turmoil from 1765 to the 1770s were remarkably free of serious personal violence, aside from organized warfare. The Boston Massacre of five people hardly qualifies as a massacre by twentieth-century war zone standards. Tarring and feathering was rough stuff, but it did not cause death. The American Revolution, even in its aspects that resemble a civil war, stopped short of the kind of massive bloodshed and torture of civilians against civilians that would characterize revolutions from the 1789 French Revolution onward.

of taking on unpopular causes, although he was continually sensitive about the wounds and imagined insults his advocacy cost him. Samuel Adams respected his cousin's decision to take the case, for there was a tactical benefit as well: It showed that the Boston leadership was not lawless but could be seen as defenders of British liberty and law.

Preston was fully acquitted of all responsibility for the Boston Massacre, as were all but two of the soldiers, who were convicted of manslaughter and then branded on the thumbs and released. John Adams was very satisfied with the outcome. It was, he wrote, "one of the most gallant, generous, manly, and disinterested Actions of my whole Life, and one of the best Pieces of Service I ever rendered my Country. Judgment of Death against those Soldiers would have been as foul a Stain upon this Country as the Executions of the Quakers or Witches, anciently." Samuel Adams was not displeased with the trial outcome either. Nothing materialized in the trial testimony to fix blame for the massacre on anyone at all—not on the soldiers, or on any crowd participants, or on the leaders of the Sons of Liberty. The defense lawyers were no doubt men of integrity, but they were at the same time very sympathetic to the patriot side. They astutely chose to defend without pointing the finger of blame elsewhere. To this day, the question of who was responsible for the Boston Massacre remains obscure.

The years from 1767 to 1770 propelled the growing crisis into deeper and murkier channels. The nebulous Townshend duties lacked the symbolic punch of the Stamp Act, and the decision to try the tactics of nonimportation and nonconsumption created serious divisions in the American population. A military occupation of Boston brought the first fatalities in the coming Revolution, but, electrifying as that was to Bostonians, colonists distant from that city could still indulge the luxury of thinking that the crisis was perhaps not all that serious.

The Tea Party and the Coercive Acts

In the same week as the Boston Massacre, the new British prime minister, Frederick North, contemplated the decrease in trade caused by the Townshend duties and recommended repeal. A skillful politician, Lord North took office in 1770 and kept it for twelve years; at last George III had stability at the helm. Lord North sought peace with the colonies and prosperity for British merchants, so all the Townshend duties were removed, except the tax on tea, which served as a pointed reminder of Parliament's ultimate power. Leniency in repealing the Stamp Act, North believed, had invited Americans "to insult our authority, to dispute our rights, and to aim at independent government." North hoped to cool tensions without sacrificing principles.

Those few Americans who could not abide the symbolism of the tea tax turned to smuggled Dutch tea. The renewal of trade and the return of cooperation between England and the colonies gave men like Thomas Hutchinson hope that the worst of the crisis was behind them. For nearly two years, it looked as though Hutchinson's hope might be realized.

The Calm before the Storm

With the repeal of the Townshend duties, there was little desire to continue nonimportation agreements. Artisans in cities and planters in the Chesapeake tried to extend the boycott, to protest the remaining duty on tea, but the lure of trade and profits was too strong for the merchants to withstand. By fall 1770, nonimportation was a dead issue in Boston, Philadelphia, New York, and Baltimore. What was more, the leaders of the popular movement seemed to be losing their power. Samuel Adams, for example, ran for a minor local office in Boston and lost to a conservative merchant. And trade boomed in 1770 and 1771.

In 1772, however, several incidents brought the conflict with England into focus again. One was the burning of a Royal Navy ship off the coast of Rhode Island. The *Gaspée* had been harassing local vessels for some time in a search for customs violators. Local newspapers unkindly characterized the British commander as a pirate, a hog stealer, and a chicken thief. In June 1772, the ship was chasing down suspected smugglers when it ran aground in shallow waters. Some irate Rhode Islanders seized the opportunity to board the *Gaspée*. They wrecked the interior and then burned the hull, allowing the crew to leave first—not unharmed, however, for the despised commander was shot in the groin. A royal investigating commission could not identify any suspects to arrest (even though one young man had been seen the next day sporting the commander's lace-trimmed beaver hat). But the commission announced it would send suspects, if it found any, back to England for trial for high treason; burning the *Gaspée* was an act of war against the king.

This decision seemed to fly in the face of the traditional English right to a trial by a jury of one's peers. When the news of the *Gaspée* investigation spread, it was greeted with disbelief in other colonies. Patrick Henry, Thomas Jefferson, and Richard Henry Lee from the Virginia House of Burgesses proposed that a network of standing committees be established to link the colonies and pass along alarming news. By mid-1773, every colony except Pennsylvania had a "committee of correspondence." The British handling of the *Gaspée* incident had backfired, for it provoked the first serious effort to create semiofficial links among the American colonial governments.

Another British action in 1772 led to a second important communications network. Just as Charles Townshend had tried to free royal governors from colonial control by paying their salaries, now Lord North proposed to do the same for the superior court justices, paying their salaries out of the tea duty instead of allowing colonial assemblies to set the stipends. The Boston town meeting took particular exception to this idea, which threatened to subvert justice itself by putting judges in the pockets of their new paymasters. Samuel Adams tried to persuade Thomas Hutchinson to call a meeting of the Massachusetts assembly to respond to the salary issue, and Hutchinson predictably refused. So Adams proposed that each Massachusetts town set up a committee of correspondence to exchange vital information about unfolding political events. In December 1772, the Boston committee of correspondence sent out a letter to other towns describing the judges' salary policy as the latest move in a British plot to undermine traditional English "liberties" in the colonies. First there was unjust taxation, followed by a military occupation and massacre. This latest policy would "compleat our Slavery," claimed the Boston committee.

By spring 1773, half of the towns in Massachusetts had set up their own committees of correspondence and were busily doing exactly what Samuel Adams had envisioned: debating issues, voting on resolutions, and responding to circular letters from the more radical Boston group. The institution of such committees thus provided a forum for politicizing ordinary townspeople and served as a substitute for the usual flow of political power and information through the colony's royal government.

The third and final incident that irrevocably shattered the relative calm of the early 1770s was the Tea Act of 1773. Lord North had thus far avoided conflict by ignoring the colonies. In the spring of 1773, his attention was turned to a major but seriously troubled English joint stock company, the East India Company; many members of Parliament were among its stockholders, as was Thomas Hutchinson. Americans had been drinking moderate amounts of English tea and paying the tea duty without objection, but they were also smuggling large quantities of Dutch tea, and the East India Company was experiencing sagging sales. So Lord North proposed special legislation giving favored status to the East India Company, allowing it to sell its tea through special agents, appointed by the government, rather than through public auction to independent merchants. The hope was that the price of the East India tea, even with the duty, would then fall below that of the smuggled Dutch tea, creating an incentive for Americans to obey the law as well as boosting sales for the East India Company.

The Boston Tea Party

In the fall of 1773, news of the Tea Act reached the colonies. Parliamentary legislation to make tea inexpensive struck many colonists as a subtle and therefore evil plot to trick Americans into buying large quantities of the dutied tea. The real goal, some argued, was the increased revenue, which would then be used to pay the royal governors and judges. The Tea Act was thus a sudden and painful reminder of Parliament's claim to the power to tax and legislate for the colonies.

As with the Stamp Act and the Townshend duties, the colonists' strategy was crucial. Nonimportation was not a viable option, because the trade was too lucrative to expect colonial merchants to give it up willingly. Consumer boycotts of tea had proved ineffective since 1770, chiefly because it was extremely hard to distinguish between dutied tea (the object of the boycott) and smuggled tea (illegal but politically clean) once it was in the teapot. Like the Stamp Act, the Tea Act mandated special agents to handle the tea sales, and that requirement provided one convenient target for colonists' actions. A revived patriot group in New York City publicly identified the tea agents and pressured them to resign. In Philadelphia, the Sons of Liberty held a mass meeting and resolved that any merchant who handled East India tea was "an enemy to his country." They also issued threats to tar and feather anyone who assisted the landing of the tea ships; the first captain who arrived with tea took that warning to heart and turned his ship around. In

Charleston, South Carolina, tea ships did arrive and unload in December 1773, but the tea agents had resigned their positions, under pressure from the local Sons of Liberty, so there was no way to sell the cargo. After twenty days, the governor impounded the tea for nonpayment of duty, and it rotted in storage cellars.

The Boston Sons of Liberty were slower to act than their compatriots in other cities, but their action—more direct and illegal than anywhere else—ultimately provoked the most alarming reprisals from England. The first ship bearing 114 chests of tea arrived in Boston in late November 1773, and the next day the city was showered with notices calling for "manly opposition to the machinations of tyranny." As mass meetings engaging up to six thousand people debated the fate of the tea, two more ships arrived. They cleared customs and unloaded their other cargoes, but the tea remained on board. The owner of one ship, a Quaker from the island of Nantucket, off the Massachusetts coast, readily agreed to return the tea to England. But he found he was stuck in a legalistic nightmare of the sort that only a Thomas Hutchinson would scrupulously enforce: Because the ship had already entered the harbor, it could not get clearance to leave without first paying the tea duty. And there was a twenty-day limit on the stay allowed in the harbor, by which time either the duty had to be paid or the tea would be confiscated and sold by the authorities. The ever stiff-necked Governor Hutchinson would not bend the rules.

It took three hours to dump 342 chests of tea into Boston harbor. Bostonians quickly dubbed the event the Boston Tea Party, a jolly name that blunted the massive illegal destruction of property.

For the full twenty days, pressure built in Boston. Daily mass meetings energized the citizenry not only from Boston but from surrounding towns, alerted by the committees of correspondence. On the final day, December 16, the Quaker shipowner made one last effort to obtain a pass to leave the harbor and reported his failure to a large gathering at the Old South Church in Boston, presided over by Samuel Adams. At that point, Adams declared to the crowd, "This meeting can do nothing more to save the country." Perhaps the meeting could not,

but some people at the meeting had already concocted a plan to end the stalemate. At Adams's words, whoops rang out, and a large part of the crowd moved to Griffin's Wharf, where the three ships were anchored. Some five dozen men dressed as Indians destroyed the tea while a crowd of two thousand watched. It took three hours to dump 342 chests of tea into Boston harbor; the total weight was ninety thousand pounds, and it was worth £10,000 sterling. Bostonians quickly dubbed the event the Boston Tea Party, a jolly name that blunted the massive illegal destruction of property.

TEA DESTROYED BY INDIANS
A broadside was a one-page printed notice that could be tacked up on walls. This broadside of 1773 relates lively verses about the Boston Tea Party, useful for episodes of planned or spontaneous public singing. Notice the use of racial and gender stereotypes in the first verse in the references to manliness, fair Liberty, foreign Indians, and savage Moors.
Courtesy of the Massachusetts Historical Society ©.

The Coercive Acts

Lord North's response was swift and stern. Within
three months he persuaded Parliament to issue the
first of the Coercive Acts, a series of four laws meant
to punish Massachusetts for the Tea Party. The laws
were soon known as the Intolerable Acts in America, along with a fifth one not aimed at Massachusetts alone, the Quebec Act.

The first, the Boston Port Act, closed Boston
harbor to all shipping traffic as of June 1, 1774, for
as long as the destroyed tea was not paid for. In effect, England was obliterating the commercial life
of the city.

The second, called the Massachusetts Government Act, altered the colony's charter (in itself an
unprecedented step, underscoring Parliament's
claim to supremacy over Massachusetts): The royal
governor's powers were greatly augmented; the
council became an appointive, not elective, body;
and no town meeting beyond the annual spring
election of town selectmen could be held unless the
governor expressly permitted it. Not only Boston
but every Massachusetts town felt the punitive
sting. The act was meant to undermine local control of politics.

The third of the Coercive Acts, the Impartial
Administration of Justice Act, stipulated that any

royal official accused of a capital crime—for example, Captain Preston and his soldiers at the Boston Massacre—would now be tried in a court in England. It did not matter that Preston in fact got a fair trial in Boston. What this act ominously suggested was that down the road, there might be more Captain Prestons and soldiers firing into crowds.

The fourth of the Coercive Acts was a new amendment to the 1765 Quartering Act, permitting military commanders to lodge soldiers wherever necessary, even in private households. For Boston this was no idle gesture, for in a related move, Lord North appointed General Thomas Gage, commander of the Royal Army in New York, to be the new governor of Massachusetts. Thomas Hutchinson was out, relieved at long last of his duties, and military rule, including soldiers, returned once more to Boston.

The fifth Intolerable Act, the Quebec Act, had little to do with the first four but, ill-timed, it greatly fed the alarm of Americans. It confirmed the continuation of French civil law, government form, and Catholicism for Quebec, all an affront to Protestant New Englanders denied their own representative government. The act also gave Quebec control of disputed lands (and hence control of the lucrative fur trade) throughout the Ohio River valley, lands claimed variously by Virginia, Pennsylvania, and Connecticut.

If England could step on Massachusetts and change its charter, suspend government, inaugurate military rule, and on top of that give Ohio to Catholic Quebec, then what liberties were possibly secure?

When the Boston Port Act was passed, many merchants in Boston and other cities favored simply paying reparations for the tea. But with the rapid issuance of further punitive acts, alarm spread. If England could step on Massachusetts and change its charter, suspend government, inaugurate military rule, and on top of that give Ohio to Catholic Quebec, then what liberties were possibly secure?

In Virginia, the House of Burgesses proposed a day of fasting and prayer in sympathy with Massachusetts for the Port Act. Despite the moderate na-

ture of this proposal, the governor, John Murray, Lord Dunmore, dissolved the house for its gesture of solidarity with rebellious Massachusetts. If the burgesses were complacent about their liberties before that moment, they could not be now. Eighty-nine of them met in the Raleigh Tavern in Williamsburg, just as they had done in 1769 in the Townshend duties crisis, and in this unauthorized form passed resolutions on parliamentary and colonial rights. Via the committees of correspondence, they urged all the other colonial assemblies to meet in Philadelphia in the fall of 1774 to respond to the crisis.

The First Continental Congress

Every colony except Georgia sent delegates to Philadelphia for the meeting of the First Continental Congress in September 1774. In six colonies, specially reconstituted assemblies made the delegate selections, for, as in Virginia, the royal governors were dissolving the official bodies as fast as they could. The gathering in Philadelphia included the leading patriots, such as Samuel and John Adams from Massachusetts and George Washington and Patrick Henry from Virginia. A few colonies sent men who were cool to provoking a crisis with England, like Pennsylvania's Joseph Galloway, whose mission was to slow down the revolutionary momentum. Whatever their views, most of the delegates were the leading statesmen of their localities. John Adams wrote to his wife, Abigail, that "the magnanimity and public spirit which I see here make me blush for the sordid, venal herd which I have seen in my own Province."

Two difficult tasks confronted the congress: The delegates wanted to agree on exactly what liberties they claimed as English subjects and what rights Parliament held over them, and they needed to make a unified response to the Coercive Acts. Some delegates wanted a total ban on trade with England, to force a repeal of the Coercive Acts, but others—especially from the southern colonies heavily dependent on the export of tobacco and rice—could not afford such a comprehensive stoppage. Samuel Adams and Patrick Henry were more than eager for a ringing denunciation of all parliamentary control, whereas the conservative Joseph Galloway proposed a plan (quickly defeated) to create a colonial miniparliament in America to assist the British Parliament in ruling the colonies.

The congress met for seven weeks in Carpenter's Hall, Philadelphia, and eventually hammered out a declaration of rights, couched in traditional language: "We ask only for peace, liberty and security. We wish no diminution of royal prerogatives, we demand no new rights." Yet the rights assumed already to exist were in fact radical, from England's point of view. Chief among them was the claim that Americans were not represented in Parliament and so each colonial government had the sole right to legislate for and tax its own people. The one slight concession to England was a carefully worded agreement that the colonists would "cheerfully consent" to trade regulations, for the larger good of the empire—so long as trade regulation was not a covert means of raising revenue. By consenting to this one power, however, the patriots were implying their right to revoke consent at any time. To express their displeasure with the Boston Port Act, the delegates also agreed to a staggered and limited ban on trade—imports prohibited this year, exports the following year, and rice totally exempted, to keep South Carolinians happy. As with previous attempts to curtail trade, they developed an enforcement strategy for the boycott, in the form of a Continental Association, which would have chapters in each town. Local associations, variously called committees of public safety or of inspection, would monitor all commerce and confront suspected violators of the boycott. Its work done, the congress disbanded on October 26, 1774, with a vote to reconvene the following May in a Second Continental Congress.

The committees of public safety, the committees of correspondence, the regrouped colonial assemblies, and the Continental Congresses were all functioning political bodies without any formal constitutional authority. British officials did not recognize them as legitimate, but many Americans who supported the patriot cause instantly accepted them. A key reason for the stability of such unauthorized bodies throughout the Revolutionary period was that they were composed of the same men, by and large, who had composed the official bodies now disbanded.

England's severe reaction to the Boston Tea Party finally succeeded in making many colonists from New Hampshire to Georgia realize that the problems of British rule went far beyond questions of taxation. The Coercive Acts infringed on liberty and denied self-government; they could not be ignored. With one colony subordinated to military rule now, and a British army at the ready in Boston, the threat of a general war was at the doorstep.

Domestic Insurrections

Before the Second Continental Congress could meet, war began in Massachusetts. General Thomas Gage, military commander and new governor, thought he had a domestic insurrection on his hands that needed only a show of force to quiet it. The Americans saw things differently: They were defending their homes and liberties against an intrusive power that was trying to enslave them. To the south, a different and inverted version of the same story began to unfold, as thousands of enslaved black men and women seized an unprecedented opportunity to mount a different kind of domestic insurrection, against planter-patriots who looked over their shoulders uneasily whenever they called out for liberty from the British.

Lexington and Concord

Over the winter of 1774–1775 the Continental Association enforced the import ban with enthusiasm. Some hoped the collapse of the Coercive Acts was just around the corner. Others, more pessimistic, started accumulating arms and ammunition. Militiamen started to drill and train. In Massachusetts, gunpowder and shot were stored in strategic places, and special militia units calling themselves "minutemen" prepared to be ready on a minute's notice to respond to unusual movements of the British soldiers now occupying Boston.

Thomas Gage felt the increased tensions and experienced something close to panic. He knew that a single aggressive show of force on his part would plunge the country into war, and so he wrote to Lord North asking for twenty thousand reinforcements. The people, he informed North, were "numerous, worked up to a fury, and not a Boston rabble but the freeholders and farmers of the country." The "disease" of rebellion is now "so universal there is no knowing where to apply a remedy." With the men he had, he had secured Boston's port and closed it to traffic, but his force was inadequate to stop smuggling at nearby peninsulas and islands in Boston harbor. Gage had set up cannon on the narrow neck of land connecting Boston to the mainland, and he was attempting to acquire maps of the countryside by sending out scouts disguised as civilians. To the king, Gage strongly suggested that the Coercive Acts should be repealed, simply to defuse a very tense situation. But his advice was

BRITISH TROOPS IN CONCORD CENTER
*In this contemporary engraving by Amos Doolittle, two British officers seek the high ground of
the cemetery in Concord, Massachusetts, to orient themselves to the unfamiliar town at around
9 A.M. on April 19, 1775. Their troops march in formation, fresh from the skirmish at Lexington.
American militiamen had amassed at the Old North Bridge, off to the right about a mile from the
town center. The officer with the telescope is undoubtedly scanning for them.*
Miriam and Ira D. Walsh Division of Art, Prints and Photographs, The New York Public Library. Astor, Lenox and
Tilden Foundations.

spurned as an unacceptable admission of failure. Instead, on April 14, 1775, Gage got orders from England: Arrest troublemaking leaders and stop things
before the Americans got better organized.

For four days, Gage worked quickly to orches-
trate a surprise attack on an ammunition storage
site at Concord, a village about eighteen miles west
of Boston. Boats along the Charles River were
quickly pulled ashore in Boston and caulked, in
preparation for troop movement across the water.
On the evening of April 18, just before midnight,
British soldiers in the small boats crossed the wide
expanse of river in the direction of Concord. Boston
silversmith Paul Revere and another close observer,
William Dawes, raced ahead to wake the minutemen. At 4:30 A.M., about 70 sleepy American men
assembled on the village green at Lexington, about
five miles east of Concord, unsure of what awaited
them. When the British soldiers arrived, their commander barked out, "Lay down your arms, you
damned rebels, and disperse." The militiamen hesitated and then began to comply, turning to leave
the green, but then someone fired—who it was has
never been clear. In the next two minutes, more fir-

ing left eight Americans dead and ten wounded.
Only one British soldier was slightly wounded.

The British units then moved on to Concord,
along a narrow wooded road, no longer under cover
of dark or with any pretense of surprise. Three companies of minutemen nervously occupied the center of Concord but offered no challenge to the British
troops as they wheeled into town and moved north,
away from the center, toward a particular house
thought to hold the ammunition supply. But no
weapons were in fact located there. The British
turned back to the town but encountered several
hundred minutemen at the Old North Bridge over
the Concord River. Again some shots were exchanged, resulting in the deaths of two Americans
and three British soldiers.

By now both sides were very apprehensive. The
British had failed to find the expected powder magazine, and the Americans had failed to thwart the
British incursion. As the British retreated to Boston
along the narrow road, militia units attacked from
the sides in the bloodiest fighting of the day. In the
end, 273 British soldiers were wounded or dead; the
toll for the Americans stood at about 95.

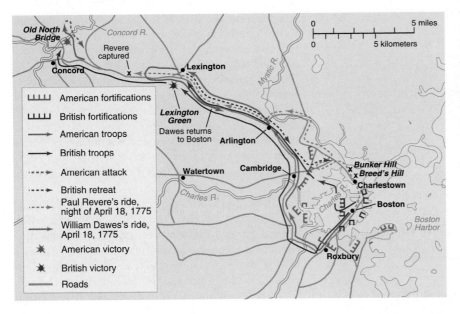

MAP 6.3
Lexington and Concord, April 1775
Under pressure from England, British forces at Boston staged a raid on a suspected rebel arms supply in Concord, Massachusetts, starting the first battle of the Revolutionary War.

Map legend:
- American fortifications
- British fortifications
- American troops
- British troops
- American attack
- British retreat
- Paul Revere's ride, night of April 18, 1775
- William Dawes's ride, April 18, 1775
- American victory
- British victory
- Roads

Another Rebellion against Slavery

News of the battles of Lexington and Concord spread rapidly. Within eight days, Virginians had heard of the fighting, and, as Thomas Jefferson reflected, "A phrenzy of revenge seems to have seized all ranks of people." The royal governor of Virginia, Lord Dunmore, had just removed a large quantity of gunpowder from the Williamsburg powder house, and in the dead of night he had it placed on a ship, out of reach of any frenzied Virginians. Next, Dunmore threatened to arm the slaves, if necessary, to ward off any attacks by colonists. To the British ministry he wrote, "My declaration that I would arm and set free such slaves as should assist me if I was attacked has stirred up fears in them [the colonists] which cannot easily subside as they know how vulnerable they are in that particular."

This was clearly Dunmore's ace card, for he understood full well how to produce panic among the planters. Yet he did not play the card until November 1775, when he issued an official proclamation promising freedom to defecting, able-bodied slaves who would fight for the British. Dunmore's dilemma was that while he wanted to scare the planters, he had no intention of liberating all slaves or of starting a real slave rebellion. So his offer was limited to able-bodied men. Female, young, and elderly slaves were not welcome behind British lines, and many were sent back to face irate masters. Astute blacks noticed that Dunmore neglected to free his own slaves. A Virginia barber named Caesar declared that "he did not know any one foolish enough to believe him [Dunmore], for if he intended to do so, he ought first to set his own free."

In the northern colonies as well, slaves clearly recognized the evolving political struggle with England as an ideal moment to bid for freedom. A twenty-one-year-old Boston domestic slave employed sarcasm in a 1774 newspaper essay to call attention to the hypocrisy of local slave owners: "How well the Cry for Liberty, and the reverse Disposition for exercise of oppressive Power over others agree,—I humbly think it does not require the Penetration of a Philosopher to Determine." This assertive young woman, Phillis Wheatley, had already gained international fame through a book of poems published in London in 1773. Kidnapped from Africa at age eight, sold to a Boston merchant named John Wheatley in 1761, fully literate in English within sixteen months and Latin by age twelve, Phillis Wheatley became an accomplished poet by age sixteen. She earned the regard of both Governor Thomas Hutchinson and merchant John Hancock, whose testimonials endorsed her book and affirmed her remarkable life story. Possibly neither Hutchinson nor Hancock fully appreciated the irony of their endorsement, however, for Wheatley's poems spoke of "Fair Freedom" as the "Goddess long desir'd" by Africans enslaved in America. At the urging of his wife, John Wheatley freed the young poet in 1775.

Wheatley's poetic ideas about freedom found concrete expression among other discontented

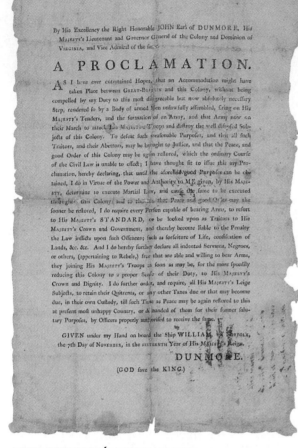

LORD DUNMORE'S PROCLAMATION
In November 1775, Lord Dunmore of Virginia offered free-dom to "all indented Servants, Negroes, or others (apper-taining to Rebels)" who would help put down the rebellion. Dunmore issued multiple printed copies in broadside form from the safety of a ship anchored at Norfolk, Virginia.
Special Collections. University of Virginia Library.

planter reported that "the insolence of the Negroes in this county is come to such a height, that we are under a necessity of disarming them. . . . We took about eighty guns, some bayonets, swords, etc." In North Carolina, whites mounted night patrols to en-force a 9 P.M. curfew for all slaves. In July, a planned uprising was uncovered, and scores of slaves were arrested. No one seemed to see any irony in the fact that it was the revolutionary committee of public safety that dealt severely with this quest for liberty: Each conspiring slave suffered eighty lashes on the back and had both ears cropped.

In Orange County, Virginia, a twenty-four-year-old member of the committee of public safety named James Madison worried about the implica-tions of a recently uncovered slave plot: "Lately a few of those unhappy wretches met together and chose a leader who was to conduct them when the English troops should arrive—which they thought would be very soon and that by revolting to them they should be rewarded with their freedom. Their intentions were soon discovered and the proper pre-cautions taken to prevent the Infection." Madison well understood the contagion of ideas about lib-erty and slavery, so potent to blacks and whites as well: "It is prudent such attempts should be con-cealed as well as suppressed."

Probably for that reason, Lord Dunmore's proclamation to encourage slave defection was not reported in many southern newspapers, for fear it would spread the news to slaves. Blacks, however, did not depend on newspapers for their informa-tion. John Adams was assured by southern dele-gates to the Continental Congress that a proclama-tion like Dunmore's would quickly draw twenty thousand slaves in South Carolina because "the Ne-groes have a wonderful art of communicating In-telligence among themselves; it will run several hundreds of miles in a week or fortnight." The con-tagion of liberty spread quickly by newspaper, by word of mouth, and even by drumbeat.

In 1775, probably several thousand slaves in Virginia took Lord Dunmore up on his offer. The numbers grew in 1776 and 1777, and by 1778 as many as thirty thousand black Virginians had de-fected from slavery. Possibly as many as eighty thousand southern blacks over the course of the Revolutionary War voted against slavery with their feet. Many of them did not find the liberation they were seeking. The British army used them for me-nial labor and failed to feed or clothe them ade-quately. Disease, especially smallpox, devastated encampments of runaways, and the British offered

groups. Some slaves in Boston petitioned Thomas Gage, promising to fight for the British if he would liberate them. Gage turned them down. In Ulster County, New York, along the Hudson River, two blacks were overheard discussing gunpowder, and thus unraveled a plot that involved at least twenty slaves in four villages, discovered to have gun-powder and shot stashed away.

The numerical preponderance of black slaves in the southern colonies deepened white fears of re-bellion. In Maryland, soon after the news of the Lex-ington battle arrived, slaves exhibited impatience with their status, in light of the revolutionary move-ment unfolding around them. One Maryland no medical help. More than five hundred blacks died of smallpox on an island off the Virginia coast in 1776. Twenty years later the skeletons were still there, where the refugees had been abandoned.

In South Carolina, Sullivan's Island became a refugee camp for escaped slaves. Located near Charleston, the island was one of the few secure places held by the British in 1775, and it became a magnet for fleeing slaves. One black man went there after delivering to his white master a grand speech. The master reported, "Though he is my Property, he has the audacity to tell me, he will be free, that he will serve no Man, and that he will be conquered or governed by no Man." But the Charleston committee of public safety decided otherwise. The encampment held an estimated five hundred slaves and in the committee's view its existence undermined public order. In December 1775, the Charleston revolutionaries organized a surprise raid on the island. About fifty blacks were killed, their tents were burned, and hundreds were sent back to slavery.

Without self-government, some argued, Americans would be reduced to slavery. Thousands of actual slaves grasped the implications of these ideas and seized the moment.

Lexington and Concord marked the military beginnings of the American Revolution. The minutemen fought to protect their towns from invasion and to protest the undermining of traditional English rights to liberty and property, which had ceased to exist in Massachusetts. Without self-government, some argued, Americans would be reduced to slavery. Thousands of actual slaves grasped the implications of these ideas and seized the moment offered by Lord Dunmore in Virginia. Far fewer of the white population of the colonies could extend their own revolutionary rhetoric that far.

Conclusion: How Far Does Liberty Go?

The French and Indian War set the stage for the imperial crisis of the 1760s and 1770s by driving a wedge of suspicion between England and its colonies and by creating a huge deficit in the British treasury. The years from 1763 to 1775 brought repeated attempts by the British government to rein in the colonies and make them subordinate, paying partners in the larger scheme of empire.

American resistance grew slowly over those years. In 1765, at the time of the Stamp Act, the issue for men like Samuel Adams and Patrick Henry was unjust taxation, by a government body—Parliament—that did not adequately represent American interests. For a few years, American and British leaders talked past each other, with different understandings of what constituted adequate representation and of the different forms taxation could take. But as the misunderstandings escalated, so did the level of tension and, eventually, violence. British troops originally intended to protect the colonists from Indians were drafted into police duties in the cities. British efforts to make Americans pay for their own protection looked to the Americans like confiscation of their property, an infringement of a basic liberty.

By 1775, events propelled Adams, Henry, and a host of American leaders to the conclusion that a concerted effort was afoot to deprive Americans of all their liberties. The first liberty threatened was the right to self-taxation, the next was their right to live free of an occupying army, and finally came their right to self-rule. It appeared to them that England was trying to enslave them, and they used the term "abject slavery" very often to describe the ultimate and most horrible stage of being unfree, deprived of all liberty and property, the status to be avoided at all costs. Thousands of minutemen amassed around Concord in the spring of 1775, prepared to fight to the death to assert these American liberties. April 19 marked the start of their rebellion.

Another rebellion under way in 1775 was doomed to be short-circuited. This uprising involved black Americans who had experienced over the course of a century and a half the condition of being abject slaves deprived of all liberties and rights. They now listened to shouts of "Liberty!" in the Stamp Act crowds and appropriated the language of revolution swirling around them that spoke to their deepest needs and hopes. Defiance of authority was indeed contagious.

The emerging leaders of the patriot cause were mindful of a delicate balance they felt they had to strike. To energize the American public about the crisis with England, they had to politicize masses of men—and eventually women too—and infuse them with a keen sense of their rights and liberties, now presumably threatened by British policies. But in so doing, they became fearful of the unintended consequences of teaching a vocabulary of rights and liberties. They worried that the rhetoric of enslavement might go too far.

The question of how far the crisis could be stretched before something snapped was largely unexamined in 1765. Patriot leaders in the year of the Stamp Act were amazed to find Parliament passing unprecedented tax laws that seemed to strike at the heart of the ancient liberties of English subjects. What they wanted was a correction, a return to the status quo ante. But the course of actions in the decade up to 1775 convinced many that no return to the old ways was possible. A challenge to Parliament's right to tax had led, step by step, to a challenge to Parliament's right to legislate over the colonies in any matter. If Parliament's sovereignty was set aside, then who actually had authority over the American colonies? By 1775, with the outbreak of fighting and the specter of slave rebellions, American leaders turned to the king for the answer to that question.

CHRONOLOGY

1745 Massachusetts and British soldiers capture French fortress Louisbourg in Nova Scotia.

1747 Ohio Company of Virginia formed.

1748 Treaty of Aix-la-Chapelle.

1754 French and Indian War begins in America.
Albany Congress proposes Plan of Union and courts Iroquois support.

1755 General Braddock defeated by French and Indians in Pennsylvania.

1757 William Pitt, prime minister in Britain, fully commits to war effort.

1758 Louisbourg recaptured by British and American forces.

1759 Quebec falls to British.

1760 George III becomes king.

1763 Treaty of Paris ends French and Indian War.
Pontiac's uprising provokes fear and destruction in western frontier settlements.
Proclamation of 1763 prohibits settlement west of Appalachians.

1764 The Revenue (Sugar) Act lowers tax on foreign molasses to promote compliance with trade duty.

1764 Currency Act prohibits issuance of colonial paper money.

1765 Stamp Act imposes tax on documents.
May. Patrick Henry sponsors Virginia Resolves.
August. Crowd actions in Boston inaugurate Sons of Liberty.
October. Stamp Act Congress meets in New York City.

1766 Stamp Act repealed; Declaratory Act asserts Parliament's control over colonies.

1767 Townshend duties reinstate revenue-raising taxes.

1768 **Fall.** British troops stationed in Boston.

1769 Year of nonimportation agreements; Daughters of Liberty appear.

1770 **March 5.** Boston Massacre.
Townshend duties repealed; Lord North comes to power.

1772 **June.** *Gaspée* attacked off Rhode Island.
Committees of Correspondence formed.

1773 Tea Act lowers price of tea to tempt American boycotters.
December 16. Boston Tea Party.

1774 Parliament passes Coercive Acts (Intolerable Acts): Boston Port Act, Massa-

chusetts Government Act, Impartial Administration of Justice Act, Quartering Act, Quebec Act.
September. First Continental Congress meets. Continental Association formed.

1775 **April 19.** Battles of Lexington and Concord.
Virginia's Lord Dunmore promises freedom to defecting slaves.

BIBLIOGRAPHY

GENERAL WORKS
Edward Countryman, *The American Revolution* (1985).

Marc Egnal, *A Mighty Empire: The Origins of the American Revolution* (1988).

Lawrence H. Gipson, *The Coming of the Revolution, 1763–1775* (1954).

Jack P. Greene, ed., *The American Revolution: Its Character and Limits* (1987).

Merrill Jensen, *The Founding of a Nation: A History of the American Revolution, 1763–1776* (1968).

Bernhard Knollenberg, *Origin of the American Revolution, 1759–1766* (1960).

Bernhard Knollenberg, *Growth of the American Revolution, 1766–1775* (1975).

James Kirby Martin, *In the Course of Human Events: An Interpretive Exploration of the American Revolution* (1979).

Robert Middlekauff, *The Glorious Cause: The American Revolution, 1763–1789* (1982).

Edmund S. Morgan, *The Challenge of the American Revolution* (1976).

Gordon Wood, *The Radicalism of the American Revolution* (1992).

Esmond Wright, *The Causes and Consequences of the American Revolution* (1966).

Alfred F. Young, *The American Revolution: Explorations in the History of American Radicalism* (1976).

NATIVE AMERICANS AND THE FRENCH AND INDIAN WAR
Fred Anderson, *A People's Army: Massachusetts Soldiers and Society in the Seven Years' War* (1984).

Francis Jennings, *Empire of Fortune: Crowns, Colonies, and Tribes in the Seven Years War in America* (1988).

Douglas E. Leach, *Roots of Conflict: British Armed Forces and Colonial Americans, 1677–1763* (1986).

Michael N. McConnell, *A Country Between: The Upper Ohio Valley and Its Peoples, 1724–1774* (1992).

Richard Middleton, *The Bells of Victory: The Pitt-Newcastle Ministry and the Conduct of the Seven Years' War, 1757–1762* (1985).

Howard H. Peckham, *Pontiac and the Indian Uprising* (1947).

Jack M. Sosin, *Whitehall and the Wilderness: The Middle West in British Colonial Policy, 1760–1775* (1961).

Richard White, *The Middle Ground: Indians, Empires, and Republics in the Great Lakes Region, 1650–1815* (1991).

THE BRITISH VIEW OF EMPIRE
Bernard Bailyn, *The Origins of American Politics* (1968).

Thomas C. Barrow, *Trade and Empire: The British Customs Service in America, 1660–1775* (1967).

John Brewer, *Party Ideology and Popular Politics at the Accession of George III* (1976).

John Brooke, *King George III* (1972).

John L. Bullion, *A Great and Necessary Measure: George Grenville and the Genesis of the Stamp Act, 1763–1765* (1983).

Ian R. Christie, *Crisis of Empire: Great Britain and the American Colonies, 1754–1783* (1966).

Bernard Donoughue, *British Politics and the American Revolution: The Path to War, 1773–1775* (1964).

Jack P. Greene, *Peripheries and Center: Constitutional Development in the Extended Politics of the British Empire and the United States, 1607–1788* (1986).

James A. Henretta, *"Salutary Neglect": Colonial Administration under the Duke of Newcastle* (1972).

Michael Kammen, *A Rope of Sand: Colonial Agents, British Politics, and the American Revolution* (1968).

Michael Kammen, *Empire and Interest: The American Colonies and the Politics of Mercantilism* (1970).

Philip Lawson, *George Grenville: A Political Life* (1984).

James L. McKelvey, *George III and Lord Bute* (1973).

Alison Gilbert Olson, *Making the Empire Work: London and American Interest Groups, 1690–1790* (1992).

Alan Rogers, *Empire and Liberty: American Resistance to British Authority, 1755–1763* (1974).

John Sainsbury, *Disaffected Patriots: London Supporters of Revolutionary America, 1769–1782* (1987).

Carl Ubbelohde, *The Vice-Admiralty Courts and the American Revolution* (1960).

THE REVOLUTIONARY CRISIS OF THE 1760S–1770S

David Ammerman, *In the Common Cause: American Response to the Coercive Acts of 1774* (1975).

Bernard Bailyn, *The Ideological Origins of the American Revolution* (1967).

Bernard Bailyn, *The Ordeal of Thomas Hutchinson* (1974).

Bernard Bailyn, *Faces of Revolution: Personalities and Themes in the Struggle for American Independence* (1990).

Richard R. Beeman, *Patrick Henry* (1974).

Ruth H. Bloch, *Visionary Republic: Millennial Themes in American Thought, 1750–1800* (1985).

John L. Brooke, *The Heart of the Commonwealth: Society and Political Culture in Worcester County, Massachusetts, 1713–1861* (1989).

Joseph A. Ernst, *Money and Politics in America, 1755–1775* (1973).

John E. Ferling, *The First of Men: A Life of George Washington* (1988).

David Hackett Fischer, *Paul Revere's Ride* (1994).

Jay Fliegelman, *Prodigals and Pilgrims: The American Revolution against Patriarchal Authority, 1750–1800* (1982).

Dirk Hoerder, *Crowd Action in Revolutionary Massachusetts, 1765–1780* (1977).

Thomas A. Lewis, *For King and Country: The Maturing of George Washington, 1748–1760* (1993).

Paul K. Longmore, *The Invention of George Washington* (1988).

Pauline Maier, *From Resistance to Revolution: Colonial Radicals and the Development of American Opposition to Britain, 1765–1776* (1972).

Pauline Maier, *The Old Revolutionaries: Political Lives in the Age of Samuel Adams* (1980).

Edmund S. Morgan, *The Genius of George Washington* (1980).

Edmund S. Morgan, *Inventing the People: The Rise of Popular Sovereignty in England and America* (1988).

Edmund S. Morgan and Helen M. Morgan, *The Stamp Act Crisis: Prologue to Revolution* (1962).

Gary B. Nash, *The Urban Crucible: Social Change, Political Consciousness, and the Origins of the American Revolution* (1979).

Peter Shaw, *American Patriots and the Rituals of Revolution* (1981).

Peter D. G. Thomas, *The Townshend Duties Crisis: The Second Phase of the American Revolution, 1767–1773* (1987).

Peter D. G. Thomas, *Tea Party to Independence: The Third Phase of the American Revolution, 1773–1776* (1991).

Peter D. G. Thomas, *The Revolution in America: Britain and Her Colonies, 1763–1776* (1992).

John W. Tyler, *Smugglers and Patriots: Boston Merchants and the Advent of the American Revolution* (1986).

Ann Fairfax Withington, *Toward a More Perfect Union: Virtue and the Formation of American Republics* (1991).

Hiller B. Zobel, *The Boston Massacre* (1970).

WOMEN

Richard Buel and Joy Day Buel, *The Way of Duty: A Woman and Her Family in Revolutionary America* (1984).

Ronald Hoffman and Peter J. Albert, eds., *Women in the Age of the American Revolution* (1989).

Linda Kerber, *Women of the Republic: Intellect and Ideology in Revolutionary America* (1980).

Mary Beth Norton, *Liberty's Daughters: The Revolutionary Experience of American Women, 1750–1800* (1980).

SLAVERY

Ira Berlin and Ronald Hoffman, *Slavery and Freedom in the Age of the American Revolution* (1983).

Jeffrey Crow, *The Black Experience in Revolutionary North Carolina* (1977).

David Brion Davis, *The Problem of Slavery in the Age of Revolution, 1770–1823* (1975).

Sylvia Frey, *Water from the Rock: Black Resistance in a Revolutionary Age* (1991).

Winthrop D. Jordan, *White over Black: American Attitudes toward the Negro, 1550–1812* (1968).

Sidney Kaplan and Emma Nogrady Kaplan, *The Black Presence in the Era of the American Revolution* (1973; rev. ed., 1989).

Duncan J. Macleod, *Slavery, Race, and the American Revolution* (1974).

Benjamin Quarles, *The Negro in the American Revolution* (1961).

Donald L. Robinson, *Slavery in the Structure of American Politics, 1765–1820* (1971).

REGIONAL STUDIES

Richard R. Beeman, *The Evolution of the Southern Backcountry: A Case Study of Lunenburg County, Virginia, 1746–1832* (1984).

T. H. Breen, *Tobacco Culture: The Mentality of the Great Tidewater Planters on the Eve of the American Revolution* (1985).

Richard D. Brown, *Revolutionary Politics in Massachusetts: The Boston Committee of Correspondence and the Towns, 1772–1774* (1970).

Richard Bushman, *King and People in Provincial Massachusetts* (1985).

Edward Countryman, *A People in Revolution: The American Revolution and Political Society in New York, 1760–1790* (1981).

Jere R. Daniell, *Experiment in Republicanism: New Hampshire Politics and the Revolution, 1741–1794* (1970).

A. Roger Ekirch, *"Poor Carolina": Politics and Society in North Carolina, 1729–1776* (1981).

Larry R. Gerlach, *Prologue to Independence: New Jersey in the Coming of the Revolution* (1976).

Paul Gilje, *Road to Mobocracy: Popular Disorder in New York City, 1763–1834* (1987).

Jack P. Greene, *The Quest for Power: The Lower Houses of Assembly of the Southern Royal Colonies, 1689–1776* (1963).

Robert A. Gross, *The Minutemen and Their World* (1976).

Ronald Hoffman, *A Spirit of Dissension: Economics, Politics, and the Revolution in Maryland* (1973).

Rhys Isaac, *The Transformation of Virginia, 1740–1790* (1982).

Richard M. Jellison, ed., *Society, Freedom, and Conscience: The Coming of the Revolution in Virginia, Massachusetts, and New York* (1976).

Davis S. Lovejoy, *Rhode Island Politics and the Revolution, 1760–1776* (1958).

Stephen E. Lucas, *Portents of Rebellion: Rhetoric and Revolution in Philadelphia, 1765–1776* (1976).

Bernard Mason, *The Road to Independence: The Revolutionary Movement in New York, 1773–1777* (1966).

John A. Neuenschwander, *The Middle Colonies and the Coming of the American Revolution* (1973).

William Pencak, *Politics and Revolution in Provincial Massachusetts* (1981).

Steven Rossman, *Arms, Country, and Class: The Philadelphia Militia and the "Lower Sort" during the American Revolution* (1987).

Richard A. Ryerson, *The Revolution Is Now Begun: The Radical Committees of Philadelphia, 1765–1776* (1978).

Albert H. Tillson, *Gentry and Common Folk: Political Culture on a Virginia Frontier, 1740–1789* (1991).

Richard Walsh, *Charleston's Sons of Liberty: A Study of the Artisans, 1763–1789* (1959).

But to soften her criticism of men (whom she characterized as "Naturally Tyrannical"), she slipped into a humorous tone, borrowing the language of the male revolutionaries to dress up a pretended threat: "If particular care and attention is not paid to the Ladies we are determined to foment a Rebellion, and will not hold ourselves bound by any Laws in which we have no voice, or Representation."

Abigail assumed that the Continental Congress would be drawing up a new code of laws, but she was directing her advice to the wrong political body. Criminal and civil law (including family law, which dictated the legal subservience of wives to husbands) was the concern of the men founding state governments in 1775 and 1776, and they simply adopted traditional British family law. John Adams, of course, did respond to his wife's provocative idea, but he dismissed it as a "saucy" suggestion: "As to your extraordinary Code of Laws, I cannot but Laugh." The Revolution had perhaps unleashed discontent among other dependent groups, he allowed; children, apprentices, students, Indians, and blacks had grown "disobedient" and "insolent." "But your Letter was the first Intimation that another Tribe more numerous and powerful than all the rest were grown discontented." Men were too smart to repeal their "Masculine Systems," John assured her, for otherwise they would find themselves living under a "despotism of the petticoat."

This clever exchange between husband and wife in 1776 says much about the cautious, limited radicalism of the American Revolution. Both John and Abigail Adams understood (Abigail probably far more than John) that ungluing the hierarchical bond between the king and his subjects potentially unglued other kinds of social inequalities. John was surely joking in listing the groups made unruly in the spirit of a challenge to authority, for children, apprentices, and students were hardly rebellious in the 1770s. But it would soon prove to be an uncomfortable joke, because Indians and blacks did take up the cause of their own liberty during the Revolution, and the great majority of them saw their liberty best served by joining the British side in the war.

The Continental Congress did not concern itself with codes of laws or with the rights and privileges of citizens. Its members were much too busy with more immediate tasks: raising an army, financing a war, putting together a pro-independence coalition, and exploring diplomatic alliances with foreign countries. For the next six years, the war for

ABIGAIL ADAMS
Abigail Smith Adams was twenty-two when she sat for this pastel portrait in 1766. A wife for two years and a mother for one, Adams exhibits a steady, intelligent gaze. Pearls and a lace collar anchor her femininity, while her facial expression projects a confidence and maturity not often credited to young women of the 1760s.
Courtesy of the Massachusetts Historical Society ©.

America engrossed everyone's attention. In part, it was a classic war with professional armies and textbook battles. But it was also a civil war in America, at times even a brutal guerrilla war, of committed rebels versus those who stayed loyal to England.

Only in one glorious moment did the congress issue a ringing statement about social hierarchy and how it would be rearranged in America after submission to the king was undone. That was on July 4, 1776, when the Declaration of Independence asserted in its preamble that "all men are created equal." This striking phrase went completely unremarked in the two days of congressional debate spent tinkering with the language of the Declaration. The solvent to dissolve social inequalities in America was created at that moment, but none of the men at the congress, or even Abigail Adams up in Braintree, fully realized it at the time.

The Second Continental Congress

On May 10, 1775, nearly one month after the onset of fighting at Lexington and Concord, the Second Continental Congress assembled in Philadelphia. The congress immediately set to work on two crucial and seemingly contradictory tasks: to raise and supply an army and to negotiate a reconciliation with England. But as the war progressed and hopes of reconciliation faded, delegates at the congress began to ponder the treasonous act of declaring independence.

Assuming Political Authority

Like the First Continental Congress, the second had no legal authority for existing. Neither did most of the legislatures that had selected the delegates to go to Philadelphia. Like the Virginia House of Burgesses, which by late 1775 had reconstituted itself as the Virginia Convention, the political leadership of one colony after another subverted British authority by simply assuming power on its own.

The same pattern was replicated in town after town as well: Men who had once been the selectmen or town councillors now called themselves the committee of public safety, of inspection, or of correspondence and took it upon themselves to be the ruling body of the town. The inspiration for such creative government came initially from the Coercive Acts that had crippled town government in Massachusetts in 1774. Government by committee spread to other colonies when the First Continental Congress implemented the Continental Association and recommended that local committees of public safety form to enforce economic boycotts of British goods.

Royal administrators found there was little they could do to stop such actions, with no police force and a militia of, at best, uncertain loyalty. For their own protection, governors packed their bags and headed for British naval vessels in the coastal harbors. The governor of New York tried to run his office from shipboard for several months. Other governors gave up and sailed for England, and by the end of 1775 no royal governor commanded any political authority whatsoever. On the colonial level, royal authority was virtually dead, a feat accomplished with hardly a single act of violence.

The new holders of political authority were not really new to politics, for they had run the colonial assemblies before 1775. To the British, these men looked like rebels and revolutionaries, but to the other colonists, they looked like the customary legislative leaders.

The delegates to the Second Continental Congress likewise were well-established political figures likely to command respect and authority, even though the body they served in existed beyond the bounds of legitimate power. John Hancock, a wealthy Boston merchant and an active member of the Massachusetts assembly, presided over the deliberations of the congress. Some of the delegates had attended the First Continental Congress in 1774 and already knew each other. But that did not mean that they were of similar minds about the political issues facing them; nor was each man consistent over time in his views. The Adams cousins, John and Samuel, would soon diverge sharply in political beliefs, but in 1775 they sat together at the radical end of the political spectrum, favoring independence from England. John Dickinson, a returning delegate from Pennsylvania, was no longer the same eager revolutionary who had dashed off *Letters from a Farmer* back in 1767. He was now a moderate, prepared to block any radical action that would interfere with a reconciliation with England.

George Washington and Benjamin Franklin cut sharply contrasting figures among the delegates. Washington daily wore his old military uniform from the French and Indian War, a conspicuous nonverbal statement about his views on the coming conflict. Franklin, in contrast, was feared by some to be a British spy. He had returned from an eleven-year residence in England just five days before the congress met. His long sojourn abroad, plus his long silences in the congress in the first months, made his loyalty suspect. James Madison, a young Virginian just making his entry into political life, heard the gossip about Franklin and jumped to a hasty conclusion: "The least suspicion of his guilt amounts very nearly to a proof of its reality." The men of the Second Continental Congress were still in the process of getting to trust each other. Mutual suspicions flourished easily when the undertaking was so dangerous, opinions were so varied, and a misstep could spell disaster.

Despite their prior experience in the First Continental Congress, most of the delegates were not yet prepared to break with England. Total independence was an alarming idea to many, and some legislatures, chiefly those in the middle colonies such as New York and Pennsylvania, had instructed their delegates to oppose any such move. Some felt that government without a monarchical element was surely unworkable and that continued allegiance to the king was essential. Others feared that the colonies would always need the protection of England against their traditional enemies, France and Spain, and that independence would therefore be suicidal. Colonies that traded actively with England feared undermining their economies. Nor were the vast majority of ordinary Americans ready or able to envision independence from the British monarchy. From the Stamp Act to the Coercive Acts, the decade-long constitutional struggle with England had turned on the issue of parliamentary power. During that decade almost no one questioned the legitimacy of the monarchy.

The few men at the Continental Congress who did think that independence was desirable were, not surprisingly, the Massachusetts delegates. Their colony had been stripped of civil government under the Coercive Acts and their capital was occupied by the British army. Even so, these men knew that it was premature to push for a decisive break with England before others were ready. John Adams wrote to Abigail in June 1775: "America is a great, unwieldy body. Its progress must be slow. It is like a large fleet sailing under convoy. The fleetest sailors must wait for the dullest and slowest."

Raising an Army

As slow as the American colonies were in sailing toward political independence, they needed to take swift action to coordinate a military defense, for the Massachusetts countryside was under the threat of further attack. The congress feared that New England militia units were inadequate to defend against the British army in Boston, thought to be over ten thousand strong. (In truth, the contingent of redcoats numbered only five thousand in late spring 1775.) All the delegates in the congress, even the hesitant moderates, agreed that a military buildup was necessary, a feeling shared widely in the colonies. Voluntary militia units from New York to Georgia collected arms and were drilling on village greens in anticipation.

The next military encounter after Lexington and Concord was hardly a defensive maneuver, however. In May 1775, Connecticut militiamen (led by Captain Benedict Arnold) and riflemen from the Green Mountains in what is now Vermont (led by Ethan Allen) attacked Fort Ticonderoga in northern New York, situated along the water route to Que-

bec. The British had held the fort as a military storage depot since the French and Indian War; the fifty soldiers who manned it surrendered with little resistance. The capture of the fort netted sixty cannons, which were relocated south of Boston and trained on the occupied city. Fort Ticonderoga gave the Americans control of the major water link between New York and Canada; it was thus destined to be a contested spot in short order, for the British wanted it back.

In June, the congress took further steps to prepare for war. Needing money to purchase gunpowder and other military supplies, the congress authorized a currency issue of $2 million. The Continental dollars were merely paper; they did not represent gold or silver, for the congress owned no precious metals. The delegates somewhat naively expected that the currency would be accepted as valuable on trust as it spread in the population through the hands of soldiers, farmers, munitions suppliers, and beyond. They assumed it would eventually be retired from circulation through local taxation.

On June 14, the congress voted to create an army, which mainly meant proclaiming that the New England soldiers dug in around Boston *were* the American army, henceforth called the Continental army and directed and paid by the congress. The congress also called for ten companies of riflemen from Virginia, Maryland, and Pennsylvania to join the New England troops. Rifles were the weapon of choice in frontier regions, for their long, specially grooved barrels allowed marksmen to hit small targets at 150 or 200 yards. In contrast, the militias and the British regular army fought with muskets, which were straight-bore weapons and hence much less accurate, with a range of only about 50 yards. To maximize firepower, musketmen worked as a unit in rows three deep. Men in the front row knelt and fired simultaneously in the direction of the target; in the hail of shots surely some would hit. The second row of men readied themselves to fire, and the men in the third row, who had been in the front row moments before, regrouped and reloaded on signal. Musketmen had to move like a well-oiled machine, and their precision required weeks of drill. But it was the riflemen who were most feared by the British soldiers, at least at first. A joke circulated that the entire Continental army should be outfitted in western hunting shirts, to make the redcoats think they were all riflemen. However, the riflemen's propensity for solitary, freelance shooting and their frontier distaste for the discipline of army life did not mesh well with eighteenth-century military styles. The Continental army made relatively little use of them after the first two years of the war.

Choosing a commander in chief to lead the army presented the congress with an opportunity to demonstrate yet again that this was no local war of a single rebellious colony. The most obvious candidate for the job was Artemus Ward, a Connecticut man with leadership experience from the French and Indian War who was already commanding the soldiers massed around Boston. But John Adams, working closely with southern delegates, argued that the commander ought to be from a distant colony to demonstrate widespread commitment to the war beyond New England. Virginia planter George Washington actually had far less experience commanding soldiers than did Ward, and he was not much known beyond his native region. But the forty-three-year-old Washington, who looked every bit the part of commander in his old military uniform, was unanimously chosen to lead the Continental army.

> In just two months, the Second Continental Congress had taken on the major functions of a legitimate government, both military and financial, without any legal basis for its authority.

Next, a committee of the congress drew up a document called "A Declaration of the Causes and Necessity of Taking Up Arms," which rehearsed familiar arguments about the tyranny of Parliament and the need to defend traditional English liberties. This document was first drafted by a young Virginia planter, Thomas Jefferson, a newcomer to the congress and a radical on the question of independence. The moderate John Dickinson complained that the declaration was offensive to England and would shut the door to reconciliation. Jefferson later wrote that Dickinson "was so honest a man, and so able a one, that he was greatly indulged even by those who could not feel his scruples. We therefore requested him to take the paper, and put it into a form he could approve." Dickinson toned it down; however, he still left much of Jefferson's highly charged language about choosing "to die freemen rather than to live slaves." Even a man as reluctant

for independence as Dickinson acknowledged the necessity of military defense against an invading army.

In just two months, the Second Continental Congress had created an army, declared war, and issued its own currency. It had taken on the major functions of a legitimate government, both military and financial, without any legal basis for its authority, for it had not—and would not for a full year yet—declare independence from the legitimate authority of the king. Equally unnoticed, the congress's assumption of governance lacked any real power to compel compliance by Americans. Enthusiasm for the cause drew recruits to the army, and optimism kept the newly printed Continental dollars afloat at full value for a time. But when that initial enthusiasm waned, the congress and the war effort fell on hard times.

Pursuing Both War and Peace

Three days after the congress voted to raise the Continental army, the bloodiest battle of the entire Revolution occurred. The British commander in Boston, Thomas Gage, had recently received troop reinforcements, three talented major generals (William Howe, John Burgoyne, and Henry Clinton), and new instructions to root out the rebels around Boston. But before Gage could take the offensive, Massachusetts and Connecticut militias fortified the hilly terrain of Charlestown, a peninsula just north of Boston, on the night of June 16, 1775.

The British generals could have nipped off the peninsula where it met the mainland, to box in the Americans. But General Howe insisted on a bold frontal assault, across the water and up the hill, more intimidating but potentially costly. Howe's forces numbered about 2,500 men, and he loaded them with equipment and food weighing more than seventy-five pounds each. They crossed from Boston to the Charlestown shore, protected by eight artillery pieces aimed at the American lines. (See Map 6.3, page 231.)

The Americans had perhaps 1,400 men atop Breed's Hill in hastily dug trenches. In close rank, the British soldiers, burdened with their heavy packs, moved up the hill. The Americans held their fire until the British were about twenty yards away; their commander, Colonel William Prescott, a veteran of the Louisbourg campaign in the French and Indian War, had instructed them to wait until the redcoats were close enough to "see the whites of their eyes." At that distance the musket volley was

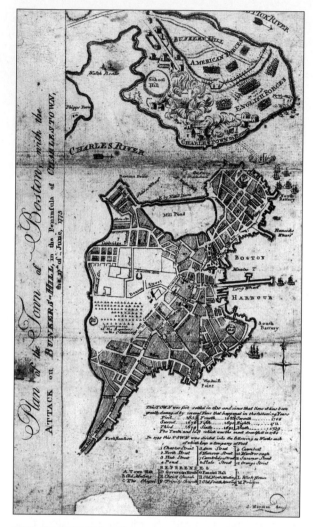

**MAP OF BOSTON, CHARLESTOWN, SHOWING
THE BUNKER HILL BATTLE**

*A contemporary map refers to significant Boston land-
marks ("Government House," Old South Meeting House,
Faneuil Hall) and then shifts to a representation of
Charlestown, north across the Charles River, to portray
the Battle of Bunker Hill in the thick of fighting.*
Courtesy of The Bostonian Society, Old State House.

On the third assault, the British took the hill,
mainly because the American ammunition supply
gave out, and the defenders quickly retreated across
the Charlestown neck. The Battle of Bunker Hill (it
was named for another Charlestown hill) was thus
a British victory, but an expensive one. The dead
numbered 226 on the British side, with more than
800 wounded; the Americans suffered 140 dead, 271
wounded, and 30 captured. As General Clinton later
remarked, "It was a dear bought victory; another
such would have ruined us."

Clinton wanted to pursue the fleeing Americans to their headquarters at Cambridge, a few
miles away, but Howe overruled him and pulled the
army back to Boston. There they sat, penned up, unwilling to risk more forays into the countryside.
Their food had to be shipped in by British naval vessels. Gage bewailed his position. "I wish this place
was burned," he wrote to a friend, "the only use is
its harbour, which may be said to be material; but
in all other respects it's the worst place either to act
offensively from, or defensively." If Gage had had
any grasp of the basic instability of the American
units gathered at Cambridge, he might have pushed
westward and perhaps decisively defeated the core
of the Continental army in its infancy. Instead the
British lingered in Boston, abandoning it without a
fight nine months later.

A week after Bunker Hill, General Washington
hurried to Cambridge to take charge of the new
Continental army. He found enthusiastic but undis-
ciplined troops. Sanitation was an unknown concept, with inadequate numbers of latrines fouling
the campground and posing severe risk of disease.
Drunkenness on duty was common. Washington
was amazed to find that a large number of the soldiers were on furlough, their leaders oddly lax
about comings and goings. Washington attributed
the disarray to the New England custom of letting
militia units elect their own officers, a custom he felt
undermined deference and respect. A captain from
a Connecticut regiment was spotted shaving one of
his own men, an inappropriate gesture of personal
service on the part of a superior officer. But in civilian life the captain was a barber; he had been chosen as an officer by the men of his town, who saw
nothing strange in his practicing his trade in the
camp. Washington moved quickly to establish military discipline and respect for hierarchy, staging
whippings and frequent courts-martial to impress
on the soldiers the importance of his policy. "Discipline is the soul of the army," he stated; officers
must be zealous, the men properly obedient.

sure and deadly, and the British turned back. Twice
more General Howe sent his men up the hill to receive the same blast of firepower; the third time he
permitted them to remove their packs, but the men
encountered another obstacle—the bodies felled in
the two previous attempts. The eight artillery pieces
proved worthless; the British had ferried across the
wrong size cannon balls.

Another immediate problem was getting men to sign up for longer enlistments. Militia units expected only three-month obligations, but Washington knew that no extended campaign could work with three-month soldiers. The Continental army required one-year enlistments, but by December 1775 only four thousand additional men had signed up. Washington wanted an army of twenty thousand, but he had fewer than half that number.

While military plans moved into high gear, the Second Continental Congress pursued its second, contradictory objective, reconciliation with England. Delegates from the middle colonies, especially Pennsylvania, Delaware, and New York, whose merchants depended on trade with England, urged that channels for negotiation remain open. Congressional moderates led by John Dickinson engineered an appeal to the king, called the Olive Branch Petition, in July 1775. The petition affirmed loyalty to the monarchy and resorted to a convenient fiction of blaming all the troubles on bad advice from the king's ministers and on Parliament. It proposed that the American colonial assemblies be recognized as individual parliaments, all under the umbrella of the monarchy. That Dickinson himself could write both the "Declaration on the Causes and Necessity of Taking Up Arms" and the Olive Branch Petition within a few days of each other shows how ambivalent the American position was in the summer of 1775.

By late fall 1775, however, reconciliation was out of the question. King George rejected the Olive Branch Petition and heatedly condemned the Americans, calling them rebels, traitors, and enemies. It was thereafter hard to maintain the illusion that ministers and not the king himself were to blame for the conflict. But still the Continental Congress shied away from an official declaration of independence. In January 1776, Dickinson and other moderates convinced the congress to issue a statement "respecting Independency," to reassure the king that independence was not the goal of the Americans. This document, rambling and overlong, justified resistance to England while denying independence, a tricky position to maintain. Dickinson ended the statement with what he probably imagined was a desperate plea for indulgence from England: "Though an independent empire is not our wish . . . it may be the fate of our countrymen and ourselves." Far from interpreting this statement as a plea, British officials read it accurately as a sign of resignation: Moderates like Dickinson could no longer keep a lid on revolutionary sentiments.

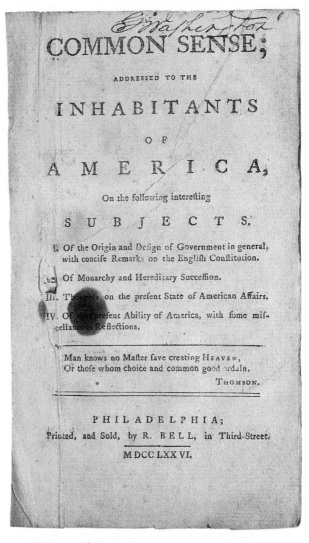

WASHINGTON'S INSCRIBED COPY OF *COMMON SENSE*
Thomas Paine's incendiary pamphlet Common Sense *was widely read after its publication in Philadelphia in January 1776. Copies were passed from hand to hand and read aloud in public. Virginian George Washington, a member of the Second Continental Congress, inscribed his name on the title page to declare his ownership of Paine's booklet.*
Boston Athenaeum.

Thomas Paine and the Case for Independence

One day after Dickinson tried to reassure himself and whoever else would listen that independence was not the goal of the congress, a pamphlet titled *Common Sense* appeared in Philadelphia. Thomas Paine, its author, was an English artisan and coffeehouse intellectual who had befriended Benjamin Franklin in London. Paine came to America in the fall of 1774 with letters of introduction from Franklin to some of Philadelphia's printers. He landed a job with the *Pennsylvania Magazine* and soon met delegates from the Second Continental Congress. With their encouragement, he wrote *Common Sense* to lay out a lively and compelling case for complete independence.

"One of the strongest natural proofs of the folly of hereditary right in kings," Thomas Paine wrote, "is that nature disapproves it; otherwise she would not so frequently turn it into ridicule by giving mankind an ass *for a lion."*

In simple yet forceful language, Paine elaborated on the absurdities of the British monarchy. Why should one man, by accident of birth, claim extensive power over others? he asked. A king might be foolish or wicked. "One of the strongest natural proofs of the folly of hereditary right in kings," Paine wrote, "is that nature disapproves it; otherwise she would not so frequently turn it into ridicule by giving mankind an *ass for a lion*." The king was nothing but a "brute," a "crowned ruffian," and the descendant of a French bastard.

Calling the king of England an ass broke through the automatic deference most Americans still had for the monarchy. And by moving the focus from Parliament to the king, Paine succeeded in making a case for independence. To replace monarchy, he advocated republican government, based on the consent of the people. Rulers, according to Paine, were only representatives of the people, and the best form of government relied on frequent elections to achieve the most direct democracy possible.

Paine's pamphlet sold more than 150,000 copies in a matter of weeks. Newspapers reprinted it, men read it aloud in taverns and coffeehouses, Abigail Adams passed it around to neighbors. Another of John Adams's correspondents wrote him in late February that ninety-nine out of a hundred New Englanders desired an official declaration of independence. But then New England had two armies on its doorstep. The middle and southern colonies

remained uncertain; their hesitation prompted Samuel Adams to suggest that one military engagement to the south of New England would do the trick.

One factor hastening official independence was the advantage of an alliance with France. France could provide military supplies as well as naval power, but not without firm assurance that the Americans would separate from England. News that the British were negotiating for German mercenary soldiers further solidified support for independence. By May, all but four colonies were agitating for a declaration. The exceptions were Pennsylvania, Maryland, New York, and South Carolina, the latter two containing large loyalist populations.

Finally on June 7, 1776, the Virginia delegation introduced a resolution calling for independence: "Resolved, That these United Colonies are, and of right ought to be, free and independent States, that they are absolved from all allegiance to the British Crown, and that all political connection between them and the State of Great Britain is, and ought to be, totally dissolved." Here was the assertion everyone had been anticipating, some with impatience, others with dread. (See Texts in Historical Context, page 248.) The moderates still commanded enough support to postpone a vote on the measure until July. Thomas Jefferson and others formed a committee to draft a longer document explaining the justification for independence. In the meantime, the abstaining delegations went home to consult with their assemblies. Probably no one doubted that once a vote was taken, the measure would pass. But political sense dictated that the positive vote should be nearly unanimous, to present a united front to England.

On July 1, the first vote was taken on the resolution of June 7. Pennsylvania and South Carolina voted against it, while the two-man Delaware delegation was split and the New Yorkers abstained. On July 2, after a night of politicking, a second vote shifted South Carolina and Pennsylvania into the pro-independence camp, and a newly elected delegate from Delaware rode all night to cast the deciding pro-independence vote. The New Yorkers still abstained, as required by their assembly's instructions, but since they had not voted negatively, the congress could truthfully claim that the resolution for independence had passed without a negative vote. John Adams predicted that "the second day of July, 1776, will be the most memorable

DECLARATION OF INDEPENDENCE READ TO A CROWD
Printed copies of the Declaration of Independence were read aloud in public places throughout America in the weeks after July 4, 1776, often accompanied by carefully orchestrated celebrations.
Historical Society of Pennsylvania.

The congress merely glanced at the political philosophy, finding nothing exceptional in it; the ideas about natural rights and the consent of the governed were seen as "self-evident truths," just as the document claimed. In itself, this absence of comment showed a remarkable transformation in political thinking since the end of the French and Indian War. The single phrase declaring the natural equality of "all men" was also passed over without comment; no one elaborated on its radical implications.

What the congress did wrangle over were the specific grievances. Jefferson included an impassioned statement blaming the king for slavery, which delegates from Georgia and South Carolina struck out. They had no intention of denouncing their labor system as an evil practice. Northern delegates were also relieved to drop it, for influential merchants from Boston and Newport, Rhode Island, were deeply implicated in the overseas trade of Africans. But the congress let stand another of Jefferson's grievances, blaming the king for mobilizing "the merciless Indian Savages" into bloody frontier warfare. Following the same strategy as that of Paine's *Common Sense*, Jefferson intended to fix blame on the king himself for everything wrong in America.

On July 4, the corrections to Jefferson's text were complete and the delegates formally affixed their signatures to it. Four men, including John Dickinson, declined to sign; several others "signed with regret . . . and with many doubts," according to John Adams. The document was then printed and distributed by the thousands. It was read aloud in cities and towns. In New York, a crowd listened and then toppled a lead statue of George III on horseback to melt it down for bullets. On July 15, the New York delegation switched from abstention to endorsement, making the vote on independence truly unanimous.

Printed copies of the Declaration of Independence did not include the signers' names, for they had committed treason, a crime punishable by death. At the moment of signing, they had indulged in gallows humor. When Benjamin Franklin paused before signing to look over the Declaration, John Hancock teased him, "Come, come, sir. We must be unanimous. No pulling different ways. We must all hang together." Franklin replied, "Indeed we must all hang together. Otherwise we shall most assuredly hang separately." The overweight Benjamin Harrison from Virginia remarked to the extremely slight Elbridge Gerry of Massachusetts, "When the

epocha in the history of America. I am apt to believe that it will be celebrated, by succeeding generations, as the great anniversary festival. . . . It ought to be solemnized with pomp and parade, with shows, games, sports, guns, bells, bonfires and illuminations, from one end of this continent to the other, from this time forward, forevermore." He was right about the celebration, if wrong about the date.

On July 2 and 3, the congress turned to the document drafted by Thomas Jefferson. Jefferson began with a preamble that articulated philosophical principles about natural rights, equality, the right of revolution, and the consent of the governed as the only true basis for government. He then listed more than two dozen specific grievances against King George.

The Issue of Independence

In May and June 1776, talk of independence gripped Americans everywhere. When would it come? What would it mean? Why was the congress so slow to declare it? Town meetings all over Massachusetts were voting for immediate action; with war already on their doorstep, they saw no reason to delay. In contrast, political leaders in New York City were ambivalent and divided, and they did their best to avert calls for action. Independence-minded planters in Virginia worried that the common people might take a completely different meaning from the rush for independence. And merchants everywhere expressed anxiety that a declaration would kill all chances at reconciliation. While congress no doubt hoped that the July 4 Declaration of Independence would help unite the country, the reality was that disunity was fearfully evident.

Men of Scituate debated independence on June 4, 1776, and conveyed their remarks to their town representative.

DOCUMENT 1. The Town Meeting of Scituate, Massachusetts, Pledges to Fight for Independence

The Inhabitants of this Town being called together on the recommendation of our General Assembly to Signify our minds on the great point of Independence on Great-Britain, think fit to Instruct you on that head.

The Ministry of that Kingdom, having formed a design of Subjecting the Colonies to a distant, external and absolute power in all Cases whatsoever, wherein the Colonies have not, nor in the nature of things can have any share by Representation, have, for a course of years past, exerted their utmost Art and Endeavours to put the same plan, so destructive to both Countries, into Execution. But finding it, through the noble and virtuous opposition of the Sons of Freedom, impracticable by means of mere political Artifice and Corruption, they have at

length had a fatal Recourse to a Standing Army, so repugnant to the nature of a free Government, to fire and Sword, to Bloodshed and Devastation, calling in the aid of foreign Troops, as well as endeavouring to stir up the Savages of the wilderness to exercise their barbarities upon us, being determined, by all appearances, if practicable, to extirpate the Americans from the face of the Earth, unless they tamely resign the Rights of humanity, and to repeople this once happy Country with the ready Sons of Vassalage, if such can be found.

We therefor, Apprehending such a subjection utterly inconsistant with the just rights and blessings of Society, unanimously Instruct you to endeavour that our Delegates in Congress be informed, in case that Representative Body of the Continent should think fit to declare the Colonies Independant of Great Britain, of our readiness and determination to assist with the our Lives and Fortunes in Support of that, we apprehend, necessary Measure.

In New York, a group of craftsmen drafted their own document justifying independence. They delivered it to the assembly and encountered a chilly reception.

DOCUMENT 2. Minutes of the New York Assembly, June 3, 1776

A number of citizens, who style themselves a Committee of Mechanicks, having come into the Congress-Chamber . . . and delivered at the Chair a paper which they style an Address, the House was ordered to be cleared, in order that the said paper may be inspected, to discover whether it is proper for this Congress to receive the same. . . . The door was opened, and the said citizens were desired to come into the Chamber, . . . the said paper being read by Lewis Thibou.

They therein set forth that they are devoted friends to their bleeding country; that they are afflicted by beholding her struggling under heavy loads of oppression and tyranny; . . . that their Prince is deaf to petitions for redressing our grievances; that one year has not sufficed to satisfy the rage of a cruel Ministry in their bloody pursuits, designed to reduce us to be slaves, and to be taxed by them without our consent; that, therefore, they rather wish to separate from such oppressors; and declare that, if this Congress should think proper to instruct their Delegates in Continental Congress to cause these United Colonies to become independent of Great Britain, it would give them the highest satisfaction.

We are of opinion that the Continental Congress alone have that enlarged view of our political circumstances which will enable them to decide upon those measures which are necessary for the general welfare. We cannot presume . . . to make or declare any resolutions upon so momentous a concern; but are determined patiently to await and firmly to abide by whatever a majority of that august body shall think needful.

In Virginia, ordinary citizens circulated petitions pressing for a Declaration of Independence in May 1776. Landon Carter, a wealthy and worried planter, feared that what they meant by independence might be far more radical than he could accept. In a letter to George Washington on May 9, Carter expressed his concerns.

Document 3. Virginian Landon Carter Warns Fellow Planter George Washington

I need only tell you of one definition that I heard of Independency: It was expected to be a form of Government that, by being independent of the rich men, every man would then be able to do as he pleased. . . . One of the Delegates [to the Virginia assembly] I heard exclaim against the Patrolling law, because a poor man was made to pay for keeping a rich man's slaves in order. I shamed the fool so much for it that he slunk away; but he got elected by it. . . . I know who I am writing to, and therefore I am not quite so confined in my expressions. . . . And from hence it is that our independency is to arise! Papers, it seems, are everywhere circulating about for poor ignorant creatures to sign, as directions to their Delegates to endeavour at an independency. In vain do we ask to let it be explained what is designed by it!

Even after July 4, many merchants remained dubious about the wisdom of independence. The Philadelphia merchant Joseph Reed wrote to Robert Morris on July 18.

Document 4. Merchants Joseph Reed and Robert Morris Exchange Fading Hopes for Reconciliation

I fear the die is irrevocably cast, and that we must play out the game, however doubtful and desperate. . . . My private judgment led me to think that if the two great cardinal points of exemption from British taxation and charge of internal government could have been secured, our happiness and prosperity would have been best promoted by preserving the dependence. The Declaration of Independence is a new and very strong objection to entering into any negotiation. . . . But I fancy there are numbers, and some of them firm in the interests of America, who would think an overture ought not to be rejected.

Robert Morris replied to Reed on July 21.

I am sorry to say there are some amongst us that cannot bear the thought of Reconciliation on any terms. I cannot help Condemning this disposition as it must be founded in keen Resentment or on interested Views. . . . I have uniformly voted against & opposed the declaration of Independance because in my poor oppinion it was an improper time and will neither promote the interest or redound to the honor of America, for it has caused division when we wanted Union.

Document 1. Henry S. Commager and Richard B. Morris, eds., *The Spirit of Seventy-Six* (1958; reprint, 1975), 298–99. Original in the Massachusetts Archives, CLVI, 103.

Document 2. Peter Force, *American Archives,* Fourth Series, vol. 6 (1846), 1362–63.

Document 3. Peter Force, *American Archives,* Fourth Series, vol. 6 (1846), 389–92.

Document 4. John H. Hazelton, *The Declaration of Independence: Its History* (1906), 226–28.

hanging scene comes to be exhibited, my friend, I shall have all the advantage over you. With me it will be over in a minute. But you, you'll be dancing on air an hour after I'm gone!" Independence had finally been launched, but the outcome was far from certain; a small dose of caution was perfectly in order.

The First Two Years of War

Both sides had cause to approach the war for America with caution and trepidation. The Americans faced the mightiest military power in the world, and many thought it was foolhardy to expect victory. Further, pockets of loyalism remained strong; the country was not united. But the British faced serious obstacles as well. Their utter disdain for the fighting abilities of the Americans had to be reevaluated in light of their costly Bunker Hill victory. The logistics of supplying an army across three thousand miles of water were daunting. Each soldier required a minimum of two pounds of food per day, consisting of salted meat and grains, which amounted to a third of a ton per year per man—plus oats for the many horses. Since the British goal was to regain allegiance, not to destroy and conquer, the army was often constrained in its actions.

The American Military Forces

Americans claimed that the initial months of war were purely defensive, triggered by the British army's invasion. But quickly the war also became a rebellion, an overthrowing of long-established authority. As both defenders and rebels, Americans were generally highly motivated to fight, and the potential manpower that could be mobilized was in theory very great.

The recruitment pool, able-bodied men aged sixteen to sixty, already had some military training arising out of the American tradition of militia service. From the earliest decades of settlement, local defense rested with a militia requiring service from nearly every man. There were some exceptions: Apprentices and servants (including blacks in many colonies) were generally exempted, as were friendly Indians, vagabonds, ministers, important politicians, and, in New England, Harvard and Yale students. All other men were required to assemble regularly, usually several times a year, to practice the

complicated and deft maneuvers of mass musket firing with their own guns. In many communities, muster day was a holiday, the hours of parading capped off with hearty drinking and picnicking.

The militia style of warfare was well suited to American defensive needs; for two centuries the main threat to public safety came from occasional Indian attacks. In the mid-eighteenth century, southern militias trained with potential slave rebellions in mind (and hence the general rule that friendly Indians and blacks could not serve). In cities, militias became a police force in rare times of civil disorder. Americans prided themselves on their citizen defense units, which they liked to contrast with the expensive and potentially repressive standing professional armies in Europe.

But now an army was necessary. Militias worked well in limited circumstances, and they continued to function in local theaters of war, but they were not appropriate for extended wars and military campaigns far from home. The congress formed the Continental army and set enlistment at one year, but army leaders soon learned that that was not enough time to train soldiers and carry out campaigns. A three-year enlistment earned a new soldier a twenty-dollar bonus, paid up front, while men who committed for the duration—however long the war took—were promised a postwar land grant of one hundred acres. To make this inducement effective, of course, recruits had to believe that the Americans would win. By early 1777, the army was the largest it would ever be—29,000 troops; it was still not enough.

The Continental Congress assigned troop quotas to each state, and state assemblies directed communities to produce certain numbers. The local committees of public safety began to function like draft boards. From 1778 to the end of the war, draftees tended to be the marginal men in a community, such as servants or the unemployed; thus the army had a very different look from the state militias. In some towns, suspected loyalists were drafted first, either as an effective way to smoke them out or as a way to punish them for their British sympathies. Although it proved hard to get adequate numbers of men to enlist, the total number of individual enlistments over the course of the war totaled 231,950 men, or roughly one-quarter of the white male population over age sixteen.

Women also served in the Continental army. They were needed to do the everyday cooking and washing, and after battle they nursed wounded men. The professional British army established a

TECHNOLOGY IN AMERICA
The Committee of Safety Musket and Standardized Firearms

In the early months of war, soldiers had fought with hunting guns or antiquated firearms from the French and Indian War. These guns were often in ill repair and also required many different sizes of ammunition, a highly inconvenient state of affairs. In April 1775, Committees of Safety were directed by the Continental Congress to order standardized muskets from the five hundred gunsmiths operating from the Carolinas to New England. Each state authorized one main Committee of Safety to oversee arms acquisition and to swap and trade guns or parts with other states' committees; the plan was the earliest American example of systematic weapons procurement. The Congress insisted on precise specifications: 3/4-inch bore, a 44-inch barrel, and an 18-inch bayonet. Each musket, made of brass, iron, and wood parts, weighed around 10 pounds; soldiers also carried a powder horn of gunpowder and enough bullets for 20 or 30 rounds of fire.

Despite this effort to acquire standardized muskets, a perpetual shortage of firearms meant that American soldiers often fought with whatever weapon was available. A Prussian general, who volunteered his expertise to the Continental army, arrived at Valley Forge in 1778 and was shocked to find "muskets, carbines, fowling pieces, and rifles" all in the same company of troops. Not until the first two decades of the nineteenth century would the United States begin to manufacture firearms whose components were machine-tooled rather than hand-crafted under a system known as interchangeable parts. Firearms in the field — in Indian wars and the War of 1812 — could be fully uniform and easily repaired with standardized parts. The concept of machine-tooled parts that grew out of the need for standardized firearms would ultimately revolutionize manufacturing techniques in many industries.

The Historical Society of York County, Pennsylvania.

---

ratio of one woman to every ten men; in the Continental army, the ratio was set at one woman to fifteen men. Close to twenty thousand women served during the war, probably most of them wives of men in service. Children tagged along as well, and babies were born in the camps and on the road.

Black Americans were at first excluded from the Continental army, a rule that slave owner George Washington made on his fifth day as commander in chief. (Blacks had already fought at Concord and Bunker Hill, in the militias; they were allowed to continue their service when their units became the foundation of the Continental army.) But as manpower needs increased, the northern states began to welcome free blacks into service; even slaves could serve in some states, with their masters' permission. About five thousand black men served in the Revolutionary War on the rebel side, mostly from the northern states. (At least ten times that number of enslaved southern blacks disobeyed their owners and ran off to join the British.) Black Continental

soldiers sometimes were segregated into separate units; two battalions from Rhode Island were entirely black. Just under three hundred blacks joined regiments from Connecticut. While some of these were draftees, others were clearly men inspired by the ideals of freedom being voiced in a war against tyranny. For example, five Connecticut blacks gave "Liberty" as their surname at the time of enlistment, and another eighteen said their name was "Freedom" or "Freeman." The assumption that blacks in uniform were freemen must have encouraged enslaved blacks to join, in the hopes they could slip over the line to real freedom after the war. A white doctor in Westfield, Massachusetts, volunteered his slave Gilliam to go in his place when he was drafted, but then he discovered that Gilliam had already enlisted on his own. The doctor appealed to recover his human property but was turned down. Northern states as well as Maryland and Virginia allowed masters to send slaves as substitutes for themselves, but South Carolina and Georgia understood all too

The American army was at times raw and inexperienced, and much of the time woefully undermanned. It never had the precision and discipline of European professional armies. But it was never as bad as the British continually assumed. Early intelligence reports confidently informed the British high command that the Continental army was relying heavily on Irishmen (who were presumed to be little more than savages) and was basically "a contemptible body of vagrants, deserters, and thieves." The British were to learn that it was a serious mistake to underrate the enemy.

The British Strategy

The American strategy was relatively straightforward—to repulse and defeat an invading army. The British strategy was not nearly so clear. England wanted to put down a rebellion and restore monarchical power in the colonies, but the question was how to accomplish this. A decisive defeat of the Continental army was essential but not sufficient to end the rebellion, for there were all those militiamen around the countryside to contend with. An armed and highly motivated insurgent population promised to be a tough enemy for England.

Furthermore, there was no single political nerve center whose capture would spell certain victory. The Continental Congress floated from place to place, staying just out of reach of the British. During the course of the war, the British captured and for a time occupied every major port city—Boston, New York, Newport, Philadelphia, and Charleston —but with no significant gain. The British needed these harbor cities for their constant caravan of supply ships, but capturing them brought no real loss to the Americans, 95 percent of whom lived in the countryside.

England's delicate task was to restore the old governments, not to destroy an enemy country. Hence, the British generals were usually reluctant to ravage the countryside, confiscate food, or burn villages and towns. There were thirteen distinct political entities to capture, pacify, and then restore to the crown, and they were spread out in a very long line from New Hampshire to Georgia. Clearly a large land army was required for the job. Without the willingness to seize food from the locals, such an army needed hundreds of supply ships that could keep several months' worth of food in storage.

Another ingredient of the British strategy was the assumption (quite untested) that large numbers

BLACK REVOLUTIONARY WAR SAILOR
Thousands of black men served on the patriot side as soldiers and sailors, usually at the rank of private or ordinary seaman. Their names are preserved in regiment records and crew lists; rarely, however, were their faces preserved. This 1780 portrait by an unknown artist shows an unnamed man, sword and scabbard at hand, dressed in military finery with a ship in view to establish his naval connection. His clothing suggests he was an officer.
Collection of A. A. McBurney.

well the contradiction, and the risk, of forcing or allowing enslaved blacks to fight for the cause of white people's liberty. Blacks from the Deep South were thus prohibited from becoming Continentals.

Military service helped to politicize Americans during the early stages of the war. In early 1776, independence was a new and risky idea, treasonous from the British point of view. But as the war heated up and leaders and recruiters demanded commitment, some apathetic Americans discovered that apathy had its dangers as well. Anyone who refused to serve ran the risk of being called a traitor to the cause. Military service established one's credentials as a patriot; it became a prime way of defining and demonstrating political allegiance.

of Americans remained loyal to the king and would come to the aid of the British army. Without substantial numbers of loyal subjects, the plan to restore old royal governments made no sense.

The British plan focused on New York, the state judged to harbor the greatest number of loyal subjects—perhaps as much as half the population—and therefore presumably the easiest to subdue and restore. New York offered a geographic advantage as well: Control of the Hudson River would allow the British to isolate the most troublesome states, those in New England. Armies could descend from Canada and move up from New York City along the Hudson River into western Massachusetts. Between a naval blockade on the eastern coast and army raids in the west, Massachusetts would be driven to surrender. Or so the British hoped.

England's delicate task was to restore the old governments, not to destroy an enemy country.

South of New York, in New Jersey and Pennsylvania, the British expected to find large pockets of loyalist strength to secure their advances. Rebellious citizens were to be convinced to sign loyalty oaths to the crown. Virginia was a problem, like Massachusetts, but the British were confident that the Carolinas contained many loyalists and that they could thus isolate and subdue Virginia. The overall plan was a divide-and-conquer approach to recapturing the thirteen colonies.

There were some in England who bravely questioned the wisdom of going to war to win back America. Why hold on to the colonies if they were so troublesome? Quite likely the established commercial ties would remain intact even without political control; the financial advantages of the colonial trade relationship, these critics argued, did not outweigh the costs of war. But this economic analysis did not factor in a key preoccupation of King George and his ministers: Losing the colonies was a severe blow to the glorious dreams of a British empire to rival those of France and Spain.

Quebec, New York, and New Jersey

While Washington disciplined his troops in Massachusetts, an American expedition was launched in late 1775 to capture the British cities Montreal and Quebec, a clear sign that the war was not merely a

defensive reaction to the invasion of Massachusetts. The two cities were symbolic as well as strategic goals, having been sites of contest in the French-British wars of the 1740s and 1750s. Some Americans even mistakenly expected that the French at Quebec would welcome them as a liberating army. American commanders moved swiftly north to attack before British reinforcements could arrive. A force of New York Continentals commanded by General Richard Montgomery took Montreal easily in September 1775 and then advanced on Quebec. Meanwhile, a second contingent of Continentals led by Colonel Benedict Arnold moved through Maine on the Kennebec River to Quebec, a punishing trek through rain and snow with woefully inadequate food and boats; many men died. Arnold's fierce determination to get to Quebec was heroic, but in human costs the campaign was a tragedy. Arnold and Montgomery jointly attacked Quebec in December but suffered heavy losses. Montgomery was killed, and for months afterward the "Ghost of Montgomery" became a favorite pseudonym for anyone who penned an article pressing for independence. Arnold sustained a wound in his leg and, despite the failure to take Quebec, was hailed a hero because of his courage in the face of terrible odds.

The main action of the first year of war came not in Canada, however, but in New York, the state deemed crucial to England. In August 1776, some 20,000 fresh British troops (including 8,000 German mercenary soldiers, called Hessians) landed on Staten Island, south of New York City. They were joined by regiments withdrawn from Boston by General Howe and shipped down from Nova Scotia, bringing the total to nearly 45,000 soldiers. General Washington had anticipated that New York would be Howe's target and had moved his army, numbering about 20,000, from Massachusetts to an area of heightened, fortified ground on Long Island.

The Battle of Long Island, in late August 1776, pitted the well-trained British redcoats against a very green Continental army. Howe advanced 15,000 men from three directions on the American fortifications. The American troops panicked and ran off to a second line of fortifications on Brooklyn Heights, leaving behind their blankets, guns, ammunition, and packs. Washington was furious. In one day, August 27, the Continental army sustained 1,500 casualties (dead and wounded), while the British suffered only 370. It was a terrible defeat and a severe blow to morale. More such blows would follow in the days and weeks ahead.

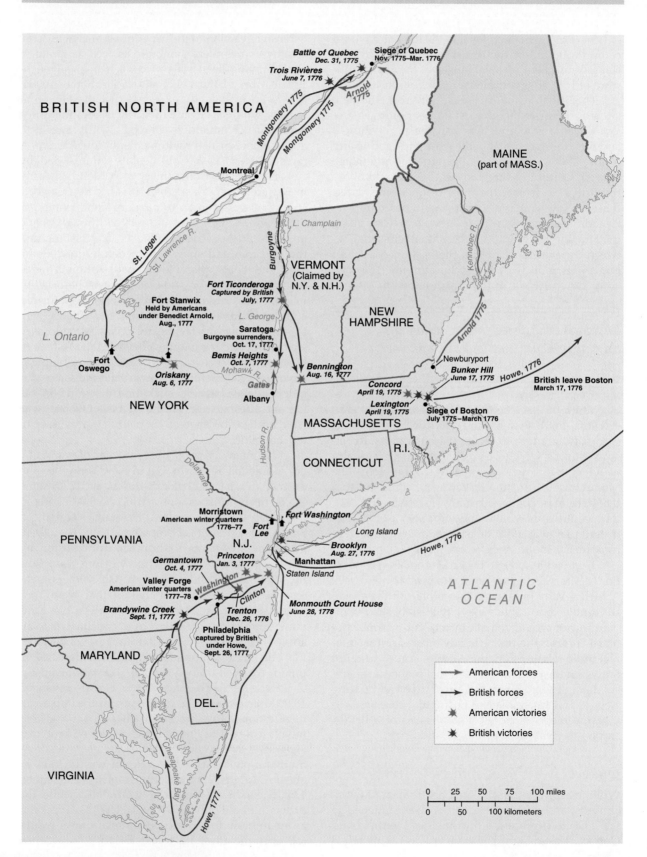

BRITISH NORTH AMERICA

Battle of Quebec
Dec. 31, 1775

Siege of Quebec
Nov. 1775–Mar. 1776

Trois Rivières
June 7, 1776

Montgomery 1775

Arnold 1775

Montreal

St. Leger

St. Lawrence R.

L. Champlain

Burgoyne

VERMONT
(Claimed by
N.Y. & N.H.)

NEW
HAMPSHIRE

Kennebec R.

MAINE
(part of MASS.)

Fort Ticonderoga
Captured by British
July, 1777

Fort Stanwix
Held by Americans
under Benedict Arnold,
Aug., 1777

L. Ontario

L. George

Saratoga
Burgoyne surrenders,
Oct. 17, 1777

Bemis Heights
Oct. 7, 1777

Fort
Oswego

Oriskany
Aug. 6, 1777

Mohawk R.

Gates

NEW YORK

Albany

Arnold 1775

Newburyport

Bennington
Aug. 16, 1777

Concord
April 19, 1775

Howe, 1776

Bunker Hill
June 17, 1775

British leave Boston
March 17, 1776

Lexington
April 19, 1775

Siege of Boston
July 1775–March 1776

MASSACHUSETTS

Hudson R.

CONNECTICUT

R.I.

Delaware R.

Morristown
American winter quarters
1776–77

Fort Washington

Long Island

*Fort
Lee*

Howe, 1776

PENNSYLVANIA

N.J.

Brooklyn
Aug. 27, 1776

Germantown
Oct. 4, 1777

Princeton
Jan. 3, 1777

Manhattan

Washington

Staten Island

ATLANTIC
OCEAN

Valley Forge
American winter quarters
1777–78

Clinton

Brandywine Creek
Sept. 11, 1777

Trenton
Dec. 26, 1776

Monmouth Court House
June 28, 1778

Philadelphia
captured by British
under Howe,
Sept. 26, 1777

MARYLAND

DEL.

Chesapeake Bay

Howe, 1777

VIRGINIA

American forces

British forces

American victories

British victories

| 0 | 25 | 50 | 75 | 100 miles |
| 0 | | 50 | | 100 kilometers |

MAP 7.1

The War in the North, 1775–1778

After the early battles in Massachusetts in 1775, rebel forces invaded Canada but failed to capture Quebec. A large British army landed in New York in August 1776, turning New Jersey into a continual site of battle in 1777 and 1778. Burgoyne arrived to secure Canada and made his attempt to pinch off New England along the Hudson River line, but he was stopped at Saratoga in 1777 in the key battle of the early war years.

If General Howe had pressed a direct frontal attack on the Continentals at Brooklyn Heights, he probably would have wiped out the army altogether. Instead Howe, perhaps remembering the costly victory of Bunker Hill, waited for ships with artillery. Washington meanwhile evacuated his troops to Manhattan Island in the dead of night, under cover of an unusually thick fog. Hundreds of small, unlighted boats ferried silently across the East River, and in the morning an amazed Howe discovered that Brooklyn Heights had been abandoned.

Washington knew it would be hard to hold Manhattan against a British attack. One of his generals recommended burning the city; two-thirds of the buildings belonged to loyalists anyway, and burning it would prevent the British from housing troops there. Washington vetoed this idea, preferring instead to strip it of ammunition and supplies and leave quickly.

But the British advanced before Washington could leave. They sailed up the East River with booming cannons. Connecticut troops had been stationed at Kip's Bay, a probable landing spot, but these soldiers were no match for the sound of cannons. They had been in the army less than a week; when the British arrived, they ran, scrambling over fields and fences to get away. One of them, a youth named Joseph Plumb Martin, later recalled running off with two other men to a house "in which were two women and some small children, all crying most bitterly." They asked the women for some "spirits" and after imbibing a glass of rum each, they "bid them goodbye, [and] betook ourselves to the highway again."

Meanwhile, four thousand British troops landed on Manhattan and started moving inland, looking for an enemy to engage. Washington rode up and commanded the fleeing men to assume defensive positions, but no one obeyed him. The disheartened Virginian lingered on the field of nonbattle, muttering about the "scum" in his army;

his aides swooped in and led him to safety. Howe had again failed to press his advantage, for the capture of General Washington would have been a significant victory for the British. Instead Howe stopped to take cake and wine with the wife of a Quaker merchant named Robert Murray, an avowed pacifist and presumed loyalist. The gracious Mrs. Murray invited the British officers in and detained them more than two hours while the American army was making its hasty exit up the west side of Manhattan Island.

Another woman demonstrated more extreme means to make Manhattan inhospitable to the British. As the redcoats rolled in, fire broke out and raged for two days, burning a quarter of the city. Washington had vetoed arson as an official strategy, but a private citizen carried it out anyway. The British traced the fire to a soot-covered woman in a cellar full of incendiary devices. A member of Parliament pointed to the violent act of this "miserable woman" to illustrate the stubborn tenacity the British could expect to encounter in subduing America: "Knowing that she would be condemned to die, upon being asked her purpose, [she] said, 'to fire the city!' and was determined to omit no opportunity of doing what her country called for."

From September to November, the two armies juggled for position and engaged in limited fighting. In November, Howe finally attacked and captured two critical forts on either side of the Hudson River, Fort Washington and Fort Lee, taking thousands of prisoners. Washington retreated quickly across New Jersey into Pennsylvania. The British army followed him; at one point, Howe was only one hour behind Washington, but he rested his men for a day and widened the gap. As Howe moved through New Jersey, the Continental Congress, meeting in Philadelphia, fled to Baltimore.

Yet again, Howe unaccountably failed to take advantage of the situation. He could have attacked Washington's army at Philadelphia and probably would have taken the city. Instead he parked his German troops in winter quarters along the Delaware River and returned himself to New York City, to be close to his supply ships. Perhaps he knew that many of the Continental soldiers' enlistment periods ended on December 31, so he felt confident that the Americans would not attack him. But he was wrong. On Christmas—a holiday Germans celebrated with much more spirit (and spirits) than did Americans—Washington recrossed the Delaware River at night with 2,400 men and made a quick capture of the unsuspecting (and largely hungover)

German soldiers at Trenton. The victory was impressively executed, and it did much to restore the sagging morale of the patriot side. For the next two weeks, Washington remained on the offensive, dancing just ahead of the British army, capturing supplies in a clever attack on British units at Princeton on January 3. Soon he was safe in Morristown, in northern New Jersey, settled in for the winter.

All in all, in the first year of declared war, the rebellious Americans had a few isolated moments to feel proud of but also much to worry about. The very inexperienced Continental army had barely hung on in the New York campaign. Washington had shown exceptional daring as well as admirable restraint, but what really saved the American army may have been the repeated reluctance of the British to follow through militarily when they had the advantage.

The Home Front

Battlefields alone did not determine the outcome of the war. Struggles on the home front were equally important. Many years later, John Adams insisted that "the revolution was in the minds and hearts of the people" long before "hostilities commenced," but that was wishful misremembering on his part. In 1776, each community contained small numbers of highly committed people on both sides, and far larger numbers who were either apolitical or uncertain about whether independence was worth a war. The contest for the "minds and hearts" of the many neutrals thus figured as a major factor, and both persuasion and force were used. Revolutionaries who took control of local government often used it to punish loyalists and intimidate neutrals. On their side, loyalists worked to reestablish British authority. The struggle to secure political allegiance was complicated greatly by the wartime instability of the economy. The creative financing of the fledgling government brought hardships as well as opportunities, forcing Americans to confront new manifestations of virtue and corruption.

Patriotism at the Local Level

Committees of correspondence, of public safety, and of inspection dominated the political landscape in patriot communities. These committees took on more than customary local governance; they enforced boycotts, picked army draftees, and policed suspected traitors. Committees of inspection visited homes to search for contraband goods and auctioned off confiscated property. In some places, committees even regulated public amusements deemed inappropriate to the revolutionary mood, banning horse racing, gaming, cockfighting, plays, and other entertainments.

Some citizens, loyalists especially, were dismayed by what seemed to them to be excessive or arbitrary power taken on by committees. On occasion, secret and resourceful loyalists managed to get elected to these committees in order to subvert them. Others were open with their denunciations. A man in Westchester, New York, described his response to intrusions by committees: "Do as you please; if you like it better, choose your committee or suffer it to be chosen by a half dozen fools in your neighborhood—open your doors to them—let them examine your tea-cannisters and molasses-jugs, and your wives' and daughters' petty coats—bow and cringe and tremble and quake—fall down and worship our sovereign lord the mob. . . . Should any pragmatical committee-gentleman come to my house and give himself airs, I shall show him the door, and if he does not soon take himself away, a good hickory cudgel shall teach him better manners." Excessive or not, the powers of the local committees were rarely challenged. Committees of safety and of correspondence became the local governing agencies, and their persuasive powers convinced many middle-of-the-road citizens that neutrality was not a comfortable option.

Another group new to political life—white women—increasingly demonstrated a capacity for patriotism at the local level as wartime hardships dramatically altered their own work routines. Like Abigail Adams on her Braintree farm, many wives with husbands away on military or political service found themselves taking on masculine duties. Their increased competence to tend farms and make business decisions appears to have encouraged some to assert competence in political matters as well. Eliza Wilkinson managed a plantation on the South Carolina coast and talked revolutionary politics with her women friends. "None were greater politicians than the several knots of ladies who met together," she remarked, alert to the unusual turn female conversations had taken. "We commenced perfect statesmen."

Women from prominent Philadelphia families went a step beyond political talk to action. In 1780, they formed the Ladies Association, going door to door collecting a substantial sum of money, which

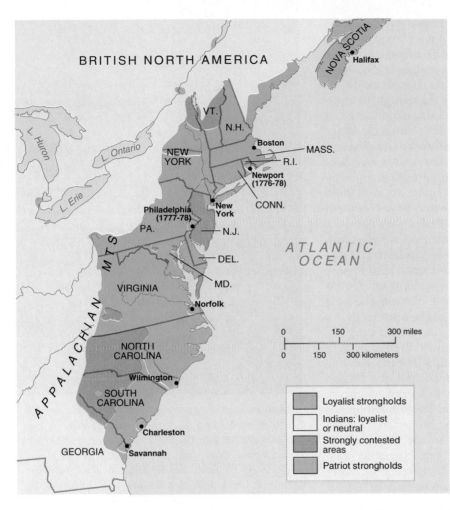

BRITISH NORTH AMERICA

ATLANTIC OCEAN

	Loyalist strongholds
	Indians: loyalist or neutral
	Strongly contested areas
	Patriot strongholds

MAP 7.2
Loyalist Strength and Rebel Support
The exact number of loyalists can never be known. No one could have made an honest count at the time; in addition, political allegiance often shifted with the winds. This map shows the pockets of loyalist strength that the British relied on—the lower Hudson valley, the Carolina piedmont, and the areas most hotly contested by both sides: New Jersey and the Mohawk River Valley, regions repeatedly torn by battles and skirmishes.

they planned to distribute directly to Continental soldiers in the field as a gift of appreciation. A published broadside, "The Sentiments of an American Woman," defended their female patriotism against anticipated male criticism by recalling heroic biblical women and famous female monarchs of the past. "The time is arrived to display the same sentiments which animated us at the beginning of the Revolution, when we renounced the use of teas . . . [and] when our republican and laborious hands spun the flax." The Philadelphia women were right to expect criticism. General Washington rejected their monetary gift and instead requested that the women buy material and sew shirts for the soldiers, an offering he deemed more appropriately feminine.

The Loyalists

Between 20 and 30 percent of the American population remained openly loyal to the British monarchy in 1776, and another 20 to 40 percent could be described as neutral. Such a large population base could have sustained the British Empire in America, if only the British army leaders had known how to use it.

In general, loyalists were people who still found the idea of the British Empire, with all its historical, cultural, and economic ties, an appealing vision. They were convinced that American prosperity and stability depended on British rule and on a government anchored by monarchy and aristocracy. Perhaps most of all, they feared democratic tyranny. Like Abigail Adams, they understood that dissolving the automatic respect that submissive subjects had for their king could potentially lead to a society where all deference and hierarchy came unglued. Adams welcomed this chance to identify tyranny in unequal power relations, as between men and women; loyalists feared it. Patriots seemed to them to be unscrupulous, violent, self-interested men, men of ambition and malice who simply wanted power for themselves.

The most visible and dedicated loyalists (also called Tories by their enemies) were royal officials, not only top officeholders like Thomas Hutchinson in Massachusetts, but also local judges and customs officers. Wealthy merchants with commercial ties to England were made uneasy by the thought of abandoning the trade protections of navigation acts and the British navy. Urban lawyers of a conservative temperament found it impossible to imagine forgoing the stability of British law and order. New Yorker Peter Van Schaack committed a long essay to his private journal justifying his loyalism on those grounds: "If it be asked how we come to be subject to the authority of the British Parliament, I answer, by the same compact which entitles us to the benefits of the British constitution and its laws; and that we derive advantage even from some kind of subordination, is evident, because, without such a controlling common umpire, the colonies must become independent states, which would be introductive of anarchy and confusion among ourselves."

The early-eighteenth-century grants of religious liberty to grateful groups like the Palatine Germans in upstate New York and the French Huguenots in the Carolinas influenced some of them to remain loyal to Britain. Two other religious enclaves, the Quakers and the Moravians, located in Pennsylvania and North Carolina, were pacifists by religious conviction and were therefore often treated as though they were loyalists. Very recent immigrants, notably the Scots who had settled the North Carolina piedmont in the early 1770s, felt gratitude to the crown for providing royal land grants.

Some were loyalists merely as a product of oppositional politics with leading patriot men. For example, backcountry farmers in the Carolinas gravitated toward loyalism out of resentment over the political and economic power of the lowlands gentry. Southern slaves had their own resentments against the white slave-owning class. Many thousands in Virginia responded to Lord Dunmore's promise of eventual freedom if they would defect and aid the British, and more still in South Carolina ran off to Charleston to seek refuge with the British army when it occupied the city.

Many, indeed most, Indians eventually supported the British side. Some tribes, like the powerful Iroquois Nation in New York, had strong economic ties to the empire. One young Mohawk leader, Thayendanegea (known to Americans as Joseph Brant), traveled to England in 1775 to complain to King George about how the king's subjects

JOSEPH BRANT
The Mohawk leader Thayendanegea, called Joseph Brant, had been educated in English ways at Eleazar Wheelock's New England school (which became Dartmouth College in 1769). In 1775, Brant traveled to England with another warrior to negotiate Mohawk support for the British. There he had his portrait painted by George Romney. The thirty-four-year-old Brant wears a feudal gorget around his neck over his English shirt (compare with Washington, page 201), along with Indian armbands and headdress.
National Gallery of Canada, Ottawa.

repeatedly deceived the Mohawks. "It is very hard when we have let the King's subjects have so much of our lands for so little value," he wrote, "they should want to cheat us in this manner of the small spots we have left for our women and children to live on. We are tired out in making complaints & getting no redress." Thayendanegea negotiated his people's support for the king in exchange for protection from encroaching settlers, under a revived implementation of the Proclamation Act of 1763. On his return, Thayendanegea toured the western portions of New York and Pennsylvania, building Indian support for the British on the grounds that the Americans were a serious threat to the Indians' "own Country and Liberty." Another rationale for extensive Indian loyalism was the widespread assumption that England would surely win the war, and it was always better to side with the winners.

Pockets of loyalism thus existed everywhere. The largest pockets were in the middle colonies and the backcountry of the South. But even New England towns at the heart of turmoil, like Concord, Massachusetts, had a small and increasingly silenced core of loyalists who refused to countenance armed revolution.

The loyalists were most vocal between 1774 and 1776, when the possibility of a full-scale rebellion from England was still uncertain. Loyalists challenged the emerging patriot side using pamphlets, broadsides (single-sheet flyers designed to be publicly posted), and newspapers; every major city had one or sometimes two loyalist printers. In New York City in 1776, some loyalists circulated a broadside titled "A Declaration of Dependence," a direct answer to the Continental Congress's July 4 manifesto. "So far from having given the least countenance or encouragement, to the most unnatural, unprovoked Rebellion that ever disgraced the annals of Time," they wrote, "we have on the contrary, steadily and uniformly opposed it, in every Stage of its rise and progress at the risque of our Lives and Fortunes."

Speeches and rallies amplified the spread of loyalism in backcountry areas where print culture had not fully penetrated. Loyalist ministers used their pulpits, while other defenders of the empire staged rallies or disrupted patriot gatherings. At an open-air rally in backcountry South Carolina in 1775, a loyalist elbowed his way to the platform to remind the audience of the superior might of the British army and of the damage to trade that would surely follow any attempt at independence. But his winning argument was to invoke the backcountry's fears and resentments of the coastal planters' wealth and political power: It is ironic, he said, that "the charge of our intending to enslave you should come oftenest from the mouths of those lawyers who in your southern provinces, at least, have long made you slaves to themselves."

Who Is a Traitor?

The rough treatment that loyalists experienced at the hands of the revolutionaries seemed to substantiate their worst fears. In June 1775, the First Continental Congress passed a resolution declaring loyalists to be traitors. Over the next year, state after state wrote laws defining treasonable acts and their punishments. Anyone who joined the British army or supplied it with food or ammunition was said to have committed treason. In some states, it was treason to discourage men from enlisting in the Continental army or to say or print anything that could undermine patriot morale. New Hampshire actually made it treasonable to maintain a personal belief in the legitimacy of British authority. Punishments ranged from house arrest and suspension of voting privileges to dire penalties such as confiscation of property and deportation. And sometimes self-appointed committees of Tory hunters bypassed the judicial niceties and terrorized loyalists, raiding their houses or tarring and feathering them.

"They call me a brainless Tory, but tell me . . . which is better—to be ruled by one tyrant three thousand miles away, or by three thousand tyrants not a mile away?"

A question rarely asked in the heat of the revolutionary moment was whether the wives of loyalists were traitors as well. When loyalist families fled the country, they usually fled together, and property held in the name of the family patriarch was then confiscated. But what if the wife stayed? One Connecticut woman brought witnesses before a justice of the peace to testify that she was "a steady and true and faithful friend to the American states in opposition to her husband, who has been of quite a different character." In such cases, the court typically allowed the woman to keep her dower rights (one-third of the property, the amount she was due if widowed) and confiscated the rest. But even when the wife fled with her husband, was she necessarily a traitor? Could she have independent political beliefs apart from her husband's? If he ordered her to flee with him, was she not obligated to go? (The centuries-old English legal doctrine of *feme covert*, specifying the rights and duties of married women, held that a wife was a nonperson under law and that her husband was responsible for her actions.) Such questions came up in several lawsuits after the Revolution, where descendants of refugee loyalists sued to regain property that had entered the family through the mother's line of inheritance. In one well-publicized case in Massachusetts in 1805, the issue of female responsibility for political acts was debated by some of the best legal minds of the time. The outcome confirmed the traditional view of women as political blank slates; the son of loyalist

DEATH OF JANE MCCREA
This 1804 painting by John Vanderlyn memorializes the martyr legend of Jane McCrea. McCrea lived with her patriot family in upstate New York, but in July 1777 she fled to join her fiancé, a loyalist fighting with Burgoyne's army. She was murdered en route, allegedly by Iroquois allies of the British. The American General Horatio Gates sent Burgoyne an accusatory letter. "The miserable fate of Miss McCrea was particularly aggravated by her being dressed to meet her promised husband," Gates wrote, "but she met her murderers employed by you." Gates skillfully used the story of the vulnerable, innocent maiden dressed in alluring clothes as propaganda to inspire his soldiers' drive for victory at Saratoga. Vanderlyn's painting, and a half dozen similar pictorial representations, emphasized McCrea's helplessness and sexuality. Yet had McCrea been a man, her flight would have been traitorous. What explains this different treatment of a woman? Wadsworth Atheneum, Hartford.

refugee Anna Martin recovered her property on the grounds that she had no independent will to be a loyalist.

Tarring and feathering, property confiscation, deportation, terrorism—to the loyalists, such denials of liberty of conscience and of freedom to own private property proved that democratic tyranny was more to be feared than the monarchical variety. A Boston loyalist, Mather Byles, aptly expressed this point: "They call me a brainless Tory, but tell me . . . which is better—to be ruled by one tyrant three thousand miles away, or by three thousand tyrants not a mile away?" Byles, a minister, was later sentenced to deportation. "Discord and tyranny, in the guise of liberty, stalk forth among us," complained an embittered New York loyalist in 1775.

Throughout the war, probably seven to eight thousand loyalists fled to England, while twenty-eight thousand found closer haven in Canada. But many chose to remain in the new United States and tried to manage to swing with the changing political fortunes of their communities as best they could. In some places, that proved extremely hard to manage. In New Jersey, for example, three thousand Jerseyites felt protected enough by the occupying British army in 1776 to swear an oath of allegiance to the king. Even a man who just months before had signed the Declaration of Independence, Richard Stockton, came forward to beg pardon for his action. What those three thousand publicly sworn loyalists could not foresee was that General Howe would draw back to New York City and leave them at the mercy of local patriot committees. British strategy depended on using loyalists to hold occupied territory, but the New Jersey experience showed just how poorly that strategy was put into practice.

Financial Instability and Corruption

Wars cost money—to pay soldiers; to pay suppliers for food, clothing, and housing; to pay manufacturers for muskets, cannon, and gunpowder. The Continental Congress printed money, but within a few short years its value had deteriorated, since there were no reserves of gold or silver held by the congress to back the currency. In practice, the currency was worth only what a buyer and seller agreed it was worth. The dollar eventually bottomed out at one-fortieth of its face value; a loaf of bread that once sold for two and a half cents now sold for a dollar. States too were printing their own paper money to pay for wartime expenses, further complicating the economy.

Soon the congress had to resort to other means to procure needed supplies and labor. One method was to borrow hard money (not paper) from wealthy men, who in return would get certificates of debt (also called public securities) promising repayment with interest. In effect, the wealthy men had bought government bonds. To pay soldiers, the Congress offered land bounties, which amounted to a promise of a tangible form of wealth. In short order, public securities and land bounties became a form of negotiable currency too. For example, a soldier with no paycheck or cash might sell his land bounty certificate to get food for his family. These certificates also fluctuated in value, mainly depreciating.

Depreciating currency inevitably led to rising prices, as sellers compensated for the falling value of the money. The wartime economy of the late 1770s, with its unreliable currency and inflation in prices, was unprecedented and extremely demoralizing to Americans everywhere. Prices of goods and labor in the prewar decades had generally been stable and predictable. So local committees of public safety in 1778 began to fix prices. A committee would decree the price of flour, bread, and other essentials for one month in an effort to impose some brief stability. Such short-run expectations for holding down prices testifies to the wild character of the economy.

Inevitably, some Americans turned this rollercoaster situation to their advantage. Money that fell fast in value needed to be spent quickly; being in debt was suddenly advantageous because the debt could be repaid weeks later in devalued currency. A brisk black market sprang up in prohibited luxury imports, such as tea, sugar, textiles, and wines. No matter that these items came from Britain. As one Virginia lawyer said, "Such is the Spirit to trade, that if Beelzebub [the devil] was to appear with a Cargoe—the people would deal with him." The governor of New Jersey sarcastically observed that the best way to get good wine imported to America might be to declare war on Portugal. A New Hampshire delegate to the congress denounced the extravagance that flew in the face of the virtuous homespun association agreements of just a few years before: "We are a crooked and perverse generation, longing for the fineries and follies of those Egyptian task masters from whom we have so lately freed ourselves."

The Campaigns of 1777: Highs and Lows

In early 1777, the Continental army had a bleak road ahead. Washington had shown considerable skill in avoiding outright military defeat, but the small victories in New Jersey lent only faint optimism to the American side. The British still intended to pursue their plan to isolate New England by controlling the waterway between Canada and New York City. The large numbers of British regular soldiers who arrived to reinforce Quebec in May 1776 gave the British the manpower they needed to start the northern squeeze on the Hudson River valley.

Burgoyne's Army

General John Burgoyne commanded the British troops in Canada in 1777. Familiar with America, he had served in the French and Indian War and again under General Thomas Gage in Boston in 1775. Between war stints, Burgoyne wrote treatises on the use of artillery and occupied a seat in Parliament; he also dabbled in playwriting and acquired a reputation for being a high-living gambler.

Burgoyne had an army of 7,800 uniformed soldiers, plus another 1,000 assorted "camp followers" such as wives, cooks, laundresses, and musicians, and 400 Indians to serve as scouts. This very large army did not travel light. In addition to food supplies for more than 9,000 people, Burgoyne the cannon expert insisted on bringing lots of heavy artillery. The artillery required more than 400 horses to haul it, and the horses in turn required hay. Burgoyne also traveled with more than thirty personal trunks of such useful wilderness amenities as elegant clothing and fine wines. Not for nothing was his nickname "Gentleman Johnny."

Burgoyne's instructions were to capture Albany, a town 150 miles north of New York City near the intersection of the Hudson and Mohawk Rivers. But his first goal was Fort Ticonderoga. About 3,000 American troops held the fort, but they had not anticipated a major invasion from Canada so soon, and they were low on food and supplies. After spying the approaching artillery power, the Americans crept away one dark early morning, without offering a fight. Fort Ticonderoga was back in British hands.

The British gave immediate chase, moving south toward Albany. But Burgoyne lost ground quickly because he insisted on moving his entire army, camp followers and all, taking a land route instead of traveling on Lake George. Local farmers created obstacles by felling trees in his path. Burgoyne lost a critical month hacking his way down the road, and meanwhile his supply lines back to Canada were severely stretched. Soldiers sent out to forage food were beaten back by militia units from New Hampshire and Vermont. The general's opinion, that "the great bulk of the country is undoubtedly with the Congress in principle and zeal," could not have been welcome news to the British government.

Saratoga

The logical second step in isolating New England should have been to advance troops up the Hudson from New York City. General Howe still held Manhattan, and American surveillance indicated that he was readying his men for a major troop movement. George Washington, in New Jersey, was sure Howe would go north to meet Burgoyne. With disbelief he watched while Howe loaded his men on ships in August 1777 and sailed south. Howe had decided to try to capture Philadelphia. Not until Howe's ships had entered the mouth of the Chesapeake Bay did Washington fully accept that Howe was not going to help Burgoyne. Another British general in New York, Henry Clinton, was dismayed by

Howe's decision and later flatly called it a mistake. Clinton promised to send reinforcements to Burgoyne, but he could not get them to Albany in time.

In addition, British troops were supposed to move east from the Great Lakes down the Mohawk River, joined by Indians of Joseph Brant's Iroquois League. The British believed that the Palatine Germans of the Mohawk valley were heavily loyalist, so they expected little trouble moving forward. Fort Stanwix, left over from the French and Indian War, marked the western gateway to the Mohawk valley, and it was guarded by 750 Continental soldiers. Local militias hastily assembled to reinforce the small garrison of Continentals; despite widespread Palatine loyalism, many Germans were fiercely devoted to the rebel cause. The Mohawk valley was a particularly bloody example of the Revolution as civil war, as neighbors fought neighbors over the course of several years, even when the British army was not around. The rebel militia unit moving toward Stanwix met with ambushing Indians in a narrow ravine and suffered great losses (200 killed and another 200 taken prisoner). Fort Stanwix was spared a similar fate only because General Benedict Arnold, still highly esteemed for his heroism in Quebec, arrived with reinforcements (bolstered by a well-circulated but false rumor of even more reinforcements to come), and this scared the British into retreating. Burgoyne, camped forty miles north of Albany, thus did not have the expected help. He was isolated and stuck; his food supplies were dwindling, and his men were deserting.

The Continentals at Albany, now under the new command of General Horatio Gates, advanced to Saratoga, a small farming community on the Hudson River north of Albany. Gates had 7,000 men, including Arnold's division, several New York militia units and some Virginia riflemen, whose hunting shirts and wild turkey calls intimidated the British.

Burgoyne decided to attack first, since every day his army weakened, and retreat was unthinkable and humiliating. The first Battle of Saratoga joined both armies in a classic military engagement, with the two sides facing each other and pressing forward. By day's end, Burgoyne's army claimed the victory, but the loss of men (600 dead and wounded) made it costly; the relative unimportance of the battle location made it a dubious victory.

Three weeks later, a repeat engagement at Saratoga cost Burgoyne another 600 men and most of his cannon as well. Burgoyne tried to retreat, but Gates's army blocked his path. With food running out and many wounded and demoralized men, Bur-

WASHINGTON'S TENT
When in the field, General Washington traveled with three tents, one each for sleeping, eating, and storage. Pictured here is his sleeping tent, containing a cot and a folding table.
Collection of the New York Historical Society.

goyne finally officially surrendered to the Americans on October 17, 1777.

Americans on the side of the rebellion were jubilant. This was the first decisive victory for the Continental army. Almost overnight, a popular dance called "General Burgoyne's Surrender" swept through the country, and bookies in the major cities set odds at five to one that the war would be won in just six months. Both the American leaders, Gates and Arnold, were lauded as the heroes of Saratoga.

General Howe, meanwhile, had succeeded in taking Philadelphia in September 1777. Washington had moved his army south of the city to defend it, but he lost a crucial battle at Brandywine Creek. The Continental Congress had departed nine days earlier for Lancaster, sixty miles west. The British government figured that Burgoyne's surrender was evenly balanced by the capture of Philadelphia and thus proposed a negotiated settlement—not including independence—to end the war. But the Americans refused; they danced "Burgoyne's Surrender" and remained optimistic about eventual victory.

The optimism was not well founded, however, in the winter of 1777–1778; spirits ran high, but finances and supplies ran precariously low. Washington moved his troops into winter quarters at Valley Forge, a day's march west of occupied Philadelphia. Quartered in drafty sheds, the men lacked blankets, boots, and stockings. Washington complained to the congress that nearly three thousand of his men were "unfit for duty because they are bare foot and otherwise naked"; without blankets, large numbers were forced to "set up all Night by fires, instead of taking comfortable rest in a natural way." Food was also scarce. Standard rations dwindled for a time to "firecake," a tasteless pancake made with plain flour and water only, and in one week in February there were no food rations at all. Local farms had produced adequate food that year, but Washington was sure that the farmers were selling their grain to the British, who could pay with the king's silver. Washington claimed that such Americans were worse than the enemy and expressed a grim desire to hang the whole lot. His young aide-de-camp Alexander Hamilton openly wondered if the country was even worth fighting for, so corrupt did it seem.

The evidence of corruption indeed appeared abundant. Army suppliers too often provided defective food, clothing, and gunpowder. Washington's men unfolded a shipment of blankets only to discover that they were a quarter of their customary size. Barrels of flour arrived short-weighted, with "the Center Scooped out and the sides standing." Teamsters who hauled barrels of preserved salted meat might drain out the brine to lighten their load and then refill the barrels later, allowing the meat to rot in transit. Selfishness and greed seemed to infect the American side. A new slang vocabulary identified this new breed of war enthusiasts: "Sharpers," "cheats," and "mushroom gentlemen" were war profiteers, wheeling and dealing in an unstable economy. As one Continental officer said, "The people at home are destroying the Army by their conduct much faster than Howe and all his army can possibly do by fighting us."

The French Alliance

On their own, the Americans could not have defeated England. Essential help arrived as a result of the victory at Saratoga, which convinced the French to enter the war. Two days after news reached the French court, the Americans and French drafted a formal alliance against England and signed it in February 1778. France recognized the United States as an independent nation and promised full military and commercial support throughout the war. The most crucial support was the French navy,

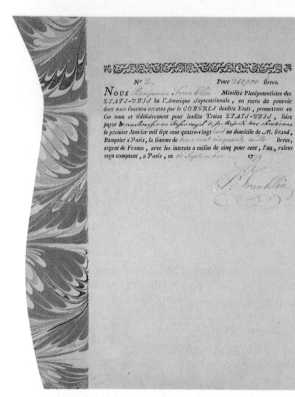

PROMISSORY NOTES NEGOTIATED BY FRANKLIN
Benjamin Franklin, in France in 1778, negotiated loans from the French government to the United States. The preprinted loan form calls Franklin a "Minister Plenipotentiary" with authority to act on behalf of the thirteen (united states); the fact that the form is printed suggests that the French anticipated making several, or many, such loans; this one is numbered 2. It called for repayment in 1779 at five percent interest.
American Philosophical Society Library.

American shipping without restriction, a favor that was most useful in the French West Indies. Most important, France anticipated participation in the war by gearing up its navy in the two years prior to 1778, building new and repairing old warships, so that when the treaty was finally signed, France could be an instant combatant.

> *Even defeat was not a full disaster for France, if the war took many years and drained England of men, money, and psychological energy.*

French sympathies for the Americans were secured through the artful diplomacy of Benjamin Franklin, who lived in Paris for several years as the agent of the Continental Congress. Franklin's deft social skills, impressive scientific knowledge, and rustic charm smoothed his way at court and kept French interest in the American cause high.

Yet monarchical France was understandably cautious about endorsing a democratic revolution that attacked the principles of kingship. The main attraction of an alliance for France was simply the opportunity to defeat England, its archrival. A victory would also open pathways to trade. A French minister, the count of Vergennes, predicted that "the power that will first recognize the independence of the Americans will be the one that will reap the fruits of this war." France coveted the British West Indies, which might fall to them in a victory. And even defeat was not a full disaster for France, if the war took many years and drained England of men, money, and psychological energy. The French alliance proved to be essential for American victory, but it by no means meant that the parties to the alliance shared close goals.

The French navy arrived off the coast of Virginia in July 1778, bearing arms and supplies, and then moved north to threaten (but not attack) the British in New York, occupying the harbor for a week. In August, the allied ships went farther north to Newport, Rhode Island, also held by the British, and engaged in limited battle before heading on to Boston, now returned to American rule. By 1781, the French proved indispensable to the American victory, but the first months of the alliance brought no dramatic victories, inducing grumbling from some Americans that the partnership would prove worthless. "These murmurings the governing powers

which now could challenge England's transatlantic pipeline of supplies and troops.

France had been waiting for a promising American victory to justify a formal declaration of war, for it was foolish as well as dangerous to ally openly with a loser. Yet since 1776, France had aided the Americans in every way short of becoming official partners in war. It had provided military goods—cannons, muskets, gunpowder—funneled through a dummy private firm secretly financed by the French government. Highly trained French military experts had "volunteered" to help the American army in the field with technical advice and military strategy. The marquis de Lafayette, a young nobleman, was one of several French officers advising Washington in 1777. France had opened its ports to

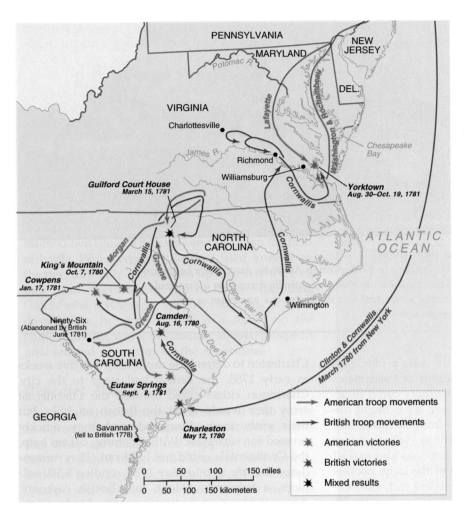

M A P 7.3
*The War in the South,
1780–1781*
*After taking Charleston in
1780, the British advanced
into South Carolina and the
foothill region of North Carolina, leaving a bloody civil
war in their wake. Cornwallis
next invaded Virginia but was
overpowered by American and
French forces at Yorktown in
1781 in the final battle of the
Revolutionary War.*

prudently endeavored to suppress, that they might
not give offence to their new allies," observed a
British captain. Indeed, by late fall of 1778, the
French fleet had sailed off for the West Indies.

The Southern Strategy:
1778–1781

When France joined the war, some British officials
paused to consider whether the fight was worth
continuing. A troop commander, arguing for an immediate negotiated settlement, shrewdly observed
that "we are far from an anticipated peace, because
the bitterness of the rebels is too widespread, and
in regions where we are masters the rebellious spirit
is still in them. The land is too large, and there are
too many people. The more land we win, the weaker
our army gets in the field." The commander of the

British navy argued for abandoning the war, and
even Lord North, the prime minister of King
George's cabinet, was believed to be in favor of ending it quickly. But the king was determined to crush
the rebellion, the French notwithstanding, and he
encouraged the development of a new strategy for
victory. It was a brilliant but desperate plan.

Georgia and South Carolina

The new strategy shelved the plan to isolate New
England and instead focused on the South, thought
to be easier to recapture for the crown. The entry of
the French navy into the war pulled the center of
gravity southward, because of France's interest in
the British West Indies. Some British strategists even
argued that the thirteen rebel colonies should be
written off entirely, in favor of defending the much
more valuable sugar islands. But the southern
colonies, with their tobacco, rice, and indigo crops,

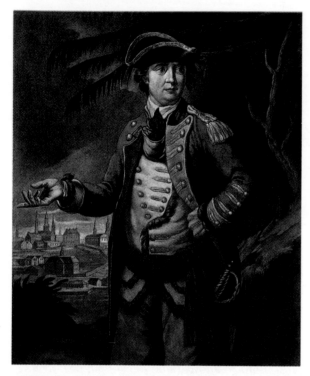

BENEDICT ARNOLD
Benedict Arnold in 1776, when he was the hero of the Quebec campaign.
Anne S. K. Brown Military Collection, Providence, R.I.

the British commander in New York, Henry Clinton, know that with sufficient reward—say, £8,000—he would deliver a major prize that would tip victory England's way.

The ever-hesitant General Clinton remained cautious about Arnold for more than a year. Arnold had named an enormous sum for his reward, and it was not at all clear what he could deliver from his inactive duty in Philadelphia. Meanwhile, to show good faith, Arnold passed along whatever he learned from Washington—about the arrival of the French fleet, about the weak state of Charleston's defenses, even about a planned invasion of Canada that was actually disinformation on Washington's part. Arnold's main task throughout 1779 and early 1780 was to acquire an active command that would be worth something to the British, in addition to quietly closing out his property holdings in Connecticut and Philadelphia in anticipation of flight.

Arnold lobbied Washington for the command of West Point, a fortress guarding a critical narrows in the Hudson River about sixty miles north of New York City. West Point was being fortified to protect against the original and still ultimate British goal, controlling the Hudson and isolating New England. Its easy seizure would be worth a lot to the British; it might well mean instant victory. Arnold's plan was to invite the British to attack and to make their victory effortless by giving them full information on the Americans' defense plans.

Granted command in the spring of 1780, Arnold proceeded to slow down the fortification efforts while entering into serious negotiations with the British about the exact terms of his payoff. He demanded to meet an emissary from Clinton in person, to argue the terms; Clinton hesitated for weeks, knowing the danger. Finally Clinton sent a trusted aide, Major John André, behind enemy lines at night, and Arnold, ever true to character, detained him until daybreak haggling over the payment. Arnold then sent him back unescorted and burdened with drawings and plans for the fort's defense. Near the British line, André was halted by three Americans, and when he offered to bribe them for his release with his gold watch, his horse, and a large sum of money, they quickly became suspicious. The discovery of the fortress plans on his person sealed his doom, and word of his arrest went upriver, to Arnold and to General Washington nearby. Arnold escaped to the British in New York only minutes ahead of the arrival of a consternated Washington. Major André was tried as a spy and hanged ten days later, in October 1780, much lamented by his British friends and by American officers as well, who were moved by his honorable acceptance of the gallows. Arnold was safe but not sound in New York City, surrounded by British officers who now despised him for luring their esteemed young aide into the danger that caused his death and, equally, for failing to deliver West Point, the prize that would have made Clinton victorious.

News of the Arnold treason spread quickly throughout America. Arnold represented all of the patriots' worst fears: greedy self-interest like that of the war profiteers, unprincipled abandonment of the war aims like that of the turncoat Tories of the South, a final fleeing panic like that of the terrified soldiers with Gates at the Battle of Camden. But instead of symbolizing and magnifying all that was troubling about the American side of the war, the treachery of Arnold became celebrated in a kind of displacement of the anxieties of the moment. Vilifying Arnold allowed Americans to stake out a wide distance between themselves and this truly evil man. Parades and effigy burnings in many cities equated Arnold with the devil, and his opponents as therefore men of virtue. It inspired a renewal of patriotism at what had been a particularly low moment. Smoking out Arnold worked to cleanse the American war effort.

The Other Southern War: Guerrillas

Both Gates's defeat at Camden and the treason of Benedict Arnold revitalized rebel support in western South Carolina, an area that Cornwallis had believed to be pacified and loyal. The backcountry of the South soon became the site of a guerrilla war. In hit-and-run attacks, both sides burned and ravaged not only enemy property but the property of anyone claiming to be neutral. The loyalist militia units organized by the British were met by fierce rebel militia units who now figured they had little to lose. It did not help matters that Cornwallis had hanged several men captured at Camden who had signed loyalty oaths but had gone over to the rebel militia. Bloody, extreme tactics only escalated the violence. Guerrilla warfare soon spread to Georgia and North Carolina. In South Carolina, some 6,000 men became active partisan fighters, and they entered into at least twenty-six engagements with loyalist units. Some of these were classic battles; but on other occasions the fighters were more like bandits than soldiers. Both sides murdered enemies, committed atrocities, and plundered property, clear deviations from standard military practice.

The British southern strategy counted on sufficient loyalist strength—in terms of both numbers of people and the respect and authority they could command—to hold reconquered territory as the army moved north. The backcountry civil war proved this assumption false. The Americans won few major battles in the South, but they ultimately succeeded by dogging the British forces, nipping at their heels, harassing them, preventing them from foraging for food. Cornwallis boldly moved the war into North Carolina in late 1780, not because he thought South Carolina was secure—it was not—but because the North Carolinians were supplying the South Carolina rebels with arms and men. As he wrote to Clinton (who was safely resting in New York City), "It may be doubted by some whether the invasion of North Carolina may be a prudent measure; but I am convinced it is a necessary one, and that if we do not attack that province, we must give up both South Carolina and Georgia, and retire within the walls of Charleston." Cornwallis headed north, but news of a brutal defeat—a massacre, actually—of loyalist units in western South

Carolina at Kings Mountain, at the hands of 1,400 frontier riflemen, sent him hurrying back. The British were stretched too thin to hold even two of their onetime colonies.

Surrender at Yorktown

In the early months of 1781, Cornwallis set out to try his North Carolina plan again; if successful, it would isolate South Carolina and Georgia. For months, he moved his army around the state, taking land but not holding it. In February 1781, Cornwallis proclaimed, prematurely, that North Carolina was reconquered, a move calculated to increase loyalist support. But few loyalists could be found who were willing to take up arms against the energized rebel forces.

Cornwallis decided to push the war further north, into Virginia. He captured Williamsburg, which had been the capital until the previous year. Then he raided Charlottesville, where Virginia's revolutionary government was meeting, and seized members of the assembly; Governor Thomas Jefferson narrowly avoided capture. (More than a dozen of Jefferson's slaves ran off to seek refuge with the British army.) As late as the start of September, Cornwallis was not wrong to think he had the upper hand in Virginia.

What changed the picture dramatically was an infusion of French military support. A large French army under the command of the comte de Rochambeau had joined Washington in Rhode Island in mid-1780. News that a large fleet had sailed from France in the spring of 1781 set in motion Washington's plan to defeat the British. The fleet was bound for the Chesapeake Bay, so Washington and Rochambeau fixed their attention on Cornwallis's campaign in Virginia. Bypassing New York (where Clinton had been expecting an attack), thousands of American and French soldiers headed south in the last week of August 1781, traveling on four separate roads to confuse the British.

British intelligence about the French fleet movement had been delayed, and by the time British ships arrived at the mouth of the Chesapeake, the French had already taken control of it. A five-day naval battle in early September sent the British ships limping away and left the French in clear command of the bay and the Virginia and North Carolina coasts. This proved to be the decisive factor in ending the war, because it eliminated a water escape route for Cornwallis's land army, encamped at Yorktown, Virginia.

THOMAS NELSON HOUSE

The finest house in Yorktown belonged to Thomas Nelson, the American governor of Virginia in 1781. During the British occupation of Yorktown, Nelson recommended that American guns be trained directly on his home, on the presumption that Cornwallis had made it his headquarters. Fifteen years later an artist sketched the damaged house, still unrepaired and surrounded by British defensive earthworks.

The Library of Virginia.

General Cornwallis and his 7,500 troops now faced a combined French and American army numbering over 16,000. Thousands of civilian sightseers also flocked around, attracted to the scene by the army's long parade south. For twelve days, the Americans and French laid siege to the British fortifications at Yorktown, bombarding the British with cannon and shells. Quickly Cornwallis ran low on food and ammunition. An American observer keeping a diary noted that "the enemy, from want of forage, are killing off their horses in great numbers. Six or seven hundred of these valuable animals have been killed, and their carcasses are almost continually floating down the river." Realizing escape was impossible, Cornwallis signaled his intention to surrender.

On October 19, 1781, the British leaders formally capitulated. Cornwallis claimed "indisposition" and sent a subordinate as substitute. The defeated troops marched through a double line of American and French soldiers to relinquish their weapons; an American diarist reported that "their mortification could not be concealed. . . . Many of the soldiers manifested a sullen temper, throwing their arms on the pile with violence as if determined to render them useless." Washington allowed Cornwallis his personal liberty, and he sailed off to New York City with as many loyalists as could fit on one ship. The remaining British soldiers were packed off to prison camps in Virginia and Maryland.

What had begun as a promising southern strategy by the British in 1778 had turned into a discouraging defeat by 1781. British attacks in the South energized American resistance, as did the timely exposure of Benedict Arnold's treason. The arrival of the French fleet sealed the fate of Cornwallis at Yorktown, and the military war quickly came to a halt.

The Losers and the Winners

The surrender at Yorktown proved to be the end of the war, but it took some time for the principals to realize that. The peace treaty was nearly two years in the making, and in the meantime both the American and the British armies remained in the field, in case the treaty fell through.

Peace Slowly Dawns

Cornwallis had surrendered his army at Yorktown, but he had no authority to end the war. Clinton continued to hold New York City with many thousands of soldiers; Charleston and Savannah, too, stayed under British control, although the British had been chased out of the rest of the South. King George tenaciously clung to the idea of pursuing the war, but the sentiment for peace was growing in Parliament. A vote taken soon after Cornwallis's surrender showed that only a bare majority favored continuing the war. A resolution to end the war a few months later lost by only a single vote, and five days later the necessary majority was rounded up. The war had become unpopular among the British citizenry in general, and support for it dwindled until finally the king had to realize it was over.

The Continental Congress appointed three commissioners, Benjamin Franklin, John Adams, and John Jay of New York, to negotiate the settlement. It took more than six months to come to preliminary agreement. The Americans met with the British negotiator in Paris, ostensibly so that they could consult with their ally France. But France had different and conflicting interests from the Americans, and the British tried playing the two allies off against each other. The French would have been quite content to divide up the colonies, awarding New York, the Carolinas, and Georgia to the British; the Americans wanted not only all thirteen colonies but Canada as well.

In late November 1782, eighty-two articles of peace were agreed to. The first article went to the heart of the matter: "His Britannic Majesty acknowledges the said United States to be free Sovereign and independent States." Other articles described the boundaries of the new country: a northern line separating Canada, which remained British, a western line along the Mississippi River, and a southern line sectioning off Florida, which England soon handed over to Spain in a separate treaty. Creditors on both sides were entitled to collect debts owed them, in sterling money; this was an important provision for British merchants, especially those in the southern trade, who claimed that commercial debts owed them had gone uncollected during the war. A legalistic provision dealt with loyalist property: The Continental Congress agreed to recommend that state legislatures restore confiscated property to the loyalists. But since the congress had no power to compel the states to return property, no property was returned under this provision. England agreed to withdraw its troops in a timely fashion; more than a decade later, this article would still not be fully satisfied.

The final, official peace treaty—the Treaty of Paris—was signed nearly a year later, on September 2, 1783. The Americans were waiting for a separate peace agreement between the British and the French. Meanwhile, the British army continued to occupy three cities (New York, Charleston, and Savannah) and a string of forts in western New York, Pennsylvania, and the Ohio country. The logistical problems of evacuating the army from the cities proved to be nearly as difficult as sending and supplying the army during the war. There simply were not enough ships to remove all the soldiers, artillery, and stores of food, let alone the thousands of loyalists who rightly feared for their safety once the British were gone.

The final evacuation proceeded in stages. It took 129 ships to do the job from Charleston; small boats and even canoes had to be pressed into service to take loyalists—whites and blacks—from upriver settlements down the coast to St. Augustine, Florida. In the fall of 1783, hundreds of ships converged on New York City to load the headquarters of the British after their seven-year occupation. More than 27,000 soldiers and 30,000 loyalists left New York for Nova Scotia, where a second convoy took many on to England. In a final act of mischief, on the November day when the last ships left, the losing side raised the British flag at the southern tip of Manhattan, cut away the ropes used to hoist it, and greased the flagpole.

Why the British Lost

England began the war for America with a conviction that it could not lose. What a later century termed "the arrogance of power" afflicted British officials and caused them to underestimate their task. But they had some grounds for confidence. They had the strongest and best-trained army and navy in the world; they were familiar with the

American landscape from the French and Indian War; and they outnumbered their opponents in uniform. They easily captured the capital and every other port city of consequence in America. Probably one-fifth of the population was loyalist, and another two-fifths were undecided. Why, then, did they lose?

One continuing problem the British faced was the practical one of food and supplies. Instead of the six-month food supply the generals wanted, reserves typically hovered at the level of a thirty-to-sixty-day supply; at one grim moment in 1780, General Clinton was down to only six days of food before a resupply arrived. Uncertainty about food helps explain the repeated reluctance of Howe and Clinton to push aggressively into the interior in pursuit of the Continental army. Yet it does not fully explain other moments when British commanders refused to coordinate their operations and come to one another's aid, as when Burgoyne at Saratoga was left to his fate, and likewise Cornwallis at Yorktown. Personal jealousies among the commanders appear to have interfered with the larger goal of winning the war.

A second obstacle to British success was their continual misuse of loyalist energies. Any plan to repacify the colonies required the cooperation of the loyalists as well as new support from the many neutrals. But again and again, the British failed to back the loyalists, leaving them to the mercy of vengeful rebels. In the South, they allowed loyalist militias to engage in vicious guerrilla warfare that drove away potential converts among the rest of the population. There was no real program to court the neutrals and to show them that the stability of British rule was preferable to the rebel government. If the British had been more lenient and forgiving, they might have succeeded in retaking the South. But perhaps the central problem was that there simply were not enough loyalists, and the British did nothing to augment their numbers.

The French alliance looms large in any explanation of the British defeat. The artillery and ammunition they supplied throughout the war, even before 1778, were critical necessities for the Continental army. In 1780, the French army brought a fresh infusion of troops to a war-weary America, and the French navy made the Yorktown victory possible. The symbolic impact of the major naval defeat in the Chesapeake, just before the Yorktown siege, dissolved the pro-war spirit in England and forced the king to admit defeat.

Finally, the British abdicated civil power in the colonies in 1775 and 1776, when royal officials were forced to flee to safety, and they never really regained it. For nearly seven years, the Americans of necessity created their own government structures, from the Continental Congress to local committees and militias. Staffed by many who before 1775 had been the political elites, these new government agencies had remarkably little trouble establishing their credentials and authority to rule. The single effort in Georgia to appoint a new royal governor was not successful, and the British did not try to repeat the experiment. The basic British goal in the war—to turn back the clock to imperial rule—receded into impossibility as the war dragged on.

Conclusion: The Dynamic of Equality and Liberty

The war for America had taken five and a half years to fight, from Lexington to Yorktown; negotiations and the evacuation took two more. It remains the second longest war in American history, second only to the Vietnam War. It profoundly disrupted the lives of Americans everywhere, from Canada to Georgia. It was a war for independence from England, but it was also much more. It was a war that required men and women to think about politics and the legitimacy of authority. New government structures had to be forged to replace the vacuum left by the departing British. The precise disagreement with England about representation and political participation had profound implications for the kinds of governance the Americans would choose to adopt, both in the short-run moment of emergency, as extralegal committees and bodies took charge, and in the longer run of the late 1770s and early 1780s when state constitutions began to be written and the Continental Congress pondered its own legitimacy. The rhetoric employed to justify the revolution against England put words like *liberty, tyranny, slavery, independence,* and *equality* into common usage. But these words carried deeper meanings than a mere complaint over taxation without representation, meanings that came to the surface as Americans struggled to articulate what kind of new government they should institute. As Abigail Adams and others saw, the Revolution unleashed a dynamic of equality and liberty. That it was largely unintended and unwanted by the revolutionary leaders of 1776 made it all the more potent a force in American life in the decades to come.

CHRONOLOGY

1775 **May 10.** Second Continental Congress convenes in Philadelphia.

May. Fort Ticonderoga falls to American forces.

June 14. Continental Congress creates Continental army.

June 17. Battle of Bunker Hill.

July. Congress offers the Olive Branch Petition in attempt at reconciliation with king.

American armies march on Montreal and Quebec.

1776 **January 1.** Americans lose assault on Quebec.

January. Thomas Paine's *Common Sense* published.

March. British evacuate Boston.

July 4. Declaration of Independence adopted.

August 27. Battle of Long Island.

September 15. British take Manhattan.

September 21. Part of New York City burned.

November. Americans retreat to Philadelphia.

December 26. Washington surprises British and Hessians at Trenton.

1777 **January.** Washington winters at Morristown, New Jersey.

July. Burgoyne takes Fort Ticonderoga for British.

August 6. Fort Stanwix ambush.

September. British occupy Philadelphia.

October 17. Burgoyne surrenders at Saratoga.

December. Washington goes into winter quarters at Valley Forge, Pennsylvania.

1778 **February.** France enters war on American side.

July–August. French fleet threatens New York and Newport, Rhode Island.

December. Savannah, Georgia, falls to British.

1779 **January–June.** Skirmishes in South Carolina and Georgia.

October. British evacuate Newport.

1780 Philadelphia Ladies Association raises money for soldiers.

March–May. British lay siege to Charleston, South Carolina.

July. Rochambeau and French army arrive at Newport.

August 16. Battle of Camden, South Carolina, dims hopes for Americans.

September–October. Benedict Arnold's treason exposed.

September–December. Guerrilla warfare in South.

October 7. Battle of Kings Mountain, South Carolina.

1781 **January 17.** Battle of Cowpens, South Carolina.

May–August. Cornwallis in Virginia.

August. Cornwallis occupies Yorktown, Virginia.

September 5. French fleet takes Chesapeake Bay.

September 28–October 19. Siege of Yorktown.

October 19. Cornwallis surrenders.

1783 Treaty of Paris ends war.

BIBLIOGRAPHY

GENERAL WORKS

John R. Alden, *The American Revolution, 1775–1783* (1954).

Edward Countryman, *The American Revolution* (1985).

Don Higginbotham, *The War of Independence: Military Attitudes, Policies, and Practices, 1763–1789* (1983).

Don Higginbotham, *George Washington and the American Military Tradition* (1985).

Don Higginbotham, *War and Society in Revolutionary America: The Wider Dimensions of Conflict* (1988).

Ronald Hoffman and Peter J. Albert, *Arms and Independence: The Military Character of the American Revolution* (1984).

Piers Mackesy, *The War for America, 1775–1783* (1964).

James Kirby Martin, *In the Course of Human Events: An Interpretive Exploration of the Revolution* (1979).

Robert Middlekauff, *The Glorious Cause: The American Revolution, 1763–1789* (1982).

Charles Royster, *A Revolutionary People at War: The Continental Army and American Character, 1775–1783* (1979).

John Shy, *A People Numerous and Armed: Reflections on the Military Struggle for American Independence* (rev. ed., 1990).

James L. Stokesbury, *A Short History of the American Revolution* (1991).

THE WARTIME CONFEDERATION

John Alden, *George Washington* (1984).

Joseph J. Ellis, *Passionate Sage: The Character and Legacy of John Adams* (1993).

E. James Ferguson, *The Power of the Purse: A History of American Public Finance: 1776–1790* (1961).

John Ferling, *John Adams: A Life* (1992).

Jay Fliegelman, *Declaring Independence: Jefferson, Natural Language, and the Culture of Performance* (1993).

Eric Foner, *Tom Paine and Revolutionary America* (1976).

Edith Gelles, *Portia: The World of Abigail Adams* (1992).

James H. Hutson, *John Adams and the Diplomacy of the American Revolution* (1980).

Jackson Turner Main, *The Sovereign States, 1775–1783* (1973).

Jerrilyn Greene Marston, *King and Congress: The Transfer of Political Legitimacy, 1774–1776* (1987).

Jack N. Rakove, *The Beginnings of National Politics: An Interpretive History of the Continental Congress* (1979).

John Phillip Reid, *A Constitutional History of the American Revolution: The Authority of Rights* (1986).

Peter Shaw, *The Character of John Adams* (1976).

William C. Stinchcombe, *The American Revolution and the French Alliance* (1969).

Garry Wills, *Inventing America: Jefferson's Declaration of Independence* (1978).

Lynne Withey, *Dearest Friend: A Life of Abigail Adams* (1981).

THE LOYALISTS

Bernard Bailyn, *The Ordeal of Thomas Hutchinson* (1974).

Wallace Brown, *The Good Americans: The Loyalists in the American Revolution* (1969).

Robert M. Calhoon, *The Loyalists of Revolutionary America, 1760–1781* (1973).

Robert M. Calhoon, *The Loyalist Perception and Other Essays* (1989).

John Ferling, *The Loyalist Mind: Joseph Galloway and the American Revolution* (1977).

Malcolm Frieberg, *Prelude to Purgatory: Thomas Hutchinson in Provincial Massachusetts Politics, 1760–1770* (1990).

Adele Hast, *Loyalism in Revolutionary Virginia* (1982).

Neil MacKinnon, *This Unfriendly Soil: The Loyalist Experience in Nova Scotia, 1783–1791* (1986).

William N. Nelson, *The American Tory* (1961).

Mary Beth Norton, *The British-Americans: The Loyalist Exiles in England, 1774–1789* (1972).

William Pencak, *America's Burke: The Mind of Thomas Hutchinson* (1982).

Janice Potter, *The Liberty We Seek: Loyalist Ideology in Colonial New York and Massachusetts* (1983).

James W. St. G. Walker, *The Black Loyalists: The Search for a Promised Land in Nova Scotia and Sierra Leone, 1783–1870* (1976).

THE WAR IN THE NORTH

Rodney Atwood, *The Hessians* (1980).

Michael A. Bellesiles, *Revolutionary Outlaws: Ethan Allen and the Struggle for Independence on the Early American Frontier* (1993).

Clare Brandt, *The Man in the Mirror: A Life of Benedict Arnold* (1994).

Richard Buel Jr., *Dear Liberty: Connecticut's Mobilization for the Revolutionary War* (1980).

E. Wayne Carp, *To Starve the Army at Pleasure: Continental Army Administration and American Political Culture, 1775–1783* (1984).

Edward Countryman, *A People in Revolution: The American Revolution and Political Society in New York, 1760–1790* (1981).

John C. Dann, ed., *The Revolution Remembered: Eyewitness Accounts of the War for Independence* (1980).

Gregory E. Dowd, *A Spirited Resistance: The North American Indian Struggle for Unity, 1745–1815* (1992).

William M. Fowler Jr., *Rebels under Sail: The American Navy during the Revolution* (1976).

Sylvia Frey, *The British Soldier in America: A Social History of Military Life in the Revolutionary Period* (1965).

Barbara Graymont, *The Iroquois in the American Revolution* (1972).

Robert Gross, *The Minutemen and Their World* (1976).

Ira D. Gruber, *The Howe Brothers and the American Revolution* (1972).

Richard J. Hargrove Jr., *General John Burgoyne* (1983).

Sidney Kaplan and Emma Nogrady Kaplan, *The Black Presence in the Era of the American Revolution* (1989).

Isabel T. Kelsay, *Joseph Brant, 1743–1807* (1984).

Richard M. Ketchum, *The Winter Soldiers* (1973).

Donald R. Lennon and Charles E. Bennett, *A Quest for Glory: Robert Howe and the American Revolution* (1991).

James Kirby Martin and Edward Mark Lender, *A Respectable Army: The Military Origins of the Republic, 1763–1789* (1982).

Paul David Nelson, *General Horatio Gates* (1976).

Dave R. Palmer, *The Way of the Fox: American Strategy in the War for America, 1775–1783* (1975).

Gary A. Puckrein, *The Black Regiment in the American Revolution* (1978).

Willard Sterne Randall, *Benedict Arnold: Patriot and Traitor* (1990).

John Shy, *Toward Lexington: The Role of the British Army in the Coming of the American Revolution* (1965).

John A. Tilley, *The British Navy and the American Revolution* (1987).

Anthony F. C. Wallace, *The Death and Rebirth of the Seneca* (1969).

Donald Wallace White, *A Village at War: Chatham, New Jersey, and the American Revolution* (1979).

Robert K. Wright Jr., *The Continental Army* (1983).

DIPLOMACY

Jonathan R. Dull, *A Diplomatic History of the American Revolution* (1985).

R. Ernest Dupuy et al., *The American Revolution: A Global War* (1977).

Ronald Hoffman and Peter Albert, eds., *Peace and the Peacemakers: The Treaty of 1783* (1986).

Reginald Horsman, *The Diplomacy of the New Republic, 1776–1815* (1985).

James H. Hutson, *John Adams and the Diplomacy of the American Revolution* (1980).

Lee Kennett, *The French Forces in America, 1780–1783* (1977).

Richard Morris, *The Peacemakers: The Great Powers and American Independence* (1965).

THE SOUTHERN STRATEGY

R. Arthur Bowler, *Logistics and the Failure of the British Army in America, 1775–1783* (1975).

Jeffrey J. Crow and Larry Tise, eds., *The Southern Experience in the American Revolution* (1978).

John Ferling, ed., *The World Turned Upside Down: The American Victory in the War of Independence* (1988).

M. Thomas Hatley, *The Dividing Paths: Cherokees and South Carolinians through the Era of Revolution* (1993).

W. Robert Higgins, ed., *The Revolutionary War in the South* (1979).

Ronald Hoffman, Thad W. Tate, and Peter J. Albert, eds., *An Uncivil War: The Southern Backcountry during the American Revolution* (1985).

Henry Lumpkin, *From Savannah to Yorktown* (1981).

Jerome J. Nadelhaft, *The Disorders of War: The Revolution in South Carolina* (1981).

James H. O'Donnell III, *Southern Indians in the American Revolution* (1973).

John S. Pancake, *This Destructive War: The British Campaign in the Carolinas, 1780–1782* (1985).

Hugh Rankin, *The North Carolina Continentals* (1971).

John E. Selby, *The Revolution in Virginia, 1775–1783* (1988).

Timothy Silver, *A New Face on the Countryside: Indians, Colonists, and Slaves in South Atlantic Forests, 1500–1800* (1990).

Russell F. Weigley, *The Partisan War: The South Carolina Campaign of 1780–1782* (1970).

By the 1780s, Mercy Warren's confidence in her political judgment had grown. So had her anxiety about the direction of the newly independent Republic, which "resembled the conduct of a restless, vigorous youth, prematurely emancipated from the authority of a parent, but without the experience necessary to direct him to act with dignity or discretion." First came years of disagreement among the states over the ownership of western lands, followed by bickering over taxation and the war debt. At times it seemed to Mercy and James that the country was on the brink of total disaster.

To make matters worse, severe economic chaos clouded much of the 1780s. No currency could keep value for long; prices fluctuated wildly, and speculators grew rich while other people grew poor. Mercy Warren worried that the simplicity, virtue, and self-sacrifice cherished by the sturdy American patriots of 1776 had vanished overnight, replaced by a greed to profit from the uncertain economy and a selfish desire to indulge in luxury. A bewildered Warren wrote, "Such a total change of manners in so short a period, I believe was never known in the history of man. Rapacity and profusion, pride and servility, and almost every vice is contrasted in the same heart."

By the mid-1780s, the Massachusetts state government embarked on a course the Warrens disapproved of, taxing inhabitants at high rates to retire the state debt. But they equally disapproved of citizens' armed protests against taxes. Mercy Warren considered such protesters "incendiary and turbulent" and "too ignorant to distinguish between an opposition to regal despotism and a resistance to a government recently established by themselves."

When a group of American leaders responded to such protests by drafting a new constitution for the Republic, Mercy Warren, now thoroughly alarmed, took up her pen again to denounce the "many-headed monster" that threatened individual liberties. Her unsigned nineteen-page pamphlet gained wide circulation.

By 1788, Mercy Warren's views had lost out and the Constitution had been ratified. The Warrens also lost their own little indulgence, their new house; the financial instability of the 1780s forced them to sell it. They returned to Plymouth, where Mercy spent the next fifteen years polishing her three-volume *History of the Rise, Progress, and Termination of the American Revolution*. Finally published in 1805, the work credited its author, "Mrs. Mercy Warren," on the title page. Here she was finally at liberty to claim her political views as her own, backed up by quo-

MERCY OTIS WARREN
The Boston artist John Singleton Copley painted Mercy Warren when she was thirty-six. The blue satin gown adorned with point lace sleeves and silk braid conveys a message of proper—and prosperous—femininity. Mercy Warren's warm and intelligent face bears a gentle yet appraising expression.
Bequest of Winslow Warren, Courtesy, Museum of Fine Arts, Boston.

tations from leading participants and footnotes from documents of record. The work's public reception, however, fell far short of its genuine merit. Her onetime friend and mentor John Adams objected strongly to her treatment of him and the other proponents of the Constitution. "History is not the Province of the Ladies," he fumed. But Mercy Otis Warren's own life proved him wrong.

The Articles of Confederation

For five years, from independence in 1776 until 1781, the Second Continental Congress continued to meet in Philadelphia and other cities. It existed as an extralegal body, without any formal constitutional basis, while its members groped to establish a government on principles congruent with the themes of the Revolution. With monarchy gone, where did sovereignty lie? If people could not be taxed except by their representatives, where did the power of taxation lie? What was the nature of representation? If distant governments inevitably lost sight of the interests of the people, what was the proper size for a political entity? And just who were "the people" anyway?

The initial answers to these questions took the form of a plan called the Articles of Confederation. The plan, however, proved to be controversial and difficult to implement. By the time the Articles were finally ratified, in 1781, they were virtually obsolete.

Congress and Confederation

The Second Continental Congress had assumed power in May 1775, when the British attack on Lexington and Concord required a unified colonial response. Only as they fashioned the Declaration of Independence a year later did the delegates consider the need for a written document that would specify what powers the congress had, by what authority it existed, and how it was to be constituted. Several men briefly tried drafting such a document; but finally it was John Dickinson, the moderate conciliator from Pennsylvania, who chaired the committee entrusted with this important task. Dubious as he was about the prospects of independence, Dickinson was intrigued by the assignment of setting forth the powers and structure of the congress.

Dickinson's draft of the Articles of Confederation reveals the wide scope of agreement that existed about how the congress should function. The delegates thought of themselves as a harmonious body, fairly well unified by their opposition to England. Most agreed that the congress should handle functions such as pursuing war and peace, conducting foreign relations, regulating trade, and running a postal service.

Dickinson's draft called for a congress with those powers plus the authority to issue bills of credit and to borrow money, to settle all disputes between states, and to administer the unsettled western lands. It was these final two points—the preeminent authority of the congress over the states and over western lands—that proved to be the major sources of disagreement over the draft. Some states, such as Virginia and Connecticut, had very old colonial charters that located their western boundaries many hundreds of miles to the west. States without extensive land grants could not abide

such grandiose claims. Dickinson's Articles granted the congress final authority on this and many other matters.

Off and on over the next sixteen months, the congress tinkered with the Articles; its immediate attention, however, was focused on the war. When the possibility of a French alliance began to materialize in 1777, the delegates returned to the task of hammering out the Articles. They reasoned that some sort of government, however imperfect, was better than no official government at all; they wanted to look like a serious country to the French. And there were growing problems, too, that called for a constitution. As things stood, the congress could tell the states to raise men, money, and supplies for the war, but no one had any clear idea what to do if a state ignored the request.

A final version of the Articles of Confederation emerged in November 1777. Dickinson had resigned from the congress many months before and was not there to argue for his expansive version of the congress's powers. What resulted, after amendment, was a document that clearly identified the union as a loose confederation of states. Gone was the provision giving the congress control of state boundaries and western lands. Also absent was the statement of congress's superior authority. Instead, the Articles opened with two carefully crafted declarations about state powers and the nature of the union. Each state retained all powers and rights not expressly delegated to the congress, and the union was characterized as "a firm league of friendship" existing mainly to foster a common defense. There was no national executive office (that is, no president) and no national judiciary.

The structure of the government closely paralleled that of the existing Continental Congress. The confederation was embodied in a congress, composed of two to seven delegates from each state. The actual number was not critical, since each state delegation cast a single vote; in a confederation of thirteen equal states, Rhode Island's vote was the equal of Virginia's. The Articles specified that the delegates be selected annually by the state legislature, with only two limitations: No one could serve more than three years out of any six, and no one could hold another government office at the same time. Thus was established the principle of rotation in office and an end to the practice of plural office-holding.

Routine decisions in congress required a simple majority of seven states; for momentous powers, such as declaring war, nine states needed to agree. But to approve or amend the Articles required the unanimous consent of the thirteen states —not just of the thirteen delegations in the congress, but of the thirteen state legislatures. The congressional delegates undoubtedly thought they were guaranteeing that no individual state could be railroaded by the other twelve in fundamental constitutional matters. But what this requirement really did was to hamstring the government. One renegade state could—and did—hold the rest of the country hostage to its demands.

In general, the lack of centralized authority in the confederation government was exactly what many state leaders wanted in the late 1770s.

On the delicate question of deriving revenue to run the government, specifically to finance the war, the Articles provided an ingenious but ultimately troublesome solution. Each state was to contribute to the common treasury in proportion to the current property value of the state's land. Large and populous states would contribute more than small or sparsely populated states whose land was not settled and improved. The actual taxes would be levied by the state legislatures, not by the congress, to preserve the Revolution's principle of taxation only by direct representatives. However, no mechanism was created to compel states to contribute their fair share.

In general, the lack of centralized authority in the confederation government was exactly what many state leaders wanted in the late 1770s. A league of states with rotating personnel, no executive branch, no power of taxation, and a requirement of unanimity for any major change seemed to be a good way to avoid the potential tyranny of government. But soon the inherent weaknesses of these features became apparent.

The Problem of Western Lands

Once approved by the congress, the Articles of Confederation had to be approved unanimously by the state legislatures. Newspapers published the plan, but there was little public debate because the war monopolized the news. No pamphlets appeared debating the pros and cons of the Articles, and hardly any politicking went on in state legislatures. The congress scheduled only five days for the final debate and promptly dismissed all but one of the thirty-six amendments proposed by the various state legislatures.

The one proposed change that took time to debate was a plea by five states to give the congress administrative control of the western lands up to the Mississippi River as a national domain that could eventually constitute new states. Not surprisingly, these five states were small, with charters granting them boundaries at most a few hundred miles from the coast: Maryland, Delaware, New Jersey, Rhode Island, and Pennsylvania. Though Pennsylvania was much larger than the others, about one-fifth of its area was simultaneously claimed by Connecticut, whose charter set its western boundary unimaginably far west. Connecticut's claim was not an empty threat. By the late 1770s, Connecticut families were moving into the area of the upper Susquehanna River in Pennsylvania, leading to violent skirmishes with the Pennsylvanians also staking out land claims there.

By contrast, the charters of the states with more land specified ambitious but vague western boundaries. Virginia's charter dated from 1624, a time when the royal grantors lacked realistic knowledge of the geography and demography of the American continent. Consequently, Virginia could claim, on paper anyway, to own territory west to the Mississippi River and north to Lake Superior, taking in present-day West Virginia, Kentucky, Ohio, Indiana, Illinois, Michigan, and Wisconsin. Connecticut was sure that its territory cut through Virginia's domain, and Massachusetts claimed a strip of present-day New York, Michigan, and Wisconsin. The Carolinas and Georgia drew their western boundaries at the Mississippi River. A great portion of the contested western lands actually fell under the control of another group not party to the disputes in the Continental Congress: the many thousands of Indians who inhabited that region, who would have been very surprised to learn that they lived in Virginia or Connecticut territory.

The five smaller states were not entirely without western claims of their own. Ambitious individual investors from Maryland, New Jersey, and Pennsylvania had purchased large tracts of land in the Ohio valley from Indians in the 1760s, and they wanted the confederated government to confirm their ownership and make the rest into a national domain. Many of these speculators were also leading politicians in their state governments. While wearing their political hats, they tried to make their arguments as principled as possible. Maryland leg-

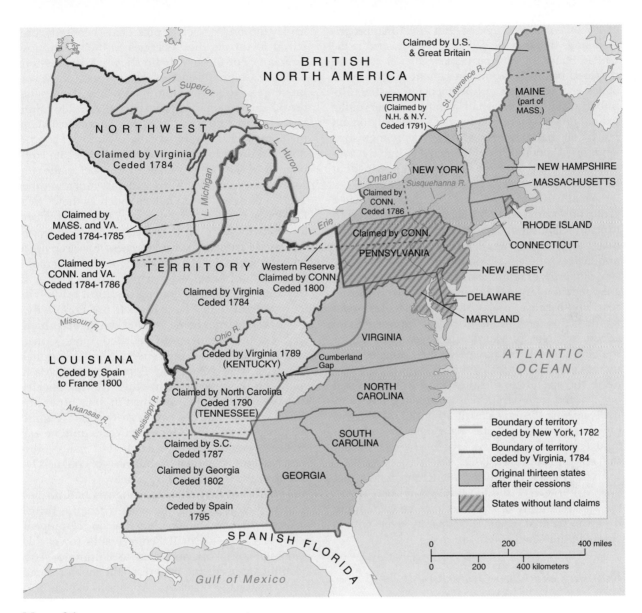

M A P 8.1
Cession of Western Lands, 1782–1802
The thirteen new states found it hard to ratify the Articles of Confederation without settling their conflicting land claims in the west, an area larger than the original states and occupied by Indian tribes.

islators, for example, protested the unfairness of allowing Virginia a wealth of unsettled land. With it, Virginia would easily meet its financial obligations to the confederated government through land sales, while states like Maryland had no alternative to painful taxation of its citizens.

The other eight states were ready to sign the Articles of Confederation as approved by the con-

gress. Rhode Island, Pennsylvania, and New Jersey finally capitulated and signed, "not from a Conviction of the Equality and Justness of it," said a New Jersey delegate, "but merely from an absolute Necessity there was of complying to save the Continent." But Delaware and Maryland continued to hold out for many months, insisting on a national domain policy. In a compromise move, near the end of 1779 the congress agreed that any "unappropriated lands that may be ceded or relinquished to the United States, by any particular state, . . . shall be disposed of for the common benefit of the United States and be settled and formed into distinct Republican States, which shall become members of the federal union." Here finally was a national domain policy; all that was needed now was relinquished land. It was enough to pull Delaware into the confederation; Maryland remained the single holdout for more than a year.

Finally, in early 1781, the logjam broke when a group of Virginians led by Thomas Jefferson agreed to cede all lands to the confederation except the area that later became West Virginia. The compromise undercut Virginia's economic interests but made sense in terms of republican principles. Such a large area, Jefferson argued, could not be governed successfully because the seat of state government would be too far from its citizens to represent them adequately. Not all Marylanders were pleased, for the offer failed to acknowledge the claims of speculators who had purchased land from Indians. Indeed, the speculators' claims took so long to sort out that the confederation government did not formally acquire Virginia's territory until 1784. But Virginia's offer removed the main obstacle to Maryland's ratification, and the Articles at long last went into effect in February 1781.

The western lands issue demonstrated that powerful interests divided the thirteen new states; the apparent unity of purpose inspired by fighting the war against England papered over sizable cracks in the new confederation.

Running the New Government

No fanfare greeted the long-awaited inauguration of the new government. The congress continued to sputter along, its problems far from solved by the signing of the Articles. Day-to-day activities were often hampered by the lack of a quorum. The Articles required representation from seven states to conduct business, with a minimum of two men for each state's delegation. But some days fewer than fourteen men showed up.

State legislatures were slow to select delegates; those appointed were often reluctant to attend. (James Warren of Massachusetts, Mercy's husband, was chosen twice by his state to be a delegate, yet he failed to show up for even one session.) The confederation congress at times seemed deadlocked or

irrelevant, and so active politicians generally preferred to devote their energies to their state governments. For those who did show up, the sessions could be seemingly endless. The urgency of the war prevented recess for more than a few days; what breaks there were came unexpectedly and involuntarily, when a quorum failed to materialize. Many members were lawyers, so debates often got bogged down in procedural intricacies. One delegate complained of the "time it takes to transact matters in so large an Assembly filled with lawyers and other gentlemen who love to talk as much as they." John Dickinson had left the congress in July 1776, happy to avoid the vote on the Declaration of Independence. He compared his eagerness to leave office with the eagerness of a groom on his wedding night: "No youthful Lover ever stript off his Cloathes to step into Bed to his blooming beautiful bride with more delight than I have cast off my Popularity."

Absence from home worked the greatest hardship on the middle-aged married men. Consequently, some of the most effective and committed delegates were young bachelors like James Madison, who was twenty-eight when he was selected to serve from Virginia, and men in their fifties and sixties whose families were grown, like Samuel Adams. Adams served for seven years until he was finally overcome by exhaustion. But many other men had barely learned the business of congress before they were on their way home.

It did not help that the congress had no permanent home. During the war, when the British army threatened Philadelphia, the congress repeatedly relocated, to small Pennsylvania towns like Lancaster and York and then to Baltimore. After hostilities ceased, the congress still moved about, from Trenton to Princeton to Annapolis to New York City, seeking a congenial home base.

To address the inherent difficulties of an inefficient congress with long-winded delegates and rapid turnover, some members advanced the idea of a standing committee system. Executive boards of war, finance, and foreign affairs were created to handle the purely administrative functions of government, but still the congress got bogged down in tedious details. A major reorganization in 1781 created executive departments run by secretaries. When the secretaries were ambitious—as was Robert Morris, a wealthy Philadelphia merchant who served as superintendent of finance—they could exercise considerable executive power. The Articles of Confederation had deliberately refrained from setting up an executive branch, but a modest one was being invented by necessity.

Because of the pressing needs of running a war machine, the confederation government got a slow start on writing its justifying document, the Articles. Then the difficulties over the ownership of western lands slowed down ratification for years. By the time the Articles were fully functioning, yet another problem emerged. Much more exciting political work was going on at the state level, especially during the creative burst of state constitution–writing in the late 1770s. Before 1776, the cream of political talent in the country was attracted to the Continental Congress, but between 1776 and 1780 the talent flowed to the state governments.

The Sovereign States

In the first decade of independence, the states were sovereign and all-powerful. Only a few functions, like that of declaring war and peace, had been transferred to the confederation government. Familiar and close to home, state governments claimed the allegiance of their citizens. As Americans discarded their English identity, they thought of themselves instead as Virginians or New Yorkers or Pennsylvanians. Few people, even among the wealthy, traveled far from home, so their primary affiliation was local. State government was thus the arena where the Revolution's innovations would first be tried.

The State Constitutions

Unlike the Continental Congress, almost every state legislature made it a top priority to pass a written constitution without delay. In May 1776, the congress in Philadelphia recommended that all the states draw up constitutions based on "the authority of the people." By 1778, ten of the thirteen states had produced documents spelling out the liberties, rights, and obligations of citizens and rulers. Two more states, Connecticut and Rhode Island, simply adopted and updated their original colonial charters.

The idea of a written constitution laying out the powers and duties of government was essentially new. When the British invoked their own ancient and venerable constitution, they were referring to a collection of traditions, customs, and privileges, nowhere written down. Americans felt they had been injured by the unwritten nature of British traditions; liberties they had assumed they were entitled to had been denied them. They wanted a written contract whose basic principles could not be easily altered by the particular government in power at the moment.

A shared feature of all the state constitutions was the conviction that government ultimately rests on the consent of the governed. Political writers in the late 1770s embraced the concept of republicanism as the underpinning of the new governments. Republicanism meant more than just the practice of popular elections and representative institutions. For some, it invoked a way of thinking about who leaders should be—ideally autonomous, virtuous, public-minded citizens who placed civic values above private interests. For others, it suggested direct democracy, delivered best by a political structure that put the fewest obstacles before the will of the people. For all, it meant that the primary end of government was to promote the people's welfare. "The word *republic*," wrote Thomas Paine, "means the *public good,* or the good of the whole, in contradistinction to the despotic form, which makes the good of the sovereign, or of one man, the only object of the government."

Widespread agreement about the virtues of republican government went hand in hand with another axiom of political theory, the idea that republics could succeed only in relatively small units. A government run for and by the people had to be near at hand, so the people could make sure their interests were being served. If a republic was too large, the people's representatives would be out of touch with their constituents—perhaps even unknown to them. It was on these grounds that Virginia was willing to give up its western land claim. Distant governments could easily become tyrannical governments; that was the lesson of the 1760s.

It followed, then, that the best form of government was the one that allowed maximum voice to the people. Nearly every state continued the colonial practice of a two-chamber assembly. Under British rule, the upper chamber had consisted of a small council of handpicked elites who helped the royal governor rule over an elected lower assembly; in contrast, the newly formed states greatly augmented the powers of the lower house. Two states, Pennsylvania and Georgia, established a unicameral, or one-house, legislature; why even bother with an upper house if its main function was to curb the lower house elected by the people?

Virtually all of the state constitutions went to great lengths to restrain and subdivide power. They severely limited the powers of the governor, identified in most people's minds with the royal governors of colonial days. Governors could no longer convene or dismiss legislatures at will, and they were stripped of veto power over legislation. They were also deprived of informal means of influence. No longer could governors make land grants, once a surefire way of buying loyalty. State constitutions devised elaborate mechanisms—such as New York's Council of Appointments—to take job patronage away from the executive. Most states also restricted the governor to a short term of office, usually one year, with limited eligibility for reelection. In fact, legislatures usually chose the governor; his very job security depended on close cooperation with that body. Little wonder that the two unicameral states, Pennsylvania and Georgia, decided to abolish the office of governor altogether.

The legislatures' lower houses were the centerpieces of the new republican governments, and most states made them very responsive to popular majorities. Annual elections and guaranteed rotation in office prevented anyone from monopolizing power; if a representative displeased his constituents, he could be out of office in a matter of months. Daily governance of the state rested with the lower house, whose most important decisions were economic. Each state was trying to finance its war effort, and each legislature had to make crucial decisions about printing, borrowing, taxing, and spending money.

Six of the state constitutions included bills of rights. These were lists of basic individual rights that governments could not abridge, not even democratic governments that expressed the voice of the majority. Virginia debated and passed the first bill of rights in June 1776, and many of the other states borrowed from it, with alterations. Its language also bears a close resemblance to the wording of the Declaration of Independence that Thomas Jefferson was composing that same June in Philadelphia: "That all men are by nature equally free and independent, and have certain inherent rights, of which, when they enter into a state of society, they cannot by any compact deprive or divest their posterity; namely, the enjoyment of life and liberty, with the means of acquiring and possessing property, and pursuing and obtaining happiness and safety." Thus life, liberty, property, and the pursuit of happiness and safety were defined as inherent rights, along with more specific rights to freedom of speech, freedom of the press, and trial by jury.

Who Are "the People"?

When the Continental Congress called for state constitutions based on "the authority of the people," and when the Virginia bill of rights granted "all men" certain rights, who was meant by "the people"? Who exactly were the citizens of this new country, and how far did the principle of democratic government extend? Different people answered this question differently, but in the 1770s certain limits to full political participation by all Americans were widely agreed upon among the lawmakers and constitution writers.

Every state set property qualifications for voters and candidates alike. Although the precise threshold for qualifying varied from state to state, the idea prevailed everywhere that the propertied classes were the only legitimate participants in government. In nearly every state, property qualifications for public office were structured so that the highest offices—the governorship and membership in the upper house—would draw only on the richest segment of the population. In Maryland, for example, a candidate for the lower house had to own real or personal property worth £500; candidates for governor had to be worth £5,000; these were very large sums of money, restricting candidacy to the very upper stratum. Voters in Maryland had to own fifty acres of land or £30, a sum that would screen out perhaps a third of adult white males. In the most democratic state, Pennsylvania, voters and candidates alike needed only to be taxpayers—that is, to own enough property to owe taxes.

The justification for restricting political participation to property owners was so widely accepted that it rarely needed to be explained. Only property owners were presumed to possess the necessary independence of mind to make wise political choices. Are not propertyless men, asked John Adams, "too little acquainted with public affairs to form a right judgment, and too dependent upon other men to have a will of their own?" Like women and children, he reasoned, such men were dependent on others and would "talk and vote as they are directed by some man of property, who has attached their minds to his interest." Adams and others assumed that only property owners would feel a keen sense of community and thus be able to think clearly about the common interest. Besides, it did not seem right to give a propertyless man a voice in decisions to levy taxes if he was not going to be paying taxes himself.

Probably one-quarter to one-half of all adult white males were disfranchised by property qualifications, depending on the state. Not all of them took their nonvoter status quietly. One Maryland man wondered what was so special about being worth £30: "Every poor man has a life, a personal liberty, and a right to his earnings; and is in danger of being injured by government in a variety of ways." Why then restrict such a man from voting for his representatives? Others pointed out that propertyless men were fighting and dying in the Revolutionary War; surely they were expressing an active concern about politics that did not spring solely from property ownership. A company of Maryland militiamen dramatized their demand for the vote by marching on a polling place in 1776; all of them together owned less than £40, but they felt they had a right to the vote. Finally, a very few radical voices challenged the notion that owning property automatically transformed men into good citizens. Perhaps it did the opposite: The richest men might well be greedy and selfish, the worst kind of citizen. A writer in a Rhode Island newspaper in 1775 even advanced the idea that there should be an absolute legal limit on property holding, to prevent unhealthy concentrations of power, influence, and wealth.

If suffrage is brought up for debate, John Adams warned, "there will be no end of it. New claims will arise; women will demand a vote . . . and every man who has not a farthing, will demand an equal voice with any other."

But ideas like this were clearly outside the mainstream. The men who wrote the new constitutions were themselves men of property and material substance, and they viewed the Revolution as an effort to guarantee people the right to own property and to prevent unjust governments from appropriating it through taxation. John Adams urged the framers of the Massachusetts constitution not even to discuss the scope of suffrage but simply to adopt the traditional colonial property qualifications. If it is brought up for debate, he warned, "there will be

no end of it. New claims will arise; women will demand a vote; lads from twelve to twenty-one will think their rights not enough attended to; and every man who has not a farthing, will demand an equal voice with any other." Adams was astute enough to anticipate complaints about excluding women, youth, and poor men from political life, but it did not even occur to him to worry about another excluded group: slaves.

Equality and Slavery

Restrictions on political participation did not mean that propertyless people enjoyed no civil rights and liberties. The inalienable rights enumerated in the various state bills of rights were meant to apply to all individuals who had, as the Virginia bill so carefully phrased it, "enter[ed] into a state of society." No matter how poor, a free person was entitled to life, liberty, property, and freedom of conscience. Unfree people, however, were another matter.

The author of the Virginia bill of rights was George Mason, a plantation owner with 118 slaves. When he penned the sentence "all men are by nature equally free and independent," he did not have his slaves in mind. He was doubtless invoking this principle of equality to argue that Americans were the equals of the British and could not be denied the liberties of British citizens. Other members of the Virginia legislature who debated his proposed bill were less sure of the meaning of the phrase. The discussion lengthened and became heated, and one impatient member reported that "a number of absurd or unmeaning alterations have been proposed" for that one line. The difficulty, specifically, was that some feared that the words could be construed to apply to slaves. These aristocratic slaveholders were finally put at ease by the addition of the phrase specifying that rights belonged only to people who had entered civil society. As one wrote, with relief, "Slaves, not being constituent members of our society, could never pretend to any benefit from such a maxim." They let Mason's sentence remain in the Virginia constitution, smug in their faith that it could not upset their slave-based society and economy.

One month later, the Declaration of Independence used essentially the same phrase about equality in its preamble, this time without the modifying clause about entering society. Most white people probably assumed, like Mason, that it referred to a comparison of American and British citizens. Two state constitutions also included the inspiring language about equality, again without modifying or limiting it as in Virginia. One was Pennsylvania, whose constitution drafters embraced some of the most radical thoughts about democracy and politics. The other was Massachusetts, whose framers were more cautious and ambivalent. In Massachusetts, debate on the meaning of equality filtered down to the level of town meetings; Massachusetts alone had decided that, to be a truly democratic document, the state constitution needed to be ratified town by town. So ordinary citizens had the opportunity to comment on the meaning of the sentence "All men are born free and equal." One town, Hardwick, sent back the suggestion that the sentence be reworded to read "All men, whites and blacks, are born free and equal." The suggestion fell on deaf ears.

The only other state to include language about equality in its constitution was Vermont, whose 1777 constitution explicitly made slavery illegal and based its logic on the equality phrase. (Vermont had almost no slaves within its borders. Its statehood was not recognized until 1791 because New York and New Hampshire, each of whom claimed the Vermont land as its own, had many friends in the Continental Congress.) This reluctance to adopt the phrase in state bills of rights and constitutions probably means that after 1776, its radical implications for domestic institutions, however unanticipated and unwelcomed, were being recognized.

Nevertheless, the ideals of the Revolution—natural equality, rights to life and liberty, republicanism—began to eat away at the institution of slavery. In some cases, enslaved blacks themselves challenged their legal status. In 1777, some Massachusetts slaves petitioned the state legislature, claiming a "natural & unalienable right to that freedom which the great Parent of the Universe hath bestowed equally on all mankind." They modestly asked for freedom for their children at age twenty-one and were turned down. In 1779, similar petitions in Connecticut and New Hampshire met with no success. Seven Massachusetts freemen, including the mariner brothers Paul and John Cuffe, refused to pay taxes for three years on the grounds that they could not vote and so were not represented. The Cuffe brothers landed in jail in 1780 for tax evasion, but their petition to the state legislature spurred the extension of suffrage to taxpaying free blacks in that state.

Another way to bring the issue before the lawmakers was to sue in court. In 1781, a Massachu-

PAUL CUFFE'S SILHOUETTE
Captain Paul Cuffe of Martha's Vineyard, off the Massachusetts coast, was the son of a Wampanoag Indian woman and an African father who had purchased his own freedom from a Quaker owner. Cuffe studied navigation and went to sea at age sixteen during the American Revolution (enduring several months of capture by the British). After the war, he and his brother petitioned for tax relief, a move that foreshadowed Cuffe's life of dedication to racial questions. In his thirty-year career as shipbuilder and master mariner, Captain Cuffe traveled extensively. By 1812, when this engraving with silhouette was made, Cuffe had explored the African country of Sierra Leone as a possible site for resettlement of American blacks and had met with African kings, English dukes, and an American president.
Library of Congress.

setts black man named Quok Walker ran away from his master, who pursued and beat him. Walker pressed charges for assault and battery, and his lawyers argued in court that he was in fact a free man, given the assertion in the Massachusetts constitution that "all men are born free and equal." Walker won the assault case and was set free, a decision confirmed in an appeal to the state's superior court in 1783. Several similar court cases followed, and by 1789 judges agreed that slavery had indeed been abolished by judicial decision in Massachusetts.

Pennsylvania was the first state to prohibit slavery by statute, in 1780. Gradual emancipation laws were passed in Rhode Island and Connecticut, in 1784; New York and New Jersey passed such laws in 1785 and 1786, respectively. Gradual emancipation illustrates the tension between radical and conservative implications of republican ideology. Republican government was designed to protect people's liberties and property; yet slaves were both people and property. Gradual emancipation balanced the civil rights of blacks and the property rights of their owners by delaying the promise of freedom. Most such laws declared that children born after a certain date would be free at a particular age, usually twenty-one or twenty-eight.

In the Upper South—Maryland and Virginia—general emancipation bills were debated and defeated. Slavery was too deeply entrenched and too important to the economy to abolish. However, legal restrictions were eased on individual acts of emancipation, under new manumission laws that governed private grants of freedom. Virginia's law passed in 1782, and two years later the number of free blacks in the state had doubled. Clearly, a significant number of white Virginians were struggling to square their consciences with revolutionary ideals. By 1790, close to ten thousand Virginia slaves had been freed under this law. Most remained in Virginia and formed free black communities complete with schools and churches, a visible alternative to the system of slavery.

> *Every state from Pennsylvania northward acknowledged that the enslavement of blacks was fundamentally inconsistent with revolutionary ideology; "all men are created equal" was beginning to acquire real force as a basic principle.*

Lawmakers in the Carolinas and Georgia never discussed liberalizing manumission, let alone emancipation. Freedom for slaves was unthinkable for Deep South whites. Yet more than ten thousand slaves from South Carolina—more than in all the northern states combined—achieved immediate freedom in 1783 by leaving with the British army from Charleston, and another six thousand set sail under the British flag from Savannah, Georgia. In sheer numbers alone, this was by far the largest emancipation of blacks in the entire country. Some went to Canada, some to England, and a small number relocated in the 1790s to Sierra Leone, on the west coast of Africa. Another three thousand made a similar escape with the British from New York. In both Charleston and New York, the British were extremely legalistic about who was entitled to go. Slaves belonging to loyalists were refused passage, as were slaves who had escaped from a master who happened to live within the British lines. The British intent in promising freedom during the war to some blacks was to inconvenience the enemy, not to liberate black men and women. This distinction tripped up a woman named Mercy, who fled her patriot owner in Westchester County, New York, only to be denied passage out of Manhattan with the British because her county had been held by the British since 1776.

Legal emancipation affected fewer blacks in the North, simply because there were fewer of them to begin with. Nevertheless, the symbolic importance of the North's gradual emancipation was enormous. Every state from Pennsylvania northward acknowledged that the enslavement of blacks was fundamentally inconsistent with revolutionary ideology; "all men are created equal" was beginning to acquire real force as a basic principle. On some level, southerners also understood this, but their inability to imagine a free biracial society prevented them from taking action. George Washington owned 390 slaves and freed not one of them in the 1780s, even when his friend the French general Lafayette urged him to do so as a model for others. (When Washington lived in Philadelphia as president in the 1790s, he brought house slaves with him, but he carefully rotated them back to Virginia to prevent any from remaining long enough to qualify as legal residents of a free state.) In his will, Washington provided for the eventual freedom of his slaves—but only after his wife, Martha, died. From the 1780s on, the North was associated with freedom and the South with slavery. This geographical pattern would have profound consequences for the next two centuries of American history.

All the states individually created constitutions and had them in place before the confederation ratified its Articles. Citizens looked primarily to their states for the blessings of liberty, for the right to self-rule, and for most government functions that affected their lives. The sharp variations that emerged in the state constitutions reflected a wide range of interpretations of republicanism. The differences—in voting rights, in slavery—did not cause much difficulty under the loose confederation government.

The Critical Period

Historians often refer to the years from 1781 to 1788 as "the critical period." A sense of crisis indeed gripped some—but not all—of the revolutionary leaders when they contemplated the inadequacies of the Articles of Confederation. The confederation government had been purposely constructed to be weak and secondary to state governments, but there were dangers in such weakness. Other leaders defended the weak Articles as the best guarantee of individual liberty, because the real issues of governance then were dealt with at the state level, closer to the people's inspection. Political theorizing about the proper relation among citizen, state, and confederation remained active and controversial throughout the decade as the new government confronted questions of finance, territorial expansion, and civil disorder.

Financial Chaos and Paper Money

Seven years of war produced a booming but chaotic economy in the 1780s. The confederation and the individual states had run up huge war debts, financed by printing paper money and borrowing from private sources. Some $400 to $500 million in paper currency had been injected into the economy, and prices and wages fluctuated wildly. Private debt and rapid expenditure flourished; why save money when it is plunging in value? Newspapers of the era bemoaned the rampant spending on imported luxury items—hats, silks, laces, china, rum, tea—indulged in even by ordinary people. Instead of celebrating a rising standard of living, some political economists of the 1780s warned that the economy was headed for a disastrous fall. Ordinary families knew that trouble was on the horizon too. Private debt actions quadrupled in many localities over the prewar levels, and debtors' prisons became crowded. Twenty-eight men in the Worcester, Massachusetts, county debtors' jail complained to the court one December of their "Suffering Condition Occasioned by the Rapid Augmentation of their Number, the Smallness of the Gaol,—and the Coldness of the Weather." A serious postwar depression settled in by the mid-1780s and did not lift until the 1790s.

Capable minds disagreed about the source of the depression. Some people blamed paper money for undermining the economy through turbulent inflation. By 1781, Continental dollars had lost almost all value: It took 146 of them to buy what a dollar had bought in 1775. Several state legislatures continued to print their own currency well into the 1780s. Rhode Island, where supporters of paper money gained control of the government in 1786, passed strict legal-tender laws requiring that the state currency be accepted at full face value, which was a real boon for debtors, who were mostly farmers. Creditors, who were most often big merchants, suffered; they called the state "Rogues' Island."

The confederation government was itself in a terrible financial fix in 1781, and desperate times required desperate measures. Six years earlier, a financial wizard from Philadelphia named Robert Morris had been a delegate to the Continental Congress. Morris had single-handedly bought huge amounts of supplies and equipment for the army

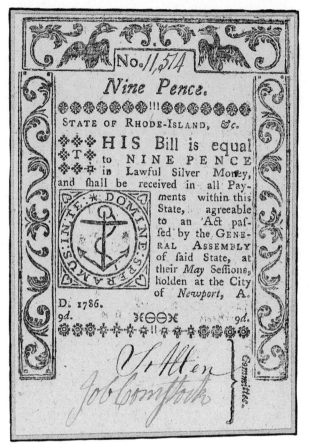

RHODE ISLAND MONEY
Rhode Island's paper money in 1786 stated directly on each bill that an act passed in May by the state assembly required the acceptance of such paper for all payments at face value.
Rhode Island Historical Society.

from overseas sources, fronting the money himself out of his considerable fortune and shipping in much-needed arms from the French (still nominally neutral in the war) disguised in crates addressed to his private Philadelphia firm. Morris resigned from the congress in 1778 under a cloud of suspicion that he had unfairly profited from his public service efforts; indeed, he left public life several million dollars richer than he had entered it, and the stark contrast between his riches—advertised by his fancy carriage, opulent clothes, and swank dinner parties—and the starving troops a few miles away at Valley Forge that winter was more than some could stomach.

But in 1781, the congress needed his financial services again, and Pennsylvania obliged by select-

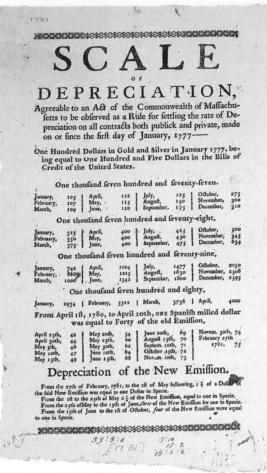

SCALE OF DEPRECIATION

This complicated chart shows the monthly value of United States Continental dollars from 1777 to February 1781, as stipulated by the government of Massachusetts. For example, in March 1780, it took $3,736 Continental dollars to equal the buying power of $100 in gold or silver, up from $3,322 the month before. Such a chart was needed when debtors and creditors settled accounts contracted at one point in time and paid off later in greatly depreciated dollars.
Courtesy, American Antiquarian Society.

ing him as a delegate to the congress. Morris accepted but made it a condition that he be allowed to pursue his private business simultaneously. From 1781 to 1784, Morris served as superintendent of finance for the confederation, applying his considerable talents to the confederation's economic problems. Not everyone was pleased. Mercy's husband, James Warren, wrote to John Adams: "Morris is a King, and more than a King. He has the Keys of the Treasury at his Command, Appropriates Money as

he pleases, and every Body must look up to him for Justice and for Favour."

Morris first sought a way to augment the revenue of the confederation government. He proposed a 5 percent impost—that is, a tax imposed on goods imported into the country. There was no authority in the Articles of Confederation for any such tax. States lucky enough to have port cities already collected their own impost, paid by the merchants who bought the duties cargoes; the merchants then passed the tax on to consumers in the form of higher prices for the goods. (Consumers in portless New Jersey, whose imported goods came through Philadelphia or New York, were thus involuntarily helping those neighbors to retire their state debt.) Morris's impost plan required a constitutional amendment to the Articles reached unanimously by the thirteen states. Despite general agreement that the financial situation of the central government was desperate, unanimous agreement proved impossible. In 1781, Morris came close, but not close enough. The states with bustling ports were reluctant to give up the right to impose their own taxes; Rhode Island, with its active wharves at Newport and Providence, absolutely refused to agree. When Morris pushed the impost amendment again in 1783, it was New York (whose premier port had just been newly freed from British occupation) that now refused.

Morris's next idea for shoring up the economy was the creation of a private bank, the Bank of North America, which would enjoy a special relationship with the confederation government. It would hold the government's hard-money deposits (insofar as there were any deposits to make) as well as private deposits, and it would make short-term loans to the government. Private investors owned the bank; specifically, Morris and three close friends bought 40 percent of the bank stock, and Morris also controlled the sizable chunk of stock held by the confederation government. The bank's contribution to economic stability came in the form of banknotes, pieces of paper inscribed with a dollar value. The fundamental difference between banknotes and paper money was that the banknotes were to be backed by hard money in the bank's vaults; thus, they would not depreciate. Morris invited any holder of a banknote to visit the bank and claim the hard money. In fact, however, more banknotes were issued than there was hard money; Morris was counting on the probability that relatively few people would test his claim—it was enough that people had confidence it was true. Morris hoped that the new circulating medium of banknotes would perform the functions of paper money without any of its drawbacks. Congress agreed and voted to approve the bank in 1781.

The Bank of North America, located in Philadelphia, had limited success curing the confederation's economic woes. In the short run, the bank supplied the government with a currency that held its value, but it issued so little that the impact remained very small. The bank enriched Morris and his associates and made enemies among other financial interests in Philadelphia; when its charter expired in 1786, the state of Pennsylvania refused to renew it. By that time, Morris was out of the Continental Congress because of a three-year limit for holding office. Morris continued to be active in politics well into the 1790s, but he lost all his wealth in a complete financial reversal and ended his career in debtors' prison.

If Morris could not resuscitate the economy in the 1780s, probably no one could have. Because the Articles of Confederation reserved most economic functions to the states, congress was helpless to tax trade, control inflation, curb the flow of state-issued paper money, or pay the mounting public debt. But the confederation had acquired one source of potential enormous wealth: the huge territory ceded by Virginia, which in 1784 became the national domain.

Land Ordinances and the Northwest Territory

The Continental Congress appointed Thomas Jefferson to draft a policy for handling the national domain. Jefferson embraced this task as an unparalleled opportunity to embed an extravagant version of revolutionary ideals, highlighting rationalism and economic democracy, into the permanent landscape of America. He proposed dividing the territory north of the Ohio River and east of the Mississippi—called the Northwest Territory—into ten new states. Each state would be subdivided into townships ten miles square, and each township would consist of one hundred sections one mile square. Jefferson became so enamored of his decimal-based brainchild that he even proposed to lengthen the mile to make one square mile equal to 1,000 acres; the traditional square mile contains 640 acres.

Three other features of Jefferson's proposal illustrate how innovative this precision-minded, scientific intellectual from Virginia could be. First, he

THOMAS JEFFERSON
This miniature shows Thomas Jefferson at age forty-five, during his years as a diplomat in Paris. The American artist John Trumbull visited France in 1788 and painted Jefferson's likeness in this five-by-four-inch format so he could later copy it into his planned large canvas depicting the signing of the Declaration of Independence. Jefferson requested three replicas of the miniature to bestow as gifts, a common and intimate item of exchange. One went to his daughter Martha, another to an American woman in London, and the third to Maria Cosway, a British artist of whom the widower Jefferson had grown very fond during his stay in France.
Monticello.

advocated giving the land to settlers, rather than selling it, on the grounds that the improved lands would so enrich the country through property taxes over the years that there was no need to make the settlers contribute to the government's coffers twice. His aim was to encourage rapid and democratic settlement of the land, to build a nation of freeholders (as opposed to renters), and to avoid speculative frenzy. Second, Jefferson insisted that the new states have representative governments enjoying equal

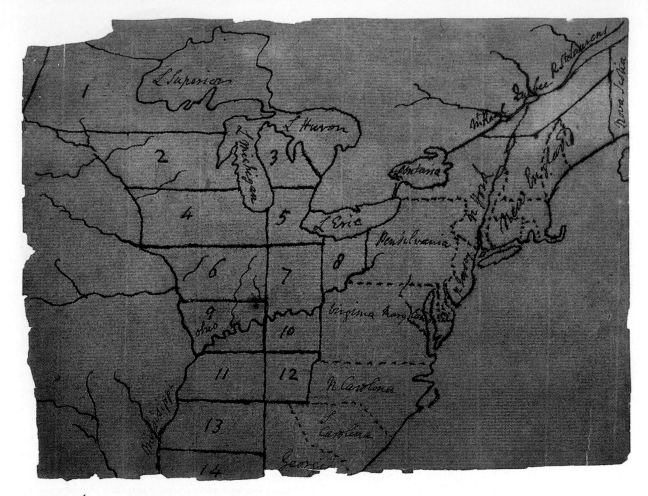

JEFFERSON'S MAP OF THE NORTHWEST TERRITORY
Thomas Jefferson sketched out borders for ten new states in his initial plan for the Northwest Territory in 1784. Straight lines and right angles held a strong appeal for him. But such regularity ignored inconvenient geographical features like rivers and even more inconvenient political features like Indian territorial claims, most unlikely to be ceded by treaty in orderly blocks of land. Jefferson also submitted ten distinctive names for the states. Number 9, for example, was Polypotamia, or "land of many rivers" in Greek.
William L. Clements Library.

status with the original states once they reached a certain minimum population. The United States had freed itself from a colonial empire, and Jefferson did not want the new nation to become a colonial power itself. Finally, Jefferson's draft prohibited slavery and involuntary servitude from all of the ten new states.

The congress cheerfully adopted parts of Jefferson's plan in the Ordinance of 1784: the rectangular grid, the decimal mile, and the ten states, which Jefferson proposed naming Sylvania, Michi-

gania, Cherronesus, Assenisipia, Metropotamia, Illinoia, Washington, Saratoga, Polypotamia, and Pelisipia. (The congress's 1784 legislation simply ignored the names, a telling reminder that Thomas Jefferson's suggestions were sometimes rejected.) The congress accepted the guarantee of self-government and equality with the original states, although there was some grumbling about wild frontiersmen who perhaps were not worthy of self-government. What the congress found too radical to swallow was the proposal to give away the land;

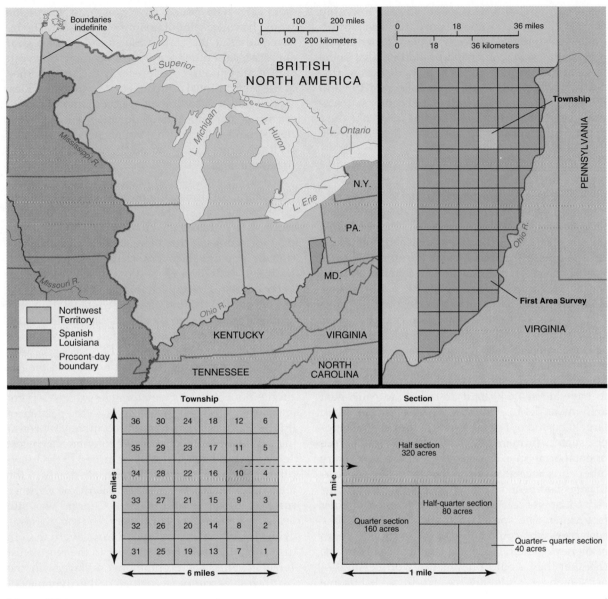

M A P **8.2**
The Northwest Territory and Ordinance of 1785
Surveyors mapping the eastern edge of the Northwest Territory followed the Land Ordinance of
1785, using the stars as well as polls and chains (standard surveying equipment) to run long
boundary lines. The result was a blanket of six-mile square townships, further subdivided into
one-mile squares containing sixteen forty-acre farms.

the national domain was the confederated government's only source of independent wealth. And the slavery prohibition failed to be included by only one state's vote.

A year later, the congress reconsidered the land act and passed a new version, called the Ordinance of 1785. The decimal theme and the stretched-out mile, though intellectually elegant, were too impractical. The new plan called for walkable townships six miles square, each containing thirty-six sections; a one-mile section was once again 640 acres, and a quarter section offered an adequate-sized farm of 160 acres. One lot in each township was set aside for educational purposes. The 1785 ordinance also revised Jefferson's plan for ten neatly rectangular states, after it was noticed that some would have no river access at all, a disastrous disadvantage. The new ordinance called for three to five states whose boundaries would conform to natural geographical features like the Great Lakes and major rivers instead of abstractly drawn survey lines.

Imposing a relentlessly regular township grid on the irregular hills, valleys, rivers, and lakes of the Northwest Territory created more solvable problems. Though even in size, the land squares were not all equally valuable. How should they be priced for sale? The 1785 ordinance established land offices to sell the land at public auction; the minimum price was $1 an acre, but the auction mechanism allowed for market forces to drive up the prices of the most desirable land. Two further restrictions applied: Land was sold in minimum parcels of 640 acres each, and payment had to be in hard money or in certificates of debt issued by the confederation government.

To join in the land boom, a purchaser thus had to have at least 640 hard dollars or an equivalent amount in debt certificates. These certificates had largely passed out of the hands of the original holders, such as farmers who had sold food to the Continental army in exchange for the IOUs. Like every other currency substitute in the war years, debt certificates had been circulated, depreciated, and purchased by speculators at a small fraction of their face value. The speculators tended to be wealthy easterners who could afford to tie up a modest sum of money in the depreciated certificates, taking the risk that they would plummet to worthlessness— or somehow suddenly be worth a handsome amount. The Land Ordinance of 1785 made good their bet.

Even before the land was surveyed, the congress, gravely in need of revenue, sold one and a half million acres to a group of investors called the Ohio Company. Speculators who rushed to purchase usually had no intention of settling on the land themselves but were holding it for subsequent resale. They could thus avoid direct contact with the most serious obstacle to speedy settlement of the Northwest Territory: the dozens of Indian tribes that occupied the land. Treaties signed at Fort Stanwix in 1784 and Fort McIntosh in 1785 coerced partial cessions of land from Iroquois, Delaware, Huron, and Miami tribes, but a united Indian meeting near

Detroit in 1786 issued an ultimatum: No cession would be valid without unanimous consent. The Indians advised the United States to "prevent your surveyors and other people from coming upon our side of the Ohio river"—precisely the land claimed as the new national domain. For two more decades, violent and terrible Indian wars in Ohio and Indiana would continue to impede settlement, as the nation struggled to find an Indian policy consistent with the drive to cash in on the wealth of the national domain.

In 1787, a third land act, called the Northwest Ordinance, confirmed the promise of eventual self-government when the white male population reached five thousand, but it devised an interim plan for sparsely settled territories with a congressionally appointed governor. The other landmark feature of the 1787 act was a prohibition on slavery in the entire region, which this time passed without any debate. For the first time, the confederation government presumed to dictate the domestic institutions of a part of the United States. The congress would not have dreamed of applying a similar prohibition to an existing state, but nothing in the Articles restricted the congress's power over new territories not yet states. Something less than a fervent antislavery sentiment was at work in the passage of this provision, as shown by an accompanying warning that fugitive slaves escaping into the Northwest Territory could be caught and returned to their lawful owners. And the prohibition applied only to the area north of the Ohio River; plenty of territory south of the river and west of Georgia was still available for the spread of slavery. The congress was evidently less interested in curbing slavery than in discouraging blacks from coming to the Northwest Territory. Still, the prohibition on slavery in the Northwest Territory perpetuated the dynamic of gradual emancipation in the North: A North-South sectionalism, based on slavery, was slowly taking shape.

Shays's Rebellion

Without an impost amendment, the confederation turned to the states to contribute revenue voluntarily. The states were struggling with their own war debts; since heavy taxation tends to create disgruntled constituents, some legislatures were hesitant to push too hard. There were some who favored heavy taxation: The holders of the public debt certificates wanted to be paid, and wealthy people in general hoped taxation would counteract the alarming depreciation of paper money that was eroding their net worth. But the vast majority of ordinary Americans preferred low taxes, cheap money, easy credit, and stay laws (laws restraining creditors from foreclosing on debtors). And popularly elected representatives, facing annual elections, liked to give people what they wanted.

Western farmers had learned from their experience in the American Revolution how to respond to oppressive taxation.

Massachusetts, however, had a tough-minded, fiscally conservative upper house with veto power over its lower house. The upper house, dominated by the commercial centers of eastern Massachusetts, vetoed the cheap-money legislation the lower house tried to pass. Its goal was to retire the state debt by raising taxes; to make matters worse, the upper house insisted that taxes be paid in hard money, not cheap paper. Farmers in the western half of the state found such taxes nearly impossible to pay, and by 1786 sheriffs routinely descended on tax delinquents to confiscate their salable property (such as livestock), foreclose on their real estate, and ultimately throw them in jail.

However, the western farmers had learned from their experience in the American Revolution how to respond to oppressive taxation. They called conventions to discuss their grievances and circulated petitions demanding tax reductions and debt relief legislation. At least eight towns called for the abolition of the profession of law, since sharp lawyers seemed to be lurking everywhere, handling foreclosure and jailing proceedings as well as dominating the legislature. As more and more defaulting taxpayers were hauled into court for nonpayment, groups of men marched on the county courthouses to shut them down. In the fall of 1786, armed men threatened the courts in three western Massachusetts counties. The leader of this tax revolt was a farmer and onetime captain in the Continental army, Daniel Shays; about 2,500 other men joined him in arms, while many more attended the town conventions and cheered the Shaysites from the sidelines.

The governor of Massachusetts, James Bowdoin, who had once organized protests against British taxes, did not hesitate now to characterize the Shaysites as illegal rebels and to call out the militia. Another former rebel, Samuel Adams, took the

lead in defining the protest movement as a treasonous rebellion: "County conventions and popular committees served an excellent purpose when they were first in practice," he wrote. "But as we now have constitutional and regular governments and all our men in authority depend upon the annual and free elections of the people, we are safe without them." Safe without them—and apparently unsafe with them, for Adams took the extreme position that "the man who dares rebel against the laws of a republic ought to suffer death."

Why did the protesting farmers so upset the aging tax protesters of an earlier era? The Shaysites were a threat to men like Adams and Bowdoin because their very existence challenged the idea that popularly elected governments would always be fair and just. The revolutionary generation, and particularly its most democratically inclined members, had given little thought to the possibility that popular majorities, embodied in a state legislature, could be oppressive, just as monarchs could. The farmers now felt they were an oppressed minority in Massachusetts with no hope of altering the composition of the state legislature (especially given its dominance by the eastern seaboard population cen-

SILVER BOWL FOR ANTI-SHAYS GENERAL
The militia of Springfield in western Massachusetts presented its leader, General William Shepard, with this silver bowl to honor his victory over the insurgents in Shays's Rebellion. Presentational silver conveyed a double message. It announced gratitude and praise in engraved words, and it transmitted considerable monetary value in the silver itself. General Shepard could display his trophy on a shelf, use it as a punch bowl, will it to descendants to keep his famous moment alive in memory, or melt it down in hard times. Not only is Shepard's name commemorated on the silver; SHAYS too appears in the last line, there for the ages to remember.
Yale University Art Gallery, Mabel Brady Garvan Collection.

ters). Adams's advice that they wait patiently until the next election did not begin to give them hope.

Bowdoin sent more than four thousand soldiers to quell the rebellion, paying them with money raised quickly and privately among worried eastern seaboard merchants. The militia met the protesters at Springfield in January 1787 and dispersed the ragtag dissidents back to their homes. The leaders fled the state, but more than a thousand men were rounded up and thrown in jail. The legislature passed the Disqualifying Act prohibiting the rebels from ever again voting, holding public office, working as schoolmasters, or operating taverns. The first two prohibitions denied the men a political voice, and the second two denied them occupations in which they could instruct or influence others.

Samuel Adams's absolute faith in republican institutions made him recoil from the Shaysites; men from the opposite and more conservative side of the political spectrum recoiled for very different reasons. The men of wealth who chipped in to pay for the militia worried that a dangerous leveling influence was at work. In Massachusetts and throughout the country, men who were already worried that the confederation might fail to hold together speculated about what Shays's Rebellion portended. Perhaps there were similar "combustibles" in other states, awaiting the spark that would set off a dreadful political conflagration. Lawyer and diplomat John Jay in New York wrote to George Washington, "Our affairs seem to lead to some crisis, some revolution—something I cannot foresee or conjecture. I am uneasy and apprehensive; more so than during the war." Planter Charles Pinckney of South Carolina characterized the threat as one of "anarchy—or what's worse, pure democracy." For such men, it was entirely possible to be a supporter of republican government and still disdain a democracy based on majority rule. Benjamin Franklin, in his eighties, shrewdly observed that in 1776 Americans had feared "an excess of power in the rulers," whereas now the problem was "a defect of obedience" in the subjects. A merchant in Philadelphia saw more ominous implications in the fears inspired by domestic insurrection: "A Convulsion of some kind seems to be desirable," he wrote, for it is "the only chance we have of restoration to political health."

The years of unstable finances were of course directly related to the cause of Shays's Rebellion. Rigid efforts to pay off a state debt, in an economy already hit with the burdens of a precarious cur-

rency, had ignited a spark of tax rebellion again, producing an ironic predicament for old rebels now taking a hard line against civil disorder. To some, the sense of crisis in the confederation had greatly deepened.

The Federal Constitution

Events in the fall of 1786 provoked an odd mixture of fear and hope that the government under the Articles of Confederation was losing its grip on power. Efforts to augment the financial powers of the government had nearly ground to a halt, and some people worried that the country would have to hit bottom before fully realizing the crisis it was in. A small circle of Virginians decided to try one last time to augment the powers of the Articles. Their call for a meeting to discuss trade regulation led, more quickly than they could have imagined in 1786, to a total reworking of the national government.

From Annapolis to Philadelphia

The Virginians took their lead from James Madison, now thirty-five years old and still a bachelor with time on his hands. Madison was the eldest son of a wealthy planter from the Piedmont region of Virginia. A Princeton graduate, bookish and solitary by nature, Madison was a bright and avid student of politics. He entered active political life as a member of Virginia's extralegal assembly in 1776 and found that it suited him; by 1779, he had been chosen to represent his state at the Continental Congress. His father's money and his lack of dependents freed him from the obligations that made other delegates yearn to get back to private life. After four diligent years in the congress, he returned to the Virginia assembly, where he tried hard to secure his state's cooperation in keeping the Confederation afloat.

Madison's strategy was to prompt the states to consider a relatively modest modification of the Articles, giving the congress power to regulate trade. He persuaded the Virginia legislature to call for a meeting of the states, bypassing the confederation's congress. Even if unsuccessful, such a meeting would establish a precedent for new pathways to alter the Articles. State legislatures were invited to send representatives to the meeting, set for Annapolis, Maryland, in September 1786.

JAMES MADISON,
PORTRAIT BY CHARLES WILLSON PEALE
This miniature portrait was made of James Madison in
1783 when he was in his early thirties. The natural hair
and smooth face emphasized his youthful looks.
Library of Congress.

Only five of the nine states that agreed to participate actually sent representatives. Like Madison, the dozen men who attended were deeply troubled by a sense of impending crisis. They decided to reschedule the meeting for Philadelphia in May 1787, again inviting the state legislatures to reappoint representatives. One representative, lawyer Alexander Hamilton of New York, defined the agenda of the meeting much more ambitiously: "to devise such further provisions as shall appear to them necessary to render the constitution of the Federal Government adequate to the exigencies of the Union."

Alexander Hamilton by character was suited for such bold steps. Only thirty years old, he had risen far and fast through a series of bold undertakings. The bright son of a struggling single mother on a small West Indies island, Hamilton at age sixteen impressed an American trader, who rescued him from obscurity and sent him to school first in

New Jersey and then King's College (soon renamed Columbia College) in New York City. Hamilton was nineteen when the Continental army swept through in 1776, and the youth joined General Washington's staff and served at the great man's side through much of the Revolution. After the war, Hamilton studied law, married into a wealthy New York mercantile family, and sat in the Continental Congress for two years. Despite his stigmatized childhood, he identified fully with the elite classes and their fear of democratic disorder.

Support for Hamilton's expanded agenda for the Philadelphia meeting was augmented by the urgent crisis unfolding that fall in Massachusetts, Shays's Rebellion. Some states worried that the confederated government lacked authority to quell domestic rebellions and so welcomed major revisions to the Articles. Others worried about the dangers of major revisions and so sent representatives to scuttle revisionist efforts. The ambitious scope of the Hamilton agenda thus ensured a good turnout of delegates. States that could ignore a pesky proposal on trade regulation could not afford to ignore this meeting. After five months, the congress of the confederation government reluctantly endorsed the Philadelphia meeting, limiting the agenda to "the sole and express purpose of revising the Articles of Confederation."

It took more than a week for a quorum to assemble in Philadelphia. Meanwhile, Madison and the other Virginians settled into lodging houses and used the time to draw up a fifteen-point plan for a completely restructured federal government. They intended to seize the initiative at the convention and keep it.

The fifty-five men who assembled at Philadelphia that spring to consider the shortcomings of the Articles of Confederation were by no means a representative cross section of Americans, or even of the political leadership of the states. They were generally those most concerned about weaknesses in the present government. Alexander Hamilton, for example, lobbied to be a delegate to Philadelphia; the New York legislature warily sent him, but in the company of two firm opponents of fundamental revisions to the Articles, so that his vote would not carry the delegation. In general, however, few attended who were unalterably opposed to revising the Articles. Patrick Henry, author of the Virginia Resolves in 1765 and more recently the governor of his state, refused to go, saying he "smelled a rat." Rhode Island, ever the odd state out in the 1780s,

States Constitution. Proponents of the competing plans pooled the plans' common features—a government with three branches and supreme power over the states—and agreed on a bicameral legislature in which the lower house, the House of Representatives, would be apportioned by population and the upper house, called the Senate, would represent each state. But instead of one vote per state in the upper house, as the New Jersey Plan favored, the compromise plan provided two senators who voted independently of each other.

Representation by population turned out to be an ambiguous concept once it was subjected to rigorous discussion. Who counted? Were slaves, for example, people or property? As people, they added weight to the southern delegations in the House of Representatives, but as property they added to the tax burdens of those states. What emerged was the remarkable compromise known as the three-fifths clause: All free persons plus "three-fifths of all other Persons" constituted the numerical base for the apportionment of representatives.

Using "all other persons" as a euphemism for slaves indicates the discomfort delegates felt in acknowledging the existence of slavery in a republican document. The words *slave* and *slavery* appear nowhere in the Constitution, but the slave labor system figured in two other places in addition to the three-fifths clause. Trade regulation, for example, a power of the new Congress, naturally included regulation of the slave trade. South Carolina and Georgia delegates wanted assurance that the slave trade would not be curbed by a coalition of northern free states combining with Maryland and Virginia, two slave states with an abundance of native-born slaves. The result was another compromise, again in euphemistic language: "The Migration or Importation of such Persons as any of the States now shall think proper to admit, shall not be prohibited by the Congress prior to the Year one thousand eight hundred and eight." A third provision on slavery guaranteed the return of fugitive slaves: "No person, held to Service or Labour in one State, under the Laws thereof, escaping into another, shall, in Consequence of any Law or Regulation therein, be discharged from such Service or Labour but shall be delivered up on Claim of the party to whom such Service or Labour may be due." Slavery was nowhere named, but it was recognized, guaranteed, and thereby perpetuated by the U.S. Constitution.

Plenty of fine-tuning followed the Great Compromise of mid-July, but the most difficult problem —that of representation—had been solved. The small states worked to consolidate power in the Senate, where their weight would be proportionately greater than in the lower house, and Madison slowly recovered from the crushing sense of defeat he experienced at first. He had entered the convention convinced that the major flaw in the old government was that it had relied on unreliable states, and he feared that the Great Compromise perpetuated that flaw. But as the respective powers of the House and Senate were hammered out, he lent his support to the package as the most reasonable of political outcomes. After the convention, he would become one of the most prominent defenders of the Constitution, Senate and all.

Democracy versus Republicanism

In deciding the crucial details of the Constitution, the delegates made a distinction between democracy and republicanism that had been absent from the political vocabulary a decade earlier. When state constitutions were written, the two words were often used interchangeably to refer to a government that rested ultimately on popular consent. At the Philadelphia convention, however, pure democracy was taken to be a dangerous thing. As a Connecticut delegate put it, "The people . . . should have as little to do as may be about the Government. They want [lack] information and are constantly liable to be misled." A Massachusetts delegate declared that "the evils we experience flow from the excess of democracy." Edmund Randolph of Virginia similarly criticized "the turbulence and follies of democracy." The delegates still claimed to favor republican institutions, but they created a government that gave direct voice to the people only in the House and that granted a check on that voice to the Senate, which would be composed of men more removed from the control of the people.

In the final document, senators held office for six years and had the privilege of unlimited reelection. They were to be elected not by direct popular vote but by the state legislatures. In a country that was itself only eleven years old, a guaranteed six years in office was a very long time. Senators were thus protected from the whims of democratic majorities; the men at Philadelphia assumed that tumultuous, fickle passion characterized democracies. Long terms also fostered experience and maturity in office. Madison and the other men who had served in the confederation congress had seen the ineptitude and inconvenience caused by the revolving door concept of public service.

Similarly, the presidency evolved during the Philadelphia convention into a powerful office out of the reach of direct democracy. The delegates devised an elaborate mechanism, called the electoral college, whose only function was to elect the president and vice president. Each state's legislature chose the electors, amounting in number to the sum of representatives and senators for each state, an interesting melding of the two principles of representation. What resulted was a president who owed his office not to the Congress, the states, or the people, but to an ephemeral body of distinguished citizens who could vote their own judgment on the candidates.

Madison's proposal to grant the new government sweeping powers in all areas where the states were incompetent was too vague to survive debate. Instead, the convention carefully listed the powers of Congress and of the president. The president could initiate policy and propose legislation; he could veto acts of Congress; he could command the military and direct the foreign policy of the country; and he could make appointments to numerous lesser executive offices and to the entire judiciary, subject only to the approval of the Senate. Congress held the purse strings: the power to levy taxes, to regulate trade, and to coin money and control the currency. States were expressly forbidden to issue paper money. Two further powers of Congress—to "provide for the common defence and general Welfare" of the country and "to make all laws which shall be necessary and proper" for carrying out the enumerated powers—provided elastic language that came closest to Madison's wish to grant sweeping powers to the new government.

The framers had developed a far more complex form of a federal government than that provided by the Articles of Confederation. In curbing the excesses of democracy, they did not assume that states and their leaders would always be virtuous and wise. They devised a government with limits and checks on all branches. They set forth a powerful president who could veto Congress, but then gave Congress power to override his vetoes. They set up a national judiciary to settle disputes between states and citizens of different states. They made each branch of government as independent from every other branch as they could, by basing election on different universes of voters—voting citizens, state legislators, the electoral college.

The Constitution was a product of lengthy debate and compromise; no one was entirely satisfied with every line. Madison himself, who was later called the Father of the Constitution, remained unsure that the most serious flaws of the Articles had been expunged. But when the final vote was taken at the Philadelphia convention in September 1787, only three dissenters refused to endorse the Constitution. The thirty-nine who signed it (thirteen others had gone home early) no doubt wondered how to sell this plan, with its powerful executive and Congress and its deliberate limits on pure democracy, to the American public. The Constitution specified a mechanism for ratification that avoided the dilemma faced earlier by the confederation government: Nine states, not all thirteen, had to ratify it, and special ratifying conventions instead of state legislatures would make the crucial decision. The innovation of debating the Constitution in special bodies elected only for that purpose had been used once before, for the Massachusetts state constitution. It drew attention to a major theme of the proposed plan: that the national government was no longer a league of states, but a government for all the people. Equally important practical considerations motivated the choice of popular ratifying conventions: No one could expect state legislatures to cede their powers willingly to the new government, so it was convenient to bypass them entirely. But who could predict how the people, acting through the ratifying conventions, would react?

Ratification of the Constitution

Had a popular vote been taken on the Constitution in the late fall of 1787, it would probably have been rejected. In the three most populous states—Virginia, Massachusetts, and New York—substantial majorities opposed a powerful new national government. North Carolina and Rhode Island refused to call conventions. In only a few of the eight remaining states could the proponents of the Constitution count on an easy victory. To secure the agreement of nine states, they faced a formidable task.

The Federalists

The proponents of the Constitution plotted their course carefully and moved into action swiftly. To silence the charge that they had illegally bypassed the confederation government (which indeed they had, by failing to adhere to the legal procedure for

Was the New United States a Christian Country?

REBECCA SAMUEL, a Jewish resident of Virginia, conveyed her excitement about the new U.S. Constitution when she wrote her German parents in 1791 that finally "Jew and Gentile are as one" in the realm of politics and citizenship. Other voices were distinctly less favorable. An Antifederalist pamphlet warned that the pope could become president; another feared that "a Turk, a Jew, a Roman Catholic, and what is worse than all, a Universalist, may be President."

The document that produced such wildly different readings was indeed remarkable in its handling of religion. The Constitution did not invoke Christianity as a state religion. It made no reference to an almighty being, and it specifically promised, in Article 6, section 3, that "no religious test shall ever be required as a qualification to any office or public trust under the United States." The six largest congregations of Jews—numbering about two thousand and located in Newport, New York, Philadelphia, Baltimore, Charleston, and Savannah—were delighted with this nearly unprecedented statement of political equality and wrote George Washington to express their hearty thanks.

But more than a few Christian leaders were stunned at the Constitution's near silence on religion. It seemed to represent a complete turnabout from the state constitutions of the 1770s and 1780s. A New Yorker warned that, "should the Citizens of America be as irreligious as her Constitution, we will have reason to tremble, lest the Governor of the universe . . . crush us to atoms." A delegate to North Carolina's ratifying convention played on anti-immigrant fears by predicting that the Constitution was "an invitation for Jews and pagans of every kind to come among us." A concerned Presbyterian minister asked Alexander Hamilton why God was not in the Constitution, and Hamilton reportedly quipped, "Indeed, Doctor, we forgot it."

Measured against the practices of state governments, Hamilton's observation is hardly credible. The men who wrote and debated the state and federal constitutions from 1775 to 1787 actively thought about principles of inclusion and exclusion when they defined citizenship, voting rights, and office-holding. They carefully considered property ownership, race, gender, and age in formulating rules about who could participate. And they also thought about religious qualifications.

Most leaders of the 1780s took for granted that Christianity was the one true faith and the essential foundation of morality. All but two state constitutions assumed the primacy of Protestantism, and a third of them collected public taxes to support Christian churches. Every state but New York required a Christian oath as a condition for office-holding. For example, every member of Pennsylvania's legislature swore to "acknowledge the Scripture of the Old and New Testament to be given by divine inspiration." North Carolina's rule was even more restrictive, since it omitted Catholics: "No person who shall deny the being of God or the truth of the Protestant religion, or the divine authority of the Old or New Testaments" could hold office. In South Carolina all *voters* had to be Protestants.

Other common political practices affirmed that the United States was a Christian country. Governors proclaimed days of public thanksgiving in the name of the Holy Trinity; chaplains led legislatures in Christian prayer. Jurors and witnesses in court swore to Christian oaths. New England states passed Sabbath laws prohibiting all work or travel on Sunday. Blasphemy laws punished people who cursed the Christian God or Jesus.

These laws and customs continued, even though close to half the state constitutions included the right to freedom of religion as an explicit guarantee. But freedom of religion meant only that difference would be tolerated; it did not guarantee political equality.

How then did the U.S. Constitution come to be such a break from the immediate past? Had the framers really just forgotten about religion?

Not James Madison of Virginia. Madison arrived at the 1787 convention fresh from a hard-won victory in Virginia to establish religious liberty. At the end of 1786, he had finally secured passage of a bill written by Thomas Jefferson seven years earlier, called the Virginia Statute of Religious Freedom. "All men shall be free to profess, and by argument to maintain, their opinions in matters of religion, and that the same shall in no wise diminish, enlarge, or affect their civil capacities," the bill read. Madison had convinced both the Episco-

palians and the Baptist dissenters, at war with each other over state support, that to grant either or even both churches tax money would be to concede to the state forever the authority to endorse one religion—and by implication to crush another. The statute separated church from state to protect religion. Further, it went beyond mere toleration to guarantee that religious choice was independent of civil rights. Jefferson was proud that his law protected "the Jew and the Gentile, the Christian and Mahometan, the Hindoo, and infidel of every denomination."

In Madison's judgment, it was best for the U.S. Constitution to say as little as possible about religion, especially since state laws reflected a variety of positions. When Antifederalists demanded a bill of rights, Madison drew up a list for the First Congress to consider. Two items dealt with religion, but only one was approved. One became part of the First Amendment: "Congress shall make no law respecting an establishment of religion, or prohibiting the free exercise thereof." In a stroke, Madison set

religious worship and the privileging of any one church beyond Congress's power. Significantly, his second proposal failed to pass: "No State shall violate the equal rights of conscience." Evidently, the states wanted to be able to keep their Christian-only rules without federal interference. Different faiths would be tolerated—but not guaranteed equal standing. And the very same session of Congress proceeded to hire Christian chaplains and proclaim days of thanksgiving.

Gradually, states deleted restrictive laws, but as late as 1840, Jews still could not hold public office in four states. Into the twentieth century, some states maintained Sunday laws that forced business closings on the Christian Sabbath, working enormous hardship on those whose religion required Saturday closings. The guarantee of freedom of religion was embedded in state and federal founding documents in the 1770s and 1780s, but it has taken many years to fulfill Jefferson's vision of what true religious liberty meant: the freedom for religious belief to be independent of civil status.

amending the government and overstepping their charge to revise only the Articles), they sent the new document to the Continental Congress for approval. The congress, at first reluctant, finally resolved to send the Constitution to the states for their consideration. It helped that James Madison was then a member of the congress and was able to speak persuasively for the plan.

Had a popular vote been taken on the Constitution in the late fall of 1787, it would probably have been rejected.

The pro-Constitution forces shrewdly secured another advantage by calling themselves Federalists. By all logic, this label was more suitable for the backers of the confederation concept, since the Latin root of the word *federal* means "league." The new Federalists, however, preempted the term and its positive Revolutionary-era associations and applied it to a comparatively nonfederalist plan to diminish the power of the states in a national government. Their opponents cast around for a label to identify themselves; Republican Federalist was tried, but that was too close to their opponents' name. In the end, they became known as Antifederalists, a label that made them sound defensive and negative, lacking a program of their own.

The Federalists identified the states most likely to ratify quickly, and they immediately scheduled special local elections to select delegates to ratifying conventions in those states. Delaware managed to push through elections, convention, and unanimous ratification by early December, before the Antifederalists had barely begun a campaign. Pennsylvania, New Jersey, and Georgia quickly followed. In the latter two states, voter turnout was extremely low; apathy favored the Federalists. These early victories established a Federalist momentum that enhanced their chances for further success.

Delaware and New Jersey were small and relatively weak states that lived in the shadows of more powerful neighbors; a government that would regulate trade and set taxes according to population was an attractive proposition to them. Georgia had a different reason for favoring a powerful national government: It sat at the southernmost end of the country, bordered by hostile Indians and Spanish Florida. "If a weak State with the Indians on its back and the Spaniards on its flank does not see the ne-

cessity of a General Government there must I think be wickedness or insanity in the way," said Federalist George Washington.

Another three states to ratify with relative ease were Connecticut, Maryland, and South Carolina. As in Pennsylvania, merchants, lawyers, and urban artisans in general favored the new Constitution, as did large landowners and slaveholders. This tendency for the established political elite to be Federalist enhanced the prospects of Federalist victory, for they already had power disproportionate to their numbers. Antifederalists in these states tended to be rural, western and noncommercial, men whose access to news was limited and whose participation in state government was tenuous.

Massachusetts was the only early state to ratify in which the Federalists encountered difficulty. The popular vote gave a twenty-delegate advantage to the Antifederalists, whose strength came mainly from the western areas, home to Shays's Rebellion. Easterners opposed it too: Mercy Otis Warren weighed in with her Antifederalist pamphlet, authored by "a Columbian Patriot," a sustained analysis of the dangers of corruption invited by the proposed government. One rural delegate from the town of Sutton voiced widely shared suspicions: "These lawyers and men of learning and money men that talk so finely, and gloss over matters so smoothly, to make us poor illiterate people swallow down the pill, expect to get into Congress themselves; they expect to be the managers of the Constitution and get all the power and all the money into their own hands, and then they will swallow up all us little folks." But another delegate from Berkshire County, in the western part of the state, showed signs of compromise: "I am a plain man . . . not used to speak in public," he began. But he had read the Constitution "over and over. I had been a member of the convention to form our own state constitution, and had learnt something of the checks and balances of power, and I found them all here. . . . These men of learning are all embarked on the same cause with us, and we must all sink or swim together, and shall we throw the Constitution overboard because it does not please us alike?" The Antifederalist lead was slowly eroded by a vigorous newspaper campaign. The final vote in the early 1788 ratifying convention was 187 to 168; it was the closest squeak yet for the Federalists. The victory was accomplished only with promises that amendments to the Constitution suggested by the Massachusetts Antifederalists would be taken up at the first Congress.

THE TENSIONS OF 1787
A New Haven engraver named Amos Doolittle captured the tensions of 1787. A wagon named
Connecticut *sinks in the mud. To the left, under sunshine, men spouting nationalist ideas try to*
pull it out: "Pay Commutation" (pensions to veteran officers), "Comply with Congress." To the
right, under severe weather, localist men call out "Tax Luxury," "Success to Shays," and "The
People Are Opres'd."
The Connecticut Historical Society, Hartford.

By May 1788, eight states had ratified; only one more was needed. The Federalists knew that North Carolina and Rhode Island were hopeless, and New Hampshire looked nearly as bleak. More worrisome was their failure to win over the largest and most important states. Because Virginia and New York both had articulate and prominent Antifederalist leaders, the goal in those states was to move slowly and overcome the opposition by forceful debate. It was in those states that the Antifederalists emerged distinctly and coherently as opponents of the Constitution.

The Antifederalists

Antifederalists were a composite group, united mainly in their desire to block the Constitution. A good part of Antifederalist strength came from rural and backcountry sources, in areas with a long tradition of suspicion of the motives of the eastern elites. Yet clearly many Antifederalist leaders came from the same social background as Federalist leaders; economic class alone did not differentiate them. Antifederalism drew strength in states already on a sure economic footing, like New York, that could afford to remain independent entities. Probably the biggest appeal of antifederalism lay in the long-nurtured fear of the danger that distant power might infringe on people's liberties. The language of the 1760s and 1770s revolutionary movement was not easily forgotten or set aside.

But by the time eight states had ratified, the Antifederalists faced a far harder task than they had at first imagined. First, they were no longer defending the status quo, now that the momentum lay with the Federalists. Second, it was difficult to defend the confederation government with its admitted flaws. Even so, they remained genuinely fearful that the new plan of government would lead to disaster. The innovation of superimposing a republican government on thirteen states was unprecedented in history. According to prevailing political philosophy, such an experiment must fail: Republican governments had to stay close to the people, to reflect their needs and interests. A distant government whose workings could not be observed and checked might easily become corrupt or tyrannical.

The new government was indeed distant. The House of Representatives was the only directly democratic element of the government, yet one member represented some thirty thousand people. How could such a representative really know or communicate with his constituency, the Antifederalists wanted to know? And how could the constituents judge his service to them? The status quo was preferable, as one Antifederalist explained: "The members of our state legislatures are annually elected—they are subject to instructions—they are

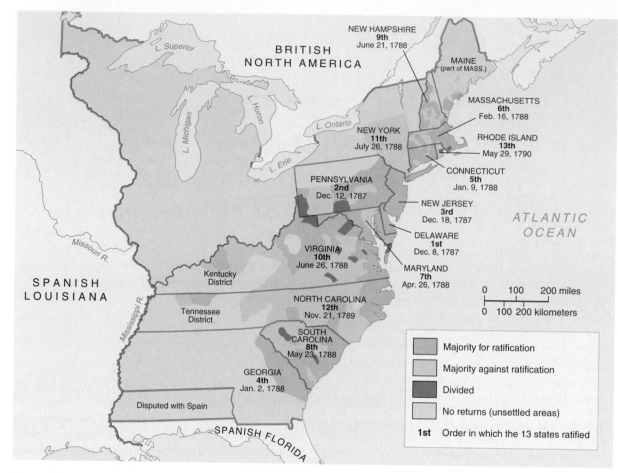

MAP 8.3
Ratification of the Constitution, 1788–1790
Populated areas cast votes for delegates to state ratification conventions. This map shows Anti-federalist strength generally concentrated in backcountry, noncoastal and nonurban areas, but with significant exceptions (for example, Rhode Island).

chosen within small circles—they are sent but a small distance from their respective homes. Their conduct is constantly known to their constituents. They frequently see, and are seen, by the men whose servants they are."

Under the new system, the Antifederalists were convinced, the elected representatives would always turn out to be members of the elite—that is, prominent members of the gentry with name recognition among voters. Such men "will be ignorant of the sentiments of the middling and much more of the lower class of citizens, strangers to their ability, unacquainted with their wants, difficulties, and distress," worried a Maryland man. None of this would be a problem under a confederation system,

according to the Antifederalists, because real power would continue to reside in the closely watched state governments. But the new Constitution eclipsed state power.

The Federalists generally agreed with the Antifederalist assumption that the elite would be favored for election to Congress, not to mention the Senate and the presidency. That was precisely what they hoped. The Federalists wanted power to flow to intelligent, virtuous, public-spirited leaders, like themselves. They did not envision a government constituted of every class of people. "Fools and knaves have voice enough in government already," according to a New York Federalist, without being guaranteed representation in proportion to the total population of fools. Alexander Hamilton claimed that mechanics and laborers preferred to have their social betters represent them. The Federalists were sure that a natural aristocracy of talented, educated, virtuous statesmen stood ready to take up the reins of government. The Antifederalists challenged the notion that any class of men could be free of selfish interests. Society was too heterogeneous; it was foolish to expect that "lawyers and planters" could be "adequate judges of tradesmen's concerns." They feared that the Federalists were merely resurrecting rule by an aristocracy of wealth.

Antifederalists also fretted over other features of the Constitution besides its undermining of state governments and its undemocratic principles. Proponents of paper money understood well that the Constitution would prohibit further issues of currency by the states. A particularly mistrustful objection was the fear that authorizing Congress to regulate the time, place, and manner of congressional elections would lead to such abuses as allowing only one polling place per state and thus deliberately inconveniencing distant western voters. The most widespread and quite reasonable objection to the Constitution was its lack of any guarantees of individual liberties. Unlike nearly half of the state constitutions, the proposed Constitution did not contain a bill of rights.

The decisive ninth vote for ratification was delivered by tiny New Hampshire, once assumed to be securely Antifederalist. Federalists there succeeded in getting the convention postponed from February to June and in the interim conducted an intense lobbying effort on specific delegates. The Constitution passed in New Hampshire with a ten-vote margin.

The Big Holdouts: Virginia and New York

Four states still remained outside the new union, and a glance at a map demonstrated the necessity of pressing the Federalist case in Virginia and New York. Though Virginia was home to Madison and Washington, an influential Antifederalist group led by Patrick Henry and George Mason made the outcome uncertain. Mason had been present throughout the Philadelphia convention and was one of the three delegates who refused to sign the Constitution; this made him an especially effective opponent. The Federalists finally won his support with

a carefully worded resolution declaring certain individual rights and republican principles inviolate in the new government and listing twenty specific amendments that Antifederalist Virginians desired. But the vote to ratify was not explicitly contingent on those amendments. The Antifederalists' escape clause was an assertion that, when a government derives its power from the people, the people can always take back any power the federal government uses to injure them. By a 10-vote margin, out of 168 votes cast, the Federalists got their ratification.

The New York ratifying convention was in session when news of the Virginia vote arrived, carried by express couriers traveling day and night. As in Virginia, powerful New York politicians opposed the Constitution. George Clinton, governor of the state, represented agrarian interests in upstate New York, but more central to his antifederalism was a sense that a state as large and powerful as New York did not need to relinquish so much authority to the new federal government.

New York was also home to some of the most persuasive and resourceful Federalists, such as Alexander Hamilton. Hamilton collaborated with James Madison and New York lawyer John Jay on a series of essays on the political philosophy of the new Constitution, starting in October 1787. Ultimately numbering eighty-five, the essays were published in New York newspapers and later republished as *The Federalist Papers.* The essays brilliantly set out the failures of the Articles of Confederation and offered an analysis of the complex nature of federalism. In one of the most compelling essays in *The Federalist Papers,* Madison argued for successful large-scale republican government, a direct challenge to one of the Antifederalists' most heartfelt convictions. Whereas the Antifederalists assumed that a true republic could succeed only in a small, homogeneous area, Madison argued that a large and diverse population was itself a guarantee of liberty. In such a state, no single faction or self-interested group could ever be large enough to subvert the freedom of other groups. "The smaller the society, the fewer will probably be the distinct parties and interests, the more frequently will a majority be found of the same party; and the smaller the compass within which they are placed, the more easily will they . . . execute their plans of oppression. Extend the sphere, and you take in a greater variety of parties and interests; you make it less probable that a majority of the whole will have a common motive to invade the rights of other citizens." Madison called this a "republican remedy for the diseases most incident to republican government."

New York's ratifying convention met at Poughkeepsie, halfway between New York City and Albany, deep in the heart of Antifederalist country. A clear majority of the delegates were Antifederalist, but newspaper debate and heavy lobbying produced some switches in votes. At one point, Hamilton threatened that New York City would secede from the state and join the union by itself if upstate farmers held out. The last-minute arrival of news from Virginia finally tipped the balance in favor of ratification.

New York's ratification assured the solidity and legitimacy of the new government. It took another year and a half for the Antifederalists in North Carolina to come around, and fiercely independent Rhode Island, still full of "rogues" to the Federalists, held out until May 1790, and even then barely ratified, by a two-vote margin.

In less than twelve months, the U.S. Constitution was both written and ratified. An amazingly short time by twentieth-century standards, it is equally remarkable for the late eighteenth century with its horsepowered transportation and hand-printed communications. The Federalists had faced a formidable task, but by building momentum and assuring a bill of rights, they carried the day.

Conclusion: Decade of Decision

Thus ended one of the most intellectually tumultuous and creative decades in American history. Americans experimented with ideas and drew up plans to embody their evolving and conflicting notions of how a society and a government ought to be formulated. Widespread agreement supported the concept of a republican government, one in which the people are sovereign and government leaders derive their power and authority from the people. State constitutions, the Articles of Confederation, and finally the federal Constitution wrestled with different conceptions of the degree of democracy—of the amount of direct control of government by the people—that was workable in American society and consistent with the ideal of republicanism.

The decade began in 1776 with a confederation government that could barely be ratified, so cumbersome were its procedures to ensure unanimity. Unanimity was thought desirable, so that no state could be squeezed or stepped on by others. But it also proved to be unworkable. As the decade progressed, Americans came to see that diversity of opinion was not only an unavoidable reality; it was a hidden strength of the new society beginning to take shape.

The Federalists still hoped for a society in which men of exceptional wisdom would rule and would intuitively discern the best path for public policy. In their vision of leadership they looked backward, to a society of hierarchy, rank, and benevolent rule by an aristocracy of talent. Meanwhile, however, they created a government with thoroughly forward-looking checks and balances as a guard against corruption, which they figured would most likely emanate from the people. The Antifederalists, by contrast, looked backward to an old order of small-scale direct democracy and local control, based on the virtue of people who could hold their potentially corruptible rulers to account. They envisioned a larger world of contentious, heterogeneous, self-interested leaders who needed to be held in check. In the 1790s, these two conceptions of republicanism and of leadership would be tested in real life.

CHRONOLOGY

1775	**May.** Second Continental Congress begins.
1778	State constitutions completed.
1776	Virginia adopts bill of rights.
	John Dickinson of Pennsylvania drafts Articles of Confederation.
1777	**November.** Final draft of Articles of Confederation approved by congress and sent to states.
1780	Pennsylvania abolishes slavery.
1781	Articles of Confederation finally ratified.
	Creation of executive departments; Robert Morris appointed superintendent of finance.
	Bank of North America formed.
	Quok Walker, a slave, sues for his freedom in Massachusetts.
1782	Virginia relaxes state manumission law.
1783	Treaty of Paris signed.
1784	Gradual emancipation laws passed in Rhode Island and Connecticut.
	Treaty of Fort Stanwix with Iroquois.
1785	Gradual emancipation in New York.
1786	Gradual emancipation in New Jersey.
	Bank of North America expires.
	Virginia adopts Statute of Religious Freedom.
	Shays's Rebellion in western Massachusetts.
	Annapolis meeting proposes convention to revise Articles of Confederation.
1787	Northwest Ordinance allows self-government and prohibits slavery in Northwest Territory.
	May–September. Constitutional convention meets in Philadelphia.
1788	United States Constitution is ratified.

BIBLIOGRAPHY

GENERAL WORKS

John P. Diggins, *The Lost Soul of American Politics: Virtue, Self-Interest, and the Foundations of Liberalism* (1984).

Joseph J. Ellis, *After the Revolution: Profiles of Early American Culture* (1979).

Merrill Jensen, *The New Nation: A History of the United States During the Confederation, 1781–1789* (1950).

James Kirby Martin, *Men in Rebellion: Higher Governmental Leaders and the Coming of the Revolution* (1973).

Forrest McDonald, *E Pluribus Unum: The Formation of the American Republic, 1776–1790* (1965).

Edmund S. Morgan, *Inventing the People: The Rise of Popular Sovereignty in England and America* (1988).

Richard B. Morris, *Witnesses at the Creation: Hamilton, Madison, Jay, and the Constitution* (1985).

Richard B. Morris, *The Forging of the Union, 1781–1789* (1987).

John Phillip Reid, *The Concept of Liberty in the Age of the American Revolution* (1988).

Robert E. Shalhope, *The Roots of Democracy: American Thought and Culture, 1760–1800* (1990).

Richard Sinopoli, *The Foundations of American Citizenship: Liberalism, the Constitution, and Civic Virtue* (1992).

Gerald Stourzh, *Alexander Hamilton and the Idea of Republican Government* (1970).

Gordon Wood, *The Creation of the American Republic, 1776–1787* (1969).

Alfred F. Young, ed., *Beyond the American Revolution: Explorations in the History of American Radicalism* (1993).

Rosemarie Zagarri, *The Politics of Size: Representation in the United States, 1776–1850* (1987).

Rosemarie Zagarri, *A Woman's Dilemma: Mercy Otis Warren and the American Revolution* (1995).

THE CONFEDERATION GOVERNMENT

Joseph L. Davis, *Sectionalism in American Politics, 1774–1787* (1977).

Daniel M. Friedenberg, *Life, Liberty, and the Pursuit of Land: The Plunder of Early America* (1992).

J. James Henderson, *Party Politics in the Continental Congress* (1974).

Reginald Horsman, *The Frontier in the Formative Years, 1783–1815* (1970).

Merrill Jensen, *The Articles of Confederation: An Interpretation of the Social-Constitutional History of the American Revolution, 1774–1781* (1940).

Jackson Turner Main, *Political Parties before the Constitution* (1973).

Peter S. Onuf, *The Origins of the Federal Republic: Jurisdictional Controversies in the United States, 1775–1787* (1983).

Peter S. Onuf, *Statehood and Union: A History of the Northwest Ordinance* (1987).

Peter S. Onuf and Cathy D. Matson, *A Union of Interests: Political and Economic Thought in Revolutionary America* (1990).

Jack N. Rakove, *The Beginnings of National Politics: An Interpretive History of the Continental Congress* (1979).

THE SOVEREIGN STATES AND CITIZENSHIP

Willi Paul Adams, *The First American Constitutions: Republican Ideology and the Making of the State Constitutions in the Revolutionary Era* (1980).

Edward Countryman, *A People in Revolution: The American Revolution and Political Society in New York, 1760–1790* (1981).

Robert Dinkin, *Voting in Revolutionary America* (1982).

Elisha P. Douglass, *Rebels and Democrats* (1965).

Eric Foner, *Tom Paine and Revolutionary America* (1976).

Van Beck Hall, *Politics without Parties: Massachusetts, 1780–1791* (1972).

Ronald Hoffman and Peter J. Albert, eds., *Sovereign States in an Age of Uncertainty* (1981).

Linda Kerber, *Women of the Republic: Intellect and Ideology in Revolutionary America* (1980).

James H. Kettner, *The Development of American Citizenship, 1608–1870* (1978).

Donald Lutz, *Popular Consent and Popular Control: Whig Political Theory in the Early State Constitutions* (1980).

Jackson Turner Main, *The Sovereign States, 1775–1783* (1973).

Richard P. McCormick, *Experiment in Independence: New Jersey in the Critical Period, 1781–1789* (1950).

Gary B. Nash and Jean R. Sonderlund, *Freedom by Degrees: Emancipation in Pennsylvania and Its Aftermath* (1991).

Steven E. Patterson, *Political Parties in Revolutionary Massachusetts* (1973).

Irwin H. Polishook, *Rhode Island and the Union, 1774–1795* (1969).

Marylynn Salmon, *Women and the Law of Property in Early America* (1986).

Robert J. Taylor, *Western Massachusetts in the Revolution* (1954).

Patricia Watlington, *The Partisan Spirit: Kentucky Politics, 1779–1792* (1972).

Chilton Williamson, *American Suffrage: From Property to Democracy, 1760–1860* (1960).

Alfred Young, *The Democratic-Republicans of New York: The Origins, 1763–1797* (1967).

Arthur Zilversmit, *The First Emancipation* (1967).

THE CRITICAL PERIOD

William G. Anderson, *The Price of Liberty: The Public Debt of the American Revolution* (1983).

Robert A. Becker, *Revolution, Reform, and the Politics of American Taxation, 1763–1783* (1980).

Thomas M. Doerflinger, *A Vigorous Spirit of Enterprise: Merchants and Economic Development in Revolutionary Philadelphia* (1986).

E. James Ferguson, *The Power of the Purse: A History of American Public Finance, 1776–1790* (1961).

Dall W. Forsythe, *Taxation and Political Change in the Young Nation, 1781–1833* (1977).

Robert A. Gross, ed., *In Debt to Shays: The Bicentennial of an Agrarian Rebellion* (1993).

David P. Szatmary, *Shays' Rebellion: The Making of an Agrarian Insurrection* (1980).

THE CONSTITUTION AND RATIFICATION

John K. Alexander, *The Selling of the Constitutional Convention: A History of News Coverage* (1990).

Charles Beard, *An Economic Interpretation of the Constitution* (1913).

Richard Beeman, Stephen Botein, and Edward C. Carter II, eds., *Beyond Confederation: Origins of the Constitution and American National Identity* (1987).

Herman Belz, Ronald Hoffman, and Peter J. Albert, eds., *To Form a More Perfect Union: The Critical Ideas of the Constitution* (1992).

Richard B. Bernstein and Kym S. Rice, *Are We to Be a Nation? The Making of the Constitution* (1987).

Steven R. Boyd, *The Politics of Opposition: Antifederalists and the Acceptance of the Constitution* (1979).

M. E. Bradford, *Original Intentions: On the Making and Ratification of the United States Constitution* (1993).

Irving Brant, *James Madison: The Nationalist, 1780–1787* (1948).

Robert E. Brown, *Charles Beard and the Constitution* (1956).

Roger H. Brown, *Redeeming the Republic: Federalists, Taxation, and the Origins of the Constitution* (1993).

Patrick T. Conley and John P. Kaminski, eds., *The Bill of Rights and the States: The Colonial and Revolutionary Origins of American Liberties* (1992).

Linda Grant DePauw, *The Eleventh Pillar: New York State and the Federal Constitution* (1966).

Michael Allen Gillespie and Michael Lienesch, eds., *Ratifying the Constitution* (1989).

A. E. Dick Howard, ed., *The United States Constitution: Roots, Rights, and Responsibilities* (1992).

Calvin C. Jillson, *Constitution Making: Conflict and Consensus in the Federal Convention of 1787* (1988).

Michael Kammen, *A Machine That Would Go of Itself: The Constitution in American Culture* (1986).

Ralph Ketcham, *James Madison* (1971).

Ralph Ketcham, *Framed for Posterity: The Enduring Philosophy of the Constitution* (1993).

Peter B. Knupfer, *The Union As It Is: Constitutional Unionism and Sectional Compromise, 1787–1861* (1991).

Donald S. Lutz, *Origins of American Constitutionalism* (1988).

Staughton Lynd, *Class Conflict, Slavery, and the United States Constitution* (1967).

Jackson Turner Main, *The Anti-Federalists: Critics of the Constitution* (1961).

Forrest McDonald, *We the People: The Economic Origins of the Constitution* (1958).

Forrest McDonald, *Novus Ordo Seclorum: The Intellectual Origins of the Constitution* (1985).

William Lee Miller, *The Business of May Next: James Madison and the Founding* (1992).

Ellen Franken Paul and Howard Dickman, eds., *Liberty, Property, and the Foundations of the American Constitution* (1989).

Jack N. Rakove, *James Madison and the Creation of the American Republic* (1990).

Jack N. Rakove, *Original Meanings: Politics and Ideas in the Making of the Constitution* (1996).

John Phillip Reid, *Constitutional History of the American Revolution: The Authority of Rights* (1986).

John Phillip Reid, *Constitutional History of the American Revolution: The Authority to Tax* (1987).

Robert A. Rutland, *The Ordeal of the Constitution: The Antifederalists and the Ratification Struggle of 1787–1788* (1966).

Stephen L. Schechter, *The Reluctant Pillar: New York and the Adoption of the Federal Constitution* (1985).

Garry Wills, *Explaining America: The Federalist* (1981).

RELIGION

Ruth H. Bloch, *Visionary Republic: Millennial Themes in American Thought, 1756–1800* (1985).

Morton Borden, *Jews, Turks, and Infidels* (1984).

Naomi W. Cohen, *Jews in Christian America: The Pursuit of Religious Equality* (1992).

Nathan O. Hatch, *The Sacred Cause of Liberty: Republican Thought and the Millennium in Revolutionary New England* (1977).

Jacob Marcus, *The American Colonial Jew: A Study in Acculturation* (1967).

Jacob Marcus, *United States Jewry, 1776–1985* (1989).

sion down Broadway while a crowd of thirty thousand applauded wildly. A week later, he took the oath of office on a balcony of the newly built Federal Hall overlooking Broad and Wall Streets. A festive red-and-white striped canopy framed the scene and directed the crowd's visual attention. His voice could not be heard, of course, but guns fired in the harbor minutes later announced his inauguration to the world.

The clear meaning of the inaugural pageantry was something very like hero worship for Washington as an individual. But the question, as yet unresolved, was whether the office of the presidency itself would be grandly heroic. The arches, the crowds, the gun salutes, the grand entry on a white horse—all this was an uneasy reminder of the trappings of monarchy.

In its first month, Congress debated the proper form of address for the president, raising explicitly the issue of how kingly this new presidency was to be. Vice President John Adams insisted on the dignity of a regal title. He preferred "His Highness, the President of the United States of America and Protector of Their Liberties," but he was willing to compromise on "His Majesty, the President." Virginia representative James Madison soundly ridiculed Adams. "His Highness" was as distasteful and unnecessary as "splendid tinsel and gorgeous robes," Madison complained. A few other representatives joked that the plump vice president should be called "His Rotundity." (Adams did not enjoy universal support; he had won the vice presidency by only thirty-four of the possible sixty-nine electoral votes.)

Yet Washington himself was known to favor being addressed as "His High Mightiness," so Adams was not altogether out of step. Significantly, the representatives targeted the vice president for ridicule, not the great man himself. Several former Antifederalists sitting in Congress held out for a less exalted title. The final version was simply "President of the United States of America," and the established form of address became "Mr. President," a subdued yet dignified title in a society where only independent, property-owning adult white males could presume to be called "Mister."

Washington's genius in establishing the presidency lay in his capacity for implanting his own reputation for integrity into the office itself. He was not a particularly brilliant thinker, nor was he a shrewd political strategist. He was not even a very congenial man. In the political language of the day,

GEORGE WASHINGTON BY JOSEPH WRIGHT
George Washington wears a laurel wreath, the traditional mark of honor in ancient times. Carved in beeswax in 1784, the work elevates Washington to the status of a Greek or Roman hero.
Courtesy of the Mount Vernon Ladies Association.

he was virtuous. Washington cultivated a personal style that was aloof, resolute, and dignified, to the point of appearing wooden at times. He encouraged pomp and ceremony to create respect for the authority of his office, traveling with no fewer than six horses drawing his coach, hosting formal balls, and surrounding himself with servants in livery. He even held weekly levees, as European monarchs did, hour-long audiences granted to a group of distinguished visitors. At these events, Washington, attired in black velvet, a feathered hat, and polished sword, accepted formal bows and avoided the egalitarian familiarity of handshakes. But he always managed, perhaps just barely, to avoid the extreme of royal splendor.

The thirteen American states had just come through a difficult decade, swinging between a distrust of executive power on the one hand and a fear of the turbulent effects of party politics on the other. Washington's reputation for integrity boosted confidence that executive power could be compatible with the public good. And his strong pronouncements about the evils of divisive factions and "party animosities" raised hopes that at last America was on a steady course.

National harmony proved to be elusive, however. Political parties developed in the 1790s, despite the best intentions of the decade's statesmen. The surprise was that factions emerged within the camp of the 1788 Federalists. Men who had worked together to ratify the Constitution found that the process of implementing it exposed serious disagreement. Economic policy and foreign affairs proved to be the two most significant fissures that split the political leadership of the 1790s. The disagreements were articulated around particular events and particular policies, but at heart they arose out of fundamentally opposing ideological stances about the value of democracy, the nature of leadership, and the limits of federal power. By 1800, these divisions had crystallized into full-fledged political parties, the Federalists and the Republicans.

The Search for Stability

Conventional wisdom today praises the development of a two-party system: Parties organize conflict, legitimize disagreement, and mediate among competing political strategies. Yet they were entirely unanticipated by the writers of the Constitution. James Madison had argued in *The Federalist Papers* in 1788 that a superior feature of the national government was precisely that its extensive size would prevent small, selfish factions from becoming dangerously dominant. No one was prepared for the intense and passionate polarization of the 1790s.

Instead, leaders in the early 1790s sought stability to heal divisions of the 1780s. Veneration for the president provided one powerful source of unity, and George Washington commanded near-universal respect. People trusted him to initiate the untested and perhaps elastic powers of the presidency. But a sterling leader alone was not enough to bring stability to the country. Schemes to promote national harmony and public virtue abounded in the 1790s. Passage of the Bill of Rights in 1791 lessened the scars of the battle over ratification of the Constitution. The private virtue of women was mobilized to bolster the public virtue of male citizens; republicanism was forcing a rethinking of women's relation to the state. Finally, politicians and writers took up numbers and statistics to chart the progress of the nation and confer legitimacy on republican institutions. The economic growth revealed by the numbers offered assurance that the hard times and political instability of the 1780s were now in the past.

SUIT WORN BY WASHINGTON AT SECOND INAUGURAL

At his first inauguration, Washington wore a suit of plain brown cloth woven in Connecticut to symbolize the independence of America from European manufacturers. Four years later at his second inauguration, in 1793, the president chose this suit of French black velvet. Possibly he felt that American independence was now adequately established, whereas presidential authority required the boost of a luxury fabric. The suit is elegant and dignified yet simple, avoiding all but a hint of monarchical opulence.

Courtesy of the Chicago Historical Society, Hope B. McCormick Costume Center. Gift of Virginia Lewis Mitchell, Laura Landon Mitchell, and Neville Mitchell Smith.

Washington's Cabinet

At first President Washington had relatively little to do. Major decisions, like establishing the executive departments and the federal court system, fell to the initiative of Congress. Washington fretted about his competency—"I feel an insuperable diffidence in my own abilities," he wrote to a South Carolina friend in May—and fended off the dozens of job seekers who sought his approval and appointment. He set up a fixed social schedule; in addition to his Tuesday levees for male guests, he established a Friday night tea party and a Wednesday dinner at 4 P.M. for selected guests of both sexes. He also made it a rule never to accept a dinner invitation to someone else's table.

Within four months, Congress had created the departments of war, treasury, and state, and now Washington could begin his work. His antiparty assumptions guided his choices; he did not require any political test for office. Instead he picked talented and experienced individuals, not lackeys, to head the departments. Their deep philosophical differences did not trouble him. For the Department of War, he chose Henry Knox, who had headed the same department in the confederation government. For the Treasury, he quickly turned to Alexander Hamilton of New York, known for his general brilliance as well as financial genius. Washington knew that this post, the most important one in the government, would require the adept political skills Hamilton clearly had. Revenue problems excited discontent and division and had largely been the cause of the failure of the confederation government. To lead the Department of State, the foreign policy arm of the executive branch, Washington chose Thomas Jefferson, who had just returned from a four-year stint as minister to France. The Franco-American alliance that had won the Revolutionary War was complicated now by the early stages of a democratic revolution sweeping France in the summer of 1789. No one understood the immediate intricacy of diplomatic relations better than Jefferson.

Beyond the three executive departments, Washington had legal appointments at his disposal. He turned to Virginian Edmund Randolph to be the first attorney general. In 1787, Randolph had presented the Virginia Plan on Madison's behalf at the Philadelphia convention, so clearly he was friendly to the idea of a powerful government. Yet Randolph had turned Antifederalist for a time; he was one of only three at the convention who had refused to sign the final Constitution, largely because he pre-ferred a ratification process that gave more voice to the voters to advocate for change. John Jay, the New York lawyer who vigorously defended the Constitution along with Madison and Hamilton in the *Federalist Papers,* became the first chief justice of the Supreme Court, a job with slight duties in the first few years.

> *No one anticipated that fundamental disagreements leading to two decades of party turbulence would emerge from the brilliant but explosive mix of Washington's first cabinet.*

Washington liked and trusted all these men, and by 1793, in his second term, he was meeting regularly with them, thereby establishing the precedent of a presidential cabinet. (Vice President Adams did not join these meetings; his only official duty was to preside over the Senate, a job he found "a punishment" because he could not actually participate in legislative debates. He complained to his wife, Abigail, "My country has in its wisdom contrived for me the most insignificant office.") No one anticipated that fundamental disagreements leading to two decades of party turbulence would emerge from the brilliant but explosive mix of Washington's first cabinet.

The Bill of Rights

Most members of the First Congress, which convened in April 1789, had been ardent supporters of ratification, so for a time harmony prevailed. In a spirit of conciliation, they turned to the work of constructing a bill of rights. Many Antifederalists had complained about the absence of guarantees of individual liberties and limitations to federal power, and seven states had ratified the Constitution on the express condition that a bill of rights be swiftly incorporated. Many state constitutions protected freedom of speech, press, religion, peaceable assembly, and the right to petition and to have jury trials, so it seemed to Antifederalists that the federal government could do no less.

In the final days of the 1787 Philadelphia convention, only one voice at the meeting (the Virginian George Mason's) had called for a bill of rights. James Madison and the other delegates decided that an enumeration of rights was unnecessary. Perhaps a general fatigue after the four months of wrangling contributed to their hasty dismissal. But the complaint surfaced continually in the ratification process. Alexander Hamilton tried to answer it in one of the *Federalist Papers*. Enumerating individual rights was actually dangerous, he claimed: "Why declare that things shall not be done which there is no power to do?" This was little comfort to uneasy Antifederalists, who saw it as circular reasoning.

By 1789, James Madison had reversed himself and prepared a set of amendments to satisfy the Antifederalists. He still did not think that the lack of a bill of rights was a serious flaw in the Constitution; in his view, the real threat to individual liberties came not so much from government as from popular majorities acting with the sanction of law. He hoped that a clear, solemn statement of fundamental rights would help fix these truths in the public mind and would contribute to public virtue.

Members of the First Congress had little quarrel with any of the particular rights Madison specified in his first draft. No one wanted a government that could force citizens to incriminate themselves or to quarter soldiers in peacetime. But with more pressing items on the congressional agenda, such as how best to raise money for the new government, Congress sidelined Madison's proposals for five months. And even then, the eventual debate was lackluster and indifferent. Some of the members quibbled over details, and one provided a moment of humor by asking, in exasperation, if every possible right had been listed, pointing out one somehow overlooked: that "a man should have a right to wear his hat."

Final agreement from both House and Senate on the first ten amendments to the Constitution came in September 1789. Numbers one through eight dealt with individual liberties, and nine and ten concerned the boundary between federal and state authority. The amendments did have the immediate effect of cementing a sense of national unity. The process of ratifying the amendments in the states took another two years, but there was no serious doubt about the outcome. North Carolina and Rhode Island, the two holdout states, came into the Union in large part because the most credible argument against joining had now been deflated.

But not everyone was entirely satisfied. Amendments that would change the structural details of the new government, ardently desired by some Antifederalists, were never considered by Congress. Madison had no intention of reopening debates settled at the Philadelphia convention, about the length of term for the president or the power to levy excise taxes or the power of Congress to maintain a peacetime army.

The Right to Vote

Significantly, no one complained about another striking omission in the Bill of Rights: the right to vote. Only much later did voting come to be seen as a fundamental liberty requiring protection by constitutional amendment—indeed, by four additional amendments. The 1788 Constitution deliberately left all decisions about defining voters to individual states, precisely to promote stability in the new federal government. Any uniform federal voting law would run the double risk of excluding some who could already vote in state elections or including too many new voters somehow deemed undesirable in the more restrictive states.

Most states maintained property qualifications of varying degree. The assumption held that only property owners would be independent enough to vote in perfect freedom. Slaves, servants, apprentices, tenants, children, wives, and a new and growing class of propertyless wage laborers at the lower end of the social scale were thought to lack the necessary independence of mind, being subject to pressure from masters, husbands, and bosses. And, since a major purpose of government was to secure private property, as many leaders of the revolutionary generation thought, then it made sense to them to restrict participation to those who actually owned property. Or so they reasoned. Widening the circle of voters could lead to major disruptions, if, for instance, the many have-nots decided to tax the rich heavily.

The Constitution counted on the states to set limits on voters. Only one state expanded its pool of voters beyond the customary bounds, and that was at first unintentional. The New Jersey constitution of 1776 enfranchised "all free inhabitants" worth "over 50 pounds." The lawmakers simply forgot to specify the words *white* and *male,* so deeply was it implanted in their minds that voters would of course be white men. But in the 1780s, unmarried women and free blacks who met the property qualification quietly began to participate in elections in a few towns. (Married women owned no property, for by law their husbands held title to everything, so they were still excluded under this law.) What began as an oversight soon became acceptable: A revised election law of 1790 used the words *he or she* in reference to voters, thus making

ciation during the 1780s were more than most ordinary people with rudimentary arithmetic skills could handle. But under the Constitution, the federal government alone had the power to coin money, and other currencies were phased out. Thomas Jefferson drew up a plan basing federal money for the first time on the decimal system. Dollars, dimes, cents, and half-cents were far easier to reckon with than pence and shillings. "The policy of tyrants," said one author of a new arithmetic text, is "to keep their accounts in as intricate and perplexing a method as possible," so that no one could figure out taxes and public debts. "But Republican money ought to be simple, and adapted to the meanest capacity." Decimal money enabled the average farmer or mechanic to participate more fully in the widening world of commerce.

Sources of Economic Change

Following a decade of severe economic instability, the 1790s ushered in a period of prosperity and sustained economic growth. New agricultural opportunities, transportation improvements, and innovations in finance were beginning to transform not only the economy but the way ordinary men and women thought about their work and their chances for bettering their lives. The simplified monetary system and serious attention to arithmetic training allowed many more people to participate confidently in the world of commercial exchange.

Commercial Agriculture

From at least the mid-eighteenth century, most farmers had participated in market transactions at local stores and in nearby towns. Self-sufficiency was simply not possible in a society where a taste for some of the luxuries of life had taken hold. For example, a store in the village of Brookfield, in central Massachusetts, stocked fine cloth—velvets and silks—from England and India; watch chains and shoe buckles; teapots and dishware; raisins, allspice, salt, sugar, and tea. Rarely was cash actually exchanged at the moment of purchase. Instead, the store owner recorded transactions in his account book, keeping a running total of each customer's debt, which was periodically paid off in either cash or, more likely, "country goods," meaning a surplus of cheese, butter, or grain from the farmer's own production.

This pattern of local market exchange was altered in the 1790s, when dramatic increases in the international price of grain motivated farmers to step up their grain production. Food prices were generally rising in Europe in the late eighteenth century, driven up by demand caused by marked population growth. After 1793, prices rose even more sharply, when France and England entered into two decades of conflict known as the Napoleonic Wars. Soon all the major European powers were embroiled in war, leaving the United States, the only neutral shipper, with a monopoly on the Atlantic trade. Thomas Paine in his 1776 pamphlet *Common Sense* had predicted that America could count on prosperity as long as "eating is the custom of Europe," and his prediction was borne out in the 1790s. American grain farmers from the Connecticut River valley in the North to the Chesapeake region in the South responded to the attractive European market by putting more acres under cultivation. In Virginia and Maryland, soil worn out by tobacco cultivation could be renewed by a switch to wheat production. The increase in overseas grain trade generated a host of new jobs in related areas as the number of millers, coopers, and ship and wagon builders expanded. The grain trade generated moral pride as well: American production was concentrated on food, a basic human need, not on luxury items.

A second type of commercial agriculture also embarked on a new course after 1793. Limited amounts of smooth-seed cotton had long been grown in the low-lying coastal areas of the southern states, but this variety of cotton did not prosper in the drier, inland regions. Green-seed cotton, in contrast, grew well inland throughout the South but contained many rough seeds that adhered tenaciously to the cotton fibers. Typically, it took an entire day to clean a pound of cotton by hand. Southern cotton growers were thus intent on finding a way to diminish the laborious task; some states even offered bounties for the invention of an efficient mechanical way to separate the rough seeds from the cotton.

In 1793, a clever young Yale graduate named Eli Whitney, visiting friends at a Georgia plantation, turned his mechanical talents to the task. His invention, the cotton gin, could clean fifty pounds of cotton per day. Whitney improved and patented his machine in 1794, but not before imitators eagerly leaped into the business of making cotton gins. The English textile industry provided a ready market for all cotton grown; the demand was high, and now supply could meet it. The figures of cotton production tell the whole story: 138,228 pounds of cotton were grown in the South in 1792; two years later, the number was 1,601,000, eleven times as much. In 1795, production amounted to 6,272,000 pounds, a fourfold increase over just the year before; and by 1800, the figure was 35 million pounds of cotton. Cotton fever had gripped the South, with momentous and chilling consequences for the one million enslaved black Americans living there.

Transportation

The prosperous cash economy made possible by grain exports and cotton culture was initially confined to areas within easy reach of the port cities— farming regions usually within thirty miles of navigable waterways or the coast. Poor roads presented the single biggest obstacle to the spread of commercial farming, because of the high cost of transporting goods over muddy or rutted paths barely wide enough for a wagon. The only major continuous road existing at the beginning of the 1790s was the Post Road, running near the East Coast for 1,600 miles from Maine to Georgia. It consisted of local country roads, linked together in the 1780s, and it carried an ever-increasing load of passenger traffic in stagecoaches as well as freight and the U.S. mail.

In the 1790s, east-to-west road building commenced. In 1794, the Lancaster Turnpike, the first private toll road in the nation, connected Philadelphia with Lancaster, sixty-five miles west, and, later, with Pittsburgh in western Pennsylvania. Soon another turnpike connected Boston with Albany, New York. Private companies under charter by state governments financed these projects; the company built the roadbed, often made of solid stone covered by gravel, and collected fees from all vehicles. Some surfaces were made of planks or felled logs placed side by side, which prevented mudhole problems but shook up passengers frightfully. From Albany, a new highway moved along the Mohawk River valley, pushing west into land once held by the powerful Iroquois until the Revolutionary War forced them farther west. In the Upper South, a major road extended southwest down the Shenandoah Valley between the crest of the Blue Ridge Mountains and the Appalachians. In the west, a road named Zane's Trace moved across southern Ohio in 1796; and another road linked Richmond, Virginia, with the Tennessee towns of Knoxville and Nashville in the interior. An early Ohio law reveals the primitive character of these western roads compared with state-of-the-art gravel turnpikes in the

STAGE COACH ADVERTISEMENT
Stagecoach lines advertised their schedules and terms in newspapers. This is from the New York Journal and Patriotic Register *for August 21, 1793. It promises to accommodate passengers in the most agreeable manner and to reach Philadelphia in "about" twenty-four hours.*
Courtesy, American Antiquarian Society.

East: The law prohibited stumps in the roadway higher than one foot. Western roads greatly facilitated the migration of settlers, but they were too slow to allow an economical movement of heavy, bulky agricultural products like grain. Consequently, western farmers usually opted to distill their surplus farm produce into a much more compact form—wheat and rye whiskeys—for transport to eastern markets.

By 1800, a dense network of dirt, gravel, or plank roadways connected cities and towns in southern New England and the Middle Atlantic states, while isolated roadways and old Indian trails fanned out to the west. Commercial stage lines connected major eastern cities, offering four-day travel time between Boston and New York and an exhausting but speedy thirty-six-hour trip between New York and Philadelphia. Whereas in 1790 only three stagecoach companies operated out of Boston, in 1800 there were twenty-four. On the roads far-

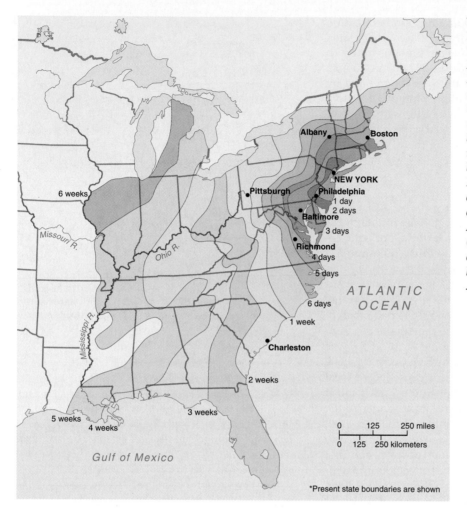

MAP 9.1
Travel Times from New York City in 1800
Notice that the first week of travel out of New York extends over a much greater distance than subsequent weeks because of poor or nonexistent roads in the west, mountain barriers, and Indian dangers. River corridors in either west or east speeded up travel — if one were going downriver. Also note that travel by sea (north and south along the coast) was much faster than land travel.

ther west, the sons and daughters of eastern farm families trekked by the thousands in search of fresh homesteads, and four new states—Vermont, Kentucky, Tennessee, and Ohio—became sufficiently populated to join the Union by 1800. In that year, Kentucky had more settlers than did five of the original thirteen states.

South of the Potomac River, road building and commercial stagecoach travel remained in a primitive state, chiefly because of low passenger demand. Two-thirds of the southern population—the enslaved blacks and the poorer whites—could not travel, and the elite of the planter class generally owned their own coaches and wagons. Growers of cotton and tobacco continued to rely on the many southern rivers to move produce to market, which reinforced the economic dominance of property owners fronting on the eastern waterways.

Merchants and Capital

The surge in the overseas grain and cotton trades stimulated the growth of the commercial classes in the seacoast cities of the new nation. At the pinnacle of the business community were the merchants, often men with multiple financial dealings. The word *merchant* had a more specific meaning in the late eighteenth century than now, for it designated a person involved in both wholesale and retail operations. Someone who merely retailed goods to the public was a shopkeeper. The richest merchants had lines of trade stretching across the Atlantic. Not only did they buy and sell foreign goods, they typically owned some fraction of the ships that carried the goods. With each ship owned by four to six merchants, the risk of financial catastrophe from the loss of a ship was thus spread out over several firms.

In the 1780s, states could and did erect trade barriers, but the creation of the new federal government finally removed all obstacles to interstate business alliances and guaranteed the free movement of goods across state borders. The horizons of the business community widened, and the volume of trade mushroomed. New investment opportunities beckoned, not only in mercantile trades but also in such areas as the chartering of turnpike companies and stagecoach lines or the development of spinning factories or woolen mills in New England.

These opportunities required a larger and longer commitment of capital than did a joint venture for a single cargo in a ship. The need for investment capital was met by the development of commercial banking, a financial innovation that had not existed in America before the Revolution. During the 1790s, the number of banks multiplied nearly tenfold, from three at the beginning of the decade to twenty-nine in 1800. (By 1810, there were more than one hundred banks.) Banks drew in money chiefly through the sale of stock. They then made loans in the form of banknotes, paper currency issued by the bank and backed by the gold and silver paid in by stockholders. Because they issued two or three times as much money in banknotes as they held in hard money, banks were really creating new money for the economy.

Rich merchants in particular embraced banking schemes with enthusiasm. In one feverish week in New York City in 1792, three rival banks were proposed, with aimed-for stock subscriptions totaling about $4 million. Isaac Roosevelt, the president of the Bank of New York, typified the multiventure involvement of this new breed of merchants who were developing innovative and complex financial dealings. Roosevelt owned a sugar refinery, financed overseas shipping, and speculated heavily in confiscated loyalist real estate. As president of the leading New York bank, he had ready access to investments (buying stock in the bank) as well as access to credit. Not everyone in New York was appreciative of the virtues of commercial banking, however. When Roosevelt and his fellow merchants applied for a state charter for their bank, one New York newspaper condemned the bank for being "an odious combination of wealthy men."

Hamilton's Political Economy

In late 1790, the government moved from New York to Philadelphia, a more centrally located city with a merchant class no less enterprising than that in New York. This too was a temporary home; the long-range plan entailed construction of the capital on the Potomac River between Maryland and Virginia, independent of any state. (See Historical Question, page 324.) Many Philadelphians, hoping to derail the Potomac plan, welcomed the government officials with lavish displays of the social attractions of their city. A whirl of entertainments caused Abigail Adams, the vice president's wife, to complain about the "continued scene of parties upon parties," but the outward friendliness could not mask the growing political rifts over economic policy. A different sort of party scene, even more upsetting than the social whirl, was in the making. At the center of growing controversy was the head of the Treasury, Alexander Hamilton.

TABLE 9.1

GROWTH OF THE U.S. POSTAL SERVICE, **1790-1820**

Year	Number of Post Offices	Miles of Post Road	Letters (millions)	Newspapers Mailed (millions)
1790	75	1,875	.3	.5
1800	903	20,817	2.0	1.9
1810	2,300	36,406	3.9	n.a.
1820	4,500	72,492	8.9	6.0

Postal rates set in 1792 favored newspapers over letters to promote the spread of information: letters cost 6 cents to a dollar, newspapers cost either 1 or 1.5 cents. The number of newspapers posted at first exceeded that of letters, and never fell far behind.

Source: Richard R. John, *Spreading the News: The American Postal System from Franklin to Morse* (1995).

The Public Debt and Taxes

The youthful Hamilton was clearly something of a prodigy. At age twenty, he had been indispensable to George Washington during the Revolutionary War; at age twenty-six, he had gained admission to the bar after only three months of study. At age thirty, he had had enough credibility in New York to be chosen for the Philadelphia convention. His vigorous defense of the Constitution's political philosophy in the *Federalist Papers* and his tactical maneuvering in the ratification process made it clear that he had a brilliant political future. At age thirty-four, he joined President Washington's first cabinet as "First Lord of the Treasury," as he once styled himself. To rectify the instabilities of the 1780s economy, Hamilton proposed a three-part plan.

He first turned his attention to the very large public debt, a sum amounting to $52 million. About $11.7 million was owed to foreign creditors, while a tangled web of IOUs and interest-bearing public securities amounted to a further $40.4 million of domestic indebtedness. The debt dated from the difficult war years, when the government needed supplies and manpower but had no independent source of revenue. In the 1780s, the actual paper IOUs and certificates of debt had fallen in value, in some states to as little as one-twentieth of the original value; this drop reflected the widespread belief that the confederation government could never make good on them. In recent years, wealthy speculators were buying the IOUs cheaply and quietly, betting that they might rise in value in the long run.

Even though the 1787 Constitution contained a clause specifically guaranteeing that all debts contracted under the previous government "shall be as valid against the United States under this Constitution, as under the Confederation," a close reading of those words reveals an ambiguity. The public debt of the confederation government may have been valid, but it was not being honored before the Constitution; that document therefore made no new promises. But neither did it repudiate the debt, for that would have been a blow to the country's integrity. The question now was open: What exactly should be done about the debt?

Hamilton's answer, elaborated in his *Report on Public Credit* in January 1790, was that the debt, both foreign and domestic, be funded at full value. This meant that an old IOU or a certificate of debt would be rolled over into a new bond, at the same value, with a schedule of regular interest payments from government to holder and a promise to retire the

ALEXANDER HAMILTON
Alexander Hamilton in 1792 at age thirty-seven, painted by John Trumbull.
Yale University Art Gallery.

debt in forty years, using government income from import taxes. Thus there would still be a public debt, but it would be secure, supported by the confidence of Americans in their new government. The old fluctuating certificates would be retired, traded in for the new bonds, which would circulate as a stable medium of exchange, injecting new and more valuable money into the economy. "A national debt if not excessive will be to us a national blessing; it will be a powerfull cement of our union," Hamilton wrote to another financier.

Probably about 2 percent of the white population held the largest portions of the debt. Now these influential men would have a direct stake in the new government, support that Hamilton regarded as essential to the country's stability. He was also providing those same few men with more than $40 million released for new investment, a distinct improvement over the old depreciated bonds, which had circulated in daily transactions at only a small fraction of their face value.

If the *Report on Public Credit* had only gone this far, it would have been somewhat controversial. But

Hamilton took a much bolder step by adding into the federal debt another $25 million still owed by some state governments to individuals. All the states had obtained supplies during the war by issuing IOUs to farmers, merchants, and moneylenders. Some states, such as Virginia and New York, had paid off these debts entirely, while others, like Massachusetts, had accomplished partial success through heavy and painful taxation of the inhabitants; about half the states had made little headway. Hamilton called for the federal government to assume these state debts and add them to the federal debt. Hamilton's "assumption plan" in effect consolidated federal power over the states.

The assumption of state debts required the federal government to exercise even stronger powers of taxation. To meet the interest payments on a national debt swollen to some $77 million, Hamilton did not propose raising import duties, for that would have been unacceptable to the merchant class whose support he was seeking. Instead, he convinced Congress in 1791 to pass a hefty excise tax on distilled spirits, amounting to 25 percent of the eventual market value of the whiskey, to be paid by the farmer when he brought his grain to the distillery. Members of Congress favored the tax, especially those from New England where the favorite drink was rum, an imported beverage already taxed under the import duty laws. A New Hampshire representative pointed out that the country would be "drinking down the national debt," an idea he evidently thought was good.

"A national debt if not excessive will be to us a national blessing; it will be a powerful cement of our union," Hamilton wrote.

Congress passed Hamilton's funding and assumption plans, but not without first considering a serious objection. Congressman James Madison agreed on paying full value to an original holder of the debt, but he objected to the windfall profits that would go to speculators. He also strenuously objected to assumption of all the states' debts. A large debt is dangerous, Madison warned, especially because the government must tax heavily to service the interest on the debt, and so money flows out of the pockets of ordinary people and moves to the purses of the few rich creditors. Madison's plan to differentiate between original and new holders of

the debt was too complex and probably unworkable because the government lacked records of the original transactions. Other representatives complained that even original holders could be like speculators, if they had made their loans to the government in the form of the virtually worthless Continental dollars. Madison's amendments were voted down, and the debt was funded Hamilton's way. Madison and Hamilton, so recently allies in writing the *Federalist Papers,* were very quickly becoming opponents.

Secretary of State Jefferson, too, was fearful of Hamilton's schemes. Cabinet meetings had become disagreeable and uncomfortable, a situation that prompted President Washington to rebuke them both. Hamilton misread the motives of Madison and Jefferson, thinking they were rivals for his power. Jefferson had a clearer picture of the problem: "No man is more ardently intent to see the public debt soon and sacredly paid off than I am. This exactly marks the difference between Colonel Hamilton's views and mine, that I would wish the debt paid tomorrow; he wishes it never to be paid, but always to be a thing where with to corrupt and manage the legislature." Jefferson feared that rich speculators with a financial stake in the government would meddle with the Congress, just as he suspected that Hamilton was already corrupted. In a letter to the president in 1792, Jefferson characterized Hamilton as "the man who has the shuffling of millions backwards & forwards from paper into money & money into paper, from Europe to America, & America to Europe, the dealing out of Treasury-secrets among his friends in what time & measure he pleases, and who never slips an occasion of making friends with his means."

The First Bank of the United States

A second major element of Hamilton's economic plan was his proposal for a national Bank of the United States, which he presented to the Congress in December 1790. Believing that banks were the "nurseries of national wealth," Hamilton modeled his plan on the Bank of England: a private corporation that worked primarily for the public good. In Hamilton's plan, 20 percent of the bank's stock would be bought by the federal government. In effect, the bank would become the fiscal agent of the new government, holding and handling its revenue money derived from import duties, land sales, and the whiskey excise tax. The other 80 percent of the bank's capital would come from private investors, who could buy stock in the bank with either hard money (silver or gold) or federal securities. By its size and privilege of being the only national bank, the bank would help stabilize the economy by exerting prudent control over credit, interest rates, and the value of the currency. Five of the twenty-five directors of the bank would be appointed by the government, to look out for the public interest. Hamilton had extraordinarily good faith in the virtue of the other twenty directors, who would be chosen from among the private stockholders and thus be merchants drawn from the world of commerce and high finance.

Madison tried to stop the bank plan in Congress, but he could not muster the necessary support. Again he complained that the rich would have undue influence in the government's finances and in setting economic policy. Jefferson advised Washington that creating a national bank was unconstitutional, because there was nothing about chartering banks in the list of specified powers granted to Congress by the Constitution. Hamilton, however, argued that the same list specified many powers to regulate commerce and ended with a broad grant of the right "to make all Laws which shall be necessary and proper for carrying into execution the foregoing Powers." Washington considered both arguments for two weeks and then agreed with Hamilton. He scrapped a statement vetoing the bank, which he had asked Madison to draft, and signed the bank bill in February 1791, chartering the bank for twenty years.

When the bank's stock—the 80 percent that was to be privately held—went on sale in New York City in July, it sold out in a few hours, touching off an immediate mania of speculation in the resale of stock shares. A discouraged Madison reported that "the Coffee House is an eternal buzz with the gamblers" meeting over hot drinks to trade stock shares. Two months later, the gamblers had moved their game to an office and formally organized as the New York Stock Exchange, for the more efficient buying and selling of bank stock.

The Report on Manufactures

The third component of Hamilton's plan was set out in December 1791 in the *Report on Manufactures*, a proposal to encourage the production of American-made goods. Manufacturing was in its infancy in 1790, the result of years of dependence on British imports. Hamilton recognized that a balanced and self-reliant economy required the United States to produce its own cloth and iron products. His plan mobilized the new powers of the federal government to impose tariffs and grant subsidies to encourage the growth of local manufacturing. Tariffs were a tricky business, however, for Hamilton had to be careful not to undercut his important merchant allies who made their money trading with England and whose trade, in turn, generated over half the government's income. A high tariff would either seriously dampen that trade or would force merchants into smuggling, a practice well known from the days of British rule. So Hamilton favored a moderate tariff, with extra bounties paid to American manufacturers to encourage production.

The *Report on Manufactures* was the one Hamiltonian plan that was not approved by Congress. Hamilton himself was somewhat indifferent and did not push hard for its adoption. Much of the work of drafting the report had been done by his assistant Tench Coxe, a Pennsylvanian who had headed a group called the Manufacturing Society of Philadelphia. Hamilton was far more interested in a financial investment he helped set up earlier in 1791, the Society to Encourage Useful Manufactures, which funneled capital from merchant investors into stock purchases in new textile factories being built in Paterson, New Jersey. The plan was friendly primarily to investors and secondarily to manufacturers, and then only large-scale manufacturers. In the late 1790s, the small manufacturers of America—the cotton spinners, the cloth weavers, the gun makers, and paper manufacturers—favored Hamilton's opponent, the emerging Republican Party of Jefferson and Madison, as the more likely source of protective trade tariffs.

The Whiskey Rebellion

Hamilton may have been a financial genius, but he still could make serious political mistakes, as his excise tax on whiskey showed. Many more voters were grain farmers and whiskey drinkers than were merchants. Western farmers with an abundance of wheat and rye suddenly faced high taxes at the distillery when they presented their grains for processing. The tax was up-front money that could not be recovered until the product was transported to market and sold. Cash-short farmers deeply resented their assigned role in Hamilton's plan for economic recovery.

In 1791, angry grain farmers in the western parts of Pennsylvania, Virginia, Maryland, and the Carolinas and throughout Kentucky conveyed to

WHISKEY REBELLION "FIRE COPPER"
This forty-gallon "fire copper" produced Monongahela rye whiskey in the 1790s in western Pennsylvania. Mashed rye grain was mixed and heated with mash from a previously distilled brew. The distiller next added yeast and water and let the mixture ferment for several days. The mixture was then heated to 175 degrees, the boiling point of alcohol, in this three-foot copper vessel (called a still, as in distilling). Alcohol-laden vapor from the boiling brew cooled and condensed in a spiral copper tubing that dripped whiskey into a jug. High-proof, expensive whiskey required a second processing in the still to concentrate the vapors. The owner of this fire copper was James Miller, whose nephew Oliver Miller Jr. was an early fatality in the Whiskey Rebellion.
Oliver Miller Homestead/Photo by Andrew Wagner; Courtesy of American History Magazine.

Congress their resentment of Hamilton's tax. Marginal farmers stood to lose the most under the law; one man who petitioned Congress explained that he already had handed over half his grain as payment to the local distillery for distilling his rye, and now the distiller was paying the tax on the whole quantity of whiskey out of the farmer's remaining half alone. This "reduces the balance to less than one-third of the original quantity. If this is not an oppressive tax, I am at a loss to describe what is so." Many such petitions of protest arrived at Congress, which produced modest modifications in the tax in 1792; but even so, discontent was rampant.

Simple evasion of the law was the most common response. And indeed, the tax proved hard to collect. Federally appointed tax inspectors soon learned the unpleasant consequences, as crowds threatened to tar and feather them. A congressional representative from Pennsylvania, William Findley, observed that "it is well known that in some counties, as well of Virginia as of Pennsylvania, men have not, and cannot be induced by any consider-

ation to accept of the excise offices." With no tax collectors, by late 1792 the tax was dead in northwest Virginia, western North Carolina, and all of Kentucky. Even in Philadelphia, the nation's capital, major distilleries right under Hamilton's nose were evading the tax by underreporting their production by nearly half. With embarrassment, Hamilton admitted to Congress that the revenue yield from the tax was far less than anticipated. But rather than abandon the law, he tightened up on the prosecution of tax evaders.

In western Pennsylvania, Hamilton had one ally, a stubborn tax collector who had refused to quit even after a group of spirited farmers had burned an effigy of him and after his deputies had received ominous midnight visits from men wearing disguises. In late May 1794, this tax collector filed charges against seventy-five farmers and distillers for tax evasion. In mid-July, the collector and a federal marshal were ambushed in Allegheny County by a group of forty men, and during the next two days the tax collector's house was burned to the ground by a crowd estimated at five hundred. At the end of July, seven thousand farmers staged a march on Pittsburgh to express their hostility to the hated tax.

An angry Hamilton convinced President Washington to respond with a show of force. Washington nationalized the Pennsylvania militia, and the aged ex-general donned his old military garb and set out, with Hamilton at his side urging him on, at the head of fifteen thousand soldiers. This was as large a force as had served in any single campaign of the Continental army, when the enemy was the British army. Their goal now was to quell the "rebellion," as Hamilton called it, in the counties around Pittsburgh. Since a one-day demonstration of seven thousand farmers is not exactly a full-scale rebellion, it was undoubtedly Hamilton's plan to make an example of western Pennsylvania that would send a message to other noncomplying regions.

By the time the military force arrived, in late September, the demonstrators had all gone home. No battles were fought, and no fire was exchanged. Twenty men were rounded up as rebels and charged with high treason, but only two were convicted, and both were soon pardoned by President Washington, with the faint excuse that one was insane and the other dimwitted.

At the core of the Whiskey Rebellion lay the question of what citizens can and cannot do when they think a law is unjust and what governments can and cannot do when groups of citizens resort to extralegal and even violent means to express their grievances.

Had the government overreacted? Or was Hamilton right to think that the whiskey rioters posed a serious threat to the stability of the federal government? At issue was more than the hardships of western farmers short on money and resentful of taxes, and more than Hamilton's need to get the debt funded and to restore confidence in the nation's economy. At the core of the Whiskey Rebellion lay the question of what citizens can and cannot do when they think a law is unjust and what governments can and cannot do when groups of citizens resort to extralegal and even violent means to express their grievances.

The long colonial tradition of crowd action to protest unfair practices or to express public opinion had worked comfortably in a political culture where ordinary people had limited formal access to power. But in a republic, laws were passed by the supposed representatives of the people, not by tyrannical kings or distant parliaments. Burning effigies of stamp tax collectors in 1765 made sense as an effective contribution to the political process. In contrast, burning effigies of whiskey tax collectors in 1792 appeared to many to be an unlawful rejection of the will of the people as expressed through Congress. Hamilton thought so, and that is why he convinced the president to lead an army west. This was his chance to replay Shays's Rebellion of 1786, this time with a federal government empowered to raise armies and put down rebellions.

The whiskey rebels, however, recognized oppressive taxes for what they were and felt entitled to resort to protest and demonstration. Representative government had not worked to their benefit. The Whiskey Rebellion was an early example of what would prove to be a long-term conflict, the tension between minority rights and majority rule.

Conflicts West and East

Washington's second term began in 1793, after a smooth and again unanimous reelection. But as the Whiskey Rebellion demonstrated, the widespread admiration for the individual man did not translate to complete domestic tranquillity. While the whiskey rebels challenged federal leadership from within the country, considerable disorder threatened the United States from external sources as well. To the west, a powerful confederation of Indian tribes in the Ohio country resisted white encroachment as thousands of settlers moved onto their tribal lands. The result was a brutal war. At the same time, conflicts between the major European powers forced Americans to take sides and nearly thrust the country into another war, this time across the Atlantic.

To the West: The Indians

By the Treaty of Paris of 1783, England had given up all land east of the Mississippi River to the United States. But unfortunately this land was not entirely England's to give; the English neglected to consult their allies in the Revolutionary War, the In-

George Washington,

PRESIDENT of the

UNITED STATES of AMERICA,

To all to whom thefe Prefents shall come:

KNOW YE, That the nation of Indians called the _Kaskaskia_ ———— inhabiting the town of _Kaskaskia_ ————

and other towns, villages and lands of the fame community ———— pawnee villages, lands, hunting-grounds and other rights and property in the peace and under the protection of the United States of America: And all perfons, citizens of the United States are hereby warned not to commit any injury, trefpaís or molef-tation whatever on the perfons, lands, hunting-grounds, or other rights or property of the faid Indians: And they and all others are in like manner forbidden to purchafe, accept, agree or treat for, with the faid Indians directly or indirectly, the title or occupation of any lands held or claimed by them; and I do hereby call upon all perfons in authority under the United States, and all citizens thereof in their feveral capacities, to be aiding and affifting to the profecution and punifhment according to law of all perfons who fhall be found offending in the premifes.

GIVEN under my Hand and the Seal of the United States this _Seventh_ day of _May_ in the year of our Lord one thoufand feven hundred and ninety-_three_ and of the Independence of the United States of America the _feventeenth._

G Washington

WASHINGTON'S PROCLAMATION ABOUT THE KASKASKIA INDIANS' LAND
The president's name, in bold print, prefaces a warning that American citizens were forbid-den to injure Indians or tres-pass their lands in the North-west Territory. When the federal government signed treaties with tribes ceding land, it often guaranteed pro-tections for land not ceded. This poster of 1793 announced federal protection for the Kaskaskia Indians in central Illinois Territory. The warn-ings were not very effective, however. Washington wrote in 1796, "I believe scarcely any thing short of a Chinese Wall, or line of Troops will restrain Land Jobbers, and the In-croachment of Settlers, upon Indian Territory."
Chicago Historical Society.

dian tribes who inhabited 25,000 square miles of that very land. As recently as 1768, England had for-mally guaranteed the Indians their rights to all land north of the Ohio River, but the Treaty of Paris sim-ply ignored that obligation.

British commanders at forts in the Great Lakes region at first concealed the terms of the 1783 treaty from local natives, the Chippewas, Potawatomis, and Ottawas. They perhaps hoped that the thirteen unsteady states would fail to create a viable coun-try, and then the British forts could simply continue with the fur trade as before. When the commander at Fort Niagara finally told the Iroquois neighbors about the treaty terms, the Indians expressed as-tonishment. They "look upon our conduct to them as treacherous and cruel. They told me they never

could believe that our king could pretend to cede to America what was not his own to give." In south-ern Ohio, British Indian agents assured the Shawnees and Delawares that England had relin-quished only political control to the United States but that Indians still had the right to occupy the land over the claims of American settlers. Such con-fusion and misrepresentation only aggravated an al-ready volatile situation.

A doubled American population, from 2.5 mil-lion in 1770 to 5 million in 1790, created an insistent pressure for western land. Several thousand settlers a year moved down the Ohio River in the mid-1780s, some bound for tranquil Kentucky but many others eyeing the fresh forests and fields north of the Ohio River. For seven months in the fall and

TREATY OF GREENVILLE
General Anthony Wayne meets with Chief Little Turtle of the Miamis and Chief Tarhe the Crane of the Wyandots to negotiate the Treaty of Greenville in 1795.
Chicago Historical Society.

winter of 1786–87, an officer at an American garrison counted 177 boats, 2,689 people, 1,333 horses, 766 cattle, and 102 wagons moving west; the increasing flow of traffic was also observed by wary Indians. By the late 1780s, government land sales in eastern Ohio commenced.

Even western Ohio was not safe from American incursions. Downriver, at the site of present-day Cincinnati, an outpost named Fort Washington was constructed in 1789 and put under the command of General Arthur St. Clair, a military man who was also named governor of the entire Northwest Territory. If the Indians had any initial hope that American military outposts would function as the British forts had, as tiny way stations in the fur trade, they soon realized their mistake. St. Clair's mission was to displace the Indians and clear the way for permanent American settlement in Ohio. He first tried peaceful tactics: He got an assortment of Indians to sign a treaty yielding land near the Muskingum River, in eastern Ohio. But the signing Indians were not chiefs authorized to undertake negotiations, so the dubious treaty did nothing to improve the chances for peace in the region.

Bloody frontier raids and skirmishes between settlers and Indians led the United States to expand its military force. Finally, St. Clair took direct action. In the fall of 1791, more than two thousand men (and two hundred women camp followers) marched north from Fort Washington to engage in battle with Miami and Shawnee Indians. The Miami chief Little Turtle and the Shawnee chief Blue Jacket anticipated the army and attacked first, at daybreak on November 4, at the headwaters of the Wabash River in western Ohio. The ferocious battle was a total disaster for the Americans. The dead and wounded amounted to 55 percent of the force before noon; only three of the women escaped alive. It was the worst defeat in the entire history of the U.S.-Indian wars. The Indians captured valuable guns and artillery and scalped and dismembered the bodies of the dead and dying. They pursued fleeing survivors for miles into the forest. The grisly tales of St. Clair's Defeat—the battle has no other official name—became instantly infamous, increasing, if this were possible, the level of sheer terror that Americans brought to their confrontation with the Indians.

President Washington responded by doubling the American military presence in Ohio, attracting the new recruits by significant pay raises for all soldiers. He appointed a new commander, General Anthony Wayne of Pennsylvania. Wayne, an officer in the Continental army during the Revolution, had earned the nickname "Mad Anthony" for his headstrong and rambunctious style of leadership. He was a heavy drinker, inclined to incautious decisions, and intolerant of disobedient soldiers. About the Indians he wrote, "I have always been of the opinion that we never should have a permanent peace with those Indians until they were made to experience our superiority."

The hasty Wayne was persuaded to delay the full thrust of his campaign for a year, while federal negotiators resumed talks with some tribes. The victory over St. Clair had given the Indians a momentary sense of bargaining strength, so they held out in peace talks for the removal of all American settlers in western Ohio. But the main function served by the delay was to allow time for the U.S. forces to train and rearm. With some 3,500 men, Wayne established two new military camps, Fort Greenville and Fort Recovery, deep in Indian territory in western Ohio.

Finally, in December 1793, Wayne was ready to seize the initiative. Moving north from Fort

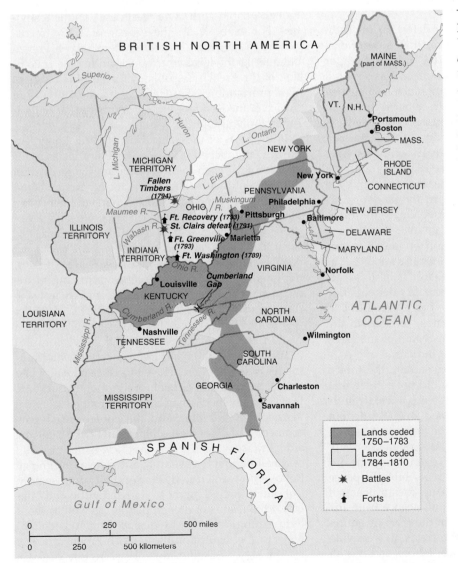

MAP 9.2
Western Expansion and Indian Land Cessions to 1810
By the first decade of the nineteenth century, the period of intense Indian wars had resulted in significant cessions of land to the U.S. government by treaty. The battles of the 1790s concentrated in Ohio, and in 1803 the region was pacified sufficiently to become the seventeenth state in the Union.

Greenville, Wayne's army camped on the very site of St. Clair's defeat in 1791. His troops faced a chilling task: They had to pile up the hundreds of skeletons and broken muskets littering the ground in order to pitch their tents. By spring, Wayne's army had engaged in several skirmishes with the Shawnees and Delawares. The decisive action came in August 1794 at the Battle of Fallen Timbers, near the Maumee River at a spot where a recent severe rainstorm had felled many trees. The confederated Indians—mainly Ottawas, Potawatomis, and Delawares, numbering around 800—first ambushed the Americans, but they were underarmed, many having only tomahawks. Wayne's well-disciplined troops made effective use of their guns and bayonets, and in just over an hour the Indians had retreated and scattered.

Fallen Timbers was a major defeat for the Indians. The Americans had also destroyed cornfields and villages on the march north, and with winter approaching, the Indians' confidence was sapped. They reentered negotiations in a much less powerful bargaining position. In 1795, about a thousand Indians representing a confederacy of nearly a dozen tribes met with Wayne and other American emissaries to work out the Treaty of Greenville. Wayne flourished a copy of the 1783 treaty with the British to prove the Americans' right to the land. He then offered $25,000 worth of treaty goods (calico shirts, yard goods, axes, knives, baling wire, blankets, kettles, mirrors, ribbons, thimbles, and abundant wine and liquor casks) and promised an annual shipment worth $10,000 of more goods—but always first deducting a rather large freight charge. The government's idea was to create a dependency on American goods to keep the Indians friendly. In exchange, the Indians ceded most of Ohio to the Americans; only the northwest region of the territory was reserved solely to the Indians.

One Indian leader held off signing the treaty. Little Turtle of the Miami tribe did not believe that the British had any right to give his tribal lands away in the first place. He argued with Wayne, but to no avail. Finally he signed the document, saying with a heavy heart that as the last to sign the treaty he would be the last to break it, even though he did not agree with its terms. The treaty brought peace to the region, but it did not bring back a peaceful life to the Miamis. The annual allowance from the United States too often came in the form of liquor. "More of us have died since the Treaty of Greenville than we lost by the years of war before, and it is all owing to the introduction of liquor among us," said Little Turtle in 1800. "This liquor that they introduce into our country is more to be feared than the gun and tomahawk."

Across the Atlantic: France and England

In 1793 and 1794, while the nation battled Indians in Ohio, other conflicts stirred far to the east, across the Atlantic. Since 1789, a violent revolution had been raging in France. At first, the general American reaction was positive, for it was flattering to think that the American Revolution had inspired imitation in France. Monarchy and privilege were overthrown in the name of republicanism; towns throughout America celebrated the victory of the French people with civic feasts and public festivities. For example, in the winter of 1793, townspeople in Augusta, Maine, gathered for a French banquet at the local courthouse under the tricolor flag of the French Republic. Citizens stuck a giant sign proclaiming "France, Liberty, Equality" into the ice of the Kennebec River and bathed it with illumination all night.

But news of the beheading of King Louis XVI quickly dampened the uncritical enthusiasm for everything French. Now Americans were divided in their sentiments. Those who fondly remembered the excitement and risk of the American Revolution were apt to regard France with the same kind of optimism. However, the reluctant revolutionaries of the 1770s and 1780s, who had worried about excessive democracy and social upheaval in America, deplored the far greater violence occurring in the name of republicanism as France moved into the revolutionary period known as the Reign of Terror.

Until 1793, support for the French Revolution could remain a matter of personal conviction. But in that year, England and France went to war, turning the question of French versus British loyalty into a very delicate and critical foreign policy question. France had helped America substantially during the American Revolution, and the confederated government had signed an alliance in 1778 promising aid if France were ever under attack. Americans still optimistic about the eventual outcome of the French Revolution wanted to deliver on that promise now. But others, including those shaken by the guillotining of thousands of French people, as well as those with strong commercial ties to England, sought ways to stay neutral in the English-French war.

In May 1793, President Washington issued a Neutrality Proclamation, with friendly assurances to both sides. His aim was to cool the tensions abroad and protect American interests in both countries. But tensions at home flared in response to official neutrality. "The cause of France is the cause of man, and neutrality is desertion," wrote H. H. Brackenridge, a western Pennsylvanian, to the president, voicing the sentiments of thousands who were still partial to France. Dozens of popular, pro-French political clubs sprang up around the country, called Democratic or Republican Societies. The societies mobilized farmers and mechanics, issued circular letters, injected pro-French and anti-British feelings into local elections, and in general heightened the degree of popular participation and public interest in foreign policy. The activities of these societies also made Washington and Hamilton intensely uncomfortable, for they vented opposition to the policies of the president. The evils of party spirit seemed to be gaining momentum.

The Neutrality Proclamation was in theory a fine idea, in view of Washington's goal of staying out of European wars. Yet American ships continued to trade between the French West Indies and France, carrying primarily grains, sugar, and other foodstuffs. In late 1793 and early 1794, England expressed displeasure with the limited American interpretation of neutrality by capturing more than three hundred of these ships in the vicinity of the West Indies. A crisis was provoked, and even pro-British politicians like Hamilton agreed that it was necessary to make a formal agreement with England. Washington sent John Jay, the chief justice of the Supreme Court and a man known to have very strong pro-British sentiments, to negotiate a treaty.

The Jay Treaty

John Jay's assignment was to secure agreement about general commercial ties between the two countries and to negotiate compensation for the seizure of American ships. In addition, he was supposed to resolve several long-standing problems dating from the end of the Revolutionary War. Southern planters wanted reimbursement for the slaves lured away by the British army during the war, and western settlers wanted England to vacate the western forts still occupied for their strategic proximity to the Indian fur trade.

Jay returned from his diplomatic mission with a treaty that almost no one liked because of several major concessions to the British. First, the treaty made no direct provision for the captured ships or the lost property in slaves. Instead, it set up commissions and complicated, lengthy procedures to settle liability charges. Second, although the Jay Treaty arranged for the evacuation of the western forts, it granted the British eighteen more months to withdraw while guaranteeing them continued rights in the fur trade. Many Americans felt that the British had already retained the forts for twelve years too long; a continued British presence in the Great Lakes region would only offer their Indian allies hope of making Michigan into the next territory of terror, as Ohio had been. Finally, the Jay Treaty called for repayment with interest of the debts some American planters still owed to British firms dating from the Revolutionary War years. In exchange for granting such generous terms to England, Jay secured some favorable commercial agreements for the United States, but even there the results were mixed. The Jay Treaty was widely regarded by many as exchanging the country's strong moral bargaining power (the outrage over the seized ships) for an improved trading status beneficial to only a handful of merchants in the overseas trade. The treaty did stave off war with England, which had been a distinct possibility in view of the hundreds of ships the British had captured. However, peace was bought at a high price, according to pro-French Americans.

John Jay returned from his diplomatic mission with a treaty that almost no one liked.

Washington sent the Jay Treaty to the Senate for approval. (Under the Constitution, only the Senate has treaty-making powers.) He tried to keep its terms secret, but a newspaper editor got hold of it and printed it, with damning commentary. In short order, powerful opposition to the treaty emerged from Maine to Georgia. In Massachusetts, graffiti appeared on a wall: "Damn John Jay! Damn everyone who won't damn John Jay! Damn everyone who won't stay up all night damning John Jay!" A newspaper in New Jersey used accessible gender imagery to explain to its readers the implications of the Jay Treaty: "The nation has been secretly, I will not say treacherously, divorced from France, and most clandestinely married to Great Britain: we are taken from the embraces of a loving wife, and find ourselves in the arms of a detestable and abandoned whore, covered with crimes, rottenness, and corruption."

The Jay Treaty passed the Senate in 1795 by a vote of twenty to ten. Some representatives in the House, led by Madison, tried to undermine the Senate's approval by insisting on a chance to vote on the funding provisions of the treaty, on the grounds that the House controlled all money bills. Finally in 1796, the House approved funds to implement the various commissions mandated by the treaty, but the vote was close, with approval squeaking by with just a three-vote margin. The cleavage of votes in both houses of Congress divided along the same lines as the Hamilton-Jefferson split on economic policy.

Federalists and Republicans

The assumption that a division into political parties was a sign of failure was soon put to a severe test. In Washington's second term, consistent voting blocs first appeared in Congress on economic issues. By the time of the Jay Treaty, party labels—Federalist and Republican—had come into use, and rival newspapers were beginning to identify with one or the other label. Washington's decision not to run for a third term opened the floodgates to serious partisan electioneering. Both the Federalists and Republicans scurried to win the highest executive office for one of their own.

The Election of 1796

Washington struggled to appear to be above party politics, and in his farewell address of September 1796, he stressed the need to maintain a "unity of government" reflecting a unified body politic. He also urged the country to "steer clear of permanent alliances with any portion of the foreign world." The leading contenders for his position, John Adams of Massachusetts and Thomas Jefferson of Virginia, in theory both agreed with him: Political parties were deplorable, and neutrality toward England and France was essential. But around them raged a party contest split along pro-English versus pro-French lines.

Adams and Jefferson were not adept politicians in the modern sense. They were men of intellect and integrity rather than of persuasion and intrigue. Jefferson had resigned as secretary of state in 1793, partly to escape conflict with Alexander Hamilton. He retired to Monticello, his home in the Virginia foothills, and claimed to be devoting himself to

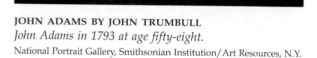

JOHN ADAMS BY JOHN TRUMBULL
John Adams in 1793 at age fifty-eight.
National Portrait Gallery, Smithsonian Institution/Art Resources, N.Y.

farming, even to the extent of shunning newspapers. Adams's job as vice president kept him closer to the political action, but his personality often kept people at a distance. He was temperamental, thin-skinned, and quick to take offense. A friend once listed his shortcomings as a politician: "He can't dance, drink, game, flatter, promise, dress, swear with gentlemen, and small talk and flirt with the ladies."

While the two principal contestants sat above the fray, the leading Federalists and Republicans met to choose candidates. To run with Adams, the Federalists picked Thomas Pinckney of South Carolina; the Republicans agreed on Aaron Burr of New York to pair with Jefferson. The Constitution did not anticipate parties and tickets. Instead, each electoral college voter could cast two votes, on only one ballot; the top vote-getter became president and the next highest assumed the vice presidency. (This procedural flaw was corrected by the Eleventh Amendment to the Constitution, adopted in 1804.) With only one ballot, careful maneuvering was required to make sure the chief rivals for the presidency did not land in the top two spots.

Into that maneuverable moment stepped Alexander Hamilton. Hamilton had resigned from the Treasury in 1795 to return to his law practice, but he still exercised great influence over Washington. Hamilton did not trust Adams, who was too independent to take orders directly from Hamilton and who had committed the sin of not warmly embracing Hamilton's various economic plans. Hamilton's preferred candidate was Pinckney, and he tried to influence electors to throw their support to the South Carolinian. But his plan backfired: Adams was elected president with seventy-one votes, and Jefferson came in second with sixty-eight votes and thus became vice president. Pinckney got fifty-nine votes, while Burr trailed with thirty.

John Adams's Presidency

Adams's inaugural speech before Congress echoed the themes of Washington's farewell address. Adams emphasized his determination to rise above party strife and put the interests of all the people ahead of party loyalty. He promised to be neutral in foreign affairs and lifted Republican hopes by noting his great respect for the French people based on seven years' residence there. As he began the speech, Adams watched the aging George Washington in the audience. Later he told his wife, Abigail, that he imagined that the old man was taunting him: "I am fairly out and you fairly in! See which of us will be happiest!" Adams had desperately wanted to be president, but now he was uneasy about managing the job.

President Adams's first mistake was to retain the same cabinet members in office at the end of Washington's administration. Adams probably thought that continuity would help some of the Washington magic rub off on him. But as it happened, the three cabinet officers—Secretary of State Timothy Pickering, Secretary of the Treasury Oliver Wolcott, and Secretary of War James McHenry—had no magic to lend him. They were mediocre appointments, in office mainly because Hamilton had recommended them to Washington. Even worse, all three were in Hamilton's pocket, writing him frequently for advice and passing that advice on to the unwitting Adams as their own. Thus, private citizen Hamilton exercised a great deal of power in the Adams presidency.

Vice President Jefferson, a gracious loser to Adams after the electoral college balloting, extended a conciliatory arm when the two old friends met in Philadelphia, still the capital. They had not seen each other in four years, and they took temporary lodging in the same boarding house as if expecting to work closely together. But quickly the Hamiltonian cabinet ruined the honeymoon. Jefferson's advice was spurned, and he withdrew from active counsel of the president, not wishing to be associated with what he regarded as bad policies.

The XYZ Affair

Foreign policy lay at the heart of the rift between Adams and Jefferson and between Federalists and Republicans. If the Jay Treaty heated tempers in 1795 and 1796, the French response to the treaty in 1797 was like oil added to the fire.

France read the Jay Treaty as the Republicans did: as a document giving so many concessions to the British that it made America a British satellite. In retaliation, France abandoned the terms of the 1778 wartime alliance with the United States and allowed privateers—armed private vessels—to seize American ships carrying British goods. The old principle of "free ships, free goods" (meaning that if the ship was not an enemy's and hence was free to pass, the goods on it were also free to pass) was disregarded. By March 1797, when Adams's inaugural address promised evenhanded neutrality, French privateers had already detained more than three hundred American vessels and seized the goods on board. In a related move, in the winter of 1796–97, France refused to recognize a new minister sent by President Washington, Charles Cotesworth Pinckney (brother of Thomas Pinckney, the defeated Federalist candidate for vice president). French authorities rudely chased him out of Paris, claiming his credentials and papers were not in order. In fact, Pinckney did have the right papers, but he was of the wrong political persuasion to suit the French, being a staunch Federalist.

To avenge these insults, Federalists started murmuring openly about war with France. President Adams wanted to try further negotiations, and he appointed a three-man commission to approach the French government. Two of the three appointees were Federalist hard-liners: Charles Pinckney and John Marshall, a lawyer from Virginia. The third man on the commission was a Republican-leaning moderate, Elbridge Gerry, a Massachusetts friend of John Adams. Adams dramatically called a special session of Congress in May 1797 to announce the mission to France and to recommend new expenditures for military defense. Negotiations, it appeared, would be backed by the muscle of military preparedness. Congress approved money for building three new naval frigates, for adding arms to some merchant vessels, and for improving defenses in coastal cities.

In the fall of 1797, the three Americans arrived in Paris to a cool welcome. But at least they were not chased out; instead, they waited several weeks to gain an official meeting with someone in power. Finally the French minister of foreign affairs, Talleyrand, sent three agents, unnamed and later known to the American public as X, Y, and Z, to the American commissioners with the suggestion that $250,000 might grease the wheels of diplomacy and obtain an official interview with Talleyrand. The French agents also insisted that the price of a peace treaty would be a $12 million loan to the French government. The three Americans were incensed by the suggestion of a bribe, and they departed to inform the president.

The American reaction to the XYZ affair was shock and anger. Even staunch pro-French Republicans began to reevaluate their allegiance. The Federalists' demand for military action became more insistent. Congress voted to expand both the army and the navy and repealed all prior treaties with France. In 1798, some twenty naval warships launched the United States into its first undeclared war, called the Quasi War by historians to underscore its uncertain legal status. The main scene of action was the Caribbean, where more than one hundred French privateers were captured; closer to home, a French ship was also captured off the New Jersey coast.

Adams was beginning to suspect that his cabinet was more loyal to Hamilton than to the presidency.

Abigail Adams wrote her sister, "Why, when we have the thing, should we boggle at the Name?" She was perplexed at Congress's reluctance to vote an outright declaration of war. Yet her husband the president was equally reluctant to take the offensive in war, because of the opposition it would generate among the Republicans. Better to "wage war and call it self-defence," said a Federalist senator from Massachusetts.

An enhanced navy presence was a military plan with broad support, but Hamilton, working through his puppets in the cabinet and his friends

in Congress, was equally interested in beefing up the army. The Federalist-dominated Congress obliged him by appropriating money to recruit ten thousand men immediately and a provisional army of another fifty thousand. Republicans feared—with justification—that the Federalists' real aim was to use the army against domestic dissenters. There was little chance of a land invasion by France, yet Hamilton convinced ex-president Washington (none too active a man now, only a year away from his death) to command the army and then insisted that the retired leader appoint Hamilton as second in command. President Adams was mistrustful, but his cabinet pressured for Hamilton, and Adams was too weak politically to prevail. He was, however, beginning to suspect that his cabinet was more loyal to Hamilton than to the presidency.

Even without a declaration, war fever remained strong among the Federalists, and intense antagonism grew between Federalists and Republicans. Republican newspapers launched heated attacks on Adams: One denounced him as "a person without patriotism, without philosophy, and a mock monarch." Another declared that he was "old, querulous, bald, blind, crippled, and toothless" and accused him of appointing relatives to office and of misusing public monies. On July 4, 1798, a pro-French mob roamed the streets in Philadelphia wearing hats with cockades, small ribbon florets that indicated solidarity with the radical revolutionaries of France. An alarmed Adams smuggled guns and ammunition into his house, fearing attack by a Republican mob.

Federalists too were taking offensive action. In Newburyport, Massachusetts, they staged a huge bonfire, burning issues of the state's Republican newspapers. The Virginia militia began drilling in the streets of Williamsburg. Officers in a New York militia unit drank a menacing toast on July 4, 1798: "One and but one party in the United States." A leading Federalist newspaper declared that "he who is not for us is against us." Jefferson wrote to a friend, "Men who have been intimate all their lives cross the streets to avoid meeting, and turn their heads another way, lest they should be obliged to touch their hats."

The Alien and Sedition Acts

If the United States had actually declared war on France, the pro-French Republicans could have been labeled traitors, subject to laws of treason. In-

CARTOON OF MATTHEW LYON FIGHT IN CONGRESS
The political tensions of 1798 were not merely intellectual. A February session in Congress degenerated from name-calling to a brawl. Roger Griswold, a Connecticut Federalist, called Matthew Lyon, a Vermont Republican, a coward. Lyon responded with some well-aimed spit, the first departure from the gentleman's code of honor. Griswold responded by raising his cane to Lyon, whereupon Lyon grabbed nearby fire tongs to beat back his assailant. Madison wrote to Jefferson that the two should have dueled: "No man ought to reproach another with cowardice, who is not ready to give proof of his own courage" by negotiating a duel, the honorable way to avenge insults.
Library of Congress.

deed, some Republicans suspected that the main impetus for a declaration of war was precisely the opportunity to treat dissenters as traitors. But without a declared war, Federalists had to invent another law to muffle opposition. In June and July 1798, Congress hammered out a two-part Sedition Act that mandated a heavy fine or a jail sentence for anyone engaged in conspiracies or revolts against the government. Further, it set penalties (up to $2,000) for anyone convicted of "speaking, writing, or publishing any false, scandalous, or malicious statement, with the intent to defame or bring into contempt or disrepute the President, the Congress, or the Government." In other words, spoken or written words that falsely criticized government leaders were now criminal utterances. The trick, of course, was to be able to distinguish between malicious opposition on the one hand and legitimate criticism on the other. Federalists in 1798 had a hard time with that distinction.

Along with the Sedition Act, Congress passed two Alien Acts. The first extended the waiting period required for an alien to achieve status as a naturalized citizen from five to fourteen years and required all aliens to register with the federal government. The second, called the Alien Enemies Act, empowered the president in time of war to deport or to imprison without trial any foreigner suspected of being a danger to the United States. The clear intent of the alien laws was to harass French immigrants in the United States and discourage others from coming.

One of the first persons prosecuted under the Sedition Act was an unfortunate man named Luther Baldwin, who was idling away a morning in a tavern in Newark, New Jersey, in July 1798. President

THE *NEW YORK JOURNAL* MASTHEAD
Newspapers proliferated in the 1790s. The New York Journal and Patriotic Register *supported the Republicans; it was issued twice a week. Like all newspapers until the mid-nineteenth century, it devoted page 1 to ads and routine notices. Current news came on page 2, spilling over to page 3. Page 4, the final sheet, again consisted of ads that continued in successive issues. All type was hand-set; the most efficient format allowed blocks of type to stay in place over many issues.*
Courtesy, American Antiquarian Society.

Adams was passing nearby that day, traveling from Philadelphia to his home in Massachusetts, and Newark had honored him with a display of flags, the ringing of church bells, and a sixteen-gun salute. When the guns fired, a drinking companion joked, "There goes the President, and they are firing at his ass." The truculent Baldwin replied, "I do not care if they fire through his ass." He probably roused a laugh from drinking companions, but the tavern owner reported the remark to Federalist leaders, who agreed that Baldwin had violated the law on sedition by expressing malicious contempt for the president. Baldwin was convicted in a federal court, fined $150, and sent to prison until he could pay it.

Baldwin's arrest was something of a fluke, for the real targets of the Sedition Act were the Republican newspaper editors who were free and abusive in their criticism of the Adams administration. One Federalist in Congress justified his vote for the law with reference to the Republican press: "Let gentlemen look at certain papers printed in this city and elsewhere, and ask themselves whether an unwarrantable and dangerous combination does not exist to overturn and ruin the government by publishing the most shameless falsehoods against the representatives of the people." In all, twenty-five men, almost all newspaper editors, were charged with sedition; twelve were convicted by juries.

The First Amendment in the Constitution's Bill of Rights guarantees freedom of speech and freedom of the press, and it is likely that a court today would strike down the 1798 Sedition Act as an unconstitutional abridgment of those liberties. Yet complete freedom to say or write anything has always been curtailed by considerations of truth versus falsity, malicious intent, and public safety. The Federalists truly thought that calling the president nasty names endangered the security of the government, just as shouting "Fire!" in a crowded theater endangers public safety. Today's laws distinguish between libelous speech about public figures and about private citizens, allowing greater freedom for hostile or inflammatory speech against public officials. The defendants charged with sedition in 1798 generally argued that their writings were legitimate political opinion protected by the First Amendment, and some of them won their cases on those grounds. Slowly the concept of legitimate opposition in politics was taking shape.

Jefferson and Madison strongly opposed the Alien and Sedition Acts on the grounds that they were in conflict with the Bill of Rights. The Sedition Act in particular was a direct blow to the Republican Party. The Republicans did not have the votes to revoke the acts in Congress, nor could the federal judiciary, dominated by Federalist judges, be counted on to challenge them. So Jefferson and Madison turned to the state legislatures, the only other competing political arena, to mount their opposition. They each drafted a set of resolutions condemning the Alien and Sedition Acts and had the legislatures of Virginia and Kentucky present them to the federal government in late fall 1798. The Virginia and Kentucky Resolutions tested the novel argument that state legislatures have the right to judge the constitutionality of federal laws and to nullify laws that infringe on the liberties of the people as defined in the Bill of Rights. No other legislatures joined the Virginia and Kentucky protest, and the resolutions made little dent in the application of the Alien and Sedition Acts. But the idea of a state's right to nullify federal law did not disappear; it surfaced again some thirty years later and played a role in the coming of the Civil War.

Amidst all the war hysteria, sedition fears, and party conflict in 1798, President Adams somehow managed to regain a measure of caution. Though his character tended toward the temperamental and vain and he generally stewed over personal insults, he was remarkably restrained in pursuing opponents under the Sedition Act. And he finally refused to be pushed into a hasty declaration of war by the extreme Federalists to avenge American honor. No doubt he was beginning to realize how much he had been the dupe of Hamilton. He also shrewdly realized that France was in fact not eager for war and that a peaceful settlement might be close at hand. In January 1799, a peace initiative from France

WASHINGTON'S DEATH
The death of George Washington in 1799 occasioned many memorial souvenirs. This painting on glass represents Washington as the Pater Patriae, *the father of his country. A soldier weeps, while Columbia with her shield and spear looks stunned with grief. Minerva, the goddess of war, holds the great man's portrait, and an angel trumpets his famous military victories. Nothing in the memorial notes his service as president, except the oblique statement that he was "Great in the Senate," a reference to ancient Roman government service. Curiously, the amateur artist failed to capture Washington's actual likeness.*
The Metropolitan Museum of Art, Gift of Edgar William and Bernice Chrysler Garblach, 1964 (64.309.6).

arrived, in the form of a letter assuring Adams that diplomatic channels were open again and that new commissioners would be welcomed in France. Adams accepted this overture and appointed a new negotiator; by late 1799, the Quasi War with France had subsided. But in responding to the French initiative, Adams lost the support of a significant part of his own party, thus sealing his fate as the first one-term president of the United States.

In responding to the French initiative, Adams lost the support of a significant part of his own party, thus sealing his fate as the first one-term president of the United States.

The election of 1800 was openly organized along party lines, with the self-designated national leaders of each group meeting to handpick their candidates for president and vice president. Adams ran again but was doomed to lose. When the election was over, the new president, Thomas Jefferson, mounted the inaugural platform to announce, "We are all republicans, we are all federalists." He meant that everyone was both at once, an appealing rhetoric of harmony appropriate to an inaugural address. But his formulation perpetuated a denial of the validity of party politics, a denial that ran deep in the founding generation of political leaders.

Conclusion: Parties Nonetheless

During the crisis of 1798–1799, a strong sense of peril gripped the nation, and out of that arose the initial acknowledgment of the existence of political parties. The Federalists grew out of the main core of supporters for the Constitution in 1788, and they dominated Congress and the presidency throughout the 1790s. They persisted in thinking of themselves as the legitimate, disinterested rulers who could give the country enlightened leadership; they did not like their leadership challenged. Under Hamilton's urgings, they supported economic plans to develop commerce and enhance the strength of the federal government.

But those economic plans quickly engendered opposition, initially among onetime Federalists in Congress like Madison. As opposition widened—to the whiskey tax, to the Jay Treaty, and finally to the Alien and Sedition Acts—it drew in larger numbers of citizens beyond the elected members of the federal government and began to coalesce into a widespread and still diverse group that took the name Republican. The Federalists were pro-British, pro-commerce, and ever alarmed about the potential excesses of democracy, while the Republicans celebrated, up to a point, the radical republicanism of France. Grafted into the Republican group was the 1780s Antifederalist suspicion of a powerful federal government; the Sedition Act seemed an especially clear example of what the Republicans feared.

When Jefferson offered his conciliatory assurance that the political citizens of the United States were at the same time "all republicans" and "all federalists," he was possibly thinking of widely shared ideas that undergirded political institutions in the new nation. Certainly his listeners favored republican government, where power derived from the people, and likewise they favored the unique federal system of shared governance structured by the Constitution. But by 1800, these same two words, adapted to be the proper names of parties, had come to signify competing philosophies of government. Federalists and Republicans had strong disagreements that had developed over a decade of decision making. Jefferson's speech was spoken aloud; his listeners could not hear the presence or absence of capital letters. For at least some of his listeners, Jefferson's assertion of harmony across party lines could only have seemed bizarre.

CHRONOLOGY

1789 Washington inaugurated president.
French revolution begins.
First Congress meets in New York City.

1790 Hamilton's funding and assumption plans approved.
Government moves from New York to Philadelphia.
First federal census conducted.

1791 Bill of Rights ratified by states.
Bank of the United States chartered by Congress.
St. Clair's defeat by Ohio Indians.
Congress passes whiskey tax.

1793 Washington's second term begins.
War breaks out between France and England.

1793 Washington issues Neutrality Proclamation.
Battle of Fallen Timbers; U.S. victory over Indians in Ohio.

1794 Whiskey Rebellion in western Pennsylvania.

1795 Treaty of Greenville with Indians.
Jay Treaty with England.

1796 John Adams elected president, Thomas Jefferson vice president.

1797 XYZ affair with France.

1798 Quasi War with France.
Alien and Sedition Acts.
Virginia and Kentucky Resolutions.

1800 Election campaign between Adams and Jefferson.

1801 Jefferson elected president.

BIBLIOGRAPHY

GENERAL WORKS

Rudolph M. Bell, *Party and Faction in American Politics: The House of Representatives, 1789–1801* (1973).

Richard Buel, *Securing the Revolution: Ideology in American Politics, 1789–1815* (1972).

William Nisbet Chambers, *Political Parties in a New Nation: The American Experience, 1776–1809* (1963).

Stanley Elkins and Eric McKitrick, *The Age of Federalism: The Early American Republic, 1788–1800* (1993).

John F. Hoadley, *Origins of American Political Parties, 1789–1803* (1986).

Ralph Ketcham, *Presidents above Party: The First American Presidency, 1789–1829* (1984).

John C. Miller, *The Federalist Era, 1789–1800* (1960).

John R. Nelson, *Liberty and Property: Political Economy and Policymaking in the New Nation, 1789–1812* (1987).

James Rogers Sharp, *American Politics in the Early Republic: The New Nation in Crisis* (1993).

WASHINGTON'S ADMINISTRATION

Bob Arnebeck, *Through a Fiery Trial: Building Washington, 1790–1800* (1991).

Kenneth R. Bowling, *Politics in the First Congress, 1789–1791* (1990).

Kenneth R. Bowling, *The Creation of Washington, D.C.: The Idea and Location of the American Capital* (1991).

Steven R. Boyd, ed., *The Whiskey Rebellion: Past and Present Perspectives* (1985).

Alexander DeConde, *Entangling Alliance: Politics and Diplomacy under George Washington* (1958).

James T. Flexner, *George Washington and the New Nation, 1783–1793* (1970).

James T. Flexner, *George Washington: Anguish and Farewell, 1793–1799* (1972).

Constance McLaughlin Green, *Washington: Village and Capital, 1800–1878*, vol. 1 (1962).

Forrest McDonald, *The Presidency of George Washington* (1974).

John Reps, *Washington on View: The Nation's Capital since 1790* (1991).

Robert A. Rutland, *The Birth of the Bill of Rights, 1776–1791* (1991).

Bernard Schwartz, *The Great Rights of Mankind* (1977).

Thomas P. Slaughter, *The Whiskey Rebellion: Frontier Epilogue to the American Revolution* (1986).

Leonard White, *The Federalists: A Study in Administrative History* (1948).

SOCIETY AND CULTURE

Richard D. Brown, *Knowledge Is Power: The Diffusion of Information in Early America, 1700–1865* (1989).

Patricia Cline Cohen, *A Calculating People: The Spread of Numeracy in Early America* (1983).

Nancy Cott, *The Bonds of Womanhood: Women's Sphere in New England, 1780–1835* (1977).

Cathy N. Davidson, *Revolution and the Word: The Rise of the Novel in America* (1986).

Emory Elliott, *Revolutionary Writers: Literature and Authority in the New Republic, 1725–1810* (1982).

Richard B. Kielbowicz, *News in the Mail: The Press, the Post Office, and Public Information, 1700–1860* (1989).

Laurel T. Ulrich, *A Midwife's Tale: The Life of Martha Ballard, Based on Her Diary, 1785–1812* (1990).

THE ECONOMY AND HAMILTON'S PROGRAM

Joyce Appleby, *Capitalism and a New Social Order: The Republican Vision of the 1790s* (1984).

Christopher Clark, *The Roots of Rural Capitalism: Western Massachusetts, 1780–1860* (1990).

Jacob E. Cooke, *Tench Coxe and the Early Republic* (1978).

Jacob E. Cooke, *Alexander Hamilton* (1982).

Clarence Danhof, *Change in Agriculture: The Northern United States, 1820–1870* (1969).

Robert A. Hendrickson, *The Rise and Fall of Alexander Hamilton* (1981).

James A. Henretta, *The Origins of American Capitalism: Collected Essays* (1991).

Joan Jensen, *Loosening the Bonds: Mid-Atlantic Farm Women, 1750–1850* (1986).

Allan Kulikoff, *The Agrarian Origins of American Capitalism* (1992).

James Lemon, *The Best Poor Man's Country: A Geographical Study of Early Southeastern Pennsylvania* (1972).

Winifred Rothenberg, *From Market-Places to a Market Economy: The Transformation of Rural Massachusetts, 1750–1850* (1992).

Gerald Stourzh, *Alexander Hamilton and the Idea of Republican Government* (1970).

NATIVE AMERICANS AND THE FRONTIER

Robert F. Berkhofer Jr., *Salvation and the Savage: An Analysis of Protestant Missions and American Indian Response, 1787–1862* (1965).

Colin G. Calloway, *Crown and Calumet: British-Indian Relations, 1783–1815* (1987).

Gregory E. Dowd, *A Spirited Resistance: The North American Indian Struggle for Unity, 1745–1815* (1992).

Dorothy Jones, *License for Empire: Colonialism by Treaty in Early America* (1982).

Francis Paul Prucha, *American Indian Policy in the Formative Years: The Indian Trade and Intercourse Acts, 1780–1834* (1962).

Malcolm J. Rohrbough, *The Transappalachian Frontier: People, Societies, and Institutions, 1775–1850* (1978).

Wiley Sword, *President Washington's Indian War: The Struggle for the Old Northwest, 1790–1795* (1985).

Richard White, *The Middle Ground: Indians, Empires, and Republics in the Great Lakes Region, 1650–1815* (1991).

J. Leitch Wright, *Britain and the American Frontier, 1783–1815* (1975).

FOREIGN RELATIONS

Henry Ammon, *The Genet Mission* (1973).

Albert H. Bowman, *The Struggle for Neutrality: Franco-American Diplomacy during the Federalist Era* (1974).

Jerald A. Combs, *The Jay Treaty: Political Battleground of the Founding Fathers* (1970).

Lawrence D. Cress, *Citizens in Arms: The Army and the Militia in American Society to the War of 1812* (1982).

Alexander DeConde, *The Quasi-War: The Politics and Diplomacy of the Undeclared War with France, 1797–1801* (1966).

Peter P. Hill, *French Perceptions of the Early American Republic, 1783–1793* (1988).

Daniel G. Lang, *Foreign Policy in the Early Republic* (1985).

Charles R. Ritcheson, *Aftermath of Revolution: British Policy toward the United States, 1783–1795* (1969).

William Stinchcombe, *The XYZ Affair* (1981).

Richard J. Twomey, *Jacobins and Jeffersonians: Anglo-American Radicalism in the United States, 1790–1820* (1989).

FEDERALISTS AND REPUBLICANS

Ralph A. Brown, *The Presidency of John Adams* (1975).

Joseph Charles, *The Origins of the American Party System* (1956).

Noble Cunningham, *The Jeffersonian Republicans: The Formation of Party Organization, 1789–1801* (1957).

Larry D. Eldridge, *A Distant Heritage: The Growth of Free Speech in Early America* (1994).

Joseph J. Ellis, *Passionate Sage: The Character and Legacy of John Adams* (1993).

John Ferling, *John Adams: A Life* (1992).

Richard Hofstadter, *The Idea of a Party System: The Rise of Legitimate Opposition in the United States, 1780–1840* (1969).

John R. Howe, *The Changing Political Thought of John Adams* (1966).

Richard H. Kohn, *Eagle and Sword: The Federalists and the Creation of the Military Establishment in America, 1783–1802* (1975).

Stephen G. Kurtz, *The Presidency of John Adams: The Collapse of Federalism, 1795–1800* (1957).

Leonard Levy, *Jefferson and Civil Liberties: The Darker Side* (1963).

Leonard Levy, *The Emergence of a Free Press* (1985).

Drew McCoy, *The Elusive Republic: Political Economy in Jeffersonian America* (1980).

Drew McCoy, *The Last of the Fathers: James Madison and the Republican Legacy* (1989).

Peter Shaw, *The Character of John Adams* (1976).

James Morton Smith, *Freedom's Fetters: The Alien and Sedition Laws and American Civil Liberties* (1966).

Donald H. Stewart, *The Opposition Press of the Federalist Period* (1969).

John Zvesper, *Political Philosophy and Rhetoric: A Study of the Origins of American Party Politics* (1977).

STATE HISTORIES

Richard R. Beeman, *The Old Dominion and the New Nation, 1788–1801* (1972).

Paul Goodman, *The Democratic-Republicans of Massachusetts* (1964).

Norman Risjord, *Chesapeake Politics, 1781–1800* (1978).

Charles Steffen, *The Mechanics of Baltimore: Workers and Politics in the Age of Revolution, 1763–1812* (1984).

Alan Taylor, *Liberty Men and Great Proprietors: The Revolutionary Settlement on the Maine Frontier, 1760–1820* (1990).

Alfred Young, *The Democratic-Republicans of New York: The Origins, 1763–1797* (1967).

Jefferson's intentions were scientific. He instructed Lewis to investigate Indian languages and kinship systems, to collect plant and animal specimens, and to chart the geography of the rivers and mountains of the West. The explorers were equipped with measuring devices—a quadrant, a microscope, thermometers—and an authoritative treatise on animal classification. Nine of the men kept journals. Congress had more traditional goals in mind: The expedition was to scout out possible locations for military posts, open commercial agreements for the fur trade, and seek out that centuries-old goal, a water pathway between the East and West Coasts.

The explorers left St. Louis in the spring of 1804, working their way northwest up the Missouri River on a large barge. Abandoned Indian villages, their onetime residents victims to smallpox, dotted the river's shores, grim evidence that European contact was not new in 1804. By the time the chill of October came, the men had passed through Sioux territory and arrived at what is now the central part of North Dakota, where they camped for the winter at a Mandan village. The Mandan Indians were familiar with British and French traders from Canada, but the black man York created a sensation. As happened repeatedly on the trip, Indians rubbed moistened fingers over the man's skin to see if the color was painted on. York was of imposing size and strength, yet he danced with agility and amazed the Indians that "so large a man should be active," according to Lewis.

Early next spring, they turned west, now aided by a hired guide, a French trapper accompanied by his wife, a sixteen-year-old Indian woman named Sacajawea, who had just had a baby. What first seemed to be a burden to Lewis and Clark—a mother and infant—was to prove unexpectedly helpful. Indian tribes encountered en route withdrew their suspicion that the Americans were hostile because, as Lewis wrote in his journal, "no woman ever accompanies a war party of Indians in this quarter."

When Lewis met the three Shoshone women in August, Sacajawea was not with him. Yet his friendly overtures were accepted, and the women led him to their tribe. Soon Lewis was sharing a pipe with Cameahwait, the Shoshone chief, who removed his moccasins to smoke as a gesture of trust—and insisted that a reluctant Lewis do likewise. The Indian leaders delivered many cheek-to-cheek embraces to Lewis; "we wer all carresed and be-

SACAJAWEA

Sacajawea and baby, as imagined by mid-nineteenth-century artist Edgar S. Paxson, who produced a series of paintings of grand moments on the Lewis and Clark expedition. The young Shoshone mother was also called "Janey" by the explorers, who admired her courage and fortitude. Her baby, Jean Baptiste Charbonneau, was nick-named Pompey. William Clark brought the boy to St. Louis when he was six to educate him. In the 1820s, the youth was taken to Germany by the prince of Württemberg; he returned six years later, fluent in German, French, Spanish, and English. Half Shoshone and half French, Charbonneau became a guide and interpreter for many trading expeditions throughout the West until his death in the 1860s.

Sacajawea oil painting by Edgar S. Paxson. The University of Montana Museum of Fine Arts Collection.

smeared with their grease and paint till I was heartily tired of the national hug," Lewis recorded in his journal.

When the rest of the expedition caught up, they were surprised to discover that Cameahwait was in fact Sacajawea's brother. The young mother had been kidnapped from her tribe some years before and taken captive by the Hidatsas near the Mandan village before being traded to her French husband. The Shoshone provided the needed horses and guides, and the expedition continued west, Sacajawea and infant choosing to accompany them.

The Lewis and Clark expedition reached the Pacific at the mouth of the Columbia River, in what is now Oregon, in November 1805. The party wintered there and then returned home by the same route. Upon their return they were greeted as national heroes. They had established favorable relations with dozens of Indian tribes. They had collected information on the people, soils, and geography of the West that was invaluable to later travelers. Their scientific observations of plants and animals extended the frontiers of knowledge in botany and biology. And they inspired a nation of restless explorers and solitary imitators.

The success of the Lewis and Clark expedition created a high point in Jefferson's early presidency. Other undertakings proved far more problematic. A difficult election had marred Jefferson's glory in winning the high office. Serious Indian troubles in the Northwest Territory continued to plague his administration, and soon those Indians allied with the British, mounting pressures for war. Jefferson adopted experimental economic policies to forestall war, but the War of 1812 came anyway and perilously split the United States. Jefferson's successors in office, James Madison and James Monroe, continued his policies, only to find that the combination of slavery and westward movement created the first great constitutional crisis, over Missouri statehood in 1820.

The Lewis and Clark expedition turned out to be the high point in the explorers' lives as well. Sacajawea died of a fever about ten years later in the Dakota region. Meriwether Lewis met a violent end in 1809 under mysterious circumstances, ruled a suicide at the time. Clark became governor of the Missouri Territory and struggled through the 1820 Missouri crisis. And York, who had carried a gun, danced with Indians, and attracted favorable attention, to the great benefit of his white companions on the trip, returned to slavery in Kentucky.

Jefferson's Presidency

Thomas Jefferson later called his election the "revolution of 1800." Certainly the years 1799–1800, marked by conflict and instability, had many classic ingredients of a revolutionary moment. Pervasive discontent engulfed the country, touched off by the Alien and Sedition Acts and the Quasi War with France. Newspaper invective intensified, making it seem that the very survival of the United States was at stake.

At the same time, a different and truly deadly "revolution of 1800" crystallized. A literate slave named Gabriel who worked in Richmond, Virginia's capital, followed the abusive rhetoric of the presidential campaign and figured that when white men were so badly divided, the time was right to strike for freedom. Rebellion perhaps seemed logical to Gabriel, but it took Federalists and Republicans alike by surprise.

What Jefferson probably really meant when he recalled 1800 as a moment of revolution was the new vision of republican simplicity he brought to bear on the federal government. Throughout his years in office, he aimed for a limited government, and yet he also found that circumstances sometimes required him to draw on the expansive powers of the presidency.

The "Revolution of 1800"

Although John Adams had ensured his own defeat in 1800 by reopening diplomatic channels with France, it was by no means assured that Thomas Jefferson—both Adams's vice president and his Republican opponent—would therefore win the presidency. It took seven months in 1800 for the states to select electoral college voters. Then the electoral college produced a tie vote—surprisingly, between Jefferson and his running mate, Senator Aaron Burr of New York, both with seventy-three votes. (Adams got sixty-five votes and Charles Cotesworth Pinckney of South Carolina, sixty-four.) The election was thus thrown to the House of Representatives, where a Federalist-dominated chamber would make the final choice.

Into this uncertain moment stepped Gabriel, a twenty-four-year-old blacksmith owned by Virginian Thomas Prosser. From spring to midsummer of 1800, Gabriel recruited hundreds of coconspirators from five Virginia counties to a plot to end slavery.

ity of America, were corrupt and worthless, he believed, and their promotion had no authority under the Constitution.

In Jefferson's vision, the source of true freedom in America was the independent farmer, someone who owned and worked his land, producing agricultural products both for himself and for the market. Widespread landownership, which would support unsubservient and therefore virtuous citizens, was Jefferson's cornerstone of liberty. The dependence of tenancy, on the other hand, "begets subservience and venality, suffocates the germ of virtue, and prepares fit tools for the designs of ambition." He embedded the idea of easy access to land in the various land ordinances he designed in the 1780s for the Northwest Territory. Once, he even went so far as to suggest that Virginia use its vast western domain to hand fifty acres of land, free of charge, to every landless white man. Members of the Virginia legislature, substantial landowners who had gotten their land the old-fashioned way (inheritance, shrewd marriage, or outright purchase) found his idea much too radical—free land devalued existing private property—and his idea was quickly dismissed. But Jefferson remained committed to the idea of cheaply available land; abundant, unsettled western land seemed to him to be the insurance policy that guaranteed American freedom.

In Jefferson's vision, the source of true freedom in America was the independent farmer, someone who owned and worked his land, producing agricultural products both for himself and for the market.

Fresh with distrust of Hamiltonian plans, Jefferson as president set about to dismantle as many as he could of the Federalist governmental powers. He reduced the size of the army by a third, leaving only three thousand soldiers, and cut back the navy from twenty-five to seven ships. Peacetime defense, he felt, should rest with "a well-disciplined militia," not a standing army. With the consent of Congress, he abolished all federal internal taxes, including both those based on population and the hated whiskey tax; government revenue would now derive solely from customs duties and from the sale of western lands. (This maneuver was of particular benefit to the South, where the three-fifths clause of the Constitution counted slaves for both representation and taxation. Now the South enjoyed its extra weight in the House of Representatives without having to pay any extra monies in taxes.) Jefferson's goal aimed at republican simplicity in government, and by the end of his first term he had deeply reduced Hamilton's cherished national debt.

A properly limited federal government, according to Jefferson, really had little cause to be expensive in times of peace. It was responsible for running a postal system, maintaining the federal courts, staffing lighthouses, collecting customs duties, and conducting a census once every ten years. There were a few salaries to be paid, but those were kept to a minimum. The president had just one private secretary to help him with his correspondence, and Jefferson paid him out of his own pocket. (Another 14 servants performed domestic and valet chores for the president, and they were also paid—or owned—by Jefferson.) The Department of State employed only 8 people: Secretary James Madison, 6 clerks, and a messenger. The Treasury Department was by far the largest unit, with 73 revenue commissioners, auditors, clerks, and two watchmen. The entire payroll of the executive branch of the government amounted to a mere 130 people in 1801. In the hot summer months, it shrank to just a few dozen men.

And they were all men. Albert Gallatin, who headed the Treasury, once suggested to Jefferson that they consider remedying a shortage of qualified candidates by appointing talented women, to which Jefferson brusquely replied, "The appointment of a woman to office is an innovation for which the public is not prepared, nor am I." The shortage of willing and able male employees resulted from the temporary nature of the work and the severe interruption it posed to family life and to more lucrative careers that would suffer if let go. Lawyer John Marshall, for example, served in President Adams's cabinet, traveled to France as a diplomat to negotiate the XYZ affair, and then reluctantly allowed himself to be nominated as chief justice of the Supreme Court in 1801, all the while fearing that his profitable law practice was ebbing away. He wrote his ailing wife, back home in Richmond, Virginia, "Oh God, how much time and how much happiness have I thrown away?"

The Judiciary and the Midnight Judges

Marshall was in fact genuinely surprised to be nominated for the Supreme Court, but he took the job to help out the Federalist Party. John Adams's re-

JEFFERSON'S
INDEPENDENT FARMER
*A Jeffersonian vision of rustic
virtue: a farmer plows his
field on the outskirts of Salem,
North Carolina. The farmer
wears a hat, coat, and long
trousers to protect his legs;
he also appears to be barefoot.*
Collection of the Wachovia Historical
Society.

sponse to the sweeping Republican victory in the 1800 election was to quickly appoint Federalists to the one branch of government he still controlled: the judiciary.

The federal court system took its shape from the Judiciary Act of 1789, built on the skeleton provided by the Constitution, which said only that there would be a Supreme Court and "such inferior courts as the Congress may from time to time ordain and establish." The 1789 act established six Supreme Court justices who would simultaneously preside over six circuit courts, which traveled to hear cases over a large territory. No one imagined that the Supreme Court would need to meet often, or even together, so it seemed natural to design other duties for the justices. But the travel required by circuit-riding was grueling, and the best legal minds of the day were reluctant to accept appointment to the Supreme Court. In the 1790s, the Court met infrequently, and justices issued decisions separately.

One of the last acts of the Federalist presidency and Congress was to pass the Judiciary Act of 1801, which Adams signed into law in February, his final month in office. The new act set up sixteen circuit courts, an increase of ten districts, and separated them from the Supreme Court justices. The ratio-

nale for the change was sound: More courts were in fact needed, and releasing Supreme Court justices from circuit-riding duties was a blessing for the experienced (and usually aged) judges best suited to the highest court. Under the new plan, the Supreme Court would take cases on appeal from circuit courts run not by themselves but by different judges. All of these changes were reasonable, but they had a huge drawback to the Republicans: The act produced a political windfall of new appointments for the Federalists. If he could act quickly, President Adams suddenly could appoint sixteen new judges who would hold lifetime tenure in the job, plus dozens more state attorneys, marshals, and clerks to go with each court. The Judiciary Act of 1801 also reduced the size of the Supreme Court, from six to five justices. Adams had recently appointed John Marshall, a solid Federalist, to a vacant sixth seat, but once the Judiciary Act became law, the Republican president would not be able to fill the next resigned seat.

Adams and Marshall worked feverishly in the last weeks of February. They secured agreements from 217 men to serve in judicial, diplomatic, and military posts—an astonishing number, in view of the slowness of mail and travel and an expectation of considerable refusals. The two men were still at

The Americans suggested that the United States might simply seize New Orleans, if buying it was not an option, hinting that a military alliance with the British might also be part of the plan. Finally, the French negotiator suddenly asked Livingston to name his price for the entire Louisiana Territory, stretching north to Canada. Livingston stalled, and the Frenchman floated prices ranging from $125 million to $60 million. Livingston, sensing a French eagerness to sell, shrewdly stalled some more. He pointed out that if the price was too high, "it would render the present Government [Jefferson's] unpopular, and have a tendency, at the next election, to throw the power into the hands of men who were most hostile to a connection with France. I asked him," Livingston wrote to Jefferson just hours after the meeting, "whether the few millions acquired at this expense would not be too dearly bought?" Within a few days, the French sold the entire territory for the bargain price of $15 million.

Jefferson and most of the Congress were delighted with the outcome of the diplomatic mission. Congress quickly approved the purchase and voted for a bond issue to raise money for the price. However, all but one of New England's representatives voted against it. (The one affirmative vote was that of John Quincy Adams.) Federalist-dominated New England had been willing to consider war to seize New Orleans and control navigation rights on the river. But the huge territory that came along with the city raised sudden anxiety about the ultimate geographic balance of power in the United States. So much land, sure to be carved into states one day, made some fear the eventual marginalization of New England.

Jefferson had his own reason to be reluctant about the Louisiana Purchase. The price was right, and the enormous expansion of territory fulfilled Jefferson's dream of abundant farmland for generations of Americans to come. But by what authority in the Constitution could he justify the purchase? His frequent criticism of the Hamiltonian stretching of the Constitution came back to haunt him. His legal reasoning told him he needed a constitutional amendment to fully authorize the addition of territory; more expedient minds told him the treaty-making powers of the president could be invoked to cover his action. Expediency won out. In late 1803, the American army took formal control of the Louisiana Territory, and the United States was now 828,000 square miles larger than it had been before.

Republicans in a Dangerous World

The election of 1804 proved an easy triumph for the Republican Party. Jefferson's Federalist opponent, Charles Cotesworth Pinckney of South Carolina, garnered only 14 votes in the electoral college, in contrast to 162 for the president. New England, the stronghold of federalism, was lukewarm for Jefferson, but only Connecticut's electoral votes went for Pinckney. Just months before the election, the Federalists had lost their shrewdest statesman: Alexander Hamilton, called by some "the brains of the Federalist Party," was tragically killed in a duel, gunned down by Aaron Burr. (See Historical Question, page 358.) Republicans would hold the presidency for another twenty years.

In his second term, Jefferson turned his attention to serious troubles arising out of the ongoing war between France and England, which gravely imperiled the United States. As a peaceful alternative to war, the president experimented with economic sanctions and trade embargoes. Jefferson and his successors in office faced war threats not only across the Atlantic but also in the new states of the old Northwest Territory, where a powerful new Indian confederacy challenged the westward press of American settlement.

Troubles at Sea

In the 1790s, American shipping had prospered when the two leading European powers, France and England, were at war, for they left trade routes and markets wide open for American ships to fill. England and France determined not to make that mistake again. When war broke out between them in 1803, the two powerful countries established restrictions on American trade with the enemy. England declared a vast array of goods, far beyond war materials, to be forbidden and announced a blockade of the French coast to stop American ships and to search for illegal goods. France too, starting in 1807, declared it would seize any American ship caught trading with England.

When the British started enforcing their threats in 1806, the costs were felt by many hundreds of Americans. In addition to searching for prohibited goods, British naval patrols claimed the right to seize (and impress into service) sailors whom they accused of being deserters from the British navy. In

TWO CAPTAINS AT SEA
The captains of two sailing ships confer at sea, using horns to amplify their voices, in this water-color by Benjamin Latrobe (also the architect of the Capitol). New England coastal towns like Salem, Newburyport, Portsmouth, and Portland played a major role in the shipping trade and extended their routes to China and India in the early nineteenth century, in addition to the West Indies–Europe circuit. Some schooners really were as small as these depicted, measuring fifteen to eighteen feet wide and as little as forty feet long. Jefferson's embargo worked a great hardship on the New England industry.
Maryland Historical Society, Baltimore.

fact, some deserters had fled and taken new jobs in the American merchant marine. Some had even become naturalized U.S. citizens. The impressment sweeps captured those men but also caught up hundreds of native-born Americans as well. Between 1807 and 1812, about 2,500 men were taken captive by imperious British commanders and were impressed into royal naval service. Jefferson and the American public were outraged.

One incident in particular made the usually cautious Jefferson nearly belligerent. In June 1807, an American ship, the *Chesapeake,* had picked up some British deserters, and a short time later a British frigate ordered the *Chesapeake* to stop for inspection. The *Chesapeake* refused, and the British opened fire, killing three Americans. The attackers then boarded the ship and forcibly removed four British subjects. Provocative as the incident was, what made it even more insulting was the location: The attack occurred in Chesapeake Bay, well within U.S. territory. President Jefferson assembled his cabinet to read his draft of a heated manifesto he wanted to issue to Great Britain, demanding an end to impressment. One cabinet member described the high tension of the moment: The incident, he wrote, "has excited the spirit of '76 and the whole country is literally in arms." But the country was not actually prepared for war—the much reduced army and navy presented a serious problem—and so Jefferson's cabinet toned down his challenge to England. Instead, Jefferson banned British warships from all travel in American waters. Plans were put in motion to increase the armed forces substantially, but still Jefferson preferred diplomacy as the instrument of foreign policy. He instructed James Monroe, the American ambassador in England, to pressure the government there to repudiate the policy of impressment. Monroe's efforts were unsuccessful.

The Embargo and Its Aftermath

Jefferson's initial response to the British threat against American shipping in 1806 had been to push nonimportation laws in Congress. A select list of British-made goods was declared off limits for trade. But the *Chesapeake* incident triggered much stronger measures. Jefferson and his secretary of state, James Madison, developed the idea of a total embargo on all trade.

In December 1807, Congress passed the Embargo Act, which forbade any American ships from engaging in any trade with any foreign port. It was a drastic measure, but it was intended as economic coercion substituting for a far more drastic possibility, a declaration of war. The immediate goal was to make England suffer, and all foreign ports were included in the ban so as to discourage illegal trading through secondary ports. The two Republican leaders were convinced that England needed America's trade goods, mainly agricultural products, far more than America needed British goods. Jefferson's long-standing anti-English prejudice had by now rubbed off on Madison, who belittled British imports as "superfluities or poisons," things Americans would be better off without. At his peak of personal influence, the president secured swift agreement from a Republican-dominated Congress bent on sending a signal to England.

The Embargo Act of 1807 was a total disaster. From 1790 to 1807, U.S. exports had increased fivefold, and in an instant the Embargo Act wiped out all commerce. Worse, it was ineffective as a penalty to the enemy. England did not suffer much at all; it simply turned to South American countries for agricultural supplies, unhindered now by American vessels, which were no longer on the seas. New England, the heart of the shipping industry, complained the loudest. Trade was at a standstill, and unemployment began to rise. Emergency town meetings convened to plan a course of action; protest petitions flooded Washington. Federalists in Barre, Massachusetts, pointed out that the damage to trade also hurt farmers: "We consider the interest of Agriculture and Commerce as inseparable"; the "belief that the farmer can flourish, while [the merchant] is

neglected and depressed" was a serious error, they warned. Connecticut Federalists dredged up Jefferson's own words from the 1798 Kentucky Resolutions, suggesting that state nullification of the federal embargo might be in order. States could "interpose their protecting shield between the rights and liberties of the people and the assumed power of the general government," said Connecticut's governor, Jonathan Trumbull. The South hurt mightily as well; tobacco rotted on the docks and cotton went unpicked. The wheat crop of the central and western states plummeted in value, and river traffic came to a halt. The federal government itself suffered too, for import duties were the chief source of national revenue.

> *The Embargo Act was a drastic measure, but it was intended as economic coercion substituting for a far more drastic possibility, a declaration of war.*

The Embargo Act proved difficult to police, and inevitably American shippers reacquainted themselves with their Revolutionary-era traditions of illegal smuggling. Despite the evasions, the U.S. economy was severely affected. Prices of basic agricultural products like corn fell by a third from the boom year of 1804. The Federalist Party, in danger of fading away after its very weak showing in the election of 1804, began to pick up considerable strength from the anti-Jefferson protest.

The embargo stayed in place until the last day of Jefferson's presidency, in March 1809, but it created a very rocky and bewildering final year for the administration. Congress finally repealed it and replaced it with the Non-Intercourse Act of 1809, which prohibited trade only with the two belligerent nations, England and France, and their colonial possessions. In effect, the new law opened the way for a legal, indirect trade, so the economic anguish of New England shippers and southern planters in the export trade was greatly diminished, for the moment.

Madison Gets Entangled

In mid-1808, Jefferson made it clear that he planned to follow George Washington's lead and limit his presidency to two terms. James Madison, the secretary of state for eight years and Jefferson's closest ally in the government, was the clear heir apparent.

Disgruntled Republicans from hurting tobacco regions of the South made a move to support James Monroe, another Virginia planter with wide experience as a diplomat to England, but Madison was the clear front-runner choice of the various state caucuses of Republicans. At this point, party politics, still held to be a bad thing by leading statesmen, operated through informal coalition building and statewide caucuses that orchestrated state and local elections. The Federalist caucuses, thinking they would gain strength from the unpopular Embargo Act, chose Charles Cotesworth Pinckney again. Pinckney did much better than in 1804; he received forty-seven electoral votes, nearly half the number that the winner, James Madison, got. Support for the Federalists remained centered in the New England states, where they regained a number of seats in both the House and the Senate, but Republicans still held the balance of power.

The depredations of England on American ships continued. Sailors still faced captivity and impressment, while cargoes were subject to inspection. The British claimed that their actions could be construed as enforcement of the American Non-Intercourse Act. But Madison took as insult the notion that England should presume to enforce American laws at all. He insisted that Americans were neutral in the British-French conflict and that a neutral ship must by definition be carrying a neutral cargo.

In 1810, the Non-Intercourse Act expired, and Congress replaced it with a complicated law called Macon's Bill Number 2, named for a North Carolina congressman. This law now permitted direct trade with either France or England, the lucky country being the one to first give assurance that it had lifted restrictions on American shipping. The French ruler Napoleon seized the initiative and declared that France would revoke its restrictions, on condition that the United States reinstate its embargo against England. Madison too hastily accepted Napoleon's offer without waiting to see if the French leader backed up his pledge with action. With trade to France reopened, Madison notified England that he intended to reinstate the embargo in the spring of 1811, unless England rescinded its search and seizure policy.

Unfortunately for Madison, the duplicitous French leaders continued to seize American ships. Furthermore, the British made no move to stop impressments or to repeal trade restrictions, and Madison was forced to reactivate the embargo, much to the great displeasure of the New England shipping industry. In 1811, the country was seriously divided and in a deep quandary about what to do. To some, it seemed the United States must be on the verge of war; but it was hard to decide if the enemy should be France or England. To others, war meant disaster, for it would surely finish off the grievously hurting shipping industry. Madison knew he had been duped by France, but he persisted in treating England as the bigger threat to American security.

A new Congress, elected in the fall of 1810, arrived in Washington in March 1811 just as Madison's threatened embargo was to take effect. Some of the new and much younger members were eager to avenge the insults from abroad. In particular, Henry Clay, thirty-four, from Kentucky, and John C. Calhoun, twenty-nine, from South Carolina, became the center of a group informally called the War Hawks. Though calling themselves Republicans, like Madison, these younger men had much more expansive ideas of the way the United States should meet the challenge of enemies abroad.

Indian Troubles in the West

In the atmosphere of indecision about war with European powers, news filtered east about renewed difficulties with Indian tribes in the old Northwest Territory. Since the mid-1790s, after the Battle of Fallen Timbers, a general peace had been obtained in the Ohio valley. The Treaty of Greenville had established a boundary to Indian territory that had held until recent years. But by 1810, white settlement was again encroaching north and west, through the boundary in some cases; more than 230,000 Americans now lived in the Ohio Territory. Concerned Indians were renewing their alliances with supportive British Indian agents and fur traders in Canada, who were a potential source of food and weapons. While Madison contemplated war with England, he could be certain that part of the sting of that war would be felt on the frontier, as Indians and the British reinvigorated the alliance they had shared since the 1760s.

But this time a new element emerged in the Indian strategy. A powerful and charismatic Shawnee war chief named Tecumseh was successfully building a confederacy among the many Indian tribes in the Indiana, Ohio, and Michigan region. Tecumseh's remarkable political talents were enhanced by the reputation of his visionary brother Tenskwatawa, known throughout the region as the "Prophet." Tecumseh and Tenskwatawa had lost their father and two brothers in various battles with whites in the late eighteenth century. Their widowed mother, a Creek woman who had married a Shawnee chief, had moved south when Tecumseh was ten and left him and his younger siblings in the care of an aunt. Tecumseh trained for the warrior role, while his younger brother followed a much more sedentary and embittered life of idleness and excessive drinking. But in 1805, Tenskwatawa fell into a state of near death. His wife prepared him for burial, but then the man revived and recounted a startling vision, a meeting with the Master of Life. Tenskwatawa now claimed to have prophetic powers. He urged Indians everywhere to return to the customs of their ancestors and to give up borrowed practices—using European dress, plows, firearms, bread, and alcohol—learned from the white invaders. The Prophet's teachings sparked a religious revival throughout the Ohio valley and beyond, as far as the Mississippi.

From 1805 to 1807, the Prophet's popularity spread. He preached that the Americans were children of the Evil Spirit, scum and pollution destined in the end to be destroyed. The Master of Life wished the Indians to stay forever where they were, he said, and so the Prophet led his people to a site where Tippecanoe Creek joined the Wabash River in northern Indiana and established a village called Prophetstown. Tecumseh, too, inspired followers and denounced white Americans. "Once," he said, "there was not a white man in all this country. Then it all belonged to the redmen . . . now made miserable by the white people, who are never satisfied but always encroaching on our land. . . . The only way to stop this evil, is for all the redmen to unite in claiming a common right in the soil, as it was at first, and should be now." The brothers together pledged a potent blend of spiritual regeneration and political unity that proved very attractive to tribes such as the Chippewa, Potawatomi, Delaware, Miami, Kickapoo, Wyandot, and Winnebago.

The Shawnee chief Tecumseh advised that "the only way to stop this evil, is for all the red-men to unite in claiming a common right in the soil, as it was at first, and should be now."

The American governor of the Indiana Territory, William Henry Harrison, became alarmed by the two brothers' growing power. In early 1806, he issued a challenge to the Indians near him in Indi-

TENSKWATAWA

Tenskwatawa, the Shawnee Prophet, and his brother Tecumseh led the spiritual and political efforts of a number of Indian tribes to resist land-hungry Americans moving west in the decade before the War of 1812. The Prophet is shown in a portrait by George Catlin with necklaces, metal arm- and wristbands, earrings, and a necklace that looks very similar to George Washington's gorget (see page 201).

National Museum of American Art, Washington, D.C./Art Resource, New York.

ana: Who is this man the Prophet, and why do you believe he has divine powers? Harrison proposed that the test for divinity be an ability to perform miracles, and he named a few which he was certain would be impossible. "Ask of him to make the sun stand still, or the moon to alter its course—or the dead to rise from their graves." But as it happened, an eclipse of the sun was near at hand, in June 1806, and somehow the Prophet knew that in advance. He invited doubters to come to Prophetstown on the appointed day to see the sun stand still. His apparent miracle magnified his reputation enormously.

Harrison was skeptical about the Prophet's powers, but he understood that with Tecumseh he was up against a worthy opponent. He described the Indian leader as "one of those uncommon geniuses which spring up occasionally to produce revolutions." Harrison was not about to concede defeat, however. If Tecumseh's goal was to build an Indian confederacy based on the concept that all Indian lands were held in common by all the tribes, so that no individuals or even single tribes could sell land to U.S. agents, Harrison would undermine it. In 1809, he arranged with the leaders of three tribes to cede tribal lands in a document called the Treaty of Fort Wayne, in exchange for annual payments of money. Tecumseh, discouraged and angry, began to extend his confederacy and to prepare for war.

In 1811, while Tecumseh was on a trip to Alabama to forge alliances with the Creek and Chickasaw tribes, Governor Harrison decided to march on Prophetstown, to disperse the Shawnees with the Prophet and burn their settlement. With one thousand armed men he approached Tippecanoe Creek, but the Indians attacked first. The two-hour battle resulted in about a hundred deaths—sixty-two Americans and forty Indians—before the Prophet's forces fled the area. Harrison burned the town and its food supplies. The November 1811 Battle of Tippecanoe was heralded as a glorious victory for the Americans; Harrison acquired the nickname "Tippecanoe" and used it as a patriotic rallying cry nearly thirty years later when he ran for and won the presidency in 1840. The Indians' faith in the Prophet's magical powers diminished sharply; Tenskwatawa never again enjoyed such influence.

The War of 1812

The Indian conflicts in the Northwest Territory in 1811 soon merged into the wider conflict with England known as the War of 1812. The defeat at Tippecanoe pushed Tecumseh into a renewal of the old alliance with British military commanders stationed at outposts in lower Canada. If there had been doubt before about who should be the target of a declaration of war, France or England, it was now abundantly clear, especially to westerners living near the frontier, that the British should get the honor.

The War Begins

The several dozen young War Hawks new to Congress saluted Harrison's Tippecanoe victory and continued to urge the country on to war. Mostly lawyers by profession, they came from the West and South, and they welcomed a war with England both to legitimize war with Indians and to bring an end to impressment. Many were expansionists, looking to occupy Florida and threaten Canada. Representative Felix Grundy from Tennessee, for example, rejected British maritime plundering, asserting, "I prefer war to submission." The Indian troubles in Indiana could be explained by Grundy "in one way only: Some powerful nation must have intrigued with them, and turned their peaceful disposition towards us into hostilities. . . . We shall drive the British from our Continent . . . [and] receive the Canadians as adopted brethren."

Kentuckian Henry Clay was elected Speaker of the House, an extraordinary honor in view of his youthful age and his lack of prior experience in Congress. John C. Calhoun from South Carolina got a seat on the Foreign Relations Committee. The War Hawks urged major defense expenditures; the army, for example, was quadrupled in size. Through all these war preparations, New England Federalists in Congress staunchly refused to endorse any of them, just as they had opposed the embargo in 1807.

In early 1812, President Madison called for a renewed embargo on all American shipping. Unlike the first embargo, designed to be economic coercion, this version was a two-month embargo designed to clear merchant ships off the ocean in preparation for war. (While Congress debated the embargo in secret session, Federalists leaked word of the trade stoppage to mercantile friends. The wharves of Baltimore, Philadelphia, New York City, and Boston instantly filled to capacity with ships shoving off with one last cargo. In the space of a few days, hundreds of ships set sail.) When the embargo expired in June 1812, Congress declared war on Great Britain. The vote divided on sectional lines: New England and some of the Middle Atlantic states opposed the war, while the South and West were strongly for it.

Ironically, Great Britain had just decided to repeal its authorization for British ships to search and seize American ships. News of that diplomatic breakthrough arrived too late, however; the war machine was in motion and would not be stopped. The Foreign Relations Committee issued an elaborate document titled *Report on the Causes and Reasons for War*, written mainly by Calhoun. The report went far beyond a condemnation of Britain's search and seizure policy. War was necessary, the document said, to avenge the insults of Great Britain in treating the United States as though it was a third-rate power. Extravagant language about Britain's "lust for power," "unbounded tyranny," and "mad ambition" suggested that America was actually engaged in a second revolution for independence; failure to resist and fight Great Britain would lead to a "shameful degradation" of the United States. These were fighting words, in a war that was in large measure about insult and honor.

The War Hawks proposed an invasion of Canada, Britain's colony to the north, confidently predicting victory in four weeks, before the fall elections. Instead, the war lasted thirty months, and Canada never fell. The northern invasion turned out

to be a series of strategic blunders that revealed the grave unpreparedness of the country for war. The combined strength of British soldiers and Indian allies was unexpectedly powerful, and, in addition, the United States made no attempt at the outset to create a naval presence on the Great Lakes. Detroit quickly fell to the British and Indian forces, as did Fort Dearborn (site of the future Chicago). The American plan called for a three-pronged attack by land moving toward Montreal. But all three attack routes failed, and by the fall of 1812, the war was in a dismal state.

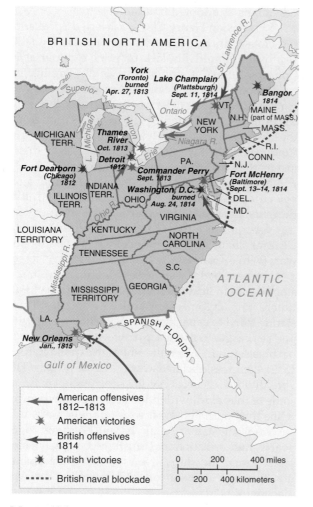

M A P 10.3
The War of 1812
Battles in this war were fought along the border of Canada and in the Chesapeake region. The most important American victory came in New Orleans, two weeks after peace had been agreed to in England.

> *The northern invasion of Canada turned out to be a series of strategic blunders that revealed the grave unpreparedness of the country for war.*

Worse, the New England states dragged their feet in raising troops, and New England merchants continued to carry on an illegal trade with Great Britain. Later in the war, Britain as a war measure blockaded the United States coastline to prevent trade—everywhere except New England. The British understood full well the potential for friendly alliance with the New England states and were pursuing a divide and conquer strategy. New Englanders drank India tea in Liverpool cups, while President Madison fumed in Washington about Federalist disloyalty.

The presidential election in fall 1812 solidified Federalist discontent with the war. Madison stood for a second term, opposed by DeWitt Clinton of New York. Clinton was only marginally identified with the Federalists; his uncle George Clinton, a venerable New York Republican, had served Madison as vice president in 1808–1812. The younger Clinton called himself a Republican, but one of a different stripe from Madison. The Federalist strongholds fell naturally into his camp. Clinton picked up all of New England's electoral votes, with the exception of Vermont's, and also took New York, New Jersey, and part of Maryland, states with significant antiwar feeling. Madison won in the electoral college, 128 to 89, but his margin of victory was considerably smaller than in the 1808 election.

In late 1812 and early 1813, Americans began to turn the tide in the war for a time. First came some reassuring victories at sea, by the navy ships *Con-*

A BOXING MATCH, or Another Bloody Nose for JOHN BULL.

WAR OF 1812: BOXING MATCH
A battle between the American
ship Enterprise *and the British*
ship Boxer *off the Maine coast*
sparked this wishful-thinking
cartoon. A bare-knuckled James
Madison has just punched King
George III, blackened his eye,
and made his nose bleed. The
king begs "Mercy, mercy on
me," and acknowledges "your
[Madison's] superior skill."
Madison asserts "we are an En-
terpriscing *Nation" capable of*
"equal force any day." This
Madison clearly does not antici-
pate the humiliating burning of
Washington in 1814.
Courtesy, American Antiquarian
Society.

slitution, *Wasp,* and *Hornet;* but little lasting gain came with these successes. Americans attacked York (now Toronto), the capital of Upper Canada, and burned it in April 1813. A few months later, Commodore Oliver Hazard Perry defeated the British fleet at the western end of Lake Erie. Emboldened by these successes, General William Henry Harrison drove an army into Lower Canada from Detroit and in October 1813 defeated British and Indian fighters at the Battle of the Thames, where the Shawnee chief Tecumseh met his death.

Another battle with Indians proved successful, yet vicious. A lanky and eccentric Tennessee general named Andrew Jackson led 2,500 Tennessee militiamen south in an attack on Creek Indians who had shown signs of allying with the Indian confederacy of the Northwest Territory. At the Battle of Horseshoe Bend in March 1814, Jackson defeated the Creeks, leaving more than 550 Indians dead, including women and children along with the warriors. A subsequent treaty with surviving Creeks opened the rich lands of northern Alabama to American settlement. Jackson next marched to Pensacola, Florida, directly against the president's orders to leave the Spanish settlers alone. (War Hawks were enthusiastic, however.) Jackson's excuse was that the Spanish had been supplying Creeks with arms. His men captured a Spanish fort in November and then withdrew.

The British Offensives of 1814

In August 1814, British ships sailed into Chesapeake Bay toward Washington, D.C. For three days, Washington dwellers were thrown into a panic, wondering what to expect. Families evacuated their children and valuables, banks removed their money, and government clerks packed up boxes of important papers to be carted away. One clerk in the State Department quickly located the Declaration of Independence and removed it to safety.

When five thousand British troops landed and marched toward the city, the only defense came from inexperienced militia units from Maryland. President Madison and his cabinet had been planning to dine together; instead they mounted horses and vainly tried to inspire the militia, who fled in disorder as the British advanced. The president's wife waited at home until she could hear the enemy troops, at which point she left hurriedly with a black servant named Sukey and a canvas portrait of George Washington quickly removed from its frame. When the British commanders entered the president's residence, they helped themselves to the meal roasting in the kitchen, toasted the king with the president's wines, and then set fire to the house. They also burned the Capitol, a newspaper office, some dockyards, and a well-stocked arsenal of weapons. Only a violent thunderstorm that night

CURIOSITY

Curiosity *is the playful title of this 1833 painting, done in New York City by a young German-born artist, Christian Mayr. Three women, possibly a mother and two daughters, have apparently just shown a gentleman caller into a room behind a large wooden door. Is it a business call on the man of the house? A courtship call on an older sister? The women, ears and eyes pressed to the door, are keen to know what is going on. Information networks often had important gender dimensions built into them in the 1830s.*

against the state and keeping a brothel. The fundamental assumption of the law of coverture was that husbands did—and ought to—control their wives.

State legislatures, when codifying their laws, generally passed up the opportunity to rewrite the laws of domestic relations, even though they were redrafting so much other law in light of republican principles. For Federalists and Republicans alike, the British common law governing women and marriage seemed fully adequate and in no need of change. As the practice of law expanded and more young men gained legal training to meet the growing needs of the population, legal treatises appeared in print offering handy compilations articulating common law principles and practices of current courts. One influential treatise on family law, published in 1816 by Tapping Reeve, founder of one of the country's leading law schools, at Litchfield, Connecticut, was titled *The Law of Baron and Feme* ("lord and woman"). Reeve's terminology was exactly the common legal usage. Lawyers never paused even to defend, much less to challenge, the assumption that unequal power relations lay at the heart of marriage.

Marriage in the early Republic was a legal event that joined two consenting persons for life under a binding contract whose terms were specified by the state. The laws of coverture defined the restrictions and duties of wives; in exchange, wives were entitled to economic support and protection by husbands. The early Republic's conception of the "republican wife and mother" (see chapter 9) in no way altered this legal framework. The virtuous wife whose obedience was earned by affection and the enlightened mother who acquired intellectual skills to transmit to her citizen sons still operated well within the boundaries of the expected female subservience and obligation to men.

The one aspect of family law that changed in the early Republic was divorce. Before the Revolution, only New England jurisdictions had recognized a right to divorce; by 1820, every state except South Carolina had set up divorce procedures. Divorce was uncommon and difficult, however, for it was obtainable only under carefully circumscribed conditions that found substantial fault with one partner, such as desertion or adultery. In many states, divorces could be obtained only by petition to the state's legislature, probably a daunting obstacle for many ordinary people. In some instances, divorcing couples were denied legal dissolution on the grounds that they had conspired to deceive authorities about their marital problems; a mutual wish to terminate a marriage was by itself insufficient grounds for divorce. A New York judge affirmed that "it would be aiming a deadly blow at public morals to decree a dissolution of the marriage contract merely because the parties requested it. Divorces should never be allowed, except for the protection of the innocent party, and for the punishment of the guilty." States were clearly invested in upholding the institution of marriage, both to protect persons they thought of as naturally dependent (women and children) and to regulate the use and inherited transmission of property. And certainly the state's enforcement of marriage as an unequal relationship played a major role in maintaining gender inequality in the nineteenth century.

Single adult women could own and convey property, make contracts, initiate suits, and pay taxes. They could not vote (except in New Jersey until 1807; see chapter 9), serve on juries, or practice law, so their civil status was limited. Single women's economic status was often limited as well: Unless a woman had inherited adequate property, being a single adult woman in Jeffersonian America was highly correlated with poverty.

Lawyers never paused even to defend, much less to challenge, the assumption that unequal power relations lay at the heart of marriage.

One form of legal action involving single women that became more prevalent in the early decades of the nineteenth century was the seduction suit. Its increased usage as a legal remedy points to a heightened social value attached to female virginity. When unmarried women lost their virginity (with pregnancy being a closely related, highly visible, and yet not legally necessary symptom of the condition), they and their relatives increasingly concluded they had lost value in the marriage market. The legal remedy to recover damages was a seduction suit, brought against the accused man—not by the woman, but by her father or master. The law squarely reflected the traditional assumption that women were a form of property owned by fathers or masters, whose injury resulted from the loss of services they suffered when girls were seduced. Seduction suits were therefore a part of property law, not family law. And yet judges and juries typically awarded successful plaintiffs large damage judgments, on the order of $800 to $1,200, figures far in excess of the annual market value of any young woman's labor. A Pennsylvania judge in 1822 observed that loss of service was merely a "technical form of action" and that the real loss being compensated was "the destruction of the family's honor." Apparently the value of a woman's sexual honor was very high. From seduction suits to coverture, the evolving American legal system expressed the nineteenth century's commonsense notions about the status, capacity, and expected behavior of men and women in society.

Free men and women, that is. None of the legal institutions that structured white gender relations applied to blacks enslaved in the South. Slaves were denied the opportunity of marriage sanctioned by the state. As property themselves, they could not freely consent to any contractual obligations, including marriage. The protective features of state-sponsored unions were thus denied to black men and women. Husbands could not guarantee support, nor could wives guarantee exclusive services, because both were controlled by a more powerful authority, the slave owner. But this also meant that slave unions did not establish unequal power relations backed by the force of law, as did free marriages.

Still, one prevalent cultural assumption about wives' incapacity apparently could apply to slave women as well as free women under coverture: the assumption that only husbands and not wives were responsible for political actions and decisions. Just as Anna Martin was not held accountable for being a loyalist in her own right, so too Nanny, the wife of Gabriel who plotted revolution in Virginia in 1800, was not arrested by Richmond authorities. Indeed, she was not even questioned about her husband's planned insurrection, nor was any other woman.

Women and Church Governance

In most Protestant denominations around 1800, white women made up the majority of congregants, as they had for some time. Although they usually outnumbered men at prayer meetings and services, the church hierarchy, consisting of ordained ministers and elders, was exclusively male, and the governance of most denominations rested in men's hands.

There were some exceptions, however. In several small evangelical groups, notably Baptist congregations in New England that had been strongly affected by the Great Awakening of the mid-eighteenth century, women served along with men on church governance committees, deciding admission of new members, voting on the hiring of ministers, participating in disciplinary proceedings, and even debating doctrinal points. The Awakening's emphasis on more egalitarian social relations worked to elevate women's authority in these Baptist congregations.

Quakers, too, another nonhierarchical religious group, had a history of recognizing that women's spiritual talents could equal men's. Quaker women who felt a special call were accorded the status of ministers, which among Quakers meant persons capable of leading and speaking in a religious meeting. Quaker governance, however, proceeded along sex-segregated lines: Separate men's and women's committees heard disciplinary cases and formulated church policy.

Between 1790 and 1820, a small and highly unusual set of women emerged who actually engaged in open preaching. Most were from the Freewill Baptist groups centered in Maine, New Hampshire, and Vermont, with a group in upstate New York via migration. Others were from small Methodist sects, and yet others rejected any formal religious affiliation. Probably fewer than a hundred such women existed, most of them single or widowed, but several dozen became known beyond their local communities because they traveled (some of them hundreds of miles), creating converts and controversy wherever they went. They spoke from the heart, without prepared speeches, often exhibiting trances and emotional religious states. Some denied they were infringing on the male domain of preaching and instead were exhorting and praying in public. But exhorting—that is, counseling or warning—was in practice sometimes hard to distinguish from preaching. Fanny Newell, a Methodist woman in Maine, described in 1809 her compulsion to speak out: "I felt such an impression to speak, that I did not dare to neglect it; but rose and exhorted the people, and had great liberty in so doing." But none of these women were ordained ministers, with official credentials to preach or perform baptisms.

Perhaps the most unusual and well known exhorting woman was Jemima Wilkinson, who called herself the "Publick Universal Friend." After a near-death experience from high fever in 1776, Wilkinson awoke to proclaim that her body was no longer female *or* male, but the incarnation of the "Spirit of Light." She dressed in men's clothes, wore her hair in a masculine style, shunned gender-specific pronouns, and preached openly in Rhode Island and Philadelphia, drawing some committed followers but also many hecklers. In the early nineteenth century, Wilkinson withdrew to a settlement called New Jerusalem in western New York with more than 250 followers, her fame sustained by periodic newspaper articles that fed a public curiosity about her lifelong transvestism and her unfeminine forcefulness.

As more women exhorters cropped up, their behavior came under increasing fire. A Baptist periodical in Massachusetts printed frequent reminders of the biblical prohibition "Let your women learn to keep silence in the churches" (1 Corinthians 14:34). An 1810 article elaborated on the logic of this prohibition: It arises "from the relation [women] bear to men, as being the weaker vessel, the derived,

WOMEN AND THE CHURCH: JEMIMA WILKINSON
Jemima Wilkinson, the Public Universal Friend, in an early woodcut, wears a clerical collar and body-obscuring robe, in keeping with the claim that the former Jemima was now a person without sex or gender. Her hair is pulled back tight on her head and curled at the neck in a masculine style of the 1790s.
Rhode Island Historical Society.

the dependent part." Therefore, for women to speak their faith in church "is not only in opposition to scripture, but to nature itself." Female preachers well knew the scriptural passages that dictated women's subordination, and they were ready with biblical interpretations of their own, as in Deborah Pierce's 1817 book *A Scriptural Vindication of Female Preaching, Prophesying, and Exhortation.*

Even though women on the radical fringes of a few denominations carved out some sort of role as exhorters, in the more mainstream religious societies women's leadership status was in decline. Even the New England Baptist communities that for a half century had allowed women to participate in church governance steadily withdrew that privilege. Between 1790 and 1810, women disappeared from church committees, their disfranchisement rarely commented on in the records. One glimpse of the tension over the issue emerges in an 1823 grievance lodged by a woman in Warren, Rhode Island, against her Baptist brethren, commenting that "the Sisters were formerly capable of executing the business of Committees, and if they were not now, they had better be cutt off from the church." Apparently the men agreed; this woman was excommunicated five months later for "disorderly conduct."

The decades from 1790 to the 1820s marked a period of unusual confusion, ferment, and creativity in American religion. New denominations blossomed, new styles of religiosity gripped adherents, and an extensive periodical press devoted to religion popularized all manner of theological and institutional innovations. In such a climate, even the age-old tradition of gender subordination came into question here and there among the most radically democratic of the churches. Yet on balance, the presumption of male authority over women was deeply entrenched in American culture. Individual churches established their respectability by reinstating patterns of dominance and subordination along gender lines.

Madison's Successors

Through the elections of 1812, 1816, and 1820, Republican Virginians extended their lock on the presidency to twenty-four years. The Federalists never recovered from the taint of disloyalty after the Hartford Convention, and the party moved into its twilight days, dying a surprisingly graceful death. In 1816, James Monroe beat Federalist Rufus King of Massachusetts for the presidency by an electoral vote of 183 to 34. When Monroe stood for reelection in 1820, the national presence of the Federalists was fully eclipsed. All but one electoral vote went to Monroe, the sole dissenting vote cast for John Quincy Adams, the son of Federalist John Adams, who wasn't even running. The unanimity of the 1820 election did not reflect voter satisfaction with the status quo, however, for barely a quarter of eligible voters bothered to vote. Apathy in federal elections was at an all-time high.

Monroe's two terms were dubbed the "Era of Good Feelings" by a contemporary newspaper.

Americans congratulated themselves on finally having achieved the perfection of the one-party state. Yet Monroe's presidency was not at all placid. A major constitutional crisis emerged over the admission of Missouri to the Union, pitting the North against the South. Foreign policy questions animated sharp disagreements as well. The election of 1824 brought forth an abundance of candidates, all claiming to be Republicans. A one-party political system was put to the test of practical circumstances; it failed and then fractured.

The Missouri Compromise

The faith that good and wise statesmen could find broad areas of agreement was put to the test in 1819 and 1820 over the question of admitting Missouri to the Union. The origins of the crisis lay in a seemingly routine event: Missouri applied for statehood. In the years since 1815, four other states had joined the Union (Indiana, Mississippi, Illinois, and Alabama), reflecting the fast westward flow of population now unimpeded by any Indian confederacy. Generally the constitutional pathway from territory to statehood operated smoothly, as it had since the 1790s.

What was different about Missouri was that while it shared a northern geography with the lower portions of Illinois, Indiana, Ohio, and Pennsylvania, it already contained a significant number of slaves. Many southern whites had been migrating across the Mississippi River from Virginia, Kentucky, and Tennessee, bringing their slaves with them to stake claim to the rich soil of this part of the Louisiana Purchase. The ten thousand slaves taken there by owners amounted to about one-sixth of the territory's population.

The first sign that Missouri's unusual combination of geography and demography would cause trouble arose in February 1819, when white Missourians petitioned Congress for statehood. On that occasion, a New York representative named James Tallmadge Jr. proposed two amendments to the Missouri statehood bill: that slaves thereafter born in Missouri would be free at age twenty-five and that no new slaves could be imported into the state. The combined effect of the two conditions, if federally imposed, was to abolish slavery in Missouri. Tallmadge's plan would mean that by 1844 the only slaves in Missouri would be the survivors of the existing ten thousand now in residence; in another generation, when they died out, Missouri would be entirely a free state. The gradual emancipation fea-

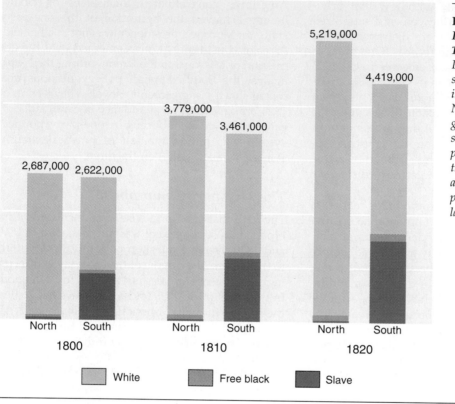

FIGURE **10.1**
Population Trends,
1800–1820
Population in the northern
states grew more rapidly than
in the South, increasing the
North's representation in Con-
gress. Slaves remained a sub-
stantial part of the South's
population. By the Constitu-
tion's three-fifths clause, slaves
augmented southern political
power, even though they
lacked all rights of citizenship.

ture very much resembled the plan New York had adopted in 1785. It did not strip slave owners of their current property, even giving them full use of the labor of newborn slaves well into their prime productive years, at which point a profit-minded owner could simply sell his property in the South rather than let twenty-fifth birthdays rob him of his investment. In the short run, this was hardly a radical plan to eradicate slavery and deprive individual owners of their property.

Nevertheless, southerners in Congress loudly protested Tallmadge's amendments. Under gradual emancipation, owners would not lose their shirts, but they would, in losing slaves and thus slavery, lose their distinctive manner of livelihood. Even larger loomed the question of Missouri as an eventual free state, a prospect gravely alarming to the South. Just as southern economic power rested on slave labor, southern political power also drew extra strength from enumerated slave bodies: The Constitution's three-fifths clause ordained that representation in Congress was based on the total population, with each slave counting as three-fifths of a white person. In 1820, the South as a region had seventeen more representatives in Congress than it would have had if only whites had figured in the population basis. Without slaves, the South's political power would be much diminished. Hence, southerners argued that the federal government had no authority to alter social systems in new states.

In 1820, the South as a region had seventeen more representatives in Congress than it would have had if only whites had figured in the population basis. Without slaves, the South's political power would be much diminished.

Both of Tallmadge's amendments passed in the House of Representatives, but with a close and sharply sectional vote of North against South (with a few northern Republicans taking the side of the South). The debate was ferocious and explosive, nearly a complete dress rehearsal of all the main ar-

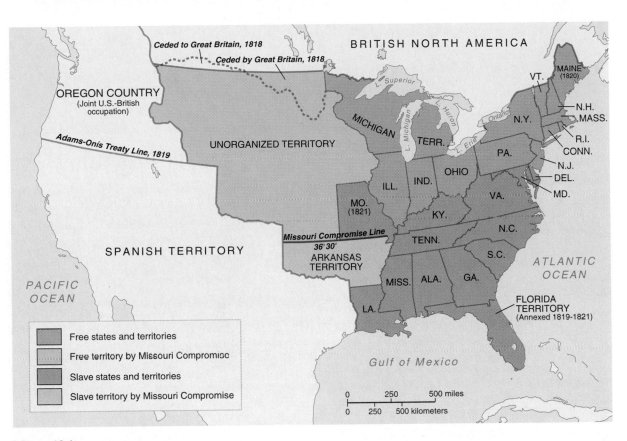

MAP 10.4
The Missouri Compromise, 1820
After a difficult battle in Congress, Missouri entered the Union in 1821 as part of a package of compromises. Maine was admitted as a free state to balance slavery in Missouri; and a line drawn at latitude 36°30' put most of the rest of the Louisiana Territory off limits to slavery in the future.

guments that would surface a generation later in the 1850s struggle leading to civil war. A Georgia representative predicted that the Missouri slavery question had started "a fire which all the waters of the ocean could not extinguish. It can be extinguished only in blood."

The Senate, with an even number of slave and free states, voted down the amendments, with some border states joining the proslavery line. The deadlock of House versus Senate meant that the total package of Missouri statehood was set aside for the next congressional term.

When it came up again in 1820, it was clear that the passions ignited in 1819 had not cooled in the least. It took a northern senator of southern origins (Jesse Thomas, formerly of Maryland, who now lived in Illinois with his five black "apprentices") to

come up with the pieces of a compromise, a plan with something for everyone. One new element was that Maine now wanted statehood. Thomas proposed a dual admission, Maine as a free state and Missouri as a slave state, to maintain the balance of power in the Senate. To make the North feel less alarmed about such a northern-reaching state being part of the slave South, Thomas proposed that the southern latitude of Missouri, 36'30", become a permanent line dividing slave from free. All of the Louisiana Territory north of that line—except Missouri—would be closed to slavery. Senator Thomas's plan passed in the Senate.

The northern-dominated House was not so easily persuaded, but in the end the compromise passed. The North secured a large area where federal prohibition of slavery was guaranteed and got

A VIEW OF ST. LOUIS FROM AN ILLINOIS TOWN
Just fifteen years after the Missouri Compromise, St. Louis was already a booming city, having gotten its start in the eighteenth century as a French fur trading village. It was incorporated as a town in 1809 and chartered as a city in 1822. In this 1835 view, commercial buildings and steamships line the riverfront; a ferry on the Illinois shore prepares to transport travelers across the Mississippi River. Black laborers (in the foreground) handle loading tasks. The Illinois side is a free state; Missouri, where their ferry lands, is a slave state.
The Saint Louis Art Museum.
Private Collection of Dorothy Ziern Hanon and Joseph B. Hanon.

Maine as an immediate counterbalance to Missouri. The South got Missouri without any interference with slavery. The whole package passed only because seventeen northern representatives decided that minimizing sectional conflict was in the best interests of the United States and so voted with the South for the unrestricted entry of Missouri.

President Monroe and Thomas Jefferson, retired to his home in Charlottesville, Virginia, worried that the schism over admitting Missouri meant that a Federalist Party was regrouping to challenge the Republicans, and that a new party division would fracture along sectional lines, the free North versus the slave South. But even ex-Federalists agreed that this was too dangerous a fault line to let shape national politics. When new parties did develop in the 1830s, they took pains to bridge geography, each party developing a presence in both North and South. Monroe and Jefferson also worried about the future of slavery. Each understood slavery to be deeply problematic, but, as Jefferson said, "We have the wolf by the ears, and we can neither hold him, nor safely let him go. Justice is in one scale, and self-preservation in the other."

A HOUSE IN MAGNOLIA, FLORIDA
*The artist who completed this 1829 watercolor of a balconied home was a thirteen-year-old boy named
George Washington Sully, whose family moved to the Florida Panhandle in the first decade of U.S. own-
ership of the territory. Many frontier settlements were springing up and real estate speculation flourished.
Magnolia, along the St. Marks River, attracted three hundred settlers in less than a decade, lured by four
brothers from Maine who had originally purchased the land. In 1835, Magnolia was bypassed by an early
Florida railroad, and within two years it was a virtual ghost town. George Sully's watercolor suggests the
grand intentions so quickly abandoned by the early settlers. His family moved to New Orleans.*
Collection of Samuel H. and Roberta Vickers/The Florida Collection.

The Monroe Doctrine

While the Congress struggled to compromise on
north-south divisions internal to the country, President Monroe was challenged by external issues of
foreign policy. In 1816, American troops led by General Andrew Jackson invaded the northern part of
Spanish Florida in pursuit of hostile Seminole Indians, who had been welcoming escaped slaves across
the border into territory owned by Spain. Jackson
declared himself the commander of northern
Florida in 1817, and he demonstrated his power in
1818 by executing two British men who he claimed
were dangerous enemies.

In asserting rule over the territory, and surely
in executing the two British subjects on Spanish
land, Jackson had gone too far. Privately, President
Monroe was grievously distressed and considered
court-martialing Jackson. But Jackson's immense
popularity as a war hero dissuaded Monroe. Instead, John Quincy Adams, the secretary of state,
opened negotiations with Spain to acquire the territory. The result was a treaty that delivered Florida
to the United States in 1819. In exchange, the Amer-

icans agreed to abandon any claim to Texas or Cuba, which was taken in the South as a considerable concession, since southerners had eyed both places as potential slave states. Adams's treaty also established a boundary between New Spain to the west and the Louisiana Territory.

Spain at that moment was preoccupied with its other colonies in South America, several of which were on the verge of breaking away. One after another—Chile, Colombia, Peru, and finally Mexico —declared themselves independent in the early 1820s. For a time, it appeared that Spain, perhaps joined by allies France and Prussia, might try to regain the lost colonies. Britain proposed an alliance with the United States to block any such effort, but Monroe was wary of an alliance with the adversary of the War of 1812.

Instead, Monroe formulated his own declaration of principles on South America. In December 1823, he incorporated into his annual message to Congress several passages enunciating what would come to be known, decades later, as the Monroe Doctrine. Basically, his message had two parts: noncolonization and nonintervention. He asserted that "the American Continents, by the free and independent condition which they have assumed and maintain, are henceforth not to be considered as subjects for future colonization by any European power." Any new attempt to interfere in the Western Hemisphere or to control or subvert the newly independent countries would be regarded as "the manifestation of an unfriendly disposition towards the United States."

Monroe articulated these policy goals without any real force to back them up in 1823. The American navy was not up to the task of defending Chile or Peru against Spain or France. Monroe did not even have the backing of Congress for his statement; it was merely his idea of a sound policy laid out in a public message. It is doubtful that Monroe saw his message as an implied promise or threat to make the United States the policeman of the Western Hemisphere or to assert U.S. dominance over South America, both usages to which the Monroe Doctrine was put many years later. In exchange for noninterference by Europeans, Monroe pledged that the United States would stay out of European struggles.

The Election of 1824

Monroe was the last president to wear a powdered wig and knee breeches. In late-eighteenth-century style, he had assembled a cabinet that contained

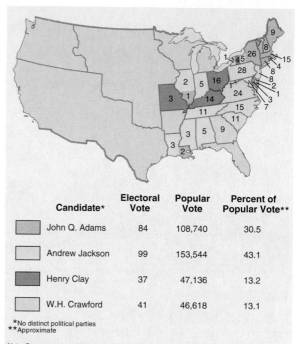

Candidate*	Electoral Vote	Popular Vote	Percent of Popular Vote**
John Q. Adams	84	108,740	30.5
Andrew Jackson	99	153,544	43.1
Henry Clay	37	47,136	13.2
W.H. Crawford	41	46,618	13.1

*No distinct political parties
**Approximate

Note: Because no candidate garnered a majority in the electoral college, the election was decided in the House of Representatives. Although Clay was eliminated from the running, as Speaker of the House he influenced the final decision in favor of Adams.

MAP 10.5
The Election of 1824

men of sharply different philosophies. Secretary of State John Quincy Adams represented the urban Northeast, South Carolinian John C. Calhoun spoke for the commercial planter aristocracy as secretary of war, and William H. Crawford of Georgia, secretary of the treasury, was a throwback to early Jeffersonian states' rights and limited federal power.

Well before the end of Monroe's second term, this group of rather different Republicans began to maneuver for the presidency. Since Jefferson's term, the secretary of state had always been the successor. Adams thus thought he had some presumptive right to run, after his eight years heading the State Department. But four other men vied for the office, and the prolonged politicking created bitter feelings.

Since 1800, the congressional caucuses of each party had met to identify and lend their considerable but still informal authority to the leading candidate from each party. In 1824, with only one party, the caucus system splintered. Some New York and Virginia representatives met and endorsed Crawford, for eight years the secretary of the treasury. Crawford perhaps best represented Monroe's old

Republican views of a limited government. Unfortunately, Crawford, then fifty-one, had just suffered a serious stroke, which left him partially paralyzed and barely able to speak.

Henry Clay, Speaker of the House, also was a declared candidate. The Kentuckian was forty-seven but had vast experience in the workings of Congress. He had also engaged in high-level diplomacy, having accompanied John Quincy Adams to Ghent to negotiate the 1814 peace treaty with Britain. Clay put forth a set of policies he called the American System, a package of protective tariffs to promote manufacturing and federal expenditures for extensive internal improvements, many of them roads and canals in the western states. John C. Calhoun, secretary of war, was another serious contender. At

forty-two, he was the youngest candidate, but he had worked in Washington since 1811, in the House and in several cabinets. A product of Yale College and then Tapping Reeve's law school in Connecticut, Calhoun combined the riches of a well-off Carolina planter with the agile mind of a bright lawyer. Like Clay, he favored internal improvements, protective tariffs, and banking measures, which he figured would earn him standing in northern urban areas.

The final candidate battling for office was an outsider: General Andrew Jackson of Tennessee. Unlike the others, Jackson had only the mere wisp of actual experience in political office, having served brief terms of service in Congress. Monroe had appointed him to be governor of the territory

THE ELECTION OF 1824: THREAD BOX FOR JOHN QUINCY ADAMS

Purchasers of this thread box confirmed their loyalty to John Quincy Adams, presidential candidate in 1824. The inside cover carried a picture of Adams, made by a lithographic process just coming into wide use in the 1820s that made possible the production of thousands of pictures from a single master stone plate. (Wood and copper plates, the earlier technology, produced prints numbering only in the hundreds before deteriorating under pressure.) The velvet pincushion on the outside cover is printed with the slogan "BE FIRM FOR ADAMS."

Collection of Janice L. and David J. Frent.

THE ELECTION OF 1824: JACKSON CUP PLATE

A ceramic saucer of 1824 doubles as an object of veneration for General Andrew Jackson in his first bid for the presidency. It shows Jackson in civilian clothes, even though his reputation was largely military. This particular image of Jackson was mass-produced on housewares, using a newly developed transfer process. Even the English pottery industry made articles for the specialized election market, attaching Jackson's face to expensive pitchers imported to America. Both the saucer and the thread box were household implements associated with women's daily lives. The thread box was, then, no longer just a thread box; it was a commodity that allowed its purchaser to imagine a partisan identity for herself, even though the rules of politics formally excluded her.

Collection of Janice L. and David J. Frent.

Conclusion: From Jefferson to Adams

The nineteenth century opened with the Jeffersonian Republicans in power, trying to undo much of the Federalist structure created in the 1790s. Jefferson's desire for a more limited government, in size, scope, and power, finally had to give way to the realities of an increasing interaction with foreign powers. Jefferson's diplomats steered between France and Spain and unexpectedly acquired the huge Louisiana Territory as a result. Jefferson and Madison struggled to steer a course between France and England, trying to avoid war with high-minded but costly trade embargoes, but eventually the country's sense of honor required a declaration of war. The War of 1812 thus had more meaning as a symbolic event than as a concrete economic or political struggle. Its conclusion at the Battle of New Orleans allowed Americans to feel they had fought a second war of independence against the mother country.

The war elevated to national prominence General Andrew Jackson, whose sudden popularity with voters in the 1824 election surprised the traditional politicians and threw the one-party rule of Republicans into a tailspin. John Quincy Adams barely secured the presidency in the early months of 1825 before the election campaign of 1828 was off and running. Appeals to the people—the mass of white male voters—would be the hallmark of all elections after 1824. It was a game at which Adams was at quite a disadvantage.

Women of course did not vote. But in the years from 1800 to 1828, subtle changes in family law, divorce law, and litigation over sexual injuries expanded by a tiny fraction their possibilities for gaining some personal autonomy. Religious societies of the early Republic offered the greatest opportunity for women to move beyond their appointed and limited sphere, but critics aplenty attacked women exhorters and developed a defense of women's natural and scriptural subservience to men.

The War of 1812 started in motion another chain of events of momentous importance in the decades to come. Jefferson's long embargo and Madison's wartime trade stoppages gave strong encouragement to American manufacturing, momentarily protected from competition with English factories. When peace resumed in 1815, the years of independent development burst forth into a period of sustained economic growth that continued nearly unabated into the mid-nineteenth century. Economic growth brought about a vast reorganization of production, consumption, and market relations, all of which built an essential foundation for the coming revolution in politics during the years of Andrew Jackson's presidency.

CHRONOLOGY

1789 Judiciary Act establishes six Supreme Court justices who preside over circuit courts.

1800 Thomas Jefferson and Aaron Burr tie in electoral college.

Gabriel's Rebellion fails in Virginia.

1801 Judiciary Act reduces Supreme Court justices to five and allows for sixteen circuit judges.

Jefferson elected president by House of Representatives.

1802 Judiciary Act of 1801 repealed.

1803 *Marbury vs. Madison* declares part of Judiciary Act of 1789 unconstitutional.

Embargoes on American shipping by both England and France.

Louisiana Purchase from France.

1804 Jefferson reelected president.

Burr-Hamilton duel.

1804–
1806 Lewis and Clark expedition.

1807 **June.** *Chesapeake* attacked and searched by British in Chesapeake Bay.

December. Embargo Act forbids all American trade with England and France and their colonies.

1808 James Madison elected president.

1809 Treaty of Fort Wayne with Indians in Indiana Territory.

Non-Intercourse Act.

1810 Macon's Bill Number 2.

1811 Battle of Tippecanoe won by William Henry Harrison's troops.

1812 **June.** War declared on Great Britain.

Madison reelected president.

1814 British attack Washington, D.C., burning several buildings.

Treaty of Ghent ends War of 1812.

Hartford Convention.

1815 Battle of New Orleans won by Andrew Jackson's forces.

1816 James Monroe elected president.

1819 Adams-Onís Treaty with Spain cedes Florida to United States.

1820 Missouri Compromise admits Missouri as slave state and Maine as free state.

Monroe reelected president.

1823 Monroe Doctrine asserts independence of Western Hemisphere from European intervention.

1824 "Corrupt bargain" election of John Quincy Adams.

BIBLIOGRAPHY

GENERAL WORKS

Joyce Appleby, *Capitalism and a New Social Order: The Republican Vision of the 1790s* (1984).

Lance Banning, *The Jeffersonian Persuasion: Evolution of a Party Ideology* (1978).

James Broussard, *The Southern Federalists, 1800–1816* (1978).

Noble E. Cunningham, *In Pursuit of Reason: The Life of Thomas Jefferson* (1987).

John R. Howe, *From the Revolution through the Age of Jackson* (1973).

Ralph Ketcham, *Presidents above Party: The First American Presidency, 1789–1829* (1984).

Marshall Smelser, *The Democratic Republic, 1801–1815* (1968).

Stephen Watts, *The Republic Reborn: War and the Making of Liberal America, 1790–1820* (1987).

James Sterling Young, *The Washington Community, 1800–1828* (1966).

JEFFERSON AND REPUBLICANS

Thomas Abernethy, *The Burr Conspiracy* (1954).

Leonard Baker, *John Marshall: A Life in Law* (1974).

Doron S. Ben-Atar, *The Origins of Jeffersonian Commercial Policy and Diplomacy* (1993).

Noble E. Cunningham, *The Jeffersonian Republicans in Power: Party Operations, 1801–1809* (1963).

Noble E. Cunningham, *The United States in 1800: Henry Adams Revisited* (1988).

Alexander DeConde, *This Affair of Louisiana* (1976).

Richard E. Ellis, *The Jeffersonian Crisis: Courts and Politics in the Young Republic* (1971).

David Hackett Fischer, *The Revolution of American Conservatism: The Federalist Party in the Era of Jeffersonian Democracy* (1965).

Morton J. Horwitz, *The Transformation of American Law, 1780–1860* (1977).

Robert M. Johnstone Jr., *Jefferson and the Presidency: Leadership in the Young Republic* (1978).

Lawrence S. Kaplan, *"Entangling Alliances with None": American Foreign Policy in the Age of Jefferson* (1987).

Ralph Ketcham, *James Madison: A Biography* (1971).

Milton Lomask, *Aaron Burr* (1982).

Dumas Malone, *Jefferson the President: First Term, 1801–1805* (1970).

Dumas Malone, *Jefferson the President: Second Term, 1805–1809* (1974).

Richard K. Matthews, *The Radical Politics of Thomas Jefferson: A Revisionist View* (1984).

Drew R. McCoy, *The Elusive Republic: Political Economy in Jeffersonian America* (1980).

Drew R. McCoy, *The Last of the Fathers: James Madison and the Republican Legacy* (1989).

R. Kent Newmyer, *The Supreme Court under Marshall and Taney* (1986).

Peter Onuf, ed., *Jeffersonian Legacies* (1993).

Merrill Peterson, *Thomas Jefferson and the New Nation: A Biography* (1970).

Willard Sterne Randall, *Thomas Jefferson: A Life* (1993).

Norman K. Risjord, *The Old Republicans: Southern Conservatism in the Age of Jefferson* (1965).

Robert A. Rutland, *The Presidency of James Madison* (1990).

Thomas C. Shevory, ed., *John Marshall's Achievement: Law, Politics, and Constitutional Interpretations* (1989).

Jack M. Sosin, *The Aristocracy of the Long Robe: The Origins of Judicial Review in America* (1989).

Francis N. Stites, *John Marshall: Defender of the Constitution* (1981).

Robert W. Tucker, *Empire of Liberty: The Statecraft of Thomas Jefferson* (1990).

G. E. White, *The Marshall Court and Cultural Change, 1815–1835* (1988).

Sean Wilentz, *Chants Democratic: New York City and the Rise of the American Working Class, 1788–1850* (1984).

LEWIS AND CLARK AND THE WEST

John Logan Allen, *Passage through the Garden: Lewis and Clark and the Image of the American Northwest* (1975).

Stephen E. Ambrose, *Undaunted Courage: Meriwether Lewis, Thomas Jefferson, and the Opening of the American West* (1996).

Andrew Cayton, *The Frontier Republic: Ideology and Politics in the Ohio Country, 1780–1825* (1986).

Paul Russell Cutright, *Lewis and Clark: Pioneering Naturalists* (1969).

Albert Furtwangler, *Acts of Discovery: Visions of America in the Lewis and Clark Journals* (1993).

David Freeman Hawke, *Those Tremendous Mountains: The Story of the Lewis and Clark Expedition* (1980).

Donald Jackson, *Thomas Jefferson and the Stony Mountains: Exploring the West from Monticello* (1981).

Robert Mitchell, ed., *Appalachian Frontiers: Settlement, Society, and Development in the Preindustrial Era* (1991).

James P. Ronda, *Lewis and Clark among the Indians* (1984).

FOREIGN POLICY AND WAR OF 1812

James M. Banner, *To the Hartford Convention: The Federalists and the Origins of Party Politics in Massachusetts, 1789–1815* (1969).

Pierre Berton, *The Invasion of Canada* (1980).

Harry L. Coles, *The War of 1812* (1965).

Clifford L. Egan, *Neither Peace nor War: Franco-American Relations, 1803–1812* (1983).

Ronald L. Hatzenbuehler and Robert L. Ivie, *Congress Declares War: Rhetoric, Leadership, and Partisanship in the Early Republic* (1983).

Donald R. Hickey, *The War of 1812: A Forgotten Conflict* (1989).

Reginald Horsman, *The Causes of the War of 1812* (1962).

Linda K. Kerber, *Federalists in Dissent: Imagery and Ideology in Jeffersonian America* (1970).

Alan Lloyd, *The Scorching of Washington: The War of 1812* (1974).

Bradford Perkins, *Prologue to War: England and the United States, 1805–1812* (1961).

Burton Spivak, *Jefferson's English Crisis: Commerce, Embargo, and the Republican Revolution* (1979).

J. C. A. Stagg, *Mr. Madison's War: Politics, Diplomacy, and Warfare in the Early American Republic, 1783–1830* (1983).

SLAVERY

David Brion Davis, *The Problem of Slavery in the Age of Revolution, 1770–1823* (1975).

Douglas Egerton, *Gabriel's Rebellion* (1993).

Sylvia Frey, *Water from the Rock* (1991).

Robert McColley, *Slavery and Jeffersonian Virginia* (1964).

Gary B. Nash, *Forging Freedom: The Formation of Philadelphia's Black Community, 1720–1840* (1988).

Albert J. Raboteau, *Slave Religion: The "Invisible Institution" in the Antebellum South* (1978).

Donald L. Robinson, *Slavery in the Structure of American Politics, 1765–1820* (1971).

Shane White, *Somewhat More Independent: The End of Slavery in New York City, 1710–1810* (1991).

NATIVE AMERICANS

Henry Warner Bowden, *American Indians and Christian Missions: Studies in Cultural Conflict* (1981).

Gregory E. Dowd, *A Spirited Resistance: The North American Indian Struggle for Unity, 1745–1815* (1992).

R. David Edmunds, *The Shawnee Prophet* (1983).

R. David Edmunds, *Tecumseh and the Quest for Indian Leadership* (1984).

Bil Gilbert, *God Gave Us This Country: Tekamthi and the First American Civil War* (1989).

H. S. Halbert and T. H. Ball, *The Creek War of 1813 and 1814* (1969).

Reginald Horsman, *Expansion and American Indian Policy, 1783–1812* (1967).

William G. McLoughlin, *Cherokees and Missionaries, 1789–1839* (1984).

James Merrell, *The Indians' New World: Catawbas and Their Neighbors from European Contact through the Era of Removal* (1989).

Paul Francis Prucha, *The Great Father: The United States Government and the American Indians* (1984).

Bernard W. Sheehan, *Seeds of Extinction: Jeffersonian Philanthropy and the American Indians* (1973).

John Sugden, *Tecumseh's Last Stand* (1985).

Anthony F. C. Wallace, *The Death and Rebirth of the Seneca* (1969).

Richard White, *The Middle Ground: Indians, Empires, and Republics in the Great Lakes Region, 1650–1815* (1991).

WOMEN AND RELIGION

Norma Basch, *In the Eyes of the Law: Women, Marriage, and Property in Nineteenth-Century New York* (1982).

John Boles, *The Great Revival, 1787–1805* (1972).

Jon Butler, *Awash in a Sea of Faith: Christianizing the American People* (1990).

Nancy Cott, *The Bonds of Womanhood* (1977).

Philip Greven, *The Protestant Temperament: Patterns of Childrearing, Religious Experience, and the Self in Early America* (1977).

Michael Grossberg, *Governing the Hearth: Law and the Family in Nineteenth-Century America* (1985).

Nathan Hatch, *The Democratization of American Christianity* (1989).

Janet Wilson James, *Changing Ideas about Women in the United States, 1776–1825* (1981).

Joan Jensen, *Loosening the Bonds: Mid-Atlantic Farm Women, 1750–1850* (1986).

Susan Juster, *Disorderly Women: Sexual Politics and Evangelicalism in Revolutionary New England* (1994).

Linda Kerber, *Women of the Republic* (1980).

Jan Lewis, *The Pursuit of Happiness: Family and Values in Jefferson's Virginia* (1983).

Carla Pestana, *Quakers and Baptists in Colonial Massachusetts* (1991).

Marylynn Salmon, *Women and the Law of Property in Early America* (1986).

Laurel Thatcher Ulrich, *A Midwife's Tale: The Life of Martha Ballard, Based on Her Diary, 1786–1812* (1990).

MONROE AND ADAMS PRESIDENCIES

Harry Ammon, *James Monroe: The Quest for National Identity* (1971).

George Dangerfield, *The Era of Good Feelings* (1952).

George Dangerfield, *The Awakening of American Nationalism, 1815–1828* (1965).

Don E. Fehrenbacher, *The South and Three Sectional Crises* (1980).

Mary W. M. Hargreaves, *The Presidency of John Quincy Adams* (1986).

Walter LaFeber, ed., *John Quincy Adams and American Continental Empire* (1965).

Shaw Livermore, *The Twilight of Federalism: The Disintegration of the Federalist Party, 1815–1830* (1962).

Ernest R. May, *The Making of the Monroe Doctrine* (1975).

Glover Moore, *The Missouri Controversy, 1819–1821* (1953).

Dexter Perkins, *Hands Off: A History of the Monroe Doctrine* (1941).

Robert V. Remini, *Andrew Jackson and the Course of American Empire, 1767–1821* (1977).

SHIP'S FIGUREHEAD OF
ANDREW JACKSON

Carved in 1834 and affixed to the bow of the revered navy frigate Constitution, *this figurehead of Andrew Jackson symbolized national pride by putting "the image of the most popular man of the West upon the favorite ship of the East," according to the commodore who commissioned it. But when Jackson introduced a new, strict banking policy, his popularity in the urban East quickly evaporated. In Boston, where the* Constitution *was docked, protesters complained that the figurehead of a tyrant corrupted their ship. On the night of July 3, 1834, the eve of the national holiday, an eighteen-year-old youth stole on board at night and decapitated the figurehead, sawing it through just below the ears. The commodore, himself alert to symbolic statements, wrapped the headless statue in a flag and sent it to New York City where woodworkers fashioned a new head in 1835. It was reattached to the ship in another port: Jackson's banking policies still rankled in urban financial centers, and naval authorities did not want to risk a second mutilation of the president's image.*

Museum of the City of New York.

ANDREW JACKSON'S AMERICA
11

1815–1840

P RESIDENT ANDREW JACKSON WAS THE DOMINANT FIGURE of his age, as even his enemies conceded. Yet his precarious and unhappy childhood little foretold the fame, fortune, and influence he would enjoy in the years from 1815 to 1840. Jackson was born to a poor Scots-Irish family in the Carolina backcountry in 1767. His father died before he was born, and his mother struggled to support three small boys. During the Revolution, young Andrew, at age thirteen, accompanied one of his brothers into battle against the British, but both were taken prisoner and caught smallpox; the brother died. His oldest brother died of a camp fever in the militia, and within the year cholera took his mother. Alone at fourteen, Jackson drifted around, drinking, gambling, brawling, and indifferently trying to find a trade.

But at seventeen he started to study law with a North Carolina lawyer, and his prospects bettered. In three years he was licensed to practice law, and he went west to Nashville, a small frontier settlement, where he immediately was appointed public prosecutor. The urban frontier provided great opportunities for a young man of Jackson's legal training and aggressive temperament. He married into a leading local family, began to acquire land and slaves, and became active in politics. When Tennessee became a state in 1796, Jackson served a term as its first representative to the U.S. Congress.

Jackson captured national attention in 1815 when he led the victorious American forces at the Battle of New Orleans. With little else to celebrate about the War of 1812, many Americans seized on the Tennessee general as the champion of the day. Songs, broadsides, and an admiring biography commemorated his heroism and cast him in a new light: His early orphanhood framed Jackson as the original self-made man, the parentless child fully responsible for his own destiny. He had little formal education and no inherited advantages, but these deficits were now transformed into virtues. Jackson seemed to have created himself, a gritty, forceful personality extracting opportunities from the dynamic, turbulent frontier.

Jackson enhanced his national reputation by fighting Creek and Seminole Indians. His unauthorized adventure into Spanish Florida in 1817–1818 angered President Monroe and triggered a congressional investigation for insubordination. But even Congress would not censure him, for, as one member said, Jackson was a Hercules, an immortal hero, and "the American people will not be pleased to see their great defender, their great avenger, sacrificed."

The New Orleans and Florida episodes proved that Jackson was a man of action. He was also strong-willed, reckless, and quick to anger. When a slave ran away from him in 1804, he advertised a fifty-dollar reward "and ten dollars extra for every hundred lashes any person will give to the amount of three hundred." He impulsively challenged men to duels on slight pretexts. His best-known fight, an 1806 pistol duel, acquired legendary status as an example of Jackson's obstinacy. His opponent was an expert marksman who could hit a silver dollar at twenty-four feet (as he demonstrated on the way to the duel site, to unnerve Jackson). Jackson deliberately let the marksman shoot first. The bullet hit him in a rib, but he masked all sign of injury under a loose cloak and immobile face. He then took careful aim at the astonished man and killed him. Such steely courage chilled his political opponents.

Jackson's image as a frontier man of action and force set him apart from the learned and privileged gentlemen from Virginia and Massachusetts who had monopolized the presidency up to 1828. When he lost the 1824 election to John Quincy Adams, an infuriated Jackson vowed to fight a rematch and started running for the office immediately. He won, in 1828 and again in 1832, capturing large majorities of voters. His appeal stretched across the urban working classes of the East, frontier voters of the West, and slaveholders in the South, who all saw something of themselves in Jackson. Once elected, he brought a combative style to politics and enlarged the powers of the presidency.

The confidence and even recklessness of Jackson's personality mirrored the new confidence of American society in the years after 1815. An entrepreneurial spirit gripped the country, producing a market revolution of unprecedented scale. Old social hierarchies appeared to be eroding; the most ordinary of men could dream of moving high on the wheel of fortune, just as Jackson had done. Stunning advances in transportation and economic productivity fueled such dreams and propelled thousands to move west and many thousands more to move to cities. Urban growth and technological change fostered the diffusion of a distinctive and vibrant public culture, spread through newspapers and the spoken word. The development of rapid print allowed popular opinions to coalesce and intensify; Jackson's sudden nationwide celebrity was a case in point.

Expanded communication transformed politics dramatically. Sharp disagreements over the best way to promote individual liberty, economic opportunity, and national prosperity in the new market economy defined salient differences between Jackson and Adams and the parties they gave rise to in the 1830s. The process of party formation brought new habits of political participation and party loyalty to many thousands more adult white males. Religion became democratized as well: An evangelical revival of national proportions brought its adherents the confidence that salvation and perfection were now available to all. For those less than perfect, the evangelicals set out to reform their unhappy ways.

As president from 1828 to 1836, Jackson presided over all these changes, fighting some and supporting others in his vigorous and volatile way. And, as with his own stubborn personality, there was a dark underside to the confidence and expansiveness of American society. Steamboats blew up, banks and businesses periodically collapsed, alcoholism rates soared, Indians were killed or relocated far west, and slavery continued to expand. The brash confidence that turned some people into Jackson-like, rugged, self-promoting individuals inspired others to think about the human costs of rapid economic expansion and thus about reforming society in dramatic ways. The common denominator was a faith that people and societies can shape their own destinies.

The Market Revolution

The return of peace in 1815 unleashed powerful economic and social forces that revolutionized the organization of the market. Said one Philadelphia editor, the war "emancipated us from our former slavish dependence on the looms and the anvils of Great Britain." Spectacular changes in transportation (termed by contemporaries "internal improvements") facilitated the movement of commodities, information, and people. Textile mills and other factories created many new jobs, especially for young unmarried women, for whom the chief opportunity in wage labor had been domestic service. Innovations in banking functions, legal practices, and tariff policies promoted swift economic growth.

This was not yet an industrial revolution, but a market revolution. The old standbys, water, wood, beasts of burden, and human muscle, still constituted the energy supply; factories were limited to sites near rapid rivers, mostly in New England. What distinguished the changes as a market revolution was the accelerated pace of economic activity, which made a new variety and volume of consumption goods available in national markets. Men and women were drawn out of old patterns of rural

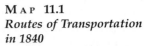

MAP 11.1
Routes of Transportation in 1840

Transportation advances by the 1830s had cut travel times significantly. Goods and people could move from New York City to Buffalo, New York, in four days via the Erie Canal, a trip that took two weeks by road in 1800. A four-week trip from New York to New Orleans in 1800 could now be accomplished in less than half that time, due to steamboats on the western rivers.

self-sufficiency and into the wider realm of market relations; labor once used for home production was now released for industrial employment. At the same time, the nation's money supply enlarged considerably, leading to speculative investments in commerce, manufacturing, transportation, and land. The changed nature and scale of production and consumption changed behavior, attitudes, and expectations.

Confidence in the commercial market was sharply punctured by the panic of 1819, but within a few years strong growth resumed for another two decades, until the panic of 1837. By the 1830s, observers noted that this boom and bust economy distributed its rewards unevenly. Disagreement about the causes and consequences of inequalities in wealth came to define a major difference between the political parties emerging in the 1830s.

Improvements in Transportation

Before 1815, transportation in the United States was so slow and difficult that it cost as much to ship freight over 30 miles of domestic roads as it did to send the same weight of cargo across the Atlantic Ocean. Mailing a one-ounce letter via the U. S. mail for a distance of 150 to 400 miles cost seventy-four cents (when, in comparison, a pound of bread cost six and a half cents). A stagecoach trip from Boston to New York took an uncomfortable four days. But between 1815 and 1840, networks of roads, canals, steamboats, and finally railroads dramatically raised the speed and lowered the cost of travel. Migrants like Andrew Jackson got to Nashville in the 1790s by walking or riding horseback for weeks along old Indian trails. But when the newly elected President Jackson went to Washington, D.C., in 1829 for his inauguration, he traveled by steamboat down the Cumberland River and up the Ohio to Pittsburgh and thence by turnpike to the capital city in a matter of days.

The benefits of improved transportation to economic development were abundantly clear: Products could be sold more cheaply in a wider market. Equally important, transportation facilitated the flow of political information; traffic in newspapers had profound consequences for Jacksonian-era elections. Travel encouraged cultural change as well. Easily accessible passenger travel lifted men and women out of their local communities, brought country merchants and their wives the excitement of a visit to urban amusements, and allowed adolescents of both sexes to obtain new forms of employment in cities or factory towns, where they lived away from home. Commercial passenger travel provided opportunities for family visits, an important counterweight to the isolating effects of the massive westward migration of settlers. These forms of travel required new rules for class and gender behavior in public, to balance the adventure and freedom inherent in escape from hometown moorings with the potential dangers such freedom entailed. Public coaches mixed respectable citizens with con artists, thieves, and seducers who were riding the roads in search of their own opportunities for gain.

The economic, political, and cultural attractions of enhanced public transport did not alone cause the building of thoroughfares. Such undertakings were very expensive, and benefits were not uniform. A canal in New York or a road in Kentucky produced no benefit for South Carolina. Transportation routes directed economic traffic in certain grooves—and of necessity bypassed others. The key questions involved the issues of who would plan, pay for, and profit from improved transportation.

Both Congress and the early Republican presidents hesitated to undertake federally sponsored road projects. Thomas Jefferson and James Madison valued improved transportation but held that federal funding for it was unconstitutional. During Jefferson's presidency, Congress approved start-up funding for the National Road, to connect Baltimore with the heart of Ohio, provided that the money came directly from the sale of Ohio public lands, the area that would benefit. By 1818, the gravel roadbed of the National Road crossed the Cumberland Gap and extended to Wheeling, West Virginia, reaching

its terminus in the 1830s at Columbus, Ohio. In the 1820s, President John Quincy Adams departed from his cautious predecessors and proposed that transportation improvements be undertaken at government expense. Essentially he adopted the pro-development view of Henry Clay's American System, a multifaceted plan to promote banking, manufacturing, and transportation. But Congress would not oblige Adams. Hence it fell largely to private investors to undertake transportation improvements. They pooled resources and chartered stagecoach, canal, and railroad companies, with significant aid from the states in the form of subsidies and guarantees of monopolistic rights.

Turnpike and roadway mileage dramatically increased after 1815, reducing the cost of land shipment of goods. Stagecoach lines proliferated in an extensive network of passenger corridors dense in the populated East and fanning out to the Mississippi River. Travel time on main routes was cut in half; Boston to New York now took two days. Not only did people, mail, and newspapers move across space, the coach itself became a site of vital information exchange with its dozen strangers locked in close contact. Foreign travelers often noted with amazement that American men relished controversial conversation topics about politics, religion, and slavery. Equally amazing to foreigners was the presence of American women traveling on public stagecoaches, often without male escorts. The English writer Harriet Martineau toured America for many months in 1834 and found the "liberty" of women on the road "highly amusing." But she also condemned women travelers in general for being "spoiled children. Screaming and trembling at the apprehension of danger are not uncommon." Martineau herself once experienced an overturned coach in New Hampshire and later a burst steamboiler on a railway in Virginia, but presumably she kept a firm grip on her fears.

Steamboats signaled an important advance in the technology of transportation. In 1807, Robert Fulton adapted a steam engine to propel a 133-foot boat, the *Clermont*. Its first voyage, up the Hudson River from New York City to Albany, took thirty-two hours against a head wind, compared with two days for the land route. Onlookers at Poughkeepsie stared in astonishment, according to one eyewitness: "Some imagined it to be a sea-monster, whilst others did not hesitate to express their belief that it was a sign of the approaching judgement," the heavy black smoke and huge flames suggesting the

TECHNOLOGY IN AMERICA
Early Steamboats

Steamboats revolutionized travel in the 1820s and 1830s. The basic technology consisted of a steam engine, powered by the steam from a furnace-heated boiler, that propelled a boat by turning a wooden paddlewheel. In concept, steam-powered travel was ingenious, but it took years of trial-and-error to reduce risks. Between 1811 and 1851, accidents destroyed nearly a thousand boats, a third of all steam vessels built in that period. More than half the accidents resulted from snags — tree trunks or other debris — which penetrated hulls and sank boats. Fires, too, were fearsome hazards in wooden boats that commonly carried highly combustible cargoes, such as raw cotton in burlap bags. The development of sheet metal, which strengthened hulls and protected wooden surfaces near the smokestacks from sparks, was a major safety advance.

But the traveling public focused its greatest apprehension on the terror of boiler explosions. As so powerfully shown in the lithograph of the steamboat *Lexington*, whose boiler blew up in Long Island Sound in January 1840, by far the greatest loss of life on steamboats came from scalding steam, flying wreckage, and the predictable fire that would engulf a boat in a matter of minutes. In the 1830s alone, eighty-nine boiler explosions caused 861 deaths and many more injuries. The cause of explosion was often mysterious: Was it excessive steam pressure or weak metal? Exactly how much pressure could plate iron fastened with rivets really withstand? Did a dangerous or explosive gas develop in the boiler when the water level fell too low? Or was it principally human error — reckless or drunk engineers (none of them licensed) or captains bent on breaking speed records or bowing to the economics of competition?

The first federal grant for scientific research was awarded in 1830 during John Quincy Adams's term, when the Franklin Institute of Philadelphia undertook to explain the causes of boiler explosions. In 1852, the U.S. Congress mandated steamboat inspection regulations to ensure public safety. After the Civil War, affordable sheet steel and the development of new welding techniques produced boilers that were much stronger.

Library of Congress.

LANDSCAPE WITH FREIGHT TRAIN AND TOW BOAT
A canal boat and train pass through a village, each transporting goods, not passengers. Three
horses on a tow path power the boat; a coal-burning locomotive steam engine drives the train.
The utility poles along the train tracks (probably telegraph wires) indicate that this anonymous
watercolor dates no earlier than the late 1840s.
Gift of Maxim Karolik. Courtesy, Museum of Fine Arts, Boston.

possible end of the world. Fulton's *Clermont* was not the first steamboat ever—there had been prototypes back to the early 1790s, both in Europe and in the United States. But Fulton linked his technology to the business and legal know-how of Robert R. Livingston, whose precocious interest in steam technology had led him to acquire from New York in 1798 a twenty-year monopoly on all steam transportation on the Hudson, if he could create a steamboat that traveled four miles per hour.

Steamboat transportation arrived in the popular consciousness in 1807 with the *Clermont;* after 1815, a steamboat craze was in full swing. By 1820, a dozen steamboats left New York City daily, churning up the Hudson to Albany in half a day or moving east on the Long Island Sound. Captains of rival companies sometimes staged impromptu races at wide sections of the Hudson, thrilling (and sometimes killing) the passengers as the boilers were pushed to their limits. Traffic soon spread to the western rivers and the Great Lakes. A voyager on one of the first steamboats to go down the Mississippi reported that the Chickasaw Indians called the vessel a "fire canoe" and considered it "an omen of evil . . . the sparks from the chimney of the boat being likened to the train of the celestial visitant" —that is, a comet, also feared as an omen of evil. By the early 1830s, more than seven hundred steamboats had been swiftly launched into operation on the Ohio and Mississippi Rivers. A journey from New

Orleans to Louisville, Kentucky, took one week, in contrast to the three months a keelboat required.

Repeatedly, boiler explosions revealed the risks of steam transport; by 1830, close to eighty vessels had been blasted out of the water. Such accidents brought terrible loss of life, since each boat carried several hundred passengers and swimming was an uncommon skill (assuming one could escape the flaming wreckage). One newspaper called for a citizens' investigation to be conducted by a committee of twenty disinterested men with mechanical genius: "The Steam Boat Oliver Evans lately exploded and scattered such abundance of boiling water, that eleven persons were scalded to death and many others dangerously wounded. Must we wait for the sacrifice of many valuable lives before one single precaution is taken to guard our wives, children, and friends, from so dreadful a calamity?" But newspaper reports of the horrors of accidents made little dent in the traveling public's excitement over fast travel.

The early practice of states granting monopolies to encourage investment in steam transportation came to seem restrictive and unfair to newcomers in the business by the 1820s. In a landmark decision of 1824, *Gibbons v. Ogden,* the Supreme Court under John Marshall ruled that navigation on the Hudson River was actually a form of interstate commerce and thus was under the jurisdiction of the federal government; state-granted monopolies were therefore declared invalid on rivers that traversed two or more states.

Canals were another major innovation of the revolution in transportation. Before 1815, a few states licensed private investors to dig canals, usually modest undertakings just a few miles in length to connect existing riverways. The virtues of entire highways made of water soon became apparent. Canals did not have to be very deep; usually four feet of water sufficed for a flat-bottomed barge. At a width of thirty to forty feet, the placid canals could accommodate two-way traffic. The barges were powered by horses or mules that trudged the towpaths along the embankment pulling the barges. The animals produced speeds of under two miles per hour, but the economy came from increased loads: The low-friction water allowed one horse to pull a fifty-ton barge. In winter, canals froze over and became smooth, stump- and rock-free highways for sleighs.

Pennsylvania in 1815 and New York in 1817 commenced major state-sponsored canal enter-

prises intended to create large regional markets for goods. Pennsylvania's Schuylkill Canal stretched 108 miles when it was completed in 1826. It was overshadowed by the impressive Erie Canal in New York, begun in 1817 and finished in 1825, which connected the 350 miles between Albany on the Hudson River with Buffalo on Lake Erie. In effect, the Erie Canal linked the port of New York City with the inland region of New York State and, via the Great Lakes, the entire Northwest Territory. Wheat and flour moved east, textiles and books moved west; by the 1830s, the cost of shipping by canal fell to less than a tenth of the cost of overland transport, and New York City developed in short order into the premier city of trade and commerce in the United States.

The Erie Canal also quickly became the principal passenger route west. As many as forty people crowded on each tiny barge and practiced the novel custom of ducking or lying down several times an hour as they passed under low bridges. The canal's well-maintained towpaths made overnight travel possible, and canal boats, like steamboats, generally provided an interior ladies' cabin where women could retreat from men and sleep undisturbed (except by the ever-present bedbugs). Such cabins had to be extremely low in height, given the shallow water; the Englishwoman Harriet Martineau found the "compressed crowd, lying packed like herrings in a barrel" so repulsive that sleeping with the men on the open decks seemed preferable—until it started to rain.

In the 1830s, private railroad companies began to give canals stiff competition, and by the mid-1840s the canal-building era was over. (Use of the canals for freight continued well into the twentieth century.) The nation's first railroad, the Baltimore and Ohio, boasted thirteen miles of track in 1829, laid out west from Baltimore grandly gesturing in the direction of Ohio. During the 1830s, three thousand more miles of track materialized nationwide, the result of a speculative fever in railroad construction masterminded by bankers, locomotive and iron manufacturers, and state legislators, who provided subsidies, charters, and land rights-of-way. Lines in the 1830s were generally short, on the order of twenty to one hundred miles; they were not yet an efficient distribution system for goods. But passengers flocked to experience the marvelous travel speeds of fifteen to twenty miles per hour, despite the frightful noise and cascades of ashes and cinders that rained on them.

Factories, Workingwomen, and Wage Labor

Transportation advances promoted a rapid expansion of manufacturing after 1815. Teamsters, wagoners, and bargemen hauled products like shoes, textiles, clocks, guns, and books into nationwide distribution. Some of the gain in manufacturing, especially in the textile industry, came from the development of water-driven machinery, built near fast-coursing rivers. (The steam power harnessed for steamboats and railroads had limited application in industry until the 1840s.) But much of the new manufacturing involved only a reorganization of production, still using the power and skill of human hands. Both mechanized and manual manufacturing pulled young women into the labor market for the first time and greatly enlarged the segment of the population earning a living by selling labor for hourly wages.

The earliest factory appeared in Pawtucket, Rhode Island, in the 1790s. British immigrant Samuel Slater designed a mechanical spinning machine that produced thread and yarn. By 1815, 169 spinning mills dotted the lower New England countryside.

Slater followed the British model of hiring whole families, including children, but the male portion of his labor force tended to disappear inconveniently at harvest time, responding to the seasonal need for increased agricultural labor. As early as 1791, Treasury Secretary Alexander Hamilton in his *Report on Manufactures* had argued that women made the ideal factory labor force. Young farm women in particular, said Hamilton, were idle and underemployed; female labor would allow American manufacturing to develop without undermining the agricultural sector, where men worked. (Hamilton's assumption that young women were idle made sense only in the context of the developing market revolution that defined productive labor as labor that generates wages. Only in a wage economy could wives' and daughters' arduous but unpaid household tasks of cooking, cleaning, sewing, and childrearing be rendered invisible.) A division of labor by sex was also attractive because it promised to save America from the worst feature of English manufacturing cities, the permanent impoverishment of whole families who worked in health-threatening, low-wage factories. Young American women, the theory ran, would gladly work for minimal wages, so long as the pay was higher than domestic service wages. After a few years they would then happily retire to marriage, their places taken by fresh recruits from the New England countryside earning a beginner's wage. There would thus be no permanent poor clustered around factories, and factory labor would stay cheap for employers.

A female labor force came to be called the "Waltham system" after 1814, when a group of Boston entrepreneurs headed by Francis Cabot Lowell consolidated and mechanized all aspects of cloth production—carding, fulling, spinning, weaving, and dyeing—in one location, in Waltham, Massachusetts, and hired young women. A decade later, the Waltham system was improved on at Lowell, Massachusetts, a new manufacturing town built along the Merrimack River at Lowell and his business group, the Boston Associates. Short canals captured the river's power enough to drive eight separate mills, which by 1830 employed more than six thousand young women. A key innovation in Lowell was the close moral supervision of the female workers, who lived in company-owned boardinghouses run by middle-aged women. Parents back on the farms were assured that their daughters would be watched and guarded. Mill owners too profited from having "an industrious, sober, orderly, and moral class of operatives," according to a local clergyman who took pride in the new city's technique for combining factory employment with high moral standards. "No persons are employed on the corporations who are addicted to intemperance, or who are known to be guilty of any immoralities of conduct," he wrote; girls dismissed for bad conduct were blacklisted. Soon the Waltham system was replicated in many towns in New Hampshire and Maine.

The mill workers welcomed the unprecedented if still limited personal freedom of living in an all-female social space, away from parents, excused from all domestic tasks, and with the exhilarating bonus of a little pocket money.

The vast majority of mill workers were women aged sixteen to twenty-three; they signed on for a minimum of a year and often worked a total of three or four, usually broken up into several periods. Pay averaged about two dollars a week plus another dollar in value for room and board. While this was

**BEDROOM OF A BOARDING-
HOUSE IN LOWELL,
MASSACHUSETTS**
*Lowell mill girls of the 1830s
lived in closely supervised
boardinghouses, four to six
persons per room (that is, two
to three per double bed, as in
this photograph of a restored
bedroom). Trunks took the
place of closets or chests of
drawers; and the roommates
took turns using the writing
table and water stand.*
Courtesy Lowell National
Historical Park.

more than what a seamstress or domestic servant could earn, it was less than young men's wages. Many of the workers contributed earnings to their families, while managing to keep a little for themselves. The work was not pleasant or easy: The women tended noisy machines like spinning jennies and power looms, quickly repairing sudden breaks in the yarn, in rooms kept hot and humid (ideal for yarn, not so comfortable for people). The hours were long, typically twelve to thirteen hours a day, six days a week, with mandatory Sunday church attendance. The boardinghouses were often crowded, sometimes with six girls to a bedroom.

Despite the discomforts, young women flocked to obtain textile jobs. Animated by the same energy that moved Andrew Jackson westward, the faith that people can shape their own destinies, the mill workers left rural farms behind and traveled to new factory towns in the hope of becoming more autonomous individuals. They welcomed the unprecedented if still limited personal freedom of living in an all-female social space, away from parents, excused from all domestic tasks, and with the exhilarating bonus of a little pocket money. In Lowell, the women workers could engage in evening self-improvement activities, like lectures, and the company established a newspaper, *The Lowell Offering*, written and edited by some of the working-women.

In the mid-1830s, worldwide changes in the cotton market impelled the mill owners to try to get more productivity from their labor force by adding more machines per worker and by lowering wages.

The workers, emboldened by their communal living arrangements and by their relative independence from the job, protested. In 1834 and again in 1836, many hundreds of them went out on strike, or "turnouts" as they termed their action. Their sense of independence derived from the fact that they were temporary, not lifelong, employees, so they could afford to challenge the owners; male workers dependent on long-term employment could take fewer risks. At mill sites all around New England, young women were the leaders in planning strikes and forming labor unions. Women strikers at a turnout in Dover, New Hampshire, in 1834 denounced their owners for trying to turn them into "slaves": "However freely the epithet of 'factory slaves' may be bestowed upon us, we will never deserve it by a base and cringing submission to proud wealth or haughty insolence." Their assertiveness surprised many; but ultimately their easy replaceability undermined their bargaining power. Still, the owners realized that an all-female labor force could not be counted on to be compliant and submissive. A decade later, while the mill women concentrated their efforts on state legislatures to get a ten-hour workday law passed, mill owners began to shift to immigrant families as their labor source. By midcentury, American factory towns came to resemble European industrial sites with their permanent working class.

Other manufacturing enterprises of the 1820s and 1830s, such as shoemaking, employed women in ever larger numbers. No new machinery transformed the actual work, but new modes of organizing the work allowed the manufacturers to step up production, control wastage and quality, and lower wages by subdividing the tasks and by hiring women. No longer did a cobbler make an entire pair of shoes. Now leather would be cut by male workers at a central shop under the shoe boss's careful eye. Men made the soles, usually in work groups of fewer than twenty. The stitching of the upper part of the shoe, called shoebinding, became women's work, performed at home as outwork so that it could mesh with women's domestic chores. Women shoebinders earned piecework wages, that is, a pay-

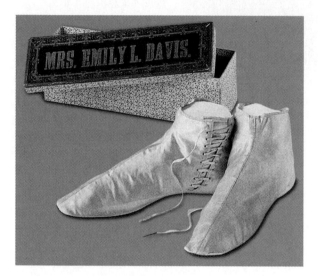

FANCY WEDDING SHOES MADE IN LYNN, MASSACHUSETTS

These shoes from Lynn, Massachusetts, were part of the wedding outfit of Emily Lucinda Alden when she married Addison Davis in 1840. The soles are flat, with no heel, and the upper shoe is hand-stitched of white satin. Nothing except the ankle lacing distinguishes right from left shoe. (All footwear from the period was made with identical rights and lefts; only usage over time differentiated each shoe.) An extraordinary clue about women and marriage is revealed in this picture. The bride affixed her name-to-be to the shoe box. Etiquette books of the 1840s, however, uniformly decreed that her correct public name should be Mrs. Addison Davis. We might surmise that Emily, on the verge of marriage, had not entirely internalized the eclipse of her own public and legal personage that marriage would soon impose on her. Another bride of 1840, Elizabeth Cady, married Henry Stanton, and had to do battle to be called Mrs. Elizabeth Cady Stanton when she became a leader of the emerging women's rights movement in 1848 (see chapter 13, pages 488 – 489).
Lynn Historical Society/photo by Lightstream.

ment per item completed. Women's wages were much smaller than men's, but their contribution to family income was now tangible, in cash. By 1830, there were more women shoebinders in Massachusetts than mill girls.

The new shoe entrepreneurs who had reorganized the industry moved to cut shoebinder wages in the economically turbulent 1830s. Unlike the mill workers, women shoebinders worked in relative isolation, a serious hindrance to organized protest. In Lynn, Massachusetts, a major shoemaking center, women turned to other female networks, mainly churches as sites of meetings and religious newspapers as forums for communication. The Lynn shoebinders who demanded higher wages in 1834 built on a collective sense of themselves as women even though they did not share daily work lives. "Equal rights should be extended to all—to the weaker sex as well as the stronger," they wrote in a document forming the Female Society of Lynn. Even so, they proceeded cautiously in blaming men: The women binders "would reluctantly impute to their employers of the other sex, any unworthy motives, or any willingness to oppress them; but there appears to be somewhere a manifest *error*, a want of justice, and reasonable compensations to the females; which calls imperiously for redress. While the prices of their labour have been reduced, the business of their employers has appeared to be improving and prosperous, enabling them to increase in wealth. *These things ought not so to be!*" The women affirmed their rights of petition and assembly and defined "freedom from want" as a natural right as well.

Yet ultimately, the Lynn shoebinders' protests of the 1830s failed to achieve wage increases for women in the industry. Isolated workers all over New England continued to accept low wages, undercutting attempts to establish a minimum rate. And even within the town of Lynn, many shoebinders shied away from organized protest, preferring to situate their work in the context of family duty instead of market relations. Such women felt they stitched uppers to help their menfolk in finishing each shoe; for them, wages represented compensation for undone domestic chores rather than calculable fractions of the market value of the shoes. The isolation and family context of shoebinding allowed shoe manufacturers to count on a pliant female labor force for several decades to come, until sewing machines and factory work sites dramatically altered the women workers' views in the 1850s.

Bankers and Lawyers

Entrepreneurs like the Boston Associates who built the Lowell factories relied on innovations in the banking system to finance their ventures. The number of state-chartered banks in the country more than doubled in the boom years 1814–1816, from fewer than 90 to 208; by 1830, there were 330, and hundreds more by 1840. Banks stimulated the economy both by making loans to businessmen, manufacturers, and real estate purchasers and by enlarging the country's money supply. Borrowers were issued loans in the form of banknotes, certificates unique to each bank. The borrowers then used the notes exactly like money, good for all transactions. Neither federal nor state governments issued paper money, so banknotes became the currency of the country.

In theory, a note could always be traded in at the bank for its equivalent in gold or silver (in a transaction known as "specie payment"). A note from a solid local bank might be worth exactly what it was written for; a ten-dollar note could purchase ten dollars' worth of goods. But if the note came from a distant or questionable bank, its value would be discounted by some fraction. The money market of Jacksonian America definitely required knowledge, caution, and trust. Many city newspapers of the 1820s and 1830s devoted considerable space to regional banking news and prevailing discount rates. But even scrupulous caution sometimes failed to detect counterfeiters, many in number, who found it inviting and rewarding to forge banknotes. Entrepreneurial skills took many forms in this era.

Bankers exercised great power over the economy in their decisions about who would get loans and what the discount rates would be. The most powerful bankers sat on the board of directors for the second Bank of the United States, chartered in 1816. The charter of the first Bank of the United States, granted by Congress in 1791 for twenty years, had expired in 1811; at the time, Madison's administration was confident that state banks could provide all needed services. But difficulties financing the War of 1812 forced the administration to change its stance. In 1816, the second bank, located again in Philadelphia, opened for business under a twenty-year charter, with eighteen branches throughout the country. The rechartering of this second bank would prove to be a major issue in Andrew Jackson's reelection campaign in 1832.

Accompanying the market revolution was a revolution in commercial law. In the decades after

OFFICE SAFE
Financial records, banknotes, and stock certificates required safekeeping in the stepped-up commercial world of the 1830s. This small office safe opened by key.
Eric Long/Smithsonian Institution.

1815, lawyers both inside and outside of state governments fashioned a legal system that advanced the interests of commercial activity and enhanced the prospects of private investment.

Of particular significance was the changing practice of legal incorporation, the chartering of businesses by states. Up to now, states chartered businesses formed to meet the public good, such as to build a bridge. Under new state laws, corporations could be formed for any reasonable purpose. New York passed the first such state incorporation law in 1811. The new laws limited the liability of the investors to the value of their original investment. Thus, if a corporation failed, the private fortunes of its investors were spared any risk. In 1800, there were perhaps twenty corporations in the United States; by 1817, there were eighteen hundred.

The legal revolution of these decades reformulated older concepts of contract to reflect the burgeoning entrepreneurial marketplace. Courts had enforced business contracts in the eighteenth century in light of notions of fairness. If a seller foolishly contracted to sell a barrel of wheat for half its true or accepted value and then had regrets, he could rely on the courts to declare the agreement void. In the nineteenth century, courts moved toward an interpretation of contracts as freely negotiated, legally binding agreements, regardless of the fairness of the outcome; the law now presumed that a price was, simply, what a buyer and seller agreed it should be.

Several landmark Supreme Court decisions clarified these concepts as they were being shaped by state courts and legislatures. One early case before the Marshall Court was *Fletcher v. Peck* (1810), a conflict involving corrupt land deals in the Yazoo land tract of western Georgia. The Georgia state legislature, under the heavy influence of bribes, had sold this land in 1795 to several land companies for the amazingly low price of one and a half cents per acre. An angry voting public unseated the corrupt state officials in the next election, and the new legislature overturned the land sales the following year —but not before the land companies had managed to sell much of the Yazoo lands for ten cents an acre to speculators in New England. The complicated situation gave rise to complicated interstate lawsuits, finally put to the Supreme Court. The Court held the inviolability of contracts: No matter how corrupt, the original state land grant constituted a binding contract. The *Fletcher* decision was one of the first in which the Supreme Court in effect invalidated a state law, the law rescinding the land sale.

A second landmark Supreme Court case on contracts and corporations was *Dartmouth College v. Woodward* (1819). The New Hampshire college was founded in 1769 by a charter granted by King George III. In 1816, the state government annulled the charter and made Dartmouth a public university; it expanded the board of trustees and fired the existing college president. The original trustees, abundantly alarmed, entered the courts to reclaim control of their institution. The Supreme Court ruled in favor of the trustees on the grounds that the original charter constituted a contract and that, once the charter was granted, the state had no right to interfere in the running of the corporation. Again, the Supreme Court had overruled a state legislative action.

In all these disputes, lawyers predominated. After the War of 1812, the majority of representatives in the U.S. Congress were lawyers, and a similar wave of legal professionals moved into state politics. Articulate, trained in legal reasoning, and able to advocate all sides of a question in the interest of winning for a client, lawyers brought formidable skills to the job of writing and enforcing the new laws governing commerce. More rustic and ordinary citizens who stood for election and entered government service found themselves at a clear disadvantage.

Working through legislatures and courts, lawyers established rights to contract without state interference and designed the model of the business corporation that would carry the United States through the commercial and industrial transformation of the nineteenth century. Lawyers outlawed the use of strikes by aggrieved employees, on the grounds that strikes constituted illegal conspiracies. They wrote the laws of eminent domain, empowering states to buy land for roads and canals, even from unwilling sellers. They drafted legislation on contributory negligence, relieving employers from responsibility for workplace injuries if it could be shown that the employees exercised inadequate caution and thus contributed to the injuries. In these ways and many others, entrepreneurial lawyers of the 1820s and 1830s created the legal foundation for an economy that gave priority to ambitious individuals interested in maximizing their own wealth.

Not everyone applauded these developments. Andrew Jackson, himself a skillful lawyer-turned-politician, spoke for a large and mistrustful segment of the population when he warned about the abuses of power "which the moneyed interest derives from a paper currency which they are able to control, from the multitude of corporations with exclusive privileges which they have succeeded in obtaining in the different states, and which are employed altogether for their benefit." Jacksonians believed that ending government-granted privileges was the way to maximize individual liberty and economic opportunity.

Booms and Busts

One aspect of the economy that the lawyer-politicians could not control was the threat of financial collapse. The boom years from 1815 to 1818 exhibited an energy and volatility that resulted in the first large-scale economic panic in U.S. history; the pattern was repeated in the 1830s. Rapidly rising consumer demand stimulated rising prices for goods, and speculative investment opportunities with high payoffs abounded —in bank stocks, western land sales, urban real estate, and commodities markets. Steep inflation made some people wealthy but created hardships for workers on fixed incomes.

When the bubble first burst in 1819, the overnight rich suddenly became the overnight poor. Some suspected that a precipitating cause of the panic of 1819 was the second Bank of the United States. For too long, the bank had neglected to exercise control over state banks, many of which had suspended specie payments—the exchange of gold or silver for banknotes—in their eagerness to make loans and expand the economic bubble. Then, in mid-1818, the Bank of the United States started to call in its loans and insisted that state banks do likewise. The contraction of the money supply created tremors throughout the economy, a foretaste of the catastrophe to come.

What made the crunch worse was a parallel financial crisis in Europe in the spring of 1819. Overseas prices of agricultural products plummeted; cotton, tobacco, and wheat suddenly fell in value by more than 50 percent. Now when the Bank of the United States and state banks tried to call in their outstanding loans, debtors involved in the commodities trade could not pay. The number of business and personal bankruptcies skyrocketed.

The intricate web of credit and debt relationships meant that almost everyone with even a toe in the new commercial economy was affected by the panic of 1819. Thousands of Americans lost their savings and property. Estimates of unemployment suggest that a half million people lost their livelihoods nationwide.

The intricate web of credit and debt relationships meant that almost everyone with even a toe in the new commercial economy was affected by the panic of 1819.

It took several years for the country to recover from the panic of 1819. Prices continued to fall and bottomed out only in 1821 and 1822. Unemployment rates slowly improved, but the emotional shock and bitterness lasted for many years. A powerful resentment against banks lingered, ready to be mobilized by politicians in the decades to come. The dangers of a system that depended on extensive credit were now clear: In one memorable, folksy formulation that gained circulation around 1820, a farmer was said to compare credit to "a man pissing in his breeches on a cold day to keep his arse

warm—very comfortable at first but I dare say. . . you know how it feels afterwards."

By the mid-1820s, the booming economy was back on track, driven by high productivity, a resumed consumer demand for goods, a greatly accelerating volume of international trade, and a restless and calculating people moving goods, human labor, and investment capital in ever larger and expanding circles of commerce. But an undercurrent of fear and anxiety about rapid economic change continued to shape the political views of many Americans.

The Tariff of 1828

The federal government promoted the booming economy—and fattened itself as well—by passing tariffs on imported goods. The first significant federal tariff had passed easily in 1816, winning support in both the North and the South. It levied an import duty of about 25 percent on cotton cloth from abroad, to shelter the new American textile mills from foreign competition. In 1824, Congress passed a much expanded tariff bill, covering iron, iron products, glass, hemp, wool, and woolen goods, at levels significantly higher than in 1816, about 33 percent on average.

This measure was opposed by some southern congressional leaders, who feared that steep tariffs would decrease overseas shipping and hurt the South's export of raw cotton. Concerns also were raised about the uneven benefits of the tariff. A high tax on imported iron might be of great financial advantage to iron-rich central Pennsylvania, but anyone who wanted to make or buy machinery, stoves, guns, or nails in Massachusetts or Georgia, places without a natural supply of iron, had to pay an extra 33 percent for imported iron. During John Quincy Adams's administration (1825–1829), tariffs began to generate heated debate.

The final and most controversial tariff of the 1820s passed in 1828. Pieces of it were added by members of Congress from every section of the country and every type of industry; in the main, it was pro-Jackson men in Congress who assembled the package and engineered support for it, loading it with duties on raw materials needed by New England. In return, protectionist New Englanders heaped on other duties. One wealthy cotton mill owner laughed that the tariff would "keep the South and West in debt to New England the next hundred years." The final bill was a strange agglomeration of dozens of tariffs, many as high as 50 percent and some in conflict with each other as economic policy. Southerners quickly dubbed it the "Tariff of Abominations" and loudly protested its passage.

The significance of the tariff of 1828 was twofold. It represented an impressive source of income for the federal government, perhaps ten times as great as income from the sale of western lands. In the 1830s, the federal government would retire all its debts and be flush with surplus money, for the first and last time in American history. But that happy eventuality was seriously undercut by the second result of the high tariff, the development of very grave sectional divisions. The traditional American lament over unjust taxation surfaced; the tariff—the only tax now collected by the federal government—was unevenly paid, and its benefits (protection for industries) were unevenly distributed. The tariff of 1828 precipitated a major constitutional crisis in 1832–1833 over one southern state's attempt to nullify it (see p. 417). Like the Missouri Compromise debates of 1819–1820, nullification of the tariff of 1828 became another dress rehearsal for the conflict that led to the Civil War.

The Spread of Democracy

Just as the market revolution held out the promise, if not the reality, of economic opportunity for anyone who worked hard, the political transformation of the 1830s held out the promise of political opportunity for hundreds of thousands of new voters. Between 1828 and 1836, the years of Andrew Jackson's presidency, the second American party system took shape, although not until 1836 would the parties have distinct names and consistent programs that transcended the particular personalities running for office. Over those years, more men could and did vote, and new methods of arousing public interest developed. In 1828, Jackson's charismatic personality defined his party. By 1836, both parties had institutionalized one of his most successful themes: that politicians had to appear to have the common touch in an era when popularity with voters drove the electoral process.

Popular Politics and Partisan Identity

The election of 1828 was the first presidential contest in which popular votes determined the outcome; in twenty-two out of twenty-four states, voters now designated electors committed to a particular candidate. More than a million voters participated, nearly three times the number in 1824, reflecting the high stakes voters perceived in the Adams-Jackson rematch. Throughout the 1830s, the number of voters rose to all-time highs. Partly this increase resulted from relaxed voting qualifications; by the mid-1830s, all but three states allowed universal white male suffrage, without property qualifications. But the higher turnout also indicated increased interest in elections. In contrast to the sleepy Monroe elections of 1816 and 1820, more than half the electorate voted in 1828, and in some states the turnout ran as high as 70 percent. By 1840, the presidential election pulled in 78 percent of the adult white male vote nationwide.

The 1828 election inaugurated new campaign styles as well. State-level candidates routinely gave speeches to woo the voters, appearing at picnics and public banquets. (Adams and Jackson still declined such activities in 1828 as too undignified; but Henry Clay of Kentucky, campaigning for Adams, earned the nicknames the "Barbecue Orator" and the "Gastronomic Cicero.") Campaign rhetoric began to change under the necessity to create popular appeal, becoming more informal and often blunt.

As party rivalry evolved, political leaders in the 1830s orchestrated public events such as rallies and parades. The Jackson camp established many Hickory Clubs, trading on Jackson's popular nickname, "Old Hickory," a common Tennessee tree suggesting resilience and toughness. (Jackson was the first presidential candidate to have an affectionate and widely used nickname.) Published compilations of voting statistics made their first appearance in statistical almanacs, allowing party leaders to calculate and strategize their party's strength. Political committees made sure their supporters got to the polls, which could be a day's ride or more away from some voters.

Beginning with the 1828 election, partisan newspapers defined issues and publicized political personalities as never before. Party leaders cultivated editors and judiciously dispensed subsidies and other favors to secure the loyalties of papers, even in remote towns and villages. In New York State, where party development was most advanced, a pro-Jackson group called the Bucktails had fifty weekly publications under its control. Papers were unabashedly open about their political affiliation, often declaring it right on the masthead. Bargain postal rates for newspapers allowed party leaders to create networks of sympathetic editors. Stories from the leading Jacksonian paper in Washington, D.C., would be reprinted two days later in a Boston or Cincinnati paper, as fast as the mail stage could carry them. Presidential campaigns now took place with accountability to a public arena that encompassed the whole nation.

Parties declined to adopt official names in 1828, still honoring the fiction of Republican Party unity. Instead, they called themselves the Jackson party or the Adams party. By the 1832 election, labels began to appear; Adams's political heir, Henry Clay, represented the National Republicans, while Jackson's supporters opted for Democratic Republicans. Both parties were still claiming the mantle of the Jefferson-to-Monroe heritage by keeping "Republican" in the name, but Clay's National Republicans looked to a large arena of national action to promote commercial development, while Jackson's Democratic Republicans confirmed by their name their promise to be responsive to the will of the majority. By 1834, a few state-level National Republicans shortened their name to the Whig Party, a term that was gradually accepted and in common use by 1836, the same year that Jackson's party became simply the Democrats. Thus, Whig and Democrat crystallized as names only at the end of an eight-year evolutionary process.

The Election of 1828 and the Character Issue

The campaign of 1828 was modern in more ways than just the drawn-out politicking and the importance of majority rule. It was also the first national election in which scandal and character questions reigned supreme in the campaign coverage, a feature of electioneering made possible by the insistent voice of partisan newspapers.

John Quincy Adams was vilified by his opponents as a hopeless elitist, a bookish academic, and perhaps a monarchist, a man out of touch with the common American, a man who looked to European culture for refinement. Much was made of the fact that Adams had a billiard table and an ivory chess set installed in the White House, widely taken to be symbols of aristocratic degeneracy. The "corrupt bargain" of 1824, alleging an election deal between Adams and Henry Clay, was publicized endlessly. Jackson men were especially happy to malign Clay because they considered him the chief architect of anti-Jackson propaganda as well as the most credible threat in future elections.

The Adams men returned fire with fire. They portrayed Jackson as the bastard son of a prostitute,

a story made remotely plausible by his fatherless childhood. Worse, the cloudy, undocumented circumstances around his marriage to Rachel Donelson Robards gave rise to the story that Jackson was a seducer and an adulterer. Jackson claimed he had married Robards in 1791, but at that time her divorce from her first husband was not yet final, necessitating a remarriage in 1794. Adams papers howled that Jackson was a sinful and impulsive man, while Adams was portrayed as a man of restraint, piety, learning, and virtue.

Editors for Adams played up Jackson's notorious violent temper, evidenced by the many duels, brawls, and canings they could recount. Jackson men, of course, used the same stories to prove the old man's strength and resolve. Critics complained of his impetuous style of military justice that resulted in his execution of six Tennessee militiamen for insubordination during the war with the Creek Indians in 1814. One ardent Jackson editor shrewdly trounced that complaint: "Pshaw! Why don't you tell the whole truth? On the 8th of January, 1815, he murdered in the coldest blood 1,500 British soldiers!" Jackson's supporters preferred to project him as a tough frontier hero who knew how to command obedience and who stood up to abusive men (like Rachel Robard's first husband) who dishonored women. In this version of events, his capacity for violence became the muscle that gave force to

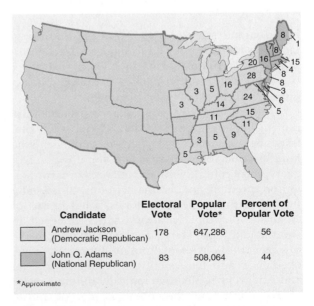

Candidate	Electoral Vote	Popular Vote*	Percent of Popular Vote
Andrew Jackson (Democratic Republican)	178	647,286	56
John Q. Adams (National Republican)	83	508,064	44

*Approximate

M A P 11.2
The Election of 1828

COFFIN HANDBILL
This 1828 campaign broadside memorialized the six soldiers Andrew Jackson ordered to be shot in 1815 for desertion. John Binns, editor of the anti-Jackson Democratic Press *in Philadelphia, wanted to horrify readers by turning Jackson into the murderer of six martyred men, each of whose name and story graced a coffin. Binn printed thousands of copies, but his "coffin handbill" soon backfired and made him the target of pro-Jackson crowds that threatened to clap him in a coffin and carry him around town.*

Louisiana State Museum.

his admirable sense of honor. And as for learning, Jackson's rough frontier education gave him a "natural sense," wrote a Boston editor, which "can never be acquired by reading books—it can only be acquired, in perfection, by reading men."

These stories were not smoke screens to obscure the "real" issues in the election. They became real issues because voters used them to comprehend the kind of public officer each man would make. Not every voter could follow the nuances of tariff policy or cared to ponder the wisdom of federally funded astronomical laboratories, a pet project of Adams's. But the character issues, conveyed in shorthand through stories about masculinity, spoke to larger questions about morality, honor, discipline, obedience, and the sanctity of contracts. Jackson and Adams presented two radically different styles of masculinity, and the voters, all men of course, concluded that the gendered behavior of these candidates foreshadowed their presidential styles and policies.

Throughout the campaign, Jackson deliberately kept his stand on economic and political issues vague; he was famous for his willingness to support a "judicious tariff," taken by different groups to mean quite different things. Adams stood by his record, mainly his promise to promote commerce through federal action, which brought him strength in New England and parts of New York. His stewardship over the passage of the 1828 tariff won him some friends in the manufacturing Northeast and among grateful hemp growers in Kentucky and sugar planters in Louisiana. Jackson's near-silence on issues like the tariff, banking, public land sales, and government patronage gave him a diffuse combination of backers, who could be sure only that he would favor western expansion and more limited federal powers than Adams.

Jackson won a sweeping victory, with 56 percent of the popular vote and 178 electoral votes (compared to Adams's 83). The general took most of the South and West and carried Pennsylvania and

New York as well. His vice president was John C. Calhoun, who had just been vice president under Adams but had broken with Adams's policies. Here was a clue that the firm lines dividing Jackson and Adams men were still fluid when it came to all offices below the presidency.

After 1828, national politicians no longer deplored the existence of political parties, as they had since the days of George Washington.

After 1828, national politicians no longer deplored the existence of political parties, as they had since the days of George Washington. They were coming to see that parties mobilized and delivered voters, sharpened the focus of differences in candidacies, and created party loyalty that surpassed individual candidates and elections. Jackson was an especially charismatic man, and his election did much to solidify voter loyalty to what would soon be called the Democratic Party. An election over personalities went far to create a party system that could withstand and override personality contests. What sounds like a contradiction makes sense because the personalities of Jackson and Adams so perfectly symbolized and defined for voters the competing ideas of the emerging parties: a moralistic, top-down party ready to make major decisions to promote economic growth competing against a contentious, energetic party ready to embrace liberty-loving individualism.

Jackson's Democratic Agenda

Between the November election and the inauguration in March 1829, Rachel Jackson died. An embittered Andrew Jackson, certain that the ugly campaign had hastened her death, went into deep mourning. His depression was worsened by constant pain from the 1806 bullet still lodged in his chest and by lead and mercury poisoning unwittingly caused by the medicines he took constantly. Sixty-two years old, he carried only 140 pounds on his six-foot-one frame. His adversaries doubted he would make it to a second term.

His supporters, however, went wild at the inauguration. Thousands cheered his ten-minute inaugural address, the shortest in history. Senator Daniel Webster of Massachusetts, allied with the emerging National Republican Party, wrote, "A monstrous crowd of people is in the City. I never saw anything like it before. Persons have come 500 miles to see Genl Jackson & they really seem to think that the country is rescued from some dreadful danger." An open reception at the White House turned into a near-riot as well-wishers jammed the premises, used windows as doors, stood on furniture for a better view of the great man, and broke thousands of dollars' worth of china and glasses.

One of Jackson's first tasks was to repair the damage to the White House. In addition to new upholstery, the president added east and west wings and installed twenty spittoons in the East Room. This extraordinary capacity for accommodating spit met the needs of the throngs that continued to arrive daily to see the president. Some came without invitation to seek jobs in the new administration. Others were tourists just calling on the old man to chat. The courteous Jackson, committed to his image as the president of the "common man," held audience with unannounced tourists throughout his two terms.

Jackson's cabinet appointments marked a departure. Whereas past presidents had tried to lessen party conflict by including men of different factions in their cabinets, Jackson would have only Jackson loyalists, a reasonable tactic followed by most later presidents. The most important position, secretary of state, he offered to Martin Van Buren, one of the shrewdest politicians of the day and newly elected governor of New York. Jackson barely knew him, but they quickly developed great mutual respect. The other principal candidate for leadership was South Carolina's John C. Calhoun, but he was installed in the ornamental post of vice president, where he impatiently chafed at the bit. The rest of Jackson's cabinet consisted of a loyal but undistinguished group of men. For advice, Jackson relied mainly on Van Buren and on a group of old Tennessee and Kentucky friends who were dubbed by the press "the kitchen cabinet."

Jackson's general agenda quickly came into focus once he was in office. He favored a Jeffersonian limited federal government, fearing that intervention in the economy inevitably favored some groups at the expense of others. He therefore opposed federal internal improvements and grants of monopolies and charters that privileged wealthy investors. In theory, he opposed protective tariffs, too, but he let stand the high tariff of 1828 since it generated revenue that reduced the federal debt. Like Jefferson, he anticipated rapid settlement of the interior of the country, where land sales would spread economic democracy to settlers. Establishing a federal Indian policy would thus have high priority.

Unlike Jefferson, however, Jackson exercised full presidential powers over Congress. Early in his first term, in 1830, he vetoed the Maysville Road bill, a highway project in Kentucky that Congress voted to support with federal dollars. In addition to his principled objection that it was unconstitutional, Jackson took satisfaction from the fact that the project he was killing was centered in Henry Clay's home state. (Clay was fast becoming the center of the opposition party.) Jackson used the veto twelve times during his tenure in office; all previous presidents, taken together, had exercised that right a total of nine times.

Cultural Shifts

Despite differences about the best or fairest way to enhance commercial development, Jackson's Democratic Republicans and Henry Clay's National Republicans shared enthusiasm for the outcome—a growing, booming economy. For increasing numbers of families, especially in the highly commercialized Northeast, the standard of living rose, consumption patterns changed, and the nature and location of work altered. All of these changes had a direct impact on the roles and duties of men and women in families and on the training of youth for the economy of the future. New ideas about gender relations appropriate to the new economy surfaced in books, periodicals, newspapers, and public behavior. In Jacksonian America, a widely shared public culture came into being, spread easily through rising levels of literacy, an explosion of print, and an increase in performance arts, both theatrical and oratorical.

The Family and Separate Spheres

The centerpiece of a new set of ideas about gender relations held that husbands found their status and authority in the new world of work, leaving wives to tend the hearth and home. Sermons, advice books, periodical articles, and novels reinforced the idea that men and women inhabited separate spheres with separate duties. "To woman it belongs . . . to elevate the intellectual character of her household [and] to kindle the fires of mental activity in childhood," wrote Mrs. A. J. Graves in a popular book titled *Advice to American Women*. For men,

in contrast, "the absorbing passion for gain, and the pressing demands of business, engross their whole attention" so that thay can converse only about bank discounts, stock jobbing, and tariffs. In particular, the private home, now the exclusive domain of women, was sentimentalized as the source of intimacy, love, and safety, an island of refuge from the cruel and competitive world of market relations. An 1830 magazine article pronounced that "it is at home, where man seeks a refuge from the vexations and embarrassments of business, . . . where is [found] the treasury of pure, disinterested love, such as is seldom found in the busy walks of a selfish and calculating world."

Some new aspects of society gave substance to this formulation of separate spheres. Men's work, especially in the manufacturing and urban North-

CELESTIA BULL'S DOMESTIC SCENE, CONNECTICUT
Celestia Bull of Winchester, Connecticut, painted this domestic scene as part of a "friendship book" for her friend Sarah Sawyer in 1826. The garlanded inscription at the top notes that "Lord Charles is fiddling . . . Lady Sarah is sewing." The billing doves make clear that this is a scene of marital bliss. Charles has the leisure to play music to his lady while she intently sews; sheet music and books lie open on the table.
Private collection. Photograph courtesy Walters-Benisek Art & Antiques, Northampton, Mass. David Stanbury Photography, Springfield, Mass.

east (not coincidentally the site of most book production), was undergoing profound change in the years after 1815. Increasingly, men's jobs brought cash to the household. Farmers and tradesmen sold products in a market, and bankers, bookkeepers, shoemakers, and canal diggers got pay envelopes. Even ministers, who used to get their allowance in country goods and cords of wood, now got cash instead. Furthermore, many men's jobs were performed outside the home, at an office or store. For nonfarm men, work indeed seemed newly disconnected from the home.

The home end of this dichotomy, however, was more complicated than the cultural prescriptions indicated. The vast majority of married white women did not hold paying jobs, but they certainly continued to find the home a site of time-consuming labor. The advice books treated household tasks as loving familial duties performed as a demonstration of feminine nurturance. Housework as *work* was thereby rendered invisible in an economy that evaluated work by its cash-generating potential.

In reality, wives directly contributed to family income in many ways. Some took in boarders, while others engaged in outwork, earning pay for shoe-binding, hatmaking, or needlework done at home. Women stretched men's dollars through thrift and recycling. Even among the most comfortable classes, the market intruded whenever wives hired domestic servants to perform the heavy household tasks no true lady would consider doing, like laundry. Most middle- and upper-income families hired servants; households striving to meet a respectable level of class display simply could not be run on the labor of one woman. A wife was therefore also an employer, facing tensions similar to those of her husband in supervising unruly, underpaid workers in the competitive world of market relations.

Why then did ideas about the sentimental, noncommercial, feminine home and the masculine world of work gain a wide acceptance in the 1830s (and well beyond)? In part, the cultural dominance of the middle and upper classes of the Northeast allowed them to assert their own experience as a universal characteristic of all society. In part, the doctrine of separate spheres functioned as all divisions of labor by gender function, to provide clear messages for how to be masculine and feminine. Men achieved a sense of manhood through work and pay; women established a sense of femininity through proper subordination to duty and service to others. The convenient fiction of this particular formulation of gender difference helped smooth the path for the first generation of Americans experiencing the market revolution. The doctrine of separate spheres ordained that men would absorb and display the values appropriate to the market economy—competition, acquisitiveness— while women would exemplify and foster older noncommercial values of loving service to family and community. Both men and women of the middle classes benefited from this bargain; men were set free to pursue wealth, while women gained moral authority within the home.

The Education and Training of Youth

The market economy and the new division of labor by sex required fresh methods of training the rising youth of both sexes. The generation that came of age in the 1820s and 1830s had opportunities for education and work unparalleled in previous generations. Northern states adopted public schooling between 1790 and the 1820s, and within another decade southern states began to provide "common schools" for white children. Most schools were one-room affairs, sometimes providing two entry doors to admit the sexes separately, another small but daily reminder of gender difference. The curriculum produced pupils able, by age twelve or fourteen, to read and to participate in marketplace calculations. Remarkably, girls received the same basic education as boys. Literacy rates for white females climbed dramatically, nearly catching up to male rates for the first time.

The fact that taxpayers paid for children's education created an incentive to seek an inexpensive teaching force. By the 1830s, northeastern school districts had replaced male teachers with young females. Like mill workers, teachers were in their late teens and regarded the work as temporary. In Massachusetts, one-fifth of all women taught school during their unmarried years. Some had acquired education in private girls' academies that were springing up to meet the middle-class ambition for polished daughters. In the 1840s, several states opened teacher training schools ("normal" schools) for women students. Only one college in the 1830s admitted women: Oberlin College in Ohio in 1837 opened a Ladies Department. The school also admitted black male students, so clearly it was unusually progressive. No other regular colleges admitted women until after the Civil War, but a handful of private "female seminaries" established

MARY JANE PATTERSON,
OBERLIN'S FIRST BLACK WOMAN GRADUATE
Mary Jane Patterson was the first black woman to earn a bachelor's degree in the United States. Oberlin College in Ohio was founded by evangelical and abolitionist activists in the 1830s; it admitted white and black, men and women to its collegiate program — although in the early years the black students were all male and the women students were all white. Patterson, the daughter of slaves, earned her degree in 1862. She taught school in Philadelphia and Washington for the next three decades, until her death in 1894.
Oberlin College Archives, Oberlin, Ohio.

suffering, and gentleness necessary to superintend the formation of character," said the author Harriet Beecher Stowe, who taught at her sister's Hartford school.

Male youths leaving the common school faced two paths. A small percentage continued at private boys' academies (numbering in the several hundreds nationwide), and a far smaller number matriculated at the country's two dozen colleges. More typically, boys left school at fourteen to train for an occupation. Some apprenticed to learn specific trades, while many others flooded to old cities like Boston and Baltimore or new towns like Rochester and Cincinnati, seeking business careers in entry-level clerkships. The new practice of separating home and work among the commercial classes meant that these employees, as young as fourteen, were unlikely to live under the direct supervision of their employers. A new form of urban housing materialized in the 1830s: the male boardinghouse.

Changes in patterns of youth employment and training meant that large numbers of youngsters in the 1830s and later had escaped the watchful eyes of their families.

Young girls also headed for the cities in unprecedented numbers, seeking work in the expanding service sectors as seamstresses and domestic servants. The female migrants generally resided with their employers; a boardinghouse for women too much resembled a brothel.

Changes in patterns of youth employment and training meant that large numbers of youngsters in the 1830s and later had escaped the watchful eyes of their families. Moralists fretted about the dangers of the situation. In the wake of a serious criminal case, a Newburyport, Massachusetts, newspaper urged parents to "inquire about the morals of the business supervisor of your child" because "a want of suitable companions and advisers for his leisure hours" could lead to the downfall of any young boy. Worthy organizations set up apprentice's libraries and lecture series to keep young people uplifted— and off the streets. An outpouring of advice books numbering in the hundreds rose to the challenge of instructing youth in the virtues of hard work and delayed gratification. Other forms of inexpensive reading matter came their way, however, not so easily screened for correct moral values. And, at loose

a rigorous curriculum that rivaled that of the best men's colleges. The three most prominent were the Troy Seminary in New York, founded by Emma Willard in 1821; the Hartford Seminary in Connecticut, founded by Catharine Beecher in 1822; and Mount Holyoke in Massachusetts, founded by Mary Lyon in 1837. These women educators argued that women made better teachers than men: "If men have more knowledge, they have less talent at communicating it. Nor have they the patience, the long-in the city with evenings free, boys and young men turned to the attractions of urban amusements like the theater.

The Penny Press of the 1830s

Cultural ideals about gender and youth spread rapidly in a climate increasingly saturated with the printed word. In the 1790s, fewer than ninety newspapers, each printing a few thousand copies per issue, provided the knowledge base of current events; by 1830, there were eight hundred papers, sixty-five of them urban dailies, and the number continued to expand.

Innovations in printing technology, as well as rising literacy rates, helped spur this rapid expansion. New steam-driven rotary presses with an automatic feed device made possible a much higher output of copies than the old-style handpresses were capable of. Circulation figures for the most successful urban newspapers of the 1830s jumped to twenty thousand. But neither literacy rates nor technology changes fully account for this revolution. It took a new style of journalism, called the penny press, published in small format with lively human interest stories, to draw thousands of new readers into the information networks of Jacksonian America.

The traditional political and commercial papers of the 1830s cost six cents and were large, often two by three feet, a size that required a table or counter for reading. They targeted the business classes with coverage of banking, shipping, and complete transcripts of political speeches. In contrast, the penny papers were cheap and small, on the order of twelve by eighteen inches, and hence convenient to read anywhere—in a crowded tenement, in a saloon, even in a privy. They featured breezy political coverage, irreverent editorializing on current events, local news and exposés, drama reviews, racetrack

LURID COVER OF A CRIME PAMPHLET, NEW YORK
Cheap and easy printing in the early nineteenth century gave rise to new genres of popular reading matter, including a large pamphlet literature detailing horrific murder stories that invited readers to contemplate the nature of evil. This woodcut cover from 1836 promises to reveal the "interesting particulars" of the murder of Ellen Jewett, a New York City prostitute axed to death in her brothel bed. The pamphlet claims to constitute "an impressive warning" to youth about the tragedies of "Dens of Infamy." But the crude picture of the female corpse, with bare legs and breasts fully exposed, suggests that alternative, less moralistic readings of the same material were certainly possible for the purchasers.
William L. Clements Library.

TABLE 11.1
THE GROWTH OF NEWSPAPERS, 1820–1840

	1820	1830	1835	1840
U.S. Population (in millions)	9.6	12.8	15.0	17.1
Number of newspapers published	500	800	1200	1400
Daily newspapers	42	65	—	138

results, and crime reporting. Before long, the traditional papers also began to attend to such forms of news.

New York was home to the first penny paper in 1833, and by 1835 there were three. By 1836, Philadelphia, Boston, and Baltimore each had penny papers selling thousands of copies. Their influence was felt far beyond the urban centers, facilitated by a regular system of newspaper exchange via the postal system. Town and village papers far from the East Coast reprinted the snappy political editorials and sensationalized crime stories, putting very undeferential ideas into the heads of readers new to politics.

Public Life and Popular Amusements

Newspapers were not the only new medium for spreading a shared American culture. Starting in the 1830s, traveling lecturers crisscrossed the country, bringing entertainment and instruction to small-town audiences. Some were organized through a central agency called the Lyceum, while others were independent operators who booked local halls and collected admissions of about twenty-five cents. Speakers gave dramatic readings of plays or poetry or lectured on history, current events, or controversial topics like advanced female education. Some speakers specialized in medical knowledge and came equipped with wax models of body parts to illustrate physiology and anatomy.

Theater blossomed in the 1830s, providing Americans with their most common form of shared entertainment. The number and size of theaters greatly increased and ticket prices dropped, putting theatergoing within the reach of many ordinary Americans. The major cities each had a half dozen or more theaters, with as many as three thousand seats apiece. With performances six nights a week, they could accommodate a large segment of the urban population (and urban visitors). Audiences mostly comprised white men of all classes, but women and blacks attended as well, in smaller numbers. The highest level of the gallery in most theaters was by custom reserved for blacks, prostitutes, and men seeking prostitutes.

Shakespeare's plays were an all-round favorite. In 1835 in Philadelphia, sixty-five separate Shakespeare productions were held. Other English and American productions of tragedies, comedies, and melodramas rotated nightly. Before and after plays, theaters provided short acts of singers, dancers, and, increasingly, minstrelsy, a blackface musical comedy first performed in New York City in 1831. White performers with blackened faces parodied everything from romance to Shakespeare, trading on (and thereby reinforcing) racist stereotypes about African Americans' speech, dress, and conduct.

Playgoing audiences were responsive and interactive. Applause was joined by hisses, jeers, whistling, and stomping; actors expected interruptions or even projectiles thrown at them. Audience response helped to shape the content of the productions. An actor in 1822 in New Orleans tried out a new song on a theater audience made up of keelboat men: "The Hunters of Kentucky," a sprightly ditty praising Jackson's militiamen for legendary (and largely mythical) heroics at the Battle of New Orleans. The rivermen made him sing it three times that night; he was immediately forced to make it a regular part of any show he appeared in. Within a few years it was a wildly popular tune, sung all over the country, a happy circumstance for Jackson's electoral fortunes.

The public culture of the theater demonstrates a fluidity of cultural styles in the 1830s. In the era of the "common man," ordinary men and women had a surprisingly well-honed acquaintance with Shakespeare, knowing the scripts so well that they could hoot and stomp when actors muffed their lines or laugh uproariously at clever satires of the Bard. Not until the 1840s and beyond would a kind of market segmentation appear in public amusements, with different theaters aiming at different audiences—some targeting the cultural elite and others the working classes.

The theater world also promoted a new vision of what a public woman could be. Traditionally, a "public woman" was a prostitute, and actresses suffered from the association; there had been no way for a woman to have a public persona without calling her sexual respectability into question. The spectacular success of theaters beginning in the 1830s made some women stars of the stage, drawing admiration, fans, and respectability around them in well-tended publicity campaigns. Women on the stage could speak commanding words in loud voices. In Shakespeare's day, boys had played the female roles precisely to prevent that undesired display of female power. But now actresses could routinely perform roles that enlarged the scope of possibilities for female behavior; some, indeed, dressed in breeches and played male parts. The trade-off, of course, was that theaters also offered actresses's bodies to the largely male audience for viewing.

Finally, the popularity of theaters exemplified a general cultural turn toward the celebration of brilliant public speech. In this golden age of oration, actors, lawyers, politicians, and ministers could hold crowds spellbound with their flawless elocution and elegant turns of phrase. Criminal trials, for example, were astonishingly short by modern standards, but the lawyers' closing arguments might continue for many hours, with crowds of spectators hanging on every word. Senator Daniel Webster of Massachusetts was the acknowledged genius of political oration, putting grown men into raptures. At a Webster speech commemorating the Pilgrims' arrival, one man in a crowd of fifteen hundred recalled that "three or four times I thought my temples would burst with the gush of blood." Ministers with gifted tongues could in the space of hours transform crowds of sinners into deeply moved believers. Skillful speakers demanded and generally got skillful, attentive listeners. Catchy slogans had little place in this oratorical style.

A widely shared national culture became possible in the 1830s as movement of books, newspapers, and people spread ideas and values. This culture was not universal, of course; it originated with the new commercial classes whose superior access to publication and transportation helped ensure the dominance of their ideas. They pioneered new ways of organizing private life, ordering gender relations, and educating the young that affirmed values appropriate to the market revolution. The culture was not monolithic either; simply getting ideas in circulation does not ensure that everyone will agree. Indeed, the proliferation of print in many instances promoted disagreement and debate. Democrats and Whigs, for example, made conflict a natural part of the political culture, and a parallel divergence in religious styles rocked the spiritual life of the country.

Democracy and Religion

An unprecedented revival of evangelical religion peaked in the early 1830s, after gathering three decades of momentum in states across the North and the upper South. Known as the Second Great Awakening, the outpouring of religious fervor changed the shape of American Protestantism. The heart of the evangelical message was that salvation was available to anyone willing to eradicate individual sin and accept faith in God's grace. Just as universal male suffrage allowed all white men to vote, democratized religion offered salvation to all who chose to embrace it.

Among the most serious adherents of evangelical Protestantism were men and women of the new mercantile classes whose self-discipline in pursuing market ambitions meshed well with the message of self-discipline in pursuit of spiritual perfection. Not content with individual perfection, many of these men and women sought to perfect society as well.

Just as universal male suffrage allowed all white men to vote, democratized religion offered salvation to all who chose to embrace it.

They provided the moral and intellectual drive behind reform movements devoted to eradicating general sins and social ills in the 1830s.

The Second Great Awakening

The earliest manifestations of an unusual outbreak of fervent piety appeared in 1801 in Kentucky. A crowd estimated from ten to twenty thousand people camped out on a hillside at Cane Ridge for a revival meeting that lasted several weeks. By the 1810s and 1820s, camp meetings had spread to the Atlantic seaboard states, finding especially enthusiastic audiences in western New York and Pennsylvania. By the 1830s, frequent regional meetings flourished in places easy to reach by public transport.

The gatherings attracted women and men hungry for a more immediate access to spiritual peace —no need to engage in years of Bible reading and soul-searching preparation. Ministers adopted an emotional style and invited audience members to an immediate experience of conversion and salvation. One eyewitness at a revival reported that "some of the people were singing, others praying, some crying for mercy in the most piteous accents. . . . At one time I saw at least 500 swept down in a moment as if a battery of a thousand guns had been opened upon them, and then immediately followed shrieks and shouts that rent the very heavens." Self-selected individuals put themselves in the line of fire by choosing to occupy the "sinners' bench" or "anxious seat" at the front of the audience.

THE BROADWAY TABERNACLE.

CHARLES G. FINNEY'S BROADWAY TABERNACLE
The Reverend Charles G. Finney took his evangelical movement to New York City in the early 1830s, operating out of existing Presbyterian churches. In 1836, the Broadway Tabernacle was built for his pastorate. In its use of space the Tabernacle resembled a theater more than a traditional church, but in one respect it departed radically from one very theaterlike tradition of churches, — the custom of charging pew rents. In effect, most churches required worshipers to purchase their seats. In contrast, Finney insisted that all seats in his house were free, unreserved, and open to all.
Oberlin College Archives, Oberlin, Ohio.

From 1800 to 1820, church membership doubled in the United States, much of it among the evangelical groups. Methodists, Baptists, and Presbyterians formed the core of the new movement, while Episcopalians, Congregationalists, Unitarians, Dutch Reformed, Lutherans, and Catholics maintained strong skepticism about the emotional enthusiasm. Women more than men were attracted to the evangelical movement, and the pattern of recruitment typically involved wives and mothers who then were able to persuade husbands and sons to join them.

The leading exemplar of the Second Great Awakening was a lawyer-turned-minister named Charles Grandison Finney. Up to his late twenties, Finney showed no religious inclinations; he had never read the Bible until shortly before his own awakening in 1821. Finney lived in western New York, where the completion of the Erie Canal in 1825 fundamentally altered the social and economic landscape overnight. Towns swelled with new inhabitants, who brought in remarkable prosperity along with other, less admirable aspects of urban growth, namely prostitution, drinking, and gaming.

Finney's genius was to see New York canal towns like Utica, Rome, and Buffalo as ripe for evangelical awakening. In Rochester, New York, Finney sustained a six-month revival through the long winter of 1830–31, generating thousands of new converts.

The message that Finney preached was directed primarily at women and men of the business classes, and, true to his training, Finney couched his message in legal metaphors. "The world is divided into two great political parties," he announced in a sermon, the party of Satan and the party of Jehovah. "Ministers should labor with sinners, as a lawyer does with a jury . . . ; and the sinner should weigh his arguments, and make up his mind as upon oath and for his life, and give a verdict upon the spot." Finney urged his listeners to take control of their own salvation, arguing that a reign of Christian perfection loomed. The promise of perfection required a public-spirited outreach to the less than perfect, to foster their salvation; Christian benevolence, or do-good action, was demanded of all believers. Evangelicals promoted Sunday schools to bring piety to children; they battled to end mail delivery, stop public transport, and close shops on Sundays to honor the Sabbath. Many women formed Missionary Societies, which printed and distributed millions of Bibles and religious tracts, taking the message of the Sunday sermon out of the pulpit and into individual parlors. Maternal Associations sprang up to promote a new style of moral mothering. Through such avenues, evangelical religion offered women expanded spheres of influence.

In 1832, Finney moved to New York City and renovated a disreputable theater on Chatham Street into a Free Presbyterian church. His dynamic, theatrical performances suited the location perfectly. A scribe took down his sermons, and the New York *Evangelist* carried his message weekly to a national readership. Finney adopted tactics of Jacksonian-era politicians to sell his cause: publicity, argumentation, rallies, and dramatic speeches. His object, he said, was to get Americans to "vote in the Lord Jesus Christ as the governor of the Universe."

The Temperance Movement

The evangelical disposition—a combination of righteousness, energy, self-discipline, and faith—animated a vigorous campaign to define alcohol as an unacceptable and dangerous self-indulgence. Millions of Americans took the pledge to abstain from strong drink, and temperance in the 1830s became a middle-class fixation.

Alcohol consumption had steadily risen in the decades before the 1830s. On the supply side, increased acreage planted in wheat, corn, and rye resulted in abundant whiskey, for it was far cheaper to transport distilled grains than to ship bulky and less valuable flour products. On the demand side, alcohol consumption rose in direct correlation to urban growth and the expansion of the wage-earning classes. Where master artisans had once handed out beverages (in moderate quantities) to their apprentices and journeymen, the reorganized wage labor force of the new market put social distance between workers and employers, who now frowned on alcohol as counterproductive to good work habits. Drinking off the job, as a leisure activity, accordingly increased.

Historians estimate that by 1830 the per capita annual consumption of alcohol for the entire population over age thirteen amounted to an astonishing 9.5 gallons of hard liquor plus 30.3 gallons of hard cider, beer, and wine. Since a substantial portion of that population abstained, the actual consumption level for serious drinkers was higher still.

Leisure-time drinking flourished in urban streets with their multitudes of saloons, barbershops, and groceries selling liquor by the glass. A lively saloon culture fostered mutual aid, job contacts, and masculine camaraderie among laborers. It also fostered excessive alcohol consumption and a new style of binge drinking that alarmed older proponents of moderate drinking.

Alcoholism was not limited to the working classes. In elite homes, sociable customs separated men and women after dinner gatherings, the men to imbibe whiskey and smoke cigars, the women to chat and sip sherry. Colleges before 1820 routinely served students a pint of ale with meals, and the army and navy made a pint of rum a standard daily ration. Middle-class sons working away from home fell under the spell of oyster bars and the port served there. The attraction of bottled, fermented drinks among all classes made a certain amount of sense, given the uncertain availability of safe drinking water and the lack of reliable refrigeration.

Organized opposition to drinking first surfaced in the 1810s among groups in New England concerned about health issues. In 1826, Lyman Beecher, the father of Catharine Beecher and Harriet Beecher Stowe and the Connecticut minister of an "awakened" church, founded the American Temperance Society, stamped with the moral condemnation of indulgent behavior. Moderate drinking was not sufficiently virtuous, Beecher preached: "The daily use

conviction that called for the eradication of sin. By the 1840s, in response to criticism, they toned down their tactics and concentrated on rescue work among downtrodden girls.

Organizing against Slavery

Even more radical than moral reform was the effort to eradicate slavery in the 1830s, which evangelicals saw as a national sin of injustice. The abolition movement, as it was called, excited fierce resistance from white Americans, North and South. The debate leading to the Missouri Compromise of 1820 showed how divisive and irreconcilable the issue was. A group of Maryland and Virginia planters had founded the American Colonization Society in 1817 to promote gradual emancipation, by which slave owners voluntarily released slaves and had them transported to Africa. By the early 1820s, several thousand African Americans were living on the West African coast in a new colony (later a country) called Liberia, created for freed slaves. (Liberia's capital was named Monrovia in honor of President James Monroe, who advocated colonization.) Not surprisingly, newly freed men and women were often not eager to move to Liberia; their African roots were three or more generations in the past. Migration across the Atlantic proved to be so gradual (and expensive) as to have a negligible impact on American slavery.

A more insistent attention to the evils of slavery emerged in 1831, dictated by the perfectionist impulse of the Second Great Awakening. Charles Finney's religious campaigns in Rochester and New York City identified slavery as a major obstacle to America's progress toward perfection. Both of those cities quickly became centers of antislavery agitation.

In Boston, an antislavery movement developed around William Lloyd Garrison, who started publishing a weekly newspaper called the *Liberator* in 1831. Garrison was then twenty-six; raised in Massachusetts, he had spent some time in Baltimore, where he absorbed a firsthand knowledge of both slavery and Quaker antislavery sentiment. Back in the North, he launched his drive for immediate abolition, promising that his paper would be "as harsh as truth, and as uncompromising as justice. On this subject, I do not wish to think, or speak, or write, with moderation. No! No! Tell a man whose house is on fire to give a moderate alarm; tell him to moderately rescue his wife from the hands of the ravisher; tell the mother to gradually extricate her

babe from the fire into which it has fallen;—but urge me not to use moderation in a cause like the present." No gradualist plan could ever be acceptable to Garrison.

Garrison's visibility in Boston built on several years of growing local antislavery sentiment. In 1829, a black Bostonian named David Walker published *An Appeal to the Colored Citizens of the World*. Walker, a forty-four-year-old freedman born in North Carolina, was a printer and an active member of the recently formed Massachusetts Colored Association. His pamphlet condemned racism, invoked the egalitarian language of the Declaration of Independence, and hinted at racial violence if whites did not change their prejudiced ways. "Wo, wo, will be to you if we have to obtain our freedom by fighting. Throw way your fears and prejudices then, and enlighten us and treat us like men, and we will like you more than we do now hate you, and tell us now no more about colonization, for America is as much our country, as it is yours." Walker's fervent *Appeal* electrified Garrison, pushing him into a more radical stance on slavery. It electrified the South as well, and several southern states prohibited its circulation.

From 1831 to 1833, a young black woman, Maria Stewart, newly widowed, staged a series of public lectures in Boston on slavery and racial prejudice. She spoke to black audiences, and while her arguments against slavery were welcomed, her voice—that of a woman—created problems. Few American-born women had yet engaged in public speaking beyond ceremonial or theatrical performance; Stewart was breaking a social taboo. Compounding her audience's discomfort was the fact that Stewart also criticized members of her own race for contributing to their oppressed condition. She faulted black women for accepting deadening domestic jobs instead of pursuing an education, while black men lacked "ambition and force" to combat racial prejudice. Boston's elite black men in the audience discouraged her career, and she retired from the platform in 1833. Garrison published her lectures, giving them wider circulation. A cresting wave of antislavery sentiment was about to break over many northeastern cities.

Southerners feared Garrison's cresting wave. Eight months after the *Liberator* started, a charismatic slave named Nat Turner led the largest and most deadly of all slave insurrections, in Southampton County, Virginia (see chapter 12). The event left the South reeling with palpable paranoia about future slave revolts. As they had with Walker's *Ap-*

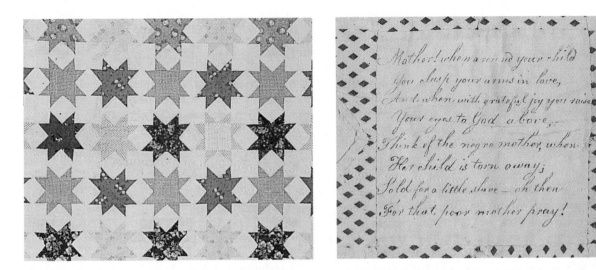

ABOLITIONIST CRIB QUILT

This crib quilt (left) was sewn by women of the Boston Female Anti-Slavery Society in 1836. Many abolitionist women produced handcrafted items for sale at antislavery fairs to raise money to support antislavery agents in the field and publication costs of abolitionist literature. The central square of this quilt (detail) reminds mothers hugging their own free babies to "Think of the negro mother, when Her child is torn away; Sold for a little slave — oh then, For that poor mother pray!"

Courtesy of Society for Preservation of New England Antiquities/photo by David Bohl.

peal, several southern states ordered local postmasters to refuse delivery of the *Liberator.*

In 1832 and 1833, the antislavery movement got organized. The New England Anti-Slavery Society coalesced in 1832 around Garrison, with a women's auxiliary run by Maria Weston Chapman, an assistant editor of the *Liberator.* The New York Anti-Slavery Society became active in 1833, as did another in Philadelphia. Within five years, there would be 1,350 local antislavery societies pocketed all over the North, with a membership totaling a quarter of a million men and women. This was a significant number, but by no means a large one in relation to the North's population.

Abolitionists borrowed revivalist techniques. Conventions drew like-minded people together, as camp meetings did, to hear speeches and debate strategy. The print media were fully enlisted, with a dozen antislavery newspapers as well as pamphlets and books in profusion. Effective public speakers were hired as agents to travel on speaking tours, like itinerant ministers. Antislavery agents inspired the formation of new local societies, but they also drew hecklers and worse in many towns.

Many northerners were not prepared to embrace the abolitionist call for emancipation, immediate or gradual. They might oppose slavery as a blot on the country's ideals or as a rival to the free labor system of the North, but at the same time most white northerners remained antiblack and therefore antiabolition. From 1834 to 1838, there were several dozen eruptions of serious mob violence against abolitionists; sometimes the violence was also viciously directed against black neighborhoods, as in New York in 1834. Garrison once grappled with a lynch mob in Boston. Antislavery headquarters in Philadelphia burned to the ground in 1838, after which the mob burned a black church and the Shelter for Colored Orphans. The depth of negative feeling for abolition sprang from deep wells of northern racism; abolitionists were called "amalgamationists," a potent label suggesting that abolitionists favored racial intermixing, both social and sexual.

Women played a prominent role in abolition, just as they had in moral reform and evangelical religion. They formed women's auxiliaries and engaged in fundraising to support agents in the field and the expenses of pamphlet publication. In the political realm, women circulated antislavery petitions, which they presented to the U.S. Congress with tens of thousands of signatures.

Garrison particularly welcomed women's activity. The *Liberator* had a women's department, featuring appeals to northern women to extend their protective feminine sympathies to their black sisters of the South. When a southern plantation daughter named Angelina Grimké wrote him about her personal repugnance for slavery, Garrison published the letter in the *Liberator* and brought her overnight fame. Grimké and her older sister Sarah, now living in Philadelphia, quickly became agents with the antislavery movement and started a speaking tour of Massachusetts in 1837 to offer personal testimony about slavery to women's groups. Grimké's powerful eyewitness speeches attracted men as well, causing the Congregational church leadership of Massachusetts to issue a warning to all its ministers not to let the Grimké sisters use their podiums. As with Maria Stewart, the Grimkés had violated a gender norm by presuming to instruct men. It certainly did not help that their message involved the most controversial political topic of the 1830s.

In the late 1830s, the cause of abolition divided the nation as no other subject did. It had its martyr: An antislavery editor in Illinois, Elijah Lovejoy, was killed by a rioting crowd that tried to destroy his printing press. Even among the abolitionists there emerged significant divisions. The Grimké sisters, radicalized by the public reaction to their speaking tour, began to write and speak about women's rights. Moderate abolitionists unwilling to push the woman question retreated from the implications of their own egalitarian rhetoric employed in their race speeches. Some radical men, like Garrison, embraced women's rights fully, working to get women leadership positions in the national antislavery group. Out of the New England antislavery movement came the first organized women's rights movement in U.S. history, in the 1840s. The more moderate New York group stayed with antislavery as a single issue and in the 1840s moved more directly into politics, founding first the Liberty Party and then the Free-Soil Party, precursors to the Republican Party of the 1850s.

The many men and women active in reform movements in the 1830s found their initial inspiration in evangelical Protestantism's dual message: Salvation was open to all and society needed to be perfected. Their activist mentality squared well with the interventionist tendencies of the party forming in opposition to Andrew Jackson's Democrats. On the whole, reformers gravitated to the Whig Party.

Jackson Defines the Democratic Party

In his eight years in office, Jackson worked to implement his vision of a politics of opportunity for all white men. He also greatly enhanced the power of the presidency. He favored rapid western land settlement, which required him to disrupt certain Indian tribes and to face down the Supreme Court when it backed some of their claims. He had a dramatic confrontation with John C. Calhoun and South Carolina when that state tried to nullify the tariff of 1828. Disapproving of all government-granted privilege, Jackson challenged what he called the "monster" Bank of the United States and took it down to defeat, along with the National Republican leadership who tried to pin the 1832 campaign to it. Jackson's legacy to his successor, Martin Van Buren, was a Democratic Party strong enough to withstand the passing of the powerful old man.

Indian Policy and the Trail of Tears

For forty years, white Americans moving west had encountered strong resistance from Indian tribes east of the Mississippi River. After 1815, improved transportation greatly accelerated the westward flow of white settlers, and states containing Indian enclaves rapidly joined the Union. When Jackson took office, fundamental questions remained unresolved: What was the legal status of the quarter of a million Indians now resident in the United States? Were they subject to state and federal law?

From the 1790s to the 1820s, the federal government negotiated treaties with tribes, just as colonies had done in the pre-independence period, on the assumption that Indians were foreign nations. The Indians asserted their own sovereignty and communal rights to their land, even though they now lived within state borders. Treaty making, however, proved a precarious practice. American negotiators found it hard to strike workable terms that whole tribes would accept when trading money or promises of security in exchange for Indian land. All too often, a few Indians with no legitimacy to speak for their tribes were persuaded to sign treaties ceding vast acreage.

After the War of 1812, Andrew Jackson as an army general negotiated many such treaties, but he

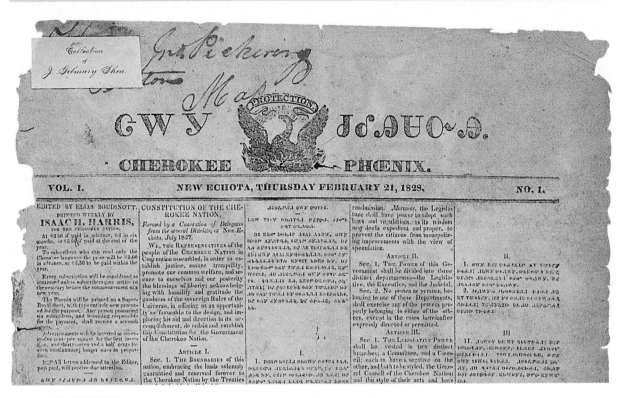

CHEROKEE PHOENIX

Around 1820, Sequoyah, about forty-five years old and nephew of a Cherokee chief, invented
written symbols to convey the Cherokee language. Each symbol represented a syllable of sound.
In 1828, the Cherokee in New Echota, Georgia, ordered custom-made type embodying the new
symbols and began printing a newspaper, the Cherokee Phoenix, *the first newspaper published*
by Native Americans, printed in both English and Cherokee.

Special Collections Division, Georgetown University Library, Washington, D.C.

privately thought it was "absurd" to assume that the Indians were foreigners. In his view, the Indians were now subjects of the United States, perhaps entitled to keep their villages and improved land but not their large hunting grounds. When he became president in 1829, he moved to implement his idea.

Others in the period from 1790 to the 1820s proposed assimilation as a more peaceable solution. Nationally organized missionary associations tried to "civilize" native peoples by converting them to Christianity. In 1819, Congress authorized $10,000 a year for interdenominational missions to instruct Indians in religion, reading and writing, and agricultural practices. Missionaries were also eager to institute their own notions of private property and correct gender relations, assumed by them to be essential features of a civilized society. They hoped to persuade Indian tribes to limit women to domestic tasks, forcing men to do agricultural tasks usually done by women. But assimilation proved to be slow going. Indian women were particularly reluctant to adopt a gender system that accorded them less power than their tribal system. The general failure of assimilation moved Jackson to a more drastic policy.

In his first message to Congress in 1829, President Jackson declared that Indians within the United States borders could not remain independent and in sovereign control of tribal lands. Congress agreed and passed the Removal Act of 1830, appropriating $500,000 to relocate tribes west of the Mississippi River.

For northern tribes, their numbers greatly diminished by years of war, gradual removal was well under way. But not all the Indians went quietly. In 1832 in western Illinois, Black Hawk, a leader of the Sac and Fox Indians, convinced his people to refuse to leave their Indian lodges when whites claimed them under a dubious treaty signed by four unauthorized Sac Indians. Federal troops sent by Jackson attacked and chased the Indians into southern Wisconsin, where, after several skirmishes and battles, Black Hawk was captured and many of his two thousand people massacred.

The southern tribes proved to be even more resistant to removal. The powerful Creek, Chickasaw, Choctaw, and Cherokee, whose lands encompassed parts of North Carolina, Tennessee, and northern Georgia, Alabama, and Mississippi, at first refused to relocate. But their land attracted cotton-hungry white settlers, and a rumor of gold on Cherokee land in Georgia in 1829 only intensified the pressure.

Ironically, the seventeen thousand members of the Cherokee tribe had "assimilated" most success-

fully, spurred by dedicated missionaries living with them. Starting in 1808, they adopted written laws, culminating in 1827 in a constitution with a bicameral legislature, an executive office, and a court system modeled on those of the United States government. The constitution defined the boundaries of their nation, which they claimed was independent of Georgia. More than two hundred of the wealthiest Cherokee had intermarried with whites and had adopted white styles of housing, dress, and cotton agriculture, including the ownership of over a thousand African American slaves. They had developed a written alphabet and published a newspaper as well as Christian prayerbooks in their language. The missionaries supported them fully in their battle first with Georgia and then with Jackson.

In 1826, Georgia asserted the dependent status of the Cherokee: "The Indians are tenants at Geor-

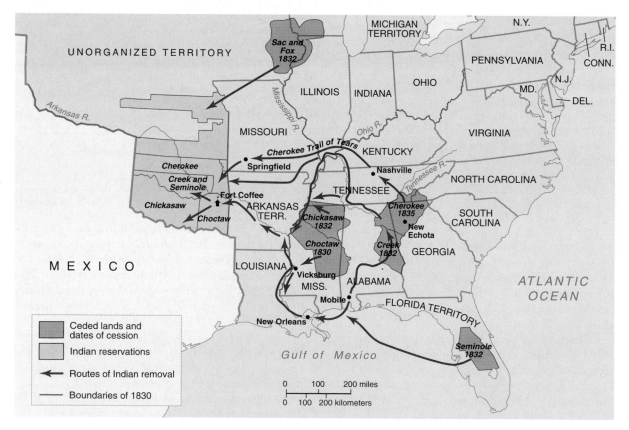

M A P 11.3

Indian Removal and the Trail of Tears, 1830s
The federal government under President Andrew Jackson pursued a vigorous policy of Indian removal in the 1830s. Southern tribes were forcibly moved west to land known as the Indian Territory, to the west of Arkansas (in present-day Oklahoma). As many as a quarter of the Cherokee Indians died in 1838 on their route, known as the Trail of Tears.

gia's will, and Georgia may at any time she pleases determine that tenancy by taking possession of the premises." President Jackson sided with Georgia, so the legal-minded Cherokee resorted to the U.S. government's weapon of choice: a team of first-rate lawyers who brought suit before the Supreme Court.

In 1831 in *Cherokee Nation v. Georgia,* the Cherokee sued to prohibit Georgia from subjecting them to state laws. Chief Justice John Marshall set aside the case on technicalities but encouraged the Cherokee to seek further legal redress. When Georgia jailed two missionaries, Samuel Worcester and Elizur Butler, under an 1830 law forbidding missionary aid to Indians without state permission, the Cherokee brought suit again. In the 1832 case, *Worcester v. Georgia,* the Supreme Court found for the missionaries and made the larger point for the Cherokee, recognizing their existence as "a distinct community, occupying its own territory, in which the laws of Georgia can have no force."

An angry President Jackson announced that he would ignore the Court's decision. "John Marshall has made his opinion, now let him enforce it," he reportedly declared. Jackson instead proceeded with the Removal Act. "If they [the Cherokee] now refuse to accept the liberal terms offered, they can only be liable for whatever evils and difficulties may arise. I feel conscious of having done my duty to my red children."

Still, the Cherokee remained in Georgia for two more years without significant violence. Then, in 1835, a small, unauthorized part of the tribe signed a treaty ceding all the tribal lands to the state, and Georgia rapidly sold off the land to whites through a state lottery. Several thousand Cherokee petitioned the U.S. Congress to ignore the bogus treaty, but their pleas went unheard.

The disputed treaty relinquished a large piece of northern Georgia in exchange for $5 million and equal acreage west of Arkansas, in present-day Oklahoma. But most of the Cherokee refused to move, and in May 1838, the deadline for voluntary evacuation, federal troops arrived to deport them. Moving in groups of a thousand each, under armed guard, the Cherokee embarked on a twelve-hundred-mile journey that came to be called the Trail of Tears. A Maine newspaperman traveling in Kentucky encountered the migration stream, some in wagons but others walking barefoot. "Even aged females, apparently, nearly ready to drop into the grave, were travelling with heavy burdens attached to the back—on the sometimes frozen ground. . . .

We learned from the inhabitants on the road where the Indians passed that they buried fourteen to fifteen at every stopping place, and they make a journey of ten miles per day only on an average." Nearly a quarter of the Cherokee died en route, from hardship and starvation. They joined fifteen thousand Creek, twelve thousand Choctaw, and five thousand Chickasaw Indians also forcibly relocated to what is now Oklahoma. In the early 1840s, the small surviving remnant of the Florida Seminole tribe was moved west, after a seven-year war that killed nearly half of them and fifteen hundred federal soldiers as well. Jackson's Indian policy proved to be costly in human life.

Jackson genuinely believed that exile to the west was necessary to save Indian culture from destruction.

In his farewell address to the nation in 1837, Jackson justified Indian removal with high-minded language about the benefit of the policy to the forlorn natives: "This unhappy race . . . are now placed in a situation where we may well hope that they will share in the blessings of civilization and be saved from the degradation and destruction to which they were rapidly hastening while they remained in the states." Jackson genuinely believed that exile to the west was necessary to save Indian culture from destruction.

Nullification: Federal Power versus States' Rights

Jackson's Indian policy happened to harmonize with the principle of states' rights: The president supported Georgia's right to ignore the Supreme Court decision in *Worcester v. Georgia.* But in another pressing question of states' rights, Jackson trounced on South Carolina's claim to ignore federal tariff policy.

South Carolina had been smarting since the "Tariff of Abominations" passed in 1828. Worldwide prices for cotton were already in sharp decline in the late 1820s and early 1830s, and the further depression of shipping caused by high tariffs hurt the South's export of agricultural products. In 1828, a group of South Carolina politicians headed by John C. Calhoun drew up a statement outlining a doctrine of nullification. The Union, they argued, was a confederation of states that had yielded some but not all power to the federal government. When Congress overstepped its powers, states had the right to nullify its acts, and as precedents they pointed to the Virginia and Kentucky Resolutions of 1798, which had attempted to invalidate the Alien and Sedition Acts. Congress had erred in using tariff policy as an instrument to benefit specific industries, the South Carolinians claimed; tariffs should be used only to raise revenue.

The 1828 statement was an assertion of principles, not a declaration of action, and it was not officially endorsed by the South Carolina legislature. Jackson ignored it, except to avoid appointing South Carolinians to high administrative office. He was stuck with Calhoun in the vice presidency, but he effectively deprived him of influence or power. Sensing futility, Calhoun resigned from the vice presidency in 1832 and accepted election by the South Carolina legislature to a seat in the U.S. Senate, where he could better protect his state's anti-tariff stance.

Tariff revisions in early 1832 had brought little relief to the South. Strained to their limit, the South Carolina leaders called a special convention on tariff law, and in November 1832 they implemented nullification by declaring the federal tariffs to be null and void in their state as of February 1, 1833.

Finally, the constitutional crisis was out in the open. Jackson opted for a dramatic confrontation. He sent armed ships to Charleston's harbor and threatened to invade the state. He pushed through Congress a bill, called the Force Bill, defining the Carolina stance as treason and authorizing military action to collect federal tariffs.

At the same time, Congress was busy patching together a revised tariff more acceptable to the South. The astute Senator Henry Clay rallied support for a moderate bill that gradually lowered tariffs by half, back to the level prevailing in 1816. Both the new tariff and the Force Bill were passed on the same day in Congress, March 1, 1833. South Carolina responded by withdrawing its nullification of the old tariff—and then nullifying the Force Bill. It was a symbolic gesture, since Jackson's show of muscle was no longer necessary. Both sides took a measure of satisfaction in the immediate outcome. Federal power had prevailed over a dangerous assertion of states' rights; and South Carolina got the lower tariff it wanted.

In the long run, however, the question of federal power versus states' rights was far from settled. The implied threat behind nullification was se-

cession, a position articulated in 1832 by some South Carolinians whose concerns went beyond tariff policy. The growing voice of antislavery activism in the North threatened the South's economic system. If and when a northern-dominated federal government decided to end slavery, the South Carolinians thought, the South must have the right to remove itself from the Union.

The Bank War and the Panic of 1837

Along with the tariff and nullification, President Jackson had another political battle on his hands over the Bank of the United States. After riding out the panic of 1819, the bank had prospered under the leadership of Philadelphian Nicholas Biddle. It handled the federal government's deposits, extended credit and loans, and issued banknotes—by 1830 the most secure and steady circulating currency in the country. With twenty-nine branches, it spread its stabilizing benefits to the whole nation. Jackson, however, did not find the bank's temperate functions sufficiently valuable to offset his criticism of the concept of a national bank. In his first and second messages to Congress, in 1829 and 1830, Jackson claimed that the bank concentrated undue economic power in the hands of a few. His Democratic allies privately hoped he would be content with anti-bank rhetoric, without taking concrete action.

Senators Henry Clay and Daniel Webster, leaders of the National Republicans, decided to force the issue. They convinced Biddle to apply for renewal of the bank's federal charter in 1832, well before the fall election, even though the twenty-year charter ran until 1836. They fully expected that Congress's renewal would force Jackson to follow through on his rhetoric with a veto. The unpopular veto would then cause Jackson to lose the election, while the bank would survive on an override vote from a new Congress swept into power in the anti-Jackson tide.

At first the plan seemed to work. Biddle applied for recharter, Congress voted to renew, and Jackson, angry over being manipulated, issued his veto. But it was a brilliantly written veto, full of fierce language about privileges of the moneyed elite who oppress the liberties of the democratic masses in order to concentrate wealth in their own hands. "Many of our rich men have not been content with equal protection and equal benefits, but have besought us to make them richer by act of Congress," Jackson wrote.

Biddle and Clay thought that Jackson's economic ideas were so absurd and his language so shocking that they distributed thousands of copies of the bank veto as campaign material for the National Republicans. A confident Henry Clay headed the ticket for the presidency. But they miscalculated. Jackson had translated the bank controversy into a language of class antagonism and egalitarian ideals that strongly resonated with many Americans. Old Hickory won the election easily, with 55 percent of the popular vote and a lopsided electoral college vote of 219 to only 49 for Clay. The Jackson party still controlled Congress, so no override was possible. The bank's fate was sealed; it would cease to exist after 1836.

But Jackson took his reelection as a mandate to destroy the bank sooner. Calling the bank a "monster," he ordered the secretary of the treasury to remove the federal deposits from Biddle's vaults, despite the fact that nearly his entire cabinet disagreed with the action. The money was redeposited into "pet banks," Democratic-leaning institutions throughout the country; because of the high tariffs and high-volume sales of public lands, this government nest egg was quite sizable. In retaliation, Biddle showed he still had formidable powers by tightening credit in the economy. He accomplished this by raising interest rates and calling in loans, which he claimed he had to do since the bank's deposits were now dangerously low. This action caused a minor recession in 1833 and actually enhanced Jackson's claim that the bank was too powerful for the good of the country.

Unleashed and unregulated, the economy went into high gear, to Jackson's dismay. Perhaps only a small part of the problem arose from irresponsible banking practices; just at this moment, an excess of silver from Mexican mines had made its way into American banks' deposits, giving bankers license to print ever more banknotes. Inflation soared from 1834 to 1837; prices of basic goods rose more than 50 percent. Real estate in hot markets like Manhattan inflated 500 percent. Southern planters bought land and slaves fast, paying as much as 30 percent interest on bank loans for their purchases. Many hundreds of new private banks were quickly chartered by the states, each bank issuing its own banknotes and setting interest rates as high as the market would bear. Entrepreneurs borrowed and invested money, much of it funneled into privately financed railroads and canals.

The market in western land sales heated up. In 1834, about 4.5 million acres of the public domain

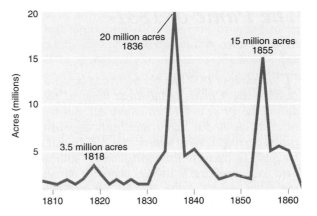

FIGURE 11.1
Western Land Sales, 1810–1860
Land sales peaked in the 1810s, 1830s, and 1850s as Americans rushed to speculate in western lands sold by the federal government. In particular the surges in 1818 and 1836 demonstrate the volatile, speculative economy that suddenly collapsed in the panics of 1819 and 1837.

had been sold, the highest annual volume since the peak year 1819. A year later, the figure rose to more than 13 million acres, and in 1836, the total reached an astonishing 20 million acres. What was most disturbing to the Jackson administration was that the purchasers were overwhelmingly eastern capitalists, not individual yeoman farmers who intended to settle on the land.

In one respect, the economy attained an admirable goal: The national debt disappeared, and, for the first and only time in American history, from 1835 to 1837 the government had a surplus of money. But much of it consisted of questionable bank currencies—bloated, diseased currencies, in Jackson's vivid terminology.

Jackson decided to restrain the economy. In 1836, the Treasury Department issued the Specie Circular, ordering that public land could be purchased only with hard money, federally coined gold and silver. In response, bankers started to reduce their loans, fearing a general contraction of the economy. Compounding the difficulty, the Bank of England also now insisted on hard-money payments for American loans, which had grown fat in the years since 1831 because of a trade imbalance. Some short-run failures in various crop markets, a downturn in the price of cotton on the international market, and the silver glut, all unrelated to Jackson's fiscal policies, fed the growing economic crisis.

FISTFIGHT BETWEEN OLD HICKORY AND BULLY NICK
This 1834 cartoon represents President Andrew Jackson squaring off to fight Nicholas Biddle, the director of the Bank of the United States. Pugilism as a semiprofessional sport gained great popularity in the 1830s; the joke here is that the aged Jackson and the aristocratic Biddle would strip to such revealing tight pants and engage in open combat. To Biddle's left are his seconds, Daniel Webster and Henry Clay; behind the president is his vice-president, Martin Van Buren. Whiskey and port lubricate the action.
The Library Company of Philadelphia.

Suddenly, the familiar events of the panic of 1819 unfolded again, with terrifying rapidity. In April 1837, a wave of banks and businesses failed, and the credit market tumbled like a house of cards. (See Texts in Historical Context, page 420.) The Specie Circular was only one precipitating cause, but the Whig Party held it and Jackson responsible for the depression. For more than five years after the panic of 1837, the United States suffered from economic hard times.

Van Buren's One-Term Presidency

The election of 1836, which preceded the panic by six months, demonstrated the transformation of the Democrats from coalition to party. The personality of Jackson had stamped the elections of 1824, 1828, and 1832, but now party apparatus was sufficiently developed to support itself. Local and state committees existed throughout the country. Democratic candidates ran in every state election, gaining success even in old Federalist states like Maine and New Hampshire. More than four hundred newspapers were affiliated as Democratic. In 1836, the Democrats repeated an innovation begun in 1832, holding a national convention that nominated Martin Van Buren of New York for president, balanced by

vice presidential candidate Richard M. Johnson of Kentucky. (Johnson was a slave owner from the West who insistently championed Sunday mail delivery and boasted that he was the actual killer of Shawnee chief Tecumseh back in 1813.)

Sophisticated party organization was Martin Van Buren's specialty. Friends nicknamed him the "Little Magician" for his consummate political skills. Another nickname, the "Red Fox of Kinderhook," honored his once red hair, his Dutch heritage, and his shrewd and calculated maneuvers. From humble origins in a Dutch village of New York's Hudson River valley, Van Buren overcame an inadequate early education and with the help of influential patrons became a lawyer. As a youth, he learned politics with Jeffersonian Republicans in New York City, and two decades later he was the acknowledged leader of a statewide coalition, the Bucktails, which pioneered many of the loyalty-enhancing techniques the Democrats used in the 1830s. After engineering a rewriting of his state's constitution in 1821, which implemented dramatic democratic reforms, Van Buren served as senator and then was elected governor just as Jackson tapped him to be secretary of state in 1828. From the State Department he moved to the vice presidency in 1832. His eight years in the volatile Jackson administration required the full measure of his political deftness, as he sought repeatedly to save Jackson both from his enemies and from his own obstinacy.

Van Buren was a backroom politician, not a popular public figure, and his candidacy gave hope to the Whigs that he might be defeatable. In many states Whigs had captured high office in 1834, shedding the awkward National Republican label and developing statewide organizations to rival those of the Democrats. However, no figure at the national level could command support in all regions; Massachusetts Senator Daniel Webster, for example, had absolutely no following in the South, a heavily pro-Jackson region. The result was that three candidates opposed Van Buren in 1836, each with a solid popular regional base. Webster could deliver New England; Tennessee Senator Hugh Lawson White attracted proslavery, pro-Jackson, but anti–Van Buren voters in the South; and the aging General William Henry Harrison of Indiana, memorable for his Indian war heroics in 1811, pulled in the western, anti-Indian vote. Only Webster and Harrison actually identified themselves as Whigs, while White, a banker, kept his affiliation ambiguous. Not one of the three candidates could have won the presidency, but together they came close to denying Van Buren a majority vote. Their combined strength pulled many Whigs into office at the state level and laid the groundwork for an alternative to the Democrats in the South, an area that had been a solid pro-Jackson block until 1836. In the end, Van Buren had 170 electoral votes, while the other three received a total of 113.

Van Buren took office in March 1837, and a month later the panic hit. The new president called a special session of Congress to consider creating an independent treasury system to fulfill some of the functions of the defunct Bank of the United States. Such a treasury system, funded by the government's deposits, would deal only in hard money, and gold and silver would thus flow out of commercial banks, restricting their issuance of paper currency. Equally important, the new system would not make loans, thus avoiding the danger of speculative meddling in the economy. In short, an independent treasury system could exert a powerful moderating influence on inflation and the credit market without itself being directly involved in the market. But Van Buren encountered strong resistance in Congress to the independent treasury, even from Democrats. It finally won approval in 1840,

but by then Van Buren's chances of a second term in office were virtually at an end. The four years had proved to be tumultuous for the economy, with federal bank policy at a stalemate while twenty-six separate state legislatures battled over controversial bank regulation.

In 1840, the Whigs settled on William Henry Harrison, aged sixty-seven, as their single candidate to oppose Van Buren. The campaign drew on voter involvement as no other presidential campaign ever had. The Whigs took tricks out of the Democrats' book: Harrison was touted as a common man, born in a log cabin, although a Virginia plantation was the real site. His Indian-fighting days, now thirty years behind him, were played up to give him an aura like that of Jackson. Whigs staged festive rallies all over the country, drumming up mass appeal with candlelight parades and song shows. (One spirited campaign tune recited "Van, Van, Van's a used up man.") Women participated in campaign rallies as they never had before. Some 78 percent of eligible voters cast ballots—the highest percentage ever in American history. Even so, the campaign was not really close. Harrison took 53 percent of the popular vote and won a resounding 234 electoral college votes, to Van Buren's 60. A Democratic editor lamented, "We have taught them how to conquer us!"

Conclusion: Democrats and Whigs

From 1828 to 1840, the Democrats put together and then held together an unlikely, tenuous, but ultimately workable coalition of rural western farmers, urban laborers, pro–state bank commercial men, and wealthy southern slave owners. What united these groups was a common vision of an America where the highest value was placed on personal liberty, free competition, and egalitarian opportunity open to all white men. Jacksonian Democrats accepted drinking and tolerated Sabbath violations, preferring not to legislate morality. Democrats of the 1830s never debated the wisdom of slavery, if they could help it.

In contrast, the Whigs were the party of activist moralism and state-sponsored entrepreneurship. Wealthy northerners and merchants from Boston to Savannah, with their appreciation for institutions like the Bank of the United States and for legislated protective tariffs, tended to be Whigs. So did the evangelical middle classes, enthused with the hope that salvation could be brought within the reach of all. Personal liberty was a fine thing, Whigs thought, but it had to be tempered by responsibility, self-discipline, and internal controls, helped along by state-sponsored controls that, for example, prohibited liquor sales or stagecoach travel on Sundays. Abolitionists tended to vote for Whigs, even though most Whig politicians shied away from antislavery ideas.

National politics in the 1830s were more heated and divisive than at any time since the 1790s, when Federalists and Republicans had defined competing visions of government. The second party system of Democrats and Whigs cut far deeper into the electorate than had the first. Partly this was a function of technological changes that brought political information to the backwoods. More generally, the mass politicization reflected the involvement of voters in an expansive economy where they stood to gain or lose, depending on the government's economic policy. Politics acquired immediacy and excitement, and four out of five white men cast a ballot in 1840.

Yet one of the deepest divisions in American society was almost completely ignored by the political parties of the 1830s, that of slavery. Indeed, the practice of coalition politics required that silence be maintained on this taboo subject, so that each party could build strength in the South. Whigs found this silence harder to maintain than Democrats, since their party contained wider divergence on the issue, stretching from ex-president John Quincy Adams, now sponsoring antislavery petitions from his Whig seat in the House of Representatives, to John C. Calhoun, nullifier, slaveholder, and Whig cabinet member in Harrison's new administration.

Slavery, however, was the defining difference in American social, economic, and political life in the nineteenth century. It could not be ignored for long by either Whigs or Democrats.

CHRONOLOGY

1807   Robert Fulton develops first commercially successful steamboat, the *Clermont*.

1810   In the case of *Fletcher v. Peck,* Supreme Court overturns a state law for first time.

1816   Second Bank of the United States chartered for twenty years.
       Import tariff imposed on foreign cotton cloth.

1817   American Colonization Society founded to promote gradual emancipation and removal of African Americans to Liberia.

1818   National Road links Baltimore and Wheeling, West Virginia.
       In *Dartmouth College v. Woodward,* Supreme Court overturns state action and reinstates Dartmouth College as private institution.

1819   Economic collapse and panic nationwide.

1824   Congress passes expanded tariff bill on variety of products—iron, glass, wool, and others.

1825   Erie Canal spans 350 miles in New York State.

1826   Schuylkill Canal—108 miles long—opens in Pennsylvania.

1828   Tariff of Abominations passed.
       Andrew Jackson elected president.

1829   First railroad, Baltimore and Ohio, consists of thirteen miles of track.
       David Walker's *Appeal* published.

1830   Indian Removal Act appropriates money to relocate Indian tribes west of Mississippi River.

1831   William Lloyd Garrison begins publishing abolitionist newspaper the *Liberator.*
       Nat Turner's rebellion in Virginia.
       Charles G. Finney stages revival in Rochester, New York.

1831	*Cherokee Nation v. Georgia* set aside by the Supreme Court, allowing Georgia to continue to subject Indians to state laws.	1833	Nullification crisis: South Carolina declares federal tariffs void in the state.

1831   *Cherokee Nation v. Georgia* set aside by the Supreme Court, allowing Georgia to continue to subject Indians to state laws.

1832   Supreme Court in *Worcester v. Georgia* recognizes Cherokee as distinct community outside legal jurisdiction of Georgia.

Jackson vetoes Bank of United States charter.

New England Anti-Slavery Society founded.

Andrew Jackson reelected president.

1833   Nullification crisis: South Carolina declares federal tariffs void in the state.

New York and Philadelphia Anti-Slavery Societies founded.

1834, 1836   Female mill workers strike in Lowell, Massachusetts.

1836   Jackson issues Specie Circular.

Martin Van Buren elected president.

1837   Economic panic.

1838   Trail of Tears—Cherokee forced to relocate west.

1840   Independent Treasury Act.

BIBLIOGRAPHY

GENERAL WORKS

Jean H. Baker, *Affairs of Party: The Political Culture of Northern Democrats in the Mid-Nineteenth Century* (1983).

Michael F. Holt, *Political Parties and American Political Development from the Age of Jackson to the Age of Lincoln* (1992).

Richard P. McCormick, *The Second American Party System: Party Formation in the Jacksonian Era* (1966).

Merrill D. Peterson, *The Great Triumvirate: Webster, Clay, and Calhoun* (1987).

Charles G. Sellers, *The Market Revolution: Jacksonian American, 1815–1846* (1991).

Peter Temin, *The Jacksonian Economy* (1969).

Ronald Walters, *American Reformers, 1815–1860* (1978).

Harry L. Watson, *Liberty and Power: The Politics of Jacksonian America* (1990).

Robert H. Wiebe, *The Opening of American Society: From the Adoption of the Constitution to the Eve of Disunion* (1984).

THE MARKET REVOLUTION

Eugene Alvarez, *Travel on Southern Antebellum Railroads, 1828–1860* (1974).

Elizabeth Blackmar, *Manhattan for Rent, 1785–1850* (1989).

Mary H. Blewett, *Men, Women, and Work: Class, Gender, and Protest in the New England Shoe Industry, 1780–1910* (1988).

Jeanne Boydston, *Home and Work: Housework, Wages, and the Ideology of Labor in the Early Republic* (1990).

Stuart Bruchey, *The Roots of American Economic Growth, 1607–1861* (1965).

Christopher Clark, *The Roots of Rural Capitalism: Worcester, Massachusetts, 1780–1860* (1990).

Thomas C. Cochran, *Frontiers of Change: Early Industrialism in America* (1981).

Clarence H. Danhof, *Change in Agriculture: The Northern United States, 1820–1870* (1969).

Alan Dawley, *Class and Community: The Industrial Revolution in Lynn* (1976).

Thomas Dublin, *Women at Work: The Transformation of Work and Community in Lowell, Massachusetts, 1826–1860* (1979).

Thomas Dublin, *Transforming Women's Work: New England Lives in the Industrial Revolution* (1994).

Albert Fishlow, *American Railroads and the Transformation of the Ante-Bellum Economy* (1965).

Tony A. Freyer, *Producers versus Capitalists: Constitutional Conflict in Antebellum America* (1994).

Erik F. Haites, James Mak, and Gary M. Walton, *Western River Transportation: The Era of Early Internal Development, 1800–1860* (1975).

Bray Hammond, *Banks and Politics in America from the Revolution to the Civil War* (1957).

Brooke Hindle, *Emulation and Invention* (1981).

Morton J. Horwitz, *The Transformation of American Law, 1780–1860* (1977).

David J. Jeremy, *Transatlantic Industrial Revolution: The Diffusion of Textile Technologies between Britain and America, 1790–1830s* (1981).

Bruce Laurie, *Artisans into Workers: Labor in Nineteenth-Century America* (1989).

Otto Mayr and Robert C. Post, eds., *Yankee Enterprise: The Rise of the American System of Manufactures* (1981).

Judith A. McGaw, *Most Wonderful Machine: Mechanization and Social Change in Berkshire Paper Making, 1815–1885* (1987).

Richard B. Stott, *Workers in the Metropolis: Class, Ethnicity, and Youth in Antebellum New York City* (1990).

George R. Taylor, *The Transportation Revolution, 1815–1860* (1951).

Peter Temin, *The Jacksonian Economy* (1969).

Christopher L. Tomlins, *Law, Labor, and Ideology in the Early American Republic* (1993).

Barbara Tucker, *Samuel Slater and the Origins of the American Textile Industry, 1790–1860* (1984).

THE SPREAD OF DEMOCRACY

Ronald P. Formisano, *The Birth of Mass Political Parties: Michigan, 1827–1861* (1971).

Paul Goodman, *Towards a Christian Republic: Antimasonry and the Great Transition in New England, 1826–1836* (1988).

Daniel W. Howe, *The Political Culture of the American Whigs* (1980).

Lawrence Frederick Kohl, *The Politics of Individualism: Parties and the American Character in the Jacksonian Era* (1989).

Robert V. Remini, *The Election of Andrew Jackson* (1963).

Robert V. Remini, *Andrew Jackson and the Course of American Freedom, 1822–1832* (1981).

Alexander Saxton, *The Rise and Fall of the White Republic: Class Politics and Mass Culture in Nineteenth-Century America* (1990).

Sean Wilentz, *Chants Democratic: New York City and the Rise of the American Working Class, 1788–1850* (1984).

CULTURE AND SOCIETY

Gerald J. Baldasty, *The Commercialization of News in the Nineteenth Century* (1992).

Stuart M. Blumin, *The Emergence of the Middle Class: Social Experience in the American City, 1760–1900* (1989).

Richard L. Bushman, *The Refinement of America: Persons, Houses, Cities* (1992).

Kenneth Cmiel, *Democratic Eloquence: The Fight over Popular Speech in Nineteenth-Century America* (1990).

Daniel A. Cohen, *Pillars of Salt, Monuments of Grace: New England Crime Literature and the Origins of American Popular Culture, 1674–1860* (1993).

Faye E. Dudden, *Women in the American Theatre: Actresses and Audiences, 1790–1870* (1994).

Ann Fabian, *Card-Sharps, Dream Books, and Bucket Shops: Gambling in Nineteenth-Century America* (1990).

Timothy J. Gilfoyle, *City of Eros: New York City, Prostitution, and the Commercialization of Sex, 1790–1920* (1992).

Karen Halttunen, *Confidence Men and Painted Women: A Study of Middle-Class Culture in America, 1830–1870* (1982).

Carl F. Kaestle, *Pillars of the Republic: Common Schools and American Society, 1780–1860* (1983).

John F. Kasson, *Rudeness and Civility: Manners in Nineteenth-Century America* (1990).

Michael P. Kramer, *Imagining Language in America: From the Revolution to the Civil War* (1991).

Lawrence W. Levine, *Highbrow/Lowbrow: The Emergence of Cultural Hierarchy in America* (1988).

Lewis Perry, *Boats against the Current: American Culture between Revolution and Modernity, 1820–1860* (1993).

Ellen K. Rothman, *Hands and Hearts: A History of Courtship in America* (1984).

E. Anthony Rotundo, *American Manhood: Transformations in Masculinity from the Revolution to the Modern Era* (1993).

Mary P. Ryan, *Women in Public: Between Banners and Ballots, 1825–1880* (1990).

Michael Schudson, *Discovering the News: A Social History of American Newspapers* (1978).

Stanley K. Schultz, *The Culture Factory: Boston Public Schools, 1789–1860* (1973).

Carroll Smith-Rosenberg, *Disorderly Conduct: Visions of Gender in Victorian America* (1985).

Christine Stansell, *City of Women: Sex and Class in New York, 1789–1860* (1986).

Ronald J. Zboray, *A Fictive People: Antebellum Development and the American Reading Public* (1993).

REFORM AND RELIGION

Robert Abzug, *Passionate Liberator: Theodore Dwight Weld and the Dilemma of Reform* (1980).

Robert Abzug, *Cosmos Crumbling: American Reform and the Religious Imagination* (1994).

R. J. M. Blackett, *Building an Antislavery Wall: Black Americans in the Atlantic Abolitionist Movement, 1830–1860* (1983).

Lawrence J. Friedman, *Gregarious Saints: Self and Community in American Abolitionism, 1830–1870* (1982).

Lori D. Ginzberg, *Women and the Work of Benevolence: Morality, Politics, and Class in the Nineteenth-Century United States* (1990).

Nathan O. Hatch, *The Democratization of American Christianity* (1989).

Blanche Glassman Hersh, *The Slavery of Sex: Feminist-Abolitionists in America* (1978).

Nancy A. Hewitt, *Women's Activism and Social Change: Rochester, New York, 1822–1872* (1984).

Barbara Meil Hobson, *Uneasy Virtue: The Politics of Prostitution and the American Reform Tradition* (1987).

Donald M. Jacobs, ed., *Courage and Conscience: Black and White Abolitionists in Boston* (1993).

Paul Johnson, *A Shopkeeper's Millennium: Society and Revivals in Rochester, New York, 1815–1837* (1978).

Gerda Lerner, *The Grimké Sisters from South Carolina: Pioneers for Woman's Rights and Abolition* (1967).

Katharine Du Pré Lumpkin, *The Emancipation of Angelina Grimké* (1974).

Donald Mathews, *Religion in the Old South* (1977).

Keith Melder, *Beginnings of Sisterhood: The American Woman's Rights Movement, 1800–1850* (1977).

Lewis Perry and Michael Fellman, eds., *Anti-Slavery Reconsidered: New Perspectives on the Abolitionists* (1979).

Mary P. Ryan, *Cradle of the Middle Class: The Family in Oneida County, New York, 1790–1865* (1981).

Carroll Smith-Rosenberg, *Religion and the Rise of the American City: The New York City Mission Movement, 1812–1870* (1971).

Dorothy Sterling, *Ahead of Her Time: Abby Kelley and the Politics of Antislavery* (1991).

Ian Tyrrell, *Sobering Up: From Temperance to Prohibition in Antebellum America, 1800–1860* (1979).

Ronald Walters, *The Antislavery Appeal: Abolitionism after 1830* (1976).

Jean Fagan Yellin and John C. Van Horne, eds., *The Abolitionist Sisterhood: Women's Political Culture in Antebellum America* (1994).

JACKSONIAN POLITICS

Irving H. Bartlett, *John C. Calhoun: A Biography* (1993).

Donald B. Cole, *The Presidency of Andrew Jackson* (1993).

Richard E. Ellis, *The Union at Risk: Jacksonian Democracy, States' Rights, and the Nullification Crisis* (1987).

Daniel Feller, *The Public Lands in Jacksonian Politics* (1984).

William W. Freehling, *Prelude to Civil War: The Nullification Controversy in South Carolina, 1816–1836* (1965).

William W. Freehling, *The Road to Disunion: Secessionists at Bay, 1776–1854* (1990).

Peter B. Knupfer, *The Union As It Is: Constitutional Unionism and Sectional Compromise, 1787–1861* (1991).

Richard B. Latner, *The Presidency of Andrew Jackson: White House Politics, 1829–1837* (1979).

John M. McFaul, *The Politics of Jacksonian Finance* (1972).

John Niven, *Martin Van Buren: The Romantic Age of American Politics* (1983).

John Niven, *John C. Calhoun and the Price of Union: A Biography* (1988).

Robert V. Remini, *Henry Clay: Statesman for the Union* (1991).

Leonard Richards, *The Life and Times of Congressman John Quincy Adams* (1986).

Arthur M. Schlesinger Jr., *The Age of Jackson* (1945).

James Roger Sharp, *The Jacksonians versus the Banks: Politics in the States after the Panic of 1837* (1970).

Glyndon G. Van Deusen, *The Jacksonian Era, 1828–1848* (1959).

Major L. Wilson, *The Presidency of Martin Van Buren* (1984).

NATIVE AMERICANS

John A. Andrew, *From Revivals to Removal: Jeremiah Evarts, the Cherokee Nation, and the Search for the Soul of America* (1992).

John R. Finger, *The Eastern Band of Cherokees, 1819–1900* (1984).

William G. McLoughlin, *Cherokees and Missionaries, 1789–1839* (1984).

Theda Perdue, *The Cherokee* (1989).

Michael Paul Rogin, *Fathers and Children: Andrew Jackson and the Subjugation of the American Indian* (1975).

Anthony F. C. Wallace, *The Long, Bitter Trail: Andrew Jackson and the Indians* (1993).

Philip Weeks, *Farewell, My Nation: The American Indian and the United States, 1820–1890* (1990).

J. Leitch Wright, *The Only Land They Knew: The Tragic Story of the American Indians in the Old South* (1981).

have been. Gullah Jack Pritchard, an Angolan, was a conjurer, a sorcerer who drew upon African traditions and distributed crab claws he claimed would protect anyone who joined the insurrection. The conspirators' plan was evidently quite simple. At midnight on July 14, 1822, they would storm Charleston's arsenal, capture its weapons, kill any white who stood in their way, and set fire to the city. The flames would signal rebels in the countryside to rush in and complete the victory. Vesey may have planned to crowd as many slaves as he could on a ship and sail away to Haiti.

But the revolt never occurred. Before the conspiracy could become full-blown insurrection, it was betrayed by other blacks, both slave and free. The first arrests came in May. One arrest led to another as suspects, prodded by torture and the threat of death, implicated others. Shaken badly by the disclosures, whites feverishly tracked down every conspirator. After three months, the authorities had arrested 131 blacks. In the end, whites banished more than two dozen blacks from the state and executed 37 others, including Denmark Vesey.

The Vesey affair not only reveals the complex calculation of blacks about how best to defend themselves—join Vesey or betray him—but also illustrates the determination of whites to beat back any challenge to their supremacy. Slave revolts were whites' worst nightmare. The Vesey affair was doubly terrifying because it occurred in the wake of the Missouri controversy of 1819–1820, with its display of powerful antislavery, antisouthern political forces. By the 1820s, the northern states had either abolished slavery or put it on the road to extinction while the southern states aggressively built the largest slave society in the New World. The division of the nation generally coincided with the "Mason-Dixon line"—the line drawn in 1763 by the English surveyors Charles Mason and Jeremiah Dixon to decide the boundary between the bickering colonies of Maryland and Pennsylvania. A half century later, the English surveyors' mark divided the free North and slave South.

Black slavery dominated southern society and shaped the South into a distinctive region. Slavery molded the experiences of all of the region's inhabitants, those who had direct personal experience with slavery and those who did not. Still, the South was too vast and sprawling to form a solid block with a uniform viewpoint. Antebellum (pre–Civil War) Southerners included diverse peoples who at times found themselves at odds with one another —not only slaves and free people, but also women and men; Indians, Africans, and Europeans; aristocrats and common folk; merchants and mule drivers; and politicians and thinkers. Nevertheless, beneath this diversity of Southerners there was also "a South," with features that arose from slavery and that distinguished it from the North. Increasingly, a sectional self-consciousness spread among most white Southerners. The South was a slave society, and most white Southerners were proud of it.

In the decades after 1820, Southerners raced westward, spreading slavery, cotton, and plantations halfway to the Pacific. Geographic expansion meant that slavery became more vigorous and profitable than ever, embraced more people, and increased the South's political power. In the end, the South's identification with slavery and insistence on its preservation culminated in the creation of a separate Confederacy that ultimately brought about what Denmark Vesey had tried in vain to achieve in 1822: the end of slavery. Curiously, some of the white Charlestonians who witnessed Vesey's execution lived to see slavery's death in 1865. But from 1820 through 1860, most white Southerners simply assumed that slavery was a permanent and valuable feature of their society, as it had been for nearly two centuries before 1820. In their eyes, slavery made the South the South—and always would.

The Southern Difference

When the Frenchman Alexis de Tocqueville visited the United States in the early 1830s, he observed that the inhabitants "constitute a single people . . . more truly a united society than some nations of Europe which lived under the same legislation and the same prince." Tocqueville identified an important truth about the young nation. Southerners and Northerners were all Americans.

The Mason-Dixon line was a surveyor's mark on a map, not a physical barrier dividing North and South. No impenetrable jungle, insurmountable mountain range, or impassable desert separated the sections. From the earliest settlements, inhabitants of southern colonies had shared a great deal with northern colonists. Much of the white population of both sections was British in origin, although non-British Europeans migrated in large numbers to the colonies in the 1700s. Most settlers were Protestants. They spoke a common language,

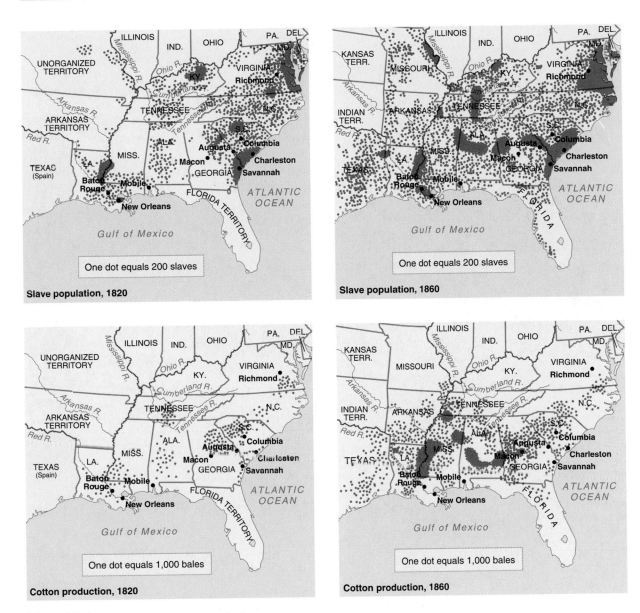

MAP 12.1
Cotton Kingdom, Slave Empire: 1820 and 1860
As the production of cotton soared, the slave population increased dramatically. Slaves continued to toil in tobacco and rice fields along the Atlantic seaboard, but increasingly they worked on cotton plantations in Alabama, Mississippi, and Louisiana.

even if a regional twang or drawl flavored their speech. They shared an exuberant pride in their victorious revolution against British rule. The creation of the new nation under the Constitution in 1789 forged strong political ties that bound all Americans. And by the mid-nineteenth century, an incip-

ient national economy was fostering economic interdependence and communication across sectional boundaries. White Americans everywhere celebrated the achievements of the prosperous, powerful young nation, and they looked forward to its seemingly boundless future.

Arise! Arise! and weep no more dry up your tears, we Shall part no more. Come rose we go to Tennessee, that happy Shore to old virginia never — never — return.

SLAVE TRADERS: SOLD TO TENNESSEE
Slave trading, or "Negro speculation" as it was called by contemporaries, was a booming business in the antebellum South. This color drawing by Lewis Miller portrays slaves on their way from Virginia to Tennessee under the watchful eyes of professional slave traders. A few children accompany the adults, some of whom presumably are their parents, but forced migrations almost always resulted in separation of black families.
Abby Aldrich Rockefeller Folk Art Center, Williamsburg, Va.

Despite these national similarities, Southerners and Northerners were different. Tocqueville believed he knew why. "I could easily prove," he asserted in 1831, "that almost all the differences which may be noticed between the character of the Americans in the Southern and Northern states have originated in slavery." A quarter century later, most Americans agreed with the Frenchman. And neither Northerners nor Southerners liked what they saw on the other side of the Mason-Dixon line. "On the subject of slavery," the Charleston *Mercury* declared, "the North and South . . . are not only two Peoples, but they are rival, hostile Peoples." Slavery made the South different, and it was the differences between the sections, not the similarities, that came to shape antebellum American history.

Cotton Kingdom, Slave Empire

In the first half of the nineteenth century, legions of Northerners and Southerners migrated west, but the southern surge westward was propelled by an insatiable hunger for more and better cotton land. The stampede began in 1815, with the end of the War of 1812 against Great Britain and with the start of Indian removal east of the Mississippi River. Eager slaveholders seeking virgin acreage for new plantations, struggling yeomen looking for patches of good land for small farms, herders and drovers pushing their hogs and cattle toward fresh pastures —anyone who was restless and ambitious felt the pull. Southern farmers pushed into the territories of Alabama, Mississippi, Louisiana, Arkansas, and elsewhere, until by midcentury the South encompassed nearly a million square miles, much of it planted in cotton.

The South's climate and geography were ideally suited for the cultivation of cotton. That fact is remarkable because as Southerners advanced a thousand miles west from the Atlantic, they encountered a variety of terrain, soil, and weather. But the short-staple (or green-seed) cotton seeds they carried with them were very adaptable. They grew in the sandy plains of the tidewater, the red clay of the Piedmont, and especially the rich soils of the black belt (named for the dark color of the soil) and the alluvial deltas. Cotton requires two hundred frost-free days from planting to picking and prefers rains that are plentiful in spring and lighter in fall, conditions found in much of the South. In less than a half century, cotton fields stretched from southern Virginia to central Texas. Production soared, and by 1860 the South produced three-fourths of the world supply. The South—especially that tier of states from South Carolina west to Texas known as the lower South—had become the cotton kingdom.

The cotton kingdom was also a slave empire. The South's cotton boom rested on the backs of slaves, who grew 75 percent of the crop on plantations, toiling in gangs in broad fields under the direct supervision of whites. As cotton agriculture expanded westward, slavery's center of gravity shifted away from the old seaboard states. Hundreds of thousands of slaves were driven toward the Southwest. Some accompanied masters who were leaving behind worn-out, eroded plantations in the East. Most, however, were victims of a brutal but thriving domestic slave trade. Traders advertised for slaves who were "hearty and well made" and marched black men, women, and children hundreds of miles to the new plantation regions of the Lower South. Cotton, slaves, and plantations moved west together.

Slavery made the South different, and it was the differences between the sections, not the similarities, that came to shape antebellum American history.

The slave population also grew enormously. Southern slaves numbered fewer than 700,000 in 1790, about 2 million in 1830, and by 1860 about 4 million, an increase of almost 600 percent in seven decades. By 1860, slavery spread from Delaware to Texas and from Missouri to Florida. The South contained more slaves than all the other slave societies in the New World combined. The extraordinary growth was not the result of huge purchases in the international slave trade. The United States outlawed the importation of slaves in 1808. Afterward, only about 50,000 slaves were smuggled into the South illegally. The main reason for the growth in the slave population was natural reproduction. By the nineteenth century, most slaves were southern-born. They were black Southerners.

The South in Black and White

In 1860, the South contained 95 percent of the nation's African American population. One in every three Southerners was black (about 4 million blacks and 8 million whites). In the Lower South, the proportion was higher, for whites and blacks lived there in almost equal numbers. In Mississippi and South Carolina blacks were the majority. In certain areas within those two states—the sea islands of South Carolina and the plantation district surrounding Vicksburg, Mississippi—blacks constituted 90 percent of the population. The contrast with the North was striking. In 1860, only one Northerner in seventy-six was black (about 250,000 blacks to 19 million whites).

The presence of large numbers of African Americans had profound consequences for the South. Southern culture—language, food, music, religion, and even accents—was shaped by blacks. But the most direct consequence of the South's biracialism was the response it stimulated in the region's white majority. Southern whites were dedicated to white supremacy. Northern whites were, too, but they lived in a society in which blacks made up only 1 percent of the population. Their commitment to white supremacy lacked the intensity and urgency felt by white Southerners, who were preoccupied with racial hierarchy. After all, white Southerners lived among millions of blacks whom they simultaneously despised and feared. They despised blacks because they considered them members of an inferior race, further degraded by their status as slaves. They feared blacks because they realized that slaves had every reason to hate their oppressors and to seek to end their oppression, as Denmark Vesey had, by any means necessary.

Attacks on slavery—from blacks within and from abolitionists without—jolted southern slaveholders into a distressing awareness that they lived in a dangerous world. In response, in the 1820s and

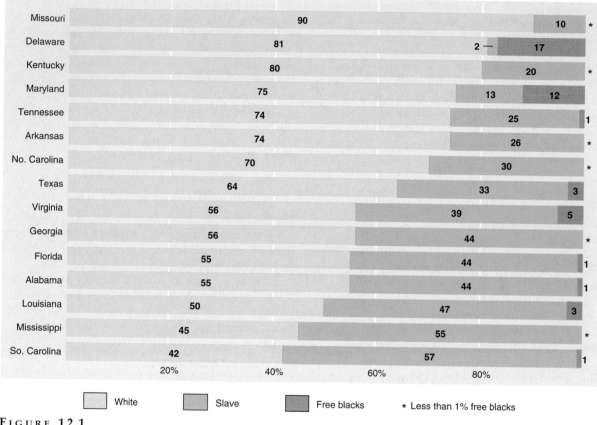

State	White	Slave	Free blacks
Missouri	90	10	*
Delaware	81	2	17
Kentucky	80	20	*
Maryland	75	13	12
Tennessee	74	25	1
Arkansas	74	26	*
No. Carolina	70	30	*
Texas	64	33	3
Virginia	56	39	5
Georgia	56	44	*
Florida	55	44	1
Alabama	55	44	1
Louisiana	50	47	3
Mississippi	45	55	*
So. Carolina	42	57	1

☐ White   ☐ Slave   ☐ Free blacks   * Less than 1% free blacks

FIGURE 12.1
Proportion of Black and White Population in the South, 1860
Despite considerable variation from state to state, blacks represented a much larger fraction of the population in the South than in the North.

1830s, southern leaders initiated fresh efforts to strengthen slavery and ward off threats. State legislatures constructed elaborate slave codes that required the total submission of slaves to their masters and to white society in general. As the Louisiana code stated, a slave "owes his master . . . a respect without bounds, and an absolute obedience." The laws underlined the authority of all whites, not just masters. Any white could stop a slave on a road and demand to see the slave's written permission to be away from his home. Any white could expect a slave to step aside to let him or her pass. Any white could "correct" slaves who did not stay "in their place" and show the proper deference.

Intellectuals joined legislators in the campaign to strengthen slavery. The South's academics, writers, and clergy constructed a proslavery argument that sought to unify the region's whites around slavery, smother any doubts that disturbed tender con-

sciences, and provide ammunition for the emerging war of words with northern abolitionists. Under the intellectuals' tutelage, the white South gradually moved away from defending slavery as a "necessary evil"—the halfhearted argument popular in Jefferson's day—and toward a full-throated, aggressive defense of slavery as a "positive good."

The presence of large numbers of African Americans had profound consequences for the South. Southern culture—language, food, music, religion, and even accents—was shaped by blacks.

Slavery's champions employed every imaginable defense. The law protected slavery, they observed, for slaves were legal property. And wasn't the security of property the bedrock of American

ATTENTION PAID A POOR SICK WHITE MAN.

ATTENTION PAID A POOR SICK NEGRO.

PROSLAVERY WOODCUTS

As antislavery critics accelerated their verbal attacks, white Southerners fought back. These 1853 woodcuts contrast the callousness of free labor with the benefits of slavery. The message was clear: While free laborers ("wage slaves") were carted directly from the factory to the poorhouse, aged and infirm slaves were made comfortable by their masters and mistresses. Proslavery polemicists asked: Which society was brutally exploitative and which cared for its laborers from cradle to grave?

Josiah Priest's *In Defense of Slavery*, Rare Book and Manuscript Department, Boston Public Library.

liberty? History also endorsed slavery. Weren't the great civilizations—those of the Hebrews, Greeks, and Romans—slave societies? In addition, the Bible, properly interpreted, sanctioned slavery. Didn't the Old Testament patriarchs own slaves? Didn't Paul in the New Testament return the runaway slave Onesimus to his master? Some proslavery spokesmen went on the offensive and attacked the economy and society of the North. The Virginian George Fitzhugh argued that behind the North's grand slogans—individualism and egalitarianism—lay a heartless philosophy: "Every man for himself, and the devil take the hindmost." Gouging capitalists exploited wage workers unmercifully, Fitzhugh said, and he contrasted the vicious capitalist-laborer relationship with the humane relations he believed prevailed between masters and slaves because slaves were valuable capital that masters sought to protect.

Since slavery was a condition Southerners reserved exclusively for African Americans, at bottom the white defense of slavery rested on claims of black inferiority. Black enslavement was both necessary and proper, defenders argued, because Africans were inferior beings. Rather than exploitative, slavery was a mass civilizing effort that lifted lowly blacks from barbarism and savagery, taught them disciplined work, and converted them to soul-saving Christianity. According to Virginian Thomas R. Dew, "the slaves of a good master are his warmest, most constant, and most devoted friends." Freeing blacks, the Charleston *Mercury* declared, would mean their destruction, as well as the destruction of southern "civilization, society, and government."

Black slavery encouraged whites to unify around race rather than to divide by class. The South Carolinian James H. Hammond argued that every society had its "mudsill" class, the poor, degraded workers who did the dirty work. Black slaves filled that niche in the South, and every white man stood above them looking down. The grubbiest, most tobacco-stained white man could proudly proclaim his superiority to blacks and his equality with the most refined southern patrician. Because slaves were not recognized as citizens in the South, Georgia attorney Thomas R. R. Cobb observed, everyone who was a citizen "feels that he belongs to an elevated class. It matters not that he is no slaveholder; he is not of the inferior race; he is a freeborn citizen." Consequently, the "poorest meets the richest as an equal; sits at his table with him; salutes him as a neighbor; meets him in every pub-

lic assembly, and stands on the same social platform." In the South, Cobb boasted, "there is no war of classes."

In reality, slavery did not create perfect harmony among whites or ease every strain along class lines. But by providing every white symbolic membership in the ruling class, racial slavery helped whites bridge differences in class, wealth, education, and culture. Slavery meant white dominance, white superiority, and white equality. Slaveless whites united with slave masters in opposition to black freedom and equality.

The Plantation Economy

Race was important in unifying white Southerners because most whites did not own slaves. The majority of the South's whites worked small farms with just the help of family members. Only about one-quarter of the white population lived in families that owned slaves. A majority of masters owned fewer than five. Small slaveholders often worked their fields shoulder to shoulder with their sons and their slaves. About 12 percent of the slave owners (about 46,000 individuals) owned twenty or more slaves, the number historians consider necessary to distinguish a planter from a farmer. Fewer than 1 percent of slaveholders (about 2,300) owned one hundred or more slaves and thus could be considered "great planters." Wade Hampton III was one of the greatest. In the 1850s, he held about three thousand slaves on plantations in South Carolina and Mississippi. Although greatly outnumbered by nonslaveholders and small slaveholders, planters dominated the southern economy. A majority (52 percent) of the South's slaves lived and worked on plantations. Plantation slaves produced more than 75 percent of the South's export crops, the backbone of the region's economy.

The majority of the South's whites worked small farms with just the help of family members. Only about one-quarter of the white population lived in families that owned slaves.

Patterns of plantation slavery established along the Atlantic seaboard persisted as Southerners raced westward in the nineteenth century. A new crop, new climates and soils, new and more primitive

TECHNOLOGY IN AMERICA
The Cotton Gin

By the 1790s, the English had succeeded in mechanizing the manufacture of cotton cloth, but they were unable to get enough raw cotton. The South could grow cotton in unimaginable quantities, but cotton that was stuck to seeds was useless in English textile mills. In 1793, Eli Whitney, a Northerner who was serving as a tutor on a Savannah River plantation, built a simple little device for separating the cotton from the seed — just wire teeth set in a wooden cylinder that, when rotated, reached through narrow slats to pull cotton fibers away from seeds, while the brush swept the fibers from the revolving teeth. Widespread use of the cotton gin (the word *gin* is simply short for *engine*) broke the bottleneck in the commercial production of cotton and eventually bound millions of African Americans to slavery.

Smithsonian Institution.

frontier conditions did not sever the South's deeply rooted connection with plantation slavery. Indeed, fresh land reinvigorated plantation slavery by providing an escape hatch for slaveholders in the Southeast who limped along on exhausted acreage and by creating a vigorous market for the East's surplus slaves. Although slavery was slowly dying elsewhere in the New World, slave plantations increased their domination of southern agriculture with each antebellum decade. And agriculture, in turn, remained the central feature of the southern economy.

Staple Agriculture

The dominant crops of southern agriculture were the five major staples grown on plantations: tobacco, hemp, sugar, rice, and cotton. All plantations had similar features, but they differed depending on the staple crop they produced.

Tobacco was the original plantation crop in North America. By the nineteenth century, however, most planters around the Chesapeake had shifted to wheat and other crops, and tobacco had moved to western Virginia and to Tennessee and Kentucky. Samuel Hairston, a Virginia tobacco planter, owned at midcentury fifteen hundred slaves and was worth more than $3 million. Work in the tobacco fields was labor-intensive. Most phases of the process—planting, transplanting, thinning, picking off caterpillars, cutting, drying, packing—required

field hands to stoop or bend down in painful labor over the tobacco plants.

Hemp, grown to make into bale rope and bagging for cotton, was the least important plantation crop and was found only in portions of Kentucky, Tennessee, and Missouri. Planters hoped to produce rope that was acceptable to the American navy, but American hemp was really not competitive in price or quality with imported hemp. It survived only because a steep tariff protected it from foreign competition. The American navy, which wanted the best, bought its rope abroad.

Large-scale sugar production began in 1795, when Étienne de Boré built a modern sugar mill in what is today New Orleans. Like hemp, sugar owed its existence to a tariff. Without protection, American sugar would have been driven from the market by cheaper sugar from tropical Latin America, especially Cuba. Labor on sugarcane plantations was reputed to be the most physically demanding in the antebellum South. Masters elsewhere would attempt to frighten obstinate slaves with the threat of selling them "down the river"—down the Mississippi River to sugar planters. During the fall, slaves worked eighteen hours a day to cut the cane and haul it to the sugar mill, where they would grind and boil it. Sugar plantations, which were confined almost entirely to Louisiana, required large sums for expensive refining equipment to turn cane juice into sugar and for large gangs of slaves. Magnolia Plantation in Plaquemines Parish contained 2,200

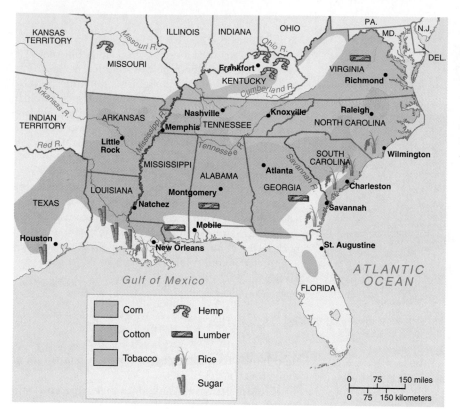

MAP 12.2
The Agricultural Economy of the South, 1860
Cotton dominated the South's agricultural economy, but the region grew a diversity of crops and was largely self-sufficient in foodstuffs.

acres and in 1861 produced sugar valued at nearly $150,000. Southerners understood the truth in the adage that "a man has to be a rich cotton planter before he can start as a poor sugar planter."

Commercial rice production began in seventeenth-century South Carolina. Like sugar, rice was confined to a small geographical area, a narrow strip of the tidewater stretching from the Carolinas into northern Georgia. Because of the need for canals, dikes, and gates to flood rice fields with water and then drain them and to protect the ripening plant from salt water, rice planting was an expensive undertaking. Like sugar planters, rice planters were one of the wealthiest groups in America. When rice planter Nathaniel Heyward died in 1851, he left two thousand slaves and five thousand acres of prime rice land, worth a total of more than $2 million. Since rice plantations required huge numbers of slaves, blacks accounted for 90 percent of the population in the coastal rice districts. For slaves, rice meant danger and extreme discomfort. Working in water and mud in the heat of a Carolina summer regularly threatened slaves with malaria, yellow fever, and other diseases.

If tobacco, hemp, sugar, and rice were princes of plantation agriculture, cotton was king. Cotton became commercially significant after the invention of the cotton gin by Eli Whitney in 1793. By the early years of the nineteenth century, cotton had displaced tobacco and had begun to dominate the southern economy. The white fluffy stuff was grown almost everywhere in the South and by almost everyone, small farmer and planter alike. It was relatively easy to grow and took little capital to get started—just enough for land, seed, and simple tools. Nonetheless, plantations produced three-quarters of the South's cotton, and planters received a disproportionate slice of the region's income. While hardscrabble farmer Jessup Snopes grew half a bale, Mississippian Frederick Stanton, who owned more than fifteen thousand prime acres, produced 3,054 bales of cotton worth $122,000 in 1859. With a record-breaking crop of 4,861,000 bales in 1859, the South's planters were, as they liked to put it, in "high cotton."

Plantations grew more than staples. Even the largest, most commercial plantations usually produced enough corn, beans, sweet potatoes, and pork to become self-sufficient in food. Two crops—cotton and corn—dovetailed particularly well. The amount of labor required to cultivate cotton varied with the growing season. In late summer, just when the pace slackened in the cotton fields, when the slaves had finished the last plowing, corn demanded their attention. In the fall, when every hand was needed to pick cotton, corn was usually already harvested. Because cultivating corn did not take time away from cultivating cotton, slaves were able to grow their own food (at almost no additional cost to the planter) and at the same time produce the South's major cash crop. Corn fed not only the slaves and the millions of white farmers who grew it, but also the South's livestock. The livestock industry was no minor affair. In 1860, the value of the animals (particularly hogs) butchered in the South exceeded that in the North.

Economic Vulnerability

Northerners claimed that slavery was a backward, inefficient form of labor, one that had been superseded by the more modern, more productive free-labor system. A whip could not stimulate continuous hard work the way individual self-interest did, economists argued. When Northerners cast their eyes southward, they seemed to find evidence that confirmed their theory. By standards that equated economic progress with diversification, industrialization, and urbanization, the Old South's economy was backward.

Judged by other criteria, however, it was productive and profitable. For those who owned slaves, slavery paid off handsomely. The rate of return for investments in cotton plantations was about 8 percent annually, a profit equal to that in most other businesses in which planters could have invested. The South was fortunate to have nearly a monopoly on the hottest commodity in the international marketplace. Because the world demand for cotton increased about 5 percent annually between 1820 and 1860, the South could extend the cotton kingdom westward a thousand miles and vastly increase production, without (in most years) glutting the market and driving down cotton prices. Not only did planters earn money from the sale of cotton and other staple crops, but they also gained from the rising values of land and slaves, from the hiring out of slaves, and, most important, from the birth of

COTTON LEVEE, NEW ORLEANS
This 1860 view of the New Orleans levee attempts to capture the magnitude of the cotton trade in the South's largest city and major port. Twelve years earlier, visitor Solon Robinson expressed his awe in words: "It must be seen to be believed; and even then, it will require an active mind to comprehend acres of cotton bales standing upon the levee, while miles of drays [carts] are constantly taking it off to the cotton presses. . . . Boats are constantly arriving, so piled up with cotton, that the lower tier of bales on deck are in the water." Amidst the mountains of cotton and forests of smokestacks, few doubted that cotton was king.
Chicago Historical Society.

slave children. Slaves were a rare kind of capital that reproduced itself. Judged by the size of planters' profits, then, the plantation economy flourished in the Old South.

Plantation slavery also benefited the national economy. Throughout the antebellum years, the products of southern plantations made up the greatest part of America's exports. By 1840, cotton alone accounted for more than 60 percent of the nation's sales abroad. Much of the profit from sales of cotton overseas returned to planters, but some did not. Cotton had to be bought, sold, insured, warehoused, and shipped before it reached the mills in Great Britain and elsewhere. Increasingly, these services were in the hands of northern middlemen, each of whom made a profit from slave-grown southern crops. As these profits were invested in the burgeoning northern economy, industrial development there received much-needed capital. Furthermore, planters provided an important market for northern textiles, shoes, agricultural tools, and other manufactured goods. Without cotton, one economist has estimated, American industrial development would have been retarded a generation.

In part because of the vitality of plantation agriculture, the economies of North and South steadily diverged. While the North developed a mixed economy—agriculture, commerce, and manufacturing—the South remained overwhelmingly agricultural. Since planters were earning healthy profits, they saw little reason to diversify. Moreover, economic change could conceivably threaten plantation slavery, the key to the social and economic order that planters dominated. Planters knew that if southern economic development followed the path blazed by the North, then manufacturing in the South would mean the rise of an urban, industrial working class without direct ties to slavery and the plantation. Would city-living factory workers accept rural planter rule and give their hearty support to slavery, or would they favor free labor, as northern workers did? Planters did not want to find out. Year after year, they funneled the profits they earned from land and slaves back into more land and slaves.

With its capital flowing into agriculture, the Old South did not develop many factories. By 1860, only 10 percent of the nation's industrial workers were in the South. Overwhelmingly, Southerners worked the land, where they produced 100 percent of the country's sugar, rice, and cotton, about 90 percent of the hemp and tobacco, and significant fractions of the nation's food crops and livestock. By 1860,

Indiana and Illinois—two midwestern states known for agriculture—had more capital invested in industry than the seven Lower South states, including Louisiana with its sugar mills.

The South was not entirely without factories, of course. They usually processed agricultural products and raw materials produced in the region. In terms of the value of the products, flour and corn milling were the most important southern manufacturing activities. Lumbering employed the most manufacturing workers. In the Upper South (that tier of slave states north and west of North Carolina), the manufacture of tobacco products grew in importance. By 1860, more than ten thousand workers in Richmond, Virginia, made snuff, cigars, and plugs of chewing tobacco. Cotton mills developed where there were cotton, water power, and cheap labor. The most famous was William Gregg's South Carolina factory, which employed three hundred workers, mostly white women and children. Still, in 1860 the region that produced 100 percent of the nation's cotton manufactured less than 7 percent of its cotton textiles.

Without significant economic diversification, the South developed fewer cities than the North. In 1860, it was the least urban region in the country. While nearly 37 percent of New England's population lived in towns, less than 12 percent of Southerners were urban dwellers. That figure would have been dramatically smaller without Maryland's 34 percent urban population (because of Baltimore) and Louisiana's 26 percent (because of New Orleans). In fact, nine southern states had 5 percent or fewer of their people in towns. Only one town in Arkansas numbered more than 2,500; rural Iowa had nine that large.

Not only were cities less common in the South, but they were also different from those in the North. They were mostly port cities on the periphery of the region and busy principally with exporting the agricultural products of plantations in the interior. The region's energetic, enterprising urban merchants provided agriculture with indispensable economic services, such as hauling, insuring, and selling the South's cotton, rice, and sugar. But as the tail of the plantation dog, southern cities did not become significant manufacturing centers or important independent centers of social and economic innovation.

Because the South had so few cities and industrial jobs, it attracted relatively small numbers of European immigrants. Seeking economic opportunity, not competition with slaves, immigrants steered well north of the South's slave-dominated, agricul-

MAP 12.3
Major Cities in 1860
By 1860, northern cities were both more numerous and larger than southern cities. In the slave states, cities were usually seaports or river ports that served the needs of agriculture, especially cotton.

tural economy. Thus in 1860, more than 3,580,000 people of foreign birth lived in the nonslave states, whereas only a little more than 550,000 lived in the slave states. Nationally, 13 percent of Americans were foreign-born. But in nine of the fifteen slave states, only 2 percent or fewer were born abroad. Immigrants who did venture below the Mason-Dixon line concentrated in cities, as they did in the North. In 1850, more than one-fifth of the inhabitants of Charleston and more than one-third of those of Mobile, Alabama, were foreign-born. But nearly nine of every ten Southerners lived in rural areas, and there foreign-born whites remained rare.

Not every Southerner celebrated the region's plantation economy. Critics railed against the excessive commitment to cotton and slaves and bemoaned the "deplorable scarcity" of factories. In his widely circulated journal *De Bow's Review*, James D. B. De Bow of New Orleans challenged southern farmers to produce more grain crops and livestock and implored southern manufacturers to make more of nearly everything. Reformers complained that Southerners were rocked in cradles manufactured in the North, were dressed in northern-made clothes, used northern plows and agricultural tools, and were buried in northern coffins. Diversification, they promised, would make the South not only economically independent but more prosperous and healthy as well.

Economic reformers attracted some attention, especially when profits in the plantation economy sagged, as they did when cotton prices temporarily

fell following the panics of 1819 and 1837. State governments encouraged economic development by helping to create banking systems that supplied credit for a wide range of projects, industrial as well as agricultural. State and local governments joined private investors in building an extensive railroad network. Alabama constructed its first railroad in 1830, just five years after the first modern railroad in the world was constructed in England and only three years after the inauguration of the first railroad in America. Thirty years later, 9,280 miles of track spanned the South.

But encouragement of a diversified economy had clear limits. State governments failed to create some of the essential services modern economies require. By midcentury, for example, no southern legislature had created a statewide public school system. Consequently, the South's illiteracy rate for whites topped 20 percent. Dominant slaveholders failed to see any benefit in educating the region's labor force. Railroads also illustrate the limits of the South's commitment to modernization. Despite the flurry of railroad building, the South's mileage in 1860 was less than half that of the North. Moreover, northern railroads crisscrossed the region connecting towns and cities and carrying manufactured goods as well as agricultural products. In the South, most rail lines ran from port cities back into farming areas and were built to export staple crops.

Northerners claimed that slavery was outmoded and doomed, but few Southerners perceived economic weakness in their region. Indeed, the planters' pockets were never fuller than at the end of the antebellum period. But planters' individual profits did not automatically translate into long-term regional economic health. When the South bet on plantation agriculture, especially cotton, it not only committed itself to slavery but also left itself vulnerable to the fickle world market. The super-heated international demand for cotton would not last forever. Compared with antebellum Northern-ers, Southerners committed less of their capital to investment in industry, transportation, and public education. Planters' decisions to reinvest in staple agriculture ensured the continuity and inertia of the plantation economy and the social and political re-lationships that were rooted in it.

Masters, Mistresses, and the Big House

Nowhere was the contrast between northern and southern life more vivid than in the plantations of the South. Located on a patchwork of cleared fields and dense forests, a plantation typically included a "big house" and slave quarters. Scattered about were numerous outbuildings, each with a special function. Near the big house were the kitchen, store-house, smokehouse (for curing and preserving meat), and hen coop. More distant were the stables, barns, toolsheds, artisans' workshops, and over-seer's house. Large plantations sometimes had sep-arate buildings for an infirmary, nursery, and chapel for the slaves. Depending on the crop, there was a tobacco shed, a rice mill, a sugar refinery, or a cot-ton gin house. Lavish or plain, plantations every-where had an underlying similarity.

The plantation was the home of masters, mis-tresses, and slaves. Slavery shaped the lives of all the plantation's inhabitants but affected each dif-ferently. Relationships were governed by a hierar-chy of rigid roles and duties. Presiding was the mas-ter, who according to both law and convention ruled his wife, children, and slaves, none of whom had many legal rights and all of whom were designated by the state as dependents under his dominion and protection.

Plantation Masters

Because planters lived off the toil of their slaves, it is not surprising that masters devoted considerable energy to plantation management. Plantations were

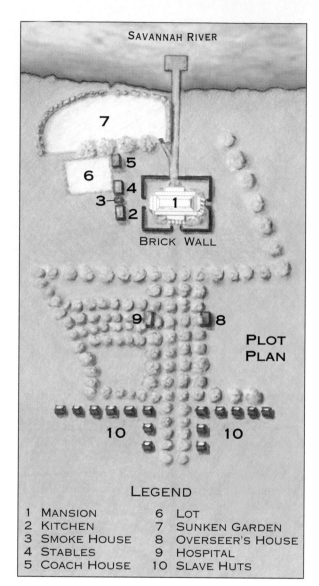

FIGURE 12.2
A Southern Plantation
Slavery determined how masters laid out their planta-tions, where they situated their mansions and the quar-ters, and what kinds of buildings they constructed.

Adapted from *Back of the Big House: The Architecture of Plantation Slavery* by John Michael Vlach. Copyright © 1993 by the University of North Carolina Press. Original illustration property of the Historic American Buildings Survey, a division of the National Park Service.

usually organized quite simply. Smaller planters su-pervised the labor of their slaves themselves. Larger planters usually hired an overseer. Overseers were either ambitious young white men—perhaps rela-tives of the planter or poor men from the neigh-borhood—or professionals who made a career of supervising slaves. Because overseers went to the fields with the slaves, planters could limit themselves to only occasional inspections and concentrated instead on marketing, finance, and general plantation affairs.

The plantation was the home of masters, mistresses, and slaves. Presiding was the master, who according to both law and convention ruled his wife, children, and slaves.

Increasingly in the nineteenth century, planters characterized the master-slave relationship in terms of what historians have called "paternalism." The concept of paternalism denied that the form of slavery practiced in the South was brutal and exploitative. Instead, it defined slavery as a set of reciprocal obligations between masters and slaves. In exchange for the slaves' labor and obedience, masters provided slaves with basic care and necessary guidance. To northern claims that they were tyrants and exploiters, slaveholders responded that they were stewards and guardians. As owners of blacks, masters argued, they had the heavy responsibility of caring for a childlike, dependent people. If slav-

ery was a burden, they said, whites shouldered it, not blacks. In 1814, Thomas Jefferson captured the essence of the ideal: "We should endeavor, with those whom fortune has thrown on our hands, to feed & clothe them well, protect them from ill usage, require such reasonable labor only as is performed voluntarily by freemen, and be led by no repugnancies to abdicate them, and our duties to them."

Paternalism was part propaganda and part self-delusion. But it was more. Indeed, there was some truth in the assertion that master-slave relationships in the South were unique. Unlike planters elsewhere in the New World, southern planters usually owned a single plantation, on which they lived. Absentee owners were not unknown, but most planters lived year-round where their slaves worked, which meant that slave management was an everyday affair and the relationship between master and slave was face to face, direct, and personal. In addition, slavery in the South reached its prime in the nineteenth century, after the nation had closed its external slave trade in 1808. Masters realized that the expansion of the slave labor force could come only from natural reproduction. Thus, masters had to provide slaves with a certain minimum level of physical welfare if they wanted more slaves, and they certainly did want more slaves.

SOUTHERN MAN WITH CHILDREN AND THEIR MAMMY
Obviously prosperous and projecting the aura of a man accustomed to giving orders and to being obeyed, this patriarch poses around 1848 with his young daughters and their nurse for a family portrait. The absent mother may have been dead, which might in part explain the inclusion of the slave woman in the family circle. But her presence also confirms her importance in the household. Fathers devoted little attention to domestic matters and left the raising of children to mothers and nurses. However important, the black woman is clearly a servant, a status indicated by both her race and her attire.
Collection of the J. Paul Getty Museum, Malibu, Calif.

One consequence was a relative improvement in slaves' material welfare. The nineteenth-century slaves' diet still consisted mainly of fatty pork and cornmeal. The cabins still had cracks large enough, slaves said, for cats to slip through. Slaves' clothing seldom amounted to much more than two crude outfits a year. Nevertheless, conditions in the quarters got better. In the fields, workdays remained sunup to sundown, but planters often provided a rest period in the heat of the day. And most owners ceased the eighteenth-century practices of punishing slaves by branding, castrating, and other forms of mutilation.

Paternalism should not be mistaken for "Ol' Massa's" kindness and goodwill. It had nothing to do with gentleness and niceness. It encouraged better treatment, but it was essentially self-interested and self-serving. Planters who accepted paternalism (and not all did) certainly did not suffer financially. Paternalism and profits went hand in hand. It made economic sense to provide at least minimal care for scarce and valuable slaves. Nor did paternalism require that planters put aside their whips. They could lay on the leather and claim that they were only fulfilling their responsibilities as guardians of their childlike, yet at times insubordinate, dependents. Paternalism gave slaves some protection against the most brutal punishments, but whipping remained the planters' essential coercion. (See Historical Question, page 444.)

Southern planters took plantation management seriously, but they did not tend to business all the time. Quite often they escaped to town to discuss the weather, to the courthouse and legislature to debate politics, and to the woods to hunt and fish. Planters had reputations as accomplished drinkers and gamblers. They enjoyed horse racing and cockfighting. Southern boys were expected to master the "manly" arts.

The Virginian Edmund Randolph argued that slavery created in white southern men a "quick and acute sense of personal liberty" and a "disdain for every abridgement of personal independence." Indeed, prickly individualism and aggressive independence became crucial features of the southern concept of honor. Social standing, political advancement, and even self-esteem rested on a reputation of honor. Defending honor became a male passion. Andrew Jackson's mother reportedly told her son, "Never tell a lie, nor take what is not your own, nor sue anybody for slander or assault and battery. *Always settle them cases yourself.*" Among planters, such advice sometimes led to duels. Duel-

ing arrived from Europe in the eighteenth century. It died out in the North, but in the South, even after legislatures banned it, gentlemen continued to defend their honor with pistols at ten paces. Honor was a tender thing, and duels were fought by Andrew Jackson, whose wife one foolish man slandered, as well as by two college students who happened at dinner to reach simultaneously for the last piece of trout.

Southerners also expected an honorable gentleman to be a proper patriarch. Nowhere in America was patriarchy more accentuated. In the South, slavery buttressed the power of husbands and fathers. Planters described the plantation as a single social unit, incorporating their "white and black families"—their personal households and the slave quarters. Reputation required that the husband possess absolute authority. Attempts by family members to assert themselves against the patriarch—the head of the family, the master of slaves—threatened slavery itself. Slaves were experts at exploiting divisions among whites, whether among masters and overseers or planters and their wives and children. Slavery simply did not allow democracy in the big house. Planters liked to think of themselves as firm but fair, strong, and ready with a pistol if necessary, the defenders of all those in their custody.

Individualistic impulses were strong among planters, but duty to family was paramount. In time, as the children of one elite family married the children of another, planters were linked to one another by ties of blood and kinship as well as ideology and economic interest. Conscious of what they shared as slaveholders, planters worked together to defend their common interests. The values of the big house—slavery, honor, male domination—washed over the boundaries of plantations and flooded all of southern life.

Plantation Mistresses

Like their northern counterparts, southern ladies were expected to possess feminine virtues of piety, purity, chastity, and obedience within the context of marriage, motherhood, and domesticity. Southerners also expected ladies to exemplify all that was best in plantation society. Countless toasts praised her as the perfect complement to her husband, the patriarch. She was physically weak, "formed only for the less laborious occupations," and thus dependent on male protection. To gain this protection, she was modest and delicate, beautiful and graceful, cultured and charming. Freed from physical labor, she cultivated fashion, polished her French, and performed magically at the piano and in the ballroom. The lady, southern men said proudly, was an "ornament."

Southern men put elite women atop a very high pedestal. But for women, the image of the lady, which rigidly prescribed proper character and behavior, was no blessing. Chivalry—the South's romantic ideal of male-female relationships—glorified the lady but simultaneously subordinated her. Chivalry's underlying assumptions about the weakness of women and the protective authority of men resembled the assumptions that underlay the paternalistic defense of slavery. Indeed, the most articulate proslavery advocates also eloquently defended the subordination of women. Just as the slaveholder's mastery was written into law, so too were the paramount rights of husbands. Once married, antebellum southern women found divorce almost impossible.

Daughters of planters confronted chivalry's demands at an early age. Their educations aimed at fitting them to take their ordained places as southern ladies. At their private boarding schools they read literature, learned languages, and struggled to master the requisite drawing-room arts. Elite women married early, usually before they were twenty. Kate Carney exaggerated only slightly when she wrote in her diary: "Today, I am seventeen, getting quite old, and am not married." Elizabeth Ruffin, who was about the same age, complained of being pushed into a wedding. Everyone, she said, seemed determined to "deter me from all the anticipated horrors of *old-maidenhood*." When they married, elite women made enormous efforts to live up to their region's lofty ideal. Caroline Merrick of Louisiana told a friend in 1859, "We owe it to our husbands, children, and friends to represent as nearly as possible the ideal which they hold so dear."

In fact, they faced an impossible task. The ideal of southern lady clashed with the daily reality of the plantation mistress. Rather than being freed from labor by servants, she discovered that having servants required her to work long hours. Like her husband, the mistress had managerial responsibilities. She managed the big house, often supervising anywhere from two or three to more than a dozen servants. One slaveholder remembered that the house he grew up in had "two cooks, two washerwomen, one dining room servant, two seamstresses, one house girl, one house boy, one carriage driver, one hostler [stableman], one gardener, [and] one er-

SOUTHERN BELLE
Lucy Petway Holcombe, a legendary Texas beauty, was twenty-six when she married twice-widowed Francis W. Pickens, a wealthy South Carolina planter, congressman, and governor. Lucy believed that she had made "a sacrifice" in marrying a man twice her age. She told her mother that she had married Pickens to pay off her father's debts and to obtain a plantation for herself. But there may have been more to her decision. She married Pickens only after her true love had been killed on a private military adventure in Cuba. Lucy had a Confederate company named after her, and her picture appeared on the Confederate hundred-dollar bill.
Orville Vernon Burton, *In My Father's House Are Many Mansions.*

rand boy." And, he added, they were "all under the supervision of my mother."

But unlike her husband, who was often insulated from the aggravations of direct supervision of slaves, the mistress had no overseer. All the house servants answered to her. She assigned them tasks each morning, directed their work throughout the day, and punished them when she found fault. In addition to supervising a complex household, she had responsibility for the henhouse and dairy. And on some plantations, she directed the slave hospi-

THE PRICE OF BLOOD

This 1868 painting by T. S. Noble depicts a transaction between a slave trader and a rich planter. The trader nervously pretends to study the contract, while the planter waits impatiently for the completion of the sale. The planter's mulatto son, who is being sold, looks away. The children of white men and slave women were property and could be sold by the father/master. But the tragedy of miscegenation extended beyond the son shown here. Who is absent from the painting? Who else's son is being sold away?

Morris Museum of Art, Augusta, Ga.

tal and nursery and rationed supplies for the slave quarters. Although she did little manual labor herself, she spent a long day engaged in decidedly unromantic chores. In addition, she bore the burdens of childbearing and child rearing. Southern ladies did not lead lives of leisure.

The mistress's life was circumscribed by the plantation, as was the slave's life. Masters used their status as slaveholders as a springboard into public affairs, but their wives served the family, not the community. Masters left the plantation when business demanded or just when they pleased, but plantation mistresses could not leave. Up to their elbows with responsibilities in the big house, they could not readily take off. Besides, white women needed

chaperones to travel. When they could, they went to church, for their faith was important to them. But women spent most days on the plantation, where they often became lonely. In 1853, Mary Kendall wrote how much she enjoyed her sister's letter: "For about three weeks I did not have the pleasure of seeing *one white female face*, there being no white family except our own upon the plantation." But sometimes a parade of family, friends, and strangers broke the isolation. Visitors were welcome, but the burden of hospitality fell on the mistress and the house slaves, not the master.

As members of slaveholding families, mistresses lived privileged lives. But they also had significant grounds for discontent, and a few independent-minded women protested. Some complained of their exhausting burdens as mistresses. Others protested their tiring and dangerous cycle of childbearing. Two decades of childbearing could mean ten or eleven children. And some women denounced slavery itself. In the early 1820s, Sarah and Angelina Grimké, daughters of a Charleston planter, fled their home for the North, where they wrote blistering attacks on slavery. Sarah's *Letters on the Equality of the Sexes* also protested the South's "image of women."

No feature of plantation life generated more rage and anguish among mistresses than miscegenation, the sexual mixing of the races. Laws prohibited interracial sex. Some masters condemned sex with slaves as immoral and practiced self-restraint. Others merely urged discretion. How many trips masters and their sons made to slave cabins is impossible to tell, but as long as slavery gave white men extraordinary power over black women, liaisons occurred. No white woman denounced the practice more scathingly than Mary Boykin Chesnut of Camden, South Carolina. She wrote in her diary: "God forgive us, but ours is a monstrous system, a wrong and iniquity. Like the patriarchs of old, our men live all in one house with their wives and their concubines; and the mulattos one sees in every family partly resemble the white children. Any lady is ready to tell you who is the father of all the mulatto children in everybody's household but her own. Those, she seems to think drop from the clouds."

But the mistress's world rested on slavery, just as the master's did. Most planters' wives—including Mary Boykin Chesnut—found ways to accept slavery. Mistresses worked hard and made enormous contributions to their husbands' estates. They raised their children, instructing, disciplining, and loving them. And when they had time, they read literature and their Bibles. They lived busy and responsible lives, but they were not considered equal to menfolk. According to the southern ideal, the white man ruled over all in his household—wife, children, and slaves.

Slaves and the Quarters

On most plantations, only a few hundred yards separated the big house and the slave quarters. The distance was short enough to assure whites easy access to the labor of blacks. Yet the distance was great enough to provide slaves with some privacy, despite increased paternalistic intrusion. Out of eyesight and earshot of the big house, slaves drew together and built lives of their own.

The rise of plantations still left a substantial minority of slaves living and working elsewhere. Most worked on small farms, where they wielded a hoe alongside another slave or two and perhaps their master. But by the mid-nineteenth century, as many as half a million slaves (one in eight) did not work in agriculture at all. They were employed in towns and cities as domestics, stevedores, day laborers, bakers, barbers, tailors, and more. Other slaves, far from urban centers, toiled as fishermen, lumbermen, railroad workers, and deckhands and stokers on riverboats. Slavery was a flexible labor system, and slaves could be found in virtually every skilled and unskilled occupation throughout the South, including the region's few factories. Nevertheless, a majority of slaves counted plantations as their homes and workplaces.

Work

Above all, what masters wanted from slaves was work. The desire for exploitable labor was the chief explanation of slavery's origin in the New World and the principal reason it persisted into the nineteenth century. Slaves understood clearly the motive for their enslavement. As ex-slave Albert Todd recalled, "Work was a religion we was taught."

Masters thought they knew what it took to make slaves work. Without close supervision and coercion, whites believed, black men and women would not labor. Whites reasoned that blacks were naturally lazy, a trait that they believed was the racial inheritance of a tropical people. On most plantations, a white man on horseback patrolled the fields to make sure slave laborers were bent over their hoes. A flick of his whip painfully reminded slackers that he believed that slaves were put on this earth to labor.

All slaves who were capable of productive labor worked. Young children were introduced to the world of work as early as age five or six. Ex-slave Carrie Hudson recalled that children who were "knee high to a duck" had to work. Some were sent to the fields to carry water to thirsty workers or to protect ripening crops from hungry birds. Others helped in the slave nursery, caring for children even younger than themselves, or in the big house, where they did simple chores, such as sweeping floors or shooing flies in the dining room. When slave boys and girls reached the age of eleven or twelve, masters sent most of them to the fields, where they learned farmwork by laboring alongside their parents. After a lifetime of labor, old women left the fields to care for the small children and spin yarn and old men to mind livestock and clean stables.

Slaves understood clearly the motive for their enslavement. As ex-slave Albert Todd recalled, "Work was a religion we was taught."

The overwhelming majority of slaves in 1860 were field hands. Planters sometimes assigned men and women to separate gangs, the women working at lighter tasks and the men doing the heavy work of clearing and breaking the land. But women also did heavy work. "I had to work hard," Nancy Boudry remembered, "plow and go and split wood just like a man." Sally Neely recalled that her owner "used the slave negro woman just like he did the slave man. He never did let the slave girl do one kind of work and the slave boy another, he worked us right on together." Although the daily tasks of slaves working in tobacco, rice, and sugar fields differed from those of slaves laboring in cotton fields, the backbreaking labor and the monotonous year-round routines made for grim similarity. As one ex-slave observed, on the plantation the "history of one day is the history of every day."

A few slaves became house servants. But only one or two in every ten worked in the big house, and virtually all of those who did (nine of ten) were women. There, under the critical eye of the white mistress, they cooked the white family's food, cleaned their house, babysat their infants, washed their clothes, and did the dozens of other tasks the master and mistress required. House servants enjoyed certain advantages, such as somewhat less physically demanding work, better food, and more comfortable quarters. But working in the big house had significant drawbacks. House servants were constantly on call. They had no time that was entirely their own. They worked in the incessant presence of whites. Since no servant could please constantly, most bore the brunt of white frustration and rage. Ex-slave Jacob Branch of Texas remembered, "My poor mama! Every washday old Missy give her a beating." No wonder some house servants wished they could trade places with field hands.

Even rarer than house servants were skilled artisans. In the cotton South, no more than one slave in twenty (almost all men) worked in a skilled trade. Most were blacksmiths and carpenters, but slaves also worked as masons, mechanics, cotton gin makers, millers, and shoemakers. Slave craftsmen took pride in their skills and often exhibited an independence of spirit that caused slaveholder James H. Hammond of South Carolina to declare in disgust that when a slave became a skilled artisan, "he is more than half freed." Skilled slave fathers often taught their crafts to their sons. "My pappy was one of the black smiths and worked in the shop," John Mathews remembered. "I had to help my pappy in the shop when I was a child and I learnt how to beat out the iron and make wagon tires, and make plows."

Rarest of all slave occupations was that of driver. Probably no more than one slave in a hundred —all men—worked in this capacity. These men were well named, for their primary task was driving other slaves to greater efforts in the fields. In some drivers' hands, the whip never rested. Ex-slave Jane Johnson of South Carolina called her driver the "meanest man, white or black, I ever see." But other drivers showed all the restraint they could. "Ole Gabe didn't like that whippin' business," West Turner of Virginia remembered, "but he couldn't help hisself. When Marsa was there, he would lay it on 'cause he had to. But when old Marsa wasn't lookin', he never would beat them slaves."

Work dominated the slaves' daylight hours. Normally, slaves worked from what they called "can to can't," from "can see" in the morning to "can't see" at night. Even with a break at noon for a meal and rest, it made for a long day. And nightfall did not necessarily mean an end of labor. After women had worked all day in the cotton patch, Pinkie Kelley remembered, we "had to shell a bushel of corn before we could go to bed, and then we was so tired we didn't have no time for nothin' and was glad to get to bed." One ex-slave remembered that no slave suffered from that "disease known as 'mattress fever.'" For slaves, Lewis Young recalled, "work, work, work, 'twas all they do."

Family, Religion, and Community

Despite the grind of exhausting labor, there was life after slaves left the fields. From dawn to dusk, slaves worked for the master. But from dusk to dawn, when the labor was done, and all day Sun-

NANCY FORT, HOUSE SERVANT
This rare portrait of a slave woman at the turn of the nineteenth century depicts a strong and dignified person. Some who worked in domestic service took pride in their superior status and identified more with the master than with the slaves. "Honey, I wan't no common eve'day slave," one former servant recalled proudly. "I [helped] de white folks in de big house." But intense interaction with whites did not necessarily breed affection. Most domestic servants remained bound by ties of kinship and friendship, as well as by common oppression, to the slave quarters.
Courtesy of Georgia Department of Archives and History.

SLAVE CARPENTER
Haywood Dixon (1826–c. 1889) was a slave carpenter who worked in Greene County, North Carolina. In this 1854 daguerreotype, he is posed with a symbol of his profession, the carpenter's square. When work was slow on the home plantation, masters could hire out their skilled craftsmen to neighbors who needed a carpenter, blacksmith, or mason.
Collection of William L. Murphy.

days and usually Saturday afternoons, slaves were left largely to themselves. Bone tired perhaps, they nonetheless used the time and space to develop and enjoy what mattered most: family, religion, and community.

In the quarters, slaves lived lives that their masters were hardly aware of. Temporarily leaving the master-slave relationship at their cabin doors, slaves became husbands and wives, mothers and fathers, sons and daughters, preachers and singers, fiddlers and hunters, storytellers and conjurers. Over the generations, they created a community and a culture of their own that buoyed them up during long hours in the fields and brought them joy and hope in the few hours they had to themselves.

One of the most important consequences of the slaves' limited autonomy was the preservation and persistence of the family. Perhaps the most serious charge abolitionists leveled against slavery was that it wrecked black family life, a telling indictment in a society that put family at the heart of decent society. Slaveholders sometimes agreed that blacks had no family life, but they placed the blame on the slaves themselves, claiming that blacks chose to lead licentious, promiscuous lives.

Contrary to both abolitionists' and slaveholders' claims, the black family survived slavery. Indeed, family was the chief fact of life in the quarters. Several factors account for the durability of the slave family. First, owners sometimes encouraged the cre-

SLAVE CABIN
Other than the well-built brick chimney, this one-room, dirt-floored cabin on a small Georgia plantation had little to recommend it. Still, it no doubt housed a family. The six children in the photograph probably lived there with their mother and perhaps with their father. It may be Sunday — the oldest children are working about the cabin rather than in the fields, while the youngest children are playing in the bare yard. "The first seven or eight years of the slave-boy's life are about as full of sweet content as those of the most favored and petted white children," recalled Frederick Douglass. The two boys in straw hats are about the age when childhood ended and "light" chores began, chores that would grow increasingly heavy over the slave's lifetime. Collection of the New-York Historical Society.

ation and maintenance of families. Some masters wanted slaves to live morally upright lives and rewarded those who married with small presents and punished those who divorced with whippings. Others encouraged slave families because of their financial interest in slave reproduction. And some masters realized that families made the quarters more stable and orderly places. It is not surprising that most runaways were young, unmarried men.

Despite occasional white encouragement, marriage and family in the quarters were primarily the result of black commitment. Masters were often indifferent to the living arrangements of their slaves, as long as the quarters were quiet. Moreover, no slave marriage was recognized by law, and therefore no master or slave was legally obligated to honor the bond. Still, plantation records show that

slave marriages were often long-lasting. Young men and women in the slave quarters fell in love, married, and set up housekeeping in cabins of their own. The primary cause of the ending of slave marriages was death, just as it was in white families. An elderly widow remembered fondly the slave husband to whom she had been married most of her life: "He was the first one and the best one and the last one." But the second most frequent cause of the end of slave marriages was sale of the husband or wife, something no white family ever had to fear. Precise figures are unavailable, but one scholar estimates that in the years 1820–1860, sales destroyed 300,000 slave marriages. Years after Moses Grandy was parted from his slave wife, he said, "I have never seen or heard of her from that day to this." And he added, "I loved her as I love my life."

Plantation records also reveal that a majority of children grew up in two-parent households, one family to a cabin. Not all fathers could live with their children—some men had been sold away and others had married women on neighboring plantations—but most fathers were present. And contrary to common belief, they were significant figures. Naming practices reveal fathers' importance. Despite slave fathers' inability to fulfill the traditional roles of provider and protector, slave parents often named their sons after their fathers. Slave fathers gained status by doing what they could to provide for their families: hunting, raising hogs, cultivating a garden, making furniture. In the eyes of slaves, an ex-bondsman recalled, "the man who does this is a great man amongst them." Still, masters sharply circumscribed the authority of slave husbands. Unlike white men, slave husbands could not exercise patriarchal dominion over their wives and children. Nevertheless, ex-slaves held both their mothers and fathers in high esteem, grateful for the refuge they had provided from the rigors of slavery.

Families were an important feature of a distinctive African American culture that flourished in the quarters. And families became the principal means of passing the slaves' culture on from generation to generation. But families were only one of the quarters' vital institutions. A second was religion. Like families, religion provided slaves with a refuge and a reason for living.

Christianity arrived late in the quarters. In the seventeenth century and for most of the eighteenth, masters cared little about the spiritual lives of their slaves, and most blacks clung to their African beliefs. Beginning about the time of the American Revolution, however, Protestant evangelical sects, particularly the Baptists and Methodists, began trying to convert slaves. Evangelicals offered an emotional "religion of the heart" to which blacks (and many whites as well) responded enthusiastically. By the mid-nineteenth century, perhaps as many as one-quarter of all slaves claimed church membership, and many of the rest would not have objected to being called Christians.

Planters began promoting Christianity in the quarters because they came to see the slaves' salvation as part of their obligation and to believe that religion made slaves more obedient. Certainly, the Christianity that masters broadcast to slaves emphasized the meeker virtues. White preachers admonished their black congregants to love God and to obey their owners. Many slaves laughed up their

BRASS ORNAMENT
Artifacts recovered by archaeologists excavating plantation sites help us understand how an African heritage was transplanted, reinterpreted, or replaced in America. This small brass ornament decorated with a clenched hand was recovered from a slave cabin at the Hermitage, the home of Andrew Jackson outside Nashville, Tennessee. Such a charm, one former slave recalled, is "what will keep de witches away."
The Hermitage: Home of President Andrew Jackson, Nashville, Tenn.

sleeves at the message. "That old white preacher just was telling us slaves to be good to our masters," a Virginia ex-slave chuckled. "We ain't cared a bit about that stuff he was telling us 'cause we wanted to sing, pray, and serve God in our own way."

Meeting in their cabins or secretly in the woods, slaves created a hidden African American Christianity that served their needs, not the masters'. Although it was illegal in the South after the 1830s to teach slaves to read, some slaves could read enough to struggle with the Bible. With the help of black preachers, they interpreted the Christian message themselves. Rather than obedience, their faith emphasized justice. God kept score, and accounts of this world would be settled in the next. "God is punishing some of them old suckers and their children right now for the way they use to treat us poor colored folks," an ex-slave declared contentedly. But the slaves' faith involved more than retribution. It also spoke to their experiences in this world. In the Old Testament they discovered Moses, who delivered his people from slavery, and in the New Testament they found Jesus, who offered salvation to all and thereby established the equality of all people. Jesus' message of equality provided a potent antidote to the planters' claim that blacks were an inferior people whom God condemned to slavery and a crucial buttress to the slaves' self-esteem.

Christianity did not entirely drive out traditional African beliefs. Some slaves saw no contradiction between their belief in Christianity and in conjurers, witches, and spirits. Depending on whether he or she was a friend or an enemy, the conjurer could make one lucky in love or give one boils. "They can take your garter or your stocking top and drop it in running water and make you run the rest of you life—you'll be in a hurry all the time," ex-slave Nancy Bradford claimed. Christian music, preaching, and rituals showed the influence of Africa, as did much of the slaves' secular activities, such as wood carving, quilt making, and story-telling.

Resistance and Rebellion

Slaves did not suffer slavery passively. They were, as whites said, "troublesome property." Slaves understood that accommodation to what they could not change was the price of survival, but in a hundred ways they protested their bondage. Theoretically, the master was all-powerful and the slave powerless. Indeed, masters had available powerful instruments of coercion. But oppressed, seemingly powerless people have always found ways to resist their oppressors. Slaves were no different. Sustained by their culture and emboldened by the slave community, slaves engaged in day-to-day resistance against their enslavers.

The spectrum of slave resistance ranged from mild to extreme. Telling a pointed story by the fireside in a slave cabin was probably the mildest form of protest. But when the weak got the better of the strong, as they did in tales of Brer Rabbit and Brer Fox ("Brer" is a contraction of "Brother"), listeners could enjoy the thrill of a vicarious victory over their masters. Trickster tales distilled the folk wisdom of Africa. The American versions taught slaves, especially young ones, how to survive the plantation regime. The tales did not always have happy endings, and slaves learned that dull-witted resisters got punished for their bungling.

Protest in the fields was more active than that around firesides. Slaves were particularly inventive in resisting their master's demand that they work. They dragged their feet getting to the fields, hoed excruciatingly slowly, put rocks in their cotton bags before putting them on the scale to be weighed, feigned illness, terribly mistreated the master's work animals, and pretended to be so thickheaded that they could not understand the simplest instruction. Slaves broke so many hoe handles that owners outfitted the hoes with oversized handles. Slaves so mistreated the work animals that masters switched from horses to mules, which could absorb more abuse. While slaves worked hard in the master's fields, they also sabotaged his interests.

One widespread form of protest that was particularly aggravating to masters was slaves attempting to escape from the plantation. Runaway slaves denied masters what they wanted most from their slaves—work. Sometimes runaways sought the ultimate prize: freedom in the North or in Canada. Over the decades, thousands of slaves, mostly from the Upper South, made it. But from the Lower South, escape to freedom was almost impossible. At most, the average runaway could hope to escape for a few weeks. Runaways usually stayed close to the plantation, keeping to the deep woods or swamps and slipping back into the quarters at night to get food. "Lying out," as it was known, usually ended when the runaway, worn out and ragged, gave up or was finally chased down by slave-hunting dogs.

Standing up to whites was an even bolder protest, and it occurred more often than we might expect. Direct confrontation rarely ended in a slave's triumph, however. An ex-slave from North Carolina remembered the night when patrollers broke up an unauthorized dance in the quarters. "Uncle Joe's son he decide they was one time to die and he started to fight," she recalled. "He say he tired standing so many beatings, he just can't stand no more." After the whites had overpowered the young man and had whipped him "for a long time, then one of them take a stick and hit him over the head, and just bust his head wide open."

While resistance was common, outright rebellion—a violent assault on slavery by large numbers of slaves—was rare. The scarcity of revolts in the antebellum South is not evidence of the slaves' contentedness. Rather, existing conditions gave rebels virtually no chance of success. Whites outnumbered blacks two to one and were heavily armed. Moreover, slaves were spread relatively thinly in the South, communication between plantations was difficult, and, with the partial exceptions of the Dismal Swamp (in Virginia and North Carolina), the Okefenokee (in Georgia and Florida), and the Everglades (in Florida), the South provided little protective wilderness into which rebels could retreat and defend themselves. Organized rebellion in the American South was virtual suicide.

Given the odds, it is perhaps surprising to find any organized rebellion. But slaves in the antebellum South did rise up. The best-known slave revolt, led by Nat Turner, occurred in 1831 in Southampton County, Virginia. All of his life, Turner believed that he "was ordained for some great purpose in the hands of the Almighty." He worked as a field hand, but he also preached to the slaves. "Ol' Prophet Nat," the slaves called him. In time, Turner became convinced that God had appointed him an instrument of divine vengeance. He set out to punish sinful white slaveholders and free their suffering slaves. Following an eclipse of the sun, which he took as a sign from the Lord, Turner and a few disciples murdered his master and his family. By the next day, some 60 other slaves, armed with axes, had joined the insurrection. White militiamen crushed the revolt in less than two days, but by then the rebels had killed about 60 white men, women, and children. In retaliation, whites killed about 120 blacks, many of them innocent bystanders. Turner managed to escape to the woods, but the authorities captured him nine weeks later. By then, 20 of his followers had been executed and 10 others exiled. Tried on November 5, 1831, Nat Turner was hanged six days later.

Antebellum southern history is also punctuated with slave conspiracies, rebellions that were suppressed before they exploded. Some so-called conspiracies were simply the product of overheated white imaginations. But in 1800, Gabriel Prosser, a slave in Richmond, planned a real rebellion that whites foiled at the last minute. And there was Denmark Vesey, the free black man in Charleston who was thwarted in 1822 in his effort to become a black Moses.

Although masters often boasted that their slaves were "instinctively contented," steady resistance and occasional rebellion proved otherwise. Slaves found challenging white authority a risky but invigorating business. By asserting themselves, they affirmed their humanity and worth. By resisting their masters' will, slaves also helped shape

their own destiny. They became actors in the plantation drama, helping to establish limits beyond which planters and overseers hesitated to go. Slaves did not have the power to end their bondage, but they remained thorns in their masters' sides.

It would be false to the historical record to minimize what the lack of freedom meant to slaves. Because the essence of slavery was the inability to shape one's own life, slavery blunted and thwarted African Americans' hopes and aspirations. Slavery broke some and crippled others. But slavery's destructive power had to contend with the resiliency of the human spirit. Slaves fought back physically, culturally, and spiritually. They not only survived bondage but created in the slave quarters a vibrant African American culture and community that would sustain them through more than two centuries of bondage and after.

Black and Free: On the Middle Ground

Not every black Southerner was a slave. In 1860, some 260,000 (approximately 6 percent) of the region's 4.1 million African Americans were free. What is surprising is not that their numbers were small but that they existed at all. "Free black" seemed a contradiction to most white Southerners. According to the dominant racial thinking, blacks were supposed to be slaves; free people were supposed to be white. Nature had decreed it and a decent society required it, proslavery theorists declared. Blacks who were free did not fit neatly into the South's idealized social order. They stood out, and whites made them objects of special scrutiny. Free blacks realized that they stood precariously between slavery and full freedom, on what a young free black artisan in Charleston characterized in 1848 as "a middle ground."

White Response to Free Blacks

Free blacks were rare in the colonial era, but their numbers swelled after the Revolution, when the natural rights philosophy of the Declaration of Independence and the egalitarian message of evangelical Protestantism joined to challenge slavery. Although probably not more than one slaveholder in a hundred freed his slaves, a brief flurry of emancipation visited the Upper South, where the ideological assault on slavery coincided with a deep depression in the tobacco economy. Other planters permitted favorite slaves to work after hours to accumulate money with which to buy their freedom. By 1810, free blacks numbered more than 100,000 and had become the fastest-growing element of the southern population. Burgeoning numbers of free blacks worried white Southerners, who, because of the cotton boom, wanted desperately to see more slaves, not more free blacks.

In the 1820s and 1830s, state legislatures acted to stem the growth of the free black population and to shrink the liberty of those blacks who had already gained their freedom. To cut down access to freedom, laws denied masters the right to free their slaves. Additional laws humiliated and restricted the South's existing free blacks by subjecting them to special taxes, requiring them to register annually with the state or to choose a white guardian, prohibiting them from interstate travel, denying them the right to have schools and to participate in politics, and requiring them to carry "freedom papers" to prove they were not slaves. Increasingly, whites subjected free blacks to many of the same laws as slaves. They could not testify under oath in a court of law or serve on juries. They were liable to punishment meted out to slaves such as whipping and the treadmill. Like slaves, free blacks were forbidden to strike whites, even to defend themselves. "Free negroes belong to a degraded caste of society," a South Carolina judge summed up in 1848. "They are in no respect on a perfect equality with the white man. . . . They ought, by law, to be compelled to demean themselves as inferiors."

The elaborate system of regulations confined most free African Americans to a constricted life of poverty and dependence, which led most whites to despise them as degraded parasites.

The elaborate system of regulations confined most free African Americans to a constricted life of poverty and dependence, which led most whites to despise them as degraded parasites. Whites pushed the majority of free blacks to the bottom of the southern social hierarchy. Typically, free blacks were rural, uneducated, unskilled agricultural laborers and domestic servants, scrambling to find work and eke out a living. Opportunities of all kinds—for

work, education, community—were slim. Planters looked upon free blacks as worthless rascals, likely to set a bad example for slaves. They believed that free blacks subverted the racial subordination that was the essence of slavery.

Achievement despite Restrictions

Despite increasingly harsh and constricting laws and stepped-up harassment and persecution, free African Americans made the most of the advantages their status offered. Unlike slaves, free blacks could legally marry. They could protect their families from arbitrary disruption by whites and pass on their heritage of freedom to their children. Freedom also meant that, unlike slaves, free blacks could choose occupations and own property. For most, however, these proved only theoretical rights, for whites allowed most free blacks few economic opportunities. Unlike whites, a majority of the antebellum South's free blacks remained propertyless.

Still, some free blacks escaped the poverty and degradation whites thrust upon them. Particularly in urban areas—especially in the cities of Charleston, Mobile, and New Orleans—a small elite of free blacks developed and even flourished. Urban whites enforced many of the restrictive laws only sporadically, allowing free blacks room to maneuver. The elite consisted overwhelmingly of light-skinned African Americans who worked at skilled trades, as tailors, carpenters, mechanics, and the like. Their customers were prominent whites— planters, merchants, judges—who appreciated their able, respectful service. The small white working class, however, resented their competition and their profitable connections with white aristocrats. The free black elite illegally operated schools for their children, illegally traveled in and out of their states, worshiped with whites (in separate seating) in the finest churches, and lived scattered about in white neighborhoods, not in separate ghettos. Though this small elite lived in proximity to dark-skinned free blacks and to slaves, they put distance between themselves and other African Americans.

Yet in one important way, the free black elite was not remote from slaves. In 1860, about 3,200 blacks owned slaves. Blacks could own blacks because, despite all of the restrictions whites placed on free African Americans, whites did not deny them the right to own property, which in the South included human property. Most owned only a few, who were sometimes family members whom they could not legally free. But others owned slaves in

MADDEN'S TAVERN
*Completed in about 1840, the tavern was built, owned, and oper-
ated by Willis Madden (1799–1879), a free black. One of the best-
known taverns in Culpeper County, Virginia, it numbered among
its patrons, who were all white, the area's most prominent citizens.
Employment for free blacks was hard to come by in the slave South,
and Madden also operated a general store and a blacksmith shop,
which provided work for his sons and relatives. Heavily damaged by
Union troops, the tavern ceased operations after the Civil War.*
Department of Historic Resources, Virginia.

large numbers, none of whom were family and all
of whom were exploited for labor.

One such free black slave owner was William
Ellison of South Carolina. Ellison was himself born
a slave in 1790, but by 1860 he was the wealthiest
free black in his state and owned more slaves than
any other free black in the South outside Louisiana.
In 1816, Ellison bought his freedom from his white
master (who may have been his father) and moved
to a booming plantation district about one hundred
miles north of Charleston. He set up business as a
cotton gin maker, a trade he had learned as a slave.
Ellison's gin business grew with the cotton boom
until by 1835 he was prosperous enough to purchase
the home of a former governor of the state. Ellison
lived in the house until his death in 1861. By then,
he had become a big planter, making a hundred

bales of cotton a year with sixty-three slaves on an
eight-hundred-acre plantation.

Not every free black was willing to accommodate to whites and enslave and exploit other blacks.
At the very time Ellison was building his slave empire, Denmark Vesey was plotting slavery's destruction. Most free blacks followed a middle
course. They neither became slaveholders nor
sought to raise a slave rebellion. They simply tried
to preserve their freedom, to deny whites what they
most wanted—a society in which all whites were
free and all blacks were slaves. Increasingly under
attack from planters who wanted to eliminate or enslave them and from white artisans who coveted
their jobs, they sought to impress whites with their
reliability, their economic progress, and their good
behavior.

The Plain Folk

Most whites in the South did not own slaves, not even one. In 1860, more than 6 million of the South's 8 million whites lived in slaveless families. Some slaveless Southerners—artisans, traders, and mechanics, for example—were urban dwellers, but their numbers were relatively small because the South had few cities. Others—storekeepers, parsons, and schoolteachers, for example—lived in the country but worked outside agriculture. But most "plain folk" were small farmers. Perhaps three out of four were yeomen, small farmers who owned their own land. As in the North, farm ownership provided a family with an economic foundation, social respectability, and political standing. Unlike their northern counterparts, however, southern yeomen lived in a region whose economy and society were dominated by unfree labor. Not even the nonslaveholding white majority escaped the influence of slavery.

In an important sense, the South had more than one white yeomanry. The huge southern landscape provided space enough for two yeoman societies, separated roughly along geographical lines. Yeomen throughout the South had a good deal in common, but the life of a small farm family in the upcountry—the area of hills and mountains—differed from the life of one in the plantation belt—the flatlands that included the black belt and delta regions.

Plantation Belt Yeomen

Plantation belt yeomen lived within the orbit of the planter class. Small landholdings actually outnumbered the larger plantations, but they were dwarfed in importance. Although only small fry, yeomen participated in the dominant cotton economy. They

GATHERING CORN

In this 1865 drawing, two white men, perhaps kinfolk or neighbors, join in harvesting corn. While one cuts and gathers the stalks, the other shucks the corn. A black man, who was probably a slave either owned or hired by one of the white men, loads the corn into a wagon. Corn was a primary crop of most antebellum yeoman farmers, even those who grew considerable cotton. Yeomen usually grew about twice the corn needed for their families and livestock and marketed the rest.
Library of Congress.

devoted a significant portion of their land to growing cotton and with family labor produced perhaps five or six 400-pound bales each year. (Large planters measured their crop in hundreds of bales.) Small farmers also grew food crops. Both their cotton and their corn tied them to planters. Unable to afford cotton gins or baling presses of their own, they relied on helpful neighborhood slave owners to gin and bale their small crops. With no link to merchants in the port cities, yeomen turned to better-connected planters to ship and sell their cotton. If a yeoman had surplus corn one season, he might find a local planter who had run short and would pay a fair price. More likely, the farmer himself would run short and would receive from the neighborly planter a few bushels to tide him over.

A dense network of personal relationships laced small farmers and planters together in patterns of reciprocity and mutual obligation. A planter sometimes sent his slaves to help a newcomer build a house or a sick farmer get in his crop. He hired out surplus slaves to ambitious yeomen who wanted to expand cotton production. He sometimes chose his overseers from among the sons of farm families in the community. Plantation mistresses sometimes nursed ailing neighbors. Family ties often spanned class lines, making rich and poor kin as well as neighbors. Yeomen shared the planters' commitment to white supremacy and actively defended black subordination. Rural counties required adult white males to ride in slave patrols, which nightly scoured country roads to make certain that no slaves were moving about without permission. On Sundays, plantation dwellers and plain folk came together in church to worship and afterward lingered to gossip and to transact small business.

Yeomen throughout the South had a good deal in common, but the life of a small farm family in the upcountry—the area of hills and mountains—differed from the life of one in the plantation belt—the flatlands that included the black belt and delta regions.

Yeomen may have envied, and at times even resented, wealthy slaveholders, but in general small farmers learned to accommodate. Planters made accommodation easier by going out of their way to provide necessary services, behave as good neighbors, and avoid direct exploitation of slaveless whites in their community. As a consequence, rather than raging at the oppression of the planter regime, the typical plantation belt yeoman sought entry into it. He dreamed of adding acreage to his farm, buying a few slaves of his own, retiring from field work, and perhaps even joining his prosperous neighbors on their shady verandas for a cool drink.

Upcountry Yeomen

The hills and mountains in the interior of the South resisted the penetration of slavery and plantations. While increasing participation in the market was a trend everywhere in the South, the western parts of Virginia, North Carolina, and South Carolina, northern Georgia and Alabama, and eastern Tennessee and Kentucky retained a quite different economy and society. The higher elevation, colder climate, rugged terrain, and poor transportation made it difficult for commercial agriculture to make headway. These regions were characterized by small farms, few slaves, food crops, and production for home consumption. For yeomen who lived in the hills and mountains, planters and slaves were not everyday acquaintances. Geographically isolated, the upcountry was a yeoman stronghold.

At the core of the distinctive upcountry culture was the independent farm family working its own

THE APPALACHIAN DULCIMER
This southern mountain folk instrument has its origins in Germany, Sweden, and Norway and may have been introduced to the Appalachians by Pennsylvania Germans. As pleasing to the eye as to the ear, dulcimers were usually crafted in "teardrop" or "figure-eight" shapes. When plucked, dulcimers emit a soft and gentle, somewhat melancholy, sound. Mountain people fashioned these instruments to accompany doleful Scottish and English ballads as well as to play lively instrumental tunes.
Collection of the Blue Ridge Institute and Museum/Ferrum College.

patch of land; raising a considerable number of hogs, cattle, and sheep; and seeking self-sufficiency and independence. Toward that end, all members of the family worked, their tasks depending on their sex and age. Husbands labored in the fields, and with their sons they cleared, plowed, planted, and cultivated primarily food crops—corn, wheat, sweet potatoes, and perhaps some fruit. Although pressed into field labor at picking or harvest time, wives and daughters worked in and about the cabin most of the year. One upcountry farmer remembered that his mother "worked in the house cooking, spinning, weaving [and doing] patchwork." In addition, the women tended the vegetable garden, kept a cow and some chickens, preserved foods, cleaned their homes, fed their families, and cared for the infants and toddlers. Male and female tasks were equally crucial to the farm's success, but as in other white southern households, the female domestic sphere was subordinated to the will of the male patriarch.

The typical upcountry yeoman also grew a little cotton or tobacco, but production for home consumption was more important than production for the market. Not much currency changed hands in the upcountry. Credit was common, as was direct barter. A yeoman might trade his small commercial crop to a country store owner for a little salt, lead shot, needles, and nails. Or he might swap extra sweet potatoes with the blacksmith for a plow or with the tanner for leather. Networks of exchange and mutual assistance tied individual homesteads to the larger community. Farm families swapped goods and work and joined together in logrolling, house- or barn-raising, and cornhusking. Strong ties to a cooperative community made the yeoman's goal of maintaining his family's independence realistic.

Plain folk did not usually associate "book learning" with the basic needs of life. In any case, the children of yeomen had limited opportunity for schooling. A northern woman visiting the South in the 1850s observed, "Education is not extended to the masses here as at the North." Private academies charged fees that yeomen could not afford, and public schools were scarce. Even where schools existed, terms were short, only about 50 or 60 days a year in the South compared with 100 to 150 days in the North. Although most people managed to pick up a basic knowledge of the "three R's," approximately one southern white man in five was illiterate in 1860, and the rate for white women was even

higher. "People here prefer talking to reading," a Virginian remarked. Telling stories, reciting ballads, and singing hymns were important activities in yeoman folk culture.

Many plain folk spent more hours in revival tents than in classrooms. By no means were all rural whites religious, but many were, and the most characteristic feature of their evangelical Christian faith was the revival. The greatest of the early-nineteenth-century revivals occurred in 1801 at Cane Ridge, Kentucky, where some twenty thousand people gathered to listen to a host of preachers who spoke day and night for a week. Ministers sought to convert and save souls by bringing individuals to a personal conviction of sin. Revivalism crossed denominational lines, but Baptists and Methodists adopted it wholeheartedly and by midcentury had become the South's largest religious groups. By emphasizing free choice and individual worth, the plain folk's religion was hopeful and affirming. Hymns and spirituals provided guides to right and wrong—praising modesty and steadfastness, condemning drinking and devilish activity like dancing. Above all, hymns spoke of eventual release from worldly sorrows and the assurance of eternal salvation:

> A few more struggles here,
> A few more partings o'er,
> A few more toils, a few more tears,
> And we shall weep no more,
> And we shall weep no more,
>   Happy thought to die no more,
> No, never, never more.

Yeomen did not have the upcountry entirely to themselves. Even the hills had some plantations and slaves. But they existed in much smaller numbers than in the plantation belt. Many upcountry counties were less than a quarter black, whereas counties in the plantation belt were more than half black. Only a small fraction of upcountry folks owned slaves, and those who did usually had only two or three. As a result, slaveholders had much less direct social and economic power, and yeomen had more. Farmers and farms, not planters and plantations, dominated upcountry culture. Yeoman domination did not mean that the upcountry opposed slavery. As long as they were free to lead their own lives, upcountry plain folk defended slavery and white supremacy just as staunchly as did other white Southerners.

Poor Whites

Northerners denied the claim that the South's white majority constituted a sturdy yeomanry—hardworking, landholding, small farmers. Instead, they charged that the institution of slavery had pushed slaveless whites to the bottom of the social and economic ladder, where they had lost heart, ambition, and energy. The majority of the South's whites, according to northern critics, were landless, shiftless, and degraded. Contemporaries called these Southerners a variety of derogatory names: snuff dippers, clay eaters, hillbillies, crackers, rednecks, and poor white trash. Even slaves were known to chant: "I'd rather be a nigger an' plow ol' Beck, / Than a white hill-billy with a long red neck." Poor whites were not just whites who were poor. The label carried a moral as well as a material meaning. It suggested not only poverty but cultural degeneracy as well. Poor whites were supposedly ignorant and inbred, sick in body and culture. According to the South's critics, slavery meant riches, esteem, and power for the few and deprivation, degradation, and impotence for the white majority.

Significant numbers of Southerners were poor, as the critics claimed. Perhaps one in four farmers was landless. Landless farm families lived as tenants, renting rather than owning land. Other poor rural Southerners worked as unskilled day laborers, hunters, herders, and fishermen. Living on the periphery of the southern economy, some barely made a go of it. Wits could declare that "poor whites were born lazy and had a relapse." In fact, poor whites subsisted on unhealthy diets, lived in miserable housing, spent summers going barefooted around animals, and, consequently, suffered high incidences of hookworm, pellagra, and other severely debilitating diseases that thrived in the South's warm, wet climate. Although impoverished, most of these Southerners were not degenerate. Instead, they were ambitious people kicking and scratching to survive and aspiring to climb into the yeomanry.

Poor whites were sometimes poor only temporarily. The Lipscomb family illustrates the possibility of upward mobility. In 1845, Smith and Sally Lipscomb and their children abandoned tired land in South Carolina for Benton County, Alabama. "Benton is a mountainous country but ther is a heep of good levil land to tend in it," Smith wrote back to his brother. Alabama, Smith declared, "will be better for the rising generation if not for ourselves

but I think it will be the best for us all that live any length of time." Indeed, primitive conditions made survival uncertain. All of the Lipscombs fell ill, but all recovered, and the entire family went to work. Because they had no money to buy land, they squatted on seven acres. With the help of neighbors, they built a twenty-two-foot-by-twenty-four-foot cabin, a detached kitchen sixteen feet square, and two stables. Each day, from daylight to dark, Smith and his sons worked the land. Nature cooperated, and they produced plenty of food and several bales of cotton. The women worked just as hard in the cabin, and Sally managed to contribute to the family's income by sewing shirts, which she sold for seventy-five cents, and knitting socks, selling for thirty-seven cents a pair. In time, the Lipscombs bought land of their own. Eventually, they joined Hebron Baptist Church and completed their transformation from landless poor whites to respectable yeomen.

The upward mobility demonstrated by the Lipscombs became rarer in the 1850s. The prosperity of the cotton economy encouraged planters to expand their operations, driving the price of land beyond the reach of poor families. Squeezed by competition with plantation slavery and pushed to the least fertile regions of the South, such as the pine barrens along the Atlantic coast, poor whites were likely to remain poor.

The Politics of Slavery

Like every other significant feature of southern society, politics showed the impress of slavery. Even after the South's politics became democratic in form for the white male population, political power remained less than evenly distributed. The nonslaveholding white majority wielded less political power than their numbers indicated. The slaveholding white minority wielded more. Self-conscious, cohesive, and with a well-developed sense of class interest, slaveholders busied themselves with party politics, campaigns, and officeholding and made demands of state governments. As a result, they received significant benefits. But most nonslaveholding whites were more concerned with preserving their liberties and keeping their taxes low. Collectively, they asked government for little of an economic nature, and they received little.

Slaveholders worried about nonslaveholders' political loyalty to slavery. Ultimately, they need not have fretted. Since the eighteenth century, the mass of whites had accepted the planters' argument that the existing social order served *all* Southerners' interests. Slavery gave the planter class enormous advantages, but the slaveless white majority gained as well. Slavery compensated every white man—no matter how poor—with membership in the South's white ruling class. It also provided the means by which nonslaveholders might someday advance into the ranks of the planters. White men in the South fought furiously about many things, but they agreed that they should take land from Indians, promote agriculture, uphold white supremacy, and defend slavery from its enemies.

The Democratization of the Political Arena

The political reforms that swept the nation in the first half of the nineteenth century reached deeply into the South. Southern politics became democratic politics—for white men. State by state, Southerners eliminated the wealth and property requirements that had restricted political participation. By the early 1850s, every state had extended suffrage to all white males who were at least twenty-one years of age. Most southern states also removed the property requirements for holding state offices. In addition, increasing numbers of local and state officials were chosen by the voters. Justices of the peace, judges, militia officers, and others had to win elections rather than the favor of the governor or legislature. To be sure, undemocratic features lingered. In several states, the plantation districts still wielded disproportionate power in the legislatures. Nevertheless, with certain exceptions, southern politics increasingly took place within a democratic political structure.

The nonslaveholding white majority wielded less political power than their numbers indicated. The slaveholding white minority wielded more.

White male suffrage ushered in an era of vigorous electoral competition. Eager voters rushed to the polls to exercise their new rights. In South Carolina, for example, in the 1810 election—the last election with voting restrictions in place—only 43 percent of white men cast ballots. But in the first election held after the state dropped its property requirement, nearly 64 percent of white men voted. And by 1824, the number of white men voting had climbed to a remarkable 76 percent. High turnouts became hallmarks of southern electoral politics. Elections in this democratic arena were spirited, even raucous. Governor John A. Wise claimed that in Virginia, "everybody talked politics everywhere." Candidates crisscrossed their electoral districts, speaking to groups several times a day for weeks on end. Voters displayed considerable political savvy and expected solid argument as well as stirring oratory. They also demanded good entertainment—barbecues and bands, rum and races. Candidates competed in producing extravaganzas, hoping to attract attention and votes.

As politics became aggressively democratic, it also grew fiercely partisan. From the 1830s to the 1850s, Whigs and Democrats battled for the electorate's favor. In most southern states, the two parties competed fairly equally. Whigs and Democrats both presented themselves as the plain white folks' best friend. All candidates declared their fervent commitment to republican equality and pledged themselves to defend the people's liberty. Each party sought to sour the other party's relationship with voters by portraying it as a collection of rich, snobbish, selfish men who had antidemocratic designs up their silk sleeves. Each, in turn, claimed for itself the mantle of humble "servant of the people."

The Whig and Democratic Parties sought to serve the people differently, however. Southern Whigs tended, as Whigs did elsewhere in the nation, to favor government intervention in the economy, and Democrats tended to oppose it. Whigs generally backed state support of banks, railroads, and corporations, arguing that government aid would stimulate the economy, enlarge opportunity, and thus increase the general welfare. Democrats emphasized the threat to individual liberty that government intervention posed, claiming that granting favors to special economic interests would result in concentrated power, which would jeopardize the common man's opportunity and equality. Beginning with the panic of 1837, the parties clashed repeatedly on concrete economic and financial issues.

No simple formula explains who was likely to become a Whig or a Democrat. Many factors came into play, but in the South, party conflict often reflected geography. Different regions within states had different economic needs, which encouraged them to tilt toward one party or the other. In North Carolina, for example, farmers in the eastern coastal plain (a region that was intersected by navigable rivers) had little need for better transportation facilities for their crops and thus displayed little interest in the Whig Party's program of expensive, government-backed internal improvements. But ambitious farmers in the western Piedmont and mountains (regions without good natural transportation) looked more favorably on state aid to internal improvements and thus on the Whig Party. Other southern states revealed similar relationships among geography, economic need, and party loyalty. Inevitably, however, party allegiance also reflected intangibles such as friendships, family histories, and neighborhood traditions.

Planter Power

Whether Whig or Democrat, southern officeholders were likely to be slave owners. The power slaveholders exerted over slaves did not translate directly into political authority over whites, however. In the nineteenth century, political power could be won only at the ballot box, and almost everywhere, nonslaveholders were in the majority. Yet year after year, proud and noisily egalitarian common men elected wealthy slaveholders.

In 1850, the percentage of slave owners in state legislatures ranged from 39 percent in Texas to more than 81 percent in North Carolina. Legislators not only tended to own slaves—they often owned large numbers. The percentage of planters (individuals with twenty or more slaves) in southern legislatures in 1850 ranged from 5.5 percent in Texas to 53.5 percent in South Carolina. In North Carolina, where only 3 percent of the state's white families belonged to the planter class, 36 percent of the legislature were planters. In Georgia's legislature, the president of the Senate owned 65 slaves and the speaker of the House of Representatives owned 122 slaves. The democratization of politics in the nineteenth century meant that more ordinary citizens served in government than in the eighteenth century, but yeomen and artisans remained rare sights in the halls of southern legislatures.

Upper-class dominance of southern politics represented, in part, the persistence of old patterns. It reflected the strength of the rural folk culture, which valued tradition, continuity, and stability. In the colonial era, yeomen had looked to the upper class for political leadership. Large planters pos-

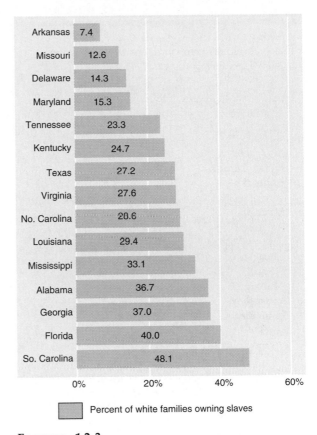

	Percent of white families owning slaves
Arkansas	7.4
Missouri	12.6
Delaware	14.3
Maryland	15.3
Tennessee	23.3
Kentucky	24.7
Texas	27.2
Virginia	27.6
No. Carolina	28.6
Louisiana	29.4
Mississippi	33.1
Alabama	36.7
Georgia	37.0
Florida	40.0
So. Carolina	48.1

FIGURE 12.3
Slave Ownership, 1860
Whites in the Lower South were much more likely to own slaves than whites in the Upper South.

sessed great wealth, education, oratorical gifts, leisure, experience in public affairs, the habit of command, and eagerness to serve. Notions of hierarchy and habits of deference declined in the nineteenth century as egalitarianism and democracy rose, but planter status remained important in the South and the surest ticket to political advancement.

But tradition was not enough to ensure planter rule. Slaveholders had to persuade the white majority that what was good for slaveholders was also good for them. Slaveless whites proved to be receptive to the planters' argument. The South had, on the whole, done well by them. Most had farms of their own. They participated as equals in a democratic political system. As white men, they enjoyed an elevated social status, above all blacks and in theory equal to all other whites. As long as slavery existed, they could dream of joining the planter class, of rising above the drudgery of field labor.

TABLE 12.1

SLAVEHOLDERS AND PLANTERS IN LEGISLATURES, 1850 AND 1860

Percent of Slaveholders

Legislature	1850	1860
Virginia	67.1	67.3
Maryland	56.3	53.4
North Carolina	51.5	85.8
Kentucky	66.4	60.6
Tennessee	41.0	66.0
Missouri	35.9	41.2
Arkansas	53.6	42.0
South Carolina	80.5	81.7
Georgia	69.7	71.6
Florida	N/D*	55.4
Alabama	66.4	76.3
Mississippi	61.5	73.4
Louisiana	42.6	63.8
Texas	38.8	54.1

Percent of Planters†

Legislature	1850	1860
Virginia	22.9	24.2
Maryland	12.6	19.3
North Carolina	22.8	36.6
Kentucky	14.9	8.4
Tennessee	7.0	14.0
Missouri	1.3	5.3
Arkansas	10.3	13.0
South Carolina	53.5	55.4
Georgia	29.8	29.0
Florida	N/D	20.0
Alabama	33.6	40.8
Mississippi	30.3	49.5
Louisiana	19.8	23.5
Texas	5.5	18.1

*N/D: not determined.

†Planters: owned 20 or more slaves.

Source: Adapted from Ralph A. Wooster, The People in Power: Courthouse and Statehouse in the Lower South, 1850–1860 (1969), 41; Politicians, Planters, and Plain Folks: Courthouse and Statehouse in the Upper South (1975), 40. Courtesy of the University of Tennessee Press.

Slaveholders took pains to win the plain folk's trust and to nurture their respect. In the plantation districts especially, where slaveholders and non-slaveholders lived side by side, planters had to act sensitively. Planters were powerful neighbors, and economic advantage lay heavily on their side. But the gentry learned that flexing their economic muscle was a poor way to win the political allegiance of common men. Instead, they developed a lighter touch, fully attentive to their own interests but aware of the personal feelings of poorer whites. One South Carolinian told his wealthy neighbor that he had a bright political future because he never thought himself "too good to sit down & talk to a poor man."

Not all of the gentry behaved astutely, however. Plain folk still encountered strutting slave owners. A slaveless farmer in Tennessee declared that in his neighborhood, "all who owned as much as one negro seemed to feel that they were in a separate and higher class than the common people." Another claimed that "Negroes and white men did the work" while slaveholders spent their time "hunting and fishing and riding around." But no slave master with political ambitions could afford to play the aristocrat. Even if he believed that the hierarchical social relations of plantations should extend to the broader community, he could not treat white men like slaves. Open elitism was political suicide.

Smart candidates found ways to convince wary yeomen of their democratic convictions and egalitarian sentiments, whether they were genuine or not. When Walter L. Steele ran for a seat in the North Carolina legislature in 1846, he commented sarcastically to a friend that he was "busily engaged in proving to the people, the soundness of my political faith, and the purity of my personal character & playing the fool to a considerable extent, as you know, all candidates are obliged to do." He detested pandering to the electorate, but he had learned to speak with a "candied tongue."

Young John A. Quitman understood what it took to win a seat in the Mississippi legislature. At one campaign stop, he amazed a boisterous crowd of small farmers by not only entering but winning contests in jumping, boxing, wrestling, and sprinting. For his finale he outshot the area's champion marksman. Then, demonstrating his deft political touch, he gave his prize, a fat ox, to the defeated rifleman. The electorate showed its approval by sending Quitman to the state capital.

The massive representation of slaveholders ensured that southern legislatures would make every

And they were as certain as any slave owner that emancipation would be catastrophic. Slaveless men found much to celebrate in the slave South and saw their slaveholding neighbors as men to respect, emulate, and elect to public office.

effort to preserve slavery. Georgia politics show how well the planters protected themselves in the political struggle. In 1850, about half of the state's revenues came from taxes on slave property, the characteristic form of planter wealth. However, the tax rate on slaves was trifling, only about one-fifth the rate on land. Moreover, planters benefited far more than other social groups from public spending, for financing railroads—which carried cotton to market—was the largest state expenditure in the late antebellum period. The legislature established low tax rates on land, the characteristic form of yeoman wealth, which meant that the typical yeomen's annual tax bill was small. Still, relative to their wealth, large slaveholders paid less than did other whites. Relative to their numbers, they got more. A sympathetic slaveholding legislature protected planters' interests and gave the impression of protecting the small farmers' interest as well.

In the 1830s, white Southerners decided that slavery was too important to debate, especially with the specter of abolitionism in the North. "So interwoven is [slavery] with our interest, our manners, our climate and our very being," one man declared in 1833, "that no change can ever possibly be effected without a civil commotion from which the heart of a patriot must turn with horror." A "cotton curtain" descended along the Mason-Dixon line that ended free speech on the slavery question. Slavery's critics were dismissed from college faculties, driven from pulpits, and hounded from political life. Sometimes they fell victim to vigilantes and mob violence. One could defend slavery; one could even delicately suggest mild reforms. But no Southerner could safely call slavery evil or sinful or advocate its destruction.

By gagging slavery's critics, slaveholders gained real advantages. In 1857, for example, Hinton Rowan Helper, a North Carolinian who moved north, published *The Impending Crisis of the South*, in which he argued that slavery denied nonslaveholding whites the opportunities for economic advancement that free-labor societies offered. Slaveholders found *The Impending Crisis* deeply disquieting, but rather than confront the book's arguments, they simply banned it. The South's small farmers, whose economic advancement had stalled in the 1850s, remained unaware of Helper's economic broadside against slavery. Instead, they heard the South's politicians, academics, and clergy celebrate slavery's benefits.

In the antebellum South, therefore, the rise of the common man occurred alongside the continuing, even growing, power of the planter class. Rather than pitting slaveholders against nonslaveholders, elections remained an effective means of binding the region's whites together. Elections affirmed the sovereignty of white men, whether genteel planter or plain folk, and the subordination of African Americans. Those twin themes played well among white women as well. Although unable to vote, white women supported equality for whites and slavery for blacks.

Conclusion: A Slave Society

Southerners and Northerners came to see the South as fundamentally different from the rest of the nation. It was a rural region with a biracial population that reflected the dominance of plantation slavery. Regional differences generally increased over time, not merely because the South became more and more dominated by slavery, but also because developments in the North rapidly propelled it in a very different direction.

Much more than racial slavery contributed to the South's distinctiveness and to the loyalty and regional identification of its whites. Southerners felt strong attachments to local communities, to extended families, to personal, face-to-face relationships, to rural life, to evangelical Protestantism, and to codes of honor and chivalry, among other things. But slavery was crucial to the South's economy, society, and culture, as well as to its developing sectional consciousness. After the 1830s, little disturbed the white consensus south of the Mason-Dixon line that racial slavery was necessary and just. By making all blacks a pariah class, all whites gained a measure of equality and harmony.

Racism did not erase all stress along class lines. Nor did the other features of southern life that helped confine class tensions: the wide availability of land, rapid economic mobility, the democratic nature of political life, the shrewd behavior of slaveholders toward poorer whites, common kinship, and rural folkways. Anxious slaveholders continued to worry that yeomen would defect from the proslavery consensus, but during the 1850s a far more ominous division emerged between the "slave states" and the "free states."

For state and local studies:

Randolph B. Campbell, *An Empire for Slavery: The Peculiar Institution in Texas, 1821–1865* (1989).

Margaret W. Creel, *"A Peculiar People": Slave Religion and Community-Culture among the Gullahs* (1988).

Charles B. Dew, *Bond of Iron: Master and Slave at Buffalo Forge* (1994).

Douglas R. Egerton, *Gabriel's Rebellion: The Virginia Slave Conspiracies of 1800 and 1802* (1993).

Charles Joyner, *Down by the Riverside: A South Carolina Slave Community* (1984).

John Lofton, *Denmark Vesey's Revolt* (1983).

Melton A. McLaurin, *Celia, a Slave* (1991).

Stephen B. Oates, *The Fires of Jubilee: Nat Turner's Fierce Rebellion* (1975).

SOCIETY AND CULTURE

Adele Logan Alexander, *Ambiguous Lives: Free Women of Color in Rural Georgia* (1991).

Harriet E. Amos, *Cotton City: Urban Development in Antebellum Mobile* (1985).

Edward L. Ayers, *Vengeance and Justice* (1984).

David Bailey, *Shadow on the Church: Southwestern Evangelical Religion and the Issue of Slavery, 1783–1860* (1985).

Fred Arthur Bailey, *Class and Tennessee's Confederate Generation* (1987).

Peter Bardaglio, *Reconstructing the Household: Families, Sex, and the Law in the Nineteenth-Century South* (1995).

Ira Berlin, *Slaves without Masters* (1974).

John B. Boles, *The Great Revival, 1787–1805* (1972).

Dickson D. Bruce Jr., *And They All Sang Hallelujah* (1974).

Dickson D. Bruce Jr., *Violence and Culture in the Antebellum South* (1979).

Orville Vernon Burton, *In My Father's House Are Many Mansions: Family and Community in Edgefield, South Carolina* (1985).

Orville Vernon Burton and Robert C. McMath Jr., eds., *Class, Conflict, and Consensus: Antebellum Southern Community Studies* (1982).

Victoria Bynum, *Unruly Women: The Politics of Social and Sexual Control in the Old South* (1992).

Randolph B. Campbell and Richard G. Lowe, *Wealth and Power in Antebellum Texas* (1977).

Bruce Collins, *White Society in the Antebellum South* (1985).

Leonard P. Curry, *The Free Black in Urban America, 1800–1850* (1981).

Carl N. Degler, *The Other South* (1974).

Paul Escott, *Power and Privilege in North Carolina, 1850–1900* (1985).

James O. Farmer Jr., *The Metaphysical Confederacy: James Henley Thornwell and the Synthesis of Southern Values* (1986).

Drew G. Faust, *A Sacred Circle: The Dilemma of the Intellectual in the Old South* (1977).

Barbara J. Fields, *Slavery and Freedom on the Middle Ground: Maryland during the Nineteenth Century* (1985).

J. Wayne Flint, *Dixie's Forgotten People* (1979).

Walter J. Fraser et al., eds., *The Web of Southern Social Relations* (1985).

David R. Goldfield, *Urban Growth in the Age of Sectionalism: Virginia, 1774–1861* (1977).

David R. Goldfield, *Cotton Fields and Skyscrapers* (rev. ed., 1989).

Stephen Hahn, *The Roots of Southern Populism* (1983).

J. William Harris, *Plain Folk and Gentry in a Slave Society* (1985).

John C. Inscoe, *Mountain Masters, Slavery, and the Sectional Crisis in Western North Carolina* (1989).

Michael P. Johnson and James L. Roark, *Black Masters* (1984).

Robert C. Kenser, *Kinship and Neighborhood in a Southern Community: Orange County, North Carolina, 1849–1881* (1987).

Lawrence H. Larsen, *The Rise of the Urban South* (1985).

Suzanne Lebsock, *The Free Women of Petersburg* (1984).

Anne C. Loveland, *Southern Evangelicals and the Social Order, 1820–1860* (1980).

Donald G. Mathews, *Religion in the Old South* (1977).

John M. McCardell, *Idea of a Southern Nation* (1979).

Stephanie McCurry, *Masters of Small Worlds: Yeoman Households, Gender Relations, and the Political Culture of the Antebellum South Carolina Low Country* (1995).

Sally G. McMillen, *Motherhood in the Old South* (1990).

Grady McWhiney, *Cracker Culture* (1988).

Gary B. Mills, *The Forgotten People: Cane River's Creoles of Color* (1984).

Thomas D. Morris, *Southern Slavery and the Law, 1619–1860* (1996).

John Solomon Otto, *The Southern Frontiers, 1607–1860* (1989).

Loren Schweninger, *Black Property Owners in the South, 1790–1915* (1990).

Bertram Wyatt-Brown, *Southern Honor* (1982).

POLITICS AND POLITICAL CULTURE

Paul H. Bergeron, *Antebellum Politics in Tennessee* (1982).

William J. Cooper Jr., *The South and the Politics of Slavery, 1828–1856* (1978).

William J. Cooper Jr., *Liberty and Slavery: Southern Politics to 1860* (1983).

Lacy K. Ford Jr., *Origins of Southern Radicalism: The South Carolina Upcountry, 1800–1860* (1988).

William M. Freehling, *Prelude to Civil War: The Nullification Controversy in South Carolina, 1816–1836* (1966).

William M. Freehling, *The Road to Disunion* (1990).

Kenneth S. Greenberg, *Masters and Statesmen: The Political Culture of American Slavery* (1985).

Thomas E. Jeffrey, *State Parties and National Politics: North Carolina, 1815–1861* (1989).

Marc W. Kruman, *Parties and Politics in North Carolina, 1836–1865* (1983).

Robert E. May, *John A. Quitman* (1985).

Craig M. Simpson, *A Good Southerner: The Life of Henry A. Wise of Virginia* (1985).

J. Mills Thornton III, *Politics and Power in a Slave Society: Alabama, 1800–1860* (1978).

Peter Wallenstein, *From Slave South to New South: Public Policy in Nineteenth-Century Georgia* (1987).

Harry L. Watson, *Jacksonian Politics and Community Conflict: The Emergence of the Second Party System in Cumberland County, North Carolina* (1981).

Ralph A. Wooster, *The People in Power: Courthouse and Statehouse in the Lower South, 1850–1860* (1969).

Ralph A. Wooster, *Politicians, Planters, and Plain Folks: Courthouse and Statehouse in the Upper South, 1850–1860* (1975).

year in all. "There was absolutely nothing to excite ambition for education," Lincoln recollected. Abraham hungered for learning. He borrowed every book he could find and read voraciously. At nineteen, he took his first trip away from home. He and a friend were hired to build a flatboat, load it with local produce, and float it down the Ohio and Mississippi to New Orleans. Lincoln earned $24 on the trip and gave the money to his father. But even with Thomas's earnings as a carpenter, that was not enough to keep the family afloat.

In 1830, Thomas decided once again to start over. For $125, considerably less than he had paid for it, he sold the Indiana farm where he and his family had labored for fourteen years. With his twenty-one-year-old son straddling one of the oxen pulling the family's three wagons, they moved two hundred miles west to the Sangamon River in central Illinois. Abraham's sister Sarah did not accompany them; in 1828, a year after her marriage to a young Indiana farmer, she had died in childbirth. Once again the Lincolns built a log cabin and moved in; once again Abraham pitched in to make "sufficient of rails to fence ten acres of ground, [then] fenced and broke the ground, and raised a crop of sown corn upon it the same year." When the spring thaw came, Thomas Lincoln picked up stakes again and moved about thirty miles east to Coles County, Illinois. But this time his son Abraham did not go along. This time Abraham set out on his own, a "friendless, uneducated, penniless boy," he wrote later, who had "separated from his father."

In 1851, after Abraham Lincoln had become a prosperous lawyer and ambitious politician who had represented his district in the Illinois legislature and the United States House of Representatives, Thomas Lincoln lay dying on his Coles County farm. Lincoln ignored letters from his step-brother, John D. Johnston, asking him to write to his father. When Thomas died, Abraham did not attend the funeral. When Lincoln heard that Johnston planned to sell out and move to Missouri, Lincoln wrote him a stinging letter that spelled out shortcomings Lincoln may also have glimpsed in his father, Thomas:

> What can you do in Missouri, better than here? Is the land any richer? Can you there, any more than here, raise corn, & wheat & oats, without work? Will any body there, any more than here, do your work for you? If you intend to go to work, there is no better place than right where you are; if you do not intend to go to work, you can not get along any where. Squirming & crawling about from place to place can

ABRAHAM LINCOLN'S HAT
Abraham Lincoln wore this stovepipe hat, made of beaver pelt, during his years as president of the United States. Stovepipe hats were worn by established, respectable, middle-class men in the 1850s. Workingmen and farmers would have felt out of place wearing such a hat, except perhaps on special occasions like weddings or funerals. Growing up in Kentucky, Indiana, and Illinois, Lincoln may have seen stovepipe hats on the leading men of his community, but he probably never owned one until he became an aspiring Illinois lawyer and politician. Wearing such a hat was a mark that one had achieved a certain success in life, in Lincoln's case the enormous social distance he had traveled from his backwoods origins to the White House. But even as president he continued a backwoods practice he began as a young postmaster in New Salem, Illinois, using his hat as a place to store letters and papers. Lincoln's law partner, William Herndon, termed Lincoln's hat "an extraordinary receptacle [that] served as his desk and memorandum book." Smithsonian Institution.

do no good. You have raised no crop this year, and what you really want is to sell the land, get the money and spend it . . . . [The] truth is, you are destitute because you have *idled* away all your time . . . . *Go to work* is the only cure for your case.

With relentless effort, Abraham Lincoln rose to the White House in 1861 from that three-sided lean-to in the Indiana wilderness in 1816. Like Lincoln, millions of Americans believed that with work they could make something of themselves, whatever their origins. From their point of view, individuals like John D. Johnston who did not work—who were improvident, foolish, or waiting for somebody else to help them—had only themselves to blame if they did not succeed. Work was a prerequisite, not a guarantee. As Thomas Lincoln's experience illustrated, the difficulties and risks were great. But as Abraham Lincoln's career showed, the possibilities were enormous. Such calculations spurred mid-nineteenth-century Americans to efforts that shaped the economic, cultural, and political contours of Lincoln's America and pushed the boundaries of the nation to the Rio Grande in the Southwest and the shores of the Pacific Ocean in the Far West. That expansion—economic, political, and geographical—also raised anew the question of slavery, a question Lincoln ultimately confronted when he became commander in chief.

Economic and Industrial Evolution

In 1801, news that Thomas Jefferson had been elected president of the United States spread as fast as a man could ride on horseback. When Jefferson traveled the hundred miles to Washington from his home at Monticello in Virginia, he had to swim his horse across the five rivers that lacked a ferry. Sixty years later, when the electoral college confirmed Abraham Lincoln's election to the White House, the news raced almost instantaneously along telegraph lines that connected Washington to the far corners of the nation. Lincoln journeyed to Washington from his home in Springfield, Illinois, by railroad. When Jefferson became president, Springfield did not exist. In 1801, the geographical center of the U.S. population lay *east* of Washington, D.C. By 1861, the geographical center of the nation's population had moved more than five hundred miles west, near Chillicothe, Ohio. The changes that occurred between the elections of Jefferson and Lincoln—changes that happened mostly within Lincoln's lifetime—signaled the economic growth that transformed the nation into a bustling transcontinental colossus.

Economic Growth, 1800–1860: An Overview

In 1800, the United States faced daunting obstacles to economic growth. Unlike England—the world leader in mechanization, factory production, and steam power—the United States produced nearly all manufactured goods by hand in small shops or at home rather than by machines in factories. Wind, water, and muscle powered production, as they had

for centuries. Nearly all of the nation's 5 million people lived east of the Appalachian Mountains. Unbroken forest stretched from the Appalachians almost to the Mississippi River. Long-distance transportation was difficult, time-consuming, and unpredictable. Travelers from New York City could book better, more comfortable passage to London, England, than to Albany, New York.

Despite these obstacles to economic change, a profound economic transformation occurred during the first six decades of the nineteenth century. (Economic changes in the early nineteenth century are discussed in chapter 11.) By 1860, Americans' per capita income was twice what it had been in 1800. At first glance that does not seem impressive evidence of economic growth. But consider that during those same years the nation's population grew sixfold, to over 31 million. Therefore, the total output of the American economy multiplied twelve times in sixty years. Fundamental changes in American society fueled this phenomenal economic growth.

The changes that occurred between the elections of Jefferson and Lincoln—changes that happened mostly within Lincoln's lifetime—signaled the economic growth that transformed the nation into a bustling transcontinental colossus.

First, the American population began a long-term shift from farms to cities that would continue well into the twentieth century. As the nation's population grew, the number of rural Americans increased from about 5 million in 1800 to more than 25 million in 1860. Farmers still made up 80 percent of the nation's population in 1860. But like Abraham Lincoln, millions of Americans left the farm to make a life in the city. The fraction of Americans who lived in urban areas grew from 6 percent in 1800 to 20 percent in 1860. In 1800, the nation had only 7 cities roughly the size of Lincoln's hometown of Springfield, Illinois (9,500 people in 1860); by 1860, there were 186 such cities. Large cities also grew. In 1800, only Philadelphia had a population over 50,000; by 1860, there were 16 such cities. People in these large cities made up 10 percent of the nation's population in 1860, compared with only 1 percent in 1800.

A second major change, closely related to the shift of population from farms to cities, was that a growing number of Americans worked in factories. In 1800, only about 3 percent of American workers were engaged in manufacturing outside the home; by 1860, almost 20 percent of the labor force worked in factories. This trend made an important contribution to the nation's economic growth because, in general, factory workers were twice as productive (in output per unit of labor input) as agricultural workers.

A third fundamental change—a change in the source of energy—permitted factories to be brought to the labor force in cities. The first American factories had to be situated on streams that supplied water power, and workers had to be attracted to the factory site. But steam power freed business owners to locate their factories anywhere workers and materials could be readily brought together. Since manufacturers needed a steady supply of cheap labor, they tended to locate factories in cities and ship in the materials of production. Steam power had other important advantages over water power. It could be generated year-round regardless of the weather, and it could be produced in greater or lesser quantities as needed for the job at hand.

Beginning around 1840, steam became harnessed to manufacturing, but the transition was slow, delayed by the continued effectiveness of water-powered factories. By 1850, steam supplied just 10 percent of the total inanimate power used in manufacturing; animal and human muscles still provided 33 times more energy for manufacturing than steam. The trend toward steam accelerated during the 1850s. By 1860, for example, Massachusetts manufacturers used steam to produce most of their wood and metal products.

The shortage of cheap, plentiful fuel was the chief obstacle to earlier use of steam in factories. During the 1830s, extensive mining began in the Pennsylvania coal fields and massive quantities of coal became available for industrial fuel. Heat from coal not only powered steam engines in factories. It also permitted new methods of iron production and metalworking required for the full-scale mechanization of production. In addition, those methods made it possible to couple steam power to land transportation in the building of railroads.

This cascade of interrelated developments—steam, coal, iron, mechanization, railroads—had begun to transform the character of the American economy by the 1850s. Historians have often referred to this transformation as an industrial revolution.

Certainly the profound changes in the American economy between 1800 and 1860 pushed the nation toward industrialization. Yet those changes did not cause a revolutionary discontinuity in the economy or society during these years. The United States remained overwhelmingly agricultural. Old methods of production continued alongside the new. Changes in production tended to be evolutionary and cumulative. In the long term—by the early twentieth century—the consequences of these and other changes were indeed revolutionary. Between 1800 and 1860, however, the American economy underwent a process that might best be termed "industrial evolution."

That process was made possible by a fourth fundamental development that propelled American economic growth. Between 1800 and 1860, the declining fraction of the population engaged in agriculture managed to grow enough food to feed themselves and the growing population in cities. Clearly, agricultural productivity (defined as crop output per unit of labor input) increased. Economic historians estimate that agricultural productivity nearly doubled during the sixty-year period. This dramatic increase contributed more than any other single factor to the economic growth of Lincoln's America. While cities, factories, and steam engines blossomed throughout the nation—especially outside the South—the roots of American economic growth lay in agriculture.

Agriculture and Land Policy

It may seem odd to consider an ax a basic agricultural tool, like a hoe or shovel. Yet farmers in Lincoln's America needed axes. Lincoln wrote that he had "an axe put into his hands" when he was eight years old and he "was almost constantly handling that most useful instrument." A French traveler observed in 1831 that "country-dwelling Americans spend half their lives cutting trees, and their children learn . . . at an early age to use the axe against the trees, their enemies." Americans had "a general feeling of hatred against trees," the Frenchman reported. Although the traveler exaggerated, his observation contained an important truth. Forests impeded agriculture. With their "most useful instrument," farmers leveled trees, cleared land for planting, and built cabins, fences, and barns.

The sheer physical labor required to convert forest to field limited agricultural productivity. Energy that might have gone to growing crops went instead to felling trees. But as farmers like Thomas

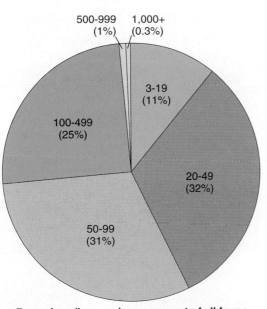

Farm sizes (in acres) as a percent of all farms

FIGURE 13.1
Farm Sizes in 1860
The United States was a nation of small farms; almost three out of four farms were under 100 acres. All but a few of the farms over 1,000 acres were located in the South.

Lincoln pushed the frontier of farming westward, they encountered thinner forests and eventually the Midwest's comparatively treeless prairie. Rich prairie soils produced somewhat higher crop yields than eastern farms, and farmers migrated to the Midwest by the tens of thousands between 1830 and 1860. The population of Indiana, Illinois, Michigan, Wisconsin, and Iowa exploded tenfold, growing from 500,000 in 1830 to more than 5 million by 1860, four times faster than the growth of the nation as a whole. During the 1850s, Illinois added more people than any other state in the Union. On the midwestern prairie, farmers could spend less time with an ax and more time at the plow or hoe. The diminished need for axes on midwestern farms significantly boosted agricultural productivity by markedly reducing the labor required to grow a bushel of corn or wheat.

Labor-saving improvements in other farm implements also hiked agricultural productivity. Abraham Lincoln pointed out that as a youngster he used his ax "less of course in plowing and harvesting seasons," when every farmer's labor needs peaked. Early in the nineteenth century, most farmers used

wooden plows, if they plowed at all. Frontier farmers commonly planted their first crop simply by dropping kernels of corn into holes chopped in the ground with an ax or a hoe. Wooden plows required strenuous efforts from the animals who pulled them and the farmers who guided them because they tended to stick to the soil rather than cut through it. They also broke easily. In 1819, Jethro Wood patented a plow that used replaceable cast-iron parts to cut and scour the soil. Wood's cast-iron plow required only half as much labor as a wooden plow, and farmers throughout the Northeast quickly adopted it or one of the many variations crafted by local blacksmiths.

But cast-iron plows proved too weak and sticky for the thick turf and dense soil of the midwestern prairie. In 1837, John Deere patented a strong, smooth steel plow that sliced through prairie soil so cleanly that farmers called it the "singing plow." Deere's steel plow underwent many improvements that made plowing less work, prairie farmers more productive, and Deere's company the leading plow manufacturer in the Midwest, turning out more than ten thousand plows a year by the late 1850s. Farmers, blacksmiths, and mechanics continually tinkered to make plows stronger, easier to use, and cheaper. In 1860 alone, the federal government issued 109 patents for plow improvements. By 1860, the energy for plowing still came from animal and human muscles, but better plows permitted that energy to break more ground and plant more crops.

Improvements in grain harvesting also multiplied farmers' productivity. Nearly all American farmers grew corn as a basic dietary staple for themselves and their animals. Corn pone, corn fritters, corn bread, corn mush, and other corn delicacies appeared on plates throughout rural America. Farmers harvested hundreds of millions of bushels of corn every year, all by hand. Labor-saving devices developed instead for the wheat harvest. Outside the South, most farmers planted wheat, and in the Midwest—where soil and climate conditions were nearly ideal—many planted mostly wheat. Wheat was more difficult than corn to grow and harvest, but it was also more desirable. More dense and less bulky than corn, wheat was more readily transported to market and sold for a much higher price.

The crucial point in wheat production came at harvest time. Once ripe, wheat had to be cut quickly before rain or wind ruined the crop or overripe grains dropped from the stalk and scattered uselessly on the ground. Early in the nineteenth century, farmers harvested wheat by cutting the stalks

HARVESTING GRAIN WITH CRADLES

This late-nineteenth-century painting shows the grain harvest during the mid-nineteenth century at Bishop Hill, Illinois, a Swedish community where the artist, Olof Krans, and his parents settled in 1850. The men swing cradles, slowly cutting a swath through the grain; the women gather the cut grain into sheaves to be hauled away later for threshing. As a well-organized community, Bishop Hill could call upon the labor of a large number of men and women at harvest time. Most farmers had only a few family members and a hired hand or two to help with the harvest. Note that although the grain field appears level enough to be ideal for a mechanical reaper, all the work is done by hand; no machine is in sight.

Bishop Hill State Historic Site, Illinois Historic Preservation Agency.

with a sharp-bladed scythe. Working hard, a farmer could scythe three-fourths of an acre of wheat a day. By 1850, most farmers had adopted scythes with cradles (a frame that projected above the scythe). Their long wooden fingers were able to gather more grain stalks to be cut by each stroke of the attached blade. A cradle allowed a farmer to harvest two or three acres of wheat a day—a considerable advance over the old-fashioned scythe—but it was heavy, backbreaking work.

Tinkerers throughout the nation tried to fashion a mechanical reaper that would make the wheat harvest easier and quicker. In 1830, Cyrus McCormick cobbled together a prototype reaper that indicated both the possibilities and the problems.

McCormick and others experimented with designs, parts, and methods of manufacturing until the late 1840s, when more than a few mechanical reapers were at work in American wheat fields. McCormick went from farm to farm touting his reaper, trying to talk farmers into buying one for $100 to $150. A mechanical reaper allowed a farmer to harvest twelve acres a day, at least when it worked. As design and manufacturing improved, reapers became more reliable and more readily repaired, and thousands of farmers decided to buy them. By 1860, about 80,000 reapers had been sold, making it possible for the new owners to harvest three or four times more wheat than with a cradle. Although reapers represented the cutting edge of agricultural technology, they still had to be powered by the muscles of a horse or an ox. Most farmers had not yet shifted their wheat harvest to animal power, so they continued to muscle the heavy cradle through their grain.

Mechanical reapers and better plows permitted farmers to produce more corn or wheat only because the labor farmers saved could be used to plow and plant more land. Neither the reapers nor the plows increased the yield of a given acre of cultivated land. Instead, they allowed more land to be brought into cultivation. Without access to fresh, uncultivated land, farmers could not have doubled the corn and wheat harvests between 1840 and 1860, as they in fact did. In the end, the agricultural productivity that fueled the nation's economy was an outgrowth of federal land policy.

From 1800 to 1860, the United States continued to be land rich and labor poor. During these years the nation became a great deal richer in land, acquiring more than a billion acres with the Louisiana Purchase and the annexation of Florida, Oregon, and vast territories following the Mexican War (discussed later in this chapter). The federal government made the land available for purchase to attract settlers and to generate revenues.

In 1800, federal land cost $2 an acre and a buyer was required to purchase at least 320 acres (half a square mile). Over the next six decades, the price of federal land dropped and the size of the minimum purchase shrank, bringing more land within reach of more farmers more readily. From 1820 to 1854, federal land cost $1.25 an acre. The minimum purchase shrank to 160 acres in 1804, to 80 acres in 1820, and to 40 acres in 1832.

Despite these reductions in price and minimum purchase requirements, millions of farmers could not afford federal land. Like Thomas Lincoln, they squatted on unclaimed federal land and carved out a farm they neither rented nor owned. These squatters sought the right (called "preemption") to buy the land they had made into a farm before the government sold it to some other buyer. In 1830, Congress passed a law guaranteeing such preemption and renewed the law until it became permanent in 1841. Although many poor farmers never accumulated enough money to purchase the land on which they squatted, they still benefited from the preemption laws. Poor squatters often sold their preemption right to somebody else who, in effect, paid them for the labor they had invested in clearing land and building a farm. That person could then exercise the squatters' right of preemption and purchase the land at the government price while the squatters moved elsewhere, often to unclaimed federal land where they renewed the cycle of squatting and preemption.

Government land policy not only aided small farmers. It also enriched wily speculators who found ways to claim large tracts of the most desirable plots and sell them to settlers at a generous markup. Nonetheless, by making land available to millions of ordinary people, the federal government achieved the goal of attracting settlers to the new territories, which in due course joined the Union as new states. Above all, federal land policy created the basic precondition for the increase in agricultural productivity that underlay the nation's impressive economic growth.

Manufacturing and Mechanization

Changes in manufacturing arose in the context of the nation's land-rich, labor-poor economy. Manufacturers in England and other European countries worked in land-poor, labor-rich economies; there, meager opportunities in agriculture kept factory laborers plentiful and wages low. In the United States, geographical expansion and government land policies buoyed agriculture, keeping millions of people on the farm and thereby limiting the supply of workers for manufacturing and elevating wages. Because of this shortage of workers, manufacturers searched constantly for ways to save labor. Mechanization offered the best prospects. But it was easier to say "mechanize" than it was actually to build a machine to do a task previously done by human hands—and to do it better, faster, cheaper, and with tireless repetition.

Because of the shortage of workers, manufacturers searched constantly for ways to save labor. Mechanization offered the best prospects.

Consider the seemingly simple process of making axes. The ax market was a manufacturer's dream since Americans needed as many axes as they could get. In the early 1830s, however, each ax still had to be crafted by a skilled metalworker who welded a steel bit (the cutting edge) to a cast-iron poll (the head), pounded the metal into a wedge shape, made a hole for the handle, and then heated, hammered, ground, and polished the ax until it was ready to be sold. Between 1836 and 1849, Elisha K. Root, a machinist who worked at the Collins ax factory in Connecticut, invented a series of sophisticated machines that carried out these steps more quickly, safely, and cheaply and that did not require skilled operators. Root's machines allowed fewer workers with less skill to turn out twenty-five times as many axes as skilled craftsmen, and the machine-made axes were of better quality.

Manufacturers had such a strong incentive to save labor that mechanization marched forward as quickly as innovative ideas like Root's could be fashioned into workable combinations of gears, levers, screws, and pulleys. Outside the textile industry (see chapter 11), homegrown machines set the pace. Early in the nineteenth century, the manufacture of firearms was mechanized, led by gun makers at the federal armories who had to keep the army supplied with rifles and pistols. The desire to make each gun as much as possible like every other encouraged gun makers to devise uniform parts that could be interchanged from one gun to another. Although the parts often were not uniform enough to be literally interchangeable, with some filing here and jimmying there they were close enough to establish the principle of interchangeable parts as a distinctive feature of American manufacturing. The practice of manufacturing and then assembling interchangeable parts spread from industry to industry and became known as the "American system." Clock makers used it; sewing machine makers used it; even ax makers used it.

Mechanization became so integral to American manufacturing by the 1830s that some machinists specialized in what came to be called the machine tool industry. That is, they built machines that made parts for other machines that, in turn, produced goods for general consumption. Nothing better illustrated the transformation in American manufacturing than this mechanization of machine making.

New England led the nation in manufacturing. Manufacturing and agriculture meshed into a dynamic national economy. New England products like clocks, guns, and axes were shipped west and south, while commodities like wheat, pork, whiskey, tobacco, and cotton flowed north and east. Manufacturers specialized in producing for the gigantic domestic market rather than for export. British goods dominated the international market and, on the whole, they were cheaper and better than American-made products. U.S. manufacturers, however, supported tariffs to minimize British competition. But their best protection from British competitors

was to be more sensitive to, more responsive to, and more eager to please their American customers, the vast majority of whom were farmers. From their side, farmers were only too happy to buy manufactured goods, if they were affordable and especially if they saved labor that could be redirected to plow more furrows and plant more seeds.

Manufacturers not only produced old things like axes in new ways; they also built entirely new labor-saving devices, like mechanical reapers and sewing machines. Both reapers and sewing machines promised far-reaching social and economic changes, the former in the field, the latter by the fireside. But neither machine began to be manufactured in considerable numbers until the 1850s. Through 1855, Cyrus McCormick had built a total of only 12,000 reapers, and the Singer Sewing Machine Company had produced just 2,500 machines. During the last half of the decade, production and sales accelerated; McCormick turned out 22,000 reapers and Singer built 33,000 sewing machines. The machines, however, had barely made a dent in the traditional methods of hand reaping and hand sewing that prevailed on most farms and in most households in 1860.

Throughout American manufacturing, hand labor continued to be an essential component of production, despite the advances in mechanization. Even in heavily mechanized industries, factories remained fairly small, few having more than twenty or thirty employees. A measure of the distinctive character of manufacturing in this predominantly agricultural economy is that by 1860 iron manufacturing—so important in virtually all phases of mechanization—was only the sixth largest industry (in value), following cotton goods, lumber, boots and shoes, flour and meal, and men's clothing, in that order. The industrial evolution under way from 1800 to 1860 would quicken later in the nineteenth century; railroads were a harbinger of that future.

Railroads: Breaking the Bonds of Nature

To a degree unequaled by any other industry, railroads incorporated the most advanced developments of the age: steam energy; massive, powerful, complicated locomotives; mile after mile of iron rails ribboned across plains, through valleys, up hills, over passes; boldly engineered bridges that vaulted rivers and chasms; unprecedented sums of money to undertake these tasks; and large, complex organizations to keep the trains running efficiently,

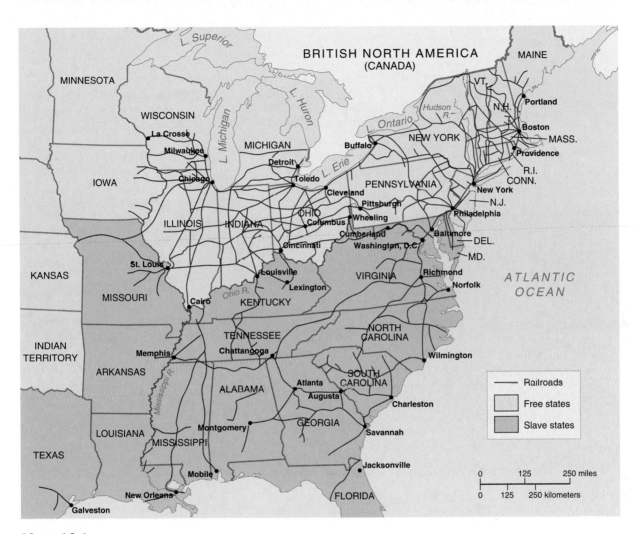

M A P 13.1
Railroads in 1860
Railroads were a crucial component of the revolutions in transportation and communications that transformed nineteenth-century America. The railroad system reflected the differences that had developed in the economies of the North and South.

safely, and on time. No wonder a Swedish visitor in 1849 noticed that American schoolboys constantly doodled sketches of locomotives, always smoking, always in motion.

Railroads captured Americans' imaginations in part because they seemed to break the bonds of nature. When canals and rivers froze in winter or became impassable during summer droughts, trains steamed ahead. When becalmed sailing ships went nowhere, locomotives kept on chugging. Heavy barges cruised along canals at two or three miles an hour, the pace of the mules that pulled them; horse-

drawn stagecoaches could go a bit faster; but steam-powered trains left both in the dust, averaging over twenty miles an hour during the 1850s. Above all, railroads offered cities not blessed with canals or navigable rivers a way to compete for the trade of the countryside. A railroad was akin to a river of iron designed not by the ancient geological whims of nature but by the contemporary commercial desires of human beings.

On July 4, 1828, Charles Carroll, the last surviving signer of the Declaration of Independence, broke ground for the Baltimore and Ohio Railroad.

RAILROAD TRAVEL

In addition to carrying people and goods more quickly and reliably than ever before, railroads also brought many Americans face to face for the first time with machinery that was much larger and more powerful than any human being. (Compare, for example, the locomotives in this painting with the handtools in the illustration on page 470.) This painting of a train leaving Rochester, New York, in 1852 contrasts the size and power of human beings and machines. The huge, lovingly portrayed, steam-belching locomotive is barely held back by some unseen brake against which the massive engine strains, ready to pull the long train through the columns of the station, out of the past and into the future. The people, in contrast, appear indistinct, passive, and dependent. They are waiting for the train rather than vice versa. Except for the two women and child in the foreground, the people face backward, and all of them avoid looking directly at the locomotive. The painting evokes the way the almost incomprehensible power of the railroads dwarfed human effort.

Rochester Historical Society.

Baltimore merchants and bankers feared that without the B&O, they would lose access to western commerce that would drain down the Ohio and Mississippi Rivers to New Orleans or float from the Great Lakes to the Hudson River along the recently completed Erie Canal. By connecting Baltimore to the Ohio River, the B&O promised to short-circuit western trade away from New Orleans, Philadelphia, and New York. Building the roadbed and laying track went slowly; by 1830, the B&O had 13 miles of track; by 1834, it had 84 miles; by 1842, the route consisted of 125 miles; and finally, by 1852, the 379 miles that connected Baltimore to Ohio were completed.

Despite the slow pace of construction, the B&O motivated leading citizens in other American cities to undertake railroad projects to bring western commerce to their own shops, markets, and wharves. In 1830, the entire nation had fewer than 100 miles of railroad track. By 1850, trains steamed along 9,000 miles of track, almost two-thirds of it in New England and the Middle Atlantic states. During the 1850s, construction exploded, especially in the Midwest. In 1856 alone, construction gangs laid more than 3,600 miles of new track. By 1860, several railroads had crossed the Mississippi River to link frontier farmers to the nation's 30,000 miles of track, approximately as much as all the rest of the world combined. (In 1857, for example, France had 3,700 miles of track; England and Wales had a total of 6,400 miles.) Chicago stood at the hub of eleven railroads, including the Illinois Central, the longest railroad in the world.

By 1860, the visions of railroad promoters that had once seemed fantastic had become commonplace realities. In 1800, a traveler needed six weeks to get from New York City to Chicago; in 1860, the trip by railroad took two days. By 1860, the volume of freight carried on railroads surpassed that shipped by canals, and railroads emerged as the iron skeleton of the nation's economy. The massive expansion of railroads in Lincoln's America helped the United States catapult into position as the world's second leading industrial power, behind Great Britain.

In addition to speeding transportation, railroads also fostered the growth of other industries. Locomotive manufacturers hardly existed in 1830, but by the 1850s they annually produced about 500 of the twenty-five-ton behemoths; by 1860, some 8,500 locomotives were in operation. Iron production grew five times faster than the population during the decades up to 1860, in part to meet the demand for rails, wheels, axles, and locomotives. Likewise, coal production more than doubled during the 1850s to provide fuel for iron furnaces and locomotive boilers. Heavy, gravity-defying iron bridges were built to carry trains across rivers; a spectacular example completed in 1855 was the suspension bridge across the Niagara River designed and built by John Roebling.

Railroads also stimulated the fledgling telegraph industry. In 1844, Samuel F. B. Morse persuasively demonstrated the potential of his telegraph by transmitting a series of dots and dashes that instantly conveyed an electronic message along forty miles of wire between Washington and Balti-

more. By 1852, more than 23,000 miles of telegraph wire hummed with messages while construction crews strung out more. By 1861, in excess of 50,000 miles of wire stretched across the continent to the Pacific. Many telegraph lines were strung alongside railroad tracks, and railroad managers soon discovered the advantages of instantaneous communication. Most railroads consisted of only one set of tracks, so careful scheduling was required to avoid disastrous head-on collisions. Telegraph messages permitted railroad managers to speed trains on their way when a track was clear and hold them when it was not. By 1860, nearly every railroad station had a clattering telegraph.

Almost all railroads were built and owned by private corporations rather than by local, state, or federal governments. In contrast, three-fourths of the total capital invested in canals by 1860 had come from government sources. By selling stocks and bonds, railroad companies had attracted well over a billion dollars in investments by 1860, more than five times the total capital invested in canals. Undergirding these private investments was massive government aid, especially federal land grants. Up to 1850, the federal government had granted a total of seven million acres of federal land to various turnpike, highway, and canal projects. In that year, Illinois senator Stephen A. Douglas obtained congressional approval for a precedent-setting grant of federal land to railroads, including the Illinois Central. The 1850 law provided a grant of six square miles of federal land for each mile of track constructed. Railroad companies quickly lined up congressional support for other lucrative land deals. By 1860, Congress had granted railroads more than twenty million acres of federal lands, establishing a generous policy that would last for decades.

The railroad boom of the 1850s was a signal of the growing industrial might of the American economy. But railroads, like other industries, succeeded because they served farms as well as cities. Passengers and freight routinely sped along tracks by 1860. But the continued significance of more traditional forms of transportation is suggested by the operation of the federal postal system, which reached into virtually every village and hamlet. By 1857, trains carried about one-third of the mail; most of the rest still went by stagecoach or horseback. In 1860, most Americans were still far more familiar with horses than with iron horses.

The economy of Lincoln's America linked axes, muscles, animals, and farms to machines, steam, railroads, and cities. Abraham Lincoln split rails as a young man and defended railroad corporations as a successful attorney. His legendary upward mobility illustrated the direction of economic change and the opportunities that change offered to enterprising individuals.

Free Labor: Promise and Reality

The impressive performance of the antebellum economy did not reward all Americans equally. Some, like Abraham Lincoln, moved far beyond their roots on hardscrabble farms to success in law, medicine, the ministry, journalism, or politics. A few, like Cyrus McCormick, became fabulously wealthy manufacturers or financiers. Many others strove to make a decent living as farmers, tradesmen, or laborers. While many prospered, many others barely kept their heads above water, and still others sank. With few exceptions, women were excluded from the opportunities open to men. Although tens of thousands of women worked as seamstresses, laundresses, domestic servants, factory hands, and teachers, both men and women tended to think of the economy of Lincoln's America as a man's world, and in particular a white man's world. Outside the South, slavery was slowly eliminated in the half century after the American Revolution, but free African Americans in the North found themselves relegated, on the whole, to dead-end jobs as laborers and servants. This discrimination against women and free blacks did not trouble most white men; with certain notable exceptions, they considered it proper and just. Instead, the varied experiences of white men—the presence of poverty in the midst of prosperity, of failure alongside success, of the bust that seemed to follow every boom—caught the attention of influential spokesmen.

The Free-Labor Ideal: Freedom plus Labor

During the decades before the Civil War, leaders throughout the North emphasized a set of ideas that seemed to explain why the changes under way in their society benefited some more than others. They referred again and again to the advantages of what they termed "free labor." (The word "free" referred to laborers who were not slaves; it did not mean laborers who worked for nothing.) By the 1850s, "free labor" identified the basic character of the economy and society taking shape in the North. Free-labor ideas contrasted northern society with the South, whose slave economy also prospered during these years. Free-labor ideas proposed a social and economic ideal that accounted for both the successes and the shortcomings of northern society.

Free-labor spokesmen celebrated hard work, self-reliance, and independence. They proclaimed that the door to success was open not just to those who inherited wealth or status but also to self-made men like Abraham Lincoln. Lincoln himself declared, "Free labor—the just and generous, and prosperous system, which opens the way for all—gives hope to all, and energy, and progress, and improvement of condition to all." Most Americans, Lincoln explained, were "men, with their families—wives, sons and daughters—[who] work for themselves, on their farms, in their houses and in their shops, taking the whole product to themselves." The free-labor system permitted these independent producers to reap what they sowed, to keep the products of their own labor. The free-labor system also benefited individuals who worked for wages, Lincoln and others pointed out. Unlike slaves, wage laborers were not fixed in perpetual bondage. Also unlike slaves, they received a wage that compensated them for their labor.

By the 1850s, "free labor" identified the basic character of the economy and society taking shape in the North.

Ultimately, the free-labor system made it possible for hired laborers to become independent property owners, proponents argued. A laborer worked for wages only temporarily. "The prudent, penniless beginner in the world," Lincoln asserted, "labors for wages awhile, saves a surplus with which to buy tools or land, for himself; then labors on his own account another while, and at length hires another new beginner to help him." Wage labor was the first rung on the ladder that reached upward toward self-employment and, eventually, to hiring others. Lincoln acknowledged that some laborers did not manage to climb the ladder of success. "If any continue through life in the condition of the hired laborer, it is not the fault of the system [of free labor]," he said, "but because of either a dependent nature which prefers it, or improvidence, folly, or singular misfortune."

A YOUNG MECHANIC
This 1848 painting shows a young boy, a mechanic or
tradesman, sitting behind the counter of a cluttered and
worn woodworking shop. The painting hints that the young
boy is an apprentice or perhaps the son of the mechanic
who owns the shop. The better-dressed boys on the opposite
side of the counter appear to be talking with the young
mechanic about whittling a new mast for their toy boat.
The barefoot young girl in the foreground appears to be the
sister of the young mechanic; her attention is focused on
the customers. The painting evokes the physical setting of
a none-too-prosperous tradesman's workshop and the social
differences that separated an open-faced young artisan and
his better-off, shadowed customers. The image suggests that
such routine encounters of the free-labor system were so
commonplace that children reenacted them in play.
Los Angeles County Museum of Art, Gift of the American Art
Council and Mr. and Mrs. J. Douglas Pardee.

The free-labor ideal affirmed an egalitarian vision of human potential. Lincoln and other spokesmen stressed the importance of universal education
to permit "heads and hands . . . [to] cooperate as
friends." Throughout the North, communities supported public schools to make the rudiments of
learning available to young children. By 1860, many
cities and towns boasted that up to 80 percent of
children aged seven to thirteen attended school, at

least for a few days each year. In rural areas, where
the labor of children was more difficult to spare,
schools typically enrolled no more than half the
school-age children. Lessons included not just arithmetic, penmanship, and a smattering of other subjects. Textbooks and teachers—most of whom were
young women—drummed into students the
virtues of the free-labor system: self-reliance, discipline, and above all hard work. "Remember that all
the ignorance, degradation, and misery in the world
is the result of indolence and vice," one textbook intoned. Free-labor ideology, whether in school or out,
emphasized labor as much as freedom.

Economic Inequality

The free-labor ideal made sense to many Americans,
especially in the North, because it seemed to describe their own experience. Lincoln frequently referred to his humble beginnings as a hired laborer
and silently invited his listeners to consider how far
he had come. In 1860, his wealth of $17,000 easily
placed him in the top 5 percent of the population.
The opportunities presented by the expanding
economy made a few men much, much richer. In
1860, the nation had about forty millionaires, including Cyrus McCormick, whose wealth exceeded
$2 million. Most Americans, however, measured
success in far more modest terms. The average
wealth (defined as real and personal property) of
adult white men in the North in 1860 barely topped
$2,000. Only about a quarter of American men pos-
sessed that much. Nearly one-half had no wealth at
all; almost 60 percent owned no land. It is difficult
to estimate the wealth of adult white women since
property possessed by married women was normally considered to belong to their husbands, but
certainly women had less wealth than men. Free
African Americans had still less; 90 percent were
propertyless.

Free-labor spokesmen considered these economic inequalities a natural outgrowth of freedom,
the inevitable result of some individuals being more
able, more willing to work, and luckier. These
inequalities suggest, however, the gap between the
promise and the performance of the free-labor ideal
in Lincoln's America. Thomas Lincoln, who had become a landowner by the time he died, was far more
characteristic of the free-labor system than his more
famous son. By 1860, a majority of American men
had yet to obtain their own land and match Thomas
Lincoln's achievement. The economic growth of
Lincoln's America permitted many men to move

from landless squatters to landowning farmers and from hired laborers to independent, self-employed producers. But many more Americans remained behind, landless and working for wages. The expanding economy, especially the availability of federal land, kept alive the aspirations at the heart of the free labor ideal. By 1860, however, those aspirations were much more widespread than the achievements promised by free-labor proponents. Even most of those who had realized their aspirations had a precarious hold on their independence; bad debts, crop failure, sickness, or death could quickly eliminate a family's gains.

Since the free-labor ideal pointed to individuals as the source of both success and failure, many Americans felt anxious about their prospects. The ambition and striving that led to high achievements could also engender a gnawing dissatisfaction with one's place in life. Seeking out new opportunities in pursuit of free-labor ideals created restless geographic mobility. Commonly up to two-thirds of the residents of a rural area moved every decade, and the population turnover in cities was even greater. Such constant coming and going weakened community ties to neighbors and friends and threw individuals even more upon their own resources for help in times of trouble. The stress on individual achievement encouraged personal introspection that often turned into intense self-doubt. The social and geographic mobility the free-labor system fostered permitted many, like Abraham Lincoln, to become quite different persons from what they had been. But such individuals, including Lincoln, sometimes suffered from a lack of confidence that they had genuinely transformed themselves. Lincoln managed to get out of the log cabin he grew up in; but that log cabin—with its economic insecurities, educational deficiencies, an illiterate mother, and a semiliterate father—remained with him, reminding him how far he had come and how few had come so far.

Immigrants and the Free-Labor Ladder

The risks and uncertainties of free labor did not deter millions of immigrants from entering the United States, especially during the 1840s and 1850s. Almost four and a half million immigrants arrived between 1840 and 1860, six times more than had come during the previous two decades. The half million immigrants who came in 1854 accounted for nearly 2 percent of the entire population, a higher proportion than in any other single year of the nation's history. By 1860, foreign-born residents made up about one-eighth of the American population, a fraction that held steady well into the twentieth century.

Nearly three out of four of the immigrants who arrived between 1840 and 1860 came from either Germany or Ireland. The vast majority of the 1.4 million Germans who entered the United States during these years were skilled tradesmen and their families. They left Germany to escape deteriorating economic conditions and to seize opportunities offered by the expanding economy of Lincoln's America, where skilled artisans had little difficulty finding work. German butchers, bakers, beer makers, carpenters, shopkeepers, machinists, and others tended to congregate in cities, particularly in the Midwest. In St. Louis, Cincinnati, and Milwaukee, German immigrants made up as much as one-third of the population; Chicago, Cleveland, Detroit, and other cities had almost as many. Roughly a quarter of German immigrants were farmers, most of whom scattered throughout the Midwest, although some settled in Texas. German immigrants did not have a common religion; some were Protestants, others Catholics, and others Jews. They did, however, share the German language and cultural roots in the Old World. That ethnic heritage spawned dozens of Little Germanies, urban neighborhoods with a distinctly middle European flavor where, for example, families relaxed in beer gardens and sang or listened to band music, even on Sundays. On the whole, German Americans settled into that middle stratum of sturdy independent producers celebrated by free-labor spokesmen; relatively few Germans occupied the bottom rung of the free-labor ladder as wage laborers or domestic servants.

Irish immigrants, in contrast, entered at the bottom of the free-labor ladder and had difficulty climbing up. Nearly 1.7 million Irish immigrants arrived between 1840 and 1860, nearly all of them desperately poor and often weakened by hunger and disease. Potato blight struck Ireland in 1845 and returned repeatedly in subsequent years, spreading a catastrophic famine throughout the island. Millions of poor farmers and hired hands depended on potatoes as their principal source of food. When the blight ruined the potatoes, tens of thousands literally starved to death; hundreds of thousands fell sick and died. The lucky ones, half-starved,

EVICTION OF IRISH TENANT
An Irish tenant (the seated man with crossed arms) and his family (two barefoot boys are shown) are evicted; their few pieces of furniture have been piled outside the cottage. The landlord or his agent (the man near the doorway) has brought four armed police to force the tenant to leave. Evictions like this were common in Ireland in the mid-nineteenth century, an example of the poverty and human suffering that pushed many Irish immigrants to the United States.
Lawrence Collection, National Library of Ireland.

crowded into the holds of ships and set out for America. As one immigrant group declared, "All we want is to get out of Ireland; we must be better anywhere than here." Death trailed after them. So many died crossing the Atlantic that ships from Ireland were often termed "coffin ships." Many more died soon after arrival. But enough survived to make the Irish the largest single immigrant group in Lincoln's America.

Roughly three out of four Irish immigrants worked as laborers or domestic servants. Irish men dug canals, loaded ships, built railroad tracks, and took what other work they could find. Irish women hired out to cook, wash and iron, mind children, and clean house. Slaveholders often preferred to hire Irish laborers for heavy, dangerous jobs rather than risk injury to their valuable slaves. Most Irish immigrants, however, congregated in cities. By 1860, Irish immigrants made up one-fourth of the population of Boston and New York City and almost one-fifth of Pittsburgh, St. Louis, and Chicago. Almost all Irish immigrants were Catholics, a fact that set them apart from the overwhelmingly Protestant native-born residents. Many natives regarded the Irish as hard-drinking, obstreperous, half-civilized folk. Such views lay behind the discrimination that often excluded Irish immigrants from better jobs; job announcements commonly stated, "No Irish need apply." Despite these preju-

dices, native residents hired Irish immigrants because they accepted low pay and worked hard.

In the labor-poor economy of Lincoln's America, Irish laborers could earn in one day wages that would require several weeks' work in Ireland, if work could be found there. In America, one immigrant explained in 1853, there was "plenty of work and plenty of wages plenty to eat and no land lords thats enough what more does a man want." But some immigrants wanted more, especially respect and decent working conditions. One immigrant recalled that Irish laborers were thought of as "nothing . . . more than dogs . . . despised and kicked about." Another immigrant who dug cellars prayed, "May heaven save me from ever again being compelled to labour so severely . . . driven like horses . . . a slave for the Americans as the generality of the Irish . . . are."

Such testimony illustrates that the realities of the free-labor system, whether for immigrants or native-born laborers, often did not match the optimistic vision outlined by Abraham Lincoln and others. If wage laborers could not realistically aspire to become independent, self-sufficient property holders—if wage laborers became a permanent rather than a temporary working class—what would become of the free-labor ideal? By 1860, a few workingmen asked such questions, but the continuing economic expansion muted their voices.

Reforming Self and Society

The emphasis on self-discipline and individual effort at the core of the free-labor ideal pervaded Lincoln's America. Many Americans believed that insufficient self-control caused the most important social problems of the era. Evangelical Protestants struggled to control individuals' propensity to sin, and temperance advocates exhorted drinkers to control their urge for alcohol. In the midst of the worldly disruptions of geographic expansion and economic change, evangelicals brought more Americans than ever before into churches. Historians estimate that church members accounted for about one-third of the American population by midcentury. Most Americans remained outside churches, as did Abraham Lincoln. But the influence of evangelical religion reached far beyond those who belonged to churches.

Church members' zeal and organization gave them considerable power. In 1851, for example, they helped push a law through the Maine legislature to prohibit the sale or manufacture of alcoholic beverages. Within four years, thirteen other states had enacted what were known as Maine laws; New England, New York, and parts of the Midwest were officially dry. In part, the Maine laws targeted the habits of German and Irish immigrants, who enjoyed tipping a glass, even on Sundays. Although the prohibition laws were eventually repealed, they illustrated the ability of the vocal evangelical minority to define propriety and Americanism. The evangelical temperament—a conviction of righteousness coupled with energy, self-discipline, and faith that the world could be improved—animated most reformers to one degree or another.

The emphasis on self-discipline and individual effort at the core of the free-labor ideal pervaded Lincoln's America.

A few activists pointed out that certain fundamental injustices lay beyond the reach of self-control. Transcendentalists and utopians believed that perfection could be attained only by rejecting the values of the larger society. Women's rights activists and abolitionists sought to reverse the subordination of women and to eliminate the enslavement of blacks by changing society. They confronted the daunting challenge of repudiating widespread assumptions about male supremacy and white supremacy and somehow subverting the entrenched institutions that reinforced those assumptions: the family and slavery.

The Pursuit of Perfection: Transcendentalists and Utopians

A group of New England writers that came to be known as transcendentalists believed that individuals should not conform to the competitive, materialistic world or to some abstract notion of religion. Instead, people should look within themselves for truth and guidance. In 1836, the leading transcendentalist, Ralph Waldo Emerson—an essayist, poet, and lecturer—proclaimed that "man has access to the entire mind of the Creator, [and] is himself the creator in the finite. This view . . . animates me to create my own world through the purification of my soul." Emerson and other transcendentalists, such as the writers Henry David Thoreau and Margaret Fuller, had supreme confidence in the powers of individual human beings to know God. Emerson declared that "the currents of the Universal Being circulate through me; I am part or particle of God." Through introspection, each person could communicate with the divine order and conduct himself or herself accordingly. Most Americans failed to lift their eyes from the mundane task of making a living. "We hear . . . too much of the results of machinery, commerce, and the useful arts," Emerson wrote. "Avarice, hesitation, and following are our diseases." The remedy for these diseases, transcendentalists believed, was not to join a reform society, or circulate petitions, or even to vote. "Every thing that tends to insulate the individual . . . tends to true . . . greatness," Emerson proclaimed. The power of the solitary individual was nearly limitless. Emerson explained that "if the single man plant himself indomitably on his instincts, and there abide, the huge world will come round to him."

Transcendentalists influenced many writers in the northern states, but they had a limited appeal to the broader society. Emerson gave lectures throughout the North during the 1840s and 1850s, spreading the infectious gospel of self-reliance more than the abstruse doctrines of transcendentalism, which novelist Herman Melville ridiculed as "oracular gibberish." In many ways, transcendentalism represented less an alternative to the values of mainstream society than an exaggerated form of the rampant individualism of the age. Melville called it "self-conceit."

Unlike transcendentalists, a few reformers tried to change the world by organizing utopian communities. Although these communities never involved more than a few thousand people, their activities demonstrated both their dissatisfactions with the larger society and their efforts to realize their visions of perfection. Like their members, the utopian communities varied considerably.

Some communities functioned essentially as retreats for those who did not want to sever their ties with the larger society. Reformers active in the peace, women's rights, antislavery, educational, and temperance movements founded Hopedale in 1842 in Milford, Massachusetts. They used the community as a home base from which they frequently traveled to spread their reform messages. Brook Farm, organized in 1841 in West Roxbury, Massachusetts, provided a haven for individual development apart from the constraints of conventional society. Brook Farm attracted literary and artistic New Englanders who agreed to balance bookish pursuits with manual labor; novelists and essayists often weeded the garden while others read poetry to them. Emerson, who declined to join, described Brook Farm as "a perpetual picnic." Despite their attractions, both Brook Farm and Hopedale had financial difficulties and collapsed within a few years.

Other communities set out to become models of perfection that they hoped would ultimately point the way toward a better life for everyone. During the 1840s, more than two dozen communities—principally in New York, New Jersey, Pennsylvania, and Ohio—organized around the ideas of Charles Fourier, a French critic of contemporary society. Members of these Fourierist communities (or phalanxes, as they were called) believed that individualism and competition were evils that denied the basic truth that "men . . . are brothers and not competitors." Fourierist phalanxes tried to replace competition with harmonious cooperation based on communal ownership of property through a system of shareholding by individual members. In addition, members were supposed to work not because they had to but because their work was satisfying and fulfilling. One former member complained that in his phalanx "there was plenty of discussion, and an abundance of variety, which is called the spice of life. This spice however constituted the greater part of the fare, as we sometimes had scarely anything to eat." Such complaints signaled the failure of the Fourierist communities to achieve their ambitious goals. Few of the phalanxes survived more than two or three years.

MARY CRAGIN, ONEIDA WOMAN
Mary Cragin, one of the founding members of the Oneida community, had a passionate sexual relationship with John Humphrey Noyes even before the community was organized. Within the bounds of complex marriage as practiced by the Oneidans, Cragin's magnetic sexuality made her a favorite partner of many men. In her journal Cragin confessed that "every evil passion was very strong in me from my childhood, sexual desire, love of dress and admiration, deceit, anger, pride." Oneida, however, transformed evil passion to holy piety. Cragin wrote, "In view of [God's] goodness to me and of his desire that I should let him fill me with himself, I yield and offer myself, to be penetrated by his spirit, and desire that love and gratitude may inspire my heart so that I shall sympathize with his pleasure in the thing, before my personal pleasure begins, knowing that it will increase my capability for happiness." After she accidentally drowned in 1851, a eulogist proclaimed that, "Her only ambition was to be the servant of love and she was beautifully and wonderfully made for the office." Oneida's sexual practices were considered outrageous and sinful by almost all other Americans. Even Oneidans did not agree with all of Noyes's ideas about sex. "There is no reason why [sex] should not be done in public as much as music and dancing," he declared. It would display the art of sex, he explained, and watching "would give pleasure to a great many of the older people who now have nothing to do with the matter." Nonetheless, public sex never caught on among Oneidans.
Oneida Community Mansion House/James Demarest.

The Oneida community went beyond the Fourierist notion of communalism. John Humphrey Noyes, the charismatic leader of Oneida, believed that individuals who had achieved salvation were literally without sin. The larger society's commitment to private property, however, made even saints greedy and selfish. Noyes believed that the root of the evil of private property lay in marriage, in men's conviction that their wives were their exclusive property. With a substantial inheritance, Noyes organized the Oneida community in New York in 1848 to permit himself and others to live according to his ideas. Oneidans practiced what Noyes called "complex marriage," which meant that sexual intercourse was permissible between any man and woman in the community who had been saved; in effect, every saved man in the community was married to every saved woman. Noyes usually reserved for himself the duties of "first husband," namely introducing sanctified young virgins to complex marriage. In time, Oneidans developed a formal procedure for the day-by-day operation of complex marriage: A member who desired intercourse with another member of the opposite sex approached a third member, who brokered the arrangement and registered it in a public community ledger. To prevent a population explosion and to promote health and self-control, Noyes insisted that Oneida men practice "male continence," that is, sexual intercourse without ejaculation. Noyes also required all members to relinquish their economic property to the community, which developed a lucrative business manufacturing animal traps. Oneida's sexual and economic communalism attracted several hundred members, but most of their neighbors considered Oneidans eccentric, heretical free lovers, adulterers, blasphemers, and worse. Yet the practices that set Oneida apart from its mainstream neighbors also strengthened the community, and it survived long after the Civil War.

Women's Rights Activists

Women participated in the many reform activities that grew out of evangelical churches. Women church members outnumbered men two to one, and they worked to put their religious ideas into practice by joining peace, temperance, antislavery, and other societies. Although women supplied much energy and membership in these societies, men normally headed the groups. Assumptions of male supremacy were so strong and pervasive that even women's rights activists feared the consequences of openly confronting them. Involvement in reform organizations gave a few women activists practical experience in such political arts as speaking in public, running a meeting, drafting resolutions, and circulating petitions. Along with such experience came confidence. Abolitionist Lydia Maria Child pointed out in 1841 that "those who urged women to become missionaries and form tract societies . . . have changed the household utensil to a living energetic being and they have no spell to turn it into a broom again." (See Texts in Historical Context, pages 490–491.)

In 1848, about one hundred living energetic beings, led by reformers Elizabeth Cady Stanton and Lucretia Mott, gathered at Seneca Falls, New York, for the first women's rights convention in the United States. None of the boldest women's rights activists in the nation was willing to chair the meeting; instead, they asked James Mott, Lucretia's husband, to assume that duty. The Seneca Falls women did not shrink, however, from proclaiming in their Declaration of Sentiments, "The history of mankind is a history of repeated injuries and usurpations on the part of man toward woman, having in direct object the establishment of an absolute tyranny over her." The Declaration of Sentiments declared that male tyranny caused women to "feel themselves aggrieved, oppressed, and fraudulently deprived of their most sacred rights." In the style of the Declaration of Independence, the Seneca Falls Declaration listed the ways women had been discriminated against. Through the tyranny of male supremacy, men "endeavored in every way that [they] could to destroy her confidence in her own powers, to lessen her self-respect, and to make her willing to lead a dependent and abject life." The Seneca Falls Declaration insisted that women "have immediate admission to all the rights and privileges which belong to them as citizens of the United States," particularly the "inalienable right to the elective franchise."

After the Seneca Falls meeting adjourned, Stanton, Mott, and others worked to gain support for woman suffrage. They wrote tracts, gave speeches, and tried to recruit other women to campaign for the cause. But it was tough going. Nearly two dozen women's rights conventions assembled in the years before the Civil War (1861–1865), repeatedly calling for suffrage. But they had difficulty receiving a respectful hearing, much less obtaining legislative action. No state came close to permitting women to vote. Politicians and editorialists hooted at the idea. Everyone knew, they sneered, that a woman's place

ABOLITIONIST MEETING
This rare daguerreotype was made by Ezra Greenleaf Weld in August 1850 at an abolitionist meeting in Cazenovia, New York. Frederick Douglass, who had escaped from slavery in Maryland twelve years earlier, is seated on the platform next to the woman at the table. One of the nation's most brilliant and eloquent abolitionists, Douglass also supported equal rights for women. The man immediately behind Douglass gesturing with his outstretched arm is Gerrit Smith, a wealthy New Yorker and militant abolitionist whose funds supported many reform activities. Note the two black women in similar clothing on either side of Smith and the white woman next to Douglass. Most mid-nineteenth-century white Americans considered such voluntary racial proximity scandalous and promiscuous. Clearly, what scandalized these respectable-appearing Americans was slavery, not biracial protest meetings.
Collection of the J. Paul Getty Museum, Malibu, Calif.

was in the home, rearing her children and civilizing her man. Nonetheless, the Seneca Falls Declaration served as a path-breaking manifesto of dissent against male supremacy and of support for women's suffrage, which would become the focus of the women's rights movement during the next seventy years.

Abolitionists and the American Ideal

During the 1840s and 1850s, abolitionists continued to struggle to draw the nation's attention to the plight of slaves and the need for emancipation. Former slaves like Frederick Douglass, Henry Bibb, and Sojourner Truth lectured to reform audiences throughout the North about the cruelties, horrors,

and indignities of slavery. Abolitionists published newspapers, held conventions, and petitioned Congress. But they never attracted a mass following among white Americans. Leading white abolitionists criticized the pervasive assumptions of black inferiority and white supremacy and affirmed their belief in human equality.

Many white Northerners became convinced that slavery was wrong, but they still believed that blacks were inferior. Many other white Northerners shared the common view of white Southerners that because blacks were inferior, slavery was necessary and even desirable. The pervasive racism among most whites in the North limited the reach of the abolitionist appeal. The geographical expansion of the nation during the 1840s (discussed later in the chapter) offered abolitionists an opportunity to link

tions of racial discrimination in virtually every arena of daily life: at work, at school, at church, in shops, in the streets, on trains, in hotels, and elsewhere. Only four New England states (Maine, Massachusetts, New Hampshire, and Vermont) permitted black men to vote; New York imposed a special property-holding requirement on black—but not white—voters, effectively excluding most black men from the franchise. All other states prohibited black voting. The pervasive racial discrimination in the North both handicapped and energized black abolitionists. Garnet said, as if he were speaking to slaves, "While you have been oppressed, we have also been partakers; nor can we be free while you are enslaved. We . . . [are] bound with you." African American leaders organized campaigns against segregation in northern communities, particularly in transportation and education. Their most notable success came in 1855 when Massachusetts integrated public schools. Elsewhere, despite their protests, white supremacy continued unabated.

Outside the public spotlight, many free African Americans in the North contributed to the antislavery cause by quietly aiding fugitive slaves. Harriet Tubman escaped from slavery in Maryland in 1849 and repeatedly risked her freedom and her life to return to the South and escort scores of slaves to freedom. Few matched Tubman's heroic courage, but when the opportunity arose, many free blacks in the North provided fugitive slaves with food, a safe place to rest, and a helping hand. A few whites also participated in this "underground railroad"

from slavery to freedom. Mainly, however, the underground railroad ran through black neighborhoods, black churches, and black homes. The underground railroad transported only a few thousand slaves to freedom. But it did illustrate the substratum of antislavery sentiment and opposition to white supremacy that unified virtually all African Americans in the North.

The ideas and activities of reformers challenged mainstream institutions and assumptions of Lincoln's America. While reformers appealed to widespread ideals of justice, equality, democracy, and freedom, they also confronted equally widespread impediments of sin, male supremacy, white supremacy, and slavery. Although reformers had limited influence in national politics, the continued geographic expansion of the nation pushed the issue of slavery to the center of national politics and confronted all Americans with the question reformers had debated for many years: What steps should be taken to bring American society into harmony with American ideals?

The Westward Movement

The 1840s ushered in an era of rapid westward movement. Until then, the overwhelming majority of Americans lived east of the Mississippi River. To the west, Native Americans inhabited the plains, prairies, and deserts to the rugged coasts of the Pa-

NORTHERN SLOPES OF THE SIERRA NEVADA BY C. S. SCHUMANN AFTER EGLOFFSTEIN, **1854.**

cific. The British claimed the Oregon Country, and the Mexican flag flew over the vast expanse of the Southwest. But by 1850, the boundaries of the United States stretched to the Pacific, and the nation had more than doubled its size. By 1860, the great migration had carried four million Americans west of the Mississippi River.

Thomas Jefferson, John Quincy Adams, and other government officials had helped clear the way for the march across the continent. The nation's revolution in transportation and communication, its swelling population, and its booming economy propelled the westward surge. But the emigrants themselves pushed to conquer the continent. Farmer-settlers craved land and stubbornly shoved ahead. Unimpressed with the claims of native people, Mexicans, and British, they simply asserted their "right" to the land. Shock troops of American empire, frontier settlers took the soil and then lobbied their government to follow them with the flag. The human cost of westward expansion was high. Two centuries of Indian wars east of the Mississippi ended during the 1830s, but the old, fierce struggle between native inhabitant and invader continued for another half century in the West.

Manifest Destiny

Most Americans believed that the superiority of their institutions and white culture bestowed on them a God-given right to spread their civilization across the continent. They imagined the West as a howling wilderness, empty and undeveloped. If they recognized Indians and Mexicans at all, they dismissed them as primitive drags on progress who would have to be redeemed, shoved aside and isolated, or exterminated. The sense of uniqueness and mission was as old as the Puritans, but by the 1840s the conviction of superiority had been bolstered by the young nation's amazing success. What right had Americans, they asked, to keep the blessings of liberty, democracy, and prosperity to themselves? The West needed the civilizing power of the hammer and plow, the ballot box and pulpit, that had transformed the East.

As important as national pride and racial arrogance were to Manifest Destiny, economic gain made up its core. Land hunger drew hundreds of thousands of average Americans westward.

In the summer of 1845, New York journalist John L. O'Sullivan coined the term "Manifest Destiny" as the latest justification for white settlers to take the land they coveted. Slight of build, pale complexioned, with thick glasses, O'Sullivan was an armchair expansionist, but he took second place to no one in his passion for conquest of the West. O'Sullivan called on Americans to resist any foreign power—British, French, or Mexican—that

Courtesy the Center for American History, the University of Texas at Austin.

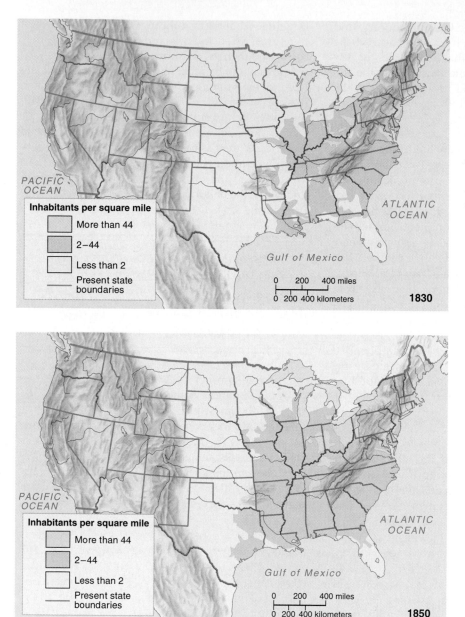

MAP 13.2
Population Advances Westward, 1830–1850
Millions of Americans moved westward in the middle decades of the nineteenth-century, crowding into the cities of the Northwest and hacking out farms and planta-tions in the great Mississippi River valley.

attempted to thwart "the fulfillment of our mani-fest destiny to overspread the continent allotted by Providence for the free development of our yearly multiplying millions." He dismissed those who raised the law as an objection to American expan-sion. What justified America's continental march, he said, was "the right of our manifest destiny to . . . possess the whole of the continent which Provi-dence has given us for the development of the great experiment of liberty and federative self-govern-ment entrusted to us." Almost overnight, the magic phrase "Manifest Destiny" swept the nation and provided an ideological shield for conquering the West.

As important as national pride and racial arro-gance were to Manifest Destiny, economic gain made up its core. Land hunger drew hundreds of thousands of average Americans westward. Some politicians, moreover, had become convinced that national prosperity depended on capturing the rich trade of the Far East. To trade with Asia, the United States needed the Pacific ports that stretched from

San Francisco to Puget Sound. No one was more eager to extend American trade in the Pacific than Missouri senator Thomas Hart Benton. Since the 1820s, he had beat the drum for western expansion, all the way to China and India. "The sun of civilization must shine across the sea: socially and commercially," he declared. The United States and Asia must "talk together, and trade together. Commerce is a great civilizer." In the 1840s, American economic expansion came wrapped in the rhetoric of uplift and civilization.

The concept of Manifest Destiny captured the temper of the nation. It gave a spine-tingling name to Americans' conviction and desire. Self-righteous and self-serving, Manifest Destiny also spoke of sincere belief. The nation looked forward to a time, contemporaries said, when the American eagle would have its beak in Canada, its talons in Mexico, and its wings flapping in the Atlantic and Pacific Oceans.

"Oregon Fever" and the Overland Trail

Oregon Country, that vast region bounded on the west by the Pacific, on the east by the Rockies, on the south by the forty-second parallel, and on the north by Russian Alaska, caused the pulse of American expansionists to race. But Americans were not alone in hungrily eyeing the Pacific Northwest. The British traced their interest (and their rights) to the voyage of Sir Francis Drake, who, they argued, discovered the Oregon coast in 1579. Americans matched the British assertion with historic claims of their own. Unable to agree on ownership, the United States and Great Britain decided in 1818 on a "joint occupation" that would leave Oregon "free and open" to settlement by both countries. A handful of American fur traders and "mountain men" roamed the region in the 1820s, but in the 1830s and 1840s, expansionists made Oregon Country an early target of Manifest Destiny.

"Oregon fever" broke out in 1833 when a Methodist journal published a fictitious letter from an Indian in the Northwest begging for the Bible. Pulpits across the East broadcast the plea, and soon earnest missionaries raced west. The Indians they encountered displayed a decided lack of enthusiasm for Christianity, but the missionaries' letters home glowed with astonishment at the bounty nature had bestowed on Oregon. By the late 1830s, settlers began to trickle along the Oregon Trail, following a path blazed by "mountain men." The first Oregon wagon trains hit the trail in 1841, and by 1843 about 1,000 emigrants a year set out from Independence, Missouri. By 1869, when the first transcontinental railroad was completed, something like 350,000 migrants had traveled west to the Pacific over the Oregon Trail.

When they traversed the vast reaches of the West, the emigrants encountered Plains Indians, whose cultures differed markedly from those of the Eastern Woodlands tribes. The quarter of a million Native Americans who populated the area between the Rocky Mountains and the Mississippi River defy easy generalization. Some were farmers who lived peaceful, sedentary lives, but a majority of Plains Indians—the Sioux, Cheyenne, Shoshoni, and Arapaho of the Central Plains and the Kiowa, Wichita, Apache, and Comanche in the Southwest—were horse-mounted, nomadic, nonagricultural peoples whose warriors symbolized the "savage Indian" in the minds of whites.

Horses, which had been brought to the continent by Spaniards in the sixteenth century, permitted the Plains tribes to become highly mobile hunters of buffalo. In time they came to depend on buffalo for most of their food, clothing, shelter, and fuel. As they followed the huge herds over the Plains, the people bumped into one another. Rival tribes learned from these encounters, but they also fought. Warfare became a crucial component of their way of life. Young men were introduced to the art of war early, learning to ride ponies at breakneck speed while firing off arrows and, later, rifles with astounding accuracy.

Plains Indians struck fear in the hearts of whites who rode on the wagon trains. But Native Americans had far more to fear from whites. Indians killed fewer than 400 emigrants on the trail between 1840 and 1860, while whites proved to be deadly to the Indians. Even though they were usually just passing through on their way to the Pacific slope, whites brought alcohol and disease, especially destructive epidemics of smallpox, measles, cholera, and scarlet fever. Moreover, whites killed the buffalo, slaughtering hundreds of thousands for fun and leaving their carcasses to rot in the sun. Buffalo still numbered some twelve million in 1860, but the herds were shrinking rapidly, intensifying conflict among the Plains Indians. Intertribal warfare weakened the Indians and made them more vulnerable to conquest.

As white migration increased, overland emigrants insisted that the federal government provide them more protection. The government responded by constructing a chain of forts along the trail. More important, the United States adopted a new Indian policy of "concentration." To clear the way, the government rescinded the "permanent" frontier it had granted the Indians west of the ninety-fifth meridian, which was only a few miles west of the Mississippi River. Then, in 1851, it called the Plains tribes to a conference at Fort Laramie, Wyoming. Some ten thousand Dakota, Sioux, Arapaho, Cheyenne, Crow, and other Indians showed up, hopeful that something could be done to protect them from the ravages of the wagon trains. Instead, government negotiators persuaded the chiefs to sign agreements restricting their people to specific areas that whites promised they would never violate. This policy of isolation became the seedbed for the subsequent policy of reservations. But whites would not keep out of Indian territory, and Indians would not easily give up their traditional way of life. Competition meant warfare for decades to come.

Still, Indians threatened emigrants less than life on the trail did. The men, women, and children who headed west each spring could count on four to six months of grueling travel through often inhospitable country. Until 1860, maps labeled the vast area between the Rockies and the Mississippi River as the "Great American Desert." With nearly two thousand miles to go and traveling no more than fifteen miles a day, the pioneers endured parching

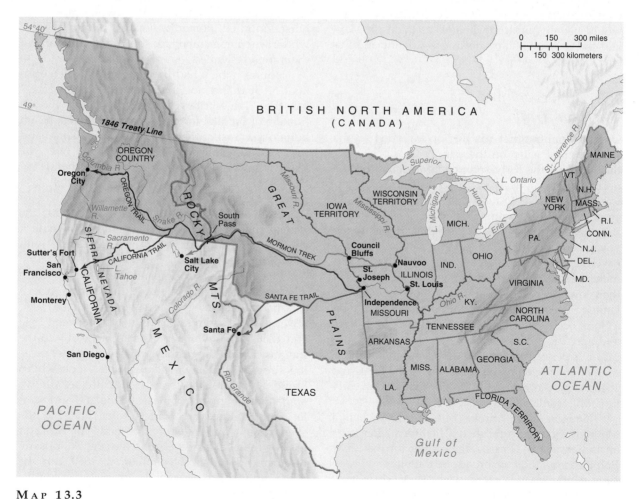

MAP 13.3
Trails to the West
In the 1830s, wagon trains began snaking their way to the Southwest and the Pacific coast. Deep ruts soon marked the most popular routes.

WI-JUN-JON, AN ASSINIBOIN CHIEF
Pennsylvania-born artist George Catlin, the painter of this 1845 dual portrait, was present in the Assiniboin village when Wi-Jun-Jon returned from Washington, D.C., wearing the military uniform that President Andrew Jackson had presented to him. His uniform and ceaseless boasting bred so much dislike and distrust that a young warrior from a nearby tribe murdered him. Catlin was convinced that the western Indian cultures that he had begun observing in the 1830s would soon disappear, and he sought to document Indian life through hundreds of paintings and prints.
Library of Congress.

heat, drought, treacherous rivers, disease, rattlesnakes, bad water, accidents, physical and emotional exhaustion, and, if the snows closed the mountain passes before they got through, freezing and starvation. Women sometimes faced the dangers of trailside childbirth. It was said that one could walk from Missouri to the Pacific stepping only on the graves of those who had failed to make it.

Everyone experienced hardships on the trail, but no one felt the burden quite as much as the women who made the trip. Since husbands usually decided to pull up stakes and go west, many wives went involuntarily. One miserable woman, trying to keep her children dry in a rainstorm and to calm them as they listened to Indian shouts, wondered "what had possessed my husband, anyway, that he should have thought of bringing us away out through this God forsaken country." Men viewed the privation as a necessary step to a new, better life; women tended to judge it by the homes, kin, and friends they had left behind to take up what one called "this wild goose chase."

Consumed with the tasks of surviving and getting to the coast, men and women abandoned eastern notions of "men's work" and "women's work." Women performed new chores, such as gathering buffalo dung for fuel. As gender boundaries faded, women also took on traditionally male work. One woman remembered learning to drive a team of oxen on the trail along the Platte River, while another told how she had managed to "crack that big whip." Some shouldered rifles to hunt or to guard their families. While women took on male tasks, men rarely reciprocated. Every emigrant woman knew the truth expressed by one young wife who found "as I was told before I started that there is no rest in such a journey."

The men who trekked westward usually sought land and, with it, the independence and economic opportunity that had eluded them in the East. But not all emigrants who reached Oregon celebrated what they found. Hezekiah Packingham, writing from the Willamette Valley in March 1847, claimed that Oregon was "a mean, dried up, and drowned country." He gave it credit for "only one or two things, and these are, good health and plenty of salmon, and Indians." Most disturbing to this single man, he found that Oregon was "rapidly filling up with young men, (but no girls)." Richard R. Howard saw things differently, in part no doubt because he was married. While he agreed that one-third of the men "are without wives," he believed that Oregon was "one of the greatest countries in the world." From "the Cascade mountains to the Pacific," he declared, "the whole country can be cultivated." His wife, he added, "was never more satisfied with a move in her life." But, he added guardedly, "she is fast recovering her health."

When women reached Oregon, they confronted a wilderness, not new homes. "I had all I could do to keep from asking George to turn around and bring me back home," one woman wrote to her mother in Missouri. Oregon, another noted, "was a hard country for a woman." Neighbors were few and far between, and the isolation weighed heavily. Moreover, things were in a "primitive state." One young wife set up housekeeping with her new husband with only one stew kettle and three knives. Necessity continued to blur the division between men's and women's work. "I am maid of all traids," one busy woman remarked in 1853. Work seemed unending. "I am a very old woman," remarked

twenty-nine-year-old Sarah Everett. "My face is thin sunken and wrinkled, my hands bony withered and hard." Pioneer life left little room for leisure or refinement. As one wife observed, "A woman that can not endure almost as much as a horse has no business here."

Despite the ordeal of the trail and the difficulties of starting from scratch, emigrants kept coming. By 1845, Oregon counted five thousand American settlers. And from the beginning, they clamored for the protection of the U.S. government.

The Mormon Migration

Not every wagon train heading west had the Pacific slope as its destination. One remarkable group of religious emigrants chose to settle in the heart of the arid West. Halting near the Great Salt Lake in what was then Mexican territory, the Mormons deliberately chose the remote site as a refuge. After years of persecution in the East, they sought religious freedom and communal security in the West. Protected by mountains and deserts, Deseret, as they called their kingdom, lay a thousand miles from the Kansas frontier.

In 1830, Joseph Smith Jr., who was only twenty-four, published *The Book of Mormon* and founded the Church of Jesus Christ of Latter-Day Saints (the Mormons). A decade earlier, the upstate New York farm boy had begun to have uncommon religious experiences. His visions and revelations were followed, he said, by a visit from an angel who led him to golden tablets buried near his home. With the aid of magic stones, he translated the mysterious language on the tablets. What was revealed was *The Book of Mormon*. It told the story of an ancient Christian civilization in the New World and predicted the appearance of an American prophet who would reestablish Jesus Christ's undefiled kingdom in America. Converts, attracted to the promise of a pure faith in the midst of antebellum America's social turmoil and rampant materialism, flocked to the new church.

"Gentile" neighbors branded Mormons heretics and resented their close-knit community, what they considered the Mormons' religious self-righteousness, and their sympathy toward abolitionists and Indians. Persecution drove Smith and his followers from New York to Ohio, then to Missouri, and finally in 1839 to Nauvoo, Illinois. Over the next five years, they built Nauvoo into a prosperous community of fifteen thousand. Visitors marveled at

GREAT SALT LAKE CITY IN 1853, LOOKING SOUTH
This 1853 sketch by Englishman Frederick Piercy reveals that only six years after its founding
Salt Lake City was already on its way to becoming a monumental city. For plans, the Mormons
looked to the ideas of their martyred prophet Joseph Smith. The city was laid out with very broad
streets—132 feet wide, said to be broad enough to allow ox-drawn wagons to turn around. It
had huge blocks—660 feet on a side—and sidewalks 20 feet wide. This would be a grand city,
the temple city, the religious capital of the Latter-Day Saints.
Library of Congress.

Nauvoo's broad streets, neat squares, and spectacular temple, but the Mormons had not outrun trouble. Dissenters within the church accused Smith of advocating plural marriage (polygamy) and published an exposé of the practice. Non-Mormons caught wind of the controversy and eventually arrested Smith and his brother. On June 27, 1844, a mob stormed the jail and shot both men dead.

The embattled church turned to an extraordinary new leader, Brigham Young, who immediately began to plan the exodus of his people. In 1846, the Mormons evacuated Nauvoo. Traveling in 3,700 wagons, twelve thousand Mormons made their way to eastern Iowa, where they established refugee camps. In 1847, Young led an advance party to their new home beside the Great Salt Lake. Young described it as a barren waste, "the paradise of the lizard, the cricket and the rattlesnake." Within ten years, however, the Mormons developed an efficient irrigation system and made the desert bloom. They accomplished the feat through cooperative labor, not the individualistic and competitive enterprise common among most emigrants. Under the stern leadership of Young and other church leaders, the Mormons built a thriving community.

In 1850, only three years after its founding, Deseret became annexed to the United States as Utah Territory. Although the Mormons professed loyalty to the Constitution, they paid little attention to distant Washington. What focused the nation's attention on the Latter-Day Saints was the announcement by Brigham Young in 1852 that many Mormons practiced polygamy. Although only one Mormon man in five had more than one wife (Young had twenty-three), Young's public statement caused an outcry that forced the government to establish its authority in Utah. In 1857, twenty-five hundred U.S. troops invaded Salt Lake City in what was known as the Mormon War. The bloodless occupation illustrates that most Americans viewed the Mormons as a threat to American morality, law, and institutions. The invasion did not dislodge the Mormon Church from its central place in Utah, however, and for years to come, most Americans perceived the Mormon settlement as a strange, and suitably isolated, place.

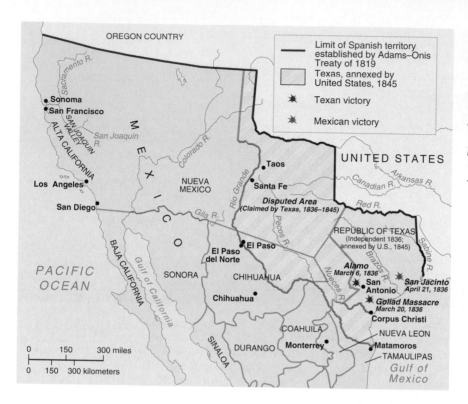

MAP 13.4
*Texas and Mexico in
the 1830s*
*As Americans spilled into
lightly populated and loosely
governed northern Mexico,
Texas and then other Mexican
provinces became contested
territory.*

The Mexican Borderlands

In the Mexican Southwest, westward-moving Anglo-American pioneers confronted northern-moving Spanish-speaking frontiersmen. On this frontier as elsewhere, cultures, interests, and aspirations collided. Since 1821, when Mexico won its independence from Spain, the Mexican flag had flown over the vast expanse that stretched from the Gulf of Mexico to the Pacific and from Oregon Country to Guatemala. Mexico's borders remained ill-defined, and its northern provinces were sparsely populated. Moreover, severe problems plagued the young nation: civil wars, economic crises, quarrels between the Roman Catholic Church and the state, and devastating raids by the Comanche, Apache, and Kiowa. Between 1833 and 1855, the presidency of Mexico changed hands thirty-six times. The central government found it increasingly difficult to defend its borderlands, especially when faced with a northern neighbor that was convinced of its superiority and bent on territorial acquisition.

The American assault began quietly. In the 1820s, Anglo-American trappers, traders, and settlers began drifting into the far northern provinces of Mexico. Santa Fe, a remote outpost in the province of New Mexico, became a magnet for

American enterprise. In 1821, a band of American traders stumbled into Santa Fe and discovered that newly independent Mexico was eager for American business. Each spring thereafter, American traders gathered at Independence, Missouri, for the long trek southwest along the Santa Fe Trail. Traders crammed their wagons with inexpensive American manufactured goods and returned with Mexican silver, furs, and mules. Trade between Mexico and the United States gradually pulled Mexico's far northern frontier into the American economic orbit.

The Mexican province of Texas attracted a flood of Americans who had settlement, not long-distance trade, on their minds. The Mexican government, which wanted to populate and develop its northern territory, granted the American Stephen F. Austin a huge tract of land, and in the 1820s he established a thriving settlement along the Brazos River. Land was cheap—only ten cents an acre—and thousands of farmers poured over the border. Most of the migrants were Southerners, who brought cotton and slaves with them. By 1835, the number of settlers—free and slave—in Texas had reached 30,000, while the Mexican population was barely 7,800. By and large, Anglo-American settlers were not Roman Catholic, did not speak Spanish, and cared little about assimilating into a culture that was so different from their own. The Mexican government realized that it had a problem on its hands; in 1829 it sought to arrest further immigration with an emancipation proclamation, which it hoped would make Texas less attractive. The settlers sidestepped the decree by calling their slaves servants, but they had other grievances, most significantly the puny voice they had in local government. General Antonio López de Santa Anna all but extinguished that voice when he seized political power and concentrated authority in Mexico City.

Faced with what they considered tyranny, the Texan settlers rebelled and declared the independent Republic of Texas. Santa Anna took the field and in March 1836 arrived at the outskirts of San Antonio with 6,000 troops. The rebels, who included the Tennessee frontiersman Davy Crockett, and the Louisiana adventurer Jim Bowie, took refuge in the old Franciscan mission the Alamo. Wave after wave of Mexicans crashed against the walls until the attackers finally broke through and killed all 186 defenders. A few weeks later in the small town of

SURVEYING TEXAS LAND
Land has always bred conflict in Texas. The new republic (1836–1845) wrestled with a confusing variety of Spanish, Mexican, and Texas claims, surveys, and titles. This painting by Theodore Gentilz in about 1844 documents the efforts of surveyor John James to settle the thorny issues. Five years later, however, Texas Governor P. H. Bell could still observe: "There is no subject which addresses itself more forcibly . . . than that of settling upon a secure and permanent basis the land titles of the country."
Courtesy, Mr. Larry Sheerin.

Goliad, Mexican forces surrounded and captured a garrison of 365 Texans. Following orders from Santa Anna, Mexican firing squads executed the men as pirates. But in April at San Jacinto, Santa Anna suffered a crushing defeat at the hands of forces under General Sam Houston. Mexico made no further military effort to bring Texas back into the fold. Texans elected Sam Houston president of their Lone Star Republic, and in 1837 the United States recognized the independence of Texas from Mexico.

The distant Mexican province of California also caught the eye of a few Americans. Spain had first extended its influence into California in 1769, when it sent a naval expedition north from Mexico to the San Francisco Bay in an effort to block Russian fur traders who were moving south along the Pacific coast from their base in Alaska. The Spanish built garrisoned towns (*presidios*), but, more important, they constructed a string of twenty-one missions, spaced a day's journey apart, along the coast from San Diego to Sonoma. Junípero Serra and other Franciscan friars converted the Indians to Christianity and drew them into the life and often hard agricultural labor of the missions. In 1824, in an effort to increase Mexican migration to thinly settled California, the Mexican government granted *ranchos*—huge estates devoted to cattle raising—to new settlers. *Rancheros* ruled over near-feudal empires worked by Indians whose condition sometimes approached that of slaves. Not satisfied, Mexican *rancheros* coveted the vast lands controlled by the Franciscan missions. In 1834, they persuaded the government to confiscate the missions and make their lands available to new settlement. Some seven hundred new *ranchos* followed, a development that accelerated the decline of California Indians. Devastated by disease, the Indians, who numbered approximately 300,000 when the Spanish arrived in California, declined by mid-nineteenth century to barely 150,000.

Despite the efforts of the Mexican government, California counted a population of only 7,000 Mexican settlers in 1840. Non-Mexican settlers numbered only 380, but among them were Americans who championed Manifest Destiny. Thomas O. Larkin, a prosperous merchant, John Marsh, a successful *ranchero* in the San Joaquin Valley, and others became boosters who sought to attract Americans from Oregon Country to California. The first overland party arrived in California in 1841. Thereafter, wagon after wagon followed the California Trail, which forked off from the Oregon Trail near the Snake River and led through the Sierra Nevada

at Lake Tahoe. As the trickle of Americans became a river, Mexican officials grew alarmed. California, they feared, would go the way of Texas. As a New York newspaper put it in 1845, "Let the tide of emigration flow toward California and the American population will soon be sufficiently numerous to play the Texas game." Indeed, many Americans in California continued to live apart, unassimilated, and to view themselves as superior to their Mexican neighbors. Not all Americans in California wanted to play the "Texas game," but many dreamed of living again under the American flag.

The U.S. government made no secret of its desire to acquire California. In 1835, President Andrew Jackson tried to purchase it. In 1842, Commodore Thomas Catesby Jones, hearing a rumor that the United States and Mexico were at war, seized the port of Monterey and ran up the American flag. The red-faced officer promptly ran it down again when he learned of his error. But his actions left no doubt about Washington's intentions. In 1846, American settlers in the Sacramento Valley took matters into their own hands. Prodded by John C. Frémont, a former army captain and explorer who had arrived in December 1845 with a party of sixty buckskin-clad frontiersmen spoiling for a fight, the Californians raised an independence movement known as the Bear Flag Revolt. By then, James K. Polk, a champion of expansion, sat in the White House.

The Politics of Expansion

Although emigrants were the advance guard of American empire, there was nothing automatic about the U.S. annexation of territory in the West. Acquiring territory required political action, and in the 1840s the difficult problems of Texas, Oregon, and the Mexican borderlands intruded into national politics. The politics of expansion thrust the United States into dangerous diplomatic crises with Great Britain and Mexico. Even more ominous, expansion became hopelessly entangled with sectionalism and the slavery question.

Tyler and the Whig Fiasco

The complicated issues of westward expansion and the nation's boundaries ended up on the desk of John Tyler when he became president in April 1841. William Henry Harrison, a Whig, had been elected president in 1840, but one month after he took of-

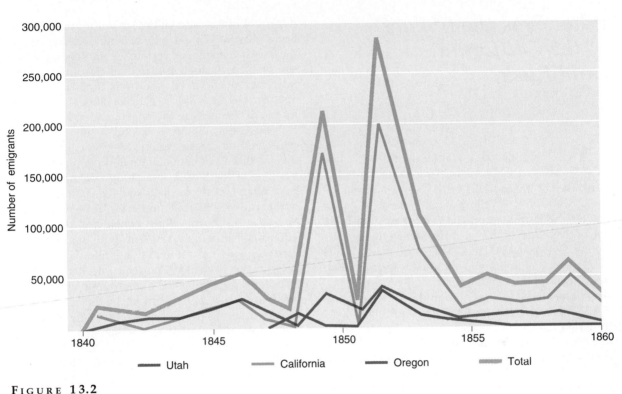

FIGURE 13.2
Emigration to the West, 1840–1860
Land drew a steady stream of emigrants westward, but gold attracted torrents of emigrants to California.

fice, he died, the victim of pneumonia caught as he delivered his long inaugural address. For the first time in American history, a president had died in office, and it was not clear whether Vice President Tyler—"His Accidency," as his opponents called him—could legally exercise the full powers of an elected president.

The politics of expansion thrust the United States into dangerous diplomatic crises with Great Britain and Mexico.

Worse for the Whigs, Tyler was really a Democrat in Whig clothing. The fifty-one-year-old Virginian was a Whig only because he had fallen out with Andrew Jackson over Jackson's strong-armed tactics during the South Carolina nullification crisis. Whigs had placed Tyler on the ballot to balance the ticket and to appeal to Southerners. Tyler had consistently opposed all the measures of the Whig Henry Clay's American System: protective tariffs,

the national bank, and internal improvements at federal expense. Tyler favored strict construction and states' rights, positions closer to John C. Calhoun and the Democrats than to Clay and the Whigs. But the Whigs never expected that Tyler would wield power. Even after Tyler moved into the White House, they assumed that he would bow to the party's leader, Kentucky senator Henry Clay.

Clay viewed the Whig victory in 1840 as "a great civil revolution." After twelve years of Democratic rule, he could hardly wait to translate Whig programs and principles into law. He knew Tyler's views but remained optimistic because, as a reporter wrote, "If [Clay] was to intimate a wish that the majority of the Senate should go to [hell] . . . , they would immediately raise a committee to ascertain the most direct and eligible route." Clay guided a raft of legislation through Congress. Tyler accepted the repeal of the Democrat's independent treasury and grudgingly approved a slightly higher tariff, but he vetoed a bill for internal improvements. Clay pressed on, emerging from Congress with a bill for a new national bank. The president

What Was the Impact of the California Gold Rush?

ON A COLD JANUARY MORNING in 1848, while James Marshall was walking along the American River in the foothills of the Sierra Nevada, he detected the glint of yellow metal in the stream. The nuggets he found set off the California gold rush, one of the wildest mining stampedes in the world's history. Between 1849 and 1852, more than 250,000 forty-niners, as the would-be miners were known, descended on the Golden State.

Marshall discovered gold in the same year that the Treaty of Guadalupe Hidalgo transferred California and other northern provinces of Mexico to the United States. Americans did not find it surprising that the discovery coincided with American acquisition. "God kept that coast for a people of the Pilgrim blood," one minister intoned. "He would not permit any other to be fully developed there." Most Americans were determined that the West would be an enclave for Anglo-American enterprise and culture.

Gold proved irresistible to easterners. Newspapers went crazy with stories about prospectors who extracted half a pan of gold from every pan of gravel they scooped from western streams. Soon, cities reverberated with men singing:

Oh Susannah, don't you cry for me;
I'm gone to California with my wash-bowl on
  my knee.

Scores of ships sailed from East Coast ports, headed either around South America to San Francisco or to Panama, where the passengers made their way by foot and canoe to the Pacific and waited for a ship to carry them north. Even larger numbers of gold seekers took riverboats to the Missouri River and then set out in wagons, on horseback, or by foot for the West.

But young men everywhere contracted gold fever. As stories of California gold circled the globe, Chinese and Germans, Mexicans and Irish, Australians and French, Chileans and Italians, and dozens of other nationalities set out to strike it rich. Louisa Knapp Clappe, wife of a minister and one of the few women in gold country, remarked that when she walked through Indian Bar, the little mining town where she lived, she heard English, French, Spanish, German, Italian, Kanaka (Hawaiian), Asian Indian, and American Indian languages. Hangtown, Hell's Delight, Gouge Eye, and a hundred other crude mining camps became temporary home to a diverse throng of nationalities and peoples.

One of the largest groups of new arrivals was the Chinese. Between 1848 and 1854, Chinese men numbering 45,000 (but almost no Chinese women) arrived in California. Most considered themselves sojourners, temporary residents who planned to return home as soon as their savings allowed. The majority came under a Chinese-controlled contract labor system in which the immigrant worked out the cost of his transportation. In the early years, most worked as wage laborers in mining. By the 1860s, they dominated railroad construction in the West. Ninety percent of the Central Pacific Railroad's 10,000 workers were Chinese. The Chinese also made up nearly one-half of San Francisco's labor force, working in the shoe, tobacco, woolen, laundry, and sewing trades. By 1870, the Chinese population had grown to 63,200, including 4,500 women. They constituted nearly 10 percent of the state's people and 25 percent of its wage-earning force.

The presence of peoples from around the world shattered the Anglo-American dream of a racially and ethnically homogeneous West, but ethnic diversity did nothing to increase the tolerance of Anglo-American prospectors. In their eyes, no "foreigner" had a right to dig gold. In 1850, the California legislature passed the Foreign Miners' Tax Law, which levied high taxes on non-Americans to drive them from the gold fields, except as hired laborers working on claims owned by Americans. Stubborn foreign miners were sometimes hauled before "Judge Lynch." One of the earliest lynchings in the gold fields was of a Frenchman and a Chilean.

Anglo-Americans considered the Chinese devious and unassimilable. They also feared that hardworking, self-denying Chinese labor would undercut white labor and drive it from the country. As a consequence, the Chinese were segregated residentially and occupationally and made ineligible for citizenship. Along with blacks and Indians, Chinese were denied public education and the

right to testify in court. In addition to exclusion, they suffered from violence. Mobs drove them from Eureka, Truckee, and other mining towns.

American prospectors swamped the *Californios,* the Spanish and Mexican settlers who had lived in California for generations. On the eve of the American takeover, *Californios* included *rancheros,* professionals, merchants, artisans, and laborers. Raging prejudice and discriminatory laws increasingly pushed Hispanics into the ranks of unskilled labor. Americans took their land, even though the federal government had pledged to protect Mexican and Spanish land titles after the cession of 1848. Anglo forty-niners branded Spanish-speaking miners, even native-born *Californios,* "foreigners" and drove them from the diggings. Mariano Vallejo, a leading *Californio,* said of the forty-niners: "The good ones were few and the wicked many."

For Native Americans, the gold rush was a catastrophe. Numbering about 150,000 in 1848, the Indian population fell to 25,000 in 1856. *Californios* had exploited the native peoples, but the forty-niners wanted to eradicate them. Starvation, disease, and a declining birthrate took a heavy toll. Indians also fell victim to wholesale murder. "That a war of extermination will continue to be waged between the

two races until the Indian race becomes extinct must be expected," declared California governor Peter W. Burnett in 1851. Nineteenth-century historian Hubert Howe Bancroft described white behavior toward Indians during the gold rush as "one of the last human hunts of civilization, and the basest and most brutal of them all." To survive, Indians moved to the most remote areas of the state and tried to stay out of the way.

The forty-niners created dazzling wealth—in 1852, eighty-one million ounces of gold, nearly one-half of the world's production. But because Anglo-Americans made the rules, not everyone shared equally. Of course, only a few prospectors—of whatever race and nationality—struck it rich. The era of the individual prospector panning in streams quickly gave way to corporate-owned deep-shaft mining. Most forty-niners eventually took up farming or other lines of work. But because of gold, an avalanche of people had roared across California. Anglo-Americans were most numerous, and Anglo dominance developed early. But the gold rush also brought a rainbow of nationalities. Anglo-American dominance and ethnic and racial diversity in the West both count among the most significant legacies of the gold rush.

promptly rejected it with a Jackson-like argument that it was "unconstitutional."

With his second veto, Tyler forfeited all claim to Whig leadership. His views on economic policy flew in the face of his party and left Clay's plan in shambles. The Whigs formally expelled Tyler from the party, and, in an unprecedented move, most of the cabinet resigned. Secretary of State Daniel Webster, however, stayed on to settle the boundary between Canada and the United States, still undetermined after fifty-six years. Britain sent Lord Ashburton to Washington, where he renewed the friendly relationship he and Webster had established in England. Observers dubbed the negotiations the "battle of the maps," but the cooperative mood led in 1842 to the Webster-Ashburton Treaty, which settled all border issues with Canada, except Oregon.

Even Webster's success could not redeem the Tyler administration. Tyler betrayed the economic principles of his supposed party, and the Whigs suffered near-complete domestic stalemate. Clay did not hesitate to compare John Tyler to Benedict Arnold. "Tyler is on his way to the Democratic camp," Clay declared. "They will give him lodgings in some outhouse, but they will never trust him. He will stand here, like Arnold in England, a monument of his own perfidy and disgrace." Writing off Tyler, Clay's followers hoisted his banner for the presidency in 1844. Clay resigned from the Senate to prepare for the race. Tyler dove into a quest for the Democratic nomination, but he needed an issue that could provide a bridge back to his former party.

Texas, Oregon, and the Election of 1844

Fending off Clay's economic program demanded most of John Tyler's energy, but the issue that stirred his blood, and that of much of the nation, was Texas. Texans had sought admission to the Union almost since their independence from Mexico in 1836, and Tyler, an ardent expansionist, knew that the acquisition of Texas would appeal strongly to southern and western Democrats. He also understood that Texas was a dangerous issue. Any suggestion of adding another slave state to the Union brought many Northerners to a boil. Andrew Jackson and his successor, Martin Van Buren, had cautiously avoided annexation because they doubted it was worth the price. Annexing Texas also risked precipitating war because Mexico had never relinquished its claim to its lost province.

Inhabitants of the Lone Star Republic lived a precarious existence. They often exchanged shots with Mexicans along the border, and they worried that Mexico would launch a new invasion. Cold-shouldered by the United States, Texans explored Great Britain's interest in recognition and trade. They discovered that the British were eager to keep Texas independent. In Britain's eyes, Texas provided a buffer against American expansion and a new market for English manufactured goods. Moreover, Britain hoped to persuade Texas to adopt gradual emancipation. Southern slaveholders accused the British of plotting to end slavery in Texas and to seal off the South's expansion to the west. Other Americans worried that Britain's real object was adding Texas to the British Empire. This fluid mix of threat, fear, and opportunity convinced Tyler to risk negotiations with Texas, and he worked vigorously to annex the republic before his term expired. His efforts pushed Texas and the slavery issue to the center of national politics.

In April 1844, after months of secret negotiations between Texas and the Tyler administration, the new secretary of state, South Carolinian John C. Calhoun, laid an annexation treaty before the Senate. But when Calhoun publicly linked annexation to the defense of slavery, he doomed the treaty. His statement strengthened the abolitionist claim that annexation was merely a proslavery plot, and howls of protest against annexation erupted everywhere north of the Mason-Dixon line. When the Senate soundly rejected the treaty, it appeared that Tyler had succeeded only in inflaming sectional conflict.

The issue of Texas had not died down by the 1844 elections. Henry Clay expected to win the Whig Party's presidential nomination and looked forward to waging his campaign on the old Whig economic issues in his American System that Tyler had frustrated. But everywhere he spoke, he confronted a barrage of questions about Texas. Finally, to appeal to northern voters, he came out against the immediate annexation of Texas. "Annexation and war with Mexico are identical," Clay declared. When news of Clay's statement reached Andrew Jackson at his plantation in Tennessee, he chuckled, "Clay [is] a dead political Duck." In Jackson's shrewd judgment, no man who opposed annexation could be elected president. But the Whig Party paid no attention, nominated Clay, and adopted a platform that proclaimed the principles of Clay's American System while remaining silent on Texas.

Among Democrats, Martin Van Buren expected to receive the party's nomination, but when he an-

TECHNOLOGY IN AMERICA
Hydraulic Mining

Individual prospectors who made the first gold strikes used a simple process known as placer mining, requiring only a decent claim and basic tools. As one awed visitor to the gold fields in 1848 observed: "No capital is required to obtain this gold, as the laboring man wants nothing but his pick and shovel and tin pan with which to dig and wash the gravel." But when these easy pickings along the rivers and streams gave out, a good deal of gold still remained trapped in quartz or buried deep in the earth, extractable only by methods far beyond the means and capacity of the average prospector.

Soon capital and technology invaded the diggings. Corporations initiated hydraulic operations to pursue the hidden veins of gold. These high-pressure streams of water blasted the ore loose and, later, other equipment was used to break down the rock and extract the precious gold. Eager to make a quick profit, the purveyors of this new technology gave little thought to its impact on the environment. The hydraulic jets demolished entire mountains, devastating stream beds and creating heaps of rubble. As big business gradually took over mining, corporations found laborers among the disillusioned forty-niners, who could earn more as wageworkers than as independent miners using pans. This scene probably shows the Timbuctoo operation near the Yuba River.
Collection of Matthew Isenburg.

A POLK SNUFFBOX

The use of political paraphernalia to appeal to the electorate is not a new phenomenon. James K. Polk, the Democratic presidential candidate in 1844, was portrayed on this fine snuffbox. In a time when almost every adult male used tobacco in one form or another, this handsome political object was sure to attract attention.

Collection of Janice L. and David J. Frent.

nounced his opposition to Texas annexation, his candidacy collapsed in the South. Van Buren's demise opened the door at the Democratic convention. After John Tyler generated little support, James K. Polk of Tennessee gained his party's presidential nomination. Fourteen years in Congress had brought Polk modest fame, but Texas lifted him into the national spotlight. Polk was as strong for annexation as Clay was against it.

In the 1844 election, Democrats sought to champion Texas annexation without splitting their party or the nation. They succeeded by yoking Texas to Oregon, thus tapping the desire for expansion in the free states of the North as well as in the slave states of the South. The Democratic platform pulled out all the stops on behalf of Manifest Destiny. It called for the "reannexation of Texas" and the "reoccupation of Oregon." The suggestion that the United States was merely reasserting its existing rights was poor history but good politics. And by "Oregon" the Democrats meant all of Oregon Country, from the northern border of Mexican California to the southern border of Russian Alaska, a huge coun-

terweight to balance massive Texas. According to the Democratic formula, Texas annexation did not give an advantage to slavery and the South. Linked to Oregon, Texas expanded America to the advantage of the entire nation.

Much to Henry Clay's discomfort, Texas, not the tariff, emerged as the dominant issue of the 1844 campaign. When Clay finally recognized the groundswell for expansion, he lost his nerve. He waffled on Texas, hinting that he might accept annexation under certain circumstances. His retreat won little support in the South and only succeeded in alienating antislavery opinion in the North. The fledgling Liberty Party, which stood firmly against annexation, denounced him as "rotten as a stagnant fish pond." The Liberty Party candidate, James G. Birney, picked up the votes of thousands of disillusioned Clay supporters. In the November election, Polk received 2,698,609 votes and Clay got only 38,180 votes fewer. But Polk's electoral majority was wider, 170 to 105. New York's 35 electoral votes proved critical to Clay's defeat. Birney received 15,000 votes in New York, but since Clay lost the state by only 5,000, a shift of just one-third of Birney's votes to Clay would have given him the state and the presidency.

The nation did not have to wait for Polk's inauguration to see results from his victory. One month after the election, President Tyler announced that the Democratic triumph provided a mandate for the annexation of Texas "promptly and immediately." After a fierce debate between antislavery and proslavery forces, Congress approved a joint resolution offering the Republic of Texas admission to the United States. On March 1, 1845, three days before Polk took office, Texas entered the Union as a slave state. Nine years after its independence, Texas achieved statehood. Almost four years after taking office, Tyler had an achievement to crow about.

Tyler had seen to Texas, but James Polk had promised Oregon, too. Settlers in the West and expansionists elsewhere demanded that the new president make good on the Democrats' campaign slogan—"Fifty-four Forty or Fight"—that is, all of Oregon, right up to Alaska ("fifty-four forty" being the southern latitude of Russian Alaska). But Polk never coveted the Northwest as he did the Southwest. Moreover, he was close to war with Mexico and could not afford a simultaneous war with Britain over its claims to Canada. After the initial bluster, therefore, Polk buried the Democrats' campaign promise and renewed an old offer to divide Oregon along the forty-ninth parallel. After some hesitation, the British accepted the compromise. Westerners cried betrayal, but most Americans celebrated the agreement that gave the nation an enormous territory peacefully. Besides, when the Senate finally approved the treaty in June 1846, the United States and Mexico were already at war.

The Mexican War

From its independence in 1821, Mexico realized that its security and success in nation building depended on harmonious relations with its northern neighbor. The United States, however, exhibited expansionist tendencies from the beginning. Aggravation between the two nations escalated to open antagonism in 1845 when the United States annexed Texas. Absorbing territory still claimed by Mexico ruptured diplomatic relations between the United States and Mexico and set the stage for war. But it was President James K. Polk's insistence on having Mexico's other northern provinces that made war certain. Polk and the expansionist crowd never doubted the justice of their quest. Justice looked very different in Mexico City. The war was not as easy as Polk anticipated, but it ended in American victory and acquisition of a new American West. Mexicans could only lament, "Poor Mexico, so far from God, so near the United States."

"Mr. Polk's War"

From the day he entered the White House, Polk craved Mexico's remaining northern provinces: California and New Mexico, land that today makes up California, Nevada, and Utah, most of New Mexico and Arizona, and parts of Wyoming and Colorado. Polk hoped to buy the territory. If the Mexicans refused to sell, however, he was willing to take what he wanted. Polk made a last-ditch effort to gain the territory peacefully by sending an envoy, John Slidell, to Mexico City to negotiate the purchase of New Mexico and California. But the Mexicans refused to sell off their country, and in March 1846 they sent Slidell packing. A furious Polk concluded that it would take military force to realize the United States' Manifest Destiny.

Polk had already ordered General Zachary Taylor to march his 4,000-man Army of Occupation of Texas from its position on the Nueces River, the southern boundary of Texas according to the Mexicans, to the banks of the Rio Grande 150 miles south, the boundary claimed by Texans. Excitement ran high as the raw, young troops entered the disputed territory. Lieutenant George G. Meade, who would command troops at Gettysburg a few years later, admitted, "I hope for a war and a speedy battle, and I think one good fight will settle the business; and really, after coming so far . . . it would hardly be the thing to come back without some laurels." Action came quickly enough. The Mexican general in Matamoros viewed the American advance as aggression and ordered Taylor back to the Nueces. Taylor refused, and on April 25, Mexican cavalry attacked a party of American soldiers, killing or wounding 16 and capturing the rest. Even before news of the battle arrived in Washington, Polk had already obtained his cabinet's approval of a war message.

Polk and the expansionist crowd never doubted the justice of their quest. Justice looked very different in Mexico City.

On May 11, 1846, the president told Congress, "Mexico has passed the boundary of the United States, has invaded our territory, and shed American blood upon American soil." Thus "war exists, and, notwithstanding all our efforts to avoid it, exists by the act of Mexico herself." Two days later, Congress passed a declaration of war and began raising an army. Despite years of saber rattling toward Mexico and Britain, the American army was pitifully small, only 7,400 soldiers. Faced with the nation's first foreign war, up against a Mexican army that numbered more than 30,000, Polk called for volunteers who would serve for six to twelve months. Men everywhere rushed to the colors. The city of Baltimore met its quota in thirty-six hours. More than 30,000 Tennesseans competed for the state's 3,000 allotted positions. Even Massachusetts, where many citizens denounced the war as a plot to extend slavery, filled its quota within a month. Eventually, more than 112,000 white Americans (blacks were banned) joined the army to fight in Mexico.

Despite the outpouring of support, the war divided the nation. Whigs displayed considerably less enthusiasm for the Mexican adventure than did Democrats. Northerners were not nearly as hot-blooded about the war as Southerners. Although some Northerners kept their opposition to themselves because they did not want to appear unpa-

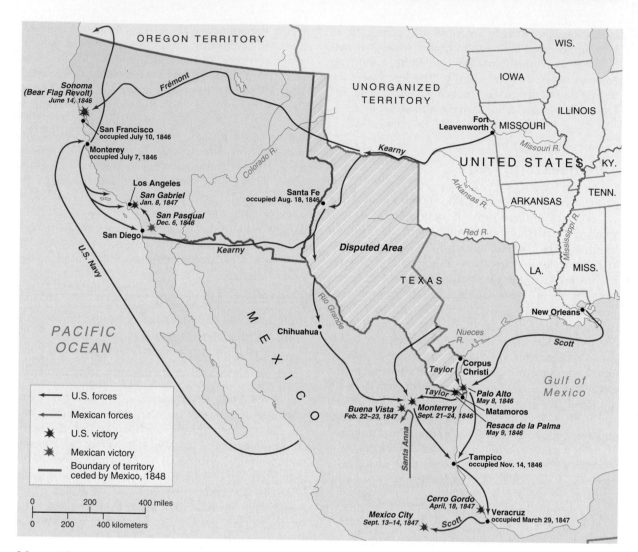

M A P 13.5
The Mexican War, 1846–1848
American and Mexican soldiers skirmished across much of northern Mexico, but the major
battles took place between the Rio Grande and Mexico City.

triotic or unwilling to support American soldiers in the field, a hard core of northern Whigs loudly condemned the war as the unwarranted bullying of a weak nation by its greedy expansionist neighbor.

In January 1848, a gangly freshman representative from Illinois rose from his back-row seat in the House of Representatives to deliver his first important speech in Congress. Abraham Lincoln took direct aim at the president and his war. Polk's defense of the war, Lincoln declared, was from beginning to end the "sheerest deception." He challenged the president's version of the incident that precipitated war and sought to disprove Polk's claim that the territory between the Nueces and the Rio Grande was indisputably American soil. He likened the president's views to "the half-insane mumbling of a fever dream" and proclaimed Polk "a bewildered, confounded, and miserably perplexed man." Before he sat down, Lincoln had questioned the president's intelligence, honesty, and sanity. President Polk simply ignored the upstart representative, but antislavery, antiwar Whigs kept up the attack throughout the conflict. In their effort to undercut national support, they labeled it "Mr. Polk's War."

Since most Americans backed the war, it was not really Polk's war, but the president acted as if it were. Although he had no military experience, he directed the war personally. Working eighteen hours a day, Polk established overall strategy and oversaw the details of military campaigns. He planned a short war in which American armies would occupy Mexico's northern provinces and defeat the Mexican army in a decisive battle or two, after which Mexico would sue for peace and the United States would keep the territory its armies occupied. But Mexico surprised Polk. Although its government was in disarray and its army poorly led, trained, and equipped, Mexico fought stubbornly rather than surrender its territory.

Taking the Borderlands

In May 1846, Zachary Taylor's troops drove south from the Rio Grande and routed the Mexican army, first on the plain of Palo Alto and then in a palm-filled ravine known as Resaca de la Palma. Taylor became an instant war hero. Sixty-two years old, "Old Rough and Ready," as he was affectionately known, had an undistinguished career behind him. But his simplicity and informality, as well as his cool behavior under fire, endeared him to his men. Polk rewarded Taylor for his victories by making him commander for the conquest of Mexico.

A second prong of the campaign to occupy Mexico's northern provinces centered on Colonel Stephen Watts Kearny, who led a 1,700-man army from Missouri into New Mexico. Without firing a shot, American forces took Santa Fe in August 1846. Kearny promptly proclaimed New Mexico American territory and with 300 troops headed for California. On the trail, incredibly, he met Kit Carson, part of John C. Frémont's buckskin army, who was hurrying east with the news of the American seizure of California. Thinking the contest already won, Kearny sent two-thirds of his men back to Santa Fe and pushed westward, with Carson as his scout. After nearly three months on the trail, Kearny's small band marched into San Diego and into a major Mexican rebellion against American rule. In January 1847, after several clashes, the American forces occupied Los Angeles. California and New Mexico were in American hands.

By then, Taylor had driven deep into the interior of Mexico. In September 1846, after a five-day siege and house-to-house fighting, he took the fortified city of Monterrey. With reinforcements and fresh supplies, Taylor pushed his 5,000 troops southwest, where the Mexican hero of the Alamo, General Antonio López de Santa Anna, was concentrating a huge army of 21,000, which he hoped would strike a decisive blow against the invaders from the north.

MEXICAN FAMILY
Mexican civilians, like this family in 1847, were vulnerable to atrocities committed by an invading army. Volunteers, a large portion of American troops, received little training and resisted military discipline. The "lawless Volunteers stop at no outrage," Brigadier General William Worth declared. "Innocent blood has been basely, cowardly, and barbarously shed in cold blood." Generals Zachary Taylor and Winfield Scott gradually tamed the "wild volunteers" by employing stern military justice.
Courtesy Amon Carter Museum, Fort Worth.

On Washington's birthday 1847, Taylor's troops met Santa Anna's at Buena Vista. Superior American artillery and accurate musket fire won the day, but the Americans suffered heavy casualties, including Henry Clay Jr., the son of the man who had opposed Texas annexation for fear it would precipitate war. But the Mexicans suffered even greater losses, and during the night Santa Anna removed his battered army from the battlefield, much to the "profound disgust of the troops," one Mexican officer remembered. "They are filled with grief that they were going to lose the benefit of all the sacrifices that they had made; that the conquered field would be abandoned, and that the victory would be given to the enemy; and finally, to affirm the idea already general in the army—that it was impossible to conquer the Americans."

The series of uninterrupted victories in northern Mexico fed the American troops' sense of superiority and very nearly led to a feeling of invincibility. "No American force has ever thought of being defeated by any amount of Mexican troops," one soldier declared. The Americans worried about other hazards, however. "I can assure you that fighting is the least dangerous & arduous part of a soldier's life," one young man said. Letters home told of torturous marches across burning, arid wastes alive with tarantulas, scorpions, and rattlesnakes. Others recounted clouds of flies, mosquitoes, and fleas. One soldier complained to his sister that "if [we] dont soon get a ship load of blood brought over we [will] be in a bad fix for the fleas and gnats have sucked all the blood out of us and eat our hides up." Dysentery, malaria, smallpox, cholera, and yellow fever were not joking matters. Of the 13,000 American soldiers who died in Mexico, only 2,000 fell to Mexican bullets and shells. Disease killed most of the others. Medicine was so primitive and conditions so harsh that army doctors could do little. As a Tennessee man observed, "nearly all who take sick die."

Victory in Mexico

Although Americans won battle after battle, President Polk's strategy misfired. Despite its loss of territory and men, Mexico determinedly refused to trade land for peace. One American soldier captured the Mexican mood: "They cannot submit to be deprived of California after the loss of Texas, and nothing but the conquest of their Capital will force them to such a humiliation." Polk had arrived at the same conclusion. Zachary Taylor had not proven

decisive enough for Polk, and the president tapped another general to carry the war to Mexico City. While Taylor occupied the north, General Winfield Scott would land his army on the Gulf coast of Mexico and march 250 miles inland to the capital. Polk's plan entailed enormous risk; it meant that Scott would have to cut himself off from supplies on the coast and lead his men deep into enemy country against a numerically superior foe.

After months of careful planning and the skillful coordination of army and navy, an amphibious landing near Veracruz put 8,600 American troops ashore in five hours without the loss of a single life. The Americans encircled the city, and after eighty-eight hours of furious shelling, Veracruz surrendered. Scott immediately began preparations for the march west. Transportation alone posed enormous problems. His army required 9,300 wagons and 17,000 pack mules, 500,000 bushels of oats and corn, and 100 pounds of blister ointment before it could begin the mountainous journey. In early April 1847, the army moved out, following the path that had been trodden more than three centuries earlier by Hernán Cortés.

Meanwhile, after the frightful defeat at Buena Vista, Santa Anna had returned to Mexico City. He rallied his ragged troops and marched them east to set a trap for Scott in the mountain pass at Cerro Gordo. But the Americans knifed through Mexican lines, almost capturing Santa Anna, who fled the field on foot. So complete was the victory that Scott gloated to Taylor, "Mexico no longer has an army." But Scott barely had one either. One-third of his troops—some 3,000 men—were volunteers whose year's service had expired. Scott had no choice but to release them and wait for reinforcements. In July 1847, with the army topping 14,000 soldiers, Scott resumed his march. Ever resilient, Santa Anna again rallied the Mexican army. Some 30,000 troops took up defensive positions on the outskirts of Mexico City, where they hurriedly began melting down church bells to cast new cannon.

In August, Scott began his assault on the Mexican capital. The fighting proved the most brutal of the war. Santa Anna backed his army into the city, fighting each step of the way. At the battle of Churubusco, the Mexicans took 4,000 casualties in a single day and the Americans more than 1,000. At Chapultepec, a castle that stood two hundred feet above the marsh that surrounded it, American troops scaled the walls and fought the Mexican defenders hand to hand. Santa Anna lost 1,800 men that day, and Scott lost more than 400. After Cha-

M A P 13.6
Territorial Expansion by 1860
*Less than a century after its founding, the United States had spread from the Atlantic seaboard
to the Pacific Ocean. War, purchase, and diplomacy had gained a continent.*

pultepec, Mexico City lay open. But during the night, Santa Anna evacuated the capital, and on September 14, 1847, General Winfield Scott rode in triumphantly. The ancient capital of the Aztecs had fallen once again to an invading army.

With Mexico City in American hands, Polk sent Nicholas P. Trist, the chief clerk in the State Department, to Mexico to negotiate the peace. When Trist arrived, he found that Santa Anna had resigned as president and had fled the country. But Trist began talks with commissioners appointed by a new Mexican president and on February 2, 1848, signed the Treaty of Guadalupe Hidalgo. Mexico agreed to give up all claims to Texas above the Rio Grande and to cede the huge provinces of New Mexico and California to the United States. The United States agreed to pay Mexico $15 million and to assume $3.25 million in claims that American citizens had against Mexico. Some Americans clamored for all of Mexico, but the treaty gave the pres-

ident what he wanted. Polk sent the treaty to the Senate, which ratified it by a vote of thirty-eight to fourteen in March 1848. The last American soldiers left Mexico a few months later.

The American triumph in the Mexican War had enormous consequences. With the northern half of Mexico in American hands, for example, California gold would never make Mexicans rich or bankroll Mexico's economic development. The war also reinforced the worst stereotypes Mexicans and Americans had of each other. A virulent anti-Yankee sentiment took root in Mexico, while deeply prejudiced views of Mexicans and Mexican culture flourished in the fertile soil of American victory. For Mexico, defeat meant national humiliation, but it also had a positive effect. It generated for the first time a genuine nationalism, no small thing in a country still trying to build a nation. In America, victory increased the sense of superiority that was already deeply ingrained.

Conclusion:
Free Labor, Free Men

Less than three-quarters of a century after its founding, the United States achieved its self-proclaimed Manifest Destiny to stretch from the Atlantic to the Pacific. In the 1840s, diplomacy and war had handed the nation 1.2 million square miles and more than 1,000 miles of Pacific coastline. To most Americans, vast geographical expansion seemed to be the natural companion of a stunning economic transformation. A cluster of interrelated developments—steam power, railroads, and the growing mechanization of agriculture and manufacturing—resulted in greater productivity, a burst of output from farms and factories, and prosperity for many.

To Northerners, their industrial evolution confirmed the choice they had made to put slavery on the road to extinction and to promote free labor as the key to independence, equality, and prosperity. Millions of Northerners, like Abraham Lincoln, could point to personal experience as evidence of the practical truth of the free-labor ideal. But millions of others had different stories to tell. Rather than producing economic equality, the free-labor system saw wealth and poverty continue to rub shoulders. Instead of social independence, more than half of the nation's free-labor workforce toiled for someone else by 1860. Free-labor enthusiasts denied that the problems were built into the system. They argued that most social ills—including poverty and dependency—sprang from individual deficiencies. Consequently, reformers usually focused on the lack of self-control and discipline, on sin and alcohol. They denied that free labor meant exploitation. Slaves, not free workers, suffered, they argued.

Differences between North and South had appeared early in the nation's history, but by midcentury the distinctive ways in which North and South organized their labor systems left their mark on all aspects of regional life. Each region was increasingly animated by economic interests, cultural values, and political aims that were antithetical to those of the other. In the midst of deepening differences between the regions, Mexican land thrust the fundamental issue of slave or free labor into the center of national life. Now that Americans had half of Mexico, they had to decide what to do with it. Would the new American West, like the United States, be half slave and half free, or would it be all one or the other? The debate about the territory taken from Mexico became a struggle over the nation's future.

CHRONOLOGY

1828	America's first railroad, the Baltimore and Ohio, breaks ground.		William Henry Harrison dies in office after one month.
1836	Texas declares independence from Mexico.	**1842**	Webster-Ashburton Treaty settles all border issues with British Canada except Oregon.
1837	John Deere patents his steel plow.		
1840s	Americans begin harnessing steam power to manufacturing.	**1844**	Democrat James K. Polk elected president on platform calling for annexation of Texas and Oregon.
	Cyrus McCormick and others create practical mechanical reapers.		Samuel F. B. Morse invents telegraph.
1841	Congress approves permanent preemption law.	**1845**	Term "Manifest Destiny" coined by New York journalist John L. O'Sullivan; used as justification for Anglo-American settlers to take land in West.
	First wagon trains set out for West on Oregon Trail.		
	Vice President John Tyler becomes president of the United States when		United States annexes Texas, which enters Union as slave state.

1846 Bear Flag Revolt, independence movement to secede from Mexico, takes place in California.

May 13. Congress declares war on Mexico.

United States and Great Britain agree to divide Oregon Country at forty-ninth parallel.

1847 Brigham Young leads advance party of Mormons to Great Salt Lake in Utah.

1848 Treaty of Guadalupe Hidalgo ends Mexican War. Mexico gives up all claims to Texas north of Rio Grande and cedes provinces of New Mexico and California to United States.

Oneida community organized in New York.

First women's rights convention in United States takes place at Seneca Falls, New York.

1849 California gold rush begins.

Harriet Tubman escapes from slavery in Maryland.

1850 Mormon community of Deseret annexed to United States as Utah Territory.

1851 Conference in Laramie, Wyoming, between U.S. government and Plains tribes marks beginning of government policy of forcing Indians onto reservations.

Maine prohibits sale or manufacture of alcoholic beverages.

1855 Massachusetts integrates public schools as result of campaigns led by African American leaders.

BIBLIOGRAPHY

GENERAL WORKS

Roy P. Basler, ed., *The Collected Works of Abraham Lincoln*, 8 vols. (1953).

Stuart Bruchey, *Enterprise: The Dynamic Economy of a Free People* (1990).

Lawrence A. Cremin, *American Education: The National Experience, 1783–1876* (1980).

David B. Danbom, *Born in the Country: A History of Rural America* (1995).

David Brion Davis, ed., *Antebellum American Culture: An Interpretive Anthology* (1979).

David Herbert Donald, *Lincoln* (1995).

John Mack Faragher, *Sugar Creek: Life on the Illinois Frontier* (1986).

Lori D. Ginzberg, *Women and the Work of Benevolence: Morality, Politics, and Class in the Nineteenth-Century United States* (1990).

Nathan O. Hatch, *The Democratization of American Christianity* (1991).

John F. Kasson, *Rudeness and Civility: Manners in Nineteenth-Century Urban America* (1990).

Bruce Laurie, *Artisans into Workers: Labor in Nineteenth-Century America* (1989).

Bruce Levine, *Half Slave and Half Free: The Roots of the Civil War* (1992).

Patricia Nelson Limerick, Clyde A. Milner II, and Charles E. Rankin, eds., *Trails: Toward a New Western History* (1991).

Clyde A. Milner II, Carol A. O'Conner, and Martha A. Sandweiss, eds., *The Oxford History of the American West* (1994).

Richard White, *"It's Your Misfortune and None of My Own": A New History of the American West* (1991).

THE ECONOMY AND FREE LABOR

James R. Beniger, *The Control Revolution: Technological and Economic Origins of the Information Society* (1986).

Allan G. Bogue, *From Prairie to Corn Belt* (1963).

Alfred D. Chandler Jr., *The Visible Hand: The Managerial Revolution in American Business* (1977).

Thomas C. Cochran, *Frontiers of Change: Early Industrialism in America* (1981).

Lee Craig, *To Sow One Acre More: Childbearing and Farm Productivity in the Antebellum North* (1993).

Stanley L. Engerman and Robert E. Gallman, eds., *Long-Term Factors in American Economic Growth* (1986).

Paul Faler, *Mechanics and Manufacturers in the Early Industrial Revolution: Lynn, Massachusetts, 1780–1860* (1981).

Albert Fishlow, *American Railroads and the Transformation of the Ante-Bellum Economy* (1965).

Robert E. Gallman and John J. Wallis, eds., *American Economic Growth and Standards of Living before the Civil War* (1992).

Paul W. Gates, *The Farmer's Age: Agriculture, 1815–1860* (1960).

Jonathan A. Glickstein, *Concepts of Free Labor in Antebellum America* (1991).

Brooke Hindle, *Emulation and Invention* (1981).

Brooke Hindle and Steven Lubar, *Engines of Change: The American Industrial Revolution, 1790–1860* (1986).

Susan E. Hirsch, *Roots of the American Working Class: The Industrialization of Crafts in Newark, 1800–1860* (1978).

Donald R. Hoke, *Ingenious Yankees: The Rise of the American System of Manufactures in the Private Sector* (1990).

David A. Hounshell, *From the American System to Mass Production, 1800–1932* (1984).

Louis C. Hunter, *A History of Industrial Power in the United States, 1780–1930*, vol. 1, *Water Power in the Century of the Steam Engine* (1979), vol. 2, *Steam Power* (1985), vol. 3, *The Transmission of Power* (1991).

Paul Israel, *From Machine Shop to Industrial Laboratory: Telegraphy and the Changing Context of American Invention, 1830–1920* (1992).

Allan Kulikoff, *The Agrarian Origins of American Capitalism* (1992).

Bruce Laurie, *Working People of Philadelphia, 1800–1850* (1980).

Judith A. McGaw, *Most Wonderful Machine: Mechanization and Social Change in Berkshire Paper Making, 1801–1885* (1987).

Jonathan Prude, *The Coming of Industrial Order: Town and Factory Life in Rural Massachusetts, 1810–1860* (1983).

Daniel T. Rodgers, *The Work Ethic in Industrial America, 1850–1920* (1978).

W. J. Rorabaugh, *The Craft Apprentice: From Franklin to the Machine Age in America* (1986).

Merritt Roe Smith, *Harpers Ferry Armory and the New Technology* (1977).

John F. Stover, *The Life and Decline of the American Railroad* (1970).

John F. Stover, *Iron Road to the West: American Railraods in the 1850s* (1978).

George Rogers Taylor, *The Transportation Revolution, 1815–1860* (1951).

ANTEBELLUM CULTURE AND REFORM

Norman Basch, *In the Eyes of the Law: Women, Marriage, and Property in Nineteenth-Century New York* (1982).

Thomas Bender, ed., *The Antislavery Debate: Capitalism and Abolition as a Problem in Historical Interpretation* (1992).

Stuart Blumin, *The Emergence of the Middle Class: Social Experience in the American City, 1790–1900* (1989).

Jeanne Boydston, *Home and Housework: Housework, Wages, and the Ideology of Labor in the Early Republic* (1990).

Christopher Clark, *The Communitarian Moment: The Radical Challenge of the Northhampton Association* (1995).

Ellen Carol DuBois, *Feminism and Suffrage: The Emergence of an Independent Women's Suffrage Movement in America, 1848–1869* (1978).

Barbara Leslie Epstein, *The Politics of Domesticity: Women, Evangelism, and Temperance in Nineteenth-Century America* (1981).

Michael Fellman, *The Unbounded Frame: Freedom and Community in Nineteenth Century American Utopianism* (1973).

George Forgie, *Patricide in the House Divided: A Psychological Interpretation of Lincoln and His Age* (1979).

Lawrence Foster, *Religion and Sexuality: Three American Communal Experiments of the Nineteenth Century* (1981).

Lawrence Foster, *Women, Family, and Utopia: Communal Experiments of the Shakers, the Oneida Community, and the Mormons* (1991).

Rhoda Golden Freeman, *The Free Negro in New York City in the Era before the Civil War* (1994).

Peter Dobkin Hall, *The Organization of American Culture, 1700–1900* (1982).

Karen Halttunen, *Confidence Men and Painted Women: A Study of Middle-Class Culture in America, 1830–1870* (1982).

Blanche Glassman Hersh, *The Slavery of Sex: Feminist Abolitionists in America* (1978).

Nancy A. Hewitt, *Women's Activism and Social Change: Rochester, New York, 1822–1872* (1984).

Sylvia D. Hoffert, *When Hens Crow: The Women's Rights Movement in Antebellum America* (1995).

Joan M. Jensen, *Loosening the Bonds: Mid-Atlantic Farm Women, 1750–1850* (1986).

Carl F. Kaestle, *Pillars of the Republic: Common Schools and American Society, 1780–1860* (1983).

John F. Kasson, *Civilizing the Machine: Technology and Republican Values in America, 1776–1900* (1976).

Mary Kelley, *Private Women, Public Stage: Literary Domesticity in Nineteenth-Century America* (1984).

Spencer Klaw, *Without Sin: The Life and Death of the Oneida Community* (1993).

Jack Larkin, *The Reshaping of Everyday Life, 1790–1840* (1988).

William J. McFeely, *Frederick Douglass* (1991).

Keith E. Melder, *Beginnings of Sisterhood: The American Women's Rights Movement, 1800–1850* (1977).

Kerby A. Miller, *Emigrants and Exiles: Ireland and the Irish Exodus to North America* (1985).

Steven Mintz, *Moralists and Modernizers: America's Pre-Civil War Reformers* (1995).

Steven Mintz and Susan Kellogg, *Domestic Revolutions: A Social History of American Family Life* (1988).

C. Peter Ripley et al., eds., *Witness for Freedom: African American Voices on Race, Slavery, and Emancipation* (1993).

W. J. Rorabaugh, *The Alcoholic Republic: An American Tradition* (1979).

John R. Stilgoe, *Borderland: Origins of the American Suburb, 1820–1939* (1988).

Shirley Yee, *Black Women Abolitionists: A Study in Activism, 1828–1860* (1992).

Jean Fagan Yellin, *Women and Sisters: The Antislavery Feminists in American Culture* (1989).

Jean Fagan Yellin and John C. Van Horne, eds., *The Abolitionist Sisterhood: Women's Political Culture in Antebellum America* (1994).

POLITICS AND EXPANSION

Nels Anderson, *Desert Saints: The Mormon Frontier in Utah* (2nd ed., 1966).

Leonard J. Arrington and Davis Bitton, *The Mormon Experience* (1979).

Irving H. Bartlett, *John C. Calhoun: A Biography* (1993).

Richard A. Bartlett, *The New Country: A Social History of the American Frontier, 1776–1890* (1974).

William A. Bowen, *The Willamette Valley: Migration and Settlement on the Oregon Frontier* (1978).

Gene M. Brack, *Mexico Views Manifest Destiny, 1821–1846* (1975).

John Faragher, *Women and Men on the Overland Trail* (1979).

William H. Goetzmann, *New Lands, New Men: America and the Second Great Age of Discovery* (1986).

Norman A. Graebner, *The Foundation of American Foreign Policy* (1985).

William Greever, *Bonanza West: The Story of the Western Mining Rushes, 1848–1900* (1963).

Thomas R. Hietala, *Manifest Design: Anxious Aggrandizement in Late Jacksonian America* (1985).

Albert L. Hurtado, *Indian Survival on the California Frontier* (1988).

Reginald Horseman, *Race and Manifest Destiny: The Origins of American Racial Anglo-Saxonism* (1981).

Robert H. Jackson and Edward Castillo, *Indians, Franciscans, and Spanish Colonization: The Impact of the Mission System on California Indians* (1995).

Julie Roy Jeffrey, *Frontier Women: The Trans-Mississippi West, 1840–1880* (1979).

Rudolph M. Lapp, *Blacks in Goldrush California* (1977).

Patricia Nelson Limerick, *The Legacy of Conquest: The Unbroken Past of the American West* (1987).

Ward McAfee and J. Cordell Robinson, eds., *Origins of the Mexican War: A Documentary Source Book*, 2 vols. (1982).

Charles J. McClain, *In Search of Equality: The Chinese Struggle against Discrimination in Nineteenth-Century America* (1994).

D. W. Meinig, *The Shaping of America: A Geographical Perspective on Five Hundred Years of History*, vol. 2, *Continental America, 1800–1867* (1993).

Frederick Merk, *Manifest Destiny and Mission in American History* (1963).

Michael C. Meyer and William L. Sherman, *The Course of Mexican History* (4th ed., 1991).

Rodman W. Paul, *Mining Frontiers of the Far West, 1848–1880* (1963).

David M. Pletcher, *The Diplomacy of Annexation: Texas, Oregon, and the Mexican War* (1973).

Glenda Riley, *The Female Frontier: A Comparative View of Women on the Prairie and the Plains* (1988).

Malcolm J. Rohrbough, *The Trans-Appalachian Frontier* (1978).

Charles Sellers, *The Market Revolution: Jacksonian America, 1815–1846* (1991).

Joel H. Silbey, *The American Political Nation, 1838–1893* (1991).

Kevin Starr, *Americans and the California Dream, 1850–1915* (1973).

Ronald Takaki, *Iron Cages: Race and Culture in Nineteenth-Century America* (1979).

John D. Unruh, *The Plains Across: The Overland Emigrants and the Trans-Mississippi West, 1840–1860* (1979).

Robert M. Utley, *The Indian Frontier of the American West, 1846–1890* (1984).

David J. Weber, *The Mexican Frontier, 1821–1846* (1982).

Sanford Wexler, ed., *Westward Expansion: An Eyewitness History* (1991).

THE MEXICAN WAR

K. Jack Bauer, *The Mexican War, 1846–1848* (1974).

Seymour V. Conner and Odie B. Faulk, *North America Divided: The Mexican War, 1846–1848* (1971).

John S. C. Eisenhower, *So Far from God: The U.S. War with Mexico, 1846–1848* (1989).

Robert W. Johannsen, *To the Halls of the Montezumas: The Mexican War in the American Imagination* (1985).

Ernest M. Lander Jr., *Reluctant Imperialists: Calhoun, the South Carolinians, and the Mexican War* (1980).

James M. McCaffrey, *Army of Manifest Destiny: The American Soldiers in the Mexican War, 1846–1848* (1992).

Ramon Eduardo Ruiz, ed., *The Mexican War: Was It Manifest Destiny?* (1963).

John H. Schroeder, *Mr. Polk's War* (1973).

Otis A. Singletary, *The Mexican War* (1960).

In other words, rather than judging the case on its merits, the justices had retaliated against the abolitionists.

But Dred and Harriet Scott and their supporters (white friends, several sympathetic lawyers, and probably some of St. Louis's free blacks) were not easily discouraged. In 1854, Dred Scott turned to the federal courts in Missouri, but lost. He and his family remained slaves. Scott then appealed to the highest court of the land—the U.S. Supreme Court. Although proslavery and antislavery forces had begun to see the potential opportunity (and danger) in the *Dred Scott* case, no one could have anticipated the sweeping decision that came down from the Supreme Court in 1857. It left the Scotts slaves, and it brought the nation closer to civil war.

What had begun as the straightforward effort of one black family to gain freedom had become entangled in the national debate over slavery. One month after the Scotts filed their first lawsuits for freedom in 1846, the United States went to war with Mexico. Three months later, Representative David Wilmot introduced a bill to prohibit slavery from any territory that might be acquired as a result of the war. After that, the nation was bitterly divided by the problem of slavery in the territories. The principle of excluding slavery from the territories set the course of national politics for the next decade and a half. South Carolina Senator John C. Calhoun saw the sad truth of Mexican land earlier than most. "Mexico is to us the forbidden fruit," he declared in May 1846. "The penalty of eating it [is] to subject our institutions to political death."

Once Mexican land thrust the issue of the expansion of slavery into national politics, no one could get it out. For a decade and a half, slavery poisoned national political debate and contaminated issues that were only distantly related. Slavery proved powerful enough to transform party politics into sectional politics. Rather than Whigs and Democrats confronting one another across party lines, Northerners and Southerners eyed one another with hostility across the Mason-Dixon line. Sectional politics worked like a blacksmith's hammer on the South's separatist impulses. A fitful tendency before the Mexican War, southern separatism gained strength with each blow. As the nation lurched from crisis to crisis, southern disaffection and alienation mounted. Year by year, the constituency for conciliation and compromise wore away. The era ended as it began—with a crisis of the Union. By 1861, men who had fought side by side at Buena Vista and Cerro Gordo trained their cannon on one another. As Abraham Lincoln predicted, "a house divided against itself cannot stand."

Fruits of War

Congress had faced the question of slavery in the national territories before the Mexican War. But history provided contradictory precedents. In 1787, Congress passed the Northwest Ordinance, which banned slavery north of the Ohio River. In 1803, when the United States acquired the Louisiana Territory, where slavery was already legal, Congress allowed slavery to remain. As part of the Missouri Compromise of 1820, Congress voted to prohibit slavery in part of the territory and allow it in the rest.

In 1846, when it appeared that the war with Mexico would mean new U.S. territories, politicians put on the table a variety of very different plans. David Wilmot proposed totally excluding slavery from the territories. President James K. Polk and others called for extending the Missouri Compromise line of 36°30' all the way to the Pacific. Southerners often advocated the uninhibited spread of slavery to all the territories. Some Northerners and Southerners joined to advocate letting the people of each territory themselves decide whether to allow slavery. When the Mexican War ended in 1848, Congress had made no headway in solving the great issue before it. Nor did the presidential election that year produce an answer. Instead, the territorial issue ripped apart the Whig and Democratic Parties, spawned a third party, and raised the political temperature of the nation to a boil. In 1850, after four years of strife, Congress patched together a settlement, one that promised to be permanent but actually proved transient.

The Wilmot Proviso and the Expansion of Slavery

Curiously, between 1846 and 1861, Americans did not focus on slavery where it existed but on the possibility that it might expand into areas where it did not exist. The Constitution confined the sectional controversy to these narrow limits. Except for a few abolitionists who strove to uproot slavery wherever they found it, most of the nation agreed that the Constitution had left the issue of slavery to the in-

PINE FOREST, OREGON
This 1844 engraving by William E. Tucker illustrates the gargantuan size of the Northwest's timber.
Some Easterners were awed by the size of nature's bounty; others calculated the board feet in a single
tree. Images such as this inspired hundreds of thousands of white men to dream of land in the West.
Library of Congress.

dividual states to decide. One by one, northern states had done away with slavery, while southern states had retained it. But what about slavery in the nation's territories? The Constitution stated that "Congress shall have Power to . . . make all needful Rules and Regulations respecting the Territory . . . belonging to the United States." The debate between the North and South about slavery, then, turned toward Congress and the definition of its authority over western lands.

The spark for the national debate was provided in August 1846 by a young Democratic representative from Pennsylvania, David Wilmot, who proposed that Congress bar slavery from all lands acquired in the war with Mexico. He modeled his proposal, which became known as the Wilmot Proviso, after the Northwest Ordinance of 1787, which banned slavery in territory north of the Ohio River.

Wilmot explained that the Mexicans had already abolished slavery in all of their territory. "God forbid," he declared, "that we should be the means of planting this institution upon it."

Although a newcomer to Congress, Wilmot had his finger on the pulse of northern sentiment. Regardless of party affiliation, Northerners wanted to stop the spread of slavery. The Wilmot Proviso rallied an interesting assortment of antislavery Northerners. Abolitionists, of course, supported "free soil," that is, territory from which slavery was prohibited. They saw slavery as a moral disaster and wanted Congress not only to deny slavery room to expand but also to destroy it where it existed. Many Whigs also stepped forward on the basis of principle. They often denounced slavery as a sin and emphasized Congress's authority to ban it from the territories.

But not all Northerners who opposed slavery's extension did so out of sympathy for slaves. Support for the Wilmot Proviso did not stem entirely, or even primarily, from humanitarian concern. The proviso also found support among Democratic politicians who feared that the Whigs would pick up voters by claiming that the Mexican War was a landgrab for slaveholders. By denying slavery a place in the territory the United States took from Mexico, Democrats could support expansion without offending antislavery constituents. A Connecticut representative declared that it was time "when the Northern democracy should make a stand. . . . We must satisfy the northern people . . . that we are not to extend the institution of slavery as a result of this war." Another Northerner declared that the "adoption of the principle of the 'Wilmot proviso' is the only way to *save* the Democratic party in the free states." Without coming out against slavery's expansion, Democrats "are destined to defeat and doomed . . . from Iowa to Maine."

Support for blocking slavery's expansion also came from Northerners—Whigs as well as Democrats—who were not so much antislavery as they were anti-South. New slave territories would eventually mean new slave states, and they wanted nothing to do with magnifying the power of Southerners in national politics. From experience they knew that proslavery Southerners often brought to Congress economic policies radically different from their own, especially in banking, internal improvements, and the tariff.

Further support came from Northerners who were hostile to slavery's expansion because they were hostile to African Americans. They wanted to reserve new lands for whites. Wilmot himself had blatantly encouraged racist support when he declared, "I would preserve for free white labor a fair country, a rich inheritance, where the sons of toil, of my own race and own color, can live without the disgrace which association with negro slavery brings upon free labor." Hundreds of thousands of white men dreamed of land in the West, and few wanted to work shoulder to shoulder with slaves or with free African Americans. It's no wonder that some called the Wilmot Proviso the White Man's Proviso.

While the specter of new slave territory alarmed diverse Northerners, the thought that slavery might be excluded outraged diverse Southerners. From the colonial era, yeoman and planter alike regarded the West as a ladder for economic and so-

cial opportunity. Southern whites never thought of expansion apart from slavery. Southerners who recognized that the arid West was less than ideal plantation country still agreed that the exclusion of slavery was a slap in the face. From Virginia to Texas, whites denounced the proviso as grossly unfair and insulting. "If by your legislation you seek to drive us from the territories of California and New Mexico . . . thereby attempting to fix a national degradation upon half the States of this Confederacy," Robert Toombs of Georgia fumed, "*I am for disunion.*" An Alabamian pointed out that at least half of the American soldiers in Mexico were Southerners. "When the war-worn soldier returns home," he asked, "is he to be told that he cannot carry his property to the country won by his blood?"

But to Southerners, territorial expansion involved even more than economic opportunity, social mobility, and honor. Southern leaders had always understood the need for political parity with the North to protect the South's interests, especially slavery. The need never seemed more urgent than in the 1840s, when the North's population and wealth was booming. James Henry Hammond of South Carolina predicted that ten new states would be carved from the acquired Mexican land. If free soil won, the North would "ride over us rough shod" in Congress, he claimed. "Our only safety is in *equality* of POWER."

In the nation's capital, foes of slavery's expansion squared off against foes of slavery's exclusion. Because Northerners had a majority in the House, they easily passed the Wilmot Proviso over the united opposition of Southerners. In the Senate, John C. Calhoun denied that Congress had constitutional authority to exclude slavery from the nation's territories. In a series of closely reasoned resolutions, he declared that the territories were the "joint and common property" of all the states, that Congress could not justly deprive any state of equal rights in the territories, and that Congress therefore could not bar citizens of one state from migrating with their property (including slaves) to the territories. Where Wilmot demanded that Congress slam shut the door to slavery, Calhoun required that Congress hold the door wide open. Because slave states outnumbered free states fifteen to fourteen, southern senators stopped the proviso.

Between these extremes there appeared to be little middle ground. One plan—to extend the Missouri Compromise line to the Pacific—generated no significant enthusiasm. But Senator Lewis Cass of

Michigan offered a compromise that he hoped would find support among moderates everywhere. He proposed the doctrine of "popular sovereignty": letting the people who actually settled the territories decide for themselves slavery's fate. This solution, Cass argued, sat squarely in the American tradition of democracy and local self-government. It had the added attraction of removing the incendiary issue of the expansion of slavery from Congress and lodging it in distant, sleepy territorial legislatures, where it would excite fewer passions.

> *Northerners who demanded no new slave territory anywhere, ever, and Southerners who demanded free entry for their slave property into all territories, or else, staked out their extreme positions.*

The most attractive feature of Cass's popular sovereignty plan was its ambiguity about the precise moment when settlers could determine slavery's fate. That imprecision made possible different predictions about the plan's consequences. Northern advocates told their constituents that the decision on slavery could be made as soon as the first territorial legislature assembled. With free-soil majorities likely, they would shut the door to slavery almost before the first slave arrived. Southern supporters, for their part, declared that popular sovereignty guaranteed that slavery would be unrestricted throughout the entire territorial period. Only at the very end, when settlers drew up a constitution and applied for statehood, could they decide the issue of slavery or freedom. By then, slavery would have sunk deep roots. The southern interpretation made popular sovereignty almost indistinguishable from Calhoun's doctrine. As long as the matter of timing remained vague, popular sovereignty provided some Northerners and some Southerners common ground.

When Congress ground to a halt in 1848, no plan had won a majority in both houses. Northerners who demanded no new slave territory anywhere, ever, and Southerners who demanded free entry for their slave property into all territories, or else, staked out their extreme positions, further polarizing the issue. Unresolved in Congress, the territorial question naturally intruded into the presidential election of 1848.

The Election of 1848

The Democratic and Whig Parties were both hurting in 1848. The territorial debate revealed free-soil factions in both parties. Antislavery northern Democrats challenged Democratic President Polk and the dominant southern element of their party. Northern Whigs split between an antislavery faction called Conscience Whigs and a more conservative group, Cotton Whigs (because many of them were textile mill owners) who sought to compromise the territorial issue to hold the party together. Conscience Whigs denounced the evil alliance of northern "lords of the loom" and southern "lords of the lash" and threatened to bolt the party.

Polk—worn out, ailing, and unable to unite the Democratic Party—chose not to seek reelection. The Democratic convention nominated Senator Lewis Cass of Michigan, the man most closely associated with the doctrine of popular sovereignty, but the party platform avoided a firm position on slavery in the territories. One angry antislavery Democratic faction, dubbed the Barnburners, nominated their own candidate, former president Martin Van Buren, on a free-soil platform.

The Whigs followed a different strategy in their effort to patch the fissures within the party over slavery. They passed over "Mr. Whig" himself—

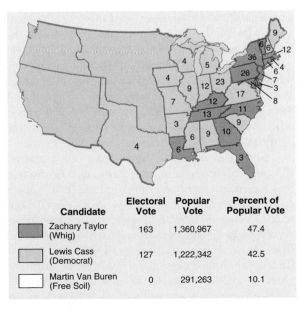

Candidate	Electoral Vote	Popular Vote	Percent of Popular Vote
Zachary Taylor (Whig)	163	1,360,967	47.4
Lewis Cass (Democrat)	127	1,222,342	42.5
Martin Van Buren (Free Soil)	0	291,263	10.1

MAP 14.1
The Election of 1848

GENERAL TAYLOR CIGAR CASE
This papier-mâché cigar case portrays General Zachary Taylor, Whig presidential candidate in 1848, in a colorful scene from the Mexican War. Shown as a dashing, elegant officer, Taylor was in fact a short, thickset, and roughly dressed Indian fighter who had spent his career commanding small frontier garrisons. The inscription reminds voters that Taylor was a victor in the first four battles fought in the war and directs attention away from the fact that in politics he was a rank amateur.
Collection of Janice L. and David J. Frent.

Henry Clay, the seventy-one-year-old founder of the party and chief spokesman for its American System. Clay carried the burden of being a three-time loser in presidential campaigns as well as the additional liability of having opposed the successful war with Mexico. Instead, the Whigs nominated the hero of Buena Vista, "Old Rough and Ready," General Zachary Taylor, and they declined to adopt any party platform, no matter how vague. The Whigs bet that a military hero who had never voted and who had no known political opinions, combined with total silence on the central issue before the country, would carry the day.

Taylor, who owned more than one hundred slaves on plantations in Mississippi and Louisiana, was hailed by Georgian Robert Toombs as a "Southern man, a slaveholder, a cotton planter." Conscience Whigs balked and looked for an alternative. As old party allegiances unraveled, the time seemed ripe for a major political realignment. Senator Charles Sumner called for "one grand Northern party of Freedom," and in the summer of 1848 antislavery Democrats and antislavery Whigs founded the Free-Soil Party. Nearly 15,000 noisy Free-Soilers gathered in Buffalo, New York, where they welded the factions together by nominating a dissident

Democrat, Martin Van Buren, for president and a Conscience Whig, Charles Francis Adams, for vice president. The platform boldly proclaimed, "Free soil, free speech, free labor, and free men."

The November election dashed the hopes of the Free-Soilers. Although they succeeded in making slavery the campaign's central issue, they could not lure enough Whigs and Democrats out of the old parties to win. The Free-Soil Party gained 291,000 votes but did not carry a single state. The major parties went through contortions to present their candidates favorably in both the North and the South, and their evasions succeeded. The Whigs' Taylor polled 1,360,000 votes to 1,222,000 for the Democrats' Cass. Taylor won the all-important electoral vote 163 to 127, carrying eight of the fifteen slave states and seven of fifteen free states. (Wisconsin had entered the Union earlier in 1848, making fifteen slave states and fifteen free states.) Northern voters proved they were not yet ready for Sumner's "one grand Northern party of Freedom," but the struggle between freedom and slavery in the territories had shaken the major parties badly.

The "Great Debate"

Zachary Taylor was very much a mystery when he entered the White House in March 1849. He had purposefully remained vague on the slavery issue throughout the campaign, and no one could claim to know what this political novice would do in office. He surprised almost everyone—and he infuriated Southerners. Who among them had imagined that the slaveholding father-in-law of Mississippi Senator Jefferson Davis would champion a free-soil solution to the problem of western land? But he did. The discovery of gold in California and the rush of 1849 made the existing military rule of California and New Mexico pitifully inadequate and the need for competent civil government urgent. Taylor sent agents west to urge settlers to frame constitutions and apply immediately for admission to the Union as states. The settlers acted quickly. Predominantly antislavery, they began writing free-state constitutions and anticipated knocking on Congress's door for admission. "For the first time," Jefferson Davis declared, "we are about permanently to destroy the balance of power between the sections."

When Congress convened in December 1849, anxious citizens packed the galleries. Latecomers spilled over into the halls and lobbies, happy even for standing room at the "Great Debate." They witnessed what proved to be one of the longest, most contentious, and most significant sessions in the history of Congress. For seven months, politicians orated, debated, buttonholed, cajoled, and threatened in efforts to fashion a solution to the problems that divided the nation.

The previous Congress had left a raft of unfinished business, and foremost was the territorial issue. In January 1850, President Taylor urged Congress to admit California as a state immediately and to admit New Mexico, which lagged behind by a few months, as soon as it applied. Southerners exploded. In their eyes, Taylor had betrayed his region. Southerners who would "consent to be thus degraded and enslaved," a North Carolinian declared, "ought to be whipped through their fields by their own negroes." Calhoun almost lost heart. "As things now stand," he said in February, the South "cannot with safety remain in the Union." The sense of emergency strengthened the movement toward southern unity that Calhoun had pushed for years. From Mississippi came a menacing call for a convention of southern states "to devise and adopt some mode of resistance to northern aggression." It would meet in Nashville on the first Monday in June 1850.

Into this rancorous scene stepped Henry Clay, recently returned to the Senate by his home state of Kentucky. His reputation preceded him: the "Great Pacificator," master of accommodation, architect of Union-saving compromises in the Missouri and nullification crises. At seventy-two, Clay remained a powerful public speaker, and he had no doubt that the South's desperate mood threatened the survival of the Union.

"Mr. President," Clay declared when he took the floor on January 29, 1850, "I hold in my hand a series of resolutions which I desire to submit to the consideration of this body. Taken together, in combination, they propose an amicable arrangement of all questions in controversy between the free and slave states, growing out of the subject of slavery." His comprehensive plan consisted of a series of proposals that sought to balance the interests of the slave and free states. Admit California as a free state, he proposed, but organize the rest of the Southwest without restrictions on slavery. Abolish the slave trade in Washington, D.C., but confirm slavery itself in the nation's capital. Require Texas to abandon its claim to parts of New Mexico, but compensate it by assuming its preannexation debt. Reassert Congress's lack of authority to interfere with the in-

JOHN C. CALHOUN
Hollow-cheeked and dark-eyed in this 1850 daguerreotype by Mathew Brady, Calhoun had only months to live. Still, his passion and indomitable will come through. British writer Harriet Martineau once described the champion of southern rights as "the cast-iron man who looks as if he had never been born and could never be extinguished."
National Portrait Gallery, Smithsonian Institution/Art Resource, N.Y.

terstate slave trade. And enact a more effective fugitive slave law. The Peacemaker offered concessions to both sections in the hope of finding a balance that would preserve the imperiled Union.

Abolitionists and "fire-eaters" (as radical southern secessionists were called) stumbled over one another in their rush to condemn Clay's plan. Senator Salmon Chase of Ohio ridiculed it as "sentiment for the North, substance for the South." Senator Henry S. Foote of Mississippi denounced it as more offensive to the South than the speeches of abolitionists William Lloyd Garrison, Wendell Phillips, and Frederick Douglass combined.

The most ominous response came from the mighty Calhoun. Too weakened by consumption to deliver his own speech, he slumped in his Senate chair, wrapped his black cloak around him, and listened as a colleague read for him his gloomy words concluding that the time for compromise had passed. Unending northern agitation on the slavery question, Calhoun said, had "snapped" many of the "cords which bind these states together in one common Union . . . and has greatly weakened all the others." The fragile political equilibrium between North and South depended on continued equal representation in the Senate, which Clay's plan for a free California destroyed. Without equality, Calhoun declared, Southerners were defenseless and could not remain in the Union. The Senate had never witnessed a more somber diagnosis of the Union's health.

After Clay and Calhoun had spoken, it was time for the third member of the "great triumvirate," Daniel Webster of Massachusetts. The Senate debate of 1850 proved to be the final scene for these three statesmen, whose careers had dominated national politics for decades. All were born during the American Revolution. Calhoun would be gone in less than a month, Clay and Webster in two years. They gave virtuoso performances, with Calhoun prophesying darkly that all was lost and Clay and Webster eloquently championing conciliation.

"Mr. President," Webster began his March 7 address, "I wish to speak today, not as a Massachusetts man, nor as a Northern man, but as an American. . . . I speak today for the preservation of the Union. 'Hear me for my cause.'" Admitting that the South had grievances that required redress, he argued forcefully that secession from the Union would mean civil war. He also appealed for an end to reckless proposals, and, to the dismay of many Northerners, he mentioned by name the Wilmot Proviso. A legal ban on slavery in the territories was unnecessary, he said, because nature prohibited the expansion of cotton and slaves into the Southwest. Why, then, "taunt" or "reproach" Southerners with the proviso? "I would not take pains to reaffirm an ordinance of nature nor to reenact the will of God," he said. Like Clay, Webster sought to balance the grievances of the North and South and build a constituency for compromise among moderates.

Free-soil forces recoiled from Webster's desertion. Theodore Parker, a Boston clergyman and abolitionist, could only conclude that "the Southern men" must have offered Webster the presidency. Senator William H. Seward of New York responded that Webster's and Clay's compromise with slavery

was "radically wrong and essentially vicious." He flatly rejected Calhoun's argument that Congress lacked constitutional authority to exclude slavery from the territories. In any case, Seward said, in the most sensational moment in his address, there was a "higher law than the Constitution"—the law of God—to ensure freedom in all the public domain. Claiming that God was a Free-Soiler did nothing to cool the superheated atmosphere of Washington.

Still, other politicians feverishly sought a solution. In May, a Senate committee (with the tireless Clay at its head) reported a bill that joined Clay's resolutions into a single comprehensive package, known as the Omnibus Bill because it was a vehicle on which "every sort of passenger" could ride. Clay bet that a majority of Congress wanted compromise and that while the omnibus contained items individuals disliked, each would vote for the package to gain an overall settlement of sectional issues. Clay's bundle of resolutions helped to take the wind out of the sails of the fire-eaters at the Nashville convention, which met in early June 1850. With the omnibus before the Senate, secessionists found it impossible to persuade delegates from nine southern states that there was no hope for the South in the Union. The convention adjourned after doing nothing more threatening than agreeing to a vague resolution in favor of southern rights.

Zachary Taylor came out against Clay's omnibus and reaffirmed his own plan for California and New Mexico. The president's opposition threatened to sink Clay's bill, but on July 9, 1850, Taylor suddenly died. Prospects for compromise soared when his successor, Vice President Millard Fillmore of New York, gave his support to Clay. Still, as critics had predicted, the omnibus strategy backfired. Clay had barely released his bill—his "dove of peace," he said—when congressional sharpshooters took aim. Free-Soilers, Conscience Whigs, and proslavery Southerners would support separate parts of Clay's bill, but they would not endorse the whole. After seventy speeches defending his plan, Clay saw it go down to defeat.

Fortunately for those who favored a settlement, Senator Stephen A. Douglas, a rising Democratic star from Illinois, stepped into Clay's shoes. He had never believed in the omnibus strategy. Instead, he broke the bill into its various parts and skillfully ushered each through Congress by fashioning a different coalition for the support of each bill. The agreement Douglas won in September 1850 was very much the one Clay had proposed in February.

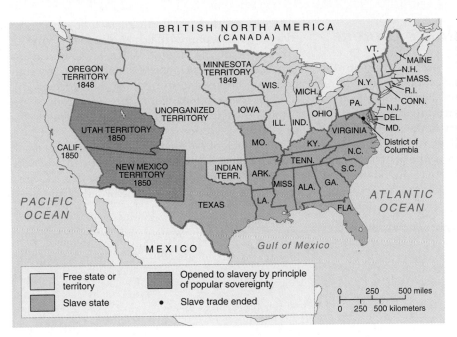

MAP 14.2
The Compromise of 1850
The patched-together sectional agreement was both clumsy and unstable. Few Americans — in either the North or the South — supported all five parts of the compromise.

California entered the Union as a free state. New Mexico and Utah became territories in which the question of slavery would be decided by popular sovereignty. Congress enacted a more stringent fugitive slave law. It ended the slave trade in the District of Columbia. Texas accepted its present-day boundary with New Mexico and received $10 million from the federal government. In September, President Fillmore signed each bill into law.

The "Compromise" of 1850

After seven months of some of the most majestic oratory and roughest infighting in Senate history, Congress completed its patchwork settlement of the sectional problem. Collectively known as the Compromise of 1850, it was hailed by President Fillmore as "the final settlement."

Unionists everywhere breathed a sigh of relief and then broke out in raucous celebration. The Union had teetered at the edge of an abyss, and Americans had snatched it back. Free-soil and southern rights forces, however, saw little to cheer about and much to regret. From 1846 to 1850, antislavery Northerners had demanded that Congress prohibit slavery's expansion into the territories. Now Congress had abandoned the Wilmot Proviso and promised noninterference with slavery in New Mexico and Utah. Similarly, proslavery Southerners steadfastly demanded equality in the Senate, and

now California's statehood ended the old balance of slave and free states.

Actually, the Compromise of 1850 was not a true compromise at all. Douglas's parliamentary skill, not a spirit of conciliation, led to legislative success. Douglas understood that true compromisers—individuals who were willing to make mutual concessions—were a decided minority. But compromisers held the balance of power between the larger blocs of Northerners and Southerners who voted along sectional lines. Only by nimbly allying the compromisers and Southerners on one bill, then the compromisers and Northerners on another, did Douglas gain the majority for each separate measure.

Nor, we now know, was the settlement "final." Congress had managed to fashion only a truce, an armistice. The settlement resolved certain pesky conflicts, and it preserved the Union and peace for the moment, no small feat given the severity of the threats. But it scarcely touched the deeper conflict over slavery. Free-Soiler Salmon Chase was correct when he told Congress, "The question of slavery in the territories has been avoided. It has not been settled."

Still, the settlement broke the deadlock between the North and the South that had paralyzed the national government for four years. Now, most Americans hoped, Congress could do business without confronting the eternal slavery question.

The Sectional Balance Undone

The words "final settlement" echoed through the halls of Congress like a magical phrase, but, in reality, the Compromise of 1850 began to come apart almost immediately. The thread that unraveled the Compromise was not slavery in the Southwest, the crux of the disagreement, but runaway slaves in New England, a component of the settlement that had received relatively little attention. Southerners made it clear from the beginning that sectional

peace depended on Northerners living up to the bargain, every part of it. But Northerners found enforcement of the fugitive slave law repulsive. It made them players in the national drama, and some found it impossible to perform the expected role. Rather than restore calm, the Compromise disrupted their lives by bringing the horrors of slavery into the North.

Millions of Northerners who never saw a runaway slave also discovered slavery in the early 1850s. Harriet Beecher Stowe's *Uncle Tom's Cabin*, a novel that vividly depicted the brutality and heart-

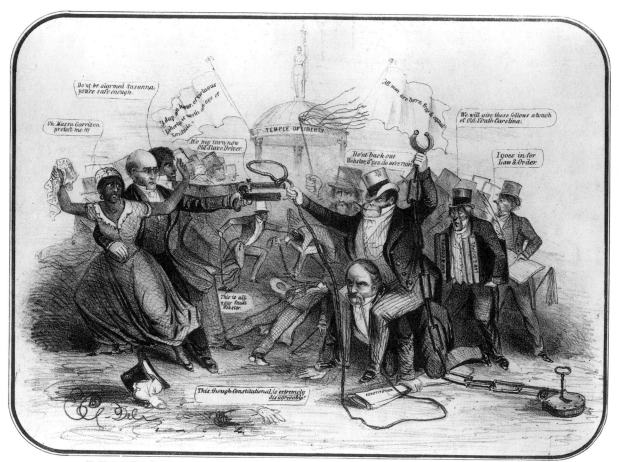

PRACTICAL ILLUSTRATION OF THE FUGITIVE SLAVE LAW.

FUGITIVE SLAVE CARTOON
In this scathing attack on the Fugitive Slave Act of 1850, a brutal southern slave catcher rides Daniel Webster, who counseled compliance with the act. With a chain in one hand and a rope in the other, the slave catcher attempts to capture a woman and take her south. The slave catchers parade the fact that they have the law on their side, but the woman's black and white defenders take up arms nevertheless. "Every slave-hunter," Frederick Douglass declared, "who meets a bloody death in this infernal business, is an argument in favor of the manhood of our race."
Library of Congress.

lessness of the South's "peculiar institution," swept the North. It aroused passions so deep that many found goodwill toward white Southerners nearly impossible. But no popular uprising forced Congress to reopen the slavery controversy. Politicians did it themselves. Four years after Congress delicately stitched the sectional compromise together, it ripped the threads out. It reopened the question of slavery in the territories, the most deadly of all sectional issues.

The Fugitive Slave Act

When Henry Clay and Daniel Webster died within four months of each other in 1852, eulogies for the statesmen emphasized a single theme: the preservation of the Union. Yet one week after Webster's death, Theodore Parker, a preacher and abolitionist, sounded a very different note. Yes, Parker said, Webster was a great man, his boyhood hero, but the truth was that Webster was a fallen angel. Among his sins, none was blacker than his March 7 speech in the Senate in 1850. "Think of him!" Parker shouted. "The Daniel Webster of Plymouth Rock advocating the 'Compromise Measures.' . . . Think of Daniel Webster become the assassin of Liberty in the Capitol! Think of him . . . scoffing at the Higher Law of God." Indeed, as Parker noted, Webster had spoken vigorously during his last two years of life for the enforcement of the Compromise, including its Fugitive Slave Act. "No man is at liberty to set up . . . his own conscience as above the law," Webster had reminded New Englanders. But Theodore Parker denounced the law as "a hateful statute of kidnappers" and headed a Boston vigilance committee that openly violated it.

The Fugitive Slave Act proved the most explosive of the Compromise measures. The issue of runaways was as old as the Constitution, which contained a provision for the return of any "person held to service or labor in one state" who escaped to another. In 1793, a federal law gave muscle to the provision by authorizing slave owners to enter other states to recapture their slave property. It also denied runaways jury trials and the right to testify in their own defense. Proclaiming the 1793 law a license to kidnap free blacks, northern states in the 1830s began passing "personal liberty laws" that provided fugitives with some protection. Many northern communities also formed vigilance committees to help runaways and to obstruct white Southerners who came north to reclaim them. Each year, a few hundred slaves escaped into free states

and found friendly northern "conductors" who put them aboard the "underground railroad," which was not a railroad at all but a series of secret "stations" (hideouts) on the way to Canada.

Furious about northern interference, Southerners in 1850 insisted that any comprehensive settlement of sectional differences include an effective fugitive slave law. They got what they wanted in the stricter law passed as part of the Compromise. To seize an alleged slave, a slaveholder or his agent simply had to appear before a commissioner appointed by the court and swear that the runaway was his. The commissioner earned ten dollars for every black returned to slavery but only five dollars for those set free. Most galling to Northerners, the law stipulated that all citizens were expected to assist officials in apprehending runaways. That required Northerners to become slave catchers. Sickened by the prospect, thousands vowed never to track down people who had risked their lives fleeing slavery.

The words "final settlement" echoed through the halls of Congress like a magical phrase, but in reality the Compromise of 1850 began to come apart almost immediately.

Within a month, slaveholders claimed runaways from the East Coast to the Great Lakes. Storms of resistance sprang up. On October 8, 1850, a slave owner claimed a black man in Detroit and had him arrested. Several hundred armed African Americans surrounded the jail. Instead of attacking, they raised five hundred dollars and offered to buy the runaway's freedom. The owner pocketed the money and quickly got out of town. An angry crowd in Boston showed less restraint. In February 1851, they overpowered federal marshals and snatched a runaway named Shadrach from a courtroom, put him on the underground railroad, and whisked him off to Montreal, Canada. Many communities, however, lost longtime African American residents. In Indiana, agents ripped one man away from his wife and children and returned him to a slave owner who claimed the man had run away nineteen years earlier.

Southerners viewed the Fugitive Slave Act as the one true concession they received in the Compromise. Now it seemed that the "fanatics of the 'higher law' creed" had whipped Northerners into a frenzy of massive resistance. Actually, the overwhelming majority of fugitives claimed before federal commissioners were reenslaved and shipped South peacefully. Spectacular rescues such as the one that saved Shadrach were rare. Still, brutal enforcement of the unpopular law had a radicalizing effect in the North, particularly in New England. Textile owner Amos A. Lawrence, a Cotton Whig eager for good relations with the South, said that "we went to bed one night old fashioned, conservative, Compromise Union Whigs & waked up stark mad Abolitionists." He exaggerated, but it did seem to Southerners that Northerners had betrayed the Compromise and the Constitution. And as a Tennessee man warned in November 1850, "If the fugitive slave bill is not enforced in the north, the moderate men of the South . . . will be overwhelmed by the 'fire-eaters.'"

Uncle Tom's Cabin

The spectacle of shackled African Americans being herded south seared the conscience of every Northerner who witnessed such a scene. But, curiously, even more Northerners were turned against slavery by a fictional account, a novel. Harriet Beecher Stowe, a Northerner who had never seen a plantation, made the South's slaves into flesh-and-blood human beings, more real than life.

The daughter of evangelist Lyman Beecher and a member of the famous clan of preachers, teachers, and reformers, Stowe despised the slave catchers. She had done a bit of writing in moments snatched from her domestic responsibilities as wife of Calvin Stowe and mother of seven children, and she decided to do something that would expose the sin of slavery. Beginning in June 1851 as a serial in an antislavery weekly, *Uncle Tom's Cabin, or Life among the Lowly* made the author famous before the final installment was printed ten months later. Published as a book in March 1852, it kept the presses running night and day. After a year, it had sold 300,000 copies and had become America's first literary blockbuster. By the end of the decade, more than three million copies had been sold at home and overseas.

Stowe's characters leaped from the page. Here was the gentle slave Uncle Tom, a Christian saint who forgave those who beat him to death; the courageous slave Eliza, who fled with her child across the frozen Ohio River; and the fiendish Simon Legree, whose Louisiana plantation was a nightmare of torture and death. Stowe aimed her

most powerful blows at slavery's destructive impact on the family. Deeply committed to the values of motherhood and domesticity, Stowe said later that her loss of a baby to cholera had taught her "what a poor slave mother may feel when her child is torn away from her." *Uncle Tom's Cabin* is especially sensitive to the anguish of slave mothers. Eliza succeeds in keeping her son from being sold away, but other mothers are not so fortunate. When told that her infant has been sold, Lucy drowns herself. Driven half mad by the sale of a son and daughter, Cassy decides "never again [to] let a child live to grow up!" She gives her third child an opiate and watches as "he slept to death." Rivers of tears flowed when Northerners read the novel aloud around their family hearths.

Responses to the novel depended on geography. In the North, common people and literary giants alike sang its praises. The poet John Greenleaf Whittier sent "ten thousand thanks for thy immortal book," and poet Henry Wadsworth Longfellow judged it "one of the greatest triumphs recorded in literary history." What northern readers accepted as truth, southern ones denounced as slander. The New Orleans *Crescent* called Stowe "part quack and part cutthroat," a fake physician who came with arsenic in one hand and a pistol in the other to treat diseases she had "never witnessed." Virginian George F. Holmes proclaimed Stowe a member of the "Woman's Rights" and "Higher Law" schools and dismissed the novel as a work of "intense fanaticism." Unfortunately, he said, this "maze of misinterpretation" had filled those who knew nothing about slavery "with hatred for that institution and those who uphold it." Holmes found only one character convincing: Simon Legree. Stowe had made Legree a transplanted Yankee.

As Legree's northern origins suggest, the novel did not indict just the South. Stowe rebuked the entire nation for tolerating the scourge of slavery. Although it is impossible to measure precisely the impact of a novel on public opinion, *Uncle Tom's Cabin* clearly helped to crystallize northern sentiment against slavery and to confirm Southerners' suspicion that they no longer had any sympathy in the free states. Other writers—ex-slaves who knew life in slave cabins firsthand—also produced stinging indictments of slavery that attacked the ignorance and moral indifference of whites. Solomon Northup's compelling *Twelve Years a Slave* (1853) sold 27,000 copies in two years, and Frederick Douglass's powerful *Narrative of the Life of Frederick Douglass, as Told by Himself* (1845) eventually sold more

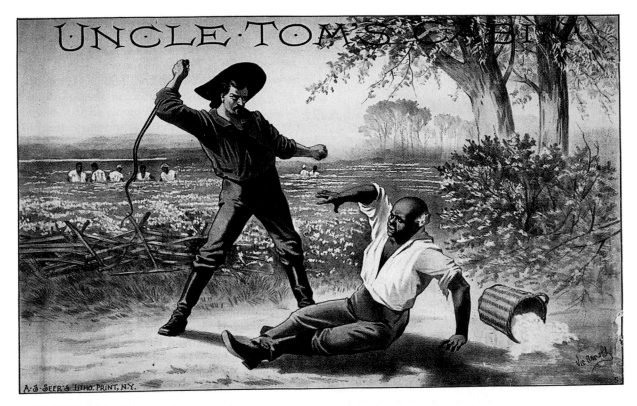

THEATER POSTER
During the 1850s, at least ten individuals, including Harriet Beecher Stowe herself, dramatized the novel Uncle Tom's Cabin. *These plays, known as "Tom Shows," drew crowds in America and Britain. Stowe's moral indictment of slavery translated well to the stage. Scenes of Eliza crossing the ice with bloodhounds in pursuit, the cruelty of Legree, and Little Eva borne to heaven on puffy clouds gripped the imagination of audiences and fueled the growing antislavery crusade.*
Smithsonian Institution.

than 30,000 copies. But no work touched the North's conscience like the novel by the woman who had never set foot on a plantation. A decade later, when Stowe visited Abraham Lincoln at the White House, he reportedly said, "So this is the little lady who made this big war."

The Election of 1852

The fugitive slave law and *Uncle Tom's Cabin* added new recruits to militant antislavery forces in the North. Heightened criticism from the free states stung white Southerners into increasingly belligerent defenses of slavery and southern society. Still, the arguments across the Mason-Dixon line failed to destroy popular support for the Compromise of 1850. Majorities in both sections continued to defend it as the "final settlement," a bulwark against

dangerous sectional forces. Evidence that allegiance was sincere and widespread came in the summer of 1852, when both the Whig and Democratic Parties adopted platforms accepting the Compromise as the settlement of the slavery question.

As national elections approached in 1852, Democrats and Whigs sought to close the rifts that had opened along sectional lines within their parties. The Democrats were more successful. As their presidential nominee, they turned to Franklin Pierce of New Hampshire. Pierce was an amiable veteran of the Mexican War and a former senator, but his most valuable asset was his well-known sympathy with southern views on public issues. His leanings caused northern critics to include him among those they contemptuously called "doughfaces," northern men with principles that were malleable enough to champion southern causes. The Whigs were less

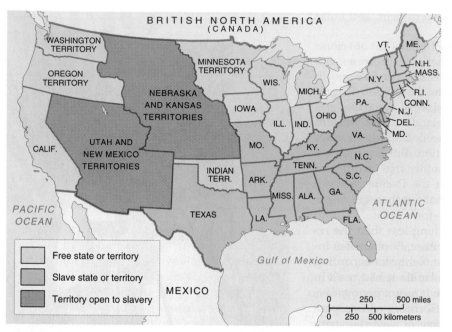

M AP 14.3
*The Kansas-Nebraska Act,
1854*
*Americans hardly thought
twice about dispossessing the
Indians of lands guaranteed
them by treaty, but many worried about the outcome of repealing the Missouri Compromise and opening up lands to
slavery.*

bill through Congress in May 1854. It passed because nine-tenths of all southern members (Whigs
and Democrats) and half of the northern Democrats
cast votes in favor. Still, ominously, half of the northern Democrats broke with their party and opposed
it. In its final form, the Kansas-Nebraska Act divided the territory into two parts: Nebraska west of
Iowa and Kansas west of the slave state of Missouri.

The Realignment of the Party System

The Kansas-Nebraska Act marked a fateful escalation of the sectional conflict. Douglas's ill-advised
measure had several consequences, none more crucial than the realignment of the nation's political
parties. Since the rise of the Whigs as an opposition
party to Andrew Jackson's Democrats in the early
1830s, Whigs and Democrats had organized and
channeled political conflict in the nation. This party
system dampened sectionalism and strengthened
the Union. To achieve national political power,
Whigs and Democrats had to retain strength in both
the North and the South. Strong northern and
southern wings required that the party compromise
and find positions acceptable to both.

The Kansas-Nebraska controversy shattered
this conservative political system. In place of two
national parties with bisectional strength, the mid-
1850s witnessed the development of one party
heavily dominated by one section and another party
entirely limited to the other section. Rather than
"national" parties, the country had what one critic
disdainfully called "geographical" parties. Not

> *In place of two national parties with bisec-
> tional strength, the mid-1850s witnessed the
> development of one party heavily dominated
> by one section and another party that was
> entirely limited to the other section.*

everyone opposed the new political system, however. Parties now had the advantage of sharpening
ideological and policy differences between the sections and no longer muffling moral issues, like slavery. But the new party system also thwarted political compromise. Instead, it promoted political
polarization. The breakup of the old party system
of the 1830s and 1840s snapped one of what John
C. Calhoun called the "cords of Union." The new
party system of the 1850s reflected the sectional division between North and South and offered little
encouragement to sectional reconciliation.

WHIG PARTY MEMBERS
On February 18, 1853, George Howe made this daguerreotype of the Log Cabin and Hard Cider Club of Portland, Maine. This Whig organization took its name and its emblem from William Henry Harrison's 1840 presidential campaign, a rousing effort to depict the tony Virginian as a man of the people. Well-heeled and respectable, these Maine shopkeepers, bankers, and farmers made up the spine of the Whig Party. Before long, these solid citizens would be looking for a new party.
Collections of the Maine Historical Society.

The breakup of the old parties had personal meaning as well as national significance. In the political universe of antebellum America, most citizens had far stronger attachments to their parties than most Americans do today. "Unflinching adherence to party is principle with them," a visiting Englishman observed in the 1850s, and "to forsake a party is regarded as an act of greatest dishonor." But many Americans had no choice but to find new parties. The parties they found had much clearer sectional profiles.

The Old Parties: Whigs and Democrats

Distress signals could be heard from the Whig camp as early as the Mexican War, when members clashed over the future of slavery in annexed Mexican lands. But the disintegration of the party dated from 1849–1850, when proslavery Southerners watched in stunned amazement as Whig President Zachary Taylor sponsored a plan for a free California. Southern Whigs felt betrayed and began to question their party affiliation. Above the Mason-Dixon line, the strains of the slavery issue split northern Whigs. The Conscience Whigs, who responded to slavery as a moral blight, gained a majority by 1852. The party could please the southern wing or the northern

wing but not both. The Whigs' miserable showing in the election of 1852 made clear that they were no longer a strong national party. By 1856, after more than two decades of contesting the Democrats, they were hardly a party at all.

The decline and eventual collapse of the Whig Party left the Democrats as the country's only national party. But the Democrats were not immune to the disruptive pressures of the territorial question. David Wilmot, after all, was a Democrat. However, Democrats discovered in popular sovereignty a doctrine that many of its members could support. Popular sovereignty very nearly undid the party as well. When Stephen Douglas applied the doctrine to that part of the Louisiana Purchase where slavery had been barred, he destroyed the dominance of the Democratic Party in the free states. Most of the northern Democrats in the House who had cast ballots in support of Douglas's Kansas-Nebraska bill were not reelected the following year. As a result, northern Democratic representation in the House fell sharply, and after 1854, the Democrats became a southern-dominated party.

Nevertheless, Democrats remained the dominant party throughout the 1850s. Gains in the South more than balanced losses in the North. During the decade, Democrats elected two presidents and won majorities in Congress in almost every election. But national power required that they maintain a north-

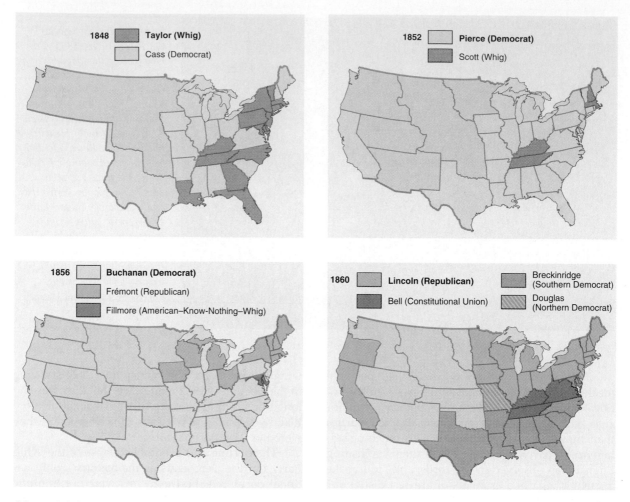

MAP 14.4
Political Realignment, 1848–1860
In 1848, slavery and sectionalism began hammering the country's party system. The Whig party was an early casualty. By 1860, national parties — those that contended for votes in both the North and the South — had been replaced by regional parties.

ern and a southern wing, which in turn required that they avoid the issue of the expansion of slavery. The fate of the Whigs constantly reminded Democrats that slavery was neither easily avoided nor compromised.

The breakup of the Whigs and the disaffection of significant numbers of northern Democrats set many Americans politically adrift. As they searched for new political harbors, they discovered that they had plenty of choices. The death of the old party system created a kaleidoscope of fresh political alternatives. The question was, Who would attract the drifters?

The New Parties: Know-Nothings and Republicans

Among the new organizations that vied to replace the Whigs as the second party in the national two-party system were splinter groups with such odd names as Anti-Nebraskaites, Fusionists, Maine Lawites, Temperance men, Rum Democrats, Hard Shell Democrats, Half Shells, Soft Shells, and others. Out of this confusion, two organizations emerged as true contenders. One grew out of the slavery controversy, a spontaneous coalition of indignant antislavery Northerners. The other major new party arose from an entirely different split in American society, that between Roman Catholic immigrants and native Protestants.

The tidal wave of immigrants that broke over America in the decade from 1845 to 1855 produced a nasty backlash among Protestant Americans, who believed they were about to drown in a sea of Irish and German Roman Catholics. The new arrivals encountered economic prejudice, ethnic hostility, and religious antagonism. Because some of them displayed a taste for whiskey and beer, they also drew the wrath of the temperance movement. When the immigrants entered American politics, largely as Democrats because they perceived that party as more tolerant of newcomers than were the Whigs, they met sharp political opposition. In the early 1850s, nativists (individuals who were anti-immigrant) began to organize, first into secret fraternal societies such as the Order of the Star-Spangled Banner, then into a political party. Recruits swore never to vote for either foreign-born or Roman Catholic candidates. The party retained its secret rit-

uals, and members promised not to reveal any information about the organization. When questioned, they said: "I know nothing." Officially, they were the American Party, but most Americans called them Know-Nothings.

Pledged to reducing the political power of immigrants, the Know-Nothings exploded onto the political stage in 1854 and 1855 with a series of dazzling successes. They captured state legislatures in the Northeast, West, and South and claimed dozens of seats in Congress. Their greatest triumph came in Massachusetts, a favorite destination for the Irish. Know-Nothings elected the Massachusetts governor, all of the state senators, all but two of the state representatives, and all of the congressmen. Know-Nothings attracted both Democrats and Whigs, but with their party crumbling, more Whigs responded to the attraction. In 1855, an individual might reasonably have concluded that the American Party had emerged as the successor to the Whigs.

But Know-Nothings were not the only new party making noise. Among the new antislavery or-

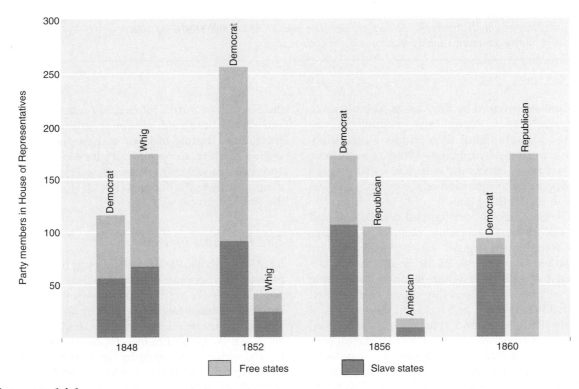

FIGURE 14.1
Changing Political Landscape, 1848–1860
The polarization of American politics between the free states and slave states occurred in little more than a decade.

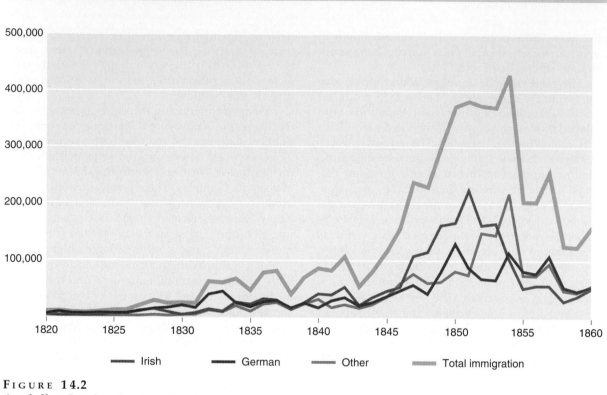

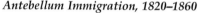

FIGURE **14.2**
Antebellum Immigration, 1820–1860
After increasing gradually for several decades, immigration shot up in the mid-1840s. Between 1848–1860, nearly 3.5 million immigrants entered the United States.

ganizations provoked by the Kansas-Nebraska Act, one called itself Republicans. Republicans attempted to unite under their banner all the dissidents and political orphans—Whigs, Free-Soilers, anti-Nebraska Democrats, even Know-Nothings—who opposed the extension of slavery into any territory of the United States.

The Republican creed tapped basic beliefs and values of the northern public. Slave labor and free labor, Republicans argued, had spawned two incompatible civilizations. In the South, slavery degraded the dignity of white labor by associating work with blacks and servility. Slavery condemned most whites, as well as blacks, to ignorance and poverty. Repression and tyranny laid heavily on every Southerner, except planter aristocrats. Those insatiable slave lords, whom antislavery Northerners called the Slave Power, now conspired to expand slavery, subvert liberty, and undermine the Constitution through the Democratic Party. Only by restricting slavery to the South, Republicans believed, could free labor flourish elsewhere. Free labor created in the North a society that was the opposite of

the South. The North hitched self-interest to effort and thus stimulated economic efficiency. It respected the dignity of labor and provided anyone willing to work an opportunity for a decent living and for advancement. Although exaggerated, these images attracted a hodgepodge of Northerners to the Republican cause.

The Election of 1856

By the mid-1850s, the Know-Nothings had emerged as the principal champion of nativism and the Republicans as the primary advocate of antislavery. Both new parties had scored astonishing successes almost overnight. Together, they had helped to break the Whigs and to bloody the Democrats. But the Republicans emerged as the Democrats' main challenger. The election of 1856 revealed that their political star was rising sharply, whereas that of the Know-Nothings was dead.

Slavery in the territories became the election's only issue. The Know-Nothings came apart when party leaders insisted on a platform that endorsed the Kansas-Nebraska Act, and most Northerners walked out. The Know-Nothings who remained nominated ex-President Millard Fillmore. The Republicans, in contrast, adopted a platform that focused almost exclusively on "making every territory free." When they labeled slavery a "relic of barbarism," Republicans announced that they had written off the South. For president, they nominated the dashing soldier and California adventurer John C. Frémont, "Pathfinder of the West." Though a celebrated explorer, he lacked political credentials. Political know-how resided in his wife, Jessie Frémont, who, as a daughter of Senator Thomas Hart Benton of Missouri, knew the political map as well as her husband knew western trails.

The Democrats, successful in 1852 in bridging sectional differences by nominating a northern man with southern principles, chose another "doughface," James Buchanan of Pennsylvania. Regarding slavery, the Democrats took refuge in the ambiguity of popular sovereignty. They portrayed Republicans as extremists whose support for the Wilmot Proviso risked pushing the South out of the Union.

The Democratic strategy helped carry the day for Buchanan, but Frémont did astonishingly well. Buchanan won 174 electoral votes against Frémont's 114 and Fillmore's 8. Frémont carried all but five of the states north of the Mason-Dixon line. The election made clear that the Whigs had disintegrated, that the Know-Nothings would not ride nativism to national power, and that the Democrats were badly strained. But the big news was the "glorious defeat" of the Republicans. Despite being a brand-new party and purely sectional, they challenged other parties for national power. Sectionalism had fashioned a third party system, one that spelled danger for the Republic.

JOHN C. AND JESSIE BENTON FRÉMONT
The election of 1856 was the first time a candidate's wife appeared on campaign items. Appropriately, the woman who made the breakthrough was Jessie Benton Frémont, as seen here on a silk ribbon with her husband, John C. Frémont, Republican Party presidential nominee. Jessie proved a valuable asset, helping to plan her husband's campaign, coauthoring his election biography, and drawing northern women into political activity as never before. Jessie Frémont was, as Abraham Lincoln observed ambivalently, "quite a female politician."
Collection of Janice L. and David J. Frent.

TABLE 14.2
THE ELECTION OF 1856

Candidate	Electoral Vote	Popular Vote	Percent of Popular Vote
James Buchanan (Democrat)	174	1,833,000	45.3
John C. Frémont (Republican)	114	1,339,000	33.1
Millard Fillmore (American)	8	872,000	21.6

Freedom under Siege

The "triumph" of the Republicans meant that the second party in the new two-party system was entirely sectional. It felt no compelling need to compromise, to conciliate, to keep a southern wing happy. Indeed, the Republican Party organized around the premise that the slaveholding South provided a profound threat to "free soil, free labor, and free men." It declared northern society healthy and upright while condemning the South as rotten and depraved. Republicans kept up a steady drumbeat of charges against the Slave Power, the most important of which was that proslavery southern Democrats threatened free men's liberties.

The Republican Party organized around the premise that the slaveholding South provided a profound threat to "free soil, free labor, and free men." It declared northern society healthy and upright while condemning the South as rotten and depraved.

Northerners who resisted the Republican message encountered disturbing new evidence in the four years following the passage of the Kansas-Nebraska Act in 1854. Events in distant Kansas Territory provided the young Republican organization with an enormous boost. Kansas reeled with violence between proslavery and antislavery settlers, which Republicans argued was southern in origin. Kansas offered a window onto southern values and intentions, they claimed. Nor was the southern fondness for the club, knife, and revolver evident only on the Kansas frontier, Republicans argued. They pointed to the brutal beating by a Southerner of a respected northern senator on the floor of Congress. Even the Supreme Court, in the Republicans' view, reflected the South's drive toward tyranny and minority rule. In 1858, the issues dividing North and South received an extraordinary airing in a senatorial contest in Illinois, when the nation's foremost Democrat debated a resourceful Republican.

"Bleeding Kansas"

Three days after the House of Representatives approved the Kansas-Nebraska Act, Senator William H. Seward of New York boldly challenged the South. "Come on then, Gentlemen of the Slave States," he cried, "since there is no escaping your challenge, I accept it in behalf of the cause of freedom. We will engage in competition for the virgin soil of Kansas, and God give the victory to the side which is stronger in numbers as it is in right." Because of Stephen Douglas, popular sovereignty would determine whether Kansas became slave or free. No one really expected New Mexico and Utah to become slave states when Congress instituted popular sovereignty there in 1850. By 1860, only twenty-nine slaves lived in arid Utah and none in New Mexico. But Kansas was different. Kansas sat on the borderline, and everyone believed it could go either way. In reality a majority of settlers sought the traditional goals of getting a farm, building a town, or speculating in real estate. But Kansas was hardly a typical frontier. Free-state and slave-state settlers each sought majorities at the ballot box, claimed God's blessing, and kept their rifles ready.

In the North, emigrant aid societies sprang up to promote settlement from the free states. The most famous, the New England Emigrant Aid Company, sponsored some 1,240 settlers in 1854 and 1855. In the South, proslavery expansionists eagerly took up Seward's challenge. Tiny rural communities from Virginia to Texas raised money to support proslavery settlers. Missourians especially thought it important to secure Kansas for slavery. Already bordered on the east by the free state of Illinois and on the north by the free state of Iowa, they did not relish another free state to the west. Plenty of western Missourians, hell-for-leather frontier types, prepared to do whatever it took to prevent abolitionists from seizing Kansas.

In theory, popular sovereignty meant an orderly tallying of ballots. In Kansas, however, elections became circuses. Thousands of Missourians, egged on by Missouri Senator David Rice Atchison, invaded Kansas. "There are eleven hundred coming over from Platte County to vote," Atchison reported, "and if that ain't enough we can send five thousand—enough to kill every God-damned abolitionist in the Territory." Not surprisingly, proslavery candidates swept the early elections. When the first territorial legislature met, it enacted laws that made the Missouri slave law look tame. It became a felony merely to argue that slavery did not legally exist in Kansas. The law prohibited antislavery men from holding office or serving on juries. Assisting a runaway slave became a capital offense. Ever-pliant President Pierce endorsed the work of the fraudulently elected proslavery legislature. Free-state men

FRAUDULENT VOTING IN KANSAS
*In this northern indictment of the corruption of popular sovereignty by Missourians, rough frontier types, with pistols and knives tucked into their belts, rush to get free whiskey and then line up at the polling place, where next to a sign, "*DOWN WITH THE ABOLITIONISTS,*" they doubtlessly voted the proslavery ticket.*
The Kansas State Historical Society, Topeka, Kansas.

did not. They elected their own legislature, which promptly banned both slaves *and* free blacks from the territory and applied for admission to the Union as a free state. Organized into two rival governments and armed to the teeth, Kansans verged on civil war.

Fighting broke out on the morning of May 21, 1856. Under banners inscribed "Southern Rights" and "South Carolina," a mob of several hundred entered the town of Lawrence, the center of free-state settlement. They wrecked the offices of antislavery newspapers and, after failing to destroy the Free State Hotel with cannon fire, burned it to the ground. Only one man died—a proslavery raider who was killed when a burning wall collapsed—but the Sack of Lawrence, as free-soil forces called it, inflamed northern opinion. The press reported dozens of bodies strewn over the town, crumpled beside hundreds of charred chimneys. In Kansas, news of Lawrence provoked one free-soil settler, John Brown, to "fight fire with fire." Announcing that "it was better that a score of bad men should die than that one man who came here to make

Kansas a Free State should be driven out," he led a posse that massacred five allegedly proslavery settlers along the Pottawatomie Creek. After that, guerrilla war engulfed the territory. (See Texts in Historical Context, pages 542–543.)

By providing graphic evidence of a dangerously aggressive Slave Power, "Bleeding Kansas" gave the fledgling Republican Party an enormous boost. The Republicans received additional encouragement from an event that occurred in the national capital. On May 19 and 20, 1856, Senator Charles Sumner of Massachusetts delivered a scathing speech entitled "The Crime against Kansas." He damned the administration, the South, and proslavery Kansans. He also indulged in a scalding personal attack on South Carolina's elderly Senator Andrew P. Butler, whom Sumner described as a "Don Quixote" who had taken as his mistress "the harlot, slavery."

Preston Brooks, a young South Carolina member of the House and a kinsman of Butler, felt compelled to defend the honor of his aged relative and of his state. For his instrument of chastisement,

Kansas: Contested Ground

*I*llinois Senator Stephen A. Douglas, author of the Kansas-Nebraska Act, promised that squatter sovereignty offered a peaceful means of settling the fate of slavery in the Kansas and Nebraska Territories. In a speech in Peoria, Illinois, Abraham Lincoln denounced opening territory that was previously free to the possibility of slavery and predicted that bloodshed, not tranquility, would result.

DOCUMENT 1. Abraham Lincoln Warns of the Consequences of Squatter Sovereignty, October 16, 1854

Some yankees, in the east, are sending emigrants to Nebraska, to exclude slavery from it; and, so far as I can judge, they expect the question to be decided by voting, in some way or other. But the Missourians are awake too. They are within a stone's throw of the contested ground. They hold meetings, and pass resolutions, in which not the slightest allusion to voting is made. They resolve that slavery already exists in the territory; that more shall go there; that they, remaining in Missouri will protect it; and that abolitionists shall be hung, or driven away. Through all this, bowie-knives and six-shooters are seen plainly enough; but never a glimpse of the ballot-box. And, really, what is to be the result of this? Each party WITHIN, having numerous and determined backers WITHOUT, is it not probable that the contest will come to blows, and bloodshed? Could there be a more apt invention to bring about collision and violence, on the slavery question, than this Ne-

braska project is? I do not charge, or believe, that such was intended by Congress; but if they had literally formed a ring, and placed champions within it to fight out the controversy, the fight could be no more likely to come off, than it is. And if this fight should begin, is it likely to take a very peaceful, Union-saving turn? Will not the first drop of blood so shed, be the real knell of the Union?

*A*s Lincoln predicted, elections became circuses, and worse. Missourians believed that they were defending home territory against an invasion of Northerners. In 1856, a congressional committee gathered evidence of intimidation and violence at Kansas polls.

DOCUMENT 2. Samuel N. Wood Recounts His Experience on Election Day, March 30, 1855

I first came into the Territory in June, 1854, from the State of Ohio. . . . I was here on the day of election of the 30th of March, 1855; it was a Friday. On the Wednesday evening before, I saw some two or three hundred men encamped on the ravine bottom near the ford, who said they were from Missouri, and were going above to some place to vote, and there would be about 1,000 more to vote at this place. The next day, Thursday, they commenced coming in here to Lawrence on horseback, on mules, in wagons and carriages. . . .

It was found pretty difficult, when the polls were opened, for any one to get to the window to vote. . . . They formed two lines of them near from the window out on the prairie . . . standing some six feet apart, and those who voted had to enter in at the outer end of these two lines, walk up to the window, and vote. . . . Soon after the voting commenced

Brooks chose something he believed appropriate for a social inferior. On May 22, armed with a walking cane, Brooks entered the Senate, where he found Sumner working at his desk. After accusing him of libel, Brooks began beating Sumner over the head with his cane. After about a minute, Sumner lay bleeding and unconscious on the Senate floor. Brooks resigned his seat in the House, only to be promptly reelected. In the North, the southern hero became the archvillain. Like Bleeding Kansas,

"Bleeding Sumner" provided the Republican Party with a potent symbol of the South's twisted and violent "civilization."

The Dred Scott Decision

As the French visitor Alexis de Tocqueville observed in the 1830s, "Scarcely any question arises in the United States that is not resolved, sooner or later, into a judicial question." Because the Constitution

I heard quite an excitement a little to the left of where I was standing. . . . I saw a man running from the house towards the river, and as many as a hundred running after him. I started after them . . . and I saw it was a Mr. Bond, of this place. There were some two or three pistol-shots fired after him. There was considerable excitement on the bank. Several of them said they must drive all the damned abolitionists off the ground. . . .

These Missourians had almost exclusive control of the polls until late in the afternoon. . . . I recollect that a man named Willis, who lived in this place at that time, came up about the middle of the afternoon to vote, when about half of these Missourians had left. When he came up they raised a cry that he was a damned abolitionist, a negro thief, &c., and hallooed "Kill him!" "Shoot him!" &c. There were several of our men on the ground, and they told them if they wanted to commence that game they could do so, and that they would find the matter would not end here in Kansas Territory; and they quieted down very much. I think Willis voted.

The Committee also received testimony from Mahala Doyle, the widow of a man who was slaughtered by John Brown's antislavery "army."

DOCUMENT 3. Mahala Doyle Testifies

I am the widow of the late James P. Doyle . . . my husband, myself, and children moved into the Territory of Kansas some time in November, A.D. 1855, and settled on Mosquito creek . . . where it empties into Pottawatomie creek . . . on Saturday, the 24th day of May, A.D. 1856, about 11 o'clock at night, after we had all retired, my husband, . . . myself, and five children . . . were all in bed, when we heard some persons come into the yard and rap at the door. . . . My husband got up and went to the door. Those outside inquired for Mr. Wilkson, and where he lived. My husband told them that he would tell them. Mr. Doyle, my husband, opened the door, and several came into the house, and said that they were from the army. My husband was a pro-slavery man. They told my husband that he and the boys must surrender, they were their prisoners. These men were armed with pistols and large knives. They first took my husband out of the house, then they took two of my sons—the two oldest ones, William and Drury. . . . My son John was spared, because I asked them in tears to spare him. In a short time afterwards I heard the report of pistols. I heard two reports, after which I heard moaning, as if a person was dying; then I heard a wild whoop. They had asked before they went away for our horses. We told them that the horses were out on the prairie. My husband and two boys, my sons, did not come back any more. I went out next morning in search of them, and found my husband and William, my son, lying dead in the road near together, about two hundred yards from the house. My other son I did not see any more until the day he was buried. . . . Fear of myself and the remaining children induced me to leave the home where we had been living. We had improved our claim a little. I left all and went to the State of Missouri.

Document 1. Roy P. Basler, ed., *The Collected Works of Abraham Lincoln* (New Brunswick, N.J.: Rutgers University Press, 1953), 2:271–72.

Document 2. *Report of the Special Committee Appointed to Investigate the Troubles in the Territory of Kansas*, 34th Cong., 1st sess., 1856, H. Doc. 200, serial 869, 140–41.

Document 3. Ibid., 1175–76.

lacked precision on the issue of slavery in the territories, political debate reflected sectional interests and party politics. Only the Supreme Court spoke definitively about the meaning of the Constitution. In 1857, in the *Dred Scott* case, the Court proved that it enjoyed no special immunity from the sectional and partisan passions that convulsed the land.

Eleven years after Dred and Harriet Scott first sued for freedom, the Supreme Court ruled in the case. The justices could have settled the immediate issue of Scott's status as a free man or slave on narrow grounds, but they saw the case as an opportunity to settle once and for all the vexing question of slavery in the territories. The justices believed that their ruling would finally remove this divisive issue from the political arena. Many Americans wanted the Supreme Court to settle the troubling territorial question. No one was more eager than Southerners, for five of the nine justices were from the South and seven were Democrats.

THE DRED SCOTT FAMILY
The Dred Scott *case in 1857 produced a fierce political storm, but it also fueled an enormous
curiosity about the family suing for freedom. Popular magazines rushed to supply the demand
with images and interviews. The correspondent for the popular* Frank Leslie's Illustrated
*met Dred Scott in St. Louis and reported: "We found him on examination to be a pure-
blooded African, perhaps fifty years of age, with a shrewd, intelligent, good-natured face, of
rather light frame, being not more than five feet six inches high."*
Library of Congress.

On the morning of March 6, 1857, seventy-nine-year-old Chief Justice Roger B. Taney read the majority decision of the Court. Taney hated Republicans and detested racial equality, and the Court's decision reflected those prejudices. First, the Court ruled that Dred Scott could not legally claim that his constitutional rights had been violated because he was not a citizen of the United States. At the time of the Constitution, Taney said, blacks "had for more than a century before been regarded as beings of an inferior order . . . so far inferior, that they had no rights which the white man was bound to respect." Second, the laws of Missouri determined Dred Scott's status, and his travels in free areas did not make him free. Third, Congress's power to make "all needful rules and regulations" for the territories did not include the right to exclude slavery. The Court then explicitly declared the Missouri Compromise unconstitutional, even though it had already been voided by the Kansas-Nebraska Act.

Republicans exploded in outrage. Taney's extreme proslavery decision ranged far beyond a determination of Dred Scott's freedom. By declaring unconstitutional the Republican program of federal exclusion of slavery in the territories, the Court had cut the ground from beneath the party. Moreover, as the *New York Tribune* lamented, the decision seemed to mean that "all our Territories are henceforth Slave Territories on the way to be ripened into Slave States." Particularly frightening to African Americans in the North was the Court's declaration that blacks were not citizens and have "no rights which the white man was bound to respect." It's no wonder that black abolitionist Frederick Douglass denounced the Dred Scott decision as "a most scandalous and devilish perversion of the Constitution."

The Republican rebuttal to Taney's decision relied heavily on the brilliant dissenting opinion of Justice Benjamin R. Curtis. Scott *was* a citizen of the United States, Curtis argued. At the time of the writing of the Constitution, free black men could vote in five states and participated in the ratification process. Scott *was* free. Because slavery was prohibited in Wisconsin, the "involuntary servitude of a slave, coming into the Territory with his master, should cease to exist." And the Missouri Compromise *was* constitutional. The Founders meant exactly what they said: Congress had the power to make "*all* needful rules and regulations" for the territories, including barring slavery.

Unswayed by Curtis's dissent, the Court's seven-to-two majority had validated the most extreme statement of the South's territorial rights.

John C. Calhoun's claim that Congress had no authority to exclude slavery now became the law of the land. One Southerner gloated that the *Dred Scott* decision was "the funeral sermon of Black Republicanism . . . crushing and annihilating the anti-slavery platform." But what southern Democrats cheered, northern Democrats found profoundly disturbing. They feared that the *Dred Scott* decision annihilated not just the Wilmot Proviso but popular sovereignty as well. If Congress did not have the authority to exclude slavery, how could Congress's creation, a territorial government, assume that right? No one was in a tighter bind than Stephen A. Douglas. Civil war raged in Kansas at that very moment because Douglas's Kansas-Nebraska Act had opened the territory to popular sovereignty. Now, contrary to Douglas's promise, it appeared that a free-soil majority could not keep slavery out. No one could exclude slavery until the moment of statehood. By draining the last drop of ambiguity out of popular sovereignty, the *Dred Scott* decision jeopardized not only Douglas's presidential ambition but the ability of the Democratic Party to hold its northern and southern wings together.

Ironically, the *Dred Scott* decision strengthened the young Republican Party by giving credence to its claim that a hostile Slave Power conspired against northern liberties. Only the capture of the Supreme Court by the "slavocracy," Republicans argued, could explain the tortured and historically inaccurate *Dred Scott* decision. Although President Buchanan praised the decision as the "final settlement . . . of the question of slavery in the Territories," the decision inflamed sectional tensions and further polarized positions. The justices' efforts had failed as dismally as the politicians' efforts. As for Dred Scott, although the Court rejected his suit, he did in the end gain his freedom. White friends, the sons of his first owner, Peter Blow, purchased and freed Scott and his family. Dred Scott died less than a year later.

Prairie Republican: Abraham Lincoln

The reigniting of sectional flames provided Republican politicians with fresh challenges and fresh opportunities. None proved more eager for them than Abraham Lincoln of Illinois. Lincoln had long since put behind him his hardscrabble, log cabin beginnings in Kentucky and Indiana. At the time of the *Dred Scott* decision, he lived in a fine two-story house in Springfield, had enough business from the

Illinois Central Railroad to be known as the "railroad lawyer," and by virtue of his marriage and successful practice associated with men of reputation and standing.

The law provided Lincoln's living, but politics was his life. "His ambition was a little engine that knew no rest," observed his law partner William Herndon. At age twenty-six, he served his first term in the Illinois state legislature. Between 1847 and 1849, he enjoyed his only term in the House of Representatives, where he fired away at "Mr. Polk's War" and cast dozens of votes for free soil but otherwise served inconspicuously. When he returned to Springfield, he pitched into his law practice but kept his eye fixed on public office. As a young man, he had chosen as his political hero the Whig Henry Clay. He deeply admired the man, his principles, and his program. On the vexing issues of Union, slavery, and race, Clay exemplified for Lincoln the reasonable moderate, the realistic pragmatist, and the effective compromiser.

But, like Whigs everywhere in the mid-1850s, Lincoln had no political home. With their party in shambles, a good many Illinois Whigs gravitated to the Know-Nothings. Mary Todd Lincoln, Lincoln's Kentucky-born wife, sympathized with the nativists, for she knew, she said, the burdens of "wild Irish" servants. But Lincoln was not a Know-Nothing. "How could I be?" he asked. "How can any one who abhors the oppression of negroes be in favor of degrading classes of white people?" Lincoln's credo—opposition to "the *extension* of slavery"—made the Democrats an impossible choice. But the Republicans made free soil their principal tenet, and in 1856 Lincoln joined the party.

The Kansas-Nebraska Act of 1854 had pushed Lincoln into new levels of political awareness and engagement. Its repeal of the Missouri Compromise —that "sacred compact"—left him "thunderstruck and stunned." Convinced that slavery was a "monstrous injustice," a "great moral wrong," and an "unqualified evil to the negro, the white man, and the State," he was certain that Douglas had jeopardized the Founders' plan to contain the spread of slavery. He admitted that the Constitution sanctioned slavery in those states where it existed; but penned in, plantation slavery would exhaust southern soil at the same time the number of slaves increased. Slaveholders would have no choice but to end slavery themselves. By providing fresh, life-giving lands, however, Douglas put slavery "on the high road to extension and perpetuity." Lincoln conveniently forgot those moments when the Founders

permitted slavery to spread westward, but he remained convinced that the "spirit of seventy-six and the spirit of Nebraska are utter antagonisms."

Lincoln realized that slavery was yoked with race. Just as he staked out the middle ground on antislavery, he also held what were, for his times, moderate racial views. Like a majority of Republicans, he defended black humanity without challenging white supremacy. He denounced slavery as immoral and believed that it should end, but he also viewed black equality as impractical and unachievable. "Negroes have natural rights . . . as other men have," he said, "although they cannot enjoy them here." Insurmountable white prejudice made it impossible to extend full citizenship and equality to blacks in America. Freeing blacks and allowing them to remain in this country would lead to race war. In Lincoln's mind, social stability and black progress required that slavery end and that blacks leave the country.

Lincoln realized that because most Northerners lacked sympathy for blacks, humanitarian concern would not mobilize them to fight for free soil. Instead, he linked northern labor's self-interest to halting slavery's advance. He described the territories as "places for poor people to go to, and better their conditions." If slavery expanded, white men would compete with slave labor. He spoke to those millions of Americans who were in lowly stations and wanted to make something of themselves: farmhands who wanted to become farm owners, clerks who aspired to be merchants, rail-splitters who dreamed of being lawyers. "The *free* labor system," he said, "opens the way for all—gives hope to all, and energy, and progress, and improvement of condition to all." In Lincoln's view, slavery's expansion threatened this freedom to succeed.

Lincoln became persuaded that slaveholders formed an aggressive and dangerous conspiracy to nationalize slavery. Evidence abounded. The Kansas-Nebraska Act repealed the restriction on slavery's advance in the territories. The *Dred Scott* decision denied Congress the right to impose fresh restrictions. The next step, Lincoln warned, would be "another Supreme Court decision, declaring that the Constitution of the United States does not permit a *State* to exclude slavery from its limits." Unless its citizens woke up, he warned, the Supreme Court would make "Illinois a slave State."

In his memorable 1858 "House Divided" speech, Lincoln declared provocatively that the nation could not "endure, permanently half slave and half free." Either opponents of slavery would arrest

DISCUSSING THE NEWS

Newspapers permitted Midwesterners to keep up-to-date. Here a farmer takes a break from his task of cutting firewood to debate the latest news with his friends. He is so engrossed that he ig-nores the little girl tugging at his pants leg and trying to get him to notice the woman waving in the doorway. Men like these increasingly accepted Lincoln's portrait of the Republican Party as the guardian of the common people's liberty and economic opportunity. When Lincoln claimed that southern slaveholders threatened free labor and democracy, they listened.

Copyright © 1971, The R.W. Norton Art Gallery, Shreveport, La. Used by permission. Painting by Arthur F. Tait.

its spread and place it on the "course of ultimate ex-tinction" or its advocates would push it forward until it became legal in "*all* the States, *old* as well as *new—North* as well as *South*." Lincoln identified Illinois's own son Stephen A. Douglas as a chief conspirator. Douglas's philosophy of not caring whether slavery was "voted down or voted up" in the territories fed a complacency that eased the way for new advances by the Slave Power.

As Lincoln developed and honed his ideas about slavery and freedom, he tried them out on audiences across the North. His words stirred many of his listeners, touching their deepest hopes and anxieties. In time, his convictions that slavery was wrong, that Congress must stop its spread, and that it must be put on the road to extinction formed the core of the Republican ideology. By 1858, he had so impressed his fellow Republicans in Illinois that they put him forward to challenge the nation's premier Democrat who was seeking reelection to the Senate.

The Lincoln-Douglas Debates

When Stephen Douglas learned that Abraham Lincoln would be his opponent for the Senate, he confided in a fellow Democrat: "I shall have my hands full. He is the strong man of the party—full of wit, facts, dates—and the best stump speaker, with his droll ways and dry jokes, in the West. He is as honest as he is shrewd, and if I beat him my victory will be hardly won."

Not only did Douglas have to contend with a formidable foe, but he also carried the weight of a burden not of his own making. The previous year, the nation's economy experienced a sharp downturn, a depression that antebellum Americans called a "panic." Prices plummeted, thousands of businesses failed, and unemployment rose. The causes of the panic of 1857 lay in the international economy, but Americans reflexively interpreted the panic in sectional terms. Northeastern businesses and industries suffered most, and Northerners blamed the southern-dominated Congress, which had just months before reduced tariff duties to their lowest levels in the nineteenth century. Given this invitation, Northerners believed, foreign competition ravaged the northern economy. Southerners, who had largely escaped hardship because cotton prices remained high, saw the panic as proof of the feebleness of a free-labor economy and the hardiness of their own system of plantation slavery. Although Illinois suffered less than the Northeast, Douglas had to go before the voters in 1858 as a member of the freshly accused, southern-dominated Democratic Party.

Douglas's response to another crisis in 1857, however, helped shore up his standing with his constituents. During the previous winter, proslavery forces in Kansas met in Lecompton, drafted a proslavery constitution, and applied for statehood. President Buchanan blessed the Lecompton constitution and instructed Congress to admit Kansas as the sixteenth slave state. Everyone knew that free-soilers outnumbered proslavery settlers two or three to one, and Republicans denounced the "Lecompton swindle." Douglas broke with the Democratic administration and came out against the proslavery constitution, not because it accepted slavery but because it violated the democratic requirement of popular sovereignty.

In choosing to defend political principle, Douglas also practiced political self-preservation. He knew that a vote for the bogus Lecompton constitution would have handed over Kansas to slavery and marked him as a southern flunky in the eyes of Illinois voters. Coming out against the constitution declared his independence from the South and, he hoped, made him acceptable at home. True, his anti-Lecompton stance cost him dearly with white Southerners, who mounted a vicious attack on him. But he had first to secure his political base in Illinois. In March 1858, despite Douglas's vigorous opposition, the Senate passed the Kansas statehood bill, but the northern majority in the House killed it. (When Kansans would reconsider the Lecompton constitution in an honest election, they would reject it six to one, and Kansas would enter the Union in 1861 as a free state.)

A relative unknown and a decided underdog in the Illinois election, Lincoln challenged the incumbent Douglas to debate him face to face. Douglas agreed, and the two met in seven communities for a legendary series of debates. To the thousands who stood straining to see and hear, they must have seemed an odd pair. Douglas was five feet four inches tall, broad, and stocky; Lincoln was six feet four inches tall, angular, and lean. Douglas was in perpetual motion, darting across the platform, shouting, and jabbing the air. Lincoln was almost lethargic, speaking deliberately, sincerely. Douglas wore the latest fashion and dazzled audiences with his flashy vests. Lincoln wore good suits but managed to look rumpled anyway. But their differences in physical appearance and style were of least importance. They showed the citizens of Illinois (and much of the nation because of national press coverage) the difference between an anti-Lecompton Democrat and a true Republican. They debated, often brilliantly, the central issue before the country: slavery and freedom.

Lincoln badgered Douglas with the question of whether he favored the spread of slavery. If not, how did he expect to stop it, since the *Dred Scott* decision declared that citizens had a right to carry their slaves into the national territories? Lincoln tried to force Douglas into the damaging admission that the Supreme Court had repudiated his territorial solution, popular sovereignty. In the debate at Freeport, Illinois, Douglas answered Lincoln's challenge by declaring that popular sovereignty still had plenty of life. Settlers could not now pass legislation barring slavery, he admitted, but they could ban slavery just as effectively by not passing protective laws.

Without "appropriate police regulations and local legislation," such as those found in slave states, he explained, slavery could not live a day, an hour. Southerners condemned Douglas's "Freeport Doctrine" and charged him with trying to steal the victory they had gained with the *Dred Scott* decision. Lincoln chastised his opponent for his "don't care" attitude, for "blowing out the moral lights around us," and for treating the great issue of slavery like just another election question.

For his part, Douglas worked the racial issue. He called Lincoln an abolitionist, a miscegenationist (one who favored marriage between the races), and a color-blind egalitarian enamored with "our colored brethren." Lincoln denied every charge. Put on the defensive, he came close to staking out positions on abolition and race that were as conservative as Douglas's. Lincoln reiterated his belief that slavery enjoyed constitutional protection where it existed. He also reaffirmed his faith in white rule. "I will say, then, that I am not, nor ever have been, in favor of bringing about in any way the social and political equality of the white and black race." But Lincoln was no negrophobe like Douglas, who told racist jokes and spit out racial epithets. Lincoln always tried to steer the debate back to what he considered the true issue: the morality and future of slavery. "Slavery is wrong," he repeated, because "a man has the right to the fruits of his own labor."

As Douglas predicted, the election was hard-fought. It was also closely contested. In the nineteenth century, citizens voted for state legislators, who in turn selected the U.S. senator. Republicans gained a slight plurality of the votes, but because of the way Illinois was apportioned, the Democrats won a majority in the legislature. The new legislature chose to return Douglas to the Senate. But the debates thrust Lincoln into the national spotlight. No one expressed Republican principles more compellingly.

The Union Collapses

Lincoln's thesis that the "slavocracy" conspired to make slavery a national institution now seems exaggerated and fantastical. But from the northern perspective, the Kansas-Nebraska Act, the Brooks-Sumner affair, the *Dred Scott* decision, the panic of 1857, and the Lecompton constitution seemed irrefutable evidence of the South's aggressiveness. Lincoln was surely right that the house was divided.

If he was also right that it must become all one thing or the other, then the tilt, Northerners increasingly agreed, was clear and frightening.

Southerners, of course, saw things differently. They were the ones who were under siege and had grievances, they declared. Which was the minority section? they asked. In a democracy, how could a minority hope to control the government? Signs were everywhere, they argued, that the North planned to use its numerical advantage to attack slavery, and not just in the territories. Republicans had already proved themselves unwilling to be bound by the Constitution as interpreted by the Supreme Court in the *Dred Scott* case. After a Northerner attempted to incite a slave insurrection in Virginia in 1859, Southerners argued that Republicans had also proven themselves unwilling to be bound by Christian decency and reverence for life.

The 1850s delivered powerful blows to Southerners' confidence that they could remain Americans and protect slavery and their way of life.

Threats of secession increasingly laced the sectional debate. Talk of leaving the Union had been heard for years, of course. In 1827, Thomas Cooper of South Carolina warned that "we shall 'ere long be compelled to calculate the value of the union; and to enquire of what use to us is this most unequal alliance." Until the final crisis, however, Southerners used secession as a ploy to gain concessions within the Union, not to destroy the Union. But the 1850s delivered powerful blows to Southerners' confidence that they could remain Americans *and* protect slavery and their way of life. When the Republican Party defeated the Democrats in 1860, many Southerners concluded that national power had shifted permanently. Still, Southerners fell short of unity. Within states and among states, they responded to the crisis differently. At the same time, generations of slavery had also created among southern whites shared values and deep commitments.

John Brown's Raid

Three years after the 1856 Pottawatomie massacre in Kansas, John Brown reemerged. Time had not dampened his zeal for abolition. More than ever, he

JOHN BROWN
Was John Brown crazy? The debate about Brown's mental state began with his contemporaries and has raged ever since. Those who argue that he was a madman have asked: Would a sane man have butchered innocent victims at Pottawatomie Creek and set out for Harpers Ferry to overthrow slavery with fewer than two dozen men? But others see a resolute and selfless hero, not a psychotic. They have asked, would New England's Secret Six (four of them Harvard men) have sworn allegiance to a lunatic?
Boston Athenaeum.

was a man on fire. He had spent thirty months begging money from New England abolitionists to support his vague plan for military operations against slavery, perhaps in Kansas, perhaps in the South itself. The rough-hewn but hypnotic Kansas fighting man captivated the genteel Easterners, particularly the Boston elite. Although he won more hearts than pocketbooks, Brown received enough in gifts to gather a small band of antislavery warriors.

On the night of October 16, 1859, John Brown took his war against slavery into the South. With only twenty-two men, including five African Americans, he crossed the Potomac River and occupied a federal arsenal at Harpers Ferry, Virginia. The invaders were quickly surrounded, first by local militia and then by Colonel Robert E. Lee, who com-

manded the U.S. marines in the area. When Brown refused to surrender, federal troops charged with bayonets. It was all over in less than thirty-six hours. Seventeen men, including two slaves, lost their lives. Ten of Brown's raiders, including two of his sons, died. Although a few of Brown's troops escaped, federal forces captured seven men, among them Brown himself, who suffered a painful but not serious sword wound.

John Brown's precise objective remains somewhat hazy, but he apparently wanted to initiate a slave insurrection. "When I strike, the bees will begin to swarm," Brown told Frederick Douglass a few months before the raid. As slaves rushed to Harpers Ferry, Brown would arm them with the pikes (long spears) that he carried with him and with weapons stolen from the arsenal. They would then fight a war of liberation. In fact, Brown neglected to inform the slaves that he had arrived, and the few who knew wanted nothing to do with the suicidal enterprise. "It was not a slave insurrection," Abraham Lincoln observed later. "It was an attempt by white men to get up a revolt among slaves, in which the slaves refused to participate. In fact, it was so absurd that the slaves, with all their ignorance, saw plainly enough it could not succeed."

If Brown had been killed during his raid, his impact on history would probably have been minor. As it was, he lived, was tried by the state of Virginia for treason and conspiracy to incite insurrection, and on December 2, 1859, was hanged. In life, "Old Brown" was a ne'er-do-well who failed at nearly everything he tried. He died, however, with courage, dignity, and composure. With his "piercing eyes" and "resolute countenance," he uttered some of the most stirring words ever to issue from a courtroom: "If it is deemed necessary that I should forfeit my life for the furtherance of the ends of justice, and mingle my blood further with the blood of my children and with the blood of millions in this slave country whose rights are disregarded by wicked, cruel, and unjust enactments, I say, let it be done."

Some Northerners grieved for John Brown. One abolitionist proclaimed Brown the "bravest and humanest man in all the country." In Boston, the essayist Ralph Waldo Emerson dubbed him "that new saint" who "will make the gallows glorious like the cross." Writer Henry David Thoreau compared him to Christ and called him "an angel of light." Some abolitionists went beyond canonizing Brown to explicitly endorsing his cause of slave rebellion. Even the abolitionist William Lloyd Garrison, who professed pacifism, announced, "I am prepared to say 'success to every slave insurrection at the South and in every slave country.'" Generally, however, abolitionists did not condone violence, and northern opinion did not celebrate bloody slave insurrection. Lincoln spoke for the majority when he endorsed Brown's antislavery stance but concluded that noble ideals could not "excuse violence, bloodshed, and treason."

In the South, the din of eulogies drowned out Lincoln's sober voice. Mississippians denounced the bloodthirsty fiend whose mission was "to incite slaves to murder helpless women and children." Especially after it came out that Brown had received financial aid from leading New England citizens (known as the Secret Six), white Southerners felt a cold fury. They contemplated what they had in common with people who "regard John Brown as a martyr and a Christian hero, rather than a murderer and robber." Many Southerners lost the capacity to distinguish between Northerners who opposed slavery, like Lincoln, and those who were willing to see it washed away in a river of blood, like Brown. Robert Toombs of Georgia announced solemnly that Southerners must "never permit this Federal government to pass into the traitorous hands of the black Republican party." At that moment, the presidential election was only months away.

Republican Victory in 1860

Calm did not follow John Brown's storm. Anxieties provoked by his raid flared for months as southern whites feverishly searched for abolitionists and tarred and feathered (or treated even worse) those they suspected. Moreover, other events in the eleven months between Brown's hanging and the presidential election heightened sectional hostility, incrimination, and estrangement.

First, a small southern business convention meeting in Nashville shocked the country (including many Southerners) by calling for the reopening of the African slave trade, closed since 1808 and considered an abomination everywhere in the Western world. Next, Chief Justice Taney whipped up new indignation when the Supreme Court ruled northern personal liberty laws unconstitutional and reaffirmed the Fugitive Slave Act. Then, in February 1860, the normally routine business of electing a Speaker of the House of Representatives turned into one of the ugliest moments in the history of Con-

gress. When Republicans and Democrats deadlocked, it looked for a while as if they would simply shoot it out. "The only persons who do not have a revolver and a knife are those who have two revolvers," observed a South Carolinian. Congress averted bloodshed when a few Know-Nothings pitched in with the Republicans to elect an old Whig. Finally, Jefferson Davis demanded that the Senate adopt a federal slave code for the territories, a goal of extreme proslavery Southerners for several years. Not only could Congress not block slavery's spread, he argued, but it must offer it all "needful protection."

The demand for a federal slave code gave notice that Southerners intended to make their extreme position binding doctrine when Democrats converged on Charleston for their convention in April 1860. Meeting only blocks from the grave of John C. Calhoun, the party immediately split along sectional lines. On home turf, encouraged by cheering galleries, southern fire-eaters denounced Stephen Douglas and demanded a platform that included federal protection of slavery in the territories. "Ours are the institutions which are at stake; ours is the property that is to be destroyed; ours is the honor at stake," shouted the Alabama extremist William Lowndes Yancey. But northern Democrats needed a platform that they could take home, and northern voters would not stomach a federal slave code. When two platforms—one with a federal slave code and one with popular sovereignty—came before the delegates, popular sovereignty won. Representatives from the entire lower South and Arkansas stomped out of the convention. The remaining delegates adjourned to meet a few weeks later in Baltimore, where they nominated Douglas for president and adopted a platform that required nothing more than congressional noninterference in the territories.

When southern Democrats met, they nominated Vice President John C. Breckinridge of Tennessee for president and approved a platform with a federal slave code. But southern moderates refused to hand over their section to Breckinridge and the fire-eaters. Senator John J. Crittenden of Kentucky and others formed a new party that would provide voters a Unionist choice. Instead of adopting a platform—which inevitably fanned controversy—the new Constitutional Union Party merely approved a vague resolution pledging "to recognize no political principle other than *the Constitution . . . the Union . . . and the Enforcement of the Laws.*"

For president they picked former Senator John Bell of Tennessee. Republicans gently mocked the new party as the "Old Gentleman's Party." Southern Democrats accused it of "insulting the intelligence of the American people" when it ignored "the slavery question. That issue must be met and settled."

The Republicans smelled victory. Four years earlier they had enjoyed a "glorious defeat." Now the Democratic Party had broken up. Still, Republicans estimated that they needed to carry nearly all the free states to win. That required that they remedy deficiencies in both their candidate and their platform. In 1856, the party had suffered from following Frémont, a "pathfinder" who got lost in the political woods, and from the perception that it was a one-idea party. Antislavery sentiment had stiffened in the North in the previous four years, but Republicans decided to broaden their appeal. This time they built a platform with more than a single plank. Free homesteads, a protective tariff, a Pacific railroad, and a guarantee of immigrant political rights defined an economic and social agenda broad enough to unify the North. Republicans did not back away from antislavery, but they did soften its expression. While recommitting themselves to stop-

ping the spread of slavery, they also denounced John Brown's raid as "among the gravest of crimes" and confirmed the security of slavery in the South. Republicans hoped that by denying that they were abolitionists they would blunt charges that a vote for the Republican Party was a vote for northern extremism and thus southern secession.

Republicans cast about for a moderate candidate to go with their evenhanded platform. The foremost Republican, William H. Seward, had enemies. His famous "higher law" doctrine and "irrepressible conflict" speech made conservatives shiver. Moreover, charges of corruption during his term as governor of New York jeopardized Republican plans to exploit the recent evidence of graft and bribery in the Buchanan administration. Several lesser-known Republicans, including Abraham Lincoln, set their sights on the nomination. Lincoln had not sat on his hands since bursting onto the national scene in 1858. A speaking tour through the Midwest and East demonstrated his clear purpose, good judgment, and solid Republican credentials. That, combined with his rock-solid reputation for integrity and his residence in Illinois, a crucial state, made him attractive to the party. Masterful maneuvering by Lincoln's managers converted his status as the second choice of many delegates into a majority on the third ballot. Defeated by Douglas in a state contest less than two years earlier, Lincoln now stood ready to take Douglas on for the presidency.

The election of 1860 was like none other in American politics. It took place in the midst of the nation's severest crisis. Moreover, four major candidates crowded the presidential field. Rather than a four-cornered contest, however, the election broke into two contests, each with two candidates. In the North, Lincoln faced Douglas, and in the South, Breckinridge confronted Bell. Southerners did not even permit Lincoln's name to appear on the ballot in ten of the fifteen slave states, so outrageous did they consider the Republican Party. After John Brown, the name "Republican" conjured up well poisoners, arsonists, and men who passed out pikes to slaves. Northerners were wrapped in myths of their own. They dismissed the threats of secession as so much bluster, "the old game of scaring and bullying the North into submission to Southern demands and Southern tyranny." Like the boy who cried wolf, fire-eaters had lost their credibility.

An unprecedented number of voters cast ballots on November 6, 1860. Approximately 82 per-

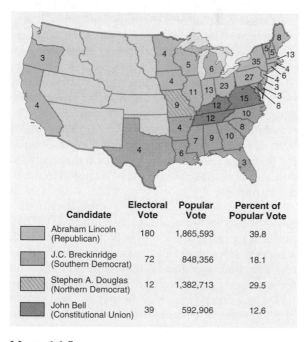

Candidate	Electoral Vote	Popular Vote	Percent of Popular Vote
Abraham Lincoln (Republican)	180	1,865,593	39.8
J.C. Breckinridge (Southern Democrat)	72	848,356	18.1
Stephen A. Douglas (Northern Democrat)	12	1,382,713	29.5
John Bell (Constitutional Union)	39	592,906	12.6

MAP 14.5
The Election of 1860

ABRAHAM LINCOLN

Lincoln actively sought the Republican presidential nomination in 1860. When in New York City to give a political address, he had his photograph taken by Mathew Brady. "While I was there I was taken to one of the places where they get up such things," Lincoln explained, sounding more innocent than he was, "and I suppose they got my shaddow, and can multiply copies indefinitely." Multiply they did. Copies of the dignified photograph of Lincoln soon replaced the less flattering drawings. Later, Lincoln credited his victory to his New York speech and to Mathew Brady.

The Lincoln Museum, Fort Wayne, Indiana. Photo: #0-17; drawing: #2024.

cent of eligible northern men and nearly 70 percent of eligible southern men went to the polls. The Republican platform succeeded in attracting a broad coalition of northern interests, and Lincoln swept all of the eighteen free states except New Jersey, which split its votes between him and Douglas. While Lincoln received only 39 percent of the popular vote, he won easily in the electoral balloting, gaining 180 votes, 28 more than he needed for victory. Douglas came in second in the popular voting, but carried only Missouri. Breckinridge was third and Bell fourth in the popular voting. Lincoln did not win simply because his opposition was splintered. Even if the votes of his three opponents were combined, Lincoln would still have won. Ominously, however, Breckinridge, running on a southern-rights platform, won the entire Lower South plus Delaware, Maryland, and North Carolina. Two fully sectionalized parties swept their regions, but the northern one won the presidency.

Lincoln did not receive a single electoral vote south of the Mason-Dixon line and had sought none. The Republican platform did not reflect the give-and-take that characterized bisectional parties.

on the territorial issue. Since the election of a Republican president, they had independence on their minds.

Finally, Lincoln arrived in Washington, forced to sneak in at night because of an assassination plot. His entrance did nothing to build confidence in a nation that doubted that this odd-looking man with almost no national political experience would be up to the task before him. The frantic search for a sectional compromise had failed. Virginia's last-minute effort to call a peace conference in Washington had not seemed promising enough to the Lower South to send delegates. The Confederate States of America acted as if it were independent and assumed that the price of secession would be censure, nothing more.

In his inaugural address, Lincoln sought to enunciate his policy. He began with reassurances to the South. He had "no lawful right" to interfere with slavery where it existed, he said again and, for emphasis, added that he had "no inclination to do so." There would be "no invasion—no using of force against or among the people anywhere." In filling federal posts, he would not "force obnoxious strangers" on the South. Conciliatory toward Southerners, he proved inflexible about the Union. The Union, he declared, is "perpetual." Secession was "anarchy" and "legally void." The Constitution required him to execute the law "in all the States." He would hold federal property, collect federal duties, and deliver the mails.

The decision for civil war or peace rested in the South's hands, he said. "You can have no conflict, without being yourselves the aggressors. *You* have no oath registered in Heaven to destroy the government, while *I* shall have the most solemn one to 'preserve, protect, and defend' it." What Southerners in Charleston held in their hands at that very moment were the cords for firing the cannons that they aimed at the federal garrison at Fort Sumter.

Conclusion: The Failure of Compromise

Northerners and Southerners had clashed as early as the writing of the Constitution. As their economies, societies, and cultures diverged in the nineteenth century, friction increased. But sectionalism shifted into a new gear in 1846 when David Wilmot proposed banning slavery in any Mexican territory won in the war. "As if by magic," a Boston newspaper observed, "it brought to a head the great question that is about to divide the American people." During the extended crisis of the Union that stretched from 1846 to 1861, the nation's attention fixed on the expansion of slavery. But from the beginning, both Northerners and Southerners recognized that the controversy had less to do with the expansion of slavery than with the future of slavery in America. The territories, then, were "merely the skirmish line of a larger and more fundamental conflict."

Lincoln doubted that the nation could endure "permanently half slave and half free." But for more than seventy years, imaginative statesmen had found compromises that, while making no improvement in the condition of millions of slaves in the South, did preserve the Union. Citizens on both sides of the Mason-Dixon line took enormous pride in the national experiment in republican democracy, and few gave up the experiment easily. But accommodation and adjustment had limits. Whites in the Deep South took Lincoln's election in 1860 as a signal that slavery and the society they had built on it were at risk in the Union, and they left. In his inaugural, Lincoln pleaded, "We are not enemies but friends. We must not be enemies." But by then, the Deep South had ceased to sing what he called "the chorus of the Union." It remained to be seen whether disunion would mean war.

CHRONOLOGY

1846   Wilmot Proviso proposes barring slavery from all lands acquired in Mexican War.

1847   John C. Calhoun challenges Wilmot Proviso on constitutional grounds, stating that Congress has no power to exclude slavery from the nation's territories.

Senator Lewis Cass offers compromise of "popular sovereignty," allowing people of territories to determine the fate of slavery.

1848   Opponents of expansion of slavery found Free-Soil Party.

General Zachary Taylor, Whig, elected president of United States, defeating Democrat Lewis Cass and Free-Soil candidate Martin Van Buren.

1850s   Vigilance committees in North challenge and sometimes thwart Fugitive Slave Act.

1850   **July 9.** President Zachary Taylor dies; succeeded by Vice President Millard Fillmore.

Senator Henry Clay proposes Omnibus Bill to avert territorial crisis over slavery; bill ultimately defeated.

Senator Stephen Douglas's compromise bills (Compromise of 1850) pass Congress, signed into law by President Fillmore.

1852   Harriet Beecher Stowe's *Uncle Tom's Cabin* published.

Democrat Franklin Pierce elected president of United States, defeating Whig Winfield Scott.

1853   Gadsden Purchase adds 45,000 square miles of territory in present-day Arizona and New Mexico.

1854   American Party (Know-Nothings) emerges, advocating nativist positions.

Kansas-Nebraska Act opens the Kansas and Nebraska Territories to popular sovereignty.

Republican Party emerges on platform opposing extension of slavery in territories.

1856   Armed conflict between proslavery and antislavery forces erupts in Kansas.

Preston Brooks of South Carolina brutally assaults Charles Sumner of Massachusetts on Senate floor.

Democrat James Buchanan elected president of United States, defeating Republican John C. Frémont.

1857   *Dred Scott* decision declares that African Americans have no constitutional rights, that Congress cannot exclude slavery in the territories, and that the Missouri Compromise is unconstitutional.

Nation experiences economic downturn, panic of 1857.

1858   In Illinois senatorial campaign, Abraham Lincoln and Stephen A. Douglas debate slavery; Douglas defeats Lincoln for the Senate seat.

1859   **October 16.** John Brown's attempt to foment slave uprising in Harpers Ferry, Virginia, further alienates South and moves nation toward war.

1860   Republican Abraham Lincoln elected president in four-way race that divides electorate along sectional lines.

December 20. South Carolina secedes from Union.

1861   Representatives of seven southern states, meeting in Montgomery, Alabama, form Confederate States of America.

BIBLIOGRAPHY

GENERAL WORKS

Eric Foner, *Politics and Ideology in the Age of the Civil War* (1980).

William W. Freehling, *The Road to Disunion* (1990).

Bruce Levine, *Half Slave and Half Free: The Roots of Civil War* (1992).

James M. McPherson, *Ordeal by Fire: The Civil War and Reconstruction* (1982).

James M. McPherson, *Battle Cry of Freedom: The Civil War Era* (1988).

Allan Nevins, *Ordeal of the Union*, 2 vols. (1947).

Allan Nevins, *The Emergence of Lincoln*, 2 vols. (1950).

Roy F. Nichols, *Disruption of American Democracy* (1949).

David M. Potter, *The Impending Crisis, 1848–1861* (1976).

Richard H. Sewell, *A House Divided: Sectionalism and Civil War, 1848–1865* (1988).

Kenneth M. Stampp, *The Imperiled Union: Essays on the Background of the Civil War* (1980).

Kenneth M. Stampp, ed., *The Causes of the Civil War* (rev. ed., 1991).

Mark W. Summers, *The Plundering Generation: Corruption and the Crisis of the Union, 1849–1861* (1987).

SLAVERY IN THE TERRITORIES

Irving H. Bartlett, *Daniel Webster and the Trial of American Nationalism, 1843–1852* (1972).

Paul B. Bergeron, *The Presidency of James K. Polk* (1987).

Eugene H. Berwanger, *The Frontier against Slavery: Western Anti-Negro Prejudice and the Slavery Extension Controversy* (1967).

Charles H. Brown, *Agents for Manifest Destiny: The Lives and Times of the Filibusters* (1979).

Don E. Fehrenbacher, *The Dred Scott Case: Its Significance in American Law and Politics* (1978).

Paul Finkelman, *An Imperfect Union: Slavery, Federalism, and Comity* (1981).

Holman Hamilton, *Prologue to Conflict: The Crisis and Compromise of 1850* (1964).

Michael F. Holt, *The Political Crisis of the 1850s* (1978).

Robert W. Johannsen, *Stephen A. Douglas* (1973).

Frederick Merk, *Slavery and the Annexation of Texas* (1972).

Chaplain W. Morrison, *Democratic Politics and Sectionalism: The Wilmot Proviso Controversy* (1967).

James Oakes, *Slavery and Freedom: An Interpretation of the Old South* (1990).

James A. Rawley, *Race and Politics: "Bleeding Kansas" and the Coming of the Civil War* (1969).

Joseph G. Rayback, *Free Soil: The Election of 1848* (1970).

Kenneth Stampp, *America in 1857: A Nation on the Brink* (1990).

Gerald W. Wolff, *The Kansas-Nebraska Bill: Party, Section, and the Coming of the Civil War* (1977).

NORTHERN SECTIONALISM

Richard H. Abbott, *Cotton and Capital: Boston Businessmen and Antislavery Reform, 1854–1868* (1991).

Tyler Anbinder, *Nativism and Slavery: The Northern Know Nothings and the Politics of the 1850s* (1992).

R. J. M. Blackett, *Building an Antislavery Wall: Black Americans in the Atlantic Abolitionist Movement, 1830–1860* (1983).

Frederick Blue, *The Free Soilers: Third Party Politics, 1848–1854* (1973).

Stanley W. Campbell, *The Slave Catchers: Enforcement of the Fugitive Slave Law, 1850–1860* (1970).

Merton L. Dillon, *The Abolitionists: The Growth of a Dissenting Minority* (1974).

David H. Donald, *Charles Sumner and the Coming of the Civil War* (1960).

Robert R. Dykstra, *Bright Radical Star: Black Freedom and White Supremacy on the Hawkeye Frontier* (1993).

Don E. Fehrenbacher, *Prelude to Greatness: Lincoln in the 1850s* (1962).

Eric Foner, *Free Soil, Free Labor, Free Men: The Ideology of the Republican Party before the Civil War* (1970).

Ronald P. Formisano, *The Birth of Mass Political Parties: Michigan, 1827–1861* (1971).

William E. Gienapp, *The Origins of the Republican Party, 1852–1856* (1987).

Len Gougeon, *Virtue's Hero: Emerson, Antislavery, and Reform* (1990).

Michael F. Holt, *Forging a Majority: The Formation of the Republican Party in Pittsburgh, 1848–1860* (1969).

Harry V. Jaffa, *Crisis of the House Divided: An Interpretation of the Lincoln-Douglas Debates* (1959).

Robert W. Johannsen, *Lincoln, the South, and Slavery: The Political Dimension* (1991).

Bruce Levine, *The Spirit of 1848: German Immigrants, Labor Conflict, and the Coming of the Civil War* (1992).

William S. McFeely, *Frederick Douglass* (1991).

Thomas D. Morris, *Free Men All: The Personal Liberty Laws of the North, 1780–1861* (1974).

Stephen B. Oates, *To Purge This Land with Blood: A Biography of John Brown* (1970).

Thomas H. O'Connor, *Lords of the Loom: The Cotton Whigs and the Coming of the Civil War* (1968).

Lewis Perry and Michael Fellman, eds., *Antislavery Reconsidered: New Perspectives on the Abolitionists* (1979).

Benjamin Quarles, *Allies for Freedom: Blacks and John Brown* (1974).

James P. Rawley, *Race and Politics: "Bleeding Kansas" and the Coming of the Civil War* (1969).

Anne C. Rose, *Victorian America and the Civil War* (1992).

Louis Ruchames, ed., *John Brown: The Making of a Revolutionary* (1959).

Richard H. Sewell, *Ballots for Freedom: Antislavery Politics in the United States, 1837–1860* (1976).

Thomas P. Slaughter, *Bloody Dawn: The Christiana Riot and Racial Violence in the Antebellum North* (1991).

James Brewer Stewart, *Joshua R. Giddings and the Tactics of Radical Politics* (1970).

James Brewer Stewart, *Holy Warriors: The Abolitionists and American Slavery* (1976).

James Brewer Stewart, *Wendell Phillips: Liberty's Hero* (1986).

Hans L. Trefousse, *The Radical Republicans: Lincoln's Vanguard for Racial Justice* (1969).

Wendy Hamand Venet, *Neither Ballots nor Bullets: Women Abolitionists and the Civil War* (1991).

Ronald G. Walters, *The Antislavery Appeal: American Abolitionism after 1830* (1976).

David Zarefsky, *Lincoln, Douglas, and Slavery: In the Crucible of Public Debate* (1990).

SOUTHERN SECTIONALISM

William L. Barney, *The Road to Secession: A New Perspective on the Old South* (1972).

John Barnwell, *Love of Order: South Carolina's First Secession Crisis* (1982).

Irving H. Bartlett, *John C. Calhoun: A Biography* (1993).

William J. Cooper Jr., *The South and the Politics of Slavery, 1828–1856* (1978).

Avery O. Craven, *The Growth of Southern Nationalism, 1848–1861* (1953).

Drew G. Faust, *James Henry Hammond and the Old South: A Design for Mastery* (1982).

Don E. Fehrenbacher, *The South and Three Sectional Crises* (1980).

Lacy K. Ford Jr., *Origins of Southern Radicalism: The South Carolina Upcountry, 1800–1860* (1988).

Thelma Jennings, *The Nashville Convention: Southern Movement for Unity, 1848–1851* (1980).

Vicki Vaughn Johnson, *The Men and the Vision of the Southern Commercial Conventions, 1845–1871* (1992).

John McCardell, *The Idea of a Southern Nation: Southern Nationalists and Southern Nationalism, 1830–1860* (1979).

John Niven, *John C. Calhoun and the Price of Union* (1988).

David M. Potter, *The South and the Sectional Conflict* (1969).

Ronald T. Takaki, *A Pro-Slavery Crusade: The Agitation to Reopen the African Slave Trade* (1971).

J. Mills Thornton III, *Politics and Power in a Slave Society: Alabama, 1800–1860* (1978).

Eric E. Walther, *The Fire-Eaters* (1992).

John M. Wiltse, *John C. Calhoun: Sectionalist, 1840–1850* (1951).

SECESSION

William L. Barney, *The Secessionist Impulse: Alabama and Mississippi in 1860* (1974).

Walter L. Buenger, *Secession and the Union in Texas* (1984).

Steven A. Channing, *Crisis of Fear: Secession in South Carolina* (1970).

Daniel W. Crofts, *Reluctant Confederates: Upper South Unionists in the Secession Crisis* (1989).

Dwight L. Dumond, *The Secession Movement, 1860–1861* (1931).

William J. Evitts, *A Matter of Allegiances: Maryland from 1850 to 1861* (1962).

John Hope Franklin, *The Militant South* (1956).

James L. Huston, *The Panic of 1857 and the Coming of the Civil War* (1987).

Michael P. Johnson, *Toward a Patriarchal Republic: The Secession of Georgia* (1977).

David M. Potter, *Lincoln and His Party in the Secession Crisis* (1942).

Kenneth M. Stampp, *And the War Came: The North and the Secession Crisis, 1860–61* (1960).

James M. Woods, *Rebellion and Realignment: Arkansas's Road to Secession* (1987).

Ralph A. Wooster, *The Secession Conventions of the South* (1962).

DAGUERREOTYPE OF DRUMMER BOY OF SHILOH

The Civil War is often called a "brother's war." Families sometimes split and offered up soldiers for both the Union and the Confederate armies. But the war was also a children's war, as this daguerreotype of the twelve-year-old John Clem, a drummer boy at the battle of Shiloh, reminds us. Beneath the lofty rhetoric of God and glory lay the heartbreak of youth destroyed and innocence lost.

Library of Congress.

THE CRUCIBLE OF WAR

15

1861–1865

I N 1838, A TWENTY-YEAR-OLD MARYLAND SLAVE by the name of Frederick Bailey fled north to freedom. The young runaway took a new name, Frederick Douglass, and might understandably have settled into obscurity, content just to avoid the slave catchers and to live quietly as a free man. Instead, he chose to wage war against slavery. An agent for the Massachusetts Anti-Slavery Society observed in 1841 that "the public have itching ears to hear a colored man speak, and particularly a *slave*." Dozens of fugitive slaves brought to northern audiences the authority of hard personal experience. None stripped away the myth of the contented slave more eloquently than Frederick Douglass. In 1845, he published his immensely popular autobiography. In 1847, he began the *North Star*, an antislavery newspaper that reached thousands. Douglass's powerful denunciations of slavery and moving pleas for emancipation made him the most famous African American in the English-speaking world.

Publicly, Douglass remained optimistic. Throughout the 1840s and 1850s, he declared repeatedly that the nation was in the "seed time" of abolition and promised that the "harvest" would soon follow. Privately, however, Douglass thought that he labored in vain. In his eyes, his two decades of speaking and writing had brought the country no closer to ending slavery. In some ways the situation had grown worse. When Douglass fled slavery in 1838, two million Americans were slaves. By 1860, the number had grown to four million. Every step forward—the birth of the Republican Party, for instance—was followed by a giant step back—such as the *Dred Scott* decision. To Douglass, the 1850s ended as they began, no closer to the eradication of slavery. "How long! How long! O Lord God of Sabbath!" he cried, "shall the crushed and bleeding bondsman wait?"

During the secession winter of 1860–1861, Douglass found himself torn between hope and despair. Abraham Lincoln's election in November had revived his optimism. "The slaveholders know that the day of their power is over," Douglass exulted. But he realized that the Republican Party's free-soil principles fell short of abolition. Republicans opposed slavery's right to expand into the national territories, not slavery's right to exist in the South. Indeed, Douglass feared that the Republicans would become "the best protectors of slavery where it now is."

When news came from Charleston in April 1861 that Southerners had fired on the American flag, Douglass celebrated the outbreak of fighting. He cheered Lincoln's vow to maintain the Union. He realized, however, that in going to war "the North only strikes for government . . . against anarchy . . . for loyalty . . . against treason and rebellion." But much earlier than most, he understood that a war to save the Union would inevitably affect slavery. The South had initiated a "war for slavery," Douglass said, and it followed that a war to crush southern independence must become a war *against* slavery. Even though "the Government is not yet on the side of the oppressed, events mightier than the Government are bringing about that result," Douglass declared. "*Friends of freedom!*" he cried, "*be up and doing;—now is your time.*"

Few Northerners, certainly not Abraham Lincoln, agreed that the outbreak of fighting marked the beginning of the end of slavery. For eighteen months, Northerners fought solely to uphold the Constitution and preserve the nation. The framers of the Constitution had dodged the question of whether sovereignty lay with the federal government or with the states. Incredibly, the nation existed for nearly three-quarters of a century without agreement about its fundamental nature. Although the nation achieved dazzling material success and physical growth, it fell short of unity and harmony. The political collision over slavery made it impossible to avoid the Constitution's ambiguity about the nature of the Union.

Even if the Civil War had not touched slavery, the war would still have transformed America. The carnage lasted four years and cost the nation 633,000 lives, nearly as many as in all of its other wars before and after. The war became a crucible that molded the modern American nation-state. The federal government emerged with new power and responsibility over national life. War furthered the emergence of a modern industrializing nation. But because the war to preserve the Union also became a war to destroy slavery, the northern victory had truly revolutionary meaning. Defeat and emancipation destroyed the slave society of the Old South and gave birth to a different society.

Years later, remembering the Civil War years, Douglass said, "It is something to couple one's name with great occasions." It *was* something—for millions of Americans. Great and terrible public events overtook private lives. Whether they battled or defended the Confederacy, whether they labored behind the lines to produce goods for northern or southern soldiers, whether they kept the home fires burning for Yankees or rebels, all Americans experienced the crucible of war. But the war affected no group more than the four million African Americans who began the war in 1861 as slaves and emerged in 1865 as free people.

FREDERICK DOUGLASS
The North's antebellum black community was avidly abolitionist. Like Frederick Douglass, however, black crusaders sometimes lost heart. "The time has gone by for colored people to talk of patriotism," Charles L. Remond said in the wake of the 1857 Dred Scott *decision. "We owe no allegiance to a country which grinds us under its iron heel and treats us like dogs." Yet, like Douglass, the black community stayed the course and helped transform a war against rebellion into a war for freedom. This photograph taken about 1847 was given by Douglass to Susan B. Anthony.*
Chester County Historical Society, West Chester, Pa.

"And the War Came"

For Abraham Lincoln the first few weeks in office were a nightmare. New to high office, he faced the worst crisis in the history of the nation. But what drove him nearly to distraction were the hordes of callers who besieged the White House. Diplomats, delegates, lobbyists, and most especially office seekers greedy for a share of the spoils of the Republican victory jammed Washington. In one hotel, three hundred men camped in the dining room, eager for a chance to see the president. It took weeks for Lincoln to dispense with the "vultures," as he called them, and to give himself fully to the grave national issue of disunion.

Lincoln revealed his strategy on March 4, 1861, in his inaugural address, which was carefully crafted to combine firmness with patience and conciliation. First, he would try to stop the contagion of secession. Eight slave states had said no to disunion, but they remained suspicious and skittish. Lincoln was determined to do nothing that would push the Upper South (North Carolina, Virginia, Maryland, Delaware, Kentucky, Tennessee, Missouri, and Arkansas) into leaving. Second, he would buy time so that emotions could cool. By reassuring the Deep South (South Carolina, Georgia, Florida, Alabama, Mississippi, Louisiana, and Texas) about the safety of slavery, he would provide Unionists there the opportunity to reassert themselves and to overturn the secession decision. Always, Lincoln expressed his uncompromising will to oppose secession and to uphold the Union.

His counterpart, Jefferson Davis, fully intended to establish the Confederate States of America as a permanent independent republic. To achieve permanence, he had to sustain the secession fever that had carried the Deep South out of the Union and to dampen reunion sentiment among antisecession elements. Even if the Deep South held firm, however, the Confederacy remained weak without additional states from the Upper South. Davis watched for opportunities to add new stars to the Confederate flag.

Neither man sought war. Both wanted to achieve their objectives peacefully. But as Lincoln later observed, "Both parties deprecated war, but one of them would *make* war rather than let the nation survive, and the other would *accept* war rather than let it perish. And the war came."

The Surrender of Fort Sumter

Fort Sumter's thick brick walls rose forty feet above the tiny island on which it perched at the entrance to Charleston harbor. Only four miles from the city, the fortress could easily be seen by strollers who took the air at the water's edge each evening. The sight infuriated good Confederates. Major Robert Anderson and some eighty U.S. soldiers occupied what Charlestonians claimed as Confederate property. The fort became a hateful symbol of the nation they had abandoned, and Southerners wanted federal troops out. But Sumter was also a symbol to Northerners, a beacon affirming federal sovereignty in the seceded states. Even President James Buchanan had understood its value. In January

1861, with uncharacteristic energy and firmness, he dispatched an unarmed merchant vessel, the *Star of the West*, to carry two hundred additional troops and provisions to the undermanned and ill-supplied federal garrison. Shots from South Carolina artillery drove the ship away before it could deliver its cargo. When Lincoln entered the White House in March, the soldiers in the fort were running dangerously short of food.

Always, Lincoln expressed his uncompromising will to oppose secession and to uphold the Union.

The situation at Fort Sumter presented Lincoln with hard choices. Without fresh supplies, Anderson would soon be starved out. Lincoln could order the fort's evacuation. That would play well in the Upper South, whose edgy slave states threatened to bolt to the Confederacy if Lincoln resorted to military force. But yielding the fort would make it appear that Lincoln accepted the Confederacy's existence. Abandonment would divide the North, batter the new Republican administration, and magnify the rebel nation's status in the eyes of the world. Lincoln decided to hold Fort Sumter. In the first week in April, he authorized a peaceful expedition to bring supplies, but not military reinforcements, to the fort. Lincoln understood that in seeking to relieve the fort he risked war. But his plan honored his inaugural promises to defend federal property and to avoid using military force unless first attacked. Masterfully, Lincoln had shifted the fateful decision of war or peace to Jefferson Davis.

On April 9, 1861, Jefferson Davis and his cabinet met to consider the situation in Charleston harbor. The territorial integrity of the Confederacy demanded the end of the federal presence, Davis argued. But his secretary of state, Robert Toombs of Georgia, pleaded against military action. "Mr. President," he declared, "at this time it is suicide, murder, and will lose us every friend at the North. You will wantonly strike a hornet's nest which extends from mountain to ocean, and legions now quiet will swarm out and sting us to death." President Davis rejected Toombs's prophecy and sent word to General Pierre Gustave T. Beauregard, the Louisianan commanding Confederate troops in Charleston, to take the fort before the relief expedition arrived. When Anderson refused Beauregard's demand to evacuate, southern cannon commenced firing.

Thirty-three hours of bombardment reduced the fort to rubble, but, miraculously, the four thousand Confederate artillery rounds did not take the life of a single Union soldier. On April 14, with the fort ablaze, Anderson offered his surrender. The Confederates had Fort Sumter, but they also had a war.

The response of the free states was thunderous. When Lincoln called for 75,000 troops to put down the rebellion, several times that many rushed to defend the flag. Lincoln asked Indiana for six regiments, and the governor wired that "without seriously repressing the ardor of the people, I can hardly stop short of twenty." A Harvard professor observed that the "whole population, men, women, and children, seem to be in the streets with Union favors and flags." Democrats responded as fervently as Republicans. Stephen A. Douglas, the recently defeated Democratic candidate for president, hurried to the White House to pledge his support. "There are only two sides to the question," he told a massive crowd in Chicago. "Every man must be for the United States or against it. There can be no neutrals in this war, *only patriots—or traitors.*" No one faced more acutely the issue of loyalty than the men and women of the Upper South.

The Upper South Chooses Sides

Lincoln's election in November 1860 had not dislodged a single one of the eight slave states in the Upper South from the Union. Throughout the winter, whites there denied that the seven seceding cotton states had sufficient cause to leave. A Tennessee man believed that secession would boomerang. It was both "unwise and impolitic," he said, and would likely bring about the "ruin and overthrow of negro slavery" and jeopardize the "freedom and liberty of the white men." But Unionism in the Upper South often came with conditions. Many antisecessionists made it clear that if the federal government resorted to military force to hold the Lower South in the Union, they would jump to the Confederate camp. In his inaugural, Lincoln had promised to maintain the Union without "bloodshed or violence . . . unless it be forced upon the national authority." Now, even though the Confederates fired first, Lincoln's call for troops confronted the Upper South with a horrendous choice: either to fight against the Lower South or to fight against the North.

Many who had only months earlier rejected secession now embraced the Confederacy. To oppose southern independence was one thing, to fight fellow Southerners was another. Thousands felt betrayed, believing that Lincoln had promised to achieve reunion peacefully by waiting patiently for Unionists to reassert themselves in the seceding states. One man furiously denounced the conflict as a "politician's war" but conceded that "this is no time now to discuss the causes, but it is the duty of all who regard Southern institutions of value to side with the South, make common cause with the Confederate States and sink or swim with them."

Some found the choice excruciating. Robert E. Lee, a career military officer and the son of one of Virginia's oldest families, observed the crisis with accelerating horror. Neither a defender of slavery nor a supporter of secession, he denounced separation as the work of cotton state hotheads. "I can anticipate no greater calamity for the country than a dissolution of the Union," he told his son in January 1861. Still, he said, "a Union that can only be maintained by swords and bayonets . . . has no charm for me." Following the bombardment of Fort Sumter, Lee was summoned from his white-columned mansion in Arlington, Virginia, to the nation's capital, where he was offered command of federal military forces. But Lee could not fight against the South. When he returned home, he learned that Virginia had left the Union. He quickly penned his resignation from the United States army and declared, "Save in defense of my native State, I never desire again to draw my sword." His beloved Virginia offered no sanctuary for his tortured allegiances. Richmond would soon be the capital of the Confederacy, Virginia would be a battleground, and Lee would again command military forces.

One by one the other states of the Upper South jumped off the fence. Within weeks, Arkansas, North Carolina, and Tennessee followed Virginia's lead. But in the border states of Delaware, Maryland, Kentucky, and Missouri, Unionism triumphed. Only in Delaware, where slaves accounted for less than 2 percent of the population, was the victory easy. In Maryland, Unionism needed a helping hand. Rather than allow the state to secede (and make Washington, D.C., a federal island in a Confederate sea), Lincoln suspended the writ of habeas corpus, essentially establishing martial law and setting aside normal constitutional guarantees such as trial before a jury of peers, and marched troops into Baltimore. Maryland's legislature, frightened by the federal invasion and aware of the strength of Union sentiment in the western counties, rejected secession.

The struggle turned violent in the West. In Missouri, the proslavery Democratic governor and the

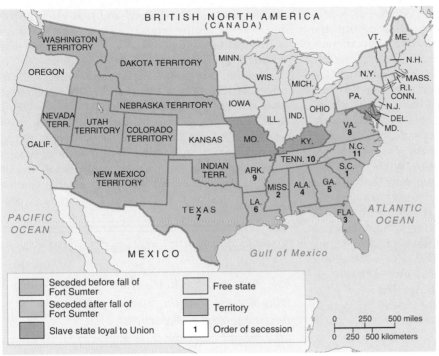

M AP 15.1
Secession
After Lincoln's election, the fifteen slave states debated what to do. Seven states quickly left the Union, four left after the firing on Fort Sumter, and four refused to go.

state legislature attempted to deliver their state to Jefferson Davis, only to be blocked by a state convention that rejected secession. Even though Unionists won, southern-sympathizing guerrilla bands roamed the state for the duration of the conflict, waging bloody war on civilians and soldiers alike. In Kentucky, Unionists narrowly defeated secession, but, as in Missouri, a prosouthern minority claimed that the state had severed its ties with the Union. The Richmond government, not particularly fastidious in counting votes, eagerly made Missouri and Kentucky the twelfth and thirteenth Confederate states. Throughout the border states, but especially in Kentucky, the Civil War was truly a "brother's war." Seven of Henry Clay's grandsons fought in the Civil War: four for the Confederacy and three for the Union.

Lincoln understood that the border states—particularly Kentucky—contained indispensable resources, population, and wealth, and they controlled major rivers and railroads. "I think to lose Kentucky is nearly the same as to lose the whole game," Lincoln said. "Kentucky gone, we can not hold Missouri, nor, as I think, Maryland. These all against us, and the job on our hands is too large for us. We would as well consent to separation at once." Although Kentucky and Missouri rejected secession, they were not securely in the Union fold. The

North could lose them through military defeat or by adopting policies that people in those states considered injurious to their interests. No interest was touchier than slavery, and skeptical inhabitants of the border states adopted a wait-and-see attitude.

Neither Lincoln's election nor the bombardment of Fort Sumter united the South. In the end, only eleven of the fifteen slave states joined the Confederate States of America. Moreover, the four seceding Upper South states contained significant populations that felt little affection for the Confederacy. Dissatisfaction was so rife in the western counties of Virginia that citizens there voted to create the separate state of West Virginia in 1863 and to remain loyal to the Union. Still, the acquisition of four new Confederate states greatly strengthened the cause of southern independence.

The Combatants

The outbreak of fighting ended drift and indecision. Although fierce struggle continued in the border states and in some areas within the seceding states of the Upper South, most whites in the South chose to defend the Confederacy. For them, Yankee "aggression" was no longer a secessionist's abstraction;

it was real, and it was at their doors. For Northerners, rebel "treason" threatened to destroy the noble experiment of republican self-government. Men rallied behind their separate battle flags, fully convinced that they were in the right and that God was on their side. Passion often overrode sober reflection in the early months of the war, but all citizens had to answer for themselves what they were fighting for and what they were fighting against.

Northerners and Southerners also had to consider what they had to fight with. While both sides claimed the lion's share of virtue, only fools argued that the South's resources and forces equaled the North's. The briefest glance at the census figures contradicted such a notion. Yankees took heart at their superior power, but the rebels believed they had advantages that nullified every northern strength. Both sides mobilized swiftly in the spring and summer of 1861, and each devised what it believed would be a winning military and diplomatic strategy.

What They Fought For

Across the South, planters, yeomen, and artisans raced to enlist and to fight Yankees. Contemporary Northerners were puzzled by the willingness of ordinary whites to fight to preserve slavery, which Alexander Stephens, vice president of the Confederacy, identified as the new nation's "cornerstone." Why should poor men who owned no slaves be willing to die to ensure that rich men could keep theirs?

Only slaveholders, of course, had a direct economic stake (estimated at some $3 billion in 1860) in preserving slavery. But all white Southerners—slaveholders and nonslaveholders alike—united in the defense of slavery. Slavery controlled blacks, whom they thought an inferior and potentially dangerous race. Moreover, the degraded and subjugated status of blacks was the basis of an elevated status for even the most humble whites. "It matters not whether slaves be actually owned by many or by few," one observer declared. "It is enough that one simply belongs to the superior and ruling race, to secure consideration and respect." Ordinary and elite whites understood the Mississippian who announced that he would rather "be exterminated" than be forced to live in the same society "with the slaves if freed."

Ordinary whites, however, did not explicitly name slavery as their reason for fighting. Instead, they emphasized defending a special southern civilization from "subjugation" and protecting hearth and home, mothers and wives, from northern hordes bent on plunder and domination. One man declared that he and his neighbors went to war "for our homes, our lives—the honor & safety of ourselves, our families & our property." Even Confederate officials shied away from publicly identifying their cause with slavery. Instead, their rhetoric overflowed with lofty abstractions such as states' rights, self-determination, and liberty. But without slavery there would have been no distinctive southern civilization, no Republican Party to threaten it, and no reason to ensure it by creating a separate nation.

Northerners and Southerners also had to consider what they had to fight with. While both sides claimed the lion's share of virtue, only fools argued that the South's resources and forces equaled the North's.

In 1861, white Southerners equated their position with that of American patriots in 1776. In both cases, they argued, a freedom-loving minority waged war to protect its liberty against the encroachments of a tyrannical central government. As one Georgia woman observed, Southerners wanted "nothing from the North but—*to be let alone*—and *they*, a people like ourselves whose republican independence was won by a rebellion, whose liberty was achieved by a secession, to think that they should attempt to coerce us—the idea is preposterous."

Northerners saw secession as an unconscionable attack on the best government on the face of the earth. The South's failure to accept the lawful election of a president and its firing on the nation's flag challenged the rule of law, the authority of the Constitution, and the ability of the people to govern themselves. Northerners believed that the South's effort to wreck the Republic threatened them in a very personal way. As an Indiana soldier told his wife, a "good government is the best thing on earth. Property is nothing without it, because it is not protected; a family is nothing without it, because they cannot be educated."

Lincoln captured the Union's special magnetism. "This is essentially a People's contest," he declared on the first Fourth of July after the war began. The Union's cause, he said, was the preservation of the government "whose leading object is, to elevate the condition of man—to lift artificial weights from all shoulders—to clear the paths of laudable pursuit for all—to afford all, an unfettered start, and a fair chance, in the race of life." In short, secession menaced the life chances of millions of eager and aspiring individuals. That is why Northerners were not willing to allow the South to go in peace. Too much was at stake. In villages, towns, and cities across the North, self-interest, as well as patriotic fervor, welded individuals to the preservation of the nation. That steel-like bond sustained men and women through four years of war.

How They Expected to Win

The balance sheet of northern and southern resources reveals enormous advantages for the Union. The twenty-three states remaining in the Union had a population of 22,300,000, while the eleven Confederate states had a population of only 9,100,000, of whom 3,670,000 (40 percent) were slaves. The North had 22,000 miles of railroads; the South had only 9,280. The states in the Union manufactured more than 90 percent of the nation's industrial goods. The North had 1,300,000 industrial workers,

the South only 110,000. The North produced 17 times as much textiles; 21 times as much coal; 24 times as many locomotives; 5 times as much tonnage in ships; and 32 times as many firearms. The list is nearly endless.

As lopsided as the inventory is, statistics do not tell the full story of the North's advantage. Not only did it have superiority in people and equipment, but it could replace both more readily than could the South. Most of the South's stockpile of war-making materiel—locomotives, rails, arms, munitions, textiles, and more—had been imported from outside the region. When an item was used up, destroyed, or captured, Southerners would have no easy way to replace it. The North's vast, expanding manufacturing and industrial economy could produce and deliver all that northern soldiers needed.

So overwhelming were the North's advantages that the question becomes why did the South make war at all? Was not the outcome written in the statistics? Was not the South's cause lost before Confederates lobbed the first rounds at Fort Sumter? The answer quite simply is no. Southerners expected to win—and for some good reasons. They came very close to doing it.

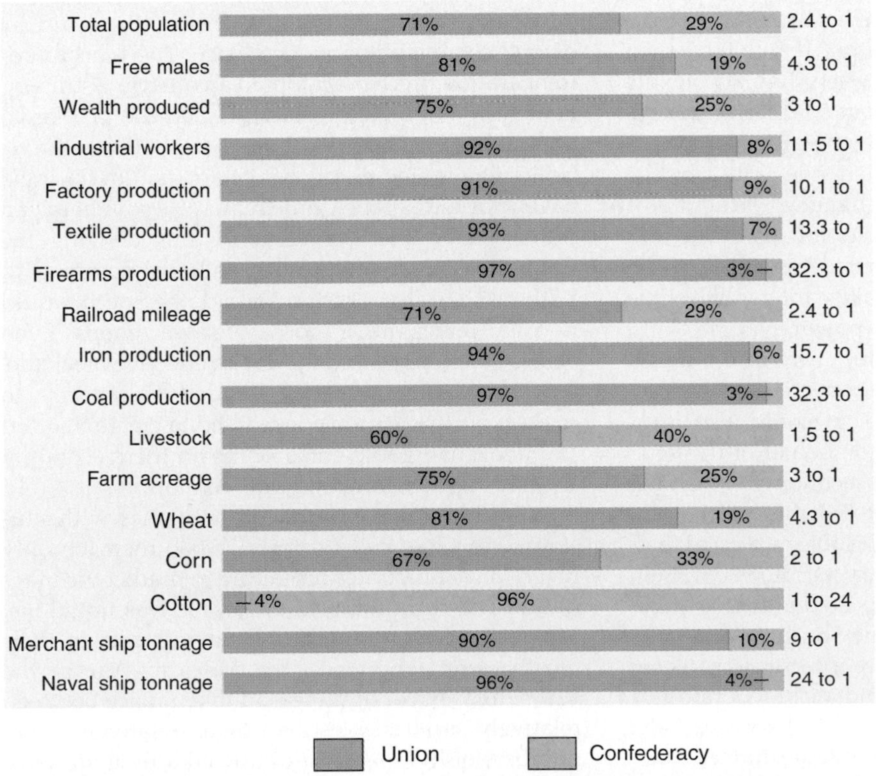

	Union	Confederacy	Ratio
Total population	71%	29%	2.4 to 1
Free males	81%	19%	4.3 to 1
Wealth produced	75%	25%	3 to 1
Industrial workers	92%	8%	11.5 to 1
Factory production	91%	9%	10.1 to 1
Textile production	93%	7%	13.3 to 1
Firearms production	97%	3%	32.3 to 1
Railroad mileage	71%	29%	2.4 to 1
Iron production	94%	6%	15.7 to 1
Coal production	97%	3%	32.3 to 1
Livestock	60%	40%	1.5 to 1
Farm acreage	75%	25%	3 to 1
Wheat	81%	19%	4.3 to 1
Corn	67%	33%	2 to 1
Cotton	4%	96%	1 to 24
Merchant ship tonnage	90%	10%	9 to 1
Naval ship tonnage	96%	4%	24 to 1

Union   Confederacy

FIGURE 15.1
Resources of the Union and Confederacy
The Union's enormous statistical advantages failed to convince Confederates that their cause was doomed.

During the secession crisis, Southerners equated their cause with that of liberty-loving American colonists, and they hugged the example of 1776 even closer when they contemplated the similarity in military situations. Southerners bucked the military odds, but hadn't the colonists, too? "Britain could not conquer three million," a Louisianan proclaimed, and "the world cannot conquer the South." David had beaten Goliath, and history brimmed with examples of smaller, weaker peoples defeating larger, stronger adversaries.

Southerners believed that they would triumph because of their region's lofty cause, superior civilization, and unsurpassed character. They genuinely thought that the South produced better men. How could anyone doubt the outcome of a contest between lean, hard, country-born rebel warriors, defending family, property, and liberty, and soft, flabby, citified Yankee mechanics waging an unconstitutional war of aggression and subjugation? No wonder Southerners would claim after the war that they had not been "whipped" but had "worn themselves out whipping Yankees."

The South's confidence also rested on its estimation of the economic clout of cotton. A war correspondent for the London *Times* found that "King Cotton" was "the fixed idea everywhere." For years, Southerners had argued that northern prosperity depended on the South's cotton. It followed then that without southern cotton, New England textile mills would stand idle. Without southern markets, northern factories would drown in their own surpluses. Without the foreign exchange earned by the overseas sales of cotton, the financial structure of the entire Yankee nation would collapse. One Virginian spoke for most Confederates when he declared that in the South's ability to "withhold the benefits of our trade, we hold a power over the North more powerful than a powerful army in the field."

King Cotton not only could decree the destruction of the North's economy but could also command European intervention on behalf of the Confederacy. After all, England's economy depended almost as much on cotton as did the North's. Indeed, some four million British subjects earned their livings from the textile industry. Of the 900 million pounds of cotton England imported annually, more than 700 million came from the South. Southerners figured that if the supply were interrupted, "sheer necessity" would make England a Confederate ally. And because the British navy ruled the seas, the North would find Britain a formidable, indeed overwhelming, foe.

Southerners' faith in the superiority of their fighting men and in the power of cotton seems naive today because that faith turned out to have been misplaced. But even hard-eyed European military observers picked the South to win. Offsetting the North's power was the South's expanse. Its huge area (750,000 square miles), with its rugged terrain and bad roads, made Lincoln's task enormous. The North, Europeans predicted, could not conquer the vast territory from the Potomac to the Rio Grande. It would require raising a massive invading army, supplying it with huge quantities of provisions and arms, and protecting supply lines that would stretch farther than any in modern history.

Indeed, the South enjoyed major advantages, and the Confederacy devised a military strategy to take advantage of them. Jefferson Davis called it an "offensive-defensive" strategy. It recognized that a victory by the North required the North to defeat and subjugate the South. A victory by the South, in contrast, required only that it stay at home, blunt northern invasions, avoid battles that risked annihilating its army, and outlast the northern will to fight. When an opportunity presented itself, the South would strike the invaders. Like the American colonists, the South could win independence by not losing the war.

If the North did nothing, the South would by default establish its independence. The Lincoln administration therefore adopted an offensive strategy. Four days after the president issued the proclamation calling for 75,000 volunteers to put down the rebellion, he issued another proclamation declaring a naval blockade of the Confederacy. He sought to pen cotton inside the Confederacy, thus denying the Confederacy use of its most valuable commodity. Without the sale of cotton abroad, the South would have far fewer dollars to pay for war goods. Even before the North could mount an effective blockade, however, Jefferson Davis decided voluntarily to cease exporting cotton. He wanted to create a cotton "famine" that would enfeeble the northern economy and precipitate European intervention.

Southerners were not the only ones with illusions. Lincoln's call for only 75,000 men for only ninety days illustrates his failure to predict the magnitude and duration of the war. He was not alone. Most Americans thought of war in terms of their most recent experience, the Mexican War in the 1840s. In Mexico, fighting had taken place between relatively small armies, had taken relatively small numbers of lives, and had inflicted only light damage on the economy.

THE ORANGE AND ALEXANDRIA RAILROAD BRIDGE
Confederate forces would burn southern railroads and bridges to slow Union advances, interdict
federal supply lines, and protect Confederate retreats. West Point trained Herman Haupt, seen
here inspecting a rebuilt bridge, was in charge of the Union's efforts at railroad construction and
repair. While the railroad had been used as an instrument of war in the Crimea in the 1850s, it
was during the Civil War that the railroad took on revolutionary importance. Railroads helped
set new standards of overland mobility, rapid maneuver, and concentration of forces.
Library of Congress.

The American Civil War, however, proved to be the first modern war, a "total war" that mobilized entire populations, harnessed the productive capacities of entire economies, and enlisted millions of troops, with single battles pitting more than 200,000 soldiers and casualties mounting into the tens of thousands. Individual bravery would play a role in the outcome, but the morale of the people, the quality of political leadership, and the ability to utilize to the fullest the industrial economy would prove critical.

Americans on the eve of the Civil War had no crystal ball with which to peer into the future. They could not know that four ghastly years of bloodletting lay just over the horizon. On the contrary, both sides anticipated relatively clean victories. Early theories and strategies, however, like the expectations of military glory and fame, quickly confronted harsh reality.

Lincoln and Davis Mobilize

Mobilization required effective political leadership, and at first glance it appeared that the South had the decided advantage. An aristocrat from a Mississippi planter family, Jefferson Davis brought to the office of Confederate president a distinguished political career, including a stint in the U.S. Senate. He was also a West Point graduate, a combat veteran of the Mexican War, and a former secretary of war. Dignified and erect, with "a jaw sawed in *steel*," Davis appeared to be everything a nation could want in a wartime leader.

In contrast, an Illinois lawyer-politician occupied the White House. He brought with him one undistinguished term in the House of Representatives, where he had opposed the Mexican War in which Davis had served gallantly. He had almost no administrative experience, and his sole brush with anything military was as a captain in the militia in the Black Hawk War, a brief struggle in Illinois in 1832 in which whites expelled the last Indians from the state. Lincoln later joked about his service in the Black Hawk War as the time when he survived bloody encounters with mosquitoes and led raids on wild onion patches. The lanky, disheveled Westerner looked anything but military or presidential in his bearing, and even his friends feared that he was in over his head.

Davis, however, proved to be less than he appeared. Even in military matters, he disappointed. Possessing little capacity for broad military strategy and yet vain about what he considered his own superior judgment, he intervened constantly in military affairs. He was an even less able political leader. Quarrelsome and proud, he had an acid tongue that made enemies the Confederacy could ill afford. Davis had a better side, but he kept it hidden from all but his family and close friends. It is true that Davis faced a daunting task. For example, state sovereignty, which was enshrined in the Confederate constitution, made Davis's task of organizing a new nation and fighting a war difficult in the extreme. His wife, Varina, reported that her husband "hardly takes time to eat his meals and works late at night," but his best efforts proved inadequate. An even more talented man might have been defeated by the Confederacy's intimidating problems.

In Lincoln, however, the North got far more than met the eye. He proved himself a master politician and a superb leader. He never allowed personal feelings to get in the way of his objectives. He shrugged off insults such as those offered by the arrogant young Union general George McClellan, who called Lincoln the "original Gorilla." When he formed his cabinet, Lincoln shrewdly appointed representatives of every Republican faction, men who were often his chief rivals and critics. He made Salmon P. Chase secretary of the treasury, knowing

that Chase intended to replace him on the Republican ticket at the next election. As secretary of state, he chose his chief opponent for the Republican nomination in 1860, William Seward, who expected to twist Lincoln around his little finger and formulate policy himself. Despite his civilian background, Lincoln displayed an innate understanding of military strategy. In time, no one proved more crucial in mapping the Union war plan. Moreover, Lincoln was an enormously eloquent man who reached out to the North's people, galvanizing them in defense of the nation he called "the last best hope of earth."

Guided by Lincoln and Davis, the North and South began gathering their armies. Southerners had the task of building almost everything from scratch, and Northerners had to mobilize their superior numbers and industrial resources for war. The puny federal army numbered only 16,000 men in 1861, most of whom were scattered over the West subjugating Indians. One-third of the officers followed Robert E. Lee's example, resigned their commissions, and headed south. The navy was in better shape. Forty-two ships were in service, and a large merchant marine would in time provide more ships and sailors. Most of the officers and men were Northerners and loyal to the Union.

The Confederacy had no navy and few shipyards for building one. But it had strong leadership in its secretary of the navy, Stephen R. Mallory, who immediately commissioned shipyards in Britain to produce several fast commerce raiders, which roamed the Atlantic preying on northern shipping. Still, the Confederate navy was never a match for the Union fleet, and the South pinned its hopes on its armies. Military companies sprang up everywhere. Since soldiers at first supplied their own uniforms, Confederate gray was just one of a rainbow of colors. Moreover, volunteers brought their own weapons, as often Bowie knives and shotguns as rifles and pistols.

From the beginning, the South exhibited more enthusiasm than ability to provide its soldiers with supplies and transportation. The Confederacy made prodigious efforts to build new factories to produce tents, shoes, blankets, and uniforms, but many soldiers spent nights with stars for a roof, huddled together for warmth, without proper clothes and sometimes without shoes. Even when factories managed to produce what soldiers needed, southern railroads—constructed to connect plantations with ports—often could not deliver what the factories made. And before long, most railroads were captured, destroyed, or in disrepair. Food production proved less of a problem, but food sometimes rotted before it reached the soldiers. The one bright spot was the Confederacy's Ordnance Bureau, headed by Josiah Gorgas, a near miracle worker when it came to manufacturing gunpowder, cannons, and rifles. In April 1864, Gorgas observed with justifiable pride: "Where three years ago we were not making a gun, a pistol nor a sabre, no shot nor shell . . . —a pound of powder—we now make all these in quantities to meet the demands of our large armies."

Recruiting and supplying huge armies required enormous public spending. Before the war, the federal government's tiny income had come primarily from tariff duties and the sale of public lands. Massive wartime expenditures made new revenues imperative. At first, both the North and the South resorted to selling war bonds, which essentially were loans from patriotic citizens. In time, both North and South began printing paper money. Inflation soared, but the South suffered more because it financed a greater part of its wartime costs through the printing press. Prices in the North rose about 80 percent during the war, while in the South inflation topped 9,000 percent. Eventually, the Union and the Confederacy turned to taxes, but the North raised one-fifth of its wartime revenue from this source, while the South raised only one-twentieth. The North proved far more able to adapt its system of public finance to extraordinary wartime conditions than did the South, and its success translated into greater economic and military might.

Within months, both sides had found men to fight and people to supply and support them. But the underlying strength of the northern economy gave the Union the decided advantage. With their military and industrial muscles beginning to ripple, Northerners became itchy for action. Northerners wanted an invasion that would once and for all smash the rebellion. Horace Greeley's *New York Tribune* began the chant: "Forward to Richmond! Forward to Richmond!"

The Battlefields, 1861–1862

During the first year and a half of the war, armies fought major campaigns in two theaters: in Virginia-Maryland in the East and in Tennessee-Kentucky in the West. With rival capitals of Richmond and Washington, D.C., only ninety miles apart and each

threatened more than once with capture, the eastern campaign was more dramatic and naturally attracted public attention. But the battles in the West proved more decisive. And while Yankee and rebel armies pounded each other on land, their navies fought it out on the seas and their diplomats sought advantage in the corridors of power in Europe. All the while, casualty lists reached appalling lengths.

Stalemate in the Eastern Theater

As one of his first important acts as commander in chief, Lincoln appointed Irvin McDowell commanding general of the army assembling outside Washington. An officer in the regular army, McDowell had no thought of taking his raw recruits into battle during the summer of 1861. But Lincoln ordered McDowell to prepare his 30,000 men for an attack on the Confederate army gathered at Manassas, a railroad junction in Virginia about thirty miles southwest of Washington. McDowell complained bitterly, but Lincoln replied, "You are green, it is true, but they are green, also; you are all green."

Repeating to the last that he did not want to go, McDowell moved his greenhorn troops out on July 16. Five days later, the Union army forded Bull Run, a branch of the Potomac, and engaged the southern forces effectively. But when federal troops failed to pin down Confederates in the Shenandoah Valley, fast-moving southern reinforcements blunted the Union attack and then counterattacked. What began as an orderly retreat turned into a panicky stampede. Demoralized soldiers ran over shocked civilians as they raced back to Washington. Thousands of dirty, disheveled, wild-eyed young soldiers served as evidence of the magnitude of the Union defeat.

By Civil War standards, casualties at Manassas (or Bull Run, as Northerners called the battle) were light, but the significance of the battle lay in the lessons Northerners and Southerners drew from it. For Southerners, it confirmed the superiority of rebel fighting men and the inevitability of Confederate nationhood. Manassas was *"one of the decisive battles of the world,"* a Georgian proclaimed. It *"has secured our independence."* While victory lifted southern conceit to new levels, defeat sobered Northerners and made them even more resolute. It was a major reversal, admitted the *New York Tribune*, but, the writer added, "Let us go to work, then, with a will." For Lincoln, Manassas was a slap in the face that awakened him to the realization that victory would be neither quick nor easy. Within four days of the disaster, the president signed bills authorizing the enlistment of one million men.

Lincoln also found a new general, replacing McDowell with the vain young George B. McClellan. Born in Philadelphia of well-to-do parents, educated in the best schools before graduating from West Point second in his class, the thirty-four-year-old McClellan believed that he was a great soldier and that Lincoln was a moron. A superb administrator and organizer, McClellan was brought to Washington as commander of the newly named Army of the Potomac. In the months following his appointment, McClellan energetically whipped his army into shape. Dispirited veterans and fresh recruits gained confidence and discipline and developed into a powerful fighting machine. The troops cheered their boyish general when he rode among them, in part no doubt because of his reluctance to send them into battle. Lincoln said McClellan had a bad case of "the slows," and, indeed, McClellan lacked decisiveness and the will to act. He defended his inactivity by claiming that his troops needed more drill or that the enemy outnumbered him—three or four to one. In actuality, McClellan commanded 120,000 troops in October 1861, while the Confederates facing him numbered only 45,000. Lincoln wanted a general who would advance, take risks, and fight, but McClellan went into winter quarters without budging from the Potomac. "If General McClellan does not want to use the army I would like to *borrow* it," Lincoln declared in frustration.

Finally, in the spring of 1862, McClellan launched his long-awaited offensive. He transported his highly polished army, now 130,000 strong, down the Chesapeake Bay to the mouth of the James River and began moving up the peninsula toward Richmond. McClellan took two and a half months to advance sixty-five miles. When he was within six miles of the Confederate capital, Confederate General Joseph Johnston hit him like a hammer. In the assault, Johnston was wounded and was replaced by Robert E. Lee, the reluctant Confederate who would become the Confederacy's most celebrated general. Lee named his command the Army of Northern Virginia.

The contrast between Lee and McClellan could hardly have been greater. McClellan overflowed with conceit and braggadocio, while Lee was courteous and reserved. But on the battlefield, where McClellan became timid and irresolute, Lee became audaciously, even recklessly, aggressive. McClellan's natural impulse was to dig in; Lee's was to attack. Lee had at his side in the peninsula campaign military men of real talent: General Thomas J. ("Stonewall") Jackson, so nicknamed for holding the line at Manassas, and James E. B. ("Jeb") Stuart, the twenty-nine-year-old cavalry commander who wore a red-lined cape, yellow sash, and hat with ostrich feather plume and rode circles around Yankee troops. Lee's assault initiated the Battle of Seven Days and began McClellan's backward march down the peninsula. By the time McClellan reached the water and the safety of the Union navy, 30,000 men had died or been wounded. Although Southerners suffered twice the casualties of Northerners, Lee had saved Richmond and achieved a strategic success. Lincoln wired McClellan to abandon the peninsula campaign and replaced him with General John Pope.

In August, just north of Richmond, Pope had his own rendezvous with Lee. At the Second Battle of Bull Run, Lee's smaller army battered Pope's forces and sent them scurrying back to Washington. Lincoln ordered Pope to Minnesota to pacify Indians and again put McClellan in command. Lincoln had not changed his mind about McClellan's capacity as a warrior. Instead, he reluctantly concluded, "There is no man in the Army who can lick these troops of ours into shape half as well as he. . . . If he can't fight himself, he excels in making others ready to fight."

Lee could fight. Sensing that he had his enemy on the ropes, he sought to land the knockout punch. Lee pushed the Army of Northern Virginia across the Potomac and invaded Maryland. A victory on northern soil would dislodge Maryland from the Union, Lee reasoned, and might even cause Lincoln to sue for peace. On September 17, 1862, McClellan's forces finally engaged Lee's army at Antietam Creek. Earlier, a Union soldier had found a copy of Lee's orders to his army wrapped around some cigars, dropped by a careless Confederate officer. McClellan had a clear picture of Lee's position, but his characteristic slowness meant that he missed a great opportunity to destroy the opposing army. Still, he did it great damage. In some of the most frenzied fighting of the war, with "solid shot . . . cracking skulls like egg-shells," the armies threw everything they had at one another. By nightfall the battlefield lay littered with 6,000 men dead or dying and 17,000 more wounded, making the Battle of Antietam the bloodiest day of the war. Badly damaged and deeply disappointed, Lee headed back to Virginia.

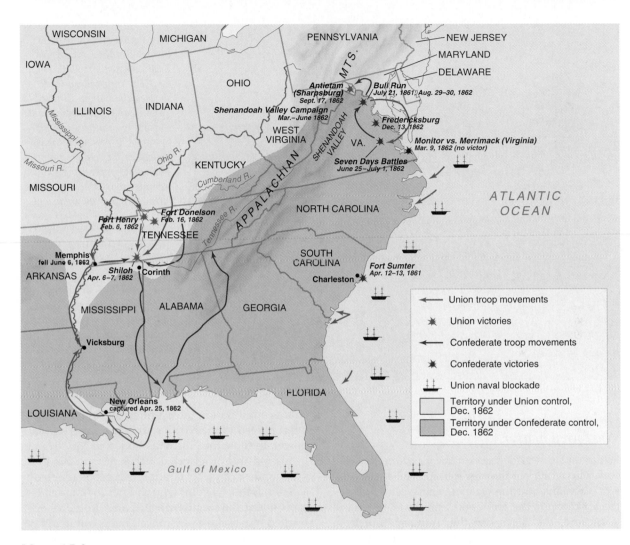

M A P 15.2
The Civil War, 1861–1862
While eyes focused on the eastern theater, especially the tiny geography between the two
capitals of Washington and Richmond, strategic victories were being won by Union troops
in the West.

But Lee remained alert for an opportunity to punish his enemy. In December, General Ambrose Burnside, yet another replacement for the ineffectual McClellan, provided the Virginian a fresh chance. At Fredericksburg, Virginia, Burnside's 122,000 Union troops faced 78,500 Confederates dug in behind a stone wall on the heights above the Rappahannock River. Half a mile of open ground lay between the armies. A Confederate artillery officer predicted that "a chicken could not live on that field when we open on it." Yet Burnside ordered a frontal assault. Wave after wave of bluecoats crashed against impregnable defenses. When the guns finally ceased, the federals counted nearly 13,000 casualties while the Confederates suffered fewer than 5,000. It was one of the Union's worst defeats.

At the end of 1862, the North seemed no nearer to taking Richmond, to whipping Lee, or to ending the rebellion than it had been when the war began. Rather than checkmate, military struggle in the East had reached a stalemate.

THE DEAD OF ANTIETAM
In October 1862, Mathew Brady opened an exhibition at his New York gallery that shocked the nation. Entitled "The Dead of Antietam" and consisting of ninety-five photographs, it presented the battlefield as the soldiers saw it. This photograph depicts Confederate troops lined up for burial. Among the thousands of visitors to the exhibit was a reporter for the New York Times, *who observed: "Mr. Brady has done something to bring to us the terrible reality and earnestness of the war. If he has not brought bodies and laid them in our door-yards and along [our] streets, he has done something very like it."* Library of Congress.

Union Victories in the Western Theater

While most eyes focused on the East, the decisive early encounters of the war took place between the Appalachians and the Ozarks. The West's rivers— the Mississippi, the Tennessee, and the Cumberland —became the keys to the military situation. Whether they were arrows into the midsection of the Union or the heart of the Confederacy depended on who drew the bow. Southerners looked northward along the rivers and spied Missouri and Kentucky, states they claimed but did not control. Looking southward, Northerners knew that by taking the Mississippi they would split Arkansas, Louisiana, and Texas from the Confederacy. And the Cumberland and Tennessee penetrated one of the Confederacy's main producers of food, mules, and iron— all vital resources.

Ulysses S. Grant became the key northern figure on the western battlefields. Although Grant had graduated from West Point, when war broke out he was a thirty-nine-year-old dry goods clerk in Galena, Illinois. Gentle at home, he became pugnacious on the battlefield. "The art of war is simple," he said. "Find out where your enemy is, get at him as soon as you can and strike him as hard as you can, and keep moving on." Grant's philosophy of

war as annihilation took a huge toll in human life, but it played to the North's strength: superior manpower. In time, the North fashioned victory from it. In his old uniform and slouch hat, with his tired, sad, nondescript face, Grant did not look much like a general. But Lincoln, who did not look much like a president, knew his worth. Later, to critics who wanted him to remove Grant from his command because of his fondness for the bottle, Lincoln would reply: *"I can't spare this man. He fights."*

Manassas disabused Lincoln of the illusion of a short war, and, after Shiloh, Grant "gave up all idea of saving the Union except by complete conquest."

In February 1862, operating in tandem with navy gunboats, Grant captured Fort Henry on the Tennessee and Fort Donelson on the Cumberland. Defeat forced the Confederates to withdraw from all of Kentucky and most of Tennessee. Without pausing to savor his victories, Grant pushed after the retreating rebels until, on April 6, General Albert Sidney Johnston's army surprised him at Shiloh Church in Tennessee. Although his troops were

badly mauled the first day, Grant remained cool and brought up reinforcements throughout the night. The next morning, the Union army counterattacked, driving the Confederates before it. The battle was terribly costly; there were 20,000 casualties, including the death of Johnston. Manassas disabused Lincoln of the illusion of a short war, and, after Shiloh, Grant "gave up all idea of saving the Union except by complete conquest."

Although no one knew it at the time, Shiloh inflicted a mortal wound to the Confederacy's bid to control the Mississippi valley. Rebel armies in the West still had plenty of fight in them, but from then on it was a downhill slide. In short order, the Yankees captured the strategic town of Corinth, Mississippi, the river city of Memphis, and New Orleans, the South's largest city. By the end of 1862, most—but not all—of the Mississippi valley lay in Union hands.

War and Diplomacy in the Atlantic Theater

With a blockade fleet of only about three dozen ships at the beginning of the war and more than 3,500 miles of southern coastline to patrol, the U.S. navy faced an impossible task. At first, rebel ships slipped in and out of port nearly at will. Yankees probably nabbed no more than one in ten. Taking on cargoes in the Caribbean, the sleek, fast blockade runners brought in vital supplies—guns and medicine—and also small quantities of luxury goods such as tea and liquor. But with the U.S. navy commissioning a new blockader almost weekly, the fleet eventually reached 150 ships on duty, and the Union navy dramatically improved its score.

Unable to build a conventional navy equal to the expanding federal fleet, the Confederates experimented with a radical new maritime design: the ironclad warship. At Norfolk, Virginia, they layered the wooden hull of the frigate *Merrimack* with two-inch-thick armor plate and armed the saltwater marvel with ten guns. Rechristened *Virginia*, it steamed out in March 1862 to engage the federal blockade fleet off Hampton Roads, Virginia. Within a few hours, it sank two large federal ships, killing at least 240 sailors. But when the *Virginia* returned the following morning to finish its work, it found the *Monitor*, a federal ironclad that had arrived from Brooklyn during the night. Alerted months earlier by rumors of the rebel invention, the federal government had built its own ironclad, a ship of even more radical design, including a revolving turret containing two eleven-inch guns. The *Monitor* and the *Virginia* hurled shells at one another for two hours, but because neither could penetrate the other's armor, the duel ended in a draw.

Both sides built other ironclads, but the Confederacy never found a way to break the blockade. Each month the blockade grew tighter until by 1865 the Union fleet intercepted about one of every two southern ships that attempted to break through. Even more significant than the ships the Union fleet captured (about 1,500 in total) were the ships that never sailed for fear of being captured. By 1863, the South had abandoned its embargo policy and desperately wanted to ship cotton to pay for imports needed to fight the war. But the growing effectiveness of the blockade meant that the South's seaborne trade declined by more than two-thirds. The federal blockade, a southern naval officer observed, "shut the Confederacy out from the world, deprived it of supplies, weakened its military and naval strength."

What they could not achieve on saltwater, Confederates sought to gain through foreign policy. According to the theory of King Cotton, however, Southerners should not have had to lift a diplomatic finger, for cotton-starved European nations supposedly had no choice but to break the blockade and recognize the Confederacy. The British and French briefly discussed joint action to lift the blockade, but it came to nothing. Although European nations granted the Confederacy "belligerent" status, which enabled it to buy goods and build ships in European ports, none recognized Confederate nationhood.

King Cotton diplomacy failed for several reasons. A bumper cotton crop in 1860 meant that the warehouses of British textile manufacturers bulged with surplus cotton throughout 1861. In 1862, when Europe began to feel the pinch of the cotton famine, manufacturers found new sources of cotton in Egypt and India. In addition, a brisk trade developed between the Union and Britain—British war materiel for American grain and flour—which helped offset the decline in textiles and encouraged Britain to remain neutral. Moreover, U.S. Secretary of State William Seward warned Europe sternly against meddling in America's civil war, which he defined as strictly an internal affair. British Foreign Minister Lord Russell agreed, observing, "They who in quarrels interpose, will often get a bloody nose." Even when the Union stepped hard on tender British toes, the British remained tolerant. In November 1861, a Union warship intercepted a British mail packet, the *Trent*, and illegally removed James Mason and John Slidell, Confederate diplo-

mats on their way to Europe. Sentiment for war flared briefly in Britain, but when Lincoln ordered the Southerners' release, the British allowed the affair to end peacefully.

Europe's temptation to intervene withered in 1862. Union military successes, especially on the rivers of the West, made Britain and France think twice about linking their fates to the Confederacy. And in the fall of 1862, Lincoln announced a new policy that made an alliance with the Confederacy an alliance with slavery. The president finally acknowledged what Frederick Douglass had predicted—that it was impossible to fight for union without fighting against slavery.

Union and Freedom

Slavery and freedom had coexisted in North America for more than two centuries when the Civil War erupted. In his inaugural address in March 1861, Abraham Lincoln solemnly announced to the nation that the war would not disturb that ancient relationship. He had "no legal right" and "no inclination" to interfere with slavery, he said. For a year and a half Lincoln insisted that emancipation was not a goal; the war was strictly to save the Union.

In the field among military commanders, in the halls of Congress, and in the White House, the truth gradually came into focus: To defeat the Confederacy, the North would have to destroy slavery.

Despite Lincoln's pronouncements, the war for union became a war for African American freedom. The transformation of northern purpose took place in fits and starts. The Lincoln administration sought to avoid the slavery issue, but rapidly evolving events made it impossible to maintain its conservative policy. Each month the war dragged on, it became clearer that the Confederate war machine depended heavily on slavery. Rebel armies used slaves to build fortifications, haul materiel, tend horses, and perform camp chores. On the home front, slaves labored in ironworks and shipyards, and they grew the food that fed both soldiers and civilians. Slavery undergirded the Confederacy as certainly as it had the Old South. In the field among military com-

SLAVE WITH CONFEDERATE SOLDIERS
The slave Scott poses in 1863 with members of a Georgia regiment. Many slaveholders took "body servants" with them to war. These slaves cooked, washed, and cleaned for the white soldiers. In 1861, James H. Langhorne reported to his sister: "Peter . . . is charmed with being with me & 'being a soldier.' I gave him my old uniform overcoat & he says he is going to have his picture taken . . . to send to the servants." Peter may have been "puttin' on ol' massa" or just glad to be free of plantation labor.
From *Milledgeville* by James C. Bonner, University of Georgia Press, 1978.

manders, in the halls of Congress, and in the White House, the truth gradually came into focus: To defeat the Confederacy, the North would have to destroy slavery. "I am a slow walker," Lincoln said, "but I never walk back."

From Slaves to Contraband

Personally, Lincoln detested human bondage, but as president he felt compelled to act prudently. He doubted his right under the Constitution to tamper with the "domestic institutions" of any state, even those in rebellion. He clung to the hope that if he avoided the slavery issue, Unionists in the South would reassert themselves and topple the Confederacy from within. Probably most important, he feared the consequences for the Union war effort. An astute politician, he worked within the limits of public opinion, and in 1861 Lincoln believed those limits were tight. The issue of black freedom was particularly explosive in the loyal border states, where slaveholders threatened to jump into the arms of the Confederacy at even the hint of emancipation. Black freedom also attracted attention in the free states. The Democratic Party gave notice that emancipation would kill the bipartisan alliance and make the war strictly a Republican affair. Democrats were as ardent for union as Republicans, but they fought against treason—period. They marched under the banner "The Constitution As It Is, the Union As It Was."

Moreover, while most white Northerners had no love of slavery, they were not about to risk their lives to satisfy abolitionist "fanaticism." "We Won't Fight to Free the Nigger," one popular banner read. They feared that emancipation would propel "two or three million semi-savages" northward, where they would crowd into white neighborhoods, compete for white jobs, and mix with white "sons and daughters." An anti-emancipation backlash, then, threatened to dislodge the loyal slave states from the Union, alienate the Democratic Party, deplete the armies, and perhaps even spark race warfare. Lincoln believed that he could not afford to jeopardize the Union coalition and proceeded cautiously.

Proponents of emancipation pressed Lincoln as relentlessly as the anti-emancipation forces. Black and white abolitionists argued that by seceding, Southerners had forfeited their right to the protection of the Constitution. Lincoln could now—as the price of treason—legally confiscate their property in slaves. When Lincoln stubbornly refused, abolitionists scalded him. Frederick Douglass labeled Lincoln "the miserable tool of traitors and rebels." Abolitionists won increasing numbers of converts during the war, especially among the radical faction of the Republican Party, which came to believe that restoring the Union with the moral evil of slavery intact would make a mockery of the sacrifices of Union soldiers.

The Republican-dominated Congress refused to leave slavery policy entirely in Lincoln's hands.

CONTRABANDS

These refugees from slavery crossed the Rappahannock River in Virginia in August 1862 to seek the sanctuary of a federal army. Most slaves fled with little more than the clothes on their backs, but not all escaped slavery empty-handed. The oxen, wagon, and goods seen here could have been procured by a number of means—purchased during slavery, "borrowed" from the former master, or gathered during flight. Refugees who possessed draft animals and a wagon had much more economic opportunity than those who had only their labor to sell.
Library of Congress.

Even the moderate majority advanced more rapidly on the slavery issue than the cautious president. In August 1861, Congress approved the First Confiscation Act, which allowed the seizure of any slave who was employed directly by the Confederate military. It also fulfilled the free-soil dream of prohibiting slavery in the territories and abolished slavery in Washington, D.C. Democrats and border state representatives voted against even these mild measures, but little by little, Congress displayed a stiffening of attitude as it cast about for a just and practical slavery policy.

Slaves, not politicians, became the most insistent force for emancipation. By escaping their masters by the tens of thousands and running away to Union lines, they placed slavery on the North's wartime agenda. Union officials could not ignore the flood of fugitives, and runaways precipitated a series of momentous decisions on the part of the military, Congress, and the president. Were the runaways now free, or were they still slaves who, according to the fugitive slave law, had to be returned to their masters? At first, most Yankee military commanders believed that administration policy required them to send the fugitives back. But Union armies needed laborers, and some officers accepted the runaways and put them to work. At Fort Monroe, Virginia, General Benjamin F. Butler not only refused to turn them over to their owners but provided them with a new status. He called them "contraband of war," meaning "confiscated property." Congress established national policy in March 1862 when it forbade the practice of returning fugitive slaves to their masters. Slaves were still not legally free, but there was a tilt toward emancipation.

Lincoln's policy of noninterference with slavery gradually crumbled. To maintain control of federal action, he proposed alternatives of his own. Lincoln assumed that the hemorrhaging of slavery in the border states, where runaways found Union lines easiest to reach, had weakened slaveholder resistance to emancipation. Consequently, he proposed a scheme that would both end slavery in the border states and honor his promise not to attack the institution. In April 1862, Congress (at Lincoln's urging) approved a voluntary emancipation program that paid slaveholders to give up their slaves. Lincoln asked masters to recognize that the war itself would kill off slavery "by mere friction and abrasion," and they would then not collect a dollar for their losses. But Lincoln badly misread border state slaveholders. They rejected the plan outright, proving that they were as stubborn about keeping their slaves as any master in the Confederacy was.

To calm Northerners' racial fears, which he considered the chief obstacle to Union acceptance of emancipation, Lincoln offered colonization, the deportation of African Americans from the United States and resettlement in Haiti, Panama, or elsewhere. In the summer of 1862, he defended colonization to a delegation of black visitors to the White House. He told them that the deep-seated racial prejudice of whites made it impossible for blacks to achieve equality in this country. For blacks to be truly free, he said, they had to emigrate to countries where opportunities existed. An African American from Philadelphia spoke for the group when he told the president, "This is our country as much as it is yours, and we will not leave it." Congress did vote a small amount of money to underwrite colonization, but after one miserable experiment on a Caribbean island, practical limitations and black opposition sank further efforts.

At the same time that he developed his own initiatives, Lincoln snuffed out actions he believed jeopardized northern unity. He was particularly alert to Union commanders who tried to dictate slavery policy from the field. In August 1861, for example, when John C. Frémont, commander of federal troops in Missouri, impetuously freed the slaves belonging to Missouri rebels, Lincoln forced the general to revoke his edict and then removed him from command. The following May, when General David Hunter issued a proclamation freeing the slaves in Georgia, Florida, and South Carolina, Lincoln countermanded his order. Events moved so rapidly, however, that Lincoln found it impossible to control federal policy on slavery. He had to hurry just to keep up.

From Contraband to Free People

On August 22, 1862, Lincoln replied to another angry abolitionist who demanded that he go after slavery. "My paramount objective in this struggle *is* to save the Union," Lincoln said deliberately, "and is *not* either to save or destroy slavery. If I could save the Union without freeing *any* slave I would

FORMER SLAVES LISTEN TO LABOR CONTRACT
In November 1861, federal forces occupied the Sea Islands near Beaufort, South Carolina. Some ten thousand slaves came under federal authority. Emancipated workers gather in 1863 to hear a white man, probably a northern labor superintendent named Josiah Fairfield, read the terms of a free-labor contract. Little was settled about their future, and these former slaves appear to listen attentively, ready to defend their interests. One freedman accused Fairfield of having a "ractified mind," meaning that he was obstinate and hot-tempered.
The South Carolina Historical Society.

do it, and if I could save it by freeing *all* the slaves I would do it; and if I could save it by freeing some and leaving others alone I would also do that." At first glance, it seemed a restatement of his old position: that union was the North's sole objective. But what marked it as a radical departure was Lincoln's refusal to say that slavery was safe. Instead, he said that he would emancipate every slave if it would preserve the nation.

By the summer of 1862, events were tumbling rapidly toward emancipation. On July 17, Congress adopted a second Confiscation Act. The first had freed slaves employed by the Confederate military, the second declared all slaves of rebel masters "forever free of their servitude." In theory, this breathtaking measure freed most of the slaves in the Confederacy, for slaveholders formed the backbone of the rebellion. Congress had traveled far since the war began. Lincoln had too, but he wanted to blaze his own path. On July 21, the president informed his cabinet that he was ready "to take some definitive steps in respect to military action and slavery." The next day, he read a draft of a preliminary emancipation proclamation that promised to free *all* slaves in the seceding states on January 1, 1863.

Lincoln described emancipation as an "act of justice," but it was not the abolitionists' appeal to conscience that finally brought him around. It was the lengthening casualty lists. The duration and difficulty of the war eroded and then ended Lincoln's policy of noninterference. Emancipation, he declared, was "a military necessity, absolutely essential to the preservation of the Union." Only freeing the slaves would "strike at the heart of the rebellion." His cabinet approved Lincoln's plan but advised him to wait for a military victory before announcing it so that critics would not call it an act of desperation. On September 22, five days after the battle at Antietam, Lincoln served notice that if the rebel states did not lay down their arms and return to the Union by January 1, 1863, their slaves "shall be then, thenceforward, and forever free."

Lincoln had taken a risk, and he had good cause to be concerned about reaction in the North. Abolitionists generally approved, but the limitations of the proclamation—it exempted the loyal border states and the Union-occupied areas of the Confederacy—caused some to ridicule the act. The London *Times* observed cynically, "Where he has no power Mr. Lincoln will set the negroes free, where he retains power he will consider them as slaves." But Lincoln had no power to free slaves in loyal

states, and invading Union armies would liberate slaves in the Confederacy as they advanced.

But it was conservative reaction Lincoln feared. By presenting emancipation as a "military necessity," he hoped he had disarmed his critics. Emancipation would shorten the war and thus save lives. Still, Democrats exploded with rage. They charged that the "shrieking and howling abolitionist faction" had captured the White House and made it "a nigger war." The fall elections were only weeks away, and Democrats sought to make political hay out of Lincoln's action. War-weariness probably had as much to do with the results as emancipation, but Democrats gained thirty-four congressional seats in 1862. When House Democrats proposed a resolution branding emancipation "a high crime against the Constitution," the Republicans, who maintained narrow majorities in both houses, beat it back. As promised, on New Year's Day, Lincoln issued the final Emancipation Proclamation. In addition to freeing the slaves in the states that were in rebellion, the edict also committed the federal government to the fullest use of African Americans to defeat the Confederate enemy.

War of Black Liberation

Even before Lincoln proclaimed freedom a Union war aim, African Americans in the North had volunteered to fight. But the War Department, doubtful of their abilities and fearful of white reaction to serving shoulder to shoulder with them, refused to make black men soldiers. Instead, the army employed black men as manual laborers; black women sometimes found employment—usually as laundresses and cooks—but less often. The navy, however, from the outset accepted blacks as sailors. They usually served in noncombatant roles, but within months a few blacks served on gun crews.

As the Union experienced manpower shortages, Northerners gradually and reluctantly turned to African Americans to fill blue uniforms. With the Militia Act of July 1862, Congress authorized enrolling blacks in "any military or naval service for which they may be found competent." Lingering resistance to black military service largely disappeared in 1863. After the Emancipation Proclamation, whites—like it or not—were fighting and dying for black freedom, and few were likely to insist that blacks remain out of harm's way behind the lines. Indeed, rather than resist black military participation, whites insisted that blacks share the

DRESS PARADE FOR THE FIRST SOUTH CAROLINA INFANTRY
The First South Carolina was the first official black regiment organized by the federal govern-
ment. Made up overwhelmingly of ex-slaves, it was led by Colonel Thomas W. Higginson, a
white Massachusetts clergyman and abolitionist. After the regiment's first skirmish with Confed-
erate soliders, Higginson celebrated his men's courage: "No officer in this regiment now doubts
that the key to the successful prosecution of this war lies in the unlimited employment of black
troops. . . . Instead of leaving their homes and families to fight they are fighting for their homes
and families."
National Archives.

danger, especially after March 1863, when Congress resorted to the draft to fill the Union army.

Black soldiers discovered that the military was far from color blind. The Union army established segregated black regiments, paid black soldiers $10 per month rather than the $13 it paid to whites, refused blacks the opportunity to become commissioned officers, punished blacks as if they were slaves, and assigned blacks to labor battalions rather than to combat units. But nothing deterred black recruits. When the war ended, 179,000 African American men had served in the Union army, approximately 10 percent of the army total. An astounding 71 percent of black men age eighteen to forty-five in the free states wore blue, a participation rate that was substantially higher than that of white men. More than 130,000 black soldiers came from the slave states, perhaps 100,000 of them ex-slaves. In time, whites allowed blacks to put down

their shovels and to shoulder rifles. At the battles of Port Hudson and Milliken's Bend on the Mississippi and at Fort Wagner in Charleston harbor, black courage under fire finally dispelled notions that African Americans could not fight. More than 38,000 black soldiers died in the Civil War (a mortality rate that was higher than that of white troops). Blacks played a crucial role in the triumph of the Union and the destruction of slavery.

From the beginning, African Americans viewed the Civil War as a revolutionary struggle for black liberation. They fought to overthrow slavery and to gain equality for their entire race. "Once let the black man get upon his person the brass letters, U.S.; let him get an eagle on his button, and a musket on his shoulder and bullets in his pocket," Frederick Douglass predicted, "and there is no power on earth which can deny that he has earned the right of citizenship." Whether or not the war changed white

TECHNOLOGY IN AMERICA
Confederate Artillery

When it came to big-gun warfare, the South was at a decided disadvantage. When the war broke out, it suffered from an almost total lack of modern field guns. The government quickly established foundries in Georgia, Mississippi, Alabama, and South Carolina, but the Confederacy's largest supplier was Richmond's Tredegar Iron Works, which had been casting cannons since 1842. Tredegar's mainstay was the powerful twelve-pounder bronze Napoleon gun. It could be fired rapidly, and at close range it was like a giant shotgun, which made it an excellent infantry killer. So reliable was it that General Lee urged that other bronze cannon be melted down to build more Napoleons. Tredegar cast an impressive 1,099 cannon — nearly half of all the artillery pieces manufactured in the Confederacy. By comparison, federal production surpassed 6,000 guns, which were consistently better in quality. The South's lack of industrial capacity, skilled labor, and strategic raw materials severely handicapped its efforts to manufacture cannon.

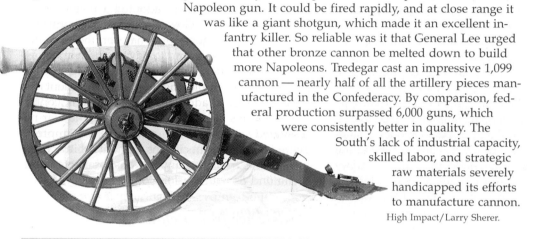

High Impact/Larry Sherer.

what Georgia Governor Joseph E. Brown denounced as the "dangerous usurpation by Congress of the reserved right of the States." A tug-of-war between Richmond and the states ensued for control of money, supplies, and soldiers, with damaging consequences for the war effort. Individual citizens also objected to the government's radical departures. They were accustomed to government that rarely intruded in what they considered private affairs. They remembered that Davis had promised to defend southern "liberty" against Republican "despotism." Luckily for Davis, the Confederate constitution provided for a single, six-year term for the president, which meant he did not have to face the voters during the war.

Hardships were widespread, but they fell most heavily on the poor, who were least able to bear them. Inflation, for example, spared no one, but it threatened the poor with starvation. Salt—necessary for preserving meat—shot up from $2 to $60 a bag during the first year of the war. Flour that cost three or four cents a pound in 1861 cost thirty-five cents in 1863. Food prices became critical when the draft depopulated yeomen farms of men, leaving the women and children to grow what they ate. A rampaging army, a drought, a sickness, a lame mule —any one calamity could cost a family a crop.

When farm wives succeeded in bringing in a harvest, government agents took 10 percent of it as a "tax-in-kind" on agriculture. Shortages, like inflation, also afflicted the entire population, but the rich lost luxuries while the poor lost necessities. Before long, some poor women and children were eating berries and boiled potato vines. In the spring of 1863, bread riots broke out in a dozen cities and villages across the South. In Richmond, a mob of nearly a thousand hungry women broke into shops and took what they needed.

Yeomen saw a profound inequality of sacrifice. They called it "a rich man's war and a poor man's fight," and they had evidence.

Severe deprivation had powerful consequences. As one southern leader observed in November 1862, "men cannot be expected to fight for the Government that permits their wives & children to starve." As things grew worse at home, women sometimes told men to choose between country and family. A Mississippi deserter explained, "We are poor men and are willing to defend our country but our families [come] first." Some wealthy individuals shared their bounty, the Confederacy made some efforts at social welfare, and the states did even more, but every effort fell short. As a result, the army leaked badly. By some estimates, when the war ended, one-third of the soldiers had already gone home.

The Confederacy also failed to persuade the suffering white majority that the war's burdens were being shared equally. Instead, yeomen saw a profound inequality of sacrifice. They called it "a rich man's war and a poor man's fight," and they had evidence. The original draft law permitted a man who had money to hire a substitute to take his place. Moreover, the "twenty-Negro law" exempted one white man on every plantation with twenty or more slaves. The government intended to provide protection for white women and to see that slaves tended the crops. But yeomen perceived rich men evading military service. A slaveless Mississippian complained to his governor about stay-at-home planters who sent their slaves into the fields to grow cotton while, in plain view, "poor soldiers' wives are plowing with *their own* hands to make a subsistence for themselves and children—while their husbands are suffering, bleeding and dying for their country." In fact, most slaveholders went off to war, but the extreme suffering of common folk fueled class animosity.

In such a long, grueling war, social strain was inevitable, but government policy aggravated stress. Officials hoped that the crucible of war would mold a region into a nation. Confederate nationalism, they believed, would provide a powerful emotional bond for southern unity. Instead, war increased discord among whites and widened divisions. War also threatened to rip the southern social fabric along its racial seam.

The Disintegration of Slavery

The legal destruction of slavery was the product of presidential proclamation, congressional legislation, and eventually constitutional amendment, but the practical destruction of slavery was the product of war, what Lincoln called war's "friction and abrasion." When the war ended in 1865, the institution had taken a heavy pounding, especially from within. More than 100,000 men fled bondage, took up arms, and attacked slavery directly. Other men and women stayed in the slave quarters, but they were not content to wait passively for blue-coated liberators. Well schooled in the slave's ways of survival, they watched and waited, alert for opportunities. Over the four years of war, they found plenty.

In dozens of ways, the war disrupted the routine, organization, and discipline of bondage. Almost immediately, it called the master away, leaving white women to assume managerial responsibilities, which they found "a new and strange business." Plantation mistresses success-

SOUTHERN WOMEN
Women such as these North Carolinians were expected to shift their energies from family to the southern cause. Most served by sewing uniforms, knitting socks, and rolling bandages at home. Some founded hospitals, others worked in them nursing the sick and wounded. Sally Tompkins, twenty-eight and unmarried in 1861, ran Richmond's Robertson Hospital, which treated more than twelve hundred sick and wounded over four years. As the war ground on, southern women had their hands full trying to keep their families fed and safe. Museum of the Confederacy.

fully oversaw the transition of the plantation from cotton to food production. As one woman wrote to a newspaper, "Do impress upon the soldiers, that they are constantly in our thoughts, that we are *working* for them, while they are *fighting* for us—and that their wants shall be supplied, as long as there is a *woman* or a *dollar* in the 'Southern Confederacy.'" But plantation mistresses could not maintain traditional standards of slave discipline. No one could. War had stifled the production of cotton, divorcing slaves from their principal work. War also meant the impressment of slaves, severing the personal relationship between masters and slaves. Moreover, military action increasingly sliced through the South's farms and plantations. Sometimes slaveholders fled, leaving behind their slaves. More often, they took their slaves with them, "refugeeing" out of the path of the Yankee invaders. But flight meant additional chaos and offered slaves more opportunities to resist bondage.

At night, slaves shared the scraps of war news and debated what it meant for their lives. From the beginning, they anticipated that a Union victory would mean freedom, but they proceeded cautiously. As the slaveholders' grip loosened, they staked claim to more freedom. Increasingly, masters complained about the slaves' "demoralization," a term that covered every sort of misbehavior—in the masters' eyes—from rudeness to rebellion. Running away to Union lines became so common that whites kept lists of their slaves' names and crossed out those who fled to "Lincoln land." Those who stayed on the plantations got to the fields late, worked more casually, and quit early. They grew less deferential to whites and more assertive.

The balance of power between master and slave gradually shifted toward the slave quarters. Some slaveholders responded violently, but most saw no alternative but to strike bargains to keep slaves at home and at work. Slaveholders offered "gifts" at harvest time, but slaves demanded more, perhaps a portion of the crop or even wages. When planters balked, slaves grew food just for their own tables. An Alabama woman reported that she had to rely on "moral suasion" to "get them to do their duty." She "begged . . . what little is done." The changes in slave behavior shocked slaveholders. They had prided themselves on "knowing" their slaves, and they learned that they did not know them at all. When the war began, a North Carolina woman praised her slaves as "diligent and respectful." When it ended, she said, "As to the idea of a *faithful servant, it is all a fiction.*"

Throughout the war, rumors of "servile insurrection" raced across the South, especially after the Emancipation Proclamation. Whites claimed that Lincoln wanted to "convert the quiet, ignorant, dependent black son of toil into a savage incendiary and brutal murderer." In fact, Lincoln worried that his proclamation might provoke black violence, but no explosion occurred. Blacks rarely took revenge for more than two centuries of slavery. Instead, they undermined white mastery and expanded control over their own lives.

The North at War

Because rebel armies generally remained within the Confederate borders, northern farms, factories, towns, and cities remained untouched by fighting. But Northerners could not avoid being touched by war. Almost every family had a son, a husband, a brother in uniform. Moreover, this war—a total war—blurred the distinction between home front and war front. As in the South, men marched off to fight, but preserving the country, either Union or Confederacy, was also women's work. During the war, traditional definitions of "manly" and "womanly" behavior tended to break down. For civilians as well as soldiers, for women as well as men, war was transforming.

The need to build and fuel the Union war machine caused the northern economy to boom. The North sent nearly two million men into the military and still increased production in almost every area. It supplied the largest army in the world with the food, weapons, munitions, clothing, and transportation it needed to crush a powerful rebellion. The boom produced impressive private wealth. But because the rewards and burdens of patriotism were not evenly distributed, the North experienced sharp, even violent, divisions. Workers confronted employers, whites confronted blacks, and Republicans confronted Democrats. Still, Northerners on the home front remained fervently attached to the ideals of their free-labor society.

The Government and the Economy

Democrats and Republicans traditionally disagreed about the best way to encourage economic growth. Democrats generally argued that in economic matters, the less government intrusion the better, while

UNION ORDNANCE, YORKTOWN, VIRGINIA
As the North successfully harnessed its enormous industrial capacity to the needs of war, cannon, mortars, and shells poured out of its factories. A fraction of that abundance is seen here in 1862 at Yorktown, ready for transportation to Union troops in the field. Two years later, Abraham Lincoln observed that the Union was "gaining strength, and may if need be maintain the contest indefinitely. . . . Material resources are now more complete and abundant than ever. . . . The national resources are unexhausted, and, as we believe, inexhaustible." Library of Congress.

Republicans advocated government support to advance enterprise and develop economic resources. Democratic domination of national politics for two decades before the war meant that the Republicans inherited a financial and economic structure that reflected the Democrats' belief in feeble government direction of the economy. There were no national banking system, no national currency, and no federal income or excise taxes.

For civilians as well as soldiers, for women as well as men, war was transforming.

The secession of eleven slave states cut the Democrats' strength in Congress in half and destroyed their capacity to resist the Republican steamroller. The Republican platform of 1860 advocated an array of federal programs to encourage economic growth, and during the war Republicans had little trouble enacting their philosophy into law. In May 1862, Congress approved the Homestead Act, which offered 160 acres of public land to settlers who would live and labor on it. In time, the Homestead Act resulted in more than a million new farms in the West. Two months later, Congress passed the Pacific Railroad Act, which provided massive federal assistance for the building of a transcontinental railroad. When completed in 1869, the railroad ran from Omaha to San Francisco. Congress also enacted a higher tariff. Republicans defended their program by pointing to the relationship between additional economic muscle and increased Union military might.

The escalating demands of the war compelled additional changes in government's role in the economy. The Legal Tender Act of February 1862 created a national currency, paper money that Northerners called "greenbacks." With passage of the National Banking Act in February 1863, Congress created a system of national banks. Republicans sought to overturn the antebellum system of decentralized state banks (each with its own banknotes) and to replace it with a national banking system with a more stable currency. It took several years, but by 1873 state banknotes had largely disappeared. Congress also enacted a series of sweeping tax laws that taxed everything from incomes to liquor to billiard tables. The Internal Revenue Act created the Bureau of Internal Revenue, the government's tax collection agency, which has become a permanent fixture. Although Salmon Chase of Ohio had no financial experience when he became secretary of the treasury, he learned quickly and built solidly. By revolutionizing the country's banking, monetary, and tax structures, the Republicans generated enormous economic and military power.

In northern agriculture and industry, the war accelerated antebellum trends. The North's 1,300,000 farms were no strangers to commercialization, mechanization, specialization, and integration into national and international markets. Still, war made a deep imprint. Two new initiatives from Washington had significant and long-term consequences. Congress created a Department of Agriculture and passed the Land-Grant College Act (also known as the Morrill Act after its sponsor, Representative Justin Morrill of Vermont), which set aside public lands to support universities that emphasized "agriculture and mechanical arts." The first task of Lincoln's administration was winning the war, but initiatives from Washington were permanently changing the nation.

Women and Work on the Home Front

With more than a million farm men called to the military, farm women stepped into new roles. In addition to their traditional labor within the farm house (and in gardens, henhouses, and cow barns), they added men's chores to their own. "I met more women driving teams on the road and saw more at work in the fields than men," a visitor to Iowa reported in the fall of 1862. Rising production figures testified to their success in plowing, planting, and harvesting. Rapid mechanization assisted farm women in their new roles. Cyrus McCormick sold 165,000 of his reapers during the war years. The combination of high prices and increased production ensured that war and prosperity walked hand in hand in the rural North.

While a few industries, such as textiles (which depended on southern cotton), declined during the war, many more grew. Huge profits prompted one Pennsylvania ironmaster to remark, "I am in no hurry for peace." The boom proved friendlier to owners than to workers, however. In industry, as in agriculture, prewar trends continued to accelerate: concentration, mechanization, growth in the size of the workplace, impersonalization, and loss of control over the pace and nature of the work. Yet with orders pouring in and a million workers siphoned off into the military, the number of jobs expanded and unemployment declined. Wages often rose, but inflation and taxes cut so deeply that workers' standard of living actually fell. Some urban laborers suffered severe hardship.

As on the farm, women in cities rushed into manufacturing jobs vacated by men and also into essentially new occupations, such as government civil service. Often, they had no choice because they could not make ends meet on their husbands' army pay. Women already made up about one-quarter of the manufacturing workforce when the war began. The fraction had increased to one-third when it ended. But as more women entered the wartime workforce, employers cut wages. By 1864, fourteen-hour days earned New York seamstresses only an average of $1.54 per week. As Cincinnati seamstresses explained to Abraham Lincoln, their wages were not enough "to sustain life." Urban workers resorted increasingly to strikes to wrench decent salaries from their employers, but protest rarely succeeded. However, tough times failed to undermine the patriotism of most workers. They remained loyal to the Union cause and took pride in their contribution to northern victory.

In everything but the actual fighting, women participated and contributed. Middle-class white women were supposed to be homebodies, nurturing families and supporting husbands, and hundreds of thousands contributed mightily to the war effort in traditional ways. Like many southern white women, they labored long hours in sewing circles, wrapped bandages, and sold homemade goods at local fairs to raise money to aid the soldiers. Unpaid labor by "lady volunteers" proved crucial in supplying the opposing war machines.

But some women expressed their patriotism in an untraditional way—as wartime nurses. Thousands of women on both sides defied prejudices about female delicacy and volunteered to nurse the wounded. Many of the northern female volunteers worked through the U.S. Sanitary Commission, a civilian organization that bought and distributed clothing, food, and medicine and recruited doctors and nurses. Nursing meant working in the midst of unspeakable sights, sounds, and smells, but it brought the profound satisfaction of displaying competence and serving well. Katherine Wormeley of Rhode Island, who served three months as a volunteer nurse on a hospital ship in 1862, recorded in her diary, "We all know in our hearts that it is thorough enjoyment to be here,—it is life."

Some volunteer nurses went on to become paid military nurses. In April 1861, Dorothea Dix, well known for her efforts to reform insane asylums, was named "Superintendent of Female Nurses," and eventually some three thousand women served under her. Most nurses worked in hospitals behind the battle lines, but some, like Clara Barton, who later founded the American Red Cross, worked in several battlefield units. At Antietam, as Barton was giving a wounded man a drink, a bullet ripped through her sleeve and struck him in the chest, killing him instantly. Several of the women who served in the war went on to lead the postwar movement to establish training schools for female nurses.

Politics and Dissent

For a moment in 1861 it looked as if the outbreak of war had silenced politics. Democrats gave the Union as full-throated a roar of allegiance as Republicans. But bipartisan unity did not last. The war and the way in which Lincoln chose to fight it set the political agenda. Within a year, Democrats were labeling the Republican administration a "reign of terror," and Republicans were calling Democrats the party of "Dixie, Davis, and the Devil." As bruising as the political struggle became, the North's two-party system actually strengthened government. In the Confederacy, which had no well-organized parties, political disagreement spiraled down into fruitless bickering, but in the Union, rival parties helped to discipline and legitimize political debate. Fear of being driven from office by their rival's victory helped to unify each party and to strengthen the political structure.

Nevertheless, Republican policy pushed the Democrats toward a dangerous alienation. Under Lincoln, the Republicans emancipated the slaves, subsidized private business, and expanded federal power at every turn. And Democrats, traditionally the party of limited government, resisted at every step. "Shall we sink down as serfs to the heartless, speculative Yankee for all time," one Democrat inquired, "swindled by his tariff, robbed by his taxes,

skinned by his railroad monopolies?" The Lincoln administration argued that the war required a loose interpretation of the Constitution, to which the Democrats countered, "The Constitution is as binding in war as in peace."

Democrats had good evidence that Lincoln did not always reach first for a copy of the Constitution when he confronted a problem. He could be very practical, especially in the realm of civil rights. In September 1862, in an effort to stifle opposition to the war, Lincoln placed under martial law any person who discouraged enlistments, resisted the draft, or engaged in "disloyal" practices. Before the war ended, his administration had imprisoned nearly fourteen thousand individuals, most in the border states. The campaign fell short of a reign of terror, for most were not northern Democratic opponents but Confederate citizens, blockade runners, and foreign nationals, and most of the arrested gained quick release. But the administration's heavy-handed tactics and habit of branding Democratic dissent as disloyal did suppress free speech.

One Democratic dissenter, ex-Congressman Clement L. Vallandigham of Ohio, proved indefatigable. "It is the desire of my heart," he announced just after the war began, "to restore the Union, the Federal Union as it was forty years ago." Consistent with that desire, he lambasted every Republican innovation, which meant most of Lincoln's conduct of the war. After the Emancipation Proclamation, which he considered abolitionist fanaticism, Vallandigham came out against the war itself. He denounced this "wicked, cruel and unnecessary war" waged "for the purpose of crushing out liberty and erecting a despotism . . . a war for the freedom of the blacks and the enslavement of the whites."

Was such talk protected by the right of free speech, or was it treason? In April 1863, General Ambrose Burnside decided that "the habit of declaring sympathy for the enemy will not be allowed" and arrested Vallandigham for treason. Lincoln had not ordered the arrest but decided to back his general, arguing that the Constitution permitted the military arrest of civilians during rebellions. "Must I shoot a simple-minded soldier boy who deserts, while I must not touch a hair of a wily agitator who induces him to desert?" Lincoln asked. Vallandigham's arrest and conviction in a military court sparked Democratic protest throughout the North. Hoping to avoid creating a martyr, Lincoln ordered Vallandigham banished to the Confederacy. In 1866, a year after the war ended, the Supreme

Court in *Ex parte Milligan* declared unconstitutional military trials of civilians where civil courts were still able to operate.

When the Republican-dominated Congress enacted the draft law in March 1863, Democrats had another grievance. As in the South, grim news from the battlefields had dried up the stream of volunteers. The North, like the South a year earlier, turned to military conscription to fill the ranks. The act required that all men between the ages of twenty and forty-five enroll and make themselves available for a lottery, which would decide who went to war. What poor men found particularly galling were provisions that allowed a draftee to hire a substitute or simply to pay a $300 fee and get out of his military obligation. As in the South, common folk could be heard chanting, "A rich man's war and a poor man's fight."

Democrats linked the draft and emancipation, arguing that Republicans employed an unconstitutional means (the draft) to achieve an unconstitutional end (emancipation). In the summer of 1863, antidraft, antiblack mobs went on rampages in northern cities. New York experienced an explosion of unprecedented proportions. Solidly Democratic Irish workingmen, crowded into stinking, disease-ridden tenements, gouged by inflation, enraged by the inequities of the draft, and dead set against fighting to free blacks, erupted in four days of rioting. Mobs attacked federal draft offices, sacked Republican newspapers, and waylaid any well-dressed man ("a $300 man") they caught on the streets. But their principal victims were blacks, whom they chased down and murdered and whose property, including the Colored Orphan Asylum, they burned. By the time police and soldiers restored order, at least 105 people lay dead.

The riots stunned black Northerners, but the racist mobs failed to achieve their purpose: the subordination of African Americans. Free black leaders had lobbied aggressively for emancipation, and after Lincoln's proclamation they fanned out over the North agitating for equality. They won small wartime successes against discrimination. Illinois and Iowa overturned laws that excluded blacks from entering the states. Illinois and Ohio began permitting blacks to testify in court. Streetcars in Washington, D.C., began allowing blacks to ride. But defeat was more common. Indiana, for example, continued to forbid blacks to vote, testify, and attend public schools, and additional blacks were not allowed to enter the state.

Grinding out Victory, 1863–1865

In the early months of 1863, the Union's prospects looked bleak, while the Confederate cause stood at high tide. But in July 1863, the tide receded. The military man who was most responsible for seeing that it never rose again was Ulysses S. Grant. Lifted up from obscurity by brilliant successes in the West in 1862 and 1863, Grant became the darling of the North. Grant was "*the* great man of the day," one man observed in July 1864, "perhaps of the age." Elevated to supreme command, Grant knit together a powerful war machine that integrated a sophisticated command structure, modern technology, and complex logistics and supply systems. But the plain arithmetic of this plain man remained unchanged: Killing more of the enemy than he kills of you equals "the complete overthrow of the rebellion." In William T. Sherman and Philip H. Sheridan he found like-minded men. The three generals set out to teach the South that war was hell. Grant instructed Sheridan "to push the enemy to the very death."

The North ground out the victory, bloody battle by bloody battle. The balance tipped in the Union's favor in 1863, but if the Confederacy was beaten, Southerners clearly did not know it.

The North ground out the victory, bloody battle by bloody battle. The balance tipped in the Union's favor in 1863, but if the Confederacy was beaten, Southerners clearly did not know it. The fighting reached new levels of ferocity in the last two years of the war. As national elections approached in the fall of 1864, a discouraged Lincoln expected a war-weary North to make him a one-term president. Instead, northern voters declared their willingness to continue the war in the defense of the ideals of union and freedom.

Vicksburg and Gettysburg

Perched on the bluffs above the eastern bank of the Mississippi River, Vicksburg, Mississippi, bristled with cannon and dared Yankee ships to try to pass.

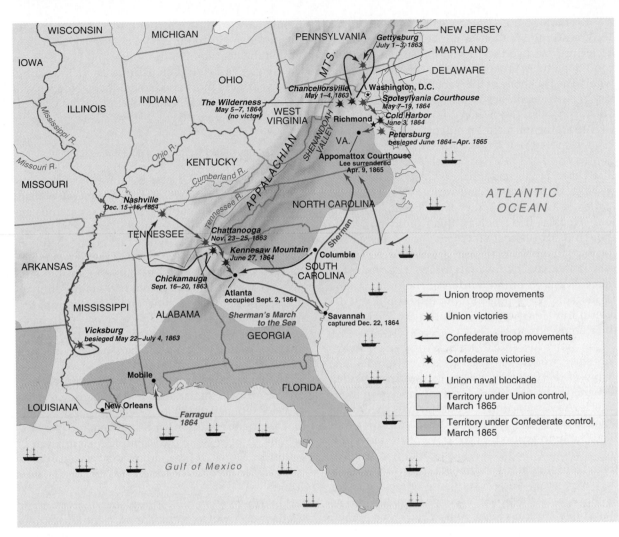

M A P 15.3
The Civil War, 1863–1865
Ulysses S. Grant's victory at Vicksburg divided the Confederacy at the Mississippi River.
William T. Sherman's march from Chattanooga to Savannah divided it again. In northern
Virginia, Robert E. Lee fought fiercely, but Grant's larger, better-supplied armies prevailed.

This Confederate stronghold stood between Union forces and complete control of the river. Since impenetrable terrain made it impossible to take the city from the north, Grant gambled on an attack from the south and east. To get his army south of Vicksburg, he marched it down the western bank of the Mississippi. After four water-logged failures, the troops made it through the swamps, but their supply wagons remained behind, up to their axles in the muck. Grant readied supply barges and several gunboats north of Vicksburg, and on the night of April 16, 1863, they ran the Confederate gauntlet. Rebel fire destroyed two ships, but the rest rendezvoused with Grant's army below the city. Union forces crossed the Mississippi River, marched northeast more than one hundred miles, wheeled sharply left, and attacked the city from the rear. When the Confederates beat back the assault, Grant began siege operations to starve out the enemy. Civilian inhabitants took to living in caves to escape incessant Union cannon bombardment and soon began eating mules and rats to survive.

Eventually, the siege took its toll. On July 4, 1863, nearly thirty thousand rebels marched out of Vicksburg, stacked their arms, and surrendered unconditionally. A Yankee captain wrote home to his wife: "The backbone of the Rebellion is this day broken. The Confederacy is divided . . . Vicksburg is ours. The Mississippi River is opened, and Gen. Grant is to be our next President."

On the same Fourth of July that a grateful nation received the news of Vicksburg, word arrived that Union forces had crushed General Lee at Gettysburg, Pennsylvania. Lee's triumph two months earlier at Chancellorsville over Joseph "Fighting Joe" Hooker had revived his confidence, even though the battle cost him his favorite commander, the incomparable Stonewall Jackson, accidentally shot in the dark by his own troops. Lee wanted to relieve Virginia of the burden of the fighting, and he felt bold enough to think that he could still deliver a morale-crunching defeat to the Yankees on their home turf.

In June, Lee's 75,000-man Army of Northern Virginia invaded Pennsylvania. On June 28, the Army of the Potomac, under its new commander, General George G. Meade, moved quickly to intercept it. Advanced units of both armies met at the small town of Gettysburg, and Union forces occupied the high ground. Three days of furious fighting, involving 165,000 soldiers, could not dislodge them from the ridges and hills. But Lee ached for a decisive victory, and on July 3 he ordered a major assault against the Union center on Cemetery Ridge. With bloodcurdling rebel yells, 12,000 men sprang forward in what became known as Pickett's Charge. The open, rolling fields provided the dug-in Yankees with three-quarters of a mile of clear vision, and they raked the mile-wide line of Confederates with cannon and rifle fire. Time and again, the rebels closed ranks and raced on, until finally their momentum failed. Gettysburg cost Lee more than one-third of his army—28,000 casualties. "It's all my fault," he said. In a drenching rain on the night of July 4, 1863, he marched his battered army back to Virginia.

The twin disasters at Vicksburg and Gettysburg proved to be the turning point of the war. The Confederacy could not replace the nearly 60,000 soldiers who were captured, wounded, or killed. Lee never launched another major offensive north of the Mason-Dixon line. No European power ever again considered intervening on behalf of the rebellion. But it is hindsight that permits us to see the pair of battles as decisive. The war dragged on nearly two

more years, and for much of the time the result remained in real doubt. The Confederacy still controlled the heartland of the South, and Lee, back on the defensive in Virginia, still had a vicious sting. War-weariness threatened to erode the North's will to win before Union armies destroyed the Confederacy's ability to go on.

Grant Takes Command

In the fall of 1863, Ulysses S. Grant burnished his already shining reputation. Union General William Rosecrans had placed his army in a dangerous situation in Chattanooga, Tennessee, where he had retreated after taking a whipping at the battle of Chickamauga. Rebels surrounded the disorganized bluecoats and threatened to starve them into submission. Grant, whom Lincoln had made commander of all Union forces between the Mississippi and the Appalachians, arrived in Chattanooga in October. Within weeks, he opened an effective supply line, broke the siege, and then (largely because troops disobeyed orders and charged wildly up Missionary Ridge) routed the Confederate army. The victory at Chattanooga had immense strategic value. It opened the door to Georgia and became the staging area for Sherman's "march to the sea" in 1864. It also confirmed Lincoln's estimation of Grant. In March 1864, the president asked him to come east to become the general in chief of all Union armies.

In Washington, Grant implemented his grand strategy of a war of annihilation. Southern armies were already worn to less than half the size of their enemy's, and Grant pressed even harder. He ordered a series of simultaneous assaults from Virginia to Louisiana. Two actions proved more significant than the others. In one, Sherman, whom Grant appointed his successor to command the western armies, plunged southeast toward Atlanta. In the other, Grant, who took control of the Army of the Potomac, went head to head with Lee for almost four straight weeks in Virginia.

Grant and Lee met in early May 1864 at the Wilderness, a dense tangle of scrub oaks and small pines that proved to be Lee's ally, for it helped offset the Yankees' numerical superiority. Often unable to see more than ten paces, the armies pounded away at each other until 18,000 Yankees and 11,000 rebels had fallen. But the savagery of the Wilderness did not compare with that at Spotsylvania Court House a few days later. Frenzied men fought hand to hand for eighteen hours in the rain. One

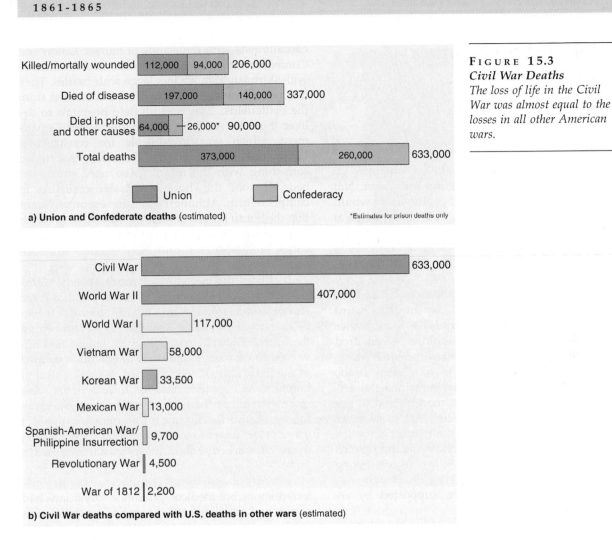

FIGURE 15.3
Civil War Deaths
The loss of life in the Civil War was almost equal to the losses in all other American wars.

Killed/mortally wounded 112,000 94,000 206,000
Died of disease 197,000 140,000 337,000
Died in prison and other causes 64,000 26,000* 90,000
Total deaths 373,000 260,000 633,000

Union   Confederacy

a) **Union and Confederate deaths** (estimated)   *Estimates for prison deaths only

Civil War 633,000
World War II 407,000
World War I 117,000
Vietnam War 58,000
Korean War 33,500
Mexican War 13,000
Spanish-American War/ Philippine Insurrection 9,700
Revolutionary War 4,500
War of 1812 2,200

b) **Civil War deaths compared with U.S. deaths in other wars** (estimated)

veteran remembered men "piled upon each other in some places four layers deep, exhibiting every ghastly phase of mutilation. Below the mass of fast-decaying corpses, the convulsive twitching of limbs and the writhing of bodies showed that there were wounded men still alive and struggling to extricate themselves from their horrible entombment." Spotsylvania cost Grant another 18,000 casualties and Lee 10,000. But the Yankee bulldog would not let go. Rather than disengage and lick his wounds, Grant kept moving and caught Lee again at Cold Harbor, where he lost 13,000 additional troops to Lee's 5,000.

Twice as many Northerners as Southerners died in the four weeks of fighting in Virginia in the spring of 1864. Yet Grant did not consider himself defeated. Since Lee had only half the number of troops, he lost proportionally as many men as Grant. And the Union commander, ever the mathematician of war, knew that the South could not replace its losses.

Moreover, the campaign had carried Grant to the outskirts of Petersburg, just south of the Confederate capital. Since most of the major railroad lines supplying Richmond ran through Petersburg, Lee had little choice but to defend the city. Grant abandoned the costly tactic of the frontal assault and began a siege, one that immobilized both armies and dragged on for nine months.

There was no pause in "Uncle Billy" Sherman's invasion of Georgia. Grant had ordered his friend to smash Confederate General Joseph E. Johnston's army and to "get into the interior of the enemy's country as far as you can, inflicting all the damage you can against their War resources." In early May, while Grant thrashed in the Wilderness, Sherman moved 100,000 men south against the 65,000 rebels in the rugged mountains of northern Georgia. Skillful maneuvering, constant skirmishing, and one pitched battle (Kennesaw Mountain) brought Sherman to Atlanta, which fell on September 1.

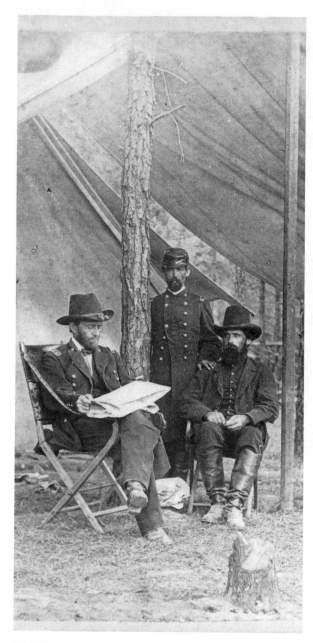

GRANT AT COLD HARBOR
Seated next to his chief of staff, John A. Rawlins, at his Cold Harbor, Virginia, headquarters, Ulysses S. Grant plots his next move against Robert E. Lee. On June 3, 1864, Grant ordered frontal assaults against entrenched Confederate forces, resulting in enormous losses. "I am disgusted with the generalship displayed," young Brigadier General Emory Upton exclaimed. "Our men have, in many cases, been foolishly and wantonly slaughtered." Grant always regretted Cold Harbor, but he kept pushing toward Richmond.
Chicago Historical Society.

Sherman was only warming up. Intending to "make Georgia howl," he marched out of Atlanta on November 15 with 62,000 battle-hardened veterans, heading for Savannah, 285 miles away. "We are not only fighting hostile armies," he said before torching Atlanta, "but a hostile people, and must make old and young, rich and poor, feel the hard hand of war." They felt it, for Sherman's troops cut a swath from 25 to 60 miles wide, and, as one veteran remembered, the Yankees "destroyed all we could not eat, stole their niggers, burned their cotton & gins, spilled their sorghum, burned & twisted their R. Roads and raised Hell generally." Sherman sought to destroy the will of the southern people to make war. A few weeks earlier, General Philip Sheridan had tried as much in the Shenandoah Valley, complying with Grant's order to turn the valley into "a barren waste . . . so that crows flying over it for the balance of this season will have to carry their provender [food] with them." When Sherman's troops entered an undefended Savannah in the third week of December, the general telegraphed Lincoln that he had "a Christmas gift" for him.

The Election of 1864

In the fall, white men in the Union states turned to the election of a president. Never before had a nation held general elections in the midst of war. "We can not have free government without elections," Lincoln explained, "and if the rebellion could force us to forgo, or postpone a national election, it might fairly claim to have already conquered and ruined us."

Lincoln's determination to hold elections is especially noteworthy because the Democratic Party smelled victory. The Union war effort had stalled during the summer. With Sherman temporarily checked outside Atlanta and Grant bogged down in the siege of Petersburg, frustration had settled over the North. Moreover, rankled by inflation, the draft, the attack on civil liberties, and the commitment to blacks, Northerners appeared ready for a change. Even Lincoln concluded in the gloomy summer of 1864, "It seems exceedingly probable that this administration will not be re-elected."

Democrats were badly divided, however. "Peace" Democrats insisted on an armistice, while "war" Democrats supported the conflict but opposed Republican means of fighting it. They tried to paper over the chasm by nominating a war candidate, General George McClellan, but adopting a peace platform that demanded that "immediate efforts be made for a cessation of hostilities." The platform also attacked emancipation and arbitrary government power, but the Republicans directed their fire at the Democrats' peace plank. Republicans labeled it a conspiracy of "Copperheads" (after a deadly, easily concealed snake) to sell out the Union and claimed that it "virtually proposed to surrender the country to the rebels in arms against us."

Lincoln was no shoo-in for renomination, much less reelection. The president had found it difficult to gain the respect of his own party. Conservatives believed he had acted precipitously in emancipating the slaves. Radicals criticized him for moving too slowly to free them and for failing to champion black equality. Members of both factions skewered him for being an inept military leader. But frightened by the strength of the peace Democrats, the Republican Party renominated Lincoln. In an effort to reach out to the largest number of voters, however, the Republicans made two changes. First, they chose a new name. As the Union Party, they made it easier for prowar Democrats to embrace Lincoln. Second, they chose a new vice presidential candidate. Dumping Hannibal Hamlin of Maine, the incumbent vice president, they turned to Andrew Johnson of Tennessee, the only southern senator to remain in Congress when his colleagues fled south in the winter of 1860–61. As a Southerner, a former slaveholder, and a former Democrat, Johnson personified the message that the party of Lincoln was broad enough to include any uncompromising Unionist.

Lincoln's pessimism about being reelected proved to be unfounded. After the fall of Atlanta in September, the political tide turned in favor of the Republicans. Lincoln received 55 percent of the popular vote, but his electoral margin was a whopping 212 to McClellan's 21. The Republicans also stormed back in the congressional elections, gaining large margins over the Democrats in the Senate and the House. The Union Party bristled with factions, but they united for a resounding victory. The victory gave Lincoln a mandate to continue the war until slavery was gone and the South had surrendered.

The Confederacy Collapses

Jefferson Davis found little to celebrate as the new year of 1865 dawned in Richmond. Military disaster littered the Confederate landscape. With the destruction of John B. Hood's army at Nashville in

RUINS OF RICHMOND
A Union soldier and a small boy in a Union cap contemplate the silence and devastation of Richmond, the Confederacy's capital. On their way out of the city on the evening of April 2, 1865, Confederate demolition squads set fire to tobacco warehouses and ammunition dumps. Huge explosions tore holes in the city, and windswept fires destroyed much of what was left standing. As one Confederate observed, "The old war-scarred city seemed to prefer annihilation to conquest."
Library of Congress.

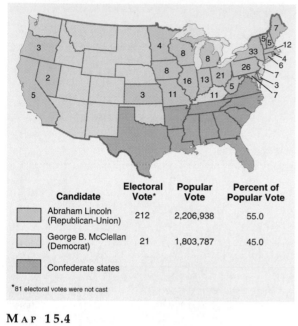

Candidate	Electoral Vote*	Popular Vote	Percent of Popular Vote
Abraham Lincoln (Republican-Union)	212	2,206,938	55.0
George B. McClellan (Democrat)	21	1,803,787	45.0
Confederate states			

*81 electoral votes were not cast

M A P 15.4
The Election of 1864

November, the interior of the Confederacy lay in Yankee hands. Sherman's troops, resting momentarily in Savannah, eyed South Carolina hungrily. Only Lee's army remained, and Grant had it pinned down in Petersburg just a few miles from Richmond. The home front grew more desperate every day. Officials reported actual starvation. Deprivation and exhaustion generated major peace movements in North Carolina, Georgia, and elsewhere. Yeomen grew surly and cursed both the planters and the government, and slaves seemed to work only when they wanted to. Southerners took out their frustration and bitterness on their president. Kinder than most, Alexander Stephens, vice president of the Confederacy, likened Davis to "my poor old blind and deaf dog."

But Davis would not accept defeat. He vowed to fight until the rebels won. And he concluded that there was one unused arrow in the Confederate quiver. Slaves would become soldiers. The Confederacy had impressed both slaves and free blacks in noncombatant military roles, but now Davis proposed arming slaves and, with a vague promise of freedom as an incentive, sending them to fight the Yankees. This bizarre notion indicates Davis's desperation, but Lee approved, and in March 1865, so did the Confederate Congress. Slaveholders in the countryside, however, refused to sacrifice slavery to

win southern nationhood. A South Carolina planter asked who gave Richmond the right "to destroy that which it was created to protect and perpetuate." "No!" cried a plantation mistress, "freedom for whites, slavery for negroes, God has so ordained it!" But before Southerners could attempt the experiment, time ran out for the Confederacy.

At the end, events came with a rush. On February 1, 1865, Sherman's troops stormed out of Savannah into South Carolina, the "cradle of the Confederacy." They twisted train rails and lit fires with even more enthusiasm than they had in Georgia. But before Sherman could push through North Carolina and arrive at the rear of Lee's army at Petersburg, where he expected to crush the Confederates between his hammer and Grant's anvil, Lee abandoned the city. Jefferson Davis fled Richmond, and the capital city fell a few days later. Grant pursued Lee for one hundred miles, until he surrendered on April 9, 1865, in a farmhouse near Appomattox Courthouse, Virginia. The beaten man arrived in an immaculate full-dress uniform, complete with sash and sword; the victor came in his usual mud-splattered private's outfit. Grant offered a generous peace. He allowed Lee's men to return home and to take their horses to help "put in a crop to carry themselves and their families through the next winter." With Lee gone, the remaining ragtag Confederate armies lost hope and gave up. After four years, the war was over.

The day after Lee's surrender, a brass band led a happy crowd of three thousand up to the White House, where they pleaded with Lincoln for a speech. He begged off and asked the band to strike up "Dixie." He knew that the rebels had claimed the tune as their own, he said, but it was one of his favorites, and now he was taking it back. The crowd roared its approval, and the band played "Dixie," following it with "Yankee Doodle." No one was more relieved than Lincoln that the war was over, but his celebration was restrained. He told his cabinet that his postwar burdens would weigh almost as heavily as those of wartime. But Lincoln had other things on his mind when he attended the theater on the evening of Good Friday, April 14, 1865. While he and his wife, Mary, enjoyed *Our American Cousin*, a British comedy, John Wilkes Booth, an actor with southern sympathies, slipped into the president's box and mortally wounded Lincoln with a single shot to his head. The man who had led the nation through the war would not lead it in its postwar search for a just peace.

Conclusion: The Second American Revolution

The Civil War had a profound effect on the nation and its people. The northern victory permanently discredited the idea of secession. It laid waste to the South. Three-fourths of southern white men of military age served in the army, and at least half of them were captured, wounded, or killed or died of disease. War raked the countryside. It destroyed two-fifths of the South's livestock, wrecked half of the farm machinery, obliterated two-thirds of the region's assessed wealth, smashed thousands of farms and plantations, blackened dozens of cities and towns, and ended slavery, the linchpin of southern society and economy. The immediate impact of the war on the North was more paradoxical. Putting down the slaveholders' rebellion cost the North a heavy price: 373,000 lives. But rather than devastating the land, the war set the countryside and cities humming with business activity.

The task of fighting the rebellion transformed the nation. Antebellum America was decentralized politically and loosely integrated economically. To bend the resources of the country to a Union victory, Congress enacted legislation that altered the nation's political and economic character. It adopted policies that established the sovereignty of the federal government and the dominance of industrial capitalism. With the South out of the Union, the Republicans laid the foundations for modern America. Moreover, the common sacrifice of northern people to save the nation created an even more fierce national loyalty. The shift in power from South to North and the creation of a national government, a national economy, and a national spirit led one historian to call the American Civil War the "Second American Revolution."

Most revolutionary of all, the war would end slavery. Because that ancient labor and racial system was entangled in almost every aspect of southern life, slavery's uprooting would mean fundamental change. But the full meaning of abolition remained unclear in 1865. The task of determining the new economic, political, and social status of four million ex-slaves would be the principal task of Reconstruction.

CHRONOLOGY

1861 **March 4.** Abraham Lincoln sworn in as sixteenth president of the United States.

April 12–13. Confederate forces attack Fort Sumter, South Carolina, in opening engagement of Civil War.

April. Dorothea Dix named superintendent of female nurses.

April–May. Four Upper South states secede and join Confederacy.

July. Union forces routed at Manassas, Virginia, in first major clash of war.

August. Congress approves First Confiscation Act, which allows seizure of any slave employed by Confederate military.

1862 **February.** Legal Tender Act creates first national currency, called "greenbacks."

February. Union forces in West under General Ulysses S. Grant capture Fort Henry and Fort Donelson and drive Confederates from Kentucky and most of Tennessee.

April. Battle of Shiloh in Tennessee results in huge casualties and ends Confederate bid to control Mississippi valley.

April. Confederate Congress passes first draft law in American history.

May. Homestead Act offers western land to those who would live and labor on it.

1862   **May–July.** General George McClellan's Union forces defeated during peninsula campaign in Virginia.

July. Congress approves second Confiscation Act, freeing all slaves of rebel masters.

July. Congress passes Militia Act, authorizing enrollment of blacks in Union military.

September 17. Battle of Antietam stops Lee's advance into Maryland, but Confederate forces escape back into Virginia.

September 22. Lincoln announces preliminary emancipation proclamation.

December. Battle of Fredericksburg results in huge Union casualties.

1863   **January 1.** Emancipation Proclamation becomes law, freeing slaves in areas still in rebellion.

February. National Banking Act creates system of national banks.

March. Congress authorizes draft.

July. Vicksburg falls to Union forces under Grant, effectively cutting Confederacy in two along Mississippi River.

July. Battle of Gettysburg results in Confederate defeat and Lee's last offensive into North.

1864   **March.** Grant appointed general in chief of all Union forces.

May–June. Grant's forces engage Confederates in Virginia in bloodiest fighting of war, from Wilderness campaign to beginnings of siege of Petersburg.

September. Atlanta falls to Union forces under General William T. Sherman.

November. Lincoln reelected president.

December. Sherman occupies Savannah after scorched-earth campaign in Georgia.

1865   **April 9.** Lee surrenders to Grant at Appomattox Courthouse, Virginia, essentially ending Confederate resistance.

April 14. Lincoln shot by John Wilkes Booth at Ford's Theatre in Washington. He dies on April 15, succeeded by Vice President Andrew Johnson.

BIBLIOGRAPHY

GENERAL WORKS

Shelby Foote, *The Civil War: A Narrative*, 3 vols. (1958–1974).

James M. McPherson, *Battle Cry of Freedom: The Civil War Era* (1988).

Allan Nevins, *The War for the Union*, 4 vols. (1971).

Peter J. Parish, *The American Civil War* (1975).

J. G. Randall and David Donald, *The Civil War and Reconstruction* (1969).

Charles P. Roland, *An American Iliad: The Story of the Civil War* (1991).

Frank E. Vandiver, *Blood Brothers: A Short History of the Civil War* (1992).

Edmund Wilson, *Patriotic Gore: Studies in the Literature of the American Civil War* (1962).

THE COMBATANTS

Michael Barton, *Goodmen: The Character of Civil War Soldiers* (1981).

Ira Berlin et al., eds., *Freedom: A Documentary History of Emancipation, 1861–1867* (1982–).

David W. Blight, *Frederick Douglass's Civil War: Keeping Faith in Jubilee* (1989).

Gabor S. Boritt, ed., *Lincoln's Generals* (1994).

Catherine Clinton and Nina Silber, eds., *Divided Houses: Gender and the Civil War* (1992).

Thomas L. Connelly, *The Marble Man: Robert E. Lee and His Image in American Society* (1977).

Dudley Cornish, *The Sable Arm: Black Troops in the Union Army, 1861–1865* (1966).

Marilyn Mayer Culpepper, *Trials and Triumphs: Women of the American Civil War* (1991).

Richard Nelson Current, *Lincoln's Loyalists: Union Soldiers from the Confederacy* (1992).

Charles B. Dew, *Ironmaker to the Confederacy: Joseph R. Anderson and the Tredegar Iron Works* (1966).

David Donald, *Lincoln* (1995).

Russell Duncan, ed., *Blue-Eyed Child of Fortune: The Civil War Letters of Colonel Robert Gould Shaw* (1992).

Byron Farwell, *Stonewall: A Biography of General Thomas J. Jackson* (1992).

Douglas Southall Freeman, *R. E. Lee,* 4 vols. (1934, 1935).

Joseph T. Glatthaar, *Forged in Battle: The Civil War Alliance of Black Soldiers and White Officers* (1990).

Frank H. Heck, *Proud Kentuckian: John C. Breckinridge, 1821–1875* (1976).

Randall C. Jimerson, *The Private Civil War: Popular Thought during the Sectional Conflict* (1988).

Gerald F. Linderman, *Embattled Courage* (1987).

John F. Marszalek, *Sherman: A Soldier's Passion for Order* (1993).

Waldo Martin, *The Mind of Frederick Douglass* (1985).

William S. McFeely, *Grant* (1981).

William S. McFeely, *Frederick Douglass* (1991).

Richard M. McMurry, *John Bell Hood and the War for Southern Independence* (1982).

James M. McPherson, *Abraham Lincoln and the Second American Revolution* (1990).

Reid Mitchell, *Civil War Soldiers: Their Expectations and Their Experiences* (1988).

Robert Manson Myers, ed., *The Children of Pride: A True Story of Georgia and the Civil War* (1972).

Mark E. Neely Jr., *The Last Best Hope of Earth: Abraham Lincoln and the Promise of America* (1993).

Stephen B. Oates, *With Malice toward None: The Life of Abraham Lincoln* (1977).

Stephen B. Oates, *A Woman of Valor: Clara Barton and the Civil War* (1994).

Benjamin M. Quarles, *The Negro in the Civil War* (1953).

Edwin S. Redkey, ed., *A Grand Army of Black Men: Letters from African-American Soldiers in the Union Army, 1861–1865* (1992).

C. Peter Ripley, ed., *Witness for Freedom: African American Voices on Race, Slavery, and Emancipation* (1993).

James I. Robertson, *Soldiers Blue and Grey* (1988).

Charles P. Roland, *Albert Sidney Johnston: Soldier of Three Republics* (1964).

William Kauffman Scarborough, ed., *The Diary of Edmund Ruffin,* 3 vols. (1972, 1976, 1989).

Stephen W. Sears, *George B. McClellan: The Young Napoleon* (1988).

Robert E. Shalhope, *Sterling Price: Portrait of a Southerner* (1971).

Craig L. Symonds, *Joseph E. Johnston: A Civil War Biography* (1992).

Emory Thomas, *Lee* (1995).

Bell I. Wiley, *The Life of Johnny Reb: The Common Soldier of the Confederacy* (1943).

Bell I. Wiley, *The Life of Billy Yank: The Common Soldier of the Union* (1952).

C. Vann Woodward, ed., *Mary Chesnut's Civil War* (1981).

MILITARY HISTORY

Richard E. Beringer et al., *Why the South Lost the Civil War* (1986).

Gabor S. Boritt, ed., *Why the Confederacy Lost* (1992).

Albert Castel, *Decision in the West: The Atlanta Campaign of 1864* (1992).

Bruce Catton, *The Centennial History of the Civil War,* 3 vols. (1961–1965).

Joseph P. Cullen, *The Peninsula Campaign, 1862: McClellan and Lee Struggle for Richmond* (1973).

Joseph P. Burke Davis, *Sherman's March* (1980).

William C. Davis, *Battle at Bull Run: A History of the First Major Campaign of the Civil War* (1977).

David H. Donald, ed., *Why the North Won the Civil War* (1961).

Michael Fellman, *Inside War: The Guerrilla Conflict in Missouri during the American Civil War* (1989).

William A. Frassanito, *Gettysburg: A Journey in Time* (1975).

Joseph T. Glatthaar, *The March to the Sea and Beyond: Sherman's Troops in the Savannah and Carolinas Campaigns* (1985).

Herman Hattaway and Archer Jones, *How the North Won* (1983).

John T. Hubbell, ed., *Battles Lost and Won: Essays from Civil War History* (1975).

Archer Jones, *Civil War Command and Strategy: The Process of Victory and Defeat* (1992).

James Pickett Jones, *Yankee Blitzkrieg: Wilson's Raid through Alabama and Georgia* (1976).

Alvin M. Josephy Jr., *The Civil War in the American West* (1991).

James Lee McDonough, *Shiloh: In Hell before Night* (1977).

James Lee McDonough, *Stones River: Bloody Winter in Tennessee* (1980).

Richard M. McMurry, *The Road Past Kennesaw: The Atlanta Campaign of 1864* (1972).

Richard M. McMurry, *John Bell Hood and the War for Southern Independence* (1982).

James M. McPherson, ed., *The Atlas of the Civil War* (1994).

Grady McWhiney and Perry D. Jamieson, *Attack and Die: Civil War Military Tactics and the Southern Heritage* (1982).

James V. Murfin, *The Gleam of Bayonets: The Battle of Antietam and the Maryland Campaign of 1862* (1965).

Howard P. Nash, *A Naval History of the Civil War* (1972).

Charles Royster, *The Destructive War: William Tecumseh Sherman, Stonewall Jackson, and the Americans* (1991).

Stephen W. Sears, *Landscape Turned Red: The Battle of Antietam* (1983).

Richard J. Sommers, *Richmond Redeemed: The Siege at Petersburg* (1981).

Wiley Sword, *Shiloh: Bloody April* (1974).

Richard Wheeler, ed., *The Siege of Vicksburg* (1978).

Steven Woodworth, *Jefferson Davis and His Generals* (1990).

Steven Woodworth, *Davis and Lee at War* (1995).

UNION AND FREEDOM

Herman Belz, *Emancipation and Equal Rights: Politics and Constitutionalism in the Civil War Era* (1978).

Ira Berlin et al., eds., *Freedom: A Documentary History of Emancipation, 1861–1867* (1982–).

Gabor S. Boritt, ed., *Lincoln, The War President* (1992).

LaWanda Cox, *Lincoln and Black Freedom: A Study in Presidential Leadership* (1981).

Robert F. Durden, *The Gray and the Black: The Confederate Debate on Emancipation* (1972).

Barbara Jean Fields, *Slavery and Freedom on the Middle Ground: Maryland during the Nineteenth Century* (1985).

John Hope Franklin, *The Emancipation Proclamation* (1963).

George M. Fredrickson, *White Supremacy: A Comparative Study in American and South African History* (1981).

Louis S. Gerteis, *From Contraband to Freedman: Federal Policy toward Southern Blacks, 1861–1865* (1973).

Janet Hermann, *The Pursuit of a Dream* (1981).

Victor B. Howard, *Black Liberation in Kentucky: Emancipation and Freedom, 1861–1884* (1983).

Peter Kolchin, *First Freedom: The Response of Alabama's Blacks to Emancipation and Reconstruction* (1972).

Leon F. Litwack, *Been in the Storm So Long: The Aftermath of Slavery* (1979).

James M. McPherson, *The Negro's Civil War: How American Negroes Felt and Acted during the War for the Union* (1965).

William F. Messner, *Freedmen and the Ideology of Free Labor: Louisiana, 1862–1865* (1978).

Clarence L. Mohr, *On the Threshold of Freedom: Masters and Slaves in Civil War Georgia* (1986).

Benjamin M. Quarles, *Lincoln and the Negro* (1962).

C. Peter Ripley, *Slaves and Freedmen in Civil War Louisiana* (1976).

Willie Lee Rose, *Rehearsal for Reconstruction: The Port Royal Experiment* (1964).

Hans L. Trefousse, *The Radical Republicans: Lincoln's Vanguard for Racial Justice* (1968).

Bell I. Wiley, *Southern Negroes, 1861–1865* (1938).

THE SOUTH AT WAR

Stephen V. Ash, *When the Yankees Came: Conflict and Chaos* (1995).

Douglas B. Ball, *Financial Failure and Confederate Defeat* (1991).

Richard E. Beringer et al., *The Elements of Confederate Defeat: Nationalism, War Aims, and Religion* (1989).

E. Merton Coulter, *The Confederate States of America, 1861–1865* (1950).

William C. Davis, *Jefferson Davis: The Man and His Hour* (1991).

Mary A. DeCredico, *Patriotism for Profit: Georgia's Urban Entrepreneurs and the Confederate War Effort* (1990).

Marshall L. DeRosa, *The Confederate Constitution of 1861: An Inquiry into American Constitutionalism* (1991).

Wayne K. Durrill, *War of Another Kind: A Southern Community in the Great Rebellion* (1990).

Clement Eaton, *A History of the Southern Confederacy* (1954).

Paul D. Escott, *After Secession: Jefferson Davis and the Failure of Confederate Nationalism* (1978).

Drew Gilpin Faust, *The Creation of Confederate Nationalism: Ideology and Identity in the Civil War South* (1988).

Drew Gilpin Faust, *Mothers of Invention: Women of the Slaveholding South in the American Civil War* (1996).

Ervin L. Jordan Jr., *Black Confederates and Afro-Yankees in Civil War Virginia* (1994).

Frank L. Owsley, *King Cotton Diplomacy: Foreign Relations of the Confederate States of America* (2nd ed. rev., 1959).

George C. Rable, *Civil Wars: Women and the Crisis of Southern Nationalism* (1989).

George C. Rable, *The Confederate Republic: A Revolution against Politics* (1994).

James L. Roark, *Masters without Slaves: Southern Planters in the Civil War and Reconstruction* (1977).

Emory M. Thomas, *The Confederacy as a Revolutionary Experience* (1971).

Emory M. Thomas, *The Confederate Nation, 1861–1865* (1979).

Bell I. Wiley, *The Plain People of the Confederacy* (1943).

THE NORTH AT WAR

Iver Bernstein, *The New York City Draft Riots* (1990).

Allan C. Bogue, *The Earnest Men: Republicans of the Civil War Senate* (1981).

Arthur C. Cole, *The Irrepressible Conflict, 1850–1865* (1934).

Emerson D. Fite, *Social and Industrial Conditions in the North during the Civil War* (1910).

George Fredrickson, *The Inner Civil War: Northern Intellectuals and the Crisis of the Union* (1965).

Paul W. Gates, *Agriculture and the Civil War* (1965).

Wood Gray, *The Hidden Civil War: The Story of the Copperheads* (1942).

Earl J. Hess, *Liberty, Virtue, and Progress: Northerners and Their War for the Union* (1988).

Alvin M. Josephy Jr., *The Civil War in the American West* (1991).

Theodore J. Karamanski, *Rally 'round the Flag: Chicago and the Civil War* (1993).

Frank L. Klement, *The Copperheads in the Middle West* (1960).

Frank L. Klement, *Dark Lanterns: Secret Political Societies, Conspiracies, and Treason Trials in the Civil War* (1984).

Ernest A. McKay, *The Civil War and New York City* (1990).

David Montgomery, *Beyond Equality: Labor and the Radical Republicans, 1862–1872* (1967).

James M. Moorhead, *American Apocalypse: Yankee Protestants and the Civil War, 1860–1869* (1978).

Eugene C. Murdock, *One Million Men: The Civil War Draft in the North* (1971).

Mark E. Neely Jr., *The Fate of Liberty: Abraham Lincoln and Civil Liberties* (1991).

Jacquelyn S. Nelson, *Indiana Quakers Confront the Civil War* (1991).

Grace Palladino, *Another Civil War: Labor, Capital, and the State in the Anthracite Regions of Pennsylvania, 1840–1868* (1990).

Philip S. Paludan, *"A People's Contest": The Union and Civil War, 1861–1865* (1988).

Philip S. Paludan, *The Presidency of Abraham Lincoln* (1994).

James A. Rawley, *The Politics of Union: Northern Politics during the Civil War* (1974).

Joel Silby, *A Respectable Minority: The Democratic Party in the Civil War Era, 1860–1868* (1977).

George W. Smith and Charles Judah, eds., *Life in the North during the Civil War* (1966).

Damon Wells, *Stephen Douglas: The Last Years, 1857–1861* (1971).

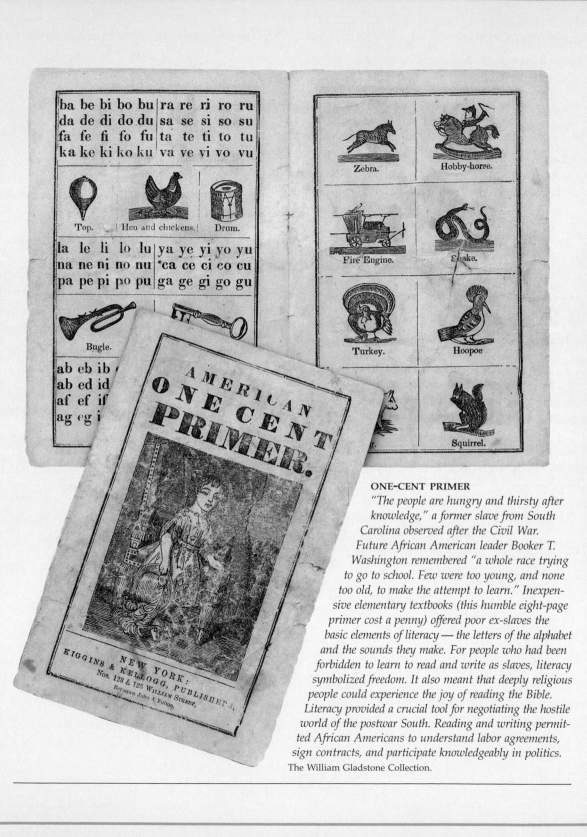

ba be bi bo bu | **ra re ri ro ru**
da de di do du | **sa se si so su**
fa fe fi fo fu | **ta te ti to tu**
ka ke ki ko ku | **va ve vi vo vu**

Top. | Hen and chickens. | Drum.

la le li lo lu | **ya ye yi yo yu**
na ne ni no nu | ***ca ce ci co cu**
pa pe pi po pu | **ga ge gi go gu**

Bugle.

ab eb ib
ab ed id
af ef if
ag eg i

Zebra. | Hobby-horse.
Fire Engine. | Snake.
Turkey. | Hoopoe
| Squirrel.

AMERICAN
ONE CENT
PRIMER.

NEW YORK:
KIGGINS & KELLOGG, PUBLISHERS,
Nos. 123 & 125 WILLIAM STREET,
Between John & Fulton.

ONE-CENT PRIMER

"The people are hungry and thirsty after knowledge," a former slave from South Carolina observed after the Civil War.
Future African American leader Booker T. Washington remembered "a whole race trying to go to school. Few were too young, and none too old, to make the attempt to learn." Inexpensive elementary textbooks (this humble eight-page primer cost a penny) offered poor ex-slaves the basic elements of literacy — the letters of the alphabet and the sounds they make. For people who had been forbidden to learn to read and write as slaves, literacy symbolized freedom. It also meant that deeply religious people could experience the joy of reading the Bible.
Literacy provided a crucial tool for negotiating the hostile world of the postwar South. Reading and writing permitted African Americans to understand labor agreements, sign contracts, and participate knowledgeably in politics.
The William Gladstone Collection.

RECONSTRUCTION

1863-1877

16

WHEN THE WAR WAS OVER, swarms of northern journalists and government officials rushed to the South to see what four years of fighting had accomplished. Ugly stories of stiff-necked defiance toward Yankees and brutal violence toward ex-slaves had drifted northward. Andrew Johnson, Abraham Lincoln's successor in the White House, asked General Carl Schurz to undertake a special fact-finding tour to assess conditions in the ex-Confederate states. Schurz, a leading antislavery lecturer and Union general, arrived in Charleston, South Carolina, the "Queen City of the South," in July 1865.

Charleston greeted the visitor with an empty harbor, rotting wharves, and gutted buildings. The city looked, Schurz observed, as if it had been struck with "the sudden and irresistible force of a thunderbolt." Cattle grazed in its weed-filled streets. Schurz met former cotton kings and rice barons who could not afford to buy breakfast. Ex-slaves, now Union soldiers, patrolled the city's streets. Schools overflowed with African American children whom it was formerly considered a crime to educate. The Citadel, the state's military school, where once "the chivalric youth of South Carolina was educated for the task of perpetuating slavery by force of arms," now housed the Fifty-fourth Massachusetts Colored Regiment.

Some whites openly expressed their hatred for the new order. Schurz came across defiant young men still "in a swearing mood" who wanted to "fight the war over again." Women in particular, he discovered, remained as "vindictive and defiant as ever." Schurz witnessed one incident in a hotel. "A day or two ago a Union officer, yielding to an impulse of politeness, handed a dish of pickles to a Southern lady at the dinner-table," he said. "A look of unspeakable scorn and indignation met him. 'So you think,' said the lady, 'a Southern woman will take a dish of pickles from a hand that is dripping with the blood of her countrymen?'"

As Schurz slowly made his way across the South to New Orleans, he concluded that most whites "accept things as they are," but he meant only that they recognized that the Confederacy was dead and legal slavery was gone. More than that, they refused to grant. When they professed loyalty to the Union, they did so with a scowl. Moreover, they had not changed their minds about slavery. "The nigger is free, to be sure," ex-slaveholders told him repeatedly, "but he will not work unless compelled to work; we must make him work somehow." Former masters "study not how to build up and develop a true system of free labor," Schurz observed, "but how to avoid it." Where there were no federal troops to stop them, they resorted to the "bowie-knife and revolver, to keep the negroes in their former subjection."

But Schurz found little evidence of black-initiated violence. "Another race . . . would probably have proceeded to cut the throats of those who were in the habit

RUINS OF PINCKNEY HOUSE, CHARLESTON, SOUTH CAROLINA
Northerners had a special hatred for Charleston. According to one inhabitant, Northerners promised: "The rebellion commenced where Charleston is, and shall end, where Charleston was." A devastating fire and three years of Yankee bombardment had almost fulfilled the promise. But in 1865, other consequences of the war alarmed white Charlestonians even more than the physical destruction. Henry Middleton told his sister in Philadelphia that no one could imagine "the utter topsy-turveying of all our institutions."
Library of Congress.

of whipping wives and mothers," he thought, but freedmen simply stood up "a little more independently before their former owners." As for former slaves' performance as free laborers, Schurz deemed it only "middling-fair." He believed he knew why. "The idea has got into the heads of the negroes that the land belongs to them," he declared. They were in no hurry, consequently, to work for whites who claimed to be landlords. Still, he concluded, "the colored man will learn sooner what he has to do as a free laborer than the white man in these parts will learn how to treat a free laborer."

Two months in the South convinced Schurz that withdrawing federal troops and restoring self-government would be a fatal error. He called the Civil War a "revolution but half accomplished." Military victory had destroyed slavery, but it had not erased proslavery ideas. Left to themselves, ex-Confederates would "introduce some new system of forced labor, not perhaps exactly slavery in its old form but something similar to it." To defend themselves, blacks would need land of their own and voting rights, Schurz concluded. Until whites "cut loose

from the past," he declared, "it will be a dangerous experiment to put Southern society upon its own legs."

As Schurz discovered, the end of the war did not mean the beginning of peace. Instead, the nation entered one of its most chaotic and conflicted eras—Reconstruction. It was not that the Civil War failed to resolve anything. Northern victory had determined once and for all the fates of secession and slavery, but out of the war emerged two new divisive questions. First, what was the status of the defeated South within the Union? Would the eleven ex-Confederate states be quickly and forgivingly welcomed back, or would they be held at arm's length and required to reform before resuming their former places? Second, what would freedom mean for ex-slaves? Would they be left to make their place in the South on their own, or would the federal government guarantee full citizenship, free labor, and equality?

Throughout Reconstruction, little was fixed, and the pace of change was swift. What seemed an unlikely possibility at one moment found majority support the next. In the months after the war, calls to extend the ballot and full citizenship to freedmen generated hysteria, but the proposals quickly became standard Republican policy and the law of the land. "These are no times of ordinary politics," Boston lawyer and reformer Wendell Phillips declared in 1867. "These are formative hours; the national purpose and thought grows and ripens in thirty days as much as ordinary years bring it forward."

In one way or another, everyone agreed that the central issue in reconstruction was the place of African Americans in American society. North and South divided over the issue, but neither region spoke with a single voice. Still, a majority of southern whites rejected black rights. Southern intransigence in turn helped northern Republicans to close ranks and shifted the party's center toward more radical definitions of black freedom. It was never simply a debate between whites, however. Blacks emerged from slavery with their own ideas, and they became active agents in the struggle to define freedom.

The political part of that struggle took place in the nation's capital and in the state legislatures and county seats of the South. But the struggle also engaged the economic and social consequences of emancipation. In masters' kitchens and in plantation fields, ex-slaves strove to leave slavery behind and to become free laborers and free people. Many whites, as Carl Schurz learned, resisted letting go of the Old South. Nevertheless, emancipation and the developments of Reconstruction had profound consequences for blacks and whites in the South and for the nation as a whole.

Wartime Reconstruction

Reconstruction did not wait for the end of war. As the odds of a northern victory increased, thinking about reunification quickened. Immediately, a question arose: Who had authority to devise a plan of reconstruction? The Founders had not anticipated such a problem, and so the Constitution stood silent. Lincoln believed firmly that reconstruction was a matter of executive responsibility. Congress just as firmly asserted its jurisdiction. Fueling the argument about who had authority to set the terms of reconstruction were significant differences about the terms themselves. Lincoln's primary aim was the restoration of national unity, which he sought through a program of speedy, forgiving political

reconciliation. Congress feared that the president's lenient program amounted to restoring the old southern ruling class to power. It wanted greater assurances of white loyalty and greater guarantees of black rights. Rival plans emerged during the war, but Lincoln and Congress managed to bridge their differences. Only continued cooperation would achieve victory over the South and abolition of slavery.

In their eagerness to formulate a plan for political reunification, neither Lincoln nor Congress gave much attention to the South's land and labor problems. But war was rapidly eroding slavery and traditional plantation agriculture, and Yankee military commanders in the Union-occupied areas of the Confederacy had no choice but to oversee the emergence of a new labor system. With little guidance from Washington, northern officials felt their way along, bumping heads with both planters and freedmen. Although hastily assembled and improvised, their labor system ultimately had more staying power than any reconstruction policy formulated in wartime Washington.

"To Bind Up the Nation's Wounds"

On March 4, 1865, President Abraham Lincoln delivered his second inaugural address. His words blazed with religious imagery as he surveyed the history of the long, deadly war and then looked ahead to peace. "With malice toward none; with charity for all; with firmness in the right, as God gives us to see the right," Lincoln said, "let us strive on to finish the work we are in; to bind up the nation's wounds . . . to do all which may achieve and cherish a just, and a lasting peace." Lincoln had contemplated reunion for nearly two years. Deep compassion for the enemy guided his thinking about peace. But kindness is not the key to understanding Lincoln's program. His reconstruction plan aimed primarily at shortening the war and ending slavery.

Lincoln believed firmly that reconstruction was a matter of executive responsibility. Congress just as firmly asserted its jurisdiction.

In his Proclamation of Amnesty and Reconstruction, issued in December 1863, when Union forces had finally gained the upper hand on the battlefield, Lincoln offered a full pardon to rebels willing to renounce secession and to accept the abolition of slavery. (Pardons were valuable because they restored all property, except slaves, and full political rights.) His offer excluded several groups of Confederates, such as high-ranking civilian and military officers, but the plan called for no mass arrests, no trials for treason, and no executions. Instead, when only 10 percent of men who had been qualified voters in 1860 had taken an oath of allegiance, they could organize a new state government. Lincoln hoped that war-sick rebels would embrace the easy terms of reunification, renew their allegiance to the Union, and abandon both slavery and secession. His plan did not require that ex-rebels extend social or political rights to ex-slaves, nor did it anticipate a program of long-term federal assistance to freedmen. Clearly, the president sought to restore the broken Union, not to reform it.

Lincoln's easy terms enraged abolitionists like Wendell Phillips, who charged that the president "makes the negro's freedom a mere sham." He "is willing that the negro should be free but seeks nothing else for him," Phillips declared. He compared Lincoln unfavorably to the most passive of the Civil War generals: "What McClellan was on the battlefield—'Do as little hurt as possible!'—Lincoln is in civil affairs—'Make as little change as possible!'" Phillips and other radicals called instead for revolutionary change, for a thoroughgoing overhaul of southern society. Their ideas proved to be too drastic for most Republicans during the war years, but Congress agreed that Lincoln's plan was inadequate. In July 1864, Congress put forward a plan of its own.

As General William T. Sherman was marching on Atlanta, Congressman Henry Winter Davis of Maryland and Senator Benjamin Wade of Ohio jointly sponsored a bill that threw out Lincoln's "10 percent plan" and demanded that a majority of voters in a conquered rebel state take the oath of allegiance before reconstruction could begin. Moreover, the Wade-Davis bill banned ex-Confederates from participating in the drafting of new state constitutions. Finally, the bill guaranteed the equality of freedmen before the law. Congress's reconstruction would be neither as quick nor as forgiving as Lincoln's. Still, the Wade-Davis bill angered radicals because it did not include a provision for black suffrage. When Lincoln exercised his right not to sign the bill and let it die instead, Wade and Davis published a manifesto charging the president with usurpation of power. They warned Lincoln to confine himself to "his executive duties—to obey and

execute, not make the laws—to suppress by arms armed rebellion, and leave political organization to Congress."

Undeterred, Lincoln continued to nurture the formation of loyal state governments under his own plan. Four states—Louisiana, Arkansas, Tennessee, and Virginia—fulfilled the president's requirements. Lincoln acknowledged that a government based on only 10 percent was not ideal, but he argued that it would be a "rallying point" for lukewarm rebels. "We shall sooner have the fowl by hatching the egg than by smashing it," Lincoln told Charles Sumner. "The eggs of crocodiles can produce only crocodiles," the Massachusetts senator retorted. Congress refused to seat representatives from the "Lincoln states." In his last public address in April 1865, Lincoln defended his plan but stressed his willingness to be flexible. For the first time he expressed publicly his endorsement of suffrage for southern blacks, at least "the very intelligent, and . . . those who serve our cause as soldiers." The announcement demonstrated that Lincoln's thinking about reconstruction was still evolving. Four days later, he was dead.

Land and Labor

Of all the problems raised by emancipation, none proved more critical than the transition from slave to free labor. Slavery had been, at bottom, a labor system, and while Republicans agreed that free labor would replace forced labor, they disagreed about what free labor would mean in the South. As Yankee armies proceeded to invade and occupy the Confederacy during the war, hundreds of thousands of slaves became free workers. Moreover, Yankee occupation meant that Union armies controlled vast territories where legal title to land had become unclear. The wartime Confiscation Acts punished "traitors" by confiscating their property. What to do with federally occupied land and how to organize labor on it engaged former slaves, former slaveholders, Union military commanders, and federal government officials long before the war ended.

From Virginia's tidewater to Louisiana's bayous, a variety of wartime labor experiments arose. The system that developed in the Mississippi valley proved to be a preview of postwar southern labor relations. Up and down the Mississippi, occupying federal troops ended slavery, which had already begun to fall apart because of slaves' resistance, and announced a new labor code. It required

THE EXECUTION OF BOOTH'S CO-CONSPIRATORS
Union troops tracked down and killed Lincoln's assassin, John Wilkes Booth, on April 26,
1865. Eight others were convicted of conspiring in the murder. On July 7, four were hanged,
including Mary Surratt. Although Surratt knew Booth and had clearly been a Confederate
sympathizer, there was no concrete evidence that she had participated in the murder plot.
Meserve-Kunhardt Collection.

planters to sign contracts with their laborers and to pay wages. The code also obligated employers to provide food, housing, and medical care. It outlawed whipping and other forms of physical punishment, but it reserved to the army the right to discipline blacks who refused to work. The code required black laborers to enter into contracts, work diligently, and remain subordinate and obedient. While the military took aim at slavery, it clearly had no intention of fomenting a social or economic revolution. Instead, it sought to restore plantation agriculture with wage labor. The effort resulted in a hybrid system of "compulsory free labor" that satisfied no one. Depending on one's point of view, it either provided too little or too much of a break with the past.

Planters complained because the new system fell short of slavery. A Louisiana sugar planter predicted that the military's plan would fail because Northerners did "not understand the Negro." Ex-slaves could not be "transformed by proclamation," he warned. Yet under the new system, blacks "are expected to perform their new obligations without coercion, & without the fear of punishment which is essential to stimulate the idle and correct the vicious." Without the right to whip, he concluded, the new labor system did not have a chance.

African Americans also criticized the new regime. They found it too reminiscent of slavery to be called "free labor." Of its many shortcomings, none disappointed ex-slaves more than the failure to provide them land of their own. "What's the use of being free if you don't own land enough to be buried in?" one man asked. "Might just as well stay a slave all your days." Freedmen were determined to become independent, and that required land. They believed they had a moral right to land because they and their ancestors had worked it without compensation for more than two centuries. Moreover, several wartime developments seemed to indicate that the federal government planned to link black freedom and landownership.

In January 1865, General Sherman had set aside for black settlement the Sea Islands off the South Carolina coast and part of the coast south of Charleston. He devised the plan to relieve himself of the burden of thousands of impoverished blacks who trailed desperately after his army. By June 1865, some 40,000 freedmen sat on 400,000 acres of "Sherman land." In addition, in March 1865, Congress established the Bureau of Refugees, Freedmen, and Abandoned Lands. The Freedmen's Bureau, as it was called, distributed food and clothing to destitute Southerners and eased the transition of blacks from slaves to free persons. But Congress also authorized the agency to divide abandoned and confiscated land into forty-acre plots, to rent them to freedmen, and eventually to sell them "with such title as the United States can convey." By June 1865, the bureau had situated nearly 10,000 black families on a half million acres that had been abandoned by fleeing South Carolina and Georgia planters. Hundreds of thousands of other ex-slaves eagerly anticipated getting farms of their own.

Despite the flurry of activity, wartime reconstruction had settled nothing. Two years of controversy had failed to produce agreement about whether the president or Congress had the authority to devise and direct policy or what proper policy should be. Lincoln had organized several new state governments, but Congress had not readmitted a single "reconstructed" state into the Union. There were hints that the price of defeat for the South would be a revolution in landholding, but the "compulsory free labor" system that emerged on plantations in the Mississippi valley suggested more continuity with antebellum traditions. Clearly, the nation faced dilemmas and difficulties almost as burdensome as those of the war.

The African American Quest for Autonomy

Although white politicians had difficulty agreeing, ex-slaves never had any doubt about what they wanted freedom to mean. They had only to contemplate what they had been denied as slaves. Slaves had to remain on their plantations; freedom

AN INDEPENDENT BLACK CHURCH
Poor freedmen found that one of the sweetest fruits of emancipation was the opportunity to worship in churches of their own. White observers characterized black worship as nothing but "visions and trances," but independent black churches did more than permit members to dance and shout if they wanted. They also promoted black education, extended relief to freedmen who could not provide for themselves, and engaged in Republican politics.
South Carolina Historical Society.

allowed blacks to go wherever they pleased. Thus, in the first heady weeks after emancipation, freedmen often abandoned their plantations just to see what was on the other side of the hill and to feel freedom under their feet. Slaves had to be at work in the fields by dawn; freedom permitted blacks to taste the forbidden pleasure of sleeping through a sunrise. Slaves had to defer to whites; freedom saw them test the etiquette of racial subordination. "Lizzie's maid passed me today when I was coming from church *without speaking to me*," huffed one plantation mistress. When she asked her own house servant to scour some kettles, the black woman snapped, "You better do it yourself. Ain't you smarter than me? You think you is—why don't you scour them yourself."

To whites, it looked like pure anarchy. Without the discipline of slavery, they said, blacks had reverted to their natural condition: lazy, irresponsible, and wild. Actually, former slaves were experimenting with freedom, in both trivial and profound ways. But poor black people could not long afford to roam the countryside, neglect work, and casually provoke whites. Soon, most were back on plantations, at work in the fields and kitchens.

But other items on ex-slaves' agenda of freedom endured. Freedmen did not easily give up their quest for economic independence. In addition, slavery had deliberately kept blacks illiterate, and freedmen emerged from bondage eager to read and write. Moreover, bondage had denied slaves secure family lives and the ability to worship openly as they saw fit. Consequently, families and religion became areas of persistent black aspiration.

Although slave marriages and family relations had existed only at the master's whim, slaves had nevertheless managed to create deep, enduring family bonds. Still, slave sales had often severed family ties. As a consequence, thousands of black men and women took to the roads in 1865 to look for relations who had been sold away. One northern newspaperman encountered a ragged freedman who had walked six hundred miles to North Carolina, where he had *heard* that his wife and children had been sold. Couples who emerged from slavery with their marriages intact often rushed to northern military chaplains to legalize their unions. (See Texts in Historical Context, page 612.)

The end of slavery saw families abandon the slave quarters and scatter over plantations, building separate cabins on the patches of land they rented. In independent households, far from whites, black families escaped white intrusion. Parents no

MARRIAGE CERTIFICATE
During the Civil War, blacks serving in the Union army married under military authority. Henry M. Turner, a black chaplain, officiated at the wedding of Elisabeth Turner and Rufus Wright. After the war, thousands of ex-slaves whose marriages had no legal standing under slavery rushed to formalize their unions.
National Archives.

longer had to endure interference in the raising of their children. Women were less vulnerable to violation by masters and their sons. Some wives were able to exchange field labor for housework. Whites claimed that they were "acting the lady," but what whites meant was that black women were not acting like slaves. Instead, they behaved like mothers and housewives, occupied with the same arduous domestic chores as poor white women. Extreme poverty eventually forced most black women back into the cotton fields (at least at picking time) or into white kitchens. Nevertheless, safe and secure families came high on every ex-slave's list of freedom's blessings.

Another hunger that freedom permitted African Americans to satisfy was independent worship. Under slavery, blacks had often, like it or not,

The Meaning of Freedom

*O*n New Year's Day 1863, President Abraham Lincoln issued the Emancipation Proclamation. It stated that "all persons held as slaves" within the states still in rebellion "are, and henceforward shall be, free." Although it did not in and of itself free any slaves, it transformed the character of the war. Despite often intolerable conditions, black people focused on the possibilities of freedom.

*J*ohn Q. A. Dennis, formerly a slave in Maryland, wrote to Secretary of War Edwin M. Stanton to ask his help in reuniting his family.

DOCUMENT 1. Letter from John Q. A. Dennis to Edwin M. Stanton

Boston July 26th 1864

Dear Sir I am Glad that I have the Honour to Write you afew line I have been in troble for about four yars my Dear wife was taken from me Nov 19th 1859 and left me with three Children and I being a Slave At the time Could Not do Anny thing for the poor little Children for my master it was took me Carry me some forty mile from them So I Could Not do for them and the man that they live with half feed them and half Cloth them & beat them like dogs & when I was admitted to go to see them it use to brake my heart & Now I say agian I am Glad to have the honour to write to you to see if you Can Do Anny thing for me or for my poor little Children I was keap in Slavy untell last Novr 1863. then the Good lord sent the Cornel borne [William Birney?] Down their in Marland in worsester Co So as I have been recently freed I have but letle to live on but I am Strieving Dear Sir but what I went too know of you Sir is is it possible for me to go & take my Children from those men that keep them in Savery if it is possible will you pleas give me a permit from your hand then I think they would let them go. . . .

Hon sir will you please excuse my Miserable writeing & answer me as soon as you can I want get the little Children out of Slavery, I being Criple would like to know of you also if I Cant be permited to rase a Shool Down there & on what turm I Could be admited to Do so No more At present Dear Hon Sir

*F*reedom also prompted ex-slaves to seek legal marriages, which under slavery had been impossible. On February 28, 1865, in Little Rock, Arkansas, A. B. Randall, the white chaplain of a black regiment, in a report to the adjutant general of the Union army, confirmed the importance of marriage to freed slaves and emphasized their conviction that emancipation was just the first step toward full freedom.

DOCUMENT 2. Report from Reverend A. B. Randall

Weddings, just now, are very popular, and abundant among the Colored People. They have just learned, of the Special Order No' 15. of Gen Thomas [Adjutant General Lorenzo Thomas] by which, they may not only be lawfully married, but have their Marriage Certificates, *Recorded*; in a *book furnished by the Government*. This is most desirable. . . . Those who were captured . . . at Ivy's Ford, on the 17th of January, by Col Brooks, had their Marriage Certificates, taken from them; and destroyed; and then were roundly cursed, for having such papers in their posession. I have married, during the month, at this Post; Twenty five couples; mostly, those, who have families; & have been living together for years. I try to dissuade single men, who are soldiers, from marrying, till their time of enlistment is out: as that course seems to me, to be most judicious.

The Colord People here, generally consider, this war not only; their *exodus*, from bondage; but the road, to Responsibility; Competency; and an honorable Citizenship—God grant that their hopes and expectations may be fully realized.

*E*arly efforts at political reconstruction prompted petitions from former slaves demanding civil and political rights. In January 1865, black Tennesseans petitioned a convention of white unionists debating the reorganization of state government.

DOCUMENT 3. Petition "to the Union Convention of Tennessee Assembled in the Capitol at Nashville, January 9th, 1865"

We the undersigned petitioners, American citizens of African descent, natives and residents of Tennessee, and devoted friends of the great National cause, do most respectfully ask a patient hearing of your honorable body in regard to matters deeply affecting the future condition of our unfortunate and long suffering race.

First of all, however, we would say that words are too weak to tell how profoundly grateful we are to the Federal Government for the good work of freedom which it is gradually carrying forward; and for the Emancipation Proclamation which has set free all the slaves in some of the rebellious States, as well as many of the slaves in Tennessee. . . .

We claim freedom, as our natural right, and ask that in harmony and co-operation with the nation at large, you should cut up by the roots the system of slavery, which is not only a wrong to us, but the source of all the evil which at present afflicts the State. For slavery, corrupt itself, corrupted nearly all, also, around it, so that it has influenced nearly all the slave States to rebel against the Federal Government, in order to set up a government of pirates under which slavery might be perpetrated.

In the contest between the nation and slavery, our unfortunate people have sided, by instinct, with the former. We have little fortune to devote to the national cause, for a hard fate has hitherto forced us to live in poverty, but we do devote to its success, our hopes, our toils, our whole heart, our sacred honor, and our lives. We will work, pray, live, and, if need be, die for the Union, as cheerfully as ever a white patriot died for his country. The color of our skin does not lessen in the least degree, our love either for God or for the land of our birth. . . .

We know the burdens of citizenship, and are ready to bear them. We know the duties of the good citizen, and are ready to perform them cheerfully, and would ask to be put in a position in which we can discharge them more effectually. We do not ask for the privilege of citizenship, wishing to shun the obligations imposed by it. . . .

This is a democracy—a government of the people. It should aim to make every man, without regard to the color of his skin, the amount of his wealth, or the character of his religious faith, feel personally interested in its welfare. Every man who lives under the Government should feel that it is his property, his treasure, the bulwark and defence of himself and his family, his pearl of great price, which he must preserve, protect, and defend faithfully at all times, on all occasions, in every possible manner.

This is not a Democratic Government if a numerous, law-abiding, industrious, and useful class of citizens, born and bred on the soil, are to be treated as aliens and enemies, as an inferior degraded class, who must have no voice in the Government which they support, protect and defend, with all their heart, soul, mind, and body, both in peace and war. . . .

. . . The nation is fighting for its life, and cannot afford to be controlled by prejudice. Had prejudice prevailed instead of principle, not a single colored soldier would have been in the Union army to-day. But principle and justice triumphed, and now near 200,000 colored patriots stand under the folds of the national flag, and brave their breasts to the bullets of the rebels. As we are in the battlefield, so we swear before heaven, by all that is dear to men, to be at the ballot-box faithful and true to the Union.

The possibility that the negro suffrage proposition may shock popular prejudice at first sight, is not a conclusive argument against its wisdom and policy. No proposition ever met with more furious or general opposition than the one to enlist colored soldiers in the United States army. The opponents of the measure exclaimed on all hands that the negro was a coward; that he would not fight; that one white man, with a whip in his hand could put to flight a regiment of them; that the experiment would end in the utter rout and ruin of the Federal army. Yet the colored man has fought so well, on almost every occasion, that the rebel government is prevented, only by its fears and distrust of being able to force him to fight for slavery as well as he fights against it, from putting half a million of negroes into its ranks.

The Government has asked the colored man to fight for its preservation and gladly has he done it. It can afford to trust him with a vote as safely as it trusted him with a bayonet.

Document 1. Ira Berlin, Joseph P. Reidy, and Leslie S. Rowland, eds., *Freedom: A Documentary History of Emancipation, 1861–1867. Series I, Volume I, The Destruction of Slavery* (Cambridge University Press, 1985), 386.

Document 2. Ira Berlin, Joseph P. Reidy, and Leslie S. Rowland, eds., *Freedom: A Documentary History of Emancipation, 1861–1867. Series II, The Black Military Experience* (Cambridge University Press, 1982), 712.

Document 3. Ibid., 811–816.

prayed with whites in biracial churches. Full expression of black spirituality could be found only in the dead of night in secret religious services. Intent on religious independence, blacks greeted freedom with a mass exodus from white churches. Some joined the newly established southern branches of all-black northern churches, such as the African Methodist Episcopal Church. Others formed black versions of the major southern denominations, Baptists and Methodists. On the eve of the war, 42,000 blacks had worshiped in biracial Methodist churches in South Carolina; by 1870, all but 600 had left. Slaves had viewed their tribulations through the lens of their deeply felt Christian faith, and freedmen comprehended the events of the Civil War and Reconstruction as people of faith. It was not surprising that ex-slaves claimed Abraham Lincoln as their Moses.

Presidential Reconstruction

Abraham Lincoln died on April 15, 1865, just hours after John Wilkes Booth had shot him at a Washington, D.C., theater. Chief Justice Salmon P. Chase immediately administered the oath of office to Vice President Andrew Johnson. Lincoln's assassination thrust the Tennessean into responsibility at a time of grave national crisis. Moreover, Congress had adjourned in March, which meant that legislators were away from Washington when Lincoln was killed. They would not reconvene until December unless the new president called Congress back into special session. But Johnson preferred to have Washington to himself while he made critical decisions about the future of the South. Like Lincoln, he believed that responsibility for restoring the Union lay with the president. Throughout the summer and fall, therefore, the "accidental president" presided over the nation without a sitting Congress. With dizzying speed, Johnson drew up and executed a plan of reconstruction.

Congress returned to the capital in December to find that, as far as the president and former Confederates were concerned, Reconstruction was over. Appalled by what they saw, members of Congress challenged the president's prerogative and policies. To most Republicans, Johnson's modest demands of ex-rebels made a mockery of the sacrifice of Union soldiers. In an 1863 speech dedicating the cemetery at Gettysburg, Lincoln had spoken of the "great task remaining before us . . . that we here highly resolve

that these dead shall not have died in vain—that this nation, under God, shall have a new birth of freedom." Instead, Johnson had acted as midwife to the rebirth of the Old South. He had achieved political reunification at the cost of black liberty. To let his program stand, Republican legislators said, would mean that the North's dead had indeed died in vain.

Johnson's Program of Reconciliation

Born in 1808 in Raleigh, North Carolina, Andrew Johnson was the son of very poor, illiterate parents. Unable to afford to send her son to school, Johnson's widowed mother apprenticed him to a tailor. Self-educated and ambitious, the young man ran away before completing his indenture and headed for Tennessee. There he worked as a tailor, accumulated a fortune in land, acquired five slaves, and built a career in politics championing the South's common white people and assailing its "illegitimate, swaggering, bastard, scrub aristocracy." According to an old political foe, "If Johnson were a snake, he would lie in the grass to bite the heels of rich men's children." The only senator from a Confederate state to remain loyal to the Union, Johnson held no grudge against the South's rebel yeomen. He believed that they had been hoodwinked by slaveholding secessionists. Less than two weeks before he became president, he made it clear what he would do to the rascals if he ever had the chance: "I would arrest them—I would try them—I would convict them and I would hang them."

Throughout the summer and fall, the "accidental president" presided over the nation without a sitting Congress. With dizzying speed, Johnson drew up and executed a plan of reconstruction.

No wonder the South's elite trembled when Lincoln died. Republicans who looked forward to drastic changes in the South celebrated their powerful new ally in the White House. In reality, however, Johnson was no friend. Indeed, he was no Republican. A Democrat all his life, Johnson occupied the White House only because the Republican Party in 1864 had needed to broaden its appeal to loyal, Union-supporting Democrats. As a Tennessee congressman and senator, Johnson had championed traditional Democratic causes, vigorously defending states' rights (but not secession) and opposing Republican efforts to expand the power of the federal government, especially in the economic realm. He had voted against almost every federal appropriation, including a bill to pave the streets of Washington.

Moreover, Johnson had been a steadfast defender of slavery. He had owned slaves until 1862, when Tennessee rebels, angry at his Unionism, confiscated them. He only grudgingly accepted emancipation. When he did, it was more because of his hatred for slaveholders than sympathy for slaves. "Damn the negroes," he said. "I am fighting those traitorous aristocrats, their masters." At a time when the nation faced its moment of truth regarding black Americans, the new president harbored unshakable racist convictions. Africans, he said, were "inferior to the white man in point of intellect —better calculated in physical structure to undergo drudgery and hardship." On the eve of his inauguration as vice president, he had reiterated his belief in a white man's government.

One month after becoming president, Johnson announced his plan of reconstruction. He presented it as a continuation of Lincoln's plan, and in some ways it was. Like Lincoln, he stressed reconciliation between the Union and the defeated Confederacy and rapid restoration of civil government in the South. He offered to pardon most ex-rebels who promised future loyalty to the Union. Like Lincoln, Johnson excluded high-ranking ex-Confederates, but he also excluded all ex-rebels with property worth more than $20,000. The Tennessee tailor was apparently taking aim at his old enemy, the planter aristocrats. Wealthy individuals would have to apply directly to the president for pardons. Johnson recognized the state governments created by Lincoln and set out his own requirements for restoring the rebel states to the Union. All that the citizens of a state had to do was to renounce the right of secession, deny that the debts of the Confederacy were legal and binding, and ratify the Thirteenth Amendment abolishing slavery, which had become part of the Constitution in December 1865. Johnson's plan ignored Lincoln's acceptance near the end of his life of some form of limited black voting.

Johnson's eagerness to normalize relations with southern states and his lack of sympathy for blacks also led him to instruct military and government officials to return to pardoned ex-Confederates all confiscated and abandoned land, even if it was in the hands of freedmen. Reformers were shocked. They had expected the president's vendetta against planters to mean the permanent confiscation of the South's plantations and the distribution of the land to loyal freedmen. Instead, his instructions canceled the promising beginnings made by General Sherman and the Freedmen's Bureau to settle blacks on land of their own. As one freedman observed, "things was hurt by Mr. Lincoln getting killed."

Johnson's reconstruction envisioned a quick and easy political reconciliation between North and South and demonstrated almost no concern for freedmen. Predictably, Republicans who sought a drastic overhaul of southern society denounced the plan. "Is there no way to arrest the insane course of the President?" asked Congressman Thaddeus Stevens. It appeared that the president was committed to surrendering blacks and the Republican Party to the "tender mercies of the rebels."

Southern Resistance and Black Codes

In the summer of 1865, delegates across the South gathered to draw up the new state constitutions required by Johnson's plan of reconstruction. They revealed that while they had been defeated, they had not been subdued. Rather than take their medicine, they choked on even the president's mild requirements. Refusing to declare their secession ordinances null and void, the South Carolina and Georgia conventions merely "repudiated" their ordinances, preserving in principle their right to secede. In addition, every state convention wrangled over the precise wording of the constitutional amendment ending slavery. In the end, Mississippi rejected the Thirteenth Amendment outright, and Alabama rejected it in part. Finally, South Carolina and Mississippi refused to repudiate their Confederate war debts. These defiant acts provoked only mild responses from Andrew Johnson. He recommended, suggested, and even pleaded, but he did not demand that Southerners comply with his lenient terms.

White Southerners learned dangerous lessons from this initial experience. By failing to draw a hard line, Johnson rekindled southern resistance. White Southerners began to think that, by standing up for themselves, they—not victorious Northerners—would shape the transition from slavery to freedom. In the fall of 1865, newly elected southern legislators set out to reverse the "retreat into barbarism" that followed emancipation.

Under the mantle of protectors of the freedmen, state governments across the South adopted a se-

ries of laws known as the black codes. Rejecting the principle of legal equality, legislators argued that ex-slaves required special laws. While emancipation had brought freedmen important rights that they had lacked as slaves—to own property, to make contracts, to marry legally, and to sue and be sued in court—the black codes made a travesty of freedom. They sought to keep blacks subordinate to whites. Scores of laws subjected blacks to every sort of discrimination. Mississippi made insulting gestures and language a criminal offense. Several states made it illegal for blacks to own a gun. Blacks were barred from jury duty. Not a single southern state granted any black—no matter how educated, wealthy, or refined—the right to vote.

At the core of the black codes, however, lay the matter of labor. Faced with the death of slavery and the disintegration of plantations, legislators sought to channel freedmen back into traditional tasks. South Carolina attempted to limit blacks to either farmwork or domestic service by requiring them to pay annual taxes of $10 to $100 to work in any other occupation. Mississippi demanded that by January of each year blacks possess written evidence of employment. An offender could be declared a vagrant and be subject to fine or involuntary plantation labor. Most states allowed judges to bind black children—orphans and others whose parents they deemed unable to support them—to white employers. Under these so-called apprenticeship laws, courts bound out thousands of black children to planter "guardians," often over the protests of their parents. Legislators bent every effort to resuscitate the traditional plantation economy and resurrect as nearly as possible the old regime.

Johnson refused to intervene decisively. A staunch defender of states' rights, he believed that the citizens of every state—even those citizens who had attempted to destroy the Union—should be free to write their own constitutions and laws. Moreover, since he shared other white Southerners' eagerness to restore white supremacy and black subordination, the black codes did not particularly offend him or seem excessive. Besides, he could point proudly to the fact that by December 1865, enough states had approved the Thirteenth Amendment to make it a part of the Constitution.

But Johnson also followed the path he believed offered him the greatest political return. A conservative Tennessee Democrat at the head of a northern Republican Party, he began to look southwards for political allies. Despite tough talk about punishing traitors, he issued more than 14,000 special pardons to wealthy or high-ranking ex-Confederates. He no doubt enjoyed the sight of former aristocrats lining up humbly to beg his pardon, but

Johnson recognized that these supplicants could also be useful politically. By pardoning planters and Confederate officials, by acquiescing in the South's black codes, and by accepting the new southern governments even when they failed to satisfy his minimal demands, he won useful allies.

If Northerners had any doubts about the mood of the South, they evaporated in the elections of 1865. To represent them in Congress, white Southerners chose former Confederates, not loyal Unionists. Of the eighty senators and representatives they sent to Washington, fifteen had served in the Confederate army, ten of them as generals. Another sixteen had served in civil and judicial posts in the Confederacy. Nine others had served in the Confederate Congress. One—Alexander Stephens—had been vice president of the Confederacy. Some had not yet even received pardons, but Johnson granted immediate clemency so that they could take office. In December, this remarkable group arrived on the steps of the nation's Capitol to be seated in Congress. As one Georgian later remarked: "It looked as though Richmond had moved to Washington."

Expansion of Black Rights and Federal Authority

Southerners had blundered monumentally. They had assumed that what Andrew Johnson was willing to accept, the northern public and Congress would accept as well. But southern intransigence compelled even moderate Republicans to conclude that ex-rebels were a "generation of vipers," still dangerous, still untrustworthy. Northerners sought evidence of a change of heart, but they searched in vain for remorse for slavery, secession, or waging a devastating war. Since white Southerners denied that they were sinners, they refused to repent. Without repentance, Northerners could not forgive.

The black codes in particular soured moderate Republicans on the South's efforts at reconstruction. The codes became a symbol of southern intentions not to accept the verdict of the battlefields, but instead to "restore all of slavery but its name." Northerners were hardly saints when it came to racial justice, but black freedom had become a hallowed war aim. The deaths of Union soldiers had sanctified it. "We tell the white men of Mississippi," the *Chicago Tribune* roared, "that the men of the North will convert the State of Mississippi into a frog pond before they will allow such laws to disgrace one foot of the soil in which the bones of our soldiers sleep and

THE LOST CAUSE
While politicians in Washington, D.C., debated the future of the South, white Southerners were coming to grips with their emotions and history. They began to refer to their failure to secede from the Union as the "Lost Cause." They enshrined the memory of certain former Confederates, especially Robert E. Lee. Lee's nobility and courage represented the white South's image of itself. This quilt from about 1870, with Lee stitched in the center, illustrates how common whites incorporated the symbols of the Lost Cause into their daily lives. The unknown maker of the quilt also included miniature Confederate flags and memorial ribbons.
Valentine Museum, Cook Collection.

over which the flag of freedom waves." Moderate Republicans generally agreed that the "first fruits of reconstruction promise a most deplorable harvest, and the sooner we gather the tares [weeds], plow the ground again and sow new seed, the better."

Moderates represented the mainstream of the Republican Party and wanted only assurance that slavery and treason were dead. They did not seek a revolution of the entire southern social order. They did not champion black equality or the confiscation of plantations or black voting, as did the Radicals, a minority faction within the Republican Party. In December 1865, however, when Congress convened in Washington, it became clear that events in the

South had succeeded in forging unity (at least temporarily) among Republican factions. Exercising Congress's right to determine the qualifications of its members, the moderate majority and the Radical minority came together to refuse to seat the southern representatives. Rather than accept Johnson's claim that the "work of restoration" was done, Congress countered his executive power. Congressional Republicans enjoyed a three-to-one majority over the Democrats, and if they could agree on a program of reconstruction, they could easily pass legislation and even override presidential vetoes.

The moderates took the initiative. Senator Lyman Trumbull of Illinois declared that the president's policy of trusting southern whites proved that the ex-slave would "be tyrannized over, abused, and virtually reenslaved without some legislation by the nation for his protection." Early in 1866, the moderates produced two bills that strengthened the federal shield. The first, the Freedmen's Bureau bill, prolonged the life of the agency established by the previous Congress. Since the end of the war, it had distributed food, supervised labor contracts, and sponsored schools for freedmen. To the cheers of southern whites and the dismay of Republican moderates, President Johnson vetoed the Freedmen's Bureau bill. The Constitution, he argued, never contemplated a "system for the support of indigent persons." Congress failed by a narrow margin to override the president's veto.

Johnson's shocking veto galvanized nearly unanimous Republican support for the moderates' second measure, the Civil Rights Act. Designed to nullify the black codes, it affirmed the rights of blacks to enjoy "full and equal benefit of all laws and proceedings for the security of person and property as is enjoyed by white citizens." Modest on its surface, the act boldly required the end of legal discrimination in state laws and represented an extraordinary expansion of black rights and federal authority. The president argued that the civil rights bill amounted to an "unconstitutional invasion of states' rights" and vetoed it. In essence, he denied that the federal government possessed authority to protect the civil rights of blacks. Had Johnson's veto stood, reconstruction would have been over, and the president would have had the final word. But in April 1866, a thoroughly aroused Republican Party again pushed a civil rights bill through Congress and overrode another presidential veto. Then in July, it sustained another Freedmen's Bureau Act. For the first time in American history, Congress had overridden presidential vetoes of major legislation.

Johnson's vetoes represented a decisive moment in reconstruction. Even moderate Republicans who wanted to avoid a break with the president concluded that he had declared war on the freedmen and the Republican Party. Jettisoning his moderate Republican political allies, he had snuggled up to conservative Democrats. Moreover, he had compounded the harm with vulgar racist statements (suggesting that a logical consequence of congressional policy would be interracial marriage), with inflammatory personal attacks (comparing certain Republicans to Judas and himself to Christ), and in general exhibiting a pugnacious, nasty temperament that made compromise and cooperation impossible. As a worried South Carolinian observed in the spring of 1866, Johnson had succeeded in uniting the Republicans and probably touched off "a fight this fall such as has never been seen."

Congressional Reconstruction

By the summer of 1866, President Andrew Johnson and Congress had dropped their gloves and stood toe to toe in a bare-knuckled contest unprecedented in American history. Johnson had made it clear that he would not budge on either constitutional questions or policy. Moderate Republicans made a major effort to resolve the dilemma of reconstruction by amending the Constitution, but the obstinacy of Johnson and white Southerners pushed Republican moderates steadily closer to the Radicals and to acceptance of additional federal intervention in the South. Each escalation of federal power brought forth new charges of congressional tyranny from the White House. Each new law produced fresh obstruction. Finally, Congress sought to end presidential interference with its prerogatives by impeaching Andrew Johnson.

Congressional reconstruction evolved haltingly and unevenly, but through it all black suffrage acted like a powerful magnet that steadily drew discussion its way. In time, white men in Congress debated whether to give the ballot to black men. Outside of Congress, blacks raised their voices on behalf of color-blind voting rights, while women argued that it was time to make voting sex-blind as well as color-blind.

The Fourteenth Amendment and Escalating Violence

In April 1866, Republican moderates introduced the Fourteenth Amendment to the Constitution, which both houses of Congress approved in June by the necessary two-thirds majority. The amendment then went to the states for ratification. Although it took two years to gather approval from the required three-fourths of the states, the Fourteenth Amendment had immediate consequences.

The most important provisions of this complex amendment made all native-born or naturalized persons American citizens and prohibited states from abridging the "privileges and immunities" of citizens, depriving them of "life, liberty, or property without due process of law," and denying them "equal protection of the laws." Lawyers have battled ever since about the meaning of this broad language, but by making blacks national citizens the amendment nullified the *Dred Scott* decision of 1857 and provided a national guarantee of equality before the law. In essence, it protected the rights of citizens against violation by their own state governments.

The Fourteenth Amendment also dealt with voting rights. Republicans revealed that while genuinely committed to black freedom, they were also alert to partisan advantage. Rather than explicitly granting the vote to blacks, as Radicals wanted, the amendment gave Congress the right to reduce the congressional representation of states that withheld suffrage from some of its adult male population. In other words, white Southerners could either allow their former slaves to vote or see their representation in Washington slashed.

Moderate Republicans soft-pedaled the voting issue because they feared that Northerners would reject any amendment that forced them to enfranchise northern blacks. At that time, only five New England states permitted black men to vote. But without the extension of voting rights to blacks, the return of the southern states to Congress would mean renewed ascendancy for the Democratic Party in the South (most southern whites were Democrats, while southern blacks could be counted on to support the party of Lincoln) and perhaps in the nation as a whole. Ironically, abolition had increased the South's representation in Congress because it had effectively ended the three-fifths compromise (a constitutional provision that had based representation on all free persons and three-fifths of all slaves). Now African Americans were free and thus whole persons in the eyes of the Constitution. Understandably, Republicans refused to sit idle while ex-rebels denied freedmen the vote and simultaneously increased by some twenty seats their power in the House of Representatives.

The Republicans drafted the Fourteenth Amendment in such a way that they could not lose. If southern whites caved in and granted voting rights to freedmen, the Republican Party, entirely a northern party since its birth, would gain valuable black votes, establish a wing in the South, and secure its national power. But if whites refused, southern representation in Congress would plunge, and Republicans would still gain immunity from southern Democratic political power. Of course, the Fourteenth Amendment's voting provision included northern states, where whites were largely hostile to black suffrage. But northern states could continue to withhold suffrage and not suffer in Washington, for their black populations were too small to count in figuring representation. Radicals labeled the Fourteenth Amendment's voting provision "hypocritical" and a "swindle," but they understood that it was the best they could get at the time.

By the summer of 1866, President Andrew Johnson and Congress had dropped their gloves and stood toe to toe in a bare-knuckled contest unprecedented in American history.

Tennessee approved the Fourteenth Amendment in July, and Congress promptly welcomed its representatives and senators back. Had Johnson counseled other southern states to ratify this relatively mild amendment and warned them that they faced the fury of an outraged Republican Party if they refused, they might have listened. Instead, Johnson advised Southerners to reject the Fourteenth Amendment and to rely on him to trounce the Republicans in the fall congressional elections.

Johnson had decided to make the Fourteenth Amendment the overriding issue of the 1866 congressional elections and to gather its white opponents into a new conservative party, the National Union Party. In August, his supporters met in Philadelphia. Democrats came, but the poor Republican turnout made it clear that rather than drawing disgruntled party members to him, Johnson had united nearly the entire Republican Party against him.

The president's strategy had already suffered a setback two weeks earlier when whites in several southern cities went on rampages against blacks. It was less an outbreak of violence than an escalation of the violence that had never ceased. In New Orleans, a mob assaulted delegates to a black suffrage convention, and thirty-four blacks died. In Memphis, white mobs hurtled through the black sections of town and killed at least forty-six people. The slaughter shocked Northerners and renewed skepticism about Johnson's claim that southern whites could be trusted. "Who doubts that the Freedmen's Bureau ought to be abolished forthwith," a New York observer declared sarcastically, "and the blacks remitted to the paternal care of their old masters, who 'understand the nigger, you know, a great deal better than the Yankees can.'"

In a last-ditch effort, Johnson took his case directly to the people. In August, he made an ill-fated "swing around the circle," which took him from Washington to Chicago and St. Louis and back to Washington. However, the president embarrassed himself and his office. When hostile crowds hurled insults, he gave as good as he got. It was Johnson at his worst—intemperate, crude, undignified. Even a friend agreed that he had "made an ass of himself." Johnson's reception on the campaign trail foretold the fate of the National Union movement in the elections. Rather than witnessing the birth of a new conservative party, the elections pitted traditional rivals: Democrats (who lined up with Johnson) against Republicans (who lined up against him). The result was an overwhelming Republican victory in which the party retained its three to one congressional majority.

Johnson had bet that Northerners would not support federal protection of black rights. He expected a racist backlash to defeat the Fourteenth Amendment and blast the Republican Party. But the cautious (and ingenious) amendment was not radical enough to drive Republican voters into Johnson's camp. Besides, the war was still fresh in northern minds. As one Republican explained, southern whites "with all their intelligence were traitors, the blacks with all their ignorance were loyal."

Radical Reconstruction and Military Rule

The elections of 1866 should have taught southern whites the folly of relying on Andrew Johnson as a guide through the thicket of reconstruction. But when Johnson continued to urge Southerners to-

ward rejection of the Fourteenth Amendment, one by one every southern state except Tennessee voted it down. "The last one of the sinful ten," thundered Representative James A. Garfield of Ohio, "has flung back into our teeth the magnanimous offer of a generous nation." In the void created by the South's rejection of the moderates' program, the Radicals seized the initiative.

Each act of defiance by southern whites had boosted the standing of the Radicals within the Republican Party. At the core was a small group of men who had cut their political teeth on the antebellum campaign against slavery, who had goaded Lincoln toward making the war a crusade for freedom, and who had carried into the postwar period the conviction that only federal power could protect the rights of the freedmen. Except for freedmen themselves, no one did more to make freedom the "mighty moral question of the age." Men like Senator Charles Sumner, that pompous but sincere Massachusetts crusader, and Thaddeus Stevens, the caustic, cadaverous representative from Pennsylvania, did not speak with a single voice, but they united in calling for civil and political equality. They insisted on extending to ex-slaves the same opportunities that northern working people enjoyed under the free-labor system. The southern states were "like clay in the hands of the potter," Stevens declared in January 1867, and he called on Congress to have "the courage to do its duty." Stevens urged that reconstruction begin all over again, that the nation return to "the point where Grant left off the work, at Appomattox Court-House."

In March 1867, after exhaustive debate, moderates joined the Radicals to overturn the Johnson state governments and initiate military rule of the South. The Military Reconstruction Act (and three subsequent acts) divided the ten unreconstructed Confederate states into five military districts. Congress placed a Union general in charge of each district and instructed him to "suppress insurrection, disorder, and violence" and to begin political reform. After the military had completed voter registration, which would include black men and exclude all those barred by the Fourteenth Amendment from holding public office, voters would elect delegates to conventions that would draw up new state constitutions. Each constitution would guarantee black suffrage. When the voters of each state had approved the constitution and the first legislature had ratified the Fourteenth Amendment, the state could submit its work to Congress. If Congress approved, the state's senators and representatives could be seated and political reunification would be accomplished.

Radicals proclaimed the provision for black suffrage "a prodigious triumph." The doggedness of the Radicals and of African Americans, along with the pigheadedness of Johnson and the white South, had swept the Republican Party far beyond the timid suffrage provisions of the Fourteenth Amendment. Republicans finally agreed with Sumner that only the voting power of ex-slaves could bring about a permanent revolution in the South. Indeed, suffrage provided blacks with a powerful instrument of change and self-protection. When combined with the disfranchisement of thousands of ex-rebels, it promised to cripple any neo-Confederate resurgence and guarantee Republican governments in the South.

Despite its bold suffrage provision, the Military Reconstruction Act of 1867 disappointed those who

advocated the confiscation and redistribution of southern plantations. No one in Washington was more distressed than Thaddeus Stevens. Unlike Sumner, who conceived of Reconstruction primarily in political terms, Stevens believed it was at bottom an economic problem. He agreed wholeheartedly with the ex-slave who said, "Give us our own land and we take care of ourselves, but without land, the old masters can hire us or starve us, as they please." Stevens envisioned confiscating the estates of traitors, breaking them up into small farms, and distributing them widely to create a loyal black yeomanry. But Johnson's offers of amnesty and pardon had reversed the small program of land transfer begun during the war. By early 1867, nearly all of the land had been returned to its ex-Confederate owners.

Congress steadfastly refused to put land into the hands of ex-slaves. Most Republicans believed

BLACK POLITICS
The Reconstruction Act of 1867 revolutionized southern politics. It also galvanized the region's African American population. One black minister remembered, "Politics got in our midst and our revival or religious work for a while began to wane." While Congress enfranchised only black men, black women participated in the debates that sprang up everywhere. Political rights meant that freedmen had access to the power of the state to advance their interests, and women, as well as men, recognized the unprecedented opportunity.
Library of Congress.

that they had already provided blacks with the critical tools: equal legal rights and the ballot. Besides, confiscation was too radical, even for some Radicals. Confiscating private property in the South, declared the *New York Times*, "strikes at the root of all property rights in both sections. It concerns Massachusetts quite as much as Mississippi." Moreover, giving land to blacks amounted to "government paternalism," most Republicans argued. In the end, it would undermine, not strengthen, black independence. Civil and political equality, a majority of Republicans believed, gave blacks "a perfectly fair chance." If they were to get forty acres, they would have to gain it themselves.

Declaring that he would rather sever his right arm than sign such a formula for "anarchy and chaos," Andrew Johnson vetoed the Military Reconstruction Act. Congress overrode his veto the very same day, dramatizing the shift in power from the executive to the legislative branch of government. With the passage of the Reconstruction Acts of 1867, congressional reconstruction was virtually completed. Congress had left white folks owning most of the South's land, but in a radical departure it had given black folks the ballot. More than any other provision, black suffrage justifies the term "radical reconstruction." In 1867, the nation began an unprecedented experiment in interracial democracy—at least in the South, for Congress's plan did not touch the North. Soon the former Confederate states would become the primary theater for political struggle. But before the spotlight swung away from Washington, the president and Congress had one more scene to play.

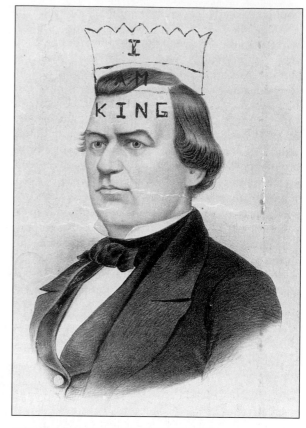

ANDREW JOHNSON, WITH ADDITIONS
This dignified 1868 portrait by Currier and Ives of President Andrew Johnson was apparently amended by a disgruntled citizen. Johnson's vetoes of several reconstruction measures passed by Congress caused his opponents to charge him with arrogant monarchical behavior.
Museum of American Political Life.

Impeaching a President

Although Johnson had lost the support of the northern people and faced a hostile Republican majority in Congress, he had no intention of yielding control of reconstruction. Ever defiant, he fought a guerrilla campaign to obstruct and delay implementation of Republican policies in the South. As president, he was responsible for enforcing the laws that Congress enacted. As commander in chief, he oversaw the military rule of the South that Congress instituted. Yet in a dozen ways he sabotaged Congress's will and encouraged white belligerence and resistance. He issued a flood of pardons to undermine efforts at political and economic change. He waged war against the Freedmen's Bureau by removing officers who sympathized too fully with ex-slaves. And he replaced Union generals eager to enforce

Congress's Reconstruction Acts with conservative men who were eager to defeat them. Johnson believed that Congress had exceeded its authority when it launched military rule and imposed black suffrage, and he claimed that he was merely defending the "violated Constitution." At bottom, however, he subverted congressional reconstruction to protect southern whites from what he considered the horrors of "Negro domination."

When Congress learned that overriding Johnson's vetoes did not assure victory, it attempted to tie the president's hands. Congress required that all orders to field commanders pass through the General of the Army, Ulysses S. Grant, who Congress believed was sympathetic to southern freedmen, Unionists, and Republicans. It also enacted the

Tenure of Office Act, which required the approval of the Senate for the removal of any government official who had been appointed with Senate consent. Republicans were seeking to protect Secretary of War Edwin M. Stanton, the lone cabinet officer who supported congressional policies. Some Republicans, however, claimed that efforts to subdue Johnson were useless. Nothing less than removing him from office could save reconstruction, they claimed, and they initiated a crusade to impeach the president. According to the Constitution, the House of Representatives can impeach and the Senate can try any federal official for "Treason, Bribery, or other high Crimes and Misdemeanors."

As long as Johnson refrained from breaking a law, however, impeachment languished. Moderates interpreted "high Crimes and Misdemeanors" to mean violation of criminal statutes, and they did not believe that the president had committed an actual crime. Radicals denounced the moderates' interpretation as excessively narrow and argued that Johnson's abuse of constitutional powers and his failure to fulfill constitutional obligations were impeachable offenses. But in August 1867, Johnson suspended Secretary of War Stanton from office. As required by the Tenure of Office Act, he requested the Senate to consent to dismissal. When the Senate balked, the president removed Stanton anyway. "Is the President crazy, or only drunk?" asked a dumbfounded Republican moderate. "I'm afraid his doings will make us all favor impeachment."

News of Johnson's open defiance of the law did indeed convince every Republican in the House to vote for a resolution impeaching the president. Chief Justice Salmon Chase presided over the Senate trial, which lasted from March until May 1868. Chase refused to allow Johnson's opponents to raise the broad issues of misuse of power, his "great crimes," and forced them to argue their case exclusively on the narrow legal grounds of Johnson's removal of Stanton. Johnson's lawyers argued that he had not committed a criminal offense, that the Tenure of Office Act was unconstitutional, and that in any case it did not apply to Stanton, who had been appointed by Lincoln. When the critical vote came, seven moderate Republicans broke with their party and joined the Democrats in voting "not guilty." With thirty-five in favor and nineteen opposed, the impeachment forces fell one vote short of the two-thirds needed to convict.

Republicans had put Johnson on trial because he threatened their efforts to remake the South. But some, including Chief Justice Chase, feared that impeachment for insufficient cause would permanently weaken the office of president. Others shied away from conviction because they feared Benjamin Wade, president pro tem of the Senate, the man who would take Johnson's place in the White House. A crusty old Ohio Radical, Wade professed ideas about monetary policy, the rights of workingmen, and female suffrage that frightened moderates. So Johnson survived, but he did not come through the ordeal unscathed. After his trial he called a truce, and for the remaining ten months of his term reconstruction proceeded unhindered by presidential interference.

The Fifteenth Amendment and Women's Demands

In February 1869, Republicans passed their last major piece of reconstruction legislation: the Fifteenth Amendment to the Constitution. The amendment prohibited states from depriving any citizen of the right to vote because of "race, color, or previous condition of servitude." The Reconstruction Acts of 1867 had already required black suffrage in the South, but the Fifteenth Amendment extended black voting to the entire nation. Some Republicans felt morally obligated to do away with the double standard between North and South. (Eleven northern states and five border states had stubbornly resisted enfranchising blacks.) Others believed that the freedman's ballot required the extra armor of a constitutional amendment to protect it from white counterattack. But partisan advantage also played an important role in the amendment's passage. Gains by northern Democrats in the 1868 elections worried Republicans, and black voters now represented the balance of power in several northern states. By giving ballots to northern blacks, Republicans could lessen their political vulnerability. As one Republican congressman observed, "party expediency and exact justice coincide for once."

Some Republicans, however, found the final wording of the Fifteenth Amendment "lame and halting." Rather than absolutely guaranteeing the right to vote, the amendment merely prohibited exclusion on grounds of race. The distinction would prove to be significant. In time, inventive white Southerners would devise tests of literacy and property and other apparently nonracial measures that would effectively disfranchise blacks and yet not violate the Fifteenth Amendment. But an amendment that guaranteed the right to vote courted defeat in the North. Rising antiforeign sentiment—against the Chinese in California and against European immigrants in the Northeast—caused states to resist giving up control of suffrage requirements. In March 1870, after three-fourths of the states had ratified it, the Fifteenth Amendment became part of the Constitution. Republicans generally breathed a sigh of relief, confident that black suffrage had been "the last great point that remained to be settled of the issues of the war."

But the Republican Party's reappraisal of suffrage had ignored completely the band of politicized and energized women who had emerged from the war demanding "the ballot for the two disenfranchised classes, negroes and women." Founding the Equal Rights Association in 1866, Susan B. Anthony and Elizabeth Cady Stanton lobbied for "a government by the people, and the whole people; for the people and the whole people." They felt betrayed when their old antislavery allies, who now occupied positions of national power, proved to be fickle and would not work for their goals. "It was the Negro's hour," Frederick Douglass later explained. The Republican Party had to avoid anything that might jeopardize black gains, Charles Sumner declared. He suggested that woman suffrage could be "the great question of the future."

It was not the first time women's expectations had been dashed. The Fourteenth Amendment had provided for punishment of any state that excluded voters on the basis of race but not on the basis of sex. It had also introduced the word *male* into the Constitution when it referred to a citizen's right to vote. Stanton had predicted that "if that word 'male' be inserted, it will take us a century at least to get it out." The Fifteenth Amendment proved to be no less disappointing. Although women fought hard to include the word *sex*, the amendment denied states the right to forbid suffrage only on the basis of race. Stanton and Anthony condemned the Republicans' "negro first" strategy and concluded that woman "must not put her trust in man."

On the eve of the Civil War, individuals who had advocated black suffrage risked ridicule in the North and their lives in the South. A decade later, in William Lloyd Garrison's words, blacks had progressed from "the auction-block to the ballot-box." Most Republicans believed that the Fifteenth Amendment completed reconstruction. "The Fifteenth Amendment," Congressman James A. Garfield of Ohio proclaimed, "confers upon the African race the care of its own destiny. It places their fortunes in their own hands." Even Wendell Phillips, that uncompromising crusader for equal-

SUSAN B. ANTHONY
Like many outspoken suffragists, Anthony, depicted here around 1850, had begun her public career in the temperance and abolitionist movements. Her continuing passions for other causes — improving working conditions for labor, for example — caused some conservatives to oppose women's political rights because they equated the suffragist cause with radicalism in general. Women could not easily overcome such views, and the long struggle for suffrage eventually drew millions of women into public life. Meserve-Kunhardt Collection.

ity, argued that the black man held "his sufficient shield in his own hands. . . . Whatever he suffers will be largely now, and in future, wholly, his own fault." In essence, northern Republicans declared victory and scratched the "Negro question" from the agenda of national politics.

The Struggle in the South

While Northerners believed they had discharged their responsibilities with the Reconstruction Acts and the amendments to the Constitution, Southerners knew that the battle had just begun. Black suffrage and large-scale rebel disfranchisement that came with congressional reconstruction had destroyed traditional southern politics and established the foundation for the rise of the Republican Party. Gathering together outsiders and outcasts from traditional society, the Republicans in the South won elections, wrote new state constitutions, and formed new state governments.

Challenging the established class for political control was dangerous business. Equally dangerous were the confrontations that took place on farms and plantations from Virginia to Texas. In the countryside, blacks sought to give practical, everyday meaning to their newly won legal and political equality. But ex-masters and other whites had their own ideas about the social and economic arrangements that should replace slavery. Freedom, then, remained contested territory, and Southerners fought pitched battles with each other to determine the boundaries of their postemancipation world.

Freedmen, Yankees, and Yeomen

African Americans made up the majority of southern Republicans. Freedmen emerged from bondage illiterate and politically inexperienced, but they understood their own interests. They realized that without the ballot they were almost powerless, and they threw themselves into the suffrage campaign. Southern blacks gained voting rights in 1867, and within months virtually every eligible black man had registered to vote. While almost all voted Republican, blacks (like whites) did not have identical political priorities. Free-born, light-skinned southern blacks were often educated, property-holding artisans who tended to be economically conservative but socially radical. Concentrated in the South's towns and cities, they showed little enthusiasm for land reform, but they ached to tear down racial barriers that inhibited their everyday lives. Ex–field hands, in contrast, showed less concern about "whites only" signs in hotels and restaurants than they did about land of their own. Blacks united, however, in their desire for education and equal treatment before the laws.

Northern whites who decided to make the South their home after the war were a second element of the South's Republican Party. Conservative white Southerners called any northern migrant a "carpetbagger," a man so poor that he could pack all his earthly belongings in a single carpet-sided suitcase and swoop southward like a buzzard to "fatten on our misfortunes." Some Northerners who moved south were scavengers, but most were rest-

less, relatively well-educated young men, often former Union officers and Freedmen's Bureau agents who looked upon the South as they did the West—as a promising place to make a living. Only a few chose politics, but in the early years of Reconstruction carpetbaggers exercised leadership in the fledgling Republican Party far beyond their limited numbers. Illinois-born Henry C. Warmoth, for example, arrived in Louisiana with the army in 1864 and within months became the state's first Republican governor. Northerners in the southern Republican Party consistently supported programs that encouraged vigorous economic development along the lines of the northern free-labor model.

> *Black suffrage and large-scale rebel disfranchisement that came with congressional reconstruction had destroyed traditional southern politics and established the foundation for the rise of the Republican Party.*

The Republican Party gained even more recruits among white Southerners. Some businessmen found Republican economic policies attractive and hoped that an infusion of northern capital, know-how, and bustle would cure the sick southern economy. But yeoman farmers in the Piedmont accounted for the vast majority of white Republicans in the South. Many were Unionists who emerged from the war with bitter memories of Confederate persecution. Some small farmers also nursed long-standing grievances against planter domination and welcomed the Republican Party because it promised to end favoritism toward plantation interests. Yeomen usually supported initiatives for public schools and for expanding economic opportunity within a reinvigorated southern economy. Approximately one out of four white Southerners voted Republican. The other three never considered joining the party of Lincoln and cursed those who did. They condemned southern-born white Republicans as traitors to their region and their race and called them "scalawags," a term for runty horses and low-down, good-for-nothing rascals.

The Republican Party in the South, then, was made up of freedmen, Yankees, and yeomen—an improbable coalition. The mix of races, regions, and classes inevitably meant friction as each group maneuvered to define the party. Despite the stress and strain, Reconstruction represents an extraordinary moment in American politics: Blacks and whites joined together to pursue political change. The Republican Party defended the political and civil equality of black Southerners and struggled to bring the South into the mainstream of American social and economic development. Formally, of course, only men participated in politics—casting ballots and holding offices—but women also played parts in the political struggle. Women joined in parades and rallies, attended stump speeches, and even campaigned. In 1868, black maids in Yazoo, Mississippi, shocked their white employers when they showed up for work boldly wearing buttons depicting the Republican candidate for president: Ulysses S. Grant.

Reconstruction politics was not for cowards. Any political act, even wearing a political button, took courage. Congress had introduced hundreds of thousands of ex-slaves into the southern electorate against the will of the white majority. Then, according to one Democrat, the Republican Party herded them to the polls like "senseless cattle." Most whites in the South condemned the entire political process as illegitimate and felt justified in doing whatever it took to stamp out Republicanism. Violence against blacks—the "white terror"—took brutal institutional form in 1866 with the formation of the Ku Klux Klan. The Klan went on a rampage of whipping, hanging, shooting, burning, and throat-cutting to defeat reconstruction and restore white supremacy. (See Historical Question, page 628.) Rapid demobilization of the Union army after the war left only twenty thousand troops to patrol the entire South, a vast territory. Without effective military protection, southern Republicans had to take care of themselves.

Democratic Equality and the General Welfare

The Reconstruction Acts required southern states to draw up new constitutions before they could be readmitted to Congress. Beginning in the fall of 1867, states held elections for delegates to constitutional conventions. About 40 percent of the white electorate stayed home, either because they had been disfranchised or because they were boycotting politics. Republicans won three-fourths of the seats. About 15 percent of the Republican delegates were Northerners who had moved south, 25 percent were African Americans, and 60 percent were white Southerners. As a British visitor observed, the elec-

tions reflected "the mighty revolution that had taken place in America." But Democrats described the conventions as zoos of "baboons, monkeys, mules . . . and other jackasses." In fact, the gatherings brought together serious, purposeful men who hammered out the legal framework for a new order.

The reconstruction constitutions introduced extensive changes into southern life. In general, changes fell into two categories: those that reduced aristocratic privilege and increased democratic equality and those that expanded the state's responsibility for the general welfare. In the first category, the constitutions adopted universal male suffrage, abolished property qualifications for holding office, and made more offices elective and fewer appointive. In the second category, they enacted prison reform; made the state responsible for caring for orphans, the insane, and the deaf and mute; and aided debtors by exempting their homes from seizure.

These forward-looking constitutions provided blueprints for a New South. But they stopped short of the specific reforms advocated by particular groups within southern Republicanism. Despite the wishes of virtually every former slave, no southern constitution confiscated and redistributed land. Despite the prediction of Unionists that unless all former Confederates were banned from politics they

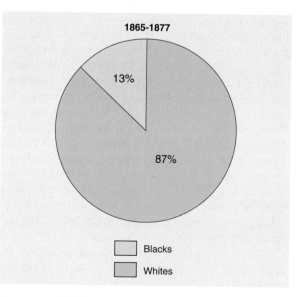

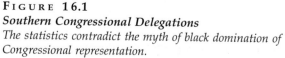

FIGURE 16.1
Southern Congressional Delegations
The statistics contradict the myth of black domination of Congressional representation.

THE STATE CONVENTION AT RICHMOND, VIRGINIA
*Between 1867 and 1869, every southern state except Tennessee held a convention to draft a
new constitution. For the first time in American history, black delegates joined whites in making laws. In Virginia, where blacks were more than 40 percent of the population, they made
up about 20 percent of the convention.*
Valentine Museum, Cook Collection.

would storm back and wreck reconstruction, no
constitution disfranchised ex-rebels wholesale. And
despite the desires of free-born blacks and others,
no constitution outlawed all forms of racial segregation.

But Democrats were blind to the limits of the
Republican program. In their eyes, they stared at
wild revolution. According to Democrats, Republican victories initiated "black and tan" (ex-slave and
mulatto) governments. But the claims of "Negro
domination" had almost no validity. Four out of five
Republican voters were black men, but more than
four out of five Republican officeholders were
white. Southerners sent fourteen black congressmen
and two black senators to Washington, but only 6
percent of Southerners in Congress during Reconstruction were black. With the exception of South
Carolina, where blacks briefly held a majority in one
house of the legislature, no state experienced
"Negro rule," despite black majorities in the populations of three states.

Democrats mocked black officeholders as ignorant field hands. Although many had only "agri-

cultural degrees" and "brick yard diplomas," most
were literate. One of Mississippi's two black U.S.
senators, free-born Hiram R. Revels, had attended
Knox College, and the other, ex-slave Blanche K.
Bruce, had learned to read while in bondage, run
away, and opened a school in Missouri. Francis Car-
dozo, South Carolina's secretary of state and secretary of the treasury, had studied at universities in
England and Scotland. But whatever their educational achievements, blacks were decidedly junior
partners in white-dominated Republican governments. Republicans sought to counter the racist attack by portraying themselves as "the poor man's
party" that promised to end the rule of the back-
ward-looking, arrogant planter aristocracy.

In almost every state, voters ratified the new
constitutions and swept Republicans into power.
After they ratified the Fourteenth Amendment, the
former Confederate states were readmitted to Congress. Southern Republicans then turned to the critical task of governing. They faced a staggering array
of problems. Wartime destruction still littered the
landscape. The war had destroyed one-third of all

What Did the Ku Klux Klan Really Want?

IN THE SUMMER OF 1866, six Confederate veterans in Pulaski, Tennessee, founded the Ku Klux Klan. Borrowing oaths and rituals from a college fraternity, the young men innocently sought fun and fellowship in a social club. But they quickly tired of playing pranks on one another and shifted to more serious matters. By the spring of 1868, when congressional Reconstruction went into effect, new groups or "dens" of the Ku Klux Klan had sprouted throughout the South.

According to former Confederate general and Georgia Democratic politician John B. Gordon, the Klan owed its popularity to the "instinct of self-preservation . . . the sense of insecurity and danger, particularly in those neighborhoods where the Negro population largely predominated." Everywhere whites looked, he said, they saw "great crime." Republican politicians organized ignorant freedmen and marched them to the polls, where they blighted honest government. Blacks drove overseers from plantations and claimed the land for themselves. Black robbers and rapists made white women cower behind barred doors. It was necessary, Gordon declared, "in order to protect our families from outrage and preserve our own lives, to have something that we could regard as a brotherhood—a combination of the best men of the country, to act purely in self-defense." According to Gordon and other conservative white Southerners, then, Klansmen were good men who stepped forward to do their duty, men who wanted nothing more than to guard their families and defend decent society from the assaults of degraded ex-slaves and a vindictive Republican Party.

Behind the Klan's high-minded and self-justifying rhetoric, however, lay another agenda. It was revealed in their actions, not their words. Klansmen embarked on a campaign to reverse history. Garbed in robes and hoods, Klansmen engaged in hit-and-run guerrilla warfare against free labor, civil equality, and political democracy. They aimed to terrorize their enemies—ex-slaves and white Republicans—into submission. As the South's chief terrorist organization between 1868 and 1871, the Klan whipped, burned, and shot in the name of white supremacy. Changes in four particular areas of southern life proved flash points for Klan violence: racial etiquette, education, labor, and politics.

The Klan punished those blacks and whites guilty of breaking the Old South's racial code. The Klan considered "impudence" a punishable offense. Asked to define "impudence" before a congressional investigating committee, one white opponent of the Klan responded: "Well, it is considered impudence for a negro not to be polite to a white man—not to pull off his hat and bow and scrape to a white man, as was done formerly." Klansmen whipped blacks for crimes that ranged from speaking disrespectfully to refusing to yield the sidewalk to raising a good crop to dressing well. Black women who "dress up and fix up like ladies" risked a midnight visit from the Klan. The Ku Klux Klan sought to restore racial subordination in every aspect of private and public life.

Klansmen also took aim at black education. White men, especially those with little schooling, found the sight of blacks in classrooms hard to stomach. Schools were easy targets, and scores of them went up in flames. Teachers, male and female, were flogged, or worse. Klansmen drove northern-born teacher Alonzo B. Corliss from North Carolina for "teaching niggers and making them like white men." In Cross Plains, Alabama, the Klan hanged an Irish-born teacher along with four black men. But not just ill-educated whites opposed black education. Planters wanted ex-slaves back in the fields, not at desks. Each student meant one less laborer. In 1869, an Alabama newspaper reported the burning of a black school and observed that it should be "a warning for them to stick hereafter to 'de shovel and de hoe,' and let their dirty-backed primers go."

Planters turned to the Klan as part of their effort to preserve plantation agriculture and restore labor discipline. An Alabama white admitted that in his area, the Klan was "intended principally for the negroes who failed to work." Masked bands

KU KLUX KLAN ROBE AND HOOD

The white robes that we associate with the Ku Klux Klan are a twentieth-century phenomenon. During Reconstruction, Klansmen donned robes of various designs and colors. It is unlikely that the man who wore this robe about 1866 — with its eye holes carefully trimmed with blue fabric — sewed it himself. Women did not participate in midnight raids, but mothers, wives, and daughters of Klansmen often shared their reactionary vision and did what they could to bring about the triumph of white supremacy.

Chicago Historical Society, Hope B. McCormick Center. Worn by Joseph Boyce Stewart, Lincoln County, Tenn., c.1866. Gift of W. G. Dithmer.

"punished Negroes whose landlords had complained of them." Sharecroppers who disputed their share at "settling up time" risked a visit from the night riders. Klansmen murdered a Georgia blacksmith who refused to do additional work for a white man until he was paid for a previous job. It was dangerous for freedmen to consider changing employers. "If we got out looking for some other place to go," an ex-slave from Texas remembered, "them KKK they would tend to Mister negro good and plenty." In Marengo County, Alabama, when the Klan heard that some local blacks were planning to leave, "the disguised men went to them and told them if they undertook it they would be killed on their way." Whites had decided that they would not be "deprived of their labor."

Above all, the Klan terrorized Republican leaders and voters. Klansmen became the military arm of the Democratic Party. They drove blacks from the polls on election day and terrorized black office-holders. Klansmen gave Andrew Flowers, a black politician in Chattanooga, a brutal beating and told him that they "did not intend any nigger to hold office in the United States." Jack Dupree, president of the Republican Club in Monroe County, Mississippi, a man known to "speak his mind," had his throat cut and was disemboweled while his wife was forced to watch.

Between 1868 and 1871, political violence reached astounding levels. Arkansas experienced nearly three hundred political killings in the three months before the fall elections in 1868, including Little Rock's U.S. congressman, J. M. Hinds. Louisiana was even bloodier. Between the local elections in the spring of 1868 and the presidential election in the fall, Louisiana experienced more than one thousand killings. Political violence often proved effective. In Georgia, Republican presidential candidate Ulysses S. Grant received no votes at all in 1868 in eleven counties, despite black majorities. The Klan murdered three scalawag members of the Georgia legislature and drove ten others from their homes. As one Georgia Republican commented after a Klan attack: "We don't call them democrats, we call them southern murderers."

It proved hard to arrest Klansmen and harder still to convict them. "If a white man kills a colored man in any of the counties of this State," observed a Florida sheriff, "you cannot convict him." By 1871, the death toll had reached thousands. Federal intervention—in the Ku Klux Klan Acts of 1870 and 1871—signaled an end to much of the Klan's power but not to counterrevolutionary violence in the South. Other groups continued the terror.

the South's livestock, and the $3 billion that was invested in slaves was gone. The South's share of the nation's wealth had fallen from 30 percent to only 12 percent. Manufacturing limped along at a fraction of prewar levels, agricultural production remained anemic, and the region's railroads had hardly advanced from the devastated condition in which Sherman had left them. Without the efforts of the Freedmen's Bureau, people would have starved. Moreover, reactionary violence and racial harassment dogged the steps of Southerners who sought reform. In this desperate context, Republicans struggled to breathe life into their new state governments.

Activity focused on three major areas. First, every state inaugurated a system of public education and began furiously building schools and training teachers. Before the Civil War, whites had deliberately kept slaves illiterate, and planter-dominated governments rarely spent tax money to educate the children of yeomen. By 1875, half of Mississippi's and South Carolina's eligible children (the majority of whom were black) attended school. Persistent underfunding meant too few schools, dilapidated facilities, and poorly trained teachers, but literacy rates rose sharply nevertheless. Although public schools were racially segregated, education remained for blacks a tangible, deeply satisfying benefit of freedom and Republican rule.

Second, states attacked racial discrimination and defended civil rights. Republicans especially resisted efforts by whites to establish separate facilities for blacks in public transportation. Texas replaced its law requiring segregation in its railroads with one that outlawed seating by race. Mississippi went further, levying fines of up to $1,000 and three years in jail for railroads, steamboats, hotels, and theaters that denied "full and equal rights" to all citizens. But passing color-blind laws was one thing; enforcing them was another. Fiercely determined that the South remain a white man's preserve, white Southerners sought to demonstrate the continued mastery of whites and the social inferiority of blacks. Segregation—the separation of blacks and whites in public places—developed at white insistence despite the law and became a feature of southern life long before the end of Reconstruction.

Third, Republican governments launched ambitious programs of economic development. They envisioned a South of diversified agriculture, roaring factories, and booming towns. Republican legislatures chartered scores of banks and industrial companies, appropriated funds to fix ruined levees

and to drain swamps, and initiated a vigorous program of internal improvements. The South went on a railroad-building binge, repairing old lines and adding some seven thousand miles of track during Reconstruction. The mania for railroads and state-sponsored economic development fell far short of solving the South's economic troubles, however. Republican spending to stimulate economic growth meant rising taxes and enormous debt that drained funds from schools and other programs.

The southern Republicans' record, then, was mixed. None of the initiatives in education, civil rights, or economic growth was an unqualified success. To their credit, the biracial Republican coalition had taken up an ambitious agenda to change the South. Success would have been difficult under the best of circumstances. As it was, money was scarce. In addition, Democrats kept up a constant drumbeat of harassment, while factionalism threatened the party from within. Moreover, corruption infected Republican governments in the South. Public morality reached new lows everywhere in the nation after the Civil War, and the chaos and disruption of the postwar South proved fertile soil for bribery, fraud, and influence peddling. Despite all of its problems and shortcomings, however, the Republican Party had made headway in its early efforts to purge the South of aristocratic privilege and racist oppression.

White Landlords, Black Sharecroppers

Reconstruction politics did not arise within a vacuum. Sharp dissatisfaction with conditions in the southern countryside politicized blacks and fueled political upheaval. On farms and plantations, freedmen confronted ex-masters who persisted in believing that blacks were unfit for free labor. A Tennessee man declared two years after the end of the war that blacks were "a trifling set of lazy devils who will never make a living without Masters." Blacks responded that if any class was lazy, it was the masters, "who lived in idleness all of their lives on stolen labor." Clashes occurred daily between ex-slaves who wished to take control of the conditions of their own labor and ex-masters who wanted to reinstitute old ways.

The system of agricultural labor that emerged in 1865 grew out of the labor program begun during the war by the federal military. When the war ended, supervision shifted to the Freedmen's Bureau, which renewed the army's campaign to restore production by binding black laborers and

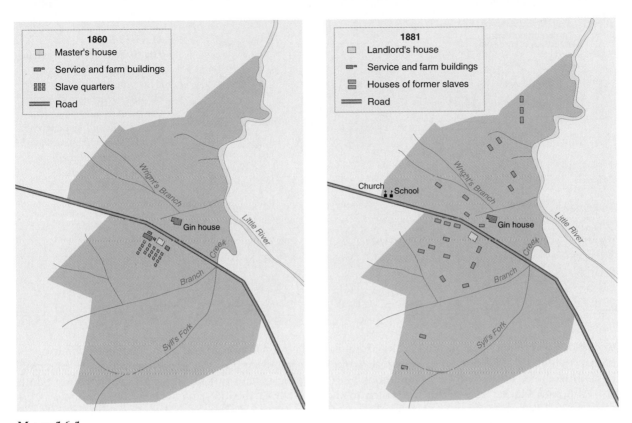

M A P 16.1

A Southern Plantation in 1860 and 1881

The maps of the Barrow plantation in Georgia illustrate some of the ways that ex-slaves expressed their freedom. Former slaves deserted the clustered living quarters behind the Big House, scattered over the plantation, built new family cabins, and farmed rented land. These ex-slaves also worked together to build a school and a church.

planters with wage contracts. Except for having to put down the whip and pay subsistence wages, planters were not required to offer many concessions to emancipation. Instead, they moved quickly to restore the antebellum world of work gangs, white overseers, field labor for black women and children, clustered cabins, minimal personal freedom, and even corporal punishment whenever they could get away with it.

Ex-slaves resisted every effort to roll back the clock. "The fact is, the colored people are very anxious to get land of their own to live upon independently," one black man remarked, "and they want money to buy stock [mules] to make crops." Disgusted planters confirmed that freedmen wanted to become "landholders" and not "hirelings." Blacks were equally determined to end planters' involvement in their personal lives. They wanted, for ex-

ample, to make their own decisions about whether women and children would labor in the fields. Indeed, within months after the war, black women (perhaps one-third of them) abandoned field labor and began working full time within their own households. Moreover, hundreds of thousands of black children enrolled in school.

The freedmen's dream of landownership never came true. Despite the ex-slaves' political agitation, Congress and southern legislatures refused to confiscate the planters' land. And without political intervention, landownership proved to be beyond the reach of all but a small fraction of blacks. Poverty-stricken freedmen were lucky to have two nickels to rub together, and few white people would offer them credit to purchase real estate. Even blacks who had money discovered that planters resisted selling them land. Whites who contemplated selling land

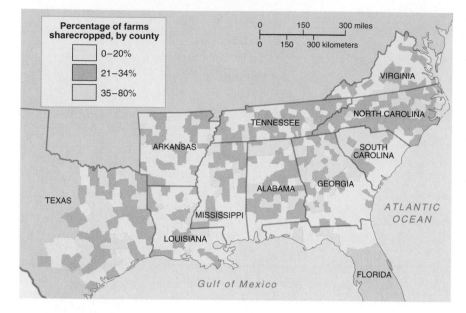

Percentage of farms sharecropped, by county
- 0–20%
- 21–34%
- 35–80%

0   150   300 miles
0   150   300 kilometers

VIRGINIA

NORTH CAROLINA

TENNESSEE

ARKANSAS

SOUTH CAROLINA

TEXAS

ALABAMA

GEORGIA

MISSISSIPPI

ATLANTIC OCEAN

LOUISIANA

FLORIDA

Gulf of Mexico

MAP 16.2
The Sharecropping System in the South, 1880
Fifteen years after the end of the Civil War, sharecropping dominated southern agriculture. White and black farmers found themselves enmeshed in a system that left them landless and impoverished.

to blacks knew they risked midnight raids from unhappy neighbors. Without land, ex-slaves would have little choice but to work on plantations.

Although blacks were forced to return to the planters' fields, freedmen resisted efforts to restore slavelike conditions. By working fewer days and shorter hours, by boycotting annual contracts, by striking, and by abandoning the most reactionary employers, they sought to force concessions. A tug-of-war between white landlords and black laborers took place on thousands of farms and plantations and out of it emerged sharecropping, a new system of southern agriculture.

Sharecropping was a compromise that offered both ex-masters and ex-slaves something but satisfied neither. Under the new system, planters divided their cotton plantations into small farms of twenty-five to thirty acres that freedmen rented, paying with a share of each year's crop, usually half. Sharecropping gave blacks more freedom than labor gangs and released them from the day-to-day supervision of whites. It meant that black families could now decide who would work, for how long, and how hard. Moreover, even half a crop seemed to promise a princely income after the subsistence of slavery and the puny wages of the Freedmen's Bureau's contract system. Still, most blacks remained dependent on the white landlord, who retained the power to expel them at the end of each season. For planters, sharecropping offered a way to resume agricultural production, but it did not allow them to reinstitute the unified plantation sys-

tem or to administer what they considered necessary discipline. An experiment at first, sharecropping spread quickly throughout the cotton South. By 1870, the old gang system, direct white supervision, and clustered black living quarters were fading memories. As increasing numbers of white yeomen lost their land in the downward spiral of postwar southern agriculture, moreover, sharecropping ensnared small white farmers as well as black farmers.

Reconstruction Collapses

By 1870, Northerners looked forward to putting "the southern problem" behind them. They had written guarantees of civil and political rights for blacks into the Constitution and enacted a program of political reunification that had restored ex-Confederate states to the Union. Now, after a decade of engagement with the public issues of war and reconstruction, they wanted to turn to their own affairs. In Washington, matters that had taken a back- seat to the southern problem—economic development, foreign policy, scandal and corruption —clamored for attention. Increasingly, practical business-minded men came to the forefront of the Republican Party, replacing the band of reformers and idealists who had been prominent in the 1860s. Civil War hero Ulysses S. Grant succeeded Andrew Johnson as president in 1869 and quickly became an issue himself, proving that brilliance on the battle-field does not necessarily translate into competence in the White House.

Each year, events in the South received less of the North's attention. Reconstruction slipped further into the background, and Northerners signaled growing unwillingness to intervene in southern affairs. While northern resolve to defend black freedom withered, southern commitment to white supremacy intensified. Throughout the South, Democrats redoubled their attack on Republican rule. Without northern protection, southern Republicans were no match for the Democrats' economic coercion, political corruption, and violence. One by one, Republican state governments fell. The election of 1876 both confirmed and completed the collapse of reconstruction.

The Grant Regime: Cronies, Corruption, and Economic Collapse

When the Civil War ended, Ulysses S. Grant was easily the most popular man in the nation, at least north of the Mason-Dixon line. But the return of peace meant that the general risked slipping back into his former obscurity. Determined to avoid that fate, he settled in Washington and plunged into reconstruction politics, playing the political game on the dangerous middle ground between President Andrew Johnson and Congress. Lesser men might not have survived the crossfire, but Grant shrewdly maneuvered between the warring factions. At first he appeared to be Johnson's man, but during the impeachment crisis he broke with the president and linked arms with Congress.

While northern resolve to defend black free-dom withered, southern commitment to white supremacy intensified.

Grant was the obvious choice for the Republican Party's presidential nomination in 1868. Radicals preferred someone with a deeper moral commitment to black equality, but Grant supported congressional reconstruction and that was enough for the Republican convention. The Democrats chose Horatio Seymour, former governor of New York. Their platform blasted congressional reconstruction as "a flagrant usurpation of power . . . unconstitutional, revolutionary, and void." Republi-

cans answered by "waving the bloody shirt," that is, they reminded the voters that the Democrats were "the party of rebellion," the party that stubbornly resisted a just peace. During the campaign, the Ku Klux Klan erupted in another reign of terror, murdering hundreds of southern Republicans. Terrorist tactics cut into Grant's tally, but he gained a narrow 300,000-vote margin in the popular vote and a substantial victory (214 votes to 80) in the electoral college.

Grant understood that most Northerners had grown weary of reconstruction. Conservative business-minded Northerners had become convinced that recurrent federal intrusion was itself a major cause of instability. Eager to invest in the South and especially to resume the profitable cotton trade, they sought order, not disruption. A growing number of northern Republican leaders began to question the wisdom of their party's alliance with the South's lower classes—its small farmers and sharecroppers. Grant's secretary of the interior, Jacob D. Cox of Ohio, proposed allying with the "thinking and influential native southerners . . . the intelligent, well-to-do, and controlling class."

The talents Grant had demonstrated on the battlefield—decisiveness, clarity, and resolution—deserted him in the White House. Unclear about his objectives, he grew tentative, unsure of himself, and bewildered. He gave the impression of a good man who was in over his head. Able advisers might have helped, but Grant surrounded himself with fumbling kinfolk and old cronies from his army days. He increasingly hobnobbed with the rich and powerful, even frequenting their expensive tailors. Grant was slow to realize that it was the desire for personal gain, not loyalty to him, that caused bankers and businessmen to cozy up to him. He also made a string of dubious appointments that led to a series of damaging scandals. Charges of corruption tainted his vice president, Schuyler Colfax, and brought down his secretary of war and secretary of the navy as well as his private secretary. Grant's dogged loyalty to liars and cheats only compounded the damage. While never personally implicated in any scandal, Grant was guilty of extreme gullibility. Before long, his administration was synonymous in many people's minds with greed, graft, and corruption.

Grant could not fairly be held responsible for the low moral tone that characterized the entire nation after the Civil War. New inventions, new technology, and new forms of business organization fed feverish growth throughout the economy. The head-

"I BEG TO REPEAT THAT THESE FRAUDS ON THE GOVERNMENT SHALL BE PROBED TO THE VERY BOTTOM."

TAMMANY RING.
CANAL RING.
WHISKEY RING.
INDIAN RING
PRESS RING.
STATE RING
COUNTY RING
TOWN RING
WARD RING

BELKNAP

FRAUD CLAIMS

BACK PAY GRAB

WHISKEY FRAUDS

BRIBERY

GRANT AND SCANDAL
This anti-Grant cartoon by the nation's most celebrated political cartoonist, Thomas Nast, shows the president falling headfirst into the barrel of fraud and corruption that tainted his administration. During Grant's eight years in the White House, many in his administration failed him. Sometimes duped, sometimes merely loyal, Grant stubbornly defended wrongdoers, even to the point of perjuring himself to keep an aide out of jail.
Library of Congress.

long advance provided enormous opportunity for graft and corruption. Democrats stole at least as brazenly as Republicans. The Tweed Ring, the Democratic political machine in New York City, pocketed some $200 million of the citizens' money. The buying and selling of politicians at the state level dwarfed federal corruption. It was said that the Standard Oil Company could do anything it wanted with the Pennsylvania legislature except refine it. The spoils system, by which victorious parties rewarded loyal workers with public office, had become a fixture of public life before Grant moved into the White House. Still, Grant was aggravatingly naive and his administration filled with rot.

In 1872, disgusted anti-Grant Republicans bolted and launched a third party, the Liberal Republicans. The Liberals promised to create a government "which the best people of this country will be proud of." They condemned the Grant regime as a riot of vulgarity—crude graft, tasteless materialism, and blatant anti-intellectualism. To clean up the mess, they proposed ending the spoils system and

replacing it with a nonpartisan civil service commission that would oversee competitive examinations for appointment to office. Moreover, they demanded that the government remove federal troops from the South and restore "home rule." Democrats especially liked the Liberal's southern policy, and the Democratic Party endorsed the Liberal presidential candidate, Horace Greeley, the longtime editor of the *New York Tribune.* Despite Grant's problems, however, the nation still felt enormous affection for the man who had saved the Union. In the 1872 election, voters gave him 56 percent of the popular vote, the most lopsided victory since Andrew Jackson swept into the White House forty-four years earlier.

Grant was not without accomplishments during his eight years as president. Ironically, he scored his greatest triumph on an issue he cared little about: the settlement of the U.S. claim against Great Britain for wartime damages caused by British-built Confederate ships. When Britain denied any wrongdoing, tempers flared. But in 1872, Hamilton Fish,

Grant's able secretary of state, skillfully orchestrated a peaceful settlement that paid the United States $15.5 million in damages.

Grant's great passion in foreign affairs—annexation of Santo Domingo in the Caribbean—ended in utter failure. Grant argued that the acquisition of this tropical land would permit the United States to expand its trade in the Caribbean and simultaneously provide a new home for the South's blacks, who were so desperately harassed by the Klan. Aggressive foreign policy had not originated with the Grant administration. Lincoln and Johnson's secretary of state, William H. Seward, had thwarted French efforts to set up a puppet empire under Maximilian in Mexico, and his purchase of Alaska ("Seward's Ice Box") from Russia in 1867 for only $7 million had fired Grant's imperial ambitions. But the Republican Party split over the president's scheme to acquire Santo Domingo, and in the end Grant could not marshal the votes needed to approve the treaty of annexation.

The Grant administration was caught up in a tangle of complicated economic problems, but by far Grant's most difficult was the depression that began in 1873. Railroads, which had fueled the postwar boom, led directly to the bust. Jay Cooke, head of a major Philadelphia bank, had poured enormous sums into railroads, became overextended with debt, and went under, initiating the panic of 1873. Like dominoes, other companies failed, and soon the nation sank into its most severe depression to that time. More than 18,000 businesses collapsed in two years, and more than one million workers lost their jobs. Urban dwellers who were lucky enough to avoid unemployment saw their wages shrivel by 25 percent while food costs declined only 5 percent. Government relief did not exist, and private charities were swamped. Desperate times arrived at the doorsteps of most working people. Industrial violence kept pace with economic hardship. The violence subsided as men and women returned to work, but only at the end of the decade did the depression lift. By then, southern Republican governments had fallen, and the experiment of reconstruction had ended.

Northern Resolve Withers

Although Northerners wanted desperately to shift their attention to the new issues, the old ones would not go away. When southern Republicans pleaded for federal protection from Klan violence, Congress enacted three laws in 1870 and 1871 that were intended to break the back of white terrorism. The severest of the three, the Ku Klux Klan Act, made interference with voting rights a felony and authorized the use of the army to enforce it. Intrepid federal marshals arrested thousands of suspected Klansmen. While the government came close to destroying the Klan, it did not end terrorism against blacks. Congress also passed the Civil Rights Act of 1875, which boldly outlawed racial discrimination in transportation, public accommodations, and juries. But federal authorities did little to enforce the law, and segregated facilities remained the rule throughout the South.

In reality, the retreat from reconstruction had begun in 1868 with Grant's election. Grant genuinely wanted to see blacks' civil and political rights protected, but he felt uneasy about an open-ended commitment that seemed to ignore constitutional limitations on federal power. Like his predecessor, he distributed pardons liberally and encouraged the passage of a general amnesty. In May 1872, Congress obliged and restored the right of officeholding to all but three hundred ex-rebels. Radicals did what they could to stiffen the North's resolve, but reform had lost its principal spokesmen. By 1874, Charles Sumner, Thaddeus Stevens, and Salmon Chase were all dead. Others, such as Benjamin Wade of Pennsylvania, had lost their seats in Congress. Still others had washed their hands of reconstruction, concluding that the quest for black equality was mistaken or hopelessly naive. Republicans who bolted to the Liberal Republican Party, for example, welcomed the South's "best people" back to power. Traditional white leaders, it seemed to them, offered the best hope for honesty, order, and prosperity.

The North's abandonment of reconstruction rested on more than weariness, greed, and disillusionment. Underlying everything was unyielding racial prejudice. Emancipation failed to uproot racism in either the South or the North. During the war, Northerners had learned to accept black freedom, but deep-seated prejudice prevented many from equating freedom with equality. Even the actions that they took on behalf of blacks often served partisan political advantage. Whether they expressed it quietly or boisterously, Northerners generally supported Indiana Senator Thomas A. Hendricks's declaration that "this is a white man's Government, made by the white man for the white man." Increasingly, when Radicals asked Northerners to remember reconstruction's victims, northern sympathy went out to white Southerners.

The U.S. Supreme Court also did its part to undermine reconstruction. From the first, Republicans had feared that the conservative Court would declare their southern policies unconstitutional. Indeed, at times the Court gave the impression of seeking to dismantle reconstruction. In the 1870s, a series of Court decisions significantly weakened the federal government's ability to protect black Southerners under the Fourteenth and Fifteenth Amendments. In the *Slaughterhouse* cases (1873), the Court distinguished between national and state citizenship and ruled that the Fourteenth Amendment protected only those rights that stemmed from the federal government. Since the Court decided that most rights derived from the states, it sharply curtailed the federal government's authority to protect black citizens. Even more devastating, the *United States v. Cruikshank* (1876) ruling said that the reconstruction amendments gave Congress power to legislate only against discrimination by states, not by individuals. The "suppression of ordinary crime," such as assault, remained a state responsibility. The Supreme Court did not declare reconstruction unconstitutional, but it gradually undermined its legal foundation.

The mood of the North found political expression in the election of 1874, when for the first time in eighteen years the Democrats gained control of the House of Representatives. Voters blamed the Grant administration for the economic hard times that had begun the previous year, but they also sent a message about reconstruction. As one Republican observed, the people had grown tired of the "negro question, with all its complications, and the reconstruction of the Southern States, with all its interminable embroilments." Voters turned to the Democrats, who had from the beginning attacked reconstruction as unconstitutional, unnatural, and unwise. After 1874, even the most stubborn Republicans knew that perpetuating reconstruction was political suicide.

Reconstruction had come apart in the North. Congress gradually abandoned it. President Grant grew increasingly unwilling to enforce it. The Supreme Court busily denied the constitutionality of significant parts of it. And the people sent unmistakable messages that they were tired of it. Rather than defend reconstruction from its southern enemies, Northerners backed away from the challenge. After the early 1870s, southern blacks faced the forces of reaction largely on their own.

White Supremacy Triumphs

Republican governments in the South attracted more bitterness and hatred than any other political regimes in American history. In the eyes of the majority of whites, each day of Republican rule produced fresh insults: Black militia patrolled town streets, black laborers negotiated contracts with former masters, black maids stood up to former mistresses, black voters cast ballots, and black legislators enacted laws. The northern retreat from reconstruction permitted southern Democrats to harness this white rage to politics. Taking the name "Redeemers," they promised to replace "bayonet

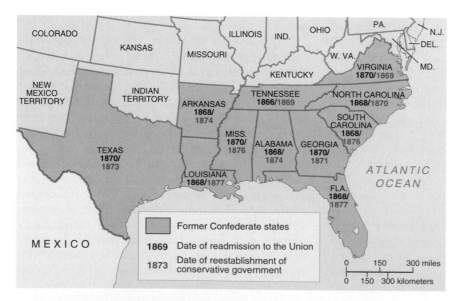

M a p 16.3
The Reconstruction of the South
Myth has it that Republican rule of the former Confederacy was not only harsh but long. In most states, however, conservative southern whites stormed back into power in only a matter of a couple of months or a very few years. By the election of 1876, Republican governments could be found in only three states. And they soon fell.

rule" (federal troops continued to be stationed in the South) with "home rule" (white southern control). They branded Republican governments a carnival of extravagance, waste, and fraud and promised that honest, thrifty Democrats would supplant the irresponsible tax-and-spend Republicans. Above all, they swore to save civilization from a descent into African "barbarism" and "negro rule." As one Redeemer put it, "We must render this either a white man's government, or convert the land into a Negro man's cemetery."

The Republican governments bore little resemblance to the Redeemer stereotypes. Nevertheless, numerous problems plagued their experiment in biracial democracy and made them vulnerable to attack. Republicans often promised more than they could deliver. Efforts to solve the massive economic problems of the devastated South often misfired. And while Democrats exaggerated in charging that "greed was unchecked and roguery unabashed," kickbacks, payoffs, and scams were common. But southern Republicans had no monopoly on corruption. During the Grant era, political dishonesty knew no particular party, region, or race.

By the early 1870s, however, Democrats understood that race was their most potent weapon. They adopted a two-pronged racial strategy to overthrow Republican governments. First, they sought to polarize the parties around color, and, second, they relentlessly intimidated black voters. They went about gathering all the South's white voters into the Democratic Party, leaving the Republicans to depend on blacks. The "straight-out" appeal to whites promised great advantage because whites made up a majority of the population in every southern state except Mississippi, South Carolina, and Louisiana.

Republican governments in the South attracted more bitterness and hatred than any other political regimes in American history.

Democrats employed several devices to dislodge whites from the Republican Party. First and foremost, they fanned the flames of racial prejudice. In South Carolina, a Democrat crowed that his party appealed to the "proud Caucasian race, whose sovereignty on earth God has proclaimed." Ostracism also proved effective. Local newspapers published the names of whites who kept company with blacks. So complete was the ostracism that one of its victims said, "No white man can live in the South in

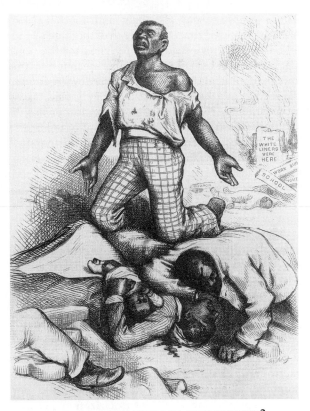

IS THIS A REPUBLICAN FORM OF GOVERNMENT?
This powerful 1876 drawing by Thomas Nast depicts the end of Reconstruction as the tragedy it was. As white supremacists in the South piled up more and more bodies, supporters of civil rights accused the Grant administration of failing to protect black Southerners and legitimately elected governments. They pointed specifically to the constitutional requirement that "[t]he United States shall guarantee to every State in this Union a Republican Form of Government, and shall protect each of them . . . against domestic violence" (Article IV, section 4).
Library of Congress.

the future and act with any other than the Democratic party unless he is willing and prepared to live a life of social isolation."

In addition, Democrats exploited the small white farmer's severe economic plight by blaming it on Republican financial policy. Government spending soared during Reconstruction, and small farmers saw their tax burden skyrocket. Farms in Mississippi were taxed at four times the prewar level. When cotton prices fell by nearly 50 percent in the 1870s, yeomen farmers found cash in short supply. To pay their taxes, one man observed, "people are selling every egg and chicken they can get."

Those unable to pay lost their land. In 1871, Mississippi reported that one-seventh of the state's land —3,300,000 acres—had been forfeited for the non-payment of taxes. The small farmer's economic distress had a racial dimension. Because few freedmen succeeded in acquiring land, they rarely paid taxes. In Georgia in 1874, blacks made up 46 percent of the population but paid only 2 percent of the taxes. From the perspective of the small white farmer, Republican rule meant not only that he was paying more taxes but that he was paying them to aid blacks. Democrats asked whether it was not time for hard-pressed yeomen to join the white man's party.

If racial pride, social isolation, and Republican financial policies proved insufficient to drive yeomen from the Republican Party, Democrats turned to terrorism. "Night riders" targeted scalawags as well as blacks for murder and assassination. By the early 1870s, then, only a fraction of southern whites any longer claimed allegiance to the party of Lincoln. White yeomen were willing for a time (as they would be again late in the century) to rise above racism and link arms with blacks to improve their common welfare, but the Republicans could not hold their allegiance. Racial polarization became a reality, and rich and poor whites united in opposition to reconstruction. Yeoman defection to the Redeemers proved a heavy blow to southern Republicanism.

The second prong of Democratic strategy—intimidation of black voters—proved equally devastating. Antiblack political violence escalated to unprecedented levels. In 1873 in Louisiana, a clash between black militiamen and gun-toting whites killed two white men and an estimated seventy black men. Half of the latter were slaughtered after they had surrendered. Although the federal government indicted more than one hundred white men, local juries failed to convict a single one.

Even before adopting the all-out white supremacist tactics of the 1870s, Democrats had already captured Virginia, Tennessee, and North Carolina. The new campaign brought fresh gains. The Redeemers regained Georgia in 1872, Texas in 1873, and Arkansas and Alabama in 1874. In 1875, Mississippi fell. The story in Mississippi was one of open, unrelenting, and often savage intimidation of black voters and their few remaining white allies. Planters warned the black sharecroppers who rented land from them: Vote Republican and find yourselves on the road. Whites used the flimsiest

pretext to hunt down and shoot blacks who kept the Republican faith. In a "riot" in Vicksburg, Mississippi, thirty-five blacks and two whites lost their lives. As the state election approached in 1875, Republican Governor Adelbert Ames appealed to Washington for federal troops to control the violence, only to hear from the attorney general that the "whole public are tired of these annual autumnal outbreaks in the South." Abandoned, Mississippi Republicans succumbed to the Democratic onslaught in the fall elections. By 1876, only three Republican state governments—in Florida, Louisiana, and South Carolina—survived.

An Election and a Compromise

The centennial year of 1876 witnessed one of the most tumultuous elections in American history. Its chaos and confusion provided a fitting conclusion to the experiment known as reconstruction. The election took place in November, but not until March 2 of the following year, at 4 A.M., did the nation know who would be inaugurated president on March 4. For four months the country suffered through a constitutional and political crisis that jeopardized the peaceful transfer of power from one administration to the next. Sixteen years after Lincoln's election, Americans feared that a presidential contest would again precipitate civil war.

The Democrats had nominated New York's reform governor, Samuel J. Tilden, who immediately targeted the corruption of the Grant administration and the despotism of Republican reconstruction. The Republicans put forward a reformer of their own, Rutherford B. Hayes, governor of Ohio. Privately, Hayes considered "bayonet rule" a mistake, but he concluded that waving the bloody shirt, as threadbare as it was, remained the Republicans' best political strategy. "It leads people away from 'hard times,' which is our deadliest foe," Hayes said lamely.

On election day, Tilden tallied 4,284,000 votes to Hayes's 4,036,000. Yet in the all-important electoral college, Tilden fell one vote short of the majority required for victory. However, the electoral votes of three states remained in doubt and thus were uncounted. Both Democrats and Republicans claimed the nineteen votes of South Carolina, Louisiana, and Florida, the only remaining Republican strongholds in the South. To win, Tilden needed only one of the contested votes. Hayes had to have all of them to take the election. The two par-

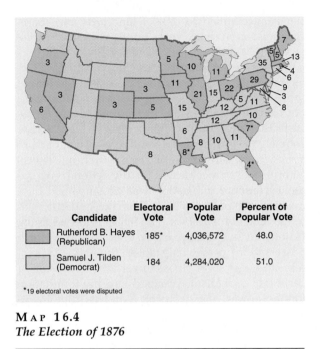

Candidate	Electoral Vote	Popular Vote	Percent of Popular Vote
Rutherford B. Hayes (Republican)	185*	4,036,572	48.0
Samuel J. Tilden (Democrat)	184	4,284,020	51.0

*19 electoral votes were disputed

MAP 16.4
The Election of 1876

ties traded charges of fraud and intimidation. To be sure, Republicans had stuffed some ballot boxes, but stepped-up violence by the Democrats had kept hundreds of thousands of southern Republicans from the polls.

Congress had to decide who had actually won the elections in the three southern states and thus who would be president. The Constitution provided little guidance. Moreover, Democrats controlled the House, and Republicans the Senate. To break the deadlock, Congress created a special electoral commission to arbitrate the disputed returns. An odd and cumbersome compromise, the commission was made up of five representatives (two Republicans, three Democrats), five senators (two Democrats, three Republicans), and five justices of the Supreme Court (two Republicans, two Democrats, and David Davis, considered to be an independent). But before the commission could meet, the Illinois legislature elected Justice Davis to the Senate. The other four justices filled his place with Justice Joseph Bradley, a fair-minded man but decidedly a Republican. The commissioners all voted the straight party line, giving every state to Hayes and putting him over the top in electoral votes.

Some outraged Democrats vowed to resist Hayes's victory. But the impasse was broken when negotiations behind the scenes between Hayes's lieutenants and some moderate southern Demo-

crats resulted in an informal understanding, known as the Compromise of 1877. In exchange for a Democratic promise not to block Hayes's inauguration and to deal fairly with the freedmen, Hayes vowed not to use the army to uphold the remaining Republican regimes. The South would also gain substantial federal subsidies for internal improvements. Less than two days later, the nation observed Hayes's peaceful inauguration.

Stubborn Tilden supporters bemoaned the "stolen election" and damned "His Fraudulency," Rutherford B. Hayes. Old-guard radicals such as William Lloyd Garrison denounced Hayes's bargain as a "policy of compromise, of credulity, of weakness, of subserviency, of surrender." But the nation as a whole celebrated. The Republic had weathered a grave crisis, and it had ended reconstruction. The last three Republican state governments fell quickly once Hayes abandoned them. The Compromise of 1877 confirmed the conservatism that had been growing in the North for years. New priorities meant that Northerners no longer wanted to intervene in the South, and, even without a deal, Hayes would probably have withdrawn the troops.

The nation's solution to this last sectional crisis marked a return to the antebellum tradition of sectional compromise. As in previous crises, whites had found a way to bridge their differences and retain the peace, and again blacks had paid the price. In 1877, Republicans followed a path of expediency and gained the presidency. Southern Democrats got home rule and a free hand in racial matters. When reconstruction ended, black Southerners were not completely subordinated to whites, but their prospects in the New South looked bleak.

Conclusion: "A Revolution but Half-Accomplished"

In 1865, when General Carl Schurz visited the South at President Andrew Johnson's behest, he discovered "a revolution but half-accomplished." Defeat had not prepared the South for an easy transition from slavery to free labor, from white racial despotism to equal justice, and from white political monopoly to biracial democracy. The old elite wanted to get "things back as near to slavery as possible," while ex-slaves and whites who had lacked power in the slave regime were eager to exploit the revolutionary implications of defeat and emancipation.

Congress pushed the revolution along. Although it refused to provide an economic underpinning to black freedom, it required defeated Confederates to accept legal equality and share political power. But conservative whites fought ferociously to recover their power and privilege. When they regained control of politics, they used the power of the state, along with private violence, to wipe out many of the gains of reconstruction. A visitor to the South in the late 1870s would have seen a landscape reminiscent of antebellum days. Blacks were back in the fields and kitchens, cotton had resumed its throne, and white Southerners again controlled the courthouses and state houses. So successful were the reactionaries that one observer concluded that the North had won the war but the South had won the peace.

But the Redeemer counterrevolution did not mean a return to slavery. Freedom meant something, and blacks knew it best. Abolition destroyed the old plantation of slavery days, and ex-slaves gained the freedom not to be whipped or sold, to send their children to school, to worship in their own churches, and to work independently on their own rented farms. The lives of impoverished sharecroppers overflowed with miseries and hardships, but even sharecropping provided more autonomy and economic welfare than bondage had. It was limited freedom, to be sure, but it was not slavery.

Emancipation set in motion the most profound upheaval in the nation's history, and nothing whites could do could entirely erase its revolutionary effects. War destroyed the richest and largest slave society in the New World. It cost masters $3 billion in lost property and destroyed the foundation of planter wealth. Slavery had defined the antebellum South, and abolition overturned the social and economic order that had dominated the region for nearly two centuries. The world of masters and slaves succumbed to that of landlords and sharecroppers. Even today, some Southerners divide history into "before the war" and "after the war."

The Civil War and emancipation mark a watershed not just in the South's history but in that of the entire nation. The scope of the revolution was not fully apparent in the 1870s, but already it was clear that the country had embarked on a new course. War had served as midwife for the birth of a modern nation-state, and for the first time sovereignty rested uncontested in the federal government. National unification was accompanied by a massive shift of power away from the landed classes to the new industrialists. The South returned to the Union, but as a junior partner. The victorious North possessed the power to establish the nation's direction, and it set its compass toward the expansion of corporate capitalism. War had laid the foundation for the power of big business and its captains in postwar America.

Still, the Civil War remained only a "half-accomplished" revolution. As such, Reconstruction represents a tragedy of enormous proportions. The nation did not fulfill the promises that it seemed to hold out to black Americans at war's end. The revolution raced forward, halted, and then slipped back, coming to rest far short of equality and justice. The failure had enduring consequences. Almost a century after reconstruction, the nation would embark on what one observer called a "second reconstruction," another effort to fulfill nineteenth-century promises. Many of the gains of the earlier reform effort had been negated, but the solid achievements of the Thirteenth, Fourteenth, and Fifteenth Amendments to the Constitution would provide a legal foundation for the renewed commitment. It is worth remembering, though, that it was only the failure of the first Reconstruction that made a modern civil rights movement necessary.

CHRONOLOGY

1863 **December.** Lincoln issues Proclamation of Amnesty and Reconstruction.

1864 **July.** Congress offers more stringent plan for reconstruction, Wade-Davis bill.

1865 **January.** General William T. Sherman sets aside land in South Carolina for black settlement.

March 4. Lincoln sworn in for second term as president of United States.

March. Congress establishes Freedmen's Bureau.

April 14. Lincoln shot, dies on April 15, is succeeded by Vice President Andrew Johnson.

Fall. Southern legislatures enact discriminatory black codes.

December. The Thirteenth Amendment abolishing slavery becomes part of U.S. Constitution.

1866   **April.** Congress approves Fourteenth Amendment making native-born blacks American citizens and guaranteeing all American citizens "equal protection under the laws." Amendment becomes part of Constitution in 1868.

April. Congress passes Civil Rights Act over President Johnson's veto.

May. Susan B. Anthony and Elizabeth Cady Stanton found Equal Rights Association to lobby for vote for women.

July. Congress extends Freedmen's Bureau over President Johnson's veto.

Summer. Ku Klux Klan founded in Tennessee.

November. Republicans triumph over Johnson in congressional elections.

1867   **March.** Congress passes Military Reconstruction Act imposing military

rule on South and requiring states to guarantee vote to black men.

1868   **March–May.** Senate impeachment trial of President Johnson results in acquittal.

November. Ulysses S. Grant elected president of the United States.

1869   **February.** Congress approves Fifteenth Amendment prohibiting racial discrimination in voting rights. Amendment becomes part of Constitution in 1870.

1871   **April.** Congress enacts Ku Klux Klan Act in effort to end white terrorism in South.

1872   **November.** President Grant reelected.

1873   Economic depression sets in for remainder of decade.

1874   **November.** Elections return Democratic majority to House of Representatives.

1875   **February.** Civil Rights Act of 1875 outlaws racial discrimination, but federal authorities do little to enforce law.

1877   **March.** Special congressional committee awards disputed electoral votes to Republican Rutherford B. Hayes, making him president of United States. Hayes agrees to pull military out of South.

BIBLIOGRAPHY

GENERAL WORKS

W. E. B. Du Bois, *Black Reconstruction in America* (1935).

Eric Foner, *Reconstruction: America's Unfinished Revolution, 1863–1877* (1988).

John Hope Franklin, *Reconstruction after the Civil War* (1961).

James M. McPherson, *Ordeal by Fire: The Civil War and Reconstruction* (1982).

Rembert W. Patrick, *The Reconstruction of the Nation* (1967).

J. G. Randall and David Donald, *The Civil War and Reconstruction* (1967).

Kenneth M. Stampp, *The Era of Reconstruction, 1865–1877* (1965).

WARTIME RECONSTRUCTION

Richard H. Abbott, *The First Southern Strategy: The Republican Party and the South, 1855–1877* (1986).

Herman Belz, *Emancipation and Equal Rights: Politics and Constitutionalism in the Civil War Era* (1978).

Ira Berlin et al., eds., *Freedom: A Documentary History of Emancipation, 1861–1867* (1982–).

Louis S. Gerteis, *From Contraband to Freedman: Federal Policy toward Southern Blacks, 1861–1865* (1973).

Peyton McCrary, *Abraham Lincoln and Reconstruction: The Louisiana Experiment* (1978).

William S. McFeely, *Yankee Stepfather: General O. O. Howard and the Freedmen* (1968).

James M. McPherson, *The Struggle for Equality: Abolitionists and the Negro in the Civil War and Reconstruction* (1964).

Willie Lee Rose, *Rehearsal for Reconstruction: The Port Royal Experiment* (1964).

Brooks D. Simpson, *Let Us Have Peace: Ulysses S. Grant and the Politics of War and Reconstruction, 1861–1868* (1991).

Hans L. Trefousse, *The Radical Republicans: Lincoln's Vanguard for Racial Justice* (1969).

PRESIDENTIAL RECONSTRUCTION

W. R. Brock, *An American Crisis: Congress and Reconstruction, 1865–1867* (1963).

Albert Castel, *The Presidency of Andrew Johnson* (1979).

LaWanda F. Cox and John H. Cox, *Politics, Principles, and Prejudice, 1865–1866* (1963).

David H. Donald, *The Politics of Reconstruction, 1863–1867* (1965).

Edward L. Gambill, *Conservative Ordeal: Northern Democrats and Reconstruction, 1865–1868* (1981).

Martin E. Mantell, *Johnson, Grant, and the Politics of Reconstruction* (1973).

Eric L. McKitrick, *Andrew Johnson and Reconstruction* (1966).

Donald G. Nieman, *To Set the Law in Motion: The Freedmen's Bureau and the Legal Rights of Blacks, 1865–1868* (1979).

J. Michael Quill, *Prelude to the Radicals: The North and Reconstruction during 1865* (1980).

Patrick W. Riddleberger, *1866: The Critical Year Revisited* (1979).

Robert D. Sawrey, *Dubious Victory: The Reconstruction Debate in Ohio* (1992).

James E. Sefton, *Andrew Johnson and the Uses of Constitutional Power* (1980).

Hans L. Trefousse, *Impeachment of a President: Andrew Johnson, the Blacks and Reconstruction* (1975).

Hans L. Trefousse, *Andrew Johnson: A Biography* (1989).

CONGRESSIONAL RECONSTRUCTION

Eric Anderson and Alfred A. Moss Jr., eds., *The Facts of Reconstruction: Essays in Honor of John Hope Franklin* (1991).

Michael Les Benedict, *The Impeachment and Trial of Andrew Johnson* (1973).

Michael Les Benedict, *A Compromise of Principle: Congressional Republicans and Reconstruction* (1974).

Richard F. Bensel, *Yankee Leviathan: The Origins of Central State Authority in America, 1859–1877* (1990).

Fawn M. Brodie, *Thaddeus Stevens: Scourge of the South* (1959).

David H. Donald, *Charles Sumner and the Rights of Man* (1970).

William Gillette, *The Right to Vote: Politics and the Passage of the Fifteenth Amendment* (1965).

Victor B. Howard, *Religion and the Radical Republican Movement, 1860–1870* (1990).

Harold M. Hyman, *A More Perfect Union: The Impact of the Civil War and Reconstruction on the Constitution* (1973).

Stanley Kutler, *The Judicial Power and Reconstruction Politics* (1968).

Michael L. Lanza, *Agrarianism and Reconstruction Politics: The Southern Homestead Act* (1990).

William S. McFeely, *Grant* (1981).

James C. Mohr, *The Radical Republicans and Reform in New York during Reconstruction* (1973).

David Montgomery, *Beyond Equality: Labor and the Radical Republicans, 1862–1872* (1967).

William E. Nelson, *The Fourteenth Amendment: From Political Principle to Judicial Doctrine* (1988).

Patrick W. Riddleberger, *George Washington Julian: Radical Republican* (1966).

Joel H. Silbey, *A Respectable Minority: The Democratic Party in the Civil War Era, 1860–1868* (1977).

Mark W. Summers, *Railroads, Reconstruction, and the Gospel of Prosperity* (1984).

Margaret S. Thompson, *The "Spider Web": Congress and Lobbying in the Age of Grant* (1985).

Hans L. Trefousse, *The Radical Republicans* (1963).

THE STRUGGLE IN THE SOUTH

James D. Anderson, *The Education of Blacks in the South, 1860–1935* (1988).

Stephen V. Ash, *Middle Tennessee Society Transformed, 1860–1870: War and Peace in the Upper South* (1988).

Dwight B. Billings Jr., *Planters and the Making of a "New South"* (1979).

Randolph B. Campbell, *A Southern Community in Crisis: Harrison County, Texas, 1850–1880* (1983).

Dan T. Carter, *When the War Was Over: The Failure of Self-Reconstruction in the South, 1865–1867* (1985).

Barry A. Crouch, *The Freedmen's Bureau and Black Texans* (1992).

Richard N. Current, *Those Terrible Carpetbaggers: A Reinterpretation* (1988).

Joseph G. Dawson III, *Army Generals and Reconstruction: Louisiana, 1862–1877* (1982).

Edmund L. Drago, *Black Politicians and Reconstruction in Georgia* (1982).

Barbara J. Fields, *Slavery and Freedom on the Middle Ground: Maryland during the Nineteenth Century* (1985).

Michael W. Fitzgerald, *The Union League Movement in the Deep South: Politics and Agricultural Change during Reconstruction* (1989).

Eric Foner, *Nothing but Freedom: Emancipation and Its Legacy* (1983).

Steven Hahn, *The Roots of Southern Populism: Yeoman Farmers and the Transformation of the Georgia Upcountry, 1850–1890* (1983).

William C. Harris, *Day of the Carpetbagger: Republican Reconstruction in Mississippi* (1979).

Janet Sharp Hermann, *The Pursuit of a Dream* (1981).

Thomas Holt, *Black over White: Negro Political Leadership in South Carolina during Reconstruction* (1977).

Elizabeth Jacoway, *Yankee Missionaries in the South* (1979).

Jacqueline Jones, *Soldiers of Light and Love: Northern Teachers and Georgia Blacks, 1865–1873* (1980).

Peter Kolchin, *First Freedom: The Responses of Alabama's Blacks to Emancipation and Reconstruction* (1972).

Leon F. Litwack, *Been in the Storm So Long: The Aftermath of Slavery* (1979).

Richard Lowe, *Republicans and Reconstruction in Virginia, 1865–1870* (1991).

Jay R. Mandle, *Not Slave, Not Free: The African American Economic Experience since the Civil War* (1992).

Donald Nieman, *To Set the Law in Motion: The Freedmen's Bureau and the Legal Rights of Blacks, 1865–1868* (1979).

Michael Perman, *Reunion without Compromise: The South and Reconstruction, 1865–1868* (1973).

Michael Perman, *The Road to Redemption: Southern Politics, 1869–1879* (1984).

Lawrence N. Powell, *New Masters: Northern Planters during the Civil War and Reconstruction* (1984).

Howard Rabinowitz, ed., *Southern Black Leaders of the Reconstruction Era* (1982).

George C. Rable, *But There Was No Peace: The Role of Violence in the Politics of Reconstruction* (1984).

Roger L. Ransom and Richard Sutch, *One Kind of Freedom: The Economic Consequences of Emancipation* (1977).

William L. Richter, *Overreached on All Sides: The Freedmen's Bureau Administrators in Texas, 1865–1868* (1991).

C. Peter Ripley, *Slaves and Freedmen in Civil War Louisiana* (1976).

James L. Roark, *Masters without Slaves: Southern Planters in the Civil War and Reconstruction* (1977).

James E. Sefton, *The United States Army and Reconstruction, 1865–1877* (1967).

Crandall A. Shifflett, *Patronage and Poverty in the Tobacco South: Louisa County, Virginia, 1860–1900* (1982).

Joe G. Taylor, *Louisiana Reconstructed* (1974).

Allen Trelease, *White Terror: The Ku Klux Klan Conspiracy and Southern Reconstruction* (1967).

Ted Tunnell, *Crucible of Reconstruction: War, Radicalism, and Race in Louisiana, 1862–1877* (1974).

Clarence E. Walker, *A Rock in a Weary Land: The African Methodist Episcopal Church during the Civil War and Reconstruction* (1982).

Peter Wallenstein, *From Slave South to New South: Public Policy in Nineteenth-Century Georgia* (1987).

Michael Wayne, *The Reshaping of Plantation Society: The Natchez District, 1860–1880* (1983).

Jonathan M. Wiener, *Social Origins of the New South, 1860–1885* (1978).

Joel Williamson, *After Slavery: The Negro in South Carolina during Reconstruction* (1966).

Sarah Woolfolk Wiggins, *The Scalawag in Alabama Politics, 1865–1881* (1977).

Gavin Wright, *Old South, New South: Revolutions in the Southern Economy since the Civil War* (1986).

COLLAPSE OF RECONSTRUCTION

William Gillette, *Retreat from Reconstruction, 1869–1879* (1979).

Otto H. Olsen, ed., *Reconstruction and Redemption in the South* (1980).

Ian Polakoff, *The Politics of Inertia: The Election of 1876 and the End of Reconstruction* (1973).

Terry L. Seip, *The South Returns to Congress: Men, Economic Measures, and Intersectional Relationships, 1868–1879* (1983).

John G. Sproat, *"The Best Men"* (1968).

C. Vann Woodward, *Reunion and Reaction: The Compromise of 1877 and the End of Reconstruction* (1951).

APPENDIX I. DOCUMENTS

THE DECLARATION OF INDEPENDENCE

In Congress, July 4, 1776,

**THE UNANIMOUS DECLARATION OF THE
THIRTEEN UNITED STATES OF AMERICA**

When in the course of human events, it becomes necessary for one people to dissolve the political bands which have connected them with another, and to assume, among the powers of the earth, the separate and equal station to which the laws of nature and of nature's God entitle them, a decent respect to the opinions of mankind requires that they should declare the causes which impel them to the separation.

We hold these truths to be self-evident, that all men are created equal; that they are endowed by their Creator with certain unalienable rights; that among these, are life, liberty, and the pursuit of happiness. That, to secure these rights, governments are instituted among men, deriving their just powers from the consent of the governed; that, whenever any form of government becomes destructive of these ends, it is the right of the people to alter or to abolish it, and to institute a new government, laying its foundation on such principles, and organizing its powers in such form, as to them shall seem most likely to effect their safety and happiness. Prudence, indeed, will dictate that governments long established, should not be changed for light and transient causes; and, accordingly, all experience hath shown, that mankind are more disposed to suffer, while evils are sufferable, than to right themselves by abolishing the forms to which they are accustomed. But, when a long train of abuses and usurpations, pursuing invariably the same object, evinces a design to reduce them under absolute despotism, it is their right, it is their duty, to throw off such government and to provide new guards for their future security. Such has been the patient sufferance of these colonies, and such is now the necessity which constrains them to alter their former systems of government. The history of the present King of Great Britain is a history of repeated injuries and usurpations, all having, in direct object, the establishment of an absolute tyranny over these States. To prove this, let facts be submitted to a candid world:

He has refused his assent to laws the most wholesome and necessary for the public good.

He has forbidden his governors to pass laws of immediate and pressing importance, unless suspended in their operation till his assent should be obtained; and, when so suspended, he has utterly neglected to attend to them.

He has refused to pass other laws for the accommodation of large districts of people, unless those people would relinquish the right of representation in the legislature; a right inestimable to them, and formidable to tyrants only.

He has called together legislative bodies at places unusual, uncomfortable, and distant from the depository of their public records, for the sole purpose of fatiguing them into compliance with his measures.

He has dissolved representative houses repeatedly for opposing, with manly firmness, his invasions on the rights of the people.

He has refused, for a long time after such dissolutions, to cause others to be elected; whereby the legislative powers, incapable of annihilation, have returned to the people at large for their exercise; the state remaining in the mean-time exposed to all the danger of invasion from without, and convulsions within.

He has endeavoured to prevent the population of these States; for that purpose, obstructing the laws for naturalization of foreigners, refusing to pass others to encourage their migration hither, and raising the conditions of new appropriations of lands.

He has obstructed the administration of justice, by refusing his assent to laws for establishing judiciary powers.

He has made judges dependent on his will alone, for the tenure of their offices, and the amount and payment of their salaries.

He has erected a multitude of new offices, and sent hither swarms of officers to harass our people, and eat out their substance.

He has kept among us, in times of peace, standing armies, without the consent of our legislature.

He has affected to render the military independent of, and superior to, the civil power.

He has combined, with others, to subject us to a jurisdiction foreign to our Constitution, and unacknowledged by our laws; giving his assent to their acts of pretended legislation:

For quartering large bodies of armed troops among us:

For protecting them by a mock trial, from punishment, for any murders which they should commit on the inhabitants of these States:

For cutting off our trade with all parts of the world:

For imposing taxes on us without our consent:

For depriving us, in many cases, of the benefit of trial by jury:

For transporting us beyond seas to be tried for pretended offences:

For abolishing the free system of English laws in a neighboring province, establishing therein an arbitrary government, and enlarging its boundaries, so as to render it at once an example and fit instrument for introducing the same absolute rule into these colonies:

For taking away our charters, abolishing our most valuable laws, and altering, fundamentally, the powers of our governments:

For suspending our own legislatures, and declaring themselves invested with power to legislate for us in all cases whatsoever.

He has abdicated government here, by declaring us out of his protection, and waging war against us.

He has plundered our seas, ravaged our coasts, burnt our towns, and destroyed the lives of our people.

He is, at this time, transporting large armies of foreign mercenaries to complete the works of death, desolation, and tyranny, already begun, with circumstances of cruelty and perfidy scarcely paralleled in the most barbarous ages, and totally unworthy the head of a civilized nation.

He has constrained our fellow citizens, taken captive on the high seas, to bear arms against their country, to become the executioners of their friends, and brethren, or to fall themselves by their hands.

He has excited domestic insurrections amongst us, and has endeavored to bring on the inhabitants of our frontiers, the merciless Indian savages, whose known rule of warfare is an undistinguished destruction of all ages, sexes, and conditions.

In every stage of these oppressions, we have petitioned for redress; in the most humble terms; our repeated petitions have been answered only by repeated injury. A prince, whose character is thus marked by every act which may define a tyrant, is unfit to be the ruler of a free people.

Nor have we been wanting in attention to our British brethren. We have warned them, from time to time, of attempts made by their legislature to extend an unwarrantable jurisdiction over us. We have reminded them of the circumstances of our emigration and settlement here. We have appealed to their native justice and magnanimity, and we have conjured them, by the ties of our common kindred, to disavow these usurpations, which would inevitably interrupt our connections and correspondence. They, too, have been deaf to the voice of justice and consanguinity. We must, therefore, acquiesce in the necessity which denounces our separation, and hold them as we hold the rest of mankind, enemies in war, in peace, friends.

We, therefore, the representatives of the United States of America, in general Congress assembled, appealing to the Supreme Judge of the world for the rectitude of our intentions, do, in the name, and by authority of the good people of these colonies, solemnly publish and declare, that these united colonies are, and of right ought to be, free and independent states: that they are absolved from all allegiance to the British Crown, and that all political connection between them and the state of Great Britain is, and ought to be, totally dissolved; and that, as free and independent states, they have full power to levy war, conclude peace, contract alliances, establish commerce, and to do all other acts and things which independent states may of right do. And, for the support of this declaration, with a firm reliance on the protection of Divine Providence, we mutually pledge to each other our lives, our fortunes, and our sacred honor.

The foregoing Declaration was, by order of Congress, engrossed, and signed by the following members:

JOHN HANCOCK

New Hampshire
Josiah Bartlett
William Whipple
Matthew Thornton

New York
William Floyd
Phillip Livingston
Francis Lewis
Lewis Morris

Massachusetts Bay
Samuel Adams
John Adams
Robert Treat Paine
Elbridge Gerry

New Jersey
Richard Stockton
John Witherspoon
Francis Hopkinson
John Hart
Abraham Clark

Rhode Island
Stephen Hopkins
William Ellery

Connecticut
Roger Sherman
Samuel Huntington
William Williams
Oliver Wolcott

Delaware
Caesar Rodney
George Read
Thomas M'Kean

Pennsylvania
Robert Morris
Benjamin Rush
Benjamin Franklin
John Morton
George Clymer
James Smith
George Taylor
James Wilson
George Ross

North Carolina
William Hooper
Joseph Hewes
John Penn

Maryland
Samuel Chase
William Paca
Thomas Stone
Charles Carroll,
   of Carrollton

Virginia
George Wythe
Richard Henry Lee
Thomas Jefferson
Benjamin Harrison
Thomas Nelson, Jr.
Francis Lightfoot Lee
Carter Braxton

South Carolina
Edward Rutledge
Thomas Heyward, Jr.
Thomas Lynch, Jr.
Arthur Middleton

Georgia
Button Gwinnett
Lyman Hall
George Walton

Resolved, That copies of the Declaration be sent to the several assemblies, conventions, and committees, or councils of safety, and to the several commanding officers of the continental troops; that it be proclaimed in each of the United States, at the head of the army.

THE CONSTITUTION OF THE UNITED STATES*

Preamble

We the people of the United States, in order to form a more perfect union, establish justice, insure domestic tranquility, provide for the common defense, promote the general welfare, and secure the blessings of liberty to ourselves and our posterity, do ordain and establish this Constitution for the United States of America.

Article I

Section 1   All legislative powers herein granted shall be vested in a Congress of the United States, which shall consist of a Senate and a House of Representatives.

Section 2   The House of Representatives shall be composed of members chosen every second year by the people of the several States, and the electors in each State shall have the qualifications requisite for electors of the most numerous branch of the State Legislature.

No person shall be a Representative who shall not have attained to the age of twenty-five years, and been seven years a citizen of the United States, and who shall not, when elected, be an inhabitant of that State in which he shall be chosen.

Representatives and direct taxes shall be apportioned among the several States which may be included within this Union, according to their respective numbers, *which shall be determined by adding to the whole number of free persons, including those bound to service for a term of years and excluding Indians not taxed, three-fifths of all other persons.* The actual enumeration shall be made within three years after the first meeting of the Congress of the United States, and within every subsequent term of ten years, in such manner as they shall by law direct. The number of Representatives shall not exceed one for every thirty thousand, but each State shall have at least one Representative; *and until such enumeration shall be made, the State of New Hampshire shall be entitled to choose three, Massachusetts eight, Rhode Island and Providence Plantations one, Connecticut five, New York six, New Jersey four, Pennsylvania eight, Delaware one, Maryland six, Virginia ten, North Carolina five, South Carolina five, and Georgia three.*

When vacancies happen in the representation from any State, the Executive authority thereof shall issue writs of election to fill such vacancies.

The House of Representatives shall choose their Speaker and other officers; and shall have the sole power of impeachment.

Section 3   The Senate of the United States shall be composed of two Senators from each State, *chosen by the legislature thereof,* for six years; and each Senator shall have one vote.

Immediately after they shall be assembled in consequence of the first election, they shall be divided as equally as may be into three classes. The seats of the Senators of the first class shall be vacated at the expiration of the second year, of the second class at the expiration of the fourth year, and of the third class at the expiration of the sixth year, so that one-third may be chosen every second year; *and if vacancies happen by resignation or otherwise, during the recess of the legislature of any State, the Executive thereof may make temporary appointments until the next meeting of the legislature, which shall then fill such vacancies.*

No person shall be a Senator who shall not have attained to the age of thirty years, and been nine years a citizen of the United States, and who shall not, when elected, be an inhabitant of that State for which he shall be chosen.

The Vice-President of the United States shall be President of the Senate, but shall have no vote, unless they be equally divided.

The Senate shall choose their other officers, and also a President *pro tempore,* in the absence of the Vice-President, or when he shall exercise the office of President of the United States.

The Senate shall have the sole power to try all impeachments. When sitting for that purpose, they shall be on oath or affirmation. When the President of the United States is tried, the Chief Justice shall preside: and no person shall be convicted without the concurrence of two-thirds of the members present.

Judgment in cases of impeachment shall not extend further than to removal from the office, and disqualification to hold and enjoy any office of honor, trust or profit under the United States: but the party convicted shall nevertheless be liable and subject to indictment, trial, judgment and punishment, according to law.

Section 4   The times, places and manner of holding elections for Senators and Representatives shall be prescribed in each State by the legislature thereof; but the Congress may at any time by law make or alter such regulations, except as to the places of choosing Senators.

---

*Passages no longer in effect are in italic type.

The Congress shall assemble at least once in every year, and such meeting *shall be on the first Monday in December, unless they shall by law appoint a different day.*

Section 5 Each house shall be the judge of the elections, returns and qualifications of its own members, and a majority of each shall constitute a quorum to do business; but a smaller number may adjourn from day to day, and may be authorized to compel the attendance of absent members, in such manner, and under such penalties, as each house may provide.

Each house may determine the rules of its proceedings, punish its members for disorderly behavior, and with the concurrence of two-thirds, expel a member.

Each house shall keep a journal of its proceedings, and from time to time publish the same, excepting such parts as may in their judgment require secrecy; and the yeas and nays of the members of either house on any question shall, at the desire of one-fifth of those present, be entered on the journal.

Neither house, during the session of Congress, shall, without the consent of the other, adjourn for more than three days, nor to any other place than that in which the two houses shall be sitting.

Section 6 The Senators and Representatives shall receive a compensation for their services, to be ascertained by law and paid out of the treasury of the United States. They shall in all cases except treason, felony and breach of the peace, be privileged from arrest during their attendance at the session of their respective houses, and in going to and returning from the same; and for any speech or debate in either house, they shall not be questioned in any other place.

No Senator or Representative shall, during the time for which he was elected, be appointed to any civil office under the authority of the United States, which shall have been created, or the emoluments whereof shall have been increased, during such time; and no person holding any office under the United States shall be a member of either house during his continuance in office.

Section 7 All bills for raising revenue shall originate in the House of Representatives; but the Senate may propose or concur with amendments as on other bills.

Every bill which shall have passed the House of Representatives and the Senate, shall, before it become a law, be presented to the President of the United States; if he approve he shall sign it, but if not he shall return it with objections to that house in which it shall have originated, who shall enter the objections at large on their journal, and proceed to reconsider it. If after such reconsideration two-thirds of that house shall agree to pass the bill, it shall be sent, together with the objections, to the other house, by which it shall likewise be reconsidered, and, if approved by two-thirds of that house, it shall become a law. But in all such cases the votes of both houses shall be determined by yeas and nays, and the names of the persons voting for and against the bill shall be entered on the journal of each house respectively. If any bill shall not be returned by the President within ten days (Sundays excepted) after it shall have been presented to him, the same shall be a law, in like manner as if he had signed it, unless the Congress by their adjournment prevent its return, in which case it shall not be a law.

Every order, resolution, or vote to which the concurrence of the Senate and House of Representatives may be necessary (except on a question of adjournment) shall be presented to the President of the United States; and before the same shall take effect, shall be approved by him, or being disapproved by him, shall be repassed by two-thirds of the Senate and House of Representatives, according to the rules and limitations prescribed in the case of a bill.

Section 8 The Congress shall have power

To lay and collect taxes, duties, imposts, and excises, to pay the debts and provide for the common defense and general welfare of the United States; but all duties, imposts and excises shall be uniform throughout the United States;

To borrow money on the credit of the United States;

To regulate commerce with foreign nations, and among the several States, and with the Indian tribes;

To establish an uniform rule of naturalization, and uniform laws on the subject of bankruptcies throughout the United States;

To coin money, regulate the value thereof, and of foreign coin, and fix the standard of weights and measures;

To provide for the punishment of counterfeiting the securities and current coin of the United States;

To establish post offices and post roads;

To promote the progress of science and useful arts by securing for limited times to authors and inventors the exclusive right to their respective writings and discoveries;

To constitute tribunals inferior to the Supreme Court;

To define and punish piracies and felonies committed on the high seas and offences against the law of nations;

To declare war, grant letters of marque and reprisal, and make rules concerning captures on land and water;

To raise and support armies, but no appropriation of money to that use shall be for a longer term than two years;

To provide and maintain a navy;

To make rules for the government and regulation of the land and naval forces;

To provide for calling forth the militia to execute the laws of the Union, suppress insurrections and repel invasions;

To provide for organizing, arming, and disciplining the militia, and for governing such part of them as may be employed in the service of the United States, reserving to the States respectively the appointment of the officers, and the authority of training the militia according to the discipline prescribed by Congress;

To exercise exclusive legislation in all cases whatsoever, over such district (not exceeding ten miles square) as may, by cession of particular States, and the acceptance of Congress, become the seat of the government of the United States, and to exercise like authority over all places purchased by the consent of the legislature of the State, in which the same shall be, for erection of forts, magazines, arsenals, dock-yards, and other needful buildings;—and

To make all laws which shall be necessary and proper for carrying into execution the foregoing powers, and all other powers vested by this Constitution in the government of the United States, or in any department or officer thereof.

Section 9 *The migration or importation of such persons as any of the States now existing shall think proper to admit shall not be prohibited by the Congress prior to the year one thousand eight hundred and eight; but a tax or duty may be imposed on such importation, not exceeding ten dollars for each person.*

The privilege of the writ of habeas corpus shall not be suspended, unless when in cases of rebellion or invasion the public safety may require it.

No bill of attainder or ex post facto law shall be passed.

No capitation, or other direct, tax shall be laid, unless in proportion to the census or enumeration herein before directed to be taken.

No tax or duty shall be laid on articles exported from any State.

No preference shall be given by any regulation of commerce or revenue to the ports of one State over those of another; nor shall vessels bound to, or from, one State be obliged to enter, clear, or pay duties in another.

No money shall be drawn from the treasury, but in consequence of appropriations made by law; and a regular statement and account of the receipts and expenditures of all public money shall be published from time to time.

No title of nobility shall be granted by the United States: and no person holding any office of profit or trust under them, shall, without the consent of the Congress, accept of any present, emolument, office, or title, of any kind whatever, from any king, prince, or foreign state.

Section 10 No State shall enter into any treaty, alliance, or confederation; grant letters of marque and reprisal; coin money; emit bills of credit; make anything but gold and silver coin a tender in payment of debts; pass any bill of attainder, ex post facto law, or law impairing the obligation of contracts, or grant any title of nobility.

No State shall, without the consent of Congress, lay any imposts or duties on imports or exports, except what may be absolutely necessary for executing its inspection laws: and the net produce of all duties and imposts, laid by any State on imports or exports, shall be for the use of the treasury of the United States; and all such laws shall be subject to the revision and control of the Congress.

No State shall, without the consent of Congress, lay any duty of tonnage, keep troops, or ships of war in time of peace, enter into any agreement or compact with another State, or with a foreign power, or engage in war, unless actually invaded, or in such imminent danger as will not admit of delay.

Article II

Section 1 The executive power shall be vested in a President of the United States of America. He shall hold his office during the term of four years, and, together with the Vice-President, chosen for the same term, be elected as follows:

Each State shall appoint, in such manner as the legislature thereof may direct, a number of electors, equal to the whole number of Senators and Representatives to which the State may be entitled in the Congress; but no Senator or Representative, or person holding an office of trust or profit under the United States, shall be appointed an elector.

The electors shall meet in their respective States, and vote by ballot for two persons, of whom one at least shall not be an inhabitant of the same State with themselves. And they shall make a list of all the persons voted for, and of the number of votes for each; which list they shall sign and certify, and transmit sealed to the seat of government of the United States, directed to the President of the Senate. The President of the Senate shall, in the presence of the Senate and House of Representatives, open all the certificates, and the votes shall then be counted. The person having the greatest number of votes shall be the President, if such number be a majority of the whole number of electors appointed; and if there be more than one who have such majority, and have an equal number of votes, then the House of Representatives shall immediately choose by ballot one of them for President; and if no person have a majority, then from the five highest on the list said house shall in like manner choose the President. But in choosing the President the votes shall be taken by States, the representation from each State having one vote; a quorum for this purpose shall consist of a member or members from two-thirds of the States, and a majority of all the States shall be necessary to a choice. In every case, after the choice of the President, the person having the greatest number of votes of the electors shall be the Vice-President. But if there should remain two or more who have equal votes, the Senate shall choose from them by ballot the Vice-President.

The Congress may determine the time of choosing the electors, and the day on which they shall give their votes; which day shall be the same throughout the United States.

No person except a natural-born citizen, *or a citizen of the United States at the time of the adoption of this Constitution*, shall be eligible to the office of President; neither shall any person be eligible to that office who shall not have attained to the age of thirty-five years, and been fourteen years a resident within the United States.

In cases of the removal of the President from office or of his death, resignation, or inability to discharge the powers and duties of the said office, the same shall devolve on the Vice-President, and the Congress may by law provide for the case of removal, death, resignation, or inability, both of the President and Vice-President, declaring what officer shall then act as President, and such officer shall act accordingly, until the disability be removed, or a President shall be elected.

The President shall, at stated times, receive for his services a compensation, which shall neither be increased nor diminished during the period for which he shall have been elected, and he shall not receive within that period any other emolument from the United States, or any of them.

Before he enter on the execution of his office, he shall take the following oath or affirmation:—"I do solemnly swear (or affirm) that I will faithfully execute the office of the President of the United States, and will to the best of my ability preserve, protect and defend the Constitution of the United States."

Section 2 The President shall be commander in chief of the army and navy of the United States, and of the militia of the several States, when called into the actual service of the United States; he may require the opinion, in writing, of the principal officer in each of the executive departments, upon any subject relating to the duties of their respective offices, and he shall have power to grant reprieves and pardons for offenses against the United States, except in cases of impeachment.

He shall have power, by and with the advice and consent of the Senate, to make treaties, provided two-thirds of the Senators present concur; and he shall nominate, and by and with the advice and consent of the Senate, shall appoint ambassadors, other public ministers and consuls, judges of the Supreme Court, and all other officers of the United States, whose appointments are not herein otherwise provided for, and which shall be established by law: but Congress may by law vest the appointment of such inferior officers, as they think proper, in the President alone, in the courts of law, or in the heads of departments.

The President shall have power to fill up all vacancies that may happen during the recess of the Senate, by granting commissions which shall expire at the end of their next session.

Section 3 He shall from time to time give to the Congress information of the state of the Union, and recommend to their consideration such measures as he shall judge necessary and expedient; he may, on extraordinary occasions, convene both houses, or either of them, and in case of disagreement between them, with respect to the time of adjournment, he may adjourn them to such time as he shall think proper; he shall receive ambassadors and other public ministers; he shall take care that the laws be faithfully executed, and shall commission all the officers of the United States.

Section 4 The President, Vice-President and all civil officers of the United States shall be removed from office on impeachment for, and on conviction of, treason, bribery, or other high crimes and misdemeanors.

Article III

Section 1 The judicial power of the United States shall be vested in one Supreme Court, and in such inferior courts as the Congress may from time to time ordain and establish. The judges, both of the Supreme and inferior courts, shall hold their offices during good behavior, and shall, at stated times, receive for their services a compensation which shall not be diminished during their continuance in office.

Section 2 The judicial power shall extend to all cases, in law and equity, arising under this Constitution, the laws of the United States, and treaties made, or which shall be made, under their authority;—to all cases affecting ambassadors, other public ministers and consuls;—to all cases of admiralty and maritime jurisdiction;—to controversies to which the United States shall be a party;—to controversies between two or more States;—*between a State and citizens of another*

State;—between citizens of different States;—between citizens of the same State claiming lands under grants of different States, and between a State, or the citizens thereof, and foreign states, citizens or subjects.

In all cases affecting ambassadors, other public ministers and consuls, and those in which a State shall be party, the Supreme Court shall have original jurisdiction. In all the other cases before mentioned, the Supreme Court shall have appellate jurisdiction, both as to law and fact, with such exceptions, and under such regulations, as the Congress shall make.

The trial of all crimes, except in cases of impeachment, shall be by jury; and such trial shall be held in the State where said crimes shall have been committed; but when not committed within any State, the trial shall be at such place or places as the Congress may by Law have directed.

Section 3   Treason against the United States shall consist only in levying war against them, or in adhering to their enemies, giving them aid and comfort. No person shall be convicted of treason unless on the testimony of two witnesses to the same overt act, or on confession in open court.

The Congress shall have power to declare the punishment of treason, but no attainder of treason shall work corruption of blood, or forfeiture except during the life of the person attainted.

Article IV

Section 1   Full faith and credit shall be given in each State to the public acts, records, and judicial proceedings of every other State. And the Congress may by general laws prescribe the manner in which such acts, records, and proceedings shall be proved, and the effect thereof.

Section 2   The citizens of each State shall be entitled to all privileges and immunities of citizens in the several States.

A person charged in any State with treason, felony, or other crime, who shall flee from justice, and be found in another State, shall on demand of the executive authority of the State from which he fled, be delivered up, to be removed to the State having jurisdiction of the crime.

No Person held to service or labor in one State, under the laws thereof, escaping into another, shall, in consequence of any law or regulation therein, be discharged from such service or labor, but shall be delivered up on claim of the party to whom such service or labor may be due.

Section 3   New States may be admitted by the Congress into this Union; but no new State shall be formed or erected within the jurisdiction of any other State; nor any State be formed by the junction of two or more States, or parts of States, without the consent of the legislatures of the States concerned as well as of the Congress.

The Congress shall have power to dispose of and make all needful rules and regulations respecting the territory or other property belonging to the United States; and nothing in this Constitution shall be so construed as to prejudice any claims of the United States, or of any particular State.

Section 4   The United States shall guarantee to every State in this Union a republican form of government, and shall protect each of them against invasion; and on application of the legislature, or of the executive (when the legislature cannot be convened), against domestic violence.

Article V

The Congress, whenever two-thirds of both houses shall deem it necessary, shall propose amendments to this Constitution, or, on the application of the legislatures of two-thirds of the several States, shall call a convention for proposing amendments, which, in either case, shall be valid to all intents and purposes, as part of this Constitution, when ratified by the legislatures of three-fourths of the several States, or by conventions in three-fourths thereof, as the one or the other mode of ratification may be proposed by the Congress; provided *that no amendments which may be made prior to the year one thousand eight hundred and eight shall in any manner affect the first and fourth clauses in the ninth section of the first article;* and that no State, without its consent, shall be deprived of its equal suffrage in the Senate.

Article VI

All debts contracted and engagements entered into, before the adoption of this Constitution, shall be as valid against the United States under this Constitution, as under the Confederation.

This Constitution, and the laws of the United States which shall be made in pursuance thereof; and all treaties made, or which shall be made, under the authority of the United States, shall be the supreme law of the land; and the judges in every State shall be bound thereby, anything in the Constitution or laws of any State to the contrary notwithstanding.

The Senators and Representatives before mentioned, and the members of the several State legislatures, and all executive and judicial officers, both of the United States and of the several States, shall be bound by oath or affirmation to support this Constitution; but no religious test shall ever be required as a qualification to any office or public trust under the United States.

Article VII

The ratification of the conventions of nine States shall be sufficient for the establishment of this Constitution between the States so ratifying the same.

Done in convention by the unanimous consent of the States present, the seventeenth day of September in the year of our Lord one thousand seven hundred and eighty-seven and of the Independence of the United States of America the twelfth. In witness whereof we have hereunto subscribed our names.

GEORGE WASHINGTON
PRESIDENT AND DEPUTY FROM VIRGINIA

New Hampshire
John Langdon
Nicholas Gilman

Massachusetts
Nathaniel Gorham
Rufus King

Connecticut
William Samuel
  Johnson
Roger Sherman

New York
Alexander Hamilton

New Jersey
William Livingston
David Brearley
William Paterson
Jonathan Dayton

Pennsylvania
Benjamin Franklin
Thomas Mifflin
Robert Morris
George Clymer
Thomas FitzSimons
Jared Ingersoll
James Wilson
Gouverneur Morris

Delaware
George Read
Gunning Bedford, Jr.
John Dickinson
Richard Bassett
Jacob Broom

Maryland
James McHenry
Daniel of
  St. Thomas Jenifer
Daniel Carroll

Virginia
John Blair
James Madison, Jr.

North Carolina
William Blount
Richard Dobbs
  Spaight
Hugh Williamson

South Carolina
John Rutledge
Charles Cotesworth
  Pinckney
Charles Pinckney
Pierce Butler

Georgia
William Few
Abraham Baldwin

AMENDMENTS TO THE CONSTITUTION WITH ANNOTATIONS
(Including the six unratified amendments)

In their effort to gain Antifederalists' support for the Constitution, Federalists frequently pointed to the inclusion of Article 5, which provides an orderly method of amending the Constitution. In contrast, the Articles of Confederation, which were universally recognized as seriously flawed, offered no means of amendment. For their part, Antifederalists argued that the amendment process was so "intricate" that one might as easily roll "sixes an hundred times in succession" as change the Constitution.

The system for amendment laid out in the Constitution requires that two-thirds of both houses of Congress agree to a proposed amendment, which must then be ratified by three-quarters of the legislatures of the states. Alternatively, an amendment may be proposed by a convention called by the legislatures of two-thirds of the states. Since 1789, members of Congress have proposed thousands of amendments. Besides the seventeen amendments added since 1789, only the six "unratified" ones included here were approved by two-thirds of both houses and sent to the states for ratification, however.

Among the many amendments that never made it out of Congress have been proposals to declare dueling, divorce, and interracial marriage unconstitutional as well as proposals to establish a national university, to acknowledge the sovereignty of Jesus Christ, and to prohibit any person from possessing wealth in excess of ten million dollars.[1]

Among the issues facing Americans today that might lead to constitutional amendment are efforts to balance the federal budget, to limit the number of terms elected officials may serve, to limit access to or prohibit abortion, to establish English as the official language of the United States, and to prohibit flag burning. None of these proposed amendments has yet garnered enough support in Congress to be sent to the states for ratification.

Although the first ten amendments to the Constitution are commonly known as the Bill of Rights, only Amendments 1–8 actually provide guarantees of individual rights. Amendments 9 and 10 deal with the structure of power within the constitutional system. The Bill of Rights was promised to appease Antifederalists who refused to ratify the Constitution without guarantees of individual liberties and limitations to federal power. After studying more than two hundred amendments recommended by the ratifying conventions of the states, Federalist James Madison presented a list of seventeen to Congress, which used Madison's list as the foundation for the twelve amendments that were sent to the states for ratification. Ten of the twelve were adopted in 1791. The first on the list of twelve, known as the Reapportionment Amendment, was never adopted (see p. A-13). The second proposed amendment was adopted in 1992 as Amendment 27 (see p. A-23).

Amendment I

Congress shall make no law respecting an establishment of religion, or prohibiting the free exercise thereof; or abridging the freedom of speech, or of the press; or the right of the people peaceably to assemble, and to petition the government for a redress of grievances.

◆◆◆

The First Amendment is a potent symbol for many Americans. Most are well aware of their rights to free speech, freedom of the press, and freedom of religion and their rights to assemble and to petition, even if they cannot cite the exact words of this amendment.

The First Amendment guarantee of freedom of religion has two clauses: the "free exercise clause," which allows individuals to practice or not practice any religion, and the "establishment clause," which prevents the federal government from discriminating against or favoring any particular religion. This clause was designed to create what Thomas Jefferson referred to as "a wall of separation between church and state." In the 1960s, the Supreme Court ruled that the First Amendment prohibits prayer (see Engel v. Vitale, *p. A-46) and Bible reading in public schools.*

Although the rights to free speech and freedom of the press are established in the First Amendment, it was not until the twentieth century that the Supreme Court began to explore the full meaning of these guarantees. In 1919, the Court ruled in Schenck v. United States *(see p. A-45) that the government could suppress free expression only where it could cite a "clear and present danger." In a decision that continues to raise controversies, the Court ruled in 1990, in* Texas v. Johnson, *that flag burning is a form of symbolic speech protected by the First Amendment.*

---

[1]Richard B. Bernstein, *Amending America*, (New York: Times Books, 1993), 177–81.

Amendment II

A well-regulated militia being necessary to the security of a free State, the right of the people to keep and bear arms shall not be infringed.

◆ ◆ ◆

Fear of a standing army under the control of a hostile government made the Second Amendment an important part of the Bill of Rights. Advocates of gun ownership claim that the amendment prevents the government from regulating firearms. Proponents of gun control argue that the amendment is designed only to protect the right of the states to maintain militia units.

In 1939, the Supreme Court ruled in United States v. Miller *that the Second Amendment did not protect the right of an individual to own a sawed-off shotgun, which it argued was not ordinary militia equipment. Since then, the Supreme Court has refused to hear Second Amendment cases, while lower courts have upheld firearms regulations. Several justices currently on the bench seem to favor a narrow interpretation of the Second Amendment, which would allow gun control legislation. The controversy over the impact of the Second Amendment on gun owners and gun control legislation will certainly continue.*

Amendment III

No soldier shall, in time of peace, be quartered in any house without the consent of the owner, nor in time of war, but in a manner to be prescribed by law.

◆ ◆ ◆

The Third Amendment was extremely important to the framers of the Constitution, but today it is nearly forgotten. American colonists were especially outraged that they were forced to quarter British troops in the years before and during the American Revolution. The philosophy of the Third Amendment has been viewed by some justices and scholars as the foundation of the modern constitutional right to privacy. One example of this can be found in Justice William O. Douglas's opinion in Griswold v. Connecticut *(see p. A-47).*

Amendment IV

The right of the people to be secure in their persons, houses, papers, and effects, against unreasonable searches and seizures, shall not be violated, and no warrants shall issue but upon probable cause, supported by oath or affirmation, and particularly describing the place to be searched, and the persons or things to be seized.

◆ ◆ ◆

In the years before the Revolution, the houses, barns, stores, and warehouses of American colonists were ransacked by British authorities under "writs of assistance" or general warrants. The British, thus empowered, searched for seditious material or smuggled goods that could then be used as evidence against colonists who were charged with a crime only after the items were found.

The first part of the Fourth Amendment protects citizens from "unreasonable" searches and seizures. The Supreme Court has interpreted this protection as well as the words search *and* seizure *in different ways at different times. At one time, the Court did not recognize electronic eavesdropping as a form of search and seizure, though it does today. At times, an "unreasonable" search has been almost any search carried out without a warrant, but in the two decades before 1969 the Court sometimes sanctioned warrantless searches that it considered reasonable based on "the total atmosphere of the case."*

The second part of the Fourth Amendment defines the procedure for issuing a search warrant and states the requirement of "Probable cause," which is generally viewed as evidence indicating that a suspect has committed an offense.

The Fourth Amendment has been controversial because the Court has sometimes excluded evidence that has been seized in violation of constitutional standards. The justification is that excluding such evidence deters violations of the amendment, but doing so may allow a guilty person to escape punishment.

Amendment V

No person shall be held to answer for a capital, or otherwise infamous crime, unless on a presentment or indictment of a grand jury, except in cases arising in the land or naval forces, or in the militia, when in actual service in time of war or public danger; nor shall any person be subject for the same offence to be twice put in jeopardy of life or limb; nor shall be compelled in any criminal case to be a witness against himself, nor be deprived of life, liberty, or property, without due process of law; nor shall private property be taken for public use without just compensation.

◆ ◆ ◆

The Fifth Amendment protects people against government authority in the prosecution of criminal offenses. It prohibits the state, first, from charging a person with a serious crime without a grand jury hearing to decide whether there is sufficient evidence to support the charge and, second, from charging a person with the same crime twice. The best-known aspect of the Fifth Amendment is that it prevents a person from being "compelled . . . to be a witness against himself." The last clause, the "takings clause," limits the power of the government to seize property.

Although invoking the Fifth Amendment is popularly viewed as a confession of guilt, a person may be innocent yet still fear prosecution. For example, during the Red-baiting era of the late 1940s and 1950s, many people who had participated in legal activities that were associated with the Communist Party claimed the Fifth Amendment privilege rather than testify before the House Un-American Activities Committee because the mood of the times cast those activities in a negative light. Since "taking the Fifth" was viewed as an admission of guilt, those people often lost their jobs or became unemployable. (See chapter 26.) Nonetheless, the right to protect oneself against self-incrimination plays an important role in guarding against the collective power of the state.

Amendment VI

In all criminal prosecutions, the accused shall enjoy the right to a speedy and public trial, by an impartial jury of the State and district wherein the crime shall have been committed, which district shall have been previously ascertained by law, and to be informed of the nature and cause of the accusation; to be confronted with the witnesses against him; to have compulsory process for obtaining witnesses in his favor, and to have the assistance of counsel for his defence.

◆ ◆ ◆

The original Constitution put few limits on the government's power to investigate, prosecute, and punish crime. This process was of great concern to the early Americans, however, and of the twenty-eight rights specified in the first eight amendments, fifteen have to do with it. Seven rights are specified in the Sixth Amendment. These include the right to a speedy trial, a public trial, a jury trial, a notice of accusation, confrontation by opposing witnesses, testimony by favorable witnesses, and the assistance of counsel.

Although this amendment originally guaranteed these rights only in cases involving the federal government, the adoption of the Fourteenth Amendment began a process of applying the protections of the Bill of Rights to the states through court cases such as Gideon v. Wainwright *(see p. A-46).*

Amendment VII

In suits at common law, where the value in controversy shall exceed twenty dollars, the right of trial by jury shall be preserved, and no fact tried by a jury shall be otherwise reexamined in any court of the United States, than according to the rules of the common law.

◆ ◆ ◆

This amendment guarantees people the same right to a trial by jury as was guaranteed by English common law in 1791. Under common law, in civil trials (those involving money damages) the role of the judge was to settle questions of law and that of the jury was to settle questions of fact. The amendment does not specify the size of the jury or its role in a trial, however. The Supreme Court has generally held that those issues be determined by English common law of 1791, which stated that a jury consists of twelve people, that a trial must be conducted before a judge who instructs the jury on the law and advises it on facts, and that a verdict must be unanimous.

Amendment VIII

Excessive bail shall not be required, nor excessive fines imposed, nor cruel and unusual punishments inflicted.

◆ ◆ ◆

The language used to guarantee the three rights in this amendment was inspired by the English Bill of Rights of 1689. The Supreme Court has not had a lot to say about "excessive fines." In recent years it has agreed that despite the provision against "excessive bail," persons who are believed to be dangerous to others can be held without bail even before they have been convicted.

Although opponents of the death penalty have not succeeded in using the Eighth Amendment to achieve the end of capital punishment, the clause regarding "cruel and unusual punishments" has been used to prohibit capital punishment in certain cases (see Furman v. Georgia, *p. A-47) and to require improved conditions in prisons.*

Amendment IX

The enumeration in the Constitution, of certain rights, shall not be construed to deny or disparage others retained by the people.

◆ ◆ ◆

Some Federalists feared that inclusion of the Bill of Rights in the Constitution would allow later generations of interpreters to claim that the people had surrendered any rights not specifically enumerated there. To guard against this, Madison added language that became the Ninth Amendment. Interest in this heretofore largely ignored amendment revived in 1965 when it was used in a concurring opinion in Griswold v. Connecticut *(see p. A-47). While Justice William O. Douglas called on the Third Amendment to support the right to privacy in deciding that case, Justice Arthur Goldberg, in the concurring opinion, argued that the right to privacy regarding contraception was an* unenumerated right that was protected by the Ninth Amendment.

In 1980, the Court ruled that the right of the press to attend a public trial was protected by the Ninth Amendment. While some scholars argue that modern judges cannot identify the unenumerated rights that the framers were trying to protect, others argue that the Ninth Amendment should be read as providing a constitutional "presumption of liberty" that allows people to act in any way that does not violate the rights of others.

Amendment X

The powers not delegated to the United States by the Constitution, nor prohibited by it to the States, are reserved to the States respectively, or to the people.

◆ ◆ ◆

The Antifederalists were especially eager to see a "reserved powers clause" explicitly guaranteeing the states control over their internal affairs. Not surprisingly, the Tenth Amendment has been a frequent battleground in the struggle over states' rights and federal supremacy. Prior to the Civil War, the Democratic Republican Party and Jacksonian Democrats invoked the Tenth Amendment to prohibit the federal government from making decisions about whether people in individual states could own slaves. The Tenth Amendment was virtually suspended during Reconstruction following the Civil War. In 1883, however, the Supreme Court declared the Civil Rights Act of 1875 unconstitutional on the grounds that it violated the Tenth Amendment. Business interests also called on the amendment to block efforts at federal regulation.

The Court was inconsistent over the next several decades as it attempted to resolve the tension between the restrictions of the Tenth Amendment and the powers the Constitution granted to Congress to regulate interstate commerce and levy taxes. The Court upheld the Pure Food and Drug Act (1906), the Meat Inspection Acts (1906 and 1907), and the White Slave Traffic Act (1910), all of which affected the states, but struck down an act prohibiting interstate shipment of goods produced through child labor. Between 1934 and 1935, a number of New Deal programs created by Franklin D. Roosevelt were declared unconstitutional on the grounds that they violated the Tenth Amendment. (See chapter 24.) As Roosevelt appointees changed the composition of the Court, the Tenth Amendment was declared to have no substantive meaning. Generally, the amendment is held to protect the rights of states to regulate internal matters such as local government, education, commerce, labor, and business, as well as matters involving families such as marriage, divorce, and inheritance within the state.

Unratified Amendment

Reapportionment Amendment (proposed by Congress September 25, 1789, along with the Bill of Rights)

After the first enumeration required by the first article of the Constitution, there shall be one Representative for every thirty thousand, until the number shall amount to one hundred, after which the proportion shall be so regulated by Congress, that there shall be not less than one hundred Representatives, nor less than one Representative for every forty thousand persons, until the number of Representatives shall amount to two hundred; after which the proportion shall be so regulated by Congress, that there shall not be less than two hundred Representatives, nor more than one Representative for every fifty thousand persons.

◆ ◆ ◆

If the Reapportionment Amendment had passed and remained in effect, the House of Representatives today would have more than 5,000 members rather than 435.

Amendment XI
[Adopted 1798]

The judicial power of the United States shall not be construed to extend to any suit in law or equity, commenced or prosecuted against one of the United States by citizens of another State, or by citizens or subjects of any foreign state.

◆ ◆ ◆

In 1793, the Supreme Court ruled in favor of Alexander Chisholm, executor of the estate of a deceased South Carolina merchant. Chisholm was suing the state of Georgia because the merchant had never been paid for provisions he had supplied during the Revolution. Many regarded this Court decision as an error that violated the intent of the Constitution.

Antifederalists had long feared a federal court system with the power to overrule a state court. When the Constitution was being drafted, Federalists had assured worried Antifederalists that section 2 of Article 3, which allows federal courts to hear cases "between a State and citizens of another State," did not mean that the federal courts were authorized to hear suits against a state by citizens of another state or a foreign country. Antifederalists and many other Americans feared a powerful federal court system because they worried that it would become like the British courts of this period, which were accountable only to the monarch. Furthermore, Chisholm v. Georgia prompted a *series of suits against state governments by creditors and suppliers who had made loans during the war.*

In addition, State legislators and Congress feared that the shaky economies of the new states, as well as the country as a whole, would be destroyed, especially if Loyalists who had fled to other countries sought reimbursement for land and property that had been seized. The day after the Supreme Court announced its decision, a resolution proposing the Eleventh Amendment, which overturned the decision in Chisholm v. Georgia, *was introduced in the U.S. Senate.*

Amendment XII
[Adopted 1804]

The electors shall meet in their respective States, and vote by ballot for President and Vice-President, one of whom, at least, shall not be an inhabitant of the same State with themselves; they shall name in their ballots the person voted for as President, and in distinct ballots the person voted for as Vice-President, and they shall make distinct lists of all persons voted for as President, and of all persons voted for as Vice-President, and of the number of votes for each, which lists they shall sign and certify, and transmit sealed to the seat of government of the United States, directed to the President of the Senate;—the President of the Senate shall, in the presence of the Senate and House of Representatives, open all the certificates and the votes shall then be counted;—the person having the greatest number of votes for President shall be the President, if such number be a majority of the whole number of electors appointed; and if no person have such majority, then from the persons having the highest numbers not exceeding three on the list of those voted for as President, the House of Representatives shall choose immediately, by ballot, the President. But in choosing the President, the votes shall be taken by States, the representation from each State having one vote; a quorum for this purpose shall consist of a member or members from two-thirds of the States, and a majority of all the States shall be necessary to a choice. And if the House of Representatives shall not choose a President whenever the right of choice shall devolve upon them, before *the fourth day of March* next following, then the Vice-President shall act as President, as in the case of the death or other constitutional disability of the President.

The person having the greatest number of votes as Vice-President shall be the Vice-President, if such number be a majority of the whole number of electors appointed; and if no person have a majority, then from the two highest numbers on the list the Senate shall choose the Vice-President; a quorum for the purpose shall consist of two-thirds of the whole number of Senators, and a majority of the whole number shall be necessary to a choice. But no person constitutionally inel-

igible to the office of President shall be eligible to that of Vice-President of the United States.

◆ ◆ ◆

The framers of the Constitution disliked political parties and assumed that none would ever form. Under the original system, electors chosen by the states would each vote for two candidates. The candidate who won the most votes would become president, while the person who won the second-highest number of votes would become vice president. Rivalries between Federalists and Antifederalists led to the formation of political parties, however, even before George Washington had left office. Though Washington was elected unanimously in 1789 and 1792, the elections of 1796 and 1800 were procedural disasters because of party maneuvering (see chapters 9 and 10). In 1796, Federalist John Adams was chosen as president, and his great rival, the Antifederalist Thomas Jefferson (whose party was called the Republican Party), became his vice president. In 1800, all the electors cast their two votes as one of two party blocs. Jefferson and his fellow Republican nominee, Aaron Burr, were tied with seventy-three votes each. The contest went to the House of Representatives, which finally elected Jefferson after thirty-six ballots. The Twelfth Amendment prevents these problems by requiring electors to vote separately for the president and vice president.

Unratified Amendment
Titles of Nobility Amendment (proposed by Congress May 1, 1810)

If any citizen of the United States shall accept, claim, receive or retain any title of nobility or honor or shall, without the consent of Congress, accept and retain any present, pension, office or emolument of any kind whatever, from any emperor, king, prince or foreign power, such person shall cease to be a citizen of the United States, and shall be incapable of holding any office of trust or profit under them, or either of them.

◆ ◆ ◆

This amendment would have extended Article 1, section 9, clause 8 of the Constitution, which prevents the awarding of titles by the United States and the acceptance of such awards from foreign powers without congressional consent. Historians speculate that general nervousness about the power of the Emperor Napoleon, who was at that time extending France's empire throughout Europe, may have prompted the proposal. Though it fell one vote short of ratification, Congress and the American people thought the proposal had been ratified and it was included in many nineteenth-century editions of the Constitution.

The Civil War and Reconstruction Amendments (Thirteenth, Fourteenth, and Fifteenth Amendments)

In the four months between the election of Abraham Lincoln and his inauguration, more than two hundred proposed constitutional amendments were presented to Congress as part of a desperate attempt to hold the rapidly dissolving Union together. Most of these were efforts to appease the southern states by protecting the right to own slaves or by disfranchising African Americans through constitutional amendment. None were able to win the votes required from Congress to send them to the states. The relatively innocuous Corwin Amendment seemed to be the only hope for preserving the Union by amending the Constitution.

The northern victors in the Civil War tried to restructure the Constitution just as the war had restructured the nation. Yet they were often divided in their goals. Some wanted to end slavery; others hoped for social and economic equality regardless of race; others hoped that extending the power of the ballot box to former slaves would help create a new political order. The debates over the Thirteenth, Fourteenth, and Fifteenth Amendments were bitter. Few of those who fought for these changes were satisfied with the amendments themselves; fewer still were satisfied with their interpretation. Although the amendments put an end to the legal status of slavery, it took nearly a hundred years after the amendments' passage before most of the descendants of former slaves could begin to experience the economic, social, and political equality the amendments had been intended to provide.

Unratified Amendment
Corwin Amendment (proposed by Congress March 2, 1861)

No amendment shall be made to the Constitution which will authorize or give to Congress the power to abolish or interfere, within any State, with the domestic institutions thereof, including that of persons held to labor or service by the laws of said State.

◆ ◆ ◆

Following the election of Abraham Lincoln, Congress scrambled to try to prevent the secession of the slaveholding states. House member Thomas Corwin of Ohio proposed the "unamendable" amendment in the hope that by protecting slavery where it existed, Congress would keep

the southern states in the Union. Lincoln indicated his support for the proposed amendment in his first inaugural address. Only Ohio and Maryland ratified the Corwin Amendment before it was forgotten.

Amendment XIII
[Adopted 1865]

Section 1 Neither slavery nor involuntary servitude, except as a punishment for crime whereof the party shall have been duly convicted, shall exist within the United States, or any place subject to their jurisdiction.

Section 2 Congress shall have power to enforce this article by appropriate legislation.

◆ ◆ ◆

Although President Lincoln had abolished slavery in the Confederacy with the Emancipation Proclamation of 1863, abolitionists wanted to rid the entire country of slavery. The Thirteenth Amendment did this in a clear and straightforward manner. In February 1865, when the proposal was approved by the House, the gallery of the House was newly opened to black Americans who had a chance at last to see their government at work. Passage of the proposal was greeted by wild cheers from the gallery as well as tears on the House floor, where congressional representatives openly embraced one another.

The problem of ratification remained, however. The Union position was that the Confederate states were part of the country of thirty-six states. Therefore, twenty-seven states were needed to ratify the amendment. When Kentucky and Delaware rejected it, backers realized that without approval from at least four former Confederate states, the amendment would fail. Lincoln's successor, President Andrew Johnson, made ratification of the Thirteenth Amendment a condition for southern states to rejoin the Union. Under those terms, all the former Confederate states except Mississippi accepted the Thirteenth Amendment, and by the end of 1865 the amendment had become part of the Constitution and slavery had been prohibited in the United States.

Amendment XIV
[Adopted 1868]

Section 1 All persons born or naturalized in the United States, and subject to the jurisdiction thereof, are citizens of the United States and of the State wherein they reside. No State shall make or enforce any law which shall abridge the privileges or immunities of citizens of the United States; nor shall any State deprive any person of life, liberty, or property, without due process of law; nor deny to any person within its jurisdiction the equal protection of the laws.

Section 2 Representatives shall be appointed among the several States according to their respective numbers, counting the whole number of persons in each State, excluding Indians not taxed. But when the right to vote at any election for the choice of Electors for President and Vice-President of the United States, Representatives in Congress, the executive and judicial officers of a State, or the members of the legislature thereof, is denied to any of the male inhabitants of such State, being twenty-one years of age and citizens of the United States, or in any way abridged, except for participation in rebellion, or other crime, the basis of representation therein shall be reduced in the proportion which the number of such male citizens shall bear to the whole number of male citizens twenty-one years of age in such State.

Section 3 No person shall be a Senator or Representative in Congress, or Elector of President and Vice-President, or hold any office, civil or military, under the United States, or under any State, who, having previously taken an oath, as a member of Congress, or as an officer of the United States, or as a member of any State legislature, or as an executive or judicial officer of any State, to support the Constitution of the United States, shall have engaged in insurrection or rebellion against the same, or given aid or comfort to the enemies thereof. Congress may, by a vote of two-thirds of each house, remove such disability.

Section 4 The validity of the public debt of the United States, authorized by law, including debts incurred for payment of pensions and bounties for services in suppressing insurrection or rebellion, shall not be questioned. But neither the United States nor any State shall assume or pay any debt or obligation incurred in aid of insurrection or rebellion against the United States, or any claim for the loss or emancipation of any slave; but all such debts, obligations, and claims shall be held illegal and void.

Section 5 The Congress shall have power to enforce, by appropriate legislation, the provisions of this article.

◆ ◆ ◆

Without Lincoln's leadership in the reconstruction of the nation following the Civil War, it soon became clear that the Thirteenth Amendment needed additional constitutional support. Less than a year after Lincoln's assassination, Andrew Johnson was ready to bring the former Confederate states back into the Union with few changes in their governments or politics. Anxious Republicans drafted the

Fourteenth Amendment to prevent that from happening. The most important provisions of this complex amendment made all native-born or naturalized persons American citizens and prohibited states from abridging the "privileges or immunities" of citizens; depriving them of "life, liberty, or property, without due process of law"; and denying them "equal protection of the laws." In essence, it made all ex-slaves citizens and protected the rights of all citizens against violation by their own state governments.

As occurred in the case of the Thirteenth Amendment, former Confederate states were forced to ratify the amendment as a condition of representation in the House and the Senate. The intentions of the Fourteenth Amendment, and how those intentions should be enforced, have been the most debated point of constitutional history. The terms due process *and* equal protection *have been especially troublesome. Was the amendment designed to outlaw racial segregation? Or was the goal simply to prevent the leaders of the rebellious South from gaining political power?*

The framers of the Fourteenth Amendment hoped Article 2 would produce black voters who would increase the power of the Republican Party. The federal government, however, never used its power to punish states for denying blacks their right to vote. Although the Fourteenth Amendment had an immediate impact in giving black Americans citizenship, it did nothing to protect blacks from the vengeance of whites once Reconstruction ended. In the late nineteenth and early twentieth centuries, section 1 of the Fourteenth Amendment was often used to protect business interests and strike down laws protecting workers on the grounds that the rights of "persons," that is, corporations, were protected by "due process." More recently, the Fourteenth Amendment has been used to justify school desegregation and affirmative action programs, as well as to dismantle such programs.

Amendment XV

[Adopted 1870]

Section 1 The right of citizens of the United States to vote shall not be denied or abridged by the United States or by any State on account of race, color, or previous condition of servitude.

Section 2 The Congress shall have power to enforce this article by appropriate legislation.

◆ ◆ ◆

The Fifteenth Amendment was the last major piece of Reconstruction legislation. While earlier Reconstruction acts had already required black suffrage in the South, the Fifteenth Amendment extended black voting rights to the entire nation. Some Republicans felt morally obligated to do away with the double standard between North and South since many northern states had stubbornly refused to enfranchise blacks. Others believed that the freedman's ballot required the extra protection of a constitutional amendment to shield it from white counterattack. But partisan advantage also played an important role in the amendment's passage, since Republicans hoped that by giving the ballot to northern blacks, they could lessen their political vulnerability.

Many women's rights advocates had fought for the amendment. They had felt betrayed by the inclusion of the word male in section 2 of the Fourteenth Amendment and were further angered when the proposed Fifteenth Amendment failed to prohibit denial of the right to vote on the grounds of sex as well as "race, color, or previous condition of servitude." In this amendment, for the first time, the federal government claimed the power to regulate the franchise, or vote. It was also the first time the Constitution placed limits on the power of the states to regulate access to the franchise. Although ratified in 1870, however, the amendment was not enforced until the twentieth century.

The Progressive Amendments (Sixteenth–Nineteenth Amendments)

No amendments were added to the Constitution between the Civil War and the Progressive Era. America was changing, however, in fundamental ways. The rapid industrialization of the United States after the Civil War led to many social and economic problems. Hundreds of amendments were proposed, but none received enough support in Congress to be sent to the states. Some scholars believe that regional differences and rivalries were so strong during this period that it was almost impossible to gain a consensus on a constitutional amendment. During the Progressive Era, however, the Constitution was amended four times in seven years.

Amendment XVI

[Adopted 1913]

The Congress shall have power to lay and collect taxes on incomes, from whatever source derived, without apportionment among the several States, and without regard to any census or enumeration.

◆ ◆ ◆

Until passage of the Sixteenth Amendment, most of the money used to run the federal government came from customs duties and taxes on specific items, such as liquor. During the Civil War, the federal government taxed incomes as an emergency measure. Pressure to enact an in-

come tax came from those who were concerned about the growing gap between rich and poor in the United States. The Populist Party began campaigning for a graduated income tax in 1892, and support continued to grow. By 1909, thirty-three proposed income tax amendments had been presented in Congress, but lobbying by corporate and other special interests had defeated them all. In June 1909, the growing pressure for an income tax, which had been endorsed by Presidents Roosevelt and Taft, finally pushed an amendment through the Senate. The required thirty-six states had ratified the amendment by February 1913.

Amendment XVII

[Adopted 1913]

Section 1 The Senate of the United States shall be composed of two Senators from each State, elected by the people thereof, for six years; and each Senator shall have one vote. The electors in each State shall have the qualifications requisite for electors of [voters for] the most numerous branch of the State legislatures.

Section 2 When vacancies happen in the representation of any State in the Senate, the executive authority of such State shall issue writs of election to fill such vacancies: Provided, that the Legislature of any State may empower the executive thereof to make temporary appointments until the people fill the vacancies by election as the Legislature may direct.

Section 3 This amendment shall not be so construed as to affect the election or term of any Senator chosen before it becomes valid as part of the Constitution.

◆ ◆ ◆

The framers of the Constitution saw the members of the House as the representatives of the people and the members of the Senate as the representatives of the states. Originally senators were to be chosen by the state legislators. According to reform advocates, however, the growth of private industry and transportation conglomerates during the Gilded Age had created a network of corruption in which wealth and power were exchanged for influence and votes in the Senate. Senator Nelson Aldrich, who represented Rhode Island in the late nineteenth and early twentieth centuries, for example, was known as "the senator from Standard Oil" because of his open support of special business interests.

Efforts to amend the Constitution to allow direct election of senators had begun in 1826, but since any proposal had to be approved by the Senate, reform seemed impossible. Progressives tried to gain influence in the Senate by instituting party caucuses and primary elections, which gave citizens the chance to express their choice of a senator who could then be officially elected by the state legislature. By 1910, fourteen of the country's thirty senators received popular votes through a state primary before the state legislature made its selection. Despairing of getting a proposal through the Senate, supporters of a direct-election amendment had begun in 1893 to seek a convention of representatives from two-thirds of the states to propose an amendment that could then be ratified. By 1905, thirty-one of forty-five states had endorsed such an amendment. Finally, in 1911, despite extraordinary opposition, a proposed amendment passed the Senate; by 1913, it had been ratified.

Amendment XVIII

[Adopted 1919; Repealed 1933 by Amendment XXI]

Section 1   After one year from the ratification of this article the manufacture, sale, or transportation of intoxicating liquors within, the importation thereof into, or the exportation thereof from the United States and all territory subject to the jurisdiction thereof, for beverage purposes, is hereby prohibited.

Section 2   The Congress and the several States shall have concurrent power to enforce this article by appropriate legislation.

Section 3   This article shall be inoperative unless it shall have been ratified as an amendment to the Constitution by the legislatures of the several States, as provided by the Constitution, within seven years from the date of the submission thereof to the States by the Congress.

◆ ◆ ◆

The Prohibition Party, formed in 1869, began calling for a constitutional amendment to outlaw alcoholic beverages in 1872. A prohibition amendment was first proposed in the Senate in 1876 and was revived eighteen times before 1913. Between 1913 and 1919, another thirty-nine attempts were made to prohibit liquor in the United States through a constitutional amendment. Prohibition became a key element of the Progressive agenda as reformers linked alcohol and drunkenness to numerous social problems, including the corruption of immigrant voters. While opponents of such an amendment argued that it was undemocratic, supporters claimed that their efforts had widespread public support. The admission of twelve "dry" western states to the Union in the early twentieth century and the spirit of sacrifice during World War I laid the groundwork for passage and ratification of the Eighteenth Amendment in 1919. Opponents added a time limit to the

amendment in the hope that they could thus block ratification, but this effort failed. (See also Amendment XXI.)

Amendment XIX

[Adopted 1920]

Section 1   The right of citizens of the United States to vote shall not be denied or abridged by the United States or by any State on account of sex.

Section 2   Congress shall have the power to enforce this article by appropriate legislation.

◆ ◆ ◆

Advocates of women's rights tried and failed to link woman suffrage to the Fourteenth and Fifteenth Amendments. Nonetheless, the effort for woman suffrage continued. Between 1878 and 1912, at least one and sometimes as many as four proposed amendments were introduced in Congress each year to grant women the right to vote. While over time women won very limited voting rights in some states, at both the state and federal levels opposition to an amendment for woman suffrage remained very strong. President Woodrow Wilson and other officials felt that the federal government should not interfere with the power of the states in this matter. Others worried that granting suffrage to women would encourage ethnic minorities to exercise their own right to vote. And many were concerned that giving women the vote would result in their abandoning traditional gender roles. In 1919, following a protracted and often bitter campaign of protest in which women went on hunger strikes and chained themselves to fences, an amendment was introduced with the backing of President Wilson. It narrowly passed the Senate (after efforts to limit the suffrage to white women failed) and was adopted in 1920 after Tennessee became the thirty-sixth state to ratify it.

Unratified Amendment

Child Labor Amendment (proposed by Congress June 2, 1924)

Section 1   The Congress shall have power to limit, regulate, and prohibit the labor of persons under eighteen years of age.

Section 2   The power of the several States is unimpaired by this article except that the operation of State laws shall be suspended to the extent necessary to give effect to legislation enacted by Congress.

◆ ◆ ◆

Throughout the late nineteenth and early twentieth centuries, alarm over the condition of child workers grew.

Opponents of child labor argued that children worked in dangerous and unhealthy conditions, that they took jobs from adult workers, that they depressed wages in certain industries, and that states that allowed child labor had an economic advantage over those that did not. Defenders of child labor claimed that children provided needed income in many families, that working at a young age developed character, and that the effort to prohibit the practice constituted an invasion of family privacy.

In 1916, Congress passed a law that made it illegal to sell goods made by children through interstate commerce. The Supreme Court, however, ruled that the law violated the limits on the power of Congress to regulate interstate commerce. Congress then tried to penalize industries that used child labor by taxing such goods. This measure was also thrown out by the courts. In response, reformers set out to amend the Constitution. The proposed amendment was ratified by twenty-eight states, but by 1925, thirteen states had rejected it. Passage of the Fair Labor Standards Act in 1938, which was upheld by the Supreme Court in 1941, made the amendment irrelevant.

Amendment XX

[Adopted 1933]

Section 1   The terms of the President and Vice President shall end at noon on the 20th day of January, and the terms of Senators and Representatives at noon on the 3rd day of January, of the years in which such terms would have ended if this article had not been ratified; and the terms of their successors shall then begin.

Section 2   The Congress shall assemble at least once in every year, and such meeting shall begin at noon on the 3d day of January, unless they shall by law appoint a different day.

Section 3   If, at the time fixed for the beginning of the term of the President, the President-elect shall have died, the Vice-President-elect shall become President. If a President shall not have been chosen before the time fixed for the beginning of his term, or if the President-elect shall have failed to qualify, then the Vice-President-elect shall act as President until a President shall have qualified; and the Congress may by law provide for the case wherein neither a President-elect nor a Vice-President-elect shall have qualified, declaring who shall then act as President, or the manner in which one who is to act shall be selected, and such person shall act accordingly until a President or Vice-President shall have qualified.

Section 4   The Congress may by law provide for the case of the death of any of the persons from whom the House of Representatives may choose a President whenever the right of choice shall have devolved upon them, and for the case of the death of any of the persons from whom the Senate may choose a Vice-President whenever the right of choice shall have devolved upon them.

Section 5   Sections 1 and 2 shall take effect on the 15th day of October following the ratification of this article.

Section 6   This article shall be inoperative unless it shall have been ratified as an amendment to the Constitution by the Legislatures of three- fourths of the several States within seven years from the date of its submission.

◆ ◆ ◆

Until 1933, presidents took office on March 4. Since elections are held in early November and electoral votes are counted in mid-December, this meant that more than three months passed between the time a new president was elected and when he took office. Moving the inauguration to January shortened the transition period and allowed Congress to begin its term closer to the time of the president's inauguration. Although this seems like a minor change, an amendment was required because the Constitution specifies terms of office. This amendment also deals with questions of succession in the event that a president- or vice president-elect dies before assuming office. Section 3 also clarifies a method for resolving a deadlock in the electoral college.

Amendment XXI

[Adopted 1933]

Section 1   The eighteenth article of amendment to the Constitution of the United States is hereby repealed.

Section 2   The transportation or importation into any State, Territory, or Possession of the United States for delivery or use therein of intoxicating liquors, in violation of the laws thereof, is hereby prohibited.

Section 3   This article shall be inoperative unless it shall have been ratified as an amendment to the Constitution by conventions in the several States, as provided in the Constitution, within seven years from the date of the submission thereof to the States by the Congress.

◆ ◆ ◆

Widespread violation of the Volstead Act, the law enacted to enforce prohibition, made the United States a nation of lawbreakers. Prohibition caused more problems than it solved by encouraging crime, bribery, and corruption.

Further, a coalition of liquor and beer manufacturers, personal liberty advocates, and constitutional scholars joined forces to challenge the amendment. By 1929, thirty proposed repeal amendments had been introduced in Congress, and the Democratic Party made repeal part of its platform in the 1932 presidential campaign. The Twenty-First Amendment was proposed in February 1933 and ratified less than a year later. The failure of the effort to enforce prohibition through a constitutional amendment has often been cited by opponents to subsequent efforts to shape public virtue and private morality.

Amendment XXII

[Adopted 1951]

Section 1   No person shall be elected to the office of the President more than twice, and no person who has held the office of President, or acted as President, for more than two years of a term to which some other person was elected President shall be elected to the office of President more than once. But this article shall not apply to any person holding the office of President when this Article was proposed by the Congress, and shall not prevent any person who may be holding the office of President, or acting as President, during the term within which this Article becomes operative from holding the office of President or acting as President during the remainder of such term.

Section 2   This article shall be inoperative unless it shall have been ratified as an amendment to the Constitution by the legislatures of three-fourths of the several States within seven years from the date of its submission to the States by the Congress.

♦ ♦ ♦

George Washington's refusal to seek a third term of office set a precedent that stood until 1912, when former President Theodore Roosevelt sought, without success, another term as an independent candidate. Democrat Franklin Roosevelt was the only president to seek and win a fourth term, though he did so amid great controversy. Roosevelt died in April 1945, a few months after the beginning of his fourth term. In 1946, Republicans won control of the House and the Senate, and early in 1947 a proposal for an amendment to limit future presidents to two four-year terms was offered to the states for ratification. Democratic critics of the Twenty-Second Amendment charged that it was a partisan posthumous jab at Roosevelt.

Since the Twenty-Second Amendment was adopted, however, the only presidents who might have been able to seek a third term, had it not existed, were Republicans Dwight Eisenhower and Ronald Reagan. Since 1826, Congress has entertained 160 proposed amendments to

limit the president to one six-year term. Such amendments have been backed by fifteen presidents, including Gerald Ford and Jimmy Carter.

Amendment XXIII

[Adopted 1961]

Section 1   The District constituting the seat of Government of the United States shall appoint in such manner as the Congress may direct: A number of electors of President and Vice-President equal to the whole number of Senators and Representatives in Congress to which the District would be entitled if it were a State, but in no event more than the least populous State; they shall be in addition to those appointed by the States, but they shall be considered for the purposes of the election of President and Vice-President, to be electors appointed by a State; and they shall meet in the District and perform such duties as provided by the twelfth article of amendment.

Section 2   The Congress shall have the power to enforce this article by appropriate legislation.

♦ ♦ ♦

When Washington, D.C., was established as a federal district, no one expected that a significant number of people would make it their permanent and primary residence. A proposal to allow citizens of the district to vote in presidential elections was approved by Congress in June 1960 and was ratified on March 29, 1961.

Amendment XXIV

[Adopted 1964]

Section 1   The right of citizens of the United States to vote in any primary or other election for President or Vice-President, for electors for President or Vice-President, or for Senator or Representative in Congress, shall not be denied or abridged by the United States or any State by reason of failure to pay any poll tax or other tax.

Section 2   The Congress shall have the power to enforce this article by appropriate legislation.

♦ ♦ ♦

In the colonial and Revolutionary eras, financial independence was seen as necessary to political independence, and the poll tax was used as a requirement for voting. By the twentieth century, however, the poll tax was used mostly to bar poor people, especially southern blacks, from voting. While conservatives complained that the amendment interfered with states' rights, liberals thought that the amendment did not go far enough because it barred the poll tax only in national elections and not in state or local elections. The amendment was ratified in 1964, however, and two years later, the Supreme Court ruled that poll taxes in state and local elections also violated the equal protection clause of the Fourteenth Amendment.

Amendment XXV

[Adopted 1967]

Section 1   In case of the removal of the President from office or of his death or resignation, the Vice-President shall become President.

Section 2   Whenever there is a vacancy in the office of the Vice-President, the President shall nominate a Vice-President who shall take office upon confirmation by a majority vote of both Houses of Congress.

Section 3   Whenever the President transmits to the President pro tempore of the Senate and the Speaker of the House of Representatives his written declaration that he is unable to discharge the powers and duties of his office, and until he transmits to them a written declaration to the contrary, such powers and duties shall be discharged by the Vice-President as Acting President.

Section 4   Whenever the Vice-President and a majority of either the principal officers of the executive departments or of such other body as Congress may by law provide, transmit to the President pro tempore of the Senate and the Speaker of the House of Representatives their written declaration that the President is unable to discharge the powers and duties of his office, the Vice-President shall immediately assume the powers and duties of the office as Acting President.

Thereafter, when the President transmits to the President pro tempore of the Senate and the Speaker of the House of Representatives his written declaration that no inability exists, he shall resume the powers and duties of his office unless the Vice-President and a majority of either the principal officers of the executive department[s] or of such other body as Congress may by law provide, transmit within four days to the President pro tempore of the Senate and the Speaker of the House of Representatives their written declaration that the President is unable to discharge the powers and duties of his office. Thereupon Congress shall decide the issue, assembling within forty-eight hours for that purpose if not in session. If the Congress, within twenty-one days after receipt of the latter written declaration, or, if Congress is not in session, within twenty-one days after Congress is required to assemble, determines by two-thirds vote of both Houses that the President is unable to discharge the powers and duties of his office, the Vice-President shall continue to discharge the same as Acting President; otherwise, the President shall resume the powers and duties of his office.

◆ ◆ ◆

The framers of the Constitution established the office of vice president because someone was needed to preside over the Senate. The first president to die in office was William Henry Harrison, in 1841. Vice President John Tyler had himself sworn in as president, setting a precedent that was followed when seven later presidents died in office. The assassination of President James A. Garfield in 1881 posed a new problem, however. After he was shot, the president was incapacitated for two months before he died; he was unable to lead the country, while his vice president, Chester A. Arthur, was unable to assume leadership. Efforts to resolve questions of succession in the event of a presidential disability thus began with the death of Garfield.

In 1963, the assassination of President John F. Kennedy galvanized Congress to action. Vice President Lyndon Johnson was a chain smoker with a history of heart trouble. According to the 1947 Presidential Succession Act, the two men who stood in line to succeed him were the seventy-two-year-old Speaker of the House and the eighty-six-year-old president of the Senate. There were serious concerns that any of these men might become incapacitated while serving as chief executive. The first time the Twenty-Fifth Amendment was used, however, was not in the case of presidential death or illness, but during the Watergate crisis. When Vice President Spiro T. Agnew was forced to resign following allegations of bribery and tax violations, President Richard M. Nixon appointed House Minority Leader Gerald R. Ford vice president. Ford became president following Nixon's resignation eight months later and named Nelson A. Rockefeller as his vice president. Thus, for more than two years, the two highest offices in the country were held by people who had not been elected to them.

Amendment XXVI

[Adopted 1971]

Section 1   The right of citizens of the United States, who are eighteen years of age or older, to vote shall not be denied or abridged by the United States or by any State on account of age.

Section 2   The Congress shall have power to enforce this article by appropriate legislation.

◆ ◆ ◆

Efforts to lower the voting age from twenty-one to eighteen began during World War II. Recognizing that those who were old enough to fight a war should have some say in the government policies that involved them in the war, Presidents Eisenhower, Johnson, and Nixon endorsed the idea. In 1970, the combined pressure of the antiwar movement and the demographic pressure of the baby boom generation led to a Voting Rights Act lowering the voting age in federal, state, and local elections.

In Oregon v. Mitchell (1970), *the state of Oregon challenged the right of Congress to determine the age at which people could vote in state or local elections. The Supreme Court agreed with Oregon. Since the Voting Rights Act was ruled unconstitutional, the Constitution had to be amended to allow passage of a law that would lower the voting age. The amendment was ratified in a little more than three months, making it the most rapidly ratified amendment in U.S. history.*

Unratified Amendment

Equal Rights Amendment (proposed by Congress March 22, 1972; seven-year deadline for ratification extended, June 30, 1982)

Section 1   Equality of rights under the law shall not be denied or abridged by the United States or by any State on account of sex.

Section 2   The Congress shall have the power to enforce, by appropriate legislation, the provisions of this article.

Section 3   This amendment shall take effect two years after the date of ratification.

◆ ◆ ◆

In 1923, soon after women had won the right to vote, Alice Paul, a leading activist in the woman suffrage movement, proposed an amendment requiring equal treatment of men and women. Opponents of the proposal argued that such an amendment would invalidate laws that protected women and would make women subject to the military draft. After the 1964 Civil Rights Act was adopted, protective workplace legislation was removed anyway.

The renewal of the women's movement, as a by-product of the civil rights and antiwar movements, led to a revival of the Equal Rights Amendment (ERA) in Congress. Disagreements over language held up congressional passage of the proposed amendment, but on March 22, 1972, the Senate approved the ERA by a vote of eighty-four to eight, and it was sent to the states. Six states ratified the

amendment within two days, and by the middle of 1973 the amendment seemed well on its way to adoption, with thirty of the needed thirty-eight states having ratified it. In the mid-1970s, however, a powerful "Stop ERA" campaign developed. The campaign portrayed the ERA as a threat to "family values" and traditional relationships between men and women. Although thirty-five states ultimately ratified the ERA, five of those state legislatures voted to rescind ratification, and the amendment was never adopted.

Unratified Amendment

D.C. Statehood Amendment (proposed by Congress August 22, 1978)

Section 1   For purposes of representation in the Congress, election of the President and Vice President, and article V of this Constitution, the District constituting the seat of government of the United States shall be treated as though it were a State.

Section 2   The exercise of the rights and powers conferred under this article shall be by the people of the District constituting the seat of government, and as shall be provided by Congress.

Section 3   The twenty-third article of amendment to the Constitution of the United States is hereby repealed.

Section 4   This article shall be inoperative, unless it shall have been ratified as an amendment to the Constitution by the legislatures of three-fourths of the several states within seven years from the date of its submission.

◆ ◆ ◆

The 1961 ratification of the Twenty-Third Amendment, giving residents of the District of Columbia the right to vote for a president and vice president, inspired an effort to give residents of the district full voting rights. In 1966, President Lyndon Johnson appointed a mayor and city council; in 1971, D.C. residents were allowed to name a nonvoting delegate to the House; and in 1981, residents were allowed to elect the mayor and city council. Congress retained the right to overrule laws that might affect commuters, the height of federal buildings, and selection of judges and prosecutors. The district's nonvoting delegate to Congress, Walter Fauntroy, lobbied fiercely for a congressional amendment granting statehood to the district. In 1978, a proposed amendment was approved and sent to the states. A number of states quickly ratified the amendment, but, like the ERA, the D.C. Statehood Amendment ran into trouble. Opponents argued that section 2 created a separate category of "nominal" statehood. They argued that the federal district should be eliminated and that the territory should be reabsorbed into the state of Maryland. Although these theoretical arguments were strong, some scholars believe that racist attitudes toward the predominantly black population of the city was also a factor leading to the defeat of the amendment.

AMENDMENT XXVII

[Adopted 1992]

No law, varying the compensation for the services of the Senators and Representatives, shall take effect, until an election of Representatives shall have intervened.

◆ ◆ ◆

While the Twenty-Sixth Amendment was the most rapidly ratified amendment in U.S. history, the Twenty-Seventh Amendment had the longest journey to ratification. First proposed by James Madison in 1789 as part of the package that included the Bill of Rights, this amendment had been ratified by only six states by 1791. In 1873, however, it was ratified by Ohio to protest a massive retroactive salary increase by the federal government. Unlike later proposed amendments, this one came with no time limit on ratification. In the early 1980s, Gregory D. Watson, a University of Texas economics major, discovered the "lost" amendment and began a single-handed campaign to get state legislators to introduce it for ratification. In 1983, it was accepted by Maine. In 1984, it passed the Colorado legislature. Ratifications trickled in slowly until May 1992, when Michigan and New Jersey became the thirty-eighth and thirty-ninth states, respectively, to ratify. This amendment prevents members of Congress from raising their own salaries without giving voters a chance to vote them out of office before they can benefit from the raises.

APPENDIX II. FACTS AND FIGURES

U.S. POLITICS AND GOVERNMENT

PRESIDENTIAL ELECTIONS

Year	Candidates	Parties	Popular Vote	Percentage of Popular Vote	Electoral Vote	Percentage of Voter Participation
1789	**GEORGE WASHINGTON (Va.)***				69	
	John Adams				34	
	Others				35	
1792	**GEORGE WASHINGTON (Va.)**				132	
	John Adams				77	
	George Clinton				50	
	Others				5	
1796	**JOHN ADAMS (Mass.)**	Federalist			71	
	Thomas Jefferson	Democratic-Republican			68	
	Thomas Pinckney	Federalist			59	
	Aaron Burr	Dem.-Rep.			30	
	Others				48	
1800	**THOMAS JEFFERSON (Va.)**	Dem.-Rep.			73	
	Aaron Burr	Dem.-Rep.			73	
	John Adams	Federalist			65	
	C.C. Pinckney	Federalist			64	
	John Jay	Federalist			1	
1804	**THOMAS JEFFERSON (Va.)**	Dem.-Rep.			162	
	C. C. Pinckney	Federalist			14	
1808	**JAMES MADISON (Va.)**	Dem.-Rep.			122	
	C. C. Pinckney	Federalist			47	
	George Clinton	Dem.-Rep.			6	
1812	**JAMES MADISON (Va.)**	Dem.-Rep.			128	
	De Witt Clinton	Federalist			89	
1816	**JAMES MONROE (Va.)**	Dem.-Rep.			183	
	Rufus King	Federalist			34	
1820	**JAMES MONROE (Va.)**	Dem.-Rep.			231	
	John Quincy Adams	Dem.-Rep.			1	
1824	**JOHN Q. ADAMS (Mass.)**	Dem.-Rep.	108,740	30.5	84	26.9
	Andrew Jackson	Dem.-Rep.	153,544	43.1	99	
	William H. Crawford	Dem.-Rep.	46,618	13.1	41	
	Henry Clay	Dem.-Rep.	47,136	13.2	37	
1828	**ANDREW JACKSON (Tenn.)**	Democratic	647,286	56.0	178	57.6
	John Quincy Adams	National Republican	508,064	44.0	83	

*State of residence when elected president.

Year	Candidates	Parties	Popular Vote	Percentage of Popular Vote	Electoral Vote	Percentage of Voter Participation
1832	**ANDREW JACKSON (Tenn.)**	Democratic	687,502	55.0	219	55.4
	Henry Clay	National Republican	530,189	42.4	49	
	John Floyd	Independent			11	
	William Wirt	Anti-Mason	33,108	2.6	7	
1836	**MARTIN VAN BUREN (N.Y.)**	Democratic	765,483	50.9	170	57.8
	W. H. Harrison	Whig			73	
	Hugh L. White	Whig	739,795	49.1	26	
	Daniel Webster	Whig			14	
	W. P. Magnum	Independent			11	
1840	**WILLIAM H. HARRISON (Ohio)**	Whig	1,274,624	53.1	234	80.2
	Martin Van Buren	Democratic	1,127,781	46.9	60	
	J. G. Birney	Liberty	7,069		—	
1844	**JAMES K. POLK (Tenn.)**	Democratic	1,338,464	49.6	170	78.9
	Henry Clay	Whig	1,300,097	48.1	105	
	J. G. Birney	Liberty	62,300	2.3	—	
1848	**ZACHARY TAYLOR (La.)**	Whig	1,360,967	47.4	163	72.7
	Lewis Cass	Democratic	1,222,342	42.5	127	
	Martin Van Buren	Free-Soil	291,263	10.1	—	
1852	**FRANKLIN PIERCE (N.H.)**	Democratic	1,601,117	50.9	254	69.6
	Winfield Scott	Whig	1,385,453	44.1	42	
	John P. Hale	Free-Soil	155,825	5.0	—	
1856	**JAMES BUCHANAN (Pa.)**	Democratic	1,832,995	45.3	174	78.9
	John C. Frémont	Republican	1,339,932	33.1	114	
	Millard Fillmore	American	871,731	21.6	8	
1860	**ABRAHAM LINCOLN (Ill.)**	Republican	1,865,593	39.8	180	81.2
	Stephen A. Douglas	Democratic	1,382,713	29.5	12	
	John C. Breckinridge	Democratic	848,356	18.1	72	
	John Bell	Union	592,906	12.6	39	
1864	**ABRAHAM LINCOLN (Ill.)**	Republican	2,206,938	55.0	212	73.8
	George B. McClellan	Democratic	1,803,787	45.0	21	
1868	**ULYSSES S. GRANT (Ill.)**	Republican	3,012,833	52.7	214	78.1
	Horatio Seymour	Democratic	2,703,249	47.3	80	
1872	**ULYSSES S. GRANT (Ill.)**	Republican	3,597,132	55.6	286	71.3
	Horace Greeley	Democratic; Liberal Republican	2,834,125	43.9	66	
1876	**RUTHERFORD B. HAYES (Ohio)**	Republican	4,036,572	48.0	185	81.8
	Samuel J. Tilden	Democratic	4,284,020	51.0	184	
1880	**JAMES A. GARFIELD (Ohio)**	Republican	4,454,416	48.5	214	79.4
	Winfield S. Hancock	Democratic	4,444,952	48.1	155	
1884	**GROVER CLEVELAND (N.Y.)**	Democratic	4,879,507	48.5	219	77.5
	James G. Blaine	Republican	4,850,293	48.2	182	
1888	**BENJAMIN HARRISON (Ind.)**	Republican	5,439,853	47.9	233	79.3
	Grover Cleveland	Democratic	5,540,309	48.6	168	
1892	**GROVER CLEVELAND (N.Y.)**	Democratic	5,555,426	46.1	277	74.7
	Benjamin Harrison	Republican	5,182,690	43.0	145	
	James B. Weaver	People's	1,029,846	8.5	22	

Year	Candidates	Parties	Popular Vote	Percentage of Popular Vote	Electoral Vote	Percentage of Voter Participation
1896	**WILLIAM McKINLEY (Ohio)**	Republican	7,104,779	51.1	271	79.3
	William J. Bryan	Democratic-People's	6,502,925	47.7	176	
1900	**WILLIAM McKINLEY (Ohio)**	Republican	7,207,923	51.7	292	73.2
	William J. Bryan	Dem.-Populist	6,358,133	45.5	155	
1904	**THEODORE ROOSEVELT (N.Y.)**	Republican	7,623,486	57.9	336	65.2
	Alton B. Parker	Democratic	5,077,911	37.6	140	
	Eugene V. Debs	Socialist	402,283	3.0	—	
1908	**WILLIAM H. TAFT (Ohio)**	Republican	7,678,908	51.6	321	65.4
	William J. Bryan	Democratic	6,409,104	43.1	162	
	Eugene V. Debs	Socialist	420,793	2.8	—	
1912	**WOODROW WILSON (N.J.)**	Democratic	6,293,454	41.9	435	58.8
	Theodore Roosevelt	Progressive	4,119,538	27.4	88	
	William H. Taft	Republican	3,484,980	23.2	8	
	Eugene V. Debs	Socialist	900,672	6.1	—	
1916	**WOODROW WILSON (N.J.)**	Democratic	9,129,606	49.4	277	61.6
	Charles E. Hughes	Republican	8,538,221	46.2	254	
	A. L. Benson	Socialist	585,113	3.2	—	
1920	**WARREN G. HARDING (Ohio)**	Republican	16,143,407	60.5	404	49.2
	James M. Cox	Democratic	9,130,328	34.2	127	
	Eugene V. Debs	Socialist	919,799	3.4	—	
1924	**CALVIN COOLIDGE (Mass.)**	Republican	15,725,016	54.0	382	48.9
	John W. Davis	Democratic	8,386,503	28.8	136	
	Robert M. LaFollette	Progressive	4,822,856	16.6	13	
1928	**HERBERT HOOVER (Calif.)**	Republican	21,391,381	58.2	444	56.9
	Alfred E. Smith	Democratic	15,016,443	40.9	87	
	Norman Thomas	Socialist	267,835	0.7	—	
1932	**FRANKLIN D. ROOSEVELT (N.Y.)**	Democratic	22,809,638	57.4	472	56.9
	Herbert Hoover	Republican	15,758,901	39.7	59	
	Norman Thomas	Socialist	881,951	2.2	—	
1936	**FRANKLIN D. ROOSEVELT (N.Y.)**	Democratic	27,751,597	60.8	523	61.0
	Alfred M. Landon	Republican	16,679,583	36.5	8	
	William Lemke	Union	882,479	1.9	—	
1940	**FRANKLIN D. ROOSEVELT (N.Y.)**	Democratic	27,244,160	54.8	449	62.5
	Wendell Willkie	Republican	22,305,198	44.8	82	
1944	**FRANKLIN D. ROOSEVELT (N.Y.)**	Democratic	25,602,504	53.5	432	55.9
	Thomas E. Dewey	Republican	22,006,285	46.0	99	
1948	**HARRY S. TRUMAN (Mo.)**	Democratic	24,105,695	49.5	303	53.0
	Thomas E. Dewey	Republican	21,969,170	45.1	189	
	J. Strom Thurmond	State-Rights Democratic	1,169,021	2.4	38	
	Henry A. Wallace	Progressive	1,156,103	2.4	—	
1952	**DWIGHT D. EISENHOWER (N.Y.)**	Republican	33,936,252	55.1	442	63.3
	Adlai Stevenson	Democratic	27,314,992	44.4	89	
1956	**DWIGHT D. EISENHOWER (N.Y.)**	Republican	35,575,420	57.6	457	60.6
	Adlai Stevenson	Democratic	26,033,066	42.1	73	
	Other	—	—		1	

Year	Candidates	Parties	Popular Vote	Percentage of Popular Vote	Electoral Vote	Percentage of Voter Participation
1960	JOHN F. KENNEDY (Mass.)	Democratic	34,227,096	49.9	303	62.8
	Richard M. Nixon	Republican	34,108,546	49.6	219	
	Other	—	—		15	
1964	LYNDON B. JOHNSON (Tex.)	Democratic	43,126,506	61.1	486	61.7
	Barry M. Goldwater	Republican	27,176,799	38.5	52	
1968	RICHARD M. NIXON (N.Y.)	Republican	31,770,237	43.4	301	60.6
	Hubert H. Humphrey	Democratic	31,270,533	42.7	191	
	George Wallace	American Indep.	9,906,141	13.5	46	
1972	RICHARD M. NIXON (N.Y.)	Republican	47,169,911	60.7	520	55.2
	George S. McGovern	Democratic	29,170,383	37.5	17	
	Other	—	—		1	
1976	JIMMY CARTER (Ga.)	Democratic	40,828,587	50.0	297	53.5
	Gerald R. Ford	Republican	39,147,613	47.9	241	
	Other	—	1,575,459	2.1	—	
1980	RONALD REAGAN (Calif.)	Republican	43,901,812	50.7	489	52.6
	Jimmy Carter	Democratic	35,483,820	41.0	49	
	John B. Anderson	Independent	5,719,722	6.6	—	
	Ed Clark	Libertarian	921,188	1.1	—	
1984	RONALD REAGAN (Calif.)	Republican	54,455,075	59.0	525	53.3
	Walter Mondale	Democratic	37,577,185	41.0	13	
1988	GEORGE BUSH (Texas)	Republican	47,946,422	54.0	426	50.2
	Michael S. Dukakis	Democratic	41,016,429	46.0	112	
1992	WILLIAM J. CLINTON (Ark.)	Democratic	44,908,254	42.3	370	55.2
	George Bush	Republican	39,102,282	37.4	168	
	H. Ross Perot	Independent	19,721,433	18.9	—	
1996	WILLIAM J. CLINTON (Ark.)	Democratic	47,401,185	49.2	379	49
	Robert Dole	Republican	39,197,469	40.7	159	
	H. Ross Perot	Independent	8,085,294	8.4	—	

PRESIDENTS, VICE PRESIDENTS, AND CABINETS

The Washington Administration (1789–1797)

Vice President	John Adams	1789–1797
Secretary of State	Thomas Jefferson	1789–1793
	Edmund Randolph	1794 1795
	Timothy Pickering	1795–1797
Secretary of Treasury	Alexander Hamilton	1789–1795
	Oliver Wolcott	1795–1797
Secretary of War	Henry Knox	1789–1794
	Timothy Pickering	1795–1796
	James McHenry	1796–1797
Attorney General	Edmund Randolph	1789–1793
	William Bradford	1794–1795
	Charles Lee	1795–1797
Postmaster General	Samuel Osgood	1789–1791
	Timothy Pickering	1791–1794
	Joseph Habersham	1795–1797

The John Adams Administration (1797–1801)

Vice President	Thomas Jefferson	1797–1801
Secretary of State	Timothy Pickering	1797–1800
	John Marshall	1800–1801
Secretary of Treasury	Oliver Wolcott	1797–1800
	Samuel Dexter	1800–1801
Secretary of War	James McHenry	1797–1800
	Samuel Dexter	1800–1801
Attorney General	Charles Lee	1797–1801
Postmaster General	Joseph Habersham	1797–1801
Secretary of Navy	Benjamin Stoddert	1798–1801

The Jefferson Administration (1801–1809)

Vice President	Aaron Burr	1801–1805
	George Clinton	1805–1809
Secretary of State	James Madison	1801–1809
Secretary of Treasury	Samuel Dexter	1801
	Albert Gallatin	1801–1809
Secretary of War	Henry Dearborn	1801–1809

Attorney General	Levi Lincoln	1801–1805
	Robert Smith	1805
	John Breckinridge	1805–1806
	Caesar Rodney	1807–1809
Postmaster General	Joseph Habersham	1801
	Gideon Granger	1801–1809
Secretary of Navy	Robert Smith	1801–1809

The Madison Administration (1809–1817)

Vice President	George Clinton	1809–1813
	Elbridge Gerry	1813–1817
Secretary of State	Robert Smith	1809–1811
	James Monroe	1811–1817
Secretary of Treasury	Albert Gallatin	1809–1813
	George Campbell	1814
	Alexander Dallas	1814–1816
	William Crawford	1816–1817
Secretary of War	William Eustis	1809–1812
	John Armstrong	1813–1814
	James Monroe	1814–1815
	William Crawford	1815–1817
Attorney General	Caesar Rodney	1809–1811
	William Pinkney	1811–1814
	Richard Rush	1814–1817
Postmaster General	Gideon Granger	1809–1814
	Return Meigs	1814–1817
Secretary of Navy	Paul Hamilton	1809–1813
	William Jones	1813–1814
	Benjamin Crowninshield	1814–1817

The Monroe Administration (1817–1825)

Vice President	Daniel Tompkins	1817–1825
Secretary of State	John Quincy Adams	1817–1825
Secretary of Treasury	William Crawford	1817–1825
Secretary of War	George Graham	1817
	John C. Calhoun	1817–1825
Attorney General	Richard Rush	1817
	William Wirt	1817–1825
Postmaster General	Return Meigs	1817–1823
	John McLean	1823–1825

Secretary of Navy	Benjamin Crowninshield	1817–1818
	Smith Thompson	1818–1823
	Samuel Southard	1823–1825

The John Quincy Adams Administration (1825–1829)

Vice President	John C. Calhoun	1825–1829
Secretary of State	Henry Clay	1825–1829
Secretary of Treasury	Richard Rush	1825–1829
Secretary of War	James Barbour	1825–1828
	Peter Porter	1828–1829
Attorney General	William Wirt	1825–1829
Postmaster General	John McLean	1825–1829
Secretary of Navy	Samuel Southard	1825–1829

The Jackson Administration (1829–1837)

Vice President	John C. Calhoun	1829–1833
	Martin Van Buren	1833–1837
Secretary of State	Martin Van Buren	1829–1831
	Edward Livingston	1831–1833
	Louis McLane	1833–1834
	John Forsyth	1834–1837
Secretary of Treasury	Samuel Ingham	1829–1831
	Louis McLane	1831–1833
	William Duane	1833
	Roger B. Taney	1833–1834
	Levi Woodbury	1834–1837
Secretary of War	John H. Eaton	1829–1831
	Lewis Cass	1831–1837
	Benjamin Butler	1837
Attorney General	John M. Berrien	1829–1831
	Roger B. Taney	1831–1833
	Benjamin Butler	1833–1837
Postmaster General	William Barry	1829–1835
	Amos Kendall	1835–1837
Secretary of Navy	John Branch	1829–1831
	Levi Woodbury	1831–1834
	Mahlon Dickerson	1834–1837

The Van Buren Administration (1837–1841)

Vice President	Richard M. Johnson	1837–1841
Secretary of State	John Forsyth	1837–1841
Secretary of Treasury	Levi Woodbury	1837–1841
Secretary of War	Joel Poinsett	1837–1841
Attorney General	Benjamin Butler	1837–1838
	Felix Grundy	1838–1840
	Henry D. Gilpin	1840–1841
Postmaster General	Amos Kendall	1837–1840
	John M. Niles	1840–1841
Secretary of Navy	Mahlon Dickerson	1837–1838
	James Paulding	1838–1841

The William Harrison Administration (1841)

Vice President	John Tyler	1841
Secretary of State	Daniel Webster	1841
Secretary of Treasury	Thomas Ewing	1841
Secretary of War	John Bell	1841
Attorney General	John J. Crittenden	1841
Postmaster General	Francis Granger	1841
Secretary of Navy	George Badger	1841

The Tyler Administration (1841–1845)

Vice President	None	
Secretary of State	Daniel Webster	1841–1843
	Hugh S. Legaré	1843
	Abel P. Upshur	1843–1844
	John C. Calhoun	1844–1845
Secretary of Treasury	Thomas Ewing	1841
	Walter Forward	1841–1843
	John C. Spencer	1843–1844
	George Bibb	1844–1845

Secretary of War	John Bell	1841
	John C. Spencer	1841–1843
	James M. Porter	1843–1844
	William Wilkins	1844–1845
Attorney General	John J. Crittenden	1841
	Hugh S. Legaré	1841–1843
	John Nelson	1843–1845
Postmaster General	Francis Granger	1841
	Charles Wickliffe	1841
Secretary of Navy	George Badger	1841
	Abel P. Upshur	1841
	David Henshaw	1843–1844
	Thomas Gilmer	1844
	John Y. Mason	1844–1845

The Polk Administration (1845–1849)

Vice President	George M. Dallas	1845–1849
Secretary of State	James Buchanan	1845–1849
Secretary of Treasury	Robert J. Walker	1845–1849
Secretary of War	William L. Marcy	1845–1849
Attorney General	John Y. Mason	1845–1846
	Nathan Clifford	1846–1848
	Isaac Toucey	1848–1849
Postmaster General	Cave Johnson	1845–1849
Secretary of Navy	George Bancroft	1845–1846
	John Y. Mason	1846–1849

The Taylor Administration (1849–1850)

Vice President	Millard Fillmore	1849–1850
Secretary of State	John M. Clayton	1849–1850
Secretary of Treasury	William Meredith	1849–1850
Secretary of War	George Crawford	1849–1850
Attorney General	Reverdy Johnson	1849–1850
Postmaster General	Jacob Collamer	1849–1850
Secretary of Navy	William Preston	1849–1850

| Secretary of Interior | Thomas Ewing | 1849–1850 |

The Fillmore Administration (1850–1853)

Vice President	None	
Secretary of State	Daniel Webster	1850–1852
	Edward Everett	1852–1853
Secretary of Treasury	Thomas Corwin	1850–1853
Secretary of War	Charles Conrad	1850–1853
Attorney General	John J. Crittenden	1850–1853
Postmaster General	Nathan Hall	1850–1852
	Sam D. Hubbard	1852–1853
Secretary of Navy	William A. Graham	1850–1852
	John P. Kennedy	1852–1853
Secretary of Interior	Thomas McKennan	1850
	Alexander Stuart	1850–1853

The Pierce Administration (1853–1857)

Vice President	William R. King	1853–1857
Secretary of State	William L. Marcy	1853–1857
Secretary of Treasury	James Guthrie	1853–1857
Secretary of War	Jefferson Davis	1853–1857
Attorney General	Caleb Cushing	1853–1857
Postmaster General	James Campbell	1853–1857
Secretary of Navy	James C. Dobbin	1853–1857
Secretary of Interior	Robert McClelland	1853–1857

The Buchanan Administration (1857–1861)

Vice President	John C. Breckinridge	1857–1861
Secretary of State	Lewis Cass	1857–1860
	Jeremiah S. Black	1860–1861

Secretary of Treasury	Howell Cobb	1857–1860
	Philip Thomas	1860–1861
	John A. Dix	1861
Secretary of War	John B. Floyd	1857–1861
	Joseph Holt	1861
Attorney General	Jeremiah S. Black	1857–1860
	Edwin M. Stanton	1860–1861
Postmaster General	Aaron V. Brown	1857–1859
	Joseph Holt	1859–1861
	Horatio King	1861
Secretary of Navy	Isaac Toucey	1857–1861
Secretary of Interior	Jacob Thompson	1857–1861

The Lincoln Administration (1861–1865)

Vice President	Hannibal Hamlin	1861–1865
	Andrew Johnson	1865
Secretary of State	William H. Seward	1861–1865
Secretary of Treasury	Samuel P. Chase	1861–1864
	William P. Fessenden	1864–1865
	Hugh McCulloch	1865
Secretary of War	Simon Cameron	1861–1862
	Edwin M. Stanton	1862–1865
Attorney General	Edward Bates	1861–1864
	James Speed	1864–1865
Postmaster General	Horatio King	1861
	Montgomery Blair	1861–1864
	William Dennison	1864–1865
Secretary of Navy	Gideon Welles	1861–1865
Secretary of Interior	Caleb B. Smith	1861–1863
	John P. Usher	1863–1865

The Andrew Johnson Administration (1865–1869)

Vice President	None	
Secretary of State	William H. Seward	1865–1869
Secretary of Treasury	Hugh McCulloch	1865–1869
Secretary of War	Edwin M. Stanton	1865–1867
	Ulysses S. Grant	1867–1868
	Lorenzo Thomas	1868
	John M. Schofield	1868–1869

Attorney General	James Speed	1865–1866
	Henry Stanbery	1866–1868
	William M. Evarts	1868–1869
Postmaster General	William Dennison	1865–1866
	Alexander Randall	1866–1869
Secretary of Navy	Gideon Welles	1865–1869
Secretary of Interior	John P. Usher	1865
	James Harlan	1865–1866
	Orville H. Browning	1866–1869

The Grant Administration (1869–1877)

Vice President	Schuyler Colfax	1869–1873
	Henry Wilson	1873–1877
Secretary of State	Elihu B. Washburne	1869
	Hamilton Fish	1869–1877
Secretary of Treasury	George S. Boutwell	1869–1873
	William Richardson	1873–1874
	Benjamin Bristow	1874–1876
	Lot M. Morrill	1876–1877
Secretary of War	John A. Rawlins	1869
	William T. Sherman	1869
	William W. Belknap	1869–1876
	Alphonso Taft	1876
	James D. Cameron	1876–1877
Attorney General	Ebenezer Hoar	1869–1870
	Amos T. Ackerman	1870–1871
	G. H. Williams	1871–1875
	Edwards Pierrepont	1875–1876
	Alphonso Taft	1876–1877
Postmaster General	John A. J. Creswell	1869–1874
	James W. Marshall	1874
	Marshall Jewell	1874–1876
	James N. Tyner	1876–1877
Secretary of Navy	Adolph E. Borie	1869
	George M. Robeson	1869–1877
Secretary of Interior	Jacob D. Cox	1869–1870
	Columbus Delano	1870–1875
	Zachariah Chandler	1875–1877

The Hayes Administration (1877–1881)

Vice President	William A. Wheeler	1877–1881
Secretary of State	William M. Evarts	1877–1881
Secretary of Treasury	John Sherman	1877–1881
Secretary of War	George W. McCrary	1877–1879
	Alex Ramsey	1879–1881
Attorney General	Charles Devens	1877–1881
Postmaster General	David M. Key	1877–1880
	Horace Maynard	1880–1881
Secretary of Navy	Richard W. Thompson	1877–1880
	Nathan Goff, Jr.	1881
Secretary of Interior	Carl Schurz	1877–1881

The Garfield Administration (1881)

Vice President	Chester A. Arthur	1881
Secretary of State	James G. Blaine	1881
Secretary of Treasury	William Windom	1881
Secretary of War	Robert T. Lincoln	1881
Attorney General	Wayne MacVeagh	1881
Postmaster General	Thomas L. James	1881
Secretary of Navy	William H. Hunt	1881
Secretary of Interior	Samuel J. Kirkwood	1881

The Arthur Administration (1881–1885)

Vice President	None	
Secretary of State	F. T. Frelinghuysen	1881–1885
Secretary of Treasury	Charles J. Folger	1881–1884
	Walter Q. Gresham	1884
	Hugh McCulloch	1884–1885
Secretary of War	Robert T. Lincoln	1881–1885
Attorney General	Benjamin H. Brewster	1881–1885
Postmaster General	Timothy O. Howe	1881–1883
	Walter Q. Gresham	1883–1884
	Frank Hatton	1884–1885
Secretary of Navy	William H. Hunt	1881–1882
	William E. Chandler	1882–1885
Secretary of Interior	Samuel J. Kirkwood	1881–1882
	Henry M. Teller	1882–1885

The Cleveland Administration (1885–1889)

Vice President	Thomas A. Hendricks	1885–1889
Secretary of State	Thomas F. Bayard	1885–1889
Secretary of Treasury	Daniel Manning	1885–1887
	Charles S. Fairchild	1887–1889
Secretary of War	William C. Endicott	1885–1889
Attorney General	Augustus H. Garland	1885–1889
Postmaster General	William F. Vilas	1885–1888
	Don M. Dickinson	1888–1889
Secretary of Navy	William C. Whitney	1885–1889
Secretary of Interior	Lucius Q. C. Lamar	1885–1888
	William F. Vilas	1888–1889
Secretary of Agriculture	Norman J. Colman	1889

The Benjamin Harrison Administration (1889–1893)

Vice President	Levi P. Morton	1889–1893
Secretary of State	James G. Blaine	1889–1892
	John W. Foster	1892–1893
Secretary of Treasury	William Windom	1889–1891
	Charles Foster	1891–1893
Secretary of War	Redfield Proctor	1889–1891
	Stephen B. Elkins	1891–1893

Attorney General	William H. H. Miller	1889–1893
Postmaster General	John Wanamaker	1889–1893
Secretary of Navy	Benjamin F. Tracy	1889–1893
Secretary of Interior	John W. Noble	1889–1893
Secretary of Agriculture	Jeremiah M. Rusk	1889–1893

The Cleveland Administration (1893–1897)

Vice President	Adlai E. Stevenson	1893–1897
Secretary of State	Walter Q. Gresham	1893–1895
	Richard Olney	1895–1897
Secretary of Treasury	John G. Carlisle	1893–1897
Secretary of War	Daniel S. Lamont	1893–1897
Attorney General	Richard Olney	1893–1895
	James Harmon	1895–1897
Postmaster General	Wilson S. Bissell	1893–1895
	William L. Wilson	1895–1897
Secretary of Navy	Hilary A. Herbert	1893–1897
Secretary of Interior	Hoke Smith	1893–1896
	David R. Francis	1896–1897
Secretary of Agriculture	Julius S. Morton	1893–1897

The McKinley Administration (1897–1901)

Vice President	Garret A. Hobart	1897–1901
	Theodore Roosevelt	1901
Secretary of State	John Sherman	1897–1898
	William R. Day	1898
	John Hay	1898–1901
Secretary of Treasury	Lyman J. Gage	1897–1901
Secretary of War	Russell A. Alger	1897–1899
	Elihu Root	1899–1901
Attorney General	Joseph McKenna	1897–1898
	John W. Griggs	1898–1901
	Philander C. Knox	1901

Postmaster General	James A. Gary	1897–1898
	Charles E. Smith	1898–1901
Secretary of Navy	John D. Long	1897–1901
Secretary of Interior	Cornelius N. Bliss	1897–1899
	Ethan A. Hitchcock	1899–1901
Secretary of Agriculture	James Wilson	1897–1901

The Theodore Roosevelt Administration (1901–1909)

Vice President	Charles Fairbanks	1905–1909
Secretary of State	John Hay	1901–1905
	Elihu Root	1905–1909
	Robert Bacon	1909
Secretary of Treasury	Lyman J. Gage	1901–1902
	Leslie M. Shaw	1902–1907
	George B. Cortelyou	1907–1909
Secretary of War	Elihu Root	1901–1904
	William H. Taft	1904–1908
	Luke E. Wright	1908–1909
Attorney General	Philander C. Knox	1901–1904
	William H. Moody	1904–1906
	Charles J. Bonaparte	1906–1909
Postmaster General	Charles E. Smith	1901–1902
	Henry C. Payne	1902–1904
	Robert J. Wynne	1904–1905
	George B. Cortelyou	1905–1907
	George von L. Meyer	1907–1909
Secretary of Navy	John D. Long	1901–1902
	William H. Moody	1902–1904
	Paul Morton	1904–1905
	Charles J. Bonaparte	1905–1906
	Victor H. Metcalf	1906–1908
	Truman H. Newberry	1908–1909
Secretary of Interior	Ethan A. Hitchcock	1901–1907
	James R. Garfield	1907–1909
Secretary of Agriculture	James Wilson	1901–1909
Secretary of Labor and Commerce	George B. Cortelyou	1903–1904
	Victor H. Metcalf	1904–1906
	Oscar S. Straus	1906–1909
	Charles Nagel	1909

The Taft Administration (1909 – 1913)

Vice President	James S. Sherman	1909–1913
Secretary of State	Philander C. Knox	1909–1913
Secretary of Treasury	Franklin MacVeagh	1909–1913
Secretary of War	Jacob M. Dickinson	1909–1911
	Henry L. Stimson	1911–1913
Attorney General	George W. Wickersham	1909–1913
Postmaster General	Frank H. Hitchcock	1909–1913
Secretary of Navy	George von L. Meyer	1909–1913
Secretary of Interior	Richard A. Ballinger	1909–1911
	Walter L. Fisher	1911–1913
Secretary of Agriculture	James Wilson	1909–1913
Secretary of Labor and Commerce	Charles Nagel	1909–1913

The Wilson Administration (1913–1921)

Vice President	Thomas R. Marshall	1913–1921
Secretary of State	William J. Bryan	1913–1915
	Robert Lansing	1915–1920
	Bainbridge Colby	1920–1921
Secretary of Treasury	William G. McAdoo	1913–1918
	Carter Glass	1918–1920
	David F. Houston	1920–1921
Secretary of War	Lindley M. Garrison	1913–1916
	Newton D. Baker	1916–1921
Attorney General	James C. McReynolds	1913–1914
	Thomas W. Gregory	1914–1919
	A. Mitchell Palmer	1919–1921
Postmaster General	Albert S. Burleson	1913–1921
Secretary of Navy	Josephus Daniels	1913–1921
Secretary of Interior	Franklin K. Lane	1913–1920
	John B. Payne	1920–1921
Secretary of Agriculture	David F. Houston	1913–1920
	Edwin T. Meredith	1920–1921
Secretary of Commerce	William C. Redfield	1913–1919
	Joshua W. Alexander	1919–1921
Secretary of Labor	William B. Wilson	1913–1921

The Harding Administration (1921–1923)

Vice President	Calvin Coolidge	1921–1923
Secretary of State	Charles E. Hughes	1921–1923
Secretary of Treasury	Andrew Mellon	1921–1923
Secretary of War	John W. Weeks	1921–1923
Attorney General	Harry M. Daugherty	1921–1923
Postmaster General	Will H. Hays	1921–1922
	Hubert Work	1922–1923
	Harry S. New	1923
Secretary of Navy	Edwin Denby	1921–1923
Secretary of Interior	Albert B. Fall	1921–1923
	Hubert Work	1923
Secretary of Agriculture	Henry C. Wallace	1921–1923
Secretary of Commerce	Herbert C. Hoover	1921–1923
Secretary of Labor	James J. Davis	1921–1923

The Coolidge Administration (1923–1929)

Vice President	Charles G. Dawes	1925–1929
Secretary of State	Charles E. Hughes	1923–1925
	Frank B. Kellogg	1925–1929
Secretary of Treasury	Andrew Mellon	1923–1929

Secretary of War	John W. Weeks	1923–1925
	Dwight F. Davis	1925–1929
Attorney General	Henry M. Daugherty	1923–1924
	Harlan F. Stone	1924–1925
	John G. Sargent	1925–1929
Postmaster General	Harry S. New	1923–1929
Secretary of Navy	Edwin Denby	1923–1924
	Curtis D. Wilbur	1924–1929
Secretary of Interior	Hubert Work	1923–1928
	Roy O. West	1928–1929
Secretary of Agriculture	Henry C. Wallace	1923–1924
	Howard M. Gore	1924–1925
	William M. Jardine	1925–1929
Secretary of Commerce	Herbert C. Hoover	1923–1928
	William F. Whiting	1928–1929
Secretary of Labor	James J. Davis	1923–1929

The Hoover Administration (1929–1933)

Vice President	Charles Curtis	1929–1933
Secretary of State	Henry L. Stimson	1929–1933
Secretary of Treasury	Andrew Mellon	1929–1932
	Ogden L. Mills	1932–1933
Secretary of War	James W. Good	1929
	Patrick J. Hurley	1929–1933
Attorney General	William D. Mitchell	1929–1933
Postmaster General	Walter F. Brown	1929–1933
Secretary of Navy	Charles F. Adams	1929–1933
Secretary of Interior	Ray L. Wilbur	1929–1933
Secretary of Agriculture	Arthur M. Hyde	1929–1933
Secretary of Commerce	Robert P. Lamont	1929–1932
	Roy D. Chapin	1932–1933
Secretary of Labor	James J. Davis	1929–1930
	William M. Doak	1930–1933

The Franklin D. Roosevelt Administration (1933–1945)

Vice President	John Nance Garner	1933–1941
	Henry A. Wallace	1941–1945
	Harry S. Truman	1945
Secretary of State	Cordell Hull	1933–1944
	Edward R. Stettinius, Jr.	1944–1945
Secretary of Treasury	William H. Woodin	1933–1934
	Henry Morgenthau, Jr.	1934–1945
Secretary of War	George H. Dern	1933–1936
	Henry A. Woodring	1936–1940
	Henry L. Stimson	1940–1945
Attorney General	Homer S. Cummings	1933–1939
	Frank Murphy	1939–1940
	Robert H. Jackson	1940–1941
	Francis Biddle	1941–1945
Postmaster General	James A. Farley	1933–1940
	Frank C. Walker	1940–1945
Secretary of Navy	Claude A. Swanson	1933–1940
	Charles Edison	1940
	Frank Knox	1940–1944
	James V. Forrestal	1944–1945
Secretary of Interior	Harold L. Ickes	1933–1945
Secretary of Agriculture	Henry A. Wallace	1933–1940
	Claude R. Wickard	1940–1945
Secretary of Commerce	Daniel C. Roper	1933–1939
	Harry L. Hopkins	1939–1940
	Jesse Jones	1940–1945
	Henry A. Wallace	1945
Secretary of Labor	Frances Perkins	1933–1945

The Truman Administration (1945–1953)

Vice President	Alben W. Barkley	1949–1953
Secretary of State	Edward R. Stettinius, Jr.	1945
	James F. Byrnes	1945–1947
	George C. Marshall	1947–1949
	Dean G. Acheson	1949–1953

Secretary of Treasury	Fred M. Vinson	1945–1946
	John W. Snyder	1946–1953
Secretary of War	Robert P. Patterson	1945–1947
	Kenneth C. Royall	1947
Attorney General	Tom C. Clark	1945–1949
	J. Howard McGrath	1949–1952
	James P. McGranery	1952–1953
Postmaster General	Frank C. Walker	1945
	Robert E. Hannegan	1945–1947
	Jesse M. Donaldson	1947–1953
Secretary of Navy	James V. Forrestal	1945–1947
Secretary of Interior	Harold L. Ickes	1945–1946
	Julius A. Krug	1946–1949
	Oscar L. Chapman	1949–1953
Secretary of Agriculture	Clinton P. Anderson	1945–1948
	Charles F. Brannan	1948–1953
Secretary of Commerce	Henry A. Wallace	1945–1946
	W. Averell Harriman	1946–1948
	Charles W. Sawyer	1948–1953
Secretary of Labor	Lewis B. Schwellenbach	1945–1948
	Maurice J. Tobin	1948–1953
Secretary of Defense	James V. Forrestal	1947–1949
	Louis A. Johnson	1949–1950
	George C. Marshall	1950–1951
	Robert A. Lovett	1951–1953

The Eisenhower Administration (1953–1961)

Vice President	Richard M. Nixon	1953–1961
Secretary of State	John Foster Dulles	1953–1959
	Christian A. Herter	1959–1961
Secretary of Treasury	George M. Humphrey	1953–1957
	Robert B. Anderson	1957–1961
Attorney General	Herbert Brownell, Jr.	1953–1958
	William P. Rogers	1958–1961
Postmaster General	Arthur E. Summerfield	1953–1961
Secretary of Interior	Douglas McKay	1953–1956
	Fred A. Seaton	1956–1961
Secretary of Agriculture	Ezra T. Benson	1953–1961
Secretary of Commerce	Sinclair Weeks	1953–1958
	Lewis L. Strauss	1958–1959
	Frederick H. Mueller	1959–1961
Secretary of Labor	Martin P. Durkin	1953
	James P. Mitchell	1953–1961
Secretary of Defense	Charles E. Wilson	1953–1957
	Neil H. McElroy	1957–1959
	Thomas S. Gates, Jr.	1959–1961
Secretary of Health, Education and Welfare	Oveta Culp Hobby	1953–1955
	Marion B. Folsom	1955–1958
	Arthur S. Flemming	1958–1961

The Kennedy Administration (1961–1963)

Vice President	Lyndon B. Johnson	1961–1963
Secretary of State	Dean Rusk	1961–1963
Secretary of Treasury	C. Douglas Dillon	1961–1963
Attorney General	Robert F. Kennedy	1961–1963
Postmaster General	J. Edward Day	1961–1963
	John A. Gronouski	1963
Secretary of Interior	Stewart L. Udall	1961–1963
Secretary of Agriculture	Orville L. Freeman	1961–1963
Secretary of Commerce	Luther H. Hodges	1961–1963
Secretary of Labor	Arthur J. Goldberg	1961–1962
	W. Willard Wirtz	1962–1963
Secretary of Defense	Robert S. McNamara	1961–1963
Secretary of Health, Education and Welfare	Abraham A. Ribicoff	1961–1962
	Anthony J. Celebrezze	1962–1963

The Lyndon Johnson Administration (1963 – 1969)

Vice President	Hubert H. Humphrey	1965–1969
Secretary of State	Dean Rusk	1963–1969
Secretary of Treasury	C. Douglas Dillon	1963–1965
	Henry H. Fowler	1965–1969
Attorney General	Robert F. Kennedy	1963–1964
	Nicholas Katzenbach	1965–1966
	Ramsey Clark	1967–1969
Postmaster General	John A. Gronouski	1963–1965
	Lawrence F. O'Brien	1965–1968
	Marvin Watson	1968–1969
Secretary of Interior	Stewart L. Udall	1963–1969
Secretary of Agriculture	Orville L. Freeman	1963–1969
Secretary of Commerce	Luther H. Hodges	1963–1964
	John T. Connor	1964–1967
	Alexander B. Trowbridge	1967–1968
	Cyrus R. Smith	1968–1969
Secretary of Labor	W. Willard Wirtz	1963–1969
Secretary of Defense	Robert F. McNamara	1963–1968
	Clark Clifford	1968–1969
Secretary of Health, Education and Welfare	Anthony J. Celebrezze	1963–1965
	John W. Gardner	1965–1968
	Wilbur J. Cohen	1968–1969
Secretary of Housing and Urban Development	Robert C. Weaver	1966–1969
	Robert C. Wood	1969
Secretary of Transportation	Alan S. Boyd	1967–1969

The Nixon Administration (1969 – 1974)

Vice President	Spiro T. Agnew	1969–1973
	Gerald R. Ford	1973–1974
Secretary of State	William P. Rogers	1969–1973
	Henry A. Kissinger	1973–1974

Secretary of Treasury	David M. Kennedy	1969–1970
	John B. Connally	1971–1972
	George P. Shultz	1972–1974
	William E. Simon	1974
Attorney General	John N. Mitchell	1969–1972
	Richard G. Kleindienst	1972–1973
	Elliot L. Richardson	1973
	William B. Saxbe	1973–1974
Postmaster General	Winton M. Blount	1969–1971
Secretary of Interior	Walter J. Hickel	1969–1970
	Rogers Morton	1971–1974
Secretary of Agriculture	Clifford M. Hardin	1969–1971
	Earl L. Butz	1971–1974
Secretary of Commerce	Maurice H. Stans	1969–1972
	Peter G. Peterson	1972–1973
	Frederick B. Dent	1973–1974
Secretary of Labor	George P. Shultz	1969–1970
	James D. Hodgson	1970–1973
	Peter J. Brennan	1973–1974
Secretary of Defense	Melvin R. Laird	1969–1973
	Elliot L. Richardson	1973
	James R. Schlesinger	1973–1974
Secretary of Health, Education and Welfare	Robert H. Finch	1969–1970
	Elliot L. Richardson	1970–1973
	Caspar W. Weinberger	1973–1974
Secretary of Housing and Urban Development	George Romney	1969–1973
	James T. Lynn	1973–1974
Secretary of Transportation	John A. Volpe	1969–1973
	Claude S. Brinegar	1973–1974

The Ford Administration (1974 – 1977)

Vice President	Nelson A. Rockefeller	1974–1977
Secretary of State	Henry A. Kissinger	1974–1977
Secretary of Treasury	William E. Simon	1974–1977

Attorney General	William Saxbe	1974–1975
	Edward Levi	1975–1977
Secretary of Interior	Rogers Morton	1974–1975
	Stanley K. Hathaway	1975
	Thomas Kleppe	1975–1977
Secretary of Agriculture	Earl L. Butz	1974–1976
	John A. Knebel	1976–1977
Secretary of Commerce	Frederick B. Dent	1974–1975
	Rogers Morton	1975–1976
	Elliot L. Richardson	1976–1977
Secretary of Labor	Peter J. Brennan	1974–1975
	John T. Dunlop	1975–1976
	W. J. Usery	1976–1977
Secretary of Defense	James R. Schlesinger	1974–1975
	Donald Rumsfeld	1975–1977
Secretary of Health, Education and Welfare	Caspar Weinberger	1974–1975
	Forrest D. Mathews	1975–1977
Secretary of Housing and Urban Development	James T. Lynn	1974–1975
	Carla A. Hills	1975–1977
Secretary of Transportation	Claude Brinegar	1974–1975
	William T. Coleman	1975–1977

The Carter Administration (1977 – 1981)

Vice President	Walter F. Mondale	1977–1981
Secretary of State	Cyrus R. Vance	1977–1980
	Edmund Muskie	1980–1981
Secretary of Treasury	W. Michael Blumenthal	1977–1979
	G. William Miller	1979–1981
Attorney General	Griffin Bell	1977–1979
	Benjamin R. Civiletti	1979–1981
Secretary of Interior	Cecil D. Andrus	1977–1981
Secretary of Agriculture	Robert Bergland	1977–1981
Secretary of Commerce	Juanita M. Kreps	1977–1979
	Philip M. Klutznick	1979–1981
Secretary of Labor	F. Ray Marshall	1977–1981
Secretary of Defense	Harold Brown	1977–1981
Secretary of Health, Education and Welfare	Joseph A. Califano	1977–1979
	Patricia R. Harris	1979
Secretary of Health and Human Services	Patricia R. Harris	1979–1981
Secretary of Education	Shirley M. Hufstedler	1979–1981
Secretary of Housing and Urban Development	Patricia R. Harris	1977–1979
	Moon Landrieu	1979–1981
Secretary of Transportation	Brock Adams	1977–1979
	Neil E. Goldschmidt	1979–1981
Secretary of Energy	James R. Schlesinger	1977–1979
	Charles W. Duncan	1979–1981

The Reagan Administration (1981 – 1989)

Vice President	George W. Bush	1981–1989
Secretary of State	Alexander M. Haig	1981–1982
	George P. Shultz	1982–1989
Secretary of Treasury	Donald Regan	1981–1985
	James A. Baker, III	1985–1988
	Nicholas Brady	1988–1989
Attorney General	William F. Smith	1981–1985
	Edwin A. Meese, III	1985–1988
	Richard Thornburgh	1988–1989
Secretary of Interior	James Watt	1981–1983
	William P. Clark, Jr.	1983–1985
	Donald P. Hodel	1985–1989
Secretary of Agriculture	John Block	1981–1986
	Richard E. Lyng	1986–1989
Secretary of Commerce	Malcolm Baldridge	1981–1987
	C. William Verity, Jr.	1987–1989
Secretary of Labor	Raymond Donovan	1981–1985
	William E. Brock	1985–1987
	Ann D. McLaughlin	1987–1989
Secretary of Defense	Caspar Weinberger	1981–1987
	Frank Carlucci	1987–1989

Secretary of Health and Human Services	Richard Schweiker	1981–1983
	Margaret Heckler	1983–1985
	Otis R. Bowen	1985–1989
Secretary of Education	Terrel H. Bell	1981–1985
	William J. Bennett	1985–1988
	Lauro F. Cavazos	1988–1989
Secretary of Housing and Urban Development	Samuel Pierce	1981–1989
Secretary of Transportation	Drew Lewis	1981–1983
	Elizabeth Dole	1983–1987
	James H. Burnley	1987–1989
Secretary of Energy	James Edwards	1981–1982
	Donald P. Hodel	1982–1985
	John S. Herrington	1985–1989

The Bush Administration (1989 – 1993)

Vice President	J. Danforth Quayle	1989–1993
Secretary of State	James A. Baker, III	1989–1992
Secretary of Treasury	Nicholas Brady	1989–1993
Attorney General	Richard Thornburgh	1989–1991
	William P. Barr	1991–1993
Secretary of Interior	Manuel Lujan	1989–1993
Secretary of Agriculture	Clayton K. Yeutter	1989–1991
	Edward Madigan	1991–1993
Secretary of Commerce	Robert Mosbacher	1989–1992
	Barbara Franklin	1992–1993
Secretary of Labor	Elizabeth Hanford Dole	1989–1991
	Lynn Martin	1991–1993
Secretary of Defense	Richard Cheney	1989–1993
Secretary of Health and Human Services	Louis W. Sullivan	1989–1993
Secretary of Education	Lauro F. Cavazos	1989–1991
	Lamar Alexander	1991–1993
Secretary of Housing and Urban Development	Jack F. Kemp	1989–1993

Secretary of Transportation	Samuel K. Skinner	1989–1992
	Andrew H. Card, Jr.	1992–1993
Secretary of Energy	James D. Watkins	1989–1993
Secretary of Veterans Affairs	Edward J. Derwinski	1989–1993

The Clinton Administration (1993 –   )

Vice President	Albert Gore	1993–
Secretary of State	Warren M. Christopher	1993–1997
	Madeleine K. Albright	1997–
Secretary of Treasury	Lloyd Bentsen	1993–1995
	Robert E. Rubin	1995–
Attorney General	Janet Reno	1993–
Secretary of Interior	Bruce Babbitt	1993–
Secretary of Agriculture	Mike Espy	1993–1995
	Dan Glickman	1995–
Secretary of Commerce	Ronald H. Brown	1993–1996
	Mickey Kantor	1996–1997
	William Daley	1997–
Secretary of Labor	Robert B. Reich	1993–1997
	Alexis Herman	1997–
Secretary of Defense	Les Aspin	1993–1994
	William J. Perry	1994–1997
	William Cohen	1997–
Secretary of Health and Human Services	Donna Shalala	1993–
Secretary of Housing and Urban Development	Henry G. Cisneros	1993–1997
	Andrew Cuomo	1997–
Secretary of Education	Richard W. Riley	1993–
Secretary of Transportation	Federico F. Peña	1993–1997
	Rodney Slater	1997–
Secretary of Energy	Hazel R. O'Leary	1993–1997
	Federico F. Peña	1997–
Secretary of Veterans Affairs	Jesse Brown	1993–

ADMISSION OF STATES TO THE UNION

State	Date of Admission	State	Date of Admission
Delaware	December 7, 1787	Michigan	January 16, 1837
Pennsylvania	December 12, 1787	Florida	March 3, 1845
New Jersey	December 18, 1787	Texas	December 29, 1845
Georgia	January 2, 1788	Iowa	December 28, 1846
Connecticut	January 9, 1788	Wisconsin	May 29, 1848
Massachusetts	February 6, 1788	California	September 9, 1850
Maryland	April 28, 1788	Minnesota	May 11, 1858
South Carolina	May 23, 1788	Oregon	February 14, 1859
New Hampshire	June 21, 1788	Kansas	January 29, 1861
Virginia	June 25, 1788	West Virginia	June 19, 1863
New York	July 26, 1788	Nevada	October 31, 1864
North Carolina	November 21, 1789	Nebraska	March 1, 1867
Rhode Island	May 29, 1790	Colorado	August 1, 1876
Vermont	March 4, 1791	North Dakota	November 2, 1889
Kentucky	June 1, 1792	South Dakota	November 2, 1889
Tennessee	June 1, 1796	Montana	November 8, 1889
Ohio	March 1, 1803	Washington	November 11, 1889
Louisiana	April 30, 1812	Idaho	July 3, 1890
Indiana	December 11, 1816	Wyoming	July 10, 1890
Mississippi	December 10, 1817	Utah	January 4, 1896
Illinois	December 3, 1818	Oklahoma	November 16, 1907
Alabama	December 14, 1819	New Mexico	January 6, 1912
Maine	March 15, 1820	Arizona	February 14, 1912
Missouri	August 10, 1821	Alaska	January 3, 1959
Arkansas	June 15, 1836	Hawaii	August 21, 1959

SUPREME COURT JUSTICES

Name	Service	Appointed by
John Jay*	1789–1795	Washington
James Wilson	1789–1798	Washington
John Blair	1789–1796	Washington
John Rutledge	1790–1791	Washington
William Cushing	1790–1810	Washington
James Iredell	1790–1799	Washington
Thomas Johnson	1791–1793	Washington
William Paterson	1793–1806	Washington
John Rutledge†	1795	Washington
Samuel Chase	1796–1811	Washington
Oliver Ellsworth	1796–1799	Washington
Bushrod Washington	1798–1829	J. Adams
Alfred Moore	1799–1804	J. Adams
John Marshall	1801–1835	J. Adams
William Johnson	1804–1834	Jefferson
Henry B. Livingston	1806–1823	Jefferson
Thomas Todd	1807–1826	Jefferson
Gabriel Duval	1811–1836	Madison
Joseph Story	1811–1845	Madison
Smith Thompson	1823–1843	Monroe
Robert Trimble	1826–1828	J. Q. Adams
John McLean	1829–1861	Jackson
Henry Baldwin	1830–1844	Jackson
James M. Wayne	1835–1867	Jackson
Roger B. Taney	1836–1864	Jackson
Philip P. Barbour	1836–1841	Jackson
John Catron	1837–1865	Van Buren
John McKinley	1837–1852	Van Buren
Peter V. Daniel	1841–1860	Van Buren
Samuel Nelson	1845–1872	Tyler
Levi Woodbury	1845–1851	Polk
Robert C. Grier	1846–1870	Polk
Benjamin R. Curtis	1851–1857	Fillmore
John A. Campbell	1853–1861	Pierce
Nathan Clifford	1858–1881	Buchanan
Noah H. Swayne	1862–1881	Lincoln
Samuel F. Miller	1862–1890	Lincoln
David Davis	1862–1877	Lincoln
Stephen J. Field	1863–1897	Lincoln
Salmon P. Chase	1864–1873	Lincoln
William Strong	1870–1880	Grant
Joseph P. Bradley	1870–1892	Grant
Ward Hunt	1873–1882	Grant
Morrison R. Waite	1874–1888	Grant
John M. Harlan	1877–1911	Hayes
William B. Woods	1880–1887	Hayes
Stanley Matthews	1881–1889	Garfield
Horace Gray	1882–1902	Arthur
Samuel Blatchford	1882–1893	Arthur
Lucious Q. C. Lamar	1888–1893	Cleveland
Melville W. Fuller	1888–1910	Cleveland
David J. Brewer	1889–1910	B. Harrison
Henry B. Brown	1890–1906	B. Harrison
George Shiras	1892–1903	B. Harrison
Howell E. Jackson	1893–1895	B. Harrison
Edward D. White	1894–1910	Cleveland
Rufus W. Peckham	1896–1909	Cleveland
Joseph McKenna	1898–1925	McKinley
Oliver W. Holmes	1902–1932	T. Roosevelt
William R. Day	1903–1922	T. Roosevelt
William H. Moody	1906–1910	T. Roosevelt
Horace H. Lurton	1910–1914	Taft
Charles E. Hughes	1910–1916	Taft
Willis Van Devanter	1910–1937	Taft
Joseph R. Lamar	1911–1916	Taft
Edward D. White	1910–1921	Taft
Mahlon Pitney	1912–1922	Taft
James C. McReynolds	1914–1941	Wilson
Louis D. Brandeis	1916–1939	Wilson
John H. Clarke	1916–1922	Wilson
William H. Taft	1921–1930	Harding
George Sutherland	1922–1938	Harding

*Chief Justices appear in bold type.
†Acting Chief Justice; Senate refused to confirm appointment.

Name	Service	Appointed by
Pierce Butler	1923–1939	Harding
Edward T. Sanford	1923–1930	Harding
Harlan F. Stone	1925–1941	Coolidge
Charles E. Hughes	1930–1941	Hoover
Owen J. Roberts	1930–1945	Hoover
Benjamin N. Cardozo	1932–1938	Hoover
Hugo L. Black	1937–1971	F. Roosevelt
Stanley F. Reed	1938–1957	F. Roosevelt
Felix Frankfurter	1939–1962	F. Roosevelt
William O. Douglas	1939–1975	F. Roosevelt
Frank Murphy	1940–1949	F. Roosevelt
Harlan F. Stone	1941–1946	F. Roosevelt
James F. Byrnes	1941–1942	F. Roosevelt
Robert H. Jackson	1941–1954	F. Roosevelt
Wiley B. Rutledge	1943–1949	F. Roosevelt
Harold H. Burton	1945–1958	Truman
Frederick M. Vinson	1946–1953	Truman
Tom C. Clark	1949–1967	Truman
Sherman Minton	1949–1956	Truman
Earl Warren	1953–1969	Eisenhower
John Marshall Harlan	1955–1971	Eisenhower
William J. Brennan Jr.	1956–1990	Eisenhower
Charles E. Whittaker	1957–1962	Eisenhower

Name	Service	Appointed by
Potter Stewart	1958–1981	Eisenhower
Byron R. White	1962–1993	Kennedy
Arthur J. Goldberg	1962–1965	Kennedy
Abe Fortas	1965–1969	Johnson
Thurgood Marshall	1967–1991	Johnson
Warren E. Burger	1969–1986	Nixon
Harry A. Blackmun	1970–1994	Nixon
Lewis F. Powell Jr.	1972–1988	Nixon
William H. Rehnquist	1972–1986	Nixon
John Paul Stevens	1975–	Ford
Sandra Day O'Connor	1981–	Reagan
William H. Rehnquist	1986–	Reagan
Antonin Scalia	1986–	Reagan
Anthony M. Kennedy	1988–	Reagan
David H. Souter	1990–	Bush
Clarence Thomas	1991–	Bush
Ruth Bader Ginsburg	1993–	Clinton
Stephen Breyer	1994–	Clinton

SIGNIFICANT SUPREME COURT CASES

Marbury v. Madison (1803)

This case established the right of the Supreme Court to review the constitutionality of laws. The decision involved judicial appointments made during the last hours of the administration of President John Adams. Some commissions, including that of William Marbury, had not yet been delivered when President Thomas Jefferson took office. Infuriated by the last-minute nature of Adams's Federalist appointments, Jefferson refused to send the undelivered commissions out, and Marbury decided to sue. The Supreme Court, presided over by John Marshall, a Federalist who had assisted Adams in the judicial appointments, ruled that although Marbury's commission was valid and the new president should have delivered it, the Court could not compel him to do so. The Court based its reasoning on a finding that the grounds of Marbury's suit, resting in the Judiciary Act of 1789, were in conflict with the Constitution.

For the first time, the Court had overturned a national law on the grounds that it was unconstitutional. John Marshall had quietly established the concept of judicial review: The Supreme Court had given itself the authority to nullify acts of the other branches of the federal government. Although the Constitution provides for judicial review, the Court had not exercised this power before and did not use it again until 1857. It seems likely that if the Court had waited until 1857 to use this power, it would have been difficult to establish.

McCulloch v. Maryland (1819)

In 1816, Congress authorized the creation of a national bank. To protect its own banks from competition with a branch of the national bank in Baltimore, the state legislature of Maryland placed a tax of 2 percent on all notes issued by any bank operating in Maryland that was not chartered by the state. McCulloch, cashier of the Baltimore branch of the Bank of the United States, was convicted for refusing to pay the tax. Under the leadership of Chief Justice John Marshall, the Court ruled that the federal government had the power to establish a bank, even though that specific authority was not mentioned in the Constitution.

Marshall maintained that the authority could be reasonably implied from Article 1, section 8, which gives Congress the power to make all laws that are necessary and proper to execute the enumerated powers. Marshall also held that Maryland could not tax the national bank because in a conflict between federal and state laws, the federal law must take precedence. Thus he established the principles of implied powers and federal supremacy, both of which set a precedent for subsequent expansion of federal power at the expense of the states.

Scott v. Sanford (1857)

Dred Scott was a slave who sued for his own and his family's freedom on the grounds, that, with his master, he had traveled to and lived in free territory that did not allow slavery. When his case reached the Supreme Court, the justices saw an opportunity to settle once and for all the vexing question of slavery in the territories. The Court's decision in this case proved that it enjoyed no special immunity from the sectional and partisan passions of the time. Five of the nine justices were from the South and seven were Democrats.

Chief Justice Roger B. Taney hated Republicans and detested racial equality; his decision reflects those prejudices. He wrote an opinion not only declaring that Scott was still a slave but also claiming that the Constitution denied citizenship or rights to blacks, that Congress had no right to exclude slavery from the territories, and that the Missouri Compromise was unconstitutional. While southern Democrats gloated over this seven-to-two decision, sectional tensions were further inflamed and the young Republican Party's claim that a hostile "slave power" was conspiring to destroy northern liberties was given further credence. The decision brought the nation closer to civil war and is generally regarded as the worst decision ever rendered by the Supreme Court.

Butchers' Benevolent Association of New Orleans v. Crescent City Livestock Landing and Slaughterhouse Co. (1873)

The *Slaughterhouse* cases, as the cases docketed under the *Butchers'* title were known, were the first legal test of the Fourteenth Amendment. To cut down on cases of cholera believed to be caused by contaminated water, the state of Louisiana prohibited the slaughter of livestock in New Orleans except in one slaughterhouse, effectively giving that slaughterhouse a monopoly. Other New Orleans butchers claimed that the state had deprived them of their occupation without due process of law, thus violating the Fourteenth Amendment.

In a five-to-four decision, the Court upheld the Louisiana law, declaring that the Fourteenth Amendment protected only the rights of federal citizenship, like voting in federal elections and interstate travel. The federal government thus was not obliged to protect basic civil rights from violation by state governments. This decison would have significant implications for African Americans and their struggle for civil rights in the twentieth century.

United States v. E. C. Knight Co. (1895)

Also known as the *Sugar Trust* case, this was among the first cases to reveal the weakness of the Sherman Antitrust Act in the hands of a pro-business Supreme Court. In 1895, American Sugar Refining Company purchased four other sugar producers, including the E. C. Knight Company, and thus took control of more than 98 percent of the sugar refining in the United States. In an effort to limit monopoly, the government brought suit against all five of the companies for violating the Sherman Antitrust Act, which outlawed trusts and other business combinations in restraint of trade. The Court dismissed the suit, however, arguing that the law applied only to commerce and not to manufacturing, defining the latter as a local concern and not part of the interstate commerce that the government could regulate.

Plessy v. Ferguson (1896)

African American Homer Plessy challenged a Louisiana law that required segregation on trains passing through the state. After ensuring that the railroad and the conductor knew that he was of mixed race (Plessy appeared to be white but under the racial code of Louisiana was classified as "colored" because he was one-eighth black), he refused to move to the "colored only" section of the coach. The Court ruled against Plessy by a vote of seven to one, declaring that "separate but equal" facilities were permissible according to section 1 of the Fourteenth Amendment, which calls upon the states to provide "equal protection of the laws" to anyone within their jurisdiction. Although the case was viewed as relatively insignificant at the time, it cast a long shadow over several decades.

Initially, the decision was viewed as a victory for segregationists, but in the 1930s and 1940s civil rights advocates referred to the doctrine of "separate but equal" in their efforts to end segregation. They argued that segregated institutions and accommodations were often *not* equal to those available to whites, and finally succeeded in overturning *Plessy* in *Brown v. Board of Education* in 1954 (see p. A-46).

Lochner v. New York (1905)

In this case, the Court ruled against a New York state law that prohibited employees from working in bakeries more than ten hours a day or sixty hours a week. The purpose of the law was to protect the health of workers, but the Court ruled that it was unconstitutional because it violated "freedom of contract" implicitly protected by the due process clause of the Fourteenth Amendment. Most of the justices believed strongly in a laissez-faire economic system that favored survival of the fittest. They felt that government protection of workers interfered with this system. In a dissenting opinion, Justice Oliver Wendell Holmes accused the majority of distorting the Constitution and of deciding the case on "an economic theory which a large part of the country does not entertain."

Muller v. Oregon (1908)

In 1905, Curt Muller, owner of a Portland, Oregon, laundry, demanded that one of his employees, Mrs. Elmer Gotcher, work more than the ten hours allowed as a maximum workday for women under Oregon law. Muller argued that the law violated his "freedom of contract" as established in prior Supreme Court decisions.

Progressive lawyer Louis D. Brandeis defended the Oregon law by arguing that a state could be justified in abridging freedom of contract when the health, safety, and welfare of workers was at issue. His innovative strategy drew on ninety-five pages of excerpts from factory and medical reports to substantiate his argument that there was a direct connection between long hours and the health of women and thus the health of the nation. In a unanimous decision, the Court upheld the Oregon law, but later generations of women fighting for equality would question the strategy of arguing that women's reproductive role entitled them to special treatment.

Schenck v. United States (1919)

During World War I, Charles Schenck and other members of the Socialist Party printed and mailed out flyers urging young men who were subject to the draft to oppose the war in Europe. In upholding the conviction of Schenck for publishing a pamphlet urging draft resistance, Justice Oliver Wendell Holmes established the "clear and present danger" test for freedom of speech. Such utterances as Schenck's during a time of national peril, Holmes wrote, could be considered the equivalent of shouting "Fire!" in a crowded theater. Congress had the right to protect the public against such an incitement to panic, the Court ruled in a unanimous decision. But the analogy was a false one. Schenck's pamphlet had little power to provoke a public firmly opposed to its message. Although Holmes later modified his position to state that the danger must relate to an immediate evil and a specific action, the "clear and present danger" test laid the groundwork for those who later sought to limit First Amendment freedoms.

Schechter Poultry Corp. v. United States (1935)

During the Great Depression, the National Industrial Recovery Act (NIRA), which was passed under President Franklin D. Roosevelt, established fair competition codes that were designed to help businesses. The Schechter brothers of New York City, who sold chickens, were convicted of violating the codes. The Supreme Court ruled that the NIRA unconstitutionally conferred legislative power on an administrative agency and overstepped the limits of federal power to regulate interstate commerce. The decision was a significant blow to the New Deal recovery program, demonstrating both historic American resistance to economic planning and the refusal of the business community to yield its autonomy unless it was forced to do so.

Brown v. Board of Education (1954)

In 1950, the families of eight Topeka, Kansas, children sued the Topeka Board of Education. The children were blacks who lived within walking distance of a whites-only school. The segregated school system required them to take a time-consuming, inconvenient, and dangerous route to get to a black school, and their parents argued that there was no reason their children should not be allowed to attend the nearest school. By the time the case reached the Supreme Court, it had been joined with similar cases regarding segregated schools in other states and the District of Columbia. A team of lawyers from the National Association for the Advancement of Colored People (NAACP), led by Thurgood Marshall (who would later be appointed to the Supreme Court), urged the Court to overturn the fifty-eight-year-old precedent established in *Plessy v. Ferguson*, which had enshrined "separate but equal" as the law of the land. A unanimous Court, led by Chief Justice Earl Warren, declared that "Separate educa-

tional facilities are inherently unequal" and thus violate the Fourteenth Amendment. In 1955, the Court called for desegregation "with all deliberate speed" but established no deadline.

Roth v. United States (1957)

In 1957, New Yorker Samuel Roth was convicted of sending obscene materials through the mail in a case that ultimately reached the Supreme Court. With a six-to-three vote, the Court reaffirmed the historical view that obscenity is not protected by the First Amendment. Yet it broke new ground by declaring that a work could be judged obscene only if, "taken as a whole," it appealed to the "prurient interest" of "the average person."

Prior to this case, work could be judged obscene if portions were thought able to "deprave and corrupt" the most susceptible part of an audience (such as children). Thus, serious works of literature such as Theodore Dreiser's *An American Tragedy*, which was banned in Boston when first published, received no protection. Although this decision continued to pose problems of definition, it did help to protect most works that attempt to convey ideas, even if those ideas have to do with sex, from the threat of obscenity laws.

Engel v. Vitale (1962)

In 1959, five parents with ten children in the New Hyde Park, New York, school system sued the school board. The parents argued that the so-called Regents' Prayer that public school students in New York recited at the start of every school day violated the doctrine of separation of church and state outlined in the First Amendment. In 1962, the Supreme Court voted six to one in favor of banning the Regents' Prayer.

The decision threw the religious community into an uproar. Many religious leaders expressed dismay and even shock; others welcomed the decision. Several efforts to introduce an amendment allowing school prayer have failed. Subsequent Supreme Court decisions have banned reading of the Bible in public schools. The Court has also declared mandatory flag saluting to be an infringement of religious and personal freedoms.

Gideon v. Wainwright (1963)

When Clarence Earl Gideon was tried for breaking into a poolroom, the state of Florida rejected his demand for a court-appointed lawyer as guaranteed by the Sixth Amendment. In 1963, the Court upheld his demand in a unanimous decision that established the obligation of states to provide attorneys for indigent defendants in felony cases. Prior to this decision, the right to an attorney had applied only to federal cases, not state cases. In its ruling in *Gideon v. Wainwright*, the Supreme Court applied the Sixth through the Fourteenth Amendments to the states. In 1972, the Supreme Court extended the right to legal representation to all cases, not just felony cases, in its decision in *Argersinger v. Hamlin*.

Griswold v. Connecticut (1965)

With a vote of seven to two, the Supreme Court reversed an "uncommonly silly law" (in the words of Justice Potter Stewart) that made it a crime for anyone in the state of Connecticut to use any drug, article, or instrument to prevent conception. *Griswold* became a landmark case because here, for the first time, the Court explicitly invested with full constitutional status "fundamental personal rights," such as the right to privacy, that were not expressly enumerated in the Bill of Rights. The majority opinion in the case held that the law infringed on the constitutionally protected right to privacy of married persons.

Although the Court had previously recognized fundamental rights not expressly enumerated in the Bill of Rights (such as the right to procreate in *Skinner v. Oklahoma* in 1942), *Griswold* was a landmark case because it was the first time the Court had justified, at length, the practice of investing such unenumerated rights with full constitutional status. Writing for the majority, Justice William O. Douglas explained that the First, Third, Fourth, Fifth, and Ninth Amendments imply "zones of privacy" that are the foundation for the general right to privacy affirmed in this case.

Miranda v. Arizona (1966)

In 1966, the Supreme Court, by a vote of five to four, upheld the case of Ernesto Miranda, who appealed a murder conviction on the grounds that police had gotten him to confess without giving him access to an attorney. The *Miranda* case was the culmination of the Court's efforts to find a meaningful way of determining whether police had used due process in extracting confessions from people accused of crimes. The *Miranda* decision upholds the Fifth Amendment protection against self-incrimination outside the courtroom and requires that suspects be given what came to be known as the Miranda warning, which advises them of their right to remain silent and warns them that anything they say might be used against them in a court of law. Suspects must also be told that they have a right to counsel.

New York Times Co. v. United States (1971)

With a six-to-three vote, the Court upheld the right of the *New York Times* and the *Washington Post* to print materials from the so-called *Pentagon Papers*, a secret government study of U.S. policy in Vietnam, leaked by dissident Pentagon official Daniel Ellsberg. Since the papers revealed deception and secrecy in the conduct of the Vietnam War, the Nixon administration had quickly obtained a court injunction against their further publication, claiming that suppression was in the interests of national security. The Supreme Court's decision overturning the injunction strengthened the First Amendment protection of freedom of the press.

Furman v. Georgia (1972)

In this case, the Supreme Court ruled five to four that the death penalty for murder or rape violated the cruel and unusual punishment clause of the Eighth Amendment because the manner in which the death penalty was meted out was irregular, "arbitrary," and "cruel." In response, most states enacted new statutes that allow the death penalty to be imposed only after a postconviction hearing at which evidence must be presented to show that "aggravating" or "mitigating" circumstances were factors in the crime. If the postconviction hearing hands down a death sentence, the case is automatically reviewed by an appellate court.

In 1976, the Court ruled in *Gregg v. Georgia* that these statutes were not unconstitutional. In 1977, the Court ruled in *Coker v. Georgia* that the death penalty for rape was "disproportionate and excessive," thus allowing the death penalty only in murder cases. Between 1977 and 1991, some 150 people were executed in the United States. Public opinion polls indicate that about 70 percent of Americans favor the death penalty for murder. Capital punishment continues to generate controversy, however, as opponents argue that there is no evidence that the death penalty deters crime and that its use reflects racial and economic bias.

Roe v. Wade (1973)

In 1973, the Court found, by a vote of seven to two, that state laws restricting access to abortion violated a woman's right to privacy guaranteed by the due process clause of the Fourteenth Amendment. The decision was based on the cases of two women living in Texas and Georgia, both states with stringent anti-abortion laws. Upholding the individual rights of both women and physicians, the Court ruled that the Constitution protects the right to abortion and that states cannot prohibit abortions in the early stages of pregnancy.

The decision stimulated great debate among legal scholars as well as the general public. Critics argued that since abortion was never addressed in the Constitution, the Court could not claim that legislation violated fundamental values of the Constitution. They also argued that since abortion was a medical procedure with an acknowledged impact on a fetus, it was inappropriate to invoke the kind of "privacy" argument that was used in *Griswold v. Connecticut* (see p. A-47), which was about contraception. Defenders suggested that the case should be argued as a case of gender discrimination, which did violate the equal protection clause of the Fourteenth Amendment. Others said that the right to privacy in sexual matters was indeed a fundamental right.

Regents of the University of California v. Bakke (1978)

When Allan Bakke, a white man, was not accepted by the University of California Medical School at Davis, he filed a lawsuit alleging that the admissions program, which set up different standards for test scores and grades for members of certain minority groups, violated the Civil Rights Act of 1964, which outlawed racial or ethnic preferences in programs supported by federal funds. Bakke further argued that the university's practice of setting aside spaces for minority applicants denied him equal protection as guaranteed by the Fourteenth Amendment. In a five-to-four decision, the Court ordered that Bakke be admitted to the medical school, yet it sanctioned affirmative action programs to attack the results of past discrimination as long as strict quotas or racial classifications were not involved.

Webster v. Reproductive Health Services (1989)

By a vote of five to four, the Court upheld several restrictions on the availability of abortions as imposed by Missouri state law. It upheld restrictions on the use of state property, including public hospitals, for abortions. It also upheld a provision requiring physicians to perform tests to determine the viability of a fetus that a doctor judged to be twenty weeks of age or older. Although the justices did not go so far as to overturn the decision in *Roe v. Wade* (see p. A-47), the ruling galvanized interest groups on both sides of the abortion issue. Opponents of abortion pressured state legislatures to place greater restrictions on abortions; those who favored availability of abortions tried to mobilize public action by presenting the decision as a major threat to the right to choose abortion.

Cipollone v. Liggett (1992)

In a seven-to-two decision, the Court ruled in favor of the family of Rose Cipollone, a woman who died of lung cancer after smoking for forty-two years. The Court rejected arguments that health warnings on cigarette packages protected tobacco manufacturers from personal injury suits filed by smokers who contract cancer and other serious illnesses.

Miller v. Johnson (1995)

In a five-to-four decision, the Supreme Court ruled that voting districts created to increase the voting power of racial minorities were unconstitutional. The decision threatens dozens of congressional, state, and local voting districts that were drawn to give minorities more representation as had been required by the Justice Department under the Voting Rights Act. If states are required to redraw voting districts, the number of black members of Congress could be sharply reduced.

Romer v. Evans (1996)

In a six-to-three decision, the Court struck down a Colorado amendment that forbade local governments from banning discrimination against homosexuals. Writing for the majority, Justice Anthony Kennedy said that forbidding communities from taking action to protect the rights of homosexuals and not of other groups unlawfully deprived gays and lesbians of opportunities that were available to others. Kennedy based the decision on the guarantee of equal protection under the law as provided by the Fourteenth Amendment.

THE AMERICAN ECONOMY

THESE FOUR "SNAPSHOTS" of the U.S. economy show significant changes over the past century and a half. In 1849, the agricultural sector was by far the largest contributor to the economy. By the turn of the century, with advances in technology and an abundance of cheap labor and raw materials, the country had experienced remarkable industrial expansion and the manufacturing industries dominated. By 1950, the service sector had increased significantly, fueled by the consumerism of the 1920s and the post-World War II years, and the economy was becoming more diversified. Note that by 1990, government's share in the economy was more than 10 percent and activity in both the trade and manufacturing sectors had declined, partly as a result of competition from Western Europe and Asia.

Main Sectors of the U.S. Economy: 1849, 1899, 1950, 1990

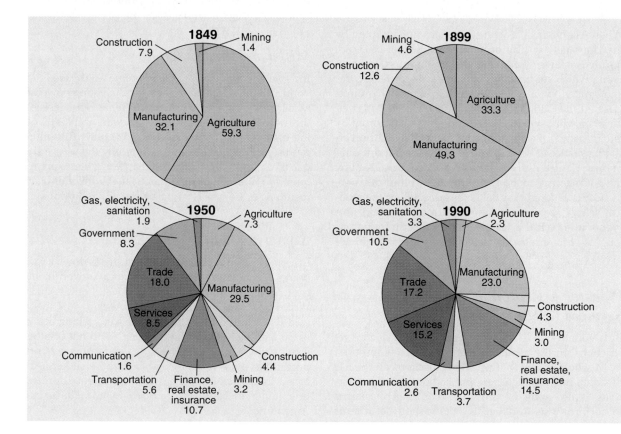

Source: Historical Statistics of the U.S., Colonial Times to 1970 (1975) and Statistical Abstract of the U.S., 1996 (1996).

Federal Spending and the Economy, 1790 – 1995

Year	Gross National Product (in billions)	Foreign Trade (in millions) Exports	Imports	Federal Budget (in billions)	Federal Surplus/Deficit (in billions)	Federal Debt (in billions)
1790	NA	20	23	0.004	0.00015	0.076
1800	NA	71	91	0.011	0.0006	0.083
1810	NA	67	85	0.008	0.0012	0.053
1820	NA	70	74	0.018	−0.0004	0.091
1830	NA	74	71	0.015	0.100	0.049
1840	NA	132	107	0.024	−0.005	0.004
1850	NA	152	178	0.040	0.004	0.064
1860	NA	400	362	0.063	−0.01	0.065
1870	7.4	451	462	0.310	0.10	2.4
1880	11.2	853	761	0.268	0.07	2.1
1890	13.1	910	823	0.318	0.09	1.2
1900	18.7	1,499	930	0.521	0.05	1.2
1910	35.3	1,919	1,646	0.694	−0.02	1.1
1920	91.5	8,664	5,784	6.357	0.3	24.3
1930	90.4	4,013	3,500	3.320	0.7	16.3
1940	99.7	4,030	7,433	9.6	−2.7	43.0
1950	284.8	10,816	9,125	43.1	−2.2	257.4
1960	503.7	19,600	15,046	92.2	0.3	286.3
1970	977.1	42,700	40,189	195.6	−2.8	371.0
1980	2,631.7	220,600	244,871	590.9	−73.8	907.7
1990	5,524.5	393,600	495,300	1,252.15	−221.1	3,233.3
1995	7,237.5	583,900	743,400	1,519.1	−163.9	4,921.0

Source: Historical Statistics of the U.S., Colonial Times to 1970 (1975) and Statistical Abstract of the U.S., 1996 (1996).

WHEN THE FEDERAL GOVERNMENT BEGAN OPERATING IN 1790, its size and expenditures were limited. Over time its functions increased, but its budget remained fairly small relative to the country's gross national product. The second half of the twentieth century witnessed a dramatic expansion in federal budget outlays. As the government's role increased and receipts could no longer offset growing expenditures, budget deficits mounted. In 1976, the federal deficit reached $65.6 billion and continued to rise, soaring as high as $290 billion in 1992, during the last year of George Bush's presidency. During the first Clinton administration, a combination of budget cuts, tax increases, declining unemployment, and economic expansion reduced the deficit by about half to approximately $145 billion.

The Federal Budget: Receipts, Outlays, and the Deficit, 1945 – 1995

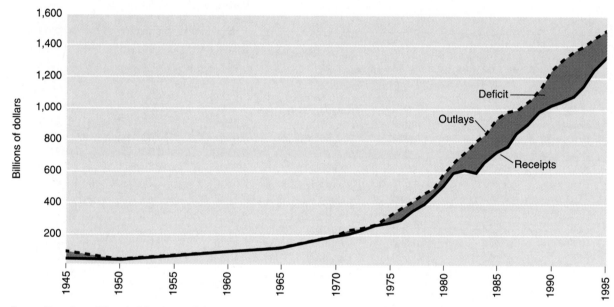

Source: Data from *Historical Statistics of the U.S., Colonial Times to 1970* (1975) and *Statistical Abstract of the U.S., 1996* (1996).

A DEMOGRAPHIC PROFILE OF THE UNITED STATES AND ITS PEOPLE

POPULATION

FROM AN ESTIMATED 4600 WHITE INHABITANTS IN 1630, the country's population grew to a total of just under 250 million in 1990. It is important to note that the U.S. census, first conducted in 1790 and the source of these figures, counted blacks, both free and slave, but did not include American Indians until 1860. The years 1790 to 1900 saw the most rapid population growth, with an average increase of 25 to 35 percent per decade. In addition to "natural" growth—birth rate exceeding death rate—immigration was also a factor in that rise, especially between 1840 and 1860, 1880 to 1890, and 1900 to 1910 (see table on page A-59). The twentieth century witnessed slower growth, partly a result of 1920s immigration restrictions, and a decline in the birth rate, especially during the Depression era and the 1960s and 1970s. The U.S. population is expected to reach almost 300 million by the year 2010.

Population Growth, 1630 – 2000

Year	Population	Percent Increase
1630	4,600	----
1640	26,600	473.3
1650	50,400	89.1
1660	75,100	49.0
1670	111,900	49.1
1680	151,500	35.4
1690	210,400	38.9
1700	250,900	19.3
1710	331,700	32.2
1720	466,200	40.5
1730	629,400	35.0
1740	905,600	43.9
1750	1,170,800	30.0
1760	1,593,600	36.1
1770	2,148,100	34.8
1780	2,780,400	29.4
1790	3,929,214	41.3
1800	5,308,483	35.1
1810	7,239,881	36.4
1820	9,638,453	33.1
1830	12,866,020	33.5
1840	17,069,453	32.7
1850	23,191,876	35.9
1860	31,443,321	35.6
1870	39,818,449	26.6
1880	50,155,783	26.0
1890	62,947,714	25.5
1900	75,994,575	20.7
1910	91,972,266	21.0
1920	105,710,620	14.9
1930	122,775,046	16.1
1940	131,669,275	7.2
1950	150,697,361	14.5
1960	179,323,175	19.0
1970	203,302,031	13.4
1980	226,542,199	11.4
1990	248,718,301	9.8
2000	274,634,000*	11.0

*Projected

Source: Historical Statistics of the U.S. (1960), Historical Statistics of the U.S. from Colonial Times to 1970 (1975), and Statistical Abstract of the U.S., 1996 (1996).

The Ten Most Populous Cities, 1700 – 1994

Year	City	Population	Year	City	Population
1700	Boston	6,700	1910	New York	4,767,000
	New York	4,900		Chicago	2,185,000
	Philadelphia	4,400		Philadelphia	1,549,000
				St. Louis	687,000
1790	Philadelphia	42,500		Boston	670,600
	New York	33,100		Cleveland, Ohio	560,700
	Boston	18,000		Baltimore	558,500
	Charleston, S.C.	16,400		Pittsburgh	533,900
	Baltimore, Md.	13,500		Detroit, Mich.	465,800
	Salem, Mass.	7,900		Buffalo, N.Y.	423,700
	Newport, R.I.	6,700			
	Providence, R.I.	6,380	1930	New York	6,930,000
	Marblehead, Mass.	5,700		Chicago	3,376,000
	Portsmouth, N.H.	4,700		Philadelphia	1,951,000
				Detroit	1,569,000
1830	New York	197,100		Los Angeles	1,238,000
	Philadelphia	161,400		Cleveland	900,400
	Baltimore	80,600		St. Louis	822,000
	Boston	61,400		Baltimore	804,900
	Charleston	30,300		Boston	781,200
	New Orleans, La.	29,700		Pittsburgh	669,800
	Cincinnati, Oh.	24,800			
	Albany, N.Y.	24,200	1950	New York	7,892,000
	Brooklyn, N.Y.	20,500		Chicago	3,621,000
	Washington, D.C.	18,800		Philadelphia	2,072,000
				Los Angeles	1,970,000
1850	New York	515,500		Detroit	1,850,000
	Philadelphia	340,000		Baltimore	949,700
	Baltimore	169,000		Cleveland	914,800
	Boston	136,800		St. Louis	856,800
	New Orleans	116,400		Washington	802,200
	Cincinnati	115,400		Boston	801,500
	Brooklyn, N.Y.	96,800			
	St. Louis, Mo.	77,900	1970	New York	7,896,000
	Albany	50,800		Chicago	3,369,000
	Pittsburgh, Pa.	46,600		Los Angeles	2,812,000
				Philadelphia	1,950,000
1870	New York	942,300		Detroit	1,514,000
	Philadelphia	674,000		Houston	1,234,000
	Brooklyn	419,900		Baltimore	905,800
	St. Louis	310,900		Dallas	844,400
	Chicago, Il.	298,900		Washington	756,700
	Baltimore	267,300		Cleveland	750,900
	Boston	250,500			
	Cincinnati	216,200			
	New Orleans	191,400			
	San Francisco, Calif.	149,500			(continues)

The Ten Most Populous Cities, 1700 – 1994 (continued)

Year	City	Population	Year	City	Population
1990	New York	7,323,000	**1994**	New York	7,333,000
	Los Angeles	3,485,000		Los Angeles	3,449,000
	Chicago	2,784,000		Chicago	2,732,000
	Houston	1,631,000		Houston	1,702,000
	Philadelphia	1,586,000		Philadelphia	1,524,000
	San Diego	1,111,000		San Diego	1,152,000
	Detroit	1,028,000		Phoenix	1,049,000
	Dallas	1,007,000		Dallas	1,023,000
	Phoenix	983,400		San Antonio	999,000
	San Antonio, Tex.	935,900		Detroit	992,000

U.S. Population, 1790 – 2010

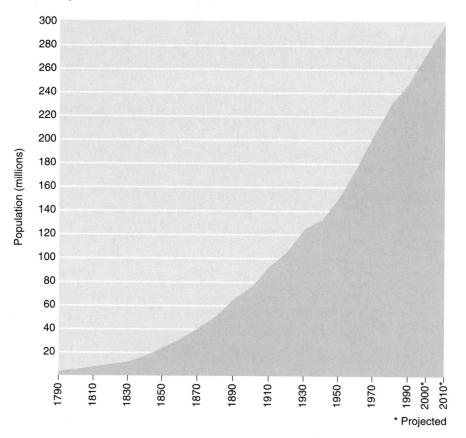

* Projected

VITAL STATISTICS

WITH SOME MINOR FLUCTUATIONS, the birth rate has been trending downward throughout the past century and a half, dipping especially low during the 1930s Depression years, when many economically hard-hit Americans postponed having children. A major exception to this decline was the steep but temporary rise nicknamed the "Baby Boom," which occurred during the relatively affluent post-World War II period. Improvements in health care and lifestyles have contributed to a decline in the death rate over the past century, which, in turn has increased life expectancy figures. Over time, as people lived longer and the birth rate declined, the median age of Americans has increased from approximately seventeen in 1820 to thirty-three in 1990, and continues to rise.

Birth Rate, 1820 – 2000

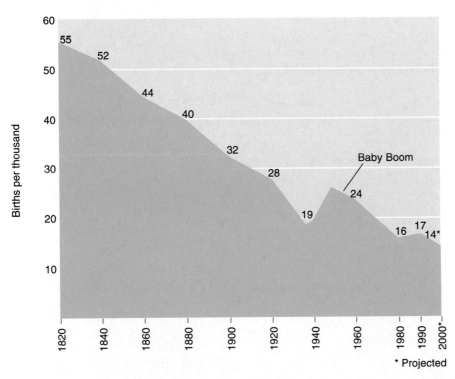

Source: Data from Historical Statistics of the U.S., Colonial Times to 1970 (1975) and Statistical Abstract of the U.S., 1996 (1996).

Death Rate, 1900 – 2000

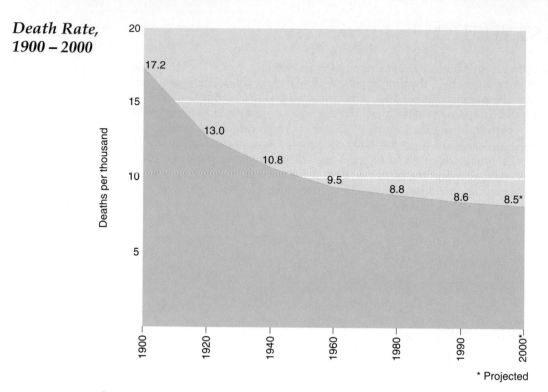

Source: *Historical Statistics of the U.S., Colonial Times to 1970* (1975) and
Statistical Abstract of the U.S., 1996 (1996).

Life Expectancy, 1900 – 2000

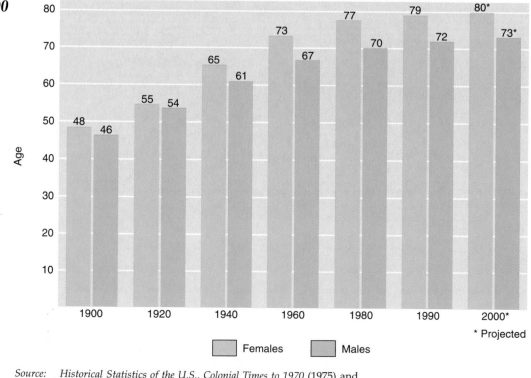

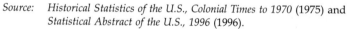

Source: *Historical Statistics of the U.S., Colonial Times to 1970* (1975) and
Statistical Abstract of the U.S., 1996 (1996).

MIGRATION AND IMMIGRATION

WE TEND TO ASSOCIATE INTERNAL MIGRATION with movement westward, yet equally significant has been the movement of the nation's population from the country to the city. In 1790, the first U.S. census recorded that approximately 95 percent of the population lived in rural areas. By 1990, that figure had fallen to less than 25 percent. The decline of the agricultural way of life, late nineteenth-century industrialization, and immigration have all contributed to increased urbanization. A more recent trend has been the migration, especially since the 1970s, of people to the "Sun Belt" states of the South and West, lured by factors as various as economic opportunities in the defense and high-tech industries and good weather. This migration has swelled the size of Sun Belt cities like Houston, Dallas, Tucson, Phoenix, and San Diego, all of which in recent years ranked among the top ten most populous U.S. cities (see the table on page A-53).

Rural and Urban Population, 1750 – 2000

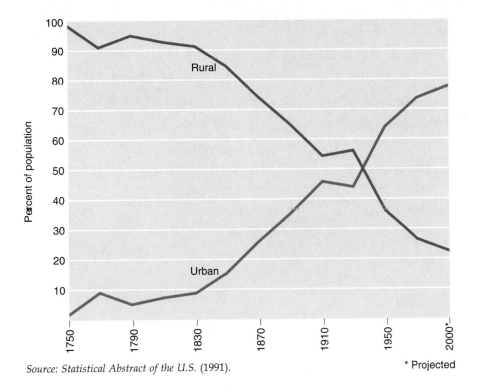

Source: Statistical Abstract of the U.S. (1991).   * Projected

Projected Change in State Populations by Percent, 1995 – 2010

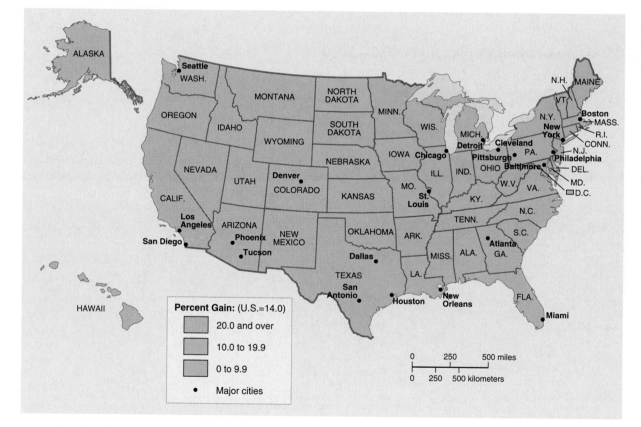

Source: Statistical Abstract of the U.S., 1996. (1996).

THE QUANTITY AND CHARACTER OF IMMIGRATION to the U.S. has varied greatly over time. During the first major influx, between 1840 and 1860, newcomers hailed primarily from Northern and Western Europe. From 1880 to 1915, when rates soared even more dramatically, the profile changed, with 80 percent of the so-called "new immigration" coming from Central, Eastern, and Southern Europe. Following World War I, strict quotas reduced the flow considerably. Note, also, the significant fall-off during the years of the Great Depression and World War II. The sources of immigration during the last half century have changed significantly, with the majority of people coming from Latin America, the Caribbean, and Asia. The latest surge during the 1980s brought more immigrants to the U.S. than in any decade except 1901–1910.

Rates of Immigration, 1820 – 1994

Year	Number	Percent of Total Population
1821–1830	151,824	1.6
1831–1840	599,125	4.6
1841–1850	1,713,521	10.0
1851–1860	2,598,214	11.2
1861–1870	2,314,824	7.4
1871–1880	2,812,191	7.1
1881–1890	5,246,613	10.5
1891–1900	3,687,546	5.8
1901–1910	8,795,386	11.6
1911–1920	5,735,811	6.2
1921–1930	4,107,209	3.9
1931–1940	528,431	0.4
1941–1950	1,035,039	0.7
1951–1960	2,515,479	1.6
1961–1970	3,321,677	1.8
1971–1980	4,493,300	2.2
1981–1990	7,338,100	3.0
1991	1,827,167	7.2
1992	973,977	3.8
1993	904,292	3.5
1994	804,416	3.0

Source: Historical Statistics of the U.S., Colonial Times to 1970 (1975), Statistical Abstract of the U.S., 1996 (1996).

Major Trends in Immigration, 1820 – 1990

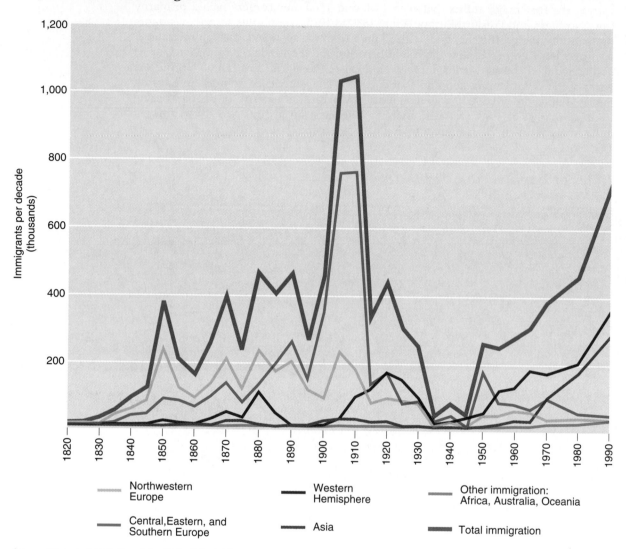

Source: *Historical Statistics of the U.S., Colonial Times to 1970* (1975) and *Statistical Abstract of the U.S., 1996* (1996).

LABOR

FOR MUCH OF THE NINETEENTH CENTURY, the United States was a nation of small farmers, with over half the population employed in agriculture. With the rise of industrialization, movement to the cities, and increasing takeover of farming by agribusiness (large-scale mechanized farming requiring little manpower), Americans increasingly moved from farming to work in manufacturing and other industries. In the twentieth century the number of people employed in services has increased; membership in labor unions peaked around 1970. Perhaps the most significant change in labor patterns has been the increase in the number of working women from approximately one sixth of the work force in 1890 to close to one half by 1994.

The Changing Nature of Work, 1810 – 1994

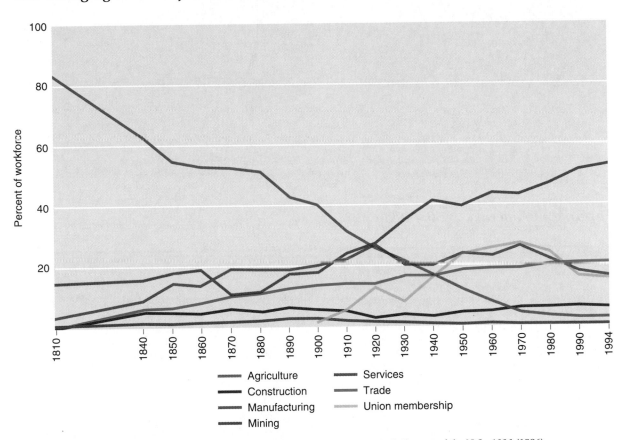

Source: *Historical Statistics of the U.S., Colonial Times to 1970* (1975) and *Statistical Abstract of the U.S., 1996* (1996).

Women in the Work Force, 1820 – 1994

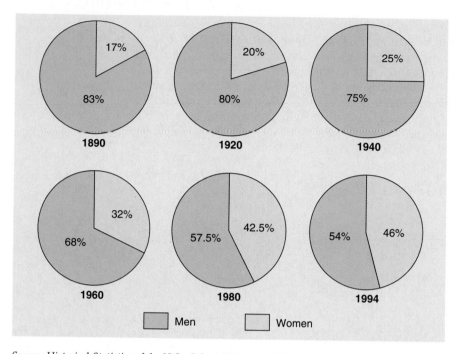

Source: *Historical Statistics of the U.S., Colonial Times to 1970* (1975) and *Statistical Abstract of the U.S., 1996* (1996).

Farming in America, 1850 – 1990

Year	Farm Population (in thousands)	Percent of Total Population	Number of Farms (in thousands)	Total Acres (in thousands)	Average Acreage Per Farm
1850	NA	NA	1,449	293,561	203
1860	NA	NA	2,044	407,213	199
1870	NA	NA	2,660	407,735	153
1880	21,973	43.8	4,009	536,082	134
1890	24,771	42.3	4,565	623,219	137
1900	29,875	41.9	5,740	841,202	147
1910	32,077	34.9	6,366	881,431	139
1920	31,974	30.1	6,454	958,677	149
1930	30,529	24.9	6,295	990,112	157
1940	30,547	23.2	6,102	1,065,114	175
1950	23,048	15.3	5,388	1,161,420	216
1960	15,635	8.7	3,962	1,176,946	297
1970	9,712	4.8	2,949	1,102,769	374
1980	6,051	2.7	2,440	1,039,000	426
1990	4,591	1.9	2,140	987,000	461

NA = Not available

Source: *Historical Statistics of the U.S., Colonial Times to 1970* (1975) and *Statistical Abstract of the U.S., 1996* (1996).

COMMUNICATIONS

THE TWENTIETH CENTURY WITNESSED the growing presence of communications technology in American homes. Especially revolutionary were radio and telephone, which connected people with the outside world in ways previously unimaginable. By 1994, telephones, radios, and televisions were standard in more than 90 percent of American homes, while more and more households had acquired cable television and video cassette recorders. The 1980s also saw the rise of the personal computer, which by 1993 could be found in nearly a quarter of American homes. As the graph shows, kids under seventeen make up a substantial percentage of computer users.

Households with Telephones, 1920 – 1994

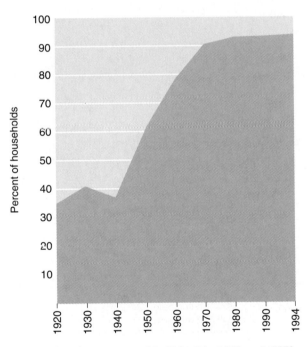

Source: Historical Statistics of the U.S., Colonial Times to 1970 (1975) and Statistical Abstract of the U.S., 1996 (1996).

Households with Radios and Television Sets, 1920 – 1970

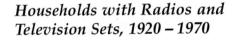
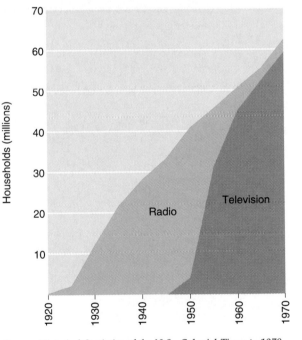

Source: Historical Statistics of the U.S., Colonial Times to 1970 (1975) and Statistical Abstract of the U.S., 1996 (1996).

Percent of Households with Radio, Television, Cable, and VCR, 1970 – 1994

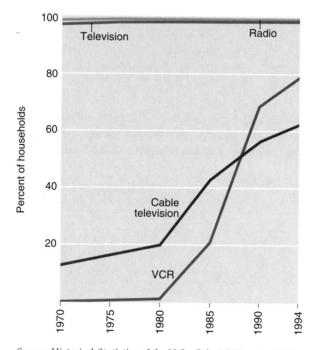

Source: Historical Statistics of the U.S., Colonial Times to 1970 (1975) and Statistical Abstract of the U.S., 1996 (1996).

Computer Use and Access, 1984 – 1993

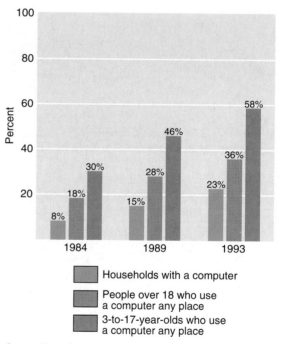

Source: Data from U.S. Bureau of the Census, Education and Social Stratification Branch, Population Division.

EDUCATION

DURING THE TWENTIETH CENTURY, there have been substantial increases in enrollments in secondary education and slower but still steady progress in degrees granted in higher education. In 1910, less than 14 percent of the population obtained high school diplomas; by 1995, that figure had risen to more than 80 percent. The number of people completing bachelor's degrees has grown steadily, from 400,000 in 1960 to just under 1.2 million in 1994, while the increasing professionalization of the workforce is reflected in the number of advanced degrees granted since 1960: Between 1960 and 1994, master's degrees awarded rose from almost 75,000 to almost 400,000, while doctoral degrees earned increased from 10,000 to 42,000.

Years of Schooling Completed, Ages 25 and Over, 1910 – 1995

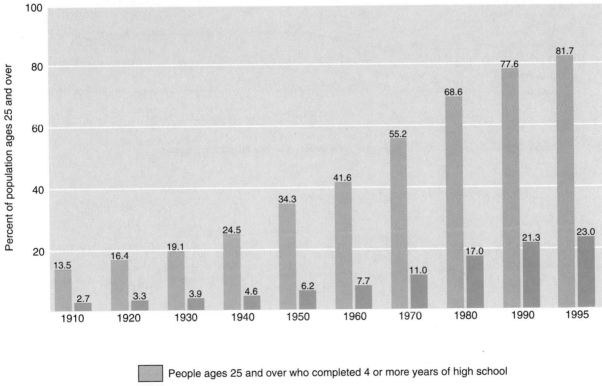

People ages 25 and over who completed 4 or more years of high school

People ages 25 and over who completed 4 or more years of college

Source: Statistics from U.S. Department of Commerce, Bureau of the Census.

Higher Education: Degrees Conferred, 1960 – 1994

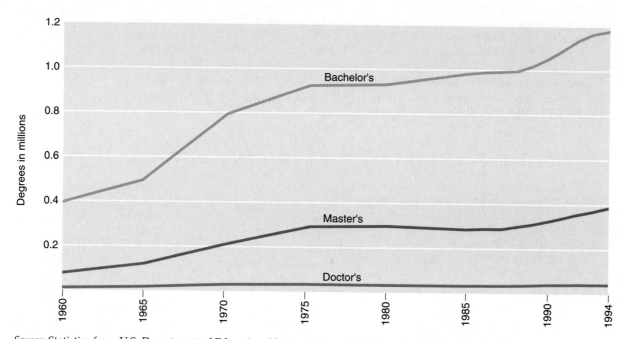

Source: Statistics from U.S. Department of Education, National Center for Education Statistics.

APPENDIX III. RESEARCH RESOURCES IN U.S. HISTORY

While doing research in history, you will use the library to track down primary and secondary sources and to answer questions that arise as you learn more about your topic. This appendix suggests helpful indexes, references, periodicals, and sources of primary documents. It also offers an overview of electronic resources available through the Internet. The materials listed here are not all carried at all libraries, but they will give you an idea of the range of sources available. Remember, too, that librarians are an extremely helpful resource. They can direct you to useful materials throughout your research process.

Bibliographies and Indexes

American Historical Association Guide to Historical Literature. 3rd ed. New York: Oxford University Press, 1995. Offers 27,000 citations to important historical literature, arranged in forty-eight sections covering theory, international history, and regional history. An indispensable guide recently updated to include current trends in historical research.

America History and Life. Santa Barbara: ABC-Clio, 1964–. Covers publications of all sorts on U.S. and Canadian history and culture in a chronological/regional format, with abstracts and alphabetical indexes. Available in computerized format. The most complete ongoing bibliography for American history.

Freidel, Frank Burt. *Harvard Guide to American History.* Cambridge: Harvard University Press, Belknap Press, 1974. Provides citations to books and articles on American history published before 1970. The first volume is arranged topically, the second chronologically. Though it does not cover current scholarship, it is a classic and remains useful for tracing older publications.

Prucha, Francis Paul. *Handbook for Research in American History: A Guide to Bibliographies and Other Reference Works.* 2nd rev. ed. Lincoln: University of Nebraska Press, 1994. Introduces a variety of research tools, including electronic ones. A good source to consult when planning an in-depth research project.

General Overviews

Dictionary of American Biography. New York: Scribner's, 1928–1937, with supplements. Gives substantial biographies of prominent Americans in history.

Dictionary of American History. New York: Scribner's, 1976. An encyclopedia of terms, places, and concepts in U.S. history; other more specialized sets include the *Encyclopedia of North American Colonies* and the *Encyclopedia of the Confederacy.*

Dictionary of Concepts in History. New York: Greenwood, 1986. Contains essays defining concepts in historiography and describing how the concepts were formed; excellent bibliographies.

Encyclopedia of American Social History. New York: Scribner's, 1993. Surveys topics such as religion, class, gender, race, popular culture, regionalism, and everyday life from pre-Columbian to modern times.

Encyclopedia of the United States in the Twentieth Century. New York: Scribner's, 1996. An ambitious overview of American cultural, social, and intellectual history in broad articles arranged topically. Each article is followed by a thorough and very useful bibliography for further research.

Specialized Information

Black Women in America: An Historical Encyclopedia. Brooklyn: Carlson, 1993. A scholarly compilation of biographical and topical articles that constitute a definitive history of African American women.

Carruth, Gordon. *The Encyclopedia of American Facts and Dates.* 9th ed. New York: HarperCollins, 1993. Covers American history chronologically from 986 to the present, offering information on treaties, battles, explorations, popular culture, philosophy, literature, and so on, mixing significant events with telling trivia. Tables allow for reviewing a year from a variety of angles. A thorough index helps pinpoint specific facts in time.

Cook, Chris. *Dictionary of Historical Terms.* 2nd ed. New York: Peter Bendrick, 1990. Covers a wide variety of terms—events, places, institutions, and topics—in history for all periods and places in a remarkably small package. A good place for quick identification of terms in the field.

Dictionary of Afro-American Slavery. New York: Greenwood, 1985. Surveys important people, events, and topics, with useful bibliographies; similar works include *Dictionary of the Vietnam War,* *Historical Dictionary of the New Deal,* and *Historical Dictionary of the Progressive Era.*

Knappman-Frost, Elizabeth. *The ABC-Clio Companion to Women's Progress in America.* Santa Barbara: ABC-Clio, 1994. Covers American women who were notable for their time as well as topics and organizations that have been significant in women's quest for equality. Each article is brief; there are a chronology and a bibliography at the back of the book.

United States. Bureau of the Census. *Historical Statistics of the United States, Colonial Times to 1970.* Washington, D.C.: Government Printing Office, 1975. Offers vital statistics, economic figures, and social data for the United States in time series. An index at the back helps locate tables by subject. For statistics since 1970, consult the annual *Statistical Abstract of the United States.*

Primary Sources

There are many routes to finding contemporary material for historical research. You may search your library catalog using the name of a prominent historical figure as an author; you may also find anthologies covering particular themes or periods in history. Consider also the following special materials for your research.

The Press

American Periodical Series, 1741–1900. Ann Arbor: University Microfilms, 1946–1979. Microfilm collection of periodicals from the colonial period to the turn of the century. An index identifies periodicals that focused on particular topics.

Herstory Microfilm Collection. Berkeley: Women's History Research Center, 1973. A microfilm collection of alternative feminist periodicals published between 1960 and 1980. Offers an interesting documentary history of the women's movement.

New York Times. New York: New York Times, 1851–. Many libraries have this newspaper on microfilm going back to its beginning in 1851. An index is available to locate specific dates and pages of news stories; it also provides detailed chronologies of events as they were reported in the news.

Readers' Guide to Periodical Literature. New York: Wilson, 1900–. This index to popular magazines started in 1900; an earlier index, *Poole's Index to Periodical Literature,* covers 1802–1906, though it does not provide such thorough indexing.

Diaries, Pamphlets, Books

The American Culture Series. Ann Arbor: University Microfilms, 1941–1974. A microfilm set, with a useful index, featuring books and pamphlets published between 1493 and 1875.

American Women's Diaries. New Canaan: Readex, 1984–. A collection of reproductions of women's diaries. There are different series for different regions of the country.

The March of America Facsimile Series. Ann Arbor: University Microfilms, 1966. A collection of more than ninety facsimiles of travel accounts to the New World published in English or English translation from the fifteenth through the nineteenth century.

Women in America from Colonial Times to the 20th Century. New York: Arno, 1974. A collection of reprints of dozens of books written by women describing women's lives and experiences in their own words.

Government Documents

Congressional Record. Washington D.C.: Government Printing Office, 1874–. Covers daily debates and proceedings of Congress. Earlier series were called *Debates and Proceedings in the Congress of the United States* and *The Congressional Globe.*

Foreign Relations of the United States. Washington D.C.: Department of State, 1861–. A collection of documents from 1861, including diplomatic papers, correspondence, and memoranda, that provides a documentary record of U.S. foreign policy.

Public Papers of the Presidents. Washington D.C.: Office of the Federal Register, 1957–. Includes major documents issued by the executive branch from the Hoover administration to the present.

Serial Set. Washington, D.C.: Government Printing Office, 1789–1969. A huge collection of congressional documents, available in many libraries on microfiche, with a useful index.

Local History Collections

State and county historical societies often house a wealth of historical documents; consider their resources when planning your research—you may find yourself working with material that no one else has analyzed before.

Internet Resources

The Internet has been a useful place for scholars to communicate and publish information in recent years. Electronic discussion lists, electronic journals, and primary texts are among the resources available for historians on the Internet. The following sources are good places to find historical information. You can also search for information on the World Wide Web using any of a number of search engines. However, bear in mind that there is no board of editors screening Internet sites for accuracy or usefulness, and the search engines generally rely on free-text searches rather than subject headings. Be critical of all of your sources, particularly those found on the Internet.

American Memory: Historical Collection from the National Digital Library Program. <http://rs6.loc.gov/amhome. html> An Internet site that features digitized primary source materials from the Library of Congress, among them African American pamphlets, civil war photographs, documents from the Continental Congress and the Constitutional Convention of 1774–1790, materials on woman suffrage, and oral histories.

Directory of Scholarly and Professional Electronic Conferences. <http://n2h2.com/KOVAKS/>. A good place to find out what electronic conversations are going on in a scholarly discipline. Includes a good search facility and instructions on how to connect to e-mail discussion lists, newsgroups, and interactive chat sites with academic content. Once identified, these conferences are good places to raise questions, find out what controversies are currently stirring the profession, and even find out about grants and jobs.

Historical Text Archive. <http://www.msstate.edu/Archives/History>. A Web interface for the oldest and largest Internet site for historical documents. Includes sections on Native American, African American, and U.S. history, in which can be found texts of the Declaration of Independence, the U.S. Constitution, the Constitution of Iroquois Nations, World War II surrender documents, photograph collections, and a great deal more. These can be used online or saved as files.

Index of Resources for Historians. <http://kuhttp.cc. ukans.edu/history/index.html>. A vast list of more than 1700 links to sites of interest to historians, arranged alphabetically by general topic. Some links are to sources for general reference information, but most are on historical topics. A good place to start an exploration of Internet resources.

MAPS, CHARTS, AND TABLES

Maps

Charts and Tables

ABOUT THE AUTHORS

James L. Roark

Born in Eunice, Louisiana, and raised in the West, James L. Roark received his B.A. from the University of California, Davis, in 1963 and his Ph.D. from Stanford University in 1973. His dissertation won the Allan Nevins Prize. He has taught at the University of Nigeria, Nsukka; the University of Nairobi, Kenya; the University of Missouri, St. Louis; and, since 1983, Emory University, where he is Samuel Candler Dobbs Professor of American History. In 1993, he received the Emory Williams Distinguished Teaching Award. He has written *Masters without Slaves: Southern Planters in the Civil War and Reconstruction* (1977). With Michael P. Johnson, he is author of *Black Masters: A Free Family of Color in the Old South* (1984) and editor of *No Chariot Let Down: Charleston's Free People of Color on the Eve of the Civil War* (1984). He has received research assistance from the American Philosophical Society and the National Endowment for the Humanities. Active in the Organization of American Historians and the Southern Historical Association, he is also a fellow of the Society of American Historians.

Michael P. Johnson

Born and raised in Ponca City, Oklahoma, Michael P. Johnson studied at Knox College, Illinois, where he received a B.A. in 1963, and at Stanford University, where he earned a Ph.D. in 1973. He is now professor of history at the Johns Hopkins University in Baltimore. His publications include *Toward a Patriarchal Republic: The Secession of Georgia* (1977); with James L. Roark *Black Masters: A Free Family of Color in the Old South* (1984) and *No Chariot Let Down: Charlestown's Free People of Color on the Eve of the Civil War* (1984); *Reading the American Past: Selected Historical Documents*, the documents reader for *The American Promise;* and articles that have appeared in the *William and Mary Quarterly,* the *Journal of Southern History, Labor History,* the *New York Review of Books,* the *New Republic,* the *Nation,* and other journals. Johnson has been awarded research fellowships by the American Council of Learned Societies and the National Endowment for the Humanities. He

has directed a National Endowment for the Humanities Summer Seminar for College Teachers and has been honored with university awards for outstanding teaching. He is an active member of the American Historical Association, the Organization of American Historians, and the Southern Historical Association.

Patricia Cline Cohen

Born in Ann Arbor, Michigan, and raised in Palo Alto, California, Patricia Cline Cohen earned a B.A. at the University of Chicago in 1968 and a Ph.D. at the University of California, Berkeley in 1977. In 1976, she joined the history faculty at the University of California at Santa Barbara. Cohen has written *A Calculating People: The Spread of Numeracy in Early America* (1982) and has published articles on numeracy, prostitution, sexual crime, and murder in journals including the *Journal of Women's History, Radical History Review,* the *William and Mary Quarterly,* and the *NWSA Journal.* Her scholarly work has received assistance from the National Endowment for the Humanities, the National Humanities Center, the American Antiquarian Society, the Schlesinger Library, and the Newberry Library. In the mid-1980s, she helped establish the Women's Studies Program on her campus, and she has been chair of the program since 1991.

Sarah Stage

Sarah Stage was born in Davenport, Iowa, and received a B.A. from the University of Iowa in 1966 and a Ph.D. in American studies from Yale University in 1975. She has taught twentieth-century U.S. history for more than twenty-five years at Williams College and the University of California, Riverside. Currently she is professor and chair of Women's Studies at Arizona State University West in Phoenix. Her books include *Female Complaints: Lydia Pinkham and the Business of Women's Medicine* (1979) and the forthcoming *Rethinking Women and Home Economics in the Twentieth Century.* Among the fellowships she has received are the Rockefeller Foundation Humanities Fellowship, the American Association of University Women dissertation fellowship, a fellowship from the Charles Warren Center for the Study of History at Harvard University, and the University of California President's Fellowship in the Humanities. She is at work on a book entitled *Women and the Progressive Impulse in American Politics, 1890–1914.*

Alan Lawson

Born in Providence, Rhode Island, Alan Lawson received his B.A. from Brown University in 1955 and his Ph.D. from the University of Michigan in 1967. Since winning the Allan Nevins Prize for his dissertation, Lawson has served on the faculties of the University of California, Irvine, Smith College, and, currently, Boston College. He has written *The Failure of Independent Liberalism* (1971) and coedited *From Revolution to Republic* (1976). While completing the forthcoming *The New Deal and the Mobilization of Progressive Experience,* he has published book chapters and essays on political economy and the cultural legacy of the New Deal. He has served as editor of the *Review of Education* and the *Intellectual History Newsletter* and contributed articles to those journals as well as to the *History Education Quarterly.* He has been active in the field of American studies as director of the Boston College American studies program and as a contributor to the *American Quarterly.* Under the auspices of the United States Information Agency, Lawson has been coordinator and lecturer for programs to instruct faculty from foreign nations in the state of American historical scholarship and teaching.

Susan M. Hartmann

Professor of history and women's studies at Ohio State University, Susan M. Hartmann grew up in St. Louis and received her B.A. from Washington University in 1961 and her Ph.D. from the University of Missouri in 1966. After specializing in the political economy of the post–World War II period and publishing *Truman and the 80th Congress* (1971), she expanded her interests to the field of women's history, publishing many articles and two books, *The Home Front and Beyond: American Women in the 1940s* (1982) and *From Margin to Mainstream: American Women and Politics since 1960* (1989). She has won research fellowships and grants from the Truman Library Institute, the Rockefeller Foundation, the National Endowment for the Humanities, and the American Council of Learned Societies. Hartmann has taught at the University of Missouri, St. Louis, and Boston University, and she has lectured on American history in Greece, France, Austria, Germany, Australia, and New Zealand. She has served on book and article award committees of the American Historical Association, the Organization of American Historians, the American Studies Association, and the National Women's Studies Association. At Ohio State she has served as director of women's studies, and in 1995 she won the Exemplary Faculty Award in the College of Humanities.

INDEX

A note about the index:

Pages containing main coverage or description of a topic or person are set in boldface for easy reference. Entries also include dates for important events and major figures.

Letters in parentheses following pages refer to:
   (i) for illustrations, including photographs and artifacts, as well as information
      contained in picture captions
   (f) for figures, including charts and graphs
   (m) for maps
   (t) for tables